Monthly Interest Amortization Tables

Covering

Interest Rates
of 5% to 28.75%

Loan Amounts
of $50 to $160,000

Terms up to 40 years

CONTEMPORARY
BOOKS, INC.
CHICAGO

Great care has been taken to ensure exact figures in the production of these tables, but there is no guarantee of accuracy assumed by the author or publisher of this book.

CONTENTS

TABLE 1. MONTHLY PAYMENT REQUIRED TO AMORTIZE A LOAN

Use this Table to find the monthly payment amount required to completely pay off a loan amount over a given loan term at a fixed rate of interest. In order to ensure complete amortization, each payment entry is rounded up to the next highest cent. When loan amounts aren't exactly equal to the amounts shown in the left-hand column of each page, simply combine the loan amounts (and their respective monthly payment amounts) to solve any problem.

Example: What monthly payment is needed to pay off a loan amount of $25,750 over a 15-year loan term at 13.75% interest?

First, find the 13.75% interest rate on page 73. Move down the 15-year column until you find a row entry for $25,750. Since there is no row entry for exactly this loan amount you must combine three row entries to get the monthly payment. The entry for $50 is $0.66, for $700 is $9.21, and for $25,000 is $328.75. The monthly payment is the sum of these three payment entries or $338.62. To obtain a high degree of accuracy combine as few row entries as possible when determining your monthly payment.

5.00% MONTHLY AMORTIZING PAYMENTS

AMOUNT OF LOAN	NUMBER OF YEARS IN TERM											
	1	2	3	4	5	6	7	8	9	10	11	12
$ 50	4.29	2.20	1.50	1.16	0.95	0.81	0.71	0.64	0.58	0.54	0.50	0.47
100	8.57	4.39	3.00	2.31	1.89	1.62	1.42	1.27	1.16	1.07	0.99	0.93
200	17.13	8.78	6.00	4.61	3.78	3.23	2.83	2.54	2.31	2.13	1.98	1.85
300	25.69	13.17	9.00	6.91	5.67	4.84	4.25	3.80	3.46	3.19	2.96	2.78
400	34.25	17.55	11.99	9.22	7.55	6.45	5.66	5.07	4.61	4.25	3.95	3.70
500	42.81	21.94	14.99	11.52	9.44	8.06	7.07	6.33	5.76	5.31	4.94	4.63
600	51.37	26.33	17.99	13.82	11.33	9.67	8.49	7.60	6.92	6.37	5.92	5.55
700	59.93	30.71	20.98	16.13	13.21	11.28	9.90	8.87	8.07	7.43	6.91	6.48
800	68.49	35.10	23.98	18.43	15.10	12.89	11.31	10.13	9.22	8.49	7.90	7.40
900	77.05	39.49	26.98	20.73	16.99	14.50	12.73	11.40	10.37	9.55	8.88	8.33
1000	85.61	43.88	29.98	23.03	18.88	16.11	14.14	12.66	11.52	10.61	9.87	9.25
2000	171.22	87.75	59.95	46.06	37.75	32.21	28.27	25.32	23.04	21.22	19.73	18.50
3000	256.83	131.62	89.92	69.09	56.62	48.32	42.41	37.98	34.56	31.82	29.60	27.75
4000	342.43	175.49	119.89	92.12	75.49	64.42	56.54	50.64	46.07	42.43	39.46	37.00
5000	428.04	219.36	149.86	115.15	94.36	80.53	70.67	63.30	57.59	53.04	49.33	46.25
6000	513.65	263.23	179.83	138.18	113.23	96.63	84.81	75.96	69.11	63.64	59.19	55.50
7000	599.26	307.10	209.80	161.21	132.10	112.74	98.94	88.62	80.63	74.25	69.06	64.75
8000	684.86	350.98	239.77	184.24	150.97	128.84	113.08	101.28	92.14	84.86	78.92	74.00
9000	770.47	394.85	269.74	207.27	169.85	144.95	127.21	113.94	103.66	95.46	88.79	83.25
10000	856.08	438.72	299.71	230.30	188.72	161.05	141.34	126.60	115.18	106.07	98.65	92.49
11000	941.69	482.59	329.68	253.33	207.59	177.16	155.48	139.26	126.70	116.68	108.51	101.74
12000	1027.29	526.46	359.66	276.36	226.46	193.26	169.61	151.92	138.21	127.28	118.38	110.99
13000	1112.90	570.33	389.63	299.39	245.33	209.37	183.75	164.58	149.73	137.89	128.24	120.24
14000	1198.51	614.20	419.60	322.42	264.20	225.47	197.88	177.24	161.25	148.50	138.11	129.49
15000	1284.12	658.08	449.57	345.44	283.07	241.58	212.01	189.90	172.76	159.10	147.97	138.74
16000	1369.72	701.95	479.54	368.47	301.94	257.68	226.15	202.56	184.28	169.71	157.84	147.99
17000	1455.33	745.82	509.51	391.50	320.82	273.79	240.28	215.22	195.80	180.32	167.70	157.24
18000	1540.94	789.69	539.48	414.53	339.69	289.89	254.42	227.88	207.32	190.92	177.57	166.49
19000	1626.55	833.56	569.45	437.56	358.56	306.00	268.55	240.54	218.83	201.53	187.43	175.73
20000	1712.15	877.43	599.42	460.59	377.43	322.10	282.68	253.20	230.35	212.14	197.29	184.98
21000	1797.76	921.30	629.39	483.62	396.30	338.21	296.82	265.86	241.87	222.74	207.16	194.23
22000	1883.37	965.18	659.36	506.65	415.17	354.31	310.95	278.52	253.39	233.35	217.02	203.48
23000	1968.98	1009.05	689.34	529.68	434.04	370.42	325.08	291.18	264.90	243.96	226.89	212.73
24000	2054.58	1052.92	719.31	552.71	452.91	386.52	339.22	303.84	276.42	254.56	236.75	221.98
25000	2140.19	1096.79	749.28	575.74	471.79	402.63	353.35	316.50	287.94	265.17	246.62	231.23
26000	2225.80	1140.66	779.25	598.77	490.66	418.73	367.49	329.16	299.45	275.78	256.48	240.48
27000	2311.41	1184.53	809.22	621.80	509.53	434.84	381.62	341.82	310.97	286.38	266.35	249.73
28000	2397.01	1228.40	839.19	644.83	528.40	450.94	395.75	354.48	322.49	296.99	276.21	258.97
29000	2482.62	1272.28	869.16	667.85	547.27	467.05	409.89	367.14	334.01	307.59	286.08	268.22
30000	2568.23	1316.15	899.13	690.88	566.14	483.15	424.02	379.80	345.52	318.20	295.94	277.47
31000	2653.84	1360.02	929.10	713.91	585.01	499.26	438.16	392.46	357.04	328.81	305.80	286.72
32000	2739.44	1403.89	959.07	736.94	603.88	515.36	452.29	405.12	368.56	339.41	315.67	295.97
33000	2825.05	1447.76	989.04	759.97	622.76	531.47	466.42	417.78	380.08	350.02	325.53	305.22
34000	2910.66	1491.63	1019.02	783.00	641.63	547.57	480.56	430.44	391.59	360.63	335.40	314.47
35000	2996.27	1535.50	1048.99	806.03	660.50	563.68	494.69	443.10	403.11	371.23	345.26	323.72
37500	3210.29	1645.18	1123.91	863.60	707.68	603.94	530.03	474.75	431.90	397.75	369.92	346.84
40000	3424.30	1754.86	1198.84	921.18	754.85	644.20	565.36	506.40	460.70	424.27	394.58	369.96
42500	3638.32	1864.54	1273.77	978.75	802.03	684.46	600.70	538.05	489.49	450.78	419.25	393.08
45000	3852.34	1974.22	1348.70	1036.32	849.21	724.73	636.03	569.70	518.29	477.30	443.91	416.21
47500	4066.36	2083.90	1423.62	1093.90	896.39	764.99	671.37	601.35	547.08	503.82	468.57	439.33
50000	4280.38	2193.57	1498.55	1151.47	943.57	805.25	706.70	633.00	575.87	530.33	493.23	462.45
52500	4494.40	2303.25	1573.48	1209.04	990.74	845.51	742.04	664.65	604.66	556.85	517.89	485.57
55000	4708.42	2412.93	1648.40	1266.62	1037.92	885.78	777.37	696.30	633.46	583.37	542.55	508.69
57500	4922.44	2522.61	1723.33	1280.19	1085.10	926.04	812.70	727.95	662.25	609.88	567.21	531.82
60000	5136.45	2632.29	1798.26	1381.76	1132.28	966.30	848.04	759.60	691.04	636.40	591.87	554.94
65000	5564.49	2851.65	1948.11	1496.91	1226.64	1046.83	918.71	822.90	748.63	689.43	641.20	601.18
70000	5992.53	3071.00	2097.97	1612.06	1320.99	1127.35	989.38	886.20	806.21	742.46	690.52	647.43
75000	6420.57	3290.36	2247.82	1727.20	1415.35	1207.87	1060.05	949.50	863.80	795.50	739.84	693.67
80000	6848.60	3509.72	2397.68	1842.35	1509.70	1288.40	1130.72	1012.80	921.39	848.53	789.16	739.92
85000	7276.64	3729.07	2547.53	1957.49	1604.06	1368.92	1201.39	1076.10	978.97	901.56	838.49	786.16
90000	7704.68	3948.43	2697.39	2072.64	1698.42	1449.45	1272.06	1139.40	1036.56	954.59	887.81	832.41
95000	8132.72	4167.79	2847.24	2187.79	1792.77	1529.97	1342.73	1202.70	1094.15	1007.63	937.13	878.65
100000	8560.75	4387.14	2997.09	2302.93	1887.13	1610.50	1413.40	1266.00	1151.73	1060.66	986.45	924.90
105000	8988.79	4606.50	3146.95	2418.08	1981.48	1691.02	1484.07	1329.30	1209.32	1113.69	1035.78	971.14
110000	9416.83	4825.86	3296.80	2533.23	2075.84	1771.55	1554.73	1392.60	1266.91	1166.73	1085.10	1017.38
115000	9844.87	5045.21	3446.66	2648.37	2170.20	1852.07	1625.40	1455.90	1324.49	1219.76	1134.42	1063.63
120000	10272.90	5264.57	3596.51	2763.52	2264.55	1932.60	1696.07	1519.20	1382.08	1272.79	1183.74	1109.87
125000	10700.94	5483.93	3746.37	2878.67	2358.91	2013.12	1766.74	1582.50	1439.66	1325.82	1233.07	1156.12
130000	11128.98	5703.29	3896.22	2993.81	2453.27	2093.65	1837.41	1645.79	1497.25	1378.86	1282.39	1202.36
135000	11557.02	5922.64	4046.08	3108.96	2547.62	2174.17	1908.08	1709.09	1554.84	1431.89	1331.71	1248.61
140000	11985.05	6142.00	4195.93	3224.11	2641.98	2254.70	1978.75	1772.39	1612.42	1484.92	1381.03	1294.85
145000	12413.09	6361.36	4345.79	3339.25	2736.33	2335.22	2049.42	1835.69	1670.01	1537.95	1430.36	1341.10
150000	12841.13	6580.71	4495.64	3454.40	2830.69	2415.74	2120.09	1898.99	1727.60	1590.99	1479.68	1387.34
155000	13269.16	6800.07	4645.49	3569.55	2925.05	2496.27	2190.76	1962.29	1785.18	1644.02	1529.00	1433.59
160000	13697.20	7019.43	4795.35	3684.69	3019.40	2576.79	2261.43	2025.59	1842.77	1697.05	1578.32	1479.83

2

AMOUNT OF LOAN	NUMBER OF YEARS IN TERM											
	13	14	15	16	17	18	19	20	25	30	35	40
$ 50	0.44	0.42	0.40	0.38	0.37	0.36	0.35	0.33	0.30	0.27	0.26	0.25
100	0.88	0.83	0.80	0.76	0.73	0.71	0.69	0.66	0.59	0.54	0.51	0.49
200	1.75	1.66	1.59	1.52	1.46	1.41	1.37	1.32	1.17	1.08	1.01	0.97
300	2.62	2.49	2.38	2.28	2.19	2.11	2.05	1.98	1.76	1.62	1.52	1.45
400	3.50	3.32	3.17	3.04	2.92	2.82	2.73	2.64	2.34	2.15	2.02	1.93
500	4.37	4.15	3.96	3.79	3.65	3.52	3.41	3.30	2.93	2.69	2.53	2.42
600	5.24	4.98	4.75	4.55	4.38	4.22	4.09	3.96	3.51	3.23	3.03	2.90
700	6.12	5.81	5.54	5.31	5.11	4.93	4.77	4.62	4.10	3.76	3.54	3.38
800	6.99	6.64	6.33	6.07	5.83	5.63	5.45	5.28	4.68	4.30	4.04	3.86
900	7.86	7.46	7.12	6.82	6.56	6.33	6.13	5.94	5.27	4.84	4.55	4.34
1000	8.74	8.29	7.91	7.58	7.29	7.04	6.81	6.60	5.85	5.37	5.05	4.83
2000	17.47	16.58	15.82	15.16	14.58	14.07	13.61	13.20	11.70	10.74	10.10	9.65
3000	26.20	24.87	23.73	22.74	21.86	21.10	20.41	19.80	17.54	16.11	15.15	14.47
4000	34.93	33.16	31.64	30.31	29.15	28.13	27.22	26.40	23.39	21.48	20.19	19.29
5000	43.66	41.45	39.54	37.89	36.44	35.16	34.02	33.00	29.23	26.85	25.24	24.11
6000	52.39	49.74	47.45	45.47	43.72	42.19	40.82	39.60	35.08	32.21	30.29	28.94
7000	61.12	58.03	55.36	53.04	51.01	49.22	47.62	46.20	40.93	37.58	35.33	33.76
8000	69.85	66.31	63.27	60.62	58.30	56.25	54.43	52.80	46.77	42.95	40.38	38.58
9000	78.58	74.60	71.18	68.20	65.58	63.28	61.23	59.40	52.62	48.32	45.43	43.40
10000	87.31	82.89	79.08	75.77	72.87	70.31	68.03	66.00	58.46	53.69	50.47	48.22
11000	96.04	91.18	86.99	83.35	80.16	77.34	74.84	72.60	64.31	59.06	55.52	53.05
12000	104.77	99.47	94.90	90.93	87.44	84.37	81.64	79.20	70.16	64.42	60.57	57.87
13000	113.50	107.76	102.81	98.50	94.73	91.40	88.44	85.80	76.00	69.79	65.61	62.69
14000	122.23	116.05	110.72	106.08	102.02	98.43	95.24	92.40	81.85	75.16	70.66	67.51
15000	130.96	124.34	118.62	113.66	109.30	105.46	102.05	99.00	87.69	80.53	75.71	72.33
16000	139.69	132.62	126.53	121.23	116.59	112.49	108.85	105.60	93.54	85.90	80.76	77.16
17000	148.43	140.91	134.44	128.81	123.88	119.52	115.65	112.20	99.39	91.26	85.80	81.98
18000	157.16	149.20	142.35	136.39	131.16	126.55	122.45	118.80	105.23	96.63	90.85	86.80
19000	165.89	157.49	150.26	143.96	138.45	133.58	129.26	125.40	111.08	102.00	95.90	91.62
20000	174.62	165.78	158.16	151.54	145.74	140.61	136.06	132.00	116.92	107.37	100.94	96.44
21000	183.35	174.07	166.07	159.12	153.02	147.64	142.86	138.60	122.77	112.74	105.99	101.27
22000	192.08	182.36	173.98	166.69	160.31	154.67	149.67	145.20	128.61	118.11	111.04	106.09
23000	200.81	190.65	181.89	174.27	167.60	161.70	156.47	151.79	134.46	123.47	116.08	110.91
24000	209.54	198.93	189.80	181.85	174.88	168.73	163.27	158.39	140.31	128.84	121.13	115.73
25000	218.27	207.22	197.70	189.43	182.17	175.76	170.07	164.99	146.15	134.21	126.18	120.55
26000	227.00	215.51	205.61	197.00	189.46	182.79	176.88	171.59	152.00	139.58	131.22	125.38
27000	235.73	223.80	213.52	204.58	196.74	189.82	183.68	178.19	157.84	144.95	136.27	130.20
28000	244.46	232.09	221.43	212.16	204.03	196.85	190.48	184.79	163.69	150.32	141.32	135.02
29000	253.19	240.38	229.34	219.73	211.32	203.88	197.29	191.39	169.54	155.68	146.36	139.84
30000	261.92	248.67	237.24	227.31	218.60	210.92	204.09	197.99	175.38	161.05	151.41	144.66
31000	270.65	256.95	245.15	234.89	225.89	217.95	210.89	204.59	181.23	166.42	156.46	149.49
32000	279.38	265.24	253.06	242.46	233.17	224.98	217.69	211.19	187.07	171.79	161.51	154.31
33000	288.11	273.53	260.97	250.04	240.46	232.01	224.50	217.79	192.92	177.16	166.55	159.13
34000	296.85	281.82	268.87	257.62	247.75	239.04	231.30	224.39	198.77	182.52	171.60	163.95
35000	305.58	290.11	276.78	265.19	255.03	246.07	238.10	230.99	204.61	187.89	176.65	168.77
37500	327.40	310.83	296.55	284.14	273.25	263.64	255.11	247.49	219.23	201.31	189.26	180.83
40000	349.23	331.55	316.32	303.08	291.47	281.22	272.12	263.99	233.84	214.73	201.88	192.88
42500	371.06	352.28	336.09	322.02	309.68	298.79	289.12	280.49	248.46	228.15	214.50	204.94
45000	392.88	373.00	355.86	340.96	327.90	316.37	306.13	296.99	263.07	241.57	227.11	216.99
47500	414.71	393.72	375.63	359.90	346.12	333.95	323.14	313.48	277.69	255.00	239.73	229.05
50000	436.53	414.44	395.40	378.85	364.33	351.52	340.14	329.98	292.30	268.42	252.35	241.10
52500	458.36	435.16	415.17	397.79	382.55	369.10	357.15	346.48	306.91	281.84	264.97	253.16
55000	480.19	455.88	434.94	416.73	400.77	386.67	374.16	362.98	321.53	295.26	277.58	265.21
57500	502.01	476.61	454.71	435.67	418.98	404.25	391.16	379.48	336.14	308.68	290.20	277.27
60000	523.84	497.33	474.48	454.61	437.20	421.83	408.17	395.98	350.76	322.10	302.82	289.32
65000	567.49	538.77	514.02	492.50	473.63	456.98	442.19	428.98	379.99	348.94	328.05	313.43
70000	611.15	580.21	553.56	530.38	510.06	492.13	476.20	461.97	409.22	375.78	353.29	337.54
75000	654.80	621.66	593.10	568.27	546.50	527.28	510.21	494.97	438.45	402.62	378.52	361.65
80000	698.45	663.10	632.64	606.15	582.93	562.43	544.23	527.97	467.68	429.46	403.76	385.76
85000	742.11	704.55	672.18	644.03	619.36	597.58	578.24	560.97	496.91	456.30	428.99	409.87
90000	785.76	745.99	711.72	681.92	655.79	632.74	612.25	593.97	526.14	483.14	454.22	433.98
95000	829.41	787.43	751.26	719.80	692.23	667.89	646.27	626.96	555.37	509.99	479.46	458.09
100000	873.06	828.88	790.80	757.69	728.66	703.04	680.28	659.96	584.60	536.83	504.69	482.20
105000	916.72	870.32	830.34	795.57	765.09	738.19	714.30	692.96	613.82	563.67	529.93	506.31
110000	960.37	911.76	869.88	833.45	801.53	773.34	748.31	725.96	643.05	590.51	555.16	530.42
115000	1004.02	953.21	909.42	871.34	837.96	808.49	782.32	758.95	672.28	617.35	580.40	554.53
120000	1047.68	994.65	948.96	909.22	874.39	843.65	816.34	791.95	701.51	644.19	605.63	578.64
125000	1091.33	1036.09	988.50	947.11	910.82	878.80	850.35	824.95	730.74	671.03	630.86	602.75
130000	1134.98	1077.54	1028.04	984.99	947.26	913.95	884.37	857.95	759.97	697.87	656.10	626.86
135000	1178.64	1118.98	1067.58	1022.87	983.69	949.10	918.38	890.95	789.20	724.71	681.33	650.97
140000	1222.29	1160.42	1107.12	1060.76	1020.12	984.25	952.39	923.94	818.43	751.56	706.57	675.08
145000	1265.94	1201.87	1146.66	1098.64	1056.56	1019.40	986.41	956.94	847.66	778.40	731.80	699.19
150000	1309.59	1243.31	1186.20	1136.53	1092.99	1054.56	1020.42	989.94	876.89	805.24	757.04	723.30
155000	1353.25	1284.75	1225.74	1174.41	1129.42	1089.71	1054.44	1022.94	906.12	832.08	782.27	747.41
160000	1396.90	1326.20	1265.27	1212.29	1165.85	1124.86	1088.45	1055.93	935.35	858.92	807.51	771.52

3

5.25%
MONTHLY AMORTIZING PAYMENTS

AMOUNT OF LOAN	NUMBER OF YEARS IN TERM											
	1	2	3	4	5	6	7	8	9	10	11	12
$ 50	4.29	2.20	1.51	1.16	0.95	0.82	0.72	0.64	0.59	0.54	0.50	0.47
100	8.58	4.40	3.01	2.32	1.90	1.63	1.43	1.28	1.17	1.08	1.00	0.94
200	17.15	8.80	6.02	4.63	3.80	3.25	2.86	2.56	2.33	2.15	2.00	1.88
300	25.72	13.20	9.03	6.95	5.70	4.87	4.28	3.84	3.50	3.22	3.00	2.82
400	34.29	17.60	12.04	9.26	7.60	6.49	5.71	5.12	4.66	4.30	4.00	3.75
500	42.87	22.00	15.05	11.58	9.50	8.12	7.13	6.39	5.82	5.37	5.00	4.69
600	51.44	26.40	18.05	13.89	11.40	9.74	8.56	7.67	6.99	6.44	6.00	5.63
700	60.01	30.79	21.06	16.20	13.30	11.36	9.98	8.95	8.15	7.52	7.00	6.57
800	68.58	35.19	24.07	18.52	15.19	12.98	11.41	10.23	9.32	8.59	8.00	7.50
900	77.15	39.59	27.08	20.83	17.09	14.60	12.83	11.51	10.48	9.66	8.99	8.44
1000	85.73	43.99	30.09	23.15	18.99	16.23	14.26	12.78	11.64	10.73	9.99	9.38
2000	171.45	87.97	60.17	46.29	37.98	32.45	28.51	25.56	23.28	21.46	19.98	18.75
3000	257.17	131.96	90.25	69.43	56.96	48.67	42.76	38.34	34.92	32.19	29.97	28.13
4000	342.89	175.94	120.34	92.58	75.95	64.89	57.01	51.12	46.56	42.92	39.96	37.50
5000	428.62	219.92	150.42	115.72	94.93	81.11	71.26	63.90	58.20	53.65	49.95	46.88
6000	514.34	263.91	180.50	138.86	113.92	97.33	85.52	76.68	69.83	64.38	59.94	56.25
7000	600.06	307.89	210.59	162.00	132.91	113.55	99.77	89.46	81.47	75.11	69.93	65.63
8000	685.78	351.87	240.67	185.15	151.89	129.77	114.02	102.24	93.11	85.84	79.92	75.00
9000	771.50	395.86	270.75	208.29	170.88	146.00	128.27	115.02	104.75	96.57	89.90	84.38
10000	857.23	439.84	300.84	231.43	189.86	162.22	142.52	127.80	116.39	107.30	99.89	93.75
11000	942.95	483.82	330.92	254.57	208.85	178.44	156.77	140.58	128.03	118.03	109.88	103.13
12000	1028.67	527.81	361.00	277.72	227.84	194.66	171.03	153.36	139.66	128.76	119.87	112.50
13000	1114.39	571.79	391.09	300.86	246.82	210.88	185.28	166.14	151.30	139.48	129.86	121.88
14000	1200.11	615.77	421.17	324.00	265.81	227.10	199.53	178.91	162.94	150.21	139.85	131.25
15000	1285.84	659.76	451.25	347.15	284.79	243.32	213.78	191.69	174.58	160.94	149.84	140.63
16000	1371.56	703.74	481.34	370.29	303.78	259.54	228.03	204.47	186.22	171.67	159.83	150.00
17000	1457.28	747.72	511.42	393.43	322.77	275.76	242.28	217.25	197.86	182.40	169.81	159.38
18000	1543.00	791.71	541.50	416.57	341.75	291.99	256.54	230.03	209.49	193.13	179.80	168.75
19000	1628.72	835.69	571.59	439.72	360.74	308.21	270.79	242.81	221.13	203.86	189.79	178.13
20000	1714.45	879.67	601.67	462.86	379.72	324.43	285.04	255.59	232.77	214.59	199.78	187.50
21000	1800.17	923.66	631.75	486.00	398.71	340.65	299.29	268.37	244.41	225.32	209.77	196.88
22000	1885.89	967.64	661.84	509.14	417.70	356.87	313.54	281.15	256.05	236.05	219.76	206.25
23000	1971.61	1011.62	691.92	532.29	436.68	373.09	327.79	293.93	267.68	246.78	229.75	215.63
24000	2057.34	1055.61	722.00	555.43	455.67	389.31	342.05	306.71	279.32	257.51	239.74	225.00
25000	2143.06	1099.59	752.09	578.57	474.65	405.53	356.30	319.49	290.96	268.23	249.72	234.38
26000	2228.78	1143.57	782.17	601.72	493.64	421.75	370.55	332.27	302.60	278.96	259.71	243.75
27000	2314.50	1187.56	812.25	624.86	512.63	437.98	384.80	345.05	314.24	289.69	269.70	253.13
28000	2400.22	1231.54	842.34	648.00	531.61	454.20	399.05	357.82	325.88	300.42	279.69	262.50
29000	2485.95	1275.52	872.42	671.14	550.60	470.42	413.30	370.60	337.51	311.15	289.68	271.87
30000	2571.67	1319.51	902.50	694.29	569.58	486.64	427.56	383.38	349.15	321.88	299.67	281.25
31000	2657.39	1363.49	932.59	717.43	588.57	502.86	441.81	396.16	360.79	332.61	309.66	290.62
32000	2743.11	1407.47	962.67	740.57	607.56	519.08	456.06	408.94	372.43	343.34	319.65	300.00
33000	2828.83	1451.46	992.75	763.71	626.54	535.30	470.31	421.72	384.07	354.07	329.63	309.37
34000	2914.56	1495.44	1022.84	786.86	645.53	551.52	484.56	434.50	395.71	364.80	339.62	318.75
35000	3000.28	1539.43	1052.92	810.00	664.51	567.75	498.81	447.28	407.34	375.53	349.61	328.12
37500	3214.58	1649.38	1128.13	867.86	711.98	608.30	534.44	479.23	436.44	402.35	374.58	351.56
40000	3428.89	1759.34	1203.34	925.71	759.44	648.85	570.07	511.18	465.54	429.17	399.56	375.00
42500	3643.19	1869.30	1278.54	983.57	806.91	689.40	605.70	543.12	494.63	455.99	424.53	398.43
45000	3857.50	1979.26	1353.75	1041.43	854.37	729.96	641.33	575.07	523.73	482.82	449.50	421.87
47500	4071.80	2089.22	1428.96	1099.28	901.84	770.51	676.96	607.02	552.82	509.64	474.47	445.31
50000	4286.11	2199.18	1504.17	1157.14	949.30	811.06	712.59	638.97	581.92	536.46	499.44	468.75
52500	4500.41	2309.14	1579.38	1215.00	996.77	851.62	748.22	670.92	611.01	563.29	524.41	492.18
55000	4714.72	2419.09	1654.58	1272.85	1044.23	892.17	783.85	702.87	640.11	590.11	549.39	515.62
57500	4929.03	2529.05	1729.79	1330.71	1091.70	932.72	819.48	734.81	669.20	616.93	574.36	539.06
60000	5143.33	2639.01	1805.00	1388.57	1139.16	973.27	855.11	766.76	698.30	643.76	599.33	562.49
65000	5571.94	2858.93	1955.42	1504.28	1234.09	1054.38	926.36	830.66	756.49	697.40	649.27	609.37
70000	6000.55	3078.85	2105.83	1619.99	1329.02	1135.49	997.62	894.55	814.68	751.05	699.22	656.24
75000	6429.16	3298.76	2256.25	1735.71	1423.95	1216.59	1068.88	958.45	872.87	804.69	749.16	703.12
80000	6857.77	3518.68	2406.67	1851.42	1518.88	1297.70	1140.14	1022.35	931.07	858.34	799.11	749.99
85000	7286.38	3738.60	2557.08	1967.14	1613.81	1378.80	1211.40	1086.24	989.26	911.98	849.05	796.86
90000	7714.99	3958.51	2707.50	2082.85	1708.74	1459.91	1282.66	1150.14	1047.45	965.63	898.99	843.74
95000	8143.60	4178.43	2857.92	2198.56	1803.67	1541.01	1353.91	1214.04	1105.64	1019.28	948.94	890.61
100000	8572.21	4398.35	3008.33	2314.28	1898.60	1622.12	1425.17	1277.93	1163.83	1072.92	998.88	937.49
105000	9000.82	4618.27	3158.75	2429.99	1993.53	1703.23	1496.43	1341.83	1222.02	1126.57	1048.82	984.36
110000	9429.43	4838.18	3309.16	2545.70	2088.46	1784.33	1567.69	1405.73	1280.21	1180.21	1098.77	1031.23
115000	9858.05	5058.10	3459.58	2661.42	2183.39	1865.44	1638.95	1469.62	1338.40	1233.86	1148.71	1078.11
120000	10286.66	5278.02	3610.00	2777.13	2278.32	1946.54	1710.21	1533.52	1396.60	1287.51	1198.66	1124.98
125000	10715.27	5497.93	3760.41	2892.84	2373.25	2027.65	1781.46	1597.42	1454.79	1341.15	1248.60	1171.86
130000	11143.88	5717.85	3910.83	3008.56	2468.18	2108.75	1852.72	1661.31	1512.98	1394.80	1298.54	1218.73
135000	11572.49	5937.77	4061.25	3124.27	2563.11	2189.86	1923.98	1725.21	1571.17	1448.44	1348.49	1265.61
140000	12001.10	6157.69	4211.66	3239.98	2658.04	2270.97	1995.24	1789.10	1629.36	1502.09	1398.43	1312.48
145000	12429.71	6377.60	4362.08	3355.70	2752.97	2352.07	2066.50	1853.00	1687.55	1555.73	1448.37	1359.35
150000	12858.32	6597.52	4512.50	3471.41	2847.90	2433.18	2137.76	1916.90	1745.74	1609.38	1498.32	1406.23
155000	13286.93	6817.44	4662.91	3587.13	2942.83	2514.28	2209.02	1980.79	1803.93	1663.03	1548.26	1453.10
160000	13715.54	7037.35	4813.33	3702.84	3037.76	2595.39	2280.27	2044.69	1862.13	1716.67	1598.21	1499.98

4

MONTHLY AMORTIZING PAYMENTS 5.25%

AMOUNT OF LOAN	NUMBER OF YEARS IN TERM											
	13	14	15	16	17	18	19	20	25	30	35	40
$ 50	0.45	0.43	0.41	0.39	0.38	0.36	0.35	0.34	0.30	0.28	0.27	0.25
100	0.89	0.85	0.81	0.78	0.75	0.72	0.70	0.68	0.60	0.56	0.53	0.50
200	1.78	1.69	1.61	1.55	1.49	1.44	1.39	1.35	1.20	1.11	1.05	1.00
300	2.66	2.53	2.42	2.32	2.23	2.15	2.09	2.03	1.80	1.66	1.57	1.50
400	3.55	3.37	3.22	3.09	2.97	2.87	2.78	2.70	2.40	2.21	2.09	2.00
500	4.43	4.21	4.02	3.86	3.72	3.59	3.48	3.37	3.00	2.77	2.61	2.50
600	5.32	5.06	4.83	4.63	4.46	4.30	4.17	4.05	3.60	3.32	3.13	3.00
700	6.21	5.90	5.63	5.40	5.20	5.02	4.86	4.72	4.20	3.87	3.65	3.50
800	7.09	6.74	6.44	6.17	5.94	5.74	5.56	5.40	4.80	4.42	4.17	4.00
900	7.98	7.58	7.24	6.94	6.68	6.45	6.25	6.07	5.40	4.97	4.69	4.49
1000	8.86	8.42	8.04	7.71	7.43	7.17	6.95	6.74	6.00	5.53	5.21	4.99
2000	17.72	16.84	16.08	15.42	14.85	14.34	13.89	13.48	11.99	11.05	10.42	9.98
3000	26.58	25.26	24.12	23.13	22.27	21.50	20.83	20.22	17.98	16.57	15.63	14.97
4000	35.44	33.68	32.16	30.84	29.69	28.67	27.77	26.96	23.97	22.09	20.83	19.96
5000	44.30	42.09	40.20	38.55	37.11	35.84	34.71	33.70	29.97	27.62	26.04	24.95
6000	53.15	50.51	48.24	46.26	44.53	43.00	41.65	40.44	35.96	33.14	31.25	29.94
7000	62.01	58.93	56.28	53.97	51.95	50.17	48.59	47.17	41.95	38.66	36.46	34.93
8000	70.87	67.35	64.32	61.68	59.37	57.33	55.53	53.91	47.94	44.18	41.66	39.91
9000	79.73	75.77	72.35	69.39	66.79	64.50	62.47	60.65	53.94	49.70	46.87	44.90
10000	88.59	84.18	80.39	77.10	74.21	71.67	69.41	67.39	59.93	55.23	52.08	49.89
11000	97.44	92.60	88.43	84.81	81.63	78.83	76.35	74.13	65.92	60.75	57.29	54.88
12000	106.30	101.02	96.47	92.52	89.05	86.00	83.29	80.87	71.91	66.27	62.49	59.87
13000	115.16	109.44	104.51	100.23	96.47	93.16	90.23	87.60	77.91	71.79	67.70	64.86
14000	124.02	117.86	112.55	107.93	103.89	100.33	97.17	94.34	83.90	77.31	72.91	69.85
15000	132.88	126.27	120.59	115.64	111.31	107.50	104.11	101.08	89.89	82.84	78.12	74.84
16000	141.74	134.69	128.63	123.35	118.74	114.66	111.05	107.82	95.88	88.36	83.32	79.82
17000	150.59	143.11	136.66	131.06	126.16	121.83	117.99	114.56	101.88	93.88	88.53	84.81
18000	159.45	151.53	144.70	138.77	133.58	128.99	124.93	121.30	107.87	99.40	93.74	89.80
19000	168.31	159.95	152.74	146.48	141.00	136.16	131.87	128.04	113.86	104.92	98.95	94.79
20000	177.17	168.36	160.78	154.19	148.42	143.33	138.81	134.77	119.85	110.45	104.15	99.78
21000	186.03	176.78	168.82	161.90	155.84	150.49	145.75	141.51	125.85	115.97	109.36	104.77
22000	194.88	185.20	176.86	169.61	163.26	157.66	152.69	148.25	131.84	121.49	114.57	109.76
23000	203.74	193.62	184.90	177.32	170.68	164.82	159.63	154.99	137.83	127.01	119.78	114.75
24000	212.60	202.03	192.94	185.03	178.10	171.99	166.57	161.73	143.82	132.53	124.98	119.73
25000	221.46	210.45	200.97	192.74	185.52	179.16	173.51	168.47	149.82	138.06	130.19	124.72
26000	230.32	218.87	209.01	200.45	192.94	186.32	180.45	175.20	155.81	143.58	135.40	129.71
27000	239.18	227.29	217.05	208.16	200.36	193.49	187.39	181.94	161.80	149.10	140.61	134.70
28000	248.03	235.71	225.09	215.86	207.78	200.65	194.33	188.68	167.79	154.62	145.81	139.69
29000	256.89	244.12	233.13	223.57	215.20	207.82	201.27	195.42	173.79	160.14	151.02	144.68
30000	265.75	252.54	241.17	231.28	222.62	214.99	208.21	202.16	179.78	165.67	156.23	149.67
31000	274.61	260.96	249.21	238.99	230.04	222.15	215.15	208.90	185.77	171.19	161.44	154.65
32000	283.47	269.38	257.25	246.70	237.47	229.32	222.09	215.64	191.76	176.71	166.64	159.64
33000	292.32	277.80	265.28	254.41	244.89	236.48	229.03	222.37	197.76	182.23	171.85	164.63
34000	301.18	286.21	273.32	262.12	252.31	243.65	235.97	229.11	203.75	187.76	177.06	169.62
35000	310.04	294.63	281.36	269.83	259.73	250.82	242.91	235.85	209.74	193.28	182.27	174.61
37500	332.19	315.68	301.46	289.10	278.28	268.73	260.26	252.70	224.72	207.08	195.28	187.08
40000	354.33	336.72	321.56	308.38	296.83	286.65	277.61	269.54	239.70	220.89	208.30	199.55
42500	376.48	357.77	341.65	327.65	315.38	304.56	294.96	286.39	254.69	234.69	221.32	212.02
45000	398.62	378.81	361.75	346.92	333.93	322.48	312.31	303.23	269.67	248.50	234.34	224.50
47500	420.77	399.86	381.85	366.20	352.49	340.39	329.66	320.08	284.65	262.30	247.36	236.97
50000	442.91	420.90	401.94	385.47	371.04	358.31	347.01	336.93	299.63	276.11	260.38	249.44
52500	465.06	441.95	422.04	404.74	389.59	376.22	364.36	353.77	314.61	289.91	273.40	261.91
55000	487.20	462.99	442.14	424.02	408.14	394.14	381.71	370.62	329.59	303.72	286.41	274.38
57500	509.35	484.03	462.23	443.29	426.69	412.05	399.06	387.47	344.57	317.52	299.43	286.86
60000	531.49	505.08	482.33	462.56	445.24	429.97	416.41	404.31	359.55	331.33	312.45	299.33
65000	575.79	547.17	522.53	501.11	482.35	465.80	451.11	438.00	389.52	358.94	338.49	324.27
70000	620.08	589.26	562.72	539.65	519.45	501.63	485.81	471.70	419.48	386.55	364.53	349.21
75000	664.37	631.35	602.91	578.20	556.55	537.46	520.51	505.39	449.44	414.16	390.56	374.16
80000	708.66	673.44	643.11	616.75	593.66	573.29	555.21	539.08	479.40	441.77	416.60	399.10
85000	752.95	715.53	683.30	655.29	630.76	609.12	589.91	572.77	509.37	469.38	442.64	424.04
90000	797.24	757.62	723.49	693.84	667.86	644.95	624.61	606.46	539.33	496.99	468.67	448.99
95000	841.53	799.71	763.69	732.39	704.97	680.78	659.31	640.16	569.29	524.60	494.71	473.93
100000	885.82	841.80	803.88	770.93	742.07	716.61	694.00	673.85	599.25	552.21	520.75	498.88
105000	930.11	883.89	844.08	809.48	779.17	752.44	728.71	707.54	629.22	579.82	546.79	523.82
110000	974.40	925.98	884.27	848.03	816.28	788.27	763.41	741.23	659.18	607.43	572.82	548.76
115000	1018.69	968.06	924.46	886.57	853.38	824.10	798.11	774.93	689.14	635.04	598.86	573.71
120000	1062.98	1010.15	964.66	925.12	890.48	859.93	832.81	808.62	719.10	662.65	624.90	598.65
125000	1107.27	1052.24	1004.85	963.67	927.59	895.76	867.51	842.31	749.06	690.26	650.93	623.59
130000	1151.57	1094.33	1045.05	1002.21	964.69	931.59	902.22	876.00	779.03	717.87	676.97	648.54
135000	1195.86	1136.42	1085.24	1040.76	1001.79	967.42	936.92	909.69	808.99	745.48	703.01	673.48
140000	1240.15	1178.51	1125.43	1079.30	1038.90	1003.25	971.62	943.39	838.95	773.09	729.05	698.42
145000	1284.44	1220.60	1165.63	1117.85	1076.00	1039.08	1006.32	977.08	868.91	800.70	755.08	723.37
150000	1328.73	1262.69	1205.82	1156.40	1113.10	1074.91	1041.02	1010.77	898.88	828.31	781.12	748.31
155000	1373.02	1304.78	1246.02	1194.94	1150.20	1110.74	1075.72	1044.46	928.84	855.92	807.16	773.25
160000	1417.31	1346.87	1286.21	1233.49	1187.31	1146.57	1110.42	1078.16	958.80	883.53	833.19	798.20

5

5.50% MONTHLY AMORTIZING PAYMENTS

AMOUNT OF LOAN	NUMBER OF YEARS IN TERM											
	1	2	3	4	5	6	7	8	9	10	11	12
$ 50	4.30	2.21	1.51	1.17	0.96	0.82	0.72	0.65	0.59	0.55	0.51	0.48
100	8.59	4.41	3.02	2.33	1.92	1.64	1.44	1.29	1.18	1.09	1.02	0.96
200	17.17	8.82	6.04	4.66	3.83	3.27	2.88	2.58	2.36	2.18	2.03	1.91
300	25.76	13.23	9.06	6.98	5.74	4.91	4.32	3.87	3.53	3.26	3.04	2.86
400	34.34	17.64	12.08	9.31	7.65	6.54	5.75	5.16	4.71	4.35	4.05	3.81
500	42.92	22.05	15.10	11.63	9.56	8.17	7.19	6.45	5.88	5.43	5.06	4.76
600	51.51	26.46	18.12	13.96	11.47	9.81	8.63	7.74	7.06	6.52	6.07	5.71
700	60.09	30.87	21.14	16.28	13.38	11.44	10.06	9.03	8.24	7.60	7.08	6.66
800	68.67	35.28	24.16	18.61	15.29	13.08	11.50	10.32	9.41	8.69	8.10	7.61
900	77.26	39.69	27.18	20.94	17.20	14.71	12.94	11.61	10.59	9.77	9.11	8.56
1000	85.84	44.10	30.20	23.26	19.11	16.34	14.38	12.90	11.76	10.86	10.12	9.51
2000	171.68	88.20	60.40	46.52	38.21	32.68	28.75	25.80	23.52	21.71	20.23	19.01
3000	257.52	132.29	90.59	69.77	57.31	49.02	43.12	38.70	35.28	32.56	30.35	28.51
4000	343.35	176.39	120.79	93.03	76.41	65.36	57.49	51.60	47.04	43.42	40.46	38.01
5000	429.19	220.48	150.98	116.29	95.51	81.69	71.86	64.50	58.80	54.27	50.57	47.51
6000	515.03	264.58	181.18	139.54	114.61	98.03	86.23	77.40	70.56	65.12	60.69	57.02
7000	600.86	308.67	211.38	162.80	133.71	114.37	100.60	90.30	82.32	75.97	70.80	66.52
8000	686.70	352.77	241.57	186.06	152.81	130.71	114.97	103.20	94.08	86.83	80.92	76.02
9000	772.54	396.87	271.77	209.31	171.92	147.05	129.34	116.10	105.84	97.68	91.03	85.52
10000	858.37	440.96	301.96	232.57	191.02	163.38	143.71	129.00	117.60	108.53	101.14	95.02
11000	944.21	485.06	332.16	255.83	210.12	179.72	158.08	141.90	129.36	119.38	111.26	104.52
12000	1030.05	529.15	362.36	279.08	229.22	196.06	172.45	154.80	141.12	130.24	121.37	114.03
13000	1115.88	573.25	392.55	302.34	248.32	212.40	186.82	167.70	152.88	141.09	131.49	123.53
14000	1201.72	617.34	422.75	325.60	267.42	228.74	201.19	180.60	164.64	151.94	141.60	133.03
15000	1287.56	661.44	452.94	348.85	286.52	245.07	215.56	193.49	176.40	162.79	151.71	142.53
16000	1373.39	705.54	483.14	372.11	305.62	261.41	229.93	206.39	188.16	173.65	161.83	152.03
17000	1459.23	749.63	513.34	395.37	324.72	277.75	244.30	219.29	199.92	184.50	171.94	161.53
18000	1545.07	793.73	543.53	418.62	343.83	294.09	258.67	232.19	211.68	195.35	182.06	171.04
19000	1630.90	837.82	573.73	441.88	362.93	310.42	273.04	245.09	223.44	206.20	192.17	180.54
20000	1716.74	881.92	603.92	465.13	382.03	326.76	287.41	257.99	235.20	217.06	202.28	190.04
21000	1802.58	926.01	634.12	488.39	401.13	343.10	301.78	270.89	246.96	227.91	212.40	199.54
22000	1888.41	970.11	664.31	511.65	420.23	359.44	316.15	283.79	258.72	238.76	222.51	209.04
23000	1974.25	1014.21	694.51	534.90	439.33	375.78	330.52	296.69	270.48	249.62	232.63	218.54
24000	2060.09	1058.30	724.71	558.16	458.43	392.11	344.89	309.59	282.24	260.47	242.74	228.05
25000	2145.92	1102.40	754.90	581.42	477.53	408.45	359.26	322.49	294.00	271.32	252.85	237.55
26000	2231.76	1146.49	785.10	604.67	496.64	424.79	373.63	335.39	305.76	282.17	262.97	247.05
27000	2317.60	1190.59	815.29	627.93	515.74	441.13	388.00	348.29	317.52	293.03	273.08	256.55
28000	2403.43	1234.68	845.49	651.19	534.84	457.47	402.37	361.19	329.28	303.88	283.20	266.05
29000	2489.27	1278.78	875.69	674.44	553.94	473.80	416.74	374.09	341.04	314.73	293.31	275.55
30000	2575.11	1322.87	905.88	697.70	573.04	490.14	431.11	386.98	352.80	325.58	303.42	285.06
31000	2660.95	1366.97	936.08	720.96	592.14	506.48	445.48	399.88	364.56	336.44	313.54	294.06
32000	2746.78	1411.07	966.27	744.21	611.24	522.82	459.85	412.78	376.32	347.29	323.65	304.06
33000	2832.62	1455.16	996.47	767.47	630.34	539.16	474.22	425.68	388.08	358.14	333.76	313.56
34000	2918.46	1499.26	1026.67	790.73	649.44	555.49	488.59	438.58	399.84	368.99	343.88	323.06
35000	3004.29	1543.35	1056.86	813.98	668.55	571.83	502.96	451.48	411.60	379.85	353.99	332.57
37500	3218.88	1653.59	1132.35	872.12	716.30	612.68	538.88	483.73	441.00	406.98	379.28	356.32
40000	3433.48	1763.83	1207.84	930.26	764.05	653.52	574.81	515.98	470.40	434.11	404.56	380.07
42500	3648.07	1874.07	1283.33	988.41	811.80	694.37	610.73	548.23	499.80	461.24	429.85	403.83
45000	3862.66	1984.31	1358.82	1046.55	859.56	735.21	646.66	580.47	529.20	488.37	455.13	427.58
47500	4077.25	2094.55	1434.31	1104.69	907.31	776.05	682.58	612.72	558.60	515.50	480.42	451.34
50000	4291.84	2204.79	1509.80	1162.83	955.06	816.90	718.51	644.97	588.00	542.64	505.70	475.09
52500	4506.44	2315.03	1585.29	1220.97	1002.82	857.74	754.43	677.22	617.40	569.77	530.99	498.85
55000	4721.03	2425.27	1660.78	1279.11	1050.57	898.59	790.36	709.47	646.80	596.90	556.27	522.60
57500	4935.62	2535.51	1736.27	1337.25	1098.32	939.43	826.28	741.72	676.20	624.03	581.56	546.35
60000	5150.21	2645.74	1811.76	1395.39	1146.07	980.28	862.21	773.96	705.60	651.16	606.84	570.11
65000	5579.40	2866.22	1962.74	1511.68	1241.58	1061.97	934.06	838.46	764.40	705.43	657.41	617.62
70000	6008.58	3086.70	2113.72	1627.96	1337.09	1143.66	1005.91	902.96	823.20	759.69	707.98	665.13
75000	6437.76	3307.18	2264.70	1744.24	1432.59	1225.35	1077.76	967.45	882.00	813.95	758.55	712.63
80000	6866.95	3527.66	2415.68	1860.52	1528.10	1307.04	1149.61	1031.95	940.80	868.22	809.12	760.14
85000	7296.13	3748.14	2566.66	1976.81	1623.60	1388.73	1221.46	1096.45	999.60	922.48	859.69	807.65
90000	7725.32	3968.61	2717.64	2093.09	1719.11	1470.41	1293.31	1160.94	1058.40	976.74	910.26	855.16
95000	8154.50	4189.09	2868.62	2209.37	1814.62	1552.10	1365.16	1225.44	1117.20	1031.00	960.83	902.67
100000	8583.68	4409.57	3019.60	2325.65	1910.12	1633.79	1437.01	1289.94	1176.00	1085.27	1011.40	950.18
105000	9012.87	4630.05	3170.57	2441.93	2005.63	1715.48	1508.86	1354.43	1234.80	1139.53	1061.97	997.69
110000	9442.05	4850.53	3321.55	2558.22	2101.13	1797.17	1580.71	1418.93	1293.60	1193.79	1112.54	1045.19
115000	9871.24	5071.01	3472.53	2674.50	2196.64	1878.86	1652.56	1483.43	1352.40	1248.06	1163.11	1092.70
120000	10300.42	5291.48	3623.51	2790.78	2292.14	1960.55	1724.41	1547.92	1411.20	1302.32	1213.68	1140.21
125000	10729.60	5511.96	3774.49	2907.06	2387.65	2042.24	1796.26	1612.42	1470.00	1356.58	1264.25	1187.72
130000	11158.79	5732.44	3925.47	3023.35	2483.16	2123.93	1868.11	1676.92	1528.80	1410.85	1314.82	1235.23
135000	11587.97	5952.92	4076.45	3139.63	2578.66	2205.62	1939.96	1741.41	1587.60	1465.11	1365.39	1282.74
140000	12017.15	6173.40	4227.43	3255.91	2674.17	2287.31	2011.81	1805.91	1646.40	1519.37	1415.96	1330.25
145000	12446.34	6393.88	4378.41	3372.19	2769.67	2369.00	2083.66	1870.41	1705.20	1573.64	1466.53	1377.75
150000	12875.52	6614.35	4529.39	3488.48	2865.18	2450.69	2155.51	1934.90	1764.00	1627.90	1517.09	1425.26
155000	13304.71	6834.83	4680.37	3604.76	2960.69	2532.38	2227.36	1999.40	1822.80	1682.16	1567.66	1472.77
160000	13733.89	7055.31	4831.35	3721.04	3056.19	2614.07	2299.21	2063.90	1881.60	1736.43	1618.23	1520.28

AMOUNT OF LOAN	NUMBER OF YEARS IN TERM											
	13	14	15	16	17	18	19	20	25	30	35	40
$ 50	0.45	0.43	0.41	0.40	0.38	0.37	0.36	0.35	0.31	0.29	0.27	0.26
100	0.90	0.86	0.82	0.79	0.76	0.74	0.71	0.69	0.62	0.57	0.54	0.52
200	1.80	1.71	1.64	1.57	1.52	1.47	1.42	1.38	1.23	1.14	1.08	1.04
300	2.70	2.57	2.46	2.36	2.27	2.20	2.13	2.07	1.85	1.71	1.62	1.55
400	3.60	3.42	3.27	3.14	3.03	2.93	2.84	2.76	2.46	2.28	2.15	2.07
500	4.50	4.28	4.09	3.93	3.78	3.66	3.54	3.44	3.08	2.84	2.69	2.58
600	5.40	5.13	4.91	4.71	4.54	4.39	4.25	4.13	3.69	3.41	3.23	3.10
700	6.30	5.99	5.72	5.50	5.29	5.12	4.96	4.82	4.30	3.98	3.76	3.62
800	7.19	6.84	6.54	6.28	6.05	5.85	5.67	5.51	4.92	4.55	4.30	4.13
900	8.09	7.70	7.36	7.06	6.81	6.58	6.38	6.20	5.53	5.12	4.84	4.65
1000	8.99	8.55	8.18	7.85	7.56	7.31	7.08	6.88	6.15	5.68	5.38	5.16
2000	17.98	17.10	16.35	15.69	15.12	14.61	14.16	13.76	12.29	11.36	10.75	10.32
3000	26.97	25.65	24.52	23.53	22.67	21.91	21.24	20.64	18.43	17.04	16.12	15.48
4000	35.95	34.20	32.69	31.38	30.23	29.22	28.32	27.52	24.57	22.72	21.49	20.64
5000	44.94	42.75	40.86	39.22	37.79	36.52	35.40	34.40	30.71	28.39	26.86	25.79
6000	53.93	51.29	49.03	47.06	45.34	43.82	42.48	41.28	36.85	34.07	32.23	30.95
7000	62.91	59.84	57.20	54.91	52.90	51.13	49.56	48.16	42.99	39.75	37.60	36.11
8000	71.90	68.39	65.37	62.75	60.45	58.43	56.64	55.04	49.13	45.43	42.97	41.27
9000	80.89	76.94	73.54	70.59	68.01	65.73	63.71	61.91	55.27	51.11	48.34	46.42
10000	89.87	85.49	81.71	78.44	75.57	73.04	70.79	68.79	61.41	56.78	53.71	51.58
11000	98.86	94.04	89.88	86.28	83.12	80.34	77.87	75.67	67.55	62.46	59.08	56.74
12000	107.85	102.58	98.06	94.12	90.68	87.64	84.95	82.55	73.70	68.14	64.45	61.90
13000	116.83	111.13	106.23	101.96	98.23	94.95	92.03	89.43	79.84	73.82	69.82	67.06
14000	125.82	119.68	114.40	109.81	105.79	102.25	99.11	96.31	85.98	79.50	75.19	72.21
15000	134.81	128.23	122.57	117.65	113.35	109.55	106.19	103.19	92.12	85.17	80.56	77.37
16000	143.79	136.78	130.74	125.49	120.90	116.86	113.27	110.07	98.26	90.85	85.93	82.53
17000	152.78	145.33	138.91	133.34	128.46	124.16	120.35	116.95	104.40	96.53	91.30	87.69
18000	161.77	153.87	147.08	141.18	136.01	131.46	127.42	123.82	110.54	102.21	96.67	92.84
19000	170.75	162.42	155.25	149.02	143.57	138.77	134.50	130.70	116.68	107.88	102.04	98.00
20000	179.74	170.97	163.42	156.87	151.13	146.07	141.58	137.58	122.82	113.56	107.41	103.16
21000	188.73	179.52	171.59	164.71	158.68	153.37	148.66	144.46	128.96	119.24	112.78	108.32
22000	197.71	188.07	179.76	172.55	166.24	160.67	155.74	151.34	135.10	124.92	118.15	113.47
23000	206.70	196.61	187.93	180.39	173.80	167.98	162.82	158.22	141.25	130.60	123.52	118.63
24000	215.69	205.16	196.11	188.24	181.35	175.28	169.90	165.10	147.39	136.27	128.89	123.79
25000	224.67	213.71	204.28	196.08	188.91	182.58	176.98	171.98	153.53	141.95	134.26	128.95
26000	233.66	222.26	212.45	203.92	196.46	189.89	184.06	178.86	159.67	147.63	139.63	134.11
27000	242.65	230.81	220.62	211.77	204.02	197.19	191.13	185.73	165.81	153.31	145.00	139.26
28000	251.63	239.36	228.79	219.61	211.58	204.49	198.21	192.61	171.96	158.99	150.37	144.42
29000	260.62	247.90	236.96	227.45	219.13	211.80	205.29	199.49	178.09	164.66	155.74	149.58
30000	269.61	256.45	245.13	235.30	226.69	219.10	212.37	206.37	184.23	170.34	161.11	154.74
31000	278.60	265.00	253.30	243.14	234.24	226.40	219.45	213.25	190.37	176.02	166.48	159.89
32000	287.58	273.55	261.47	250.98	241.80	233.71	226.53	220.13	196.51	181.70	171.85	165.05
33000	296.57	282.10	269.64	258.83	249.36	241.01	233.61	227.01	202.65	187.38	177.22	170.21
34000	305.56	290.65	277.81	266.67	256.91	248.31	240.69	233.89	208.79	193.05	182.59	175.37
35000	314.54	299.19	285.98	274.51	264.47	255.62	247.77	240.77	214.94	198.73	187.96	180.52
37500	337.01	320.56	306.41	294.12	283.36	273.87	265.46	257.96	230.29	212.93	201.39	193.42
40000	359.48	341.94	326.84	313.73	302.25	292.13	283.16	275.16	245.64	227.12	214.81	206.31
42500	381.94	363.31	347.27	333.33	321.14	310.39	300.86	292.36	260.99	241.32	228.24	219.21
45000	404.41	384.68	367.69	352.94	340.03	328.65	318.55	309.55	276.34	255.51	241.66	232.10
47500	426.88	406.05	388.12	372.55	358.92	346.91	336.25	326.75	291.70	269.70	255.09	245.00
50000	449.34	427.42	408.55	392.16	377.81	365.16	353.95	343.95	307.05	283.90	268.51	257.89
52500	471.81	448.79	428.97	411.76	396.70	383.42	371.65	361.15	322.40	298.09	281.94	270.78
55000	494.28	470.16	449.40	431.37	415.59	401.68	389.34	378.34	337.75	312.29	295.36	283.68
57500	516.75	491.53	469.83	450.98	434.48	419.94	407.04	395.54	353.11	326.48	308.79	296.57
60000	539.21	512.90	490.26	470.59	453.37	438.19	424.74	412.74	368.46	340.68	322.21	309.47
65000	584.15	555.64	531.11	509.80	491.15	474.71	460.13	447.13	399.16	369.07	349.07	335.26
70000	629.08	598.38	571.96	549.02	528.93	511.23	495.53	481.53	429.87	397.46	375.92	361.04
75000	674.01	641.12	612.82	588.23	566.71	547.74	530.92	515.92	460.57	425.85	402.77	386.83
80000	718.95	683.87	653.67	627.45	604.49	584.26	566.31	550.31	491.27	454.24	429.62	412.62
85000	763.88	726.61	694.53	666.66	642.27	620.77	601.71	584.71	521.98	482.63	456.47	438.41
90000	808.82	769.35	735.38	705.88	680.05	657.29	637.10	619.10	552.68	511.02	483.32	464.20
95000	853.75	812.09	776.23	745.09	717.83	693.81	672.50	653.50	583.39	539.40	510.17	489.99
100000	898.68	854.83	817.09	784.31	755.61	730.32	707.89	687.89	614.09	567.79	537.02	515.78
105000	943.62	897.57	857.94	823.52	793.39	766.84	743.29	722.29	644.80	596.18	563.87	541.57
110000	988.55	940.31	898.80	862.74	831.18	803.35	778.68	756.68	675.50	624.57	590.72	567.35
115000	1033.49	983.05	939.65	901.95	868.96	839.87	814.07	791.08	706.21	652.96	617.57	593.14
120000	1078.42	1025.80	980.51	941.17	906.74	876.38	849.47	825.47	736.91	681.35	644.42	618.93
125000	1123.35	1068.54	1021.36	980.38	944.52	912.90	884.86	859.86	767.61	709.74	671.28	644.72
130000	1168.29	1111.28	1062.21	1019.60	982.30	949.42	920.26	894.26	798.32	738.13	698.13	670.51
135000	1213.22	1154.02	1103.07	1058.82	1020.08	985.93	955.65	928.65	829.02	766.52	724.98	696.29
140000	1258.15	1196.76	1143.92	1098.03	1057.86	1022.45	991.05	963.05	859.73	794.91	751.83	722.08
145000	1303.09	1239.50	1184.78	1137.25	1095.64	1058.96	1026.44	997.44	890.43	823.30	778.68	747.87
150000	1348.02	1282.24	1225.63	1176.46	1133.42	1095.48	1061.83	1031.84	921.14	851.69	805.53	773.66
155000	1392.96	1324.98	1266.48	1215.68	1171.20	1132.00	1097.23	1066.23	951.84	880.08	832.38	799.45
160000	1437.89	1367.73	1307.34	1254.89	1208.98	1168.51	1132.62	1100.62	982.54	908.47	859.23	825.24

MONTHLY AMORTIZING PAYMENTS

AMOUNT OF LOAN	NUMBER OF YEARS IN TERM											
	1	2	3	4	5	6	7	8	9	10	11	12
$ 50	4.30	2.22	1.52	1.17	0.97	0.83	0.73	0.66	0.60	0.55	0.52	0.49
100	8.60	4.43	3.04	2.34	1.93	1.65	1.45	1.31	1.19	1.10	1.03	0.97
200	17.20	8.85	6.07	4.68	3.85	3.30	2.90	2.61	2.38	2.20	2.05	1.93
300	25.79	13.27	9.10	7.02	5.77	4.94	4.35	3.91	3.57	3.30	3.08	2.89
400	34.39	17.69	12.13	9.35	7.69	6.59	5.80	5.21	4.76	4.40	4.10	3.86
500	42.98	22.11	15.16	11.69	9.61	8.23	7.25	6.52	5.95	5.49	5.13	4.82
600	51.58	26.53	18.19	14.03	11.54	9.88	8.70	7.82	7.13	6.59	6.15	5.78
700	60.17	30.95	21.22	16.36	13.46	11.52	10.15	9.12	8.32	7.69	7.17	6.75
800	68.77	35.37	24.25	18.70	15.38	13.17	11.60	10.42	9.51	8.79	8.20	7.71
900	77.36	39.79	27.28	21.04	17.30	14.81	13.05	11.72	10.70	9.88	9.22	8.67
1000	85.96	44.21	30.31	23.38	19.22	16.46	14.49	13.03	11.89	10.98	10.25	9.63
2000	171.91	88.42	60.62	46.75	38.44	32.92	28.98	26.05	23.77	21.96	20.49	19.26
3000	257.86	132.63	90.93	70.12	57.66	49.37	43.47	39.07	35.65	32.94	30.73	28.89
4000	343.81	176.84	121.24	93.49	76.87	65.83	57.96	52.09	47.53	43.91	40.97	38.52
5000	429.76	221.05	151.55	116.86	96.09	82.28	72.45	65.11	59.42	54.89	51.21	48.15
6000	515.71	265.25	181.86	140.23	115.31	98.74	86.94	78.13	71.30	65.87	61.45	57.78
7000	601.67	309.46	212.17	163.60	134.52	115.19	101.43	91.15	83.18	76.84	71.69	67.41
8000	687.62	353.67	242.48	186.97	153.74	131.65	115.92	104.17	95.06	87.82	81.93	77.04
9000	773.57	397.88	272.78	210.34	172.96	148.10	130.41	117.19	106.95	98.80	92.17	86.67
10000	859.52	442.09	303.09	233.71	192.17	164.56	144.90	130.21	118.83	109.77	102.41	96.30
11000	945.47	486.29	333.40	257.08	211.39	181.01	159.38	143.23	130.71	120.75	112.65	105.93
12000	1031.42	530.50	363.71	280.45	230.61	197.47	173.87	156.25	142.59	131.73	122.89	115.56
13000	1117.38	574.71	394.02	303.82	249.82	213.92	188.36	169.27	154.48	142.70	133.13	125.19
14000	1203.33	618.92	424.33	327.19	269.04	230.38	202.85	182.29	166.36	153.68	143.37	134.82
15000	1289.28	663.13	454.64	350.56	288.26	246.83	217.34	195.31	178.24	164.66	153.61	144.45
16000	1375.23	707.33	484.95	373.93	307.47	263.29	231.83	208.33	190.12	175.64	163.85	154.08
17000	1461.18	751.54	515.25	397.30	326.69	279.74	246.32	221.35	202.01	186.61	174.09	163.71
18000	1547.13	795.75	545.56	420.68	345.91	296.20	260.81	234.37	213.89	197.59	184.33	173.34
19000	1633.08	839.96	575.87	444.05	365.12	312.65	275.30	247.39	225.77	208.57	194.57	182.97
20000	1719.04	884.17	606.18	467.42	384.34	329.11	289.79	260.41	237.65	219.54	204.81	192.60
21000	1804.99	928.37	636.49	490.79	403.56	345.56	304.27	273.43	249.54	230.52	215.05	202.23
22000	1890.94	972.58	666.80	514.16	422.77	362.02	318.76	286.45	261.42	241.50	225.29	211.86
23000	1976.89	1016.79	697.11	537.53	441.99	378.47	333.25	299.47	273.30	252.47	235.53	221.49
24000	2062.84	1061.00	727.42	560.90	461.21	394.93	347.74	312.49	285.18	263.45	245.77	231.12
25000	2148.79	1105.21	757.72	584.27	480.42	411.38	362.23	325.51	297.07	274.43	256.01	240.75
26000	2234.75	1149.41	788.03	607.64	499.64	427.84	376.72	338.53	308.95	285.40	266.25	250.38
27000	2320.70	1193.62	818.34	631.01	518.86	444.29	391.21	351.55	320.83	296.38	276.49	260.00
28000	2406.65	1237.83	848.65	654.38	538.07	460.75	405.70	364.57	332.71	307.36	286.73	269.63
29000	2492.60	1282.04	878.96	677.75	557.29	477.20	420.19	377.59	344.60	318.34	296.97	279.26
30000	2578.55	1326.25	909.27	701.12	576.51	493.66	434.68	390.61	356.48	329.31	307.21	288.89
31000	2664.50	1370.45	939.58	724.49	595.72	510.11	449.16	403.63	368.36	340.29	317.45	298.52
32000	2750.46	1414.66	969.89	747.86	614.94	526.57	463.65	416.65	380.24	351.27	327.69	308.15
33000	2836.41	1458.87	1000.20	771.23	634.16	543.02	478.14	429.67	392.13	362.24	337.93	317.78
34000	2922.36	1503.08	1030.50	794.60	653.38	559.48	492.63	442.69	404.01	373.22	348.17	327.41
35000	3008.31	1547.29	1060.81	817.98	672.59	575.93	507.12	455.71	415.89	384.20	358.41	337.04
37500	3223.19	1657.81	1136.58	876.40	720.63	617.07	543.34	488.26	445.60	411.64	384.01	361.12
40000	3438.07	1768.33	1212.36	934.83	768.68	658.21	579.57	520.81	475.30	439.08	409.61	385.19
42500	3652.95	1878.85	1288.13	993.25	816.72	699.35	615.79	553.36	505.01	466.52	435.21	409.26
45000	3867.83	1989.37	1363.90	1051.68	864.76	740.49	652.01	585.91	534.72	493.97	460.81	433.34
47500	4082.70	2099.89	1439.67	1110.11	912.80	781.62	688.23	618.46	564.42	521.41	486.41	457.41
50000	4297.58	2210.41	1515.44	1168.53	960.84	822.76	724.46	651.01	594.13	548.85	512.01	481.49
52500	4512.46	2320.93	1591.22	1226.96	1008.89	863.90	760.68	683.56	623.84	576.29	537.61	505.56
55000	4727.34	2431.45	1666.99	1285.39	1056.93	905.04	796.90	716.11	653.54	603.74	563.21	529.63
57500	4942.22	2541.97	1742.76	1343.81	1104.97	946.18	833.12	748.66	683.25	631.18	588.81	553.71
60000	5157.10	2652.49	1818.53	1402.24	1153.01	987.31	869.35	781.21	712.95	658.62	614.41	577.78
65000	5586.86	2873.53	1970.08	1519.09	1249.09	1069.59	941.79	846.31	772.37	713.50	665.61	625.93
70000	6016.61	3094.57	2121.62	1635.95	1345.18	1151.86	1014.24	911.41	831.78	768.39	716.81	674.08
75000	6446.37	3315.61	2273.16	1752.80	1441.26	1234.14	1086.68	976.51	891.19	823.27	768.01	722.23
80000	6876.13	3536.65	2424.71	1869.65	1537.35	1316.42	1159.13	1041.61	950.60	878.16	819.21	770.37
85000	7305.89	3757.69	2576.25	1986.50	1633.43	1398.69	1231.51	1106.71	1010.02	933.04	870.41	818.52
90000	7735.65	3978.73	2727.80	2103.36	1729.51	1480.97	1304.02	1171.81	1069.43	987.93	921.61	866.67
95000	8165.40	4199.77	2879.34	2220.21	1825.60	1563.24	1376.46	1236.91	1128.84	1042.81	972.81	914.82
100000	8595.16	4420.81	3030.88	2337.06	1921.68	1645.52	1448.91	1302.01	1188.25	1097.70	1024.01	962.97
105000	9024.92	4641.85	3182.43	2453.92	2017.77	1727.79	1521.35	1367.11	1247.67	1152.58	1075.21	1011.11
110000	9454.68	4862.89	3333.97	2570.77	2113.85	1810.07	1593.80	1432.21	1307.08	1207.47	1126.41	1059.26
115000	9884.43	5083.93	3485.52	2687.62	2209.93	1892.35	1666.24	1497.31	1366.49	1262.35	1177.61	1107.41
120000	10314.19	5304.97	3637.06	2804.47	2306.02	1974.62	1738.69	1562.41	1425.90	1317.24	1228.81	1155.56
125000	10743.95	5526.01	3788.60	2921.33	2402.10	2056.90	1811.13	1627.51	1485.32	1372.12	1280.01	1203.71
130000	11173.71	5747.05	3940.15	3038.18	2498.18	2139.17	1883.58	1692.61	1544.73	1427.00	1331.21	1251.86
135000	11603.47	5968.09	4091.69	3155.03	2594.27	2221.45	1956.02	1757.71	1604.14	1481.89	1382.41	1300.00
140000	12033.22	6189.13	4243.24	3271.89	2690.35	2303.72	2028.47	1822.81	1663.55	1536.77	1433.61	1348.15
145000	12462.98	6410.17	4394.78	3388.74	2786.44	2386.00	2100.91	1887.91	1722.97	1591.66	1484.81	1396.30
150000	12892.74	6631.21	4546.32	3505.59	2882.52	2468.27	2173.36	1953.01	1782.38	1646.54	1536.01	1444.45
155000	13322.50	6852.25	4697.87	3622.45	2978.60	2550.55	2245.80	2018.11	1841.79	1701.43	1587.21	1492.60
160000	13752.26	7073.29	4849.41	3739.30	3074.69	2632.83	2318.25	2083.21	1901.20	1756.31	1638.41	1540.74

MONTHLY AMORTIZING PAYMENTS 5.75%

AMOUNT OF LOAN	NUMBER OF YEARS IN TERM											
	13	14	15	16	17	18	19	20	25	30	35	40
$ 50	0.46	0.44	0.42	0.40	0.39	0.38	0.37	0.36	0.32	0.30	0.28	0.27
100	0.92	0.87	0.84	0.80	0.77	0.75	0.73	0.71	0.63	0.59	0.56	0.54
200	1.83	1.74	1.67	1.60	1.54	1.49	1.45	1.41	1.26	1.17	1.11	1.07
300	2.74	2.61	2.50	2.40	2.31	2.24	2.17	2.11	1.89	1.76	1.67	1.60
400	3.65	3.48	3.33	3.20	3.08	2.98	2.89	2.81	2.52	2.34	2.22	2.14
500	4.56	4.34	4.16	3.99	3.85	3.73	3.61	3.52	3.15	2.92	2.77	2.67
600	5.47	5.21	4.99	4.79	4.62	4.47	4.34	4.22	3.78	3.51	3.33	3.20
700	6.39	6.08	5.82	5.59	5.39	5.21	5.06	4.92	4.41	4.09	3.88	3.74
800	7.30	6.95	6.65	6.39	6.16	5.96	5.78	5.62	5.04	4.67	4.43	4.27
900	8.21	7.82	7.48	7.19	6.93	6.70	6.50	6.32	5.67	5.26	4.99	4.80
1000	9.12	8.68	8.31	7.98	7.70	7.45	7.22	7.03	6.30	5.84	5.54	5.33
2000	18.24	17.36	16.61	15.96	15.39	14.89	14.44	14.05	12.59	11.68	11.08	10.66
3000	27.35	26.04	24.92	23.94	23.08	22.33	21.66	21.07	18.88	17.51	16.61	15.99
4000	36.47	34.72	33.22	31.92	30.78	29.77	28.88	28.09	25.17	23.35	22.15	21.32
5000	45.59	43.40	41.53	39.90	38.47	37.21	36.10	35.11	31.46	29.18	27.68	26.65
6000	54.70	52.08	49.83	47.87	46.16	44.66	43.32	42.13	37.75	35.02	33.22	31.98
7000	63.82	60.76	58.13	55.85	53.86	52.10	50.54	49.15	44.04	40.86	38.75	37.31
8000	72.94	69.44	66.44	63.83	61.55	59.54	57.76	56.17	50.33	46.69	44.29	42.64
9000	82.05	78.12	74.74	71.81	69.24	66.98	64.98	63.19	56.62	52.53	49.82	47.96
10000	91.17	86.80	83.05	79.79	76.93	74.42	72.20	70.21	62.92	58.36	55.36	53.29
11000	100.29	95.48	91.35	87.76	84.63	81.86	79.42	77.23	69.21	64.20	60.89	58.62
12000	109.40	104.16	99.65	95.74	92.32	89.31	86.63	84.26	75.50	70.03	66.43	63.95
13000	118.52	112.84	107.96	103.72	100.01	96.75	93.85	91.28	81.79	75.87	71.96	69.28
14000	127.64	121.52	116.26	111.70	107.71	104.19	101.07	98.30	88.08	81.71	77.50	74.61
15000	136.75	130.20	124.57	119.68	115.40	111.63	108.29	105.32	94.37	87.54	83.03	79.94
16000	145.87	138.88	132.87	127.65	123.09	119.07	115.51	112.34	100.66	93.38	88.57	85.27
17000	154.99	147.56	141.17	135.63	130.78	126.51	122.73	119.36	106.95	99.21	94.10	90.60
18000	164.10	156.24	149.48	143.61	138.48	133.96	129.95	126.38	113.24	105.05	99.64	95.92
19000	173.22	164.92	157.78	151.59	146.17	141.40	137.17	133.40	119.54	110.88	105.17	101.25
20000	182.33	173.60	166.09	159.57	153.86	148.84	144.39	140.42	125.83	116.72	110.71	106.58
21000	191.45	182.28	174.39	167.54	161.56	156.28	151.61	147.44	132.12	122.56	116.24	111.91
22000	200.57	190.96	182.70	175.52	169.25	163.72	158.83	154.46	138.41	128.39	121.78	117.24
23000	209.68	199.64	191.00	183.50	176.94	171.16	166.04	161.48	144.70	134.23	127.31	122.57
24000	218.80	208.32	199.30	191.48	184.63	178.61	173.26	168.51	150.99	140.06	132.85	127.90
25000	227.92	217.00	207.61	199.46	192.33	186.05	180.48	175.53	157.28	145.90	138.38	133.23
26000	237.03	225.68	215.91	207.43	200.02	193.49	187.70	182.55	163.57	151.73	143.92	138.56
27000	246.15	234.36	224.22	215.41	207.71	200.93	194.92	189.57	169.86	157.57	149.45	143.88
28000	255.27	243.04	232.52	223.39	215.41	208.37	202.14	196.59	176.15	163.41	154.99	149.21
29000	264.38	251.72	240.82	231.37	223.10	215.81	209.36	203.61	182.45	169.24	160.52	154.54
30000	273.50	260.40	249.13	239.35	230.79	223.26	216.58	210.63	188.74	175.08	166.06	159.87
31000	282.62	269.08	257.43	247.33	238.48	230.70	223.80	217.65	195.03	180.91	171.59	165.20
32000	291.73	277.76	265.74	255.30	246.18	238.14	231.02	224.67	201.32	186.75	177.13	170.53
33000	300.85	286.44	274.04	263.28	253.87	245.58	238.24	231.69	207.61	192.58	182.66	175.86
34000	309.97	295.12	282.34	271.26	261.56	253.02	245.46	238.71	213.90	198.42	188.20	181.19
35000	319.08	303.80	290.65	279.24	269.26	260.46	252.67	245.73	220.19	204.26	193.73	186.52
37500	341.87	325.50	311.41	299.18	288.49	279.07	270.72	263.29	235.92	218.84	207.57	199.84
40000	364.66	347.19	332.17	319.13	307.72	297.67	288.77	280.84	251.65	233.43	221.41	213.16
42500	387.46	368.89	352.93	339.07	326.95	316.28	306.82	298.39	267.38	248.02	235.24	226.48
45000	410.25	390.59	373.69	359.02	346.18	334.88	324.87	315.94	283.10	262.61	249.08	239.80
47500	433.04	412.29	394.45	378.96	365.42	353.49	342.91	333.49	298.83	277.20	262.92	253.13
50000	455.83	433.99	415.21	398.91	384.65	372.09	360.96	351.05	314.56	291.79	276.76	266.45
52500	478.62	455.69	435.97	418.85	403.88	390.69	379.01	368.60	330.29	306.38	290.59	279.77
55000	501.41	477.39	456.73	438.80	423.11	409.30	397.06	386.15	346.01	320.97	304.43	293.09
57500	524.20	499.09	477.49	458.74	442.35	427.90	415.10	403.70	361.74	335.56	318.27	306.42
60000	546.99	520.79	498.25	478.69	461.58	446.51	433.15	421.26	377.47	350.15	332.11	319.74
65000	592.58	564.19	539.77	518.58	500.04	483.72	469.25	456.36	408.92	379.33	359.78	346.38
70000	638.16	607.59	581.29	558.47	538.51	520.92	505.34	491.46	440.38	408.51	387.46	373.03
75000	683.74	650.99	622.81	598.36	576.97	558.13	541.44	526.57	471.83	437.68	415.13	399.67
80000	729.32	694.38	664.33	638.25	615.44	595.34	577.53	561.67	503.29	466.86	442.81	426.32
85000	774.91	737.78	705.85	678.14	653.90	632.55	613.63	596.78	534.75	496.04	470.48	452.96
90000	820.49	781.18	747.37	718.03	692.36	669.76	649.73	631.88	566.20	525.22	498.16	479.60
95000	866.07	824.58	788.89	757.92	730.83	706.97	685.82	666.98	597.66	554.40	525.83	506.25
100000	911.65	867.98	830.42	797.81	769.29	744.17	721.92	702.09	629.11	583.58	553.51	532.89
105000	957.24	911.38	871.94	837.70	807.76	781.38	758.01	737.19	660.57	612.76	581.18	559.54
110000	1002.82	954.78	913.46	877.59	846.22	818.59	794.11	772.30	692.02	641.94	608.86	586.18
115000	1048.40	998.18	954.98	917.48	884.69	855.80	830.20	807.40	723.48	671.11	636.53	612.83
120000	1093.98	1041.57	996.50	957.37	923.15	893.01	866.30	842.51	754.93	700.29	664.21	639.47
125000	1139.56	1084.97	1038.02	997.26	961.62	930.22	902.39	877.61	786.39	729.47	691.88	666.11
130000	1185.15	1128.37	1079.54	1037.15	1000.08	967.43	938.49	912.71	817.84	758.65	719.56	692.76
135000	1230.73	1171.77	1121.06	1077.05	1038.54	1004.63	974.59	947.82	849.30	787.83	747.23	719.40
140000	1276.31	1215.17	1162.58	1116.94	1077.01	1041.84	1010.68	982.92	880.75	817.01	774.91	746.05
145000	1321.89	1258.57	1204.10	1156.83	1115.47	1079.05	1046.78	1018.03	912.21	846.19	802.58	772.69
150000	1367.48	1301.97	1245.62	1196.72	1153.94	1116.26	1082.87	1053.13	943.66	875.36	830.26	799.34
155000	1413.06	1345.37	1287.14	1236.61	1192.40	1153.47	1118.97	1088.23	975.12	904.54	857.93	825.98
160000	1458.64	1388.76	1328.66	1276.50	1230.87	1190.68	1155.06	1123.34	1006.58	933.72	885.61	852.63

9

6.00%   MONTHLY AMORTIZING PAYMENTS

AMOUNT OF LOAN	NUMBER OF YEARS IN TERM											
	1	2	3	4	5	6	7	8	9	10	11	12
$ 50	4.31	2.22	1.53	1.18	0.97	0.83	0.74	0.66	0.61	0.56	0.52	0.49
100	8.61	4.44	3.05	2.35	1.94	1.66	1.47	1.32	1.21	1.12	1.04	0.98
200	17.22	8.87	6.09	4.70	3.87	3.32	2.93	2.63	2.41	2.23	2.08	1.96
300	25.82	13.30	9.13	7.05	5.80	4.98	4.39	3.95	3.61	3.34	3.12	2.93
400	34.43	17.73	12.17	9.40	7.74	6.63	5.85	5.26	4.81	4.45	4.15	3.91
500	43.04	22.17	15.22	11.75	9.67	8.29	7.31	6.58	6.01	5.56	5.19	4.88
600	51.64	26.60	18.26	14.10	11.60	9.95	8.77	7.89	7.21	6.67	6.23	5.86
700	60.25	31.03	21.30	16.44	13.54	11.61	10.23	9.20	8.41	7.78	7.26	6.84
800	68.86	35.46	24.34	18.79	15.47	13.26	11.69	10.52	9.61	8.89	8.30	7.81
900	77.46	39.89	27.38	21.14	17.40	14.92	13.15	11.83	10.81	10.00	9.34	8.79
1000	86.07	44.33	30.43	23.49	19.34	16.58	14.61	13.15	12.01	11.11	10.37	9.76
2000	172.14	88.65	60.85	46.98	38.67	33.15	29.22	26.29	24.02	22.21	20.74	19.52
3000	258.20	132.97	91.27	70.46	58.00	49.72	43.83	39.43	36.02	33.31	31.11	29.28
4000	344.27	177.29	121.69	93.95	77.34	66.30	58.44	52.57	48.03	44.41	41.47	39.04
5000	430.34	221.61	152.11	117.43	96.67	82.87	73.05	65.71	60.03	55.52	51.84	48.80
6000	516.40	265.93	182.54	140.92	116.00	99.44	87.66	78.85	72.04	66.62	62.21	58.56
7000	602.47	310.25	212.96	164.40	135.33	116.02	102.26	92.00	84.05	77.72	72.57	68.31
8000	688.54	354.57	243.38	187.89	154.67	132.59	116.87	105.14	96.05	88.82	82.94	78.07
9000	774.60	398.89	273.80	211.37	174.00	149.16	131.48	118.28	108.06	99.92	93.31	87.83
10000	860.67	443.21	304.22	234.86	193.33	165.73	146.09	131.42	120.06	111.03	103.68	97.59
11000	946.74	487.53	334.65	258.34	212.67	182.31	160.70	144.56	132.07	122.13	114.04	107.35
12000	1032.80	531.85	365.07	281.83	232.00	198.88	175.31	157.70	144.07	133.23	124.41	117.11
13000	1118.87	576.17	395.49	305.31	251.33	215.45	189.92	170.84	156.08	144.33	134.78	126.87
14000	1204.94	620.49	425.91	328.80	270.66	232.03	204.52	183.99	168.09	155.43	145.14	136.62
15000	1291.00	664.81	456.33	352.28	290.00	248.60	219.13	197.13	180.09	166.54	155.51	146.38
16000	1377.07	709.13	486.76	375.77	309.33	265.17	233.74	210.27	192.10	177.64	165.88	156.14
17000	1463.13	753.46	517.18	399.25	328.66	281.74	248.35	223.41	204.10	188.74	176.24	165.90
18000	1549.20	797.78	547.60	422.74	348.00	298.32	262.96	236.55	216.11	199.84	186.61	175.66
19000	1635.27	842.10	578.02	446.22	367.33	314.89	277.57	249.69	228.11	210.94	196.98	185.42
20000	1721.33	886.42	608.44	469.71	386.66	331.46	292.18	262.83	240.12	222.05	207.35	195.18
21000	1807.40	930.74	638.87	493.19	405.99	348.04	306.78	275.98	252.13	233.15	217.71	204.93
22000	1893.47	975.06	669.29	516.68	425.33	364.61	321.39	289.12	264.13	244.25	228.08	214.69
23000	1979.53	1019.38	699.71	540.16	444.66	381.18	336.00	302.26	276.14	255.35	238.45	224.45
24000	2065.60	1063.70	730.13	563.65	463.99	397.75	350.61	315.40	288.14	266.45	248.81	234.21
25000	2151.67	1108.02	760.55	587.13	483.33	414.33	365.22	328.54	300.15	277.56	259.18	243.97
26000	2237.73	1152.34	790.98	610.62	502.66	430.90	379.83	341.68	312.15	288.66	269.55	253.73
27000	2323.80	1196.66	821.40	634.10	521.99	447.47	394.44	354.82	324.16	299.76	279.91	263.48
28000	2409.87	1240.98	851.82	657.59	541.32	464.05	409.04	367.97	336.17	310.86	290.28	273.24
29000	2495.93	1285.30	882.24	681.07	560.66	480.62	423.65	381.11	348.17	321.96	300.65	283.00
30000	2582.00	1329.62	912.66	704.56	579.99	497.19	438.26	394.25	360.18	333.07	311.02	292.76
31000	2668.06	1373.94	943.09	728.04	599.32	513.76	452.87	407.39	372.18	344.17	321.38	302.52
32000	2754.13	1418.26	973.51	751.53	618.65	530.34	467.48	420.53	384.19	355.27	331.75	312.28
33000	2840.20	1462.59	1003.93	775.01	637.99	546.91	482.09	433.67	396.19	366.37	342.12	322.04
34000	2926.26	1506.91	1034.35	798.50	657.32	563.48	496.70	446.81	408.20	377.47	352.48	331.79
35000	3012.33	1551.23	1064.77	821.98	676.65	580.06	511.30	459.96	420.21	388.58	362.85	341.55
37500	3227.50	1662.03	1140.83	880.69	724.99	621.49	547.83	492.81	450.22	416.33	388.77	365.95
40000	3442.66	1772.83	1216.88	939.41	773.32	662.92	584.35	525.66	480.23	444.09	414.69	390.35
42500	3657.83	1883.63	1292.94	998.12	821.65	704.35	620.87	558.52	510.25	471.84	440.60	414.74
45000	3872.99	1994.43	1368.99	1056.83	869.98	745.78	657.39	591.37	540.26	499.60	466.52	439.14
47500	4088.16	2105.23	1445.05	1115.54	918.31	787.22	693.91	624.22	570.28	527.35	492.44	463.53
50000	4303.33	2216.04	1521.10	1174.26	966.65	828.65	730.43	657.08	600.29	555.11	518.36	487.93
52500	4518.49	2326.84	1597.16	1232.97	1014.98	870.08	766.95	689.93	630.31	582.86	544.27	512.33
55000	4733.66	2437.64	1673.21	1291.68	1063.31	911.51	803.48	722.78	660.32	610.62	570.19	536.72
57500	4948.82	2548.44	1749.27	1350.39	1111.64	952.95	840.00	755.64	690.34	638.37	596.11	561.12
60000	5163.99	2659.24	1825.32	1409.11	1159.97	994.38	876.52	788.49	720.35	666.13	622.03	585.52
65000	5594.32	2880.84	1977.43	1526.53	1256.64	1077.24	949.56	854.20	780.38	721.64	673.86	634.31
70000	6024.66	3102.45	2129.54	1643.96	1353.30	1160.11	1022.60	919.91	840.41	777.16	725.70	683.10
75000	6454.99	3324.05	2281.65	1761.38	1449.97	1242.97	1095.65	985.61	900.44	832.66	777.53	731.89
80000	6885.32	3545.65	2433.76	1878.81	1546.63	1325.84	1168.69	1051.32	960.46	888.17	829.37	780.69
85000	7315.65	3767.26	2585.87	1996.23	1643.29	1408.70	1241.73	1117.03	1020.49	943.68	881.20	829.48
90000	7745.98	3988.86	2737.98	2113.66	1739.96	1491.56	1314.77	1182.73	1080.52	999.19	933.04	878.27
95000	8176.32	4210.46	2890.09	2231.08	1836.62	1574.43	1387.82	1248.44	1140.55	1054.70	984.87	927.06
100000	8606.65	4432.07	3042.20	2348.51	1933.29	1657.29	1460.86	1314.15	1200.58	1110.21	1036.71	975.86
105000	9036.98	4653.67	3194.31	2465.93	2029.95	1740.16	1533.90	1379.86	1260.61	1165.72	1088.54	1024.65
110000	9467.31	4875.27	3346.42	2583.36	2126.61	1823.02	1606.95	1445.56	1320.64	1221.23	1140.38	1073.44
115000	9897.64	5096.88	3498.53	2700.78	2223.28	1905.89	1679.99	1511.27	1380.67	1276.74	1192.21	1122.23
120000	10327.98	5318.48	3650.64	2818.21	2319.94	1988.75	1753.03	1576.98	1440.69	1332.25	1244.05	1171.03
125000	10758.31	5540.08	3802.75	2935.63	2416.61	2071.62	1826.07	1642.68	1500.72	1387.76	1295.88	1219.82
130000	11188.64	5761.68	3954.86	3053.06	2513.27	2154.48	1899.12	1708.39	1560.75	1443.27	1347.72	1268.61
135000	11618.97	5983.29	4106.97	3170.48	2609.93	2237.34	1972.16	1774.10	1620.78	1498.78	1399.55	1317.40
140000	12049.31	6204.89	4259.08	3287.91	2706.60	2320.21	2045.20	1839.81	1680.81	1554.29	1451.39	1366.20
145000	12479.64	6426.49	4411.19	3405.33	2803.26	2403.07	2118.25	1905.51	1740.84	1609.80	1503.23	1414.99
150000	12909.97	6648.10	4563.30	3522.76	2899.93	2485.94	2191.29	1971.22	1800.87	1665.31	1555.06	1463.78
155000	13340.30	6869.70	4715.41	3640.18	2996.59	2568.80	2264.33	2036.93	1860.90	1720.82	1606.90	1512.57
160000	13770.63	7091.30	4867.51	3757.61	3093.25	2651.67	2337.37	2102.63	1920.92	1776.33	1658.73	1561.37

10

AMOUNT OF LOAN	NUMBER OF YEARS IN TERM											
	13	14	15	16	17	18	19	20	25	30	35	40
$ 50	0.47	0.45	0.43	0.41	0.40	0.38	0.37	0.36	0.33	0.30	0.29	0.28
100	0.93	0.89	0.85	0.82	0.79	0.76	0.74	0.72	0.65	0.60	0.58	0.56
200	1.85	1.77	1.69	1.63	1.57	1.52	1.48	1.44	1.29	1.20	1.15	1.11
300	2.78	2.65	2.54	2.44	2.35	2.28	2.21	2.15	1.94	1.80	1.72	1.66
400	3.70	3.53	3.38	3.25	3.14	3.04	2.95	2.87	2.58	2.40	2.29	2.21
500	4.63	4.41	4.22	4.06	3.92	3.80	3.69	3.59	3.23	3.00	2.86	2.76
600	5.55	5.29	5.07	4.87	4.70	4.55	4.42	4.30	3.87	3.60	3.43	3.31
700	6.48	6.17	5.91	5.69	5.49	5.31	5.16	5.02	4.52	4.20	4.00	3.86
800	7.40	7.05	6.76	6.50	6.27	6.07	5.89	5.74	5.16	4.80	4.57	4.41
900	8.33	7.94	7.60	7.31	7.05	6.83	6.63	6.45	5.80	5.40	5.14	4.96
1000	9.25	8.82	8.44	8.12	7.84	7.59	7.37	7.17	6.45	6.00	5.71	5.51
2000	18.50	17.63	16.88	16.23	15.67	15.17	14.73	14.33	12.89	12.00	11.41	11.01
3000	27.75	26.44	25.32	24.35	23.50	22.75	22.09	21.50	19.33	17.99	17.11	16.51
4000	36.99	35.25	33.76	32.46	31.33	30.33	29.45	28.66	25.78	23.99	22.81	22.01
5000	46.24	44.07	42.20	40.58	39.16	37.91	36.81	35.83	32.22	29.98	28.51	27.52
6000	55.49	52.88	50.64	48.69	46.99	45.49	44.17	42.99	38.66	35.98	34.22	33.02
7000	64.74	61.69	59.07	56.81	54.82	53.08	51.53	50.16	45.11	41.97	39.92	38.52
8000	73.98	70.50	67.51	64.92	62.65	60.66	58.89	57.32	51.55	47.97	45.62	44.02
9000	83.23	79.32	75.95	73.03	70.48	68.24	66.25	64.48	57.99	53.96	51.32	49.52
10000	92.48	88.13	84.39	81.15	78.32	75.82	73.61	71.65	64.44	59.96	57.02	55.03
11000	101.72	96.94	92.83	89.26	86.15	83.40	80.97	78.81	70.88	65.96	62.73	60.53
12000	110.97	105.75	101.27	97.38	93.98	90.98	88.33	85.98	77.32	71.95	68.43	66.03
13000	120.22	114.57	109.71	105.49	101.81	98.57	95.70	93.14	83.76	77.95	74.13	71.53
14000	129.47	123.38	118.14	113.61	109.64	106.15	103.06	100.31	90.21	83.94	79.83	77.03
15000	138.71	132.19	126.58	121.72	117.47	113.73	110.42	107.47	96.65	89.94	85.53	82.54
16000	147.96	141.00	135.02	129.84	125.30	121.31	117.78	114.63	103.09	95.93	91.24	88.04
17000	157.21	149.82	143.46	137.95	133.13	128.89	125.14	121.80	109.54	101.93	96.94	93.54
18000	166.46	158.63	151.90	146.06	140.96	136.47	132.50	128.96	115.98	107.92	102.64	99.04
19000	175.70	167.44	160.34	154.18	148.79	144.06	139.86	136.13	122.42	113.92	108.34	104.55
20000	184.95	176.25	168.78	162.29	156.63	151.64	147.22	143.29	128.87	119.92	114.04	110.05
21000	194.20	185.06	177.21	170.41	164.46	159.22	154.58	150.46	135.31	125.91	119.74	115.55
22000	203.44	193.88	185.65	178.52	172.29	166.80	161.94	157.62	141.75	131.91	125.45	121.05
23000	212.69	202.69	194.09	186.64	180.12	174.38	169.30	164.78	148.19	137.90	131.15	126.55
24000	221.94	211.50	202.53	194.75	187.95	181.96	176.66	171.95	154.64	143.90	136.85	132.06
25000	231.19	220.31	210.97	202.86	195.78	189.55	184.03	179.11	161.08	149.89	142.55	137.56
26000	240.43	229.13	219.41	210.98	203.61	197.13	191.39	186.28	167.52	155.89	148.25	143.06
27000	249.68	237.94	227.85	219.09	211.44	204.71	198.75	193.44	173.97	161.88	153.96	148.56
28000	258.93	246.75	236.28	227.21	219.27	212.29	206.11	200.61	180.41	167.88	159.66	154.06
29000	268.17	255.56	244.72	235.32	227.10	219.87	213.47	207.77	186.85	173.87	165.36	159.57
30000	277.42	264.38	253.16	243.44	234.94	227.45	220.83	214.93	193.30	179.87	171.06	165.07
31000	286.67	273.19	261.60	251.55	242.77	235.04	228.19	222.10	199.74	185.87	176.76	170.57
32000	295.92	282.00	270.04	259.67	250.60	242.62	235.55	229.26	206.18	191.86	182.47	176.07
33000	305.16	290.81	278.48	267.78	258.43	250.20	242.91	236.43	212.62	197.86	188.17	181.58
34000	314.41	299.63	286.92	275.89	266.26	257.78	250.27	243.59	219.07	203.85	193.87	187.08
35000	323.66	308.44	295.35	284.01	274.09	265.36	257.63	250.76	225.51	209.85	199.57	192.58
37500	346.78	330.47	316.45	304.29	293.67	284.32	276.04	268.67	241.62	224.84	213.83	206.34
40000	369.89	352.50	337.55	324.58	313.25	303.27	294.44	286.58	257.73	239.83	228.08	220.09
42500	393.01	374.53	358.64	344.87	332.82	322.22	312.84	304.49	273.83	254.81	242.34	233.85
45000	416.13	396.56	379.74	365.15	352.40	341.18	331.24	322.40	289.94	269.80	256.59	247.60
47500	439.25	418.59	400.84	385.44	371.98	360.13	349.64	340.31	306.05	284.79	270.85	261.36
50000	462.37	440.62	421.93	405.72	391.56	379.09	368.05	358.22	322.16	299.78	285.10	275.11
52500	485.48	462.65	443.03	426.01	411.13	398.04	386.45	376.13	338.26	314.77	299.35	288.87
55000	508.60	484.68	464.13	446.30	430.71	416.99	404.85	394.04	354.37	329.76	313.61	302.62
57500	531.72	506.72	485.22	466.58	450.29	435.95	423.25	411.95	370.48	344.75	327.86	316.38
60000	554.84	528.75	506.32	486.87	469.87	454.90	441.65	429.86	386.59	359.74	342.12	330.13
65000	601.08	572.81	548.51	527.44	509.02	492.81	478.46	465.69	418.80	389.71	370.63	357.64
70000	647.31	616.87	590.70	568.01	548.18	530.72	515.26	501.51	451.02	419.69	399.14	385.15
75000	693.55	660.93	632.90	608.58	587.33	568.63	552.07	537.33	483.23	449.67	427.65	412.67
80000	739.78	704.99	675.09	649.16	626.49	606.53	588.87	573.15	515.45	479.65	456.16	440.18
85000	786.02	749.06	717.28	689.73	665.64	644.44	625.68	608.97	547.66	509.62	484.67	467.69
90000	832.26	793.12	759.48	730.30	704.80	682.35	662.48	644.79	579.88	539.60	513.18	495.20
95000	878.49	837.18	801.67	770.87	743.95	720.26	699.28	680.61	612.09	569.58	541.69	522.71
100000	924.73	881.24	843.86	811.44	783.11	758.17	736.09	716.44	644.31	599.56	570.19	550.22
105000	970.96	925.30	886.05	852.01	822.26	796.08	772.89	752.26	676.52	629.53	598.70	577.73
110000	1017.20	969.36	928.25	892.59	861.42	833.98	809.70	788.08	708.74	659.51	627.21	605.24
115000	1063.44	1013.43	970.44	933.16	900.57	871.89	846.50	823.90	740.95	689.49	655.72	632.75
120000	1109.67	1057.49	1012.63	973.73	939.73	909.80	883.30	859.72	773.17	719.47	684.23	660.26
125000	1155.91	1101.55	1054.83	1014.30	978.88	947.71	920.11	895.54	805.38	749.44	712.74	687.77
130000	1202.15	1145.61	1097.02	1054.87	1018.04	985.62	956.91	931.37	837.60	779.42	741.25	715.28
135000	1248.38	1189.67	1139.21	1095.45	1057.19	1023.52	993.72	967.19	869.81	809.40	769.76	742.79
140000	1294.62	1233.74	1181.40	1136.02	1096.35	1061.43	1030.52	1003.01	902.03	839.38	798.27	770.30
145000	1340.85	1277.80	1223.60	1176.59	1135.50	1099.34	1067.33	1038.83	934.24	869.35	826.78	797.81
150000	1387.09	1321.86	1265.79	1217.16	1174.66	1137.25	1104.13	1074.65	966.46	899.33	855.29	825.33
155000	1433.33	1365.92	1307.98	1257.73	1213.81	1175.16	1140.93	1110.47	998.67	929.31	883.80	852.84
160000	1479.56	1409.98	1350.18	1298.31	1252.97	1213.06	1177.74	1146.29	1030.89	959.29	912.31	880.35

6.25% MONTHLY AMORTIZING PAYMENTS

AMOUNT OF LOAN	NUMBER OF YEARS IN TERM											
	1	2	3	4	5	6	7	8	9	10	11	12
$ 50	4.31	2.23	1.53	1.18	0.98	0.84	0.74	0.67	0.61	0.57	0.53	0.50
100	8.62	4.45	3.06	2.36	1.95	1.67	1.48	1.33	1.22	1.13	1.05	0.99
200	17.24	8.89	6.11	4.72	3.89	3.34	2.95	2.66	2.43	2.25	2.10	1.98
300	25.86	13.34	9.17	7.08	5.84	5.01	4.42	3.98	3.64	3.37	3.15	2.97
400	34.48	17.78	12.22	9.44	7.78	6.68	5.90	5.31	4.86	4.50	4.20	3.96
500	43.10	22.22	15.27	11.80	9.73	8.35	7.37	6.64	6.07	5.62	5.25	4.95
600	51.71	26.67	18.33	14.16	11.67	10.02	8.84	7.96	7.28	6.74	6.30	5.94
700	60.33	31.11	21.38	16.52	13.62	11.69	10.32	9.29	8.50	7.86	7.35	6.93
800	68.95	35.55	24.43	18.88	15.56	13.36	11.79	10.62	9.71	8.99	8.40	7.92
900	77.57	40.00	27.49	21.24	17.51	15.03	13.26	11.94	10.92	10.11	9.45	8.90
1000	86.19	44.44	30.54	23.60	19.45	16.70	14.73	13.27	12.13	11.23	10.50	9.89
2000	172.37	88.87	61.08	47.20	38.90	33.39	29.46	26.53	24.26	22.46	20.99	19.78
3000	258.55	133.31	91.61	70.80	58.35	50.08	44.19	39.80	36.39	33.69	31.49	29.67
4000	344.73	177.74	122.15	94.40	77.80	66.77	58.92	53.06	48.52	44.92	41.98	39.56
5000	430.91	222.17	152.68	118.00	97.25	83.46	73.65	66.32	60.65	56.15	52.48	49.45
6000	517.09	266.61	183.22	141.60	116.70	100.15	88.38	79.59	72.78	67.37	62.97	59.34
7000	603.27	311.04	213.75	165.20	136.15	116.84	103.11	92.85	84.91	78.60	73.47	69.22
8000	689.46	355.47	244.29	188.80	155.60	133.53	117.83	106.11	97.04	89.83	83.96	79.11
9000	775.64	399.91	274.82	212.40	175.05	150.23	132.56	119.38	109.17	101.06	94.46	89.00
10000	861.82	444.34	305.36	236.00	194.50	166.92	147.29	132.64	121.30	112.29	104.95	98.89
11000	948.00	488.77	335.89	259.60	213.95	183.61	162.02	145.90	133.43	123.51	115.45	108.78
12000	1034.18	533.21	366.43	283.20	233.40	200.30	176.75	159.17	145.56	134.74	125.94	118.67
13000	1120.36	577.64	396.96	306.80	252.85	216.99	191.48	172.43	157.69	145.97	136.44	128.55
14000	1206.54	622.07	427.50	330.40	272.29	233.68	206.21	185.69	169.82	157.20	146.93	138.44
15000	1292.73	666.51	458.04	354.00	291.74	250.37	220.94	198.96	181.95	168.43	157.43	148.33
16000	1378.91	710.94	488.57	377.60	311.19	267.06	235.66	212.22	194.08	179.65	167.92	158.22
17000	1465.09	755.37	519.11	401.20	330.64	283.75	250.39	225.48	206.21	190.88	178.42	168.11
18000	1551.27	799.81	549.64	424.80	350.09	300.45	265.12	238.75	218.34	202.11	188.91	178.00
19000	1637.45	844.24	580.18	448.40	369.54	317.14	279.85	252.01	230.47	213.34	199.41	187.88
20000	1723.63	888.67	610.71	472.00	388.99	333.83	294.58	265.27	242.60	224.57	209.90	197.77
21000	1809.81	933.11	641.25	495.60	408.44	350.52	309.31	278.54	254.73	235.79	220.40	207.66
22000	1896.00	977.54	671.78	519.20	427.89	367.21	324.04	291.80	266.86	247.02	230.89	217.55
23000	1982.18	1021.97	702.32	542.80	447.34	383.90	338.77	305.07	278.99	258.25	241.39	227.44
24000	2068.36	1066.41	732.85	566.40	466.79	400.59	353.49	318.33	291.12	269.48	251.88	237.33
25000	2154.54	1110.84	763.39	590.00	486.24	417.28	368.22	331.59	303.25	280.71	262.38	247.21
26000	2240.72	1155.27	793.92	613.60	505.69	433.98	382.95	344.86	315.38	291.93	272.87	257.10
27000	2326.90	1199.71	824.46	637.20	525.14	450.67	397.68	358.12	327.51	303.16	283.37	266.99
28000	2413.08	1244.14	854.99	660.80	544.58	467.36	412.41	371.38	339.64	314.39	293.86	276.88
29000	2499.27	1288.57	885.53	684.40	564.03	484.05	427.14	384.65	351.77	325.62	304.36	286.77
30000	2585.45	1333.01	916.07	708.00	583.48	500.74	441.87	397.91	363.90	336.85	314.85	296.66
31000	2671.63	1377.44	946.60	731.60	602.93	517.43	456.59	411.17	376.03	348.07	325.35	306.54
32000	2757.81	1421.87	977.14	755.20	622.38	534.12	471.32	424.44	388.16	359.30	335.84	316.43
33000	2843.99	1466.31	1007.67	778.80	641.83	550.81	486.05	437.70	400.29	370.53	346.34	326.32
34000	2930.17	1510.74	1038.21	802.40	661.28	567.50	500.78	450.96	412.42	381.76	356.83	336.21
35000	3016.35	1555.17	1068.74	826.00	680.73	584.20	515.51	464.23	424.55	392.99	367.33	346.10
37500	3231.81	1666.26	1145.08	885.00	729.35	625.92	552.33	497.39	454.87	421.06	393.57	370.82
40000	3447.26	1777.34	1221.42	944.00	777.98	667.65	589.15	530.54	485.20	449.13	419.80	395.54
42500	3662.71	1888.42	1297.76	1003.00	826.60	709.38	625.97	563.70	515.52	477.20	446.04	420.26
45000	3878.17	1999.51	1374.10	1062.00	875.22	751.11	662.80	596.86	545.84	505.27	472.28	444.98
47500	4093.62	2110.59	1450.43	1121.00	923.84	792.83	699.62	630.02	576.17	533.34	498.52	469.70
50000	4309.07	2221.67	1526.77	1180.00	972.47	834.56	736.44	663.18	606.49	561.41	524.75	494.42
52500	4524.53	2332.76	1603.11	1239.00	1021.09	876.29	773.26	696.34	636.82	589.48	550.99	519.14
55000	4739.98	2443.84	1679.45	1298.00	1069.71	918.02	810.08	729.50	667.14	617.55	577.23	543.87
57500	4955.43	2554.92	1755.79	1356.99	1118.34	959.75	846.91	762.66	697.47	645.62	603.46	568.59
60000	5170.89	2666.01	1832.13	1415.99	1166.96	1001.47	883.73	795.81	727.79	673.69	629.70	593.31
65000	5601.79	2888.17	1984.80	1533.99	1264.21	1084.93	957.37	862.13	788.44	729.83	682.18	642.75
70000	6032.70	3110.34	2137.48	1651.99	1361.45	1168.39	1031.01	928.45	849.09	785.97	734.65	692.19
75000	6463.61	3332.51	2290.16	1769.99	1458.70	1251.84	1104.66	994.77	909.74	842.11	787.13	741.63
80000	6894.52	3554.67	2442.83	1887.99	1555.95	1335.30	1178.30	1061.08	970.39	898.25	839.60	791.07
85000	7325.42	3776.84	2595.51	2005.99	1653.19	1418.75	1251.94	1127.40	1031.03	954.39	892.08	840.52
90000	7756.33	3999.01	2748.19	2123.99	1750.44	1502.21	1325.59	1193.72	1091.68	1010.53	944.55	889.96
95000	8187.24	4221.17	2900.86	2241.99	1847.68	1585.66	1399.23	1260.04	1152.33	1066.67	997.03	939.40
100000	8618.14	4443.34	3053.54	2359.99	1944.93	1669.12	1472.87	1326.35	1212.98	1122.81	1049.50	988.84
105000	9049.05	4665.51	3206.22	2477.99	2042.18	1752.58	1546.52	1392.67	1273.63	1178.95	1101.97	1038.28
110000	9479.96	4887.67	3358.89	2595.99	2139.42	1836.03	1620.16	1458.99	1334.28	1235.09	1154.45	1087.73
115000	9910.86	5109.84	3511.57	2713.98	2236.67	1919.49	1693.81	1525.31	1394.93	1291.23	1206.92	1137.17
120000	10341.77	5332.01	3664.25	2831.98	2333.92	2002.94	1767.45	1591.62	1455.58	1347.37	1259.40	1186.61
125000	10772.68	5554.17	3816.92	2949.98	2431.16	2086.40	1841.09	1657.94	1516.22	1403.51	1311.87	1236.05
130000	11203.58	5776.34	3969.60	3067.98	2528.41	2169.86	1914.74	1724.26	1576.87	1459.65	1364.35	1285.49
135000	11634.49	5998.51	4122.28	3185.98	2625.66	2253.31	1988.38	1790.58	1637.52	1515.79	1416.82	1334.93
140000	12065.40	6220.67	4274.95	3303.98	2722.90	2336.77	2062.02	1856.89	1698.17	1571.93	1469.30	1384.38
145000	12496.31	6442.84	4427.63	3421.98	2820.15	2420.22	2135.67	1923.21	1758.82	1628.07	1521.77	1433.82
150000	12927.21	6665.01	4580.31	3539.98	2917.39	2503.68	2209.31	1989.53	1819.47	1684.21	1574.25	1483.26
155000	13358.12	6887.17	4732.98	3657.98	3014.64	2587.13	2282.95	2055.85	1880.12	1740.35	1626.72	1532.70
160000	13789.03	7109.34	4885.66	3775.98	3111.89	2670.59	2356.60	2122.16	1940.77	1796.49	1679.20	1582.14

MONTHLY AMORTIZING PAYMENTS 6.25%

AMOUNT OF LOAN	NUMBER OF YEARS IN TERM											
	13	14	15	16	17	18	19	20	25	30	35	40
$ 50	0.47	0.45	0.43	0.42	0.40	0.39	0.38	0.37	0.33	0.31	0.30	0.29
100	0.94	0.90	0.86	0.83	0.80	0.78	0.76	0.74	0.66	0.62	0.59	0.57
200	1.88	1.79	1.72	1.66	1.60	1.55	1.51	1.47	1.32	1.24	1.18	1.14
300	2.82	2.69	2.58	2.48	2.40	2.32	2.26	2.20	1.98	1.85	1.77	1.71
400	3.76	3.58	3.43	3.31	3.19	3.09	3.01	2.93	2.64	2.47	2.35	2.28
500	4.69	4.48	4.29	4.13	3.99	3.87	3.76	3.66	3.30	3.08	2.94	2.84
600	5.63	5.37	5.15	4.96	4.79	4.64	4.51	4.39	3.96	3.70	3.53	3.41
700	6.57	6.27	6.01	5.78	5.58	5.41	5.26	5.12	4.62	4.32	4.11	3.98
800	7.51	7.16	6.86	6.61	6.38	6.18	6.01	5.85	5.28	4.93	4.70	4.55
900	8.45	8.06	7.72	7.43	7.18	6.96	6.76	6.58	5.94	5.55	5.29	5.11
1000	9.38	8.95	8.58	8.26	7.98	7.73	7.51	7.31	6.60	6.16	5.88	5.68
2000	18.76	17.90	17.15	16.51	15.95	15.45	15.01	14.62	13.20	12.32	11.75	11.36
3000	28.14	26.84	25.73	24.76	23.92	23.17	22.52	21.93	19.80	18.48	17.62	17.04
4000	37.52	35.79	34.30	33.01	31.89	30.90	30.02	29.24	26.39	24.63	23.49	22.71
5000	46.90	44.74	42.88	41.26	39.86	38.62	37.52	36.55	32.99	30.79	29.36	28.39
6000	56.28	53.68	51.45	49.52	47.83	46.34	45.03	43.86	39.59	36.95	35.23	34.07
7000	65.65	62.63	60.03	57.77	55.80	54.07	52.53	51.17	46.18	43.11	41.10	39.75
8000	75.04	71.57	68.60	66.02	63.77	61.79	60.04	58.48	52.78	49.26	46.97	45.42
9000	84.42	80.52	77.17	74.27	71.74	69.51	67.54	65.79	59.38	55.42	52.84	51.10
10000	93.80	89.47	85.75	82.52	79.71	77.23	75.04	73.10	65.97	61.58	58.71	56.78
11000	103.17	98.41	94.32	90.78	87.68	84.96	82.55	80.41	72.57	67.73	64.58	62.46
12000	112.55	107.36	102.90	99.03	95.65	92.68	90.05	87.72	79.17	73.89	70.45	68.13
13000	121.93	116.30	111.47	107.28	103.62	100.40	97.56	95.03	85.76	80.05	76.32	73.81
14000	131.31	125.25	120.04	115.53	111.59	108.13	105.06	102.33	92.36	86.21	82.20	79.49
15000	140.69	134.20	128.62	123.78	119.56	115.85	112.56	109.64	98.96	92.36	88.07	85.17
16000	150.07	143.14	137.19	132.04	127.53	123.57	120.07	116.95	105.55	98.52	93.94	90.84
17000	159.45	152.09	145.77	140.29	135.50	131.29	127.57	124.26	112.15	104.68	99.81	96.52
18000	168.83	161.03	154.34	148.54	143.47	139.02	135.08	131.57	118.75	110.83	105.68	102.20
19000	178.21	169.98	162.92	156.79	151.44	146.74	142.58	138.88	125.34	116.99	111.55	107.88
20000	187.59	178.93	171.49	165.04	159.41	154.46	150.08	146.19	131.94	123.15	117.42	113.55
21000	196.96	187.87	180.06	173.30	167.38	162.19	157.59	153.50	138.54	129.31	123.29	119.23
22000	206.34	196.82	188.64	181.55	175.35	169.91	165.09	160.81	145.13	135.46	129.16	124.91
23000	215.72	205.77	197.21	189.80	183.33	177.63	172.60	168.12	151.73	141.62	135.03	130.59
24000	225.10	214.71	205.79	198.05	191.30	185.36	180.10	175.43	158.33	147.78	140.90	136.26
25000	234.48	223.66	214.36	206.30	199.27	193.08	187.60	182.74	164.92	153.93	146.77	141.94
26000	243.86	232.60	222.93	214.56	207.24	200.80	195.11	190.05	171.52	160.09	152.64	147.62
27000	253.24	241.55	231.51	222.81	215.21	208.52	202.61	197.36	178.12	166.25	158.52	153.29
28000	262.62	250.50	240.08	231.06	223.18	216.25	210.12	204.66	184.71	172.41	164.39	158.97
29000	272.00	259.44	248.66	239.31	231.15	223.97	217.62	211.97	191.31	178.56	170.26	164.65
30000	281.38	268.39	257.23	247.56	239.12	231.69	225.12	219.28	197.91	184.72	176.13	170.33
31000	290.76	277.33	265.81	255.82	247.09	239.42	232.63	226.59	204.50	190.88	182.00	176.00
32000	300.13	286.28	274.38	264.07	255.06	247.14	240.13	233.90	211.10	197.03	187.87	181.68
33000	309.51	295.23	282.95	272.32	263.03	254.86	247.64	241.21	217.70	203.19	193.74	187.36
34000	318.89	304.17	291.53	280.57	271.00	262.58	255.14	248.52	224.29	209.35	199.61	193.04
35000	328.27	313.12	300.10	288.82	278.97	270.31	262.64	255.83	230.89	215.51	205.48	198.71
37500	351.72	335.48	321.54	309.45	298.90	289.62	281.40	274.10	247.38	230.90	220.16	212.91
40000	375.17	357.85	342.97	330.08	318.82	308.92	300.16	292.38	263.87	246.29	234.84	227.10
42500	398.61	380.21	364.41	350.71	338.75	328.23	318.92	310.65	280.36	261.68	249.51	241.29
45000	422.06	402.58	385.85	371.34	358.68	347.54	337.68	328.92	296.86	277.08	264.19	255.49
47500	445.51	424.94	407.28	391.97	378.60	366.84	356.44	347.20	313.35	292.47	278.87	269.68
50000	468.96	447.31	428.72	412.60	398.53	386.15	375.20	365.47	329.84	307.86	293.54	283.87
52500	492.40	469.68	450.15	433.23	418.45	405.46	393.96	383.74	346.33	323.26	308.22	298.07
55000	515.85	492.04	471.59	453.86	438.38	424.77	412.72	402.02	362.82	338.65	322.90	312.26
57500	539.30	514.41	493.02	474.49	458.31	444.07	431.48	420.29	379.31	354.04	337.57	326.46
60000	562.75	536.77	514.46	495.12	478.23	463.38	450.24	438.56	395.81	369.44	352.25	340.65
65000	609.64	581.50	557.33	536.38	518.08	502.00	487.76	475.11	428.79	400.22	381.60	369.04
70000	656.54	626.23	600.20	577.64	557.94	540.61	525.28	511.65	461.77	431.01	410.96	397.42
75000	703.43	670.96	643.07	618.90	597.79	579.23	562.80	548.20	494.76	461.79	440.31	425.81
80000	750.33	715.69	685.94	660.16	637.64	617.84	600.32	584.75	527.74	492.58	469.67	454.20
85000	797.22	760.42	728.81	701.42	677.49	656.45	637.84	621.29	560.72	523.36	499.02	482.58
90000	844.12	805.15	771.69	742.68	717.35	695.07	675.36	657.84	593.71	554.15	528.37	510.97
95000	891.01	849.88	814.56	783.94	757.20	733.68	712.88	694.39	626.69	584.94	557.73	539.36
100000	937.91	894.62	857.43	825.20	797.05	772.30	750.40	730.93	659.67	615.72	587.08	567.74
105000	984.80	939.35	900.30	866.46	836.90	810.91	787.92	767.48	692.66	646.51	616.44	596.13
110000	1031.70	984.08	943.17	907.72	876.75	849.53	825.44	804.03	725.64	677.29	645.79	624.52
115000	1078.60	1028.81	986.04	948.98	916.61	888.14	862.96	840.57	758.62	708.08	675.14	652.91
120000	1125.49	1073.54	1028.91	990.24	956.46	926.76	900.48	877.12	791.61	738.87	704.50	681.29
125000	1172.39	1118.27	1071.78	1031.50	996.31	965.37	938.00	913.67	824.59	769.65	733.85	709.68
130000	1219.28	1163.00	1114.65	1072.76	1036.16	1003.99	975.52	950.21	857.58	800.44	763.20	738.07
135000	1266.18	1207.73	1157.53	1114.02	1076.02	1042.60	1013.04	986.76	890.56	831.22	792.56	766.45
140000	1313.07	1252.46	1200.40	1155.28	1115.87	1081.22	1050.56	1023.30	923.54	862.01	821.91	794.84
145000	1359.97	1297.19	1243.27	1196.54	1155.72	1119.83	1088.08	1059.85	956.53	892.79	851.27	823.23
150000	1406.86	1341.92	1286.14	1237.80	1195.57	1158.45	1125.60	1096.40	989.51	923.58	880.62	851.61
155000	1453.76	1386.65	1329.01	1279.06	1235.43	1197.06	1163.12	1132.94	1022.49	954.37	909.97	880.00
160000	1500.65	1431.38	1371.88	1320.32	1275.28	1235.67	1200.64	1169.49	1055.48	985.15	939.33	908.39

13

6.50%   MONTHLY AMORTIZING PAYMENTS

AMOUNT OF LOAN	NUMBER OF YEARS IN TERM											
	1	2	3	4	5	6	7	8	9	10	11	12
$ 50	4.32	2.23	1.54	1.19	0.98	0.85	0.75	0.67	0.62	0.57	0.54	0.51
100	8.63	4.46	3.07	2.38	1.96	1.69	1.49	1.34	1.23	1.14	1.07	1.01
200	17.26	8.91	6.13	4.75	3.92	3.37	2.97	2.68	2.46	2.28	2.13	2.01
300	25.89	13.37	9.20	7.12	5.87	5.05	4.46	4.02	3.68	3.41	3.19	3.01
400	34.52	17.82	12.26	9.49	7.83	6.73	5.94	5.36	4.91	4.55	4.25	4.01
500	43.15	22.28	15.33	11.86	9.79	8.41	7.43	6.70	6.13	5.68	5.32	5.01
600	51.78	26.73	18.39	14.23	11.74	10.09	8.91	8.04	7.36	6.82	6.38	6.02
700	60.41	31.19	21.46	16.61	13.70	11.77	10.40	9.38	8.58	7.95	7.44	7.02
800	69.04	35.64	24.52	18.98	15.66	13.45	11.88	10.71	9.81	9.09	8.50	8.02
900	77.67	40.10	27.59	21.35	17.61	15.13	13.37	12.05	11.03	10.22	9.57	9.02
1000	86.30	44.55	30.65	23.72	19.57	16.81	14.85	13.39	12.26	11.36	10.63	10.02
2000	172.60	89.10	61.30	47.43	39.14	33.62	29.70	26.78	24.51	22.71	21.25	20.04
3000	258.89	133.64	91.95	71.15	58.70	50.43	44.55	40.16	36.77	34.07	31.88	30.06
4000	345.19	178.19	122.60	94.86	78.27	67.24	59.40	53.55	49.02	45.42	42.50	40.08
5000	431.49	222.74	153.25	118.58	97.84	84.05	74.25	66.94	61.28	56.78	53.12	50.10
6000	517.78	267.28	183.90	142.29	117.40	100.86	89.10	80.32	73.53	68.13	63.75	60.12
7000	604.08	311.83	214.55	166.01	136.97	117.67	103.95	93.71	85.79	79.49	74.37	70.14
8000	690.38	356.38	245.20	189.72	156.53	134.48	118.80	107.09	98.04	90.84	85.00	80.16
9000	776.67	400.92	275.85	213.44	176.10	151.29	133.65	120.48	110.30	102.20	95.62	90.18
10000	862.97	445.47	306.50	237.15	195.67	168.10	148.50	133.87	122.55	113.55	106.24	100.20
11000	949.27	490.01	337.14	260.87	215.23	184.91	163.35	147.25	134.80	124.91	116.87	110.22
12000	1035.56	534.56	367.79	284.58	234.80	201.72	178.20	160.64	147.06	136.26	127.49	120.24
13000	1121.86	579.11	398.44	308.30	254.36	218.53	193.05	174.03	159.31	147.62	138.11	130.25
14000	1208.15	623.65	429.09	332.01	273.93	235.34	207.90	187.41	171.57	158.97	148.74	140.27
15000	1294.45	668.20	459.74	355.73	293.50	252.15	222.75	200.80	183.82	170.33	159.36	150.29
16000	1380.75	712.75	490.39	379.44	313.06	268.96	237.60	214.18	196.08	181.68	169.99	160.31
17000	1467.04	757.29	521.04	403.16	332.63	285.77	252.45	227.57	208.33	193.04	180.61	170.33
18000	1553.34	801.84	551.69	426.87	352.20	302.58	267.29	240.96	220.59	204.39	191.23	180.35
19000	1639.64	846.38	582.34	450.59	371.76	319.39	282.14	254.34	232.84	215.75	201.86	190.37
20000	1725.93	890.93	612.99	474.30	391.33	336.20	296.99	267.73	245.10	227.10	212.48	200.39
21000	1812.23	935.48	643.63	498.02	410.89	353.01	311.84	281.12	257.35	238.46	223.10	210.41
22000	1898.53	980.02	674.28	521.73	430.46	369.82	326.69	294.50	269.60	249.81	233.73	220.43
23000	1984.82	1024.57	704.93	545.45	450.03	386.63	341.54	307.89	281.86	261.17	244.35	230.45
24000	2071.12	1069.12	735.58	569.16	469.59	403.44	356.39	321.27	294.11	272.52	254.98	240.47
25000	2157.42	1113.66	766.23	592.88	489.16	420.25	371.24	334.66	306.37	283.87	265.60	250.49
26000	2243.71	1158.21	796.88	616.59	508.72	437.06	386.09	348.05	318.62	295.23	276.22	260.50
27000	2330.01	1202.75	827.53	640.31	528.29	453.87	400.94	361.43	330.88	306.58	286.85	270.52
28000	2416.30	1247.30	858.18	664.02	547.86	470.68	415.79	374.82	343.13	317.94	297.47	280.54
29000	2502.60	1291.85	888.83	687.74	567.42	487.49	430.64	388.21	355.39	329.29	308.09	290.56
30000	2588.90	1336.39	919.48	711.45	586.99	504.30	445.49	401.59	367.64	340.65	318.72	300.58
31000	2675.19	1380.94	950.12	735.17	606.56	521.11	460.34	414.98	379.89	352.00	329.34	310.60
32000	2761.49	1425.49	980.77	758.88	626.12	537.92	475.19	428.36	392.15	363.36	339.97	320.62
33000	2847.79	1470.03	1011.42	782.60	645.69	554.73	490.04	441.75	404.40	374.71	350.59	330.64
34000	2934.08	1514.58	1042.07	806.31	665.25	571.54	504.89	455.14	416.66	386.07	361.21	340.66
35000	3020.38	1559.12	1072.72	830.03	684.82	588.35	519.74	468.52	428.91	397.42	371.84	350.68
37500	3236.12	1670.49	1149.34	889.32	733.74	630.38	556.86	501.99	459.55	425.81	398.40	375.73
40000	3451.86	1781.86	1225.97	948.60	782.65	672.40	593.98	535.45	490.19	454.20	424.96	400.77
42500	3667.60	1893.22	1302.59	1007.89	831.57	714.43	631.11	568.92	520.82	482.58	451.52	425.82
45000	3883.34	2004.59	1379.21	1067.18	880.48	756.45	668.23	602.39	551.46	510.97	478.07	450.87
47500	4099.08	2115.95	1455.83	1126.47	929.40	798.48	705.35	635.85	582.09	539.36	504.63	475.92
50000	4314.83	2227.32	1532.46	1185.75	978.31	840.50	742.48	669.32	612.73	567.74	531.19	500.97
52500	4530.57	2338.68	1609.08	1245.04	1027.23	882.53	779.60	702.78	643.37	596.13	557.75	526.01
55000	4746.31	2450.05	1685.70	1304.33	1076.14	924.55	816.72	736.25	674.00	624.52	584.31	551.06
57500	4962.05	2561.41	1762.32	1363.61	1125.06	966.58	853.85	769.71	704.64	652.91	610.87	576.11
60000	5177.79	2672.78	1838.95	1422.90	1173.97	1008.60	890.97	803.18	735.28	681.29	637.43	601.16
65000	5609.27	2895.51	1992.19	1541.48	1271.80	1092.65	965.22	870.11	796.55	738.07	690.55	651.25
70000	6040.75	3118.24	2145.44	1660.05	1369.64	1176.70	1039.47	937.04	857.82	794.84	743.67	701.35
75000	6472.24	3340.97	2298.68	1778.63	1467.47	1260.75	1113.71	1003.97	919.09	851.61	796.79	751.45
80000	6903.72	3563.71	2451.93	1897.20	1565.30	1344.80	1187.96	1070.90	980.37	908.39	849.91	801.54
85000	7335.20	3786.44	2605.17	2015.78	1663.13	1428.85	1262.21	1137.83	1041.64	965.16	903.03	851.64
90000	7766.68	4009.17	2758.42	2134.35	1760.96	1512.90	1336.45	1204.77	1102.91	1021.94	956.14	901.73
95000	8198.16	4231.90	2911.66	2252.93	1858.79	1596.95	1410.70	1271.70	1164.18	1078.71	1009.26	951.83
100000	8629.65	4454.63	3064.91	2371.50	1956.62	1681.00	1484.95	1338.63	1225.46	1135.48	1062.38	1001.93
105000	9061.13	4677.36	3218.15	2490.08	2054.45	1765.05	1559.20	1405.56	1286.73	1192.26	1115.50	1052.02
110000	9492.61	4900.09	3371.40	2608.65	2152.28	1849.10	1633.44	1472.49	1348.00	1249.03	1168.62	1102.12
115000	9924.09	5122.82	3524.64	2727.22	2250.11	1933.15	1707.69	1539.42	1409.27	1305.81	1221.74	1152.21
120000	10355.58	5345.56	3677.89	2845.80	2347.94	2017.20	1781.94	1606.35	1470.55	1362.58	1274.86	1202.31
125000	10787.06	5568.29	3831.13	2964.37	2445.77	2101.25	1856.18	1673.28	1531.82	1419.35	1327.98	1252.41
130000	11218.54	5791.02	3984.38	3082.95	2543.60	2185.30	1930.43	1740.22	1593.09	1476.13	1381.09	1302.50
135000	11650.02	6013.75	4137.62	3201.52	2641.44	2269.35	2004.68	1807.15	1654.36	1532.90	1434.21	1352.60
140000	12081.50	6236.48	4290.87	3320.10	2739.27	2353.40	2078.93	1874.08	1715.64	1589.68	1487.33	1402.69
145000	12512.99	6459.21	4444.11	3438.67	2837.10	2437.44	2153.17	1941.01	1776.91	1646.45	1540.45	1452.79
150000	12944.47	6681.94	4597.36	3557.25	2934.93	2521.49	2227.42	2007.94	1838.18	1703.22	1593.57	1502.89
155000	13375.95	6904.67	4750.60	3675.82	3032.76	2605.54	2301.67	2074.87	1899.45	1760.00	1646.69	1552.98
160000	13807.43	7127.41	4903.85	3794.40	3130.59	2689.59	2375.91	2141.80	1960.73	1816.77	1699.81	1603.08

14

AMOUNT OF LOAN	NUMBER OF YEARS IN TERM											
	13	14	15	16	17	18	19	20	25	30	35	40
$ 50	0.48	0.46	0.44	0.42	0.41	0.40	0.39	0.38	0.34	0.32	0.31	0.30
100	0.96	0.91	0.88	0.84	0.82	0.79	0.77	0.75	0.68	0.64	0.61	0.59
200	1.91	1.82	1.75	1.68	1.63	1.58	1.53	1.50	1.36	1.27	1.21	1.18
300	2.86	2.73	2.62	2.52	2.44	2.36	2.30	2.24	2.03	1.90	1.82	1.76
400	3.81	3.64	3.49	3.36	3.25	3.15	3.06	2.99	2.71	2.53	2.42	2.35
500	4.76	4.55	4.36	4.20	4.06	3.94	3.83	3.73	3.38	3.17	3.03	2.93
600	5.71	5.45	5.23	5.04	4.87	4.72	4.59	4.48	4.06	3.80	3.63	3.52
700	6.66	6.36	6.10	5.88	5.68	5.51	5.36	5.22	4.73	4.43	4.23	4.10
800	7.61	7.27	6.97	6.72	6.49	6.30	6.12	5.97	5.41	5.06	4.84	4.69
900	8.57	8.18	7.84	7.56	7.31	7.08	6.89	6.72	6.08	5.69	5.44	5.27
1000	9.52	9.09	8.72	8.40	8.12	7.87	7.65	7.46	6.76	6.33	6.05	5.86
2000	19.03	18.17	17.43	16.79	16.23	15.74	15.30	14.92	13.51	12.65	12.09	11.71
3000	28.54	27.25	26.14	25.18	24.34	23.60	22.95	22.37	20.26	18.97	18.13	17.57
4000	38.05	36.33	34.85	33.57	32.45	31.47	30.60	29.83	27.01	25.29	24.17	23.42
5000	47.56	45.41	43.56	41.96	40.56	39.33	38.25	37.28	33.77	31.61	30.21	29.28
6000	57.08	54.49	52.27	50.35	48.67	47.20	45.90	44.74	40.52	37.93	36.25	35.13
7000	66.59	63.57	60.98	58.74	56.78	55.06	53.54	52.20	47.27	44.25	42.30	40.99
8000	76.10	72.65	69.69	67.13	64.89	62.93	61.19	59.65	54.02	50.57	48.34	46.84
9000	85.61	81.73	78.40	75.52	73.01	70.80	68.84	67.11	60.77	56.89	54.38	52.70
10000	95.12	90.81	87.12	83.91	81.12	78.66	76.49	74.56	67.53	63.21	60.42	58.55
11000	104.64	99.90	95.83	92.30	89.23	86.53	84.14	82.02	74.28	69.53	66.46	64.41
12000	114.15	108.98	104.54	100.69	97.34	94.39	91.79	89.47	81.03	75.85	72.50	70.26
13000	123.66	118.06	113.25	109.08	105.45	102.26	99.44	96.93	87.78	82.17	78.55	76.11
14000	133.17	127.14	121.96	117.48	113.56	110.12	107.08	104.39	94.53	88.49	84.59	81.97
15000	142.68	136.22	130.67	125.87	121.67	117.99	114.73	111.84	101.29	94.82	90.63	87.82
16000	152.20	145.30	139.38	134.26	129.78	125.85	122.38	119.30	108.04	101.14	96.67	93.68
17000	161.71	154.38	148.09	142.65	137.90	133.72	130.03	126.75	114.79	107.46	102.71	99.53
18000	171.22	163.46	156.80	151.04	146.01	141.59	137.68	134.21	121.54	113.78	108.75	105.39
19000	180.73	172.54	165.52	159.43	154.12	149.45	145.33	141.66	128.29	120.10	114.79	111.24
20000	190.24	181.62	174.23	167.82	162.23	157.32	152.98	149.12	135.05	126.42	120.84	117.10
21000	199.75	190.71	182.94	176.21	170.34	165.18	160.62	156.58	141.80	132.74	126.88	122.95
22000	209.27	199.79	191.65	184.60	178.45	173.05	168.27	164.03	148.55	139.06	132.92	128.81
23000	218.78	208.87	200.36	192.99	186.56	180.91	175.92	171.49	155.30	145.38	138.96	134.66
24000	228.29	217.95	209.07	201.38	194.67	188.78	183.57	178.94	162.05	151.70	145.00	140.51
25000	237.80	227.03	217.78	209.77	202.79	196.65	191.22	186.40	168.81	158.02	151.04	146.37
26000	247.31	236.11	226.49	218.16	210.90	204.51	198.87	193.85	175.56	164.34	157.09	152.22
27000	256.83	245.19	235.20	226.56	219.01	212.38	206.52	201.31	182.31	170.66	163.13	158.08
28000	266.34	254.27	243.92	234.95	227.12	220.24	214.16	208.77	189.06	176.98	169.17	163.93
29000	275.85	263.35	252.63	243.34	235.23	228.11	221.81	216.22	195.82	183.30	175.21	169.79
30000	285.36	272.43	261.34	251.73	243.34	235.97	229.46	223.68	202.57	189.63	181.25	175.64
31000	294.87	281.51	270.05	260.12	251.45	243.84	237.11	231.13	209.32	195.95	187.29	181.50
32000	304.39	290.60	278.76	268.51	259.56	251.70	244.76	238.59	216.07	202.27	193.33	187.35
33000	313.90	299.68	287.47	276.90	267.67	259.57	252.41	246.04	222.82	208.59	199.38	193.21
34000	323.41	308.76	296.18	285.29	275.79	267.44	260.06	253.50	229.58	214.91	205.42	199.06
35000	332.92	317.84	304.89	293.68	283.90	275.30	267.70	260.96	236.33	221.23	211.46	204.91
37500	356.70	340.54	326.67	314.66	304.18	294.97	286.83	279.59	253.21	237.03	226.56	219.55
40000	380.48	363.24	348.45	335.64	324.45	314.63	305.95	298.23	270.09	252.83	241.67	234.19
42500	404.26	385.95	370.23	356.61	344.73	334.29	325.07	316.87	286.97	268.63	256.77	248.82
45000	428.04	408.65	392.00	377.59	365.01	353.96	344.19	335.51	303.85	284.44	271.87	263.46
47500	451.82	431.35	413.78	398.57	385.29	373.62	363.31	354.15	320.73	300.24	286.98	278.10
50000	475.60	454.05	435.56	419.54	405.57	393.29	382.43	372.79	337.61	316.04	302.08	292.73
52500	499.38	476.76	457.34	440.52	425.84	412.95	401.55	391.43	354.49	331.84	317.19	307.37
55000	523.16	499.46	479.11	461.50	446.12	432.61	420.68	410.07	371.37	347.64	332.29	322.01
57500	546.94	522.16	500.89	482.47	466.40	452.28	439.80	428.71	388.25	363.44	347.39	336.64
60000	570.72	544.86	522.67	503.45	486.68	471.94	458.92	447.35	405.13	379.25	362.50	351.28
65000	618.28	590.27	566.22	545.40	527.23	511.27	497.16	484.63	438.89	410.85	392.71	380.55
70000	665.84	635.67	609.78	587.36	567.79	550.60	535.40	521.91	472.65	442.45	422.91	409.82
75000	713.40	681.08	653.34	629.31	608.35	589.93	573.65	559.18	506.41	474.06	453.12	439.10
80000	760.96	726.48	696.89	671.27	648.90	629.25	611.89	596.46	540.17	505.66	483.33	468.37
85000	808.52	771.89	740.45	713.22	689.46	668.58	650.13	633.74	573.93	537.26	513.54	497.64
90000	856.08	817.29	784.00	755.17	730.01	707.91	688.38	671.02	607.69	568.87	543.74	526.92
95000	903.64	862.70	827.56	797.13	770.57	747.24	726.62	708.30	641.45	600.47	573.95	556.19
100000	951.20	908.10	871.11	839.08	811.13	786.57	764.86	745.58	675.21	632.07	604.16	585.46
105000	998.75	953.51	914.67	881.03	851.68	825.89	803.10	782.86	708.97	663.68	634.37	614.73
110000	1046.31	998.91	958.22	922.99	892.24	865.22	841.35	820.14	742.73	695.28	664.57	644.01
115000	1093.87	1044.32	1001.78	964.94	932.79	904.55	879.59	857.41	776.49	726.88	694.78	673.28
120000	1141.43	1089.72	1045.33	1006.90	973.35	943.88	917.83	894.69	810.25	758.49	724.99	702.55
125000	1188.99	1135.13	1088.89	1048.85	1013.91	983.21	956.07	931.97	844.01	790.09	755.20	731.83
130000	1236.55	1180.53	1132.44	1090.80	1054.46	1022.53	994.32	969.25	877.77	821.69	785.41	761.10
135000	1284.11	1225.93	1176.00	1132.76	1095.02	1061.86	1032.56	1006.53	911.53	853.30	815.61	790.37
140000	1331.67	1271.34	1219.56	1174.71	1135.57	1101.19	1070.80	1043.81	945.30	884.90	845.82	819.64
145000	1379.23	1316.74	1263.11	1216.66	1176.13	1140.52	1109.05	1081.09	979.06	916.50	876.03	848.92
150000	1426.79	1362.15	1306.67	1258.62	1216.69	1179.85	1147.29	1118.36	1012.82	948.11	906.24	878.19
155000	1474.35	1407.55	1350.22	1300.57	1257.24	1219.17	1185.53	1155.64	1046.58	979.71	936.44	907.46
160000	1521.91	1452.96	1393.78	1342.53	1297.80	1258.50	1223.77	1192.92	1080.34	1011.31	966.65	936.74

AMOUNT OF LOAN	NUMBER OF YEARS IN TERM											
	1	2	3	4	5	6	7	8	9	10	11	12
$ 50	4.33	2.24	1.54	1.20	0.99	0.85	0.75	0.68	0.62	0.58	0.54	0.51
100	8.65	4.47	3.08	2.39	1.97	1.70	1.50	1.36	1.24	1.15	1.08	1.02
200	17.29	8.94	6.16	4.77	3.94	3.39	3.00	2.71	2.48	2.30	2.16	2.04
300	25.93	13.40	9.23	7.15	5.91	5.08	4.50	4.06	3.72	3.45	3.23	3.05
400	34.57	17.87	12.31	9.54	7.88	6.78	5.99	5.41	4.96	4.60	4.31	4.07
500	43.21	22.33	15.39	11.92	9.85	8.47	7.49	6.76	6.20	5.75	5.38	5.08
600	51.85	26.80	18.46	14.30	11.82	10.16	8.99	8.11	7.43	6.89	6.46	6.10
700	60.49	31.27	21.54	16.69	13.78	11.86	10.48	9.46	8.67	8.04	7.53	7.11
800	69.13	35.73	24.62	19.07	15.75	13.55	11.98	10.81	9.91	9.19	8.61	8.13
900	77.78	40.20	27.69	21.45	17.72	15.24	13.48	12.16	11.15	10.34	9.68	9.14
1000	86.42	44.66	30.77	23.84	19.69	16.93	14.98	13.51	12.39	11.49	10.76	10.16
2000	172.83	89.32	61.53	47.67	39.37	33.86	29.95	27.02	24.77	22.97	21.51	20.31
3000	259.24	133.98	92.29	71.50	59.06	50.79	44.92	40.53	37.15	34.45	32.27	30.46
4000	345.65	178.64	123.06	95.33	78.74	67.72	59.89	54.04	49.53	45.93	43.02	40.61
5000	432.06	223.30	153.82	119.16	98.42	84.65	74.86	67.55	61.91	57.42	53.77	50.76
6000	518.47	267.96	184.58	142.99	118.11	101.58	89.83	81.06	74.29	68.90	64.53	60.91
7000	604.89	312.62	215.35	166.82	137.79	118.51	104.80	94.57	86.67	80.38	75.28	71.06
8000	691.30	357.28	246.11	190.65	157.47	135.44	119.77	108.08	99.05	91.86	86.03	81.21
9000	777.71	401.94	276.87	214.48	177.16	152.37	134.74	121.59	111.43	103.35	96.79	91.36
10000	864.12	446.60	307.63	238.31	196.84	169.30	149.71	135.10	123.81	114.83	107.54	101.52
11000	950.53	491.26	338.40	262.14	216.52	186.23	164.68	148.61	136.19	126.31	118.29	111.67
12000	1036.94	535.92	369.16	285.97	236.21	203.16	179.65	162.12	148.57	137.79	129.05	121.82
13000	1123.36	580.58	399.92	309.80	255.89	220.08	194.62	175.63	160.95	149.28	139.80	131.97
14000	1209.77	625.24	430.69	333.63	275.57	237.01	209.60	189.14	173.33	160.76	150.55	142.12
15000	1296.18	669.89	461.45	357.46	295.26	253.94	224.57	202.65	185.71	172.24	161.31	152.27
16000	1382.59	714.55	492.21	381.29	314.94	270.87	239.54	216.16	198.09	183.72	172.06	162.42
17000	1469.00	759.21	522.97	405.12	334.62	287.80	254.51	229.67	210.47	195.21	182.81	172.57
18000	1555.41	803.87	553.74	428.95	354.31	304.73	269.48	243.18	222.85	206.69	193.57	182.72
19000	1641.82	848.53	584.50	452.78	373.99	321.66	284.45	256.69	235.23	218.17	204.32	192.87
20000	1728.24	893.19	615.26	476.61	393.67	338.59	299.42	270.20	247.61	229.65	215.07	203.03
21000	1814.65	937.85	646.03	500.44	413.36	355.52	314.39	283.71	259.99	241.14	225.83	213.18
22000	1901.06	982.51	676.79	524.27	433.04	372.45	329.36	297.22	272.37	252.62	236.58	223.33
23000	1987.47	1027.17	707.55	548.10	452.72	389.38	344.33	310.73	284.75	264.10	247.34	233.48
24000	2073.88	1071.83	738.32	571.94	472.41	406.31	359.30	324.24	297.13	275.58	258.09	243.63
25000	2160.29	1116.49	769.08	595.77	492.09	423.24	374.27	337.75	309.51	287.07	268.84	253.78
26000	2246.71	1161.15	799.84	619.60	511.77	440.16	389.24	351.26	321.89	298.55	279.60	263.93
27000	2333.12	1205.81	830.60	643.43	531.46	457.09	404.22	364.77	334.27	310.03	290.35	274.08
28000	2419.53	1250.47	861.37	667.26	551.14	474.02	419.19	378.27	346.65	321.51	301.10	284.23
29000	2505.94	1295.13	892.13	691.09	570.83	490.95	434.16	391.78	359.03	332.99	311.86	294.38
30000	2592.35	1339.78	922.89	714.92	590.51	507.88	449.13	405.29	371.41	344.48	322.61	304.54
31000	2678.76	1384.44	953.66	738.75	610.19	524.81	464.10	418.80	383.79	355.96	333.36	314.69
32000	2765.17	1429.10	984.42	762.58	629.88	541.74	479.07	432.31	396.17	367.44	344.12	324.84
33000	2851.59	1473.76	1015.18	786.41	649.56	558.67	494.04	445.82	408.55	378.92	354.87	334.99
34000	2938.00	1518.42	1045.94	810.24	669.24	575.60	509.01	459.33	420.93	390.41	365.62	345.14
35000	3024.41	1563.08	1076.71	834.07	688.93	592.53	523.98	472.84	433.31	401.89	376.38	355.29
37500	3240.44	1674.73	1153.61	893.65	738.13	634.85	561.41	506.62	464.26	430.60	403.26	380.67
40000	3456.47	1786.38	1230.52	953.22	787.34	677.17	598.84	540.39	495.21	459.30	430.14	406.05
42500	3672.50	1898.03	1307.43	1012.80	836.55	719.50	636.26	574.16	526.16	488.01	457.03	431.42
45000	3888.52	2009.67	1384.34	1072.37	885.76	761.82	673.69	607.94	557.11	516.71	483.91	456.80
47500	4104.55	2121.32	1461.24	1131.95	934.97	804.14	711.12	641.71	588.06	545.42	510.80	482.18
50000	4320.58	2232.97	1538.15	1191.53	984.18	846.47	748.54	675.49	619.01	574.13	537.68	507.56
52500	4536.61	2344.62	1615.06	1251.10	1033.39	888.79	785.97	709.26	649.96	602.83	564.56	532.93
55000	4752.64	2456.27	1691.97	1310.68	1082.60	931.11	823.40	743.04	680.91	631.54	591.45	558.31
57500	4968.67	2567.92	1768.87	1370.25	1131.80	973.43	860.82	776.81	711.86	660.24	618.33	583.69
60000	5184.70	2679.56	1845.78	1429.83	1181.01	1015.76	898.25	810.58	742.81	688.95	645.21	609.07
65000	5616.76	2902.86	1999.59	1548.98	1279.43	1100.40	973.10	878.13	804.71	746.36	698.98	659.82
70000	6048.81	3126.16	2153.41	1668.13	1377.85	1185.05	1047.96	945.68	866.61	803.77	752.75	710.58
75000	6480.87	3349.45	2307.22	1787.29	1476.26	1269.70	1122.81	1013.23	928.51	861.19	806.52	761.33
80000	6912.93	3572.75	2461.04	1906.44	1574.68	1354.34	1197.67	1080.78	990.41	918.60	860.28	812.09
85000	7344.99	3796.05	2614.85	2025.59	1673.10	1438.99	1272.52	1148.32	1052.31	976.01	914.05	862.84
90000	7777.04	4019.34	2768.67	2144.74	1771.52	1523.63	1347.37	1215.87	1114.21	1033.42	967.82	913.60
95000	8209.10	4242.64	2922.48	2263.90	1869.93	1608.28	1422.23	1283.42	1176.11	1090.83	1021.59	964.35
100000	8641.16	4465.94	3076.30	2383.05	1968.35	1692.93	1497.08	1350.97	1238.01	1148.25	1075.35	1015.11
105000	9073.22	4689.23	3230.11	2502.20	2066.77	1777.57	1571.94	1418.52	1299.91	1205.66	1129.12	1065.86
110000	9505.27	4912.53	3383.93	2621.35	2165.19	1862.22	1646.79	1486.07	1361.81	1263.07	1182.89	1116.62
115000	9937.33	5135.83	3537.74	2740.50	2263.60	1946.86	1721.64	1553.61	1423.71	1320.48	1236.66	1167.37
120000	10369.39	5359.12	3691.56	2859.66	2362.02	2031.51	1796.50	1621.16	1485.61	1377.89	1290.42	1218.13
125000	10801.45	5582.42	3845.37	2978.81	2460.44	2116.16	1871.35	1688.71	1547.51	1435.31	1344.19	1268.88
130000	11233.51	5805.72	3999.18	3097.96	2558.85	2200.80	1946.20	1756.26	1609.41	1492.72	1397.96	1319.64
135000	11665.56	6029.01	4153.00	3217.11	2657.27	2285.45	2021.06	1823.81	1671.31	1550.13	1451.73	1370.39
140000	12097.62	6252.31	4306.81	3336.26	2755.69	2370.09	2095.91	1891.35	1733.21	1607.54	1505.49	1421.15
145000	12529.68	6475.61	4460.63	3455.42	2854.11	2454.74	2170.77	1958.90	1795.11	1664.95	1559.26	1471.90
150000	12961.74	6698.90	4614.44	3574.57	2952.52	2539.39	2245.62	2026.45	1857.01	1722.37	1613.03	1522.66
155000	13393.79	6922.20	4768.26	3693.72	3050.94	2624.03	2320.47	2094.00	1918.91	1779.78	1666.80	1573.41
160000	13825.85	7145.50	4922.07	3812.87	3149.36	2708.68	2395.33	2161.55	1980.81	1837.19	1720.56	1624.17

16

MONTHLY AMORTIZING PAYMENTS 6.75%

AMOUNT OF LOAN	13	14	15	16	17	18	19	20	25	30	35	40
$ 50	0.49	0.47	0.45	0.43	0.42	0.41	0.39	0.39	0.35	0.33	0.32	0.31
100	0.97	0.93	0.89	0.86	0.83	0.81	0.78	0.77	0.70	0.65	0.63	0.61
200	1.93	1.85	1.77	1.71	1.66	1.61	1.56	1.53	1.39	1.30	1.25	1.21
300	2.90	2.77	2.66	2.56	2.48	2.41	2.34	2.29	2.08	1.95	1.87	1.82
400	3.86	3.69	3.54	3.42	3.31	3.21	3.12	3.05	2.77	2.60	2.49	2.42
500	4.83	4.61	4.43	4.27	4.13	4.01	3.90	3.81	3.46	3.25	3.11	3.02
600	5.79	5.54	5.31	5.12	4.96	4.81	4.68	4.57	4.15	3.90	3.73	3.63
700	6.76	6.46	6.20	5.98	5.78	5.61	5.46	5.33	4.84	4.55	4.35	4.23
800	7.72	7.38	7.08	6.83	6.61	6.41	6.24	6.09	5.53	5.19	4.98	4.83
900	8.69	8.30	7.97	7.68	7.43	7.21	7.02	6.85	6.22	5.84	5.60	5.44
1000	9.65	9.22	8.85	8.54	8.26	8.01	7.80	7.61	6.91	6.49	6.22	6.04
2000	19.30	18.44	17.70	17.07	16.51	16.02	15.59	15.21	13.82	12.98	12.43	12.07
3000	28.94	27.66	26.55	25.60	24.76	24.03	23.39	22.82	20.73	19.46	18.65	18.11
4000	38.59	36.87	35.40	34.13	33.02	32.04	31.18	30.42	27.64	25.95	24.86	24.14
5000	48.23	46.09	44.25	42.66	41.27	40.05	38.98	38.02	34.55	32.43	31.08	30.17
6000	57.88	55.31	53.10	51.19	49.52	48.06	46.77	45.63	41.46	38.92	37.29	36.21
7000	67.53	64.52	61.95	59.72	57.78	56.07	54.57	53.23	48.37	45.41	43.50	42.24
8000	77.17	73.74	70.80	68.25	66.03	64.08	62.36	60.83	55.28	51.89	49.72	48.27
9000	86.82	82.96	79.65	76.78	74.28	72.09	70.16	68.44	62.19	58.38	55.93	54.31
10000	96.46	92.17	88.50	85.31	82.54	80.10	77.95	76.04	69.10	64.86	62.15	60.34
11000	106.11	101.39	97.35	93.84	90.79	88.11	85.75	83.65	76.01	71.35	68.36	66.37
12000	115.75	110.61	106.19	102.37	99.04	96.12	93.54	91.25	82.91	77.84	74.57	72.41
13000	125.40	119.83	115.04	110.91	107.30	104.13	101.33	98.85	89.82	84.32	80.79	78.44
14000	135.05	129.04	123.89	119.44	115.55	112.14	109.13	106.46	96.73	90.81	87.00	84.47
15000	144.69	138.26	132.74	127.97	123.80	120.15	116.92	114.06	103.64	97.29	93.22	90.51
16000	154.34	147.48	141.59	136.50	132.06	128.16	124.72	121.66	110.55	103.78	99.43	96.54
17000	163.98	156.69	150.44	145.03	140.31	136.17	132.51	129.27	117.46	110.27	105.65	102.58
18000	173.63	165.91	159.29	153.56	148.56	144.18	140.31	136.87	124.37	116.75	111.86	108.61
19000	183.28	175.13	168.14	162.09	156.82	152.19	148.10	144.47	131.28	123.24	118.07	114.64
20000	192.92	184.34	176.99	170.62	165.07	160.20	155.90	152.08	138.19	129.72	124.29	120.68
21000	202.57	193.56	185.84	179.15	173.32	168.21	163.69	159.68	145.10	136.21	130.50	126.71
22000	212.21	202.78	194.69	187.68	181.58	176.22	171.49	167.29	152.01	142.70	136.72	132.74
23000	221.86	211.99	203.53	196.21	189.83	184.23	179.28	174.89	158.91	149.18	142.93	138.78
24000	231.50	221.21	212.38	204.74	198.08	192.24	187.07	182.49	165.82	155.67	149.14	144.81
25000	241.15	230.43	221.23	213.28	206.34	200.25	194.87	190.10	172.73	162.15	155.36	150.84
26000	250.80	239.65	230.08	221.81	214.59	208.26	202.66	197.70	179.64	168.64	161.57	156.88
27000	260.44	248.86	238.93	230.34	222.84	216.27	210.46	205.30	186.55	175.13	167.79	162.91
28000	270.09	258.08	247.78	238.87	231.10	224.28	218.25	212.91	193.46	181.61	174.00	168.94
29000	279.73	267.30	256.63	247.40	239.35	232.28	226.05	220.51	200.37	188.10	180.22	174.98
30000	289.38	276.51	265.48	255.93	247.60	240.29	233.84	228.11	207.28	194.58	186.43	181.01
31000	299.02	285.73	274.33	264.46	255.86	248.30	241.64	235.72	214.19	201.07	192.64	187.05
32000	308.67	294.95	283.18	272.99	264.11	256.31	249.43	243.32	221.10	207.56	198.86	193.08
33000	318.32	304.16	292.03	281.52	272.36	264.32	257.23	250.93	228.01	214.04	205.07	199.11
34000	327.96	313.38	300.87	290.05	280.62	272.33	265.02	258.53	234.91	220.53	211.29	205.15
35000	337.61	322.60	309.72	298.58	288.87	280.34	272.81	266.13	241.82	227.01	217.50	211.18
37500	361.72	345.64	331.85	319.91	309.50	300.37	292.30	285.14	259.10	243.23	233.04	226.26
40000	385.84	368.68	353.97	341.24	330.14	320.39	311.79	304.15	276.37	259.44	248.57	241.35
42500	409.95	391.72	376.09	362.56	350.77	340.41	331.27	323.16	293.64	275.66	264.11	256.43
45000	434.07	414.77	398.21	383.89	371.40	360.44	350.76	342.17	310.92	291.87	279.64	271.52
47500	458.18	437.81	420.34	405.22	392.04	380.46	370.25	361.18	328.19	308.09	295.18	286.60
50000	482.30	460.85	442.46	426.55	412.67	400.49	389.73	380.19	345.46	324.30	310.71	301.68
52500	506.41	483.89	464.58	447.87	433.30	420.51	409.22	399.20	362.73	340.52	326.25	316.77
55000	530.52	506.94	486.71	469.20	453.93	440.54	428.71	418.21	380.01	356.73	341.78	331.85
57500	554.64	529.98	508.83	490.53	474.57	460.56	448.19	437.21	397.28	372.95	357.32	346.94
60000	578.75	553.02	530.95	511.85	495.20	480.58	467.68	456.22	414.55	389.16	372.85	362.02
65000	626.98	599.11	575.20	554.51	536.47	520.63	506.65	494.24	449.10	421.59	403.93	392.19
70000	675.21	645.19	619.44	597.16	577.73	560.68	545.62	532.26	483.64	454.02	435.00	422.35
75000	723.44	691.27	663.69	639.82	619.00	600.73	584.60	570.28	518.19	486.45	466.07	452.52
80000	771.67	737.36	707.93	682.47	660.27	640.78	623.57	608.30	552.73	518.88	497.14	482.69
85000	819.90	783.44	752.18	725.12	701.53	680.82	662.54	646.31	587.28	551.31	528.21	512.86
90000	868.13	829.53	796.42	767.78	742.80	720.87	701.51	684.33	621.83	583.74	559.28	543.03
95000	916.36	875.61	840.67	810.43	784.07	760.92	740.49	722.35	656.37	616.17	590.35	573.19
100000	964.59	921.70	884.91	853.09	825.33	800.97	779.46	760.37	690.92	648.60	621.42	603.36
105000	1012.81	967.78	929.16	895.74	866.60	841.02	818.43	798.39	725.46	681.03	652.49	633.53
110000	1061.04	1013.87	973.41	938.39	907.86	881.07	857.41	836.41	760.01	713.46	683.56	663.70
115000	1109.27	1059.95	1017.65	981.05	949.13	921.11	896.38	874.42	794.55	745.89	714.63	693.87
120000	1157.50	1106.04	1061.90	1023.70	990.40	961.16	935.35	912.44	829.10	778.32	745.70	724.03
125000	1205.73	1152.12	1106.14	1066.36	1031.66	1001.21	974.32	950.46	863.64	810.75	776.78	754.20
130000	1253.96	1198.21	1150.39	1109.01	1072.93	1041.26	1013.30	988.48	898.19	843.18	807.85	784.37
135000	1302.19	1244.29	1194.63	1151.66	1114.20	1081.31	1052.27	1026.50	932.74	875.61	838.92	814.54
140000	1350.42	1290.38	1238.88	1194.32	1155.46	1121.36	1091.24	1064.51	967.28	908.04	869.99	844.70
145000	1398.65	1336.46	1283.12	1236.97	1196.73	1161.40	1130.21	1102.53	1001.83	940.47	901.06	874.87
150000	1446.88	1382.54	1327.37	1279.63	1237.99	1201.45	1169.19	1140.55	1036.37	972.90	932.13	905.04
155000	1495.10	1428.63	1371.61	1322.28	1279.26	1241.50	1208.16	1178.57	1070.92	1005.33	963.20	935.21
160000	1543.33	1474.71	1415.86	1364.93	1320.53	1281.55	1247.13	1216.59	1105.46	1037.76	994.27	965.38

MONTHLY AMORTIZING PAYMENTS

AMOUNT OF LOAN	NUMBER OF YEARS IN TERM											
	1	2	3	4	5	6	7	8	9	10	11	12
$ 50	4.33	2.24	1.55	1.20	1.00	0.86	0.76	0.69	0.63	0.59	0.55	0.52
100	8.66	4.48	3.09	2.40	1.99	1.71	1.51	1.37	1.26	1.17	1.09	1.03
200	17.31	8.96	6.18	4.79	3.97	3.41	3.02	2.73	2.51	2.33	2.18	2.06
300	25.96	13.44	9.27	7.19	5.95	5.12	4.53	4.10	3.76	3.49	3.27	3.09
400	34.62	17.91	12.36	9.58	7.93	6.82	6.04	5.46	5.01	4.65	4.36	4.12
500	43.27	22.39	15.44	11.98	9.91	8.53	7.55	6.82	6.26	5.81	5.45	5.15
600	51.92	26.87	18.53	14.37	11.89	10.23	9.06	8.19	7.51	6.97	6.54	6.18
700	60.57	31.35	21.62	16.77	13.87	11.94	10.57	9.55	8.76	8.13	7.62	7.20
800	69.23	35.82	24.71	19.16	15.85	13.64	12.08	10.91	10.01	9.29	8.71	8.23
900	77.88	40.30	27.79	21.56	17.83	15.35	13.59	12.28	11.26	10.45	9.80	9.26
1000	86.53	44.78	30.88	23.95	19.81	17.05	15.10	13.64	12.51	11.62	10.89	10.29
2000	173.06	89.55	61.76	47.90	39.61	34.10	30.19	27.27	25.02	23.23	21.77	20.57
3000	259.59	134.32	92.64	71.84	59.41	51.15	45.28	40.91	37.52	34.84	32.66	30.86
4000	346.11	179.10	123.51	95.79	79.21	68.20	60.38	54.54	50.03	46.45	43.54	41.14
5000	432.64	223.87	154.39	119.74	99.01	85.25	75.47	68.17	62.54	58.06	54.43	51.42
6000	519.17	268.64	185.27	143.68	118.81	102.30	90.56	81.81	75.04	69.67	65.31	61.71
7000	605.69	313.41	216.14	167.63	138.61	119.35	105.65	95.44	87.55	81.28	76.19	71.99
8000	692.22	358.19	247.02	191.57	158.41	136.40	120.75	109.07	100.06	92.89	87.08	82.28
9000	778.75	402.96	277.90	215.52	178.22	153.45	135.84	122.71	112.56	104.50	97.96	92.56
10000	865.27	447.73	308.78	239.47	198.02	170.50	150.93	136.34	125.07	116.11	108.85	102.84
11000	951.80	492.50	339.65	263.41	217.82	187.54	166.02	149.98	137.57	127.72	119.73	113.13
12000	1038.33	537.28	370.53	287.36	237.62	204.59	181.12	163.61	150.08	139.34	130.61	123.41
13000	1124.85	582.05	401.41	311.31	257.42	221.64	196.21	177.24	162.59	150.95	141.50	133.69
14000	1211.38	626.82	432.28	335.25	277.22	238.69	211.30	190.88	175.09	162.56	152.38	143.98
15000	1297.91	671.59	463.16	359.20	297.02	255.74	226.40	204.51	187.60	174.17	163.27	154.26
16000	1384.43	716.37	494.04	383.14	316.82	272.79	241.49	218.14	200.11	185.78	174.15	164.55
17000	1470.96	761.14	524.92	407.09	336.63	289.84	256.58	231.78	212.61	197.39	185.03	174.83
18000	1557.49	805.91	555.79	431.04	356.43	306.89	271.67	245.41	225.12	209.00	195.92	185.11
19000	1644.01	850.68	586.67	454.98	376.23	323.94	286.77	259.05	237.62	220.61	206.80	195.40
20000	1730.54	895.46	617.55	478.93	396.03	340.99	301.86	272.68	250.13	232.22	217.69	205.68
21000	1817.07	940.23	648.42	502.88	415.83	358.03	316.95	286.31	262.64	243.83	228.57	215.97
22000	1903.59	985.00	679.30	526.82	435.63	375.08	332.04	299.95	275.14	255.44	239.46	226.25
23000	1990.12	1029.77	710.18	550.77	455.43	392.13	347.14	313.58	287.65	267.05	250.34	236.53
24000	2076.65	1074.55	741.06	574.71	475.23	409.18	362.23	327.21	300.16	278.67	261.22	246.82
25000	2163.17	1119.32	771.93	598.66	495.03	426.23	377.32	340.85	312.66	290.28	272.11	257.10
26000	2249.70	1164.09	802.81	622.61	514.84	443.28	392.41	354.48	325.17	301.89	282.99	267.38
27000	2336.23	1208.86	833.69	646.55	534.64	460.33	407.51	368.12	337.67	313.50	293.88	277.67
28000	2422.75	1253.64	864.56	670.50	554.44	477.38	422.60	381.75	350.18	325.11	304.76	287.95
29000	2509.28	1298.41	895.44	694.45	574.24	494.43	437.69	395.38	362.69	336.72	315.64	298.24
30000	2595.81	1343.18	926.32	718.39	594.04	511.48	452.79	409.02	375.19	348.33	326.53	308.52
31000	2682.33	1387.95	957.20	742.34	613.84	528.52	467.88	422.65	387.70	359.94	337.41	318.80
32000	2768.86	1432.73	988.07	766.28	633.64	545.57	482.97	436.28	400.21	371.55	348.30	329.09
33000	2855.39	1477.50	1018.95	790.23	653.44	562.62	498.06	449.92	412.71	383.16	359.18	339.37
34000	2941.91	1522.27	1049.83	814.18	673.25	579.67	513.16	463.55	425.22	394.77	370.06	349.65
35000	3028.44	1567.05	1080.70	838.12	693.05	596.72	528.25	477.19	437.72	406.38	380.95	359.94
37500	3244.76	1678.98	1157.90	897.99	742.55	639.34	565.98	511.27	468.99	435.41	408.16	385.65
40000	3461.07	1790.91	1235.09	957.85	792.05	681.97	603.71	545.35	500.26	464.44	435.37	411.36
42500	3677.39	1902.84	1312.28	1017.72	841.56	724.59	641.44	579.44	531.52	493.47	462.58	437.07
45000	3893.71	2014.77	1389.47	1077.59	891.06	767.21	679.18	613.52	562.79	522.49	489.79	462.78
47500	4110.03	2126.70	1466.67	1137.45	940.56	809.83	716.91	647.61	594.05	551.52	517.00	488.49
50000	4326.34	2238.63	1543.86	1197.32	990.06	852.46	754.64	681.69	625.32	580.55	544.21	514.20
52500	4542.66	2350.57	1621.05	1257.19	1039.57	895.08	792.37	715.78	656.58	609.57	571.42	539.91
55000	4758.98	2462.50	1698.25	1317.05	1089.07	937.70	830.10	749.86	687.85	638.60	598.63	565.61
57500	4975.29	2574.43	1775.44	1376.91	1138.57	980.32	867.83	783.94	719.12	667.63	625.84	591.32
60000	5191.61	2686.36	1852.63	1436.78	1188.08	1022.95	905.57	818.03	750.38	696.66	653.05	617.03
65000	5624.24	2910.22	2007.02	1556.51	1287.08	1108.19	981.03	886.20	812.91	754.71	707.47	668.45
70000	6056.88	3134.09	2161.40	1676.24	1386.09	1193.44	1056.49	954.37	875.44	812.76	761.89	719.87
75000	6489.51	3357.95	2315.79	1795.97	1485.09	1278.68	1131.96	1022.53	937.98	870.82	816.31	771.29
80000	6922.14	3581.81	2470.17	1915.70	1584.10	1363.93	1207.42	1090.70	1000.51	928.87	870.73	822.71
85000	7354.78	3805.67	2624.56	2035.44	1683.11	1449.17	1282.88	1158.87	1063.04	986.93	925.15	874.13
90000	7787.41	4029.54	2778.94	2155.17	1782.11	1534.42	1358.35	1227.04	1125.57	1044.98	979.57	925.55
95000	8220.05	4253.40	2933.33	2274.90	1881.12	1619.66	1433.81	1295.21	1188.10	1103.04	1033.99	976.97
100000	8652.68	4477.26	3087.71	2394.63	1980.12	1704.91	1509.27	1363.38	1250.63	1161.09	1088.42	1028.39
105000	9085.31	4701.13	3242.10	2514.36	2079.13	1790.15	1584.74	1431.55	1313.16	1219.14	1142.84	1079.81
110000	9517.95	4924.99	3396.49	2634.09	2178.14	1875.40	1660.20	1499.71	1375.70	1277.20	1197.26	1131.22
115000	9950.58	5148.85	3550.87	2753.82	2277.14	1960.64	1735.66	1567.88	1438.23	1335.25	1251.68	1182.64
120000	10383.21	5372.71	3705.26	2873.55	2376.15	2045.89	1811.13	1636.05	1500.76	1393.31	1306.10	1234.06
125000	10815.85	5596.58	3859.64	2993.29	2475.15	2131.13	1886.59	1704.22	1563.29	1451.36	1360.52	1285.48
130000	11248.48	5820.44	4014.03	3113.02	2574.16	2216.38	1962.05	1772.39	1625.82	1509.42	1414.94	1336.90
135000	11681.12	6044.30	4168.41	3232.75	2673.17	2301.62	2037.52	1840.56	1688.35	1567.47	1469.36	1388.32
140000	12113.75	6268.17	4322.80	3352.48	2772.17	2386.87	2112.98	1908.73	1750.88	1625.52	1523.78	1439.74
145000	12546.38	6492.03	4477.18	3472.21	2871.18	2472.11	2188.44	1976.89	1813.42	1683.58	1578.20	1491.16
150000	12979.02	6715.89	4631.57	3591.94	2970.18	2557.36	2263.91	2045.06	1875.95	1741.63	1632.62	1542.58
155000	13411.65	6939.75	4785.96	3711.67	3069.19	2642.60	2339.37	2113.23	1938.48	1799.69	1687.04	1594.00
160000	13844.28	7163.62	4940.34	3831.40	3168.20	2727.85	2414.83	2181.40	2001.01	1857.74	1741.46	1645.41

AMOUNT OF LOAN	NUMBER OF YEARS IN TERM											
	13	14	15	16	17	18	19	20	25	30	35	40
$ 50	0.49	0.47	0.45	0.44	0.42	0.41	0.40	0.39	0.36	0.34	0.32	0.32
100	0.98	0.94	0.90	0.87	0.84	0.82	0.80	0.78	0.71	0.67	0.64	0.63
200	1.96	1.88	1.80	1.74	1.68	1.64	1.59	1.56	1.42	1.34	1.28	1.25
300	2.94	2.81	2.70	2.61	2.52	2.45	2.39	2.33	2.13	2.00	1.92	1.87
400	3.92	3.75	3.60	3.47	3.36	3.27	3.18	3.11	2.83	2.67	2.56	2.49
500	4.90	4.68	4.50	4.34	4.20	4.08	3.98	3.88	3.54	3.33	3.20	3.11
600	5.87	5.62	5.40	5.21	5.04	4.90	4.77	4.66	4.25	4.00	3.84	3.73
700	6.85	6.55	6.30	6.08	5.88	5.71	5.56	5.43	4.95	4.66	4.48	4.36
800	7.83	7.49	7.20	6.94	6.72	6.53	6.36	6.21	5.66	5.33	5.12	4.98
900	8.81	8.42	8.09	7.81	7.56	7.34	7.15	6.98	6.37	5.99	5.75	5.60
1000	9.79	9.36	8.99	8.68	8.40	8.16	7.95	7.76	7.07	6.66	6.39	6.22
2000	19.57	18.71	17.98	17.35	16.80	16.32	15.89	15.51	14.14	13.31	12.78	12.43
3000	29.35	28.07	26.97	26.02	25.19	24.47	23.83	23.26	21.21	19.96	19.17	18.65
4000	39.13	37.42	35.96	34.69	33.59	32.63	31.77	31.02	28.28	26.62	25.56	24.86
5000	48.91	46.78	44.95	43.37	41.99	40.78	39.71	38.77	35.34	33.27	31.95	31.08
6000	58.69	56.13	53.93	52.04	50.38	48.94	47.66	46.52	42.41	39.92	38.34	37.29
7000	68.47	65.48	62.92	60.71	58.78	57.09	55.60	54.28	49.48	46.58	44.72	43.51
8000	78.25	74.84	71.91	69.38	67.18	65.25	63.54	62.03	56.55	53.23	51.11	49.72
9000	88.03	84.19	80.90	78.05	75.57	73.40	71.48	69.78	63.62	59.88	57.50	55.93
10000	97.81	93.55	89.89	86.73	83.97	81.56	79.42	77.53	70.68	66.54	63.89	62.15
11000	107.59	102.90	98.88	95.40	92.37	89.71	87.37	85.29	77.75	73.19	70.28	68.36
12000	117.37	112.25	107.86	104.07	100.76	97.87	95.31	93.04	84.82	79.84	76.67	74.58
13000	127.15	121.61	116.85	112.74	109.16	106.02	103.25	100.79	91.89	86.49	83.06	80.79
14000	136.94	130.96	125.84	121.41	117.56	114.18	111.19	108.55	98.95	93.15	89.44	87.01
15000	146.72	140.32	134.83	130.09	125.95	122.33	119.13	116.30	106.02	99.80	95.83	93.22
16000	156.50	149.67	143.82	138.76	134.35	130.49	127.08	124.05	113.09	106.45	102.22	99.43
17000	166.28	159.02	152.81	147.43	142.75	138.64	135.02	131.81	120.16	113.11	108.61	105.65
18000	176.06	168.38	161.79	156.10	151.14	146.80	142.96	139.56	127.23	119.76	115.00	111.86
19000	185.84	177.73	170.78	164.77	159.54	154.95	150.90	147.31	134.29	126.41	121.39	118.08
20000	195.62	187.09	179.77	173.45	167.94	163.11	158.84	155.06	141.36	133.07	127.78	124.29
21000	205.40	196.44	188.76	182.12	176.33	171.26	166.79	162.82	148.43	139.72	134.16	130.51
22000	215.18	205.79	197.75	190.79	184.73	179.42	174.73	170.57	155.50	146.37	140.55	136.72
23000	224.96	215.15	206.74	199.46	193.13	187.57	182.67	178.32	162.56	153.02	146.94	142.93
24000	234.74	224.50	215.72	208.13	201.52	195.73	190.61	186.08	169.63	159.68	153.33	149.15
25000	244.52	233.86	224.71	216.81	209.92	203.88	198.55	193.83	176.70	166.33	159.72	155.36
26000	254.30	243.21	233.70	225.48	218.32	212.04	206.50	201.58	183.77	172.98	166.11	161.58
27000	264.09	252.56	242.69	234.15	226.71	220.19	214.44	209.34	190.84	179.64	172.50	167.79
28000	273.87	261.92	251.68	242.82	235.11	228.35	222.38	217.09	197.90	186.29	178.88	174.01
29000	283.65	271.27	260.67	251.50	243.51	236.50	230.32	224.84	204.97	192.94	185.27	180.22
30000	293.43	280.63	269.65	260.17	251.90	244.66	238.26	232.59	212.04	199.60	191.66	186.43
31000	303.21	289.98	278.64	268.84	260.30	252.81	246.20	240.35	219.11	206.25	198.05	192.65
32000	312.99	299.33	287.63	277.51	268.70	260.97	254.15	248.10	226.17	212.90	204.44	198.86
33000	322.77	308.69	296.62	286.18	277.09	269.12	262.09	255.85	233.24	219.55	210.83	205.08
34000	332.55	318.04	305.61	294.86	285.49	277.28	270.03	263.61	240.31	226.21	217.22	211.29
35000	342.33	327.40	314.59	303.53	293.89	285.43	277.97	271.36	247.38	232.86	223.60	217.51
37500	366.78	350.78	337.07	325.21	314.88	305.82	297.83	290.74	265.05	249.49	239.58	233.04
40000	391.23	374.17	359.54	346.89	335.87	326.21	317.68	310.12	282.72	266.13	255.55	248.58
42500	415.69	397.55	382.01	368.57	356.86	346.59	337.54	329.51	300.39	282.76	271.52	264.11
45000	440.14	420.94	404.48	390.25	377.85	366.98	357.39	348.89	318.06	299.39	287.49	279.65
47500	464.59	444.32	426.95	411.93	398.84	387.37	377.25	368.27	335.73	316.02	303.46	295.18
50000	489.04	467.71	449.42	433.61	419.84	407.76	397.10	387.65	353.39	332.66	319.43	310.72
52500	513.49	491.09	471.89	455.29	440.83	428.14	416.96	407.04	371.06	349.29	335.40	326.26
55000	537.95	514.48	494.36	476.97	461.82	448.53	436.81	426.42	388.73	365.92	351.38	341.79
57500	562.40	537.86	516.83	498.65	482.81	468.92	456.67	445.80	406.40	382.55	367.35	357.33
60000	586.85	561.25	539.30	520.33	503.80	489.31	476.52	465.18	424.07	399.19	383.32	372.86
65000	635.75	608.02	584.24	563.69	545.78	530.08	516.23	503.95	459.41	432.45	415.26	403.94
70000	684.66	654.79	629.18	607.05	587.77	570.86	555.94	542.71	494.75	465.72	447.20	435.01
75000	733.56	701.56	674.13	650.41	629.75	611.63	595.65	581.48	530.09	498.98	479.15	466.08
80000	782.46	748.33	719.07	693.77	671.73	652.41	635.36	620.24	565.43	532.25	511.09	497.15
85000	831.37	795.10	764.01	737.13	713.72	693.18	675.07	659.01	600.77	565.51	543.03	528.22
90000	880.27	841.87	808.95	780.49	755.70	733.96	714.78	697.77	636.11	598.78	574.98	559.29
95000	929.18	888.64	853.89	823.85	797.69	774.73	754.49	736.54	671.45	632.04	606.92	590.36
100000	978.08	935.41	898.83	867.21	839.67	815.51	794.20	775.30	706.78	665.31	638.86	621.44
105000	1026.98	982.18	943.77	910.57	881.65	856.28	834.07	814.07	742.12	698.57	670.80	652.51
110000	1075.89	1028.95	988.72	953.93	923.63	897.06	873.62	852.83	777.46	731.84	702.75	683.58
115000	1124.79	1075.72	1033.66	997.29	965.61	937.83	913.33	891.60	812.80	765.10	734.69	714.65
120000	1173.69	1122.49	1078.60	1040.65	1007.60	978.61	953.04	930.36	848.14	798.37	766.63	745.72
125000	1222.60	1169.26	1123.54	1084.02	1049.58	1019.38	992.75	969.13	883.48	831.63	798.58	776.79
130000	1271.50	1216.03	1168.48	1127.38	1091.56	1060.16	1032.46	1007.89	918.82	864.90	830.52	807.87
135000	1320.41	1262.80	1213.42	1170.74	1133.55	1100.93	1072.16	1046.66	954.16	898.16	862.46	838.94
140000	1369.31	1309.57	1258.36	1214.10	1175.53	1141.71	1111.87	1085.42	989.50	931.43	894.40	870.01
145000	1418.21	1356.34	1303.31	1257.46	1217.51	1182.48	1151.58	1124.19	1024.83	964.69	926.35	901.08
150000	1467.12	1403.11	1348.25	1300.82	1259.50	1223.26	1191.29	1162.95	1060.17	997.96	958.29	932.15
155000	1516.02	1449.88	1393.19	1344.18	1301.48	1264.03	1231.00	1201.72	1095.51	1031.22	990.23	963.22
160000	1564.92	1496.65	1438.13	1387.54	1343.46	1304.81	1270.71	1240.48	1130.85	1064.49	1022.18	994.30

19

MONTHLY AMORTIZING PAYMENTS

AMOUNT OF LOAN	NUMBER OF YEARS IN TERM											
	1	2	3	4	5	6	7	8	9	10	11	12
$ 50	4.34	2.25	1.55	1.21	1.00	0.86	0.77	0.69	0.64	0.59	0.56	0.53
100	8.67	4.49	3.10	2.41	2.00	1.72	1.53	1.38	1.27	1.18	1.11	1.05
200	17.33	8.98	6.20	4.82	3.99	3.44	3.05	2.76	2.53	2.35	2.21	2.09
300	26.00	13.47	9.30	7.22	5.98	5.16	4.57	4.13	3.79	3.53	3.31	3.13
400	34.66	17.96	12.40	9.63	7.97	6.87	6.09	5.51	5.06	4.70	4.41	4.17
500	43.33	22.45	15.50	12.04	9.96	8.59	7.61	6.88	6.32	5.88	5.51	5.21
600	51.99	26.94	18.60	14.44	11.96	10.31	9.13	8.26	7.58	7.05	6.61	6.26
700	60.65	31.43	21.70	16.85	13.95	12.02	10.66	9.64	8.85	8.22	7.72	7.30
800	69.32	35.91	24.80	19.25	15.94	13.74	12.18	11.01	10.11	9.40	8.82	8.34
900	77.98	40.40	27.90	21.66	17.93	15.46	13.70	12.39	11.37	10.57	9.92	9.38
1000	86.65	44.89	31.00	24.07	19.92	17.17	15.22	13.76	12.64	11.75	11.02	10.42
2000	173.29	89.78	61.99	48.13	39.84	34.34	30.44	27.52	25.27	23.49	22.04	20.84
3000	259.93	134.66	92.98	72.19	59.76	51.51	45.65	41.28	37.90	35.23	33.05	31.26
4000	346.57	179.55	123.97	96.25	79.68	68.68	60.87	55.04	50.54	46.97	44.07	41.68
5000	433.22	224.44	154.96	120.32	99.60	85.85	76.08	68.80	63.17	58.71	55.08	52.09
6000	519.86	269.32	185.95	144.38	119.52	103.02	91.30	82.56	75.80	70.45	66.10	62.51
7000	606.50	314.21	216.95	168.44	139.44	120.19	106.51	96.31	88.44	82.19	77.11	72.93
8000	693.14	359.09	247.94	192.50	159.36	137.36	121.73	110.07	101.07	93.93	88.13	83.35
9000	779.78	403.98	278.93	216.57	179.28	154.53	136.94	123.83	113.70	105.67	99.15	93.76
10000	866.43	448.87	309.92	240.63	199.20	171.70	152.16	137.59	126.34	117.41	110.16	104.18
11000	953.07	493.75	340.91	264.69	219.12	188.87	167.37	151.35	138.97	129.15	121.18	114.60
12000	1039.71	538.64	371.90	288.75	239.04	206.04	182.59	165.11	151.60	140.89	132.19	125.02
13000	1126.35	583.52	402.89	312.82	258.96	223.21	197.80	178.86	164.24	152.63	143.21	135.43
14000	1212.99	628.41	433.89	336.88	278.88	240.38	213.02	192.62	176.87	164.37	154.22	145.85
15000	1299.64	673.30	464.88	360.94	298.80	257.54	228.23	206.38	189.50	176.11	165.24	156.27
16000	1386.28	718.18	495.87	385.00	318.71	274.71	243.45	220.14	202.14	187.85	176.25	166.69
17000	1472.92	763.07	526.86	409.07	338.63	291.88	258.66	233.90	214.77	199.59	187.27	177.10
18000	1559.56	807.95	557.85	433.13	358.55	309.05	273.88	247.66	227.40	211.33	198.29	187.52
19000	1646.20	852.84	588.84	457.19	378.47	326.22	289.09	261.42	240.04	223.07	209.30	197.94
20000	1732.85	897.73	619.84	481.25	398.39	343.39	304.31	275.17	252.67	234.81	220.32	208.36
21000	1819.49	942.61	650.83	505.32	418.31	360.56	319.52	288.93	265.30	246.55	231.33	218.77
22000	1906.13	987.50	681.82	529.38	438.23	377.73	334.74	302.69	277.94	258.29	242.35	229.19
23000	1992.77	1032.38	712.81	553.44	458.15	394.90	349.95	316.45	290.57	270.03	253.36	239.61
24000	2079.41	1077.27	743.80	577.50	478.07	412.07	365.17	330.21	303.20	281.77	264.38	250.03
25000	2166.06	1122.16	774.79	601.57	497.99	429.24	380.38	343.97	315.84	293.51	275.40	260.44
26000	2252.70	1167.04	805.78	625.63	517.91	446.41	395.60	357.72	328.47	305.25	286.41	270.86
27000	2339.34	1211.93	836.78	649.69	537.83	463.58	410.81	371.48	341.10	316.99	297.43	281.28
28000	2425.98	1256.81	867.77	673.75	557.75	480.75	426.03	385.24	353.74	328.73	308.44	291.70
29000	2512.62	1301.70	898.76	697.81	577.67	497.91	441.25	399.00	366.37	340.47	319.46	302.11
30000	2599.27	1346.59	929.75	721.88	597.59	515.08	456.46	412.76	379.00	352.21	330.47	312.53
31000	2685.91	1391.47	960.74	745.94	617.51	532.25	471.68	426.52	391.64	363.95	341.49	322.95
32000	2772.55	1436.36	991.73	770.00	637.42	549.42	486.89	440.28	404.27	375.69	352.50	333.37
33000	2859.19	1481.24	1022.73	794.06	657.34	566.59	502.11	454.03	416.90	387.43	363.52	343.78
34000	2945.83	1526.13	1053.72	818.13	677.26	583.76	517.32	467.79	429.54	399.17	374.54	354.20
35000	3032.48	1571.02	1084.71	842.19	697.18	600.93	532.54	481.55	442.17	410.91	385.55	364.62
37500	3249.08	1683.23	1162.19	902.35	746.98	643.85	570.57	515.95	473.75	440.26	413.09	390.66
40000	3465.69	1795.45	1239.67	962.50	796.78	686.78	608.61	550.34	505.34	469.61	440.63	416.71
42500	3682.29	1907.66	1317.14	1022.66	846.58	729.70	646.65	584.74	536.92	498.96	468.17	442.75
45000	3898.90	2019.88	1394.62	1082.81	896.38	772.62	684.69	619.14	568.50	528.31	495.71	468.80
47500	4115.50	2132.09	1472.10	1142.97	946.17	815.55	722.73	653.53	600.09	557.66	523.25	494.84
50000	4332.11	2244.31	1549.58	1203.13	995.97	858.47	760.76	687.93	631.67	587.01	550.79	520.88
52500	4548.71	2356.52	1627.06	1263.28	1045.77	901.39	798.80	722.32	663.25	616.36	578.32	546.93
55000	4765.32	2468.74	1704.54	1323.44	1095.57	944.32	836.84	756.72	694.84	645.71	605.86	572.97
57500	4981.92	2580.95	1782.02	1383.59	1145.37	987.24	874.88	791.12	726.42	675.06	633.40	599.01
60000	5198.53	2693.17	1859.50	1443.75	1195.17	1030.16	912.92	825.51	758.00	704.41	660.94	625.06
65000	5631.74	2917.60	2014.45	1564.06	1294.76	1116.01	988.99	894.30	821.17	763.11	716.02	677.15
70000	6064.95	3142.03	2169.41	1684.37	1394.36	1201.86	1065.07	963.10	884.33	821.81	771.10	729.23
75000	6498.16	3366.46	2324.37	1804.69	1493.96	1287.70	1141.14	1031.89	947.50	880.51	826.18	781.32
80000	6931.37	3590.89	2479.33	1925.00	1593.55	1373.55	1217.22	1100.68	1010.67	939.21	881.25	833.41
85000	7364.58	3815.32	2634.28	2045.31	1693.15	1459.40	1293.30	1169.47	1073.83	997.91	936.33	885.50
90000	7797.79	4039.75	2789.24	2165.62	1792.75	1545.24	1369.37	1238.27	1137.00	1056.61	991.41	937.59
95000	8231.00	4264.18	2944.20	2285.93	1892.34	1631.09	1445.45	1307.06	1200.17	1115.31	1046.49	989.67
100000	8664.21	4488.61	3099.16	2406.25	1991.94	1716.94	1521.52	1375.85	1263.33	1174.02	1101.57	1041.76
105000	9097.42	4713.04	3254.12	2526.56	2091.54	1802.78	1597.60	1444.64	1326.50	1232.72	1156.64	1093.85
110000	9530.63	4937.47	3409.07	2646.87	2191.13	1888.63	1673.68	1513.44	1389.67	1291.42	1211.72	1145.94
115000	9963.84	5161.90	3564.03	2767.18	2290.73	1974.48	1749.75	1582.23	1452.83	1350.12	1266.80	1198.02
120000	10397.05	5386.33	3718.99	2887.49	2390.33	2060.32	1825.83	1651.02	1516.00	1408.82	1321.88	1250.11
125000	10830.26	5610.76	3873.95	3007.81	2489.93	2146.17	1901.90	1719.81	1579.16	1467.52	1376.96	1302.20
130000	11263.47	5835.19	4028.90	3128.12	2589.52	2232.01	1977.98	1788.60	1642.33	1526.22	1432.03	1354.29
135000	11696.68	6059.62	4183.86	3248.43	2689.12	2317.86	2054.05	1857.40	1705.50	1584.92	1487.11	1406.38
140000	12129.89	6284.05	4338.82	3368.74	2788.72	2403.71	2130.13	1926.19	1768.66	1643.62	1542.19	1458.46
145000	12563.10	6508.48	4493.78	3489.05	2888.31	2489.55	2206.21	1994.98	1831.83	1702.32	1597.27	1510.55
150000	12996.31	6732.91	4648.73	3609.37	2987.91	2575.40	2282.28	2063.77	1895.00	1761.02	1652.34	1562.64
155000	13429.52	6957.34	4803.69	3729.68	3087.51	2661.25	2358.36	2132.57	1958.16	1819.72	1707.42	1614.73
160000	13862.73	7181.77	4958.65	3849.99	3187.10	2747.09	2434.43	2201.36	2021.33	1878.42	1762.50	1666.81

MONTHLY AMORTIZING PAYMENTS 7.25%

AMOUNT OF LOAN	NUMBER OF YEARS IN TERM											
	13	14	15	16	17	18	19	20	25	30	35	40
$ 50	0.50	0.48	0.46	0.45	0.43	0.42	0.41	0.40	0.37	0.35	0.33	0.32
100	1.00	0.95	0.92	0.89	0.86	0.84	0.81	0.80	0.73	0.69	0.66	0.64
200	1.99	1.90	1.83	1.77	1.71	1.67	1.62	1.59	1.45	1.37	1.32	1.28
300	2.98	2.85	2.74	2.65	2.57	2.50	2.43	2.38	2.17	2.05	1.97	1.92
400	3.97	3.80	3.66	3.53	3.42	3.33	3.24	3.17	2.90	2.73	2.63	2.56
500	4.96	4.75	4.57	4.41	4.28	4.16	4.05	3.96	3.62	3.42	3.29	3.20
600	5.96	5.70	5.48	5.29	5.13	4.99	4.86	4.75	4.34	4.10	3.94	3.84
700	6.95	6.65	6.40	6.18	5.98	5.82	5.67	5.54	5.06	4.78	4.60	4.48
800	7.94	7.60	7.31	7.06	6.84	6.65	6.48	6.33	5.79	5.46	5.26	5.12
900	8.93	8.55	8.22	7.94	7.69	7.48	7.29	7.12	6.51	6.14	5.91	5.76
1000	9.92	9.50	9.13	8.82	8.55	8.31	8.10	7.91	7.23	6.83	6.57	6.40
2000	19.84	18.99	18.26	17.63	17.09	16.61	16.19	15.81	14.46	13.65	13.13	12.80
3000	29.76	28.48	27.39	26.45	25.63	24.91	24.28	23.72	21.69	20.47	19.70	19.20
4000	39.67	37.97	36.52	35.26	34.17	33.21	32.37	31.62	28.92	27.29	26.26	25.59
5000	49.59	47.47	45.65	44.08	42.71	41.51	40.46	39.52	36.15	34.11	32.83	31.99
6000	59.51	56.96	54.78	52.89	51.25	49.82	48.55	47.43	43.37	40.94	39.39	38.39
7000	69.42	66.45	63.91	61.71	59.79	58.12	56.64	55.33	50.60	47.76	45.96	44.78
8000	79.34	75.94	73.03	70.52	68.33	66.42	64.73	63.24	57.83	54.58	52.52	51.18
9000	89.26	85.43	82.16	79.34	76.88	74.72	72.82	71.14	65.06	61.40	59.09	57.58
10000	99.17	94.93	91.29	88.15	85.42	83.02	80.91	79.04	72.29	68.22	65.65	63.97
11000	109.09	104.42	100.42	96.97	93.96	91.32	89.00	86.95	79.51	75.04	72.22	70.37
12000	119.01	113.91	109.55	105.78	102.50	99.63	97.09	94.85	86.74	81.87	78.78	76.77
13000	128.92	123.40	118.68	114.59	111.04	107.93	105.18	102.75	93.97	88.69	85.35	83.16
14000	138.84	132.90	127.81	123.41	119.58	116.23	113.27	110.66	101.20	95.51	91.91	89.56
15000	148.76	142.39	136.93	132.22	128.12	124.53	121.37	118.56	108.43	102.33	98.48	95.96
16000	158.67	151.88	146.06	141.04	136.66	132.83	129.46	126.47	115.65	109.15	105.04	102.35
17000	168.59	161.37	155.19	149.85	145.21	141.13	137.55	134.37	122.88	115.97	111.60	108.75
18000	178.51	170.86	164.32	158.67	153.75	149.44	145.64	142.27	130.11	122.80	118.17	115.15
19000	188.42	180.36	173.45	167.48	162.29	157.74	153.73	150.18	137.34	129.62	124.73	121.54
20000	198.34	189.85	182.58	176.30	170.83	166.04	161.82	158.08	144.57	136.44	131.30	127.94
21000	208.26	199.34	191.71	185.11	179.37	174.34	169.91	165.98	151.79	143.26	137.86	134.34
22000	218.17	208.83	200.83	193.93	187.91	182.64	178.00	173.89	159.02	150.08	144.43	140.73
23000	228.09	218.33	209.96	202.74	196.45	190.94	186.09	181.79	166.25	156.91	150.99	147.13
24000	238.01	227.82	219.09	211.55	204.99	199.25	194.18	189.70	173.48	163.73	157.56	153.53
25000	247.92	237.31	228.22	220.37	213.54	207.55	202.27	197.60	180.71	170.55	164.12	159.92
26000	257.84	246.80	237.35	229.18	222.08	215.85	210.36	205.50	187.93	177.37	170.69	166.32
27000	267.76	256.29	246.48	238.00	230.62	224.15	218.45	213.41	195.16	184.19	177.25	172.72
28000	277.67	265.79	255.61	246.81	239.16	232.45	226.54	221.31	202.39	191.01	183.82	179.11
29000	287.59	275.28	264.74	255.63	247.70	240.75	234.63	229.21	209.62	197.84	190.38	185.51
30000	297.51	284.77	273.86	264.44	256.24	249.06	242.73	237.12	216.85	204.66	196.95	191.91
31000	307.42	294.26	282.99	273.26	264.78	257.36	250.82	245.02	224.08	211.48	203.51	198.30
32000	317.34	303.75	292.12	282.07	273.32	265.66	258.91	252.93	231.30	218.30	210.07	204.70
33000	327.26	313.25	301.25	290.89	281.87	273.96	267.00	260.83	238.53	225.12	216.64	211.10
34000	337.17	322.74	310.38	299.70	290.41	282.26	275.09	268.73	245.76	231.94	223.20	217.49
35000	347.09	332.23	319.51	308.52	298.95	290.57	283.18	276.64	252.99	238.77	229.77	223.89
37500	371.88	355.96	342.33	330.55	320.30	311.32	303.41	296.40	271.06	255.82	246.18	239.88
40000	396.67	379.69	365.15	352.59	341.65	332.07	323.63	316.16	289.13	272.88	262.59	255.87
42500	421.47	403.42	387.97	374.62	363.01	352.83	343.86	335.91	307.20	289.93	279.00	271.87
45000	446.26	427.15	410.79	396.66	384.36	373.58	364.09	355.67	325.27	306.98	295.42	287.86
47500	471.05	450.88	433.61	418.70	405.71	394.34	384.31	375.43	343.34	324.04	311.83	303.85
50000	495.84	474.61	456.44	440.73	427.07	415.09	404.54	395.19	361.41	341.09	328.24	319.84
52500	520.63	498.34	479.26	462.77	448.42	435.85	424.77	414.95	379.48	358.15	344.65	335.83
55000	545.42	522.07	502.08	484.81	469.77	456.60	444.99	434.71	397.55	375.20	361.06	351.82
57500	570.22	545.81	524.90	506.84	491.13	477.35	465.22	454.47	415.62	392.26	377.47	367.82
60000	595.01	569.54	547.72	528.88	512.48	498.11	485.45	474.23	433.69	409.31	393.89	383.81
65000	644.59	617.00	593.37	572.95	555.18	539.62	525.90	513.75	469.83	443.42	426.71	415.79
70000	694.17	664.46	639.01	617.03	597.89	581.13	566.35	553.27	505.97	477.53	459.53	447.78
75000	743.76	711.92	684.65	661.10	640.60	622.63	606.81	592.79	542.11	511.64	492.36	479.76
80000	793.34	759.38	730.30	705.17	683.30	664.14	647.26	632.31	578.25	545.75	525.18	511.74
85000	842.93	806.84	775.94	749.24	726.01	705.65	687.71	671.82	614.39	579.85	558.00	543.73
90000	892.51	854.30	821.58	793.32	768.71	747.16	728.17	711.34	650.53	613.96	590.83	575.71
95000	942.09	901.76	867.22	837.39	811.42	788.67	768.62	750.86	686.67	648.07	623.65	607.69
100000	991.68	949.22	912.87	881.46	854.13	830.18	809.07	790.38	722.81	682.18	656.47	639.68
105000	1041.26	996.68	958.51	925.54	896.83	871.69	849.53	829.90	758.95	716.29	689.30	671.66
110000	1090.84	1044.14	1004.15	969.61	939.54	913.19	889.98	869.42	795.09	750.40	722.12	703.64
115000	1140.43	1091.61	1049.80	1013.68	982.25	954.70	930.43	908.94	831.23	784.51	754.94	735.63
120000	1190.01	1139.07	1095.44	1057.75	1024.95	996.21	970.89	948.46	867.37	818.62	787.77	767.61
125000	1239.59	1186.53	1141.08	1101.83	1067.66	1037.72	1011.34	987.97	903.51	852.73	820.59	799.59
130000	1289.18	1233.99	1186.73	1145.90	1110.36	1079.23	1051.79	1027.49	939.65	886.83	853.41	831.58
135000	1338.76	1281.45	1232.37	1189.97	1153.07	1120.74	1092.25	1067.01	975.79	920.94	886.24	863.56
140000	1388.34	1328.91	1278.01	1234.05	1195.78	1162.25	1132.70	1106.53	1011.93	955.05	919.06	895.55
145000	1437.93	1376.37	1323.66	1278.12	1238.48	1203.75	1173.15	1146.05	1048.07	989.16	951.88	927.53
150000	1487.51	1423.83	1369.30	1322.19	1281.19	1245.26	1213.61	1185.57	1084.22	1023.27	984.71	959.51
155000	1537.10	1471.29	1414.94	1366.26	1323.89	1286.77	1254.06	1225.09	1120.36	1057.38	1017.53	991.50
160000	1586.68	1518.75	1460.59	1410.34	1366.60	1328.28	1294.51	1264.61	1156.50	1091.49	1050.35	1023.48

MONTHLY AMORTIZING PAYMENTS

AMOUNT OF LOAN	NUMBER OF YEARS IN TERM											
	1	2	3	4	5	6	7	8	9	10	11	12
$ 50	4.34	2.25	1.56	1.21	1.01	0.87	0.77	0.70	0.64	0.60	0.56	0.53
100	8.68	4.50	3.12	2.42	2.01	1.73	1.54	1.39	1.28	1.19	1.12	1.06
200	17.36	9.00	6.23	4.84	4.01	3.46	3.07	2.78	2.56	2.38	2.23	2.12
300	26.03	13.50	9.34	7.26	6.02	5.19	4.61	4.17	3.83	3.57	3.35	3.17
400	34.71	18.00	12.45	9.68	8.02	6.92	6.14	5.56	5.11	4.75	4.46	4.23
500	43.38	22.50	15.56	12.09	10.02	8.65	7.67	6.95	6.39	5.94	5.58	5.28
600	52.06	27.00	18.67	14.51	12.03	10.38	9.21	8.34	7.66	7.13	6.69	6.34
700	60.74	31.50	21.78	16.93	14.03	12.11	10.74	9.72	8.94	8.31	7.81	7.39
800	69.41	36.00	24.89	19.35	16.04	13.84	12.28	11.11	10.21	9.50	8.92	8.45
900	78.09	40.50	28.00	21.77	18.04	15.57	13.81	12.50	11.49	10.69	10.04	9.50
1000	86.76	45.00	31.11	24.18	20.04	17.30	15.34	13.89	12.77	11.88	11.15	10.56
2000	173.52	90.00	62.22	48.36	40.08	34.59	30.68	27.77	25.53	23.75	22.30	21.11
3000	260.28	135.00	93.32	72.54	60.12	51.88	46.02	41.66	38.29	35.62	33.45	31.66
4000	347.03	180.00	124.43	96.72	80.16	69.17	61.36	55.54	51.05	47.49	44.60	42.21
5000	433.79	225.00	155.54	120.90	100.19	86.46	76.70	69.42	63.81	59.36	55.75	52.77
6000	520.55	270.00	186.64	145.08	120.23	103.75	92.03	83.31	76.57	71.23	66.89	63.32
7000	607.31	315.00	217.75	169.26	140.27	121.04	107.37	97.19	89.33	83.10	78.04	73.87
8000	694.06	360.00	248.85	193.44	160.31	138.33	122.71	111.08	102.09	94.97	89.19	84.42
9000	780.82	405.00	279.96	217.62	180.35	155.62	138.05	124.96	114.85	106.84	100.34	94.98
10000	867.58	450.00	311.07	241.79	200.38	172.91	153.39	138.84	127.62	118.71	111.49	105.53
11000	954.34	495.00	342.17	265.97	220.42	190.20	168.73	152.73	140.38	130.58	122.63	116.08
12000	1041.09	540.00	373.28	290.15	240.46	207.49	184.06	166.61	153.14	142.45	133.78	126.63
13000	1127.85	585.00	404.39	314.33	260.50	224.78	199.40	180.50	165.90	154.32	144.93	137.18
14000	1214.61	630.00	435.49	338.51	280.54	242.07	214.74	194.38	178.66	166.19	156.08	147.74
15000	1301.37	675.00	466.60	362.69	300.57	259.36	230.08	208.26	191.42	178.06	167.23	158.29
16000	1388.12	720.00	497.70	386.87	320.61	276.65	245.42	222.15	204.18	189.93	178.37	168.84
17000	1474.88	765.00	528.81	411.05	340.65	293.94	260.76	236.03	216.94	201.80	189.52	179.39
18000	1561.64	810.00	559.92	435.23	360.69	311.23	276.09	249.91	229.70	213.67	200.67	189.95
19000	1648.40	855.00	591.02	459.40	380.73	328.52	291.43	263.80	242.46	225.54	211.82	200.50
20000	1735.15	900.00	622.13	483.58	400.76	345.81	306.77	277.68	255.23	237.41	222.97	211.05
21000	1821.91	945.00	653.24	507.76	420.80	363.10	322.11	291.57	267.99	249.28	234.11	221.60
22000	1908.67	990.00	684.34	531.94	440.84	380.39	337.45	305.45	280.75	261.15	245.26	232.15
23000	1995.43	1035.00	715.45	556.12	460.88	397.68	352.79	319.33	293.51	273.02	256.41	242.71
24000	2082.18	1080.00	746.55	580.30	480.92	414.97	368.12	333.22	306.27	284.89	267.56	253.26
25000	2168.94	1124.99	777.66	604.48	500.95	432.26	383.46	347.10	319.03	296.76	278.71	263.81
26000	2255.70	1169.99	808.77	628.66	520.99	449.55	398.80	360.99	331.79	308.63	289.85	274.36
27000	2342.46	1214.99	839.87	652.84	541.03	466.84	414.14	374.87	344.55	320.50	301.00	284.92
28000	2429.21	1259.99	870.98	677.01	561.07	484.13	429.48	388.75	357.31	332.37	312.15	295.47
29000	2515.97	1304.99	902.09	701.19	581.11	501.42	444.81	402.64	370.07	344.24	323.30	306.02
30000	2602.73	1349.99	933.19	725.37	601.14	518.71	460.15	416.52	382.84	356.11	334.45	316.57
31000	2689.48	1394.99	964.30	749.55	621.18	536.00	475.49	430.40	395.60	367.98	345.59	327.13
32000	2776.24	1439.99	995.40	773.73	641.22	553.29	490.83	444.29	408.36	379.85	356.74	337.68
33000	2863.00	1484.99	1026.51	797.91	661.26	570.58	506.17	458.17	421.12	391.72	367.89	348.23
34000	2949.76	1529.99	1057.62	822.09	681.30	587.87	521.51	472.06	433.88	403.59	379.04	358.78
35000	3036.51	1574.99	1088.72	846.27	701.33	605.16	536.84	485.94	446.64	415.46	390.19	369.33
37500	3253.41	1687.49	1166.49	906.71	751.43	648.38	575.19	520.65	478.54	445.14	418.06	395.71
40000	3470.30	1799.99	1244.25	967.16	801.52	691.61	613.54	555.36	510.45	474.81	445.93	422.10
42500	3687.20	1912.49	1322.02	1027.61	851.62	734.83	651.88	590.07	542.35	504.49	473.80	448.48
45000	3904.09	2024.99	1399.78	1088.06	901.71	778.06	690.23	624.78	574.25	534.16	501.67	474.86
47500	4120.98	2137.49	1477.55	1148.50	951.81	821.29	728.57	659.49	606.15	563.84	529.54	501.24
50000	4337.88	2249.98	1555.32	1208.95	1001.90	864.51	766.92	694.20	638.06	593.51	557.41	527.62
52500	4554.77	2362.48	1633.08	1269.40	1052.00	907.74	805.26	728.91	669.96	623.19	585.28	554.00
55000	4771.66	2474.98	1710.85	1329.84	1102.09	950.96	843.61	763.62	701.86	652.86	613.15	580.38
57500	4988.56	2587.48	1788.61	1390.29	1152.19	994.19	881.96	798.33	733.76	682.54	641.02	606.76
60000	5205.45	2699.98	1866.38	1450.74	1202.28	1037.41	920.30	833.04	765.67	712.22	668.89	633.14
65000	5639.24	2924.98	2021.91	1571.63	1302.47	1123.86	996.99	902.46	829.47	771.57	724.63	685.90
70000	6073.02	3149.98	2177.44	1692.53	1402.66	1210.31	1073.68	971.88	893.28	830.92	780.37	738.66
75000	6506.81	3374.97	2332.97	1813.42	1502.85	1296.76	1150.38	1041.30	957.08	890.27	836.11	791.42
80000	6940.60	3599.97	2488.50	1934.32	1603.04	1383.21	1227.07	1110.71	1020.89	949.62	891.85	844.19
85000	7374.39	3824.97	2644.03	2055.21	1703.23	1469.66	1303.76	1180.13	1084.69	1008.97	947.59	896.95
90000	7808.17	4049.97	2799.56	2176.11	1803.42	1556.12	1380.45	1249.55	1148.50	1068.32	1003.33	949.71
95000	8241.96	4274.97	2955.10	2297.00	1903.61	1642.57	1457.14	1318.97	1212.30	1127.67	1059.07	1002.47
100000	8675.75	4499.96	3110.63	2417.90	2003.80	1729.02	1533.83	1388.38	1276.11	1187.02	1114.81	1055.23
105000	9109.53	4724.96	3266.16	2538.79	2103.99	1815.47	1610.53	1457.80	1339.91	1246.37	1170.55	1107.99
110000	9543.32	4949.96	3421.69	2659.69	2204.18	1901.92	1687.22	1527.23	1403.72	1305.72	1226.29	1160.75
115000	9977.11	5174.96	3577.22	2780.58	2304.37	1988.37	1763.91	1596.65	1467.52	1365.08	1282.03	1213.52
120000	10410.90	5399.96	3732.75	2901.47	2404.56	2074.82	1840.60	1666.07	1531.33	1424.43	1337.77	1266.28
125000	10844.68	5624.95	3888.28	3022.37	2504.75	2161.27	1917.29	1735.49	1595.13	1483.78	1393.51	1319.04
130000	11278.47	5849.95	4043.81	3143.26	2604.94	2247.72	1993.98	1804.91	1658.94	1543.13	1449.25	1371.80
135000	11712.26	6074.95	4199.34	3264.16	2705.13	2334.17	2070.67	1874.33	1722.74	1602.48	1504.99	1424.56
140000	12146.04	6299.95	4354.88	3385.05	2805.32	2420.62	2147.36	1943.75	1786.55	1661.83	1560.73	1477.32
145000	12579.83	6524.95	4510.41	3505.95	2905.51	2507.07	2224.05	2013.17	1850.35	1721.18	1616.47	1530.08
150000	13013.62	6749.94	4665.94	3626.84	3005.70	2593.52	2300.75	2082.59	1914.16	1780.53	1672.21	1582.84
155000	13447.40	6974.94	4821.47	3747.73	3105.89	2679.97	2377.44	2152.00	1977.96	1839.88	1727.95	1635.61
160000	13881.19	7199.94	4977.00	3868.63	3206.08	2766.42	2454.13	2221.42	2041.77	1899.23	1783.69	1688.37

AMOUNT OF LOAN	NUMBER OF YEARS IN TERM											
	13	14	15	16	17	18	19	20	25	30	35	40
$ 50	0.51	0.49	0.47	0.45	0.44	0.43	0.42	0.41	0.37	0.35	0.34	0.33
100	1.01	0.97	0.93	0.90	0.87	0.85	0.83	0.81	0.74	0.70	0.68	0.66
200	2.02	1.93	1.86	1.80	1.74	1.69	1.65	1.62	1.48	1.40	1.35	1.32
300	3.02	2.89	2.79	2.69	2.61	2.54	2.48	2.42	2.22	2.10	2.03	1.98
400	4.03	3.86	3.71	3.59	3.48	3.38	3.30	3.23	2.96	2.80	2.70	2.64
500	5.03	4.82	4.64	4.48	4.35	4.23	4.13	4.03	3.70	3.50	3.38	3.30
600	6.04	5.78	5.57	5.38	5.22	5.07	4.95	4.84	4.44	4.20	4.05	3.95
700	7.04	6.75	6.49	6.28	6.09	5.92	5.77	5.64	5.18	4.90	4.72	4.61
800	8.05	7.71	7.42	7.17	6.95	6.76	6.60	6.45	5.92	5.60	5.40	5.27
900	9.05	8.67	8.35	8.07	7.82	7.61	7.42	7.26	6.66	6.30	6.07	5.93
1000	10.06	9.64	9.28	8.96	8.69	8.45	8.25	8.06	7.39	7.00	6.75	6.59
2000	20.11	19.27	18.55	17.92	17.38	16.90	16.49	16.12	14.78	13.99	13.49	13.17
3000	30.17	28.90	27.82	26.88	26.07	25.35	24.73	24.17	22.17	20.98	20.23	19.75
4000	40.22	38.53	37.09	35.84	34.75	33.80	32.97	32.23	29.56	27.97	26.97	26.33
5000	50.27	48.16	46.36	44.80	43.44	42.25	41.21	40.28	36.95	34.97	33.72	32.91
6000	60.33	57.79	55.63	53.75	52.13	50.70	49.45	48.34	44.34	41.96	40.46	39.49
7000	70.38	67.43	64.90	62.71	60.81	59.15	57.69	56.40	51.73	48.95	47.20	46.07
8000	80.43	77.06	74.17	71.67	69.50	67.60	65.93	64.45	59.12	55.94	53.94	52.65
9000	90.49	86.69	83.44	80.63	78.19	76.05	74.17	72.51	66.51	62.93	60.69	59.23
10000	100.54	96.32	92.71	89.59	86.88	84.50	82.41	80.56	73.90	69.93	67.43	65.81
11000	110.60	105.95	101.98	98.55	95.56	92.95	90.65	88.62	81.29	76.92	74.17	72.39
12000	120.65	115.58	111.25	107.50	104.25	101.40	98.89	96.68	88.68	83.91	80.91	78.97
13000	130.70	125.21	120.52	116.46	112.94	109.85	107.14	104.73	96.07	90.90	87.66	85.55
14000	140.76	134.85	129.79	125.42	121.62	118.30	115.38	112.79	103.46	97.90	94.40	92.13
15000	150.81	144.48	139.06	134.38	130.31	126.75	123.62	120.84	110.85	104.89	101.14	98.72
16000	160.86	154.11	148.33	143.34	139.00	135.20	131.86	128.90	118.24	111.88	107.88	105.30
17000	170.92	163.74	157.60	152.30	147.69	143.65	140.10	136.96	125.63	118.87	114.63	111.88
18000	180.97	173.37	166.87	161.25	156.37	152.10	148.34	145.01	133.02	125.86	121.37	118.46
19000	191.03	183.00	176.14	170.21	165.06	160.55	156.58	153.07	140.41	132.86	128.11	125.04
20000	201.08	192.63	185.41	179.17	173.75	169.00	164.82	161.12	147.80	139.85	134.85	131.62
21000	211.13	202.27	194.68	188.13	182.43	177.45	173.06	169.18	155.19	146.84	141.60	138.20
22000	221.19	211.90	203.95	197.09	191.12	185.90	181.30	177.24	162.58	153.83	148.34	144.78
23000	231.24	221.53	213.22	206.05	199.81	194.35	189.54	185.29	169.97	160.82	155.08	151.36
24000	241.29	231.16	222.49	215.00	208.50	202.80	197.78	193.35	177.36	167.82	161.82	157.94
25000	251.35	240.79	231.76	223.96	217.18	211.25	206.02	201.40	184.75	174.81	168.57	164.52
26000	261.40	250.42	241.03	232.92	225.87	219.70	214.27	209.46	192.14	181.80	175.31	171.10
27000	271.46	260.05	250.30	241.88	234.56	228.15	222.51	217.52	199.53	188.79	182.05	177.68
28000	281.51	269.69	259.57	250.84	243.24	236.60	230.75	225.57	206.92	195.79	188.79	184.26
29000	291.56	279.32	268.84	259.80	251.93	245.05	238.99	233.63	214.31	202.78	195.54	190.85
30000	301.62	288.95	278.11	268.75	260.62	253.50	247.23	241.68	221.70	209.77	202.28	197.43
31000	311.67	298.58	287.38	277.71	269.30	261.95	255.47	249.74	229.09	216.76	209.02	204.01
32000	321.72	308.21	296.65	286.67	277.99	270.40	263.71	257.79	236.48	223.75	215.76	210.59
33000	331.78	317.84	305.92	295.63	286.68	278.85	271.95	265.85	243.87	230.75	222.51	217.17
34000	341.83	327.47	315.19	304.59	295.37	287.30	280.19	273.91	251.26	237.74	229.25	223.75
35000	351.88	337.11	324.46	313.54	304.05	295.75	288.43	281.96	258.65	244.73	235.99	230.33
37500	377.02	361.18	347.63	335.94	325.77	316.87	309.03	302.10	277.13	262.21	252.85	246.78
40000	402.15	385.26	370.81	358.34	347.49	337.99	329.64	322.24	295.60	279.69	269.70	263.23
42500	427.29	409.34	393.99	380.73	369.21	359.12	350.24	342.38	314.08	297.17	286.56	279.69
45000	452.42	433.42	417.16	403.13	390.92	380.24	370.84	362.52	332.55	314.65	303.41	296.14
47500	477.56	457.50	440.34	425.52	412.64	401.37	391.44	382.66	351.03	332.13	320.27	312.59
50000	502.69	481.58	463.51	447.92	434.36	422.49	412.04	402.80	369.50	349.61	337.13	329.04
52500	527.82	505.66	486.69	470.31	456.08	443.62	432.65	422.94	387.98	367.09	353.98	345.49
55000	552.96	529.73	509.86	492.71	477.80	464.74	453.25	443.08	406.45	384.57	370.84	361.94
57500	578.09	553.81	533.04	515.11	499.51	485.86	473.85	463.22	424.92	402.05	387.66	378.40
60000	603.23	577.89	556.21	537.50	521.23	506.99	494.45	483.36	443.40	419.53	404.55	394.85
65000	653.50	626.05	602.56	582.29	564.67	549.24	535.66	523.64	480.35	454.49	438.26	427.75
70000	703.76	674.21	648.91	627.08	608.10	591.49	576.86	563.92	517.30	489.46	471.97	460.65
75000	754.03	722.36	695.26	671.88	651.54	633.73	618.06	604.20	554.25	524.42	505.69	493.56
80000	804.30	770.52	741.61	716.67	694.97	675.98	659.27	644.48	591.20	559.38	539.40	526.46
85000	854.57	818.68	787.97	761.46	738.41	718.23	700.47	684.76	628.15	594.34	573.11	559.37
90000	904.84	866.83	834.32	806.25	781.84	760.48	741.68	725.04	665.10	629.30	606.82	592.27
95000	955.11	914.99	880.67	851.04	825.28	802.73	782.88	765.32	702.05	664.26	640.54	625.17
100000	1005.38	963.15	927.02	895.83	868.71	844.98	824.08	805.60	739.00	699.22	674.25	658.08
105000	1055.64	1011.31	973.37	940.62	912.15	887.23	865.29	845.88	775.95	734.18	707.96	690.98
110000	1105.91	1059.46	1019.72	985.42	955.59	929.48	906.49	886.16	812.90	769.14	741.67	723.88
115000	1156.18	1107.62	1066.07	1030.21	999.02	971.72	947.70	926.44	849.84	804.10	775.38	756.79
120000	1206.45	1155.78	1112.42	1075.00	1042.46	1013.97	988.90	966.72	886.79	839.06	809.10	789.69
125000	1256.72	1203.93	1158.77	1119.79	1085.89	1056.22	1030.10	1007.00	923.74	874.02	842.81	822.59
130000	1306.99	1252.09	1205.12	1164.58	1129.33	1098.47	1071.31	1047.28	960.69	908.98	876.52	855.50
135000	1357.26	1300.25	1251.47	1209.37	1172.76	1140.72	1112.51	1087.56	997.64	943.94	910.23	888.40
140000	1407.52	1348.41	1297.82	1254.16	1216.20	1182.97	1153.72	1127.84	1034.59	978.91	943.94	921.30
145000	1457.79	1396.56	1344.17	1298.96	1259.63	1225.22	1194.92	1168.12	1071.54	1013.87	977.66	954.21
150000	1508.06	1444.72	1390.52	1343.75	1303.07	1267.46	1236.12	1208.39	1108.49	1048.83	1011.37	987.11
155000	1558.33	1492.88	1436.87	1388.54	1346.50	1309.71	1277.33	1248.67	1145.44	1083.79	1045.08	1020.01
160000	1608.60	1541.03	1483.22	1433.33	1389.94	1351.96	1318.53	1288.95	1182.39	1118.75	1078.79	1052.92

23

MONTHLY AMORTIZING PAYMENTS

AMOUNT OF LOAN	NUMBER OF YEARS IN TERM											
	1	2	3	4	5	6	7	8	9	10	11	12
$ 50	4.35	2.26	1.57	1.22	1.01	0.88	0.78	0.71	0.65	0.61	0.57	0.54
100	8.69	4.52	3.13	2.43	2.02	1.75	1.55	1.41	1.29	1.21	1.13	1.07
200	17.38	9.03	6.25	4.86	4.04	3.49	3.10	2.81	2.58	2.41	2.26	2.14
300	26.07	13.54	9.37	7.29	6.05	5.23	4.64	4.21	3.87	3.61	3.39	3.21
400	34.75	18.05	12.49	9.72	8.07	6.97	6.19	5.61	5.16	4.81	4.52	4.28
500	43.44	22.56	15.62	12.15	10.08	8.71	7.74	7.01	6.45	6.01	5.65	5.35
600	52.13	27.07	18.74	14.58	12.10	10.45	9.28	8.41	7.74	7.21	6.77	6.42
700	60.82	31.58	21.86	17.01	14.11	12.19	10.83	9.81	9.03	8.41	7.90	7.49
800	69.50	36.10	24.98	19.44	16.13	13.93	12.37	11.21	10.32	9.61	9.03	8.56
900	78.19	40.61	28.10	21.87	18.15	15.68	13.92	12.61	11.61	10.81	10.16	9.62
1000	86.88	45.12	31.23	24.30	20.16	17.42	15.47	14.01	12.89	12.01	11.29	10.69
2000	173.75	90.23	62.45	48.60	40.32	34.83	30.93	28.02	25.78	24.01	22.57	21.38
3000	260.62	135.35	93.67	72.89	60.48	52.24	46.39	42.03	38.67	36.01	33.85	32.07
4000	347.50	180.46	124.89	97.19	80.63	69.65	61.85	56.04	51.56	48.01	45.13	42.76
5000	434.37	225.57	156.11	121.48	100.79	87.06	77.31	70.05	64.45	60.01	56.41	53.44
6000	521.24	270.69	187.33	145.78	120.95	104.47	92.78	84.06	77.34	72.01	67.69	64.13
7000	608.12	315.80	218.55	170.08	141.10	121.88	108.24	98.07	90.23	84.01	78.97	74.82
8000	694.99	360.91	249.77	194.37	161.26	139.30	123.70	112.08	103.12	96.01	90.26	85.51
9000	781.86	406.03	281.00	218.67	181.42	156.71	139.16	126.09	116.01	108.01	101.54	96.20
10000	868.73	451.14	312.22	242.96	201.57	174.12	154.62	140.10	128.90	120.02	112.82	106.88
11000	955.61	496.25	343.44	267.26	221.73	191.53	170.09	154.11	141.79	132.02	124.10	117.57
12000	1042.48	541.37	374.66	291.55	241.89	208.94	185.55	168.12	154.68	144.02	135.38	128.26
13000	1129.35	586.48	405.88	315.85	262.05	226.35	201.01	182.13	167.57	156.02	146.66	138.95
14000	1216.23	631.59	437.10	340.15	282.20	243.76	216.47	196.14	180.46	168.02	157.94	149.64
15000	1303.10	676.71	468.32	364.44	302.36	261.18	231.93	210.15	193.35	180.02	169.22	160.32
16000	1389.97	721.82	499.54	388.74	322.52	278.59	247.40	224.16	206.24	192.02	180.51	171.01
17000	1476.84	766.93	530.76	413.03	342.67	296.00	262.86	238.17	219.13	204.02	191.79	181.70
18000	1563.72	812.05	561.99	437.33	362.83	313.41	278.32	252.18	232.02	216.02	203.07	192.39
19000	1650.59	857.16	593.21	461.62	382.99	330.82	293.78	266.19	244.91	228.03	214.35	203.08
20000	1737.46	902.27	624.43	485.92	403.14	348.23	309.24	280.20	257.79	240.03	225.63	213.76
21000	1824.34	947.39	655.65	510.22	423.30	365.64	324.71	294.21	270.68	252.03	236.91	224.45
22000	1911.21	992.50	686.87	534.51	443.46	383.06	340.17	308.22	283.57	264.03	248.19	235.14
23000	1998.08	1037.61	718.09	558.81	463.62	400.47	355.63	322.23	296.46	276.03	259.47	245.83
24000	2084.95	1082.73	749.31	583.10	483.77	417.88	371.09	336.24	309.35	288.03	270.76	256.52
25000	2171.83	1127.84	780.53	607.40	503.93	435.29	386.55	350.25	322.24	300.03	282.04	267.20
26000	2258.70	1172.95	811.76	631.69	524.09	452.70	402.02	364.26	335.13	312.03	293.32	277.89
27000	2345.57	1218.07	842.98	655.99	544.24	470.11	417.48	378.27	348.02	324.03	304.60	288.58
28000	2432.45	1263.18	874.20	680.29	564.40	487.52	432.94	392.28	360.91	336.03	315.88	299.27
29000	2519.32	1308.29	905.42	704.58	584.56	504.94	448.40	406.29	373.80	348.04	327.16	309.95
30000	2606.19	1353.41	936.64	728.88	604.71	522.35	463.86	420.30	386.69	360.04	338.44	320.64
31000	2693.06	1398.52	967.86	753.17	624.87	539.76	479.33	434.31	399.58	372.04	349.72	331.33
32000	2779.94	1443.63	999.08	777.47	645.03	557.17	494.79	448.32	412.47	384.04	361.01	342.02
33000	2866.81	1488.75	1030.30	801.76	665.18	574.58	510.25	462.33	425.36	396.04	372.29	352.71
34000	2953.68	1533.86	1061.52	826.06	685.34	591.99	525.71	476.34	438.25	408.04	383.57	363.39
35000	3040.56	1578.97	1092.75	850.36	705.50	609.40	541.17	490.35	451.14	420.04	394.85	374.08
37500	3257.74	1691.76	1170.80	911.10	755.89	652.93	579.83	525.38	483.36	450.04	423.05	400.80
40000	3474.92	1804.54	1248.85	971.83	806.28	696.46	618.48	560.40	515.58	480.05	451.26	427.52
42500	3692.10	1917.32	1326.90	1032.57	856.68	739.99	657.14	595.43	547.81	510.05	479.46	454.24
45000	3909.28	2030.11	1404.96	1093.31	907.07	783.52	695.79	630.45	580.03	540.05	507.66	480.96
47500	4126.47	2142.89	1483.01	1154.05	957.46	827.05	734.45	665.48	612.26	570.06	535.87	507.68
50000	4343.65	2255.67	1561.06	1214.79	1007.85	870.58	773.10	700.50	644.48	600.06	564.07	534.40
52500	4560.83	2368.46	1639.12	1275.53	1058.25	914.10	811.76	735.53	676.70	630.06	592.27	561.12
55000	4778.01	2481.24	1717.17	1336.27	1108.64	957.63	850.41	770.55	708.93	660.06	620.48	587.84
57500	4995.20	2594.02	1795.22	1397.01	1159.03	1001.16	889.07	805.58	741.15	690.07	648.68	614.56
60000	5212.38	2706.81	1873.27	1457.75	1209.42	1044.69	927.72	840.60	773.37	720.07	676.88	641.28
65000	5646.74	2932.37	2029.38	1579.23	1310.21	1131.75	1005.03	910.65	837.82	780.07	733.29	694.72
70000	6081.11	3157.94	2185.49	1700.71	1410.99	1218.80	1082.34	980.70	902.27	840.08	789.70	748.16
75000	6515.47	3383.51	2341.59	1822.19	1511.78	1305.86	1159.65	1050.75	966.72	900.08	846.10	801.60
80000	6949.84	3609.07	2497.70	1943.66	1612.56	1392.92	1236.96	1120.80	1031.16	960.09	902.51	855.04
85000	7384.20	3834.64	2653.80	2065.14	1713.35	1479.98	1314.27	1190.85	1095.61	1020.10	958.91	908.48
90000	7818.56	4060.21	2809.91	2186.62	1814.13	1567.03	1391.58	1260.90	1160.06	1080.10	1015.32	961.92
95000	8252.93	4285.77	2966.02	2308.10	1914.92	1654.09	1468.89	1330.95	1224.51	1140.11	1071.73	1015.36
100000	8687.29	4511.34	3122.12	2429.58	2015.70	1741.15	1546.20	1401.00	1288.95	1200.12	1128.13	1068.80
105000	9121.66	4736.91	3278.23	2551.06	2116.49	1828.20	1623.51	1471.05	1353.40	1260.12	1184.54	1122.24
110000	9556.02	4962.47	3434.33	2672.54	2217.27	1915.26	1700.82	1541.10	1417.85	1320.12	1240.95	1175.68
115000	9990.39	5188.04	3590.44	2794.02	2318.06	2002.32	1778.13	1611.15	1482.30	1380.13	1297.35	1229.12
120000	10424.75	5413.61	3746.54	2915.49	2418.84	2089.38	1855.44	1681.20	1546.74	1440.13	1353.76	1282.56
125000	10859.12	5639.17	3902.65	3036.97	2519.62	2176.43	1932.75	1751.25	1611.19	1500.14	1410.17	1336.00
130000	11293.48	5864.74	4058.76	3158.45	2620.41	2263.49	2010.06	1821.30	1675.64	1560.14	1466.57	1389.43
135000	11727.84	6090.31	4214.86	3279.93	2721.19	2350.55	2087.37	1891.35	1740.09	1620.15	1522.98	1442.87
140000	12162.21	6315.87	4370.97	3401.41	2821.98	2437.60	2164.68	1961.40	1804.53	1680.15	1579.39	1496.31
145000	12596.57	6541.44	4527.07	3522.89	2922.76	2524.66	2241.99	2031.45	1868.98	1740.16	1635.79	1549.75
150000	13030.94	6767.01	4683.18	3644.37	3023.55	2611.72	2319.30	2101.50	1933.43	1800.16	1692.20	1603.19
155000	13465.30	6992.58	4839.29	3765.84	3124.33	2698.78	2396.61	2171.55	1997.88	1860.17	1748.60	1656.63
160000	13899.67	7218.14	4995.39	3887.32	3225.12	2785.83	2473.92	2241.60	2062.32	1920.18	1805.01	1710.07

AMOUNT OF LOAN	NUMBER OF YEARS IN TERM											
	13	14	15	16	17	18	19	20	25	30	35	40
$ 50	0.51	0.49	0.48	0.46	0.45	0.43	0.42	0.42	0.38	0.36	0.35	0.34
100	1.02	0.98	0.95	0.92	0.89	0.86	0.84	0.83	0.76	0.72	0.70	0.68
200	2.04	1.96	1.89	1.83	1.77	1.72	1.68	1.65	1.52	1.44	1.39	1.36
300	3.06	2.94	2.83	2.74	2.66	2.58	2.52	2.47	2.27	2.15	2.08	2.03
400	4.08	3.91	3.77	3.65	3.54	3.44	3.36	3.29	3.03	2.87	2.77	2.71
500	5.10	4.89	4.71	4.56	4.42	4.30	4.20	4.11	3.78	3.59	3.47	3.39
600	6.12	5.87	5.65	5.47	5.31	5.16	5.04	4.93	4.54	4.30	4.16	4.06
700	7.14	6.85	6.59	6.38	6.19	6.02	5.88	5.75	5.29	5.02	4.85	4.74
800	8.16	7.82	7.54	7.29	7.07	6.88	6.72	6.57	6.05	5.74	5.54	5.42
900	9.18	8.80	8.48	8.20	7.96	7.74	7.56	7.39	6.80	6.45	6.23	6.09
1000	10.20	9.78	9.42	9.11	8.84	8.60	8.40	8.21	7.56	7.17	6.93	6.77
2000	20.39	19.55	18.83	18.21	17.67	17.20	16.79	16.42	15.11	14.33	13.85	13.54
3000	30.58	29.32	28.24	27.31	26.51	25.80	25.18	24.63	22.66	21.50	20.77	20.30
4000	40.77	39.09	37.66	36.42	35.34	34.40	33.57	32.84	30.22	28.66	27.69	27.07
5000	50.96	48.86	47.07	45.52	44.18	43.00	41.97	41.05	37.77	35.83	34.61	33.84
6000	61.16	58.64	56.48	54.62	53.01	51.60	50.36	49.26	45.32	42.99	41.54	40.60
7000	71.35	68.41	65.89	63.73	61.84	60.20	58.75	57.47	52.88	50.15	48.46	47.37
8000	81.54	78.18	75.31	72.83	70.68	68.80	67.14	65.68	60.43	57.32	55.38	54.13
9000	91.73	87.95	84.72	81.93	79.51	77.40	75.54	73.89	67.98	64.48	62.30	60.90
10000	101.92	97.72	94.13	91.04	88.35	86.00	83.93	82.10	75.54	71.65	69.22	67.67
11000	112.11	107.49	103.55	100.14	97.18	94.59	92.32	90.31	83.09	78.81	76.14	74.43
12000	122.31	117.27	112.96	109.24	106.02	103.19	100.71	98.52	90.64	85.97	83.07	81.20
13000	132.50	127.04	122.37	118.35	114.85	111.79	109.10	106.73	98.20	93.14	89.99	87.97
14000	142.69	136.81	131.78	127.45	123.68	120.39	117.50	114.94	105.75	100.30	96.91	94.73
15000	152.88	146.58	141.20	136.55	132.52	128.99	125.89	123.15	113.30	107.47	103.83	101.50
16000	163.07	156.35	150.61	145.66	141.35	137.59	134.28	131.36	120.86	114.63	110.75	108.26
17000	173.26	166.13	160.02	154.76	150.19	146.19	142.67	139.57	128.41	121.80	117.67	115.03
18000	183.46	175.90	169.43	163.86	159.02	154.79	151.07	147.78	135.96	128.96	124.60	121.80
19000	193.65	185.67	178.85	172.97	167.86	163.39	159.46	155.99	143.52	136.12	131.52	128.56
20000	203.84	195.44	188.26	182.07	176.69	171.99	167.85	164.19	151.07	143.29	138.44	135.33
21000	214.03	205.21	197.67	191.17	185.52	180.58	176.24	172.40	158.62	150.45	145.36	142.10
22000	224.22	214.98	207.09	200.27	194.36	189.18	184.63	180.61	166.18	157.62	152.28	148.86
23000	234.41	224.76	216.50	209.38	203.19	197.78	193.03	188.82	173.73	164.78	159.21	155.63
24000	244.61	234.53	225.91	218.48	212.03	206.38	201.42	197.03	181.28	171.94	166.13	162.39
25000	254.80	244.30	235.32	227.58	220.86	214.98	209.81	205.24	188.84	179.11	173.05	169.16
26000	264.99	254.07	244.74	236.69	229.69	223.58	218.20	213.45	196.39	186.27	179.97	175.93
27000	275.18	263.84	254.15	245.79	238.53	232.18	226.60	221.66	203.94	193.44	186.89	182.69
28000	285.37	273.61	263.56	254.89	247.36	240.78	234.99	229.87	211.50	200.60	193.81	189.46
29000	295.56	283.39	272.97	264.00	256.20	249.38	243.38	238.08	219.05	207.76	200.74	196.22
30000	305.76	293.16	282.39	273.10	265.03	257.98	251.77	246.29	226.60	214.93	207.66	202.99
31000	315.95	302.93	291.80	282.20	273.87	266.58	260.16	254.50	234.16	222.09	214.58	209.76
32000	326.14	312.70	301.21	291.31	282.70	275.17	268.56	262.71	241.71	229.26	221.50	216.52
33000	336.33	322.47	310.63	300.41	291.53	283.77	276.95	270.92	249.26	236.42	228.42	223.29
34000	346.52	332.25	320.04	309.51	300.37	292.37	285.34	279.13	256.82	243.59	235.34	230.06
35000	356.72	342.02	329.45	318.62	309.20	300.97	293.73	287.34	264.37	250.75	242.27	236.82
37500	382.19	366.45	352.98	341.37	331.29	322.47	314.71	307.86	283.25	268.66	259.57	253.74
40000	407.67	390.88	376.52	364.13	353.37	343.97	335.69	328.38	302.14	286.57	276.88	270.66
42500	433.15	415.31	400.05	386.89	375.46	365.46	356.68	348.91	321.02	304.48	294.18	287.57
45000	458.63	439.73	423.58	409.65	397.54	386.96	377.66	369.43	339.90	322.39	311.48	304.49
47500	484.11	464.16	447.11	432.41	419.63	408.46	398.64	389.96	358.79	340.30	328.79	321.40
50000	509.59	488.59	470.64	455.16	441.72	429.96	419.62	410.48	377.67	358.21	346.09	338.31
52500	535.07	513.02	494.17	477.92	463.80	451.45	440.60	431.00	396.55	376.12	363.40	355.23
55000	560.55	537.45	517.71	500.68	485.89	472.95	461.58	451.53	415.44	394.03	380.70	372.15
57500	586.03	561.88	541.24	523.44	507.97	494.45	482.56	472.05	434.32	411.94	398.01	389.06
60000	611.51	586.31	564.77	546.20	530.06	515.95	503.54	492.57	453.20	429.85	415.31	405.98
65000	662.47	635.17	611.83	591.71	574.23	558.94	545.50	533.62	490.97	465.67	449.92	439.81
70000	713.43	684.03	658.90	637.23	618.40	601.94	587.46	574.67	528.74	501.49	484.53	473.64
75000	764.38	732.89	705.96	682.74	662.57	644.93	629.42	615.72	566.50	537.31	519.14	507.47
80000	815.34	781.75	753.03	728.26	706.74	687.93	671.38	656.76	604.27	573.13	553.75	541.30
85000	866.30	830.61	800.09	773.77	750.91	730.92	713.35	697.81	642.03	608.96	588.35	575.13
90000	917.26	879.46	847.15	819.29	795.08	773.92	755.31	738.86	679.80	644.78	622.96	608.96
95000	968.22	928.32	894.22	864.81	839.26	816.91	797.27	779.91	717.57	680.60	657.57	642.79
100000	1019.18	977.18	941.28	910.32	883.43	859.91	839.23	820.95	755.33	716.42	692.18	676.62
105000	1070.14	1026.04	988.34	955.84	927.60	902.90	881.19	862.00	793.10	752.24	726.79	710.46
110000	1121.09	1074.90	1035.41	1001.35	971.77	945.90	923.15	903.05	830.87	788.06	761.40	744.29
115000	1172.05	1123.76	1082.47	1046.87	1015.94	988.89	965.11	944.10	868.63	823.88	796.01	778.12
120000	1223.01	1172.62	1129.54	1092.39	1060.11	1031.89	1007.07	985.14	906.40	859.70	830.62	811.95
125000	1273.97	1221.48	1176.60	1137.90	1104.28	1074.88	1049.03	1026.19	944.17	895.52	865.22	845.78
130000	1324.93	1270.34	1223.66	1183.42	1148.45	1117.88	1091.00	1067.24	981.93	931.34	899.83	879.61
135000	1375.89	1319.19	1270.73	1228.93	1192.62	1160.88	1132.96	1108.29	1019.70	967.16	934.44	913.44
140000	1426.85	1368.05	1317.79	1274.45	1236.80	1203.87	1174.92	1149.33	1057.47	1002.98	969.05	947.27
145000	1477.80	1416.91	1364.85	1319.96	1280.97	1246.87	1216.88	1190.38	1095.23	1038.80	1003.66	981.10
150000	1528.76	1465.77	1411.92	1365.48	1325.14	1289.86	1258.84	1231.43	1133.00	1074.62	1038.27	1014.93
155000	1579.72	1514.63	1458.98	1411.00	1369.31	1332.86	1300.80	1272.48	1170.76	1110.44	1072.88	1048.77
160000	1630.68	1563.49	1506.05	1456.51	1413.48	1375.85	1342.76	1313.52	1208.53	1146.26	1107.49	1082.60

MONTHLY AMORTIZING PAYMENTS

AMOUNT OF LOAN	NUMBER OF YEARS IN TERM											
	1	2	3	4	5	6	7	8	9	10	11	12
$ 50	4.35	2.27	1.57	1.23	1.02	0.88	0.78	0.71	0.66	0.61	0.58	0.55
100	8.70	4.53	3.14	2.45	2.03	1.76	1.56	1.42	1.31	1.22	1.15	1.09
200	17.40	9.05	6.27	4.89	4.06	3.51	3.12	2.83	2.61	2.43	2.29	2.17
300	26.10	13.57	9.41	7.33	6.09	5.26	4.68	4.25	3.91	3.64	3.43	3.25
400	34.80	18.10	12.54	9.77	8.12	7.02	6.24	5.66	5.21	4.86	4.57	4.33
500	43.50	22.62	15.67	12.21	10.14	8.77	7.80	7.07	6.51	6.07	5.71	5.42
600	52.20	27.14	18.81	14.65	12.17	10.52	9.36	8.49	7.82	7.28	6.85	6.50
700	60.90	31.66	21.94	17.09	14.20	12.28	10.92	9.92	9.12	8.50	8.00	7.58
800	69.60	36.19	25.07	19.54	16.23	14.03	12.47	11.31	10.42	9.71	9.14	8.66
900	78.29	40.71	28.21	21.98	18.25	15.78	14.03	12.73	11.72	10.92	10.28	9.75
1000	86.99	45.23	31.34	24.42	20.28	17.54	15.59	14.14	13.02	12.14	11.42	10.83
2000	173.98	90.46	62.68	48.83	40.56	35.07	31.18	28.28	26.04	24.27	22.84	21.65
3000	260.97	135.69	94.01	73.24	60.83	52.60	46.76	42.42	39.06	36.40	34.25	32.48
4000	347.96	180.91	125.35	97.66	81.11	70.14	62.35	56.55	52.08	48.54	45.67	43.30
5000	434.95	226.14	156.69	122.07	101.39	87.67	77.94	70.69	65.10	60.67	57.08	54.13
6000	521.94	271.37	188.02	146.48	121.66	105.20	93.52	84.83	78.12	72.80	68.50	64.95
7000	608.92	316.60	219.36	170.90	141.94	122.74	109.11	98.96	91.14	84.93	79.91	75.78
8000	695.91	361.82	250.70	195.31	162.22	140.27	124.69	113.10	104.15	97.07	91.33	86.60
9000	782.90	407.05	282.03	219.72	182.49	157.80	140.28	127.24	117.17	109.20	102.74	97.43
10000	869.89	452.28	313.37	244.13	202.77	175.34	155.87	141.37	130.19	121.33	114.16	108.25
11000	956.88	497.51	344.71	268.55	223.05	192.87	171.45	155.51	143.21	133.47	125.57	119.07
12000	1043.87	542.73	376.04	292.96	243.32	210.40	187.04	169.65	156.23	145.60	136.99	129.90
13000	1130.85	587.96	407.38	317.37	263.60	227.94	202.63	183.78	169.25	157.73	148.41	140.72
14000	1217.84	633.19	438.71	341.79	283.87	245.47	218.21	197.92	182.27	169.86	159.82	151.55
15000	1304.83	678.41	470.05	366.20	304.15	263.00	233.80	212.06	195.29	182.00	171.24	162.37
16000	1391.82	723.64	501.39	390.61	324.43	280.54	249.38	226.19	208.30	194.13	182.65	173.20
17000	1478.81	768.87	532.72	415.02	344.70	298.07	264.97	240.33	221.32	206.26	194.07	184.02
18000	1565.80	814.10	564.06	439.44	364.98	315.60	280.56	254.47	234.34	218.39	205.48	194.85
19000	1652.79	859.32	595.40	463.85	385.26	333.14	296.14	268.60	247.36	230.53	216.90	205.67
20000	1739.77	904.55	626.73	488.26	405.53	350.67	311.73	282.74	260.38	242.66	228.31	216.50
21000	1826.76	949.78	658.07	512.68	425.81	368.20	327.32	296.88	273.40	254.79	239.73	227.32
22000	1913.75	995.01	689.41	537.09	446.09	385.74	342.90	311.01	286.42	266.93	251.14	238.14
23000	2000.74	1040.23	720.74	561.50	466.36	403.27	358.49	325.15	299.44	279.06	262.56	248.97
24000	2087.73	1085.46	752.08	585.92	486.64	420.80	374.07	339.29	312.45	291.19	273.98	259.79
25000	2174.72	1130.69	783.41	610.33	506.91	438.34	389.66	353.42	325.47	303.32	285.39	270.62
26000	2261.70	1175.91	814.75	634.74	527.19	455.87	405.25	367.56	338.49	315.46	296.81	281.44
27000	2348.69	1221.14	846.09	659.15	547.47	473.40	420.83	381.70	351.51	327.59	308.22	292.27
28000	2435.68	1266.37	877.42	683.57	567.74	490.94	436.42	395.83	364.53	339.72	319.64	303.09
29000	2522.67	1311.60	908.76	707.98	588.02	508.47	452.01	409.97	377.55	351.86	331.05	313.92
30000	2609.66	1356.82	940.10	732.39	608.30	526.00	467.59	424.11	390.57	363.99	342.47	324.74
31000	2696.65	1402.05	971.43	756.81	628.57	543.54	483.18	438.24	403.59	376.12	353.88	335.57
32000	2783.63	1447.28	1002.77	781.22	648.85	561.07	498.76	452.38	416.60	388.25	365.30	346.39
33000	2870.62	1492.51	1034.11	805.63	669.13	578.60	514.35	466.52	429.62	400.39	376.71	357.21
34000	2957.61	1537.73	1065.44	830.04	689.40	596.14	529.94	480.65	442.64	412.52	388.13	368.04
35000	3044.60	1582.96	1096.78	854.46	709.68	613.67	545.52	494.79	455.66	424.65	399.55	378.86
37500	3262.07	1696.03	1175.12	915.49	760.37	657.50	584.49	530.13	488.21	454.98	428.08	405.92
40000	3479.54	1809.10	1253.46	976.52	811.06	701.33	623.45	565.47	520.75	485.32	456.62	432.99
42500	3697.01	1922.16	1331.80	1037.55	861.75	745.17	662.42	600.81	553.30	515.65	485.16	460.05
45000	3914.48	2035.23	1410.14	1098.59	912.44	789.00	701.38	636.16	585.85	545.98	513.70	487.11
47500	4131.96	2148.30	1488.48	1159.62	963.13	832.83	740.35	671.50	618.39	576.31	542.24	514.17
50000	4349.43	2261.37	1566.82	1220.65	1013.82	876.67	779.32	706.84	650.94	606.64	570.78	541.23
52500	4566.90	2374.44	1645.16	1281.68	1064.52	920.50	818.28	742.18	683.49	636.97	599.32	568.29
55000	4784.37	2487.51	1723.51	1342.72	1115.21	964.33	857.25	777.52	716.03	667.31	627.85	595.35
57500	5001.84	2600.57	1801.85	1403.75	1165.90	1008.17	896.21	812.86	748.58	697.64	656.39	622.42
60000	5219.31	2713.64	1880.19	1464.78	1216.59	1052.00	935.18	848.21	781.13	727.97	684.93	649.48
65000	5654.25	2939.78	2036.87	1586.84	1317.97	1139.67	1013.11	918.89	846.22	788.63	742.01	703.60
70000	6089.20	3165.92	2193.55	1708.91	1419.35	1227.33	1091.04	989.57	911.32	849.30	799.09	757.72
75000	6524.14	3392.05	2350.23	1830.97	1520.73	1315.00	1168.97	1060.26	976.41	909.96	856.16	811.84
80000	6959.08	3618.19	2506.91	1953.04	1622.12	1402.66	1246.90	1130.94	1041.50	970.63	913.24	865.97
85000	7394.02	3844.32	2663.60	2075.10	1723.50	1490.33	1324.83	1201.62	1106.60	1031.29	970.32	920.09
90000	7828.96	4070.46	2820.28	2197.17	1824.88	1578.00	1402.76	1272.31	1171.69	1091.95	1027.40	974.21
95000	8263.91	4296.60	2976.96	2319.23	1926.26	1665.66	1480.70	1342.99	1236.78	1152.62	1084.47	1028.33
100000	8698.85	4522.73	3133.64	2441.30	2027.64	1753.33	1558.63	1413.67	1301.88	1213.28	1141.55	1082.46
105000	9133.79	4748.87	3290.32	2563.36	2129.03	1841.00	1636.56	1484.36	1366.97	1273.94	1198.63	1136.58
110000	9568.73	4975.01	3447.01	2685.43	2230.41	1928.66	1714.49	1555.04	1432.06	1334.61	1255.70	1190.70
115000	10003.67	5201.14	3603.69	2807.49	2331.79	2016.33	1792.42	1625.72	1497.16	1395.27	1312.78	1244.83
120000	10438.62	5427.28	3760.37	2929.56	2433.17	2103.99	1870.35	1696.41	1562.25	1455.94	1369.86	1298.95
125000	10873.56	5653.42	3917.05	3051.62	2534.55	2191.66	1948.28	1767.09	1627.34	1516.60	1426.94	1353.07
130000	11308.50	5879.55	4073.73	3173.68	2635.94	2279.33	2026.21	1837.77	1692.44	1577.26	1484.01	1407.19
135000	11743.44	6105.69	4230.41	3295.75	2737.32	2366.99	2104.14	1908.46	1757.53	1637.93	1541.09	1461.32
140000	12178.39	6331.83	4387.10	3417.81	2838.70	2454.66	2182.08	1979.14	1822.63	1698.59	1598.17	1515.44
145000	12613.33	6557.96	4543.78	3539.88	2940.08	2542.32	2260.01	2049.82	1887.72	1759.26	1655.24	1569.56
150000	13048.27	6784.10	4700.46	3661.94	3041.46	2629.99	2337.94	2120.51	1952.81	1819.92	1712.32	1623.68
155000	13483.21	7010.24	4857.14	3784.01	3142.85	2717.66	2415.87	2191.19	2017.91	1880.58	1769.40	1677.81
160000	13918.15	7236.37	5013.82	3906.07	3244.23	2805.32	2493.80	2261.87	2083.00	1941.25	1826.48	1731.93

AMOUNT OF LOAN	NUMBER OF YEARS IN TERM											
	13	14	15	16	17	18	19	20	25	30	35	40
$ 50	0.52	0.50	0.48	0.47	0.45	0.44	0.43	0.42	0.39	0.37	0.36	0.35
100	1.04	1.00	0.96	0.93	0.90	0.88	0.86	0.84	0.78	0.74	0.72	0.70
200	2.07	1.99	1.92	1.85	1.80	1.75	1.71	1.68	1.55	1.47	1.43	1.40
300	3.10	2.98	2.87	2.78	2.70	2.63	2.57	2.51	2.32	2.21	2.14	2.09
400	4.14	3.97	3.83	3.70	3.60	3.50	3.42	3.35	3.09	2.94	2.85	2.79
500	5.17	4.96	4.78	4.63	4.50	4.38	4.28	4.19	3.86	3.67	3.56	3.48
600	6.20	5.95	5.74	5.55	5.39	5.25	5.13	5.02	4.64	4.41	4.27	4.18
700	7.24	6.94	6.69	6.48	6.29	6.13	5.99	5.86	5.41	5.14	4.98	4.87
800	8.27	7.94	7.65	7.40	7.19	7.00	6.84	6.70	6.18	5.88	5.69	5.57
900	9.30	8.93	8.61	8.33	8.09	7.88	7.70	7.53	6.95	6.61	6.40	6.26
1000	10.34	9.92	9.56	9.25	8.99	8.75	8.55	8.37	7.72	7.34	7.11	6.96
2000	20.67	19.83	19.12	18.50	17.97	17.50	17.10	16.73	15.44	14.68	14.21	13.91
3000	31.00	29.74	28.67	27.75	26.95	26.25	25.64	25.10	23.16	22.02	21.31	20.86
4000	41.33	39.66	38.23	37.00	35.94	35.00	34.19	33.46	30.88	29.36	28.42	27.82
5000	51.66	49.57	47.79	46.25	44.92	43.75	42.73	41.83	38.60	36.69	35.52	34.77
6000	61.99	59.48	57.34	55.50	53.90	52.50	51.28	50.19	46.31	44.03	42.62	41.72
7000	72.32	69.40	66.90	64.75	62.88	61.25	59.82	58.56	54.03	51.37	49.72	48.68
8000	82.65	79.31	76.46	74.00	71.87	70.00	68.37	66.92	61.75	58.71	56.83	55.63
9000	92.98	89.22	86.01	83.25	80.85	78.75	76.91	75.29	69.47	66.04	63.93	62.58
10000	103.31	99.14	95.57	92.50	89.83	87.50	85.46	83.65	77.19	73.38	71.03	69.54
11000	113.64	109.05	105.13	101.75	98.81	96.25	94.00	92.01	84.90	80.72	78.13	76.49
12000	123.97	118.96	114.68	111.00	107.80	105.00	102.55	100.38	92.62	88.06	85.24	83.44
13000	134.30	128.88	124.24	120.25	116.78	113.75	111.09	108.74	100.34	95.39	92.34	90.40
14000	144.64	138.79	133.80	129.49	125.76	122.50	119.64	117.11	108.06	102.73	99.44	97.35
15000	154.97	148.70	143.35	138.74	134.74	131.25	128.18	125.47	115.78	110.07	106.54	104.30
16000	165.30	158.62	152.91	147.99	143.73	140.00	136.73	133.84	123.50	117.41	113.65	111.25
17000	175.63	168.53	162.47	157.24	152.71	148.75	145.27	142.20	131.21	124.74	120.75	118.21
18000	185.96	178.44	172.02	166.49	161.69	157.50	153.82	150.56	138.93	132.08	127.85	125.16
19000	196.29	188.36	181.58	175.74	170.67	166.25	162.36	158.93	146.65	139.42	134.95	132.11
20000	206.62	198.27	191.14	184.99	179.66	175.00	170.91	167.29	154.37	146.76	142.06	139.07
21000	216.95	208.18	200.69	194.24	188.64	183.75	179.45	175.66	162.09	154.10	149.16	146.02
22000	227.28	218.10	210.25	203.49	197.62	192.50	188.00	184.02	169.80	161.43	156.26	152.97
23000	237.61	228.01	219.80	212.74	206.60	201.25	196.54	192.39	177.52	168.77	163.37	159.93
24000	247.94	237.92	229.36	221.99	215.59	210.00	205.09	200.75	185.24	176.11	170.47	166.88
25000	258.27	247.83	238.92	231.24	224.57	218.75	213.63	209.12	192.96	183.45	177.57	173.83
26000	268.60	257.75	248.47	240.49	233.55	227.50	222.18	217.48	200.68	190.78	184.67	180.79
27000	278.93	267.66	258.03	249.73	242.53	236.24	230.72	225.84	208.40	198.12	191.78	187.74
28000	289.27	277.57	267.59	258.98	251.52	244.99	239.27	234.21	216.11	205.46	198.88	194.69
29000	299.60	287.49	277.14	268.23	260.50	253.74	247.81	242.57	223.83	212.80	205.98	201.65
30000	309.93	297.40	286.70	277.48	269.48	262.49	256.36	250.94	231.55	220.13	213.08	208.60
31000	320.26	307.31	296.26	286.73	278.46	271.24	264.90	259.30	239.27	227.47	220.19	215.55
32000	330.59	317.23	305.81	295.98	287.45	279.99	273.45	267.67	246.99	234.81	227.29	222.50
33000	340.92	327.14	315.37	305.23	296.43	288.74	281.99	276.03	254.70	242.15	234.39	229.46
34000	351.25	337.05	324.93	314.48	305.41	297.49	290.54	284.39	262.42	249.48	241.49	236.41
35000	361.58	346.97	334.48	323.73	314.39	306.24	299.08	292.76	270.14	256.82	248.60	243.36
37500	387.41	371.75	358.37	346.85	336.85	328.12	320.44	313.67	289.44	275.17	266.35	260.75
40000	413.23	396.53	382.27	369.98	359.31	349.99	341.81	334.58	308.73	293.51	284.11	278.13
42500	439.06	421.32	406.16	393.10	381.76	371.86	363.17	355.49	328.03	311.85	301.87	295.51
45000	464.89	446.10	430.05	416.22	404.22	393.74	384.53	376.40	347.32	330.20	319.62	312.90
47500	490.72	470.88	453.94	439.34	426.68	415.61	405.89	397.31	366.62	348.54	337.38	330.28
50000	516.54	495.66	477.83	462.47	449.13	437.49	427.26	418.23	385.91	366.89	355.14	347.66
52500	542.37	520.45	501.72	485.59	471.59	459.36	448.62	439.14	405.21	385.23	372.89	365.04
55000	568.20	545.23	525.61	508.71	494.05	481.23	469.98	460.05	424.50	403.58	390.65	382.43
57500	594.02	570.01	549.50	531.84	516.50	503.11	491.34	480.96	443.80	421.92	408.41	399.81
60000	619.85	594.80	573.40	554.96	538.96	524.98	512.71	501.87	463.09	440.26	426.16	417.19
65000	671.50	644.36	621.18	601.21	583.87	568.73	555.43	543.69	501.69	476.95	461.67	451.96
70000	723.16	693.93	668.96	647.45	628.78	612.48	598.16	585.51	540.28	513.64	497.19	486.72
75000	774.81	743.49	716.74	693.70	673.70	656.23	640.88	627.34	578.87	550.33	532.70	521.49
80000	826.46	793.06	764.53	739.95	718.61	699.98	683.61	669.16	617.46	587.02	568.21	556.25
85000	878.12	842.63	812.31	786.19	763.52	743.72	726.33	710.98	656.05	623.70	603.73	591.02
90000	929.77	892.19	860.09	832.44	808.44	787.47	769.06	752.80	694.64	660.39	639.24	625.79
95000	981.43	941.76	907.87	878.68	853.35	831.22	811.78	794.62	733.23	697.08	674.75	660.55
100000	1033.08	991.32	955.66	924.93	898.26	874.97	854.51	836.45	771.82	733.77	710.27	695.32
105000	1084.73	1040.89	1003.44	971.18	943.17	918.72	897.23	878.27	810.41	770.46	745.78	730.08
110000	1136.39	1090.46	1051.22	1017.42	988.09	962.46	939.96	920.09	849.00	807.15	781.29	764.85
115000	1188.04	1140.02	1099.00	1063.67	1033.00	1006.21	982.68	961.91	887.59	843.83	816.81	799.61
120000	1239.69	1189.59	1146.79	1109.92	1077.91	1049.96	1025.41	1003.73	926.18	880.52	852.32	834.38
125000	1291.35	1239.15	1194.57	1156.16	1122.83	1093.71	1068.13	1045.56	964.78	917.21	887.83	869.14
130000	1343.00	1288.72	1242.35	1202.41	1167.74	1137.46	1110.86	1087.38	1003.37	953.90	923.34	903.91
135000	1394.65	1338.28	1290.14	1248.65	1212.65	1181.20	1153.58	1129.20	1041.96	990.59	958.86	938.68
140000	1446.31	1387.85	1337.92	1294.90	1257.56	1224.95	1196.31	1171.02	1080.55	1027.28	994.37	973.44
145000	1497.96	1437.42	1385.70	1341.15	1302.48	1268.70	1239.03	1212.84	1119.14	1063.96	1029.88	1008.21
150000	1549.62	1486.98	1433.48	1387.39	1347.39	1312.45	1281.76	1254.67	1157.73	1100.65	1065.40	1042.97
155000	1601.27	1536.55	1481.27	1433.64	1392.30	1356.20	1324.48	1296.49	1196.32	1137.34	1100.91	1077.74
160000	1652.92	1586.11	1529.05	1479.89	1437.22	1399.95	1367.21	1338.31	1234.91	1174.03	1136.42	1112.50

8.25%   MONTHLY AMORTIZING PAYMENTS

AMOUNT OF LOAN	NUMBER OF YEARS IN TERM											
	1	2	3	4	5	6	7	8	9	10	11	12
$ 50	4.36	2.27	1.58	1.23	1.02	0.89	0.79	0.72	0.66	0.62	0.58	0.55
100	8.72	4.54	3.15	2.46	2.04	1.77	1.58	1.43	1.32	1.23	1.16	1.10
200	17.43	9.07	6.30	4.91	4.08	3.54	3.15	2.86	2.63	2.46	2.32	2.20
300	26.14	13.61	9.44	7.36	6.12	5.30	4.72	4.28	3.95	3.68	3.47	3.29
400	34.85	18.14	12.59	9.82	8.16	7.07	6.29	5.71	5.26	4.91	4.63	4.39
500	43.56	22.68	15.73	12.27	10.20	8.83	7.86	7.14	6.58	6.14	5.78	5.49
600	52.27	27.21	18.88	14.72	12.24	10.60	9.43	8.56	7.89	7.36	6.94	6.58
700	60.98	31.74	22.02	17.18	14.28	12.36	11.00	9.99	9.21	8.59	8.09	7.68
800	69.69	36.28	25.17	19.63	16.32	14.13	12.57	11.42	10.52	9.82	9.25	8.77
900	78.40	40.81	28.31	22.08	18.36	15.90	14.14	12.84	11.84	11.04	10.40	9.87
1000	87.11	45.35	31.46	24.54	20.40	17.66	15.72	14.27	13.15	12.27	11.56	10.97
2000	174.21	90.69	62.91	49.07	40.80	35.32	31.43	28.53	26.30	24.54	23.11	21.93
3000	261.32	136.03	94.36	73.60	61.19	52.97	47.14	42.80	39.45	36.80	34.66	32.89
4000	348.42	181.37	125.81	98.13	81.59	70.63	62.85	57.06	52.60	49.07	46.21	43.85
5000	435.53	226.71	157.26	122.66	101.99	88.28	78.56	71.33	65.75	61.33	57.76	54.82
6000	522.63	272.05	188.72	147.19	122.38	105.94	94.27	85.59	78.90	73.60	69.31	65.78
7000	609.73	317.39	220.17	171.72	142.78	123.59	109.98	99.85	92.05	85.86	80.86	76.74
8000	696.84	362.74	251.62	196.25	163.18	141.25	125.69	114.12	105.19	98.13	92.41	87.70
9000	783.94	408.08	283.07	220.78	183.57	158.91	141.40	128.38	118.34	110.39	103.96	98.66
10000	871.05	453.42	314.52	245.31	203.97	176.56	157.12	142.65	131.49	122.66	115.51	109.63
11000	958.15	498.76	345.98	269.84	224.36	194.22	172.83	156.91	144.64	134.92	127.06	120.59
12000	1045.25	544.10	377.43	294.37	244.76	211.87	188.54	171.17	157.79	147.19	138.61	131.55
13000	1132.36	589.44	408.88	318.90	265.16	229.53	204.25	185.44	170.94	159.45	150.16	142.51
14000	1219.46	634.78	440.33	343.43	285.55	247.18	219.96	199.70	184.09	171.72	161.71	153.47
15000	1306.57	680.13	471.78	367.96	305.95	264.84	235.67	213.97	197.24	183.98	173.26	164.44
16000	1393.67	725.47	503.23	392.49	326.35	282.49	251.38	228.23	210.38	196.25	184.81	175.40
17000	1480.77	770.81	534.69	417.02	346.74	300.15	267.09	242.49	223.53	208.51	196.36	186.36
18000	1567.88	816.15	566.14	441.55	367.14	317.81	282.80	256.76	236.68	220.78	207.91	197.32
19000	1654.98	861.49	597.59	466.08	387.53	335.46	298.52	271.02	249.83	233.04	219.46	208.28
20000	1742.09	906.83	629.04	490.61	407.93	353.12	314.23	285.29	262.98	245.31	231.01	219.25
21000	1829.19	952.17	660.49	515.14	428.33	370.77	329.94	299.55	276.13	257.58	242.57	230.21
22000	1916.29	997.52	691.95	539.67	448.72	388.43	345.65	313.81	289.28	269.84	254.12	241.17
23000	2003.40	1042.86	723.40	564.21	469.12	406.08	361.36	328.08	302.42	282.11	265.67	252.13
24000	2090.50	1088.20	754.85	588.74	489.52	423.74	377.07	342.34	315.57	294.37	277.22	263.09
25000	2177.61	1133.54	786.30	613.27	509.91	441.39	392.78	356.61	328.72	306.64	288.77	274.06
26000	2264.71	1178.88	817.75	637.80	530.31	459.05	408.49	370.87	341.87	318.90	300.32	285.02
27000	2351.81	1224.22	849.20	662.33	550.70	476.71	424.20	385.14	355.02	331.17	311.87	295.98
28000	2438.92	1269.56	880.66	686.86	571.10	494.36	439.91	399.40	368.17	343.43	323.42	306.94
29000	2526.02	1314.91	912.11	711.39	591.50	512.02	455.63	413.66	381.32	355.70	334.97	317.91
30000	2613.13	1360.25	943.56	735.92	611.89	529.67	471.34	427.93	394.47	367.96	346.52	328.87
31000	2700.23	1405.59	975.01	760.45	632.29	547.33	487.05	442.19	407.61	380.23	358.07	339.83
32000	2787.34	1450.93	1006.46	784.98	652.69	564.98	502.76	456.46	420.76	392.49	369.62	350.79
33000	2874.44	1496.27	1037.92	809.51	673.08	582.64	518.47	470.72	433.91	404.76	381.17	361.75
34000	2961.54	1541.61	1069.37	834.04	693.48	600.29	534.18	484.98	447.06	417.02	392.72	372.72
35000	3048.65	1586.95	1100.82	858.57	713.87	617.95	549.89	499.25	460.21	429.29	404.27	383.68
37500	3266.41	1700.31	1179.45	919.90	764.86	662.09	589.17	534.91	493.08	459.95	433.15	411.08
40000	3484.17	1813.66	1258.08	981.22	815.86	706.23	628.45	570.57	525.95	490.62	462.02	438.49
42500	3701.93	1927.01	1336.71	1042.55	866.85	750.37	667.73	606.23	558.82	521.28	490.90	465.89
45000	3919.69	2040.37	1415.34	1103.87	917.84	794.51	707.00	641.89	591.70	551.94	519.78	493.30
47500	4137.45	2153.72	1493.97	1165.20	968.83	838.64	746.28	677.55	624.57	582.60	548.65	520.70
50000	4355.21	2267.07	1572.60	1226.53	1019.82	882.78	785.56	713.21	657.44	613.27	577.53	548.11
52500	4572.97	2380.43	1651.23	1287.85	1070.81	926.92	824.84	748.87	690.31	643.93	606.41	575.51
55000	4790.73	2493.78	1729.86	1349.18	1121.80	971.06	864.11	784.53	723.18	674.59	635.28	602.92
57500	5008.49	2607.14	1808.48	1410.51	1172.79	1015.20	903.39	820.19	756.05	705.26	664.16	630.32
60000	5226.25	2720.49	1887.11	1471.83	1223.78	1059.34	942.67	855.85	788.93	735.92	693.05	657.73
65000	5661.77	2947.20	2044.37	1594.48	1325.76	1147.62	1021.22	927.17	854.67	797.25	750.79	712.54
70000	6097.29	3173.90	2201.63	1717.14	1427.74	1235.89	1099.78	998.49	920.41	858.57	808.54	767.35
75000	6532.81	3400.61	2358.89	1839.79	1529.72	1324.17	1178.33	1069.81	986.16	919.90	866.29	822.16
80000	6968.33	3627.32	2516.15	1962.44	1631.71	1412.45	1256.89	1141.13	1051.90	981.23	924.04	876.97
85000	7403.85	3854.02	2673.41	2085.09	1733.69	1500.73	1335.45	1212.45	1117.64	1042.55	981.80	931.78
90000	7839.37	4080.73	2830.67	2207.74	1835.67	1589.01	1414.00	1283.77	1183.39	1103.88	1039.55	986.59
95000	8274.89	4307.44	2987.93	2330.40	1937.65	1677.28	1492.56	1355.09	1249.13	1165.20	1097.30	1041.40
100000	8710.41	4534.14	3145.19	2453.05	2039.63	1765.56	1571.11	1426.41	1314.87	1226.53	1155.05	1096.21
105000	9145.93	4760.85	3302.45	2575.70	2141.61	1853.84	1649.67	1497.73	1380.62	1287.86	1212.81	1151.02
110000	9581.45	4987.56	3459.71	2698.35	2243.59	1942.12	1728.22	1569.05	1446.36	1349.18	1270.56	1205.83
115000	10016.97	5214.27	3616.96	2821.01	2345.57	2030.39	1806.78	1640.37	1512.10	1410.51	1328.31	1260.64
120000	10452.49	5440.97	3774.22	2943.66	2447.55	2118.67	1885.33	1711.69	1577.85	1471.84	1386.06	1315.45
125000	10888.01	5667.68	3931.48	3066.31	2549.54	2206.95	1963.89	1783.01	1643.59	1533.16	1443.82	1370.26
130000	11323.53	5894.39	4088.74	3188.96	2651.52	2295.23	2042.44	1854.33	1709.33	1594.49	1501.57	1425.07
135000	11759.05	6121.09	4246.00	3311.61	2753.50	2383.50	2121.00	1925.66	1775.08	1655.82	1559.32	1479.88
140000	12194.57	6347.80	4403.26	3434.27	2855.48	2471.78	2199.55	1996.98	1840.82	1717.14	1617.07	1534.70
145000	12630.09	6574.51	4560.52	3556.92	2957.46	2560.06	2278.11	2068.30	1906.56	1778.47	1674.83	1589.51
150000	13065.61	6801.21	4717.78	3679.57	3059.44	2648.34	2356.66	2139.62	1972.31	1839.79	1732.58	1644.32
155000	13501.13	7027.92	4875.04	3802.22	3161.42	2736.62	2435.22	2210.94	2038.05	1901.12	1790.33	1699.13
160000	13936.66	7254.63	5032.30	3924.88	3263.41	2824.89	2513.77	2282.26	2103.79	1962.45	1848.08	1753.94

28

AMOUNT OF LOAN	NUMBER OF YEARS IN TERM											
	13	14	15	16	17	18	19	20	25	30	35	40
$ 50	0.53	0.51	0.49	0.47	0.46	0.45	0.44	0.43	0.40	0.38	0.37	0.36
100	1.05	1.01	0.98	0.94	0.92	0.90	0.87	0.86	0.79	0.76	0.73	0.72
200	2.10	2.02	1.95	1.88	1.83	1.79	1.74	1.71	1.58	1.51	1.46	1.43
300	3.15	3.02	2.92	2.82	2.74	2.68	2.61	2.56	2.37	2.26	2.19	2.15
400	4.19	4.03	3.89	3.76	3.66	3.57	3.48	3.41	3.16	3.01	2.92	2.86
500	5.24	5.03	4.86	4.70	4.57	4.46	4.35	4.27	3.95	3.76	3.65	3.58
600	6.29	6.04	5.83	5.64	5.48	5.35	5.22	5.12	4.74	4.51	4.38	4.29
700	7.33	7.04	6.80	6.58	6.40	6.24	6.09	5.97	5.52	5.26	5.10	5.00
800	8.38	8.05	7.77	7.52	7.31	7.13	6.96	6.82	6.31	6.02	5.83	5.72
900	9.43	9.06	8.74	8.46	8.22	8.02	7.83	7.67	7.10	6.77	6.56	6.43
1000	10.48	10.06	9.71	9.40	9.14	8.91	8.70	8.53	7.89	7.52	7.29	7.15
2000	20.95	20.12	19.41	18.80	18.27	17.81	17.40	17.05	15.77	15.03	14.57	14.29
3000	31.42	30.17	29.11	28.19	27.40	26.71	26.10	25.57	23.66	22.54	21.86	21.43
4000	41.89	40.23	38.81	37.59	36.53	35.61	34.80	34.09	31.54	30.06	29.14	28.57
5000	52.36	50.28	48.51	46.99	45.67	44.51	43.50	42.61	39.43	37.57	36.43	35.71
6000	62.83	60.34	58.21	56.38	54.80	53.41	52.20	51.13	47.31	45.08	43.71	42.85
7000	73.30	70.39	67.91	65.78	63.93	62.32	60.90	59.65	55.20	52.59	51.00	49.99
8000	83.77	80.45	77.62	75.18	73.06	71.22	69.60	68.17	63.08	60.11	58.28	57.14
9000	94.24	90.51	87.32	84.57	82.19	80.12	78.30	76.69	70.97	67.62	65.57	64.28
10000	104.71	100.56	97.02	93.97	91.33	89.02	87.00	85.21	78.85	75.13	72.85	71.42
11000	115.18	110.62	106.72	103.37	100.46	97.92	95.70	93.73	86.73	82.64	80.14	78.56
12000	125.65	120.67	116.42	112.76	109.59	106.82	104.39	102.25	94.62	90.16	87.42	85.70
13000	136.12	130.73	126.12	122.16	118.72	115.72	113.09	110.77	102.50	97.67	94.71	92.84
14000	146.60	140.78	135.82	131.56	127.85	124.63	121.79	119.29	110.39	105.18	101.99	99.98
15000	157.07	150.84	145.53	140.95	136.99	133.53	130.49	127.81	118.27	112.69	109.28	107.13
16000	167.54	160.90	155.23	150.35	146.12	142.43	139.19	136.34	126.16	120.21	116.56	114.27
17000	178.01	170.95	164.93	159.75	155.25	151.33	147.89	144.86	134.04	127.72	123.85	121.41
18000	188.48	181.01	174.63	169.14	164.38	160.23	156.59	153.38	141.93	135.23	131.13	128.55
19000	198.95	191.06	184.33	178.54	173.52	169.13	165.29	161.90	149.81	142.75	138.42	135.69
20000	209.42	201.12	194.03	187.94	182.65	178.03	173.99	170.42	157.70	150.26	145.70	142.83
21000	219.89	211.17	203.73	197.33	191.78	186.94	182.69	178.94	165.58	157.77	152.99	149.97
22000	230.36	221.23	213.44	206.73	200.91	195.84	191.39	187.46	173.46	165.28	160.27	157.12
23000	240.83	231.29	223.14	216.12	210.04	204.74	200.08	195.98	181.35	172.80	167.56	164.26
24000	251.30	241.34	232.84	225.52	219.18	213.64	208.78	204.50	189.23	180.31	174.84	171.40
25000	261.77	251.40	242.54	234.92	228.31	222.54	217.48	213.02	197.12	187.82	182.13	178.54
26000	272.24	261.45	252.24	244.31	237.44	231.44	226.18	221.54	205.00	195.33	189.41	185.68
27000	282.72	271.51	261.94	253.71	246.57	240.34	234.88	230.06	212.89	202.85	196.70	192.82
28000	293.19	281.56	271.64	263.11	255.70	249.25	243.58	238.58	220.77	210.36	203.98	199.96
29000	303.66	291.62	281.35	272.50	264.84	258.15	252.28	247.10	228.66	217.87	211.27	207.11
30000	314.13	301.67	291.05	281.90	273.97	267.05	260.98	255.62	236.54	225.38	218.55	214.25
31000	324.60	311.73	300.75	291.30	283.10	275.95	269.68	264.15	244.42	232.90	225.84	221.39
32000	335.07	321.79	310.45	300.69	292.23	284.85	278.38	272.67	252.31	240.41	233.12	228.53
33000	345.54	331.84	320.15	310.09	301.37	293.75	287.08	281.19	260.19	247.92	240.41	235.67
34000	356.01	341.90	329.85	319.49	310.50	302.66	295.77	289.71	268.08	255.44	247.69	242.81
35000	366.48	351.95	339.55	328.88	319.63	311.56	304.47	298.23	275.96	262.95	254.98	249.95
37500	392.66	377.09	363.81	352.37	342.46	333.81	326.22	319.53	295.67	281.73	273.19	267.81
40000	418.84	402.23	388.06	375.87	365.29	356.06	347.97	340.83	315.39	300.51	291.40	285.66
42500	445.01	427.37	412.31	399.36	388.12	378.32	369.72	362.13	335.10	319.29	309.61	303.51
45000	471.19	452.51	436.57	422.85	410.95	400.57	391.46	383.43	354.81	338.07	327.83	321.37
47500	497.37	477.65	460.82	446.34	433.78	422.83	413.21	404.74	374.52	356.86	346.04	339.22
50000	523.54	502.79	485.08	469.83	456.61	445.08	434.96	426.04	394.23	375.64	364.25	357.07
52500	549.72	527.93	509.33	493.32	479.44	467.33	456.71	447.34	413.94	394.42	382.46	374.93
55000	575.90	553.07	533.58	516.81	502.27	489.59	478.46	468.64	433.65	413.20	400.68	392.78
57500	602.07	578.21	557.84	540.30	525.10	511.84	500.20	489.94	453.36	431.98	418.89	410.63
60000	628.25	603.34	582.09	563.80	547.93	534.09	521.95	511.24	473.08	450.76	437.10	428.49
65000	680.60	653.62	630.60	610.78	593.59	578.60	565.45	553.85	512.50	488.33	473.52	464.20
70000	732.96	703.90	679.10	657.76	639.25	623.11	608.94	596.45	551.92	525.89	509.95	499.90
75000	785.31	754.18	727.61	704.74	684.92	667.62	652.44	639.05	591.34	563.45	546.37	535.61
80000	837.67	804.46	776.12	751.73	730.58	712.12	695.93	681.66	630.77	601.02	582.80	571.32
85000	890.02	854.74	824.62	798.71	776.24	756.63	739.43	724.26	670.19	638.58	619.22	607.02
90000	942.37	905.01	873.13	845.69	821.90	801.14	782.92	766.86	709.61	676.14	655.65	642.73
95000	994.73	955.29	921.64	892.67	867.56	845.65	826.42	809.47	749.03	713.71	692.07	678.44
100000	1047.08	1005.57	970.15	939.66	913.22	890.15	869.91	852.07	788.46	751.27	728.50	714.14
105000	1099.44	1055.85	1018.65	986.64	958.88	934.66	913.41	894.67	827.88	788.83	764.92	749.85
110000	1151.79	1106.13	1067.16	1033.62	1004.54	979.17	956.91	937.28	867.30	826.40	801.35	785.56
115000	1204.14	1156.41	1115.67	1080.60	1050.20	1023.67	1000.40	979.88	906.72	863.96	837.77	821.26
120000	1256.50	1206.68	1164.17	1127.59	1095.86	1068.18	1043.90	1022.48	946.15	901.52	874.19	856.97
125000	1308.85	1256.96	1212.68	1174.57	1141.52	1112.69	1087.39	1065.09	985.57	939.09	910.62	892.68
130000	1361.20	1307.24	1261.19	1221.55	1187.18	1157.20	1130.89	1107.69	1024.99	976.65	947.04	928.39
135000	1413.56	1357.52	1309.69	1268.53	1232.84	1201.70	1174.38	1150.29	1064.41	1014.21	983.47	964.09
140000	1465.91	1407.80	1358.20	1315.52	1278.50	1246.21	1217.88	1192.90	1103.84	1051.78	1019.89	999.80
145000	1518.27	1458.08	1406.71	1362.50	1324.17	1290.72	1261.37	1235.50	1143.26	1089.34	1056.32	1035.51
150000	1570.62	1508.35	1455.22	1409.48	1369.83	1335.23	1304.87	1278.10	1182.68	1126.90	1092.74	1071.21
155000	1622.97	1558.63	1503.72	1456.46	1415.49	1379.73	1348.36	1320.71	1222.10	1164.47	1129.17	1106.92
160000	1675.33	1608.91	1552.23	1503.45	1461.15	1424.24	1391.86	1363.31	1261.53	1202.03	1165.59	1142.63

MONTHLY AMORTIZING PAYMENTS

AMOUNT OF LOAN	NUMBER OF YEARS IN TERM											
	1	2	3	4	5	6	7	8	9	10	11	12
$ 50	4.37	2.28	1.58	1.24	1.03	0.89	0.80	0.72	0.67	0.62	0.59	0.56
100	8.73	4.55	3.16	2.47	2.06	1.78	1.59	1.44	1.33	1.24	1.17	1.12
200	17.45	9.10	6.32	4.93	4.11	3.56	3.17	2.88	2.66	2.48	2.34	2.23
300	26.17	13.64	9.48	7.40	6.16	5.34	4.76	4.32	3.99	3.72	3.51	3.34
400	34.89	18.19	12.63	9.86	8.21	7.12	6.34	5.76	5.32	4.96	4.68	4.45
500	43.61	22.73	15.79	12.33	10.26	8.89	7.92	7.20	6.64	6.20	5.85	5.56
600	52.34	27.28	18.95	14.79	12.31	10.67	9.51	8.64	7.97	7.44	7.02	6.67
700	61.06	31.82	22.10	17.26	14.37	12.45	11.09	10.08	9.30	8.68	8.19	7.78
800	69.78	36.37	25.26	19.72	16.42	14.23	12.67	11.52	10.63	9.92	9.35	8.89
900	78.50	40.92	28.42	22.19	18.47	16.01	14.26	12.96	11.96	11.16	10.52	10.00
1000	87.22	45.46	31.57	24.65	20.52	17.78	15.84	14.40	13.28	12.40	11.69	11.11
2000	174.44	90.92	63.14	49.30	41.04	35.56	31.68	28.79	26.56	24.80	23.38	22.21
3000	261.66	136.37	94.71	73.95	61.55	53.34	47.51	43.18	39.84	37.20	35.06	33.31
4000	348.88	181.83	126.28	98.60	82.07	71.12	63.35	57.57	53.12	49.60	46.75	44.41
5000	436.10	227.28	157.84	123.25	102.59	88.90	79.19	71.97	66.40	62.00	58.44	55.51
6000	523.32	272.74	189.41	147.89	123.10	106.68	95.02	86.36	79.68	74.40	70.12	66.61
7000	610.54	318.19	220.98	172.54	143.62	124.45	110.86	100.75	92.96	86.79	81.81	77.71
8000	697.76	363.65	252.55	197.19	164.14	142.23	126.70	115.14	106.24	99.19	93.50	88.81
9000	784.98	409.11	284.11	221.84	184.65	160.01	142.53	129.53	119.52	111.59	105.18	99.91
10000	872.20	454.56	315.68	246.49	205.17	177.79	158.37	143.93	132.80	123.99	116.87	111.01
11000	959.42	500.02	347.25	271.14	225.69	195.57	174.21	158.32	146.08	136.39	128.56	122.11
12000	1046.64	545.47	378.82	295.78	246.20	213.35	190.04	172.71	159.36	148.79	140.24	133.21
13000	1133.86	590.93	410.38	320.43	266.72	231.12	205.88	187.10	172.64	161.19	151.93	144.31
14000	1221.08	636.38	441.95	345.08	287.24	248.90	221.72	201.49	185.92	173.58	163.61	155.41
15000	1308.30	681.84	473.52	369.73	307.75	266.68	237.55	215.89	199.20	185.98	175.30	166.51
16000	1395.52	727.30	505.09	394.38	328.27	284.46	253.39	230.28	212.47	198.38	186.99	177.61
17000	1482.74	772.75	536.65	419.03	348.79	302.24	269.23	244.67	225.75	210.78	198.67	188.71
18000	1569.96	818.21	568.22	443.67	369.30	320.02	285.06	259.06	239.03	223.18	210.36	199.82
19000	1657.18	863.66	599.79	468.32	389.82	337.79	300.90	273.46	252.31	235.58	222.05	210.92
20000	1744.40	909.12	631.36	492.97	410.34	355.57	316.73	287.85	265.59	247.98	233.73	222.02
21000	1831.62	954.57	662.92	517.62	430.85	373.35	332.57	302.24	278.87	260.37	245.42	233.12
22000	1918.84	1000.03	694.49	542.27	451.37	391.13	348.41	316.63	292.15	272.77	257.11	244.22
23000	2006.06	1045.49	726.06	566.92	471.89	408.91	364.24	331.02	305.43	285.17	268.79	255.32
24000	2093.28	1090.94	757.63	591.56	492.40	426.69	380.08	345.42	318.71	297.57	280.48	266.42
25000	2180.50	1136.40	789.19	616.21	512.92	444.46	395.92	359.81	331.99	309.97	292.16	277.52
26000	2267.72	1181.85	820.76	640.86	533.43	462.24	411.75	374.20	345.27	322.37	303.85	288.62
27000	2354.94	1227.31	852.33	665.51	553.95	480.02	427.59	388.59	358.55	334.77	315.54	299.72
28000	2442.16	1272.76	883.90	690.16	574.47	497.80	443.43	402.98	371.83	347.16	327.22	310.82
29000	2529.38	1318.22	915.46	714.81	594.98	515.58	459.26	417.38	385.11	359.56	338.91	321.92
30000	2616.60	1363.68	947.03	739.45	615.50	533.36	475.10	431.77	398.39	371.96	350.60	333.02
31000	2703.82	1409.13	978.60	764.10	636.02	551.13	490.94	446.16	411.66	384.36	362.28	344.12
32000	2791.04	1454.59	1010.17	788.75	656.53	568.91	506.77	460.55	424.94	396.76	373.97	355.22
33000	2878.26	1500.04	1041.73	813.40	677.05	586.69	522.61	474.95	438.22	409.16	385.66	366.32
34000	2965.48	1545.50	1073.30	838.05	697.57	604.47	538.45	489.34	451.50	421.56	397.34	377.42
35000	3052.70	1590.95	1104.87	862.70	718.08	622.25	554.28	503.73	464.78	433.95	409.03	388.52
37500	3270.75	1704.59	1183.79	924.32	769.37	666.69	593.87	539.71	497.98	464.95	438.24	416.28
40000	3488.80	1818.23	1262.71	985.94	820.67	711.14	633.46	575.69	531.18	495.95	467.46	444.03
42500	3706.85	1931.87	1341.63	1047.56	871.96	755.59	673.06	611.67	564.38	526.94	496.68	471.78
45000	3924.90	2045.51	1420.54	1109.18	923.25	800.03	712.65	647.65	597.58	557.94	525.89	499.53
47500	4142.94	2159.15	1499.46	1170.80	974.54	844.48	752.24	683.63	630.77	588.94	555.11	527.28
50000	4360.99	2272.79	1578.38	1232.42	1025.83	888.92	791.83	719.61	663.97	619.93	584.32	555.03
52500	4579.04	2386.43	1657.30	1294.04	1077.12	933.37	831.42	755.59	697.17	650.93	613.54	582.78
55000	4797.09	2500.07	1736.22	1355.66	1128.41	977.82	871.01	791.57	730.37	681.93	642.76	610.54
57500	5015.14	2613.71	1815.14	1417.28	1179.71	1022.26	910.60	827.55	763.57	712.92	671.97	638.29
60000	5233.19	2727.35	1894.06	1478.90	1231.00	1066.71	950.19	863.53	796.77	743.92	701.19	666.04
65000	5669.29	2954.62	2051.89	1602.14	1333.58	1155.60	1029.38	935.49	863.16	805.91	759.62	721.54
70000	6105.39	3181.90	2209.73	1725.39	1436.16	1244.49	1108.56	1007.45	929.56	867.90	818.05	777.04
75000	6541.49	3409.18	2367.57	1848.63	1538.74	1333.38	1187.74	1079.41	995.96	929.90	876.48	832.55
80000	6977.59	3636.46	2525.41	1971.87	1641.33	1422.26	1266.92	1151.38	1062.35	991.89	934.92	888.05
85000	7413.69	3863.74	2683.25	2095.11	1743.91	1511.17	1346.11	1223.34	1128.75	1053.88	993.35	943.55
90000	7849.79	4091.02	2841.08	2218.35	1846.49	1600.06	1425.29	1295.30	1195.15	1115.88	1051.78	999.06
95000	8285.88	4318.29	2998.92	2341.59	1949.08	1688.95	1504.47	1367.26	1261.54	1177.87	1110.21	1054.56
100000	8721.98	4545.57	3156.76	2464.84	2051.66	1777.84	1583.65	1439.22	1327.94	1239.86	1168.64	1110.06
105000	9158.08	4772.85	3314.60	2588.08	2154.24	1866.74	1662.84	1511.18	1394.34	1301.85	1227.08	1165.56
110000	9594.18	5000.13	3472.43	2711.32	2256.82	1955.63	1742.02	1583.14	1460.73	1363.85	1285.51	1221.07
115000	10030.28	5227.41	3630.27	2834.56	2359.41	2044.52	1821.20	1655.10	1527.13	1425.84	1343.94	1276.57
120000	10466.38	5454.69	3788.11	2957.80	2461.99	2133.41	1900.38	1727.06	1593.53	1487.83	1402.37	1332.07
125000	10902.48	5681.96	3945.95	3081.04	2564.57	2222.30	1979.57	1799.02	1659.92	1549.83	1460.80	1387.57
130000	11338.58	5909.24	4103.78	3204.28	2667.15	2311.19	2058.75	1870.98	1726.32	1611.82	1519.24	1443.08
135000	11774.68	6136.52	4261.62	3327.53	2769.74	2400.09	2137.93	1942.94	1792.72	1673.81	1577.67	1498.58
140000	12210.77	6363.80	4419.46	3450.77	2872.32	2488.98	2217.11	2014.90	1859.11	1735.80	1636.10	1554.08
145000	12646.87	6591.08	4577.30	3574.01	2974.90	2577.87	2296.30	2086.86	1925.51	1797.80	1694.53	1609.59
150000	13082.97	6818.36	4735.14	3697.25	3077.48	2666.76	2375.48	2158.82	1991.91	1859.79	1752.96	1665.09
155000	13519.07	7045.63	4892.97	3820.49	3180.07	2755.65	2454.66	2230.78	2058.30	1921.78	1811.40	1720.59
160000	13955.17	7272.91	5050.81	3943.73	3282.65	2844.55	2533.84	2302.75	2124.70	1983.78	1869.83	1776.09

AMOUNT OF LOAN	NUMBER OF YEARS IN TERM											
	13	14	15	16	17	18	19	20	25	30	35	40
$ 50	0.54	0.51	0.50	0.48	0.47	0.46	0.45	0.44	0.41	0.39	0.38	0.37
100	1.07	1.02	0.99	0.96	0.93	0.91	0.89	0.87	0.81	0.77	0.75	0.74
200	2.13	2.04	1.97	1.91	1.86	1.82	1.78	1.74	1.62	1.54	1.50	1.47
300	3.19	3.06	2.96	2.87	2.79	2.72	2.66	2.61	2.42	2.31	2.25	2.20
400	4.25	4.08	3.94	3.82	3.72	3.63	3.55	3.48	3.23	3.08	2.99	2.94
500	5.31	5.10	4.93	4.78	4.65	4.53	4.43	4.34	4.03	3.85	3.74	3.67
600	6.37	6.12	5.91	5.73	5.57	5.44	5.32	5.21	4.84	4.62	4.49	4.40
700	7.43	7.14	6.90	6.69	6.50	6.34	6.20	6.08	5.64	5.39	5.23	5.14
800	8.49	8.16	7.88	7.64	7.43	7.25	7.09	6.95	6.45	6.16	5.98	5.87
900	9.56	9.18	8.87	8.60	8.36	8.15	7.97	7.82	7.25	6.93	6.73	6.60
1000	10.62	10.20	9.85	9.55	9.29	9.06	8.86	8.68	8.06	7.69	7.47	7.34
2000	21.23	20.40	19.70	19.09	18.57	18.11	17.71	17.36	16.11	15.38	14.94	14.67
3000	31.84	30.60	29.55	28.64	27.85	27.17	26.57	26.04	24.16	23.07	22.41	22.00
4000	42.45	40.80	39.39	38.18	37.14	36.22	35.42	34.72	32.21	30.76	29.88	29.33
5000	53.06	51.00	49.24	47.73	46.42	45.28	44.28	43.40	40.27	38.45	37.35	36.66
6000	63.68	61.20	59.09	57.27	55.70	54.33	53.13	52.07	48.32	46.14	44.82	43.99
7000	74.29	71.40	68.94	66.82	64.99	63.39	61.99	60.75	56.37	53.83	52.29	51.32
8000	84.90	81.60	78.78	76.36	74.27	72.44	70.84	69.43	64.42	61.52	59.75	58.65
9000	95.51	91.80	88.63	85.91	83.55	81.50	79.70	78.11	72.48	69.21	67.22	65.98
10000	106.12	102.00	98.48	95.45	92.83	90.55	88.55	86.79	80.53	76.90	74.69	73.31
11000	116.73	112.20	108.33	105.00	102.12	99.61	97.40	95.47	88.58	84.59	82.16	80.65
12000	127.35	122.40	118.17	114.54	111.40	108.66	106.26	104.14	96.63	92.27	89.63	87.98
13000	137.96	132.59	128.02	124.09	120.68	117.71	115.11	112.82	104.68	99.96	97.10	95.31
14000	148.57	142.79	137.87	133.63	129.97	126.77	123.97	121.50	112.74	107.65	104.57	102.64
15000	159.18	152.99	147.72	143.18	139.25	135.82	132.82	130.18	120.79	115.34	112.03	109.97
16000	169.79	163.19	157.56	152.72	148.53	144.88	141.68	138.86	128.84	123.03	119.50	117.30
17000	180.41	173.39	167.41	162.27	157.81	153.93	150.53	147.53	136.89	130.72	126.97	124.63
18000	191.02	183.59	177.26	171.81	167.10	162.99	159.39	156.21	144.95	138.41	134.44	131.96
19000	201.63	193.79	187.11	181.36	176.38	172.04	168.24	164.89	153.00	146.10	141.91	139.29
20000	212.24	203.99	196.95	190.90	185.66	181.10	177.09	173.57	161.05	153.79	149.38	146.62
21000	222.85	214.19	206.80	200.45	194.95	190.15	185.95	182.25	169.10	161.48	156.85	153.95
22000	233.46	224.39	216.65	209.99	204.23	199.21	194.80	190.93	177.15	169.17	164.31	161.29
23000	244.08	234.59	226.50	219.54	213.51	208.26	203.66	199.60	185.21	176.86	171.78	168.62
24000	254.69	244.78	236.34	229.08	222.80	217.31	212.51	208.28	193.26	184.54	179.25	175.95
25000	265.30	254.98	246.19	238.63	232.08	226.37	221.37	216.96	201.31	192.23	186.72	183.28
26000	275.91	265.18	256.04	248.17	241.36	235.42	230.22	225.64	209.36	199.92	194.19	190.61
27000	286.52	275.38	265.88	257.72	250.64	244.48	239.08	234.32	217.42	207.61	201.66	197.94
28000	297.14	285.58	275.73	267.26	259.93	253.53	247.93	243.00	225.47	215.30	209.13	205.27
29000	307.75	295.78	285.58	276.81	269.21	262.59	256.78	251.67	233.52	222.99	216.59	212.60
30000	318.36	305.98	295.43	286.35	278.49	271.64	265.64	260.35	241.57	230.68	224.06	219.93
31000	328.97	316.18	305.27	295.90	287.78	280.70	274.49	269.03	249.63	238.37	231.53	227.26
32000	339.58	326.38	315.12	305.44	297.06	289.75	283.35	277.71	257.68	246.06	239.00	234.60
33000	350.19	336.58	324.97	314.99	306.34	298.81	292.20	286.39	265.73	253.75	246.47	241.93
34000	360.81	346.78	334.82	324.53	315.62	307.86	301.06	295.06	273.78	261.44	253.94	249.26
35000	371.42	356.98	344.66	334.08	324.91	316.92	309.91	303.74	281.83	269.12	261.41	256.59
37500	397.95	382.47	369.28	357.94	348.11	339.55	332.05	325.44	301.97	288.35	280.08	274.92
40000	424.48	407.97	393.90	381.80	371.32	362.19	354.18	347.13	322.10	307.57	298.75	293.24
42500	451.01	433.47	418.52	405.66	394.53	384.82	376.32	368.83	342.23	326.79	317.42	311.57
45000	477.54	458.97	443.14	429.53	417.74	407.46	398.46	390.53	362.36	346.02	336.09	329.90
47500	504.07	484.47	467.76	453.39	440.94	430.10	420.59	412.22	382.49	365.24	354.76	348.22
50000	530.59	509.96	492.37	477.25	464.15	452.73	442.73	433.92	402.62	384.46	373.44	366.55
52500	557.12	535.46	516.99	501.11	487.36	475.37	464.86	455.61	422.75	403.68	392.11	384.88
55000	583.65	560.96	541.61	524.98	510.57	498.01	487.00	477.31	442.88	422.91	410.78	403.21
57500	610.18	586.46	566.23	548.84	533.77	520.64	509.14	499.00	463.01	442.13	429.45	421.53
60000	636.71	611.96	590.85	572.70	556.98	543.28	531.27	520.70	483.14	461.35	448.12	439.86
65000	689.77	662.95	640.09	620.42	603.39	588.55	575.54	564.09	523.40	499.80	485.46	476.52
70000	742.83	713.95	689.32	668.15	649.81	633.83	619.82	607.48	563.66	538.24	522.81	513.17
75000	795.89	764.94	738.56	715.87	696.22	679.10	664.09	650.87	603.93	576.69	560.15	549.83
80000	848.95	815.94	787.80	763.60	742.64	724.37	708.36	694.26	644.19	615.14	597.49	586.48
85000	902.01	866.94	837.03	811.32	789.05	769.64	752.63	737.65	684.45	653.58	634.84	623.13
90000	955.07	917.93	886.27	859.05	835.47	814.92	796.91	781.05	724.71	692.03	672.18	659.79
95000	1008.13	968.93	935.51	906.77	881.88	860.19	841.18	824.44	764.97	730.47	709.52	696.44
100000	1061.18	1019.92	984.74	954.50	928.30	905.46	885.45	867.83	805.23	768.92	746.87	733.10
105000	1114.24	1070.92	1033.98	1002.22	974.71	950.74	929.72	911.22	845.49	807.36	784.21	769.75
110000	1167.30	1121.92	1083.22	1049.95	1021.13	996.01	974.00	954.61	885.75	845.81	821.55	806.41
115000	1220.36	1172.91	1132.46	1097.67	1067.54	1041.28	1018.27	998.00	926.02	884.26	858.89	843.06
120000	1273.42	1223.91	1181.69	1145.39	1113.96	1086.55	1062.54	1041.39	966.28	922.70	896.24	879.72
125000	1326.48	1274.90	1230.93	1193.12	1160.37	1131.83	1106.81	1084.78	1006.54	961.15	933.58	916.37
130000	1379.54	1325.90	1280.17	1240.84	1206.78	1177.10	1151.08	1128.18	1046.80	999.59	970.92	953.03
135000	1432.60	1376.90	1329.40	1288.57	1253.20	1222.37	1195.36	1171.57	1087.06	1038.04	1008.27	989.68
140000	1485.66	1427.89	1378.64	1336.29	1299.61	1267.65	1239.63	1214.96	1127.32	1076.48	1045.61	1026.34
145000	1538.71	1478.89	1427.88	1384.02	1346.03	1312.92	1283.90	1258.35	1167.58	1114.93	1082.95	1062.99
150000	1591.77	1529.88	1477.11	1431.74	1392.44	1358.19	1328.17	1301.74	1207.85	1153.38	1120.30	1099.65
155000	1644.83	1580.88	1526.35	1479.47	1438.86	1403.46	1372.45	1345.13	1248.11	1191.82	1157.64	1136.30
160000	1697.89	1631.87	1575.59	1527.19	1485.27	1448.74	1416.72	1388.52	1288.37	1230.27	1194.98	1172.96

AMOUNT OF LOAN	NUMBER OF YEARS IN TERM											
	1	2	3	4	5	6	7	8	9	10	11	12
$ 50	4.37	2.28	1.59	1.24	1.04	0.90	0.80	0.73	0.68	0.63	0.60	0.57
100	8.74	4.56	3.17	2.48	2.07	1.80	1.60	1.46	1.35	1.26	1.19	1.13
200	17.47	9.12	6.34	4.96	4.13	3.59	3.20	2.91	2.69	2.51	2.37	2.25
300	26.21	13.68	9.51	7.43	6.20	5.38	4.79	4.36	4.03	3.76	3.55	3.38
400	34.94	18.23	12.68	9.91	8.26	7.17	6.39	5.81	5.37	5.02	4.73	4.50
500	43.67	22.79	15.85	12.39	10.32	8.96	7.99	7.27	6.71	6.27	5.92	5.62
600	52.41	27.35	19.02	14.86	12.39	10.75	9.58	8.72	8.05	7.52	7.10	6.75
700	61.14	31.90	22.18	17.34	14.45	12.54	11.18	10.17	9.39	8.78	8.28	7.87
800	69.87	36.46	25.35	19.82	16.51	14.33	12.77	11.62	10.73	10.03	9.46	9.00
900	78.61	41.02	28.52	22.29	18.58	16.12	14.37	13.07	12.07	11.28	10.65	10.12
1000	87.34	45.58	31.69	24.77	20.64	17.91	15.97	14.53	13.42	12.54	11.83	11.24
2000	174.68	91.15	63.37	49.54	41.28	35.81	31.93	29.05	26.83	25.07	23.65	22.48
3000	262.01	136.72	95.06	74.30	61.92	53.71	47.89	43.57	40.24	37.60	35.47	33.72
4000	349.35	182.29	126.74	99.07	82.55	71.61	63.85	58.09	53.65	50.14	47.30	44.96
5000	436.68	227.86	158.42	123.84	103.19	89.51	79.82	72.61	67.06	62.67	59.12	56.20
6000	524.02	273.43	190.11	148.60	123.83	107.42	95.78	87.13	80.47	75.20	70.94	67.44
7000	611.35	319.00	221.79	173.37	144.47	125.32	111.74	101.65	93.88	87.73	82.77	78.68
8000	698.69	364.57	253.47	198.14	165.10	143.22	127.70	116.17	107.29	100.27	94.59	89.92
9000	786.03	410.14	285.16	222.90	185.74	161.12	143.67	130.69	120.70	112.80	106.41	101.16
10000	873.36	455.71	316.84	247.67	206.38	179.02	159.63	145.21	134.11	125.33	118.24	112.40
11000	960.70	501.28	348.52	272.44	227.01	196.92	175.59	159.73	147.52	137.86	130.06	123.64
12000	1048.03	546.85	380.21	297.20	247.65	214.83	191.55	174.26	160.93	150.40	141.88	134.88
13000	1135.37	592.42	411.89	321.97	268.29	232.73	207.52	188.78	174.34	162.93	153.71	146.12
14000	1222.70	637.99	443.57	346.74	288.93	250.63	223.48	203.30	187.76	175.46	165.53	157.36
15000	1310.04	683.56	475.26	371.50	309.56	268.53	239.44	217.82	201.17	188.00	177.35	168.60
16000	1397.37	729.13	506.94	396.27	330.20	286.43	255.40	232.34	214.58	200.53	189.18	179.84
17000	1484.71	774.70	538.62	421.04	350.84	304.33	271.37	246.86	227.99	213.06	201.00	191.08
18000	1572.05	820.27	570.31	445.80	371.48	322.24	287.33	261.38	241.40	225.59	212.82	202.32
19000	1659.38	865.84	601.99	470.57	392.11	340.14	303.29	275.90	254.81	238.13	224.65	213.56
20000	1746.72	911.41	633.68	495.34	412.75	358.04	319.25	290.42	268.22	250.66	236.47	224.80
21000	1834.05	956.98	665.36	520.10	433.39	375.94	335.22	304.94	281.63	263.19	248.29	236.04
22000	1921.39	1002.55	697.04	544.87	454.02	393.84	351.18	319.46	295.04	275.72	260.11	247.28
23000	2008.72	1048.12	728.73	569.63	474.66	411.74	367.14	333.98	308.45	288.26	271.94	258.52
24000	2096.06	1093.69	760.41	594.40	495.30	429.65	383.10	348.51	321.86	300.79	283.76	269.76
25000	2183.39	1139.26	792.09	619.17	515.94	447.55	399.07	363.03	335.27	313.32	295.58	281.00
26000	2270.73	1184.83	823.78	643.93	536.57	465.45	415.03	377.55	348.68	325.85	307.41	292.24
27000	2358.07	1230.40	855.46	668.70	557.21	483.35	430.99	392.07	362.10	338.39	319.23	303.48
28000	2445.40	1275.97	887.14	693.47	577.85	501.25	446.95	406.59	375.51	350.92	331.05	314.72
29000	2532.74	1321.54	918.83	718.23	598.48	519.15	462.92	421.11	388.92	363.45	342.88	325.96
30000	2620.07	1367.11	950.51	743.00	619.12	537.06	478.88	435.63	402.33	375.99	354.70	337.20
31000	2707.41	1412.68	982.19	767.77	639.76	554.96	494.84	450.15	415.74	388.52	366.52	348.44
32000	2794.74	1458.25	1013.88	792.53	660.40	572.86	510.80	464.67	429.15	401.05	378.35	359.68
33000	2882.08	1503.82	1045.56	817.30	681.03	590.76	526.77	479.19	442.56	413.58	390.17	370.92
34000	2969.41	1549.39	1077.24	842.07	701.67	608.66	542.73	493.71	455.97	426.12	401.99	382.16
35000	3056.75	1594.96	1108.93	866.83	722.31	626.56	558.69	508.23	469.38	438.65	413.82	393.40
37500	3275.09	1708.88	1188.14	928.75	773.90	671.32	598.60	544.54	502.91	469.98	443.37	421.50
40000	3493.43	1822.81	1267.35	990.67	825.49	716.07	638.50	580.84	536.44	501.31	472.93	449.60
42500	3711.77	1936.74	1346.55	1052.58	877.09	760.83	678.41	617.14	569.96	532.64	502.49	477.70
45000	3930.11	2050.66	1425.76	1114.50	928.68	805.58	718.32	653.44	603.49	563.98	532.05	505.80
47500	4148.45	2164.59	1504.97	1176.41	980.27	850.34	758.22	689.74	637.02	595.31	561.61	533.90
50000	4366.78	2278.51	1584.18	1238.33	1031.87	895.09	798.13	726.05	670.54	626.64	591.16	562.00
52500	4585.12	2392.44	1663.39	1300.25	1083.46	939.84	838.04	762.35	704.07	657.97	620.72	590.10
55000	4803.46	2506.36	1742.60	1362.16	1135.05	984.60	877.94	798.65	737.60	689.30	650.28	618.20
57500	5021.80	2620.29	1821.81	1424.08	1186.65	1029.35	917.85	834.95	771.12	720.63	679.84	646.30
60000	5240.14	2734.21	1901.02	1486.00	1238.24	1074.11	957.75	871.26	804.65	751.97	709.40	674.40
65000	5676.82	2962.06	2059.43	1609.83	1341.43	1163.62	1037.57	943.86	871.70	814.63	768.51	730.60
70000	6113.50	3189.91	2217.85	1733.66	1444.61	1253.12	1117.38	1016.46	938.76	877.29	827.63	786.80
75000	6550.17	3417.76	2376.27	1857.49	1547.80	1342.63	1197.19	1089.07	1005.81	939.96	886.74	843.00
80000	6986.85	3645.61	2534.69	1981.33	1650.98	1432.14	1277.00	1161.67	1072.87	1002.62	945.86	899.20
85000	7423.53	3873.47	2693.10	2105.16	1754.17	1521.65	1356.82	1234.28	1139.92	1065.28	1004.97	955.40
90000	7860.21	4101.32	2851.52	2228.99	1857.36	1611.16	1436.63	1306.88	1206.97	1127.95	1064.09	1011.60
95000	8296.89	4329.17	3009.94	2352.82	1960.54	1700.67	1516.44	1379.48	1274.03	1190.61	1123.21	1067.80
100000	8733.56	4557.02	3168.36	2476.66	2063.73	1790.18	1596.25	1452.09	1341.08	1253.27	1182.32	1124.00
105000	9170.24	4784.87	3326.77	2600.49	2166.91	1879.68	1676.07	1524.69	1408.14	1315.94	1241.44	1180.20
110000	9606.92	5012.72	3485.19	2724.32	2270.10	1969.19	1755.88	1597.30	1475.19	1378.60	1300.55	1236.40
115000	10043.60	5240.57	3643.61	2848.15	2373.29	2058.70	1835.69	1669.90	1542.24	1441.26	1359.67	1292.60
120000	10480.28	5468.42	3802.03	2971.99	2476.47	2148.21	1915.50	1742.51	1609.30	1503.93	1418.79	1348.80
125000	10916.95	5696.27	3960.44	3095.82	2579.66	2237.72	1995.32	1815.11	1676.35	1566.59	1477.90	1405.00
130000	11353.63	5924.12	4118.86	3219.65	2682.85	2327.23	2075.13	1887.71	1743.40	1629.25	1537.02	1461.20
135000	11790.31	6151.97	4277.28	3343.48	2786.03	2416.74	2154.94	1960.32	1810.46	1691.92	1596.13	1517.40
140000	12226.99	6379.82	4435.70	3467.32	2889.22	2506.24	2234.75	2032.92	1877.51	1754.58	1655.25	1573.60
145000	12663.67	6607.67	4594.11	3591.15	2992.40	2595.75	2314.57	2105.53	1944.57	1817.24	1714.36	1629.80
150000	13100.34	6835.52	4752.53	3714.98	3095.59	2685.26	2394.38	2178.13	2011.62	1879.91	1773.48	1686.00
155000	13537.02	7063.37	4910.95	3838.81	3198.78	2774.77	2474.19	2250.74	2078.67	1942.57	1832.60	1742.20
160000	13973.70	7291.22	5069.37	3962.65	3301.96	2864.28	2554.00	2323.34	2145.73	2005.23	1891.71	1798.40

AMOUNT OF LOAN	NUMBER OF YEARS IN TERM											
	13	14	15	16	17	18	19	20	25	30	35	40
$ 50	0.54	0.52	0.50	0.49	0.48	0.47	0.46	0.45	0.42	0.40	0.39	0.38
100	1.08	1.04	1.00	0.97	0.95	0.93	0.91	0.89	0.83	0.79	0.77	0.76
200	2.16	2.07	2.00	1.94	1.89	1.85	1.81	1.77	1.65	1.58	1.54	1.51
300	3.23	3.11	3.00	2.91	2.84	2.77	2.71	2.66	2.47	2.37	2.30	2.26
400	4.31	4.14	4.00	3.88	3.78	3.69	3.61	3.54	3.29	3.15	3.07	3.01
500	5.38	5.18	5.00	4.85	4.72	4.61	4.51	4.42	4.12	3.94	3.83	3.77
600	6.46	6.21	6.00	5.82	5.67	5.53	5.41	5.31	4.94	4.73	4.60	4.52
700	7.53	7.25	7.00	6.79	6.61	6.45	6.31	6.19	5.76	5.51	5.36	5.27
800	8.61	8.28	8.00	7.76	7.55	7.37	7.21	7.07	6.58	6.30	6.13	6.02
900	9.68	9.31	9.00	8.73	8.50	8.29	8.11	7.96	7.40	7.09	6.89	6.77
1000	10.76	10.35	10.00	9.70	9.44	9.21	9.02	8.84	8.23	7.87	7.66	7.53
2000	21.51	20.69	19.99	19.39	18.87	18.42	18.03	17.68	16.45	15.74	15.31	15.05
3000	32.27	31.04	29.99	29.09	28.31	27.63	27.04	26.52	24.67	23.61	22.97	22.57
4000	43.02	41.38	39.98	38.78	37.74	36.84	36.05	35.35	32.89	31.47	30.62	30.09
5000	53.77	51.72	49.98	48.48	47.18	46.05	45.06	44.19	41.11	39.34	38.27	37.61
6000	64.53	62.07	59.97	58.17	56.61	55.26	54.07	53.03	49.33	47.21	45.93	45.14
7000	75.28	72.41	69.97	67.87	66.05	64.47	63.08	61.86	57.56	55.07	53.58	52.66
8000	86.04	82.76	79.96	77.56	75.48	73.68	72.09	70.70	65.78	62.94	61.23	60.18
9000	96.79	93.10	89.96	87.26	84.92	82.89	81.10	79.54	74.00	70.81	68.89	67.70
10000	107.54	103.44	99.95	96.95	94.35	92.09	90.12	88.38	82.22	78.68	76.54	75.22
11000	118.30	113.79	109.94	106.64	103.79	101.30	99.13	97.21	90.44	86.54	84.19	82.74
12000	129.05	124.13	119.94	116.34	113.22	110.51	108.14	106.05	98.66	94.41	91.85	90.27
13000	139.80	134.47	129.93	126.03	122.66	119.72	117.15	114.89	106.88	102.28	99.50	97.79
14000	150.56	144.82	139.93	135.73	132.09	128.93	126.16	123.72	115.11	110.14	107.16	105.31
15000	161.31	155.16	149.92	145.42	141.53	138.14	135.17	132.56	123.33	118.01	114.81	112.83
16000	172.07	165.51	159.92	155.12	150.96	147.35	144.18	141.40	131.55	125.88	122.46	120.35
17000	182.82	175.85	169.91	164.81	160.40	156.56	153.19	150.24	139.77	133.74	130.12	127.87
18000	193.57	186.19	179.91	174.51	169.83	165.77	162.20	159.07	147.99	141.61	137.77	135.40
19000	204.33	196.54	189.90	184.20	179.27	174.97	171.22	167.91	156.21	149.48	145.42	142.92
20000	215.08	206.88	199.89	193.89	188.70	184.18	180.23	176.75	164.43	157.35	153.08	150.44
21000	225.83	217.22	209.89	203.59	198.14	193.39	189.24	185.58	172.66	165.21	160.73	157.96
22000	236.59	227.57	219.88	213.28	207.57	202.60	198.25	194.42	180.88	173.08	168.38	165.48
23000	247.34	237.91	229.88	222.98	217.01	211.81	207.26	203.26	189.10	180.95	176.04	173.00
24000	258.10	248.26	239.87	232.67	226.44	221.02	216.27	212.10	197.32	188.81	183.69	180.53
25000	268.85	258.60	249.87	242.37	235.88	230.23	225.28	220.93	205.54	196.68	191.35	188.05
26000	279.60	268.94	259.86	252.06	245.31	239.44	234.29	229.77	213.76	204.55	199.00	195.57
27000	290.36	279.29	269.86	261.76	254.75	248.65	243.30	238.61	221.98	212.41	206.65	203.09
28000	301.11	289.63	279.85	271.45	264.18	257.85	252.32	247.44	230.21	220.28	214.31	210.61
29000	311.87	299.97	289.85	281.14	273.62	267.06	261.33	256.28	238.43	228.15	221.96	218.13
30000	322.62	310.32	299.84	290.84	283.05	276.27	270.34	265.12	246.65	236.02	229.61	225.66
31000	333.37	320.66	309.83	300.53	292.49	285.48	279.35	273.96	254.87	243.88	237.27	233.18
32000	344.13	331.01	319.83	310.23	301.92	294.69	288.36	282.79	263.09	251.75	244.92	240.70
33000	354.88	341.35	329.82	319.92	311.36	303.90	297.37	291.63	271.31	259.62	252.57	248.22
34000	365.63	351.69	339.82	329.62	320.79	313.11	306.38	300.47	279.53	267.48	260.23	255.74
35000	376.39	362.04	349.81	339.31	330.23	322.32	315.39	309.30	287.76	275.35	267.88	263.26
37500	403.27	387.90	374.80	363.55	353.81	345.34	337.92	331.40	308.31	295.02	287.02	282.07
40000	430.16	413.76	399.78	387.78	377.40	368.36	360.45	353.49	328.86	314.69	306.15	300.87
42500	457.04	439.61	424.77	412.02	400.99	391.38	382.98	375.58	349.42	334.35	325.28	319.68
45000	483.93	465.47	449.76	436.26	424.58	414.41	405.50	397.67	369.97	354.02	344.42	338.48
47500	510.81	491.33	474.74	460.49	448.16	437.43	428.03	419.77	390.52	373.69	363.55	357.29
50000	537.70	517.19	499.73	484.73	471.75	460.45	450.56	441.86	411.08	393.36	382.69	376.09
52500	564.58	543.05	524.72	508.96	495.34	483.47	473.09	463.95	431.63	413.02	401.82	394.89
55000	591.46	568.91	549.70	533.20	518.92	506.49	495.61	486.05	452.18	432.69	420.95	413.70
57500	618.35	594.77	574.69	557.44	542.51	529.52	518.14	508.14	472.74	452.36	440.09	432.50
60000	645.23	620.63	599.67	581.67	566.10	552.54	540.67	530.23	493.29	472.03	459.22	451.31
65000	699.00	672.35	649.65	630.15	613.27	598.58	585.73	574.42	534.40	511.36	497.49	488.92
70000	752.77	724.07	699.62	678.62	660.45	644.63	630.78	618.60	575.51	550.70	535.76	526.52
75000	806.54	775.79	749.59	727.09	707.62	690.67	675.84	662.79	616.61	590.03	574.03	564.13
80000	860.31	827.51	799.56	775.56	754.80	736.72	720.89	706.97	657.72	629.37	612.30	601.74
85000	914.08	879.22	849.54	824.03	801.97	782.76	765.95	751.16	698.83	668.70	650.56	639.35
90000	967.85	930.94	899.51	872.51	849.15	828.81	811.00	795.34	739.93	708.04	688.83	676.96
95000	1021.62	982.66	949.48	920.98	896.32	874.85	856.06	839.53	781.04	747.37	727.10	714.57
100000	1075.39	1034.38	999.45	969.45	943.49	920.90	901.11	883.72	822.15	786.71	765.37	752.18
105000	1129.15	1086.10	1049.43	1017.92	990.67	966.94	946.17	927.90	863.26	826.04	803.64	789.78
110000	1182.92	1137.82	1099.40	1066.40	1037.84	1012.98	991.22	972.09	904.36	865.38	841.90	827.39
115000	1236.69	1189.54	1149.37	1114.87	1085.02	1059.03	1036.28	1016.27	945.47	904.71	880.17	865.00
120000	1290.46	1241.26	1199.34	1163.34	1132.19	1105.07	1081.34	1060.46	986.58	944.05	918.44	902.61
125000	1344.23	1292.98	1249.32	1211.81	1179.37	1151.12	1126.39	1104.64	1027.68	983.38	956.71	940.22
130000	1398.00	1344.69	1299.29	1260.29	1226.54	1197.16	1171.45	1148.83	1068.79	1022.72	994.98	977.83
135000	1451.77	1396.41	1349.26	1308.76	1273.72	1243.21	1216.50	1193.01	1109.90	1062.05	1033.25	1015.44
140000	1505.54	1448.13	1399.23	1357.23	1320.89	1289.25	1261.56	1237.20	1151.01	1101.39	1071.51	1053.04
145000	1559.31	1499.85	1449.21	1405.70	1368.06	1335.30	1306.61	1281.39	1192.11	1140.72	1109.78	1090.65
150000	1613.08	1551.57	1499.18	1454.18	1415.24	1381.34	1351.67	1325.57	1233.22	1180.06	1148.05	1128.26
155000	1666.85	1603.29	1549.15	1502.65	1462.41	1427.39	1396.72	1369.76	1274.33	1219.39	1186.32	1165.87
160000	1720.61	1655.01	1599.12	1551.12	1509.59	1473.43	1441.78	1413.94	1315.43	1258.73	1224.59	1203.48

9.00% MONTHLY AMORTIZING PAYMENTS

AMOUNT OF LOAN	NUMBER OF YEARS IN TERM											
	1	2	3	4	5	6	7	8	9	10	11	12
$ 50	4.38	2.29	1.59	1.25	1.04	0.91	0.81	0.74	0.68	0.64	0.60	0.57
100	8.75	4.57	3.18	2.49	2.08	1.81	1.61	1.47	1.36	1.27	1.20	1.14
200	17.50	9.14	6.36	4.98	4.16	3.61	3.22	2.94	2.71	2.54	2.40	2.28
300	26.24	13.71	9.54	7.47	6.23	5.41	4.83	4.40	4.07	3.81	3.59	3.42
400	34.99	18.28	12.72	9.96	8.31	7.22	6.44	5.87	5.42	5.07	4.79	4.56
500	43.73	22.85	15.90	12.45	10.38	9.02	8.05	7.33	6.78	6.34	5.99	5.70
600	52.48	27.42	19.08	14.94	12.46	10.82	9.66	8.80	8.13	7.61	7.18	6.83
700	61.22	31.98	22.26	17.42	14.54	12.62	11.27	10.26	9.49	8.87	8.38	7.97
800	69.97	36.55	25.44	19.91	16.61	14.43	12.88	11.73	10.84	10.14	9.57	9.11
900	78.71	41.12	28.62	22.40	18.69	16.23	14.49	13.19	12.19	11.41	10.77	10.25
1000	87.46	45.69	31.80	24.89	20.76	18.03	16.09	14.66	13.55	12.67	11.97	11.39
2000	174.91	91.37	63.60	49.78	41.52	36.06	32.18	29.31	27.09	25.34	23.93	22.77
3000	262.36	137.06	95.40	74.66	62.28	54.08	48.27	43.96	40.63	38.01	35.89	34.15
4000	349.81	182.74	127.20	99.55	83.04	72.11	64.36	58.61	54.18	50.68	47.85	45.53
5000	437.26	228.43	159.00	124.43	103.80	90.13	80.45	73.26	67.72	63.34	59.81	56.91
6000	524.71	274.11	190.80	149.32	124.56	108.16	96.54	87.91	81.26	76.01	71.77	68.29
7000	612.17	319.80	222.60	174.20	145.31	126.18	112.63	102.56	94.81	88.68	83.73	79.67
8000	699.62	365.48	254.40	199.09	166.07	144.21	128.72	117.21	108.35	101.35	95.69	91.05
9000	787.07	411.17	286.20	223.97	186.83	162.23	144.81	131.86	121.89	114.01	107.65	102.43
10000	874.52	456.85	318.00	248.86	207.59	180.26	160.90	146.51	135.43	126.68	119.61	113.81
11000	961.97	502.54	349.80	273.74	228.35	198.29	176.98	161.16	148.98	139.35	131.57	125.19
12000	1049.42	548.22	381.60	298.63	249.11	216.31	193.07	175.81	162.52	152.02	143.53	136.57
13000	1136.87	593.91	413.40	323.51	269.86	234.34	209.16	190.46	176.06	164.68	155.50	147.95
14000	1224.33	639.59	445.20	348.40	290.62	252.36	225.25	205.11	189.61	177.35	167.46	159.33
15000	1311.78	685.28	477.00	373.28	311.38	270.39	241.34	219.76	203.15	190.02	179.42	170.71
16000	1399.23	730.96	508.80	398.17	332.14	288.41	257.43	234.41	216.69	202.69	191.38	182.09
17000	1486.68	776.65	540.60	423.05	352.90	306.44	273.52	249.06	230.23	215.35	203.34	193.47
18000	1574.13	822.33	572.40	447.94	373.66	324.46	289.61	263.71	243.78	228.02	215.30	204.85
19000	1661.58	868.02	604.20	472.82	394.41	342.49	305.70	278.36	257.32	240.69	227.26	216.23
20000	1749.05	913.70	636.00	497.71	415.17	360.52	321.79	293.01	270.86	253.36	239.22	227.61
21000	1836.49	959.38	667.80	522.59	435.93	378.54	337.88	307.66	284.41	266.02	251.18	238.99
22000	1923.94	1005.07	699.60	547.48	456.69	396.57	353.96	322.31	297.95	278.69	263.14	250.37
23000	2011.39	1050.75	731.40	572.36	477.45	414.59	370.05	336.96	311.49	291.36	275.10	261.75
24000	2098.84	1096.44	763.20	597.25	498.21	432.62	386.14	351.61	325.03	304.03	287.06	273.13
25000	2186.29	1142.12	795.00	622.13	518.96	450.64	402.23	366.26	338.58	316.69	299.03	284.51
26000	2273.74	1187.81	826.80	647.02	539.72	468.67	418.32	380.91	352.12	329.36	310.99	295.89
27000	2361.19	1233.49	858.60	671.90	560.48	486.69	434.41	395.56	365.66	342.03	322.95	307.27
28000	2448.65	1279.18	890.40	696.79	581.24	504.72	450.50	410.21	379.21	354.70	334.91	318.65
29000	2536.10	1324.86	922.20	721.67	602.00	522.75	466.59	424.86	392.75	367.36	346.87	330.03
30000	2623.55	1370.55	954.00	746.56	622.76	540.77	482.68	439.51	406.29	380.03	358.83	341.41
31000	2711.00	1416.23	985.80	771.44	643.51	558.80	498.77	454.16	419.84	392.70	370.79	352.79
32000	2798.45	1461.92	1017.60	796.33	664.27	576.82	514.86	468.81	433.38	405.37	382.75	364.17
33000	2885.90	1507.60	1049.40	821.21	685.03	594.85	530.94	483.46	446.92	418.04	394.71	375.56
34000	2973.36	1553.29	1081.20	846.10	705.79	612.87	547.03	498.11	460.46	430.70	406.67	386.94
35000	3060.81	1598.97	1113.00	870.98	726.55	630.90	563.12	512.76	474.01	443.37	418.63	398.32
37500	3279.44	1713.18	1192.49	933.19	778.44	675.96	603.35	549.39	507.86	475.04	448.54	426.77
40000	3498.06	1827.39	1271.99	995.41	830.34	721.03	643.57	586.01	541.72	506.71	478.44	455.22
42500	3716.69	1941.61	1351.49	1057.62	882.24	766.09	683.79	622.64	575.58	538.38	508.34	483.67
45000	3935.32	2055.82	1430.99	1119.83	934.13	811.15	724.01	659.26	609.44	570.05	538.24	512.12
47500	4153.95	2170.03	1510.49	1182.04	986.03	856.22	764.24	695.89	643.29	601.71	568.14	540.57
50000	4372.58	2284.24	1589.99	1244.26	1037.92	901.28	804.46	732.52	677.15	633.38	598.05	569.02
52500	4591.21	2398.45	1669.49	1306.47	1089.82	946.35	844.68	769.14	711.01	665.05	627.95	597.47
55000	4809.84	2512.67	1748.99	1368.68	1141.71	991.41	884.90	805.77	744.86	696.72	657.85	625.92
57500	5028.46	2626.88	1828.49	1430.89	1193.61	1036.47	925.13	842.39	778.72	728.39	687.75	654.37
60000	5247.09	2741.09	1907.99	1493.11	1245.51	1081.54	965.35	879.02	812.58	760.06	717.65	682.82
65000	5684.35	2969.51	2066.99	1617.53	1349.30	1171.66	1045.80	952.27	880.29	823.40	777.46	739.72
70000	6121.61	3197.94	2225.99	1741.96	1453.09	1261.79	1126.24	1025.52	948.01	886.74	837.26	796.63
75000	6558.87	3426.36	2384.98	1866.38	1556.88	1351.92	1206.69	1098.77	1015.72	950.07	897.07	853.53
80000	6996.12	3654.78	2543.98	1990.81	1660.67	1442.05	1287.13	1172.02	1083.44	1013.41	956.87	910.43
85000	7433.38	3883.21	2702.98	2115.23	1764.47	1532.18	1367.58	1245.27	1151.15	1076.75	1016.67	967.33
90000	7870.64	4111.63	2861.98	2239.66	1868.26	1622.30	1448.02	1318.52	1218.87	1140.09	1076.48	1024.23
95000	8307.90	4340.06	3020.98	2364.08	1972.05	1712.43	1528.47	1391.77	1286.58	1203.42	1136.28	1081.13
100000	8745.15	4568.48	3179.98	2488.51	2075.84	1802.56	1608.91	1465.03	1354.30	1266.76	1196.09	1138.04
105000	9182.41	4796.90	3338.98	2612.93	2179.63	1892.69	1689.36	1538.28	1422.01	1330.10	1255.89	1194.94
110000	9619.67	5025.33	3497.98	2737.36	2283.42	1982.81	1769.80	1611.53	1489.72	1393.44	1315.69	1251.84
115000	10056.92	5253.75	3656.97	2861.78	2387.22	2072.94	1850.25	1684.78	1557.44	1456.78	1375.50	1308.74
120000	10494.18	5482.17	3815.97	2986.21	2491.01	2163.07	1930.69	1758.03	1625.15	1520.11	1435.30	1365.64
125000	10931.44	5710.60	3974.97	3110.64	2594.80	2253.20	2011.14	1831.28	1692.87	1583.45	1495.11	1422.54
130000	11368.70	5939.02	4133.97	3235.06	2698.59	2343.32	2091.59	1904.53	1760.58	1646.79	1554.91	1479.44
135000	11805.95	6167.45	4292.97	3359.49	2802.38	2433.45	2172.03	1977.78	1828.30	1710.13	1614.71	1536.35
140000	12243.21	6395.87	4451.97	3483.91	2906.17	2523.58	2252.48	2051.03	1896.01	1773.47	1674.52	1593.25
145000	12680.47	6624.29	4610.97	3608.34	3009.97	2613.71	2332.92	2124.28	1963.73	1836.80	1734.32	1650.15
150000	13117.73	6852.72	4769.96	3732.76	3113.76	2703.84	2413.37	2197.54	2031.44	1900.14	1794.13	1707.05
155000	13554.98	7081.14	4928.96	3857.19	3217.55	2793.96	2493.81	2270.79	2099.16	1963.48	1853.93	1763.95
160000	13992.24	7309.56	5087.96	3981.61	3321.34	2884.09	2574.26	2344.04	2166.87	2026.82	1913.73	1820.85

34

AMOUNT OF LOAN	NUMBER OF YEARS IN TERM											
	13	14	15	16	17	18	19	20	25	30	35	40
$ 50	0.55	0.53	0.51	0.50	0.48	0.47	0.46	0.45	0.42	0.41	0.40	0.39
100	1.09	1.05	1.02	0.99	0.96	0.94	0.92	0.90	0.84	0.81	0.79	0.78
200	2.18	2.10	2.03	1.97	1.92	1.88	1.84	1.80	1.68	1.61	1.57	1.55
300	3.27	3.15	3.05	2.96	2.88	2.81	2.76	2.70	2.52	2.42	2.36	2.32
400	4.36	4.20	4.06	3.94	3.84	3.75	3.67	3.60	3.36	3.22	3.14	3.09
500	5.45	5.25	5.08	4.93	4.80	4.69	4.59	4.50	4.20	4.03	3.92	3.86
600	6.54	6.30	6.09	5.91	5.76	5.62	5.51	5.40	5.04	4.83	4.71	4.63
700	7.63	7.35	7.10	6.90	6.72	6.56	6.42	6.30	5.88	5.64	5.49	5.40
800	8.72	8.40	8.12	7.88	7.68	7.50	7.34	7.20	6.72	6.44	6.28	6.18
900	9.81	9.45	9.13	8.87	8.63	8.43	8.26	8.10	7.56	7.25	7.06	6.95
1000	10.90	10.49	10.15	9.85	9.59	9.37	9.17	9.00	8.40	8.05	7.84	7.72
2000	21.80	20.98	20.29	19.70	19.18	18.73	18.34	18.00	16.79	16.10	15.68	15.43
3000	32.70	31.47	30.43	29.54	28.77	28.10	27.51	27.00	25.18	24.14	23.52	23.15
4000	43.59	41.96	40.58	39.39	38.36	37.46	36.68	35.99	33.57	32.19	31.36	30.86
5000	54.49	52.45	50.72	49.23	47.95	46.83	45.85	44.99	41.96	40.24	39.20	38.57
6000	65.39	62.94	60.86	59.08	57.53	56.19	55.02	53.99	50.36	48.28	47.04	46.29
7000	76.28	73.43	71.00	68.92	67.12	65.56	64.19	62.99	58.75	56.33	54.88	54.00
8000	87.18	83.92	81.15	78.77	76.71	74.92	73.36	71.98	67.14	64.37	62.72	61.71
9000	98.08	94.41	91.29	88.61	86.30	84.29	82.53	80.98	75.53	72.42	70.56	69.43
10000	108.97	104.90	101.43	98.46	95.89	93.65	91.69	89.98	83.92	80.47	78.40	77.14
11000	119.87	115.39	111.57	108.30	105.47	103.01	100.86	98.97	92.32	88.51	86.24	84.85
12000	130.77	125.88	121.72	118.15	115.06	112.38	110.03	107.97	100.71	96.56	94.08	92.57
13000	141.66	136.37	131.86	127.99	124.65	121.74	119.20	116.97	109.10	104.61	101.92	100.28
14000	152.56	146.86	142.00	137.84	134.24	131.11	128.37	125.97	117.49	112.65	109.76	108.00
15000	163.46	157.35	152.14	147.68	143.83	140.47	137.54	134.96	125.88	120.70	117.60	115.71
16000	174.35	167.84	162.29	157.53	153.41	149.84	146.71	143.96	134.28	128.74	125.44	123.42
17000	185.25	178.32	172.43	167.37	163.00	159.20	155.88	152.96	142.67	136.79	133.28	131.14
18000	196.15	188.81	182.57	177.22	172.59	168.57	165.05	161.96	151.06	144.84	141.12	138.85
19000	207.04	199.30	192.72	187.06	182.18	177.93	174.22	170.95	159.45	152.88	148.96	146.56
20000	217.94	209.79	202.86	196.91	191.77	187.29	183.38	179.95	167.84	160.93	156.80	154.28
21000	228.84	220.28	213.00	206.75	201.35	196.66	192.55	188.95	176.24	168.98	164.64	161.99
22000	239.73	230.77	223.14	216.60	210.94	206.02	201.72	197.94	184.63	177.02	172.48	169.70
23000	250.63	241.26	233.29	226.44	220.53	215.39	210.89	206.94	193.02	185.07	180.32	177.42
24000	261.53	251.75	243.43	236.29	230.12	224.75	220.06	215.94	201.41	193.11	188.16	185.13
25000	272.43	262.24	253.57	246.13	239.71	234.12	229.23	224.94	209.80	201.16	196.00	192.85
26000	283.32	272.73	263.71	255.98	249.29	243.48	238.40	233.93	218.20	209.21	203.84	200.56
27000	294.22	283.22	273.86	265.82	258.88	252.85	247.57	242.93	226.59	217.25	211.68	208.27
28000	305.12	293.71	284.00	275.67	268.47	262.21	256.74	251.93	234.98	225.30	219.52	215.99
29000	316.01	304.20	294.14	285.51	278.06	271.57	265.91	260.93	243.37	233.35	227.36	223.70
30000	326.91	314.69	304.28	295.36	287.65	280.94	275.07	269.92	251.76	241.39	235.20	231.41
31000	337.81	325.18	314.43	305.20	297.23	290.30	284.24	278.92	260.16	249.44	243.04	239.13
32000	348.70	335.67	324.57	315.05	306.82	299.67	293.41	287.92	268.55	257.48	250.88	246.84
33000	359.60	346.15	334.71	324.90	316.41	309.03	302.58	296.91	276.94	265.53	258.72	254.55
34000	370.50	356.64	344.86	334.74	326.00	318.40	311.75	305.91	285.33	273.58	266.56	262.27
35000	381.39	367.13	355.00	344.59	335.59	327.76	320.92	314.91	293.72	281.62	274.40	269.98
37500	408.64	393.36	380.35	369.20	359.56	351.17	343.84	337.40	314.70	301.74	294.00	289.27
40000	435.88	419.58	405.71	393.81	383.53	374.58	366.76	359.90	335.68	321.85	313.60	308.55
42500	463.12	445.80	431.07	418.42	407.50	397.99	389.69	382.39	356.66	341.97	333.20	327.83
45000	490.36	472.03	456.42	443.04	431.47	421.41	412.61	404.88	377.64	362.09	352.80	347.12
47500	517.60	498.25	481.78	467.65	455.44	444.82	435.53	427.37	398.62	382.20	372.40	366.40
50000	544.85	524.47	507.14	492.26	479.41	468.23	458.45	449.87	419.60	402.32	392.00	385.69
52500	572.09	550.70	532.49	516.88	503.38	491.64	481.38	472.36	440.58	422.43	411.60	404.97
55000	599.33	576.92	557.85	541.49	527.35	515.05	504.30	494.85	461.56	442.55	431.20	424.25
57500	626.57	603.14	583.21	566.10	551.32	538.46	527.22	517.35	482.54	462.66	450.80	443.54
60000	653.81	629.37	608.56	590.71	575.29	561.87	550.14	539.84	503.52	482.78	470.40	462.82
65000	708.30	681.81	659.28	639.94	623.23	608.69	595.99	584.83	545.48	523.01	509.60	501.39
70000	762.78	734.26	709.99	689.17	671.17	655.52	641.83	629.81	587.44	563.24	548.80	539.96
75000	817.27	786.71	760.70	738.39	719.11	702.34	687.68	674.80	629.40	603.47	588.00	578.53
80000	871.75	839.16	811.42	787.62	767.05	749.16	733.52	719.79	671.36	643.70	627.20	617.09
85000	926.23	891.60	862.13	836.84	814.99	795.98	779.37	764.77	713.32	683.93	666.40	655.66
90000	980.72	944.05	912.84	886.07	862.93	842.81	825.21	809.76	755.28	724.17	705.60	694.23
95000	1035.20	996.50	963.56	935.30	910.87	889.63	871.06	854.74	797.24	764.40	744.80	732.80
100000	1089.69	1048.94	1014.27	984.52	958.81	936.45	916.90	899.73	839.20	804.63	784.00	771.37
105000	1144.17	1101.39	1064.98	1033.75	1006.75	983.27	962.75	944.72	881.16	844.86	823.20	809.93
110000	1198.65	1153.84	1115.70	1082.97	1054.69	1030.09	1008.59	989.70	923.12	885.09	862.40	848.50
115000	1253.14	1206.28	1166.41	1132.20	1102.63	1076.92	1054.44	1034.69	965.08	925.32	901.60	887.07
120000	1307.62	1258.73	1217.12	1181.42	1150.57	1123.74	1100.28	1079.68	1007.04	965.55	940.80	925.64
125000	1362.11	1311.18	1267.84	1230.65	1198.51	1170.56	1146.13	1124.66	1049.00	1005.78	980.00	964.21
130000	1416.59	1363.62	1318.55	1279.88	1246.45	1217.38	1191.97	1169.65	1090.96	1046.01	1019.20	1002.77
135000	1471.07	1416.07	1369.26	1329.10	1294.39	1264.21	1237.82	1214.64	1132.92	1086.24	1058.40	1041.34
140000	1525.56	1468.52	1419.98	1378.33	1342.33	1311.03	1283.66	1259.62	1174.88	1126.48	1097.60	1079.91
145000	1580.04	1520.96	1470.69	1427.55	1390.27	1357.85	1329.51	1304.61	1216.84	1166.71	1136.79	1118.48
150000	1634.53	1573.41	1521.40	1476.78	1438.21	1404.67	1375.35	1349.59	1258.80	1206.94	1175.99	1157.05
155000	1689.01	1625.86	1572.12	1526.00	1486.15	1451.49	1421.20	1394.58	1300.76	1247.17	1215.19	1195.62
160000	1743.49	1678.31	1622.83	1575.23	1534.09	1498.32	1467.04	1439.57	1342.72	1287.40	1254.39	1234.18

MONTHLY AMORTIZING PAYMENTS

AMOUNT OF LOAN	NUMBER OF YEARS IN TERM											
	1	2	3	4	5	6	7	8	9	10	11	12
$ 50	4.38	2.29	1.60	1.26	1.05	0.91	0.82	0.74	0.69	0.65	0.61	0.58
100	8.76	4.58	3.20	2.51	2.09	1.82	1.63	1.48	1.37	1.29	1.21	1.16
200	17.52	9.16	6.39	5.01	4.18	3.63	3.25	2.96	2.74	2.57	2.42	2.31
300	26.28	13.74	9.58	7.51	6.27	5.45	4.87	4.44	4.11	3.85	3.63	3.46
400	35.03	18.32	12.77	10.01	8.36	7.26	6.49	5.92	5.48	5.13	4.84	4.61
500	43.79	22.90	15.96	12.51	10.44	9.08	8.11	7.40	6.84	6.41	6.05	5.77
600	52.55	27.48	19.15	15.01	12.53	10.89	9.73	8.87	8.21	7.69	7.26	6.92
700	61.30	32.06	22.35	17.51	14.62	12.71	11.36	10.35	9.58	8.97	8.47	8.07
800	70.06	36.64	25.54	20.01	16.71	14.52	12.98	11.83	10.95	10.25	9.68	9.22
900	78.82	41.22	28.73	22.51	18.80	16.34	14.60	13.31	12.31	11.53	10.89	10.37
1000	87.57	45.80	31.92	25.01	20.88	18.15	16.22	14.79	13.68	12.81	12.10	11.53
2000	175.14	91.60	63.84	50.01	41.76	36.30	32.44	29.57	27.36	25.61	24.20	23.05
3000	262.71	137.40	95.75	75.02	62.64	54.45	48.65	44.35	41.03	38.41	36.30	34.57
4000	350.27	183.20	127.67	100.02	83.52	72.60	64.87	59.13	54.71	51.22	48.40	46.09
5000	437.84	229.00	159.59	125.02	104.40	90.75	81.09	73.91	68.38	64.02	60.50	57.61
6000	525.41	274.80	191.50	150.03	125.28	108.90	97.30	88.69	82.06	76.82	72.60	69.13
7000	612.98	320.60	223.42	175.03	146.16	127.05	113.52	103.47	95.74	89.63	84.70	80.66
8000	700.54	366.40	255.33	200.04	167.04	145.20	129.73	118.25	109.41	102.43	96.80	92.18
9000	788.11	412.20	287.25	225.04	187.92	163.35	145.95	133.03	123.09	115.23	108.90	103.70
10000	875.68	458.00	319.17	250.04	208.80	181.50	162.17	147.81	136.76	128.04	121.00	115.22
11000	963.25	503.80	351.08	275.05	229.68	199.65	178.38	162.59	150.44	140.84	133.10	126.74
12000	1050.81	549.60	383.00	300.05	250.56	217.80	194.60	177.37	164.11	153.64	145.20	138.26
13000	1138.38	595.40	414.92	325.06	271.44	235.95	210.82	192.15	177.79	166.45	157.30	149.79
14000	1225.95	641.20	446.83	350.06	292.32	254.10	227.03	206.93	191.47	179.25	169.40	161.31
15000	1313.52	687.00	478.75	375.06	313.20	272.25	243.25	221.71	205.14	192.05	181.49	172.83
16000	1401.08	732.80	510.66	400.07	334.08	290.40	259.46	236.49	218.82	204.86	193.59	184.35
17000	1488.65	778.60	542.58	425.07	354.96	308.55	275.68	251.27	232.49	217.66	205.69	195.87
18000	1576.22	824.40	574.50	450.08	375.84	326.70	291.90	266.05	246.17	230.46	217.79	207.39
19000	1663.79	870.20	606.41	475.08	396.72	344.85	308.11	280.83	259.84	243.27	229.89	218.91
20000	1751.35	916.00	638.33	500.08	417.60	363.00	324.33	295.61	273.52	256.07	241.99	230.44
21000	1838.92	961.80	670.25	525.09	438.48	381.15	340.55	310.39	287.20	268.87	254.09	241.96
22000	1926.49	1007.59	702.16	550.09	459.36	399.30	356.76	325.17	300.87	281.68	266.19	253.48
23000	2014.06	1053.39	734.08	575.10	480.24	417.45	372.98	339.95	314.55	294.48	278.29	265.00
24000	2101.62	1099.19	765.99	600.10	501.12	435.60	389.19	354.73	328.22	307.28	290.39	276.52
25000	2189.19	1144.99	797.91	625.10	522.00	453.75	405.41	369.51	341.90	320.09	302.49	288.04
26000	2276.76	1190.79	829.83	650.11	542.88	471.90	421.63	384.29	355.58	332.89	314.59	299.57
27000	2364.33	1236.59	861.74	675.11	563.76	490.05	437.84	399.07	369.25	345.69	326.69	311.09
28000	2451.89	1282.39	893.66	700.11	584.64	508.20	454.06	413.85	382.93	358.50	338.79	322.61
29000	2539.46	1328.19	925.58	725.12	605.52	526.35	470.28	428.63	396.60	371.30	350.88	334.13
30000	2627.03	1373.99	957.49	750.12	626.40	544.50	486.49	443.41	410.28	384.10	362.98	345.65
31000	2714.60	1419.79	989.41	775.13	647.28	562.65	502.71	458.19	423.95	396.91	375.08	357.17
32000	2802.16	1465.59	1021.32	800.13	668.16	580.80	518.92	472.97	437.63	409.71	387.18	368.70
33000	2889.73	1511.39	1053.24	825.13	689.04	598.95	535.14	487.75	451.31	422.51	399.28	380.22
34000	2977.30	1557.19	1085.16	850.14	709.92	617.10	551.36	502.53	464.98	435.32	411.38	391.74
35000	3064.87	1602.99	1117.07	875.14	730.80	635.25	567.57	517.31	478.66	448.12	423.48	403.26
37500	3283.78	1717.49	1196.86	937.65	783.00	680.62	608.11	554.26	512.85	480.13	453.73	432.06
40000	3502.70	1831.99	1276.65	1000.16	835.20	726.00	648.65	591.21	547.04	512.14	483.98	460.87
42500	3721.62	1946.49	1356.44	1062.67	887.40	771.37	689.20	628.16	581.23	544.14	514.23	489.67
45000	3940.54	2060.98	1436.23	1125.18	939.60	816.75	729.74	665.11	615.41	576.15	544.47	518.48
47500	4159.46	2175.48	1516.03	1187.69	991.80	862.12	770.28	702.07	649.60	608.16	574.72	547.28
50000	4378.38	2289.98	1595.82	1250.20	1044.00	907.50	810.82	739.02	683.79	640.17	604.97	576.08
52500	4597.30	2404.48	1675.61	1312.71	1096.20	952.87	851.36	775.97	717.98	672.18	635.22	604.89
55000	4816.21	2518.98	1755.40	1375.22	1148.40	998.25	891.90	812.92	752.17	704.18	665.47	633.69
57500	5035.13	2633.48	1835.19	1437.73	1200.60	1043.62	932.44	849.87	786.36	736.19	695.71	662.49
60000	5254.05	2747.98	1914.98	1500.24	1252.80	1089.00	972.98	886.82	820.55	768.20	725.96	691.30
65000	5691.89	2976.97	2074.56	1625.26	1357.20	1179.75	1054.06	960.72	888.93	832.22	786.46	748.91
70000	6129.73	3205.97	2234.14	1750.28	1461.60	1270.50	1135.14	1034.62	957.31	896.23	846.96	806.51
75000	6567.56	3434.97	2393.72	1875.30	1566.00	1361.24	1216.22	1108.52	1025.69	960.25	907.45	864.12
80000	7005.40	3663.97	2553.30	2000.32	1670.40	1451.99	1297.30	1182.42	1094.07	1024.27	967.95	921.73
85000	7443.24	3892.97	2712.88	2125.34	1774.80	1542.74	1378.39	1256.32	1162.45	1088.28	1028.45	979.34
90000	7881.08	4121.96	2872.46	2250.36	1879.20	1633.49	1459.47	1330.22	1230.82	1152.30	1088.94	1036.95
95000	8318.91	4350.96	3032.05	2375.38	1983.60	1724.24	1540.55	1404.13	1299.20	1216.32	1149.44	1094.55
100000	8756.75	4579.96	3191.63	2500.40	2087.99	1814.99	1621.63	1478.03	1367.58	1280.33	1209.93	1152.16
105000	9194.59	4808.96	3351.21	2625.42	2192.39	1905.74	1702.71	1551.93	1435.96	1344.35	1270.43	1209.77
110000	9632.42	5037.95	3510.79	2750.44	2296.79	1996.49	1783.79	1625.83	1504.34	1408.36	1330.93	1267.38
115000	10070.26	5266.95	3670.37	2875.46	2401.19	2087.24	1864.87	1699.73	1572.72	1472.38	1391.42	1324.98
120000	10508.10	5495.95	3829.95	3000.48	2505.59	2177.99	1945.95	1773.63	1641.10	1536.40	1451.92	1382.59
125000	10945.94	5724.95	3989.53	3125.50	2609.99	2268.74	2027.04	1847.53	1709.48	1600.41	1512.42	1440.20
130000	11383.77	5953.94	4149.11	3250.51	2714.39	2359.49	2108.12	1921.43	1777.86	1664.43	1572.91	1497.81
135000	11821.61	6182.94	4308.69	3375.53	2818.79	2450.24	2189.20	1995.33	1846.23	1728.45	1633.41	1555.42
140000	12259.45	6411.94	4468.27	3500.55	2923.19	2540.99	2270.28	2069.24	1914.61	1792.46	1693.91	1613.02
145000	12697.29	6640.94	4627.86	3625.57	3027.59	2631.74	2351.36	2143.14	1982.99	1856.48	1754.40	1670.63
150000	13135.12	6869.93	4787.44	3750.59	3131.99	2722.48	2432.44	2217.04	2051.37	1920.50	1814.90	1728.24
155000	13572.96	7098.93	4947.02	3875.61	3236.39	2813.23	2513.52	2290.94	2119.75	1984.51	1875.40	1785.85
160000	14010.80	7327.93	5106.60	4000.63	3340.79	2903.98	2594.60	2364.84	2188.13	2048.53	1935.89	1843.46

MONTHLY AMORTIZING PAYMENTS 9.25%

AMOUNT OF LOAN	NUMBER OF YEARS IN TERM											
	13	14	15	16	17	18	19	20	25	30	35	40
$ 50	0.56	0.54	0.52	0.50	0.49	0.48	0.47	0.46	0.43	0.42	0.41	0.40
100	1.11	1.07	1.03	1.00	0.98	0.96	0.94	0.92	0.86	0.83	0.81	0.80
200	2.21	2.13	2.06	2.00	1.95	1.91	1.87	1.84	1.72	1.65	1.61	1.59
300	3.32	3.20	3.09	3.00	2.93	2.86	2.80	2.75	2.57	2.47	2.41	2.38
400	4.42	4.26	4.12	4.00	3.90	3.81	3.74	3.67	3.43	3.30	3.22	3.17
500	5.53	5.32	5.15	5.00	4.88	4.77	4.67	4.58	4.29	4.12	4.02	3.96
600	6.63	6.39	6.18	6.00	5.85	5.72	5.60	5.50	5.14	4.94	4.82	4.75
700	7.73	7.45	7.21	7.00	6.82	6.67	6.53	6.42	6.00	5.76	5.62	5.54
800	8.84	8.51	8.24	8.00	7.80	7.62	7.47	7.33	6.86	6.59	6.43	6.33
900	9.94	9.58	9.27	9.00	8.77	8.57	8.40	8.25	7.71	7.41	7.23	7.12
1000	11.05	10.64	10.30	10.00	9.75	9.53	9.33	9.16	8.57	8.23	8.03	7.91
2000	22.09	21.28	20.59	20.00	19.49	19.05	18.66	18.32	17.13	16.46	16.06	15.82
3000	33.13	31.91	30.88	30.00	29.23	28.57	27.99	27.48	25.70	24.69	24.09	23.72
4000	44.17	42.55	41.17	39.99	38.97	38.09	37.32	36.64	34.26	32.91	32.11	31.63
5000	55.21	53.19	51.46	49.99	48.72	47.61	46.65	45.80	42.82	41.14	40.14	39.54
6000	66.25	63.82	61.76	59.99	58.46	57.13	55.97	54.96	51.39	49.37	48.17	47.44
7000	77.29	74.46	72.05	69.98	68.20	66.65	65.30	64.12	59.95	57.59	56.20	55.35
8000	88.33	85.09	82.34	79.98	77.94	76.17	74.63	73.27	68.52	65.82	64.22	63.26
9000	99.37	95.73	92.63	89.98	87.69	85.70	83.96	82.43	77.08	74.05	72.25	71.16
10000	110.41	106.37	102.92	99.97	97.43	95.22	93.29	91.59	85.64	82.27	80.28	79.07
11000	121.45	117.00	113.22	109.97	107.17	104.74	102.61	100.75	94.21	90.50	88.31	86.98
12000	132.49	127.64	123.51	119.97	116.91	114.26	111.94	109.91	102.77	98.73	96.33	94.88
13000	143.54	138.27	133.80	129.97	126.66	123.78	121.27	119.07	111.33	106.95	104.36	102.79
14000	154.58	148.91	144.09	139.96	136.40	133.30	130.60	128.23	119.90	115.18	112.39	110.70
15000	165.62	159.55	154.38	149.96	146.14	142.82	139.93	137.39	128.46	123.41	120.42	118.60
16000	176.66	170.18	164.68	159.96	155.88	152.34	149.25	146.54	137.03	131.63	128.44	126.51
17000	187.70	180.82	174.97	169.95	165.62	161.87	158.58	155.70	145.59	139.86	136.47	134.42
18000	198.74	191.45	185.26	179.95	175.37	171.39	167.91	164.86	154.15	148.09	144.50	142.32
19000	209.78	202.09	195.55	189.95	185.11	180.91	177.24	174.02	162.72	156.31	152.53	150.23
20000	220.82	212.73	205.84	199.94	194.85	190.43	186.57	183.18	171.28	164.54	160.55	158.14
21000	231.86	223.36	216.14	209.94	204.59	199.95	195.89	192.34	179.85	172.77	168.58	166.04
22000	242.90	234.00	226.43	219.94	214.34	209.47	205.22	201.50	188.41	180.99	176.61	173.95
23000	253.94	244.63	236.72	229.94	224.08	218.99	214.55	210.65	196.97	189.22	184.64	181.86
24000	264.98	255.27	247.01	239.93	233.82	228.51	223.88	219.81	205.54	197.45	192.66	189.76
25000	276.02	265.91	257.30	249.93	243.56	238.03	233.21	228.97	214.10	205.67	200.69	197.67
26000	287.07	276.54	267.59	259.93	253.31	247.56	242.54	238.13	222.66	213.90	208.72	205.58
27000	298.11	287.18	277.89	269.92	263.05	257.08	251.86	247.29	231.23	222.13	216.75	213.48
28000	309.15	297.81	288.18	279.92	272.79	266.60	261.19	256.45	239.79	230.35	224.77	221.39
29000	320.19	308.45	298.47	289.92	282.53	276.12	270.52	265.61	248.36	238.58	232.80	229.30
30000	331.23	319.09	308.76	299.91	292.28	285.64	279.85	274.77	256.92	246.81	240.83	237.20
31000	342.27	329.72	319.05	309.91	302.02	295.16	289.18	283.92	265.48	255.03	248.86	245.11
32000	353.31	340.36	329.35	319.91	311.76	304.68	298.50	293.08	274.05	263.26	256.88	253.02
33000	364.35	350.99	339.64	329.91	321.50	314.20	307.83	302.24	282.61	271.49	264.91	260.92
34000	375.39	361.63	349.93	339.90	331.24	323.73	317.16	311.40	291.17	279.71	272.94	268.83
35000	386.43	372.27	360.22	349.90	340.99	333.25	326.49	320.56	299.74	287.94	280.97	276.74
37500	414.03	398.86	385.95	374.89	365.34	357.05	349.81	343.46	321.15	308.51	301.03	296.50
40000	441.64	425.45	411.68	399.88	389.79	380.85	373.13	366.35	342.56	329.08	321.10	316.27
42500	469.24	452.04	437.41	424.88	414.05	404.66	396.45	389.25	363.97	349.64	341.17	336.04
45000	496.84	478.63	463.14	449.87	438.41	428.46	419.77	412.15	385.38	370.21	361.24	355.80
47500	524.44	505.22	488.87	474.86	462.77	452.26	443.09	435.04	406.79	390.78	381.31	375.57
50000	552.04	531.81	514.60	499.85	487.12	476.06	466.41	457.94	428.20	411.34	401.38	395.34
52500	579.65	558.40	540.33	524.85	511.48	499.87	489.73	480.84	449.61	431.91	421.45	415.10
55000	607.25	584.99	566.06	549.84	535.83	523.67	513.05	503.73	471.02	452.48	441.51	434.87
57500	634.85	611.58	591.79	574.83	560.19	547.47	536.37	526.63	492.42	473.04	461.58	454.63
60000	662.45	638.17	617.52	599.82	584.55	571.28	559.69	549.53	513.83	493.61	481.65	474.40
65000	717.66	691.35	668.98	649.81	633.26	618.88	606.33	595.32	556.65	534.74	521.79	513.93
70000	772.86	744.53	720.44	699.79	681.97	666.49	652.97	641.11	599.47	575.88	561.93	553.47
75000	828.06	797.71	771.90	749.78	730.68	714.09	699.61	686.91	642.29	617.01	602.06	593.00
80000	883.27	850.89	823.36	799.76	779.39	761.70	746.25	732.70	685.11	658.15	642.20	632.53
85000	938.47	904.07	874.82	849.75	828.10	809.31	792.89	778.49	727.93	699.28	682.34	672.07
90000	993.68	957.25	926.28	899.73	876.82	856.91	839.53	824.29	770.75	740.41	722.47	711.60
95000	1048.88	1010.43	977.74	949.72	925.53	904.52	886.17	870.08	813.57	781.55	762.61	751.13
100000	1104.08	1063.61	1029.20	999.70	974.24	952.12	932.81	915.87	856.39	822.68	802.75	790.67
105000	1159.29	1116.79	1080.66	1049.69	1022.95	999.73	979.45	961.67	899.21	863.81	842.89	830.20
110000	1214.49	1169.97	1132.12	1099.67	1071.66	1047.34	1026.09	1007.46	942.03	904.95	883.02	869.73
115000	1269.69	1223.15	1183.58	1149.66	1120.38	1094.94	1072.73	1053.25	984.84	946.08	923.16	909.26
120000	1324.90	1276.33	1235.04	1199.64	1169.09	1142.55	1119.37	1099.05	1027.66	987.22	963.30	948.80
125000	1380.10	1329.51	1286.50	1249.63	1217.80	1190.15	1166.01	1144.84	1070.48	1028.35	1003.44	988.33
130000	1435.31	1382.69	1337.95	1299.61	1266.51	1237.76	1212.66	1190.63	1113.30	1069.48	1043.57	1027.86
135000	1490.51	1435.87	1389.41	1349.60	1315.22	1285.37	1259.30	1236.43	1156.12	1110.62	1083.71	1067.40
140000	1545.71	1489.05	1440.87	1399.58	1363.93	1332.97	1305.94	1282.22	1198.94	1151.75	1123.85	1106.93
145000	1600.92	1542.23	1492.33	1449.57	1412.65	1380.58	1352.58	1328.01	1241.76	1192.88	1163.98	1146.46
150000	1656.12	1595.41	1543.79	1499.55	1461.36	1428.18	1399.22	1373.81	1284.58	1234.02	1204.12	1186.00
155000	1711.33	1648.59	1595.25	1549.54	1510.07	1475.79	1445.86	1419.60	1327.40	1275.15	1244.26	1225.53
160000	1766.53	1701.77	1646.71	1599.52	1558.78	1523.40	1492.50	1465.39	1370.22	1316.29	1284.40	1265.06

37

MONTHLY AMORTIZING PAYMENTS

AMOUNT OF LOAN	NUMBER OF YEARS IN TERM											
	1	2	3	4	5	6	7	8	9	10	11	12
$ 50	4.39	2.30	1.61	1.26	1.06	0.92	0.82	0.75	0.70	0.65	0.62	0.59
100	8.77	4.60	3.21	2.52	2.11	1.83	1.64	1.50	1.39	1.30	1.23	1.17
200	17.54	9.19	6.41	5.03	4.21	3.66	3.27	2.99	2.77	2.59	2.45	2.34
300	26.31	13.78	9.61	7.54	6.31	5.49	4.91	4.48	4.15	3.89	3.68	3.50
400	35.08	18.37	12.82	10.05	8.41	7.31	6.54	5.97	5.53	5.18	4.90	4.67
500	43.85	22.96	16.02	12.57	10.51	9.14	8.18	7.46	6.91	6.47	6.12	5.84
600	52.62	27.55	19.22	15.08	12.61	10.97	9.81	8.95	8.29	7.77	7.35	7.00
700	61.38	32.15	22.43	17.59	14.71	12.80	11.45	10.44	9.67	9.06	8.57	8.17
800	70.15	36.74	25.63	20.10	16.81	14.62	13.08	11.93	11.05	10.36	9.80	9.34
900	78.92	41.33	28.83	22.62	18.91	16.45	14.71	13.42	12.43	11.65	11.02	10.50
1000	87.69	45.92	32.04	25.13	21.01	18.28	16.35	14.92	13.81	12.94	12.24	11.67
2000	175.37	91.83	64.07	50.25	42.01	36.55	32.69	29.83	27.62	25.88	24.48	23.33
3000	263.06	137.75	96.10	75.37	63.01	54.83	49.04	44.74	41.43	38.82	36.72	35.00
4000	350.74	183.66	128.14	100.50	84.01	73.10	65.38	59.65	55.24	51.76	48.96	46.66
5000	438.42	229.58	160.17	125.62	105.01	91.38	81.72	74.56	69.05	64.70	61.20	58.32
6000	526.11	275.49	192.20	150.74	126.02	109.65	98.07	89.47	82.86	77.64	73.44	69.99
7000	613.79	321.41	224.24	175.87	147.02	127.93	114.41	104.38	96.67	90.58	85.68	81.65
8000	701.47	367.32	256.27	200.99	168.02	146.20	130.76	119.29	110.48	103.52	97.91	93.31
9000	789.16	413.24	288.30	226.11	189.02	164.48	147.10	134.20	124.29	116.46	110.15	104.98
10000	876.84	459.15	320.33	251.24	210.02	182.75	163.44	149.11	138.10	129.40	122.39	116.64
11000	964.52	505.06	352.37	276.36	231.03	201.03	179.79	164.02	151.91	142.34	134.63	128.31
12000	1052.21	550.98	384.40	301.48	252.03	219.30	196.13	178.94	165.72	155.28	146.87	139.97
13000	1139.89	596.89	416.43	326.61	273.03	237.58	212.48	193.85	179.53	168.22	159.11	151.63
14000	1227.57	642.81	448.47	351.73	294.03	255.85	228.82	208.76	193.34	181.16	171.35	163.30
15000	1315.26	688.72	480.50	376.85	315.03	274.13	245.16	223.67	207.15	194.10	183.58	174.96
16000	1402.94	734.64	512.53	401.98	336.03	292.40	261.51	238.58	220.95	207.04	195.82	186.62
17000	1490.62	780.55	544.57	427.10	357.04	310.67	277.85	253.49	234.76	219.98	208.06	198.29
18000	1578.31	826.47	576.60	452.22	378.04	328.95	294.20	268.40	248.57	232.92	220.30	209.95
19000	1665.99	872.38	608.63	477.34	399.04	347.22	310.54	283.31	262.38	245.86	232.54	221.62
20000	1753.68	918.29	640.66	502.47	420.04	365.50	326.88	298.22	276.19	258.80	244.78	233.28
21000	1841.36	964.21	672.70	527.59	441.04	383.77	343.23	313.13	290.00	271.74	257.02	244.94
22000	1929.04	1010.12	704.73	552.71	462.05	402.05	359.57	328.04	303.81	284.68	269.26	256.61
23000	2016.73	1056.04	736.76	577.84	483.05	420.32	375.92	342.96	317.62	297.62	281.49	268.27
24000	2104.41	1101.95	768.80	602.96	504.05	438.60	392.26	357.87	331.43	310.56	293.73	279.93
25000	2192.09	1147.87	800.83	628.08	525.05	456.87	408.60	372.78	345.24	323.50	305.97	291.60
26000	2279.78	1193.78	832.86	653.21	546.05	475.15	424.95	387.69	359.05	336.44	318.21	303.26
27000	2367.46	1239.70	864.89	678.33	567.06	493.42	441.29	402.60	372.86	349.38	330.45	314.93
28000	2455.14	1285.61	896.93	703.45	588.06	511.70	457.64	417.51	386.67	362.32	342.69	326.59
29000	2542.83	1331.53	928.96	728.58	609.06	529.97	473.98	432.42	400.48	375.26	354.93	338.25
30000	2630.51	1377.44	960.99	753.70	630.06	548.25	490.32	447.33	414.29	388.20	367.16	349.92
31000	2718.19	1423.35	993.03	778.82	651.06	566.52	506.67	462.24	428.10	401.14	379.40	361.58
32000	2805.88	1469.27	1025.06	803.95	672.06	584.80	523.01	477.15	441.90	414.08	391.64	373.24
33000	2893.56	1515.18	1057.09	829.07	693.07	603.07	539.36	492.06	455.71	427.02	403.88	384.91
34000	2981.24	1561.10	1089.13	854.19	714.07	621.34	555.70	506.98	469.52	439.96	416.12	396.57
35000	3068.93	1607.01	1121.16	879.31	735.07	639.62	572.04	521.89	483.33	452.90	428.36	408.24
37500	3288.14	1721.80	1201.24	942.12	787.57	685.31	612.90	559.16	517.86	485.25	458.95	437.39
40000	3507.35	1836.58	1281.32	1004.93	840.08	730.99	653.76	596.44	552.38	517.60	489.55	466.55
42500	3726.55	1951.37	1361.41	1067.74	892.58	776.68	694.62	633.72	586.90	549.94	520.15	495.71
45000	3945.76	2066.16	1441.49	1130.55	945.09	822.37	735.48	670.99	621.43	582.29	550.74	524.87
47500	4164.97	2180.94	1521.57	1193.35	997.59	868.05	776.34	708.27	655.95	614.64	581.34	554.03
50000	4384.18	2295.73	1601.65	1256.16	1050.10	913.74	817.20	745.55	690.47	646.99	611.94	583.19
52500	4603.39	2410.52	1681.73	1318.97	1102.60	959.43	858.06	782.83	725.00	679.34	642.53	612.35
55000	4822.60	2525.30	1761.82	1381.78	1155.11	1005.11	898.92	820.10	759.52	711.69	673.13	641.51
57500	5041.81	2640.09	1841.90	1444.59	1207.61	1050.80	939.78	857.38	794.04	744.04	703.73	670.67
60000	5261.02	2754.87	1921.98	1507.39	1260.12	1096.49	980.64	894.66	828.57	776.39	734.32	699.83
65000	5699.43	2984.45	2082.15	1633.01	1365.13	1187.86	1062.36	969.21	897.61	841.09	795.52	758.15
70000	6137.85	3214.02	2242.31	1758.62	1470.14	1279.23	1144.08	1043.77	966.66	905.79	856.71	816.47
75000	6576.27	3443.59	2402.48	1884.24	1575.14	1370.61	1225.80	1118.32	1035.71	970.49	917.90	874.78
80000	7014.69	3673.16	2562.64	2009.86	1680.15	1461.98	1307.52	1192.88	1104.75	1035.19	979.10	933.10
85000	7453.10	3902.74	2722.81	2135.47	1785.16	1553.35	1389.24	1267.43	1173.80	1099.88	1040.29	991.42
90000	7891.52	4132.31	2882.97	2261.09	1890.17	1644.73	1470.96	1341.98	1242.85	1164.58	1101.48	1049.74
95000	8329.94	4361.88	3043.14	2386.70	1995.18	1736.10	1552.68	1416.54	1311.89	1229.28	1162.68	1108.06
100000	8768.36	4591.45	3203.30	2512.32	2100.19	1827.47	1634.40	1491.09	1380.94	1293.98	1223.87	1166.38
105000	9206.77	4821.03	3363.46	2637.93	2205.20	1918.85	1716.12	1565.65	1449.99	1358.68	1285.06	1224.70
110000	9645.19	5050.60	3523.63	2763.55	2310.21	2010.22	1797.84	1640.20	1519.03	1423.38	1346.26	1283.02
115000	10083.61	5280.17	3683.79	2889.17	2415.22	2101.59	1879.56	1714.76	1588.08	1488.08	1407.45	1341.33
120000	10522.03	5509.74	3843.96	3014.78	2520.23	2192.97	1961.28	1789.31	1657.13	1552.78	1468.64	1399.65
125000	10960.44	5739.32	4004.12	3140.40	2625.24	2284.34	2043.00	1863.87	1726.18	1617.47	1529.84	1457.97
130000	11398.86	5968.89	4164.29	3266.01	2730.25	2375.71	2124.72	1938.42	1795.22	1682.17	1591.03	1516.29
135000	11837.28	6198.46	4324.45	3391.63	2835.26	2467.09	2206.44	2012.97	1864.27	1746.87	1652.22	1574.61
140000	12275.70	6428.03	4484.62	3517.24	2940.27	2558.46	2288.16	2087.53	1933.32	1811.57	1713.42	1632.93
145000	12714.11	6657.61	4644.78	3642.86	3045.27	2649.84	2369.88	2162.08	2002.36	1876.27	1774.61	1691.25
150000	13152.53	6887.18	4804.95	3768.48	3150.28	2741.21	2451.60	2236.64	2071.41	1940.97	1835.80	1749.56
155000	13590.95	7116.75	4965.11	3894.09	3255.29	2832.58	2533.32	2311.19	2140.46	2005.67	1897.00	1807.88
160000	14029.37	7346.32	5125.28	4019.71	3360.30	2923.96	2615.04	2385.75	2209.50	2070.37	1958.19	1866.20

MONTHLY AMORTIZING PAYMENTS 9.50%

AMOUNT OF LOAN	NUMBER OF YEARS IN TERM											
	13	14	15	16	17	18	19	20	25	30	35	40
$ 50	0.56	0.54	0.53	0.51	0.50	0.49	0.48	0.47	0.44	0.43	0.42	0.41
100	1.12	1.08	1.05	1.02	0.99	0.97	0.95	0.94	0.88	0.85	0.83	0.82
200	2.24	2.16	2.09	2.03	1.98	1.94	1.90	1.87	1.75	1.69	1.65	1.63
300	3.36	3.24	3.14	3.05	2.97	2.91	2.85	2.80	2.63	2.53	2.47	2.44
400	4.48	4.32	4.18	4.06	3.96	3.88	3.80	3.73	3.50	3.37	3.29	3.25
500	5.60	5.40	5.23	5.08	4.95	4.84	4.75	4.67	4.37	4.21	4.11	4.06
600	6.72	6.48	6.27	6.09	5.94	5.81	5.70	5.60	5.25	5.05	4.93	4.87
700	7.84	7.55	7.31	7.11	6.93	6.78	6.65	6.53	6.12	5.89	5.76	5.68
800	8.95	8.63	8.36	8.12	7.92	7.75	7.60	7.46	6.99	6.73	6.58	6.49
900	10.07	9.71	9.40	9.14	8.91	8.72	8.54	8.39	7.87	7.57	7.40	7.30
1000	11.19	10.79	10.45	10.15	9.90	9.68	9.49	9.33	8.74	8.41	8.22	8.11
2000	22.38	21.57	20.89	20.30	19.80	19.36	18.98	18.65	17.48	16.82	16.44	16.21
3000	33.56	32.36	31.33	30.45	29.70	29.04	28.47	27.97	26.22	25.23	24.65	24.31
4000	44.75	43.14	41.77	40.60	39.60	38.72	37.96	37.29	34.95	33.64	32.87	32.41
5000	55.93	53.92	52.22	50.75	49.49	48.40	47.45	46.61	43.69	42.05	41.09	40.51
6000	67.12	64.71	62.66	60.90	59.39	58.08	56.94	55.93	52.43	50.46	49.30	48.61
7000	78.31	75.49	73.10	71.05	69.29	67.76	66.42	65.25	61.16	58.86	57.52	56.71
8000	89.49	86.27	83.54	81.20	79.19	77.44	75.91	74.58	69.90	67.27	65.73	64.81
9000	100.68	97.06	93.99	91.35	89.09	87.12	85.40	83.90	78.64	75.68	73.95	72.91
10000	111.86	107.84	104.43	101.50	98.98	96.80	94.89	93.22	87.37	84.09	82.17	81.01
11000	123.05	118.63	114.87	111.65	108.88	106.48	104.38	102.54	96.11	92.50	90.38	89.11
12000	134.23	129.41	125.31	121.80	118.78	116.15	113.87	111.86	104.85	100.91	98.60	97.21
13000	145.42	140.19	135.75	131.95	128.68	125.83	123.35	121.18	113.59	109.32	106.81	105.31
14000	156.61	150.98	146.20	142.10	138.57	135.51	132.84	130.50	122.32	117.72	115.03	113.41
15000	167.79	161.76	156.64	152.25	148.47	145.19	142.33	139.82	131.06	126.13	123.25	121.51
16000	178.98	172.54	167.08	162.40	158.37	154.87	151.82	149.15	139.80	134.54	131.46	129.61
17000	190.16	183.33	177.52	172.55	168.27	164.55	161.31	158.47	148.53	142.95	139.68	137.72
18000	201.35	194.11	187.97	182.70	178.17	174.23	170.80	167.79	157.27	151.36	147.90	145.82
19000	212.53	204.89	198.41	192.85	188.06	183.91	180.28	177.11	166.01	159.77	156.11	153.92
20000	223.72	215.68	208.85	203.00	197.96	193.59	189.77	186.43	174.74	168.18	164.33	162.02
21000	234.91	226.46	219.29	213.15	207.86	203.27	199.26	195.75	183.48	176.58	172.54	170.12
22000	246.09	237.25	229.73	223.30	217.76	212.95	208.75	205.07	192.22	184.99	180.76	178.22
23000	257.28	248.03	240.18	233.45	227.65	222.62	218.24	214.40	200.96	193.40	188.98	186.32
24000	268.46	258.81	250.62	243.60	237.55	232.30	227.73	223.72	209.69	201.81	197.19	194.42
25000	279.65	269.60	261.06	253.75	247.45	241.98	237.21	233.04	218.43	210.22	205.41	202.52
26000	290.83	280.38	271.50	263.90	257.35	251.66	246.70	242.36	227.17	218.63	213.62	210.62
27000	302.02	291.16	281.95	274.05	267.25	261.34	256.19	251.68	235.90	227.04	221.84	218.72
28000	313.21	301.95	292.39	284.20	277.14	271.02	265.68	261.00	244.64	235.44	230.06	226.82
29000	324.39	312.73	302.83	294.35	287.04	280.70	275.17	270.32	253.38	243.85	238.27	234.92
30000	335.58	323.52	313.27	304.50	296.94	290.38	284.66	279.64	262.11	252.26	246.49	243.02
31000	346.76	334.30	323.71	314.65	306.84	300.06	294.15	288.97	270.85	260.67	254.70	251.12
32000	357.95	345.08	334.16	324.80	316.73	309.74	303.63	298.29	279.59	269.08	262.92	259.22
33000	369.13	355.87	344.60	334.95	326.63	319.42	313.12	307.61	288.32	277.49	271.14	267.33
34000	380.32	366.65	355.04	345.10	336.53	329.09	322.61	316.93	297.06	285.90	279.35	275.43
35000	391.51	377.43	365.48	355.25	346.43	338.77	332.10	326.25	305.80	294.30	287.57	283.53
37500	419.47	404.39	391.59	380.63	371.17	362.97	355.82	349.55	327.64	315.33	308.11	303.78
40000	447.43	431.35	417.69	406.00	395.92	387.17	379.54	372.86	349.48	336.35	328.65	324.03
42500	475.40	458.31	443.80	431.38	420.66	411.37	403.26	396.16	371.33	357.37	349.19	344.28
45000	503.36	485.27	469.91	456.75	445.41	435.57	426.98	419.46	393.17	378.39	369.73	364.53
47500	531.33	512.23	496.01	482.13	470.15	459.76	450.70	442.77	415.01	399.41	390.27	384.78
50000	559.29	539.19	522.12	507.50	494.90	483.96	474.42	466.07	436.85	420.43	410.81	405.04
52500	587.26	566.15	548.22	532.87	519.64	508.16	498.15	489.37	458.70	441.45	431.35	425.29
55000	615.22	593.11	574.33	558.25	544.38	532.36	521.87	512.68	480.54	462.47	451.89	445.54
57500	643.18	620.07	600.43	583.62	569.13	556.55	545.59	535.98	502.38	483.50	472.43	465.79
60000	671.15	647.03	626.54	609.00	593.87	580.75	569.31	559.28	524.22	504.52	492.97	486.04
65000	727.08	700.94	678.75	659.75	643.36	629.15	616.75	605.89	567.91	546.56	534.05	526.55
70000	783.01	754.86	730.96	710.50	692.85	677.54	664.19	652.50	611.59	588.60	575.13	567.05
75000	838.93	808.78	783.17	761.25	742.34	725.94	711.63	699.10	655.28	630.65	616.21	607.55
80000	894.86	862.70	835.38	812.00	791.83	774.33	759.08	745.71	698.96	672.69	657.29	648.05
85000	950.79	916.62	887.60	862.75	841.32	822.73	806.52	792.32	742.65	714.73	698.37	688.56
90000	1006.72	970.54	939.81	913.50	890.81	871.13	853.96	838.92	786.33	756.77	739.46	729.06
95000	1062.65	1024.45	992.02	964.25	940.30	919.52	901.40	885.53	830.02	798.82	780.54	769.56
100000	1118.58	1078.37	1044.23	1014.99	989.79	967.92	948.84	932.14	873.70	840.86	821.62	810.07
105000	1174.51	1132.29	1096.44	1065.74	1039.27	1016.31	996.29	978.74	917.39	882.90	862.70	850.57
110000	1230.43	1186.21	1148.65	1116.49	1088.76	1064.71	1043.73	1025.35	961.07	924.94	903.78	891.07
115000	1286.36	1240.13	1200.86	1167.24	1138.25	1113.10	1091.17	1071.96	1004.76	966.99	944.86	931.58
120000	1342.29	1294.05	1253.07	1217.99	1187.74	1161.50	1138.61	1118.56	1048.44	1009.03	985.94	972.08
125000	1398.22	1347.97	1305.29	1268.74	1237.23	1209.89	1186.05	1165.17	1092.13	1051.07	1027.02	1012.58
130000	1454.15	1401.88	1357.50	1319.49	1286.72	1258.29	1233.50	1211.78	1135.81	1093.12	1068.10	1053.09
135000	1510.08	1455.80	1409.71	1370.24	1336.21	1306.69	1280.94	1258.38	1179.50	1135.16	1109.18	1093.59
140000	1566.01	1509.72	1461.92	1420.99	1385.70	1355.08	1328.38	1304.99	1223.18	1177.20	1150.26	1134.09
145000	1621.93	1563.64	1514.13	1471.74	1435.19	1403.48	1375.82	1351.60	1266.87	1219.24	1191.34	1174.59
150000	1677.86	1617.56	1566.34	1522.49	1484.68	1451.87	1423.26	1398.20	1310.55	1261.29	1232.42	1215.10
155000	1733.79	1671.48	1618.55	1573.24	1534.17	1500.27	1470.71	1444.81	1354.23	1303.33	1273.50	1255.60
160000	1789.72	1725.39	1670.76	1623.99	1583.65	1548.66	1518.15	1491.41	1397.92	1345.37	1314.58	1296.10

39

MONTHLY AMORTIZING PAYMENTS

AMOUNT OF LOAN	NUMBER OF YEARS IN TERM											
	1	2	3	4	5	6	7	8	9	10	11	12
$ 50	4.39	2.31	1.61	1.27	1.06	0.93	0.83	0.76	0.70	0.66	0.62	0.60
100	8.78	4.61	3.22	2.53	2.12	1.85	1.65	1.51	1.40	1.31	1.24	1.19
200	17.56	9.21	6.43	5.05	4.23	3.69	3.30	3.01	2.79	2.62	2.48	2.37
300	26.34	13.81	9.65	7.58	6.34	5.53	4.95	4.52	4.19	3.93	3.72	3.55
400	35.12	18.42	12.86	10.10	8.45	7.37	6.59	6.02	5.58	5.24	4.96	4.73
500	43.90	23.02	16.08	12.63	10.57	9.21	8.24	7.53	6.98	6.54	6.19	5.91
600	52.68	27.62	19.29	15.15	12.68	11.05	9.89	9.03	8.37	7.85	7.43	7.09
700	61.46	32.23	22.51	17.67	14.79	12.89	11.54	10.53	9.77	9.16	8.67	8.27
800	70.24	36.83	25.72	20.20	16.90	14.73	13.18	12.04	11.16	10.47	9.91	9.45
900	79.02	41.43	28.94	22.72	19.02	16.57	14.83	13.54	12.55	11.77	11.15	10.63
1000	87.80	46.03	32.15	25.25	21.13	18.41	16.48	15.05	13.95	13.08	12.38	11.81
2000	175.60	92.06	64.30	50.49	42.25	36.81	32.95	30.09	27.89	26.16	24.76	23.62
3000	263.40	138.09	96.45	75.73	63.38	55.21	49.42	45.13	41.84	39.24	37.14	35.43
4000	351.20	184.12	128.60	100.98	84.50	73.61	65.89	60.17	55.78	52.31	49.52	47.23
5000	439.00	230.15	160.75	126.22	105.63	92.01	82.37	75.22	69.72	65.39	61.90	59.04
6000	526.80	276.18	192.90	151.46	126.75	110.41	98.84	90.26	83.67	78.47	74.28	70.85
7000	614.60	322.21	225.05	176.70	147.87	128.81	115.31	105.30	97.61	91.54	86.66	82.65
8000	702.40	368.24	257.20	201.95	169.00	147.21	131.78	120.34	111.55	104.62	99.04	94.46
9000	790.20	414.27	289.35	227.19	190.12	165.61	148.26	135.38	125.50	117.70	111.41	106.27
10000	878.00	460.30	321.50	252.43	211.25	184.01	164.73	150.43	139.44	130.78	123.79	118.07
11000	965.80	506.33	353.65	277.67	232.37	202.41	181.20	165.47	153.39	143.85	136.17	129.88
12000	1053.60	552.36	385.80	302.92	253.50	220.81	197.67	180.51	167.33	156.93	148.55	141.69
13000	1141.40	598.39	417.95	328.16	274.62	239.21	214.14	195.55	181.27	170.01	160.93	153.49
14000	1229.20	644.42	450.10	353.40	295.74	257.61	230.62	210.60	195.22	183.08	173.31	165.30
15000	1317.00	690.45	482.25	378.65	316.87	276.01	247.09	225.64	209.16	196.16	185.69	177.11
16000	1404.80	736.48	514.40	403.89	337.99	294.41	263.56	240.68	223.10	209.24	198.07	188.91
17000	1492.60	782.51	546.55	429.13	359.12	312.81	280.03	255.72	237.05	222.31	210.45	200.72
18000	1580.40	828.54	578.70	454.37	380.24	331.21	296.51	270.76	250.99	235.39	222.82	212.53
19000	1668.20	874.57	610.85	479.62	401.37	349.61	312.98	285.81	264.93	248.47	235.20	224.33
20000	1756.00	920.60	643.00	504.86	422.49	368.01	329.45	300.85	278.88	261.55	247.58	236.14
21000	1843.80	966.63	675.15	530.10	443.61	386.41	345.92	315.89	292.82	274.62	259.96	247.95
22000	1931.60	1012.66	707.30	555.34	464.74	404.81	362.40	330.93	306.77	287.70	272.34	259.75
23000	2019.40	1058.69	739.45	580.59	485.86	423.21	378.87	345.98	320.71	300.78	284.72	271.56
24000	2107.20	1104.72	771.60	605.83	506.99	441.61	395.34	361.02	334.65	313.85	297.10	283.37
25000	2195.00	1150.75	803.75	631.07	528.11	460.01	411.81	376.06	348.60	326.93	309.48	295.18
26000	2282.80	1196.78	835.90	656.31	549.24	478.41	428.28	391.10	362.54	340.01	321.85	306.98
27000	2370.60	1242.80	868.05	681.56	570.36	496.81	444.76	406.14	376.48	353.08	334.23	318.79
28000	2458.40	1288.83	900.20	706.80	591.48	515.21	461.23	421.19	390.43	366.16	346.61	330.60
29000	2546.20	1334.86	932.35	732.04	612.61	533.61	477.70	436.23	404.37	379.24	358.99	342.40
30000	2633.99	1380.89	964.50	757.29	633.73	552.01	494.17	451.27	418.31	392.32	371.37	354.21
31000	2721.79	1426.92	996.65	782.53	654.86	570.41	510.65	466.31	432.26	405.39	383.75	366.02
32000	2809.59	1472.95	1028.80	807.77	675.98	588.81	527.12	481.36	446.20	418.47	396.13	377.82
33000	2897.39	1518.98	1060.95	833.01	697.11	607.21	543.59	496.40	460.15	431.55	408.51	389.63
34000	2985.19	1565.01	1093.10	858.26	718.23	625.61	560.06	511.44	474.09	444.62	420.89	401.44
35000	3072.99	1611.04	1125.25	883.50	739.35	644.01	576.54	526.48	488.03	457.70	433.26	413.24
37500	3292.49	1726.12	1205.63	946.61	792.16	690.01	617.72	564.09	522.89	490.39	464.21	442.76
40000	3511.99	1841.19	1286.00	1009.71	844.97	736.01	658.90	601.69	557.75	523.09	495.16	472.28
42500	3731.49	1956.26	1366.38	1072.82	897.79	782.01	700.08	639.30	592.61	555.78	526.11	501.79
45000	3950.99	2071.34	1446.75	1135.93	950.60	828.01	741.26	676.90	627.47	588.47	557.05	531.31
47500	4170.49	2186.41	1527.13	1199.03	1003.41	874.01	782.44	714.51	662.33	621.16	588.00	560.82
50000	4389.99	2301.49	1607.50	1262.14	1056.22	920.01	823.62	752.12	697.19	653.86	618.95	590.35
52500	4609.49	2416.56	1687.88	1325.25	1109.03	966.01	864.80	789.72	732.05	686.55	649.89	619.86
55000	4828.99	2531.63	1768.25	1388.35	1161.84	1012.01	905.98	827.33	766.91	719.24	680.84	649.38
57500	5048.49	2646.71	1848.63	1451.46	1214.65	1058.01	947.16	864.93	801.77	751.93	711.79	678.90
60000	5267.98	2761.78	1929.00	1514.57	1267.46	1104.01	988.34	902.54	836.62	784.63	742.74	708.41
65000	5706.98	2991.93	2089.75	1640.78	1373.08	1196.01	1070.70	977.75	906.34	850.01	804.63	767.45
70000	6145.98	3222.08	2250.50	1766.99	1478.70	1288.01	1153.07	1052.96	976.06	915.40	866.52	826.48
75000	6584.98	3452.23	2411.25	1893.21	1584.32	1380.01	1235.43	1128.17	1045.78	980.78	928.42	885.52
80000	7023.98	3682.37	2572.00	2019.42	1689.94	1472.01	1317.79	1203.38	1115.50	1046.17	990.31	944.55
85000	7462.98	3912.52	2732.75	2145.63	1795.57	1564.01	1400.15	1278.59	1185.22	1111.55	1052.21	1003.58
90000	7901.97	4142.67	2893.50	2271.85	1901.19	1656.01	1482.51	1353.80	1254.93	1176.94	1114.10	1062.62
95000	8340.97	4372.82	3054.25	2398.06	2006.81	1748.01	1564.87	1429.01	1324.65	1242.32	1175.99	1121.65
100000	8779.97	4602.97	3215.00	2524.27	2112.43	1840.01	1647.23	1504.23	1394.37	1307.71	1237.89	1180.69
105000	9218.97	4833.12	3375.75	2650.49	2218.05	1932.01	1729.60	1579.44	1464.09	1373.09	1299.78	1239.72
110000	9657.97	5063.26	3536.50	2776.70	2323.67	2024.01	1811.96	1654.65	1533.81	1438.48	1361.68	1298.75
115000	10096.97	5293.41	3697.25	2902.91	2429.29	2116.01	1894.32	1729.86	1603.53	1503.86	1423.57	1357.79
120000	10535.96	5523.56	3858.00	3029.13	2534.91	2208.01	1976.68	1805.07	1673.24	1569.25	1485.47	1416.82
125000	10974.96	5753.71	4018.75	3155.34	2640.54	2300.01	2059.04	1880.28	1742.96	1634.63	1547.36	1475.86
130000	11413.96	5983.86	4179.50	3281.55	2746.16	2392.01	2141.40	1955.49	1812.68	1700.02	1609.25	1534.89
135000	11852.96	6214.00	4340.25	3407.77	2851.78	2484.01	2223.76	2030.70	1882.40	1765.40	1671.15	1593.92
140000	12291.96	6444.15	4501.00	3533.98	2957.40	2576.01	2306.13	2105.91	1952.12	1830.79	1733.04	1652.96
145000	12730.96	6674.30	4661.75	3660.20	3063.02	2668.01	2388.49	2181.12	2021.84	1896.17	1794.94	1711.99
150000	13169.95	6904.45	4822.50	3786.41	3168.64	2760.01	2470.85	2256.34	2091.55	1961.56	1856.83	1771.03
155000	13608.95	7134.60	4983.25	3912.62	3274.26	2852.01	2553.21	2331.55	2161.27	2026.94	1918.73	1830.06
160000	14047.95	7364.74	5144.00	4038.84	3379.88	2944.01	2635.57	2406.76	2230.99	2092.33	1980.62	1889.09

AMOUNT OF LOAN	NUMBER OF YEARS IN TERM											
	13	14	15	16	17	18	19	20	25	30	35	40
$ 50	0.57	0.55	0.53	0.52	0.51	0.50	0.49	0.48	0.45	0.43	0.43	0.42
100	1.14	1.10	1.06	1.04	1.01	0.99	0.97	0.95	0.90	0.86	0.85	0.83
200	2.27	2.19	2.12	2.07	2.02	1.97	1.93	1.90	1.79	1.72	1.69	1.66
300	3.40	3.28	3.18	3.10	3.02	2.96	2.90	2.85	2.68	2.58	2.53	2.49
400	4.54	4.38	4.24	4.13	4.03	3.94	3.86	3.80	3.57	3.44	3.37	3.32
500	5.67	5.47	5.30	5.16	5.03	4.92	4.83	4.75	4.46	4.30	4.21	4.15
600	6.80	6.56	6.36	6.19	6.04	5.91	5.79	5.70	5.35	5.16	5.05	4.98
700	7.94	7.66	7.42	7.22	7.04	6.89	6.76	6.64	6.24	6.02	5.89	5.81
800	9.07	8.75	8.48	8.25	8.05	7.88	7.72	7.59	7.13	6.88	6.73	6.64
900	10.20	9.84	9.54	9.28	9.05	8.86	8.69	8.54	8.03	7.74	7.57	7.47
1000	11.34	10.94	10.60	10.31	10.06	9.84	9.65	9.49	8.92	8.60	8.41	8.30
2000	22.67	21.87	21.19	20.61	20.11	19.68	19.30	18.98	17.83	17.19	16.82	16.60
3000	34.00	32.80	31.79	30.92	30.17	29.52	28.95	28.46	26.74	25.78	25.22	24.89
4000	45.33	43.73	42.38	41.22	40.22	39.36	38.60	37.95	35.65	34.37	33.63	33.19
5000	56.66	54.67	52.97	51.52	50.28	49.20	48.25	47.43	44.56	42.96	42.03	41.48
6000	67.99	65.60	63.57	61.83	60.33	59.03	57.90	56.92	53.47	51.55	50.44	49.78
7000	79.33	76.53	74.16	72.13	70.39	68.87	67.55	66.40	62.38	60.15	58.85	58.07
8000	90.66	87.46	84.75	82.44	80.44	78.71	77.20	75.89	71.30	68.74	67.25	66.37
9000	101.99	98.40	95.35	92.74	90.49	88.55	86.85	85.37	80.21	77.33	75.66	74.67
10000	113.32	109.33	105.94	103.04	100.55	98.39	96.50	94.86	89.12	85.92	84.06	82.96
11000	124.65	120.26	116.53	113.35	110.60	108.23	106.15	104.34	98.03	94.51	92.47	91.26
12000	135.98	131.19	127.13	123.65	120.66	118.06	115.80	113.83	106.94	103.10	100.88	99.55
13000	147.32	142.13	137.72	133.96	130.71	127.90	125.45	123.31	115.85	111.70	109.28	107.85
14000	158.65	153.06	148.32	144.26	140.77	137.74	135.10	132.80	124.76	120.29	117.69	116.14
15000	169.98	163.99	158.91	154.56	150.82	147.58	144.75	142.28	133.68	128.88	126.09	124.44
16000	181.31	174.92	169.50	164.87	160.88	157.42	154.40	151.77	142.59	137.47	134.50	132.73
17000	192.64	185.85	180.10	175.17	170.93	167.25	164.05	161.25	151.50	146.06	142.91	141.03
18000	203.97	196.79	190.69	185.48	180.98	177.09	173.70	170.74	160.41	154.65	151.31	149.33
19000	215.31	207.72	201.28	195.78	191.04	186.93	183.35	180.22	169.32	163.24	159.72	157.62
20000	226.64	218.65	211.88	206.08	201.09	196.77	193.00	189.71	178.23	171.84	168.12	165.92
21000	237.97	229.58	222.47	216.39	211.15	206.61	202.65	199.19	187.14	180.43	176.53	174.21
22000	249.30	240.52	233.06	226.69	221.20	216.45	212.30	208.68	196.06	189.02	184.93	182.51
23000	260.63	251.45	243.66	237.00	231.26	226.28	221.95	218.16	204.97	197.61	193.34	190.80
24000	271.96	262.38	254.25	247.30	241.31	236.12	231.60	227.65	213.88	206.20	201.75	199.10
25000	283.30	273.31	264.85	257.60	251.36	245.96	241.25	237.13	222.79	214.79	210.15	207.39
26000	294.63	284.25	275.44	267.91	261.42	255.80	250.90	246.62	231.70	223.39	218.56	215.69
27000	305.96	295.18	286.03	278.21	271.47	265.64	260.55	256.10	240.61	231.98	226.96	223.99
28000	317.29	306.11	296.63	288.51	281.53	275.47	270.20	265.59	249.52	240.57	235.37	232.28
29000	328.62	317.04	307.22	298.82	291.58	285.31	279.85	275.07	258.43	249.16	243.78	240.58
30000	339.95	327.98	317.81	309.12	301.64	295.15	289.50	284.56	267.35	257.75	252.18	248.87
31000	351.29	338.91	328.41	319.43	311.69	304.99	299.15	294.05	276.26	266.34	260.59	257.17
32000	362.62	349.84	339.00	329.73	321.75	314.83	308.80	303.53	285.17	274.93	268.99	265.46
33000	373.95	360.77	349.59	340.03	331.80	324.67	318.45	313.02	294.08	283.53	277.40	273.76
34000	385.28	371.70	360.19	350.34	341.85	334.50	328.10	322.50	302.99	292.12	285.81	282.05
35000	396.61	382.64	370.78	360.64	351.91	344.34	337.75	331.99	311.90	300.71	294.21	290.35
37500	424.94	409.97	397.27	386.40	377.04	368.94	361.88	355.70	334.18	322.19	315.23	311.09
40000	453.27	437.30	423.75	412.16	402.18	393.53	386.00	379.41	356.46	343.67	336.24	331.83
42500	481.60	464.63	450.23	437.92	427.32	418.13	410.13	403.12	378.74	365.15	357.26	352.57
45000	509.93	491.96	476.72	463.68	452.45	442.72	434.25	426.84	401.02	386.62	378.27	373.31
47500	538.26	519.29	503.20	489.44	477.59	467.32	458.38	450.55	423.30	408.10	399.28	394.05
50000	566.59	546.62	529.69	515.20	502.72	491.92	482.50	474.26	445.57	429.58	420.30	414.78
52500	594.92	573.95	556.17	540.96	527.86	516.51	506.63	497.98	467.85	451.06	441.31	435.52
55000	623.24	601.28	582.65	566.72	553.00	541.11	530.75	521.69	490.13	472.54	462.33	456.26
57500	651.57	628.62	609.14	592.48	578.13	565.70	554.87	545.40	512.41	494.02	483.34	477.00
60000	679.90	655.95	635.62	618.24	603.27	590.30	579.00	569.12	534.69	515.50	504.36	497.74
65000	736.56	710.61	688.59	669.76	653.54	639.49	627.25	616.54	579.24	558.46	546.39	539.22
70000	793.22	765.27	741.56	721.28	703.81	688.68	675.50	663.97	623.80	601.41	588.42	580.70
75000	849.88	819.93	794.53	772.80	754.07	737.87	723.75	711.39	668.36	644.37	630.45	622.17
80000	906.54	874.59	847.50	824.32	804.36	787.06	772.00	758.82	712.91	687.33	672.48	663.65
85000	963.19	929.25	900.46	875.84	854.63	836.25	820.25	806.24	757.47	730.29	714.51	705.13
90000	1019.85	983.92	953.43	927.36	904.90	885.44	868.50	853.67	802.03	773.24	756.54	746.61
95000	1076.51	1038.58	1006.40	978.88	955.17	934.63	916.75	901.10	846.59	816.20	798.56	788.09
100000	1133.17	1093.24	1059.37	1030.40	1005.44	983.83	965.00	948.52	891.14	859.16	840.59	829.56
105000	1189.83	1147.90	1112.34	1081.92	1055.72	1033.02	1013.25	995.95	935.70	902.12	882.62	871.04
110000	1246.48	1202.56	1165.30	1133.44	1105.99	1082.21	1061.49	1043.37	980.26	945.07	924.65	912.52
115000	1303.14	1257.23	1218.27	1184.96	1156.26	1131.40	1109.74	1090.80	1024.81	988.03	966.68	954.00
120000	1359.80	1311.89	1271.24	1236.47	1206.53	1180.59	1157.99	1138.23	1069.37	1030.99	1008.71	995.48
125000	1416.46	1366.55	1324.21	1287.99	1256.80	1229.78	1206.24	1185.65	1113.93	1073.95	1050.74	1036.95
130000	1473.12	1421.21	1377.18	1339.51	1307.08	1279.00	1254.49	1233.08	1158.48	1116.91	1092.77	1078.43
135000	1529.77	1475.87	1430.14	1391.03	1357.35	1328.16	1302.74	1280.50	1203.04	1159.86	1134.80	1119.91
140000	1586.43	1530.53	1483.11	1442.55	1407.62	1377.35	1350.99	1327.93	1247.60	1202.82	1176.83	1161.39
145000	1643.09	1585.20	1536.08	1494.07	1457.89	1426.54	1399.24	1375.35	1292.15	1245.78	1218.86	1202.86
150000	1699.75	1639.86	1589.05	1545.59	1508.16	1475.74	1447.49	1422.78	1336.71	1288.74	1260.89	1244.34
155000	1756.41	1694.52	1642.02	1597.11	1558.44	1524.93	1495.74	1470.21	1381.27	1331.69	1302.92	1285.82
160000	1813.07	1749.18	1694.99	1648.63	1608.71	1574.12	1543.99	1517.63	1425.82	1374.65	1344.95	1327.30

41

MONTHLY AMORTIZING PAYMENTS

AMOUNT OF LOAN	NUMBER OF YEARS IN TERM											
	1	2	3	4	5	6	7	8	9	10	11	12
$ 50	4.40	2.31	1.62	1.27	1.07	0.93	0.84	0.76	0.71	0.67	0.63	0.60
100	8.80	4.62	3.23	2.54	2.13	1.86	1.67	1.52	1.41	1.33	1.26	1.20
200	17.59	9.23	6.46	5.08	4.25	3.71	3.33	3.04	2.82	2.65	2.51	2.40
300	26.38	13.85	9.69	7.61	6.38	5.56	4.99	4.56	4.23	3.97	3.76	3.59
400	35.17	18.46	12.91	10.15	8.50	7.42	6.65	6.07	5.64	5.29	5.01	4.79
500	43.96	23.08	16.14	12.69	10.63	9.27	8.31	7.59	7.04	6.61	6.26	5.98
600	52.75	27.69	19.37	15.22	12.75	11.12	9.97	9.11	8.45	7.93	7.52	7.18
700	61.55	32.31	22.59	17.76	14.88	12.97	11.63	10.63	9.86	9.26	8.77	8.37
800	70.34	36.92	25.82	20.30	17.00	14.83	13.29	12.14	11.27	10.58	10.02	9.57
900	79.13	41.54	29.05	22.83	19.13	16.68	14.95	13.66	12.68	11.90	11.27	10.76
1000	87.92	46.15	32.27	25.37	21.25	18.53	16.61	15.18	14.08	13.22	12.52	11.96
2000	175.84	92.29	64.54	50.73	42.50	37.06	33.21	30.35	28.16	26.44	25.04	23.91
3000	263.75	138.44	96.81	76.09	63.75	55.58	49.81	45.53	42.24	39.65	37.56	35.86
4000	351.67	184.58	129.07	101.46	84.99	74.11	66.41	60.70	56.32	52.87	50.08	47.81
5000	439.58	230.73	161.34	126.82	106.24	92.63	83.01	75.88	70.40	66.08	62.60	59.76
6000	527.50	276.87	193.61	152.18	127.49	111.16	99.61	91.05	84.48	79.30	75.12	71.71
7000	615.42	323.02	225.88	177.54	148.73	129.69	116.21	106.22	98.56	92.51	87.64	83.66
8000	703.33	369.16	258.14	202.91	169.98	148.21	132.81	121.40	112.63	105.73	100.16	95.61
9000	791.25	415.31	290.41	228.27	191.23	166.74	149.42	136.57	126.71	118.94	112.68	107.56
10000	879.16	461.45	322.68	253.63	212.48	185.26	166.02	151.75	140.79	132.16	125.20	119.51
11000	967.08	507.60	354.94	278.99	233.72	203.79	182.62	166.92	154.87	145.37	137.72	131.46
12000	1055.00	553.74	387.21	304.36	254.97	222.32	199.22	182.09	168.95	158.59	150.24	143.41
13000	1142.91	599.89	419.48	329.72	276.22	240.84	215.82	197.27	183.03	171.80	162.76	155.37
14000	1230.83	646.03	451.75	355.08	297.46	259.37	232.42	212.44	197.11	185.02	175.28	167.32
15000	1318.74	692.18	484.01	380.44	318.71	277.89	249.02	227.62	211.19	198.23	187.80	179.27
16000	1406.66	738.32	516.28	405.81	339.96	296.42	265.62	242.79	225.26	211.45	200.32	191.22
17000	1494.58	784.47	548.55	431.17	361.20	314.94	282.23	257.97	239.34	224.66	212.84	203.17
18000	1582.49	830.61	580.81	456.53	382.45	333.47	298.83	273.14	253.42	237.88	225.36	215.12
19000	1670.41	876.76	613.08	481.89	403.70	352.00	315.43	288.31	267.50	251.09	237.88	227.07
20000	1758.32	922.90	645.35	507.26	424.95	370.52	332.03	303.49	281.58	264.31	250.40	239.02
21000	1846.24	969.05	677.62	532.62	446.19	389.05	348.63	318.66	295.66	277.52	262.92	250.97
22000	1934.15	1015.19	709.88	557.98	467.44	407.57	365.23	333.84	309.74	290.74	275.44	262.92
23000	2022.07	1061.34	742.15	583.34	488.69	426.10	381.83	349.01	323.81	303.95	287.96	274.87
24000	2109.99	1107.48	774.42	608.71	509.93	444.63	398.43	364.18	337.89	317.17	300.48	286.82
25000	2197.90	1153.63	806.68	634.07	531.18	463.15	415.03	379.36	351.97	330.38	313.00	298.77
26000	2285.82	1199.77	838.95	659.43	552.43	481.68	431.64	394.53	366.05	343.60	325.52	310.73
27000	2373.73	1245.92	871.22	684.79	573.68	500.20	448.24	409.71	380.13	356.81	338.04	322.68
28000	2461.65	1292.06	903.49	710.16	594.92	518.73	464.84	424.88	394.21	370.03	350.56	334.63
29000	2549.57	1338.21	935.75	735.52	616.17	537.25	481.44	440.06	408.29	383.24	363.08	346.58
30000	2637.48	1384.35	968.02	760.88	637.42	555.78	498.04	455.23	422.37	396.46	375.60	358.53
31000	2725.40	1430.50	1000.29	786.25	658.66	574.31	514.64	470.40	436.44	409.67	388.12	370.48
32000	2813.31	1476.64	1032.55	811.61	679.91	592.83	531.24	485.58	450.52	422.89	400.64	382.43
33000	2901.23	1522.79	1064.82	836.97	701.16	611.36	547.84	500.75	464.60	436.10	413.16	394.38
34000	2989.15	1568.93	1097.09	862.33	722.40	629.88	564.45	515.93	478.68	449.32	425.68	406.33
35000	3077.06	1615.08	1129.36	887.70	743.65	648.41	581.05	531.10	492.76	462.53	438.20	418.28
37500	3296.85	1730.44	1210.02	951.10	796.77	694.72	622.55	569.04	527.96	495.57	469.50	448.16
40000	3516.64	1845.80	1290.69	1014.51	849.89	741.04	664.05	606.97	563.15	528.61	500.80	478.04
42500	3736.43	1961.16	1371.36	1077.91	903.00	787.35	705.56	644.91	598.35	561.65	532.10	507.91
45000	3956.22	2076.53	1452.03	1141.32	956.12	833.67	747.06	682.84	633.55	594.68	563.40	537.79
47500	4176.01	2191.89	1532.70	1204.73	1009.24	879.98	788.56	720.78	668.74	627.72	594.70	567.67
50000	4395.80	2307.25	1613.36	1268.13	1062.36	926.30	830.06	758.71	703.94	660.76	626.00	597.54
52500	4615.59	2422.61	1694.03	1331.54	1115.47	972.61	871.57	796.65	739.14	693.80	657.30	627.42
55000	4835.38	2537.98	1774.70	1394.95	1168.59	1018.93	913.07	834.58	774.33	726.83	688.60	657.30
57500	5055.17	2653.34	1855.37	1458.35	1221.71	1065.24	954.57	872.52	809.53	759.87	719.90	687.18
60000	5274.96	2768.70	1936.04	1521.76	1274.83	1111.56	996.08	910.45	844.73	792.91	751.20	717.05
65000	5714.54	2999.43	2097.37	1648.57	1381.06	1204.18	1079.08	986.33	915.12	858.98	813.80	776.81
70000	6154.12	3230.15	2258.71	1775.39	1487.30	1296.81	1162.09	1062.20	985.51	925.06	876.40	836.56
75000	6593.70	3460.87	2420.04	1902.20	1593.53	1389.44	1245.09	1138.07	1055.91	991.14	939.00	896.31
80000	7033.28	3691.60	2581.38	2029.01	1699.77	1482.07	1328.10	1213.94	1126.30	1057.21	1001.60	956.07
85000	7472.86	3922.32	2742.72	2155.82	1806.00	1574.70	1411.11	1289.81	1196.69	1123.29	1064.19	1015.82
90000	7912.43	4153.05	2904.05	2282.64	1912.24	1667.33	1494.11	1365.68	1267.09	1189.36	1126.79	1075.58
95000	8352.01	4383.77	3065.39	2409.45	2018.47	1759.96	1577.12	1441.55	1337.48	1255.44	1189.39	1135.33
100000	8791.59	4614.50	3226.72	2536.26	2124.71	1852.59	1660.12	1517.42	1407.87	1321.51	1251.99	1195.08
105000	9231.17	4845.22	3388.06	2663.08	2230.94	1945.22	1743.13	1593.29	1478.27	1387.59	1314.59	1254.84
110000	9670.75	5075.95	3549.40	2789.89	2337.18	2037.85	1826.14	1669.16	1548.66	1453.66	1377.19	1314.59
115000	10110.33	5306.67	3710.73	2916.70	2443.42	2130.48	1909.14	1745.03	1619.05	1519.74	1439.79	1374.35
120000	10549.91	5537.40	3872.07	3043.52	2549.65	2223.11	1992.15	1820.90	1689.45	1585.81	1502.39	1434.10
125000	10989.49	5768.12	4033.40	3170.33	2655.89	2315.73	2075.15	1896.78	1759.84	1651.89	1564.99	1493.85
130000	11429.07	5998.85	4194.74	3297.14	2762.12	2408.36	2158.16	1972.65	1830.23	1717.96	1627.59	1553.61
135000	11868.65	6229.57	4356.08	3423.95	2868.36	2500.99	2241.16	2048.52	1900.63	1784.04	1690.19	1613.36
140000	12308.23	6460.29	4517.41	3550.77	2974.59	2593.62	2324.17	2124.39	1971.02	1850.12	1752.79	1673.11
145000	12747.81	6691.02	4678.75	3677.58	3080.83	2686.25	2407.18	2200.26	2041.41	1916.19	1815.39	1732.87
150000	13187.39	6921.74	4840.08	3804.39	3187.06	2778.88	2490.18	2276.13	2111.81	1982.27	1877.99	1792.62
155000	13626.97	7152.47	5001.42	3931.21	3293.30	2871.51	2573.19	2352.00	2182.20	2048.34	1940.59	1852.38
160000	14066.55	7383.19	5162.75	4058.02	3399.53	2964.14	2656.19	2427.87	2252.59	2114.42	2003.19	1912.13

MONTHLY AMORTIZING PAYMENTS 10.00%

AMOUNT OF LOAN	13	14	15	16	17	18	19	20	25	30	35	40
NUMBER OF YEARS IN TERM												
$ 50	0.58	0.56	0.54	0.53	0.52	0.50	0.50	0.49	0.46	0.44	0.43	0.43
100	1.15	1.11	1.08	1.05	1.03	1.00	0.99	0.97	0.91	0.88	0.86	0.85
200	2.30	2.22	2.15	2.10	2.05	2.00	1.97	1.94	1.82	1.76	1.72	1.70
300	3.45	3.33	3.23	3.14	3.07	3.00	2.95	2.90	2.73	2.64	2.58	2.55
400	4.60	4.44	4.30	4.19	4.09	4.00	3.93	3.87	3.64	3.52	3.44	3.40
500	5.74	5.55	5.38	5.23	5.11	5.00	4.91	4.83	4.55	4.39	4.30	4.25
600	6.89	6.65	6.45	6.28	6.13	6.00	5.89	5.80	5.46	5.27	5.16	5.10
700	8.04	7.76	7.53	7.33	7.15	7.00	6.87	6.76	6.37	6.15	6.02	5.95
800	9.19	8.87	8.60	8.37	8.17	8.00	7.86	7.73	7.27	7.03	6.88	6.80
900	10.34	9.98	9.68	9.42	9.20	9.00	8.84	8.69	8.18	7.90	7.74	7.65
1000	11.48	11.09	10.75	10.46	10.22	10.00	9.82	9.66	9.09	8.78	8.60	8.50
2000	22.96	22.17	21.50	20.92	20.43	20.00	19.63	19.31	18.18	17.56	17.20	16.99
3000	34.44	33.25	32.24	31.38	30.64	30.00	29.44	28.96	27.27	26.33	25.80	25.48
4000	45.92	44.33	42.99	41.84	40.85	40.00	39.26	38.61	36.35	35.11	34.39	33.97
5000	57.40	55.42	53.74	52.30	51.07	50.00	49.07	48.26	45.44	43.88	42.99	42.46
6000	68.88	66.50	64.48	62.76	61.28	60.00	58.88	57.91	54.53	52.66	51.59	50.95
7000	80.35	77.58	75.23	73.22	71.49	69.99	68.69	67.56	63.61	61.44	60.18	59.45
8000	91.83	88.66	85.97	83.68	81.70	79.99	78.51	77.21	72.70	70.21	68.78	67.94
9000	103.31	99.74	96.72	94.14	91.91	89.99	88.32	86.86	81.79	78.99	77.38	76.43
10000	114.79	110.83	107.47	104.60	102.13	99.99	98.13	96.51	90.88	87.76	85.97	84.92
11000	126.27	121.91	118.21	115.05	112.34	109.99	107.94	106.16	99.96	96.54	94.57	93.41
12000	137.75	132.99	128.96	125.51	122.55	119.99	117.76	115.81	109.05	105.31	103.17	101.90
13000	149.23	144.07	139.70	135.97	132.76	129.98	127.57	125.46	118.14	114.09	111.76	110.39
14000	160.70	155.15	150.45	146.43	142.97	139.98	137.38	135.11	127.22	122.87	120.36	118.89
15000	172.18	166.24	161.20	156.89	153.19	149.98	147.19	144.76	136.31	131.64	128.96	127.38
16000	183.66	177.32	171.94	167.35	163.40	159.98	156.99	154.41	145.40	140.42	137.55	135.87
17000	195.14	188.40	182.69	177.81	173.61	169.98	166.82	164.06	154.48	149.19	146.15	144.36
18000	206.62	199.48	193.43	188.27	183.82	179.98	176.63	173.71	163.57	157.97	154.75	152.85
19000	218.10	210.56	204.18	198.73	194.03	189.98	186.44	183.36	172.66	166.74	163.34	161.34
20000	229.57	221.65	214.93	209.19	204.25	199.97	196.26	193.01	181.75	175.52	171.94	169.83
21000	241.05	232.73	225.67	219.64	214.46	209.97	206.07	202.66	190.83	184.30	180.54	178.33
22000	252.53	243.81	236.42	230.10	224.67	219.97	215.88	212.31	199.92	193.07	189.13	186.82
23000	264.01	254.89	247.16	240.56	234.88	229.97	225.69	221.96	209.01	201.85	197.73	195.31
24000	275.49	265.97	257.91	251.02	245.10	239.97	235.51	231.61	218.09	210.62	206.33	203.80
25000	286.97	277.06	268.66	261.48	255.31	249.97	245.32	241.26	227.18	219.40	214.92	212.29
26000	298.45	288.14	279.40	271.94	265.52	259.96	255.13	250.91	236.27	228.17	223.52	220.78
27000	309.92	299.22	290.15	282.40	275.73	269.96	264.94	260.56	245.35	236.95	232.12	229.27
28000	321.40	310.30	300.89	292.86	285.94	279.96	274.76	270.21	254.44	245.73	240.71	237.77
29000	332.88	321.38	311.64	303.32	296.16	289.96	284.57	279.86	263.53	254.50	249.31	246.26
30000	344.36	332.47	322.39	313.78	306.37	299.96	294.38	289.51	272.62	263.28	257.91	254.75
31000	355.84	343.55	333.13	324.23	316.58	309.96	304.20	299.16	281.70	272.05	266.50	263.24
32000	367.32	354.63	343.88	334.69	326.79	319.95	314.01	308.81	290.79	280.83	275.10	271.73
33000	378.79	365.71	354.62	345.15	337.00	329.95	323.82	318.46	299.88	289.60	283.70	280.22
34000	390.27	376.79	365.37	355.61	347.22	339.95	333.63	328.11	308.96	298.38	292.29	288.71
35000	401.75	387.88	376.12	366.07	357.43	349.95	343.45	337.76	318.05	307.16	300.89	297.21
37500	430.45	415.58	402.98	392.22	382.96	374.95	367.98	361.89	340.77	329.09	322.38	318.43
40000	459.14	443.29	429.85	418.37	408.49	399.94	392.51	386.01	363.49	351.03	343.87	339.66
42500	487.84	470.99	456.71	444.51	434.02	424.94	417.04	410.14	386.20	372.97	365.37	360.89
45000	516.54	498.70	483.58	470.66	459.55	449.93	441.57	434.26	408.92	394.91	386.86	382.12
47500	545.23	526.40	510.44	496.81	485.08	474.93	466.10	458.39	431.64	416.85	408.35	403.35
50000	573.93	554.11	537.31	522.96	510.61	499.93	490.63	482.52	454.36	438.79	429.84	424.58
52500	602.63	581.81	564.17	549.10	536.14	524.92	515.17	506.64	477.07	460.73	451.33	445.81
55000	631.32	609.52	591.04	575.25	561.67	549.92	539.70	530.77	499.79	482.67	472.82	467.04
57500	660.02	637.22	617.90	601.40	587.20	574.92	564.23	554.89	522.51	504.61	494.32	488.26
60000	688.71	664.93	644.77	627.55	612.73	599.91	588.76	579.02	545.23	526.55	515.81	509.49
65000	746.11	720.34	698.50	679.84	663.79	649.90	637.82	627.27	590.66	570.43	558.79	551.95
70000	803.50	775.75	752.23	732.14	714.85	699.90	686.89	675.52	636.10	614.31	601.78	594.41
75000	860.89	831.16	805.96	784.43	765.91	749.89	735.95	723.77	681.53	658.18	644.76	636.86
80000	918.28	886.57	859.69	836.73	816.97	799.88	785.01	772.02	726.97	702.06	687.74	679.32
85000	975.68	941.98	913.42	889.02	868.03	849.87	834.08	820.27	772.40	745.94	730.73	721.78
90000	1033.07	997.39	967.15	941.32	919.09	899.86	883.14	868.52	817.84	789.82	773.71	764.24
95000	1090.46	1052.80	1020.88	993.61	970.15	949.86	932.20	916.78	863.27	833.70	816.69	806.69
100000	1147.85	1108.21	1074.61	1045.91	1021.22	999.85	981.26	965.03	908.71	877.58	859.68	849.15
105000	1205.25	1163.62	1128.34	1098.20	1072.28	1049.84	1030.33	1013.28	954.14	921.46	902.66	891.61
110000	1262.64	1219.03	1182.07	1150.50	1123.34	1099.83	1079.39	1061.53	999.58	965.33	945.64	934.07
115000	1320.03	1274.44	1235.80	1202.79	1174.40	1149.83	1128.45	1109.78	1045.01	1009.21	988.63	976.52
120000	1377.42	1329.85	1289.53	1255.09	1225.46	1199.82	1177.52	1158.03	1090.45	1053.09	1031.61	1018.98
125000	1434.82	1385.26	1343.26	1307.38	1276.52	1249.81	1226.58	1206.28	1135.88	1096.97	1074.60	1061.44
130000	1492.21	1440.67	1396.99	1359.68	1327.58	1299.80	1275.64	1254.53	1181.32	1140.85	1117.58	1103.89
135000	1549.60	1496.08	1450.72	1411.97	1378.64	1349.79	1324.70	1302.78	1226.75	1184.73	1160.56	1146.35
140000	1606.99	1551.49	1504.45	1464.27	1429.70	1399.79	1373.77	1351.04	1272.19	1228.61	1203.55	1188.81
145000	1664.38	1606.90	1558.18	1516.56	1480.76	1449.78	1422.83	1399.29	1317.62	1272.48	1246.53	1231.27
150000	1721.78	1662.31	1611.91	1568.86	1531.82	1499.77	1471.89	1447.54	1363.06	1316.36	1289.51	1273.72
155000	1779.17	1717.72	1665.64	1621.15	1582.88	1549.76	1520.96	1495.79	1408.49	1360.24	1332.50	1316.18
160000	1836.56	1773.13	1719.37	1673.45	1633.94	1599.75	1570.02	1544.04	1453.93	1404.12	1375.48	1358.64

MONTHLY AMORTIZING PAYMENTS

AMOUNT OF LOAN	NUMBER OF YEARS IN TERM											
	1	2	3	4	5	6	7	8	9	10	11	12
$ 50	4.41	2.32	1.62	1.28	1.07	0.94	0.84	0.77	0.72	0.67	0.64	0.61
100	8.81	4.63	3.24	2.55	2.14	1.87	1.68	1.54	1.43	1.34	1.27	1.21
200	17.61	9.26	6.48	5.10	4.28	3.74	3.35	3.07	2.85	2.68	2.54	2.42
300	26.41	13.88	9.72	7.65	6.42	5.60	5.02	4.60	4.27	4.01	3.80	3.63
400	35.22	18.51	12.96	10.20	8.55	7.47	6.70	6.13	5.69	5.35	5.07	4.84
500	44.02	23.14	16.20	12.75	10.69	9.33	8.37	7.66	7.11	6.68	6.34	6.05
600	52.82	27.76	19.44	15.29	12.83	11.20	10.04	9.19	8.53	8.02	7.60	7.26
700	61.63	32.39	22.67	17.84	14.96	13.06	11.72	10.72	9.96	9.35	8.87	8.47
800	70.43	37.01	25.91	20.39	17.10	14.93	13.39	12.25	11.38	10.69	10.13	9.68
900	79.23	41.64	29.15	22.94	19.24	16.79	15.06	13.78	12.80	12.02	11.40	10.89
1000	88.04	46.27	32.39	25.49	21.38	18.66	16.74	15.31	14.22	13.36	12.67	12.10
2000	176.07	92.53	64.77	50.97	42.75	37.31	33.47	30.62	28.43	26.71	25.33	24.20
3000	264.10	138.79	97.16	76.45	64.12	55.96	50.20	45.93	42.65	40.07	37.99	36.29
4000	352.13	185.05	129.54	101.94	85.49	74.61	66.93	61.23	56.86	53.42	50.65	48.39
5000	440.17	231.31	161.93	127.42	106.86	93.27	83.66	76.54	71.08	66.77	63.31	60.48
6000	528.20	277.57	194.31	152.90	128.23	111.92	100.39	91.85	85.29	80.13	75.98	72.58
7000	616.23	323.83	226.70	178.38	149.60	130.57	117.12	107.15	99.51	93.48	88.64	84.67
8000	704.26	370.09	259.08	203.87	170.97	149.22	133.85	122.46	113.72	106.84	101.30	96.77
9000	792.29	416.35	291.47	229.35	192.34	167.87	150.58	137.77	127.93	120.19	113.96	108.87
10000	880.33	462.61	323.85	254.83	213.71	186.53	167.31	153.07	142.15	133.54	126.62	120.96
11000	968.36	508.87	356.24	280.32	235.08	205.18	184.04	168.38	156.36	146.90	139.28	133.06
12000	1056.39	555.13	388.62	305.80	256.45	223.83	200.77	183.69	170.58	160.25	151.95	145.15
13000	1144.42	601.39	421.01	331.28	277.82	242.48	217.50	198.99	184.79	173.61	164.61	157.25
14000	1232.46	647.65	453.39	356.76	299.19	261.14	234.23	214.30	199.01	186.96	177.27	169.34
15000	1320.49	693.91	485.78	382.25	320.56	279.79	250.96	229.61	213.22	200.31	189.93	181.44
16000	1408.52	740.17	518.16	407.73	341.93	298.44	267.70	244.91	227.44	213.67	202.59	193.54
17000	1496.55	786.43	550.54	433.21	363.30	317.09	284.43	260.22	241.65	227.02	215.25	205.63
18000	1584.58	832.69	582.93	458.70	384.67	335.74	301.16	275.53	255.86	240.38	227.92	217.73
19000	1672.62	878.95	615.31	484.18	406.04	354.40	317.89	290.83	270.08	253.73	240.58	229.82
20000	1760.65	925.21	647.70	509.66	427.41	373.05	334.62	306.14	284.29	267.08	253.24	241.92
21000	1848.68	971.47	680.08	535.14	448.78	391.70	351.35	321.45	298.51	280.44	265.90	254.01
22000	1936.71	1017.73	712.47	560.63	470.15	410.35	368.08	336.75	312.72	293.79	278.56	266.11
23000	2024.75	1063.99	744.85	586.11	491.52	429.00	384.81	352.06	326.94	307.14	291.23	278.20
24000	2112.78	1110.25	777.24	611.59	512.89	447.66	401.54	367.37	341.15	320.50	303.89	290.30
25000	2200.81	1156.51	809.62	637.08	534.26	466.31	418.27	382.67	355.37	333.85	316.55	302.40
26000	2288.84	1202.78	842.01	662.56	555.63	484.96	435.00	397.98	369.58	347.21	329.21	314.49
27000	2376.87	1249.04	874.39	688.04	577.00	503.61	451.73	413.29	383.79	360.56	341.87	326.59
28000	2464.91	1295.30	906.78	713.52	598.37	522.27	468.46	428.59	398.01	373.91	354.53	338.68
29000	2552.94	1341.56	939.16	739.01	619.74	540.92	485.19	443.90	412.22	387.27	367.20	350.78
30000	2640.97	1387.82	971.55	764.49	641.11	559.57	501.92	459.21	426.44	400.62	379.86	362.87
31000	2729.00	1434.08	1003.93	789.97	662.48	578.22	518.65	474.51	440.65	413.98	392.52	374.97
32000	2817.04	1480.34	1036.32	815.46	683.85	596.87	535.39	489.82	454.87	427.33	405.18	387.07
33000	2905.07	1526.60	1068.70	840.94	705.22	615.53	552.12	505.13	469.08	440.68	417.84	399.16
34000	2993.10	1572.86	1101.08	866.42	726.59	634.18	568.85	520.44	483.30	454.04	430.50	411.26
35000	3081.13	1619.12	1133.47	891.90	747.96	652.83	585.58	535.74	497.51	467.39	443.17	423.35
37500	3301.21	1734.77	1214.43	955.61	801.39	699.46	627.40	574.01	533.05	500.78	474.82	453.59
40000	3521.29	1850.42	1295.39	1019.32	854.82	746.09	669.23	612.28	568.58	534.16	506.48	483.83
42500	3741.37	1966.07	1376.35	1083.02	908.24	792.72	711.06	650.54	604.12	567.55	538.13	514.07
45000	3961.45	2081.72	1457.32	1146.73	961.67	839.35	752.88	688.81	639.65	600.93	569.78	544.31
47500	4181.53	2197.37	1538.28	1210.44	1015.09	885.98	794.71	727.08	675.19	634.32	601.44	574.55
50000	4401.62	2313.02	1619.24	1274.15	1068.52	932.61	836.54	765.34	710.73	667.70	633.09	604.79
52500	4621.70	2428.68	1700.20	1337.85	1121.94	979.24	878.36	803.61	746.26	701.08	664.75	635.03
55000	4841.78	2544.33	1781.16	1401.56	1175.37	1025.87	920.19	841.88	781.80	734.47	696.40	665.27
57500	5061.86	2659.98	1862.12	1465.27	1228.80	1072.50	962.02	880.14	817.33	767.85	728.06	695.50
60000	5281.94	2775.63	1943.09	1528.98	1282.22	1119.13	1003.84	918.41	852.87	801.24	759.71	725.74
65000	5722.10	3006.93	2105.01	1656.39	1389.07	1212.40	1087.50	994.95	923.94	868.01	823.02	786.22
70000	6162.26	3238.23	2266.93	1783.80	1495.92	1305.66	1171.15	1071.48	995.01	934.78	886.33	846.70
75000	6602.42	3469.53	2428.86	1911.22	1602.77	1398.92	1254.80	1148.01	1066.09	1001.55	949.64	907.18
80000	7042.58	3700.84	2590.78	2038.63	1709.63	1492.18	1338.46	1224.55	1137.16	1068.32	1012.95	967.66
85000	7482.74	3932.14	2752.70	2166.04	1816.48	1585.44	1422.11	1301.08	1208.23	1135.09	1076.25	1028.14
90000	7922.90	4163.44	2914.63	2293.46	1923.33	1678.70	1505.76	1377.61	1279.30	1201.86	1139.56	1088.61
95000	8363.06	4394.74	3076.55	2420.87	2030.18	1771.96	1589.42	1454.15	1350.37	1268.63	1202.87	1149.09
100000	8803.23	4626.04	3238.47	2548.29	2137.03	1865.22	1673.07	1530.68	1421.45	1335.40	1266.18	1209.57
105000	9243.39	4857.35	3400.40	2675.70	2243.88	1958.48	1756.72	1607.22	1492.52	1402.16	1329.49	1270.05
110000	9683.55	5088.65	3562.32	2803.11	2350.73	2051.74	1840.38	1683.75	1563.59	1468.93	1392.80	1330.53
115000	10123.71	5319.95	3724.24	2930.53	2457.59	2145.00	1924.03	1760.28	1634.66	1535.70	1456.11	1391.00
120000	10563.87	5551.25	3886.17	3057.94	2564.44	2238.26	2007.68	1836.82	1705.74	1602.47	1519.42	1451.48
125000	11004.03	5782.55	4048.09	3185.36	2671.29	2331.52	2091.34	1913.35	1776.81	1669.24	1582.72	1511.96
130000	11444.19	6013.86	4210.01	3312.77	2778.14	2424.79	2174.99	1989.89	1847.88	1736.01	1646.03	1572.44
135000	11884.35	6245.16	4371.94	3440.18	2884.99	2518.05	2258.64	2066.42	1918.95	1802.78	1709.34	1632.92
140000	12324.51	6476.46	4533.86	3567.60	2991.84	2611.31	2342.30	2142.95	1990.02	1869.55	1772.65	1693.40
145000	12764.67	6707.76	4695.78	3695.01	3098.69	2704.57	2425.95	2219.49	2061.10	1936.32	1835.96	1753.87
150000	13204.84	6939.06	4857.71	3822.43	3205.54	2797.83	2509.60	2296.02	2132.17	2003.09	1899.27	1814.35
155000	13645.00	7170.37	5019.63	3949.84	3312.40	2891.09	2593.25	2372.55	2203.24	2069.86	1962.58	1874.83
160000	14085.16	7401.67	5181.56	4077.26	3419.25	2984.35	2676.91	2449.09	2274.31	2136.63	2025.89	1935.31

MONTHLY AMORTIZING PAYMENTS 10.25%

AMOUNT OF LOAN	NUMBER OF YEARS IN TERM											
	13	14	15	16	17	18	19	20	25	30	35	40
$ 50	0.59	0.57	0.55	0.54	0.52	0.51	0.50	0.50	0.47	0.45	0.44	0.44
100	1.17	1.13	1.09	1.07	1.04	1.02	1.00	0.99	0.93	0.90	0.88	0.87
200	2.33	2.25	2.18	2.13	2.08	2.04	2.00	1.97	1.86	1.80	1.76	1.74
300	3.49	3.37	3.27	3.19	3.12	3.05	3.00	2.95	2.78	2.69	2.64	2.61
400	4.66	4.50	4.36	4.25	4.15	4.07	4.00	3.93	3.71	3.59	3.52	3.48
500	5.82	5.62	5.45	5.31	5.19	5.08	4.99	4.91	4.64	4.49	4.40	4.35
600	6.98	6.74	6.54	6.37	6.23	6.10	5.99	5.89	5.56	5.38	5.28	5.22
700	8.14	7.87	7.63	7.44	7.26	7.12	6.99	6.88	6.49	6.28	6.16	6.09
800	9.31	8.99	8.72	8.50	8.30	8.13	7.99	7.86	7.42	7.17	7.04	6.96
900	10.47	10.11	9.81	9.56	9.34	9.15	8.98	8.84	8.34	8.07	7.91	7.82
1000	11.63	11.24	10.90	10.62	10.38	10.16	9.98	9.82	9.27	8.97	8.79	8.69
2000	23.26	22.47	21.80	21.24	20.75	20.32	19.96	19.64	18.53	17.93	17.58	17.38
3000	34.88	33.70	32.70	31.85	31.12	30.48	29.93	29.45	27.80	26.89	26.37	26.07
4000	46.51	44.94	43.60	42.47	41.49	40.64	39.91	39.27	37.06	35.85	35.16	34.76
5000	58.14	56.17	54.50	53.08	51.86	50.80	49.89	49.09	46.32	44.81	43.95	43.45
6000	69.76	67.40	65.40	63.70	62.23	60.96	59.86	58.90	55.59	53.77	52.74	52.13
7000	81.39	78.63	76.30	74.31	72.60	71.12	69.84	68.72	64.85	62.73	61.52	60.82
8000	93.02	89.87	87.20	84.93	82.97	81.28	79.82	78.54	74.12	71.69	70.31	69.51
9000	104.64	101.10	98.10	95.54	93.34	91.44	89.79	88.35	83.38	80.65	79.10	78.20
10000	116.27	112.33	109.00	106.16	103.71	101.60	99.77	98.17	92.64	89.62	87.89	86.89
11000	127.89	123.56	119.90	116.77	114.09	111.76	109.75	107.99	101.91	98.58	96.68	95.58
12000	139.52	134.80	130.80	127.39	124.46	121.92	119.72	117.80	111.17	107.54	105.47	104.26
13000	151.15	146.03	141.70	138.00	134.83	132.08	129.70	127.62	120.43	116.50	114.26	112.95
14000	162.77	157.26	152.60	148.62	145.20	142.24	139.67	137.44	129.70	125.46	123.04	121.64
15000	174.40	168.50	163.50	159.23	155.57	152.40	149.65	147.25	138.96	134.42	131.83	130.33
16000	186.03	179.73	174.40	169.85	165.94	162.56	159.63	157.07	148.23	143.38	140.62	139.02
17000	197.65	190.96	185.30	180.46	176.31	172.72	169.60	166.88	157.49	152.34	149.41	147.70
18000	209.28	202.19	196.20	191.08	186.68	182.88	179.58	176.70	166.75	161.30	158.20	156.39
19000	220.90	213.43	207.10	201.69	197.05	193.04	189.56	186.52	176.02	170.26	166.99	165.08
20000	232.53	224.66	218.00	212.31	207.42	203.20	199.53	196.33	185.28	179.23	175.78	173.77
21000	244.16	235.89	228.89	222.92	217.79	213.36	209.51	206.15	194.55	188.19	184.56	182.46
22000	255.78	247.12	239.79	233.54	228.17	223.52	219.49	215.97	203.81	197.15	193.35	191.15
23000	267.41	258.36	250.69	244.15	238.54	233.68	229.46	225.78	213.07	206.11	202.14	199.83
24000	279.04	269.59	261.59	254.77	248.91	243.84	239.44	235.60	222.34	215.07	210.93	208.52
25000	290.66	280.82	272.49	265.38	259.28	254.00	249.42	245.42	231.60	224.03	219.72	217.21
26000	302.29	292.06	283.39	276.00	269.65	264.16	259.39	255.23	240.86	232.99	228.51	225.90
27000	313.91	303.29	294.29	286.62	280.02	274.32	269.37	265.05	250.13	241.95	237.30	234.59
28000	325.54	314.52	305.19	297.23	290.39	284.48	279.34	274.87	259.39	250.91	246.08	243.27
29000	337.17	325.76	316.09	307.85	300.76	294.64	289.32	284.68	268.66	259.87	254.87	251.96
30000	348.79	336.99	326.99	318.46	311.13	304.80	299.30	294.50	277.92	268.84	263.66	260.65
31000	360.42	348.22	337.89	329.08	321.50	314.96	309.27	304.31	287.18	277.80	272.45	269.34
32000	372.05	359.45	348.79	339.69	331.87	325.12	319.25	314.13	296.45	286.76	281.24	278.03
33000	383.67	370.68	359.69	350.31	342.25	335.28	329.23	323.95	305.71	295.72	290.03	286.72
34000	395.30	381.92	370.59	360.92	352.62	345.44	339.20	333.76	314.98	304.68	298.82	295.40
35000	406.92	393.15	381.49	371.54	362.99	355.60	349.18	343.58	324.24	313.64	307.60	304.09
37500	435.99	421.23	408.74	398.07	388.91	381.00	374.12	368.12	347.40	336.04	329.58	325.81
40000	465.06	449.31	435.99	424.61	414.84	406.40	399.06	392.66	370.56	358.45	351.55	347.53
42500	494.12	477.39	463.23	451.15	440.77	431.80	424.00	417.20	393.72	380.85	373.52	369.25
45000	523.19	505.48	490.48	477.69	466.70	457.20	448.94	441.74	416.88	403.25	395.49	390.97
47500	552.25	533.56	517.73	504.23	492.62	482.60	473.89	466.29	440.04	425.65	417.46	412.69
50000	581.32	561.64	544.98	530.76	518.55	508.00	498.83	490.83	463.20	448.06	439.43	434.41
52500	610.38	589.72	572.23	557.30	544.48	533.39	523.77	515.37	486.36	470.46	461.40	456.13
55000	639.45	617.80	599.48	583.84	570.41	558.79	548.71	539.91	509.52	492.86	483.38	477.86
57500	668.52	645.88	626.73	610.38	596.33	584.19	573.65	564.45	532.68	515.26	505.35	499.58
60000	697.58	673.97	653.98	636.92	622.26	609.59	598.59	588.99	555.83	537.67	527.32	521.30
65000	755.71	730.13	708.47	689.99	674.11	660.39	648.47	638.07	602.15	582.47	571.26	564.74
70000	813.84	786.29	762.97	743.07	725.97	711.19	698.35	687.16	648.47	627.28	615.20	608.18
75000	871.98	842.46	817.47	796.14	777.82	761.99	748.24	736.24	694.79	672.08	659.15	651.62
80000	930.11	898.62	871.97	849.22	829.68	812.79	798.12	785.32	741.11	716.89	703.09	695.06
85000	988.24	954.78	926.46	902.30	881.53	863.59	848.00	834.40	787.43	761.69	747.03	738.50
90000	1046.37	1010.95	980.96	955.37	933.39	914.39	897.88	883.48	833.75	806.50	790.98	781.94
95000	1104.50	1067.11	1035.46	1008.45	985.24	965.19	947.77	932.57	880.07	851.30	834.92	825.38
100000	1162.63	1123.27	1089.96	1061.52	1037.10	1015.99	997.65	981.65	926.39	896.11	878.86	868.82
105000	1220.76	1179.44	1144.45	1114.60	1088.95	1066.78	1047.53	1030.73	972.71	940.91	922.80	912.26
110000	1278.90	1235.60	1198.95	1167.68	1140.81	1117.58	1097.41	1079.81	1019.03	985.72	966.75	955.71
115000	1337.03	1291.76	1253.45	1220.75	1192.66	1168.38	1147.29	1128.89	1065.35	1030.52	1010.69	999.15
120000	1395.16	1347.93	1307.95	1273.83	1244.51	1219.18	1197.18	1177.98	1111.66	1075.33	1054.63	1042.59
125000	1453.29	1404.09	1362.44	1326.90	1296.37	1269.98	1247.06	1227.06	1157.98	1120.13	1098.57	1086.03
130000	1511.42	1460.26	1416.94	1379.98	1348.22	1320.78	1296.94	1276.14	1204.30	1164.94	1142.52	1129.47
135000	1569.55	1516.42	1471.44	1433.06	1400.08	1371.58	1346.82	1325.22	1250.62	1209.74	1186.46	1172.91
140000	1627.68	1572.58	1525.94	1486.13	1451.93	1422.38	1396.70	1374.31	1296.94	1254.55	1230.40	1216.35
145000	1685.82	1628.75	1580.43	1539.21	1503.79	1473.18	1446.59	1423.39	1343.26	1299.35	1274.35	1259.79
150000	1743.95	1684.91	1634.93	1592.28	1555.64	1523.98	1496.47	1472.47	1389.58	1344.16	1318.29	1303.23
155000	1802.08	1741.07	1689.43	1645.36	1607.50	1574.77	1546.35	1521.55	1435.90	1388.96	1362.23	1346.67
160000	1860.21	1797.24	1743.93	1698.44	1659.35	1625.57	1596.23	1570.63	1482.22	1433.77	1406.17	1390.11

MONTHLY AMORTIZING PAYMENTS

AMOUNT OF LOAN	NUMBER OF YEARS IN TERM											
	1	2	3	4	5	6	7	8	9	10	11	12
$ 50	4.41	2.32	1.63	1.29	1.08	0.94	0.85	0.78	0.72	0.68	0.65	0.62
100	8.82	4.64	3.26	2.57	2.15	1.88	1.69	1.55	1.44	1.35	1.29	1.23
200	17.63	9.28	6.51	5.13	4.30	3.76	3.38	3.09	2.88	2.70	2.57	2.45
300	26.45	13.92	9.76	7.69	6.45	5.64	5.06	4.64	4.31	4.05	3.85	3.68
400	35.26	18.56	13.01	10.25	8.60	7.52	6.75	6.18	5.75	5.40	5.13	4.90
500	44.08	23.19	16.26	12.81	10.75	9.39	8.44	7.73	7.18	6.75	6.41	6.13
600	52.89	27.83	19.51	15.37	12.90	11.27	10.12	9.27	8.62	8.10	7.69	7.35
700	61.71	32.47	22.76	17.93	15.05	13.15	11.81	10.81	10.05	9.45	8.97	8.57
800	70.52	37.11	26.01	20.49	17.20	15.03	13.49	12.36	11.49	10.80	10.25	9.80
900	79.34	41.74	29.26	23.05	19.35	16.91	15.18	13.90	12.92	12.15	11.53	11.02
1000	88.15	46.38	32.51	25.61	21.50	18.78	16.87	15.45	14.36	13.50	12.81	12.25
2000	176.30	92.76	65.01	51.21	42.99	37.56	33.73	30.89	28.71	26.99	25.61	24.49
3000	264.45	139.13	97.51	76.82	64.49	56.34	50.59	46.33	43.06	40.49	38.42	36.73
4000	352.60	185.51	130.01	102.42	85.98	75.12	67.45	61.77	57.41	53.98	51.22	48.97
5000	440.75	231.89	162.52	128.02	107.47	93.90	84.31	77.21	71.76	67.47	64.03	61.21
6000	528.90	278.26	195.02	153.63	128.97	112.68	101.17	92.65	86.11	80.97	76.83	73.45
7000	617.05	324.64	227.52	179.23	150.46	131.46	118.03	108.09	100.46	94.46	89.64	85.69
8000	705.19	371.01	260.02	204.83	171.96	150.24	134.89	123.53	114.81	107.95	102.44	97.94
9000	793.34	417.39	292.53	230.44	193.45	169.02	151.75	138.97	129.16	121.45	115.25	110.18
10000	881.49	463.77	325.03	256.04	214.94	187.80	168.61	154.41	143.51	134.94	128.05	122.42
11000	969.64	510.14	357.53	281.64	236.44	206.57	185.47	169.85	157.86	148.43	140.85	134.66
12000	1057.79	556.52	390.03	307.25	257.93	225.35	202.33	185.29	172.22	161.93	153.66	146.90
13000	1145.94	602.89	422.54	332.85	279.43	244.13	219.19	200.73	186.57	175.42	166.46	159.14
14000	1234.09	649.27	455.04	358.45	300.92	262.91	236.05	216.17	200.92	188.91	179.27	171.38
15000	1322.23	695.65	487.54	384.06	322.41	281.69	252.92	231.61	215.27	202.41	192.07	183.63
16000	1410.38	742.02	520.04	409.66	343.91	300.47	269.78	247.05	229.62	215.90	204.88	195.87
17000	1498.53	788.40	552.55	435.26	365.40	319.25	286.64	262.49	243.97	229.39	217.68	208.11
18000	1586.68	834.77	585.05	460.87	386.90	338.03	303.50	277.93	258.32	242.89	230.49	220.35
19000	1674.83	881.15	617.55	486.47	408.39	356.81	320.36	293.37	272.67	256.38	243.29	232.59
20000	1762.98	927.53	650.05	512.07	429.88	375.58	337.22	308.81	287.02	269.87	256.09	244.83
21000	1851.13	973.90	682.56	537.68	451.38	394.36	354.08	324.25	301.37	283.37	268.90	257.07
22000	1939.27	1020.28	715.06	563.28	472.87	413.14	370.94	339.69	315.72	296.86	281.70	269.32
23000	2027.42	1066.65	747.56	588.88	494.36	431.92	387.80	355.13	330.07	310.36	294.51	281.56
24000	2115.57	1113.03	780.06	614.49	515.86	450.70	404.66	370.57	344.43	323.85	307.31	293.80
25000	2203.72	1159.41	812.57	640.09	537.35	469.48	421.52	386.01	358.78	337.34	320.12	306.04
26000	2291.87	1205.78	845.07	665.69	558.85	488.26	438.38	401.45	373.13	350.84	332.92	318.28
27000	2380.02	1252.16	877.57	691.30	580.34	507.04	455.24	416.89	387.48	364.33	345.73	330.52
28000	2468.17	1298.53	910.07	716.90	601.83	525.82	472.10	432.33	401.83	377.82	358.53	342.76
29000	2556.31	1344.91	942.58	742.50	623.33	544.60	488.96	447.77	416.18	391.32	371.33	355.01
30000	2644.46	1391.29	975.08	768.11	644.82	563.37	505.83	463.21	430.53	404.81	384.14	367.25
31000	2732.61	1437.66	1007.58	793.71	666.32	582.15	522.69	478.65	444.88	418.30	396.94	379.49
32000	2820.76	1484.04	1040.08	819.31	687.81	600.93	539.55	494.09	459.23	431.80	409.75	391.73
33000	2908.91	1530.41	1072.59	844.92	709.30	619.71	556.41	509.53	473.58	445.29	422.55	403.97
34000	2997.06	1576.79	1105.09	870.52	730.80	638.49	573.27	524.97	487.93	458.78	435.36	416.21
35000	3085.21	1623.17	1137.59	896.12	752.29	657.27	590.13	540.41	502.29	472.28	448.16	428.45
37500	3305.58	1739.11	1218.85	960.13	806.03	704.22	632.28	579.01	538.16	506.01	480.17	459.06
40000	3525.95	1855.05	1300.10	1024.14	859.76	751.16	674.43	617.61	574.04	539.74	512.18	489.66
42500	3746.32	1970.99	1381.36	1088.15	913.50	798.11	716.58	656.21	609.92	573.48	544.19	520.26
45000	3966.69	2086.93	1462.61	1152.16	967.23	845.05	758.74	694.81	645.79	607.21	576.21	550.87
47500	4187.06	2202.87	1543.87	1216.17	1020.97	892.01	800.89	733.41	681.67	640.95	608.22	581.47
50000	4407.44	2318.81	1625.13	1280.17	1074.70	938.95	843.04	772.01	717.55	674.68	640.23	612.08
52500	4627.81	2434.75	1706.38	1344.18	1128.43	985.90	885.19	810.61	753.43	708.41	672.24	642.68
55000	4848.18	2550.69	1787.64	1408.19	1182.17	1032.85	927.34	849.21	789.30	742.15	704.25	673.28
57500	5068.55	2666.63	1868.90	1472.20	1235.90	1079.80	969.49	887.81	825.18	775.88	736.26	703.89
60000	5288.92	2782.57	1950.15	1536.21	1289.64	1126.74	1011.65	926.41	861.06	809.61	768.27	734.49
65000	5729.66	3014.45	2112.66	1664.22	1397.11	1220.64	1095.95	1003.61	932.81	877.08	832.29	795.70
70000	6170.41	3246.33	2275.18	1792.24	1504.58	1314.53	1180.25	1080.81	1004.57	944.55	896.32	856.90
75000	6611.15	3478.21	2437.69	1920.26	1612.05	1408.43	1264.56	1158.01	1076.32	1012.02	960.34	918.11
80000	7051.89	3710.09	2600.20	2048.28	1719.52	1502.32	1348.86	1235.21	1148.07	1079.48	1024.36	979.32
85000	7492.64	3941.97	2762.71	2176.29	1826.99	1596.22	1433.16	1312.41	1219.83	1146.95	1088.38	1040.52
90000	7933.38	4173.85	2925.22	2304.31	1934.46	1690.11	1517.47	1389.61	1291.58	1214.42	1152.41	1101.73
95000	8374.12	4405.73	3087.74	2432.33	2041.93	1784.01	1601.77	1466.81	1363.34	1281.89	1216.43	1162.94
100000	8814.87	4637.61	3250.25	2560.34	2149.40	1877.90	1686.07	1544.01	1435.09	1349.35	1280.45	1224.15
105000	9255.61	4869.49	3412.76	2688.36	2256.86	1971.80	1770.38	1621.21	1506.85	1416.82	1344.47	1285.35
110000	9696.35	5101.37	3575.27	2816.38	2364.33	2065.69	1854.68	1698.41	1578.60	1484.29	1408.50	1346.56
115000	10137.09	5333.25	3737.79	2944.39	2471.80	2159.59	1938.98	1775.61	1650.35	1551.76	1472.52	1407.77
120000	10577.84	5565.13	3900.30	3072.41	2579.27	2253.48	2023.29	1852.81	1722.11	1619.22	1536.54	1468.97
125000	11018.58	5797.01	4062.81	3200.43	2686.74	2347.38	2107.59	1930.01	1793.86	1686.69	1600.56	1530.18
130000	11459.32	6028.89	4225.32	3328.44	2794.21	2441.27	2191.89	2007.21	1865.62	1754.16	1664.58	1591.39
135000	11900.07	6260.77	4387.83	3456.46	2901.68	2535.17	2276.20	2084.41	1937.37	1821.63	1728.61	1652.59
140000	12340.81	6492.65	4550.35	3584.48	3009.15	2629.06	2360.50	2161.61	2009.13	1889.09	1792.63	1713.80
145000	12781.55	6724.53	4712.86	3712.50	3116.62	2722.96	2444.80	2238.81	2080.88	1956.56	1856.65	1775.01
150000	13222.30	6956.41	4875.37	3840.51	3224.09	2816.85	2529.11	2316.01	2152.63	2024.03	1920.67	1836.22
155000	13663.04	7188.29	5037.88	3968.53	3331.56	2910.75	2613.41	2393.21	2224.39	2091.50	1984.70	1897.42
160000	14103.78	7420.17	5200.40	4096.55	3439.03	3004.64	2697.71	2470.41	2296.14	2158.96	2048.72	1958.63

AMOUNT OF LOAN	NUMBER OF YEARS IN TERM											
	13	14	15	16	17	18	19	20	25	30	35	40
$ 50	0.59	0.57	0.56	0.54	0.53	0.52	0.51	0.50	0.48	0.46	0.45	0.45
100	1.18	1.14	1.11	1.08	1.06	1.04	1.02	1.00	0.95	0.92	0.90	0.89
200	2.36	2.28	2.22	2.16	2.11	2.07	2.03	2.00	1.89	1.83	1.80	1.78
300	3.54	3.42	3.32	3.24	3.16	3.10	3.05	3.00	2.84	2.75	2.70	2.67
400	4.72	4.56	4.43	4.31	4.22	4.13	4.06	4.00	3.78	3.66	3.60	3.56
500	5.89	5.70	5.53	5.39	5.27	5.17	5.08	5.00	4.73	4.58	4.50	4.45
600	7.07	6.84	6.64	6.47	6.32	6.20	6.09	6.00	5.67	5.49	5.39	5.34
700	8.25	7.97	7.74	7.55	7.38	7.23	7.10	6.99	6.61	6.41	6.29	6.22
800	9.43	9.11	8.85	8.62	8.43	8.26	8.12	7.99	7.56	7.32	7.19	7.11
900	10.60	10.25	9.95	9.70	9.48	9.30	9.13	8.99	8.50	8.24	8.09	8.00
1000	11.78	11.39	11.06	10.78	10.54	10.33	10.15	9.99	9.45	9.15	8.99	8.89
2000	23.56	22.77	22.11	21.55	21.07	20.65	20.29	19.97	18.89	18.30	17.97	17.78
3000	35.33	34.16	33.17	32.32	31.60	30.97	30.43	29.96	28.33	27.45	26.95	26.66
4000	47.11	45.54	44.22	43.09	42.13	41.29	40.57	39.94	37.77	36.59	35.93	35.55
5000	58.88	56.93	55.27	53.87	52.66	51.62	50.71	49.92	47.21	45.74	44.91	44.43
6000	70.66	68.31	66.33	64.64	63.19	61.94	60.85	59.91	56.66	54.89	53.89	53.32
7000	82.43	79.70	77.38	75.41	73.72	72.26	70.99	69.89	66.10	64.04	62.87	62.20
8000	94.21	91.08	88.44	86.18	84.25	82.58	81.14	79.88	75.54	73.18	71.86	71.09
9000	105.98	102.46	99.49	96.96	94.78	92.91	91.28	89.86	84.98	82.33	80.84	79.98
10000	117.76	113.85	110.54	107.73	105.31	103.23	101.42	99.84	94.42	91.48	89.82	88.86
11000	129.53	125.23	121.60	118.50	115.84	113.55	111.56	109.83	103.86	100.63	98.80	97.75
12000	141.31	136.62	132.65	129.27	126.37	123.87	121.70	119.81	113.31	109.77	107.78	106.63
13000	153.08	148.00	143.71	140.05	136.91	134.19	131.84	129.79	122.75	118.92	116.76	115.52
14000	164.86	159.39	154.76	150.82	147.44	144.52	141.98	139.78	132.19	128.07	125.74	124.40
15000	176.63	170.77	165.81	161.59	157.97	154.84	152.13	149.76	141.63	137.22	134.73	133.29
16000	188.41	182.15	176.87	172.36	168.50	165.16	162.27	159.74	151.07	146.36	143.71	142.18
17000	200.18	193.54	187.92	183.14	179.03	175.48	172.41	169.73	160.52	155.51	152.69	151.06
18000	211.96	204.92	198.98	193.91	189.56	185.81	182.55	179.71	169.96	164.66	161.67	159.95
19000	223.73	216.31	210.03	204.68	200.09	196.13	192.69	189.70	179.40	173.81	170.65	168.83
20000	235.51	227.69	221.08	215.45	210.62	206.45	202.83	199.68	188.84	182.95	179.63	177.72
21000	247.28	239.08	232.14	226.23	221.15	216.77	212.97	209.66	198.28	192.10	188.61	186.60
22000	259.06	250.46	243.19	237.00	231.68	227.10	223.12	219.65	207.72	201.25	197.59	195.49
23000	270.83	261.84	254.25	247.77	242.21	237.42	233.26	229.63	217.17	210.40	206.58	204.38
24000	282.61	273.23	265.30	258.54	252.74	247.74	243.40	239.62	226.61	219.54	215.56	213.26
25000	294.38	284.61	276.35	269.32	263.28	258.06	253.54	249.60	236.05	228.69	224.54	222.15
26000	306.16	296.00	287.41	280.09	273.81	268.38	263.68	259.58	245.49	237.84	233.52	231.03
27000	317.93	307.38	298.46	290.86	284.34	278.71	273.82	269.57	254.93	246.98	242.50	239.92
28000	329.71	318.77	309.52	301.63	294.87	289.03	283.96	279.55	264.38	256.13	251.48	248.80
29000	341.48	330.15	320.57	312.41	305.40	299.35	294.11	289.54	273.82	265.28	260.46	257.69
30000	353.26	341.54	331.62	323.18	315.93	309.67	304.25	299.52	283.26	274.43	269.45	266.58
31000	365.03	352.92	342.68	333.95	326.46	320.00	314.39	309.50	292.70	283.57	278.43	275.46
32000	376.81	364.30	353.73	344.72	336.99	330.32	324.53	319.49	302.14	292.72	287.41	284.35
33000	388.58	375.69	364.79	355.50	347.52	340.64	334.67	329.47	311.58	301.87	296.39	293.23
34000	400.36	387.07	375.84	366.27	358.05	350.96	344.81	339.45	321.03	311.02	305.37	302.12
35000	412.13	398.46	386.89	377.04	368.58	361.28	354.95	349.44	330.47	320.16	314.35	311.00
37500	441.57	426.92	414.53	403.97	394.91	387.09	380.31	374.40	354.07	343.03	336.81	333.22
40000	471.01	455.38	442.16	430.90	421.24	412.90	405.66	399.36	377.68	365.90	359.26	355.43
42500	500.44	483.84	469.80	457.83	447.56	438.70	431.01	424.32	401.28	388.77	381.71	377.65
45000	529.88	512.30	497.43	484.76	473.89	464.51	456.37	449.28	424.89	411.64	404.17	399.86
47500	559.32	540.76	525.07	511.70	500.22	490.31	481.72	474.24	448.49	434.51	426.62	422.08
50000	588.76	569.22	552.70	538.63	526.55	516.12	507.07	499.19	472.10	457.37	449.07	444.29
52500	618.19	597.68	580.34	565.56	552.87	541.92	532.43	524.15	495.70	480.24	471.53	466.50
55000	647.63	626.14	607.97	592.49	579.20	567.73	557.78	549.11	519.30	503.11	493.98	488.72
57500	677.07	654.60	635.61	619.42	605.53	593.54	583.13	574.07	542.91	525.98	516.43	510.93
60000	706.51	683.07	663.24	646.35	631.85	619.34	608.49	599.03	566.51	548.85	538.89	533.15
65000	765.38	739.99	718.51	700.21	684.51	670.95	659.20	648.95	613.72	594.59	583.79	577.58
70000	824.26	796.91	773.78	754.07	737.16	722.56	709.90	698.87	660.93	640.32	628.70	622.00
75000	883.13	853.83	829.05	807.94	789.82	774.18	760.61	748.79	708.14	686.06	673.61	666.43
80000	942.01	910.75	884.32	861.80	842.47	825.79	811.32	798.71	755.35	731.80	718.51	710.86
85000	1000.88	967.67	939.59	915.66	895.12	877.40	862.02	848.63	802.56	777.53	763.42	755.29
90000	1059.76	1024.60	994.86	969.52	947.78	929.01	912.73	898.55	849.77	823.27	808.33	799.72
95000	1118.63	1081.52	1050.13	1023.39	1000.43	980.62	963.44	948.47	896.98	869.01	853.23	844.15
100000	1177.51	1138.44	1105.40	1077.25	1053.09	1032.23	1014.14	998.38	944.19	914.74	898.14	888.58
105000	1236.38	1195.36	1160.67	1131.11	1105.74	1083.84	1064.85	1048.30	991.40	960.48	943.05	933.00
110000	1295.26	1252.28	1215.94	1184.97	1158.39	1135.46	1115.56	1098.22	1038.60	1006.22	987.95	977.43
115000	1354.13	1309.20	1271.21	1238.83	1211.05	1187.07	1166.26	1148.14	1085.81	1051.96	1032.86	1021.86
120000	1413.01	1366.13	1326.48	1292.70	1263.70	1238.68	1216.97	1198.06	1133.02	1097.69	1077.77	1066.29
125000	1471.88	1423.05	1381.75	1346.56	1316.36	1290.29	1267.68	1247.98	1180.23	1143.43	1122.67	1110.72
130000	1530.76	1479.97	1437.02	1400.42	1369.01	1341.90	1318.39	1297.90	1227.43	1189.17	1167.58	1155.15
135000	1589.63	1536.89	1492.29	1454.28	1421.66	1393.51	1369.09	1347.82	1274.65	1234.90	1212.49	1199.57
140000	1648.51	1593.81	1547.56	1508.14	1474.32	1445.12	1419.80	1397.74	1321.86	1280.64	1257.39	1244.00
145000	1707.38	1650.73	1602.83	1562.01	1526.97	1496.74	1470.51	1447.66	1369.07	1326.38	1302.30	1288.43
150000	1766.26	1707.66	1658.10	1615.87	1579.63	1548.35	1521.21	1497.57	1416.28	1372.11	1347.21	1332.86
155000	1825.13	1764.58	1713.37	1669.73	1632.28	1599.96	1571.92	1547.49	1463.49	1417.85	1392.11	1377.29
160000	1884.01	1821.50	1768.64	1723.59	1684.93	1651.57	1622.63	1597.41	1510.70	1463.59	1437.02	1421.72

MONTHLY AMORTIZING PAYMENTS

AMOUNT OF LOAN	NUMBER OF YEARS IN TERM											
	1	2	3	4	5	6	7	8	9	10	11	12
$ 50	4.42	2.33	1.64	1.29	1.09	0.95	0.85	0.78	0.73	0.69	0.65	0.62
100	8.83	4.65	3.27	2.58	2.17	1.90	1.70	1.56	1.45	1.37	1.30	1.24
200	17.66	9.30	6.53	5.15	4.33	3.79	3.40	3.12	2.90	2.73	2.59	2.48
300	26.48	13.95	9.79	7.72	6.49	5.68	5.10	4.68	4.35	4.10	3.89	3.72
400	35.31	18.60	13.05	10.29	8.65	7.57	6.80	6.23	5.80	5.46	5.18	4.96
500	44.14	23.25	16.32	12.87	10.81	9.46	8.50	7.79	7.25	6.82	6.48	6.20
600	52.96	27.90	19.58	15.44	12.98	11.35	10.20	9.35	8.70	8.19	7.77	7.44
700	61.79	32.55	22.84	18.01	15.14	13.24	11.90	10.91	10.15	9.55	9.07	8.68
800	70.62	37.20	26.10	20.58	17.30	15.13	13.60	12.46	11.60	10.91	10.36	9.92
900	79.44	41.85	29.36	23.16	19.46	17.02	15.30	14.02	13.04	12.28	11.66	11.15
1000	88.27	46.50	32.63	25.73	21.62	18.91	17.00	15.58	14.49	13.64	12.95	12.39
2000	176.54	92.99	65.25	51.45	43.24	37.82	33.99	31.15	28.98	27.27	25.90	24.78
3000	264.80	139.48	97.87	77.18	64.86	56.72	50.98	46.73	43.47	40.91	38.85	37.17
4000	353.07	185.97	130.49	102.90	86.48	75.63	67.97	62.30	57.96	54.54	51.80	49.56
5000	441.33	232.46	163.11	128.63	108.09	94.54	84.96	77.87	72.45	68.17	64.74	61.95
6000	529.60	278.96	195.73	154.35	129.71	113.44	101.95	93.45	86.93	81.81	77.69	74.33
7000	617.86	325.45	228.35	180.07	151.33	132.35	118.94	109.02	101.42	95.44	90.64	86.72
8000	706.13	371.94	260.97	205.80	172.95	151.26	135.94	124.60	115.91	109.08	103.59	99.11
9000	794.39	418.43	293.59	231.52	194.57	170.16	152.93	140.17	130.40	122.71	116.54	111.50
10000	882.66	464.92	326.21	257.25	216.18	189.07	169.92	155.74	144.89	136.34	129.48	123.89
11000	970.92	511.42	358.83	282.97	237.80	207.97	186.91	171.32	159.37	149.98	142.43	136.27
12000	1059.19	557.91	391.45	308.70	259.42	226.88	203.90	186.89	173.86	163.61	155.38	148.66
13000	1147.45	604.40	424.07	334.42	281.04	245.79	220.89	202.47	188.35	177.25	168.33	161.05
14000	1235.72	650.89	456.69	360.14	302.66	264.69	237.88	218.04	202.84	190.88	181.28	173.44
15000	1323.98	697.38	489.31	385.87	324.27	283.60	254.87	233.61	217.33	204.51	194.22	185.83
16000	1412.25	743.87	521.93	411.59	345.89	302.51	271.87	249.19	231.81	218.15	207.17	198.21
17000	1500.51	790.37	554.55	437.32	367.51	321.41	288.86	264.76	246.30	231.78	220.12	210.60
18000	1588.78	836.86	587.17	463.04	389.13	340.32	305.85	280.34	260.79	245.41	233.07	222.99
19000	1677.04	883.35	619.79	488.77	410.75	359.22	322.84	295.91	275.28	259.05	246.02	235.38
20000	1765.31	929.84	652.41	514.49	432.36	378.13	339.83	311.48	289.77	272.68	258.96	247.77
21000	1853.57	976.33	685.03	540.21	453.98	397.04	356.82	327.06	304.25	286.32	271.91	260.15
22000	1941.84	1022.83	717.65	565.94	475.60	415.94	373.81	342.63	318.74	299.95	284.86	272.54
23000	2030.10	1069.32	750.28	591.66	497.22	434.85	390.80	358.20	333.23	313.58	297.81	284.93
24000	2118.37	1115.81	782.90	617.39	518.84	453.76	407.80	373.78	347.72	327.22	310.76	297.32
25000	2206.63	1162.30	815.52	643.11	540.45	472.66	424.79	389.35	362.21	340.85	323.70	309.71
26000	2294.90	1208.79	848.14	668.84	562.07	491.57	441.78	404.93	376.69	354.49	336.65	322.09
27000	2383.16	1255.29	880.76	694.56	583.69	510.47	458.77	420.50	391.18	368.12	349.60	334.48
28000	2471.43	1301.78	913.38	720.28	605.31	529.38	475.76	436.07	405.67	381.75	362.55	346.87
29000	2559.69	1348.27	946.00	746.01	626.93	548.29	492.75	451.65	420.16	395.39	375.50	359.26
30000	2647.96	1394.76	978.62	771.73	648.54	567.19	509.74	467.22	434.65	409.02	388.44	371.65
31000	2736.22	1441.25	1011.24	797.46	670.16	586.10	526.73	482.80	449.13	422.65	401.39	384.03
32000	2824.49	1487.74	1043.86	823.18	691.78	605.01	543.73	498.37	463.62	436.29	414.34	396.42
33000	2912.75	1534.24	1076.48	848.91	713.40	623.91	560.72	513.94	478.11	449.92	427.29	408.81
34000	3001.02	1580.73	1109.10	874.63	735.02	642.82	577.71	529.52	492.60	463.56	440.24	421.20
35000	3089.28	1627.22	1141.72	900.35	756.63	661.72	594.70	545.09	507.09	477.19	453.18	433.59
37000	3309.95	1743.45	1223.27	964.67	810.68	708.99	637.18	584.03	543.31	511.28	485.55	464.56
40000	3530.61	1859.68	1304.82	1028.98	864.72	756.26	679.66	622.96	579.53	545.36	517.92	495.53
42500	3751.27	1975.91	1386.37	1093.29	918.77	803.52	722.13	661.90	615.75	579.44	550.29	526.50
45000	3971.93	2092.14	1467.93	1157.60	972.81	850.79	764.61	700.83	651.97	613.53	582.66	557.47
47500	4192.60	2208.37	1549.48	1221.91	1026.86	898.05	807.09	739.77	688.19	647.61	615.03	588.44
50000	4413.26	2324.60	1631.03	1286.22	1080.90	945.32	849.57	778.70	724.41	681.70	647.40	619.40
52500	4633.92	2440.83	1712.58	1350.53	1134.95	992.58	892.05	817.63	760.63	715.78	679.77	650.38
55000	4854.58	2557.06	1794.13	1414.84	1188.99	1039.85	934.52	856.57	796.85	749.87	712.14	681.35
57500	5075.25	2673.29	1875.68	1479.15	1243.04	1087.12	977.00	895.50	833.07	783.95	744.51	712.32
60000	5295.91	2789.52	1957.23	1543.46	1297.08	1134.38	1019.48	934.44	869.29	818.04	776.88	743.29
65000	5737.24	3021.98	2120.33	1672.08	1405.17	1228.91	1104.44	1012.31	941.73	886.21	841.62	805.23
70000	6178.56	3254.43	2283.44	1800.70	1513.26	1323.44	1189.39	1090.18	1014.17	954.38	906.36	867.17
75000	6619.89	3486.89	2446.54	1929.33	1621.35	1417.98	1274.35	1168.05	1086.61	1022.55	971.10	929.11
80000	7061.21	3719.35	2609.64	2057.95	1729.44	1512.51	1359.31	1245.92	1159.05	1090.71	1035.84	991.05
85000	7502.54	3951.81	2772.74	2186.57	1837.53	1607.04	1444.26	1323.79	1231.49	1158.88	1100.58	1052.99
90000	7943.86	4184.27	2935.85	2315.19	1945.62	1701.57	1529.22	1401.66	1303.93	1227.05	1165.32	1114.93
95000	8385.19	4416.73	3098.95	2443.81	2053.71	1796.10	1614.18	1479.53	1376.37	1295.22	1230.06	1176.87
100000	8826.51	4649.19	3262.05	2572.43	2161.80	1890.63	1699.13	1557.40	1448.81	1363.39	1294.80	1238.81
105000	9267.84	4881.65	3425.15	2701.05	2269.89	1985.16	1784.09	1635.26	1521.25	1431.56	1359.54	1300.75
110000	9709.16	5114.11	3588.26	2829.68	2377.98	2079.70	1869.04	1713.13	1593.69	1499.73	1424.28	1362.69
115000	10150.49	5346.57	3751.36	2958.30	2486.07	2174.23	1954.00	1791.00	1666.13	1567.90	1489.02	1424.63
120000	10591.82	5579.03	3914.46	3086.92	2594.16	2268.76	2038.96	1868.87	1738.57	1636.07	1553.76	1486.57
125000	11033.14	5811.49	4077.56	3215.54	2702.25	2363.29	2123.91	1946.74	1811.01	1704.24	1618.50	1548.51
130000	11474.47	6043.95	4240.66	3344.16	2810.34	2457.82	2208.87	2024.61	1883.45	1772.41	1683.24	1610.45
135000	11915.79	6276.41	4403.77	3472.78	2918.43	2552.35	2293.83	2102.48	1955.89	1840.58	1747.98	1672.39
140000	12357.12	6508.86	4566.87	3601.40	3026.52	2646.88	2378.78	2180.35	2028.33	1908.75	1812.72	1734.33
145000	12798.44	6741.32	4729.97	3730.03	3134.61	2741.42	2463.74	2258.22	2100.77	1976.92	1877.46	1796.27
150000	13239.77	6973.78	4893.07	3858.65	3242.70	2835.95	2548.70	2336.09	2173.21	2045.09	1942.20	1858.21
155000	13681.09	7206.24	5056.18	3987.27	3350.79	2930.48	2633.65	2413.96	2245.65	2113.25	2006.94	1920.15
160000	14122.42	7438.70	5219.28	4115.89	3458.88	3025.01	2718.61	2491.83	2318.09	2181.42	2071.68	1982.09

MONTHLY AMORTIZING PAYMENTS 10.75%

AMOUNT OF LOAN	NUMBER OF YEARS IN TERM											
	13	14	15	16	17	18	19	20	25	30	35	40
$ 50	0.60	0.58	0.57	0.55	0.54	0.53	0.52	0.51	0.49	0.47	0.46	0.46
100	1.20	1.16	1.13	1.10	1.07	1.05	1.04	1.02	0.97	0.94	0.92	0.91
200	2.39	2.31	2.25	2.19	2.14	2.10	2.07	2.04	1.93	1.87	1.84	1.82
300	3.58	3.47	3.37	3.28	3.21	3.15	3.10	3.05	2.89	2.81	2.76	2.73
400	4.77	4.62	4.49	4.38	4.28	4.20	4.13	4.07	3.85	3.74	3.68	3.64
500	5.97	5.77	5.61	5.47	5.35	5.25	5.16	5.08	4.82	4.67	4.59	4.55
600	7.16	6.93	6.73	6.56	6.42	6.30	6.19	6.10	5.78	5.61	5.51	5.46
700	8.35	8.08	7.85	7.66	7.49	7.35	7.22	7.11	6.74	6.54	6.43	6.36
800	9.54	9.23	8.97	8.75	8.56	8.39	8.25	8.13	7.70	7.47	7.35	7.27
900	10.74	10.39	10.09	9.84	9.63	9.44	9.28	9.14	8.66	8.41	8.26	8.18
1000	11.93	11.54	11.21	10.94	10.70	10.49	10.31	10.16	9.63	9.34	9.18	9.09
2000	23.85	23.08	22.42	21.87	21.39	20.98	20.62	20.31	19.25	18.67	18.36	18.17
3000	35.78	34.62	33.63	32.80	32.08	31.46	30.93	30.46	28.87	28.01	27.53	27.26
4000	47.70	46.15	44.84	43.73	42.77	41.95	41.23	40.61	38.49	37.34	36.71	36.34
5000	59.63	57.69	56.05	54.66	53.46	52.43	51.54	50.77	48.11	46.68	45.88	45.42
6000	71.55	69.23	67.26	65.59	64.16	62.92	61.85	60.92	57.73	56.01	55.06	54.51
7000	83.48	80.76	78.47	76.52	74.85	73.41	72.16	71.07	67.35	65.35	64.23	63.59
8000	95.40	92.30	89.68	87.45	85.54	83.89	82.46	81.22	76.97	74.68	73.41	72.68
9000	107.33	103.84	100.89	98.38	96.23	94.38	92.77	91.38	86.59	84.02	82.58	81.76
10000	119.25	115.37	112.10	109.31	106.92	104.86	103.08	101.53	96.21	93.35	91.76	90.84
11000	131.18	126.91	123.31	120.24	117.61	115.35	113.39	111.68	105.84	102.69	100.93	99.93
12000	143.10	138.45	134.52	131.17	128.31	125.84	123.69	121.83	115.46	112.02	110.11	109.01
13000	155.03	149.99	145.73	142.10	139.00	136.32	134.00	131.98	125.08	121.36	119.28	118.10
14000	166.95	161.52	156.94	153.03	149.69	146.81	144.31	142.14	134.70	130.69	128.46	127.18
15000	178.88	173.06	168.15	163.97	160.38	157.29	154.62	152.29	144.32	140.03	137.63	136.26
16000	190.80	184.60	179.36	174.90	171.07	167.78	164.92	162.44	153.94	149.36	146.81	145.35
17000	202.72	196.13	190.57	185.83	181.77	178.26	175.23	172.59	163.56	158.70	155.98	154.43
18000	214.65	207.67	201.78	196.76	192.46	188.75	185.54	182.75	173.18	168.03	165.16	163.52
19000	226.57	219.21	212.99	207.69	203.15	199.24	195.85	192.90	182.80	177.37	174.33	172.60
20000	238.50	230.74	224.19	218.62	213.84	209.72	206.15	203.05	192.42	186.70	183.51	181.68
21000	250.42	242.28	235.40	229.55	224.53	220.21	216.46	213.20	202.04	196.04	192.68	190.77
22000	262.35	253.82	246.61	240.48	235.22	230.69	226.77	223.36	211.67	205.37	201.86	199.85
23000	274.27	265.36	257.82	251.41	245.92	241.18	237.08	233.51	221.29	214.71	211.03	208.94
24000	286.20	276.89	269.03	262.34	256.61	251.67	247.38	243.66	230.91	224.04	220.21	218.02
25000	298.12	288.43	280.24	273.27	267.30	262.15	257.69	253.81	240.53	233.38	229.38	227.10
26000	310.05	299.97	291.45	284.20	277.99	272.64	268.00	263.96	250.15	242.71	238.56	236.19
27000	321.97	311.50	302.66	295.13	288.68	283.12	278.31	274.12	259.77	252.04	247.73	245.27
28000	333.90	323.04	313.87	306.06	299.37	293.61	288.61	284.27	269.39	261.38	256.91	254.36
29000	345.82	334.58	325.08	317.00	310.07	304.09	298.92	294.42	279.01	270.71	266.08	263.44
30000	357.75	346.11	336.29	327.93	320.76	314.58	309.23	304.57	288.63	280.05	275.26	272.52
31000	369.67	357.65	347.50	338.86	331.45	325.07	319.54	314.73	298.25	289.38	284.43	281.61
32000	381.59	369.19	358.71	349.79	342.14	335.55	329.84	324.88	307.87	298.72	293.61	290.69
33000	393.52	380.72	369.92	360.72	352.83	346.04	340.15	335.03	317.50	308.05	302.78	299.78
34000	405.44	392.26	381.13	371.65	363.52	356.52	350.46	345.18	327.12	317.39	311.96	308.86
35000	417.37	403.80	392.34	382.58	374.22	367.01	360.77	355.34	336.74	326.72	321.13	317.94
37500	447.18	432.64	420.36	409.91	400.95	393.22	386.54	380.72	360.79	350.06	344.07	340.65
40000	476.99	461.48	448.38	437.23	427.68	419.44	412.30	406.10	384.84	373.40	367.01	363.36
42500	506.80	490.33	476.41	464.56	454.41	445.65	438.07	431.48	408.89	396.73	389.94	386.07
45000	536.62	519.17	504.43	491.89	481.14	471.87	463.84	456.86	432.95	420.07	412.88	408.78
47500	566.43	548.01	532.46	519.21	507.86	498.08	489.61	482.24	457.00	443.41	435.82	431.49
50000	596.24	576.85	560.48	546.54	534.59	524.30	515.38	507.62	481.05	466.75	458.76	454.20
52500	626.05	605.70	588.50	573.87	561.32	550.51	541.15	533.00	505.10	490.08	481.69	476.91
55000	655.86	634.54	616.53	601.19	588.05	576.73	566.92	558.38	529.16	513.42	504.63	499.62
57500	685.67	663.38	644.55	628.52	614.78	602.94	592.68	583.76	553.21	536.76	527.57	522.33
60000	715.49	692.22	672.57	655.85	641.51	629.16	618.45	609.14	577.26	560.09	550.51	545.04
65000	775.11	749.91	728.62	710.50	694.97	681.59	669.99	659.90	625.37	606.77	596.38	590.46
70000	834.73	807.59	784.67	765.15	748.43	734.01	721.53	710.67	673.47	653.44	642.26	635.88
75000	894.36	865.28	840.72	819.81	801.89	786.44	773.07	761.43	721.57	700.12	688.13	681.30
80000	953.98	922.96	896.76	874.46	855.35	838.87	824.60	812.19	769.68	746.79	734.01	726.72
85000	1013.60	980.65	952.81	929.11	908.81	891.30	876.14	862.95	817.78	793.46	779.88	772.14
90000	1073.23	1038.33	1008.86	983.77	962.27	943.73	927.68	913.71	865.89	840.14	825.76	817.56
95000	1132.85	1096.02	1064.91	1038.42	1015.72	996.16	979.21	964.47	913.99	886.81	871.63	862.98
100000	1192.47	1153.70	1120.95	1093.07	1069.18	1048.59	1030.75	1015.23	962.10	933.49	917.51	908.40
105000	1252.10	1211.39	1177.00	1147.73	1122.64	1101.02	1082.29	1066.00	1010.20	980.16	963.38	953.82
110000	1311.72	1269.07	1233.05	1202.38	1176.10	1153.45	1133.83	1116.76	1058.31	1026.83	1009.26	999.24
115000	1371.34	1326.76	1289.10	1257.04	1229.56	1205.88	1185.36	1167.52	1106.41	1073.51	1055.13	1044.66
120000	1430.97	1384.44	1345.14	1311.69	1283.02	1258.31	1236.90	1218.28	1154.52	1120.18	1101.01	1090.08
125000	1490.59	1442.12	1401.19	1366.34	1336.48	1310.74	1288.44	1269.04	1202.62	1166.86	1146.88	1135.50
130000	1550.21	1499.81	1457.24	1421.00	1389.94	1363.17	1339.98	1319.80	1250.73	1213.53	1192.76	1180.92
135000	1609.84	1557.49	1513.28	1475.65	1443.40	1415.59	1391.51	1370.56	1298.83	1260.20	1238.63	1226.34
140000	1669.46	1615.18	1569.33	1530.30	1496.85	1468.02	1443.05	1421.33	1346.93	1306.88	1284.51	1271.76
145000	1729.08	1672.86	1625.38	1584.96	1550.31	1520.45	1494.59	1472.09	1395.04	1353.55	1330.38	1317.18
150000	1788.71	1730.55	1681.43	1639.61	1603.77	1572.88	1546.13	1522.85	1443.14	1400.23	1376.26	1362.60
155000	1848.33	1788.23	1737.47	1694.26	1657.23	1625.31	1597.66	1573.61	1491.25	1446.90	1422.13	1408.02
160000	1907.95	1845.92	1793.52	1748.92	1710.69	1677.74	1649.20	1624.37	1539.35	1493.58	1468.01	1453.44

49

MONTHLY AMORTIZING PAYMENTS

AMOUNT OF LOAN	NUMBER OF YEARS IN TERM											
	1	2	3	4	5	6	7	8	9	10	11	12
$ 50	4.42	2.34	1.64	1.30	1.09	0.96	0.86	0.79	0.74	0.69	0.66	0.63
100	8.84	4.67	3.28	2.59	2.18	1.91	1.72	1.58	1.47	1.38	1.31	1.26
200	17.68	9.33	6.55	5.17	4.35	3.81	3.43	3.15	2.93	2.76	2.62	2.51
300	26.52	13.99	9.83	7.76	6.53	5.72	5.14	4.72	4.39	4.14	3.93	3.77
400	35.36	18.65	13.10	10.34	8.70	7.62	6.85	6.29	5.86	5.52	5.24	5.02
500	44.20	23.31	16.37	12.93	10.88	9.52	8.57	7.86	7.32	6.89	6.55	6.27
600	53.03	27.97	19.65	15.51	13.05	11.43	10.28	9.43	8.78	8.27	7.86	7.53
700	61.87	32.63	22.92	18.10	15.22	13.33	11.99	11.00	10.24	9.65	9.17	8.78
800	70.71	37.29	26.20	20.68	17.40	15.23	13.70	12.57	11.71	11.03	10.48	10.03
900	79.55	41.95	29.47	23.27	19.57	17.14	15.42	14.14	13.17	12.40	11.79	11.29
1000	88.39	46.61	32.74	25.85	21.75	19.04	17.13	15.71	14.63	13.78	13.10	12.54
2000	176.77	93.22	65.48	51.70	43.49	38.07	34.25	31.42	29.26	27.56	26.19	25.08
3000	265.15	139.83	98.22	77.54	65.23	57.11	51.37	47.13	43.88	41.33	39.28	37.61
4000	353.53	186.44	130.96	103.39	86.97	76.14	68.49	62.84	58.51	55.11	52.37	50.15
5000	441.91	233.04	163.70	129.23	108.72	95.18	85.62	78.55	73.13	68.88	65.47	62.68
6000	530.29	279.65	196.44	155.08	130.46	114.21	102.74	94.26	87.76	82.66	78.56	75.22
7000	618.68	326.26	229.18	180.92	152.20	133.24	119.86	109.96	102.39	96.43	91.65	87.75
8000	707.06	372.87	261.91	206.77	173.94	152.28	136.98	125.67	117.01	110.21	104.74	100.29
9000	795.44	419.48	294.65	232.61	195.69	171.31	154.11	141.38	131.64	123.98	117.84	112.82
10000	883.82	466.08	327.39	258.46	217.43	190.35	171.23	157.09	146.26	137.76	130.93	125.36
11000	972.20	512.69	360.13	284.31	239.17	209.38	188.35	172.80	160.89	151.53	144.02	137.90
12000	1060.58	559.30	392.87	310.15	260.91	228.41	205.47	188.51	175.52	165.31	157.11	150.43
13000	1148.97	605.91	425.61	336.00	282.66	247.45	222.60	204.21	190.14	179.08	170.21	162.97
14000	1237.35	652.51	458.35	361.84	304.40	266.48	239.72	219.92	204.77	192.86	183.30	175.50
15000	1325.73	699.12	491.09	387.69	326.14	285.52	256.84	235.63	219.39	206.63	196.39	188.04
16000	1414.11	745.73	523.82	413.53	347.88	304.55	273.96	251.34	234.02	220.41	209.48	200.57
17000	1502.49	792.34	556.56	439.38	369.63	323.58	291.09	267.05	248.64	234.18	222.57	213.11
18000	1590.87	838.95	589.30	465.22	391.37	342.62	308.21	282.76	263.27	247.96	235.67	225.64
19000	1679.26	885.55	622.04	491.07	413.11	361.65	325.33	298.47	277.90	261.73	248.76	238.18
20000	1767.64	932.16	654.78	516.92	434.85	380.69	342.45	314.17	292.52	275.51	261.85	250.72
21000	1856.02	978.77	687.52	542.76	456.60	399.72	359.58	329.88	307.15	289.28	274.94	263.25
22000	1944.40	1025.38	720.26	568.61	478.34	418.75	376.70	345.59	321.77	303.06	288.04	275.79
23000	2032.78	1071.99	753.00	594.45	500.08	437.79	393.82	361.30	336.40	316.83	301.13	288.32
24000	2121.16	1118.59	785.73	620.30	521.82	456.82	410.94	377.01	351.03	330.61	314.22	300.86
25000	2209.55	1165.20	818.47	646.14	543.57	475.86	428.07	392.72	365.65	344.38	327.31	313.39
26000	2297.93	1211.81	851.21	671.99	565.31	494.89	445.19	408.42	380.28	358.16	340.41	325.93
27000	2386.31	1258.42	883.95	697.83	587.05	513.93	462.31	424.13	394.90	371.93	353.50	338.46
28000	2474.69	1305.02	916.69	723.68	608.79	532.96	479.43	439.84	409.53	385.71	366.59	351.00
29000	2563.07	1351.63	949.43	749.53	630.54	551.99	496.56	455.55	424.15	399.48	379.68	363.54
30000	2651.45	1398.24	982.17	775.37	652.28	571.03	513.68	471.26	438.78	413.26	392.78	376.07
31000	2739.84	1444.85	1014.91	801.22	674.02	590.06	530.80	486.97	453.41	427.03	405.87	388.61
32000	2828.22	1491.46	1047.64	827.06	695.76	609.10	547.92	502.67	468.03	440.81	418.96	401.14
33000	2916.60	1538.06	1080.38	852.91	717.50	628.13	565.05	518.38	482.66	454.58	432.05	413.68
34000	3004.98	1584.67	1113.12	878.75	739.25	647.16	582.17	534.09	497.28	468.36	445.14	426.21
35000	3093.36	1631.28	1145.86	904.60	760.99	666.20	599.29	549.80	511.91	482.13	458.24	438.75
37500	3314.32	1747.80	1227.71	969.21	815.35	713.78	642.10	589.07	548.47	516.57	490.97	470.09
40000	3535.27	1864.32	1309.55	1033.83	869.70	761.37	684.90	628.34	585.04	551.01	523.70	501.43
42500	3756.23	1980.84	1391.40	1098.44	924.06	808.95	727.71	667.61	621.60	585.44	556.43	532.77
45000	3977.18	2097.36	1473.25	1163.05	978.41	856.54	770.51	706.88	658.17	619.88	589.16	564.10
47500	4198.13	2213.88	1555.09	1227.67	1032.77	904.12	813.32	746.16	694.73	654.32	621.89	595.44
50000	4419.09	2330.40	1636.94	1292.28	1087.13	951.71	856.13	785.43	731.30	688.76	654.62	626.78
52500	4640.04	2446.92	1718.79	1356.89	1141.48	999.29	898.93	824.70	767.86	723.19	687.35	658.12
55000	4861.00	2563.44	1800.63	1421.51	1195.84	1046.88	941.74	863.97	804.43	757.63	720.08	689.46
57500	5081.95	2679.96	1882.48	1486.12	1250.19	1094.46	984.55	903.24	840.99	792.07	752.82	720.80
60000	5302.90	2796.48	1964.33	1550.74	1304.55	1142.05	1027.35	942.51	877.56	826.51	785.55	752.14
65000	5744.81	3029.51	2128.02	1679.96	1413.26	1237.22	1112.96	1021.05	950.69	895.38	851.01	814.82
70000	6186.72	3262.55	2291.72	1809.19	1521.97	1332.39	1198.58	1099.59	1023.82	964.26	916.47	877.49
75000	6628.63	3495.59	2455.41	1938.42	1630.69	1427.56	1284.19	1178.14	1096.94	1033.13	981.93	940.17
80000	7070.54	3728.63	2619.10	2067.65	1739.40	1522.73	1369.80	1256.68	1170.07	1102.01	1047.39	1002.85
85000	7512.45	3961.67	2782.80	2196.87	1848.11	1617.90	1455.41	1335.22	1243.20	1170.88	1112.85	1065.53
90000	7954.35	4194.71	2946.49	2326.10	1956.82	1713.07	1541.02	1413.76	1316.33	1239.76	1178.32	1128.20
95000	8396.26	4427.75	3110.18	2455.33	2065.54	1808.24	1626.64	1492.31	1389.46	1308.63	1243.78	1190.88
100000	8838.17	4660.79	3273.88	2584.56	2174.25	1903.41	1712.25	1570.85	1462.59	1377.51	1309.24	1253.56
105000	9280.08	4893.83	3437.57	2713.78	2282.96	1998.58	1797.86	1649.39	1535.72	1446.38	1374.70	1316.24
110000	9721.99	5126.87	3601.26	2843.01	2391.67	2093.75	1883.47	1727.93	1608.85	1515.26	1440.16	1378.92
115000	10163.90	5359.91	3764.96	2972.24	2500.38	2188.92	1969.09	1806.47	1681.98	1584.13	1505.63	1441.59
120000	10605.80	5592.95	3928.65	3101.47	2609.10	2284.09	2054.70	1885.02	1755.11	1653.01	1571.09	1504.27
125000	11047.71	5825.98	4092.34	3230.70	2717.81	2379.26	2140.31	1963.56	1828.24	1721.88	1636.55	1566.95
130000	11489.62	6059.02	4256.04	3359.92	2826.52	2474.44	2225.92	2042.10	1901.37	1790.76	1702.01	1629.63
135000	11931.53	6292.06	4419.73	3489.15	2935.23	2569.61	2311.53	2120.64	1974.50	1859.63	1767.47	1692.30
140000	12373.44	6525.10	4583.43	3618.38	3043.94	2664.78	2397.15	2199.18	2047.63	1928.51	1832.93	1754.98
145000	12815.35	6758.14	4747.12	3747.61	3152.66	2759.95	2482.76	2277.73	2120.75	1997.38	1898.40	1817.66
150000	13257.25	6991.18	4910.81	3876.83	3261.37	2855.12	2568.37	2356.27	2193.88	2066.26	1963.86	1880.34
155000	13699.16	7224.22	5074.51	4006.06	3370.08	2950.29	2653.98	2434.81	2267.01	2135.13	2029.32	1943.02
160000	14141.07	7457.26	5238.20	4135.29	3478.79	3045.46	2739.59	2513.35	2340.14	2204.01	2094.78	2005.69

AMOUNT OF LOAN	NUMBER OF YEARS IN TERM											
	13	14	15	16	17	18	19	20	25	30	35	40
$ 50	0.61	0.59	0.57	0.56	0.55	0.54	0.53	0.52	0.50	0.48	0.47	0.47
100	1.21	1.17	1.14	1.11	1.09	1.07	1.05	1.04	0.99	0.96	0.94	0.93
200	2.42	2.34	2.28	2.22	2.18	2.14	2.10	2.07	1.97	1.91	1.88	1.86
300	3.63	3.51	3.41	3.33	3.26	3.20	3.15	3.10	2.95	2.86	2.82	2.79
400	4.84	4.68	4.55	4.44	4.35	4.27	4.19	4.13	3.93	3.81	3.75	3.72
500	6.04	5.85	5.69	5.55	5.43	5.33	5.24	5.17	4.91	4.77	4.69	4.65
600	7.25	7.02	6.82	6.66	6.52	6.40	6.29	6.20	5.89	5.72	5.63	5.57
700	8.46	8.19	7.96	7.77	7.60	7.46	7.34	7.23	6.87	6.67	6.56	6.50
800	9.67	9.36	9.10	8.88	8.69	8.53	8.38	8.26	7.85	7.62	7.50	7.43
900	10.87	10.53	10.23	9.99	9.77	9.59	9.43	9.29	8.83	8.58	8.44	8.36
1000	12.08	11.70	11.37	11.10	10.86	10.66	10.48	10.33	9.81	9.53	9.37	9.29
2000	24.16	23.39	22.74	22.19	21.71	21.31	20.95	20.65	19.61	19.05	18.74	18.57
3000	36.23	35.08	34.10	33.28	32.57	31.96	31.43	30.97	29.41	28.57	28.11	27.85
4000	48.31	46.77	45.47	44.37	43.42	42.61	41.90	41.29	39.21	38.10	37.48	37.14
5000	60.38	58.46	56.83	55.46	54.27	53.26	52.38	51.61	49.01	47.62	46.85	46.42
6000	72.46	70.15	68.20	66.55	65.13	63.91	62.85	61.94	58.81	57.14	56.22	55.70
7000	84.53	81.84	79.57	77.64	75.98	74.56	73.33	72.26	68.61	66.67	65.59	64.99
8000	96.61	93.53	90.93	88.73	86.84	85.21	83.80	82.58	78.41	76.19	74.96	74.27
9000	108.68	105.22	102.30	99.82	97.69	95.86	94.28	92.90	88.22	85.71	84.33	83.55
10000	120.76	116.91	113.66	110.91	108.54	106.51	104.75	103.22	98.02	95.24	93.70	92.83
11000	132.83	128.60	125.03	122.00	119.40	117.16	115.23	113.55	107.82	104.76	103.07	102.12
12000	144.91	140.29	136.40	133.09	130.25	127.81	125.70	123.87	117.62	114.28	112.44	111.40
13000	156.98	151.98	147.76	144.18	141.10	138.46	136.18	134.19	127.42	123.81	121.81	120.68
14000	169.06	163.67	159.13	155.27	151.96	149.11	146.65	144.51	137.22	133.33	131.18	129.97
15000	181.13	175.36	170.49	166.36	162.81	159.76	157.12	154.83	147.02	142.85	140.55	139.25
16000	193.21	187.05	181.86	177.45	173.67	170.41	167.60	165.16	156.82	152.38	149.92	148.53
17000	205.28	198.74	193.23	188.54	184.52	181.06	178.07	175.48	166.62	161.90	159.29	157.82
18000	217.36	210.43	204.59	199.63	195.37	191.71	188.55	185.80	176.43	171.42	168.66	167.10
19000	229.44	222.13	215.96	210.72	206.23	202.36	199.02	196.12	186.23	180.95	178.03	176.38
20000	241.51	233.82	227.32	221.81	217.08	213.01	209.50	206.44	196.03	190.47	187.40	185.66
21000	253.59	245.51	238.69	232.90	227.93	223.67	219.97	216.76	205.83	199.99	196.77	194.95
22000	265.66	257.20	250.06	243.99	238.79	234.32	230.45	227.09	215.63	209.52	206.14	204.23
23000	277.74	268.89	261.42	255.08	249.64	244.97	240.92	237.41	225.43	219.04	215.51	213.51
24000	289.81	280.58	272.79	266.17	260.50	255.62	251.40	247.73	235.23	228.56	224.87	222.80
25000	301.89	292.27	284.15	277.26	271.35	266.27	261.87	258.05	245.03	238.09	234.24	232.08
26000	313.96	303.96	295.52	288.35	282.20	276.92	272.35	268.37	254.83	247.61	243.61	241.36
27000	326.04	315.65	306.89	299.44	293.06	287.57	282.82	278.70	264.64	257.13	252.98	250.64
28000	338.11	327.34	318.25	310.53	303.91	298.22	293.29	289.02	274.44	266.66	262.35	259.93
29000	350.19	339.03	329.62	321.62	314.77	308.87	303.77	299.34	284.24	276.18	271.72	269.21
30000	362.26	350.72	340.98	332.71	325.62	319.52	314.24	309.66	294.04	285.70	281.09	278.49
31000	374.34	362.41	352.35	343.80	336.47	330.17	324.72	319.98	303.84	295.23	290.46	287.78
32000	386.41	374.10	363.72	354.89	347.33	340.82	335.19	330.31	313.64	304.75	299.83	297.06
33000	398.49	385.79	375.08	365.98	358.18	351.47	345.67	340.63	323.44	314.27	309.20	306.34
34000	410.56	397.48	386.45	377.07	369.03	362.12	356.14	350.95	333.24	323.79	318.57	315.63
35000	422.64	409.17	397.81	388.16	379.89	372.77	366.62	361.27	343.04	333.32	327.94	324.91
37500	452.83	438.40	426.23	415.88	407.02	399.40	392.80	387.08	367.55	357.13	351.36	348.12
40000	483.02	467.63	454.64	443.61	434.16	426.02	418.99	412.88	392.05	380.93	374.79	371.32
42500	513.20	496.85	483.06	471.33	461.29	452.65	445.18	438.69	416.55	404.74	398.21	394.53
45000	543.39	526.08	511.47	499.06	488.43	479.28	471.36	464.49	441.06	428.55	421.64	417.74
47500	573.58	555.31	539.89	526.78	515.56	505.90	497.55	490.29	465.56	452.36	445.06	440.94
50000	603.77	584.53	568.30	554.51	542.70	532.53	523.74	516.10	490.06	476.17	468.48	464.15
52500	633.96	613.76	596.72	582.23	569.83	559.16	549.92	541.90	514.56	499.97	491.91	487.36
55000	664.15	642.98	625.13	609.96	596.96	585.78	576.11	567.71	539.07	523.78	515.33	510.57
57500	694.33	672.21	653.55	637.68	624.10	612.41	602.30	593.51	563.57	547.59	538.76	533.77
60000	724.52	701.44	681.96	665.41	651.23	639.03	628.48	619.32	588.07	571.40	562.18	556.98
65000	784.90	759.89	738.79	720.86	705.50	692.29	680.86	670.93	637.08	619.02	609.03	603.40
70000	845.27	818.34	795.62	776.31	759.77	745.54	733.23	722.54	686.08	666.63	655.88	649.81
75000	905.65	876.80	852.45	831.76	814.04	798.79	785.60	774.15	735.09	714.25	702.72	696.23
80000	966.03	935.25	909.28	887.21	868.31	852.04	837.98	825.76	784.10	761.86	749.57	742.64
85000	1026.40	993.70	966.11	942.66	922.58	905.30	890.35	877.37	833.10	809.48	796.42	789.06
90000	1086.78	1052.15	1022.94	998.11	976.85	958.55	942.72	928.97	882.11	857.10	843.27	835.47
95000	1147.16	1110.61	1079.77	1053.56	1031.12	1011.80	995.10	980.58	931.11	904.71	890.11	881.88
100000	1207.53	1169.06	1136.60	1109.01	1085.39	1065.05	1047.47	1032.19	980.12	952.33	936.96	928.30
105000	1267.91	1227.51	1193.43	1164.46	1139.65	1118.31	1099.84	1083.80	1029.12	999.94	983.81	974.71
110000	1328.29	1285.96	1250.26	1219.91	1193.92	1171.56	1152.22	1135.41	1078.13	1047.56	1030.66	1021.13
115000	1388.66	1344.42	1307.09	1275.36	1248.19	1224.81	1204.59	1187.02	1127.14	1095.18	1077.51	1067.54
120000	1449.04	1402.87	1363.92	1330.81	1302.46	1278.06	1256.96	1238.63	1176.14	1142.79	1124.35	1113.96
125000	1509.41	1461.32	1420.75	1386.26	1356.73	1331.32	1309.33	1290.24	1225.15	1190.41	1171.20	1160.37
130000	1569.79	1519.78	1477.58	1441.71	1411.00	1384.57	1361.71	1341.85	1274.15	1238.03	1218.05	1206.79
135000	1630.17	1578.23	1534.41	1497.16	1465.27	1437.82	1414.08	1393.46	1323.16	1285.64	1264.90	1253.20
140000	1690.54	1636.68	1591.24	1552.61	1519.54	1491.07	1466.45	1445.07	1372.16	1333.26	1311.75	1299.62
145000	1750.92	1695.13	1648.07	1608.06	1573.81	1544.33	1518.83	1496.68	1421.17	1380.87	1358.59	1346.03
150000	1811.30	1753.59	1704.90	1663.51	1628.08	1597.58	1571.20	1548.29	1470.17	1428.49	1405.44	1392.45
155000	1871.67	1812.04	1761.73	1718.96	1682.34	1650.83	1623.57	1599.90	1519.18	1476.11	1452.29	1438.86
160000	1932.05	1870.49	1818.56	1774.41	1736.61	1704.08	1675.95	1651.51	1568.19	1523.72	1499.14	1485.28

MONTHLY AMORTIZING PAYMENTS

AMOUNT OF LOAN	NUMBER OF YEARS IN TERM											
	1	2	3	4	5	6	7	8	9	10	11	12
$ 50	4.43	2.34	1.65	1.30	1.10	0.96	0.87	0.80	0.74	0.70	0.67	0.64
100	8.85	4.68	3.29	2.60	2.19	1.92	1.73	1.59	1.48	1.40	1.33	1.27
200	17.70	9.35	6.58	5.20	4.38	3.84	3.46	3.17	2.96	2.79	2.65	2.54
300	26.55	14.02	9.86	7.80	6.57	5.75	5.18	4.76	4.43	4.18	3.98	3.81
400	35.40	18.69	13.15	10.39	8.75	7.67	6.91	6.34	5.91	5.57	5.30	5.08
500	44.25	23.37	16.43	12.99	10.94	9.59	8.63	7.93	7.39	6.96	6.62	6.35
600	53.10	28.04	19.72	15.59	13.13	11.50	10.36	9.51	8.86	8.36	7.95	7.62
700	61.95	32.71	23.01	18.18	15.31	13.42	12.08	11.10	10.34	9.75	9.27	8.88
800	70.80	37.38	26.29	20.78	17.50	15.33	13.81	12.68	11.82	11.14	10.60	10.15
900	79.65	42.06	29.58	23.38	19.69	17.25	15.53	14.26	13.29	12.53	11.92	11.42
1000	88.50	46.73	32.86	25.97	21.87	19.17	17.26	15.85	14.77	13.92	13.24	12.69
2000	177.00	93.45	65.72	51.94	43.74	38.33	34.51	31.69	29.53	27.84	26.48	25.37
3000	265.50	140.18	98.58	77.91	65.61	57.49	51.77	47.54	44.30	41.76	39.72	38.06
4000	354.00	186.90	131.43	103.87	87.47	76.65	69.02	63.38	59.06	55.67	52.96	50.74
5000	442.50	233.62	164.29	129.84	109.34	95.82	86.28	79.22	73.83	69.59	66.19	63.42
6000	530.99	280.35	197.15	155.81	131.21	114.98	103.53	95.07	88.59	83.51	79.43	76.11
7000	619.49	327.07	230.01	181.77	153.08	134.14	120.78	110.91	103.36	97.42	92.67	88.79
8000	707.99	373.80	262.86	207.74	174.94	153.30	138.04	126.75	118.12	111.34	105.91	101.48
9000	796.49	420.52	295.72	233.71	196.81	172.47	155.29	142.60	132.88	125.26	119.14	114.16
10000	884.99	467.24	328.58	259.68	218.68	191.63	172.55	158.44	147.65	139.17	132.38	126.84
11000	973.49	513.97	361.43	285.64	240.55	210.79	189.80	174.28	162.41	153.09	145.62	139.53
12000	1061.98	560.69	394.29	311.61	262.41	229.95	207.06	190.13	177.18	167.01	158.86	152.21
13000	1150.48	607.42	427.15	337.58	284.28	249.12	224.31	205.97	191.94	180.92	172.09	164.90
14000	1238.98	654.14	460.01	363.54	306.15	268.28	241.56	221.82	206.71	194.84	185.33	177.58
15000	1327.48	700.86	492.86	389.51	328.01	287.44	258.82	237.66	221.47	208.76	198.57	190.26
16000	1415.98	747.59	525.72	415.48	349.88	306.60	276.07	253.50	236.24	222.68	211.81	202.95
17000	1504.48	794.31	558.58	441.45	371.75	325.77	293.33	269.35	251.00	236.59	225.04	215.63
18000	1592.97	841.04	591.44	467.41	393.62	344.93	310.58	285.19	265.76	250.51	238.28	228.32
19000	1681.47	887.76	624.29	493.38	415.48	364.09	327.83	301.03	280.53	264.43	251.52	241.00
20000	1769.97	934.48	657.15	519.35	437.35	383.25	345.09	316.88	295.29	278.34	264.76	253.68
21000	1858.47	981.21	690.01	545.31	459.22	402.41	362.34	332.72	310.06	292.26	277.99	266.37
22000	1946.97	1027.93	722.86	571.28	481.09	421.58	379.60	348.56	324.82	306.18	291.23	279.05
23000	2035.47	1074.66	755.72	597.25	502.95	440.74	396.85	364.41	339.59	320.09	304.47	291.74
24000	2123.96	1121.38	788.58	623.22	524.82	459.90	414.11	380.25	354.35	334.01	317.71	304.42
25000	2212.46	1168.10	821.44	649.18	546.69	479.06	431.36	396.09	369.12	347.93	330.94	317.10
26000	2300.96	1214.83	854.29	675.15	568.56	498.23	448.61	411.94	383.88	361.84	344.18	329.79
27000	2389.46	1261.55	887.15	701.12	590.42	517.39	465.87	427.78	398.64	375.76	357.42	342.47
28000	2477.96	1308.28	920.01	727.08	612.29	536.55	483.12	443.63	413.41	389.68	370.66	355.16
29000	2566.46	1355.00	952.86	753.05	634.16	555.71	500.38	459.47	428.17	403.59	383.89	367.84
30000	2654.95	1401.72	985.72	779.02	656.02	574.88	517.63	475.31	442.94	417.51	397.13	380.52
31000	2743.45	1448.45	1018.58	804.99	677.89	594.04	534.88	491.16	457.70	431.43	410.37	393.21
32000	2831.95	1495.17	1051.44	830.95	699.76	613.20	552.14	507.00	472.47	445.35	423.61	405.89
33000	2920.45	1541.90	1084.29	856.92	721.63	632.36	569.39	522.84	487.23	459.26	436.84	418.57
34000	3008.95	1588.62	1117.15	882.89	743.49	651.53	586.65	538.69	502.00	473.18	450.08	431.26
35000	3097.45	1635.34	1150.01	908.85	765.36	670.69	603.90	554.53	516.76	487.10	463.32	443.94
37500	3318.69	1752.15	1232.15	973.77	820.03	718.59	647.04	594.14	553.67	521.89	496.41	475.65
40000	3539.94	1868.96	1314.29	1038.69	874.70	766.50	690.17	633.75	590.58	556.68	529.51	507.36
42500	3761.18	1985.77	1396.44	1103.61	929.37	814.41	733.31	673.36	627.49	591.47	562.60	539.07
45000	3982.43	2102.58	1478.58	1168.52	984.03	862.31	776.44	712.97	664.40	626.27	595.69	570.78
47500	4203.67	2219.39	1560.72	1233.44	1038.70	910.22	819.58	752.58	701.31	661.06	628.79	602.49
50000	4424.92	2336.20	1642.87	1298.36	1093.37	958.12	862.71	792.18	738.23	695.85	661.88	634.20
52500	4646.17	2453.01	1725.01	1363.28	1148.04	1006.03	905.85	831.79	775.14	730.64	694.97	665.91
55000	4867.41	2569.82	1807.15	1428.20	1202.71	1053.94	948.98	871.40	812.05	765.43	728.07	697.62
57500	5088.66	2686.63	1889.30	1493.11	1257.38	1101.84	992.12	911.01	848.96	800.23	761.16	729.33
60000	5309.90	2803.44	1971.44	1558.03	1312.04	1149.75	1035.26	950.62	885.87	835.02	794.26	761.04
65000	5752.40	3037.06	2135.73	1687.87	1421.38	1245.56	1121.53	1029.84	959.69	904.60	860.44	824.46
70000	6194.89	3270.68	2300.01	1817.70	1530.72	1341.37	1207.80	1109.06	1033.51	974.19	926.63	887.88
75000	6637.38	3504.30	2464.30	1947.54	1640.05	1437.18	1294.07	1188.27	1107.34	1043.79	992.82	951.30
80000	7079.87	3737.92	2628.58	2077.37	1749.39	1532.99	1380.34	1267.49	1181.16	1113.36	1059.01	1014.72
85000	7522.36	3971.54	2792.87	2207.21	1858.73	1628.81	1466.61	1346.71	1254.98	1182.94	1125.19	1078.14
90000	7964.85	4205.16	2957.16	2337.04	1968.06	1724.62	1552.88	1425.93	1328.80	1252.53	1191.38	1141.56
95000	8407.34	4438.78	3121.44	2466.88	2077.40	1820.43	1639.15	1505.15	1402.62	1322.11	1257.57	1204.98
100000	8849.84	4672.40	3285.73	2596.71	2186.74	1916.24	1725.42	1584.36	1476.45	1391.69	1323.76	1268.40
105000	9292.33	4906.02	3450.01	2726.55	2296.07	2012.05	1811.69	1663.58	1550.27	1461.28	1389.94	1331.82
110000	9734.82	5139.64	3614.30	2856.39	2405.41	2107.87	1897.96	1742.80	1624.09	1530.86	1456.13	1395.24
115000	10177.31	5373.26	3778.59	2986.22	2514.75	2203.68	1984.23	1822.02	1697.91	1600.45	1522.32	1458.66
120000	10619.80	5606.88	3942.87	3116.06	2624.08	2299.49	2070.51	1901.24	1771.73	1670.03	1588.51	1522.08
125000	11062.29	5840.50	4107.16	3245.89	2733.42	2395.30	2156.78	1980.45	1845.56	1739.62	1654.70	1585.50
130000	11504.79	6074.12	4271.45	3375.73	2842.76	2491.11	2243.05	2059.67	1919.38	1809.20	1720.88	1648.92
135000	11947.28	6307.74	4435.73	3505.56	2952.09	2586.93	2329.32	2138.89	1993.20	1878.79	1787.07	1712.34
140000	12389.77	6541.36	4600.02	3635.40	3061.43	2682.74	2415.59	2218.11	2067.02	1948.37	1853.26	1775.76
145000	12832.26	6774.98	4764.30	3765.23	3170.76	2778.55	2501.86	2297.32	2140.84	2017.95	1919.45	1839.17
150000	13274.75	7008.60	4928.59	3895.07	3280.10	2874.36	2588.13	2376.54	2214.67	2087.54	1985.63	1902.59
155000	13717.24	7242.22	5092.88	4024.91	3389.44	2970.17	2674.40	2455.76	2288.49	2157.12	2051.82	1966.01
160000	14159.74	7475.84	5257.16	4154.74	3498.77	3065.98	2760.67	2534.98	2362.31	2226.71	2118.01	2029.43

MONTHLY AMORTIZING PAYMENTS 11.25%

AMOUNT OF LOAN	NUMBER OF YEARS IN TERM											
	13	14	15	16	17	18	19	20	25	30	35	40
$ 50	0.62	0.60	0.58	0.57	0.56	0.55	0.54	0.53	0.50	0.49	0.48	0.48
100	1.23	1.19	1.16	1.13	1.11	1.09	1.07	1.05	1.00	0.98	0.96	0.95
200	2.45	2.37	2.31	2.26	2.21	2.17	2.13	2.10	2.00	1.95	1.92	1.90
300	3.67	3.56	3.46	3.38	3.31	3.25	3.20	3.15	3.00	2.92	2.87	2.85
400	4.90	4.74	4.61	4.51	4.41	4.33	4.26	4.20	4.00	3.89	3.83	3.80
500	6.12	5.93	5.77	5.63	5.51	5.41	5.33	5.25	5.00	4.86	4.79	4.75
600	7.34	7.11	6.92	6.76	6.62	6.49	6.39	6.30	5.99	5.83	5.74	5.69
700	8.56	8.30	8.07	7.88	7.72	7.58	7.46	7.35	6.99	6.80	6.70	6.64
800	9.79	9.48	9.22	9.01	8.82	8.66	8.52	8.40	7.99	7.78	7.66	7.59
900	11.01	10.67	10.38	10.13	9.92	9.74	9.58	9.45	8.99	8.75	8.61	8.54
1000	12.23	11.85	11.53	11.26	11.02	10.82	10.65	10.50	9.99	9.72	9.57	9.49
2000	24.46	23.70	23.05	22.51	22.04	21.64	21.29	20.99	19.97	19.43	19.13	18.97
3000	36.69	35.54	34.58	33.76	33.06	32.45	31.93	31.48	29.95	29.14	28.70	28.45
4000	48.91	47.39	46.10	45.01	44.07	43.27	42.58	41.98	39.93	38.86	38.26	37.94
5000	61.14	59.23	57.62	56.26	55.09	54.09	53.22	52.47	49.92	48.57	47.83	47.42
6000	73.37	71.08	69.15	67.51	66.11	64.90	63.86	62.96	59.90	58.28	57.39	56.90
7000	85.59	82.92	80.67	78.76	77.12	75.72	74.51	73.45	69.88	67.99	66.96	66.38
8000	97.82	94.77	92.19	90.01	88.14	86.53	85.15	83.95	79.86	77.71	76.52	75.87
9000	110.05	106.61	103.72	101.26	99.16	97.35	95.79	94.44	89.85	87.42	86.09	85.35
10000	122.27	118.46	115.24	112.51	110.17	108.17	106.43	104.93	99.83	97.13	95.65	94.83
11000	134.50	130.30	126.76	123.76	121.19	118.98	117.08	115.42	109.81	106.84	105.22	104.31
12000	146.73	142.15	138.29	135.01	132.21	129.80	127.72	125.92	119.79	116.56	114.78	113.80
13000	158.95	153.99	149.81	146.26	143.22	140.62	138.36	136.41	129.78	126.27	124.35	123.28
14000	171.18	165.84	161.33	157.51	154.24	151.43	149.01	146.90	139.76	135.98	133.91	132.76
15000	183.41	177.68	172.86	168.76	165.26	162.25	159.65	157.39	149.74	145.69	143.48	142.24
16000	195.63	189.53	184.38	180.01	176.27	173.06	170.29	167.89	159.72	155.41	153.04	151.73
17000	207.86	201.37	195.90	191.26	187.29	183.88	180.93	178.38	169.71	165.12	162.61	161.21
18000	220.09	213.22	207.43	202.51	198.31	194.70	191.58	188.87	179.69	174.83	172.17	170.69
19000	232.31	225.06	218.95	213.76	209.33	205.51	202.22	199.36	189.67	184.54	181.74	180.17
20000	244.54	236.91	230.47	225.01	220.34	216.33	212.86	209.86	199.65	194.26	191.30	189.66
21000	256.77	248.75	242.00	236.26	231.36	227.15	223.51	220.35	209.64	203.97	200.87	199.14
22000	268.99	260.60	253.52	247.51	242.38	237.96	234.15	230.84	219.62	213.68	210.43	208.62
23000	281.22	272.44	265.04	258.76	253.39	248.78	244.79	241.33	229.60	223.40	220.00	218.10
24000	293.45	284.29	276.57	270.01	264.41	259.59	255.43	251.83	239.58	233.11	229.56	227.59
25000	305.67	296.13	288.09	281.26	275.43	270.41	266.08	262.32	249.56	242.82	239.13	237.07
26000	317.90	307.98	299.61	292.51	286.44	281.23	276.72	272.81	259.55	252.53	248.69	246.55
27000	330.13	319.82	311.14	303.76	297.46	292.04	287.36	283.30	269.53	262.25	258.26	256.03
28000	342.35	331.67	322.66	315.01	308.48	302.86	298.01	293.80	279.51	271.96	267.82	265.52
29000	354.58	343.51	334.18	326.26	319.49	313.67	308.65	304.29	289.49	281.67	277.39	275.00
30000	366.81	355.36	345.71	337.51	330.51	324.49	319.29	314.78	299.48	291.38	286.95	284.48
31000	379.03	367.20	357.23	348.77	341.53	335.31	329.93	325.27	309.46	301.10	296.52	293.96
32000	391.26	379.05	368.76	360.02	352.54	346.12	340.58	335.77	319.44	310.81	306.08	303.45
33000	403.49	390.89	380.28	371.27	363.56	356.94	351.22	346.26	329.42	320.52	315.65	312.93
34000	415.72	402.74	391.80	382.52	374.58	367.76	361.86	356.75	339.41	330.23	325.21	322.41
35000	427.94	414.58	403.33	393.77	385.60	378.57	372.51	367.24	349.39	339.95	334.78	331.90
37500	458.51	444.20	432.13	421.89	413.14	405.61	399.11	393.48	374.34	364.23	358.69	355.60
40000	489.08	473.81	460.94	450.02	440.68	432.65	425.72	419.71	399.30	388.51	382.60	379.31
42500	519.64	503.42	489.75	478.14	468.22	459.69	452.33	445.94	424.26	412.79	406.51	403.01
45000	550.21	533.03	518.56	506.27	495.76	486.73	478.94	472.17	449.21	437.07	430.43	426.72
47500	580.78	562.65	547.37	534.40	523.31	513.77	505.54	498.40	474.17	461.35	454.34	450.43
50000	611.34	592.26	576.18	562.52	550.85	540.82	532.15	524.63	499.12	485.64	478.25	474.13
52500	641.91	621.87	604.99	590.65	578.39	567.86	558.76	550.86	524.08	509.92	502.16	497.84
55000	672.48	651.48	633.79	618.77	605.93	594.90	585.36	577.10	549.04	534.20	526.08	521.55
57500	703.04	681.10	662.60	646.90	633.48	621.94	611.97	603.33	573.99	558.48	549.99	545.25
60000	733.61	710.71	691.41	675.02	661.02	648.98	638.58	629.56	598.95	582.76	573.90	568.96
65000	794.75	769.94	749.03	731.28	716.10	703.06	691.79	682.02	648.86	631.32	621.73	616.37
70000	855.88	829.16	806.65	787.53	771.19	757.14	745.01	734.48	698.77	679.89	669.55	663.79
75000	917.01	888.39	864.26	843.78	826.27	811.22	798.22	786.95	748.68	728.45	717.38	711.20
80000	978.15	947.61	921.88	900.03	881.35	865.30	851.44	839.41	798.60	777.01	765.20	758.61
85000	1039.28	1006.84	979.50	956.28	936.44	919.38	904.65	891.87	848.51	825.58	813.02	806.02
90000	1100.41	1066.06	1037.12	1012.53	991.52	973.46	957.86	944.34	898.42	874.14	860.85	853.44
95000	1161.55	1125.29	1094.73	1068.79	1046.61	1027.54	1011.08	996.80	948.33	922.70	908.67	900.85
100000	1222.68	1184.51	1152.35	1125.04	1101.69	1081.63	1064.29	1049.26	998.24	971.27	956.50	948.26
105000	1283.82	1243.74	1209.97	1181.29	1156.78	1135.71	1117.51	1101.72	1048.16	1019.83	1004.32	995.68
110000	1344.95	1302.96	1267.58	1237.54	1211.86	1189.79	1170.72	1154.19	1098.07	1068.39	1052.15	1043.09
115000	1406.08	1362.19	1325.20	1293.79	1266.95	1243.87	1223.94	1206.65	1147.98	1116.96	1099.97	1090.50
120000	1467.22	1421.41	1382.81	1350.04	1322.03	1297.95	1277.15	1259.11	1197.89	1165.52	1147.80	1137.91
125000	1528.35	1480.64	1440.44	1406.30	1377.11	1352.03	1330.37	1311.58	1247.80	1214.08	1195.62	1185.33
130000	1589.49	1539.87	1498.05	1462.55	1432.20	1406.11	1383.58	1364.04	1297.72	1262.64	1243.45	1232.74
135000	1650.62	1599.09	1555.67	1518.80	1487.28	1460.19	1436.79	1416.50	1347.63	1311.21	1291.27	1280.15
140000	1711.75	1658.32	1613.29	1575.05	1542.37	1514.27	1490.01	1468.96	1397.54	1359.77	1339.10	1327.57
145000	1772.89	1717.54	1670.90	1631.30	1597.45	1568.35	1543.22	1521.43	1447.45	1408.33	1386.92	1374.98
150000	1834.02	1776.77	1728.52	1687.55	1652.54	1622.44	1596.44	1573.89	1497.36	1456.90	1434.75	1422.39
155000	1895.15	1835.99	1786.14	1743.81	1707.62	1676.52	1649.65	1626.35	1547.28	1505.46	1482.57	1469.80
160000	1956.29	1895.22	1843.76	1800.06	1762.70	1730.60	1702.87	1678.81	1597.19	1554.02	1530.40	1517.22

53

11.50% MONTHLY AMORTIZING PAYMENTS

AMOUNT OF LOAN	NUMBER OF YEARS IN TERM											
	1	2	3	4	5	6	7	8	9	10	11	12
$ 50	4.44	2.35	1.65	1.31	1.10	0.97	0.87	0.80	0.75	0.71	0.67	0.65
100	8.87	4.69	3.30	2.61	2.20	1.93	1.74	1.60	1.50	1.41	1.34	1.29
200	17.73	9.37	6.60	5.22	4.40	3.86	3.48	3.20	2.99	2.82	2.68	2.57
300	26.59	14.06	9.90	7.83	6.60	5.79	5.22	4.80	4.48	4.22	4.02	3.85
400	35.45	18.74	13.20	10.44	8.80	7.72	6.96	6.40	5.97	5.63	5.36	5.14
500	44.31	23.43	16.49	13.05	11.00	9.65	8.70	7.99	7.46	7.03	6.70	6.42
600	53.17	28.11	19.79	15.66	13.20	11.58	10.44	9.59	8.95	8.44	8.04	7.70
700	62.04	32.79	23.09	18.27	15.40	13.51	12.18	11.19	10.44	9.85	9.37	8.99
800	70.90	37.48	26.39	20.88	17.60	15.44	13.91	12.79	11.93	11.25	10.71	10.27
900	79.76	42.16	29.68	23.49	19.80	17.37	15.65	14.39	13.42	12.66	12.05	11.55
1000	88.62	46.85	32.98	26.09	22.00	19.30	17.39	15.98	14.91	14.06	13.39	12.84
2000	177.24	93.69	65.96	52.18	43.99	38.59	34.78	31.96	29.81	28.12	26.77	25.67
3000	265.85	140.53	98.93	78.27	65.98	57.88	52.16	47.94	44.72	42.18	40.16	38.50
4000	354.47	187.37	131.91	104.36	87.98	77.17	69.55	63.92	59.62	56.24	53.54	51.34
5000	443.08	234.21	164.89	130.45	109.97	96.46	86.94	79.90	74.52	70.30	66.92	64.17
6000	531.70	281.05	197.86	156.54	131.96	115.75	104.32	95.88	89.43	84.36	80.31	77.00
7000	620.31	327.89	230.84	182.63	153.95	135.04	121.71	111.86	104.33	98.42	93.69	89.84
8000	708.93	374.73	263.81	208.72	175.95	154.33	139.10	127.84	119.23	112.48	107.07	102.67
9000	797.54	421.57	296.79	234.81	197.94	173.63	156.48	143.82	134.14	126.54	120.46	115.50
10000	886.16	468.41	329.77	260.90	219.93	192.92	173.87	159.80	149.04	140.60	133.84	128.34
11000	974.77	515.25	362.74	286.98	241.92	212.21	191.26	175.78	163.95	154.66	147.22	141.17
12000	1063.39	562.09	395.72	313.07	263.92	231.50	208.64	191.76	178.85	168.72	160.61	154.00
13000	1152.00	608.93	428.69	339.16	285.91	250.79	226.03	207.74	193.75	182.78	173.99	166.84
14000	1240.62	655.77	461.67	365.25	307.90	270.08	243.42	223.72	208.66	196.84	187.37	179.67
15000	1329.23	702.61	494.65	391.34	329.89	289.37	260.80	239.70	223.56	210.90	200.76	192.50
16000	1417.85	749.45	527.62	417.43	351.89	308.66	278.19	255.67	238.46	224.96	214.14	205.34
17000	1506.46	796.29	560.60	443.52	373.88	327.95	295.57	271.65	253.37	239.02	227.52	218.17
18000	1595.08	843.13	593.57	469.61	395.87	347.25	312.96	287.63	268.27	253.08	240.91	231.00
19000	1683.69	889.97	626.55	495.70	417.86	366.54	330.35	303.61	283.17	267.14	254.29	243.84
20000	1772.31	936.81	659.53	521.79	439.86	385.83	347.73	319.59	298.08	281.20	267.68	256.67
21000	1860.92	983.65	692.50	547.87	461.85	405.12	365.12	335.57	312.98	295.26	281.06	269.50
22000	1949.54	1030.49	725.48	573.96	483.84	424.41	382.51	351.55	327.89	309.31	294.44	282.33
23000	2038.15	1077.33	758.45	600.05	505.83	443.70	399.89	367.53	342.79	323.37	307.83	295.17
24000	2126.77	1124.17	791.43	626.14	527.83	462.99	417.28	383.51	357.69	337.43	321.21	308.00
25000	2215.38	1171.01	824.41	652.23	549.82	482.28	434.67	399.49	372.60	351.49	334.59	320.83
26000	2304.00	1217.85	857.38	678.32	571.81	501.58	452.05	415.47	387.50	365.55	347.98	333.67
27000	2392.61	1264.69	890.36	704.41	593.81	520.87	469.44	431.45	402.40	379.61	361.36	346.50
28000	2481.23	1311.53	923.33	730.50	615.80	540.16	486.83	447.43	417.31	393.67	374.74	359.33
29000	2569.84	1358.37	956.31	756.59	637.79	559.45	504.21	463.41	432.21	407.73	388.13	372.17
30000	2658.46	1405.21	989.29	782.68	659.78	578.74	521.60	479.39	447.11	421.79	401.51	385.00
31000	2747.07	1452.05	1022.26	808.76	681.78	598.03	538.99	495.37	462.02	435.85	414.89	397.83
32000	2835.69	1498.90	1055.24	834.85	703.77	617.32	556.37	511.34	476.92	449.91	428.28	410.67
33000	2924.30	1545.74	1088.21	860.94	725.76	636.61	573.76	527.32	491.83	463.97	441.66	423.50
34000	3012.92	1592.58	1121.19	887.03	747.75	655.90	591.14	543.30	506.73	478.03	455.04	436.33
35000	3101.53	1639.42	1154.17	913.12	769.75	675.20	608.53	559.28	521.63	492.09	468.43	449.17
37500	3323.07	1756.52	1236.61	978.34	824.73	723.42	652.00	599.23	558.89	527.24	501.89	481.25
40000	3544.61	1873.62	1319.05	1043.57	879.71	771.65	695.46	639.18	596.15	562.39	535.35	513.33
42500	3766.14	1990.72	1401.49	1108.79	934.69	819.88	738.93	679.13	633.41	597.54	568.80	545.41
45000	3987.68	2107.82	1483.93	1174.01	989.67	868.11	782.40	719.08	670.67	632.68	602.26	577.50
47500	4209.22	2224.92	1566.37	1239.23	1044.65	916.33	825.86	759.03	707.93	667.83	635.72	609.58
50000	4430.76	2342.02	1648.81	1304.46	1099.64	964.56	869.33	798.97	745.19	702.98	669.18	641.66
52500	4652.30	2459.12	1731.25	1369.68	1154.62	1012.79	912.79	838.92	782.45	738.13	702.64	673.75
55000	4873.83	2576.22	1813.69	1434.90	1209.60	1061.02	956.26	878.87	819.71	773.28	736.10	705.83
57500	5095.37	2693.32	1896.13	1500.12	1264.58	1109.25	999.73	918.82	856.97	808.43	769.56	737.91
60000	5316.91	2810.42	1978.57	1565.35	1319.56	1157.47	1043.19	958.77	894.22	843.58	803.02	769.99
65000	5759.98	3044.63	2143.45	1695.79	1429.52	1253.93	1130.12	1038.66	968.74	913.88	869.93	834.16
70000	6203.06	3278.83	2308.33	1826.24	1539.49	1350.39	1217.06	1118.56	1043.26	984.17	936.85	898.33
75000	6646.13	3513.03	2473.21	1956.68	1649.45	1446.84	1303.99	1198.46	1117.78	1054.47	1003.77	962.49
80000	7089.21	3747.23	2638.09	2087.13	1759.41	1543.30	1390.92	1278.35	1192.30	1124.77	1070.69	1026.66
85000	7532.28	3981.43	2802.97	2217.57	1869.38	1639.75	1477.85	1358.25	1266.82	1195.07	1137.60	1090.82
90000	7975.36	4215.63	2967.85	2348.02	1979.34	1736.21	1564.79	1438.15	1341.33	1265.36	1204.52	1154.99
95000	8418.44	4449.83	3132.73	2478.46	2089.30	1832.66	1651.72	1518.05	1415.85	1335.66	1271.44	1219.16
100000	8861.51	4684.04	3297.61	2608.91	2199.27	1929.12	1738.65	1597.94	1490.37	1405.96	1338.36	1283.32
105000	9304.59	4918.24	3462.49	2739.35	2309.23	2025.58	1825.58	1677.84	1564.89	1476.26	1405.27	1347.49
110000	9747.66	5152.44	3627.37	2869.80	2419.19	2122.03	1912.52	1757.74	1639.41	1546.55	1472.19	1411.65
115000	10190.74	5386.64	3792.25	3000.24	2529.15	2218.49	1999.45	1837.63	1713.93	1616.85	1539.11	1475.82
120000	10633.81	5620.84	3957.13	3130.69	2639.12	2314.94	2086.38	1917.53	1788.44	1687.15	1606.03	1539.98
125000	11076.89	5855.04	4122.01	3261.13	2749.08	2411.40	2173.31	1997.43	1862.96	1757.45	1672.94	1604.15
130000	11519.96	6089.25	4286.89	3391.58	2859.04	2507.86	2260.24	2077.32	1937.48	1827.75	1739.86	1668.32
135000	11963.04	6323.45	4451.77	3522.02	2969.01	2604.31	2347.18	2157.22	2012.00	1898.04	1806.78	1732.48
140000	12406.11	6557.65	4616.65	3652.47	3078.97	2700.77	2434.11	2237.12	2086.52	1968.34	1873.70	1796.65
145000	12849.19	6791.85	4781.53	3782.91	3188.93	2797.22	2521.04	2317.01	2161.04	2038.64	1940.61	1860.81
150000	13292.26	7026.05	4946.41	3913.36	3298.90	2893.68	2607.97	2396.91	2235.55	2108.94	2007.53	1924.98
155000	13735.34	7260.25	5111.29	4043.80	3408.86	2990.13	2694.91	2476.81	2310.07	2179.23	2074.45	1989.15
160000	14178.41	7494.46	5276.17	4174.25	3518.82	3086.59	2781.84	2556.70	2384.59	2249.53	2141.37	2053.31

54

AMOUNT OF LOAN	13	14	15	16	17	18	19	20	25	30	35	40
$ 50	0.62	0.61	0.59	0.58	0.56	0.55	0.55	0.54	0.51	0.50	0.49	0.49
100	1.24	1.21	1.17	1.15	1.12	1.10	1.09	1.07	1.02	1.00	0.98	0.97
200	2.48	2.41	2.34	2.29	2.24	2.20	2.17	2.14	2.04	1.99	1.96	1.94
300	3.72	3.61	3.51	3.43	3.36	3.30	3.25	3.20	3.05	2.98	2.93	2.91
400	4.96	4.81	4.68	4.57	4.48	4.40	4.33	4.27	4.07	3.97	3.91	3.88
500	6.19	6.01	5.85	5.71	5.60	5.50	5.41	5.34	5.09	4.96	4.89	4.85
600	7.43	7.21	7.01	6.85	6.71	6.59	6.49	6.40	6.10	5.95	5.86	5.81
700	8.67	8.41	8.18	7.99	7.83	7.69	7.57	7.47	7.12	6.94	6.84	6.78
800	9.91	9.61	9.35	9.13	8.95	8.79	8.65	8.54	8.14	7.93	7.81	7.75
900	11.15	10.81	10.52	10.28	10.07	9.89	9.74	9.60	9.15	8.92	8.79	8.72
1000	12.38	12.01	11.69	11.42	11.19	10.99	10.82	10.67	10.17	9.91	9.77	9.69
2000	24.76	24.01	23.37	22.83	22.37	21.97	21.63	21.33	20.33	19.81	19.53	19.37
3000	37.14	36.01	35.05	34.24	33.55	32.95	32.44	32.00	30.50	29.71	29.29	29.05
4000	49.52	48.01	46.73	45.65	44.73	43.94	43.25	42.66	40.66	39.62	39.05	38.74
5000	61.90	60.01	58.41	57.06	55.91	54.92	54.07	53.33	50.83	49.52	48.81	48.42
6000	74.28	72.01	70.10	68.47	67.09	65.90	64.88	63.99	60.99	59.42	58.57	58.10
7000	86.66	84.01	81.78	79.89	78.27	76.89	75.69	74.66	71.16	69.33	68.33	67.78
8000	99.04	96.01	93.46	91.30	89.45	87.87	86.50	85.32	81.32	79.23	78.09	77.47
9000	111.42	108.01	105.14	102.71	100.63	98.85	97.31	95.98	91.49	89.13	87.85	87.15
10000	123.80	120.01	116.82	114.12	111.81	109.83	108.13	106.65	101.65	99.03	97.62	96.83
11000	136.18	132.01	128.51	125.53	123.00	120.82	118.94	117.31	111.82	108.94	107.38	106.52
12000	148.56	144.01	140.19	136.94	134.18	131.80	129.75	127.98	121.98	118.84	117.14	116.20
13000	160.93	156.01	151.87	148.36	145.36	142.78	140.56	138.64	132.15	128.74	126.90	125.88
14000	173.31	168.01	163.55	159.77	156.54	153.77	151.38	149.31	142.31	138.65	136.66	135.56
15000	185.69	180.01	175.23	171.18	167.72	164.75	162.19	159.97	152.48	148.55	146.42	145.25
16000	198.07	192.01	186.92	182.59	178.90	175.73	173.00	170.63	162.64	158.45	156.18	154.93
17000	210.45	204.01	198.60	194.00	190.08	186.72	183.81	181.30	172.80	168.35	165.94	164.61
18000	222.83	216.01	210.28	205.41	201.26	197.70	194.62	191.96	182.97	178.26	175.70	174.30
19000	235.21	228.02	221.96	216.83	212.44	208.68	205.44	202.63	193.13	188.16	185.47	183.98
20000	247.59	240.02	233.64	228.24	223.62	219.66	216.25	213.29	203.30	198.06	195.23	193.66
21000	259.97	252.02	245.32	239.65	234.81	230.65	227.06	223.96	213.46	207.97	204.99	203.34
22000	272.35	264.02	257.01	251.06	245.99	241.63	237.87	234.62	223.63	217.87	214.75	213.03
23000	284.73	276.02	268.69	262.47	257.17	252.61	248.68	245.28	233.79	227.77	224.51	222.71
24000	297.11	288.02	280.37	273.68	268.35	263.60	259.50	255.95	243.96	237.67	234.27	232.39
25000	309.48	300.02	292.05	285.09	279.53	274.58	270.31	266.61	254.12	247.58	244.03	242.08
26000	321.86	312.02	303.73	296.71	290.71	285.56	281.12	277.28	264.29	257.48	253.79	251.76
27000	334.24	324.02	315.42	308.12	301.89	296.54	291.93	287.94	274.45	267.38	263.55	261.44
28000	346.62	336.02	327.10	319.53	313.07	307.53	302.75	298.61	284.62	277.29	273.32	271.12
29000	359.00	348.02	338.78	330.94	324.25	318.51	313.56	309.27	294.78	287.19	283.08	280.81
30000	371.38	360.02	350.46	342.35	335.43	329.49	324.37	319.93	304.95	297.09	292.84	290.49
31000	383.76	372.02	362.14	353.77	346.61	340.48	335.18	330.60	315.11	307.00	302.60	300.17
32000	396.14	384.02	373.83	365.18	357.80	351.46	345.99	341.26	325.28	316.90	312.36	309.86
33000	408.52	396.02	385.51	376.59	368.98	362.44	356.81	351.93	335.44	326.80	322.12	319.54
34000	420.90	408.02	397.19	388.00	380.16	373.43	367.62	362.59	345.60	336.70	331.88	329.22
35000	433.28	420.02	408.87	399.41	391.34	384.41	378.43	373.26	355.77	346.61	341.64	338.90
37500	464.22	450.03	438.08	427.94	419.29	411.87	405.46	399.92	381.18	371.36	366.05	363.11
40000	495.17	480.03	467.28	456.47	447.24	439.32	432.49	426.58	406.59	396.12	390.45	387.32
42500	526.12	510.03	496.49	485.00	475.20	466.78	459.52	453.24	432.00	420.88	414.85	411.52
45000	557.07	540.03	525.69	513.53	503.15	494.24	486.55	479.90	457.42	445.64	439.25	435.73
47500	588.02	570.04	554.90	542.06	531.10	521.70	513.58	506.56	482.83	470.39	463.66	459.94
50000	618.96	600.03	584.10	570.59	559.05	549.15	540.61	533.22	508.24	495.15	488.06	484.15
52500	649.91	630.03	613.30	599.12	587.01	576.61	567.64	559.88	533.65	519.91	512.46	508.35
55000	680.86	660.04	642.51	627.65	614.96	604.07	594.67	586.54	559.06	544.67	536.86	532.56
57500	711.81	690.04	671.71	656.17	642.91	631.52	621.71	613.20	584.47	569.42	561.27	556.77
60000	742.76	720.04	700.92	684.70	670.86	658.98	648.74	639.86	609.89	594.18	585.67	580.97
65000	804.65	780.04	759.33	741.76	726.77	713.90	702.80	693.18	660.71	643.69	634.47	629.39
70000	866.55	840.04	817.74	798.82	782.67	768.81	756.86	746.51	711.53	693.21	683.28	677.80
75000	928.44	900.05	876.15	855.88	838.58	823.73	810.92	799.83	762.36	742.72	732.09	726.22
80000	990.34	960.05	934.56	912.94	894.48	878.64	864.98	853.15	813.18	792.24	780.89	774.63
85000	1052.24	1020.05	992.97	970.00	950.39	933.56	919.04	906.47	864.00	841.75	829.70	823.04
90000	1114.13	1080.05	1051.38	1027.05	1006.29	988.47	973.10	959.79	914.83	891.27	878.50	871.46
95000	1176.03	1140.06	1109.79	1084.11	1062.20	1043.39	1027.16	1013.11	965.65	940.78	927.31	919.87
100000	1237.92	1200.06	1168.19	1141.17	1118.10	1098.30	1081.22	1066.43	1016.47	990.30	976.11	968.29
105000	1299.82	1260.06	1226.60	1198.23	1174.01	1153.22	1135.28	1119.76	1067.30	1039.81	1024.92	1016.70
110000	1361.71	1320.07	1285.01	1255.29	1229.91	1208.13	1189.34	1173.08	1118.12	1089.33	1073.72	1065.12
115000	1423.61	1380.07	1343.42	1312.34	1285.82	1263.04	1243.41	1226.40	1168.94	1138.84	1122.53	1113.53
120000	1485.51	1440.07	1401.83	1369.40	1341.72	1317.96	1297.47	1279.72	1219.77	1188.35	1171.33	1161.94
125000	1547.40	1500.07	1460.24	1426.46	1397.63	1372.87	1351.53	1333.04	1270.59	1237.87	1220.14	1210.36
130000	1609.30	1560.08	1518.65	1483.52	1453.53	1427.79	1405.59	1386.36	1321.41	1287.38	1268.94	1258.77
135000	1671.19	1620.08	1577.06	1540.58	1509.43	1482.70	1459.65	1439.69	1372.24	1336.90	1317./75	1307.19
140000	1733.09	1680.08	1635.47	1597.64	1565.34	1537.62	1513.71	1493.01	1423.06	1386.41	1366.56	1355.60
145000	1794.99	1740.09	1693.88	1654.69	1621.24	1592.53	1567.77	1546.33	1473.88	1435.93	1415.36	1404.01
150000	1856.88	1800.09	1752.29	1711.75	1677.15	1647.45	1621.83	1599.65	1524.71	1485.44	1464.17	1452.43
155000	1918.78	1860.09	1810.70	1768.81	1733.05	1702.36	1675.89	1652.97	1575.53	1534.96	1512.97	1500.84
160000	1980.67	1920.09	1869.11	1825.87	1788.96	1757.28	1729.95	1706.29	1626.36	1584.47	1561./8	1549.26

MONTHLY AMORTIZING PAYMENTS

AMOUNT OF LOAN	NUMBER OF YEARS IN TERM											
	1	2	3	4	5	6	7	8	9	10	11	12
$ 50	4.44	2.35	1.66	1.32	1.11	0.98	0.88	0.81	0.76	0.72	0.68	0.65
100	8.88	4.70	3.31	2.63	2.22	1.95	1.76	1.62	1.51	1.43	1.36	1.30
200	17.75	9.40	6.62	5.25	4.43	3.89	3.51	3.23	3.01	2.85	2.71	2.60
300	26.62	14.09	9.93	7.87	6.64	5.83	5.26	4.84	4.52	4.27	4.06	3.90
400	35.50	18.79	13.24	10.49	8.85	7.77	7.01	6.45	6.02	5.69	5.42	5.20
500	44.37	23.48	16.55	13.11	11.06	9.72	8.76	8.06	7.53	7.11	6.77	6.50
600	53.24	28.18	19.86	15.73	13.28	11.66	10.52	9.67	9.03	8.53	8.12	7.79
700	62.12	32.87	23.17	18.35	15.49	13.60	12.27	11.29	10.54	9.95	9.48	9.09
800	70.99	37.57	26.48	20.97	17.70	15.54	14.02	12.90	12.04	11.37	10.83	10.39
900	79.86	42.27	29.79	23.60	19.91	17.48	15.77	14.51	13.54	12.79	12.18	11.69
1000	88.74	46.96	33.10	26.22	22.12	19.43	17.52	16.12	15.05	14.21	13.54	12.99
2000	177.47	93.92	66.20	52.43	44.24	38.85	35.04	32.24	30.09	28.41	27.07	25.97
3000	266.20	140.88	99.29	78.64	66.36	58.27	52.56	48.35	45.14	42.61	40.60	38.95
4000	354.93	187.83	132.39	104.85	88.48	77.69	70.08	64.47	60.18	56.82	54.13	51.94
5000	443.66	234.79	165.48	131.06	110.60	97.11	87.60	80.58	75.22	71.02	67.66	64.92
6000	532.40	281.75	198.58	157.27	132.71	116.53	105.12	96.70	90.27	85.22	81.19	77.90
7000	621.13	328.70	231.67	183.48	154.83	135.95	122.64	112.82	105.31	99.43	94.72	90.89
8000	709.86	375.66	264.77	209.70	176.95	155.37	140.16	128.93	120.35	113.63	108.25	103.87
9000	798.59	422.62	297.86	235.91	199.07	174.79	157.68	145.05	135.40	127.83	121.78	116.85
10000	887.32	469.57	330.96	262.12	221.19	194.21	175.20	161.16	150.44	142.03	135.31	129.84
11000	976.06	516.53	364.05	288.33	243.31	213.63	192.72	177.28	165.48	156.24	148.84	142.82
12000	1064.79	563.49	397.15	314.54	265.42	233.05	210.24	193.39	180.53	170.44	162.37	155.80
13000	1153.52	610.44	430.24	340.75	287.54	252.47	227.76	209.51	195.57	184.64	175.90	168.79
14000	1242.25	657.40	463.34	366.96	309.66	271.89	245.28	225.63	210.62	198.85	189.43	181.77
15000	1330.98	704.36	496.43	393.17	331.78	291.31	262.79	241.74	225.66	213.05	202.96	194.75
16000	1419.72	751.31	529.53	419.39	353.90	310.73	280.31	257.86	240.70	227.25	216.49	207.74
17000	1508.45	798.27	562.62	445.60	376.02	330.15	297.83	273.97	255.75	241.46	230.02	220.72
18000	1597.18	845.23	595.72	471.81	398.13	349.57	315.35	290.09	270.79	255.66	243.55	233.70
19000	1685.91	892.18	628.81	498.02	420.25	368.99	332.87	306.21	285.83	269.86	257.08	246.69
20000	1774.64	939.14	661.91	524.23	442.37	388.41	350.39	322.32	300.88	284.06	270.61	259.67
21000	1863.37	986.10	695.00	550.44	464.49	407.83	367.91	338.44	315.92	298.27	284.14	272.65
22000	1952.11	1033.05	728.10	576.65	486.61	427.25	385.43	354.55	330.96	312.47	297.67	285.64
23000	2040.84	1080.01	761.19	602.86	508.73	446.67	402.95	370.67	346.01	326.67	311.20	298.62
24000	2129.57	1126.97	794.29	629.08	530.84	466.10	420.47	386.78	361.05	340.88	324.73	311.60
25000	2218.30	1173.93	827.38	655.29	552.96	485.52	437.99	402.90	376.10	355.08	338.26	324.59
26000	2307.03	1220.88	860.48	681.50	575.08	504.94	455.51	419.02	391.14	369.28	351.79	337.57
27000	2395.77	1267.84	893.57	707.71	597.20	524.36	473.03	435.13	406.18	383.48	365.32	350.55
28000	2484.50	1314.80	926.67	733.92	619.32	543.78	490.55	451.25	421.23	397.69	378.85	363.54
29000	2573.23	1361.75	959.76	760.13	641.44	563.20	508.07	467.36	436.27	411.89	392.38	376.52
30000	2661.96	1408.71	992.86	786.34	663.55	582.62	525.58	483.48	451.31	426.09	405.91	389.50
31000	2750.69	1455.67	1025.95	812.55	685.67	602.04	543.10	499.59	466.36	440.30	419.44	402.49
32000	2839.43	1502.62	1059.05	838.77	707.79	621.46	560.62	515.71	481.40	454.50	432.97	415.47
33000	2928.16	1549.58	1092.14	864.98	729.91	640.88	578.14	531.83	496.44	468.70	446.50	428.45
34000	3016.89	1596.54	1125.24	891.19	752.03	660.30	595.66	547.94	511.49	482.91	460.03	441.44
35000	3105.62	1643.49	1158.33	917.40	774.15	679.72	613.18	564.06	526.53	497.11	473.57	454.42
37500	3327.45	1760.89	1241.07	982.93	829.44	728.27	656.98	604.35	564.14	532.62	507.39	486.88
40000	3549.28	1878.28	1323.81	1048.46	884.74	776.82	700.78	644.64	601.75	568.12	541.22	519.34
42500	3771.11	1995.67	1406.54	1113.98	940.03	825.37	744.58	684.93	639.36	603.63	575.04	551.79
45000	3992.94	2113.06	1489.28	1179.51	995.33	873.92	788.37	725.22	676.97	639.14	608.87	584.25
47500	4214.77	2230.45	1572.02	1245.04	1050.63	922.48	832.17	765.51	714.58	674.64	642.69	616.71
50000	4436.60	2347.85	1654.76	1310.57	1105.92	971.03	875.97	805.79	752.19	710.15	676.52	649.17
52500	4658.43	2465.24	1737.49	1376.10	1161.22	1019.58	919.77	846.08	789.79	745.66	710.35	681.63
55000	4880.26	2582.63	1820.23	1441.62	1216.51	1068.13	963.57	886.37	827.40	781.17	744.17	714.08
57500	5102.09	2700.02	1902.97	1507.15	1271.81	1116.68	1007.37	926.66	865.01	816.67	778.00	746.54
60000	5323.92	2817.41	1985.71	1572.68	1327.10	1165.23	1051.16	966.95	902.62	852.18	811.82	779.00
65000	5767.58	3052.20	2151.18	1703.74	1437.70	1262.33	1138.76	1047.53	977.84	923.20	879.47	843.92
70000	6211.24	3286.98	2316.66	1834.79	1548.29	1359.44	1226.36	1128.11	1053.06	994.21	947.13	908.83
75000	6654.90	3521.77	2482.13	1965.85	1658.88	1456.54	1313.95	1208.69	1128.28	1065.23	1014.78	973.75
80000	7098.56	3756.55	2647.61	2096.91	1769.47	1553.64	1401.55	1289.27	1203.49	1136.24	1082.43	1038.67
85000	7542.21	3991.33	2813.08	2227.96	1880.06	1650.74	1489.15	1369.85	1278.71	1207.26	1150.08	1103.58
90000	7985.87	4226.12	2978.56	2359.02	1990.65	1747.84	1576.74	1450.43	1353.93	1278.27	1217.73	1168.50
95000	8429.53	4460.90	3144.03	2490.07	2101.25	1844.95	1664.34	1531.01	1429.15	1349.28	1285.38	1233.41
100000	8873.19	4695.69	3309.51	2621.13	2211.84	1942.05	1751.94	1611.58	1504.37	1420.30	1353.03	1298.33
105000	9316.85	4930.47	3474.98	2752.19	2322.43	2039.15	1839.53	1692.16	1579.58	1491.31	1420.69	1363.25
110000	9760.51	5165.25	3640.46	2883.24	2433.02	2136.25	1927.13	1772.74	1654.80	1562.33	1488.34	1428.16
115000	10204.17	5400.04	3805.93	3014.30	2543.61	2233.35	2014.73	1853.32	1730.02	1633.34	1555.99	1493.08
120000	10647.83	5634.82	3971.41	3145.36	2654.20	2330.46	2102.32	1933.90	1805.24	1704.36	1623.64	1558.00
125000	11091.49	5869.61	4136.88	3276.41	2764.80	2427.56	2189.92	2014.48	1880.46	1775.37	1691.29	1622.91
130000	11535.15	6104.39	4302.36	3407.47	2875.39	2524.66	2277.52	2095.06	1955.67	1846.39	1758.94	1687.83
135000	11978.81	6339.17	4467.83	3538.52	2985.98	2621.76	2365.11	2175.64	2030.89	1917.40	1826.59	1752.74
140000	12422.47	6573.96	4633.31	3669.58	3096.57	2718.87	2452.71	2256.22	2106.11	1988.42	1894.25	1817.66
145000	12866.13	6808.74	4798.78	3800.64	3207.16	2815.97	2540.31	2336.80	2181.33	2059.43	1961.90	1882.58
150000	13309.79	7043.53	4964.26	3931.69	3317.75	2913.07	2627.90	2417.37	2256.55	2130.45	2029.55	1947.49
155000	13753.45	7278.31	5129.73	4062.75	3428.34	3010.17	2715.50	2497.95	2331.76	2201.46	2097.20	2012.41
160000	14197.11	7513.09	5295.21	4193.81	3538.94	3107.27	2803.10	2578.53	2406.98	2272.48	2164.85	2077.33

MONTHLY AMORTIZING PAYMENTS
11.75%

AMOUNT OF LOAN	13	14	15	16	17	18	19	20	25	30	35	40
					NUMBER OF YEARS IN TERM							
$ 50	0.63	0.61	0.60	0.58	0.57	0.56	0.55	0.55	0.52	0.51	0.50	0.50
100	1.26	1.22	1.19	1.16	1.14	1.12	1.10	1.09	1.04	1.01	1.00	0.99
200	2.51	2.44	2.37	2.32	2.27	2.24	2.20	2.17	2.07	2.02	2.00	1.98
300	3.76	3.65	3.56	3.48	3.41	3.35	3.30	3.26	3.11	3.03	2.99	2.97
400	5.02	4.87	4.74	4.63	4.54	4.47	4.40	4.34	4.14	4.04	3.99	3.96
500	6.27	6.08	5.93	5.79	5.68	5.58	5.50	5.42	5.18	5.05	4.98	4.95
600	7.52	7.30	7.11	6.95	6.81	6.70	6.59	6.51	6.21	6.06	5.98	5.94
700	8.78	8.51	8.29	8.11	7.95	7.81	7.69	7.59	7.25	7.07	6.98	6.92
800	10.03	9.73	9.48	9.26	9.08	8.93	8.79	8.67	8.28	8.08	7.97	7.91
900	11.28	10.95	10.66	10.42	10.22	10.04	9.89	9.76	9.32	9.09	8.97	8.90
1000	12.54	12.16	11.85	11.58	11.35	11.16	10.99	10.84	10.35	10.10	9.96	9.89
2000	25.07	24.32	23.69	23.15	22.70	22.31	21.97	21.68	20.70	20.19	19.92	19.77
3000	37.60	36.48	35.53	34.73	34.04	33.46	32.95	32.52	31.05	30.29	29.88	29.66
4000	50.13	48.63	47.37	46.30	45.39	44.61	43.94	43.35	41.40	40.38	39.84	39.54
5000	62.67	60.79	59.21	57.87	56.74	55.76	54.92	54.19	51.74	50.48	49.79	49.42
6000	75.20	72.95	71.05	69.45	68.08	66.91	65.90	65.03	62.09	60.57	59.75	59.31
7000	87.73	85.10	82.89	81.02	79.43	78.06	76.88	75.86	72.44	70.66	69.71	69.19
8000	100.26	97.26	94.74	92.60	90.77	89.21	87.87	86.70	82.79	80.76	79.67	79.07
9000	112.80	109.42	106.58	104.17	102.12	100.36	98.85	97.54	93.14	90.85	89.63	88.96
10000	125.33	121.57	118.42	115.74	113.47	111.51	109.83	108.38	103.48	100.95	99.58	98.84
11000	137.86	133.73	130.26	127.32	124.81	122.66	120.81	119.21	113.83	111.04	109.54	108.73
12000	150.39	145.89	142.10	138.89	136.16	133.81	131.80	130.05	124.18	121.13	119.50	118.61
13000	162.93	158.05	153.94	150.47	147.50	144.96	142.78	140.89	134.53	131.23	129.46	128.49
14000	175.46	170.20	165.78	162.04	158.85	156.12	153.76	151.72	144.88	141.32	139.42	138.38
15000	187.99	182.36	177.62	173.61	170.20	167.27	164.74	162.56	155.22	151.42	149.37	148.26
16000	200.52	194.52	189.47	185.19	181.54	178.42	175.73	173.40	165.57	161.51	159.33	158.14
17000	213.06	206.67	201.31	196.76	192.89	189.57	186.71	184.24	175.92	171.60	169.29	168.03
18000	225.59	218.83	213.15	208.34	204.23	200.72	197.69	195.07	186.27	181.70	179.25	177.91
19000	238.12	230.99	224.99	219.91	215.58	211.87	208.67	205.91	196.62	191.79	189.21	187.79
20000	250.65	243.14	236.83	231.48	226.93	223.02	219.66	216.75	206.96	201.89	199.16	197.68
21000	263.19	255.30	248.67	243.06	238.27	234.17	230.64	227.58	217.31	211.98	209.12	207.56
22000	275.72	267.46	260.51	254.63	249.62	245.32	241.62	238.42	227.66	222.08	219.08	217.45
23000	288.25	279.62	272.36	266.21	260.96	256.47	252.60	249.26	238.01	232.17	229.04	227.33
24000	300.78	291.77	284.20	277.78	272.31	267.62	263.59	260.09	248.36	242.26	239.00	237.21
25000	313.32	303.93	296.04	289.35	283.66	278.77	274.57	270.93	258.70	252.36	248.95	247.10
26000	325.85	316.09	307.88	300.93	295.00	289.92	285.55	281.77	269.05	262.45	258.91	256.98
27000	338.38	328.24	319.72	312.50	306.35	301.07	296.53	292.61	279.40	272.55	268.87	266.86
28000	350.91	340.40	331.56	324.08	317.69	312.23	307.52	303.44	289.75	282.64	278.83	276.75
29000	363.45	352.56	343.40	335.65	329.04	323.38	318.50	314.28	300.10	292.73	288.79	286.63
30000	375.98	364.71	355.24	347.22	340.39	334.53	329.48	325.12	310.44	302.83	298.74	296.51
31000	388.51	376.87	367.09	358.80	351.73	345.68	340.46	335.95	320.79	312.92	308.70	306.40
32000	401.04	389.03	378.93	370.37	363.08	356.83	351.45	346.79	331.14	323.02	318.66	316.28
33000	413.58	401.18	390.77	381.95	374.43	367.98	362.43	357.63	341.49	333.11	328.62	326.17
34000	426.11	413.34	402.61	393.52	385.77	379.13	373.41	368.47	351.84	343.20	338.57	336.05
35000	438.64	425.50	414.45	405.09	397.12	390.28	384.39	379.30	362.18	353.30	348.53	345.93
37500	469.97	455.89	444.05	434.03	425.48	418.16	411.85	406.40	388.05	378.53	373.43	370.64
40000	501.30	486.28	473.66	462.96	453.85	446.03	439.31	433.49	413.92	403.77	398.32	395.35
42500	532.64	516.68	503.26	491.90	482.21	473.91	466.76	460.58	439.79	429.00	423.22	420.06
45000	563.97	547.07	532.86	520.83	510.58	501.79	494.22	487.67	465.66	454.24	448.11	444.77
47500	595.30	577.46	562.47	549.77	538.94	529.66	521.67	514.77	491.53	479.47	473.01	469.48
50000	626.63	607.85	592.07	578.70	567.31	557.54	549.13	541.86	517.40	504.71	497.90	494.19
52500	657.96	638.25	621.67	607.64	595.67	585.42	576.59	568.95	543.27	529.95	522.80	518.90
55000	689.29	668.64	651.28	636.57	624.04	613.29	604.04	596.04	569.14	555.18	547.69	543.61
57500	720.62	699.03	680.88	665.51	652.40	641.17	631.50	623.14	595.01	580.42	572.59	568.31
60000	751.95	729.42	710.48	694.44	680.77	669.05	658.96	650.23	620.88	605.65	597.48	593.02
65000	814.62	790.21	769.69	752.31	737.50	724.80	713.87	704.41	672.62	656.12	647.27	642.44
70000	877.28	850.99	828.90	810.18	794.23	780.56	768.78	758.60	724.36	706.59	697.06	691.86
75000	939.94	911.78	888.10	868.05	850.96	836.31	823.69	812.79	776.10	757.06	746.85	741.28
80000	1002.60	972.56	947.31	925.92	907.69	892.06	878.61	866.97	827.84	807.53	796.64	790.70
85000	1065.27	1033.35	1006.52	983.80	964.42	947.82	933.52	921.16	879.58	858.00	846.43	840.11
90000	1127.93	1094.13	1065.72	1041.66	1021.15	1003.57	988.43	975.34	931.32	908.47	896.22	889.53
95000	1190.59	1154.92	1124.93	1099.53	1077.88	1059.32	1043.34	1029.53	983.06	958.94	946.01	938.95
100000	1253.25	1215.70	1184.14	1157.40	1134.61	1115.08	1098.26	1083.71	1034.80	1009.41	995.80	988.37
105000	1315.91	1276.49	1243.34	1215.27	1191.34	1170.83	1153.17	1137.90	1086.54	1059.89	1045.59	1037.79
110000	1378.58	1337.27	1302.55	1273.14	1248.07	1226.58	1208.08	1192.08	1138.28	1110.36	1095.38	1087.21
115000	1441.24	1398.06	1361.76	1331.01	1304.80	1282.34	1262.99	1246.27	1190.02	1160.83	1145.17	1136.62
120000	1503.90	1458.84	1420.96	1388.88	1361.53	1338.09	1317.91	1300.45	1241.76	1211.30	1194.96	1186.04
125000	1566.56	1519.63	1480.17	1446.75	1418.26	1393.85	1372.82	1354.64	1293.50	1261.77	1244.75	1235.46
130000	1629.23	1580.41	1539.38	1504.62	1474.99	1449.60	1427.73	1408.82	1345.24	1312.24	1294.54	1284.88
135000	1691.89	1641.20	1598.58	1562.49	1531.72	1505.35	1482.64	1463.01	1396.98	1362.71	1344.33	1334.30
140000	1754.55	1701.98	1657.79	1620.36	1588.45	1561.11	1537.56	1517.19	1448.72	1413.18	1394.12	1383.71
145000	1817.21	1762.76	1717.00	1678.23	1645.18	1616.86	1592.47	1571.38	1500.46	1463.65	1443.91	1433.13
150000	1879.88	1823.55	1776.20	1736.10	1701.91	1672.61	1647.38	1625.57	1552.20	1514.12	1493.70	1482.55
155000	1942.54	1884.33	1835.41	1793.97	1758.64	1728.37	1702.29	1679.75	1603.94	1564.59	1543.49	1531.97
160000	2005.20	1945.12	1894.62	1851.84	1815.37	1784.12	1757.21	1733.94	1655.68	1615.06	1593.28	1581.39

12.00%

MONTHLY AMORTIZING PAYMENTS

AMOUNT OF LOAN	NUMBER OF YEARS IN TERM											
	1	2	3	4	5	6	7	8	9	10	11	12
$ 50	4.45	2.36	1.67	1.32	1.12	0.98	0.89	0.82	0.76	0.72	0.69	0.66
100	8.89	4.71	3.33	2.64	2.23	1.96	1.77	1.63	1.52	1.44	1.37	1.32
200	17.77	9.42	6.65	5.27	4.45	3.92	3.54	3.26	3.04	2.87	2.74	2.63
300	26.66	14.13	9.97	7.91	6.68	5.87	5.30	4.88	4.56	4.31	4.11	3.95
400	35.54	18.83	13.29	10.54	8.90	7.83	7.07	6.51	6.08	5.74	5.48	5.26
500	44.43	23.54	16.61	13.17	11.13	9.78	8.83	8.13	7.60	7.18	6.84	6.57
600	53.31	28.25	19.93	15.81	13.35	11.74	10.60	9.76	9.12	8.61	8.21	7.89
700	62.20	32.96	23.26	18.44	15.58	13.69	12.36	11.38	10.63	10.05	9.58	9.20
800	71.08	37.66	26.58	21.07	17.80	15.65	14.13	13.01	12.15	11.48	10.95	10.51
900	79.97	42.37	29.90	23.71	20.03	17.60	15.89	14.63	13.67	12.92	12.32	11.83
1000	88.85	47.08	33.22	26.34	22.25	19.56	17.66	16.26	15.19	14.35	13.68	13.14
2000	177.70	94.15	66.43	52.67	44.49	39.11	35.31	32.51	30.37	28.70	27.36	26.27
3000	266.55	141.23	99.65	79.01	66.74	58.66	52.96	48.76	45.56	43.05	41.04	39.41
4000	355.40	188.30	132.86	105.34	88.98	78.21	70.62	65.02	60.74	57.39	54.72	52.54
5000	444.25	235.37	166.08	131.67	111.23	97.76	88.27	81.27	75.93	71.74	68.39	65.68
6000	533.10	282.45	199.29	158.01	133.47	117.31	105.92	97.52	91.11	86.09	82.07	78.81
7000	621.95	329.52	232.51	184.34	155.72	136.86	123.57	113.77	106.29	100.43	95.75	91.94
8000	710.80	376.59	265.72	210.68	177.96	156.41	141.23	130.03	121.48	114.78	109.43	105.08
9000	799.64	423.67	298.93	237.01	200.21	175.96	158.88	146.28	136.66	129.13	123.11	118.21
10000	888.49	470.74	332.15	263.34	222.45	195.51	176.53	162.53	151.85	143.48	136.78	131.35
11000	977.34	517.81	365.36	289.68	244.69	215.06	194.19	178.79	167.03	157.82	150.46	144.48
12000	1066.19	564.89	398.58	316.01	266.94	234.61	211.84	195.04	182.22	172.17	164.14	157.62
13000	1155.04	611.96	431.79	342.34	289.18	254.16	229.49	211.29	197.40	186.52	177.82	170.75
14000	1243.89	659.03	465.01	368.68	311.43	273.71	247.14	227.54	212.58	200.86	191.50	183.88
15000	1332.74	706.11	498.22	395.01	333.67	293.26	264.80	243.80	227.77	215.21	205.17	197.02
16000	1421.59	753.18	531.43	421.35	355.92	312.81	282.45	260.05	242.95	229.56	218.85	210.15
17000	1510.43	800.25	564.65	447.68	378.16	332.36	300.10	276.30	258.14	243.91	232.53	223.29
18000	1599.28	847.33	597.86	474.01	400.41	351.91	317.75	292.56	273.32	258.25	246.21	236.42
19000	1688.13	894.40	631.08	500.35	422.65	371.46	335.41	308.81	288.51	272.60	259.88	249.55
20000	1776.98	941.47	664.29	526.68	444.89	391.01	353.06	325.06	303.69	286.95	273.56	262.69
21000	1865.83	988.55	697.51	553.02	467.14	410.56	370.71	341.31	318.87	301.29	287.24	275.82
22000	1954.68	1035.62	730.72	579.35	489.38	430.11	388.37	357.57	334.06	315.64	300.92	288.96
23000	2043.53	1082.69	763.93	605.68	511.63	449.66	406.02	373.82	349.24	329.99	314.60	302.09
24000	2132.38	1129.77	797.15	632.02	533.87	469.21	423.67	390.07	364.43	344.34	328.27	315.23
25000	2221.22	1176.84	830.36	658.35	556.12	488.76	441.32	406.33	379.61	358.68	341.95	328.36
26000	2310.07	1223.92	863.58	684.68	578.36	508.31	458.98	422.58	394.80	373.03	355.63	341.49
27000	2398.92	1270.99	896.79	711.02	600.61	527.86	476.63	438.83	409.98	387.38	369.31	354.63
28000	2487.77	1318.06	930.01	737.35	622.85	547.41	494.28	455.08	425.16	401.72	382.99	367.76
29000	2576.62	1365.14	963.22	763.69	645.09	566.96	511.93	471.34	440.35	416.07	396.66	380.90
30000	2665.47	1412.21	996.43	790.02	667.34	586.51	529.59	487.59	455.53	430.42	410.34	394.03
31000	2754.32	1459.28	1029.65	816.35	689.58	606.06	547.24	503.84	470.72	444.76	424.02	407.16
32000	2843.17	1506.36	1062.86	842.69	711.83	625.61	564.89	520.10	485.90	459.11	437.70	420.30
33000	2932.02	1553.43	1096.08	869.02	734.07	645.16	582.55	536.35	501.08	473.46	451.37	433.43
34000	3020.86	1600.50	1129.29	895.36	756.32	664.71	600.20	552.60	516.27	487.81	465.05	446.57
35000	3109.71	1647.58	1162.51	921.69	778.56	684.26	617.85	568.85	531.45	502.15	478.73	459.70
37500	3331.83	1765.26	1245.54	987.52	834.17	733.14	661.98	609.49	569.41	538.07	512.93	492.54
40000	3553.96	1882.94	1328.58	1053.36	889.78	782.01	706.11	650.12	607.37	573.89	547.12	525.37
42500	3776.08	2000.63	1411.61	1119.19	945.39	830.89	750.25	690.75	645.33	609.70	581.31	558.21
45000	3998.20	2118.31	1494.65	1185.03	1001.01	879.76	794.38	731.38	683.30	645.62	615.51	591.04
47500	4220.32	2235.99	1577.68	1250.86	1056.62	928.64	838.51	772.01	721.26	681.49	649.70	623.88
50000	4442.44	2353.68	1660.72	1316.70	1112.23	977.51	882.64	812.65	759.22	717.36	683.90	656.71
52500	4664.57	2471.36	1743.76	1382.53	1167.84	1026.39	926.77	853.28	797.18	753.23	718.09	689.55
55000	4886.69	2589.05	1826.79	1448.37	1223.45	1075.27	970.91	893.91	835.14	789.10	752.29	722.39
57500	5108.81	2706.73	1909.83	1514.20	1279.06	1124.14	1015.04	934.54	873.10	824.96	786.48	755.22
60000	5330.93	2824.41	1992.86	1580.04	1334.67	1173.02	1059.17	975.18	911.06	860.83	820.68	788.06
65000	5775.18	3059.78	2158.94	1711.70	1445.89	1270.77	1147.43	1056.44	986.98	932.57	889.07	853.73
70000	6219.42	3295.15	2325.01	1843.37	1557.12	1368.52	1235.70	1137.70	1062.90	1004.30	957.46	919.40
75000	6663.66	3530.52	2491.08	1975.04	1668.34	1466.27	1323.96	1218.97	1138.82	1076.04	1025.85	985.07
80000	7107.91	3765.88	2657.15	2106.71	1779.56	1564.02	1412.22	1300.23	1214.74	1147.77	1094.24	1050.74
85000	7552.15	4001.25	2823.22	2238.38	1890.78	1661.77	1500.49	1381.50	1290.66	1219.51	1162.62	1116.41
90000	7996.40	4236.62	2989.29	2370.05	2002.01	1759.52	1588.75	1462.76	1366.59	1291.24	1231.01	1182.08
95000	8440.64	4471.98	3155.36	2501.72	2113.23	1857.27	1677.01	1544.02	1442.51	1362.98	1299.40	1247.75
100000	8884.88	4707.35	3321.44	2633.39	2224.45	1955.02	1765.28	1625.29	1518.43	1434.71	1367.79	1313.42
105000	9329.13	4942.72	3487.51	2765.06	2335.67	2052.78	1853.54	1706.55	1594.35	1506.45	1436.18	1379.10
110000	9773.37	5178.09	3653.58	2896.73	2446.89	2150.53	1941.81	1787.82	1670.27	1578.19	1504.57	1444.77
115000	10217.62	5413.45	3819.65	3028.40	2558.12	2248.28	2030.07	1869.08	1746.19	1649.92	1572.96	1510.44
120000	10661.86	5648.82	3985.72	3160.07	2669.34	2346.03	2118.33	1950.35	1822.11	1721.66	1641.35	1576.11
125000	11106.10	5884.19	4151.79	3291.73	2780.56	2443.78	2206.60	2031.61	1898.03	1793.39	1709.74	1641.78
130000	11550.35	6119.56	4317.87	3423.40	2891.78	2541.53	2294.86	2112.87	1973.96	1865.13	1778.13	1707.45
135000	11994.59	6354.92	4483.94	3555.07	3003.01	2639.28	2383.12	2194.14	2049.88	1936.86	1846.52	1773.12
140000	12438.84	6590.29	4650.01	3686.74	3114.23	2737.03	2471.39	2275.40	2125.80	2008.60	1914.91	1838.79
145000	12883.08	6825.66	4816.08	3818.41	3225.45	2834.78	2559.65	2356.67	2201.72	2080.33	1983.30	1904.46
150000	13327.32	7061.03	4982.15	3950.08	3336.67	2932.53	2647.91	2437.93	2277.64	2152.07	2051.69	1970.13
155000	13771.57	7296.39	5148.22	4081.75	3447.89	3030.28	2736.18	2519.20	2353.56	2223.80	2120.08	2035.80
160000	14215.81	7531.76	5314.29	4213.42	3559.12	3128.04	2824.44	2600.46	2429.48	2295.54	2188.47	2101.48

58

MONTHLY AMORTIZING PAYMENTS 12.00%

AMOUNT OF LOAN	NUMBER OF YEARS IN TERM											
	13	14	15	16	17	18	19	20	25	30	35	40
$ 50	0.64	0.62	0.61	0.59	0.58	0.57	0.56	0.56	0.53	0.52	0.51	0.51
100	1.27	1.24	1.21	1.18	1.16	1.14	1.12	1.11	1.06	1.03	1.02	1.01
200	2.54	2.47	2.41	2.35	2.31	2.27	2.24	2.21	2.11	2.06	2.04	2.02
300	3.81	3.70	3.61	3.53	3.46	3.40	3.35	3.31	3.16	3.09	3.05	3.03
400	5.08	4.93	4.81	4.70	4.61	4.53	4.47	4.41	4.22	4.12	4.07	4.04
500	6.35	6.16	6.01	5.87	5.76	5.66	5.58	5.51	5.27	5.15	5.08	5.05
600	7.62	7.39	7.21	7.05	6.91	6.80	6.70	6.61	6.32	6.18	6.10	6.06
700	8.89	8.63	8.41	8.22	8.06	7.93	7.81	7.71	7.38	7.21	7.11	7.06
800	10.15	9.86	9.61	9.39	9.21	9.06	8.93	8.81	8.43	8.23	8.13	8.07
900	11.42	11.09	10.81	10.57	10.37	10.19	10.04	9.91	9.48	9.26	9.14	9.08
1000	12.69	12.32	12.01	11.74	11.52	11.32	11.16	11.02	10.54	10.29	10.16	10.09
2000	25.38	24.63	24.01	23.48	23.03	22.64	22.31	22.03	21.07	20.58	20.32	20.17
3000	38.06	36.95	36.01	35.22	34.54	33.96	33.47	33.04	31.60	30.86	30.47	30.26
4000	50.75	49.26	48.01	46.95	46.05	45.28	44.62	44.05	42.13	41.15	40.63	40.34
5000	63.44	61.58	60.01	58.69	57.57	56.60	55.77	55.06	52.67	51.44	50.78	50.43
6000	76.12	73.89	72.02	70.43	69.08	67.92	66.93	66.07	63.20	61.72	60.94	60.51
7000	88.81	86.21	84.02	82.17	80.59	79.24	78.08	77.08	73.73	72.01	71.09	70.60
8000	101.50	98.52	96.02	93.90	92.10	90.56	89.24	88.09	84.26	82.29	81.25	80.68
9000	114.18	110.83	108.02	105.64	103.61	101.88	100.39	99.10	94.80	92.58	91.40	90.77
10000	126.87	123.15	120.02	117.38	115.13	113.20	111.54	110.11	105.33	102.87	101.56	100.85
11000	139.56	135.46	132.02	129.11	126.64	124.52	122.70	121.12	115.86	113.15	111.72	110.94
12000	152.24	147.78	144.03	140.85	138.15	135.84	133.85	132.14	126.39	123.44	121.87	121.02
13000	164.93	160.09	156.03	152.59	149.66	147.16	145.01	143.15	136.92	133.72	132.03	131.11
14000	177.62	172.41	168.03	164.33	161.18	158.48	156.16	154.16	147.46	144.01	142.18	141.19
15000	190.30	184.72	180.03	176.06	172.69	169.80	167.31	165.17	157.99	154.30	152.34	151.28
16000	202.99	197.03	192.03	187.80	184.20	181.12	178.47	176.18	168.52	164.58	162.49	161.36
17000	215.68	209.35	204.03	199.54	195.71	192.44	189.62	187.19	179.05	174.87	172.65	171.45
18000	228.36	221.66	216.04	211.28	207.22	203.76	200.77	198.20	189.59	185.16	182.80	181.53
19000	241.05	233.98	228.04	223.01	218.74	215.08	211.93	209.21	200.12	195.44	192.96	191.62
20000	253.74	246.29	240.04	234.75	230.25	226.40	223.08	220.22	210.65	205.73	203.11	201.70
21000	266.42	258.61	252.04	246.49	241.76	237.71	234.24	231.23	221.18	216.01	213.27	211.79
22000	279.11	270.92	264.04	258.22	253.27	249.03	245.39	242.24	231.71	226.30	223.43	221.87
23000	291.80	283.23	276.04	269.96	264.78	260.35	256.54	253.25	242.25	236.59	233.58	231.96
24000	304.48	295.55	288.05	281.70	276.30	271.67	267.70	264.27	252.78	246.87	243.74	242.04
25000	317.17	307.86	300.05	293.44	287.81	282.99	278.85	275.28	263.31	257.16	253.89	252.13
26000	329.86	320.18	312.05	305.17	299.32	294.31	290.01	286.29	273.84	267.44	264.05	262.21
27000	342.54	332.49	324.05	316.91	310.83	305.63	301.16	297.30	284.38	277.73	274.20	272.30
28000	355.23	344.81	336.05	328.65	322.35	316.95	312.31	308.31	294.91	288.02	284.36	282.38
29000	367.92	357.12	348.05	340.39	333.86	328.27	323.47	319.32	305.44	298.30	294.51	292.47
30000	380.60	369.43	360.06	352.12	345.37	339.59	334.62	330.33	315.97	308.59	304.67	302.55
31000	393.29	381.75	372.06	363.86	356.88	350.91	345.77	341.34	326.50	318.87	314.82	312.64
32000	405.98	394.06	384.06	375.60	368.39	362.23	356.93	352.35	337.04	329.16	324.98	322.72
33000	418.66	406.38	396.06	387.33	379.91	373.55	368.08	363.36	347.57	339.45	335.14	332.81
34000	431.35	418.69	408.06	399.07	391.42	384.87	379.24	374.37	358.10	349.73	345.29	342.89
35000	444.04	431.01	420.06	410.81	402.93	396.19	390.39	385.39	368.63	360.02	355.45	352.98
37500	475.75	461.79	450.07	440.15	431.71	424.49	418.27	412.91	394.96	385.73	380.84	378.19
40000	507.47	492.58	480.07	469.50	460.49	452.79	446.16	440.44	421.29	411.45	406.22	403.40
42500	539.19	523.36	510.08	498.84	489.27	481.08	474.04	467.97	447.63	437.17	431.61	428.62
45000	570.90	554.15	540.08	528.18	518.05	509.38	501.93	495.49	473.96	462.88	457.00	453.83
47500	602.62	584.93	570.08	557.52	546.83	537.68	529.81	523.02	500.29	488.60	482.39	479.04
50000	634.34	615.72	600.09	586.87	575.61	565.98	557.70	550.55	526.62	514.31	507.78	504.25
52500	666.05	646.51	630.09	616.21	604.39	594.28	585.58	578.08	552.95	540.03	533.17	529.47
55000	697.77	677.29	660.10	645.55	633.17	622.58	613.47	605.60	579.28	565.74	558.56	554.68
57500	729.49	708.08	690.10	674.90	661.95	650.88	641.35	633.13	605.61	591.46	583.95	579.89
60000	761.20	738.86	720.11	704.24	690.73	679.18	669.24	660.66	631.94	617.17	609.33	605.10
65000	824.64	800.43	780.11	762.93	748.30	735.77	725.01	715.71	684.60	668.60	660.11	655.53
70000	888.07	862.01	840.12	821.61	805.86	792.37	780.77	770.77	737.26	720.03	710.89	705.95
75000	951.50	923.58	900.13	880.30	863.42	848.97	836.54	825.82	789.92	771.46	761.67	756.38
80000	1014.94	985.16	960.14	938.99	920.98	905.57	892.31	880.87	842.58	822.90	812.44	806.80
85000	1078.37	1046.72	1020.15	997.67	978.54	962.16	948.08	935.93	895.25	874.33	863.22	857.23
90000	1141.80	1108.29	1080.16	1056.36	1036.10	1018.76	1003.85	990.98	947.91	925.76	914.00	907.65
95000	1205.24	1169.86	1140.16	1115.04	1093.66	1075.36	1059.62	1046.04	1000.57	977.19	964.78	958.08
100000	1268.67	1231.43	1200.17	1173.73	1151.22	1131.96	1115.39	1101.09	1053.23	1028.62	1015.55	1008.50
105000	1332.10	1293.01	1260.18	1232.42	1208.78	1188.55	1171.16	1156.15	1105.89	1080.05	1066.33	1058.93
110000	1395.54	1354.58	1320.19	1291.10	1266.34	1245.15	1226.93	1211.20	1158.55	1131.48	1117.11	1109.35
115000	1458.97	1416.15	1380.20	1349.79	1323.90	1301.75	1282.70	1266.25	1211.21	1182.91	1167.89	1159.78
120000	1522.40	1477.72	1440.21	1408.48	1381.46	1358.35	1338.47	1321.31	1263.87	1234.34	1218.66	1210.20
125000	1585.84	1539.29	1500.22	1467.16	1439.02	1414.94	1394.24	1376.36	1316.54	1285.77	1269.44	1260.63
130000	1649.27	1600.86	1560.22	1525.85	1496.59	1471.54	1450.01	1431.42	1369.20	1337.20	1320.22	1311.05
135000	1712.70	1662.43	1620.23	1584.53	1554.15	1528.14	1505.78	1486.47	1421.86	1388.63	1371.00	1361.48
140000	1776.14	1724.01	1680.24	1643.22	1611.71	1584.74	1561.54	1541.53	1474.52	1440.06	1421.77	1411.90
145000	1839.57	1785.58	1740.25	1701.91	1669.27	1641.33	1617.31	1596.58	1527.18	1491.49	1472.55	1462.33
150000	1903.00	1847.15	1800.26	1760.59	1726.83	1697.93	1673.08	1651.63	1579.84	1542.92	1523.33	1512.75
155000	1966.44	1908.72	1860.27	1819.28	1784.39	1754.53	1728.85	1706.69	1632.50	1594.35	1574.11	1563.18
160000	2029.87	1970.29	1920.27	1877.97	1841.95	1811.13	1784.62	1761.74	1685.16	1645.79	1624.88	1613.60

MONTHLY AMORTIZING PAYMENTS

AMOUNT OF LOAN	NUMBER OF YEARS IN TERM											
	1	2	3	4	5	6	7	8	9	10	11	12
$ 50	4.45	2.36	1.67	1.33	1.12	0.99	0.89	0.82	0.77	0.73	0.70	0.67
100	8.90	4.72	3.34	2.65	2.24	1.97	1.78	1.64	1.54	1.45	1.39	1.33
200	17.80	9.44	6.67	5.30	4.48	3.94	3.56	3.28	3.07	2.90	2.77	2.66
300	26.69	14.16	10.01	7.94	6.72	5.91	5.34	4.92	4.60	4.35	4.15	3.99
400	35.59	18.88	13.34	10.59	8.95	7.88	7.12	6.56	6.14	5.80	5.54	5.32
500	44.49	23.60	16.67	13.23	11.19	9.85	8.90	8.20	7.67	7.25	6.92	6.65
600	53.38	28.32	20.01	15.88	13.43	11.81	10.68	9.84	9.20	8.70	8.30	7.98
700	62.28	33.04	23.34	18.52	15.66	13.78	12.46	11.48	10.73	10.15	9.68	9.31
800	71.18	37.76	26.67	21.17	17.90	15.75	14.23	13.12	12.27	11.60	11.07	10.63
900	80.07	42.48	30.01	23.82	20.14	17.72	16.01	14.76	13.80	13.05	12.45	11.96
1000	88.97	47.20	33.34	26.46	22.38	19.69	17.79	16.40	15.33	14.50	13.83	13.29
2000	177.94	94.39	66.67	52.92	44.75	39.37	35.58	32.79	30.66	28.99	27.66	26.58
3000	266.90	141.58	100.01	79.38	67.12	59.05	53.37	49.18	45.98	43.48	41.48	39.86
4000	355.87	188.77	133.34	105.83	89.49	78.73	71.15	65.57	61.31	57.97	55.31	53.15
5000	444.83	235.96	166.67	132.29	111.86	98.41	88.94	81.96	76.63	72.46	69.14	66.43
6000	533.80	283.15	200.01	158.75	134.23	118.09	106.73	98.35	91.96	86.95	82.96	79.72
7000	622.77	330.34	233.34	185.20	156.60	137.77	124.51	114.74	107.28	101.45	96.79	93.01
8000	711.73	377.53	266.68	211.66	178.97	157.45	142.30	131.13	122.61	115.94	110.62	106.29
9000	800.70	424.72	300.01	238.12	201.34	177.13	160.09	147.52	137.93	130.43	124.44	119.58
10000	889.66	471.91	333.34	264.57	223.71	196.81	177.87	163.91	153.26	144.92	138.27	132.86
11000	978.63	519.10	366.68	291.03	246.09	216.49	195.66	180.30	168.59	159.42	152.09	146.15
12000	1067.59	566.29	400.01	317.49	268.46	236.17	213.45	196.69	183.91	173.91	165.92	159.44
13000	1156.56	613.48	433.34	343.94	290.83	255.85	231.23	213.08	199.24	188.40	179.75	172.72
14000	1245.53	660.67	466.68	370.40	313.20	275.53	249.02	229.47	214.56	202.89	193.57	186.01
15000	1334.49	707.86	500.01	396.86	335.57	295.21	266.81	245.86	229.89	217.38	207.40	199.29
16000	1423.46	755.05	533.35	423.31	357.94	314.89	284.59	262.25	245.21	231.88	221.23	212.58
17000	1512.42	802.24	566.68	449.77	380.31	334.57	302.38	278.64	260.54	246.37	235.05	225.87
18000	1601.39	849.43	600.01	476.23	402.68	354.25	320.17	295.03	275.86	260.86	248.88	239.15
19000	1690.35	896.62	633.35	502.68	425.05	373.93	337.95	311.42	291.19	275.35	262.70	252.44
20000	1779.32	943.81	666.68	529.14	447.42	393.61	355.74	327.82	306.52	289.84	276.53	265.72
21000	1868.29	991.00	700.02	555.60	469.80	413.29	373.53	344.21	321.84	304.34	290.36	279.01
22000	1957.25	1038.19	733.35	582.05	492.17	432.97	391.31	360.60	337.17	318.83	304.18	292.30
23000	2046.22	1085.38	766.68	608.51	514.54	452.66	409.10	376.99	352.49	333.32	318.01	305.58
24000	2135.18	1132.57	800.02	634.97	536.91	472.34	426.89	393.38	367.82	347.81	331.84	318.87
25000	2224.15	1179.76	833.35	661.42	559.28	492.02	444.67	409.77	383.14	362.30	345.66	332.15
26000	2313.12	1226.95	866.68	687.88	581.65	511.70	462.46	426.16	398.47	376.80	359.49	345.44
27000	2402.08	1274.14	900.02	714.34	604.02	531.38	480.25	442.55	413.79	391.29	373.31	358.73
28000	2491.05	1321.33	933.35	740.79	626.39	551.06	498.03	458.94	429.12	405.78	387.14	372.01
29000	2580.01	1368.52	966.69	767.25	648.76	570.74	515.82	475.33	444.45	420.27	400.97	385.30
30000	2668.98	1415.71	1000.02	793.71	671.13	590.42	533.61	491.72	459.77	434.76	414.79	398.58
31000	2757.94	1462.90	1033.35	820.16	693.51	610.10	551.39	508.11	475.10	449.26	428.62	411.87
32000	2846.91	1510.09	1066.69	846.62	715.88	629.78	569.18	524.50	490.42	463.75	442.45	425.16
33000	2935.88	1557.29	1100.02	873.08	738.25	649.46	586.97	540.89	505.75	478.24	456.27	438.44
34000	3024.84	1604.48	1133.36	899.53	760.62	669.14	604.75	557.28	521.07	492.73	470.10	451.73
35000	3113.81	1651.67	1166.69	925.99	782.99	688.82	622.54	573.67	536.40	507.22	483.92	465.01
37500	3336.22	1769.64	1250.02	992.13	838.92	738.02	667.01	614.65	574.71	543.45	518.49	498.23
40000	3558.64	1887.62	1333.36	1058.28	894.84	787.22	711.47	655.63	613.03	579.68	553.06	531.44
42500	3781.05	2005.59	1416.69	1124.42	950.77	836.42	755.94	696.60	651.34	615.91	587.62	564.66
45000	4003.47	2123.57	1500.03	1190.56	1006.70	885.62	800.41	737.58	689.65	652.14	622.19	597.87
47500	4225.88	2241.54	1583.36	1256.70	1062.63	934.83	844.87	778.55	727.97	688.37	656.75	631.09
50000	4448.29	2359.52	1666.70	1322.84	1118.55	984.03	889.34	819.53	766.28	724.60	691.32	664.30
52500	4670.71	2477.50	1750.03	1388.98	1174.48	1033.23	933.81	860.51	804.60	760.83	725.88	697.52
55000	4893.12	2595.47	1833.37	1455.13	1230.41	1082.43	978.27	901.48	842.91	797.06	760.45	730.73
57500	5115.54	2713.45	1916.70	1521.27	1286.34	1131.63	1022.74	942.46	881.22	833.29	795.01	763.95
60000	5337.95	2831.42	2000.04	1587.41	1342.26	1180.83	1067.21	983.44	919.54	869.52	829.58	797.16
65000	5782.78	3067.37	2166.70	1719.69	1454.12	1279.23	1156.14	1065.39	996.17	941.98	898.71	863.59
70000	6227.61	3303.33	2333.37	1851.98	1565.97	1377.64	1245.07	1147.34	1072.79	1014.44	967.84	930.02
75000	6672.44	3539.28	2500.04	1984.26	1677.83	1476.04	1334.01	1229.29	1149.42	1086.90	1036.97	996.45
80000	7117.27	3775.24	2666.71	2116.55	1789.68	1574.44	1422.94	1311.25	1226.05	1159.36	1106.11	1062.88
85000	7562.10	4011.18	2833.38	2248.83	1901.54	1672.84	1511.88	1393.20	1302.68	1231.82	1175.24	1129.31
90000	8006.93	4247.13	3000.05	2381.11	2013.39	1771.24	1600.81	1475.15	1379.30	1304.28	1244.37	1195.74
95000	8451.75	4483.08	3166.72	2513.40	2125.25	1869.65	1689.74	1557.10	1455.93	1376.74	1313.50	1262.17
100000	8896.58	4719.04	3333.39	2645.68	2237.10	1968.05	1778.68	1639.06	1532.56	1449.20	1382.63	1328.59
105000	9341.41	4954.99	3500.06	2777.96	2348.96	2066.45	1867.61	1721.01	1609.19	1521.66	1451.76	1395.03
110000	9786.24	5190.94	3666.73	2910.25	2460.81	2164.85	1956.54	1802.96	1685.82	1594.12	1520.89	1461.46
115000	10231.07	5426.89	3833.40	3042.53	2572.67	2263.26	2045.48	1884.91	1762.44	1666.58	1590.02	1527.89
120000	10675.90	5662.84	4000.07	3174.82	2684.52	2361.66	2134.41	1966.87	1839.07	1739.04	1659.16	1594.32
125000	11120.73	5898.79	4166.74	3307.10	2796.38	2460.06	2223.34	2048.82	1915.70	1811.50	1728.29	1660.75
130000	11565.56	6134.74	4333.40	3439.38	2908.23	2558.46	2312.28	2130.77	1992.33	1883.96	1797.42	1727.18
135000	12010.39	6370.70	4500.07	3571.67	3020.09	2656.86	2401.21	2212.72	2068.95	1956.42	1866.55	1793.61
140000	12455.21	6606.65	4666.74	3703.95	3131.94	2755.27	2490.14	2294.68	2145.58	2028.88	1935.68	1860.04
145000	12900.04	6842.60	4833.41	3836.23	3243.80	2853.67	2579.08	2376.63	2222.21	2101.34	2004.81	1926.47
150000	13344.87	7078.55	5000.08	3968.52	3355.65	2952.07	2668.01	2458.58	2298.84	2173.80	2073.94	1992.90
155000	13789.70	7314.50	5166.75	4100.80	3467.51	3050.47	2756.94	2540.53	2375.47	2246.26	2143.08	2059.33
160000	14234.53	7550.45	5333.42	4233.09	3579.36	3148.88	2845.88	2622.49	2452.09	2318.72	2212.21	2125.76

AMOUNT OF LOAN	NUMBER OF YEARS IN TERM											
	13	14	15	16	17	18	19	20	25	30	35	40
$ 50	0.65	0.63	0.61	0.60	0.59	0.58	0.57	0.56	0.54	0.53	0.52	0.52
100	1.29	1.25	1.22	1.20	1.17	1.15	1.14	1.12	1.08	1.05	1.04	1.03
200	2.57	2.50	2.44	2.39	2.34	2.30	2.27	2.24	2.15	2.10	2.08	2.06
300	3.86	3.75	3.65	3.58	3.51	3.45	3.40	3.36	3.22	3.15	3.11	3.09
400	5.14	4.99	4.87	4.77	4.68	4.60	4.54	4.48	4.29	4.20	4.15	4.12
500	6.43	6.24	6.09	5.96	5.84	5.75	5.67	5.60	5.36	5.24	5.18	5.15
600	7.71	7.49	7.30	7.15	7.01	6.90	6.80	6.72	6.44	6.29	6.22	6.18
700	8.99	8.74	8.52	8.34	8.18	8.05	7.93	7.83	7.51	7.34	7.25	7.21
800	10.28	9.98	9.74	9.53	9.35	9.20	9.07	8.95	8.58	8.39	8.29	8.23
900	11.56	11.23	10.95	10.72	10.52	10.35	10.20	10.07	9.65	9.44	9.32	9.26
1000	12.85	12.48	12.17	11.91	11.68	11.49	11.33	11.19	10.72	10.48	10.36	10.29
2000	25.69	24.95	24.33	23.81	23.36	22.98	22.66	22.38	21.44	20.96	20.71	20.58
3000	38.53	37.42	36.49	35.71	35.04	34.47	33.98	33.56	32.16	31.44	31.07	30.87
4000	51.37	49.90	48.66	47.61	46.72	45.96	45.31	44.75	42.87	41.92	41.42	41.15
5000	64.21	62.37	60.82	59.51	58.40	57.45	56.64	55.93	53.59	52.40	51.77	51.44
6000	77.06	74.84	72.98	71.41	70.08	68.94	67.96	67.12	64.31	62.88	62.13	61.73
7000	89.90	87.31	85.15	83.32	81.76	80.43	79.29	78.30	75.03	73.36	72.48	72.01
8000	102.74	99.79	97.31	95.22	93.44	91.92	90.61	89.49	85.74	83.84	82.83	82.30
9000	115.58	112.26	109.47	107.12	105.12	103.41	101.94	100.68	96.46	94.32	93.19	92.59
10000	128.42	124.73	121.63	119.02	116.80	114.90	113.27	111.86	107.18	104.79	103.54	102.87
11000	141.26	137.20	133.80	130.92	128.48	126.39	124.59	123.05	117.90	115.27	113.90	113.16
12000	154.11	149.68	145.96	142.82	140.16	137.88	135.92	134.23	128.61	125.75	124.25	123.45
13000	166.95	162.15	158.12	154.72	151.83	149.37	147.25	145.42	139.33	136.23	134.60	133.73
14000	179.79	174.62	170.29	166.63	163.51	160.85	158.57	156.60	150.05	146.71	144.96	144.02
15000	192.63	187.09	182.45	178.53	175.19	172.34	169.90	167.79	160.77	157.19	155.31	154.31
16000	205.47	199.57	194.61	190.43	186.87	183.83	181.22	178.98	171.48	167.67	165.66	164.59
17000	218.31	212.04	206.78	202.33	198.55	195.32	192.55	190.16	182.20	178.15	176.02	174.88
18000	231.16	224.51	218.94	214.23	210.23	206.81	203.88	201.35	192.92	188.63	186.37	185.17
19000	244.00	236.98	231.10	226.13	221.91	218.30	215.20	212.53	203.64	199.11	196.73	195.46
20000	256.84	249.46	243.26	238.04	233.59	229.79	226.53	223.72	214.35	209.58	207.08	205.74
21000	269.68	261.93	255.43	249.94	245.27	241.28	237.86	234.90	225.07	220.06	217.43	216.03
22000	282.52	274.40	267.59	261.84	256.95	252.77	249.18	246.09	235.79	230.54	227.79	226.32
23000	295.36	286.87	279.75	273.74	268.63	264.26	260.51	257.27	246.51	241.02	238.14	236.60
24000	308.21	299.35	291.92	285.64	280.31	275.75	271.83	268.46	257.22	251.50	248.49	246.89
25000	321.05	311.82	304.08	297.54	291.99	287.24	283.16	279.65	267.94	261.98	258.85	257.18
26000	333.89	324.29	316.24	309.44	303.66	298.73	294.49	290.83	278.66	272.46	269.20	267.46
27000	346.73	336.76	328.41	321.35	315.34	310.22	305.81	302.02	289.38	282.94	279.56	277.75
28000	359.57	349.24	340.57	333.25	327.02	321.70	317.14	313.20	300.09	293.42	289.91	288.04
29000	372.42	361.71	352.73	345.15	338.70	333.19	328.46	324.39	310.81	303.89	300.26	298.32
30000	385.26	374.18	364.89	357.05	350.38	344.68	339.79	335.57	321.53	314.37	310.62	308.61
31000	398.10	386.65	377.06	368.95	362.06	356.17	351.12	346.76	332.25	324.85	320.97	318.90
32000	410.94	399.13	389.22	380.85	373.74	367.66	362.44	357.95	342.96	335.33	331.32	329.18
33000	423.78	411.60	401.38	392.75	385.42	379.15	373.77	369.13	353.68	345.81	341.68	339.47
34000	436.62	424.07	413.55	404.66	397.10	390.64	385.10	380.32	364.40	356.29	352.03	349.76
35000	449.47	436.54	425.71	416.56	408.78	402.13	396.42	391.50	375.12	366.77	362.38	360.05
37500	481.57	467.73	456.12	446.31	437.98	430.85	424.74	419.47	401.91	392.97	388.27	385.76
40000	513.67	498.91	486.52	476.07	467.17	459.58	453.05	447.43	428.70	419.16	414.15	411.48
42500	545.78	530.09	516.93	505.82	496.37	488.30	481.37	475.39	455.50	445.36	440.04	437.20
45000	577.88	561.27	547.34	535.57	525.57	517.02	509.68	503.36	482.29	471.56	465.92	462.91
47500	609.99	592.45	577.75	565.33	554.77	545.75	538.00	531.32	509.08	497.76	491.81	488.63
50000	642.09	623.63	608.15	595.08	583.97	574.47	566.31	559.29	535.88	523.95	517.69	514.35
52500	674.20	654.81	638.56	624.83	613.16	603.19	594.63	587.25	562.67	550.15	543.57	540.07
55000	706.30	685.99	668.97	654.59	642.36	631.91	622.95	615.22	589.46	576.35	569.46	565.78
57500	738.40	717.18	699.38	684.34	671.56	660.64	651.26	643.18	616.26	602.55	595.34	591.50
60000	770.51	748.36	729.78	714.10	700.76	689.36	679.58	671.14	643.05	628.74	621.23	617.22
65000	834.72	810.72	790.60	773.60	759.15	746.81	736.21	727.07	696.64	681.14	673.00	668.65
70000	898.93	873.08	851.41	833.11	817.55	804.25	792.84	783.00	750.23	733.53	724.76	720.09
75000	963.13	935.45	912.23	892.62	875.95	861.70	849.47	838.93	803.81	785.93	776.53	771.52
80000	1027.34	997.81	973.04	952.13	934.34	919.15	906.10	894.86	857.40	838.32	828.30	822.95
85000	1091.55	1060.17	1033.86	1011.63	992.74	976.59	962.73	950.78	910.99	890.72	880.07	874.39
90000	1155.76	1122.53	1094.67	1071.14	1051.14	1034.04	1019.36	1006.71	964.57	943.11	931.84	925.82
95000	1219.97	1184.90	1155.49	1130.65	1109.53	1091.49	1075.99	1062.64	1018.16	995.51	983.61	977.26
100000	1284.18	1247.26	1216.30	1190.16	1167.93	1148.93	1132.62	1118.57	1071.75	1047.90	1035.38	1028.69
105000	1348.39	1309.62	1277.12	1249.66	1226.32	1206.38	1189.26	1174.50	1125.34	1100.30	1087.14	1080.13
110000	1412.59	1371.98	1337.93	1309.17	1284.72	1263.82	1245.89	1230.43	1178.92	1152.69	1138.91	1131.56
115000	1476.80	1434.35	1398.75	1368.68	1343.12	1321.27	1302.52	1286.35	1232.51	1205.09	1190.68	1182.99
120000	1541.01	1496.71	1459.56	1428.19	1401.51	1378.72	1359.15	1342.28	1286.10	1257.48	1242.45	1234.43
125000	1605.22	1559.07	1520.38	1487.69	1459.91	1436.16	1415.78	1398.21	1339.68	1309.88	1294.22	1285.86
130000	1669.43	1621.44	1581.19	1547.20	1518.30	1493.61	1472.41	1454.14	1393.27	1362.27	1345.99	1337.30
135000	1733.64	1683.80	1642.01	1606.71	1576.70	1551.06	1529.04	1510.07	1446.86	1414.67	1397.76	1388.73
140000	1797.85	1746.16	1702.82	1666.22	1635.10	1608.50	1585.67	1566.00	1500.45	1467.06	1449.52	1440.17
145000	1862.06	1808.52	1763.64	1725.72	1693.49	1665.95	1642.30	1621.92	1554.03	1519.46	1501.29	1491.60
150000	1926.26	1870.89	1824.45	1785.23	1751.89	1723.40	1698.93	1677.85	1607.62	1571.85	1553.06	1543.03
155000	1990.47	1933.25	1885.27	1844.74	1810.28	1780.84	1755.57	1733.78	1661.21	1624.24	1604.83	1594.47
160000	2054.68	1995.61	1946.08	1904.25	1868.68	1838.29	1812.20	1789.71	1714.80	1676.64	1656.60	1645.90

MONTHLY AMORTIZING PAYMENTS

AMOUNT OF LOAN	NUMBER OF YEARS IN TERM											
	1	2	3	4	5	6	7	8	9	10	11	12
$ 50	4.46	2.37	1.68	1.33	1.13	1.00	0.90	0.83	0.78	0.74	0.70	0.68
100	8.91	4.74	3.35	2.66	2.25	1.99	1.80	1.66	1.55	1.47	1.40	1.35
200	17.82	9.47	6.70	5.32	4.50	3.97	3.59	3.31	3.10	2.93	2.80	2.69
300	26.73	14.20	10.04	7.98	6.75	5.95	5.38	4.96	4.65	4.40	4.20	4.04
400	35.64	18.93	13.39	10.64	9.00	7.93	7.17	6.62	6.19	5.86	5.60	5.38
500	44.55	23.66	16.73	13.29	11.25	9.91	8.97	8.27	7.74	7.32	6.99	6.72
600	53.45	28.39	20.08	15.95	13.50	11.89	10.76	9.92	9.29	8.79	8.39	8.07
700	62.36	33.12	23.42	18.61	15.75	13.87	12.55	11.58	10.83	10.25	9.79	9.41
800	71.27	37.85	26.77	21.27	18.00	15.85	14.34	13.23	12.38	11.72	11.19	10.76
900	80.18	42.58	30.11	23.93	20.25	17.84	16.13	14.88	13.93	13.18	12.58	12.10
1000	89.09	47.31	33.46	26.58	22.50	19.82	17.93	16.53	15.47	14.64	13.98	13.44
2000	178.17	94.62	66.91	53.16	45.00	39.63	35.85	33.06	30.94	29.28	27.96	26.88
3000	267.25	141.93	100.37	79.74	67.50	59.44	53.77	49.59	46.41	43.92	41.93	40.32
4000	356.34	189.23	133.82	106.32	90.00	79.25	71.69	66.12	61.88	58.56	55.91	53.76
5000	445.42	236.54	167.27	132.90	112.49	99.06	89.61	82.65	77.34	73.19	69.88	67.20
6000	534.50	283.85	200.73	159.48	134.99	118.87	107.53	99.18	92.81	87.83	83.86	80.64
7000	623.59	331.16	234.18	186.06	157.49	138.68	125.45	115.71	108.28	102.47	97.83	94.08
8000	712.67	378.46	267.63	212.64	179.99	158.49	143.37	132.24	123.75	117.11	111.81	107.51
9000	801.75	425.77	301.09	239.22	202.49	178.31	161.30	148.76	139.21	131.74	125.78	120.95
10000	890.83	473.08	334.54	265.80	224.98	198.12	179.22	165.29	154.68	146.38	139.76	134.39
11000	979.92	520.39	367.99	292.38	247.48	217.93	197.14	181.82	170.15	161.02	153.73	147.83
12000	1069.00	567.69	401.45	318.96	269.98	237.74	215.06	198.35	185.62	175.66	167.71	161.27
13000	1158.08	615.00	434.90	345.54	292.48	257.55	232.98	214.88	201.08	190.29	181.69	174.71
14000	1247.17	662.31	468.36	372.12	314.98	277.36	250.90	231.41	216.55	204.93	195.66	188.15
15000	1336.25	709.61	501.81	398.70	337.47	297.17	268.82	247.94	232.02	219.57	209.64	201.58
16000	1425.33	756.92	535.26	425.28	359.97	316.98	286.74	264.47	247.49	234.21	223.61	215.02
17000	1514.41	804.23	568.72	451.86	382.47	336.80	304.67	280.99	262.95	248.84	237.59	228.46
18000	1603.50	851.54	602.17	478.44	404.97	356.61	322.59	297.52	278.42	263.48	251.56	241.90
19000	1692.58	898.84	635.62	505.02	427.47	376.42	340.51	314.05	293.89	278.12	265.54	255.34
20000	1781.66	946.15	669.08	531.60	449.96	396.23	358.43	330.58	309.36	292.76	279.51	268.78
21000	1870.75	993.46	702.53	558.18	472.46	416.04	376.35	347.11	324.82	307.39	293.49	282.22
22000	1959.83	1040.77	735.98	584.76	494.96	435.85	394.27	363.64	340.29	322.03	307.46	295.65
23000	2048.91	1088.07	769.44	611.34	517.46	455.66	412.19	380.17	355.76	336.67	321.44	309.09
24000	2137.99	1135.38	802.89	637.92	539.96	475.47	430.11	396.70	371.23	351.31	335.42	322.53
25000	2227.08	1182.69	836.35	664.50	562.45	495.28	448.04	413.23	386.69	365.95	349.39	335.97
26000	2316.16	1230.00	869.80	691.08	584.95	515.10	465.96	429.75	402.16	380.58	363.37	349.41
27000	2405.24	1277.30	903.25	717.66	607.45	534.91	483.88	446.28	417.63	395.22	377.34	362.85
28000	2494.33	1324.61	936.71	744.24	629.95	554.72	501.80	462.81	433.10	409.86	391.32	376.29
29000	2583.41	1371.92	970.16	770.82	652.45	574.53	519.72	479.34	448.56	424.50	405.29	389.72
30000	2672.49	1419.22	1003.61	797.40	674.94	594.34	537.64	495.87	464.03	439.13	419.27	403.16
31000	2761.57	1466.53	1037.07	823.98	697.44	614.15	555.56	512.40	479.50	453.77	433.24	416.60
32000	2850.66	1513.84	1070.52	850.56	719.94	633.96	573.48	528.93	494.97	468.41	447.22	430.04
33000	2939.74	1561.15	1103.97	877.14	742.44	653.77	591.41	545.46	510.43	483.05	461.19	443.48
34000	3028.82	1608.45	1137.43	903.72	764.93	673.59	609.33	561.98	525.90	497.68	475.17	456.92
35000	3117.91	1655.76	1170.88	930.30	787.43	693.40	627.25	578.51	541.37	512.32	489.15	470.36
37500	3340.61	1774.03	1254.52	996.75	843.68	742.92	672.05	619.84	580.04	548.92	524.08	503.95
40000	3563.32	1892.30	1338.15	1063.20	899.92	792.45	716.85	661.16	618.71	585.51	559.02	537.55
42500	3786.03	2010.57	1421.78	1129.65	956.17	841.98	761.66	702.48	657.38	622.10	593.96	571.14
45000	4008.73	2128.83	1505.42	1196.10	1012.41	891.51	806.46	743.80	696.04	658.70	628.90	604.74
47500	4231.44	2247.10	1589.05	1262.55	1068.66	941.04	851.26	785.12	734.71	695.29	663.84	638.34
50000	4454.15	2365.37	1672.69	1329.00	1124.90	990.56	896.07	826.45	773.38	731.89	698.78	671.93
52500	4676.86	2483.64	1756.32	1395.45	1181.15	1040.09	940.87	867.77	812.05	768.48	733.72	705.53
55000	4899.56	2601.91	1839.95	1461.90	1237.39	1089.62	985.67	909.09	850.72	805.07	768.65	739.13
57500	5122.27	2720.18	1923.59	1528.35	1293.64	1139.15	1030.48	950.41	889.39	841.67	803.59	772.72
60000	5344.98	2838.44	2007.22	1594.80	1349.88	1188.68	1075.28	991.73	928.06	878.26	838.53	806.32
65000	5790.39	3074.98	2174.49	1727.70	1462.37	1287.73	1164.89	1074.38	1005.40	951.45	908.41	873.51
70000	6235.81	3311.52	2341.76	1860.60	1574.86	1386.79	1254.49	1157.02	1082.73	1024.64	978.29	940.71
75000	6681.22	3548.05	2509.03	1993.50	1687.35	1485.84	1344.10	1239.67	1160.07	1097.83	1048.16	1007.90
80000	7126.63	3784.59	2676.30	2126.40	1799.84	1584.90	1433.70	1322.31	1237.41	1171.01	1118.04	1075.09
85000	7572.05	4021.13	2843.56	2259.30	1912.33	1683.96	1523.31	1404.95	1314.75	1244.20	1187.92	1142.28
90000	8017.46	4257.66	3010.83	2392.20	2024.82	1783.01	1612.92	1487.60	1392.08	1317.39	1257.79	1209.48
95000	8462.88	4494.20	3178.10	2525.10	2137.31	1882.07	1702.52	1570.24	1469.42	1390.58	1327.67	1276.67
100000	8908.29	4730.74	3345.37	2658.00	2249.80	1981.12	1792.13	1652.89	1546.76	1463.77	1397.55	1343.86
105000	9353.71	4967.27	3512.64	2790.90	2362.29	2080.18	1881.74	1735.53	1624.10	1536.95	1467.43	1411.06
110000	9799.12	5203.81	3679.90	2923.80	2474.78	2179.23	1971.34	1818.17	1701.44	1610.14	1537.30	1478.25
115000	10244.53	5440.35	3847.17	3056.70	2587.27	2278.29	2060.95	1900.82	1778.77	1683.33	1607.18	1545.44
120000	10689.95	5676.88	4014.44	3189.60	2699.76	2377.35	2150.55	1983.46	1856.11	1756.52	1677.06	1612.63
125000	11135.36	5913.42	4181.71	3322.50	2812.25	2476.40	2240.16	2066.11	1933.45	1829.71	1746.93	1679.83
130000	11580.78	6149.96	4348.98	3455.40	2924.74	2575.46	2329.77	2148.75	2010.79	1902.90	1816.81	1747.02
135000	12026.19	6386.49	4516.24	3588.30	3037.23	2674.51	2419.37	2231.39	2088.12	1976.08	1886.69	1814.21
140000	12471.61	6623.03	4683.51	3721.20	3149.72	2773.57	2508.98	2314.04	2165.46	2049.27	1956.57	1881.41
145000	12917.02	6859.56	4850.78	3854.10	3262.21	2872.63	2598.58	2396.68	2242.80	2122.46	2026.44	1948.60
150000	13362.43	7096.10	5018.05	3987.00	3374.70	2971.68	2688.19	2479.33	2320.14	2195.65	2096.32	2015.79
155000	13807.85	7332.64	5185.32	4119.90	3487.19	3070.74	2777.80	2561.97	2397.48	2268.84	2166.20	2082.98
160000	14253.26	7569.17	5352.59	4252.80	3599.68	3169.79	2867.40	2644.61	2474.81	2342.02	2236.07	2150.18

MONTHLY AMORTIZING PAYMENTS   12.50%

AMOUNT OF LOAN	13	14	15	16	17	18	19	20	25	30	35	40
$ 50	0.65	0.64	0.62	0.61	0.60	0.59	0.58	0.57	0.55	0.54	0.53	0.53
100	1.30	1.27	1.24	1.21	1.19	1.17	1.15	1.14	1.10	1.07	1.06	1.05
200	2.60	2.53	2.47	2.42	2.37	2.34	2.30	2.28	2.19	2.14	2.12	2.10
300	3.90	3.79	3.70	3.63	3.56	3.50	3.45	3.41	3.28	3.21	3.17	3.15
400	5.20	5.06	4.94	4.83	4.74	4.67	4.60	4.55	4.37	4.27	4.23	4.20
500	6.50	6.32	6.17	6.04	5.93	5.84	5.75	5.69	5.46	5.34	5.28	5.25
600	7.80	7.58	7.40	7.25	7.11	7.00	6.90	6.82	6.55	6.41	6.34	6.30
700	9.10	8.85	8.63	8.45	8.30	8.17	8.05	7.96	7.64	7.48	7.39	7.35
800	10.40	10.11	9.87	9.66	9.48	9.33	9.20	9.09	8.73	8.54	8.45	8.40
900	11.70	11.37	11.10	10.87	10.67	10.50	10.35	10.23	9.82	9.61	9.50	9.45
1000	13.00	12.64	12.33	12.07	11.85	11.67	11.50	11.37	10.91	10.68	10.56	10.49
2000	26.00	25.27	24.66	24.14	23.70	23.33	23.00	22.73	21.81	21.35	21.11	20.98
3000	39.00	37.90	36.98	36.21	35.55	34.99	34.50	34.09	32.72	32.02	31.66	31.47
4000	52.00	50.53	49.31	48.27	47.39	46.65	46.00	45.45	43.62	42.70	42.22	41.96
5000	64.99	63.16	61.63	60.34	59.24	58.31	57.50	56.81	54.52	53.37	52.77	52.45
6000	77.99	75.80	73.96	72.41	71.09	69.97	69.00	68.17	65.43	64.04	63.32	62.94
7000	90.99	88.43	86.28	84.47	82.94	81.63	80.50	79.53	76.33	74.71	73.87	73.43
8000	103.99	101.06	98.61	96.54	94.78	93.29	92.00	90.90	87.23	85.39	84.43	83.92
9000	116.98	113.69	110.93	108.61	106.63	104.95	103.50	102.26	98.14	96.06	94.98	94.41
10000	129.98	126.32	123.26	120.67	118.48	116.61	115.00	113.62	109.04	106.73	105.53	104.90
11000	142.98	138.95	135.58	132.74	130.32	128.27	126.50	124.98	119.94	117.40	116.08	115.39
12000	155.98	151.59	147.91	144.81	142.17	139.93	138.00	136.34	130.85	128.08	126.64	125.88
13000	168.97	164.22	160.23	156.87	154.02	151.59	149.50	147.70	141.75	138.75	137.19	136.36
14000	181.97	176.85	172.56	168.94	165.87	163.25	161.00	159.06	152.65	149.42	147.74	146.85
15000	194.97	189.48	184.88	181.01	177.71	174.91	172.50	170.43	163.56	160.09	158.29	157.34
16000	207.97	202.11	197.21	193.07	189.56	186.57	184.00	181.79	174.46	170.77	168.85	167.83
17000	220.97	214.74	209.53	205.14	201.41	198.23	195.50	193.15	185.37	181.44	179.40	178.32
18000	233.96	227.38	221.86	217.21	213.26	209.89	207.00	204.51	196.27	192.11	189.95	188.81
19000	246.96	240.01	234.18	229.27	225.10	221.55	218.50	215.87	207.17	202.78	200.50	199.30
20000	259.96	252.64	246.51	241.34	236.95	233.21	230.00	227.23	218.08	213.46	211.06	209.79
21000	272.96	265.27	258.83	253.41	248.80	244.87	241.49	238.59	228.98	224.13	221.61	220.28
22000	285.95	277.90	271.16	265.47	260.64	256.53	252.99	249.96	239.88	234.80	232.16	230.77
23000	298.95	290.53	283.49	277.54	272.49	268.19	264.49	261.32	250.79	245.47	242.71	241.26
24000	311.95	303.17	295.81	289.61	284.34	279.85	275.99	272.68	261.69	256.15	253.27	251.75
25000	324.95	315.80	308.14	301.67	296.19	291.51	287.49	284.04	272.59	266.82	263.82	262.23
26000	337.94	328.43	320.46	313.74	308.03	303.17	298.99	295.40	283.50	277.49	274.37	272.72
27000	350.94	341.06	332.79	325.81	319.88	314.83	310.49	306.76	294.40	288.16	284.92	283.21
28000	363.94	353.69	345.11	337.87	331.73	326.49	321.99	318.12	305.30	298.84	295.48	293.70
29000	376.94	366.32	357.44	349.94	343.58	338.15	333.49	329.49	316.21	309.51	306.03	304.19
30000	389.93	378.96	369.76	362.01	355.42	349.81	344.99	340.85	327.11	320.18	316.58	314.68
31000	402.93	391.59	382.09	374.07	367.27	361.47	356.49	352.21	338.01	330.85	327.13	325.17
32000	415.93	404.22	394.41	386.14	379.12	373.13	367.99	363.57	348.92	341.53	337.69	335.66
33000	428.93	416.85	406.74	398.21	390.96	384.79	379.49	374.93	359.82	352.20	348.24	346.15
34000	441.93	429.48	419.06	410.27	402.81	396.45	390.99	386.29	370.73	362.87	358.79	356.64
35000	454.92	442.11	431.39	422.34	414.66	408.11	402.49	397.65	381.63	373.55	369.34	367.13
37500	487.42	473.69	462.20	452.51	444.28	437.26	431.24	426.06	408.89	400.23	395.73	393.35
40000	519.91	505.27	493.01	482.67	473.90	466.41	459.99	454.46	436.15	426.91	422.11	419.57
42500	552.41	536.85	523.83	512.84	503.51	495.56	488.73	482.86	463.41	453.59	448.49	445.80
45000	584.90	568.43	554.64	543.01	533.13	524.71	517.48	511.27	490.66	480.27	474.87	472.02
47500	617.39	600.01	585.45	573.17	562.75	553.86	546.23	539.67	517.92	506.95	501.25	498.24
50000	649.89	631.59	616.27	603.34	592.37	583.01	574.98	568.08	545.18	533.63	527.63	524.46
52500	682.38	663.17	647.08	633.51	621.99	612.16	603.73	596.48	572.44	560.32	554.01	550.69
55000	714.88	694.75	677.89	663.67	651.60	641.31	632.48	624.88	599.70	587.00	580.39	576.91
57500	747.37	726.33	708.71	693.84	681.22	670.46	661.23	653.29	626.96	613.68	606.78	603.13
60000	779.86	757.91	739.52	724.01	710.84	699.61	689.98	681.69	654.22	640.36	633.16	629.36
65000	844.85	821.06	801.14	784.34	770.08	757.91	747.47	738.50	708.74	693.72	685.92	681.80
70000	909.84	884.22	862.77	844.67	829.31	816.21	804.97	795.30	763.25	747.09	738.68	734.25
75000	974.83	947.38	924.40	905.01	888.55	874.51	862.47	852.11	817.77	800.45	791.45	786.69
80000	1039.82	1010.54	986.02	965.34	947.79	932.81	919.97	908.92	872.29	853.81	844.21	839.14
85000	1104.81	1073.70	1047.65	1025.67	1007.02	991.11	977.46	965.72	926.81	907.17	896.97	891.59
90000	1169.79	1136.86	1109.27	1086.01	1066.26	1049.41	1034.96	1022.53	981.32	960.54	949.73	944.03
95000	1234.78	1200.01	1170.90	1146.34	1125.49	1107.71	1092.46	1079.34	1035.84	1013.90	1002.50	996.48
100000	1299.77	1263.17	1232.53	1206.67	1184.73	1166.01	1149.96	1136.15	1090.36	1067.26	1055.26	1048.92
105000	1364.76	1326.33	1294.15	1267.01	1243.97	1224.31	1207.45	1192.95	1144.88	1120.63	1108.02	1101.37
110000	1429.75	1389.49	1355.78	1327.34	1303.20	1282.61	1264.95	1249.76	1199.39	1173.99	1160.78	1153.82
115000	1494.74	1452.65	1417.41	1387.68	1362.44	1340.91	1322.45	1306.57	1253.91	1227.35	1213.55	1206.26
120000	1559.72	1515.81	1479.03	1448.01	1421.68	1399.21	1379.95	1363.37	1308.43	1280.71	1266.31	1258.71
125000	1624.71	1578.97	1540.66	1508.34	1480.91	1457.51	1437.44	1420.18	1362.95	1334.08	1319.07	1311.15
130000	1689.70	1642.12	1602.28	1568.68	1540.15	1515.81	1494.94	1476.99	1417.47	1387.44	1371.84	1363.60
135000	1754.69	1705.28	1663.91	1629.01	1599.38	1574.11	1552.44	1533.79	1471.98	1440.80	1424.60	1416.05
140000	1819.68	1768.44	1725.54	1689.34	1658.62	1632.41	1609.94	1590.60	1526.50	1494.17	1477.36	1468.49
145000	1884.67	1831.60	1787.16	1749.68	1717.86	1690.71	1667.43	1647.41	1581.02	1547.53	1530.12	1520.94
150000	1949.65	1894.76	1848.79	1810.01	1777.09	1749.01	1724.93	1704.22	1635.54	1600.89	1582.89	1573.38
155000	2014.64	1957.92	1910.41	1870.34	1836.33	1807.31	1782.43	1761.02	1690.05	1654.25	1635.65	1625.83
160000	2079.63	2021.07	1972.04	1930.68	1895.57	1865.61	1839.93	1817.83	1744.57	1707.62	1688.41	1678.28

63

AMOUNT OF LOAN	NUMBER OF YEARS IN TERM											
	1	2	3	4	5	6	7	8	9	10	11	12
$ 50	4.47	2.38	1.68	1.34	1.14	1.00	0.91	0.84	0.79	0.74	0.71	0.68
100	8.93	4.75	3.36	2.68	2.27	2.00	1.81	1.67	1.57	1.48	1.42	1.36
200	17.85	9.49	6.72	5.35	4.53	3.99	3.62	3.34	3.13	2.96	2.83	2.72
300	26.77	14.23	10.08	8.02	6.79	5.99	5.42	5.01	4.69	4.44	4.24	4.08
400	35.69	18.97	13.43	10.69	9.06	7.98	7.23	6.67	6.25	5.92	5.66	5.44
500	44.61	23.72	16.79	13.36	11.32	9.98	9.03	8.34	7.81	7.40	7.07	6.80
600	53.53	28.46	20.15	16.03	13.58	11.97	10.84	10.01	9.37	8.88	8.48	8.16
700	62.45	33.20	23.51	18.70	15.84	13.96	12.64	11.67	10.93	10.35	9.89	9.52
800	71.37	37.94	26.86	21.37	18.11	15.96	14.45	13.34	12.49	11.83	11.31	10.88
900	80.29	42.69	30.22	24.04	20.37	17.95	16.26	15.01	14.05	13.31	12.72	12.24
1000	89.21	47.43	33.58	26.71	22.63	19.95	18.06	16.67	15.62	14.79	14.13	13.60
2000	178.41	94.85	67.15	53.41	45.26	39.89	36.12	33.34	31.23	29.57	28.26	27.19
3000	267.61	142.28	100.73	80.12	67.88	59.83	54.17	50.01	46.84	44.36	42.38	40.78
4000	356.81	189.70	134.30	106.82	90.51	79.77	72.23	66.68	62.45	59.14	56.51	54.37
5000	446.01	237.13	167.87	133.52	113.13	99.72	90.29	83.34	78.06	73.92	70.63	67.97
6000	535.21	284.55	201.45	160.23	135.76	119.66	108.34	100.01	93.67	88.71	84.76	81.56
7000	624.41	331.98	235.02	186.93	158.38	139.60	126.40	116.68	109.28	103.49	98.88	95.15
8000	713.61	379.40	268.59	213.63	181.01	159.54	144.46	133.35	124.89	118.28	113.01	108.74
9000	802.81	426.83	302.17	240.34	203.63	179.49	162.51	150.01	140.50	133.06	127.13	122.33
10000	892.01	474.25	335.74	267.04	226.26	199.43	180.57	166.68	156.11	147.84	141.26	135.93
11000	981.21	521.67	369.32	293.74	248.88	219.37	198.62	183.35	171.72	162.63	155.38	149.52
12000	1070.41	569.10	402.89	320.45	271.51	239.31	216.68	200.02	187.33	177.41	169.51	163.11
13000	1159.61	616.52	436.46	347.15	294.13	259.26	234.74	216.69	202.94	192.20	183.63	176.70
14000	1248.81	663.95	470.04	373.86	316.76	279.20	252.79	233.35	218.55	206.98	197.76	190.29
15000	1338.01	711.37	503.61	400.56	339.38	299.14	270.85	250.02	234.16	221.76	211.89	203.89
16000	1427.21	758.80	537.18	427.26	362.01	319.08	288.91	266.69	249.77	236.55	226.01	217.48
17000	1516.41	806.22	570.76	453.97	384.64	339.03	306.96	283.36	265.38	251.33	240.14	231.07
18000	1605.61	853.65	604.33	480.67	407.26	358.97	325.02	300.02	280.99	266.12	254.26	244.66
19000	1694.81	901.07	637.90	507.37	429.89	378.91	343.08	316.69	296.60	280.90	268.39	258.25
20000	1784.01	948.49	671.48	534.08	452.51	398.85	361.13	333.36	312.21	295.68	282.51	271.85
21000	1873.21	995.92	705.05	560.78	475.14	418.80	379.19	350.03	327.82	310.47	296.64	285.44
22000	1962.41	1043.34	738.63	587.48	497.76	438.74	397.24	366.69	343.43	325.25	310.76	299.03
23000	2051.61	1090.77	772.20	614.19	520.39	458.68	415.30	383.36	359.04	340.04	324.89	312.62
24000	2140.81	1138.19	805.77	640.89	543.01	478.62	433.36	400.03	374.65	354.82	339.01	326.21
25000	2230.01	1185.62	839.35	667.59	565.64	498.57	451.41	416.70	390.26	369.60	353.14	339.81
26000	2319.21	1233.04	872.92	694.30	588.26	518.51	469.47	433.37	405.87	384.39	367.26	353.40
27000	2408.41	1280.47	906.49	721.00	610.89	538.45	487.53	450.03	421.48	399.17	381.39	366.99
28000	2497.61	1327.89	940.07	747.71	633.51	558.39	505.58	466.70	437.09	413.96	395.52	380.58
29000	2586.81	1375.31	973.64	774.41	656.14	578.33	523.64	483.37	452.70	428.74	409.64	394.17
30000	2676.01	1422.74	1007.21	801.11	678.76	598.28	541.69	500.04	468.31	443.52	423.77	407.77
31000	2765.21	1470.16	1040.79	827.82	701.39	618.22	559.75	516.70	483.92	458.31	437.89	421.36
32000	2854.41	1517.59	1074.36	854.52	724.01	638.16	577.81	533.37	499.53	473.09	452.02	434.95
33000	2943.61	1565.01	1107.94	881.22	746.64	658.10	595.86	550.04	515.14	487.88	466.14	448.54
34000	3032.81	1612.44	1141.51	907.93	769.27	678.05	613.92	566.71	530.75	502.66	480.27	462.13
35000	3122.01	1659.86	1175.08	934.63	791.89	697.99	631.98	583.38	546.36	517.44	494.39	475.73
37500	3345.01	1778.42	1259.02	1001.39	848.45	747.85	677.12	625.04	585.39	554.40	529.71	509.71
40000	3568.01	1896.98	1342.95	1068.15	905.02	797.70	722.26	666.71	624.41	591.36	565.02	543.69
42500	3791.01	2015.55	1426.89	1134.91	961.58	847.56	767.40	708.38	663.44	628.32	600.33	577.67
45000	4014.01	2134.11	1510.82	1201.67	1018.14	897.41	812.54	750.05	702.47	665.28	635.65	611.65
47500	4237.01	2252.67	1594.75	1268.43	1074.71	947.27	857.68	791.72	741.49	702.24	670.96	645.63
50000	4460.01	2371.23	1678.69	1335.18	1131.27	997.13	902.82	833.39	780.52	739.20	706.27	679.61
52500	4683.01	2489.79	1762.62	1401.94	1187.83	1046.98	947.96	875.06	819.54	776.16	741.59	713.59
55000	4906.01	2608.35	1846.56	1468.70	1244.40	1096.84	993.10	916.73	858.57	813.12	776.90	747.57
57500	5129.01	2726.91	1930.49	1535.46	1300.96	1146.69	1038.24	958.40	897.59	850.08	812.21	781.55
60000	5352.01	2845.47	2014.42	1602.22	1357.52	1196.55	1083.38	1000.07	936.62	887.04	847.53	815.53
65000	5798.01	3082.60	2182.29	1735.74	1470.65	1296.26	1173.67	1083.41	1014.67	960.96	918.15	883.49
70000	6244.01	3319.72	2350.16	1869.26	1583.78	1395.97	1263.95	1166.75	1092.72	1034.88	988.78	951.45
75000	6690.01	3556.84	2518.03	2002.77	1696.90	1495.69	1354.23	1250.08	1170.77	1108.80	1059.41	1019.41
80000	7136.01	3793.96	2685.90	2136.29	1810.03	1595.40	1444.51	1333.42	1248.82	1182.72	1130.04	1087.37
85000	7582.01	4031.09	2853.77	2269.81	1923.16	1695.11	1534.79	1416.76	1326.87	1256.64	1200.66	1155.33
90000	8028.01	4268.21	3021.63	2403.33	2036.28	1794.82	1625.07	1500.10	1404.93	1330.56	1271.29	1223.29
95000	8474.01	4505.33	3189.50	2536.85	2149.41	1894.53	1715.36	1583.44	1482.98	1404.48	1341.92	1291.25
100000	8920.01	4742.45	3357.37	2670.36	2262.54	1994.25	1805.64	1666.78	1561.03	1478.40	1412.54	1359.21
105000	9366.01	4979.58	3525.24	2803.88	2375.66	2093.96	1895.92	1750.12	1639.08	1552.32	1483.17	1427.17
110000	9812.01	5216.70	3693.11	2937.40	2488.79	2193.67	1986.20	1833.45	1717.13	1626.24	1553.80	1495.13
115000	10258.01	5453.82	3860.98	3070.92	2601.91	2293.38	2076.48	1916.79	1795.18	1700.16	1624.42	1563.09
120000	10704.01	5690.94	4028.84	3204.43	2715.04	2393.09	2166.76	2000.13	1873.23	1774.08	1695.05	1631.05
125000	11150.01	5928.07	4196.71	3337.95	2828.17	2492.81	2257.05	2083.47	1951.28	1848.00	1765.68	1699.01
130000	11596.01	6165.19	4364.58	3471.47	2941.29	2592.52	2347.33	2166.81	2029.34	1921.92	1836.30	1766.97
135000	12042.01	6402.31	4532.45	3604.99	3054.42	2692.23	2437.61	2250.15	2107.39	1995.84	1906.93	1834.93
140000	12488.01	6639.43	4700.32	3738.51	3167.55	2791.94	2527.89	2333.49	2185.44	2069.76	1977.56	1902.89
145000	12934.01	6876.55	4868.19	3872.02	3280.67	2891.65	2618.17	2416.82	2263.49	2143.68	2048.19	1970.85
150000	13380.01	7113.68	5036.05	4005.54	3393.80	2991.37	2708.45	2500.16	2341.54	2217.60	2118.81	2038.81
155000	13826.01	7350.80	5203.92	4139.06	3506.93	3091.08	2798.74	2583.50	2419.59	2291.52	2189.44	2106.77
160000	14272.01	7587.92	5371.79	4272.58	3620.05	3190.79	2889.02	2666.84	2497.64	2365.44	2260.07	2174.73

AMOUNT OF LOAN	NUMBER OF YEARS IN TERM											
	13	14	15	16	17	18	19	20	25	30	35	40
$ 50	0.66	0.64	0.63	0.62	0.61	0.60	0.59	0.58	0.56	0.55	0.54	0.54
100	1.32	1.28	1.25	1.23	1.21	1.19	1.17	1.16	1.11	1.09	1.08	1.07
200	2.64	2.56	2.50	2.45	2.41	2.37	2.34	2.31	2.22	2.18	2.16	2.14
300	3.95	3.84	3.75	3.67	3.61	3.55	3.51	3.47	3.33	3.27	3.23	3.21
400	5.27	5.12	5.00	4.90	4.81	4.74	4.67	4.62	4.44	4.35	4.31	4.28
500	6.58	6.40	6.25	6.12	6.01	5.92	5.84	5.77	5.55	5.44	5.38	5.35
600	7.90	7.68	7.50	7.34	7.21	7.10	7.01	6.93	6.66	6.53	6.46	6.42
700	9.21	8.96	8.75	8.57	8.42	8.29	8.18	8.08	7.77	7.61	7.53	7.49
800	10.53	10.24	10.00	9.79	9.62	9.47	9.34	9.24	8.88	8.70	8.61	8.56
900	11.84	11.52	11.24	11.01	10.82	10.65	10.51	10.39	9.99	9.79	9.68	9.63
1000	13.16	12.80	12.49	12.24	12.02	11.84	11.68	11.54	11.10	10.87	10.76	10.70
2000	26.31	25.59	24.98	24.47	24.04	23.67	23.35	23.08	22.19	21.74	21.51	21.39
3000	39.47	38.38	37.47	36.70	36.05	35.50	35.03	34.62	33.28	32.61	32.26	32.08
4000	52.62	51.17	49.96	48.94	48.07	47.33	46.70	46.16	44.37	43.47	43.01	42.77
5000	65.78	63.96	62.45	61.17	60.09	59.16	58.37	57.70	55.46	54.34	53.76	53.46
6000	78.93	76.76	74.94	73.40	72.11	71.00	70.05	69.23	66.55	65.21	64.52	64.16
7000	92.09	89.55	87.42	85.63	84.12	82.83	81.72	80.77	77.64	76.07	75.27	74.85
8000	105.24	102.34	99.91	97.87	96.13	94.66	93.40	92.31	88.73	86.94	86.02	85.54
9000	118.40	115.13	112.40	110.10	108.15	106.49	105.07	103.85	99.82	97.81	96.77	96.23
10000	131.55	127.92	124.89	122.33	120.17	118.32	116.74	115.39	110.91	108.67	107.52	106.92
11000	144.70	140.71	137.38	134.57	132.18	130.15	128.42	126.92	122.00	119.54	118.28	117.62
12000	157.86	153.51	149.87	146.80	144.20	141.99	140.09	138.46	133.09	130.41	129.03	128.31
13000	171.01	166.30	162.35	159.03	156.22	153.82	151.76	150.00	144.18	141.28	139.78	139.00
14000	184.17	179.09	174.84	171.26	168.23	165.65	163.44	161.54	155.27	152.14	150.53	149.69
15000	197.32	191.88	187.33	183.50	180.25	177.48	175.11	173.08	166.36	163.01	161.28	160.38
16000	210.48	204.67	199.82	195.73	192.26	189.31	186.79	184.61	177.45	173.88	172.04	171.08
17000	223.63	217.46	212.31	207.96	204.28	201.14	198.46	196.15	188.54	184.74	182.79	181.77
18000	236.79	230.26	224.80	220.20	216.30	212.98	210.13	207.69	199.63	195.61	193.54	192.46
19000	249.94	243.05	237.28	232.43	228.31	224.81	221.81	219.23	210.72	206.48	204.29	203.15
20000	263.09	255.84	249.77	244.66	240.33	236.64	233.48	230.77	221.82	217.34	215.04	213.84
21000	276.25	268.63	262.26	256.89	252.35	248.47	245.15	242.31	232.91	228.21	225.80	224.54
22000	289.40	281.42	274.75	269.13	264.36	260.30	256.83	253.84	244.00	239.08	236.55	235.23
23000	302.56	294.21	287.24	281.36	276.38	272.13	268.50	265.38	255.09	249.94	247.30	245.92
24000	315.71	307.01	299.73	293.59	288.39	283.97	280.18	276.92	266.18	260.81	258.05	256.61
25000	328.87	319.80	312.21	305.83	300.41	295.80	291.85	288.46	277.27	271.68	268.80	267.30
26000	342.02	332.59	324.70	318.06	312.43	307.63	303.52	300.00	288.36	282.55	279.56	278.00
27000	355.18	345.38	337.19	330.29	324.44	319.46	315.20	311.53	299.45	293.41	290.31	288.69
28000	368.33	358.17	349.68	342.52	336.46	331.29	326.87	323.07	310.54	304.28	301.06	299.38
29000	381.48	370.96	362.17	354.76	348.48	343.12	338.54	334.61	321.63	315.15	311.81	310.07
30000	394.64	383.76	374.66	366.99	360.49	354.96	350.22	346.15	332.72	326.01	322.56	320.76
31000	407.79	396.55	387.14	379.22	372.51	366.79	361.89	357.69	343.81	336.88	333.32	331.46
32000	420.95	409.34	399.63	391.46	384.52	378.62	373.57	369.22	354.90	347.75	344.07	342.15
33000	434.10	422.13	412.12	403.69	396.54	390.45	385.24	380.76	365.99	358.61	354.82	352.84
34000	447.26	434.92	424.61	415.92	408.56	402.28	396.92	392.30	377.08	369.48	365.57	363.53
35000	460.41	447.72	437.10	428.15	420.57	414.11	408.59	403.84	388.17	380.35	376.32	374.22
37500	493.30	479.69	468.32	458.74	450.61	443.69	437.77	432.68	415.90	407.51	403.20	400.95
40000	526.18	511.67	499.54	489.32	480.65	473.27	466.96	461.53	443.63	434.68	430.08	427.68
42500	559.07	543.65	530.76	519.90	510.70	502.85	496.14	490.37	471.35	461.85	456.96	454.41
45000	591.96	575.63	561.98	550.48	540.74	532.43	525.32	519.22	499.08	489.02	483.84	481.14
47500	624.84	607.61	593.20	581.06	570.78	562.01	554.51	548.07	526.80	516.18	510.72	507.87
50000	657.73	639.59	624.42	611.65	600.82	591.59	583.69	576.91	554.53	543.35	537.60	534.60
52500	690.61	671.57	655.64	642.23	630.86	621.17	612.88	605.76	582.26	570.52	564.48	561.33
55000	723.50	703.55	686.87	672.81	660.90	650.75	642.06	634.60	609.98	597.69	591.36	588.06
57500	756.39	735.53	718.09	703.39	690.94	680.33	671.25	663.45	637.71	624.85	618.24	614.79
60000	789.27	767.51	749.31	733.97	720.98	709.91	700.43	692.29	665.44	652.02	645.12	641.52
65000	855.04	831.47	811.75	795.14	781.06	769.07	758.80	749.98	720.89	706.36	698.88	694.98
70000	920.82	895.43	874.19	856.30	841.14	828.22	817.17	807.67	776.34	760.69	752.64	748.44
75000	986.59	959.38	936.63	917.47	901.22	887.38	875.54	865.36	831.79	815.02	806.40	801.90
80000	1052.36	1023.34	999.07	978.63	961.30	946.54	933.91	923.05	887.25	869.36	860.16	855.36
85000	1118.13	1087.30	1061.52	1039.80	1021.39	1005.70	992.28	980.74	942.70	923.69	913.92	908.82
90000	1183.91	1151.26	1123.96	1100.96	1081.47	1064.86	1050.64	1038.44	998.15	978.03	967.68	962.28
95000	1249.68	1215.22	1186.40	1162.12	1141.55	1124.02	1109.01	1096.13	1053.60	1032.36	1021.44	1015.74
100000	1315.45	1279.18	1248.84	1223.29	1201.63	1183.17	1167.38	1153.82	1109.06	1086.70	1075.20	1069.20
105000	1381.22	1343.14	1311.28	1284.45	1261.71	1242.33	1225.75	1211.51	1164.51	1141.03	1128.96	1122.66
110000	1447.00	1407.09	1373.73	1345.62	1321.79	1301.49	1284.12	1269.20	1219.96	1195.37	1182.72	1176.12
115000	1512.77	1471.05	1436.17	1406.78	1381.87	1360.65	1342.49	1326.89	1275.42	1249.70	1236.48	1229.58
120000	1578.54	1535.01	1498.61	1467.94	1441.95	1419.81	1400.86	1384.58	1330.87	1304.04	1290.24	1283.04
125000	1644.31	1598.97	1561.05	1529.11	1502.03	1478.97	1459.23	1442.27	1386.32	1358.37	1344.00	1336.50
130000	1710.08	1662.93	1623.49	1590.27	1562.12	1538.13	1517.60	1499.96	1441.77	1412.71	1397.76	1389.96
135000	1775.86	1726.89	1685.93	1651.44	1622.20	1597.28	1575.96	1557.65	1497.23	1467.04	1451.52	1443.42
140000	1841.63	1790.85	1748.38	1712.60	1682.28	1656.44	1634.33	1615.34	1552.68	1521.38	1505.28	1496.88
145000	1907.40	1854.80	1810.82	1773.77	1742.36	1715.60	1692.70	1673.03	1608.13	1575.71	1559.04	1550.34
150000	1973.17	1918.76	1873.26	1834.93	1802.44	1774.76	1751.07	1730.72	1663.58	1630.04	1612.80	1603.80
155000	2038.95	1982.72	1935.70	1896.09	1862.52	1833.92	1809.44	1788.41	1719.04	1684.38	1666.56	1657.26
160000	2104.72	2046.68	1998.14	1957.26	1922.60	1893.08	1867.81	1846.10	1774.49	1738.71	1720.32	1710.72

AMOUNT OF LOAN	NUMBER OF YEARS IN TERM											
	1	2	3	4	5	6	7	8	9	10	11	12
$ 50	4.47	2.38	1.69	1.35	1.14	1.01	0.91	0.85	0.79	0.75	0.72	0.69
100	8.94	4.76	3.37	2.69	2.28	2.01	1.82	1.69	1.58	1.50	1.43	1.38
200	17.87	9.51	6.74	5.37	4.56	4.02	3.64	3.37	3.16	2.99	2.86	2.75
300	26.80	14.27	10.11	8.05	6.83	6.03	5.46	5.05	4.73	4.48	4.29	4.13
400	35.73	19.02	13.48	10.74	9.11	8.03	7.28	6.73	6.31	5.98	5.72	5.50
500	44.66	23.78	16.85	13.42	11.38	10.04	9.10	8.41	7.88	7.47	7.14	6.88
600	53.60	28.53	20.22	16.10	13.66	12.05	10.92	10.09	9.46	8.96	8.57	8.25
700	62.53	33.28	23.59	18.78	15.93	14.06	12.74	11.77	11.03	10.46	10.00	9.63
800	71.46	38.04	26.96	21.47	18.21	16.06	14.56	13.45	12.61	11.95	11.43	11.00
900	80.39	42.79	30.33	24.15	20.48	18.07	16.38	15.13	14.18	13.44	12.85	12.38
1000	89.32	47.55	33.70	26.83	22.76	20.08	18.20	16.81	15.76	14.94	14.28	13.75
2000	178.64	95.09	67.39	53.66	45.51	40.15	36.39	33.62	31.51	29.87	28.56	27.50
3000	267.96	142.63	101.09	80.49	68.26	60.23	54.58	50.43	47.27	44.80	42.83	41.24
4000	357.27	190.17	134.78	107.31	91.02	80.30	72.77	67.23	63.02	59.73	57.11	54.99
5000	446.59	237.71	168.47	134.14	113.77	100.38	90.96	84.04	78.77	74.66	71.39	68.74
6000	535.91	285.26	202.17	160.97	136.52	120.45	109.16	100.85	94.53	89.59	85.66	82.48
7000	625.23	332.80	235.86	187.80	159.28	140.52	127.35	117.66	110.28	104.52	99.94	96.23
8000	714.54	380.34	269.56	214.62	182.03	160.60	145.54	134.46	126.03	119.45	114.21	109.98
9000	803.86	427.88	303.25	241.45	204.78	180.67	163.73	151.27	141.79	134.38	128.49	123.72
10000	893.18	475.42	336.94	268.28	227.54	200.75	181.92	168.08	157.54	149.32	142.77	137.47
11000	982.50	522.97	370.64	295.11	250.29	220.82	200.12	184.88	173.29	164.25	157.04	151.21
12000	1071.81	570.51	404.33	321.93	273.04	240.89	218.31	201.69	189.05	179.18	171.32	164.96
13000	1161.13	618.05	438.03	348.76	295.79	260.97	236.50	218.50	204.80	194.11	185.59	178.71
14000	1250.45	665.59	471.72	375.59	318.55	281.04	254.69	235.31	220.56	209.04	199.87	192.45
15000	1339.76	713.13	505.41	402.42	341.30	301.12	272.88	252.11	236.31	223.97	214.15	206.20
16000	1429.08	760.67	539.11	429.24	364.05	321.19	291.08	268.92	252.06	238.90	228.42	219.95
17000	1518.40	808.22	572.80	456.07	386.81	341.26	309.27	285.73	267.82	253.83	242.70	233.69
18000	1607.72	855.76	606.50	482.90	409.56	361.34	327.46	302.54	283.57	268.76	256.97	247.44
19000	1697.03	903.30	640.19	509.73	432.31	381.41	345.65	319.34	299.32	283.70	271.25	261.18
20000	1786.35	950.84	673.88	536.55	455.07	401.49	363.84	336.15	315.08	298.63	285.53	274.93
21000	1875.67	998.38	707.58	563.38	477.82	421.56	382.04	352.96	330.83	313.56	299.80	288.68
22000	1964.99	1045.93	741.27	590.21	500.57	441.64	400.23	369.76	346.58	328.49	314.08	302.42
23000	2054.30	1093.47	774.97	617.04	523.33	461.71	418.42	386.57	362.34	343.42	328.36	316.17
24000	2143.62	1141.01	808.66	643.86	546.08	481.78	436.61	403.38	378.09	358.35	342.63	329.92
25000	2232.94	1188.55	842.35	670.69	568.83	501.86	454.80	420.19	393.84	373.28	356.91	343.66
26000	2322.25	1236.09	876.05	697.52	591.58	521.93	473.00	436.99	409.60	388.21	371.18	357.41
27000	2411.57	1283.63	909.74	724.35	614.34	542.01	491.19	453.80	425.35	403.14	385.46	371.15
28000	2500.89	1331.18	943.44	751.17	637.09	562.08	509.38	470.61	441.11	418.08	399.74	384.90
29000	2590.21	1378.72	977.13	778.00	659.84	582.15	527.57	487.42	456.86	433.01	414.01	398.65
30000	2679.52	1426.26	1010.82	804.83	682.60	602.23	545.76	504.22	472.61	447.94	428.29	412.39
31000	2768.84	1473.80	1044.52	831.66	705.35	622.30	563.96	521.03	488.37	462.87	442.56	426.14
32000	2858.16	1521.34	1078.21	858.48	728.10	642.38	582.15	537.84	504.12	477.80	456.84	439.89
33000	2947.48	1568.89	1111.91	885.31	750.86	662.45	600.34	554.64	519.87	492.73	471.12	453.63
34000	3036.79	1616.43	1145.60	912.14	773.61	682.52	618.53	571.45	535.63	507.66	485.39	467.38
35000	3126.11	1663.97	1179.29	938.97	796.36	702.60	636.72	588.26	551.38	522.59	499.67	481.12
37500	3349.40	1782.82	1263.53	1006.04	853.25	752.78	682.20	630.28	590.76	559.92	535.36	515.49
40000	3572.70	1901.68	1347.76	1073.10	910.13	802.97	727.68	672.30	630.15	597.25	571.05	549.86
42500	3795.99	2020.53	1432.00	1140.17	967.01	853.15	773.16	714.31	669.53	634.58	606.74	584.22
45000	4019.28	2139.39	1516.23	1207.24	1023.89	903.34	818.64	756.33	708.92	671.90	642.43	618.59
47500	4242.58	2258.24	1600.47	1274.31	1080.78	953.52	864.12	798.35	748.30	709.23	678.12	652.95
50000	4465.87	2377.10	1684.70	1341.38	1137.66	1003.71	909.60	840.37	787.68	746.56	713.81	687.32
52500	4689.16	2495.95	1768.94	1408.45	1194.54	1053.90	955.08	882.39	827.07	783.89	749.50	721.68
55000	4912.46	2614.81	1853.17	1475.52	1251.42	1104.08	1000.56	924.40	866.45	821.21	785.19	756.05
57500	5135.75	2733.66	1937.41	1542.59	1308.31	1154.27	1046.04	966.42	905.84	858.54	820.88	790.41
60000	5359.04	2852.51	2021.64	1609.65	1365.19	1204.45	1091.52	1008.44	945.22	895.87	856.57	824.78
65000	5805.63	3090.22	2190.11	1743.79	1478.95	1304.82	1182.48	1092.48	1023.99	970.52	927.95	893.51
70000	6252.21	3327.93	2358.58	1877.93	1592.72	1405.19	1273.44	1176.51	1102.76	1045.18	999.33	962.24
75000	6698.80	3565.64	2527.05	2012.07	1706.49	1505.56	1364.40	1260.55	1181.52	1119.84	1070.71	1030.97
80000	7145.39	3803.35	2695.52	2146.20	1820.25	1605.93	1455.36	1344.59	1260.29	1194.49	1142.09	1099.71
85000	7591.97	4041.06	2863.99	2280.34	1934.02	1706.30	1546.32	1428.62	1339.06	1269.15	1213.47	1168.44
90000	8038.56	4278.77	3032.46	2414.48	2047.78	1806.67	1637.28	1512.66	1417.83	1343.80	1284.85	1237.17
95000	8485.15	4516.48	3200.93	2548.62	2161.55	1907.04	1728.24	1596.69	1496.60	1418.46	1356.24	1305.90
100000	8931.73	4754.19	3369.40	2682.75	2275.31	2007.42	1819.20	1680.73	1575.36	1493.11	1427.62	1374.63
105000	9378.32	4991.90	3537.87	2816.89	2389.08	2107.79	1910.16	1764.77	1654.13	1567.77	1499.00	1443.36
110000	9824.91	5229.61	3706.34	2951.03	2502.84	2208.16	2001.12	1848.80	1732.90	1642.42	1570.38	1512.09
115000	10271.49	5467.31	3874.81	3085.17	2616.61	2308.53	2092.08	1932.84	1811.67	1717.08	1641.76	1580.82
120000	10718.08	5705.02	4043.28	3219.30	2730.37	2408.90	2183.04	2016.88	1890.44	1791.73	1713.14	1649.56
125000	11164.66	5942.73	4211.75	3353.44	2844.14	2509.27	2274.00	2100.91	1969.20	1866.39	1784.52	1718.29
130000	11611.25	6180.44	4380.22	3487.58	2957.90	2609.64	2364.96	2184.95	2047.97	1941.04	1855.90	1787.02
135000	12057.84	6418.15	4548.69	3621.72	3071.67	2710.01	2455.92	2268.98	2126.74	2015.70	1927.28	1855.75
140000	12504.42	6655.86	4717.16	3755.85	3185.44	2810.38	2546.88	2353.02	2205.51	2090.36	1998.66	1924.48
145000	12951.01	6893.57	4885.63	3889.99	3299.20	2910.75	2637.84	2437.06	2284.28	2165.01	2070.04	1993.21
150000	13397.60	7131.28	5054.10	4024.13	3412.97	3011.12	2728.80	2521.09	2363.04	2239.67	2141.42	2061.94
155000	13844.18	7368.99	5222.57	4158.27	3526.73	3111.49	2819.76	2605.13	2441.81	2314.32	2212.80	2130.67
160000	14290.77	7606.70	5391.04	4292.40	3640.50	3211.86	2910.72	2689.17	2520.58	2388.98	2284.18	2199.41

AMOUNT OF LOAN	NUMBER OF YEARS IN TERM											
	13	14	15	16	17	18	19	20	25	30	35	40
$ 50	0.67	0.65	0.64	0.62	0.61	0.61	0.60	0.59	0.57	0.56	0.55	0.55
100	1.34	1.30	1.27	1.24	1.22	1.21	1.19	1.18	1.13	1.11	1.10	1.09
200	2.67	2.60	2.54	2.48	2.44	2.41	2.37	2.35	2.26	2.22	2.20	2.18
300	4.00	3.89	3.80	3.72	3.66	3.61	3.56	3.52	3.39	3.32	3.29	3.27
400	5.33	5.19	5.07	4.96	4.88	4.81	4.74	4.69	4.52	4.43	4.39	4.36
500	6.66	6.48	6.33	6.20	6.10	6.01	5.93	5.86	5.64	5.54	5.48	5.45
600	7.99	7.78	7.60	7.44	7.32	7.21	7.11	7.03	6.77	6.64	6.58	6.54
700	9.32	9.07	8.86	8.68	8.54	8.41	8.30	8.21	7.90	7.75	7.67	7.63
800	10.65	10.37	10.13	9.92	9.75	9.61	9.48	9.38	9.03	8.85	8.77	8.72
900	11.99	11.66	11.39	11.16	10.97	10.81	10.67	10.55	10.16	9.96	9.86	9.81
1000	13.32	12.96	12.66	12.40	12.19	12.01	11.85	11.72	11.28	11.07	10.96	10.90
2000	26.63	25.91	25.31	24.80	24.38	24.01	23.70	23.44	22.56	22.13	21.91	21.80
3000	39.94	38.86	37.96	37.20	36.56	36.02	35.55	35.15	33.84	33.19	32.86	32.69
4000	53.25	51.82	50.61	49.60	48.75	48.03	47.40	46.87	45.12	44.25	43.81	43.59
5000	66.57	64.77	63.27	62.00	60.94	60.03	59.25	58.58	56.40	55.31	54.76	54.48
6000	79.88	77.72	75.92	74.40	73.12	72.03	71.10	70.30	67.68	66.38	65.72	65.38
7000	93.19	90.67	88.57	86.80	85.31	84.04	82.95	82.02	78.95	77.44	76.67	76.27
8000	106.50	103.63	101.22	99.20	97.49	96.04	94.80	93.73	90.23	88.50	87.62	87.17
9000	119.81	116.58	113.88	111.60	109.68	108.04	106.65	105.45	101.51	99.56	98.57	98.06
10000	133.13	129.53	126.53	124.00	121.87	120.05	118.49	117.16	112.79	110.62	109.52	108.96
11000	146.44	142.48	139.18	136.40	134.05	132.05	130.34	128.88	124.07	121.69	120.48	119.85
12000	159.75	155.44	151.83	148.80	146.24	144.06	142.19	140.59	135.35	132.75	131.43	130.75
13000	173.06	168.39	164.49	161.20	158.42	156.06	154.04	152.31	146.62	143.81	142.38	141.64
14000	186.37	181.34	177.14	173.60	170.61	168.07	165.89	164.03	157.90	154.87	153.33	152.54
15000	199.69	194.29	189.79	186.00	182.80	180.07	177.74	175.74	169.18	165.93	164.28	163.43
16000	213.00	207.25	202.44	198.40	194.98	192.07	189.59	187.46	180.46	177.00	175.24	174.33
17000	226.31	220.20	215.10	210.80	207.17	204.08	201.44	199.17	191.74	188.06	186.19	185.22
18000	239.62	233.15	227.75	223.20	219.36	216.08	213.29	210.89	203.02	199.12	197.14	196.12
19000	252.93	246.11	240.40	235.60	231.54	228.09	225.14	222.60	214.29	210.18	208.09	207.01
20000	266.25	259.06	253.05	248.00	243.73	240.09	236.98	234.32	225.57	221.24	219.04	217.91
21000	279.56	272.01	265.71	260.40	255.91	252.10	248.83	246.04	236.85	232.31	230.00	228.80
22000	292.87	284.96	278.36	272.80	268.10	264.10	260.68	257.75	248.13	243.37	240.95	239.70
23000	306.18	297.92	291.01	285.20	280.29	276.10	272.53	269.47	259.41	254.43	251.90	250.59
24000	319.50	310.87	303.66	297.60	292.47	288.11	284.38	281.18	270.69	265.49	262.85	261.49
25000	332.81	323.82	316.32	310.00	304.66	300.11	296.23	292.90	281.96	276.55	273.80	272.38
26000	346.12	336.77	328.97	322.40	316.84	312.12	308.08	304.61	293.24	287.62	284.76	283.28
27000	359.43	349.73	341.62	334.80	329.03	324.12	319.93	316.33	304.52	298.68	295.71	294.17
28000	372.74	362.68	354.27	347.20	341.22	336.13	331.78	328.05	315.80	309.74	306.66	305.07
29000	386.06	375.63	366.93	359.60	353.40	348.13	343.63	339.76	327.08	320.80	317.61	315.96
30000	399.37	388.58	379.58	372.00	365.59	360.13	355.47	351.48	338.36	331.86	328.56	326.86
31000	412.68	401.54	392.23	384.40	377.78	372.14	367.32	363.19	349.63	342.93	339.51	337.75
32000	425.99	414.49	404.88	396.80	389.96	384.14	379.17	374.91	360.91	353.99	350.47	348.65
33000	439.30	427.44	417.53	409.20	402.15	396.15	391.02	386.62	372.19	365.05	361.42	359.54
34000	452.62	440.39	430.19	421.60	414.33	408.15	402.87	398.34	383.47	376.11	372.37	370.44
35000	465.93	453.35	442.84	434.00	426.52	420.16	414.72	410.06	394.75	387.17	383.32	381.33
37500	499.21	485.73	474.47	465.00	456.99	450.17	444.34	439.35	422.94	414.83	410.70	408.57
40000	532.49	518.11	506.10	496.00	487.45	480.18	473.96	468.64	451.14	442.48	438.08	435.81
42500	565.77	550.49	537.73	527.00	517.92	510.19	503.59	497.92	479.34	470.14	465.46	463.05
45000	599.05	582.87	569.36	558.00	548.38	540.20	533.21	527.21	507.53	497.79	492.84	490.29
47500	632.33	615.26	601.00	589.00	578.85	570.21	562.83	556.50	535.73	525.45	520.22	517.52
50000	665.61	647.64	632.63	620.00	609.31	600.22	592.45	585.79	563.92	553.10	547.60	544.76
52500	698.89	680.02	664.26	651.00	639.78	630.23	622.08	615.08	592.12	580.76	574.98	572.00
55000	732.17	712.40	695.89	682.00	670.24	660.24	651.70	644.37	620.32	608.41	602.36	599.24
57500	765.45	744.78	727.52	713.00	700.71	690.25	681.32	673.66	648.51	636.07	629.74	626.48
60000	798.73	777.16	759.15	744.00	731.17	720.26	710.94	702.95	676.71	663.72	657.12	653.71
65000	865.29	841.93	822.41	806.00	792.10	780.29	770.19	761.53	733.10	719.03	711.88	708.19
70000	931.85	906.69	885.67	868.00	853.04	840.31	829.43	820.11	789.49	774.34	766.64	762.66
75000	998.41	971.45	948.94	930.00	913.97	900.33	888.68	878.69	845.88	829.65	821.40	817.14
80000	1064.97	1036.22	1012.20	992.00	974.90	960.35	947.92	937.27	902.27	884.96	876.16	871.62
85000	1131.53	1100.98	1075.46	1053.99	1035.83	1020.37	1007.17	995.84	958.67	940.27	930.92	926.09
90000	1198.09	1165.74	1138.72	1115.99	1096.76	1080.39	1066.41	1054.42	1015.06	995.58	985.68	980.57
95000	1264.65	1230.51	1201.99	1177.99	1157.69	1140.42	1125.66	1113.00	1071.45	1050.89	1040.44	1035.04
100000	1331.22	1295.27	1265.25	1239.99	1218.62	1200.44	1184.90	1171.58	1127.84	1106.20	1095.20	1089.52
105000	1397.78	1360.03	1328.51	1301.99	1279.55	1260.46	1244.15	1230.16	1184.23	1161.51	1149.96	1143.99
110000	1464.34	1424.79	1391.77	1363.99	1340.48	1320.48	1303.39	1288.74	1240.62	1216.82	1204.72	1198.47
115000	1530.90	1489.56	1455.03	1425.99	1401.41	1380.50	1362.64	1347.32	1297.02	1272.13	1259.48	1252.95
120000	1597.46	1554.32	1518.30	1487.99	1462.34	1440.52	1421.88	1405.90	1353.41	1327.44	1314.24	1307.42
125000	1664.02	1619.08	1581.56	1549.99	1523.27	1500.55	1481.13	1464.47	1409.80	1382.75	1369.00	1361.90
130000	1730.58	1683.85	1644.82	1611.99	1584.20	1560.57	1540.37	1523.05	1466.19	1438.06	1423.76	1416.37
135000	1797.14	1748.61	1708.08	1673.99	1645.13	1620.59	1599.62	1581.63	1522.58	1493.37	1478.52	1470.85
140000	1863.70	1813.37	1771.34	1735.99	1706.07	1680.61	1658.86	1640.21	1578.97	1548.68	1533.28	1525.32
145000	1930.26	1878.14	1834.61	1797.99	1767.00	1740.63	1718.11	1698.79	1635.37	1603.99	1588.04	1579.80
150000	1996.82	1942.90	1897.87	1859.99	1827.93	1800.65	1777.35	1757.37	1691.76	1659.30	1642.79	1634.28
155000	2063.38	2007.66	1961.13	1921.99	1888.86	1860.68	1836.60	1815.95	1748.15	1714.61	1697.55	1688.75
160000	2129.94	2072.43	2024.39	1983.99	1949.79	1920.70	1895.84	1874.53	1804.54	1769.92	1752.31	1743.23

AMOUNT OF LOAN	NUMBER OF YEARS IN TERM											
	1	2	3	4	5	6	7	8	9	10	11	12
$ 50	4.48	2.39	1.70	1.35	1.15	1.02	0.92	0.85	0.80	0.76	0.73	0.70
100	8.95	4.77	3.39	2.70	2.29	2.03	1.84	1.70	1.59	1.51	1.45	1.40
200	17.89	9.54	6.77	5.40	4.58	4.05	3.67	3.39	3.18	3.02	2.89	2.79
300	26.84	14.30	10.15	8.09	6.87	6.07	5.50	5.09	4.77	4.53	4.33	4.18
400	35.78	19.07	13.53	10.79	9.16	8.09	7.34	6.78	6.36	6.04	5.78	5.57
500	44.72	23.83	16.91	13.48	11.45	10.11	9.17	8.48	7.95	7.54	7.22	6.96
600	53.67	28.60	20.29	16.18	13.73	12.13	11.00	10.17	9.54	9.05	8.66	8.35
700	62.61	33.37	23.68	18.87	16.02	14.15	12.83	11.87	11.13	10.56	10.10	9.74
800	71.55	38.13	27.06	21.57	18.31	16.17	14.67	13.56	12.72	12.07	11.55	11.13
900	80.50	42.90	30.44	24.26	20.60	18.19	16.50	15.26	14.31	13.58	12.99	12.52
1000	89.44	47.66	33.82	26.96	22.89	20.21	18.33	16.95	15.90	15.08	14.43	13.91
2000	178.87	95.32	67.63	53.91	45.77	40.42	36.66	33.90	31.80	30.16	28.86	27.81
3000	268.31	142.98	101.45	80.86	68.65	60.62	54.99	50.85	47.70	45.24	43.29	41.71
4000	357.74	190.64	135.26	107.81	91.53	80.83	73.32	67.79	63.60	60.32	57.72	55.61
5000	447.18	238.30	169.08	134.76	114.41	101.04	91.65	84.74	79.49	75.40	72.14	69.51
6000	536.61	285.96	202.89	161.72	137.29	121.24	109.97	101.69	95.39	90.48	86.57	83.41
7000	626.05	333.62	236.71	188.67	160.17	141.45	128.30	118.64	111.29	105.56	101.00	97.31
8000	715.48	381.28	270.52	215.62	183.06	161.66	146.63	135.58	127.19	120.64	115.43	111.22
9000	804.92	428.94	304.34	242.57	205.94	181.86	164.96	152.53	143.08	135.72	129.85	125.12
10000	894.35	476.60	338.15	269.53	228.82	202.07	183.29	169.48	158.98	150.79	144.28	139.02
11000	983.79	524.26	371.96	296.47	251.70	222.27	201.61	186.43	174.88	165.87	158.71	152.92
12000	1073.22	571.92	405.78	323.43	274.58	242.48	219.94	203.37	190.78	180.95	173.14	166.82
13000	1162.65	619.58	439.59	350.38	297.46	262.69	238.27	220.32	206.67	196.03	187.56	180.72
14000	1252.09	667.24	473.41	377.33	320.34	282.89	256.60	237.27	222.57	211.11	201.99	194.62
15000	1341.52	714.90	507.22	404.28	343.22	303.10	274.93	254.22	238.47	226.19	216.42	208.52
16000	1430.96	762.55	541.04	431.23	366.11	323.31	293.26	271.16	254.37	241.27	230.85	222.43
17000	1520.39	810.21	574.85	458.18	388.99	343.51	311.58	288.11	270.26	256.35	245.27	236.33
18000	1609.83	857.87	608.67	485.14	411.87	363.72	329.91	305.06	286.16	271.43	259.70	250.23
19000	1699.26	905.53	642.48	512.09	434.75	383.92	348.24	322.01	302.06	286.50	274.13	264.13
20000	1788.70	953.19	676.29	539.04	457.63	404.13	366.57	338.95	317.96	301.58	288.56	278.03
21000	1878.13	1000.85	710.11	565.99	480.51	424.34	384.90	355.90	333.85	316.66	302.98	291.93
22000	1967.57	1048.51	743.92	592.94	503.39	444.54	403.22	372.85	349.75	331.74	317.41	305.83
23000	2057.00	1096.17	777.74	619.90	526.27	464.75	421.55	389.80	365.65	346.82	331.84	319.74
24000	2146.44	1143.83	811.55	646.85	549.16	484.96	439.88	406.74	381.55	361.90	346.27	333.64
25000	2235.87	1191.49	845.37	673.80	572.04	505.16	458.21	423.69	397.45	376.98	360.70	347.54
26000	2325.30	1239.15	879.18	700.75	594.92	525.37	476.54	440.64	413.34	392.06	375.12	361.44
27000	2414.74	1286.81	913.00	727.70	617.80	545.57	494.87	457.58	429.24	407.14	389.55	375.34
28000	2504.17	1334.47	946.81	754.65	640.68	565.78	513.19	474.53	445.14	422.21	403.98	389.24
29000	2593.61	1382.13	980.63	781.61	663.56	585.99	531.52	491.48	461.04	437.29	418.41	403.14
30000	2683.04	1429.79	1014.44	808.56	686.44	606.19	549.85	508.43	476.93	452.37	432.83	417.04
31000	2772.48	1477.44	1048.25	835.51	709.32	626.40	568.18	525.37	492.83	467.45	447.26	430.95
32000	2861.91	1525.10	1082.07	862.46	732.21	646.61	586.51	542.32	508.73	482.53	461.69	444.85
33000	2951.35	1572.76	1115.88	889.41	755.09	666.81	604.83	559.27	524.63	497.61	476.12	458.75
34000	3040.78	1620.42	1149.70	916.36	777.97	687.02	623.16	576.22	540.52	512.69	490.54	472.65
35000	3130.22	1668.08	1183.51	943.32	800.85	707.23	641.49	593.16	556.42	527.77	504.97	486.55
37500	3353.80	1787.23	1268.05	1010.70	858.05	757.74	687.31	635.53	596.17	565.46	541.04	521.30
40000	3577.39	1906.38	1352.58	1078.07	915.26	808.26	733.13	677.90	635.91	603.16	577.11	556.06
42500	3800.98	2025.53	1437.12	1145.45	972.46	858.77	778.95	720.27	675.65	640.86	613.18	590.81
45000	4024.56	2144.68	1521.66	1212.83	1029.66	909.29	824.77	762.64	715.40	678.56	649.25	625.56
47500	4248.15	2263.82	1606.19	1280.21	1086.86	959.80	870.59	805.01	755.14	716.25	685.32	660.32
50000	4471.74	2382.97	1690.73	1347.59	1144.07	1010.32	916.41	847.38	794.89	753.95	721.39	695.07
52500	4695.32	2502.12	1775.27	1414.97	1201.27	1060.84	962.23	889.74	834.63	791.65	757.45	729.82
55000	4918.91	2621.27	1859.80	1482.35	1258.47	1111.35	1008.05	932.11	874.37	829.34	793.52	764.58
57500	5142.50	2740.42	1944.34	1549.73	1315.68	1161.87	1053.87	974.48	914.12	867.04	829.59	799.33
60000	5366.08	2859.57	2028.87	1617.11	1372.88	1212.38	1099.69	1016.85	953.86	904.74	865.66	834.08
65000	5813.25	3097.86	2197.95	1751.87	1487.29	1313.41	1191.33	1101.59	1033.35	980.13	937.80	903.59
70000	6260.43	3336.16	2367.02	1886.63	1601.69	1414.45	1282.98	1186.32	1112.84	1055.53	1009.94	973.10
75000	6707.60	3574.46	2536.09	2021.39	1716.10	1515.48	1374.62	1271.06	1192.33	1130.92	1082.08	1042.60
80000	7154.77	3812.75	2705.16	2156.14	1830.51	1616.51	1466.26	1355.80	1271.81	1206.32	1154.21	1112.11
85000	7601.95	4051.05	2874.24	2290.90	1944.91	1717.54	1557.90	1440.53	1351.30	1281.71	1226.35	1181.62
90000	8049.12	4289.35	3043.31	2425.66	2059.32	1818.57	1649.54	1525.27	1430.79	1357.11	1298.49	1251.12
95000	8496.29	4527.64	3212.38	2560.42	2173.72	1919.60	1741.18	1610.01	1510.28	1432.50	1370.63	1320.63
100000	8943.47	4765.94	3381.45	2695.18	2288.13	2020.63	1832.82	1694.75	1589.77	1507.89	1442.77	1390.14
105000	9390.64	5004.24	3550.53	2829.94	2402.54	2121.67	1924.46	1779.48	1669.25	1583.29	1514.90	1459.64
110000	9837.81	5242.53	3719.60	2964.70	2516.94	2222.70	2016.10	1864.22	1748.74	1658.68	1587.04	1529.15
115000	10284.99	5480.83	3888.67	3099.46	2631.35	2323.73	2107.74	1948.96	1828.23	1734.08	1659.18	1598.66
120000	10732.16	5719.13	4057.74	3234.21	2745.76	2424.76	2199.38	2033.69	1907.72	1809.47	1731.32	1668.16
125000	11179.33	5957.42	4226.82	3368.97	2860.16	2525.79	2291.02	2118.43	1987.21	1884.87	1803.46	1737.67
130000	11626.50	6195.72	4395.89	3503.73	2974.57	2626.82	2382.66	2203.17	2066.70	1960.26	1875.59	1807.18
135000	12073.68	6434.02	4564.96	3638.49	3088.97	2727.85	2474.31	2287.90	2146.18	2035.66	1947.73	1876.68
140000	12520.85	6672.31	4734.03	3773.25	3203.38	2828.89	2565.95	2372.64	2225.67	2111.05	2019.87	1946.19
145000	12968.02	6910.61	4903.11	3908.01	3317.79	2929.92	2657.59	2457.38	2305.16	2186.44	2092.01	2015.70
150000	13415.20	7148.91	5072.18	4042.77	3432.19	3030.95	2749.23	2542.12	2384.65	2261.84	2164.15	2085.20
155000	13862.37	7387.20	5241.25	4177.53	3546.60	3131.98	2840.87	2626.85	2464.14	2337.23	2236.28	2154.71
160000	14309.54	7625.50	5410.32	4312.28	3661.01	3233.01	2932.51	2711.59	2543.62	2412.63	2308.42	2224.21

MONTHLY AMORTIZING PAYMENTS 13.25%

AMOUNT OF LOAN	NUMBER OF YEARS IN TERM											
	13	14	15	16	17	18	19	20	25	30	35	40
$ 50	0.68	0.66	0.65	0.63	0.62	0.61	0.61	0.60	0.58	0.57	0.56	0.56
100	1.35	1.32	1.29	1.26	1.24	1.22	1.21	1.19	1.15	1.13	1.12	1.11
200	2.70	2.63	2.57	2.52	2.48	2.44	2.41	2.38	2.30	2.26	2.24	2.22
300	4.05	3.94	3.85	3.78	3.71	3.66	3.61	3.57	3.45	3.38	3.35	3.33
400	5.39	5.25	5.13	5.03	4.95	4.88	4.82	4.76	4.59	4.51	4.47	4.44
500	6.74	6.56	6.41	6.29	6.18	6.09	6.02	5.95	5.74	5.63	5.58	5.55
600	8.09	7.87	7.70	7.55	7.42	7.31	7.22	7.14	6.89	6.76	6.70	6.66
700	9.43	9.19	8.98	8.80	8.65	8.53	8.42	8.33	8.03	7.89	7.81	7.77
800	10.78	10.50	10.26	10.06	9.89	9.75	9.63	9.52	9.18	9.01	8.93	8.88
900	12.13	11.81	11.54	11.32	11.13	10.97	10.83	10.71	10.33	10.14	10.04	9.99
1000	13.48	13.12	12.82	12.57	12.36	12.18	12.03	11.90	11.47	11.26	11.16	11.10
2000	26.95	26.23	25.64	25.14	24.72	24.36	24.06	23.79	22.94	22.52	22.31	22.20
3000	40.42	39.35	38.46	37.71	37.08	36.54	36.08	35.69	34.41	33.78	33.46	33.30
4000	53.89	52.46	51.27	50.28	49.43	48.72	48.11	47.58	45.87	45.04	44.61	44.40
5000	67.36	65.58	64.09	62.84	61.79	60.89	60.13	59.48	57.34	56.29	55.77	55.50
6000	80.83	78.69	76.91	75.41	74.15	73.07	72.16	71.37	68.81	67.55	66.92	66.60
7000	94.30	91.81	89.73	87.98	86.50	85.25	84.18	83.27	80.27	78.81	78.07	77.70
8000	107.77	104.92	102.54	100.55	98.86	97.43	96.21	95.16	91.74	90.07	89.22	88.79
9000	121.24	118.03	115.36	113.12	111.22	109.61	108.23	107.05	103.21	101.32	100.38	99.89
10000	134.71	131.15	128.18	125.68	123.57	121.78	120.26	118.95	114.68	112.58	111.53	110.99
11000	148.18	144.26	141.00	138.25	135.93	133.96	132.28	130.84	126.14	123.84	122.68	122.09
12000	161.65	157.38	153.81	150.82	148.29	146.14	144.31	142.74	137.61	135.10	133.83	133.19
13000	175.12	170.49	166.63	163.39	160.65	158.32	156.33	154.63	149.08	146.36	144.99	144.29
14000	188.59	183.61	179.45	175.96	173.00	170.50	168.36	166.53	160.54	157.61	156.14	155.39
15000	202.06	196.72	192.27	188.52	185.36	182.67	180.38	178.42	172.01	168.87	167.29	166.49
16000	215.53	209.84	205.08	201.09	197.72	194.85	192.41	190.31	183.48	180.13	178.44	177.58
17000	229.01	222.95	217.90	213.66	210.07	207.03	204.43	202.21	194.94	191.39	189.60	188.68
18000	242.48	236.06	230.72	226.23	222.43	219.21	216.46	214.10	206.41	202.64	200.75	199.78
19000	255.95	249.18	243.53	238.79	234.79	231.39	228.48	226.00	217.88	213.90	211.90	210.88
20000	269.42	262.29	256.35	251.36	247.14	243.56	240.51	237.89	229.35	225.16	223.05	221.98
21000	282.89	275.41	269.17	263.93	259.50	255.74	252.53	249.79	240.81	236.42	234.21	233.08
22000	296.36	288.52	281.99	276.50	271.86	267.92	264.56	261.68	252.28	247.68	245.36	244.18
23000	309.83	301.64	294.80	289.07	284.22	280.10	276.58	273.57	263.75	258.93	256.51	255.28
24000	323.30	314.75	307.62	301.63	296.57	292.27	288.61	285.47	275.21	270.19	267.66	266.37
25000	336.77	327.87	320.44	314.20	308.93	304.45	300.63	297.36	286.68	281.45	278.82	277.47
26000	350.24	340.98	333.26	326.77	321.29	316.63	312.66	309.26	298.15	292.71	289.97	288.57
27000	363.71	354.09	346.07	339.34	333.64	328.81	324.68	321.15	309.61	303.96	301.12	299.67
28000	377.18	367.21	358.89	351.90	346.00	340.99	336.71	333.05	321.08	315.22	312.27	310.77
29000	390.65	380.32	371.71	364.47	358.36	353.16	348.73	344.94	332.55	326.48	323.43	321.87
30000	404.12	393.44	384.53	377.04	370.71	365.34	360.76	356.83	344.02	337.74	334.58	332.97
31000	417.59	406.55	397.34	389.61	383.07	377.52	372.78	368.73	355.48	348.99	345.73	344.06
32000	431.06	419.67	410.16	402.18	395.43	389.70	384.81	380.62	366.95	360.25	356.88	355.16
33000	444.53	432.78	422.98	414.74	407.78	401.87	396.83	392.52	378.42	371.51	368.03	366.26
34000	458.01	445.90	435.80	427.31	420.14	414.05	408.86	404.41	389.88	382.77	379.19	377.36
35000	471.48	459.01	448.61	439.88	432.50	426.23	420.88	416.31	401.35	394.03	390.34	388.46
37500	505.15	491.80	480.66	471.30	463.39	456.68	450.95	446.04	430.02	422.17	418.22	416.21
40000	538.83	524.58	512.70	502.72	494.28	487.12	481.01	475.78	458.69	450.31	446.10	443.95
42500	572.51	557.37	544.74	534.14	525.18	517.56	511.07	505.51	487.35	478.46	473.98	471.70
45000	606.18	590.15	576.79	565.56	556.07	548.01	541.13	535.25	516.02	506.60	501.86	499.45
47500	639.86	622.94	608.83	596.98	586.96	578.45	571.20	564.98	544.69	534.75	529.75	527.19
50000	673.53	655.73	640.87	628.40	617.85	608.90	601.26	594.72	573.36	562.89	557.63	554.94
52500	707.21	688.51	672.92	659.82	648.75	639.34	631.32	624.46	602.02	591.04	585.51	582.69
55000	740.89	721.30	704.96	691.24	679.64	669.79	661.39	654.19	630.69	619.18	613.39	610.43
57500	774.56	754.08	737.00	722.66	710.53	700.23	691.45	683.93	659.36	647.32	641.27	638.18
60000	808.24	786.87	769.05	754.08	741.42	730.68	721.51	713.66	688.03	675.47	669.15	665.93
65000	875.59	852.44	833.13	816.91	803.21	791.57	781.64	773.13	745.36	731.76	724.91	721.42
70000	942.95	918.01	897.22	879.75	864.99	852.46	841.76	832.61	802.70	788.05	780.67	776.91
75000	1010.30	983.59	961.31	942.59	926.78	913.35	901.89	892.08	860.03	844.34	836.44	832.41
80000	1077.65	1049.16	1025.39	1005.43	988.56	974.23	962.01	951.55	917.37	900.62	892.20	887.90
85000	1145.01	1114.73	1089.48	1068.27	1050.35	1035.12	1022.14	1011.02	974.70	956.91	947.96	943.39
90000	1212.36	1180.30	1153.57	1131.11	1112.13	1096.01	1082.26	1070.49	1032.04	1013.20	1003.72	998.89
95000	1279.71	1245.88	1217.65	1193.95	1173.92	1156.90	1142.39	1129.96	1089.37	1069.49	1059.49	1054.38
100000	1347.06	1311.45	1281.74	1256.79	1235.70	1217.79	1202.51	1189.44	1146.71	1125.78	1115.25	1109.87
105000	1414.42	1377.02	1345.83	1319.63	1297.49	1278.68	1262.64	1248.91	1204.04	1182.07	1171.01	1165.37
110000	1481.77	1442.59	1409.92	1382.47	1359.27	1339.57	1322.77	1308.38	1261.38	1238.36	1226.77	1220.86
115000	1549.12	1508.16	1474.00	1445.31	1421.06	1400.46	1382.89	1367.85	1318.71	1294.64	1282.53	1276.36
120000	1616.48	1573.74	1538.09	1508.15	1482.84	1461.35	1443.02	1427.32	1376.05	1350.93	1338.30	1331.85
125000	1683.83	1639.31	1602.18	1570.98	1544.63	1522.24	1503.14	1486.79	1433.38	1407.22	1394.06	1387.34
130000	1751.18	1704.88	1666.27	1633.82	1606.41	1583.13	1563.27	1546.26	1490.72	1463.51	1449.82	1442.84
135000	1818.54	1770.45	1730.35	1696.66	1668.20	1644.02	1623.39	1605.74	1548.05	1519.80	1505.58	1498.33
140000	1885.89	1836.02	1794.44	1759.50	1729.98	1704.91	1683.52	1665.21	1605.39	1576.09	1561.34	1553.82
145000	1953.24	1901.60	1858.52	1822.34	1791.77	1765.80	1743.64	1724.68	1662.38	1617.11	1609.32	—
150000	2020.59	1967.17	1922.61	1885.18	1853.55	1826.69	1803.77	1784.15	1720.06	1688.67	1672.87	1664.81
155000	2087.95	2032.74	1986.70	1948.02	1915.33	1887.57	1863.90	1843.62	1777.39	1744.95	1728.63	1720.30
160000	2155.30	2098.31	2050.78	2010.86	1977.12	1948.46	1924.02	1903.09	1834.73	1801.24	1784.39	1775.80

69

13.50% MONTHLY AMORTIZING PAYMENTS

AMOUNT OF LOAN	NUMBER OF YEARS IN TERM											
	1	2	3	4	5	6	7	8	9	10	11	12
$ 50	4.48	2.39	1.70	1.36	1.16	1.02	0.93	0.86	0.81	0.77	0.73	0.71
100	8.96	4.78	3.40	2.71	2.31	2.04	1.85	1.71	1.61	1.53	1.46	1.41
200	17.92	9.56	6.79	5.42	4.61	4.07	3.70	3.42	3.21	3.05	2.92	2.82
300	26.87	14.34	10.19	8.13	6.91	6.11	5.54	5.13	4.82	4.57	4.38	4.22
400	35.83	19.12	13.58	10.84	9.21	8.14	7.39	6.84	6.42	6.10	5.84	5.63
500	44.78	23.89	16.97	13.54	11.51	10.17	9.24	8.55	8.03	7.62	7.29	7.03
600	53.74	28.67	20.37	16.25	13.81	12.21	11.08	10.26	9.63	9.14	8.75	8.44
700	62.69	33.45	23.76	18.96	16.11	14.24	12.93	11.97	11.23	10.66	10.21	9.85
800	71.65	38.23	27.15	21.67	18.41	16.28	14.78	13.68	12.84	12.19	11.67	11.25
900	80.60	43.00	30.55	24.37	20.71	18.31	16.62	15.38	14.44	13.71	13.13	12.66
1000	89.56	47.78	33.94	27.08	23.01	20.34	18.47	17.09	16.05	15.23	14.58	14.06
2000	179.11	95.56	67.88	54.16	46.02	40.68	36.93	34.18	32.09	30.46	29.16	28.12
3000	268.66	143.34	101.81	81.23	69.03	61.02	55.40	51.27	48.13	45.69	43.74	42.18
4000	358.21	191.11	135.75	108.31	92.04	81.36	73.86	68.36	64.17	60.91	58.32	56.23
5000	447.77	238.89	169.68	135.39	115.05	101.70	92.33	85.45	80.22	76.14	72.90	70.29
6000	537.32	286.67	203.62	162.46	138.06	122.04	110.79	102.53	96.26	91.37	87.48	84.35
7000	626.87	334.44	237.55	189.54	161.07	142.38	129.26	119.62	112.30	106.60	102.06	98.41
8000	716.42	382.22	271.49	216.62	184.08	162.72	147.72	136.71	128.34	121.82	116.64	112.46
9000	805.97	430.00	305.42	243.69	207.09	183.06	166.19	153.80	144.39	137.05	131.22	126.52
10000	895.53	477.78	339.36	270.77	230.10	203.39	184.65	170.89	160.43	152.28	145.80	140.58
11000	985.08	525.55	373.29	297.84	253.11	223.73	203.12	187.97	176.47	167.51	160.38	154.63
12000	1074.63	573.33	407.23	324.92	276.12	244.07	221.58	205.06	192.51	182.73	174.96	168.69
13000	1164.18	621.11	441.16	352.00	299.13	264.41	240.05	222.15	208.56	197.96	189.54	182.75
14000	1253.73	668.88	475.10	379.07	322.14	284.75	258.51	239.24	224.60	213.19	204.12	196.81
15000	1343.29	716.66	509.03	406.15	345.15	305.09	276.98	256.33	240.64	228.42	218.70	210.86
16000	1432.84	764.44	542.97	433.23	368.16	325.43	295.44	273.42	256.68	243.64	233.28	224.92
17000	1522.39	812.21	576.90	460.30	391.17	345.77	313.91	290.50	272.72	258.87	247.86	238.98
18000	1611.94	859.99	610.84	487.38	414.18	366.11	332.37	307.59	288.77	274.10	262.44	253.03
19000	1701.49	907.77	644.78	514.46	437.19	386.45	350.84	324.68	304.81	289.33	277.02	267.09
20000	1791.05	955.55	678.71	541.53	460.20	406.78	369.30	341.77	320.85	304.55	291.60	281.15
21000	1880.60	1003.32	712.65	568.61	483.21	427.12	387.77	358.86	336.89	319.78	306.18	295.21
22000	1970.15	1051.10	746.58	595.68	506.22	447.46	406.23	375.94	352.94	335.01	320.76	309.26
23000	2059.70	1098.88	780.52	622.76	529.23	467.80	424.70	393.03	368.98	350.24	335.34	323.32
24000	2149.25	1146.65	814.45	649.84	552.24	488.14	443.16	410.12	385.02	365.46	349.92	337.38
25000	2238.81	1194.43	848.39	676.91	575.25	508.48	461.63	427.21	401.06	380.69	364.50	351.43
26000	2328.36	1242.21	882.32	703.99	598.26	528.82	480.09	444.30	417.11	395.92	379.08	365.49
27000	2417.91	1289.98	916.26	731.07	621.27	549.16	498.56	461.39	433.15	411.15	393.66	379.55
28000	2507.46	1337.76	950.19	758.14	644.28	569.50	517.02	478.47	449.19	426.37	408.24	393.61
29000	2597.01	1385.54	984.13	785.22	667.29	589.83	535.49	495.56	465.23	441.60	422.82	407.66
30000	2686.57	1433.32	1018.06	812.29	690.30	610.17	553.95	512.65	481.27	456.83	437.40	421.72
31000	2776.12	1481.09	1052.00	839.37	713.31	630.51	572.42	529.74	497.32	472.06	451.98	435.78
32000	2865.67	1528.87	1085.93	866.45	736.32	650.85	590.88	546.83	513.36	487.28	466.56	449.83
33000	2955.22	1576.65	1119.87	893.52	759.33	671.19	609.35	563.91	529.40	502.51	481.14	463.89
34000	3044.77	1624.42	1153.80	920.60	782.34	691.53	627.81	581.00	545.44	517.74	495.72	477.95
35000	3134.33	1672.20	1187.74	947.68	805.35	711.87	646.28	598.09	561.49	532.97	510.30	492.01
37500	3358.21	1791.64	1272.58	1015.37	862.87	762.72	692.44	640.81	601.59	571.03	546.75	527.15
40000	3582.09	1911.09	1357.42	1083.06	920.40	813.56	738.60	683.53	641.70	609.10	583.20	562.29
42500	3805.97	2030.53	1442.25	1150.75	977.92	864.41	784.76	726.25	681.80	647.17	619.65	597.43
45000	4029.85	2149.97	1527.09	1218.44	1035.45	915.26	830.93	768.97	721.91	685.24	656.10	632.58
47500	4253.73	2269.41	1611.93	1286.13	1092.97	966.11	877.09	811.69	762.01	723.31	692.55	667.72
50000	4477.61	2388.86	1696.77	1353.82	1150.50	1016.95	923.25	854.41	802.12	761.38	729.00	702.86
52500	4701.49	2508.30	1781.61	1421.51	1208.02	1067.80	969.41	897.13	842.23	799.45	765.45	738.01
55000	4925.37	2627.74	1866.45	1489.20	1265.55	1118.65	1015.57	939.85	882.33	837.51	801.90	773.15
57500	5149.25	2747.18	1951.28	1556.89	1323.07	1169.50	1061.74	982.57	922.44	875.58	838.35	808.29
60000	5373.13	2866.63	2036.12	1624.58	1380.60	1220.34	1107.90	1025.29	962.54	913.65	874.80	843.44
65000	5820.89	3105.51	2205.80	1759.97	1495.64	1322.04	1200.22	1110.74	1042.76	989.79	947.70	913.72
70000	6268.65	3344.40	2375.48	1895.35	1610.69	1423.73	1292.55	1196.18	1122.97	1065.93	1020.60	984.01
75000	6716.41	3583.28	2545.15	2030.73	1725.74	1525.43	1384.87	1281.62	1203.18	1142.06	1093.50	1054.29
80000	7164.17	3822.17	2714.83	2166.11	1840.79	1627.12	1477.20	1367.06	1283.39	1218.20	1166.39	1124.58
85000	7611.93	4061.05	2884.50	2301.49	1955.84	1728.82	1569.52	1452.50	1363.60	1294.34	1239.29	1194.86
90000	8059.69	4299.94	3054.18	2436.87	2070.89	1830.51	1661.85	1537.94	1443.81	1370.47	1312.19	1265.15
95000	8507.45	4538.82	3223.86	2572.26	2185.94	1932.21	1754.17	1623.38	1524.02	1446.61	1385.09	1335.44
100000	8955.21	4777.71	3393.53	2707.64	2300.99	2033.90	1846.49	1708.82	1604.24	1522.75	1457.99	1405.72
105000	9402.97	5016.59	3563.21	2843.02	2416.04	2135.60	1938.82	1794.26	1684.45	1598.89	1530.89	1476.01
110000	9850.73	5255.48	3732.89	2978.40	2531.09	2237.29	2031.14	1879.70	1764.66	1675.02	1603.79	1546.29
115000	10298.49	5494.36	3902.56	3113.78	2646.14	2338.99	2123.47	1965.14	1844.87	1751.16	1676.69	1616.58
120000	10746.25	5733.25	4072.24	3249.16	2761.19	2440.68	2215.79	2050.58	1925.08	1827.30	1749.59	1686.87
125000	11194.01	5972.13	4241.92	3384.55	2876.24	2542.38	2308.12	2136.02	2005.29	1903.43	1822.49	1757.15
130000	11641.77	6211.02	4411.59	3519.93	2991.28	2644.07	2400.44	2221.47	2085.51	1979.57	1895.39	1827.44
135000	12089.53	6449.90	4581.27	3655.31	3106.33	2745.76	2492.77	2306.91	2165.72	2055.71	1968.29	1897.72
140000	12537.29	6688.79	4750.95	3790.69	3221.38	2847.46	2585.09	2392.35	2245.93	2131.85	2041.19	1968.01
145000	12985.05	6927.67	4920.62	3926.07	3336.43	2949.15	2677.41	2477.79	2326.14	2207.98	2114.09	2038.29
150000	13432.81	7166.56	5090.30	4061.45	3451.48	3050.85	2769.74	2563.23	2406.35	2284.12	2186.99	2108.58
155000	13880.57	7405.44	5259.97	4196.84	3566.53	3152.54	2862.06	2648.67	2486.56	2360.26	2259.88	2178.87
160000	14328.33	7644.33	5429.65	4332.22	3681.58	3254.24	2954.39	2734.11	2566.78	2436.39	2332.78	2249.15

70

AMOUNT OF LOAN	NUMBER OF YEARS IN TERM											
	13	14	15	16	17	18	19	20	25	30	35	40
$ 50	0.69	0.67	0.65	0.64	0.63	0.62	0.62	0.61	0.59	0.58	0.57	0.57
100	1.37	1.33	1.30	1.28	1.26	1.24	1.23	1.21	1.17	1.15	1.14	1.14
200	2.73	2.66	2.60	2.55	2.51	2.48	2.45	2.42	2.34	2.30	2.28	2.27
300	4.09	3.99	3.90	3.83	3.76	3.71	3.67	3.63	3.50	3.44	3.41	3.40
400	5.46	5.32	5.20	5.10	5.02	4.95	4.89	4.83	4.67	4.59	4.55	4.53
500	6.82	6.64	6.50	6.37	6.27	6.18	6.11	6.04	5.83	5.73	5.68	5.66
600	8.18	7.97	7.79	7.65	7.52	7.42	7.33	7.25	7.00	6.88	6.82	6.79
700	9.55	9.30	9.09	8.92	8.78	8.65	8.55	8.46	8.16	8.02	7.95	7.92
800	10.91	10.63	10.39	10.19	10.03	9.89	9.77	9.66	9.33	9.17	9.09	9.05
900	12.27	11.95	11.69	11.47	11.28	11.12	10.99	10.87	10.50	10.31	10.22	10.18
1000	13.63	13.28	12.99	12.74	12.53	12.36	12.21	12.08	11.66	11.46	11.36	11.31
2000	27.26	26.56	25.97	25.48	25.06	24.71	24.41	24.15	23.32	22.91	22.71	22.61
3000	40.89	39.84	38.95	38.22	37.59	37.06	36.61	36.23	34.97	34.37	34.07	33.91
4000	54.52	53.11	51.94	50.95	50.12	49.41	48.81	48.30	46.63	45.82	45.42	45.22
5000	68.15	66.39	64.92	63.69	62.65	61.77	61.02	60.37	58.29	57.28	56.77	56.52
6000	81.78	79.67	77.90	76.43	75.18	74.12	73.22	72.45	69.94	68.73	68.13	67.82
7000	95.41	92.94	90.89	89.16	87.71	86.47	85.42	84.52	81.60	80.18	79.48	79.12
8000	109.04	106.22	103.87	101.90	100.23	98.82	97.62	96.59	93.26	91.64	90.83	90.43
9000	122.67	119.50	116.85	114.64	112.76	111.18	109.82	108.67	104.91	103.09	102.19	101.73
10000	136.30	132.78	129.84	127.37	125.29	123.53	122.03	120.74	116.57	114.55	113.54	113.03
11000	149.93	146.05	142.82	140.11	137.82	135.88	134.23	132.82	128.23	126.00	124.89	124.33
12000	163.56	159.33	155.80	152.85	150.35	148.23	146.43	144.89	139.88	137.45	136.25	135.64
13000	177.19	172.61	168.79	165.58	162.88	160.59	158.63	156.96	151.54	148.91	147.60	146.94
14000	190.82	185.88	181.77	178.32	175.41	172.94	170.83	169.04	163.20	160.36	158.95	158.24
15000	204.45	199.16	194.75	191.06	187.94	185.29	183.04	181.11	174.85	171.82	170.31	169.54
16000	218.08	212.44	207.74	203.79	200.46	197.64	195.24	193.18	186.51	183.27	181.66	180.85
17000	231.71	225.72	220.72	216.53	212.99	209.99	207.44	205.26	198.16	194.73	193.01	192.15
18000	245.34	238.99	233.70	229.27	225.52	222.35	219.64	217.33	209.82	206.18	204.37	203.45
19000	258.97	252.27	246.69	242.00	238.05	234.70	231.85	229.41	221.48	217.63	215.72	214.75
20000	272.60	265.55	259.67	254.74	250.58	247.05	244.05	241.48	233.13	229.09	227.07	226.06
21000	286.23	278.82	272.65	267.48	263.11	259.40	256.25	253.55	244.79	240.54	238.43	237.36
22000	299.86	292.10	285.64	280.21	275.64	271.76	268.45	265.63	256.45	252.00	249.78	248.66
23000	313.49	305.38	298.62	292.95	288.16	284.11	280.65	277.70	268.10	263.45	261.13	259.97
24000	327.12	318.65	311.60	305.69	300.69	296.46	292.86	289.77	279.76	274.90	272.49	271.27
25000	340.75	331.93	324.58	318.42	313.22	308.81	305.06	301.85	291.42	286.36	283.84	282.57
26000	354.38	345.21	337.57	331.16	325.75	321.17	317.26	313.92	303.07	297.81	295.19	293.87
27000	368.01	358.49	350.55	343.90	338.28	333.52	329.46	326.00	314.73	309.27	306.55	305.18
28000	381.64	371.76	363.53	356.63	350.81	345.87	341.66	338.07	326.39	320.72	317.90	316.48
29000	395.27	385.04	376.52	369.37	363.34	358.22	353.87	350.14	338.04	332.17	329.25	327.78
30000	408.90	398.32	389.50	382.11	375.87	370.57	366.07	362.22	349.70	343.63	340.61	339.08
31000	422.53	411.59	402.48	394.84	388.39	382.93	378.27	374.29	361.35	355.08	351.96	350.39
32000	436.16	424.87	415.47	407.58	400.92	395.28	390.47	386.36	373.01	366.54	363.31	361.69
33000	449.79	438.15	428.45	420.32	413.45	407.63	402.67	398.44	384.67	377.99	374.67	372.99
34000	463.42	451.43	441.43	433.05	425.98	419.99	414.88	410.51	396.32	389.45	386.02	384.29
35000	477.05	464.70	454.42	445.79	438.51	432.34	427.08	422.59	407.98	400.90	397.37	395.60
37500	511.13	497.90	486.87	477.63	469.83	463.22	457.58	452.77	437.12	429.53	425.76	423.85
40000	545.20	531.09	519.33	509.47	501.15	494.10	488.09	482.95	466.26	458.17	454.14	452.11
42500	579.28	564.28	551.79	541.31	532.47	524.98	518.59	513.14	495.40	486.81	482.52	480.37
45000	613.35	597.47	584.25	573.16	563.80	555.86	549.10	543.32	524.55	515.44	510.91	508.62
47500	647.43	630.67	616.71	605.00	595.12	586.74	579.61	573.51	553.69	544.08	539.29	536.88
50000	681.50	663.86	649.16	636.84	626.44	617.62	610.11	603.69	582.83	572.71	567.68	565.14
52500	715.58	697.05	681.62	668.68	657.76	648.50	640.62	633.88	611.97	601.35	596.06	593.39
55000	749.65	730.24	714.08	700.52	689.08	679.38	671.12	664.06	641.11	629.98	624.44	621.65
57500	783.73	763.44	746.54	732.36	720.40	710.26	701.63	694.25	670.25	658.62	652.83	649.91
60000	817.80	796.63	779.00	764.21	751.73	741.14	732.13	724.43	699.39	687.25	681.21	678.16
65000	885.95	863.01	843.91	827.89	814.37	802.91	793.14	784.80	757.67	744.52	737.98	734.67
70000	954.10	929.40	908.83	891.57	877.01	864.67	854.15	845.17	815.96	801.79	794.74	791.19
75000	1022.25	995.79	973.74	955.26	939.66	926.43	915.16	905.54	874.24	859.06	851.51	847.70
80000	1090.40	1062.17	1038.66	1018.94	1002.30	988.19	976.17	965.90	932.52	916.33	908.28	904.21
85000	1158.55	1128.56	1103.58	1082.62	1064.94	1049.95	1037.18	1026.27	990.80	973.61	965.04	960.73
90000	1226.70	1194.94	1168.49	1146.31	1127.59	1111.71	1098.20	1086.64	1049.09	1030.88	1021.81	1017.24
95000	1294.85	1261.33	1233.41	1209.99	1190.23	1173.47	1159.21	1147.01	1107.37	1088.15	1078.57	1073.75
100000	1363.00	1327.71	1298.32	1273.67	1252.87	1235.24	1220.22	1207.38	1165.65	1145.42	1135.35	1130.27
105000	1431.15	1394.10	1363.24	1337.36	1315.52	1297.00	1281.23	1267.75	1223.93	1202.69	1192.11	1186.78
110000	1499.30	1460.48	1428.16	1401.04	1378.16	1358.76	1342.24	1328.12	1282.21	1259.96	1248.88	1243.29
115000	1567.45	1526.87	1493.07	1464.72	1440.80	1420.52	1403.25	1388.49	1340.50	1317.23	1305.65	1299.81
120000	1635.60	1593.25	1557.99	1528.41	1503.45	1482.28	1464.26	1448.85	1398.78	1374.50	1362.41	1356.32
125000	1703.74	1659.64	1622.90	1592.09	1566.09	1544.04	1525.27	1509.22	1457.06	1431.77	1419.18	1412.83
130000	1771.89	1726.02	1687.82	1655.77	1628.73	1605.81	1586.28	1569.59	1515.34	1489.04	1475.95	1469.34
135000	1840.04	1792.41	1752.74	1719.46	1691.38	1667.57	1647.29	1629.96	1573.63	1546.31	1532.71	1525.86
140000	1908.19	1858.79	1817.65	1783.14	1754.02	1729.33	1708.30	1690.33	1631.91	1603.58	1589.48	1582.37
145000	1976.34	1925.18	1882.57	1846.82	1816.66	1791.09	1769.31	1750.70	1690.19	1660.85	1646.25	1638.88
150000	2044.49	1991.57	1947.48	1910.51	1879.31	1852.85	1830.32	1811.07	1748.47	1718.12	1703.02	1695.40
155000	2112.64	2057.95	2012.40	1974.19	1941.95	1914.61	1891.33	1871.44	1806.75	1775.39	1759.78	1751.91
160000	2180.79	2124.34	2077.31	2037.87	2004.60	1976.38	1952.34	1931.80	1865.04	1832.66	1816.55	1808.42

AMOUNT OF LOAN	NUMBER OF YEARS IN TERM											
	1	2	3	4	5	6	7	8	9	10	11	12
$ 50	4.49	2.40	1.71	1.37	1.16	1.03	0.94	0.87	0.81	0.77	0.74	0.72
100	8.97	4.79	3.41	2.73	2.32	2.05	1.87	1.73	1.62	1.54	1.48	1.43
200	17.94	9.58	6.82	5.45	4.63	4.10	3.73	3.45	3.24	3.08	2.95	2.85
300	26.91	14.37	10.22	8.17	6.95	6.15	5.59	5.17	4.86	4.62	4.42	4.27
400	35.87	19.16	13.63	10.89	9.26	8.19	7.45	6.90	6.48	6.16	5.90	5.69
500	44.84	23.95	17.03	13.61	11.57	10.24	9.31	8.62	8.10	7.69	7.37	7.11
600	53.81	28.74	20.44	16.33	13.89	12.29	11.17	10.34	9.72	9.23	8.84	8.53
700	62.77	33.53	23.84	19.05	16.20	14.34	13.03	12.07	11.34	10.77	10.32	9.95
800	71.74	38.32	27.25	21.77	18.52	16.38	14.89	13.79	12.96	12.31	11.79	11.38
900	80.71	43.11	30.66	24.49	20.83	18.43	16.75	15.51	14.57	13.84	13.26	12.80
1000	89.67	47.90	34.06	27.21	23.14	20.48	18.61	17.23	16.19	15.38	14.74	14.22
2000	179.34	95.79	68.12	54.41	46.28	40.95	37.21	34.46	32.38	30.76	29.47	28.43
3000	269.01	143.69	102.17	81.61	69.42	61.42	55.81	51.69	48.57	46.14	44.20	42.65
4000	358.68	191.58	136.23	108.81	92.56	81.89	74.41	68.92	64.76	61.51	58.94	56.86
5000	448.35	239.48	170.29	136.01	115.70	102.37	93.02	86.15	80.94	76.89	73.67	71.07
6000	538.02	287.37	204.34	163.21	138.84	122.84	111.62	103.38	97.13	92.27	88.40	85.29
7000	627.69	335.27	238.40	190.41	161.98	143.31	130.22	120.61	113.32	107.64	103.14	99.50
8000	717.36	383.16	272.46	217.61	185.12	163.78	148.82	137.84	129.51	123.02	117.87	113.72
9000	807.03	431.06	306.51	244.82	208.25	184.25	167.42	155.07	145.69	138.40	132.60	127.93
10000	896.70	478.95	340.57	272.02	231.39	204.73	186.03	172.30	161.88	153.77	147.33	142.14
11000	986.37	526.85	374.62	299.22	254.53	225.20	204.63	189.53	178.07	169.15	162.07	156.36
12000	1076.04	574.74	408.68	326.42	277.67	245.67	223.23	206.76	194.26	184.53	176.80	170.57
13000	1165.71	622.64	442.74	353.62	300.81	266.14	241.83	223.99	210.44	199.90	191.53	184.78
14000	1255.38	670.53	476.79	380.82	323.95	286.61	260.44	241.22	226.63	215.28	206.27	199.00
15000	1345.05	718.43	510.85	408.02	347.09	307.09	279.04	258.45	242.82	230.66	221.00	213.21
16000	1434.72	766.32	544.91	435.22	370.23	327.56	297.64	275.68	259.01	246.03	235.73	227.43
17000	1524.39	814.22	578.96	462.43	393.37	348.03	316.24	292.91	275.20	261.41	250.46	241.64
18000	1614.06	862.11	613.02	489.63	416.50	368.50	334.84	310.14	291.38	276.79	265.20	255.85
19000	1703.73	910.01	647.08	516.83	439.64	388.98	353.45	327.37	307.57	292.16	279.93	270.07
20000	1793.40	957.90	681.13	544.03	462.78	409.45	372.05	344.60	323.76	307.54	294.66	284.28
21000	1883.07	1005.80	715.19	571.23	485.92	429.92	390.65	361.83	339.95	322.92	309.40	298.50
22000	1972.73	1053.69	749.24	598.43	509.06	450.39	409.25	379.05	356.13	338.29	324.13	312.71
23000	2062.40	1101.59	783.30	625.63	532.20	470.86	427.86	396.28	372.32	353.67	338.86	326.92
24000	2152.07	1149.48	817.36	652.83	555.34	491.34	446.46	413.51	388.51	369.05	353.59	341.14
25000	2241.74	1197.38	851.41	680.04	578.48	511.81	465.06	430.74	404.70	384.42	368.33	355.35
26000	2331.41	1245.27	885.47	707.24	601.61	532.28	483.66	447.97	420.88	399.80	383.06	369.56
27000	2421.08	1293.17	919.53	734.44	624.75	552.75	502.26	465.20	437.07	415.18	397.79	383.78
28000	2510.75	1341.06	953.58	761.64	647.89	573.23	520.87	482.43	453.26	430.55	412.53	397.99
29000	2600.42	1388.96	987.64	788.84	671.03	593.70	539.47	499.66	469.45	445.93	427.26	412.21
30000	2690.09	1436.85	1021.69	816.04	694.17	614.17	558.07	516.89	485.64	461.31	441.99	426.42
31000	2779.76	1484.75	1055.75	843.24	717.31	634.64	576.67	534.12	501.82	476.68	456.72	440.63
32000	2869.43	1532.64	1089.81	870.44	740.45	655.11	595.27	551.35	518.01	492.06	471.46	454.85
33000	2959.10	1580.54	1123.86	897.65	763.59	675.58	613.88	568.58	534.20	507.44	486.19	469.06
34000	3048.77	1628.43	1157.92	924.85	786.73	696.06	632.48	585.81	550.39	522.81	500.92	483.28
35000	3138.44	1676.33	1191.98	952.05	809.86	716.53	651.08	603.04	566.57	538.19	515.66	497.49
37500	3362.61	1796.06	1277.12	1020.05	867.71	767.71	697.59	646.11	607.04	576.63	552.49	533.02
40000	3586.79	1915.80	1362.26	1088.05	925.56	818.89	744.09	689.19	647.51	615.07	589.32	568.56
42500	3810.96	2035.54	1447.40	1156.06	983.41	870.07	790.60	732.26	687.98	653.51	626.15	604.09
45000	4035.13	2155.27	1532.54	1224.06	1041.25	921.25	837.10	775.33	728.45	691.96	662.98	639.63
47500	4259.31	2275.01	1617.68	1292.06	1099.10	972.43	883.61	818.41	768.92	730.40	699.82	675.16
50000	4483.48	2394.75	1702.82	1360.07	1156.95	1023.61	930.11	861.48	809.39	768.84	736.65	710.70
52500	4707.66	2514.49	1787.96	1428.07	1214.79	1074.79	976.62	904.56	849.86	807.28	773.48	746.23
55000	4931.83	2634.22	1873.10	1496.07	1272.64	1125.97	1023.12	947.63	890.33	845.73	810.31	781.77
57500	5156.01	2753.96	1958.24	1564.08	1330.49	1177.15	1069.63	990.70	930.80	884.16	847.15	817.30
60000	5380.18	2873.70	2043.38	1632.08	1388.34	1228.33	1116.14	1033.78	971.27	922.61	883.98	852.83
65000	5828.52	3113.17	2213.67	1768.09	1504.03	1330.69	1209.15	1119.92	1052.20	999.49	957.64	923.90
70000	6276.87	3352.65	2383.95	1904.09	1619.72	1433.05	1302.15	1206.07	1133.14	1076.37	1031.31	994.97
75000	6725.22	3592.12	2554.23	2040.10	1735.42	1535.41	1395.17	1292.22	1214.08	1153.26	1104.97	1066.04
80000	7173.57	3831.59	2724.51	2176.10	1851.11	1637.77	1488.18	1378.37	1295.02	1230.14	1178.64	1137.11
85000	7621.92	4071.07	2894.79	2312.11	1966.81	1740.13	1581.19	1464.51	1375.96	1307.02	1252.30	1208.18
90000	8070.26	4310.54	3065.07	2448.12	2082.50	1842.50	1674.20	1550.66	1456.90	1383.91	1325.96	1279.25
95000	8518.61	4550.02	3235.36	2584.12	2198.20	1944.86	1767.21	1636.81	1537.83	1460.79	1399.63	1350.32
100000	8966.96	4789.49	3405.64	2720.13	2313.89	2047.22	1860.22	1722.96	1618.77	1537.67	1473.29	1421.39
105000	9415.31	5028.97	3575.92	2856.13	2429.58	2149.58	1953.23	1809.11	1699.71	1614.56	1546.96	1492.46
110000	9863.65	5268.44	3746.20	2992.14	2545.28	2251.94	2046.24	1895.25	1780.65	1691.44	1620.62	1563.53
115000	10312.00	5507.91	3916.49	3128.15	2660.97	2354.30	2139.26	1981.40	1861.59	1768.32	1694.29	1634.60
120000	10760.35	5747.39	4086.76	3264.15	2776.67	2456.66	2232.27	2067.55	1942.53	1845.21	1767.95	1705.66
125000	11208.70	5986.86	4257.05	3400.16	2892.36	2559.02	2325.28	2153.70	2023.46	1922.09	1841.62	1776.73
130000	11657.04	6226.34	4427.33	3536.17	3008.05	2661.38	2418.29	2239.84	2104.40	1998.97	1915.28	1847.80
135000	12105.39	6465.81	4597.61	3672.17	3123.75	2763.74	2511.30	2325.99	2185.34	2075.86	1988.94	1918.87
140000	12553.74	6705.29	4767.89	3808.18	3239.44	2866.10	2604.31	2412.14	2266.28	2152.74	2062.61	1989.94
145000	13002.09	6944.76	4938.17	3944.18	3355.14	2968.46	2697.32	2498.29	2347.22	2229.62	2136.27	2061.01
150000	13450.43	7184.23	5108.45	4080.19	3470.83	3070.82	2790.33	2584.43	2428.16	2306.51	2209.94	2132.08
155000	13898.78	7423.71	5278.74	4216.20	3586.53	3173.18	2883.34	2670.58	2509.09	2383.39	2283.60	2203.15
160000	14347.13	7663.18	5449.02	4352.20	3702.22	3275.54	2976.35	2756.73	2590.03	2460.27	2357.27	2274.22

AMOUNT OF LOAN	NUMBER OF YEARS IN TERM											
	13	14	15	16	17	18	19	20	25	30	35	40
$ 50	0.69	0.68	0.66	0.65	0.64	0.63	0.62	0.62	0.60	0.59	0.58	0.58
100	1.38	1.35	1.32	1.30	1.28	1.26	1.24	1.23	1.19	1.17	1.16	1.16
200	2.76	2.69	2.63	2.59	2.55	2.51	2.48	2.46	2.37	2.34	2.32	2.31
300	4.14	4.04	3.95	3.88	3.82	3.76	3.72	3.68	3.56	3.50	3.47	3.46
400	5.52	5.38	5.26	5.17	5.09	5.02	4.96	4.91	4.74	4.67	4.63	4.61
500	6.90	6.73	6.58	6.46	6.36	6.27	6.20	6.13	5.93	5.83	5.78	5.76
600	8.28	8.07	7.89	7.75	7.63	7.52	7.43	7.36	7.11	7.00	6.94	6.91
700	9.66	9.41	9.21	9.04	8.90	8.77	8.67	8.58	8.30	8.16	8.09	8.06
800	11.04	10.76	10.52	10.33	10.17	10.03	9.91	9.81	9.48	9.33	9.25	9.21
900	12.42	12.10	11.84	11.62	11.44	11.28	11.15	11.03	10.67	10.49	10.40	10.36
1000	13.80	13.45	13.15	12.91	12.71	12.53	12.39	12.26	11.85	11.66	11.56	11.51
2000	27.59	26.89	26.30	25.82	25.41	25.06	24.77	24.51	23.70	23.31	23.11	23.02
3000	41.38	40.33	39.45	38.72	38.11	37.59	37.15	36.77	35.54	34.96	34.67	34.53
4000	55.17	53.77	52.60	51.63	50.81	50.12	49.53	49.02	47.39	46.61	46.22	46.03
5000	68.96	67.21	65.75	64.54	63.51	62.64	61.91	61.28	59.24	58.26	57.78	57.54
6000	82.75	80.65	78.90	77.44	76.21	75.17	74.29	73.53	71.08	69.91	69.33	69.05
7000	96.54	94.09	92.05	90.35	88.91	87.70	86.67	85.78	82.93	81.56	80.89	80.55
8000	110.33	107.53	105.20	103.26	101.62	100.23	99.05	98.04	94.78	93.21	92.44	92.06
9000	124.12	120.97	118.35	116.16	114.32	112.75	111.43	110.29	106.62	104.87	104.00	103.57
10000	137.91	134.41	131.50	129.07	127.02	125.28	123.81	122.55	118.47	116.52	115.55	115.07
11000	151.70	147.85	144.65	141.98	139.72	137.81	136.19	134.80	130.32	128.17	127.11	126.58
12000	165.49	161.29	157.80	154.88	152.42	150.34	148.57	147.05	142.16	139.82	138.66	138.09
13000	179.28	174.73	170.95	167.79	165.12	162.86	160.95	159.31	154.01	151.47	150.22	149.59
14000	193.07	188.17	184.10	180.69	177.82	175.39	173.33	171.56	165.86	163.12	161.77	161.10
15000	206.86	201.61	197.25	193.60	190.52	187.92	185.71	183.82	177.70	174.77	173.33	172.61
16000	220.65	215.05	210.40	206.51	203.23	200.45	198.09	196.07	189.55	186.42	184.88	184.11
17000	234.44	228.49	223.55	219.41	215.93	212.97	210.47	208.32	201.40	198.07	196.44	195.62
18000	248.23	241.94	236.70	232.32	228.63	225.50	222.85	220.58	213.24	209.73	207.99	207.13
19000	262.02	255.38	249.85	245.23	241.33	238.03	235.23	232.83	225.09	221.38	219.55	218.64
20000	275.81	268.82	263.00	258.13	254.03	250.56	247.61	245.09	236.94	233.03	231.10	230.14
21000	289.60	282.26	276.15	271.04	266.73	263.09	259.99	257.34	248.78	244.68	242.66	241.65
22000	303.39	295.70	289.30	283.95	279.43	275.61	272.37	269.59	260.63	256.33	254.21	253.16
23000	317.18	309.14	302.45	296.85	292.13	288.14	284.75	281.85	272.48	267.98	265.77	264.66
24000	330.97	322.58	315.60	309.76	304.84	300.67	297.13	294.10	284.32	279.63	277.32	276.17
25000	344.76	336.02	328.75	322.67	317.54	313.20	309.51	306.36	296.17	291.28	288.88	287.68
26000	358.55	349.46	341.90	335.57	330.24	325.72	321.89	318.61	308.02	302.93	300.43	299.18
27000	372.34	362.90	355.05	348.48	342.94	338.25	334.27	330.86	319.86	314.59	311.99	310.69
28000	386.13	376.34	368.20	361.38	355.64	350.78	346.65	343.12	331.71	326.24	323.54	322.20
29000	399.92	389.78	381.35	374.29	368.34	363.31	359.03	355.37	343.56	337.89	335.10	333.70
30000	413.71	403.22	394.50	387.20	381.04	375.83	371.41	367.63	355.40	349.54	346.65	345.21
31000	427.50	416.66	407.65	400.10	393.75	388.36	383.79	379.88	367.25	361.19	358.21	356.72
32000	441.29	430.10	420.80	413.01	406.45	400.89	396.17	392.13	379.10	372.84	369.76	368.22
33000	455.08	443.54	433.95	425.92	419.15	413.42	408.55	404.39	390.94	384.49	381.32	379.73
34000	468.87	456.98	447.10	438.82	431.85	425.94	420.93	416.64	402.79	396.14	392.87	391.24
35000	482.66	470.42	460.25	451.73	444.55	438.47	433.31	428.90	414.64	407.79	404.42	402.74
37500	517.13	504.03	493.13	484.00	476.30	469.79	464.26	459.53	444.25	436.92	433.31	431.51
40000	551.61	537.63	526.00	516.26	508.06	501.11	495.21	490.17	473.87	466.05	462.20	460.28
42500	586.08	571.23	558.87	548.53	539.81	532.43	526.16	520.80	503.49	495.18	491.09	489.05
45000	620.56	604.83	591.75	580.79	571.56	563.75	557.11	551.44	533.10	524.31	519.97	517.81
47500	655.03	638.43	624.62	613.06	603.32	595.07	588.06	582.07	562.72	553.43	548.86	546.58
50000	689.51	672.03	657.50	645.33	635.07	626.39	619.01	612.71	592.34	582.56	577.75	575.35
52500	723.98	705.63	690.37	677.59	666.82	657.71	649.96	643.34	621.95	611.69	606.63	604.11
55000	758.46	739.24	723.25	709.86	698.58	689.03	680.91	673.98	651.57	640.82	635.52	632.88
57500	792.93	772.84	756.12	742.12	730.33	720.34	711.86	704.61	681.19	669.94	664.41	661.65
60000	827.41	806.44	789.00	774.39	762.08	751.66	742.81	735.25	710.80	699.07	693.30	690.42
65000	896.36	873.64	854.75	838.92	825.59	814.30	804.71	796.52	770.04	757.33	751.07	747.95
70000	965.31	940.84	920.50	903.45	889.10	876.94	866.61	857.79	829.27	815.58	808.84	805.48
75000	1034.26	1008.05	986.25	967.99	952.60	939.58	928.51	919.06	888.50	873.84	866.62	863.02
80000	1103.21	1075.25	1051.99	1032.52	1016.11	1002.22	990.41	980.33	947.74	932.10	924.39	920.55
85000	1172.16	1142.45	1117.74	1097.05	1079.61	1064.85	1052.31	1041.60	1006.97	990.35	982.17	978.09
90000	1241.11	1209.66	1183.49	1161.58	1143.12	1127.49	1114.21	1102.87	1066.20	1039.94	1035.62	
95000	1310.06	1276.86	1249.24	1226.11	1206.63	1190.13	1176.11	1164.14	1125.44	1106.86	1097.72	1093.16
100000	1379.01	1344.06	1314.99	1290.65	1270.13	1252.77	1238.01	1225.41	1184.67	1165.12	1155.49	1150.69
105000	1447.96	1411.26	1380.74	1355.18	1333.64	1315.41	1299.91	1286.68	1243.90	1223.37	1213.26	1208.22
110000	1516.91	1478.47	1446.49	1419.71	1397.15	1378.05	1361.81	1347.95	1303.14	1281.63	1271.04	1265.76
115000	1585.86	1545.67	1512.24	1484.24	1460.65	1440.68	1423.71	1409.22	1362.37	1339.88	1328.81	1323.29
120000	1654.81	1612.87	1577.99	1548.77	1524.16	1503.32	1485.61	1470.49	1421.60	1398.14	1386.59	1380.83
125000	1723.76	1680.08	1643.74	1613.31	1587.67	1565.96	1547.51	1531.76	1480.84	1456.40	1444.36	1438.36
130000	1792.71	1747.28	1709.49	1677.84	1651.17	1628.60	1609.41	1593.03	1540.07	1514.65	1502.14	1495.90
135000	1861.66	1814.48	1775.24	1742.37	1714.68	1691.24	1671.31	1654.30	1599.30	1572.91	1559.91	1553.43
140000	1930.61	1881.68	1840.99	1806.90	1778.19	1753.87	1733.21	1715.57	1658.54	1631.16	1617.68	1610.96
145000	1999.56	1948.89	1906.74	1871.43	1841.69	1816.51	1795.11	1776.84	1717.77	1689.42	1675.46	1668.50
150000	2068.51	2016.09	1972.49	1935.97	1905.20	1879.15	1857.01	1838.11	1777.00	1747.67	1733.23	1726.03
155000	2137.47	2083.29	2038.24	2000.50	1968.71	1941.79	1918.91	1899.38	1836.24	1805.93	1791.01	1783.57
160000	2206.42	2150.50	2103.98	2065.03	2032.21	2004.43	1980.81	1960.65	1895.47	1864.19	1848.78	1841.10

MONTHLY AMORTIZING PAYMENTS

AMOUNT OF LOAN	NUMBER OF YEARS IN TERM											
	1	2	3	4	5	6	7	8	9	10	11	12
$ 50	4.49	2.41	1.71	1.37	1.17	1.04	0.94	0.87	0.82	0.78	0.75	0.72
100	8.98	4.81	3.42	2.74	2.33	2.07	1.88	1.74	1.64	1.56	1.49	1.44
200	17.96	9.61	6.84	5.47	4.66	4.13	3.75	3.48	3.27	3.11	2.98	2.88
300	26.94	14.41	10.26	8.20	6.99	6.19	5.63	5.22	4.91	4.66	4.47	4.32
400	35.92	19.21	13.68	10.94	9.31	8.25	7.50	6.95	6.54	6.22	5.96	5.75
500	44.90	24.01	17.09	13.67	11.64	10.31	9.38	8.69	8.17	7.77	7.45	7.19
600	53.88	28.81	20.51	16.40	13.97	12.37	11.25	10.43	9.81	9.32	8.94	8.63
700	62.86	33.61	23.93	19.13	16.29	14.43	13.12	12.17	11.44	10.87	10.43	10.06
800	71.83	38.42	27.35	21.87	18.62	16.49	15.00	13.90	13.07	12.43	11.91	11.50
900	80.81	43.22	30.76	24.60	20.95	18.55	16.87	15.64	14.71	13.98	13.40	12.94
1000	89.79	48.02	34.18	27.33	23.27	20.61	18.75	17.38	16.34	15.53	14.89	14.38
2000	179.58	96.03	68.36	54.66	46.54	41.22	37.49	34.75	32.67	31.06	29.78	28.75
3000	269.37	144.04	102.54	81.98	69.81	61.82	56.23	52.12	49.01	46.58	44.66	43.12
4000	359.15	192.06	136.72	109.31	93.08	82.43	74.97	69.49	65.34	62.11	59.55	57.49
5000	448.94	240.07	170.89	136.64	116.35	103.03	93.71	86.86	81.67	77.64	74.44	71.86
6000	538.73	288.08	205.07	163.96	139.61	123.64	112.45	104.23	98.01	93.16	89.32	86.23
7000	628.51	336.10	239.25	191.29	162.88	144.25	131.19	121.61	114.34	108.69	104.21	100.60
8000	718.30	384.11	273.43	218.62	186.15	164.85	149.93	138.98	130.67	124.22	119.10	114.98
9000	808.09	432.12	307.60	245.94	209.42	185.46	168.67	156.35	147.01	139.74	133.98	129.35
10000	897.88	480.13	341.78	273.27	232.69	206.06	187.41	173.72	163.34	155.27	148.87	143.72
11000	987.66	528.15	375.96	300.60	255.96	226.67	206.15	191.09	179.68	170.80	163.76	158.09
12000	1077.45	576.16	410.14	327.92	279.22	247.27	224.89	208.46	196.01	186.32	178.64	172.46
13000	1167.24	624.17	444.31	355.25	302.49	267.88	243.63	225.83	212.34	201.85	193.53	186.83
14000	1257.02	672.19	478.49	382.58	325.76	288.49	262.37	243.21	228.68	217.38	208.42	201.20
15000	1346.81	720.20	512.67	409.90	349.03	309.09	281.11	260.58	245.01	232.90	223.30	215.57
16000	1436.60	768.21	546.85	437.23	372.30	329.70	299.85	277.95	261.34	248.43	238.19	229.95
17000	1526.39	816.22	581.02	464.56	395.57	350.30	318.59	295.32	277.68	263.96	253.08	244.32
18000	1616.17	864.24	615.20	491.88	418.83	370.91	337.33	312.69	294.01	279.48	267.96	258.69
19000	1705.96	912.25	649.38	519.21	442.10	391.51	356.07	330.06	310.35	295.01	282.85	273.06
20000	1795.75	960.26	683.56	546.53	465.37	412.12	374.81	347.44	326.68	310.54	297.74	287.43
21000	1885.53	1008.28	717.74	573.86	488.64	432.73	393.55	364.81	343.01	326.06	312.62	301.80
22000	1975.32	1056.29	751.91	601.19	511.91	453.33	412.29	382.18	359.35	341.59	327.51	316.17
23000	2065.11	1104.30	786.09	628.51	535.17	473.94	431.03	399.55	375.68	357.12	342.40	330.54
24000	2154.90	1152.31	820.27	655.84	558.44	494.54	449.77	416.92	392.01	372.64	357.28	344.92
25000	2244.68	1200.33	854.45	683.17	581.71	515.15	468.51	434.29	408.35	388.17	372.17	359.29
26000	2334.47	1248.34	888.62	710.49	604.98	535.75	487.25	451.66	424.68	403.70	387.06	373.66
27000	2424.26	1296.35	922.80	737.82	628.25	556.36	505.99	469.04	441.01	419.22	401.94	388.03
28000	2514.04	1344.37	956.98	765.15	651.52	576.97	524.73	486.41	457.35	434.75	416.83	402.40
29000	2603.83	1392.38	991.16	792.47	674.78	597.57	543.47	503.78	473.68	450.28	431.72	416.77
30000	2693.62	1440.39	1025.33	819.80	698.05	618.18	562.21	521.15	490.02	465.80	446.60	431.14
31000	2783.41	1488.40	1059.51	847.13	721.32	638.78	580.95	538.52	506.35	481.33	461.49	445.51
32000	2873.19	1536.42	1093.69	874.45	744.59	659.39	599.69	555.89	522.68	496.86	476.38	459.89
33000	2962.98	1584.43	1127.87	901.78	767.86	679.99	618.43	573.26	539.02	512.38	491.26	474.26
34000	3052.77	1632.44	1162.04	929.11	791.13	700.60	637.17	590.64	555.35	527.91	506.15	488.63
35000	3142.55	1680.46	1196.22	956.43	814.39	721.21	655.91	608.01	571.68	543.44	521.04	503.00
37500	3367.02	1800.49	1281.67	1024.75	872.56	772.72	702.76	651.44	612.52	582.25	558.25	538.93
40000	3591.49	1920.52	1367.11	1093.06	930.74	824.23	749.61	694.87	653.35	621.07	595.47	574.86
42500	3815.96	2040.55	1452.55	1161.38	988.91	875.75	796.46	738.29	694.19	659.89	632.69	610.78
45000	4040.43	2160.58	1538.00	1229.70	1047.08	927.26	843.31	781.72	735.02	698.70	669.90	646.71
47500	4264.89	2280.62	1623.44	1298.01	1105.25	978.78	890.16	825.15	775.86	737.52	707.12	682.64
50000	4489.36	2400.65	1708.89	1366.33	1163.42	1030.29	937.01	868.58	816.69	776.34	744.34	718.57
52500	4713.83	2520.68	1794.33	1434.65	1221.59	1081.81	983.86	912.01	857.52	815.15	781.55	754.50
55000	4938.30	2640.71	1879.77	1502.96	1279.76	1133.32	1030.71	955.44	898.36	853.97	818.77	790.42
57500	5162.76	2760.75	1965.22	1571.28	1337.93	1184.84	1077.56	998.87	939.19	892.79	855.99	826.35
60000	5387.23	2880.78	2050.66	1639.59	1396.10	1236.35	1124.41	1042.30	980.03	931.60	893.20	862.28
65000	5836.17	3120.84	2221.55	1776.23	1512.44	1339.38	1218.11	1129.15	1061.70	1009.24	967.64	934.14
70000	6285.10	3360.91	2392.44	1912.86	1628.78	1442.41	1311.81	1216.01	1143.36	1086.87	1042.07	1005.99
75000	6734.04	3600.97	2563.33	2049.49	1745.12	1545.44	1405.51	1302.87	1225.03	1164.50	1116.50	1077.85
80000	7182.97	3841.04	2734.22	2186.12	1861.47	1648.46	1499.21	1389.73	1306.70	1242.14	1190.94	1149.71
85000	7631.91	4081.10	2905.10	2322.76	1977.81	1751.49	1592.91	1476.58	1388.37	1319.77	1265.37	1221.56
90000	8080.85	4321.16	3075.99	2459.39	2094.15	1854.52	1686.61	1563.44	1470.04	1397.40	1339.80	1293.42
95000	8529.78	4561.23	3246.88	2596.02	2210.49	1957.55	1780.31	1650.30	1551.71	1475.04	1414.24	1365.28
100000	8978.72	4801.29	3417.77	2732.65	2326.83	2060.58	1874.01	1737.16	1633.38	1552.67	1488.67	1437.13
105000	9427.65	5041.36	3588.66	2869.29	2443.17	2163.61	1967.71	1824.01	1715.04	1630.30	1563.10	1508.99
110000	9876.59	5281.42	3759.54	3005.92	2559.51	2266.64	2061.41	1910.87	1796.71	1707.94	1637.54	1580.84
115000	10325.52	5521.49	3930.43	3142.55	2675.85	2369.67	2155.11	1997.73	1878.38	1785.57	1711.97	1652.70
120000	10774.46	5761.55	4101.32	3279.18	2792.20	2472.69	2248.81	2084.59	1960.05	1863.20	1786.40	1724.56
125000	11223.39	6001.62	4272.21	3415.81	2908.54	2575.72	2342.51	2171.44	2041.72	1940.84	1860.84	1796.41
130000	11672.33	6241.68	4443.10	3552.45	3024.88	2678.75	2436.21	2258.30	2123.39	2018.47	1935.27	1868.27
135000	12121.27	6481.74	4613.99	3689.08	3141.22	2781.78	2529.91	2345.16	2205.05	2096.10	2009.70	1940.13
140000	12570.20	6721.81	4784.87	3825.71	3257.56	2884.81	2623.61	2432.02	2286.72	2173.74	2084.14	2011.98
145000	13019.14	6961.87	4955.76	3962.34	3373.90	2987.84	2717.31	2518.87	2368.39	2251.37	2158.57	2083.84
150000	13468.07	7201.94	5126.65	4098.98	3490.24	3090.87	2811.01	2605.73	2450.06	2329.00	2233.00	2155.70
155000	13917.01	7442.00	5297.54	4235.61	3606.58	3193.89	2904.71	2692.59	2531.73	2406.63	2307.44	2227.55
160000	14365.94	7682.07	5468.43	4372.24	3722.93	3296.92	2998.41	2779.45	2613.40	2484.27	2381.87	2299.41

MONTHLY AMORTIZING PAYMENTS

14.00%

AMOUNT OF LOAN	NUMBER OF YEARS IN TERM											
	13	14	15	16	17	18	19	20	25	30	35	40
$ 50	0.70	0.69	0.67	0.66	0.65	0.64	0.63	0.63	0.61	0.60	0.59	0.59
100	1.40	1.37	1.34	1.31	1.29	1.28	1.26	1.25	1.21	1.19	1.18	1.18
200	2.80	2.73	2.67	2.62	2.58	2.55	2.52	2.49	2.41	2.37	2.36	2.35
300	4.19	4.09	4.00	3.93	3.87	3.82	3.77	3.74	3.62	3.56	3.53	3.52
400	5.59	5.45	5.33	5.24	5.15	5.09	5.03	4.98	4.82	4.74	4.71	4.69
500	6.98	6.81	6.66	6.54	6.44	6.36	6.28	6.22	6.02	5.93	5.88	5.86
600	8.38	8.17	8.00	7.85	7.73	7.63	7.54	7.47	7.23	7.11	7.06	7.03
700	9.77	9.53	9.33	9.16	9.02	8.90	8.80	8.71	8.43	8.30	8.23	8.20
800	11.17	10.89	10.66	10.47	10.30	10.17	10.05	9.95	9.64	9.48	9.41	9.37
900	12.56	12.25	11.99	11.77	11.59	11.44	11.31	11.20	10.84	10.67	10.59	10.55
1000	13.96	13.61	13.32	13.08	12.88	12.71	12.56	12.44	12.04	11.85	11.76	11.72
2000	27.91	27.21	26.64	26.16	25.75	25.41	25.12	24.88	24.08	23.70	23.52	23.43
3000	41.86	40.82	39.96	39.24	38.63	38.12	37.68	37.31	36.12	35.55	35.28	35.14
4000	55.81	54.42	53.27	52.31	51.50	50.82	50.24	49.75	48.16	47.40	47.03	46.85
5000	69.76	68.03	66.59	65.39	64.38	63.52	62.80	62.18	60.19	59.25	58.79	58.56
6000	83.71	81.63	79.91	78.47	77.25	76.23	75.36	74.62	72.23	71.10	70.55	70.27
7000	97.66	95.24	93.23	91.54	90.13	88.93	87.92	87.05	84.27	82.95	82.30	81.98
8000	111.61	108.84	106.54	104.62	103.00	101.64	100.48	99.49	96.31	94.79	94.06	93.70
9000	125.56	122.45	119.86	117.70	115.88	114.34	113.03	111.92	108.34	106.64	105.82	105.41
10000	139.52	136.05	133.18	130.77	128.75	127.04	125.59	124.36	120.38	118.49	117.57	117.12
11000	153.47	149.66	146.50	143.85	141.63	139.75	138.15	136.79	132.42	130.34	129.33	128.83
12000	167.42	163.26	159.81	156.93	154.50	152.45	150.71	149.23	144.46	142.19	141.09	140.54
13000	181.37	176.87	173.13	170.01	167.38	165.15	163.27	161.66	156.49	154.04	152.84	152.25
14000	195.32	190.47	186.45	183.08	180.25	177.86	175.83	174.10	168.53	165.89	164.60	163.96
15000	209.27	204.08	199.77	196.16	193.13	190.56	188.39	186.53	180.57	177.74	176.36	175.68
16000	223.22	217.68	213.08	209.24	206.00	203.27	200.95	198.97	192.61	189.58	188.11	187.39
17000	237.17	231.29	226.40	222.31	218.88	215.97	213.50	211.40	204.64	201.43	199.87	199.10
18000	251.12	244.89	239.72	235.39	231.75	228.67	226.06	223.84	216.68	213.28	211.63	210.81
19000	265.07	258.50	253.04	248.47	244.63	241.38	238.62	236.27	228.72	225.13	223.38	222.52
20000	279.03	272.10	266.35	261.54	257.50	254.08	251.18	248.71	240.76	236.98	235.14	234.23
21000	292.98	285.71	279.67	274.62	270.38	266.79	263.74	261.14	252.79	248.83	246.90	245.94
22000	306.93	299.31	292.99	287.70	283.25	279.49	276.30	273.58	264.83	260.68	258.65	257.66
23000	320.88	312.92	306.31	300.78	296.12	292.19	288.86	286.01	276.87	272.53	270.41	269.37
24000	334.83	326.52	319.62	313.85	309.00	304.90	301.42	298.45	288.91	284.37	282.17	281.08
25000	348.78	340.13	332.94	326.93	321.87	317.60	313.97	310.89	300.95	296.22	293.92	292.79
26000	362.73	353.73	346.26	340.01	334.75	330.30	326.53	323.32	312.98	308.07	305.68	304.50
27000	376.68	367.34	359.58	353.08	347.62	343.01	339.09	335.76	325.02	319.92	317.44	316.21
28000	390.63	380.94	372.89	366.16	360.50	355.71	351.65	348.19	337.06	331.77	329.19	327.92
29000	404.58	394.55	386.21	379.24	373.37	368.42	364.21	360.63	349.10	343.62	340.95	339.64
30000	418.54	408.15	399.53	392.31	386.25	381.12	376.77	373.06	361.13	355.47	352.71	351.35
31000	432.49	421.76	412.84	405.39	399.12	393.82	389.33	385.50	373.17	367.32	364.46	363.06
32000	446.44	435.36	426.16	418.47	412.00	406.53	401.89	397.93	385.21	379.16	376.22	374.77
33000	460.39	448.97	439.48	431.55	424.87	419.23	414.44	410.37	397.25	391.01	387.98	386.48
34000	474.34	462.57	452.80	444.62	437.75	431.94	427.00	422.80	409.28	402.86	399.73	398.19
35000	488.29	476.18	466.11	457.70	450.62	444.64	439.56	435.24	421.32	414.71	411.49	409.90
37500	523.17	510.19	499.41	490.39	482.81	476.40	470.96	466.33	451.42	444.33	440.88	439.18
40000	558.05	544.20	532.70	523.08	515.00	508.16	502.36	497.41	481.51	473.95	470.27	468.46
42500	592.92	578.21	566.00	555.78	547.18	539.92	533.75	528.50	511.60	503.58	499.67	497.74
45000	627.80	612.23	599.29	588.47	579.37	571.68	565.15	559.59	541.70	533.20	529.06	527.02
47500	662.68	646.24	632.58	621.16	611.56	603.44	596.55	590.68	571.79	562.82	558.45	556.30
50000	697.56	680.25	665.88	653.85	643.74	635.20	627.94	621.77	601.89	592.44	587.84	585.58
52500	732.43	714.26	699.17	686.55	675.93	666.96	659.34	652.85	631.98	622.06	617.23	614.85
55000	767.31	748.27	732.46	719.24	708.12	698.72	690.74	683.94	662.07	651.68	646.63	644.13
57500	802.19	782.29	765.76	751.93	740.30	730.48	722.13	715.03	692.17	681.31	676.02	673.41
60000	837.07	816.30	799.05	784.62	772.49	762.23	753.53	746.12	722.26	710.93	705.41	702.69
65000	906.82	884.32	865.64	850.01	836.86	825.75	816.32	808.29	782.45	770.17	764.19	761.25
70000	976.58	952.35	932.22	915.39	901.24	889.27	879.12	870.47	842.64	829.42	822.98	819.80
75000	1046.33	1020.37	998.81	980.78	965.61	952.79	941.91	932.65	902.83	888.66	881.76	878.36
80000	1116.09	1088.40	1065.40	1046.16	1029.99	1016.31	1004.71	994.82	963.01	947.90	940.54	936.92
85000	1185.84	1156.42	1131.99	1111.55	1094.36	1079.83	1067.50	1057.00	1023.20	1007.15	999.33	995.47
90000	1255.60	1224.45	1198.57	1176.93	1158.73	1143.35	1130.29	1119.17	1083.39	1066.39	1058.11	1054.03
95000	1325.35	1292.47	1265.16	1242.32	1223.11	1206.87	1193.09	1181.35	1143.58	1125.63	1116.89	1112.59
100000	1395.11	1360.49	1331.75	1307.70	1287.48	1270.39	1255.88	1243.53	1203.77	1184.88	1175.68	1171.15
105000	1464.86	1428.52	1398.33	1373.09	1351.86	1333.91	1318.67	1305.70	1263.95	1244.12	1234.46	1229.70
110000	1534.62	1496.54	1464.92	1438.47	1416.23	1397.43	1381.47	1367.88	1324.14	1303.36	1293.25	1288.26
115000	1604.37	1564.57	1531.51	1503.86	1480.60	1460.95	1444.26	1430.05	1384.33	1362.61	1352.03	1346.82
120000	1674.13	1632.59	1598.09	1569.24	1544.98	1524.46	1507.06	1492.23	1444.52	1421.85	1410.81	1405.37
125000	1743.88	1700.62	1664.68	1634.63	1609.35	1587.98	1569.85	1554.41	1504.71	1481.09	1469.60	1463.93
130000	1813.64	1768.64	1731.27	1700.01	1673.72	1651.50	1632.64	1616.58	1564.89	1540.34	1528.38	1522.49
135000	1883.39	1836.67	1797.86	1765.40	1738.10	1715.02	1695.44	1678.76	1625.08	1599.58	1587.16	1581.04
140000	1953.15	1904.69	1864.44	1830.78	1802.47	1778.54	1758.23	1740.93	1685.27	1658.83	1645.95	1639.60
145000	2022.90	1972.71	1931.03	1896.17	1866.85	1842.06	1821.03	1803.11	1745.46	1718.07	1704.73	1698.16
150000	2092.66	2040.74	1997.62	1961.55	1931.22	1905.58	1883.82	1865.29	1805.65	1777.31	1763.51	1756.72
155000	2162.41	2108.76	2064.20	2026.94	1995.59	1969.10	1946.61	1927.46	1865.83	1836.56	1822.30	1815.27
160000	2232.17	2176.79	2130.79	2092.32	2059.97	2032.62	2009.41	1989.64	1926.02	1895.80	1881.08	1873.83

MONTHLY AMORTIZING PAYMENTS

AMOUNT OF LOAN	NUMBER OF YEARS IN TERM											
	1	2	3	4	5	6	7	8	9	10	11	12
$ 50	4.50	2.41	1.72	1.38	1.17	1.04	0.95	0.88	0.83	0.79	0.76	0.73
100	9.00	4.82	3.43	2.75	2.34	2.08	1.89	1.76	1.65	1.57	1.51	1.46
200	17.99	9.63	6.86	5.50	4.68	4.15	3.78	3.51	3.30	3.14	3.01	2.91
300	26.98	14.44	10.29	8.24	7.02	6.23	5.67	5.26	4.95	4.71	4.52	4.36
400	35.97	19.26	13.72	10.99	9.36	8.30	7.56	7.01	6.60	6.28	6.02	5.82
500	44.96	24.07	17.15	13.73	11.70	10.37	9.44	8.76	8.25	7.84	7.53	7.27
600	53.95	28.88	20.58	16.48	14.04	12.45	11.33	10.51	9.89	9.41	9.03	8.72
700	62.94	33.70	24.01	19.22	16.38	14.52	13.22	12.26	11.54	10.98	10.53	10.18
800	71.93	38.51	27.44	21.97	18.72	16.60	15.11	14.02	13.19	12.55	12.04	11.63
900	80.92	43.32	30.87	24.71	21.06	18.67	17.00	15.77	14.84	14.11	13.54	13.08
1000	89.91	48.14	34.30	27.46	23.40	20.74	18.88	17.52	16.49	15.68	15.05	14.53
2000	179.81	96.27	68.60	54.91	46.80	41.48	37.76	35.03	32.97	31.36	30.09	29.06
3000	269.72	144.40	102.90	82.36	70.20	62.22	56.64	52.55	49.45	47.04	45.13	43.59
4000	359.62	192.53	137.20	109.81	93.60	82.96	75.52	70.06	65.93	62.71	60.17	58.12
5000	449.53	240.66	171.50	137.27	117.00	103.70	94.40	87.58	82.41	78.39	75.21	72.65
6000	539.43	288.79	205.80	164.72	140.39	124.44	113.28	105.09	98.89	94.07	90.25	87.18
7000	629.34	336.92	240.10	192.17	163.79	145.18	132.15	122.60	115.37	109.75	105.29	101.71
8000	719.24	385.05	274.40	219.62	187.19	165.92	151.03	140.12	131.85	125.42	120.33	116.24
9000	809.15	433.18	308.70	247.07	210.59	186.66	169.91	157.63	148.33	141.10	135.38	130.77
10000	899.05	481.32	343.00	274.53	233.99	207.40	188.79	175.15	164.81	156.78	150.42	145.30
11000	988.96	529.45	377.30	301.98	257.38	228.14	207.67	192.66	181.29	172.46	165.46	159.83
12000	1078.86	577.58	411.60	329.43	280.78	248.88	226.55	210.17	197.77	188.13	180.50	174.36
13000	1168.77	625.71	445.89	356.88	304.18	269.62	245.42	227.69	214.25	203.81	195.54	188.89
14000	1258.67	673.84	480.19	384.33	327.58	290.36	264.30	245.20	230.73	219.49	210.58	203.42
15000	1348.58	721.97	514.49	411.79	350.98	311.10	283.18	262.72	247.21	235.16	225.62	217.95
16000	1438.48	770.10	548.79	439.24	374.37	331.84	302.06	280.23	263.69	250.84	240.66	232.48
17000	1528.39	818.23	583.09	466.69	397.77	352.58	320.94	297.74	280.17	266.52	255.71	247.01
18000	1618.29	866.36	617.39	494.14	421.17	373.32	339.82	315.26	296.65	282.20	270.75	261.54
19000	1708.20	914.50	651.69	521.59	444.57	394.06	358.69	332.77	313.13	297.87	285.79	276.07
20000	1798.10	962.63	685.99	549.05	467.97	414.80	377.57	350.29	329.61	313.55	300.83	290.59
21000	1888.01	1010.76	720.29	576.50	491.36	435.54	396.45	367.80	346.09	329.23	315.87	305.12
22000	1977.91	1058.89	754.59	603.95	514.76	456.28	415.33	385.31	362.57	344.91	330.91	319.65
23000	2067.82	1107.02	788.89	631.40	538.16	477.02	434.21	402.83	379.05	360.58	345.95	334.18
24000	2157.72	1155.15	823.19	658.85	561.56	497.76	453.09	420.34	395.53	376.26	360.99	348.71
25000	2247.62	1203.28	857.48	686.31	584.96	518.50	471.96	437.86	412.01	391.94	376.03	363.24
26000	2337.53	1251.41	891.78	713.76	608.35	539.24	490.84	455.37	428.49	407.62	391.08	377.77
27000	2427.43	1299.54	926.08	741.21	631.75	559.98	509.72	472.89	444.98	423.29	406.12	392.30
28000	2517.34	1347.67	960.38	768.66	655.15	580.72	528.60	490.40	461.46	438.97	421.16	406.83
29000	2607.24	1395.81	994.68	796.11	678.55	601.46	547.48	507.91	477.94	454.65	436.20	421.36
30000	2697.15	1443.94	1028.98	823.57	701.95	622.20	566.36	525.43	494.42	470.32	451.24	435.89
31000	2787.05	1492.07	1063.28	851.02	725.34	642.94	585.24	542.94	510.90	486.00	466.28	450.42
32000	2876.96	1540.20	1097.58	878.47	748.74	663.68	604.11	560.45	527.38	501.68	481.32	464.95
33000	2966.86	1588.33	1131.88	905.92	772.14	684.42	622.99	577.97	543.86	517.36	496.36	479.48
34000	3056.77	1636.46	1166.18	933.37	795.54	705.16	641.87	595.48	560.34	533.03	511.41	494.01
35000	3146.67	1684.59	1200.48	960.83	818.94	725.90	660.75	613.00	576.82	548.71	526.45	508.54
37500	3371.43	1804.92	1286.22	1029.46	877.43	777.75	707.94	656.78	618.02	587.90	564.05	544.86
40000	3596.20	1925.25	1371.97	1098.09	935.93	829.60	755.14	700.57	659.22	627.10	601.65	581.18
42500	3820.96	2045.58	1457.72	1166.72	994.42	881.45	802.34	744.35	700.42	666.29	639.26	617.54
45000	4045.72	2165.90	1543.47	1235.35	1052.92	933.30	849.53	788.14	741.62	705.48	676.86	653.83
47500	4270.48	2286.23	1629.22	1303.98	1111.41	985.15	896.73	831.92	782.82	744.68	714.46	690.16
50000	4495.24	2406.56	1714.96	1372.61	1169.91	1037.00	943.92	875.71	824.02	783.87	752.06	726.48
52500	4720.01	2526.89	1800.71	1441.24	1228.40	1088.85	991.12	919.49	865.23	823.06	789.67	762.80
55000	4944.77	2647.21	1886.46	1509.87	1286.90	1140.70	1038.32	963.28	906.43	862.26	827.27	799.13
57500	5169.53	2767.54	1972.21	1578.50	1345.39	1192.55	1085.51	1007.06	947.63	901.45	864.87	835.45
60000	5394.29	2887.87	2057.96	1647.13	1403.89	1244.40	1132.71	1050.85	988.83	940.64	902.48	871.77
65000	5843.82	3128.52	2229.45	1784.39	1520.88	1348.09	1227.10	1138.42	1071.23	1019.03	977.68	944.42
70000	6293.34	3369.18	2400.95	1921.65	1637.87	1451.79	1321.49	1225.99	1153.63	1097.42	1052.89	1017.07
75000	6742.86	3609.84	2572.44	2058.91	1754.86	1555.49	1415.88	1313.56	1236.03	1175.80	1128.09	1089.72
80000	7192.39	3850.49	2743.94	2196.17	1871.85	1659.19	1510.28	1401.13	1318.44	1254.19	1203.30	1162.36
85000	7641.91	4091.15	2915.44	2333.43	1988.84	1762.89	1604.67	1488.70	1400.84	1332.58	1278.51	1235.01
90000	8091.44	4331.80	3086.93	2470.69	2105.83	1866.59	1699.06	1576.27	1483.24	1410.96	1353.71	1307.66
95000	8540.96	4572.46	3258.43	2607.95	2222.82	1970.29	1793.45	1663.84	1565.64	1489.35	1428.92	1380.31
100000	8990.48	4813.11	3429.92	2745.22	2339.81	2073.99	1887.84	1751.41	1648.04	1567.74	1504.12	1452.95
105000	9440.01	5053.77	3601.42	2882.47	2456.80	2177.69	1982.24	1838.98	1730.45	1646.12	1579.33	1525.60
110000	9889.53	5294.42	3772.91	3019.73	2573.79	2281.39	2076.63	1926.55	1812.85	1724.51	1654.53	1598.25
115000	10339.06	5535.08	3944.41	3156.99	2690.78	2385.09	2171.02	2014.12	1895.25	1802.90	1729.74	1670.90
120000	10788.58	5775.73	4115.91	3294.25	2807.77	2488.79	2265.41	2101.69	1977.65	1881.28	1804.95	1743.54
125000	11238.10	6016.39	4287.40	3431.51	2924.76	2592.49	2359.80	2189.26	2060.05	1959.67	1880.15	1816.19
130000	11687.63	6257.04	4458.90	3568.77	3041.75	2696.18	2454.20	2276.84	2142.45	2038.06	1955.36	1888.84
135000	12137.15	6497.70	4630.39	3706.03	3158.74	2799.88	2548.59	2364.41	2224.86	2116.44	2030.56	1961.49
140000	12586.68	6738.35	4801.89	3843.29	3275.73	2903.58	2642.98	2451.98	2307.26	2194.83	2105.77	2034.13
145000	13036.20	6979.01	4973.39	3980.55	3392.72	3007.28	2737.37	2539.55	2389.66	2273.22	2180.98	2106.78
150000	13485.72	7219.67	5144.88	4117.81	3509.71	3110.98	2831.76	2627.12	2472.06	2351.60	2256.18	2179.43
155000	13935.25	7460.32	5316.38	4255.07	3626.70	3214.68	2926.16	2714.69	2554.46	2429.99	2331.39	2252.08
160000	14384.77	7700.98	5487.88	4392.33	3743.70	3318.38	3020.55	2802.26	2636.87	2508.37	2406.59	2324.72

AMOUNT OF LOAN	NUMBER OF YEARS IN TERM											
	13	14	15	16	17	18	19	20	25	30	35	40
$ 50	0.71	0.69	0.68	0.67	0.66	0.65	0.64	0.64	0.62	0.61	0.60	0.60
100	1.42	1.38	1.35	1.33	1.31	1.29	1.28	1.27	1.23	1.21	1.20	1.20
200	2.83	2.76	2.70	2.65	2.61	2.58	2.55	2.53	2.45	2.41	2.40	2.39
300	4.24	4.14	4.05	3.98	3.92	3.87	3.83	3.79	3.67	3.62	3.59	3.58
400	5.65	5.51	5.40	5.30	5.22	5.16	5.10	5.05	4.90	4.82	4.79	4.77
500	7.06	6.89	6.75	6.63	6.53	6.45	6.37	6.31	6.12	6.03	5.98	5.96
600	8.47	8.27	8.10	7.95	7.83	7.73	7.65	7.58	7.34	7.23	7.18	7.15
700	9.88	9.64	9.45	9.28	9.14	9.02	8.92	8.84	8.57	8.44	8.38	8.35
800	11.30	11.02	10.79	10.60	10.44	10.31	10.20	10.10	9.79	9.64	9.57	9.54
900	12.71	12.40	12.14	11.93	11.75	11.60	11.47	11.36	11.01	10.85	10.77	10.73
1000	14.12	13.78	13.49	13.25	13.05	12.89	12.74	12.62	12.23	12.05	11.96	11.92
2000	28.23	27.55	26.98	26.50	26.10	25.77	25.48	25.24	24.46	24.10	23.92	23.84
3000	42.34	41.32	40.46	39.75	39.15	38.65	38.22	37.86	36.69	36.15	35.88	35.75
4000	56.46	55.09	53.95	53.00	52.20	51.53	50.96	50.47	48.92	48.19	47.84	47.67
5000	70.57	68.86	67.43	66.25	65.25	64.41	63.70	63.09	61.15	60.24	59.80	59.59
6000	84.68	82.63	80.92	79.50	78.30	77.29	76.44	75.71	73.38	72.29	71.76	71.50
7000	98.79	96.40	94.41	92.74	91.35	90.17	89.17	88.33	85.61	84.33	83.72	83.42
8000	112.91	110.17	107.89	105.99	104.40	103.05	101.91	100.94	97.84	96.38	95.68	95.33
9000	127.02	123.94	121.38	119.24	117.45	115.93	114.65	113.56	110.07	108.43	107.64	107.25
10000	141.13	137.71	134.86	132.49	130.50	128.81	127.39	126.18	122.30	120.47	119.60	119.17
11000	155.25	151.48	148.35	145.74	143.54	141.69	140.13	138.79	134.53	132.52	131.55	131.08
12000	169.36	165.25	161.83	158.99	156.59	154.58	152.87	151.41	146.76	144.57	143.51	143.00
13000	183.47	179.02	175.32	172.23	169.64	167.46	165.60	164.03	158.99	156.61	155.47	154.92
14000	197.58	192.79	188.81	185.48	182.69	180.34	178.34	176.65	171.21	168.66	167.43	166.83
15000	211.70	206.56	202.29	198.73	195.74	193.22	191.08	189.26	183.44	180.71	179.39	178.75
16000	225.81	220.33	215.78	211.98	208.79	206.10	203.82	201.88	195.67	192.75	191.35	190.66
17000	239.92	234.10	229.26	225.23	221.84	218.98	216.56	214.50	207.90	204.80	203.31	202.58
18000	254.04	247.87	242.75	238.48	234.89	231.86	229.30	227.11	220.13	216.85	215.27	214.50
19000	268.15	261.64	256.24	251.73	247.94	244.74	242.03	239.73	232.36	228.90	227.23	226.41
20000	282.26	275.41	269.72	264.97	260.99	257.62	254.77	252.35	244.59	240.94	239.19	238.33
21000	296.37	289.18	283.21	278.22	274.04	270.50	267.51	264.97	256.82	252.99	251.14	250.25
22000	310.49	302.95	296.69	291.47	287.08	283.38	280.25	277.58	269.05	265.04	263.10	262.16
23000	324.60	316.72	310.18	304.72	300.13	296.27	292.99	290.20	281.28	277.08	275.06	274.08
24000	338.71	330.49	323.66	317.97	313.18	309.15	305.73	302.82	293.51	289.13	287.02	285.99
25000	352.83	344.26	337.15	331.22	326.23	322.03	318.46	315.43	305.74	301.18	298.98	297.91
26000	366.94	358.03	350.64	344.46	339.28	334.91	331.20	328.05	317.97	313.22	310.94	309.83
27000	381.05	371.80	364.12	357.71	352.33	347.79	343.94	340.67	330.20	325.27	322.90	321.74
28000	395.16	385.57	377.61	370.96	365.38	360.67	356.68	353.29	342.42	337.32	334.86	333.66
29000	409.28	399.34	391.09	384.21	378.43	373.55	369.42	365.90	354.65	349.36	346.82	345.58
30000	423.39	413.11	404.58	397.46	391.48	386.43	382.16	378.52	366.88	361.41	358.78	357.49
31000	437.50	426.88	418.06	410.71	404.53	399.31	394.89	391.14	379.11	373.46	370.73	369.41
32000	451.61	440.65	431.55	423.95	417.58	412.19	407.63	403.76	391.34	385.50	382.69	381.32
33000	465.73	454.42	445.04	437.20	430.62	425.07	420.37	416.37	403.57	397.55	394.65	393.24
34000	479.84	468.19	458.52	450.45	443.67	437.95	433.11	428.99	415.80	409.60	406.61	405.16
35000	493.95	481.96	472.01	463.70	456.72	450.84	445.85	441.61	428.03	421.65	418.57	417.07
37500	529.24	516.38	505.72	496.82	489.35	483.04	477.69	473.15	458.60	451.76	448.47	446.86
40000	564.52	550.81	539.44	529.94	521.97	515.24	509.54	504.69	489.18	481.88	478.37	476.65
42500	599.80	585.23	573.15	563.06	554.59	547.44	541.38	536.24	519.75	512.00	508.26	506.44
45000	635.08	619.66	606.87	596.18	587.21	579.64	573.23	567.78	550.32	542.11	538.16	536.24
47500	670.36	654.08	640.58	629.31	619.84	611.85	605.08	599.32	580.90	572.23	568.06	566.03
50000	705.65	688.51	674.29	662.43	652.46	644.05	636.92	630.86	611.47	602.35	597.96	595.82
52500	740.93	722.93	708.01	695.55	685.08	676.25	668.77	662.41	642.04	632.47	627.85	625.61
55000	776.21	757.36	741.72	728.67	717.70	708.45	700.61	693.95	672.62	662.58	657.75	655.40
57500	811.49	791.78	775.44	761.79	750.33	740.66	732.46	725.49	703.19	692.70	687.65	685.19
60000	846.77	826.21	809.15	794.91	782.95	772.86	764.31	757.04	733.76	722.82	717.55	714.98
65000	917.34	895.06	876.58	861.15	848.20	837.26	828.00	820.12	794.91	783.05	777.34	774.56
70000	987.90	963.91	944.01	927.40	913.44	901.67	891.69	883.21	856.05	843.29	837.14	834.14
75000	1058.47	1032.76	1011.44	993.64	978.69	966.07	955.38	946.29	917.20	903.52	896.93	893.72
80000	1129.03	1101.61	1078.87	1059.88	1043.93	1030.47	1019.07	1009.38	978.35	963.75	956.73	953.30
85000	1199.59	1170.46	1146.30	1126.12	1109.18	1094.88	1082.76	1072.47	1039.49	1023.99	1016.52	1012.88
90000	1270.16	1239.31	1213.73	1192.36	1174.42	1159.28	1146.46	1135.55	1100.64	1084.22	1076.32	1072.47
95000	1340.72	1308.16	1281.16	1258.61	1239.67	1223.69	1210.15	1198.64	1161.79	1144.46	1136.11	1132.05
100000	1411.29	1377.01	1348.58	1324.85	1304.91	1288.09	1273.84	1261.72	1222.93	1204.69	1195.91	1191.63
105000	1481.85	1445.86	1416.01	1391.09	1370.16	1352.50	1337.53	1324.81	1284.08	1264.93	1255.70	1251.21
110000	1552.41	1514.71	1483.44	1457.33	1435.40	1416.90	1401.22	1387.90	1345.23	1325.16	1315.50	1310.79
115000	1622.98	1583.56	1550.87	1523.57	1500.65	1481.31	1464.92	1450.98	1406.37	1385.40	1375.29	1370.37
120000	1693.54	1652.41	1618.30	1589.82	1565.90	1545.71	1528.61	1514.07	1467.52	1445.63	1435.09	1429.95
125000	1764.11	1721.26	1685.73	1656.06	1631.14	1610.11	1592.30	1577.15	1528.66	1505.86	1494.88	1489.53
130000	1834.67	1790.11	1753.16	1722.30	1696.39	1674.52	1655.99	1640.24	1589.81	1566.10	1554.68	1549.12
135000	1905.23	1858.96	1820.59	1788.54	1761.63	1738.92	1719.68	1703.33	1650.96	1626.33	1614.47	1608.70
140000	1975.80	1927.81	1888.02	1854.79	1826.88	1803.33	1783.37	1766.41	1712.10	1686.57	1674.27	1668.28
145000	2046.36	1996.66	1955.45	1921.03	1892.12	1867.73	1847.07	1829.50	1773.25	1746.80	1734.06	1727.86
150000	2116.93	2065.51	2022.87	1987.27	1957.37	1932.14	1910.76	1892.58	1834.40	1807.04	1793.86	1787.44
155000	2187.49	2134.36	2090.30	2053.51	2022.61	1996.54	1974.45	1955.67	1895.54	1867.27	1853.65	1847.02
160000	2258.05	2203.21	2157.73	2119.75	2087.86	2060.94	2038.14	2018.76	1956.69	1927.50	1913.45	1906.60

MONTHLY AMORTIZING PAYMENTS

AMOUNT OF LOAN	NUMBER OF YEARS IN TERM											
	1	2	3	4	5	6	7	8	9	10	11	12
$ 50	4.51	2.42	1.73	1.38	1.18	1.05	0.96	0.89	0.84	0.80	0.76	0.74
100	9.01	4.83	3.45	2.76	2.36	2.09	1.91	1.77	1.67	1.59	1.52	1.47
200	18.01	9.65	6.89	5.52	4.71	4.18	3.81	3.54	3.33	3.17	3.04	2.94
300	27.01	14.48	10.33	8.28	7.06	6.27	5.71	5.30	4.99	4.75	4.56	4.41
400	36.01	19.30	13.77	11.04	9.42	8.35	7.61	7.07	6.66	6.34	6.08	5.88
500	45.02	24.13	17.22	13.79	11.77	10.44	9.51	8.83	8.32	7.92	7.60	7.35
600	54.02	28.95	20.66	16.55	14.12	12.53	11.42	10.60	9.98	9.50	9.12	8.82
700	63.02	33.78	24.10	19.31	16.47	14.62	13.32	12.37	11.64	11.09	10.64	10.29
800	72.02	38.60	27.54	22.07	18.83	16.70	15.22	14.13	13.31	12.67	12.16	11.76
900	81.03	43.43	30.98	24.83	21.18	18.79	17.12	15.90	14.97	14.25	13.68	13.22
1000	90.03	48.25	34.43	27.58	23.53	20.88	19.02	17.66	16.63	15.83	15.20	14.69
2000	180.05	96.50	68.85	55.16	47.06	41.75	38.04	35.32	33.26	31.66	30.40	29.38
3000	270.07	144.75	103.27	82.74	70.59	62.63	57.06	52.98	49.89	47.49	45.59	44.07
4000	360.10	193.00	137.69	110.32	94.12	83.50	76.07	70.63	66.52	63.32	60.79	58.76
5000	450.12	241.25	172.11	137.89	117.65	104.38	95.09	88.29	83.14	79.15	75.99	73.45
6000	540.14	289.50	206.53	165.47	141.17	125.25	114.11	105.95	99.77	94.98	91.18	88.14
7000	630.16	337.75	240.95	193.05	164.70	146.13	133.13	123.61	116.40	110.81	106.38	102.82
8000	720.19	386.00	275.37	220.63	188.23	167.00	152.14	141.26	133.03	126.63	121.58	117.51
9000	810.21	434.25	309.79	248.21	211.76	187.87	171.16	158.92	149.65	142.46	136.77	132.20
10000	900.23	482.50	344.21	275.78	235.29	208.75	190.18	176.58	166.28	158.29	151.97	146.89
11000	990.25	530.75	378.64	303.36	258.82	229.62	209.20	194.23	182.91	174.12	167.17	161.58
12000	1080.28	579.00	413.06	330.94	282.34	250.50	228.21	211.89	199.54	189.95	182.36	176.27
13000	1170.30	627.25	447.48	358.52	305.87	271.37	247.23	229.55	216.17	205.78	197.56	190.96
14000	1260.32	675.50	481.90	386.10	329.40	292.25	266.25	247.21	232.79	221.61	212.76	205.64
15000	1350.34	723.75	516.32	413.67	352.93	313.12	285.26	264.86	249.42	237.44	227.95	220.33
16000	1440.37	772.00	550.74	441.25	376.46	334.00	304.28	282.52	266.05	253.26	243.15	235.02
17000	1530.39	820.25	585.16	468.83	399.99	354.87	323.30	300.18	282.68	269.09	258.34	249.71
18000	1620.41	868.49	619.58	496.41	423.51	375.74	342.32	317.84	299.30	284.92	273.54	264.40
19000	1710.43	916.74	654.00	523.99	447.04	396.62	361.33	335.49	315.93	300.75	288.74	279.09
20000	1800.46	964.99	688.42	551.56	470.57	417.49	380.35	353.15	332.56	316.58	303.93	293.77
21000	1890.48	1013.24	722.85	579.14	494.10	438.37	399.37	370.81	349.19	332.41	319.13	308.46
22000	1980.50	1061.49	757.27	606.72	517.63	459.24	418.39	388.46	365.81	348.24	334.33	323.15
23000	2070.52	1109.74	791.69	634.30	541.16	480.12	437.40	406.12	382.44	364.06	349.52	337.84
24000	2160.55	1157.99	826.11	661.88	564.68	500.99	456.42	423.78	399.07	379.89	364.72	352.53
25000	2250.57	1206.24	860.53	689.45	588.21	521.87	475.44	441.44	415.70	395.72	379.92	367.22
26000	2340.59	1254.49	894.95	717.03	611.74	542.74	494.45	459.09	432.33	411.55	395.11	381.91
27000	2430.61	1302.74	929.37	744.61	635.27	563.61	513.47	476.75	448.95	427.38	410.31	396.59
28000	2520.64	1350.99	963.79	772.19	658.80	584.49	532.49	494.41	465.58	443.21	425.51	411.28
29000	2610.66	1399.24	998.21	799.77	682.33	605.36	551.51	512.07	482.21	459.04	440.70	425.97
30000	2700.68	1447.49	1032.63	827.34	705.85	626.24	570.52	529.72	498.84	474.87	455.90	440.66
31000	2790.70	1495.74	1067.06	854.92	729.38	647.11	589.54	547.38	515.46	490.69	471.09	455.35
32000	2880.73	1543.99	1101.48	882.50	752.91	667.99	608.56	565.04	532.09	506.52	486.29	470.04
33000	2970.75	1592.24	1135.90	910.08	776.44	688.86	627.58	582.69	548.72	522.35	501.49	484.73
34000	3060.77	1640.49	1170.32	937.66	799.97	709.74	646.59	600.35	565.35	538.18	516.68	499.41
35000	3150.79	1688.73	1204.74	965.23	823.49	730.61	665.61	618.01	581.98	554.01	531.88	514.10
37500	3375.85	1809.36	1290.79	1034.18	882.32	782.80	713.15	662.15	623.54	593.59	569.87	550.82
40000	3600.91	1929.98	1376.84	1103.12	941.14	834.98	760.70	706.30	665.11	633.15	607.86	587.54
42500	3825.96	2050.61	1462.90	1172.07	999.96	887.17	808.24	750.44	706.68	672.72	645.85	624.27
45000	4051.02	2171.23	1548.95	1241.01	1058.78	939.35	855.78	794.58	748.25	712.30	683.84	660.99
47500	4276.08	2291.85	1635.00	1309.96	1117.60	991.54	903.33	838.72	789.82	751.87	721.84	697.71
50000	4501.13	2412.48	1721.05	1378.90	1176.42	1043.73	950.87	882.87	831.39	791.44	759.83	734.43
52500	4726.19	2533.10	1807.11	1447.85	1235.24	1095.91	998.41	927.01	872.96	831.01	797.82	771.15
55000	4951.25	2653.72	1893.16	1516.79	1294.06	1148.10	1045.96	971.15	914.53	870.58	835.81	807.87
57500	5176.30	2774.35	1979.21	1585.74	1352.88	1200.28	1093.50	1015.30	956.10	910.15	873.80	844.59
60000	5401.36	2894.97	2065.26	1654.68	1411.70	1252.47	1141.04	1059.44	997.67	949.73	911.79	881.31
65000	5851.47	3136.22	2237.37	1792.57	1529.34	1356.84	1236.13	1147.73	1080.81	1028.87	987.77	954.76
70000	6301.58	3377.46	2409.47	1930.46	1646.98	1461.21	1331.22	1236.01	1163.95	1108.01	1063.76	1028.20
75000	6751.70	3618.71	2581.58	2068.35	1764.63	1565.59	1426.30	1324.30	1247.08	1187.16	1139.74	1101.64
80000	7201.81	3859.96	2753.68	2206.24	1882.27	1669.96	1521.39	1412.59	1330.22	1266.30	1215.72	1175.08
85000	7651.92	4101.21	2925.79	2344.13	1999.91	1774.33	1616.48	1500.87	1413.36	1345.44	1291.70	1248.53
90000	8102.03	4342.45	3097.89	2482.02	2117.55	1878.70	1711.56	1589.16	1496.50	1424.59	1367.68	1321.97
95000	8552.15	4583.70	3270.00	2619.91	2235.19	1983.08	1806.65	1677.44	1579.64	1503.73	1443.67	1395.41
100000	9002.26	4824.95	3442.10	2757.80	2352.83	2087.45	1901.74	1765.73	1662.78	1582.87	1519.65	1468.85
105000	9452.37	5066.19	3614.21	2895.69	2470.47	2191.82	1996.82	1854.02	1745.92	1662.02	1595.63	1542.30
110000	9902.49	5307.44	3786.31	3033.58	2588.12	2296.19	2091.91	1942.30	1829.05	1741.16	1671.61	1615.74
115000	10352.60	5548.69	3958.42	3171.47	2705.76	2400.56	2186.99	2030.59	1912.19	1820.30	1747.60	1689.18
120000	10802.71	5789.94	4130.52	3309.36	2823.40	2504.94	2282.08	2118.88	1995.33	1899.45	1823.58	1762.62
125000	11252.82	6031.18	4302.63	3447.25	2941.04	2609.31	2377.17	2207.16	2078.47	1978.59	1899.56	1836.07
130000	11702.94	6272.43	4474.73	3585.14	3058.68	2713.68	2472.25	2295.45	2161.61	2057.73	1975.54	1909.51
135000	12153.05	6513.68	4646.84	3723.03	3176.32	2818.05	2567.34	2383.73	2244.75	2136.88	2051.52	1982.95
140000	12603.16	6754.92	4818.94	3860.92	3293.96	2922.42	2662.43	2472.02	2327.89	2216.02	2127.51	2056.39
145000	13053.27	6996.17	4991.05	3998.81	3411.61	3026.80	2757.51	2560.31	2411.02	2295.16	2203.49	2129.84
150000	13503.39	7237.42	5163.15	4136.70	3529.25	3131.17	2852.60	2648.59	2494.16	2374.31	2279.47	2203.28
155000	13953.50	7478.67	5335.26	4274.59	3646.89	3235.54	2947.69	2736.88	2577.30	2453.45	2355.45	2276.72
160000	14403.61	7719.91	5507.36	4412.48	3764.53	3339.91	3042.77	2825.17	2660.44	2532.59	2431.44	2350.16

MONTHLY AMORTIZING PAYMENTS 14.50%

AMOUNT OF LOAN	13	14	15	16	17	18	19	20	25	30	35	40
$ 50	0.72	0.70	0.69	0.68	0.67	0.66	0.65	0.64	0.63	0.62	0.61	0.61
100	1.43	1.40	1.37	1.35	1.33	1.31	1.30	1.28	1.25	1.23	1.22	1.22
200	2.86	2.79	2.74	2.69	2.65	2.62	2.59	2.56	2.49	2.45	2.44	2.43
300	4.29	4.19	4.10	4.03	3.97	3.92	3.88	3.84	3.73	3.68	3.65	3.64
400	5.72	5.58	5.47	5.37	5.29	5.23	5.17	5.12	4.97	4.90	4.87	4.85
500	7.14	6.97	6.83	6.72	6.62	6.53	6.46	6.40	6.22	6.13	6.09	6.07
600	8.57	8.37	8.20	8.06	7.94	7.84	7.76	7.68	7.46	7.35	7.30	7.28
700	10.00	9.76	9.56	9.40	9.26	9.15	9.05	8.96	8.70	8.58	8.52	8.49
800	11.43	11.15	10.93	10.74	10.58	10.45	10.34	10.24	9.94	9.80	9.73	9.70
900	12.85	12.55	12.29	12.08	11.91	11.76	11.63	11.52	11.18	11.03	10.95	10.91
1000	14.28	13.94	13.66	13.43	13.23	13.06	12.92	12.80	12.43	12.25	12.17	12.13
2000	28.56	27.88	27.32	26.85	26.45	26.12	25.84	25.60	24.85	24.50	24.33	24.25
3000	42.83	41.81	40.97	40.27	39.68	39.18	38.76	38.40	37.27	36.74	36.49	36.37
4000	57.11	55.75	54.63	53.69	52.90	52.24	51.68	51.20	49.69	48.99	48.65	48.49
5000	71.38	69.69	68.28	67.11	66.13	65.30	64.60	64.00	62.11	61.23	60.81	60.61
6000	85.66	83.62	81.94	80.53	79.35	78.36	77.52	76.80	74.53	73.48	72.98	72.73
7000	99.93	97.56	95.59	93.95	92.57	91.42	90.44	89.60	86.96	85.72	85.14	84.85
8000	114.21	111.49	109.25	107.37	105.80	104.47	103.36	102.40	99.38	97.97	97.30	96.98
9000	128.48	125.43	122.90	120.79	119.02	117.53	116.27	115.20	111.80	110.22	109.46	109.10
10000	142.76	139.37	136.56	134.21	132.25	130.59	129.19	128.00	124.22	122.46	121.62	121.22
11000	157.03	153.30	150.21	147.63	145.47	143.65	142.11	140.80	136.64	134.71	133.78	133.34
12000	171.31	167.24	163.87	161.05	158.70	156.71	155.03	153.60	149.06	146.95	145.95	145.46
13000	185.58	181.17	177.52	174.47	171.92	169.77	167.95	166.40	161.49	159.20	158.11	157.58
14000	199.86	195.11	191.18	187.89	185.14	182.83	180.87	179.20	173.91	171.44	170.27	169.70
15000	214.14	209.05	204.83	201.32	198.37	195.89	193.79	192.00	186.33	183.69	182.43	181.82
16000	228.41	222.98	218.49	214.74	211.59	208.94	206.71	204.80	198.75	195.93	194.59	193.95
17000	242.69	236.92	232.14	228.16	224.82	222.00	219.62	217.60	211.17	208.18	206.75	206.07
18000	256.96	250.85	245.80	241.58	238.04	235.06	232.54	230.40	223.59	220.43	218.92	218.19
19000	271.24	264.79	259.45	255.00	251.27	248.12	245.46	243.20	236.02	232.67	231.08	230.31
20000	285.51	278.73	273.11	268.42	264.49	261.18	258.38	256.00	248.44	244.92	243.24	242.43
21000	299.79	292.66	286.76	281.84	277.71	274.24	271.30	268.80	260.86	257.16	255.40	254.55
22000	314.06	306.60	300.42	295.26	290.94	287.30	284.22	281.60	273.28	269.41	267.56	266.67
23000	328.34	320.53	314.07	308.68	304.16	300.36	297.14	294.40	285.70	281.65	279.72	278.80
24000	342.61	334.47	327.73	322.10	317.39	313.41	310.06	307.20	298.12	293.90	291.89	290.92
25000	356.89	348.41	341.38	335.52	330.61	326.47	322.97	320.00	310.55	306.14	304.05	303.04
26000	371.16	362.34	355.04	348.94	343.84	339.53	335.89	332.80	322.97	318.39	316.21	315.16
27000	385.44	376.28	368.69	362.36	357.06	352.59	348.81	345.60	335.39	330.64	328.37	327.28
28000	399.72	390.21	382.35	375.78	370.28	365.65	361.73	358.40	347.81	342.88	340.53	339.40
29000	413.99	404.15	396.00	389.21	383.51	378.71	374.65	371.20	360.23	355.13	352.69	351.52
30000	428.27	418.09	409.66	402.63	396.73	391.77	387.57	384.00	372.65	367.37	364.86	363.64
31000	442.54	432.02	423.31	416.05	409.96	404.83	400.49	396.80	385.08	379.62	377.02	375.77
32000	456.82	445.96	436.97	429.47	423.18	417.88	413.41	409.60	397.50	391.86	389.18	387.89
33000	471.09	459.89	450.62	442.89	436.41	430.94	426.32	422.40	409.92	404.11	401.34	400.01
34000	485.37	473.83	464.28	456.31	449.63	444.00	439.24	435.20	422.34	416.35	413.50	412.13
35000	499.64	487.77	477.93	469.73	462.85	457.06	452.16	448.00	434.76	428.60	425.66	424.25
37500	535.33	522.61	512.07	503.28	495.91	489.71	484.46	480.00	465.82	459.21	456.07	454.55
40000	571.02	557.45	546.21	536.83	528.97	522.35	516.76	512.00	496.87	489.83	486.47	484.86
42500	606.71	592.29	580.34	570.38	562.04	555.00	549.05	544.00	527.92	520.44	516.88	515.16
45000	642.40	627.13	614.48	603.94	595.10	587.65	581.35	576.00	558.98	551.06	547.28	545.46
47500	678.09	661.97	648.62	637.49	628.16	620.30	613.65	608.00	590.03	581.67	577.69	575.77
50000	713.77	696.81	682.76	671.04	661.22	652.94	645.94	640.00	621.09	612.28	608.09	606.07
52500	749.46	731.65	716.89	704.59	694.28	685.59	678.24	672.00	652.14	642.90	638.49	636.37
55000	785.15	766.49	751.03	738.14	727.34	718.24	710.54	704.00	683.19	673.51	668.90	666.68
57500	820.84	801.33	785.17	771.70	760.40	750.88	742.83	736.00	714.25	704.12	699.30	696.98
60000	856.53	836.17	819.31	805.25	793.46	783.53	775.13	768.00	745.30	734.74	729.71	727.28
65000	927.90	905.85	887.58	872.35	859.58	848.82	839.72	832.00	807.41	795.97	790.52	787.89
70000	999.28	975.53	955.86	939.45	925.70	914.12	904.32	896.00	869.52	857.19	851.32	848.50
75000	1070.66	1045.21	1024.13	1006.56	991.82	979.41	968.91	960.00	931.63	918.42	912.13	909.10
80000	1142.04	1114.89	1092.41	1073.66	1044.70	1033.51	1024.00	1024.00	993.74	979.65	972.94	969.71
85000	1213.41	1184.57	1160.68	1140.76	1124.07	1110.00	1098.10	1088.00	1055.84	1040.88	1033.75	1030.32
90000	1284.79	1254.25	1228.96	1207.87	1190.19	1175.29	1162.69	1152.00	1117.95	1102.11	1094.56	1090.92
95000	1356.17	1323.93	1297.23	1274.97	1256.31	1240.59	1227.29	1216.00	1180.06	1163.33	1155.37	1151.53
100000	1427.54	1393.61	1365.51	1342.08	1322.43	1305.88	1291.88	1280.00	1242.17	1224.56	1216.18	1212.14
105000	1498.92	1463.29	1433.78	1409.18	1388.55	1371.17	1356.48	1344.00	1304.28	1285.79	1276.98	1272.74
110000	1570.30	1532.97	1502.06	1476.28	1454.67	1436.47	1421.07	1408.00	1366.38	1347.02	1337.79	1333.35
115000	1641.67	1602.65	1570.33	1543.39	1520.79	1501.76	1485.66	1472.00	1428.49	1408.24	1398.60	1393.96
120000	1713.05	1672.33	1638.61	1610.49	1586.91	1567.05	1550.26	1536.00	1490.60	1469.47	1459.41	1454.56
125000	1784.43	1742.01	1706.88	1677.59	1653.04	1632.35	1614.85	1600.00	1552.71	1530.70	1520.22	1515.17
130000	1855.80	1811.69	1775.16	1744.70	1719.16	1697.64	1679.44	1664.00	1614.82	1591.93	1581.03	1575.78
135000	1927.18	1881.37	1843.43	1811.80	1785.28	1762.94	1744.04	1728.00	1676.92	1653.16	1641.84	1636.38
140000	1998.56	1951.05	1911.71	1878.90	1851.40	1828.23	1808.63	1792.00	1739.03	1714.38	1702.64	1696.99
145000	2069.93	2020.73	1979.98	1946.01	1917.52	1893.52	1873.23	1856.00	1801.14	1775.61	1763.45	1757.60
150000	2141.31	2090.41	2048.26	2013.11	1983.64	1958.82	1937.82	1920.00	1863.25	1836.84	1824.26	1818.20
155000	2212.69	2160.09	2116.53	2080.21	2049.76	2024.11	2002.41	1984.00	1925.36	1898.07	1885.07	1878.81
160000	2284.07	2229.77	2184.81	2147.32	2115.88	2089.40	2067.01	2048.00	1987.47	1959.29	1945.88	1939.42

79

MONTHLY AMORTIZING PAYMENTS

AMOUNT OF LOAN	NUMBER OF YEARS IN TERM											
	1	2	3	4	5	6	7	8	9	10	11	12
$ 50	4.51	2.42	1.73	1.39	1.19	1.06	0.96	0.90	0.84	0.80	0.77	0.75
100	9.02	4.84	3.46	2.78	2.37	2.11	1.92	1.79	1.68	1.60	1.54	1.49
200	18.03	9.68	6.91	5.55	4.74	4.21	3.84	3.57	3.36	3.20	3.08	2.97
300	27.05	14.52	10.37	8.32	7.10	6.31	5.75	5.35	5.04	4.80	4.61	4.46
400	36.06	19.35	13.82	11.09	9.47	8.41	7.67	7.13	6.72	6.40	6.15	5.94
500	45.08	24.19	17.28	13.86	11.83	10.51	9.58	8.91	8.39	8.00	7.68	7.43
600	54.09	29.03	20.73	16.63	14.20	12.61	11.50	10.69	10.07	9.59	9.22	8.91
700	63.10	33.86	24.19	19.40	16.57	14.71	13.41	12.47	11.75	11.19	10.75	10.40
800	72.12	38.70	27.64	22.17	18.93	16.81	15.33	14.25	13.43	12.79	12.29	11.88
900	81.13	43.54	31.09	24.94	21.30	18.91	17.25	16.03	15.10	14.39	13.82	13.37
1000	90.15	48.37	34.55	27.71	23.66	21.01	19.16	17.81	16.78	15.99	15.36	14.85
2000	180.29	96.74	69.09	55.41	47.32	42.02	38.32	35.61	33.56	31.97	30.71	29.70
3000	270.43	145.11	103.63	83.12	70.98	63.03	57.48	53.41	50.33	47.95	46.06	44.55
4000	360.57	193.48	138.18	110.82	94.64	84.04	76.63	71.21	67.11	63.93	61.41	59.40
5000	450.71	241.84	172.72	138.53	118.30	105.05	95.79	89.01	83.88	79.91	76.77	74.25
6000	540.85	290.21	207.26	166.23	141.96	126.06	114.95	106.81	100.66	95.89	92.12	89.09
7000	630.99	338.58	241.81	193.93	165.62	147.07	134.10	124.61	117.43	111.87	107.47	103.94
8000	721.13	386.95	276.35	221.64	189.28	168.08	153.26	142.41	134.21	127.85	122.82	118.79
9000	811.27	435.32	310.89	249.34	212.94	189.09	172.42	160.21	150.99	143.83	138.18	133.64
10000	901.41	483.68	345.44	277.05	236.59	210.10	191.57	178.02	167.76	159.81	153.53	148.49
11000	991.55	532.05	379.98	304.75	260.25	231.11	210.73	195.82	184.54	175.79	168.88	163.34
12000	1081.69	580.42	414.52	332.46	283.91	252.12	229.89	213.62	201.31	191.77	184.23	178.18
13000	1171.83	628.79	449.06	360.16	307.57	273.13	249.04	231.42	218.09	207.75	199.59	193.03
14000	1261.97	677.16	483.61	387.86	331.23	294.14	268.20	249.22	234.86	223.74	214.94	207.88
15000	1352.11	725.52	518.15	415.57	354.89	315.15	287.36	267.02	251.64	239.72	230.29	222.73
16000	1442.25	773.89	552.69	443.27	378.55	336.16	306.51	284.82	268.42	255.70	245.64	237.58
17000	1532.39	822.26	587.24	470.98	402.21	357.17	325.67	302.62	285.19	271.68	261.00	252.43
18000	1622.53	870.63	621.78	498.68	425.87	378.18	344.83	320.42	301.97	287.66	276.35	267.27
19000	1712.67	919.00	656.32	526.38	449.52	399.19	363.98	338.22	318.74	303.64	291.70	282.12
20000	1802.81	967.36	690.87	554.09	473.18	420.19	383.14	356.03	335.52	319.62	307.05	296.97
21000	1892.95	1015.73	725.41	581.79	496.84	441.20	402.30	373.83	352.29	335.60	322.41	311.82
22000	1983.09	1064.10	759.95	609.50	520.50	462.21	421.45	391.63	369.07	351.58	337.76	326.67
23000	2073.23	1112.47	794.49	637.20	544.16	483.22	440.61	409.43	385.85	367.56	353.11	341.51
24000	2163.37	1160.84	829.04	664.91	567.82	504.23	459.77	427.23	402.62	383.54	368.46	356.36
25000	2253.51	1209.20	863.58	692.61	591.48	525.24	478.92	445.03	419.40	399.52	383.82	371.21
26000	2343.66	1257.57	898.12	720.31	615.14	546.25	498.08	462.83	436.17	415.50	399.17	386.06
27000	2433.80	1305.94	932.67	748.02	638.80	567.26	517.24	480.63	452.95	431.49	414.52	400.91
28000	2523.94	1354.31	967.21	775.72	662.45	588.27	536.39	498.43	469.72	447.47	429.87	415.76
29000	2614.08	1402.68	1001.75	803.43	686.11	609.28	555.55	516.23	486.50	463.45	445.23	430.60
30000	2704.22	1451.04	1036.30	831.13	709.77	630.29	574.71	534.04	503.28	479.43	460.58	445.45
31000	2794.36	1499.41	1070.84	858.83	733.43	651.30	593.86	551.84	520.05	495.41	475.93	460.30
32000	2884.50	1547.78	1105.38	886.54	757.09	672.31	613.02	569.64	536.83	511.39	491.28	475.15
33000	2974.64	1596.15	1139.92	914.24	780.75	693.32	632.18	587.44	553.60	527.37	506.64	490.00
34000	3064.78	1644.52	1174.47	941.95	804.41	714.33	651.33	605.24	570.38	543.35	521.99	504.85
35000	3154.92	1692.88	1209.01	969.65	828.07	735.34	670.49	623.04	587.15	559.33	537.34	519.69
37500	3380.27	1813.80	1295.37	1038.91	887.21	787.86	718.38	667.54	629.09	599.28	575.72	556.81
40000	3605.62	1934.72	1381.73	1108.17	946.36	840.38	766.28	712.05	671.03	639.23	614.10	593.94
42500	3830.97	2055.64	1468.08	1177.43	1005.51	892.91	814.17	756.55	712.97	679.19	652.48	631.06
45000	4056.32	2176.56	1554.44	1246.69	1064.66	945.43	862.06	801.05	754.91	719.14	690.86	668.18
47500	4281.67	2297.48	1640.80	1315.95	1123.80	997.96	909.95	845.55	796.85	759.09	729.25	705.30
50000	4507.02	2418.40	1727.16	1385.21	1182.95	1050.48	957.84	890.06	838.79	799.04	767.63	742.42
52500	4732.38	2539.32	1813.51	1454.47	1242.10	1103.00	1005.73	934.56	880.73	838.99	806.01	779.54
55000	4957.73	2660.24	1899.87	1523.74	1301.24	1155.53	1053.63	979.06	922.67	878.95	844.39	816.66
57500	5183.08	2781.16	1986.23	1593.00	1360.39	1208.05	1101.52	1023.56	964.61	918.90	882.77	853.78
60000	5408.43	2902.08	2072.59	1662.26	1419.54	1260.57	1149.41	1068.07	1006.55	958.85	921.15	890.90
65000	5859.13	3143.92	2245.30	1800.78	1537.83	1365.62	1245.19	1157.07	1090.43	1038.75	997.91	965.14
70000	6309.83	3385.76	2418.02	1939.30	1656.13	1470.67	1340.98	1246.08	1174.31	1118.66	1074.68	1039.38
75000	6760.53	3627.60	2590.73	2077.82	1774.42	1575.72	1436.76	1335.08	1258.18	1198.56	1151.44	1113.62
80000	7211.24	3869.44	2763.45	2216.34	1892.72	1680.76	1532.55	1424.09	1342.06	1278.46	1228.20	1187.87
85000	7661.94	4111.28	2936.16	2354.86	2011.01	1785.81	1628.33	1513.09	1425.94	1358.37	1304.96	1262.11
90000	8112.64	4353.12	3108.88	2493.38	2129.31	1890.86	1724.11	1602.10	1509.82	1438.27	1381.72	1336.35
95000	8563.34	4594.96	3281.59	2631.90	2247.60	1995.91	1819.90	1691.10	1593.70	1518.18	1458.49	1410.59
100000	9014.04	4836.80	3454.31	2770.42	2365.90	2100.95	1915.68	1780.11	1677.58	1598.08	1535.25	1484.83
105000	9464.75	5078.64	3627.02	2908.94	2484.19	2206.00	2011.46	1869.11	1761.45	1677.98	1612.01	1559.07
110000	9915.45	5320.48	3799.74	3047.47	2602.48	2311.05	2107.25	1958.12	1845.33	1757.89	1688.77	1633.31
115000	10366.15	5562.32	3972.45	3185.99	2720.78	2416.10	2203.03	2047.12	1929.21	1837.79	1765.53	1707.55
120000	10816.85	5804.16	4145.17	3324.51	2839.07	2521.14	2298.82	2136.13	2013.09	1917.69	1842.30	1781.80
125000	11267.55	6046.00	4317.88	3463.03	2957.37	2626.19	2394.60	2225.13	2096.97	1997.60	1919.06	1856.04
130000	11718.26	6287.84	4490.60	3601.55	3075.66	2731.24	2490.38	2314.14	2180.85	2077.50	1995.82	1930.28
135000	12168.96	6529.68	4663.31	3740.07	3193.96	2836.29	2586.17	2403.14	2264.73	2157.41	2072.58	2004.52
140000	12619.66	6771.52	4836.03	3878.59	3312.25	2941.33	2681.95	2492.15	2348.60	2237.31	2149.35	2078.76
145000	13070.36	7013.36	5008.74	4017.11	3430.55	3046.38	2777.74	2581.15	2432.48	2317.21	2226.11	2153.00
150000	13521.06	7255.20	5181.46	4155.63	3548.84	3151.43	2873.52	2670.16	2516.36	2397.12	2302.87	2227.24
155000	13971.76	7497.04	5354.17	4294.15	3667.14	3256.47	2969.30	2759.16	2600.24	2477.02	2379.63	2301.48
160000	14422.47	7738.88	5526.89	4432.67	3785.43	3361.52	3065.09	2848.17	2684.12	2556.92	2456.39	2375.73

AMOUNT OF LOAN	NUMBER OF YEARS IN TERM											
	13	14	15	16	17	18	19	20	25	30	35	40
$ 50	0.73	0.71	0.70	0.68	0.68	0.67	0.66	0.65	0.64	0.63	0.62	0.62
100	1.45	1.42	1.39	1.36	1.35	1.33	1.31	1.30	1.27	1.25	1.24	1.24
200	2.89	2.83	2.77	2.72	2.69	2.65	2.62	2.60	2.53	2.49	2.48	2.47
300	4.34	4.24	4.15	4.08	4.03	3.98	3.93	3.90	3.79	3.74	3.71	3.70
400	5.78	5.65	5.54	5.44	5.37	5.30	5.24	5.20	5.05	4.98	4.95	4.94
500	7.22	7.06	6.92	6.80	6.71	6.62	6.55	6.50	6.31	6.23	6.19	6.17
600	8.67	8.47	8.30	8.16	8.05	7.95	7.86	7.80	7.57	7.47	7.42	7.40
700	10.11	9.88	9.68	9.52	9.39	9.27	9.17	9.09	8.84	8.72	8.66	8.63
800	11.56	11.29	11.07	10.88	10.73	10.59	10.48	10.39	10.10	9.96	9.90	9.87
900	13.00	12.70	12.45	12.24	12.07	11.92	11.79	11.69	11.36	11.21	11.13	11.10
1000	14.44	14.11	13.83	13.60	13.41	13.24	13.10	12.99	12.62	12.45	12.37	12.33
2000	28.88	28.21	27.66	27.19	26.81	26.48	26.20	25.97	25.23	24.89	24.73	24.66
3000	43.32	42.31	41.48	40.79	40.21	39.72	39.30	38.96	37.85	37.34	37.10	36.99
4000	57.76	56.42	55.31	54.38	53.61	52.95	52.40	51.94	50.46	49.78	49.46	49.31
5000	72.20	70.52	69.13	67.97	67.01	66.19	65.50	64.92	63.08	62.23	61.83	61.64
6000	86.64	84.62	82.96	81.57	80.41	79.43	78.60	77.91	75.69	74.67	74.19	73.97
7000	101.08	98.72	96.78	95.16	93.81	92.67	91.70	90.89	88.31	87.12	86.56	86.29
8000	115.51	112.83	110.61	108.76	107.21	105.90	104.80	103.87	100.92	99.56	98.92	98.62
9000	129.95	126.93	124.43	122.35	120.61	119.14	117.90	116.86	113.54	112.01	111.29	110.95
10000	144.39	141.03	138.26	135.94	134.01	132.38	131.00	129.84	126.15	124.45	123.65	123.27
11000	158.83	155.14	152.08	149.54	147.41	145.62	144.10	142.82	138.77	136.90	136.02	135.60
12000	173.27	169.24	165.91	163.13	160.81	158.85	157.20	155.81	151.38	149.34	148.38	147.93
13000	187.71	183.34	179.73	176.72	174.21	172.09	170.30	168.79	164.00	161.79	160.75	160.25
14000	202.15	197.44	193.56	190.32	187.61	185.33	183.40	181.77	176.61	174.23	173.11	172.58
15000	216.59	211.55	207.38	203.91	201.01	198.57	196.50	194.76	189.22	186.68	185.48	184.91
16000	231.02	225.65	221.21	217.51	214.41	211.80	209.60	207.74	201.84	199.12	197.84	197.23
17000	245.46	239.75	235.03	231.10	227.81	225.04	222.70	220.73	214.45	211.57	210.21	209.56
18000	259.90	253.86	248.86	244.69	241.21	238.28	235.80	233.71	227.07	224.01	222.57	221.89
19000	274.34	267.96	262.68	258.29	254.61	251.52	248.90	246.69	239.68	236.46	234.94	234.21
20000	288.78	282.06	276.51	271.88	268.01	264.75	262.00	259.68	252.30	248.90	247.30	246.54
21000	303.22	296.16	290.33	285.47	281.41	277.99	275.10	272.66	264.91	261.34	259.66	258.87
22000	317.66	310.27	304.16	299.07	294.81	291.23	288.20	285.64	277.53	273.79	272.03	271.19
23000	332.10	324.37	317.98	312.66	308.21	304.47	301.30	298.63	290.14	286.23	284.39	283.52
24000	346.53	338.47	331.81	326.26	321.61	317.70	314.40	311.61	302.76	298.68	296.76	295.85
25000	360.97	352.58	345.63	339.85	335.01	330.94	327.50	324.59	315.37	311.12	309.12	308.17
26000	375.41	366.68	359.46	353.44	348.41	344.18	340.60	337.58	327.99	323.57	321.49	320.50
27000	389.85	380.78	373.28	367.04	361.81	357.42	353.70	350.56	340.60	336.01	333.85	332.83
28000	404.29	394.88	387.11	380.63	375.21	370.65	366.80	363.54	353.22	348.46	346.22	345.15
29000	418.73	408.99	400.93	394.23	388.61	383.89	379.90	376.53	365.83	360.90	358.58	357.48
30000	433.17	423.09	414.76	407.82	402.01	397.13	393.00	389.51	378.44	373.35	370.95	369.81
31000	447.61	437.19	428.58	421.41	415.41	410.37	406.10	402.50	391.06	385.79	383.31	382.13
32000	462.04	451.30	442.41	435.01	428.81	423.60	419.20	415.48	403.67	398.24	395.68	394.46
33000	476.48	465.40	456.23	448.60	442.21	436.84	432.30	428.46	416.29	410.68	408.04	406.79
34000	490.92	479.50	470.06	462.19	455.61	450.08	445.40	441.45	428.90	423.13	420.41	419.11
35000	505.36	493.60	483.88	475.79	469.01	463.31	458.50	454.43	441.52	435.57	432.77	431.44
37500	541.46	528.86	518.44	509.77	502.51	496.41	491.25	486.89	473.05	466.68	463.68	462.26
40000	577.55	564.12	553.01	543.76	536.01	529.50	524.00	519.35	504.59	497.80	494.59	493.07
42500	613.65	599.37	587.57	577.74	569.51	562.60	556.75	551.81	536.13	528.91	525.51	523.89
45000	649.75	634.63	622.13	611.73	603.01	595.69	589.50	584.26	567.66	560.02	556.42	554.71
47500	685.84	669.89	656.69	645.71	636.52	628.79	622.25	616.72	599.20	591.13	587.33	585.52
50000	721.94	705.15	691.26	679.69	670.02	661.88	655.00	649.18	630.74	622.24	618.24	616.34
52500	758.04	740.40	725.82	713.68	703.52	694.97	687.75	681.64	662.27	653.35	649.15	647.16
55000	794.14	775.66	760.38	747.66	737.02	728.06	720.50	714.10	693.81	684.47	680.07	677.97
57500	830.23	810.92	794.94	781.65	770.52	761.16	753.25	746.56	725.35	715.58	710.98	708.79
60000	866.33	846.17	829.51	815.63	804.02	794.25	786.00	779.02	756.88	746.69	741.89	739.61
65000	938.52	916.69	898.63	883.60	871.02	860.44	851.50	843.94	819.96	808.91	803.71	801.24
70000	1010.72	987.20	967.76	951.57	938.02	926.62	917.00	908.85	883.03	871.14	865.54	862.87
75000	1082.91	1057.72	1036.88	1019.54	1005.02	992.81	982.50	973.77	946.10	933.36	927.36	924.51
80000	1155.10	1128.23	1106.01	1087.51	1072.02	1059.00	1048.00	1038.69	1009.18	995.59	989.18	986.14
85000	1227.30	1198.74	1175.13	1155.48	1139.02	1125.19	1113.50	1103.61	1072.25	1057.81	1051.01	1047.77
90000	1299.49	1269.26	1244.26	1223.45	1206.02	1191.37	1179.00	1168.52	1135.32	1120.03	1112.83	1109.41
95000	1371.68	1339.77	1313.38	1291.42	1273.03	1257.56	1244.50	1233.44	1198.40	1182.26	1174.66	1171.04
100000	1443.88	1410.29	1382.51	1359.38	1340.03	1323.75	1310.00	1298.36	1261.47	1244.48	1236.48	1232.67
105000	1516.07	1480.80	1451.63	1427.35	1407.03	1389.93	1375.50	1363.28	1324.54	1306.70	1298.30	1294.31
110000	1588.27	1551.31	1520.76	1495.32	1474.03	1456.12	1441.00	1428.20	1387.62	1368.93	1360.13	1355.94
115000	1660.46	1621.83	1589.88	1563.29	1541.03	1522.31	1506.50	1493.11	1450.69	1431.15	1421.95	1417.57
120000	1732.65	1692.34	1659.01	1631.26	1608.03	1588.50	1572.00	1558.03	1513.76	1493.38	1483.77	1479.21
125000	1804.85	1762.86	1728.13	1699.23	1675.03	1654.68	1637.50	1622.95	1576.84	1555.60	1545.60	1540.84
130000	1877.04	1833.37	1797.26	1767.20	1742.03	1720.87	1703.00	1687.87	1639.91	1617.82	1607.42	1602.47
135000	1949.23	1903.89	1866.39	1835.17	1809.03	1787.06	1768.50	1752.78	1702.98	1680.05	1669.25	1664.11
140000	2021.43	1974.40	1935.51	1903.14	1876.04	1853.24	1834.00	1817.70	1766.06	1742.27	1731.07	1725.74
145000	2093.62	2044.91	2004.64	1971.11	1943.04	1919.43	1899.50	1882.62	1829.13	1804.49	1792.89	1787.37
150000	2165.82	2115.43	2073.76	2039.07	2010.04	1985.62	1965.00	1947.54	1892.20	1866.72	1854.72	1849.01
155000	2238.01	2185.94	2142.89	2107.04	2077.04	2051.81	2030.50	2012.46	1955.28	1928.94	1916.54	1910.64
160000	2310.20	2256.46	2212.01	2175.01	2144.04	2117.99	2096.00	2077.37	2018.35	1991.17	1978.36	1972.27

15.00% MONTHLY AMORTIZING PAYMENTS

AMOUNT OF LOAN	NUMBER OF YEARS IN TERM											
	1	2	3	4	5	6	7	8	9	10	11	12
$ 50	4.52	2.43	1.74	1.40	1.19	1.06	0.97	0.90	0.85	0.81	0.78	0.76
100	9.03	4.85	3.47	2.79	2.38	2.12	1.93	1.80	1.70	1.62	1.56	1.51
200	18.06	9.70	6.94	5.57	4.76	4.23	3.86	3.59	3.39	3.23	3.11	3.01
300	27.08	14.55	10.40	8.35	7.14	6.35	5.79	5.39	5.08	4.85	4.66	4.51
400	36.11	19.40	13.87	11.14	9.52	8.46	7.72	7.18	6.77	6.46	6.21	6.01
500	45.13	24.25	17.34	13.92	11.90	10.58	9.65	8.98	8.47	8.07	7.76	7.51
600	54.16	29.10	20.80	16.70	14.28	12.69	11.58	10.77	10.16	9.69	9.31	9.01
700	63.19	33.95	24.27	19.49	16.66	14.81	13.51	12.57	11.85	11.30	10.86	10.51
800	72.21	38.79	27.74	22.27	19.04	16.92	15.44	14.36	13.54	12.91	12.41	12.01
900	81.24	43.64	31.20	25.05	21.42	19.04	17.37	16.16	15.24	14.53	13.96	13.51
1000	90.26	48.49	34.67	27.84	23.79	21.15	19.30	17.95	16.93	16.14	15.51	15.01
2000	180.52	96.98	69.34	55.67	47.58	42.30	38.60	35.90	33.85	32.27	31.02	30.02
3000	270.78	145.46	104.00	83.50	71.37	63.44	57.90	53.84	50.78	48.41	46.53	45.03
4000	361.04	193.95	138.67	111.33	95.16	84.59	77.19	71.79	67.70	64.54	62.04	60.04
5000	451.30	242.44	173.33	139.16	118.95	105.73	96.49	89.73	84.63	80.67	77.55	75.05
6000	541.55	290.92	208.00	166.99	142.74	126.88	115.79	107.68	101.55	96.81	93.06	90.06
7000	631.81	339.41	242.66	194.82	166.53	148.02	135.08	125.62	118.48	112.94	108.57	105.07
8000	722.07	387.90	277.33	222.65	190.32	169.17	154.38	143.57	135.40	129.07	124.08	120.08
9000	812.33	436.38	311.99	250.48	214.11	190.31	173.68	161.51	152.32	145.21	139.59	135.08
10000	902.59	484.87	346.66	278.31	237.90	211.46	192.97	179.46	169.25	161.34	155.10	150.09
11000	992.85	533.36	381.32	306.14	261.69	232.60	212.27	197.40	186.17	177.47	170.61	165.10
12000	1083.10	581.84	415.99	333.97	285.48	253.75	231.57	215.35	203.10	193.61	186.11	180.11
13000	1173.36	630.33	450.65	361.80	309.27	274.89	250.86	233.30	220.02	209.74	201.62	195.12
14000	1263.62	678.82	485.32	389.64	333.06	296.04	270.16	251.24	236.95	225.87	217.13	210.13
15000	1353.88	727.30	519.98	417.47	356.85	317.18	289.46	269.19	253.87	242.01	232.64	225.14
16000	1444.14	775.79	554.65	445.30	380.64	338.33	308.75	287.13	270.79	258.14	248.15	240.15
17000	1534.40	824.28	589.32	473.13	404.43	359.47	328.05	305.08	287.72	274.27	263.66	255.15
18000	1624.65	872.76	623.98	500.96	428.22	380.62	347.35	323.02	304.64	290.41	279.17	270.16
19000	1714.91	921.25	658.65	528.79	452.01	401.76	366.64	340.97	321.57	306.54	294.68	285.17
20000	1805.17	969.74	693.31	556.62	475.80	422.91	385.94	358.91	338.49	322.67	310.19	300.18
21000	1895.43	1018.22	727.98	584.45	499.59	444.05	405.24	376.86	355.42	338.81	325.70	315.19
22000	1985.69	1066.71	762.64	612.28	523.38	465.20	424.53	394.80	372.34	354.94	341.21	330.20
23000	2075.95	1115.20	797.31	640.11	547.17	486.34	443.83	412.75	389.26	371.08	356.72	345.21
24000	2166.20	1163.68	831.97	667.94	570.96	507.49	463.13	430.69	406.19	387.21	372.22	360.22
25000	2256.46	1212.17	866.64	695.77	594.75	528.63	482.42	448.64	423.11	403.34	387.73	375.22
26000	2346.72	1260.66	901.30	723.60	618.54	549.78	501.72	466.59	440.04	419.48	403.24	390.23
27000	2436.98	1309.14	935.97	751.44	642.33	570.92	521.02	484.53	456.96	435.61	418.75	405.24
28000	2527.24	1357.63	970.63	779.27	666.12	592.07	540.31	502.48	473.89	451.74	434.26	420.25
29000	2617.50	1406.12	1005.30	807.10	689.91	613.21	559.61	520.42	490.81	467.88	449.77	435.26
30000	2707.75	1454.60	1039.96	834.93	713.70	634.36	578.91	538.37	507.74	484.01	465.28	450.27
31000	2798.01	1503.09	1074.63	862.76	737.49	655.50	598.20	556.31	524.66	500.14	480.79	465.28
32000	2888.27	1551.58	1109.30	890.59	761.28	676.65	617.50	574.26	541.58	516.28	496.30	480.29
33000	2978.53	1600.06	1143.96	918.42	785.07	697.79	636.80	592.20	558.51	532.41	511.81	495.29
34000	3068.79	1648.55	1178.63	946.25	808.86	718.94	656.09	610.15	575.43	548.54	527.32	510.30
35000	3159.05	1697.04	1213.29	974.08	832.65	740.08	675.39	628.09	592.36	564.68	542.83	525.31
37500	3384.69	1818.25	1299.95	1043.66	892.13	792.94	723.63	672.96	634.67	605.01	581.60	562.83
40000	3610.34	1939.47	1386.62	1113.23	951.60	845.81	771.88	717.82	676.98	645.34	620.37	600.36
42500	3835.98	2060.69	1473.28	1182.81	1011.08	898.67	820.12	762.68	719.29	685.68	659.14	637.88
45000	4061.63	2181.90	1559.94	1252.39	1070.55	951.53	868.36	807.55	761.60	726.01	697.92	675.40
47500	4287.27	2303.12	1646.61	1321.97	1130.03	1004.39	916.60	852.41	803.91	766.35	736.69	712.92
50000	4512.92	2424.34	1733.27	1391.54	1189.50	1057.26	964.84	897.28	846.22	806.68	775.46	750.44
52500	4738.57	2545.55	1819.93	1461.12	1248.98	1110.12	1013.08	942.14	888.53	847.01	814.24	787.97
55000	4964.21	2666.77	1906.60	1530.70	1308.45	1162.98	1061.33	987.00	930.84	887.35	853.01	825.49
57500	5189.86	2787.99	1993.26	1600.27	1367.93	1215.84	1109.57	1031.87	973.15	927.68	891.78	863.01
60000	5415.50	2909.20	2079.92	1669.85	1427.40	1268.71	1157.81	1076.73	1015.47	968.01	930.55	900.53
65000	5866.80	3151.64	2253.25	1809.00	1546.35	1374.43	1254.29	1166.46	1100.09	1048.68	1008.10	975.57
70000	6318.09	3394.07	2426.58	1948.16	1665.30	1480.16	1350.78	1256.18	1184.71	1129.35	1085.65	1050.62
75000	6769.38	3636.50	2599.90	2087.31	1784.25	1585.88	1447.26	1345.91	1269.33	1210.02	1163.19	1125.66
80000	7220.67	3878.94	2773.23	2226.46	1903.20	1691.61	1543.75	1435.64	1353.95	1290.68	1240.74	1200.71
85000	7671.96	4121.37	2946.56	2365.62	2022.15	1797.33	1640.23	1525.36	1438.57	1371.35	1318.28	1275.75
90000	8123.25	4363.80	3119.88	2504.77	2141.10	1903.06	1736.71	1615.09	1523.20	1452.02	1395.83	1350.79
95000	8574.54	4606.24	3293.21	2643.93	2260.05	2008.78	1833.20	1704.82	1607.82	1532.69	1473.37	1425.84
100000	9025.84	4848.67	3466.54	2783.08	2379.00	2114.51	1929.68	1794.55	1692.44	1613.35	1550.92	1500.88
105000	9477.13	5091.10	3639.86	2922.23	2497.95	2220.23	2026.16	1884.27	1777.06	1694.02	1628.47	1575.93
110000	9928.42	5333.54	3813.19	3061.39	2616.90	2325.96	2122.65	1974.00	1861.68	1774.69	1706.01	1650.97
115000	10379.71	5575.97	3986.52	3200.54	2735.85	2431.68	2219.13	2063.73	1946.30	1855.36	1783.56	1726.01
120000	10831.00	5818.40	4159.84	3339.69	2854.80	2537.41	2315.62	2153.45	2030.93	1936.02	1861.10	1801.06
125000	11282.29	6060.84	4333.17	3478.85	2973.75	2643.13	2412.10	2243.18	2115.55	2016.69	1938.65	1876.10
130000	11733.59	6303.27	4506.50	3618.00	3092.70	2748.86	2508.58	2332.91	2200.17	2097.36	2016.19	1951.14
135000	12184.88	6545.70	4679.82	3757.16	3211.65	2854.58	2605.07	2422.63	2284.79	2178.03	2093.74	2026.19
140000	12636.17	6788.14	4853.15	3896.31	3330.60	2960.31	2701.55	2512.36	2369.41	2258.69	2171.29	2101.23
145000	13087.46	7030.57	5026.48	4035.46	3449.54	3066.03	2798.03	2602.09	2454.03	2339.36	2248.83	2176.28
150000	13538.75	7273.00	5199.80	4174.62	3568.49	3171.76	2894.52	2691.82	2538.66	2420.03	2326.38	2251.32
155000	13990.04	7515.44	5373.13	4313.77	3687.44	3277.48	2991.00	2781.54	2623.28	2500.70	2403.92	2326.36
160000	14441.33	7757.87	5546.46	4452.92	3806.39	3383.21	3087.49	2871.27	2707.90	2581.36	2481.47	2401.41

82

AMOUNT OF LOAN	NUMBER OF YEARS IN TERM											
	13	14	15	16	17	18	19	20	25	30	35	40
$ 50	0.74	0.72	0.70	0.69	0.68	0.68	0.67	0.66	0.65	0.64	0.63	0.63
100	1.47	1.43	1.40	1.38	1.36	1.35	1.33	1.32	1.29	1.27	1.26	1.26
200	2.93	2.86	2.80	2.76	2.72	2.69	2.66	2.64	2.57	2.53	2.52	2.51
300	4.39	4.29	4.20	4.14	4.08	4.03	3.99	3.96	3.85	3.80	3.78	3.76
400	5.85	5.71	5.60	5.51	5.44	5.37	5.32	5.27	5.13	5.06	5.03	5.02
500	7.31	7.14	7.00	6.89	6.79	6.71	6.65	6.59	6.41	6.33	6.29	6.27
600	8.77	8.57	8.40	8.27	8.15	8.06	7.97	7.91	7.69	7.59	7.55	7.52
700	10.23	9.99	9.80	9.64	9.51	9.40	9.30	9.22	8.97	8.86	8.80	8.78
800	11.69	11.42	11.20	11.02	10.87	10.74	10.63	10.54	10.25	10.12	10.06	10.03
900	13.15	12.85	12.60	12.40	12.22	12.08	11.96	11.86	11.53	11.38	11.32	11.28
1000	14.61	14.28	14.00	13.77	13.58	13.42	13.29	13.17	12.81	12.65	12.57	12.54
2000	29.21	28.55	28.00	27.54	27.16	26.84	26.57	26.34	25.62	25.29	25.14	25.07
3000	43.81	42.82	41.99	41.31	40.74	40.26	39.85	39.51	38.43	37.94	37.71	37.60
4000	58.42	57.09	55.99	55.08	54.31	53.67	53.13	52.68	51.24	50.58	50.28	50.13
5000	73.02	71.36	69.98	68.84	67.89	67.09	66.41	65.84	64.05	63.23	62.85	62.67
6000	87.62	85.63	83.98	82.61	81.47	80.51	79.70	79.01	76.85	75.87	75.41	75.20
7000	102.23	99.90	97.98	96.38	95.04	93.92	92.98	92.18	89.66	88.52	87.98	87.73
8000	116.83	114.17	111.97	110.15	108.62	107.34	106.26	105.35	102.46	101.16	100.55	100.26
9000	131.43	128.44	125.97	123.91	122.20	120.76	119.54	118.52	115.28	113.80	113.12	112.80
10000	146.03	142.71	139.96	137.68	135.78	134.17	132.82	131.68	128.09	126.45	125.69	125.33
11000	160.64	156.98	153.96	151.45	149.35	147.59	146.11	144.85	140.90	139.09	138.25	137.86
12000	175.24	171.25	167.96	165.22	162.93	161.01	159.39	158.02	153.70	151.74	150.82	150.39
13000	189.84	185.52	181.95	178.99	176.51	174.42	172.67	171.19	166.51	164.38	163.39	162.92
14000	204.45	199.79	195.95	192.75	190.08	187.84	185.95	184.36	179.32	177.03	175.96	175.46
15000	219.05	214.06	209.94	206.52	203.66	201.26	199.23	197.52	192.13	189.67	188.53	187.99
16000	233.65	228.33	223.94	220.29	217.24	214.68	212.52	210.69	204.94	202.32	201.10	200.52
17000	248.25	242.60	237.93	234.06	230.81	228.09	225.80	223.86	217.75	214.96	213.66	213.05
18000	262.86	256.87	251.93	247.82	244.39	241.51	239.08	237.03	230.55	227.60	226.23	225.59
19000	277.46	271.14	265.93	261.59	257.97	254.93	252.36	250.20	243.36	240.25	238.80	238.12
20000	292.06	285.41	279.92	275.36	271.55	268.34	265.64	263.36	256.17	252.89	251.37	250.65
21000	306.67	299.68	293.92	289.13	285.12	281.76	278.93	276.53	268.98	265.54	263.94	263.18
22000	321.27	313.95	307.91	302.89	298.70	295.18	292.21	289.70	281.79	278.18	276.50	275.71
23000	335.87	328.22	321.91	316.66	312.28	308.59	305.49	302.87	294.60	290.83	289.07	288.25
24000	350.47	342.49	335.91	330.43	325.85	322.01	318.77	316.03	307.40	303.47	301.64	300.78
25000	365.08	356.76	349.90	344.20	339.43	335.43	332.05	329.20	320.21	316.12	314.21	313.31
26000	379.68	371.04	363.90	357.97	353.01	348.84	345.34	342.37	333.02	328.76	326.78	325.84
27000	394.28	385.31	377.89	371.73	366.58	362.26	358.62	355.54	345.83	341.40	339.34	338.38
28000	408.89	399.58	391.89	385.50	380.16	375.68	371.90	368.71	358.64	354.05	351.91	350.91
29000	423.49	413.85	405.89	399.27	393.74	389.10	385.18	381.87	371.45	366.69	364.48	363.44
30000	438.09	428.12	419.88	413.04	407.32	402.51	398.46	395.04	384.25	379.34	377.05	375.97
31000	452.69	442.39	433.88	426.80	420.89	415.93	411.75	408.21	397.06	391.98	389.62	388.50
32000	467.30	456.66	447.87	440.57	434.47	429.35	425.03	421.38	409.87	404.63	402.19	401.04
33000	481.90	470.93	461.87	454.34	448.05	442.76	438.31	434.55	422.68	417.27	414.75	413.57
34000	496.50	485.20	475.86	468.11	461.62	456.18	451.59	447.71	435.49	429.92	427.32	426.10
35000	511.11	499.47	489.86	481.87	475.20	469.60	464.87	460.88	448.30	442.56	439.89	438.63
37500	547.61	535.14	524.85	516.29	509.14	503.14	498.08	493.80	480.32	474.17	471.31	469.96
40000	584.12	570.82	559.84	550.71	543.09	536.68	531.28	526.72	512.34	505.78	502.73	501.29
42500	620.63	606.50	594.83	585.13	577.03	570.22	564.49	559.64	544.36	537.39	534.15	532.63
45000	657.13	642.17	629.82	619.55	610.97	603.77	597.69	592.56	576.38	569.00	565.57	563.96
47500	693.64	677.85	664.81	653.97	644.91	637.31	630.90	625.48	608.40	600.62	596.99	595.29
50000	730.15	713.52	699.80	688.39	678.86	670.85	664.10	658.40	640.42	632.23	628.41	626.62
52500	766.66	749.20	734.79	722.81	712.80	704.39	697.31	691.32	672.44	663.84	659.83	657.95
55000	803.16	784.88	769.78	757.23	746.74	737.93	730.51	724.24	704.46	695.45	691.25	689.28
57500	839.67	820.55	804.77	791.65	780.68	771.48	763.72	757.16	736.48	727.06	722.67	720.61
60000	876.18	856.23	839.76	826.07	814.63	805.02	796.92	790.08	768.50	758.67	754.09	751.94
65000	949.19	927.58	909.74	894.91	882.51	872.10	863.33	855.92	832.54	821.89	816.93	814.60
70000	1022.21	998.93	979.72	963.74	950.40	939.19	929.74	921.76	896.59	885.12	879.77	877.26
75000	1095.22	1070.28	1049.70	1032.58	1018.28	1006.27	996.15	987.60	960.63	948.34	942.61	939.92
80000	1168.23	1141.64	1119.67	1101.42	1086.17	1073.36	1062.56	1053.44	1024.67	1011.56	1005.46	1002.58
85000	1241.25	1212.99	1189.65	1170.26	1154.05	1140.44	1128.97	1119.28	1088.71	1074.78	1068.30	1065.25
90000	1314.26	1284.34	1259.63	1239.10	1221.94	1207.53	1195.38	1185.12	1152.75	1138.00	1131.14	1127.91
95000	1387.28	1355.69	1329.61	1307.94	1289.82	1274.61	1261.79	1250.96	1216.79	1201.23	1193.98	1190.57
100000	1460.29	1427.04	1399.59	1376.77	1357.71	1341.70	1328.20	1316.79	1280.84	1264.45	1256.82	1253.23
105000	1533.31	1498.40	1469.57	1445.61	1425.59	1408.78	1394.61	1382.63	1344.88	1327.67	1319.66	1315.89
110000	1606.32	1569.75	1539.55	1514.45	1493.48	1475.86	1461.02	1448.47	1408.92	1390.89	1382.50	1378.55
115000	1679.34	1641.10	1609.53	1583.29	1561.36	1542.95	1527.43	1514.31	1472.96	1454.12	1445.34	1441.21
120000	1752.35	1712.45	1679.51	1652.13	1629.25	1610.03	1593.84	1580.15	1537.00	1517.34	1508.18	1503.87
125000	1825.36	1783.80	1749.49	1720.97	1697.13	1677.12	1660.25	1645.99	1601.04	1580.56	1571.02	1566.54
130000	1898.38	1855.16	1819.47	1789.81	1765.02	1744.20	1726.66	1711.83	1665.08	1643.78	1633.86	1629.20
135000	1971.39	1926.51	1889.45	1858.64	1832.90	1811.29	1793.07	1777.67	1729.13	1707.00	1696.70	1691.86
140000	2044.41	1997.86	1959.43	1927.48	1900.79	1878.37	1859.48	1843.51	1793.17	1770.23	1759.54	1754.52
145000	2117.42	2069.21	2029.41	1996.32	1968.67	1945.46	1925.89	1909.35	1857.21	1833.45	1822.38	1817.18
150000	2190.43	2140.56	2099.39	2065.16	2036.56	2012.54	1992.30	1975.19	1921.25	1896.67	1885.22	1879.84
155000	2263.45	2211.92	2169.37	2134.00	2104.44	2079.63	2058.71	2041.03	1985.29	1959.89	1948.07	1942.50
160000	2336.46	2283.27	2239.34	2202.84	2172.33	2146.71	2125.12	2106.87	2049.33	2023.12	2010.91	2005.16

MONTHLY AMORTIZING PAYMENTS

AMOUNT OF LOAN	NUMBER OF YEARS IN TERM											
	1	2	3	4	5	6	7	8	9	10	11	12
$ 50	4.52	2.44	1.74	1.40	1.20	1.07	0.98	0.91	0.86	0.82	0.79	0.76
100	9.04	4.87	3.48	2.80	2.40	2.13	1.95	1.81	1.71	1.63	1.57	1.52
200	18.08	9.73	6.96	5.60	4.79	4.26	3.89	3.62	3.42	3.26	3.14	3.04
300	27.12	14.59	10.44	8.39	7.18	6.39	5.84	5.43	5.13	4.89	4.70	4.56
400	36.16	19.45	13.92	11.19	9.57	8.52	7.78	7.24	6.83	6.52	6.27	6.07
500	45.19	24.31	17.40	13.98	11.97	10.65	9.72	9.05	8.54	8.15	7.84	7.59
600	54.23	29.17	20.88	16.78	14.36	12.77	11.67	10.86	10.25	9.78	9.40	9.11
700	63.27	34.03	24.36	19.58	16.75	14.90	13.61	12.67	11.96	11.41	10.97	10.62
800	72.31	38.89	27.84	22.37	19.14	17.03	15.55	14.48	13.66	13.03	12.54	12.14
900	81.34	43.75	31.31	25.17	21.53	19.16	17.50	16.29	15.37	14.66	14.10	13.66
1000	90.38	48.61	34.79	27.96	23.93	21.29	19.44	18.10	17.08	16.29	15.67	15.18
2000	180.76	97.22	69.58	55.92	47.85	42.57	38.88	36.19	34.15	32.58	31.34	30.35
3000	271.13	145.82	104.37	83.88	71.77	63.85	58.32	54.28	51.23	48.87	47.00	45.52
4000	361.51	194.43	139.16	111.84	95.69	85.13	77.75	72.37	68.30	65.15	62.67	60.69
5000	451.89	243.03	173.94	139.79	119.61	106.41	97.19	90.46	85.37	81.44	78.34	75.86
6000	542.26	291.64	208.73	167.75	143.53	127.69	116.63	108.55	102.45	97.73	94.00	91.03
7000	632.64	340.24	243.52	195.71	167.45	148.97	136.07	126.64	119.52	114.01	109.67	106.20
8000	723.02	388.85	278.31	223.67	191.38	170.25	155.50	144.73	136.59	130.30	125.34	121.37
9000	813.39	437.45	313.10	251.62	215.30	191.53	174.94	162.82	153.67	146.59	141.00	136.54
10000	903.77	486.06	347.88	279.58	239.22	212.82	194.38	180.91	170.74	162.87	156.67	151.71
11000	994.14	534.67	382.67	307.54	263.14	234.10	213.82	199.00	187.81	179.16	172.34	166.88
12000	1084.52	583.27	417.46	335.50	287.06	255.38	233.25	217.09	204.89	195.45	188.00	182.05
13000	1174.90	631.88	452.25	363.45	310.98	276.66	252.69	235.18	221.96	211.74	203.67	197.22
14000	1265.27	680.48	487.04	391.41	334.90	297.94	272.13	253.27	239.04	228.02	219.34	212.39
15000	1355.65	729.09	521.82	419.37	358.83	319.22	291.56	271.36	256.11	244.31	235.00	227.56
16000	1446.03	777.69	556.61	447.33	382.75	340.50	311.00	289.45	273.18	260.60	250.67	242.73
17000	1536.40	826.30	591.40	475.28	406.67	361.78	330.44	307.54	290.26	276.88	266.34	257.90
18000	1626.78	874.90	626.19	503.24	430.59	383.06	349.88	325.63	307.33	293.17	282.00	273.07
19000	1717.16	923.51	660.97	531.20	454.51	404.34	369.31	343.72	324.40	309.46	297.67	288.24
20000	1807.53	972.12	695.76	559.16	478.43	425.63	388.75	361.81	341.48	325.74	313.34	303.41
21000	1897.91	1020.72	730.55	587.12	502.35	446.91	408.19	379.90	358.55	342.03	329.00	318.58
22000	1988.28	1069.33	765.34	615.07	526.27	468.19	427.63	397.99	375.62	358.32	344.67	333.75
23000	2078.66	1117.93	800.13	643.03	550.20	489.47	447.06	416.08	392.70	374.60	360.34	348.92
24000	2169.04	1166.54	834.91	670.99	574.12	510.75	466.50	434.17	409.77	390.89	376.00	364.09
25000	2259.41	1215.14	869.70	698.95	598.04	532.03	485.94	452.26	426.85	407.18	391.67	379.26
26000	2349.79	1263.75	904.49	726.90	621.96	553.31	505.37	470.35	443.92	423.47	407.34	394.43
27000	2440.17	1312.35	939.28	754.86	645.88	574.59	524.81	488.44	460.99	439.75	423.00	409.60
28000	2530.54	1360.96	974.07	782.82	669.80	595.87	544.25	506.54	478.07	456.04	438.67	424.77
29000	2620.92	1409.56	1008.85	810.78	693.72	617.15	563.69	524.63	495.14	472.33	454.34	439.94
30000	2711.29	1458.17	1043.64	838.73	717.65	638.44	583.12	542.72	512.21	488.61	470.00	455.11
31000	2801.67	1506.78	1078.43	866.69	741.57	659.72	602.56	560.81	529.29	504.90	485.67	470.28
32000	2892.05	1555.38	1113.22	894.65	765.49	681.00	622.00	578.90	546.36	521.19	501.34	485.45
33000	2982.42	1603.99	1148.01	922.61	789.41	702.28	641.44	596.99	563.43	537.47	517.00	500.62
34000	3072.80	1652.59	1182.79	950.56	813.33	723.56	660.87	615.08	580.51	553.76	532.67	515.79
35000	3163.18	1701.20	1217.58	978.52	837.25	744.84	680.31	633.17	597.58	570.05	548.34	530.96
37500	3389.12	1822.71	1304.55	1048.42	897.06	798.04	728.90	678.39	640.27	610.77	587.50	568.88
40000	3615.06	1944.23	1391.52	1118.31	956.86	851.25	777.50	723.62	682.95	651.48	626.67	606.81
42500	3841.00	2065.74	1478.49	1188.20	1016.66	904.45	826.09	768.85	725.63	692.20	665.84	644.73
45000	4066.94	2187.25	1565.46	1258.10	1076.47	957.65	874.68	814.07	768.32	732.92	705.00	682.66
47500	4292.88	2308.77	1652.43	1327.99	1136.27	1010.85	923.28	859.30	811.00	773.63	744.17	720.58
50000	4518.82	2430.28	1739.40	1397.89	1196.07	1064.06	971.87	904.52	853.69	814.35	783.33	758.51
52500	4744.76	2551.79	1826.37	1467.78	1255.88	1117.26	1020.46	949.75	896.37	855.07	822.50	796.43
55000	4970.70	2673.31	1913.34	1537.68	1315.68	1170.46	1069.06	994.98	939.05	895.79	861.67	834.36
57500	5196.64	2794.82	2000.31	1607.57	1375.48	1223.66	1117.65	1040.20	981.74	936.50	900.83	872.28
60000	5422.58	2916.34	2087.28	1677.46	1435.29	1276.87	1166.24	1085.43	1024.42	977.22	940.00	910.21
65000	5874.47	3159.36	2261.22	1817.25	1554.89	1383.27	1263.43	1175.88	1109.79	1058.66	1018.33	986.06
70000	6326.35	3402.29	2435.16	1957.04	1674.50	1489.68	1360.61	1266.33	1195.16	1140.09	1096.67	1061.91
75000	6778.23	3645.42	2609.10	2096.83	1794.11	1596.08	1457.80	1356.78	1280.53	1221.53	1175.00	1137.76
80000	7230.11	3888.45	2783.04	2236.62	1913.71	1702.49	1554.99	1447.23	1365.89	1302.96	1253.33	1213.61
85000	7681.99	4131.47	2956.97	2376.40	2033.32	1808.89	1652.17	1537.69	1451.26	1384.39	1331.67	1289.46
90000	8133.87	4374.50	3130.91	2516.19	2152.93	1915.30	1749.36	1628.14	1536.63	1465.83	1410.00	1365.31
95000	8585.76	4617.53	3304.85	2655.98	2272.53	2021.70	1846.55	1718.59	1622.00	1547.26	1488.33	1441.16
100000	9037.64	4860.56	3478.79	2795.77	2392.14	2128.11	1943.73	1809.04	1707.37	1628.70	1566.66	1517.01
105000	9489.52	5103.58	3652.73	2935.56	2511.75	2234.51	2040.92	1899.49	1792.73	1710.13	1645.00	1592.86
110000	9941.40	5346.61	3826.67	3075.35	2631.35	2340.92	2138.11	1989.95	1878.10	1791.57	1723.33	1668.71
115000	10393.28	5589.64	4000.61	3215.13	2750.96	2447.32	2235.29	2080.40	1963.47	1873.00	1801.66	1744.56
120000	10845.16	5832.67	4174.55	3354.92	2870.57	2553.73	2332.48	2170.85	2048.84	1954.44	1880.00	1820.41
125000	11297.05	6075.69	4348.49	3494.71	2990.17	2660.13	2429.67	2261.30	2134.21	2035.87	1958.33	1896.26
130000	11748.93	6318.72	4522.43	3634.50	3109.78	2766.54	2526.85	2351.75	2219.57	2117.31	2036.66	1972.11
135000	12200.81	6561.75	4696.37	3774.29	3229.39	2872.94	2624.04	2442.20	2304.94	2198.74	2114.99	2047.96
140000	12652.69	6804.78	4870.31	3914.07	3349.00	2979.35	2721.22	2532.66	2390.31	2280.18	2193.33	2123.81
145000	13104.57	7047.80	5044.25	4053.86	3468.60	3085.75	2818.41	2623.11	2475.68	2361.61	2271.66	2199.66
150000	13556.45	7290.83	5218.19	4193.65	3588.21	3192.16	2915.60	2713.56	2561.05	2443.05	2349.99	2275.51
155000	14008.33	7533.86	5392.13	4333.44	3707.82	3298.56	3012.78	2804.01	2646.41	2524.48	2428.33	2351.36
160000	14460.22	7776.89	5566.07	4473.23	3827.42	3404.97	3109.97	2894.46	2731.78	2605.91	2506.66	2427.21

AMOUNT OF LOAN	NUMBER OF YEARS IN TERM											
	13	14	15	16	17	18	19	20	25	30	35	40
$ 50	0.74	0.73	0.71	0.70	0.69	0.68	0.68	0.67	0.66	0.65	0.64	0.64
100	1.48	1.45	1.42	1.40	1.38	1.36	1.35	1.34	1.31	1.29	1.28	1.28
200	2.96	2.89	2.84	2.79	2.76	2.72	2.70	2.68	2.61	2.57	2.56	2.55
300	4.44	4.34	4.26	4.19	4.13	4.08	4.04	4.01	3.91	3.86	3.84	3.83
400	5.91	5.78	5.67	5.58	5.51	5.44	5.39	5.35	5.21	5.14	5.11	5.10
500	7.39	7.22	7.09	6.98	6.88	6.80	6.74	6.68	6.51	6.43	6.39	6.37
600	8.87	8.67	8.51	8.37	8.26	8.16	8.08	8.02	7.81	7.71	7.67	7.65
700	10.34	10.11	9.92	9.76	9.63	9.52	9.43	9.35	9.11	9.00	8.95	8.92
800	11.82	11.56	11.34	11.16	11.01	10.88	10.78	10.69	10.41	10.28	10.22	10.20
900	13.30	13.00	12.76	12.55	12.38	12.24	12.12	12.02	11.71	11.57	11.50	11.47
1000	14.77	14.44	14.17	13.95	13.76	13.60	13.47	13.36	13.01	12.85	12.78	12.74
2000	29.54	28.88	28.34	27.89	27.51	27.20	26.93	26.71	26.01	25.69	25.55	25.48
3000	44.31	43.32	42.51	41.83	41.27	40.80	40.40	40.06	39.01	38.54	38.32	38.22
4000	59.08	57.76	56.67	55.77	55.02	54.39	53.86	53.42	52.02	51.38	51.09	50.96
5000	73.84	72.20	70.84	69.72	68.78	67.99	67.33	66.77	65.02	64.23	63.86	63.70
6000	88.61	86.64	85.01	83.66	82.53	81.59	80.79	80.12	78.02	77.07	76.64	76.43
7000	103.38	101.08	99.18	97.60	96.29	95.19	94.26	93.48	91.02	89.92	89.41	89.17
8000	118.15	115.52	113.34	111.54	110.04	108.78	107.72	106.83	104.03	102.76	102.18	101.91
9000	132.92	129.95	127.51	125.49	123.80	122.38	121.19	120.18	117.03	115.61	114.95	114.65
10000	147.68	144.39	141.68	139.43	137.55	135.98	134.65	133.53	130.03	128.45	127.72	127.39
11000	162.45	158.83	155.85	153.37	151.31	149.57	148.12	146.89	143.03	141.30	140.50	140.12
12000	177.22	173.27	170.01	167.31	165.06	163.17	161.58	160.24	156.04	154.14	153.27	152.86
13000	191.99	187.71	184.18	181.26	178.81	176.77	175.05	173.59	169.04	166.98	166.04	165.60
14000	206.75	202.15	198.35	195.20	192.57	190.37	188.51	186.95	182.04	179.83	178.81	178.34
15000	221.52	216.59	212.52	209.14	206.32	203.96	201.98	200.30	195.04	192.67	191.58	191.08
16000	236.29	231.03	226.68	223.08	220.08	217.56	215.44	213.65	208.05	205.52	204.35	203.81
17000	251.06	245.46	240.85	237.03	233.83	231.16	228.91	227.01	221.05	218.36	217.13	216.55
18000	265.83	259.90	255.02	250.97	247.59	244.75	242.37	240.36	234.05	231.21	229.90	229.29
19000	280.59	274.34	269.19	264.91	261.34	258.35	255.84	253.71	247.05	244.05	242.67	242.03
20000	295.36	288.78	283.35	278.85	275.10	271.95	269.30	267.06	260.06	256.90	255.44	254.77
21000	310.13	303.22	297.52	292.80	288.85	285.55	282.76	280.42	273.06	269.74	268.21	267.50
22000	324.90	317.66	311.69	306.74	302.61	299.14	296.23	293.77	286.06	282.59	280.99	280.24
23000	339.66	332.10	325.86	320.68	316.36	312.74	309.69	307.12	299.06	295.43	293.76	292.98
24000	354.43	346.54	340.02	334.62	330.11	326.34	323.16	320.48	312.07	308.28	306.53	305.72
25000	369.20	360.97	354.19	348.56	343.87	339.93	336.62	333.83	325.07	321.12	319.30	318.46
26000	383.97	375.41	368.36	362.51	357.62	353.53	350.09	347.18	338.07	333.96	332.07	331.19
27000	398.74	389.85	382.53	376.45	371.38	367.13	363.55	360.54	351.07	346.81	344.84	343.93
28000	413.50	404.29	396.69	390.39	385.13	380.73	377.02	373.89	364.08	359.65	357.62	356.67
29000	428.27	418.73	410.86	404.33	398.89	394.32	390.48	387.24	377.08	372.50	370.39	369.41
30000	443.04	433.17	425.03	418.28	412.64	407.92	403.95	400.59	390.08	385.34	383.16	382.15
31000	457.81	447.61	439.20	432.22	426.40	421.52	417.41	413.95	403.09	398.19	395.93	394.88
32000	472.57	462.05	453.36	446.16	440.15	435.11	430.88	427.30	416.09	411.03	408.70	407.62
33000	487.34	476.48	467.53	460.10	453.91	448.71	444.34	440.65	429.09	423.88	421.48	420.36
34000	502.11	490.92	481.70	474.05	467.66	462.31	457.81	454.01	442.09	436.72	434.25	433.10
35000	516.88	505.36	495.87	487.99	481.42	475.91	471.27	467.36	455.10	449.57	447.02	445.84
37500	553.80	541.46	531.29	522.84	515.80	509.90	504.93	500.74	487.60	481.68	478.95	477.68
40000	590.72	577.56	566.70	557.70	550.19	543.89	538.59	534.12	520.11	513.79	510.88	509.53
42500	627.64	613.65	602.12	592.56	584.57	577.88	572.26	567.51	552.61	545.90	542.81	541.37
45000	664.56	649.75	637.54	627.41	618.96	611.88	605.92	600.89	585.12	578.01	574.74	573.22
47500	701.47	685.85	672.96	662.27	653.35	645.87	639.58	634.27	617.63	610.12	606.67	605.06
50000	738.39	721.94	708.38	697.12	687.73	679.86	673.24	667.65	650.13	642.23	638.60	636.91
52500	775.31	758.04	743.80	731.98	722.12	713.86	706.90	701.04	682.64	674.35	670.53	668.75
55000	812.23	794.14	779.22	766.84	756.51	747.85	740.57	734.42	715.15	706.46	702.46	700.60
57500	849.15	830.23	814.64	801.69	790.89	781.84	774.23	767.80	747.65	738.57	734.39	732.44
60000	886.07	866.33	850.05	836.55	825.28	815.84	807.89	801.18	780.16	770.68	766.32	764.29
65000	959.91	938.52	920.89	906.26	894.05	883.82	875.21	867.95	845.17	834.90	830.17	827.98
70000	1033.75	1010.72	991.73	975.97	962.83	951.81	942.54	934.71	910.19	899.13	894.03	891.67
75000	1107.59	1082.91	1062.57	1045.68	1031.60	1019.79	1009.86	1001.48	975.20	963.35	957.89	955.36
80000	1181.43	1155.11	1133.40	1115.40	1100.37	1087.78	1077.18	1068.24	1040.21	1027.57	1021.75	1019.05
85000	1255.27	1227.30	1204.24	1185.11	1169.14	1155.76	1144.51	1135.01	1105.22	1091.79	1085.61	1082.74
90000	1329.11	1299.49	1275.08	1254.82	1237.92	1223.75	1211.83	1201.77	1170.24	1156.02	1149.47	1146.43
95000	1402.94	1371.69	1345.92	1324.53	1306.69	1291.74	1279.16	1268.54	1235.25	1220.24	1213.33	1210.12
100000	1476.78	1443.88	1416.75	1394.24	1375.46	1359.72	1346.48	1335.30	1300.26	1284.46	1277.19	1273.81
105000	1550.62	1516.07	1487.59	1463.96	1444.24	1427.71	1413.80	1402.07	1365.28	1348.69	1341.05	1337.50
110000	1624.46	1588.27	1558.43	1533.67	1513.01	1495.69	1481.13	1468.83	1430.29	1412.91	1404.91	1401.19
115000	1698.30	1660.46	1629.27	1603.38	1581.78	1563.68	1548.45	1535.60	1495.30	1477.13	1468.77	1464.88
120000	1772.14	1732.66	1700.10	1673.09	1650.55	1631.67	1615.77	1602.36	1560.31	1541.36	1532.63	1528.57
125000	1845.98	1804.85	1770.94	1742.80	1719.33	1699.65	1683.10	1669.13	1625.33	1605.58	1596.48	1592.26
130000	1919.82	1877.04	1841.78	1812.52	1788.10	1767.64	1750.42	1735.89	1690.34	1669.80	1660.34	1655.95
135000	1993.66	1949.24	1912.62	1882.23	1856.87	1835.62	1817.75	1802.66	1755.35	1734.02	1724.20	1719.64
140000	2067.49	2021.43	1983.45	1951.94	1925.65	1903.61	1885.07	1869.42	1820.37	1798.25	1788.06	1783.33
145000	2141.33	2093.63	2054.29	2021.65	1994.42	1971.59	1952.39	1936.19	1885.38	1862.47	1851.92	1847.02
150000	2215.17	2165.82	2125.13	2091.36	2063.19	2039.58	2019.72	2002.95	1950.39	1926.69	1915.78	1910.71
155000	2289.01	2238.01	2195.97	2161.08	2131.96	2107.57	2087.04	2069.72	2015.41	1990.92	1979.64	1974.40
160000	2362.85	2310.21	2266.80	2230.79	2200.74	2175.55	2154.36	2136.48	2080.42	2055.14	2043.50	2038.09

AMOUNT OF LOAN	NUMBER OF YEARS IN TERM											
	1	2	3	4	5	6	7	8	9	10	11	12
$ 50	4.53	2.44	1.75	1.41	1.21	1.08	0.98	0.92	0.87	0.83	0.80	0.77
100	9.05	4.88	3.50	2.81	2.41	2.15	1.96	1.83	1.73	1.65	1.59	1.54
200	18.10	9.75	6.99	5.62	4.82	4.29	3.92	3.65	3.45	3.29	3.17	3.07
300	27.15	14.62	10.48	8.43	7.22	6.43	5.88	5.48	5.17	4.94	4.75	4.60
400	36.20	19.49	13.97	11.24	9.63	8.57	7.84	7.30	6.89	6.58	6.33	6.14
500	45.25	24.37	17.46	14.05	12.03	10.71	9.79	9.12	8.62	8.23	7.92	7.67
600	54.30	29.24	20.95	16.86	14.44	12.86	11.75	10.95	10.34	9.87	9.50	9.20
700	63.35	34.11	24.44	19.66	16.84	15.00	13.71	12.77	12.06	11.51	11.08	10.74
800	72.40	38.98	27.93	22.47	19.25	17.14	15.67	14.59	13.78	13.16	12.66	12.27
900	81.45	43.86	31.42	25.28	21.65	19.28	17.63	16.42	15.51	14.80	14.25	13.80
1000	90.50	48.73	34.92	28.09	24.06	21.42	19.58	18.24	17.23	16.45	15.83	15.34
2000	180.99	97.45	69.83	56.17	48.11	42.84	39.16	36.48	34.45	32.89	31.65	30.67
3000	271.49	146.18	104.74	84.26	72.16	64.26	58.74	54.71	51.68	49.33	47.48	46.00
4000	361.98	194.90	139.65	112.34	96.22	85.67	78.32	72.95	68.90	65.77	63.30	61.33
5000	452.48	243.63	174.56	140.43	120.27	107.09	97.90	91.18	86.12	82.21	79.13	76.67
6000	542.97	292.35	209.47	168.51	144.32	128.51	117.48	109.42	103.35	98.65	94.95	92.00
7000	633.47	341.08	244.38	196.60	168.38	149.93	137.05	127.66	120.57	115.09	110.78	107.33
8000	723.96	389.80	279.29	224.68	192.43	171.34	156.63	145.89	137.79	131.53	126.60	122.66
9000	814.45	438.53	314.20	252.77	216.48	192.76	176.21	164.13	155.02	147.97	142.43	137.99
10000	904.95	487.25	349.11	280.85	240.54	214.18	195.79	182.36	172.24	164.42	158.25	153.33
11000	995.44	535.97	384.02	308.94	264.59	235.60	215.37	200.60	189.46	180.86	174.08	168.66
12000	1085.94	584.70	418.93	337.02	288.64	257.01	234.95	218.84	206.69	197.30	189.90	183.99
13000	1176.43	633.42	453.84	365.11	312.70	278.43	254.52	237.07	223.91	213.74	205.73	199.32
14000	1266.93	682.15	488.75	393.19	336.75	299.85	274.10	255.31	241.13	230.18	221.55	214.65
15000	1357.42	730.87	523.67	421.28	360.80	321.27	293.68	273.54	258.36	246.62	237.38	229.99
16000	1447.92	779.60	558.58	449.36	384.86	342.68	313.26	291.78	275.58	263.06	253.20	245.32
17000	1538.41	828.32	593.49	477.45	408.91	364.10	332.84	310.02	292.80	279.50	269.03	260.65
18000	1628.90	877.05	628.40	505.53	432.96	385.52	352.42	328.25	310.03	295.94	284.85	275.98
19000	1719.40	925.77	663.31	533.62	457.02	406.94	371.99	346.49	327.25	312.39	300.68	291.31
20000	1809.89	974.50	698.22	561.70	481.07	428.35	391.57	364.72	344.48	328.83	316.50	306.65
21000	1900.39	1023.22	733.13	589.79	505.12	449.77	411.15	382.96	361.70	345.27	332.32	321.98
22000	1990.88	1071.94	768.04	617.87	529.18	471.19	430.73	401.20	378.92	361.71	348.15	337.31
23000	2081.38	1120.67	802.95	645.96	553.23	492.61	450.31	419.43	396.15	378.15	363.97	352.64
24000	2171.87	1169.39	837.86	674.04	577.28	514.02	469.89	437.67	413.37	394.59	379.80	367.97
25000	2262.37	1218.12	872.77	702.13	601.33	535.44	489.46	455.90	430.59	411.03	395.62	383.31
26000	2352.86	1266.84	907.68	730.21	625.39	556.86	509.04	474.14	447.82	427.47	411.45	398.64
27000	2443.35	1315.57	942.59	758.30	649.44	578.28	528.62	492.37	465.04	443.91	427.27	413.97
28000	2533.85	1364.29	977.50	786.38	673.49	599.69	548.20	510.61	482.26	460.35	443.10	429.30
29000	2624.34	1413.02	1012.41	814.47	697.55	621.11	567.78	528.85	499.49	476.80	458.92	444.63
30000	2714.84	1461.74	1047.33	842.55	721.60	642.53	587.36	547.08	516.71	493.24	474.75	459.97
31000	2805.33	1510.47	1082.24	870.64	745.65	663.95	606.93	565.32	533.93	509.68	490.57	475.30
32000	2895.83	1559.19	1117.15	898.72	769.71	685.36	626.51	583.55	551.16	526.12	506.40	490.63
33000	2986.32	1607.91	1152.06	926.81	793.76	706.78	646.09	601.79	568.38	542.56	522.22	505.96
34000	3076.82	1656.64	1186.97	954.89	817.81	728.20	665.67	620.03	585.60	559.00	538.05	521.29
35000	3167.31	1705.36	1221.88	982.98	841.87	749.62	685.25	638.26	602.83	575.44	553.87	536.63
37500	3393.55	1827.18	1309.16	1053.19	902.00	803.16	734.19	683.85	645.89	616.54	593.43	574.96
40000	3619.78	1948.99	1396.43	1123.40	962.13	856.70	783.14	729.44	688.95	657.65	632.99	613.29
42500	3846.02	2070.80	1483.71	1193.61	1022.27	910.25	832.08	775.03	732.00	698.75	672.56	651.62
45000	4072.25	2192.61	1570.99	1263.82	1082.40	963.79	881.03	820.62	775.06	739.85	712.12	689.95
47500	4298.49	2314.42	1658.26	1334.04	1142.53	1017.34	929.98	866.21	818.12	780.96	751.68	728.28
50000	4524.73	2436.23	1745.54	1404.25	1202.66	1070.88	978.92	911.80	861.18	822.06	791.24	766.61
52500	4750.96	2558.04	1832.82	1474.46	1262.80	1124.42	1027.87	957.39	904.24	863.16	830.80	804.94
55000	4977.20	2679.85	1920.09	1544.67	1322.93	1177.97	1076.81	1002.98	947.30	904.26	870.37	843.27
57500	5203.43	2801.67	2007.37	1614.88	1383.06	1231.51	1125.76	1048.57	990.36	945.37	909.93	881.60
60000	5429.67	2923.48	2094.65	1685.10	1443.20	1285.05	1174.71	1094.16	1033.42	986.47	949.49	919.93
65000	5882.14	3167.10	2269.20	1825.52	1563.46	1392.14	1272.60	1185.34	1119.53	1068.67	1028.61	996.59
70000	6334.61	3410.72	2443.75	1965.95	1683.73	1499.23	1370.49	1276.52	1205.65	1150.88	1107.74	1073.25
75000	6787.09	3654.35	2618.31	2106.37	1803.99	1606.32	1468.38	1367.70	1291.77	1233.08	1186.86	1149.91
80000	7239.56	3897.97	2792.86	2246.79	1924.26	1713.40	1566.27	1458.88	1377.89	1315.29	1265.98	1226.57
85000	7692.03	4141.59	2967.41	2387.22	2044.53	1820.49	1664.16	1550.06	1464.00	1397.49	1345.11	1303.23
90000	8144.50	4385.21	3141.97	2527.64	2164.79	1927.58	1762.06	1641.24	1550.12	1479.70	1424.23	1379.89
95000	8596.97	4628.84	3316.52	2668.07	2285.06	2034.67	1859.95	1732.42	1636.24	1561.91	1503.36	1456.55
100000	9049.45	4872.46	3491.07	2808.49	2405.32	2141.75	1957.84	1823.60	1722.36	1644.11	1582.48	1533.21
105000	9501.92	5116.08	3665.63	2948.92	2525.59	2248.84	2055.73	1914.78	1808.48	1726.32	1661.60	1609.87
110000	9954.39	5359.70	3840.18	3089.34	2645.86	2355.93	2153.62	2005.96	1894.59	1808.52	1740.73	1686.53
115000	10406.86	5603.33	4014.73	3229.76	2766.12	2463.02	2251.51	2097.14	1980.71	1890.73	1819.85	1763.19
120000	10859.33	5846.95	4189.29	3370.19	2886.39	2570.10	2349.41	2188.32	2066.83	1972.93	1898.97	1839.85
125000	11311.81	6090.57	4363.84	3510.61	3006.65	2677.19	2447.30	2279.50	2152.95	2055.14	1978.10	1916.51
130000	11764.28	6334.20	4538.39	3651.04	3126.92	2784.28	2545.19	2370.67	2239.06	2137.34	2057.22	1993.17
135000	12216.75	6577.82	4712.95	3791.46	3247.19	2891.37	2643.08	2461.85	2325.18	2219.55	2136.35	2069.83
140000	12669.22	6821.44	4887.50	3931.89	3367.45	2998.45	2740.97	2553.03	2411.30	2301.75	2215.47	2146.49
145000	13121.70	7065.06	5062.05	4072.31	3487.72	3105.54	2838.87	2644.21	2497.42	2383.96	2294.59	2223.15
150000	13574.17	7308.69	5236.61	4212.73	3607.98	3212.63	2936.76	2735.39	2583.53	2466.16	2373.72	2299.81
155000	14026.64	7552.31	5411.16	4353.16	3728.25	3319.72	3034.65	2826.57	2669.65	2548.37	2452.84	2376.47
160000	14479.11	7795.93	5585.71	4493.58	3848.52	3426.80	3132.54	2917.75	2755.77	2630.57	2531.96	2453.13

AMOUNT OF LOAN	NUMBER OF YEARS IN TERM											
	13	14	15	16	17	18	19	20	25	30	35	40
$ 50	0.75	0.74	0.72	0.71	0.70	0.69	0.69	0.68	0.66	0.66	0.65	0.65
100	1.50	1.47	1.44	1.42	1.40	1.38	1.37	1.36	1.32	1.31	1.30	1.30
200	2.99	2.93	2.87	2.83	2.79	2.76	2.73	2.71	2.64	2.61	2.60	2.59
300	4.49	4.39	4.31	4.24	4.18	4.14	4.10	4.07	3.96	3.92	3.90	3.89
400	5.98	5.85	5.74	5.65	5.58	5.52	5.46	5.42	5.28	5.22	5.20	5.18
500	7.47	7.31	7.17	7.06	6.97	6.89	6.83	6.77	6.60	6.53	6.49	6.48
600	8.97	8.77	8.61	8.48	8.36	8.27	8.19	8.13	7.92	7.83	7.79	7.77
700	10.46	10.23	10.04	9.89	9.76	9.65	9.56	9.48	9.24	9.14	9.09	9.07
800	11.95	11.69	11.48	11.30	11.15	11.03	10.92	10.84	10.56	10.44	10.39	10.36
900	13.45	13.15	12.91	12.71	12.54	12.41	12.29	12.19	11.88	11.75	11.68	11.65
1000	14.94	14.61	14.34	14.12	13.94	13.78	13.65	13.54	13.20	13.05	12.98	12.95
2000	29.87	29.22	28.68	28.24	27.87	27.56	27.30	27.08	26.40	26.10	25.96	25.89
3000	44.81	43.83	43.02	42.36	41.80	41.34	40.95	40.62	39.60	39.14	38.93	38.84
4000	59.74	58.44	57.36	56.48	55.74	55.12	54.60	54.16	52.79	52.19	51.91	51.78
5000	74.67	73.04	71.70	70.59	69.67	68.90	68.25	67.70	65.99	65.23	64.88	64.72
6000	89.61	87.65	86.04	84.71	83.60	82.67	81.89	81.24	79.19	78.28	77.86	77.67
7000	104.54	102.26	100.38	98.83	97.54	96.45	95.54	94.78	92.39	91.32	90.84	90.61
8000	119.47	116.87	114.72	112.95	111.47	110.23	109.19	108.32	105.58	104.37	103.81	103.56
9000	134.41	131.48	129.06	127.07	125.40	124.01	122.84	121.85	118.78	117.41	116.79	116.50
10000	149.34	146.08	143.40	141.18	139.33	137.79	136.49	135.39	131.98	130.46	129.76	129.44
11000	164.27	160.69	157.74	155.30	153.27	151.57	150.14	148.93	145.18	143.50	142.74	142.39
12000	179.21	175.30	172.08	169.42	167.20	165.34	163.78	162.47	158.37	156.55	155.72	155.33
13000	194.14	189.91	186.42	183.54	181.13	179.12	177.43	176.01	171.57	169.59	168.69	168.28
14000	209.07	204.52	200.76	197.66	195.07	192.90	191.08	189.55	184.77	182.64	181.67	181.22
15000	224.01	219.12	215.10	211.77	209.00	206.68	204.73	203.09	197.97	195.68	194.64	194.16
16000	238.94	233.73	229.44	225.89	222.93	220.46	218.38	216.63	211.16	208.73	207.62	207.11
17000	253.87	248.34	243.78	240.01	236.86	234.23	232.03	230.16	224.36	221.77	220.59	220.05
18000	268.81	262.95	258.12	254.13	250.80	248.01	245.67	243.70	237.56	234.82	233.57	233.00
19000	283.74	277.56	272.46	268.24	264.73	261.79	259.32	257.24	250.76	247.86	246.55	245.94
20000	298.67	292.16	286.80	282.36	278.66	275.57	272.97	270.78	263.95	260.91	259.52	258.88
21000	313.61	306.77	301.14	296.48	292.60	289.35	286.62	284.32	277.15	273.95	272.50	271.83
22000	328.54	321.38	315.48	310.60	306.53	303.13	300.27	297.86	290.35	287.00	285.47	284.77
23000	343.47	335.99	329.82	324.72	320.46	316.90	313.91	311.40	303.55	300.04	298.45	297.72
24000	358.41	350.59	344.16	338.83	334.40	330.68	327.56	324.94	316.74	313.09	311.43	310.66
25000	373.34	365.20	358.50	352.95	348.33	344.46	341.21	338.48	329.94	326.13	324.40	323.60
26000	388.27	379.81	372.84	367.07	362.26	358.24	354.86	352.01	343.14	339.18	337.38	336.55
27000	403.21	394.42	387.18	381.19	376.19	372.02	368.51	365.55	356.34	352.22	350.35	349.49
28000	418.14	409.03	401.52	395.31	390.13	385.79	382.16	379.09	369.53	365.27	363.33	362.44
29000	433.08	423.63	415.86	409.42	404.06	399.57	395.80	392.63	382.73	378.31	376.30	375.38
30000	448.01	438.24	430.20	423.54	417.99	413.35	409.45	406.17	395.93	391.36	389.28	388.32
31000	462.94	452.85	444.54	437.66	431.93	427.13	423.10	419.71	409.13	404.41	402.26	401.27
32000	477.88	467.46	458.88	451.78	445.86	440.91	436.75	433.25	422.32	417.45	415.23	414.21
33000	492.81	482.07	473.22	465.89	459.79	454.69	450.40	446.79	435.52	430.50	428.21	427.16
34000	507.74	496.67	487.56	480.01	473.72	468.46	464.05	460.32	448.72	443.54	441.18	440.10
35000	522.68	511.28	501.90	494.13	487.66	482.24	477.69	473.86	461.92	456.59	454.16	453.04
37500	560.01	547.80	537.75	529.43	522.49	516.69	511.81	507.71	494.91	489.20	486.60	485.40
40000	597.34	584.32	573.60	564.72	557.32	551.13	545.94	541.56	527.90	521.81	519.04	517.76
42500	634.68	620.84	609.45	600.01	592.15	585.58	580.06	575.40	560.90	554.42	551.48	550.12
45000	672.01	657.36	645.30	635.31	626.99	620.02	614.18	609.25	593.89	587.04	583.92	582.48
47500	709.34	693.88	681.15	670.60	661.82	654.47	648.30	643.10	626.88	619.65	616.36	614.84
50000	746.68	730.40	717.00	705.90	696.65	688.91	682.42	676.95	659.88	652.26	648.80	647.20
52500	784.01	766.92	752.85	741.19	731.48	723.36	716.54	710.79	692.87	684.88	681.24	679.56
55000	821.35	803.44	788.70	776.49	766.32	757.81	750.66	744.64	725.86	717.49	713.68	711.92
57500	858.68	839.96	824.55	811.78	801.15	792.25	784.78	778.49	758.86	750.10	746.12	744.28
60000	896.01	876.48	860.40	847.08	835.98	826.70	818.90	812.33	791.85	782.72	778.56	776.64
65000	970.68	949.52	932.10	917.67	905.65	895.59	887.14	880.03	857.84	847.94	843.44	841.36
70000	1045.35	1022.56	1003.80	988.26	975.31	964.48	955.38	947.72	923.83	913.17	908.31	906.08
75000	1120.01	1095.60	1075.50	1058.85	1044.97	1033.37	1023.62	1015.42	989.81	978.39	973.19	970.80
80000	1194.68	1168.64	1147.20	1129.43	1114.64	1102.26	1091.87	1083.11	1055.80	1043.62	1038.07	1035.52
85000	1269.35	1241.68	1218.90	1200.02	1184.30	1171.15	1160.11	1150.80	1121.79	1108.84	1102.95	1100.24
90000	1344.02	1314.72	1290.60	1270.61	1253.97	1240.04	1228.35	1218.50	1187.78	1174.07	1167.83	1164.96
95000	1418.68	1387.76	1362.30	1341.20	1323.63	1308.93	1296.59	1286.19	1253.76	1239.30	1232.71	1229.68
100000	1493.35	1460.79	1434.00	1411.79	1393.30	1377.82	1364.83	1353.89	1319.75	1304.52	1297.59	1294.40
105000	1568.02	1533.83	1505.69	1482.38	1462.96	1446.72	1433.07	1421.58	1385.74	1369.75	1362.47	1359.12
110000	1642.69	1606.87	1577.39	1552.97	1532.63	1515.61	1501.31	1489.27	1451.72	1434.97	1427.35	1423.84
115000	1717.35	1679.91	1649.09	1623.56	1602.29	1584.50	1569.55	1556.97	1517.71	1500.20	1492.23	1488.56
120000	1792.02	1752.95	1720.79	1694.15	1671.96	1653.39	1637.80	1624.66	1583.70	1565.43	1557.11	1553.28
125000	1866.69	1825.99	1792.49	1764.74	1741.62	1722.28	1706.04	1692.36	1649.69	1630.65	1621.99	1618.00
130000	1941.35	1899.03	1864.19	1835.33	1811.29	1791.17	1774.28	1760.05	1715.67	1695.88	1686.87	1682.72
135000	2016.02	1972.07	1935.89	1905.92	1880.95	1860.06	1842.52	1827.74	1781.66	1761.10	1751.74	1747.44
140000	2090.69	2045.11	2007.59	1976.51	1950.61	1928.95	1910.76	1895.44	1847.65	1826.33	1816.62	1812.16
145000	2165.36	2118.15	2079.29	2047.10	2020.28	1997.84	1979.00	1963.13	1913.64	1891.55	1881.50	1876.88
150000	2240.02	2191.19	2150.99	2117.69	2089.94	2066.73	2047.24	2030.83	1979.62	1956.78	1946.38	1941.60
155000	2314.69	2264.23	2222.69	2188.27	2159.61	2135.63	2115.49	2098.52	2045.61	2022.01	2011.26	2006.32
160000	2389.36	2337.27	2294.39	2258.86	2229.27	2204.52	2183.73	2166.21	2111.60	2087.23	2076.14	2071.04

15.75% MONTHLY AMORTIZING PAYMENTS

AMOUNT OF LOAN	NUMBER OF YEARS IN TERM											
	1	2	3	4	5	6	7	8	9	10	11	12
$ 50	4.54	2.45	1.76	1.42	1.21	1.08	0.99	*0.92	0.87	0.83	0.80	0.78
100	9.07	4.89	3.51	2.83	2.42	2.16	1.98	1.84	1.74	1.66	1.60	1.55
200	18.13	9.77	7.01	5.65	4.84	4.32	3.95	3.68	3.48	3.32	3.20	3.10
300	27.19	14.66	10.52	8.47	7.26	6.47	5.92	5.52	5.22	4.98	4.80	4.65
400	36.25	19.54	14.02	11.29	9.68	8.63	7.89	7.36	6.95	6.64	6.40	6.20
500	45.31	24.43	17.52	14.11	12.10	10.78	9.86	9.20	8.69	8.30	8.00	7.75
600	54.37	29.31	21.03	16.93	14.52	12.94	11.84	11.03	10.43	9.96	9.60	9.30
700	63.43	34.20	24.53	19.75	16.93	15.09	13.81	12.87	12.17	11.62	11.19	10.85
800	72.50	39.08	28.03	22.57	19.35	17.25	15.78	14.71	13.90	13.28	12.79	12.40
900	81.56	43.96	31.54	25.40	21.77	19.40	17.75	16.55	15.64	14.94	14.39	13.95
1000	90.62	48.85	35.04	28.22	24.19	21.56	19.72	18.39	17.38	16.60	15.99	15.50
2000	181.23	97.69	70.07	56.43	48.38	43.11	39.44	36.77	34.75	33.20	31.97	30.99
3000	271.84	146.54	105.11	84.65	72.56	64.67	59.16	55.15	52.13	49.79	47.96	46.49
4000	362.46	195.38	140.14	112.85	96.75	86.22	78.88	73.53	69.50	66.39	63.94	61.98
5000	453.07	244.22	175.17	141.07	120.93	107.78	98.60	91.92	86.88	82.98	79.92	77.48
6000	543.68	293.07	210.21	169.28	145.12	129.33	118.32	110.30	104.25	99.58	95.91	92.97
7000	634.29	341.91	245.24	197.49	169.30	150.89	138.04	128.68	121.62	116.18	111.89	108.47
8000	724.91	390.75	280.27	225.70	193.49	172.44	157.76	147.06	139.00	132.77	127.87	123.96
9000	815.52	439.60	315.31	253.92	217.67	193.99	177.48	165.44	156.37	149.37	143.86	139.46
10000	906.13	488.44	350.34	282.13	241.86	215.55	197.20	183.83	173.75	165.96	159.84	154.95
11000	996.74	537.29	385.38	310.34	266.04	237.10	216.92	202.21	191.12	182.56	175.82*	170.45
12000	1087.36	586.13	420.41	338.55	290.23	258.66	236.64	220.59	208.49	199.16	191.81	185.94
13000	1177.97	634.97	455.44	366.77	314.42	280.21	256.36	238.97	225.87	215.75	207.79	201.44
14000	1268.58	683.82	490.48	394.98	338.60	301.77	276.08	257.35	243.24	232.35	223.78	216.93
15000	1359.19	732.66	525.51	423.19	362.79	323.32	295.80	275.74	260.62	248.94	239.76	232.43
16000	1449.81	781.50	560.54	451.40	386.97	344.88	315.52	294.12	277.99	265.54	255.74	247.92
17000	1540.42	830.35	595.58	479.62	411.16	366.43	335.24	312.50	295.36	282.13	271.73	263.42
18000	1631.03	879.19	630.61	507.83	435.34	387.98	354.96	330.88	312.74	298.73	287.71	278.91
19000	1721.64	928.04	665.65	536.04	459.53	409.54	374.68	349.26	330.11	315.33	303.69	294.41
20000	1812.26	976.88	700.68	564.25	483.71	431.09	394.40	367.65	347.49	331.92	319.68	309.90
21000	1902.87	1025.72	735.71	592.47	507.90	452.65	414.12	386.03	364.86	348.52	335.66	325.40
22000	1993.48	1074.57	770.75	620.68	532.08	474.20	433.84	404.41	382.23	365.11	351.64	340.89
23000	2084.09	1123.41	805.78	648.89	556.27	495.76	453.56	422.79	399.61	381.71	367.63	356.39
24000	2174.71	1172.25	840.81	677.10	580.46	517.31	473.28	441.17	416.98	398.31	383.61	371.88
25000	2265.32	1221.10	875.85	705.32	604.64	538.87	493.00	459.56	434.36	414.90	399.60	387.37
26000	2355.93	1269.94	910.88	733.53	628.83	560.42	512.72	477.94	451.73	431.50	415.58	402.87
27000	2446.55	1318.79	945.92	761.74	653.01	581.97	532.44	496.32	469.10	448.09	431.56	418.36
28000	2537.16	1367.63	980.95	789.95	677.20	603.53	552.16	514.70	486.48	464.69	447.55	433.86
29000	2627.77	1416.47	1015.98	818.16	701.38	625.08	571.88	533.08	503.85	481.28	463.53	449.35
30000	2718.38	1465.32	1051.02	846.38	725.57	646.64	591.60	551.47	521.23	497.88	479.51	464.85
31000	2809.00	1514.16	1086.05	874.59	749.75	668.19	611.32	569.85	538.60	514.48	495.50	480.34
32000	2899.61	1563.00	1121.08	902.80	773.94	689.75	631.04	588.23	555.98	531.07	511.48	495.84
33000	2990.22	1611.85	1156.12	931.01	798.12	711.30	650.76	606.61	573.35	547.67	527.46	511.33
34000	3080.83	1660.69	1191.15	959.23	822.31	732.86	670.48	625.00	590.72	564.26	543.45	526.83
35000	3171.45	1709.54	1226.19	987.44	846.49	754.41	690.20	643.38	608.10	580.86	559.43	542.32
37500	3397.98	1831.65	1313.77	1057.97	906.96	808.30	739.50	689.33	651.53	622.35	599.39	581.06
40000	3624.51	1953.75	1401.35	1128.50	967.42	862.18	788.80	735.29	694.97	663.84	639.35	619.80
42500	3851.04	2075.86	1488.94	1199.03	1027.89	916.07	838.10	781.24	738.40	705.33	679.31	658.53
45000	4077.57	2197.97	1576.52	1269.56	1088.35	969.95	887.40	827.20	781.84	746.82	719.27	697.27
47500	4304.10	2320.08	1664.11	1340.09	1148.81	1023.84	936.70	873.15	825.27	788.31	759.23	736.01
50000	4530.63	2442.19	1751.69	1410.63	1209.28	1077.73	986.00	919.11	868.71	829.80	799.19	774.74
52500	4757.17	2564.30	1839.28	1481.16	1269.74	1131.61	1035.30	965.06	912.14	871.29	839.14	813.48
55000	4983.70	2686.41	1926.86	1551.69	1330.20	1185.50	1084.60	1011.02	955.58	912.78	879.10	852.22
57500	5210.23	2808.52	2014.44	1622.22	1390.67	1239.38	1133.90	1056.97	999.01	954.27	919.06	890.96
60000	5436.76	2930.63	2102.03	1692.75	1451.13	1293.27	1183.20	1102.93	1042.45	995.76	959.02	929.69
65000	5889.82	3174.85	2277.20	1833.81	1572.06	1401.04	1281.80	1194.84	1129.32	1078.74	1038.94	1007.17
70000	6342.89	3419.07	2452.37	1974.87	1692.98	1508.82	1380.40	1286.75	1216.19	1161.71	1118.86	1084.64
75000	6795.95	3663.29	2627.53	2115.94	1813.91	1616.59	1479.00	1378.66	1303.06	1244.69	1198.78	1162.11
80000	7249.01	3907.50	2802.70	2257.00	1934.84	1724.36	1577.60	1470.57	1389.93	1327.67	1278.69	1239.59
85000	7702.08	4151.72	2977.87	2398.06	2055.77	1832.13	1676.20	1562.48	1476.80	1410.65	1358.61	1317.06
90000	8155.14	4395.94	3153.04	2539.12	2176.69	1939.90	1774.80	1654.39	1563.67	1493.63	1438.53	1394.54
95000	8608.20	4640.16	3328.21	2680.18	2297.62	2047.68	1873.40	1746.30	1650.54	1576.61	1518.45	1472.01
100000	9061.26	4884.38	3503.38	2821.25	2418.55	2155.45	1972.00	1838.21	1737.41	1659.59	1598.37	1549.48
105000	9514.33	5128.60	3678.55	2962.31	2539.47	2263.22	2070.60	1930.12	1824.28	1742.57	1678.28	1626.96
110000	9967.39	5372.82	3853.72	3103.37	2660.40	2370.99	2169.20	2022.03	1911.15	1825.55	1758.20	1704.43
115000	10420.45	5617.04	4028.88	3244.43	2781.33	2478.76	2267.80	2113.94	1998.02	1908.53	1838.12	1781.91
120000	10873.52	5861.25	4204.05	3385.49	2902.26	2586.54	2366.40	2205.85	2084.89	1991.51	1918.04	1859.38
125000	11326.58	6105.47	4379.22	3526.56	3023.18	2694.31	2465.00	2297.76	2171.76	2074.49	1997.96	1936.85
130000	11779.64	6349.69	4554.39	3667.62	3144.11	2802.08	2563.60	2389.67	2258.63	2157.47	2077.87	2014.33
135000	12232.71	6593.91	4729.56	3808.68	3265.04	2909.85	2662.20	2481.58	2345.50	2240.44	2157.79	2091.80
140000	12685.77	6838.13	4904.73	3949.74	3385.96	3017.63	2760.80	2573.49	2432.38	2323.42	2237.71	2169.27
145000	13138.83	7082.35	5079.90	4090.80	3506.89	3125.40	2859.40	2665.40	2519.25	2406.40	2317.63	2246.75
150000	13591.89	7326.57	5255.06	4231.87	3627.82	3233.17	2958.00	2757.31	2606.12	2489.38	2397.55	2324.22
155000	14044.96	7570.79	5430.23	4372.93	3748.75	3340.94	3056.60	2849.22	2692.99	2572.36	2477.46	2401.70
160000	14498.02	7815.00	5605.40	4513.99	3869.67	3448.71	3155.20	2941.14	2779.86	2655.34	2557.38	2479.17

AMOUNT OF LOAN	NUMBER OF YEARS IN TERM											
	13	14	15	16	17	18	19	20	25	30	35	40
$ 50	0.76	0.74	0.73	0.72	0.71	0.70	0.70	0.69	0.67	0.67	0.66	0.66
100	1.51	1.48	1.46	1.43	1.42	1.40	1.39	1.38	1.34	1.33	1.32	1.32
200	3.02	2.96	2.91	2.86	2.83	2.80	2.77	2.75	2.68	2.65	2.64	2.64
300	4.53	4.44	4.36	4.29	4.24	4.19	4.15	4.12	4.02	3.98	3.96	3.95
400	6.04	5.92	5.81	5.72	5.65	5.59	5.54	5.50	5.36	5.30	5.28	5.27
500	7.55	7.39	7.26	7.15	7.06	6.98	6.92	6.87	6.70	6.63	6.60	6.58
600	9.06	8.87	8.71	8.58	8.47	8.38	8.30	8.24	8.04	7.95	7.91	7.90
700	10.57	10.35	10.16	10.01	9.88	9.78	9.69	9.61	9.38	9.28	9.23	9.21
800	12.08	11.83	11.62	11.44	11.29	11.17	11.07	10.99	10.72	10.60	10.55	10.53
900	13.59	13.31	13.07	12.87	12.71	12.57	12.45	12.36	12.06	11.93	11.87	11.84
1000	15.10	14.78	14.52	14.30	14.12	13.96	13.84	13.73	13.40	13.25	13.19	13.16
2000	30.20	29.56	29.03	28.59	28.23	27.92	27.67	27.46	26.79	26.50	26.37	26.31
3000	45.30	44.34	43.54	42.89	42.34	41.88	41.50	41.18	40.18	39.74	39.55	39.46
4000	60.40	59.12	58.06	57.18	56.45	55.84	55.34	54.91	53.58	52.99	52.73	52.61
5000	75.50	73.89	72.57	71.48	70.57	69.80	69.17	68.63	66.97	66.24	65.91	65.76
6000	90.60	88.67	87.08	85.77	84.68	83.76	83.00	82.36	80.36	79.48	79.09	78.91
7000	105.70	103.45	101.60	100.06	98.79	97.72	96.83	96.08	93.76	92.73	92.27	92.06
8000	120.80	118.23	116.11	114.36	112.90	111.68	110.67	109.81	107.15	105.97	105.45	105.21
9000	135.90	133.01	130.62	128.65	127.01	125.64	124.50	123.53	120.54	119.22	118.63	118.36
10000	151.00	147.78	145.14	142.95	141.13	139.60	138.33	137.26	133.93	132.47	131.81	131.51
11000	166.10	162.56	159.65	157.24	155.24	153.56	152.16	150.98	147.33	145.71	144.99	144.66
12000	181.20	177.34	174.16	171.53	169.35	167.52	166.00	164.71	160.72	158.96	158.17	157.81
13000	196.30	192.12	188.68	185.83	183.46	181.48	179.83	178.43	174.11	172.21	171.35	170.96
14000	211.40	206.89	203.19	200.12	197.57	195.44	193.66	192.16	187.51	185.45	184.53	184.11
15000	226.50	221.67	217.70	214.42	211.69	209.40	207.49	205.89	200.90	198.70	197.71	197.26
16000	241.60	236.45	232.21	228.71	225.80	223.36	221.33	219.61	214.29	211.94	210.89	210.41
17000	256.70	251.23	246.73	243.00	239.91	237.32	235.16	233.34	227.68	225.19	224.07	223.56
18000	271.80	266.01	261.24	257.30	254.02	251.28	248.99	247.06	241.08	238.44	237.25	236.71
19000	286.90	280.78	275.75	271.59	268.13	265.24	262.82	260.79	254.47	251.68	250.43	249.86
20000	302.00	295.56	290.27	285.89	282.25	279.20	276.66	274.51	267.86	264.93	263.61	263.01
21000	317.10	310.34	304.78	300.18	296.36	293.16	290.49	288.24	281.26	278.17	276.79	276.16
22000	332.20	325.12	319.29	314.48	310.47	307.12	304.32	301.96	294.65	291.42	289.97	289.31
23000	347.30	339.89	333.81	328.77	324.58	321.08	318.15	315.69	308.04	304.67	303.15	302.46
24000	362.40	354.67	348.32	343.06	338.69	335.04	331.99	329.41	321.43	317.91	316.33	315.61
25000	377.50	369.45	362.83	357.36	352.81	349.00	345.82	343.14	334.83	331.16	329.51	328.76
26000	392.60	384.23	377.35	371.65	366.92	362.96	359.65	356.86	348.22	344.41	342.69	341.91
27000	407.70	399.01	391.86	385.95	381.03	376.92	373.48	370.59	361.61	357.65	355.87	355.06
28000	422.80	413.78	406.37	400.24	395.14	390.88	387.32	384.31	375.01	370.90	369.05	368.21
29000	437.90	428.56	420.88	414.53	409.25	404.84	401.15	398.04	388.40	384.14	382.23	381.36
30000	453.00	443.34	435.40	428.83	423.37	418.80	414.98	411.77	401.79	397.39	395.41	394.51
31000	468.10	458.12	449.91	443.12	437.48	432.76	428.81	425.49	415.18	410.64	408.59	407.66
32000	483.20	472.89	464.42	457.42	451.59	446.72	442.65	439.22	428.58	423.88	421.77	420.81
33000	498.30	487.67	478.94	471.71	465.70	460.68	456.48	452.94	441.97	437.13	434.95	433.96
34000	513.40	502.45	493.45	486.00	479.81	474.64	470.31	466.67	455.36	450.37	448.13	447.11
35000	528.50	517.23	507.96	500.30	493.93	488.60	484.14	480.39	468.76	463.62	461.31	460.26
37500	566.25	554.17	544.25	536.03	529.21	523.50	518.72	514.71	502.24	496.74	494.26	493.14
40000	604.00	591.12	580.53	571.77	564.50	558.40	553.31	549.02	535.72	529.85	527.21	526.01
42500	641.75	628.06	616.81	607.50	599.77	593.30	587.89	583.33	569.20	562.97	560.16	558.89
45000	679.50	665.01	653.09	643.24	635.05	628.20	622.47	617.65	602.69	596.08	593.11	591.76
47500	717.25	701.95	689.38	678.98	670.33	663.10	657.05	651.96	636.17	629.20	626.06	624.64
50000	755.00	738.90	725.66	714.71	705.61	698.00	691.63	686.27	669.65	662.31	659.01	657.51
52500	792.75	775.84	761.94	750.45	740.89	732.90	726.21	720.59	703.13	695.43	691.96	690.39
55000	830.50	812.78	798.22	786.18	776.17	767.80	760.79	754.90	736.61	728.54	724.91	723.26
57500	868.25	849.73	834.51	821.92	811.45	802.70	795.37	789.21	770.10	761.66	757.86	756.14
60000	906.00	886.67	870.79	857.65	846.73	837.60	829.96	823.53	803.58	794.78	790.81	789.01
65000	981.50	960.56	943.36	929.12	917.29	907.40	899.12	892.15	870.54	861.01	856.71	854.77
70000	1057.00	1034.45	1015.92	1000.59	987.85	977.20	968.28	960.78	937.51	927.24	922.61	920.52
75000	1132.50	1108.34	1088.49	1072.06	1058.41	1047.00	1037.44	1029.41	1004.47	993.47	988.52	986.27
80000	1208.00	1182.23	1161.05	1143.53	1128.97	1116.80	1106.61	1098.03	1071.44	1059.70	1054.42	1052.02
85000	1283.49	1256.12	1233.62	1215.00	1199.53	1186.60	1175.77	1166.66	1138.40	1125.93	1120.32	1117.77
90000	1358.99	1330.01	1306.18	1286.47	1270.09	1256.40	1244.93	1235.29	1205.37	1192.16	1186.22	1183.52
95000	1434.49	1403.90	1378.75	1357.95	1340.65	1326.20	1314.09	1303.91	1272.33	1258.39	1252.12	1249.27
100000	1509.99	1477.79	1451.31	1429.42	1411.21	1396.00	1383.26	1372.54	1339.29	1324.62	1318.02	1315.02
105000	1585.49	1551.67	1523.88	1500.89	1481.77	1465.80	1452.42	1441.17	1406.26	1390.85	1383.92	1380.77
110000	1660.99	1625.56	1596.44	1572.36	1552.33	1535.60	1521.58	1509.79	1473.22	1457.08	1449.82	1446.52
115000	1736.49	1699.45	1669.01	1643.83	1622.89	1605.40	1590.74	1578.42	1540.19	1523.31	1515.72	1512.27
120000	1811.99	1773.34	1741.57	1715.30	1693.45	1675.20	1659.91	1647.05	1607.15	1589.55	1581.62	1578.02
125000	1887.49	1847.23	1814.14	1786.77	1764.01	1745.00	1729.07	1715.67	1674.12	1655.78	1647.52	1643.77
130000	1962.99	1921.12	1886.71	1858.24	1834.57	1814.80	1798.23	1784.30	1741.08	1722.01	1713.42	1709.53
135000	2038.49	1995.01	1959.27	1929.71	1905.13	1884.60	1867.39	1852.93	1808.05	1788.24	1779.32	1775.28
140000	2113.99	2068.90	2031.84	2001.18	1975.69	1954.40	1936.56	1921.55	1875.01	1854.47	1845.22	1841.03
145000	2189.49	2142.79	2104.40	2072.65	2046.25	2024.20	2005.72	1990.18	1941.97	1920.70	1911.12	1906.78
150000	2264.99	2216.68	2176.97	2144.12	2116.81	2094.00	2074.88	2058.81	2008.94	1986.93	1977.03	1972.53
155000	2340.49	2290.56	2249.53	2215.59	2187.37	2163.80	2144.04	2127.43	2075.90	2053.16	2042.93	2038.28
160000	2415.99	2364.45	2322.10	2287.06	2257.93	2233.60	2213.21	2196.06	2142.87	2119.39	2108.83	2104.03

AMOUNT OF LOAN	NUMBER OF YEARS IN TERM											
	1	2	3	4	5	6	7	8	9	10	11	12
$ 50	4.54	2.45	1.76	1.42	1.22	1.09	1.00	0.93	0.88	0.84	0.81	0.79
100	9.08	4.90	3.52	2.84	2.44	2.17	1.99	1.86	1.76	1.68	1.62	1.57
200	18.15	9.80	7.04	5.67	4.87	4.34	3.98	3.71	3.51	3.36	3.23	3.14
300	27.22	14.69	10.55	8.51	7.30	6.51	5.96	5.56	5.26	5.03	4.85	4.70
400	36.30	19.59	14.07	11.34	9.73	8.68	7.95	7.42	7.02	6.71	6.46	6.27
500	45.37	24.49	17.58	14.18	12.16	10.85	9.94	9.27	8.77	8.38	8.08	7.83
600	54.44	29.38	21.10	17.01	14.60	13.02	11.92	11.12	10.52	10.06	9.69	9.40
700	63.52	34.28	24.61	19.84	17.03	15.19	13.91	12.98	12.27	11.73	11.31	10.97
800	72.59	39.18	28.13	22.68	19.46	17.36	15.89	14.83	14.03	13.41	12.92	12.53
900	81.66	44.07	31.65	25.51	21.89	19.53	17.88	16.68	15.78	15.08	14.53	14.10
1000	90.74	48.97	35.16	28.35	24.32	21.70	19.87	18.53	17.53	16.76	16.15	15.66
2000	181.47	97.93	70.32	56.69	48.64	43.39	39.73	37.06	35.06	33.51	32.29	31.32
3000	272.20	146.89	105.48	85.03	72.96	65.08	59.59	55.59	52.58	50.26	48.43	46.98
4000	362.93	195.86	140.63	113.37	97.28	86.77	79.45	74.12	70.11	67.01	64.58	62.64
5000	453.66	244.82	175.79	141.71	121.60	108.46	99.32	92.65	87.63	83.76	80.72	78.30
6000	544.39	293.78	210.95	170.05	145.91	130.16	119.18	111.18	105.16	100.51	96.86	93.95
7000	635.12	342.75	246.10	198.39	170.23	151.85	139.04	129.71	122.68	117.26	113.01	109.61
8000	725.85	391.71	281.26	226.73	194.55	173.54	158.90	148.24	140.21	134.02	129.15	125.27
9000	816.58	440.67	316.42	255.07	218.87	195.23	178.76	166.76	157.73	150.77	145.29	140.93
10000	907.31	489.64	351.58	283.41	243.19	216.92	198.63	185.29	175.26	167.52	161.44	156.59
11000	998.04	538.60	386.73	311.75	267.50	238.62	218.49	203.82	192.78	184.27	177.58	172.25
12000	1088.78	587.56	421.89	340.09	291.82	260.31	238.35	222.35	210.31	201.02	193.72	187.90
13000	1179.51	636.53	457.05	368.43	316.14	282.00	258.21	240.88	227.83	217.77	209.87	203.56
14000	1270.24	685.49	492.20	396.77	340.46	303.69	278.07	259.41	245.36	234.52	226.01	219.22
15000	1360.97	734.45	527.36	425.11	364.78	325.38	297.94	277.94	262.88	251.27	242.15	234.88
16000	1451.70	783.41	562.52	453.45	389.09	347.07	317.80	296.47	280.41	268.03	258.30	250.54
17000	1542.43	832.38	597.67	481.79	413.41	368.77	337.66	314.99	297.93	284.78	274.44	266.20
18000	1633.16	881.34	632.83	510.13	437.73	390.46	357.52	333.52	315.46	301.53	290.58	281.85
19000	1723.89	930.30	667.99	538.47	462.05	412.15	377.38	352.05	332.98	318.28	306.73	297.51
20000	1814.62	979.27	703.15	566.81	486.37	433.84	397.25	370.58	350.51	335.03	322.87	313.17
21000	1905.35	1028.23	738.30	595.15	510.68	455.53	417.11	389.11	368.04	351.78	339.01	328.83
22000	1996.08	1077.19	773.46	623.49	535.00	477.23	436.97	407.64	385.56	368.53	355.15	344.49
23000	2086.81	1126.16	808.62	651.83	559.32	498.92	456.83	426.17	403.09	385.29	371.30	360.14
24000	2177.55	1175.12	843.77	680.17	583.64	520.61	476.69	444.70	420.61	402.04	387.44	375.80
25000	2268.28	1224.08	878.93	708.51	607.96	542.30	496.56	463.22	438.14	418.79	403.58	391.46
26000	2359.01	1273.05	914.09	736.85	632.27	563.99	516.42	481.75	455.66	435.54	419.73	407.12
27000	2449.74	1322.01	949.24	765.19	656.59	585.68	536.28	500.28	473.19	452.29	435.87	422.78
28000	2540.47	1370.97	984.40	793.53	680.91	607.38	556.14	518.81	490.71	469.04	452.01	438.44
29000	2631.20	1419.94	1019.56	821.87	705.23	629.07	576.00	537.34	508.24	485.79	468.16	454.09
30000	2721.93	1468.90	1054.72	850.21	729.55	650.76	595.87	555.87	525.76	502.54	484.30	469.75
31000	2812.66	1517.86	1089.87	878.55	753.86	672.45	615.73	574.40	543.29	519.30	500.44	485.41
32000	2903.39	1566.82	1125.03	906.89	778.18	694.14	635.59	592.93	560.81	536.05	516.59	501.07
33000	2994.12	1615.79	1160.19	935.23	802.50	715.84	655.45	611.45	578.34	552.80	532.73	516.73
34000	3084.85	1664.75	1195.34	963.57	826.82	737.53	675.32	629.98	595.86	569.55	548.87	532.39
35000	3175.59	1713.71	1230.50	991.91	851.14	759.22	695.18	648.51	613.39	586.30	565.02	548.04
37500	3402.41	1836.12	1318.39	1062.77	911.93	813.45	744.83	694.83	657.20	628.18	605.37	587.19
40000	3629.24	1958.53	1406.29	1133.62	972.73	867.68	794.49	741.16	701.02	670.06	645.73	626.34
42500	3856.07	2080.94	1494.18	1204.47	1033.52	921.91	844.14	787.48	744.83	711.94	686.09	665.48
45000	4082.89	2203.34	1582.07	1275.32	1094.32	976.14	893.80	833.80	788.64	753.81	726.45	704.63
47500	4309.72	2325.75	1669.96	1346.17	1155.11	1030.37	943.45	880.12	832.45	795.69	766.81	743.77
50000	4536.55	2448.16	1757.86	1417.02	1215.91	1084.60	993.11	926.44	876.27	837.57	807.16	782.92
52500	4763.38	2570.57	1845.75	1487.87	1276.70	1138.83	1042.76	972.77	920.08	879.45	847.52	822.06
55000	4990.20	2692.98	1933.64	1558.72	1337.50	1193.06	1092.42	1019.09	963.89	921.33	887.88	861.21
57500	5217.03	2815.38	2021.53	1629.57	1398.29	1247.29	1142.07	1065.41	1007.71	963.21	928.24	900.35
60000	5443.86	2937.79	2109.43	1700.42	1459.09	1301.52	1191.73	1111.73	1051.52	1005.08	968.60	939.50
65000	5897.51	3182.61	2285.21	1842.12	1580.68	1409.97	1291.04	1204.38	1139.15	1088.84	1049.31	1017.79
70000	6351.17	3427.42	2461.00	1983.82	1702.27	1518.43	1390.35	1297.02	1226.77	1172.60	1130.03	1096.08
75000	6804.82	3672.24	2636.78	2125.53	1823.86	1626.89	1489.66	1389.66	1314.40	1256.35	1210.74	1174.37
80000	7258.47	3917.05	2812.57	2267.23	1945.45	1735.35	1588.97	1482.31	1402.03	1340.11	1291.46	1252.67
85000	7712.13	4161.87	2988.35	2408.93	2067.04	1843.81	1688.28	1574.95	1489.65	1423.87	1372.17	1330.96
90000	8165.78	4406.68	3164.14	2550.63	2188.63	1952.27	1787.59	1667.60	1577.28	1507.62	1452.89	1409.25
95000	8619.44	4651.50	3339.92	2692.33	2310.22	2060.73	1886.90	1760.24	1664.90	1591.38	1533.61	1487.54
100000	9073.09	4896.32	3515.71	2834.03	2431.81	2169.19	1986.21	1852.88	1752.53	1675.14	1614.32	1565.83
105000	9526.75	5141.13	3691.49	2975.73	2553.40	2277.65	2085.52	1945.53	1840.16	1758.89	1695.04	1644.12
110000	9980.40	5385.95	3867.28	3117.44	2674.99	2386.11	2184.83	2038.17	1927.78	1842.65	1775.75	1722.41
115000	10434.05	5630.76	4043.06	3259.14	2796.58	2494.57	2284.14	2130.82	2015.41	1926.41	1856.47	1800.70
120000	10887.71	5875.58	4218.85	3400.84	2918.17	2603.03	2383.45	2223.46	2103.04	2010.16	1937.19	1879.00
125000	11341.36	6120.39	4394.63	3542.54	3039.76	2711.49	2482.76	2316.10	2190.66	2093.92	2017.90	1957.29
130000	11795.02	6365.21	4570.42	3684.24	3161.35	2819.94	2582.07	2408.75	2278.29	2177.68	2098.62	2035.58
135000	12248.67	6610.02	4746.20	3825.94	3282.94	2928.40	2681.38	2501.39	2365.91	2261.43	2179.33	2113.87
140000	12702.33	6854.84	4921.99	3967.64	3404.53	3036.86	2780.69	2594.04	2453.54	2345.19	2260.05	2192.16
145000	13155.98	7099.66	5097.77	4109.35	3526.12	3145.32	2880.00	2686.68	2541.17	2428.95	2340.77	2270.45
150000	13609.63	7344.47	5273.56	4251.05	3647.71	3253.78	2979.31	2779.32	2628.79	2512.70	2421.48	2348.74
155000	14063.29	7589.29	5449.35	4392.75	3769.30	3362.24	3078.62	2871.97	2716.42	2596.46	2502.20	2427.03
160000	14516.94	7834.10	5625.13	4534.45	3890.89	3470.70	3177.94	2964.61	2804.05	2680.21	2582.91	2505.33

AMOUNT OF LOAN	NUMBER OF YEARS IN TERM											
	13	14	15	16	17	18	19	20	25	30	35	40
$ 50	0.77	0.75	0.74	0.73	0.72	0.71	0.71	0.70	0.68	0.68	0.67	0.67
100	1.53	1.50	1.47	1.45	1.43	1.42	1.41	1.40	1.36	1.35	1.34	1.34
200	3.06	2.99	2.94	2.90	2.86	2.83	2.81	2.79	2.72	2.69	2.68	2.68
300	4.59	4.49	4.41	4.35	4.29	4.25	4.21	4.18	4.08	4.04	4.02	4.01
400	6.11	5.98	5.88	5.79	5.72	5.66	5.61	5.57	5.44	5.38	5.36	5.35
500	7.64	7.48	7.35	7.24	7.15	7.08	7.01	6.96	6.80	6.73	6.70	6.68
600	9.17	8.97	8.82	8.69	8.58	8.49	8.42	8.35	8.16	8.07	8.04	8.02
700	10.69	10.47	10.29	10.13	10.01	9.90	9.82	9.74	9.52	9.42	9.37	9.35
800	12.22	11.96	11.75	11.58	11.44	11.32	11.22	11.14	10.88	10.76	10.71	10.69
900	13.75	13.46	13.22	13.03	12.87	12.73	12.62	12.53	12.23	12.11	12.05	12.03
1000	15.27	14.95	14.69	14.48	14.30	14.15	14.02	13.92	13.59	13.45	13.39	13.36
2000	30.54	29.90	29.38	28.95	28.59	28.29	28.04	27.83	27.18	26.90	26.77	26.72
3000	45.81	44.85	44.07	43.42	42.88	42.43	42.06	41.74	40.77	40.35	40.16	40.07
4000	61.07	59.80	58.75	57.89	57.17	56.57	56.07	55.66	54.36	53.80	53.54	53.43
5000	76.34	74.75	73.44	72.36	71.46	70.72	70.09	69.57	67.95	67.24	66.93	66.79
6000	91.61	89.70	88.13	86.83	85.76	84.86	84.11	83.48	81.54	80.69	80.31	80.14
7000	106.87	104.64	102.81	101.30	100.05	99.00	98.13	97.39	95.13	94.14	93.70	93.50
8000	122.14	119.59	117.50	115.77	114.34	113.14	112.14	111.31	108.72	107.59	107.08	106.86
9000	137.41	134.54	132.19	130.24	128.63	127.29	126.16	125.22	122.30	121.03	120.47	120.21
10000	152.68	149.49	146.88	144.72	142.92	141.43	140.18	139.13	135.89	134.48	133.85	133.57
11000	167.94	164.44	161.56	159.19	157.22	155.57	154.20	153.04	149.48	147.93	147.24	146.93
12000	183.21	179.39	176.25	173.66	171.51	169.71	168.21	166.96	163.07	161.38	160.62	160.28
13000	198.48	194.33	190.94	188.13	185.80	183.86	182.23	180.87	176.66	174.82	174.01	173.64
14000	213.74	209.28	205.62	202.60	200.09	198.00	196.25	194.78	190.25	188.27	187.39	187.00
15000	229.01	224.23	220.31	217.07	214.38	212.14	210.27	208.69	203.84	201.72	200.78	200.35
16000	244.28	239.18	235.00	231.54	228.68	226.28	224.28	222.61	217.43	215.17	214.16	213.71
17000	259.54	254.13	249.68	246.01	242.97	240.43	238.30	236.52	231.02	228.61	227.54	227.07
18000	274.81	269.08	264.37	260.48	257.26	254.57	252.32	250.43	244.60	242.06	240.93	240.42
19000	290.08	284.02	279.06	274.96	271.55	268.71	266.34	264.34	258.19	255.51	254.31	253.78
20000	305.35	298.97	293.75	289.43	285.84	282.85	280.35	278.26	271.78	268.96	267.70	267.13
21000	320.61	313.92	308.43	303.90	300.13	297.00	294.37	292.17	285.37	282.40	281.08	280.49
22000	335.88	328.87	323.12	318.37	314.43	311.14	308.39	306.08	298.96	295.85	294.47	293.85
23000	351.15	343.82	337.81	332.84	328.72	325.28	322.41	319.99	312.55	309.30	307.85	307.20
24000	366.41	358.77	352.49	347.31	343.01	339.42	336.42	333.91	326.14	322.75	321.24	320.56
25000	381.68	373.72	367.18	361.78	357.30	353.57	350.44	347.82	339.73	336.19	334.62	333.92
26000	396.95	388.66	381.87	376.25	371.59	367.71	364.46	361.73	353.32	349.64	348.01	347.27
27000	412.22	403.61	396.55	390.72	385.89	381.85	378.48	375.64	366.90	363.09	361.39	360.63
28000	427.48	418.56	411.24	405.20	400.18	395.99	392.49	389.56	380.49	376.54	374.78	373.99
29000	442.75	433.51	425.93	419.67	414.47	410.14	406.51	403.47	394.08	389.98	388.16	387.34
30000	458.02	448.46	440.62	434.14	428.76	424.28	420.53	417.38	407.67	403.43	401.55	400.70
31000	473.28	463.41	455.30	448.61	443.05	438.42	434.55	431.29	421.26	416.88	414.93	414.06
32000	488.55	478.36	469.99	463.08	457.35	452.56	448.56	445.21	434.85	430.33	428.32	427.41
33000	503.82	493.30	484.68	477.55	471.64	466.71	462.58	459.12	448.44	443.77	441.70	440.77
34000	519.08	508.25	499.36	492.02	485.93	480.85	476.60	473.03	462.03	457.22	455.08	454.13
35000	534.35	523.20	514.05	506.49	500.22	494.99	490.62	486.94	475.62	470.67	468.47	467.48
37500	572.52	560.57	550.77	542.67	535.95	530.35	525.66	521.73	509.59	504.29	501.93	500.87
40000	610.69	597.94	587.49	578.85	571.68	565.70	560.70	556.51	543.56	537.91	535.39	534.26
42500	648.85	635.31	624.20	615.03	607.41	601.06	595.75	591.29	577.53	571.53	568.85	567.66
45000	687.02	672.69	660.92	651.20	643.14	636.42	630.79	626.07	611.50	605.15	602.32	601.05
47500	725.19	710.06	697.64	687.38	678.87	671.77	665.83	660.85	645.48	638.76	635.78	634.44
50000	763.36	747.43	734.36	723.56	714.60	707.13	700.88	695.63	679.45	672.38	669.24	667.83
52500	801.52	784.80	771.07	759.74	750.33	742.48	735.92	730.41	713.42	706.00	702.70	701.22
55000	839.69	822.17	807.79	795.92	786.06	777.84	770.97	765.20	747.39	739.62	736.16	734.61
57500	877.86	859.54	844.51	832.09	821.79	813.20	806.01	799.98	781.37	773.24	769.62	768.00
60000	916.03	896.91	881.23	868.27	857.52	848.55	841.05	834.76	815.34	806.86	803.09	801.39
65000	992.36	971.65	954.66	940.63	928.98	919.27	911.14	904.32	883.28	874.10	870.01	868.18
70000	1068.70	1046.40	1028.10	1012.98	1000.44	989.98	981.23	973.88	951.23	941.33	936.93	934.96
75000	1145.03	1121.14	1101.53	1085.34	1071.90	1060.69	1051.31	1043.45	1019.17	1008.57	1003.86	1001.74
80000	1221.37	1195.88	1174.97	1157.69	1143.36	1131.40	1121.40	1113.01	1087.12	1075.81	1070.78	1068.52
85000	1297.70	1270.62	1248.40	1230.05	1214.82	1202.12	1191.49	1182.57	1155.06	1143.05	1137.70	1135.31
90000	1374.04	1345.37	1321.84	1302.40	1286.27	1272.83	1261.58	1252.14	1223.00	1210.29	1204.63	1202.09
95000	1450.37	1420.11	1395.27	1374.76	1357.73	1343.54	1331.66	1321.70	1290.95	1277.52	1271.55	1268.87
100000	1526.71	1494.85	1468.71	1447.12	1429.19	1414.25	1401.75	1391.26	1358.89	1344.76	1338.47	1335.65
105000	1603.04	1569.59	1542.14	1519.47	1500.65	1484.96	1471.84	1460.82	1426.84	1412.00	1405.40	1402.44
110000	1679.38	1644.33	1615.58	1591.83	1572.11	1555.68	1541.93	1530.39	1494.78	1479.24	1472.32	1469.22
115000	1755.72	1719.08	1689.01	1664.18	1643.57	1626.39	1612.01	1599.95	1562.73	1546.48	1539.24	1536.00
120000	1832.05	1793.82	1762.45	1736.54	1715.03	1697.10	1682.10	1669.51	1630.67	1613.71	1606.17	1602.78
125000	1908.39	1868.56	1835.88	1808.89	1786.49	1767.81	1752.19	1739.07	1698.62	1680.95	1673.09	1669.57
130000	1984.72	1943.30	1909.32	1881.25	1857.95	1838.53	1822.28	1808.64	1766.56	1748.19	1740.02	1736.35
135000	2061.06	2018.05	1982.75	1953.60	1929.41	1909.24	1892.36	1878.20	1834.50	1815.43	1806.94	1803.13
140000	2137.39	2092.79	2056.19	2025.96	2000.87	1979.95	1962.45	1947.76	1902.45	1882.66	1873.86	1869.91
145000	2213.73	2167.53	2129.62	2098.31	2072.33	2050.66	2032.54	2017.33	1970.39	1949.90	1940.79	1936.70
150000	2290.06	2242.27	2203.06	2170.67	2143.79	2121.38	2102.62	2086.89	2038.34	2017.14	2007.71	2003.48
155000	2366.40	2317.02	2276.49	2243.03	2215.25	2192.09	2172.71	2156.45	2106.28	2084.38	2074.63	2070.26
160000	2442.73	2391.76	2349.93	2315.38	2286.71	2262.80	2242.80	2226.01	2174.23	2151.62	2141.56	2137.04

MONTHLY AMORTIZING PAYMENTS

AMOUNT OF LOAN	NUMBER OF YEARS IN TERM											
	1	2	3	4	5	6	7	8	9	10	11	12
$ 50	4.55	2.46	1.77	1.43	1.23	1.10	1.01	0.94	0.89	0.85	0.82	0.80
100	9.09	4.91	3.53	2.85	2.45	2.19	2.01	1.87	1.77	1.70	1.64	1.59
200	18.17	9.82	7.06	5.70	4.90	4.37	4.01	3.74	3.54	3.39	3.27	3.17
300	27.26	14.73	10.59	8.55	7.34	6.55	6.01	5.61	5.31	5.08	4.90	4.75
400	36.34	19.64	14.12	11.39	9.79	8.74	8.01	7.48	7.08	6.77	6.53	6.33
500	45.43	24.55	17.65	14.24	12.23	10.92	10.01	9.34	8.84	8.46	8.16	7.92
600	54.51	29.45	21.17	17.09	14.68	13.10	12.01	11.21	10.61	10.15	9.79	9.50
700	63.60	34.36	24.70	19.93	17.12	15.29	14.01	13.08	12.38	11.84	11.42	11.08
800	72.68	39.27	28.23	22.78	19.57	17.47	16.01	14.95	14.15	13.53	13.05	12.66
900	81.77	44.18	31.76	25.63	22.01	19.65	18.01	16.81	15.91	15.22	14.68	14.25
1000	90.85	49.09	35.29	28.47	24.46	21.83	20.01	18.68	17.68	16.91	16.31	15.83
2000	181.70	98.17	70.57	56.94	48.91	43.66	40.01	37.36	35.36	33.82	32.61	31.65
3000	272.55	147.25	105.85	85.41	73.36	65.49	60.02	56.03	53.04	50.73	48.92	47.47
4000	363.40	196.34	141.13	113.88	97.81	87.32	80.02	74.71	70.71	67.63	65.22	63.29
5000	454.25	245.42	176.41	142.35	122.26	109.15	100.03	93.39	88.39	84.54	81.52	79.12
6000	545.10	294.50	211.69	170.82	146.71	130.98	120.03	112.06	106.07	101.45	97.83	94.94
7000	635.95	343.58	246.97	199.28	171.16	152.81	140.04	130.74	123.74	118.36	114.13	110.76
8000	726.80	392.67	282.25	227.75	195.61	174.64	160.04	149.41	141.42	135.26	130.43	126.58
9000	817.65	441.75	317.53	256.22	220.06	196.47	180.05	168.09	159.10	152.17	146.74	142.41
10000	908.50	490.83	352.81	284.69	244.52	218.30	200.05	186.77	176.78	169.08	163.04	158.23
11000	999.35	539.91	388.09	313.16	268.97	240.13	220.06	205.44	194.45	185.99	179.34	174.05
12000	1090.20	589.00	423.37	341.63	293.42	261.96	240.06	224.12	212.13	202.89	195.65	189.87
13000	1181.04	638.08	458.65	370.10	317.87	283.79	260.07	242.79	229.81	219.80	211.95	205.70
14000	1271.89	687.16	493.93	398.56	342.32	305.62	280.07	261.47	247.48	236.71	228.25	221.52
15000	1362.74	736.24	529.21	427.03	366.77	327.45	300.08	280.15	265.16	253.62	244.56	237.34
16000	1453.59	785.33	564.49	455.50	391.22	349.28	320.08	298.82	282.84	270.52	260.86	253.16
17000	1544.44	834.41	599.77	483.97	415.67	371.11	340.09	317.50	300.51	287.43	277.16	268.99
18000	1635.29	883.49	635.06	512.44	440.12	392.94	360.09	336.17	318.19	304.34	293.47	284.81
19000	1726.14	932.58	670.34	540.91	464.58	414.77	380.09	354.85	335.87	321.25	309.77	300.63
20000	1816.99	981.66	705.62	569.37	489.03	436.60	400.10	373.53	353.55	338.15	326.07	316.45
21000	1907.84	1030.74	740.90	597.84	513.48	458.43	420.10	392.20	371.22	355.06	342.38	332.28
22000	1998.69	1079.82	776.18	626.31	537.93	480.26	440.11	410.88	388.90	371.97	358.68	348.10
23000	2089.54	1128.91	811.46	654.78	562.38	502.09	460.11	429.56	406.58	388.88	374.98	363.92
24000	2180.39	1177.99	846.74	683.25	586.83	523.92	480.12	448.23	424.25	405.78	391.29	379.74
25000	2271.24	1227.07	882.02	711.72	611.28	545.75	500.12	466.91	441.93	422.69	407.59	395.57
26000	2362.08	1276.15	917.30	740.19	635.73	567.58	520.13	485.58	459.61	439.60	423.89	411.39
27000	2452.93	1325.24	952.58	768.65	660.18	589.41	540.13	504.26	477.29	456.51	440.20	427.21
28000	2543.78	1374.32	987.86	797.12	684.64	611.24	560.14	522.94	494.96	473.41	456.50	443.03
29000	2634.63	1423.40	1023.14	825.59	709.09	633.07	580.14	541.61	512.64	490.32	472.80	458.86
30000	2725.48	1472.48	1058.42	854.06	733.54	654.90	600.15	560.29	530.32	507.23	489.11	474.68
31000	2816.33	1521.57	1093.70	882.53	757.99	676.73	620.15	578.96	547.99	524.14	505.41	490.50
32000	2907.18	1570.65	1128.98	911.00	782.44	698.56	640.16	597.64	565.67	541.04	521.71	506.32
33000	2998.03	1619.73	1164.26	939.46	806.89	720.39	660.16	616.32	583.35	557.95	538.02	522.15
34000	3088.88	1668.81	1199.54	967.93	831.34	742.22	680.17	634.99	601.02	574.86	554.32	537.97
35000	3179.73	1717.90	1234.83	996.40	855.79	764.05	700.17	653.67	618.70	591.77	570.63	553.79
37500	3406.85	1840.60	1323.03	1067.57	916.92	818.62	750.18	700.36	662.89	634.03	611.38	593.35
40000	3633.97	1963.31	1411.23	1138.74	978.05	873.19	800.19	747.05	707.09	676.30	652.14	632.90
42500	3861.10	2086.02	1499.43	1209.92	1039.18	927.77	850.21	793.74	751.28	718.57	692.90	672.46
45000	4088.22	2208.72	1587.63	1281.09	1100.30	982.34	900.22	840.43	795.47	760.84	733.66	712.01
47500	4315.34	2331.43	1675.83	1352.26	1161.43	1036.92	950.23	887.12	839.67	803.11	774.42	751.57
50000	4542.47	2454.14	1764.03	1423.43	1222.56	1091.49	1000.24	933.81	883.86	845.38	815.18	791.13
52500	4769.59	2576.84	1852.24	1494.60	1283.69	1146.07	1050.25	980.50	928.05	887.65	855.94	830.68
55000	4996.71	2699.55	1940.44	1565.77	1344.81	1200.64	1100.26	1027.19	972.24	929.91	896.69	870.24
57500	5223.83	2822.26	2028.64	1636.94	1405.94	1255.21	1150.28	1073.88	1016.44	972.18	937.45	909.80
60000	5450.96	2944.96	2116.84	1708.11	1467.07	1309.79	1200.29	1120.57	1060.63	1014.45	978.21	949.35
65000	5905.20	3190.38	2293.24	1850.46	1589.33	1418.94	1300.31	1213.95	1149.01	1098.99	1059.73	1028.46
70000	6359.45	3435.79	2469.65	1992.80	1711.58	1528.09	1400.33	1307.33	1237.40	1183.53	1141.25	1107.58
75000	6813.70	3681.20	2646.05	2135.14	1833.84	1637.23	1500.36	1400.71	1325.78	1268.06	1222.76	1186.69
80000	7267.94	3926.62	2822.45	2277.48	1956.09	1746.38	1600.38	1494.09	1414.17	1352.60	1304.28	1265.80
85000	7722.19	4172.03	2998.85	2419.83	2078.35	1855.53	1700.41	1587.47	1502.55	1437.14	1385.80	1344.91
90000	8176.43	4417.44	3175.26	2562.17	2200.60	1964.68	1800.43	1680.85	1590.94	1521.67	1467.31	1424.02
95000	8630.68	4662.86	3351.66	2704.51	2322.86	2073.83	1900.45	1774.23	1679.33	1606.21	1548.83	1503.14
100000	9084.93	4908.27	3528.06	2846.85	2445.11	2182.98	2000.48	1867.61	1767.71	1690.75	1630.35	1582.25
105000	9539.17	5153.68	3704.47	2989.20	2567.37	2292.13	2100.50	1960.99	1856.10	1775.29	1711.87	1661.36
110000	9993.42	5399.10	3880.87	3131.54	2689.62	2401.27	2200.52	2054.37	1944.48	1859.82	1793.38	1740.47
115000	10447.66	5644.51	4057.27	3273.88	2811.88	2510.42	2300.55	2147.76	2032.87	1944.36	1874.90	1819.59
120000	10901.91	5889.92	4233.67	3416.22	2934.14	2619.57	2400.57	2241.14	2121.25	2028.90	1956.42	1898.70
125000	11356.16	6135.34	4410.08	3558.57	3056.39	2728.72	2500.59	2334.52	2209.64	2113.44	2037.93	1977.81
130000	11810.40	6380.75	4586.48	3700.91	3178.65	2837.87	2600.62	2427.90	2298.02	2197.97	2119.45	2056.92
135000	12264.65	6626.16	4762.88	3843.25	3300.90	2947.02	2700.64	2521.28	2386.41	2282.51	2200.97	2136.03
140000	12718.89	6871.58	4939.29	3985.59	3423.16	3056.17	2800.66	2614.66	2474.79	2367.05	2282.49	2215.15
145000	13173.14	7116.99	5115.69	4127.93	3545.41	3165.31	2900.69	2708.04	2563.18	2451.58	2364.00	2294.26
150000	13627.39	7362.40	5292.09	4270.28	3667.67	3274.46	3000.71	2801.42	2651.56	2536.12	2445.52	2373.37
155000	14081.63	7607.82	5468.50	4412.62	3789.92	3383.61	3100.74	2894.80	2739.95	2620.66	2527.04	2452.48
160000	14535.88	7853.23	5644.90	4554.96	3912.18	3492.76	3200.76	2988.18	2828.33	2705.20	2608.55	2531.60

AMOUNT OF LOAN	13	14	15	16	17	18	19	20	25	30	35	40
$ 50	0.78	0.76	0.75	0.74	0.73	0.72	0.72	0.71	0.69	0.69	0.68	0.68
100	1.55	1.52	1.49	1.47	1.45	1.44	1.43	1.42	1.38	1.37	1.36	1.36
200	3.09	3.03	2.98	2.93	2.90	2.87	2.85	2.83	2.76	2.73	2.72	2.72
300	4.64	4.54	4.46	4.40	4.35	4.30	4.27	4.24	4.14	4.10	4.08	4.07
400	6.18	6.05	5.95	5.86	5.79	5.74	5.69	5.65	5.52	5.46	5.44	5.43
500	7.72	7.56	7.44	7.33	7.24	7.17	7.11	7.06	6.90	6.83	6.80	6.79
600	9.27	9.08	8.92	8.79	8.69	8.60	8.53	8.47	8.28	8.19	8.16	8.14
700	10.81	10.59	10.41	10.26	10.14	10.03	9.95	9.88	9.65	9.56	9.52	9.50
800	12.35	12.10	11.89	11.72	11.58	11.47	11.37	11.29	11.03	10.92	10.88	10.86
900	13.90	13.61	13.38	13.19	13.03	12.90	12.79	12.70	12.41	12.29	12.24	12.21
1000	15.44	15.12	14.87	14.65	14.48	14.33	14.21	14.11	13.79	13.65	13.59	13.57
2000	30.87	30.24	29.73	29.30	28.95	28.66	28.41	28.21	27.58	27.30	27.18	27.13
3000	46.31	45.36	44.59	43.95	43.42	42.98	42.61	42.31	41.36	40.95	40.77	40.69
4000	61.74	60.48	59.45	58.60	57.89	57.31	56.82	56.41	55.15	54.60	54.36	54.26
5000	77.18	75.60	74.31	73.25	72.37	71.63	71.02	70.51	68.93	68.25	67.95	67.82
6000	92.61	90.72	89.18	87.90	86.84	85.96	85.22	84.61	82.72	81.90	81.54	81.38
7000	108.05	105.84	104.04	102.55	101.31	100.28	99.43	98.71	96.50	95.55	95.13	94.95
8000	123.48	120.96	118.90	117.20	115.78	114.61	113.63	112.81	110.29	109.20	108.72	108.51
9000	138.92	136.08	133.76	131.84	130.26	128.94	127.83	126.91	124.07	122.85	122.31	122.07
10000	154.35	151.20	148.62	146.49	144.73	143.26	142.04	141.01	137.86	136.50	135.90	135.63
11000	169.79	166.32	163.48	161.14	159.20	157.59	156.24	155.11	151.64	150.15	149.49	149.20
12000	185.22	181.44	178.35	175.79	173.67	171.91	170.44	169.21	165.43	163.80	163.08	162.76
13000	200.66	196.56	193.21	190.44	188.15	186.24	184.65	183.31	179.22	177.45	176.67	176.32
14000	216.09	211.68	208.07	205.09	202.62	200.56	198.85	197.41	193.00	191.10	190.26	189.89
15000	231.53	226.80	222.93	219.74	217.09	214.89	213.05	211.51	206.79	204.75	203.85	203.45
16000	246.96	241.92	237.79	234.39	231.56	229.22	227.25	225.61	220.57	218.39	217.44	217.01
17000	262.40	257.04	252.65	249.04	246.04	243.54	241.46	239.71	234.36	232.04	231.03	230.58
18000	277.83	272.16	267.52	263.68	260.51	257.87	255.66	253.81	248.14	245.69	244.62	244.14
19000	293.27	287.28	282.38	278.33	274.98	272.19	269.86	267.91	261.93	259.34	258.21	257.70
20000	308.70	302.40	297.24	292.98	289.45	286.52	284.07	282.01	275.71	272.99	271.79	271.26
21000	324.14	317.52	312.10	307.63	303.93	300.84	298.27	296.11	289.50	286.64	285.38	284.83
22000	339.57	332.64	326.96	322.28	318.40	315.17	312.47	310.22	303.28	300.29	298.97	298.39
23000	355.01	347.76	341.82	336.93	332.87	329.50	326.68	324.32	317.07	313.94	312.56	311.95
24000	370.44	362.88	356.69	351.58	347.34	343.82	340.88	338.42	330.85	327.59	326.15	325.52
25000	385.88	378.00	371.55	366.23	361.82	358.15	355.08	352.52	344.64	341.24	339.74	339.08
26000	401.31	393.12	386.41	380.87	376.29	372.47	369.29	366.62	358.43	354.89	353.33	352.64
27000	416.75	408.24	401.27	395.52	390.76	386.80	383.49	380.72	372.21	368.54	366.92	366.21
28000	432.18	423.36	416.13	410.17	405.23	401.12	397.69	394.82	386.00	382.19	380.51	379.77
29000	447.62	438.48	430.99	424.82	419.71	415.45	411.90	408.92	399.78	395.84	394.10	393.33
30000	463.05	453.60	445.86	439.47	434.18	429.78	426.10	423.02	413.57	409.49	407.69	406.89
31000	478.49	468.72	460.72	454.12	448.65	444.10	440.30	437.12	427.35	423.13	421.28	420.46
32000	493.92	483.84	475.58	468.77	463.12	458.43	454.50	451.22	441.14	436.78	434.87	434.02
33000	509.36	498.96	490.44	483.42	477.60	472.75	468.71	465.32	454.92	450.43	448.46	447.58
34000	524.79	514.08	505.30	498.07	492.07	487.08	482.91	479.42	468.71	464.08	462.05	461.15
35000	540.23	529.20	520.16	512.71	506.54	501.40	497.11	493.52	482.49	477.73	475.64	474.71
37500	578.82	567.00	557.32	549.34	542.72	537.22	532.62	528.77	516.96	511.86	509.61	508.62
40000	617.40	604.80	594.47	585.96	578.90	573.03	568.13	564.02	551.42	545.98	543.58	542.52
42500	655.99	642.60	631.63	622.58	615.08	608.85	603.64	599.27	585.89	580.10	577.56	576.43
45000	694.58	680.40	668.78	659.20	651.27	644.66	639.15	634.53	620.35	614.23	611.53	610.34
47500	733.16	718.20	705.93	695.82	687.45	680.48	674.65	669.78	654.81	648.35	645.51	644.25
50000	771.75	756.00	743.09	732.45	723.63	716.29	710.16	705.03	689.28	682.47	679.48	678.15
52500	810.34	793.80	780.24	769.07	759.81	752.10	745.67	740.28	723.74	716.60	713.45	712.06
55000	848.93	831.60	817.40	805.69	795.99	787.92	781.18	775.53	758.20	750.72	747.43	745.97
57500	887.51	869.40	854.55	842.31	832.17	823.73	816.68	810.78	792.67	784.84	781.40	779.88
60000	926.10	907.20	891.71	878.94	868.35	859.55	852.19	846.03	827.13	818.97	815.37	813.78
65000	1003.28	982.80	966.01	952.18	940.72	931.17	923.21	916.53	896.06	887.21	883.32	881.60
70000	1080.45	1058.39	1040.32	1025.42	1013.08	1002.80	994.22	987.04	964.98	955.46	951.27	949.41
75000	1157.63	1133.99	1114.63	1098.67	1085.44	1074.43	1065.24	1057.54	1033.91	1023.71	1019.22	1017.23
80000	1234.80	1209.59	1188.94	1171.91	1157.80	1146.06	1136.25	1128.04	1102.84	1091.95	1087.16	1085.04
85000	1311.98	1285.19	1263.25	1245.16	1230.16	1217.69	1207.27	1198.54	1171.77	1160.20	1155.11	1152.86
90000	1389.15	1360.79	1337.56	1318.40	1302.53	1289.32	1278.29	1269.05	1240.69	1228.45	1223.06	1220.67
95000	1466.32	1436.39	1411.86	1391.64	1374.89	1360.95	1349.30	1339.55	1309.62	1296.69	1291.01	1288.49
100000	1543.50	1511.99	1486.17	1464.89	1447.25	1432.57	1420.32	1410.05	1378.55	1364.94	1358.95	1356.30
105000	1620.67	1587.59	1560.48	1538.13	1519.61	1504.20	1491.33	1480.55	1447.47	1433.19	1426.90	1424.12
110000	1697.85	1663.19	1634.79	1611.38	1591.98	1575.83	1562.35	1551.06	1516.40	1501.43	1494.85	1491.93
115000	1775.02	1738.79	1709.10	1684.62	1664.34	1647.46	1633.36	1621.56	1585.33	1569.68	1562.80	1559.75
120000	1852.20	1814.39	1783.41	1757.87	1736.70	1719.09	1704.38	1692.06	1654.25	1637.93	1630.74	1627.56
125000	1929.37	1889.99	1857.72	1831.11	1809.06	1790.72	1775.39	1762.56	1723.18	1706.17	1698.69	1695.38
130000	2006.55	1965.59	1932.02	1904.35	1881.43	1862.34	1846.41	1833.06	1792.11	1774.42	1766.64	1763.19
135000	2083.72	2041.18	2006.33	1977.60	1953.79	1933.97	1917.43	1903.57	1861.04	1842.67	1834.59	1831.01
140000	2160.90	2116.78	2080.64	2050.84	2026.15	2005.60	1988.44	1974.07	1929.96	1910.91	1902.53	1898.82
145000	2238.07	2192.38	2154.95	2124.09	2098.51	2077.23	2059.46	2044.57	1998.89	1979.16	1970.48	1966.64
150000	2315.25	2267.98	2229.26	2197.33	2170.87	2148.86	2130.47	2115.07	2067.82	2047.41	2038.43	2034.45
155000	2392.42	2343.58	2303.57	2270.57	2243.24	2220.49	2201.49	2185.58	2136.74	2115.65	2106.38	2102.26
160000	2469.60	2419.18	2377.87	2343.82	2315.60	2292.12	2272.50	2256.08	2205.67	2183.90	2174.32	2170.08

MONTHLY AMORTIZING PAYMENTS

AMOUNT OF LOAN	NUMBER OF YEARS IN TERM											
	1	2	3	4	5	6	7	8	9	10	11	12
$ 50	4.55	2.47	1.78	1.43	1.23	1.10	1.01	0.95	0.90	0.86	0.83	0.80
100	9.10	4.93	3.55	2.86	2.46	2.20	2.02	1.89	1.79	1.71	1.65	1.60
200	18.20	9.85	7.09	5.72	4.92	4.40	4.03	3.77	3.57	3.42	3.30	3.20
300	27.30	14.77	10.63	8.58	7.38	6.60	6.05	5.65	5.35	5.12	4.94	4.80
400	36.39	19.69	14.17	11.44	9.84	8.79	8.06	7.53	7.14	6.83	6.59	6.40
500	45.49	24.61	17.71	14.30	12.30	10.99	10.08	9.42	8.92	8.54	8.24	8.00
600	54.59	29.53	21.25	17.16	14.76	13.19	12.09	11.30	10.70	10.24	9.88	9.60
700	63.68	34.45	24.79	20.02	17.21	15.38	14.11	13.18	12.49	11.95	11.53	11.20
800	72.78	39.37	28.33	22.88	19.67	17.58	16.12	15.06	14.27	13.66	13.18	12.79
900	81.88	44.29	31.87	25.74	22.13	19.78	18.14	16.95	16.05	15.36	14.82	14.39
1000	90.97	49.21	35.41	28.60	24.59	21.97	20.15	18.83	17.83	17.07	16.47	15.99
2000	181.94	98.41	70.81	57.20	49.17	43.94	40.30	37.65	35.66	34.13	32.93	31.98
3000	272.91	147.61	106.22	85.80	73.76	65.91	60.45	56.48	53.49	51.20	49.40	47.97
4000	363.88	196.81	141.62	114.39	98.34	87.88	80.60	75.30	71.32	68.26	65.86	63.95
5000	454.84	246.02	177.03	142.99	122.93	109.85	100.74	94.12	89.15	85.33	82.33	79.94
6000	545.81	295.22	212.43	171.59	147.51	131.81	120.89	112.95	106.98	102.39	98.79	95.93
7000	636.78	344.42	247.84	200.18	172.10	153.78	141.04	131.77	124.81	119.45	115.26	111.92
8000	727.75	393.62	283.24	228.78	196.68	175.75	161.19	150.60	142.64	136.52	131.72	127.90
9000	818.71	442.83	318.64	257.38	221.27	197.72	181.34	169.42	160.47	153.58	148.18	143.89
10000	909.68	492.03	354.05	285.98	245.85	219.69	201.48	188.24	178.30	170.65	164.65	159.88
11000	1000.65	541.23	389.45	314.57	270.43	241.65	221.63	207.07	196.13	187.71	181.11	175.87
12000	1091.62	590.43	424.86	343.17	295.02	263.62	241.78	225.89	213.96	204.78	197.58	191.85
13000	1182.58	639.64	460.26	371.77	319.60	285.59	261.93	244.72	231.79	221.84	214.04	207.84
14000	1273.55	688.84	495.67	400.36	344.19	307.56	282.08	263.54	249.62	238.90	230.51	223.83
15000	1364.52	738.04	531.07	428.96	368.77	329.53	302.22	282.36	267.45	255.97	246.97	239.82
16000	1455.49	787.24	566.48	457.56	393.36	351.49	322.37	301.19	285.28	273.03	263.44	255.80
17000	1546.45	836.44	601.88	486.15	417.94	373.46	342.52	320.01	303.11	290.10	279.90	271.79
18000	1637.42	885.65	637.28	514.75	442.53	395.43	362.67	338.84	320.94	307.16	296.36	287.78
19000	1728.39	934.85	672.69	543.35	467.11	417.40	382.81	357.66	338.77	324.23	312.83	303.76
20000	1819.36	984.05	708.09	571.95	491.70	439.37	402.96	376.48	356.59	341.29	329.29	319.75
21000	1910.33	1033.25	743.50	600.54	516.28	461.33	423.11	395.31	374.42	358.35	345.76	335.74
22000	2001.29	1082.46	778.90	629.14	540.86	483.30	443.26	414.13	392.25	375.42	362.22	351.73
23000	2092.26	1131.66	814.31	657.74	565.45	505.27	463.41	432.96	410.08	392.48	378.69	367.71
24000	2183.23	1180.86	849.71	686.33	590.03	527.24	483.55	451.78	427.91	409.55	395.15	383.70
25000	2274.20	1230.06	885.11	714.93	614.62	549.21	503.70	470.60	445.74	426.61	411.61	399.69
26000	2365.16	1279.27	920.52	743.53	639.20	571.17	523.85	489.43	463.57	443.67	428.08	415.68
27000	2456.13	1328.47	955.92	772.12	663.79	593.14	544.00	508.25	481.40	460.74	444.54	431.66
28000	2547.10	1377.67	991.33	800.72	688.37	615.11	564.15	527.08	499.23	477.80	461.01	447.65
29000	2638.07	1426.87	1026.73	829.32	712.96	637.08	584.29	545.90	517.06	494.87	477.47	463.64
30000	2729.03	1476.08	1062.14	857.92	737.54	659.05	604.44	564.72	534.89	511.93	493.94	479.63
31000	2820.00	1525.28	1097.54	886.51	762.13	681.01	624.59	583.55	552.72	529.00	510.40	495.61
32000	2910.97	1574.48	1132.95	915.11	786.71	702.98	644.74	602.37	570.55	546.06	526.87	511.60
33000	3001.94	1623.68	1168.35	943.71	811.29	724.95	664.89	621.20	588.38	563.12	543.33	527.59
34000	3092.90	1672.88	1203.75	972.30	835.88	746.92	685.03	640.02	606.21	580.19	559.79	543.57
35000	3183.87	1722.09	1239.16	1000.90	860.46	768.89	705.18	658.84	624.04	597.25	576.26	559.56
37500	3411.29	1845.09	1327.67	1072.39	921.92	823.81	755.55	705.90	668.61	639.91	617.42	599.53
40000	3638.71	1968.10	1416.18	1143.89	983.39	878.73	805.92	752.96	713.18	682.57	658.58	639.50
42500	3866.13	2091.10	1504.69	1215.38	1044.85	933.65	856.29	800.02	757.76	725.23	699.74	679.47
45000	4093.55	2214.11	1593.20	1286.87	1106.31	988.57	906.66	847.08	802.33	767.90	740.90	719.44
47500	4320.97	2337.12	1681.71	1358.36	1167.77	1043.49	957.03	894.14	846.91	810.56	782.06	759.40
50000	4548.39	2460.12	1770.22	1429.86	1229.23	1098.41	1007.40	941.20	891.48	853.22	823.22	799.37
52500	4775.81	2583.13	1858.74	1501.35	1290.69	1153.33	1057.77	988.26	936.05	895.88	864.39	839.34
55000	5003.23	2706.13	1947.25	1572.84	1352.15	1208.25	1108.14	1035.32	980.63	938.54	905.55	879.31
57500	5230.64	2829.14	2035.76	1644.33	1413.61	1263.17	1158.51	1082.38	1025.20	981.20	946.71	919.28
60000	5458.06	2952.15	2124.27	1715.83	1475.08	1318.09	1208.88	1129.44	1069.77	1023.86	987.87	959.25
65000	5912.90	3198.16	2301.29	1858.81	1598.00	1427.93	1309.62	1223.56	1158.92	1109.18	1070.19	1039.18
70000	6367.74	3444.17	2478.31	2001.80	1720.92	1537.77	1410.36	1317.68	1248.07	1194.50	1152.51	1119.12
75000	6822.58	3690.18	2655.33	2144.78	1843.84	1647.61	1511.10	1411.80	1337.22	1279.82	1234.83	1199.06
80000	7277.42	3936.19	2832.36	2287.77	1966.77	1757.45	1611.84	1505.92	1426.36	1365.14	1317.16	1278.99
85000	7732.25	4182.20	3009.38	2430.75	2089.69	1867.29	1712.58	1600.04	1515.51	1450.46	1399.48	1358.93
90000	8187.09	4428.22	3186.40	2573.74	2212.61	1977.13	1813.32	1694.16	1604.66	1535.79	1481.80	1438.87
95000	8641.93	4674.23	3363.42	2716.72	2335.53	2086.97	1914.05	1788.28	1693.81	1621.11	1564.12	1518.80
100000	9096.77	4920.24	3540.44	2859.71	2458.46	2196.81	2014.79	1882.40	1782.95	1706.43	1646.44	1598.74
105000	9551.61	5166.25	3717.47	3002.69	2581.38	2306.65	2115.53	1976.52	1872.10	1791.75	1728.77	1678.68
110000	10006.45	5412.26	3894.49	3145.68	2704.30	2416.49	2216.27	2070.64	1961.25	1877.07	1811.09	1758.61
115000	10461.28	5658.28	4071.51	3288.66	2827.22	2526.33	2317.01	2164.76	2050.40	1962.39	1893.41	1838.55
120000	10916.12	5904.29	4248.53	3431.65	2950.15	2636.17	2417.75	2258.88	2139.54	2047.71	1975.73	1918.49
125000	11370.96	6150.30	4425.55	3574.63	3073.07	2746.01	2518.49	2353.00	2228.69	2133.03	2058.05	1998.42
130000	11825.80	6396.31	4602.57	3717.62	3195.99	2855.85	2619.23	2447.12	2317.84	2218.35	2140.37	2078.36
135000	12280.64	6642.32	4779.60	3860.60	3318.92	2965.69	2719.97	2541.24	2406.99	2303.68	2222.70	2158.30
140000	12735.47	6888.33	4956.62	4003.59	3441.84	3075.53	2820.71	2635.36	2496.13	2389.00	2305.02	2238.23
145000	13190.31	7134.35	5133.64	4146.57	3564.76	3185.37	2921.45	2729.48	2585.28	2474.32	2387.34	2318.17
150000	13645.15	7380.36	5310.66	4289.56	3687.68	3295.21	3022.19	2823.60	2674.43	2559.64	2469.66	2398.11
155000	14099.99	7626.37	5487.68	4432.54	3810.61	3405.05	3122.93	2917.72	2763.57	2644.96	2551.98	2478.04
160000	14554.83	7872.38	5664.71	4575.53	3933.53	3514.89	3223.67	3011.84	2852.72	2730.28	2634.31	2557.98

AMOUNT OF LOAN	NUMBER OF YEARS IN TERM											
	13	14	15	16	17	18	19	20	25	30	35	40
$ 50	0.79	0.77	0.76	0.75	0.74	0.73	0.72	0.72	0.70	0.70	0.69	0.69
100	1.57	1.53	1.51	1.49	1.47	1.46	1.44	1.43	1.40	1.39	1.38	1.38
200	3.13	3.06	3.01	2.97	2.94	2.91	2.88	2.86	2.80	2.78	2.76	2.76
300	4.69	4.59	4.52	4.45	4.40	4.36	4.32	4.29	4.20	4.16	4.14	4.14
400	6.25	6.12	6.02	5.94	5.87	5.81	5.76	5.72	5.60	5.55	5.52	5.51
500	7.81	7.65	7.52	7.42	7.33	7.26	7.20	7.15	7.00	6.93	6.90	6.89
600	9.37	9.18	9.03	8.90	8.80	8.71	8.64	8.58	8.39	8.32	8.28	8.27
700	10.93	10.71	10.53	10.38	10.26	10.16	10.08	10.01	9.79	9.70	9.66	9.64
800	12.49	12.24	12.03	11.87	11.73	11.61	11.52	11.44	11.19	11.09	11.04	11.02
900	14.05	13.77	13.54	13.35	13.19	13.06	12.96	12.87	12.59	12.47	12.42	12.40
1000	15.61	15.30	15.04	14.83	14.66	14.51	14.39	14.29	13.99	13.86	13.80	13.77
2000	31.21	30.59	30.08	29.66	29.31	29.02	28.78	28.58	27.97	27.71	27.59	27.54
3000	46.82	45.88	45.12	44.49	43.97	43.53	43.17	42.87	41.95	41.56	41.39	41.31
4000	62.42	61.17	60.15	59.31	58.62	58.04	57.56	57.16	55.93	55.41	55.18	55.08
5000	78.02	76.46	75.19	74.14	73.27	72.55	71.95	71.45	69.92	69.26	68.98	68.85
6000	93.63	91.76	90.23	88.97	87.93	87.06	86.34	85.74	83.90	83.11	82.77	82.62
7000	109.23	107.05	105.26	103.80	102.58	101.57	100.73	100.03	97.88	96.97	96.57	96.39
8000	124.83	122.34	120.30	118.62	117.24	116.08	115.12	114.32	111.86	110.82	110.36	110.16
9000	140.44	137.63	135.34	133.45	131.89	130.59	129.51	128.61	125.85	124.67	124.16	123.93
10000	156.04	152.92	150.38	148.28	146.54	145.10	143.90	142.90	139.83	138.52	137.95	137.70
11000	171.64	168.22	165.41	163.11	161.20	159.61	158.29	157.18	153.81	152.37	151.74	151.47
12000	187.25	183.51	180.45	177.93	175.85	174.12	172.68	171.47	167.79	166.22	165.54	165.24
13000	202.85	198.80	195.49	192.76	190.50	188.63	187.07	185.76	181.78	180.07	179.33	179.01
14000	218.45	214.09	210.52	207.59	205.16	203.14	201.46	200.05	195.76	193.93	193.13	192.78
15000	234.06	229.38	225.56	222.41	219.81	217.65	215.85	214.34	209.74	207.78	206.92	206.55
16000	249.66	244.68	240.60	237.24	234.47	232.16	230.24	228.63	223.72	221.63	220.72	220.32
17000	265.27	259.97	255.64	252.07	249.12	246.67	244.63	242.92	237.71	235.48	234.51	234.09
18000	280.87	275.26	270.67	266.90	263.77	261.18	259.02	257.21	251.69	249.33	248.31	247.86
19000	296.47	290.55	285.71	281.72	278.43	275.69	273.40	271.50	265.67	263.18	262.10	261.63
20000	312.08	305.84	300.75	296.55	293.08	290.20	287.79	285.79	279.65	277.03	275.90	275.40
21000	327.68	321.14	315.78	311.38	307.73	304.71	302.18	300.07	293.64	290.89	289.69	289.17
22000	343.28	336.43	330.82	326.21	322.39	319.22	316.57	314.36	307.62	304.74	303.48	302.94
23000	358.89	351.72	345.86	341.03	337.04	333.73	330.96	328.65	321.60	318.59	317.28	316.71
24000	374.49	367.01	360.90	355.86	351.70	348.24	345.35	342.94	335.58	332.44	331.07	330.48
25000	390.09	382.30	375.93	370.69	366.35	362.75	359.74	357.23	349.57	346.29	344.87	344.24
26000	405.70	397.60	390.97	385.51	381.00	377.25	374.13	371.52	363.55	360.14	358.66	358.01
27000	421.30	412.89	406.01	400.34	395.66	391.76	388.52	385.81	377.53	373.99	372.46	371.78
28000	436.90	428.18	421.04	415.17	410.31	406.27	402.91	400.10	391.51	387.85	386.25	385.55
29000	452.51	443.47	436.08	430.00	424.96	420.78	417.30	414.39	405.50	401.70	400.05	399.32
30000	468.11	458.76	451.12	444.82	439.62	435.29	431.69	428.68	419.48	415.55	413.84	413.09
31000	483.72	474.06	466.15	459.65	454.27	449.80	446.08	442.96	433.46	429.40	427.64	426.86
32000	499.32	489.35	481.19	474.48	468.93	464.31	460.47	457.25	447.44	443.25	441.43	440.63
33000	514.92	504.64	496.23	489.31	483.58	478.82	474.86	471.54	461.43	457.10	455.22	454.40
34000	530.53	519.93	511.27	504.13	498.23	493.33	489.25	485.83	475.41	470.96	469.02	468.17
35000	546.13	535.22	526.30	518.96	512.89	507.84	503.64	500.12	489.39	484.81	482.81	481.94
37500	585.14	573.46	563.90	556.03	549.52	544.12	539.61	535.84	524.35	519.44	517.30	516.36
40000	624.15	611.68	601.49	593.10	586.16	580.39	575.58	571.57	559.30	554.06	551.79	550.79
42500	663.16	649.91	639.08	630.17	622.79	616.66	611.56	607.29	594.26	588.69	586.27	585.21
45000	702.17	688.14	676.67	667.23	659.42	652.94	647.53	643.01	629.22	623.32	620.76	619.64
47500	741.17	726.37	714.27	704.30	696.06	689.21	683.50	678.73	664.17	657.95	655.25	654.06
50000	780.18	764.60	751.86	741.37	732.69	725.49	719.48	714.46	699.13	692.58	689.73	688.48
52500	819.19	802.83	789.45	778.44	769.33	761.76	755.45	750.18	734.08	727.21	724.22	722.91
55000	858.20	841.06	827.04	815.51	805.96	798.03	791.42	785.90	769.04	761.84	758.70	757.33
57500	897.21	879.29	864.64	852.57	842.60	834.31	827.40	821.62	804.00	796.47	793.19	791.76
60000	936.22	917.52	902.23	889.64	879.23	870.58	863.37	857.35	838.95	831.09	827.68	826.18
65000	1014.24	993.98	977.42	963.78	952.50	943.13	935.32	928.79	908.86	900.35	896.65	895.03
70000	1092.25	1070.44	1052.60	1037.92	1025.77	1015.68	1007.27	1000.24	978.78	969.61	965.62	963.88
75000	1170.27	1146.90	1127.79	1112.05	1099.04	1088.23	1079.21	1071.68	1048.69	1038.87	1034.60	1032.72
80000	1248.29	1223.36	1202.97	1186.19	1172.31	1160.77	1151.16	1143.13	1118.60	1108.12	1103.57	1101.57
85000	1326.31	1299.82	1278.16	1260.33	1245.57	1233.32	1223.11	1214.57	1188.51	1177.38	1172.54	1170.42
90000	1404.33	1376.28	1353.34	1334.46	1318.84	1305.87	1295.06	1286.02	1258.43	1246.64	1241.51	1239.26
95000	1482.34	1452.74	1428.53	1408.60	1392.11	1378.42	1367.00	1357.46	1328.34	1315.90	1310.49	1308.12
100000	1560.36	1529.20	1503.71	1482.73	1465.38	1450.97	1438.95	1428.91	1398.25	1385.15	1379.46	1376.96
105000	1638.38	1605.66	1578.90	1556.87	1538.65	1523.51	1510.90	1500.35	1468.16	1454.41	1448.43	1445.81
110000	1716.40	1682.12	1654.08	1631.01	1611.92	1596.06	1582.84	1571.80	1538.07	1523.67	1517.40	1514.66
115000	1794.42	1758.58	1729.27	1705.14	1685.19	1668.61	1654.79	1643.24	1607.99	1592.93	1586.38	1583.51
120000	1872.43	1835.04	1804.46	1779.28	1758.46	1741.16	1726.74	1714.69	1677.90	1662.18	1655.35	1652.36
125000	1950.45	1911.50	1879.64	1853.42	1831.72	1813.71	1798.69	1786.13	1747.81	1731.44	1724.32	1721.20
130000	2028.47	1987.96	1954.83	1927.55	1904.99	1886.25	1870.63	1857.58	1817.72	1800.70	1793.30	1790.05
135000	2106.49	2064.42	2030.01	2001.69	1978.26	1958.80	1942.58	1929.02	1887.64	1869.95	1862.27	1858.90
140000	2184.50	2140.88	2105.20	2075.83	2051.53	2031.35	2014.53	2000.47	1957.55	1939.21	1931.24	1927.75
145000	2262.52	2217.34	2180.38	2149.96	2124.80	2103.90	2086.48	2071.91	2027.46	2008.47	2000.21	1996.60
150000	2340.54	2293.80	2255.57	2224.10	2198.07	2176.45	2158.42	2143.36	2097.37	2077.73	2069.19	2065.44
155000	2418.56	2370.26	2330.75	2298.24	2271.34	2248.99	2230.37	2214.80	2167.28	2146.98	2138.16	2134.29
160000	2496.58	2446.72	2405.94	2372.37	2344.61	2321.54	2302.32	2286.25	2237.20	2216.24	2207.13	2203.14

95

MONTHLY AMORTIZING PAYMENTS

AMOUNT OF LOAN	NUMBER OF YEARS IN TERM											
	1	2	3	4	5	6	7	8	9	10	11	12
$ 50	4.56	2.47	1.78	1.44	1.24	1.11	1.02	0.95	0.90	0.87	0.84	0.81
100	9.11	4.94	3.56	2.88	2.48	2.22	2.03	1.90	1.80	1.73	1.67	1.62
200	18.22	9.87	7.11	5.75	4.95	4.43	4.06	3.80	3.60	3.45	3.33	3.24
300	27.33	14.80	10.66	8.62	7.42	6.64	6.09	5.70	5.40	5.17	4.99	4.85
400	36.44	19.73	14.22	11.50	9.89	8.85	8.12	7.59	7.20	6.89	6.66	6.47
500	45.55	24.67	17.77	14.37	12.36	11.06	10.15	9.49	9.00	8.62	8.32	8.08
600	54.66	29.60	21.32	17.24	14.84	13.27	12.18	11.39	10.79	10.34	9.98	9.70
700	63.77	34.53	24.87	20.11	17.31	15.48	14.21	13.29	12.59	12.06	11.64	11.31
800	72.87	39.46	28.43	22.99	19.78	17.69	16.24	15.18	14.39	13.78	13.31	12.93
900	81.98	44.40	31.98	25.86	22.25	19.90	18.27	17.08	16.19	15.50	14.97	14.54
1000	91.09	49.33	35.53	28.73	24.72	22.11	20.30	18.98	17.99	17.23	16.63	16.16
2000	182.18	98.65	71.06	57.46	49.44	44.22	40.59	37.95	35.97	34.45	33.26	32.31
3000	273.26	147.97	106.59	86.18	74.16	66.33	60.88	56.92	53.95	51.67	49.88	48.46
4000	364.35	197.29	142.12	114.91	98.88	88.43	81.17	75.89	71.94	68.89	66.51	64.62
5000	455.44	246.62	177.65	143.63	123.60	110.54	101.46	94.87	89.92	86.11	83.14	80.77
6000	546.52	295.94	213.18	172.36	148.32	132.65	121.75	113.84	107.90	103.34	99.76	96.92
7000	637.61	345.26	248.70	201.09	173.03	154.75	142.05	132.81	125.88	120.56	116.39	113.08
8000	728.69	394.58	284.23	229.81	197.75	176.86	162.34	151.78	143.87	137.78	133.01	129.23
9000	819.78	443.91	319.76	258.54	222.47	198.97	182.63	170.76	161.85	155.00	149.64	145.38
10000	910.87	493.23	355.29	287.26	247.19	221.07	202.92	189.73	179.83	172.22	166.27	161.53
11000	1001.95	542.55	390.82	315.99	271.91	243.18	223.21	208.70	197.81	189.44	182.89	177.69
12000	1093.04	591.87	426.35	344.72	296.63	265.29	243.50	227.67	215.80	206.67	199.52	193.84
13000	1184.12	641.19	461.87	373.44	321.34	287.39	263.80	246.65	233.78	223.89	216.14	209.99
14000	1275.21	690.52	497.40	402.17	346.06	309.50	284.09	265.62	251.76	241.11	232.77	226.15
15000	1366.30	739.84	532.93	430.89	370.78	331.61	304.38	284.59	269.74	258.33	249.40	242.30
16000	1457.38	789.16	568.46	459.62	395.50	353.71	324.67	303.56	287.73	275.55	266.02	258.45
17000	1548.47	838.48	603.99	488.34	420.22	375.82	344.96	322.54	305.71	292.77	282.65	274.60
18000	1639.56	887.81	639.52	517.07	444.94	397.93	365.25	341.51	323.69	310.00	299.27	290.76
19000	1730.64	937.13	675.05	545.80	469.65	420.04	385.55	360.48	341.67	327.22	315.90	306.91
20000	1821.73	986.45	710.57	574.52	494.37	442.14	405.84	379.45	359.66	344.44	332.53	323.06
21000	1912.81	1035.77	746.10	603.25	519.09	464.25	426.13	398.43	377.64	361.66	349.15	339.22
22000	2003.90	1085.09	781.63	631.97	543.81	486.36	446.42	417.40	395.62	378.88	365.78	355.37
23000	2094.99	1134.42	817.16	660.70	568.53	508.46	466.71	436.37	413.60	396.10	382.40	371.52
24000	2186.07	1183.74	852.69	689.43	593.25	530.57	487.00	455.34	431.59	413.33	399.03	387.68
25000	2277.16	1233.06	888.22	718.15	617.96	552.68	507.29	474.32	449.57	430.55	415.66	403.83
26000	2368.24	1282.38	923.74	746.88	642.68	574.78	527.59	493.29	467.55	447.77	432.28	419.98
27000	2459.33	1331.71	959.27	775.60	667.40	596.89	547.88	512.26	485.53	464.99	448.91	436.13
28000	2550.42	1381.03	994.80	804.33	692.12	619.00	568.17	531.23	503.52	482.21	465.53	452.29
29000	2641.50	1430.35	1030.33	833.06	716.84	641.10	588.46	550.21	521.50	499.43	482.16	468.44
30000	2732.59	1479.67	1065.86	861.78	741.56	663.21	608.75	569.18	539.48	516.66	498.79	484.59
31000	2823.68	1528.99	1101.39	890.51	766.27	685.32	629.04	588.15	557.46	533.88	515.41	500.75
32000	2914.76	1578.32	1136.91	919.23	790.99	707.42	649.34	607.12	575.45	551.10	532.04	516.90
33000	3005.85	1627.64	1172.44	947.96	815.71	729.53	669.63	626.10	593.43	568.32	548.66	533.05
34000	3096.93	1676.96	1207.97	976.68	840.43	751.64	689.92	645.07	611.41	585.54	565.29	549.20
35000	3188.02	1726.28	1243.50	1005.41	865.15	773.75	710.21	664.04	629.39	602.76	581.92	565.36
37500	3415.74	1849.59	1332.32	1077.22	926.94	829.01	760.94	711.47	674.35	645.82	623.48	605.74
40000	3643.45	1972.89	1421.14	1149.04	988.74	884.28	811.67	758.90	719.31	688.87	665.05	646.12
42500	3871.17	2096.20	1509.96	1220.85	1050.53	939.55	862.40	806.33	764.26	731.93	706.61	686.50
45000	4098.88	2219.51	1598.78	1292.67	1112.33	994.81	913.13	853.76	809.22	774.98	748.18	726.89
47500	4326.60	2342.81	1687.61	1364.48	1174.13	1050.08	963.86	901.20	854.18	818.03	789.74	767.27
50000	4554.31	2466.12	1776.43	1436.30	1235.92	1105.35	1014.58	948.63	899.13	861.09	831.31	807.65
52500	4782.03	2589.42	1865.25	1508.11	1297.72	1160.62	1065.31	996.06	944.09	904.14	872.87	848.03
55000	5009.74	2712.73	1954.07	1579.93	1359.51	1215.88	1116.04	1043.49	989.04	947.20	914.44	888.42
57500	5237.46	2836.03	2042.89	1651.74	1421.31	1271.15	1166.77	1090.92	1034.00	990.25	956.00	928.80
60000	5465.17	2959.34	2131.71	1723.56	1483.11	1326.42	1217.50	1138.35	1078.96	1033.31	997.57	969.18
65000	5920.60	3205.95	2309.35	1867.19	1606.70	1436.95	1318.96	1233.21	1168.87	1119.41	1080.70	1049.95
70000	6376.04	3452.56	2487.00	2010.82	1730.29	1547.49	1420.42	1328.07	1258.78	1205.52	1163.83	1130.71
75000	6831.47	3699.17	2664.64	2154.44	1853.88	1658.02	1521.87	1422.94	1348.69	1291.63	1246.96	1211.48
80000	7286.90	3945.78	2842.28	2298.07	1977.47	1768.55	1623.33	1517.80	1438.61	1377.74	1330.09	1292.24
85000	7742.33	4192.39	3019.92	2441.70	2101.06	1879.09	1724.79	1612.66	1528.52	1463.85	1413.22	1373.00
90000	8197.76	4439.01	3197.56	2585.33	2224.66	1989.62	1826.25	1707.52	1618.43	1549.96	1496.35	1453.77
95000	8653.19	4685.62	3375.21	2728.96	2348.25	2100.16	1927.71	1802.39	1708.35	1636.06	1579.48	1534.53
100000	9108.62	4932.23	3552.85	2872.59	2471.84	2210.69	2029.16	1897.25	1798.26	1722.17	1662.61	1615.30
105000	9564.05	5178.84	3730.49	3016.22	2595.43	2321.23	2130.62	1992.11	1888.17	1808.28	1745.74	1696.06
110000	10019.48	5425.45	3908.13	3159.85	2719.02	2431.76	2232.08	2086.97	1978.08	1894.39	1828.87	1776.83
115000	10474.91	5672.06	4085.77	3303.48	2842.62	2542.29	2333.54	2181.83	2068.00	1980.50	1912.00	1857.59
120000	10930.34	5918.67	4263.42	3447.11	2966.21	2652.83	2435.00	2276.70	2157.91	2066.61	1995.13	1938.36
125000	11385.77	6165.28	4441.06	3590.74	3089.80	2763.36	2536.45	2371.56	2247.82	2152.71	2078.26	2019.12
130000	11841.20	6411.89	4618.70	3734.37	3213.39	2873.90	2637.91	2466.42	2337.73	2238.82	2161.39	2099.89
135000	12296.64	6658.51	4796.34	3878.00	3336.98	2984.43	2739.37	2561.28	2427.65	2324.93	2244.52	2180.65
140000	12752.07	6905.12	4973.99	4021.63	3460.57	3094.97	2840.83	2656.14	2517.56	2411.04	2327.65	2261.42
145000	13207.50	7151.73	5151.63	4165.26	3584.17	3205.50	2942.29	2751.01	2607.47	2497.15	2410.78	2342.18
150000	13662.93	7398.34	5329.27	4308.88	3707.76	3316.03	3043.74	2845.87	2697.38	2583.26	2493.91	2422.95
155000	14118.36	7644.95	5506.91	4452.51	3831.35	3426.57	3145.20	2940.73	2787.30	2669.36	2577.04	2503.71
160000	14573.79	7891.56	5684.55	4596.14	3954.94	3537.10	3246.66	3035.59	2877.21	2755.47	2660.17	2584.47

AMOUNT OF LOAN	NUMBER OF YEARS IN TERM											
	13	14	15	16	17	18	19	20	25	30	35	40
$ 50	0.79	0.78	0.77	0.76	0.75	0.74	0.73	0.73	0.71	0.71	0.70	0.70
100	1.58	1.55	1.53	1.51	1.49	1.47	1.46	1.45	1.42	1.41	1.40	1.40
200	3.16	3.10	3.05	3.01	2.97	2.94	2.92	2.90	2.84	2.82	2.80	2.80
300	4.74	4.64	4.57	4.51	4.46	4.41	4.38	4.35	4.26	4.22	4.20	4.20
400	6.31	6.19	6.09	6.01	5.94	5.88	5.84	5.80	5.68	5.63	5.60	5.60
500	7.89	7.74	7.61	7.51	7.42	7.35	7.29	7.24	7.09	7.03	7.00	6.99
600	9.47	9.28	9.13	9.01	8.91	8.82	8.75	8.69	8.51	8.44	8.40	8.39
700	11.05	10.83	10.65	10.51	10.39	10.29	10.21	10.14	9.93	9.84	9.80	9.79
800	12.62	12.38	12.18	12.01	11.87	11.76	11.67	11.59	11.35	11.25	11.20	11.19
900	14.20	13.92	13.70	13.51	13.36	13.23	13.12	13.04	12.77	12.65	12.60	12.58
1000	15.78	15.47	15.22	15.01	14.84	14.70	14.58	14.48	14.18	14.06	14.00	13.98
2000	31.55	30.93	30.43	30.02	29.68	29.39	29.16	28.96	28.36	28.11	28.00	27.96
3000	47.32	46.40	45.64	45.02	44.51	44.09	43.73	43.44	42.54	42.17	42.00	41.93
4000	63.10	61.86	60.86	60.03	59.35	58.78	58.31	57.92	56.72	56.22	56.00	55.91
5000	78.87	77.33	76.07	75.04	74.18	73.48	72.89	72.40	70.90	70.27	70.00	69.89
6000	94.64	92.79	91.28	90.04	89.02	88.17	87.46	86.87	85.08	84.33	84.00	83.86
7000	110.42	108.26	106.50	105.05	103.86	102.86	102.04	101.35	99.26	98.38	98.00	97.84
8000	126.19	123.72	121.71	120.06	118.69	117.56	116.62	115.83	113.44	112.44	112.00	111.82
9000	141.96	139.19	136.92	135.06	133.53	132.25	131.19	130.31	127.62	126.49	126.00	125.79
10000	157.73	154.65	152.14	150.07	148.36	146.95	145.77	144.79	141.80	140.54	140.00	139.77
11000	173.51	170.12	167.35	165.08	163.20	161.64	160.35	159.27	155.98	154.60	154.00	153.74
12000	189.28	185.58	182.56	180.08	178.03	176.34	174.92	173.74	170.16	168.65	168.00	167.72
13000	205.05	201.05	197.78	195.09	192.87	191.03	189.50	188.22	184.34	182.71	182.00	181.70
14000	220.83	216.51	212.99	210.10	207.71	205.72	204.08	202.70	198.52	196.76	196.00	195.67
15000	236.60	231.98	228.20	225.10	222.54	220.42	218.65	217.18	212.70	210.81	210.00	209.65
16000	252.37	247.44	243.42	240.11	237.38	235.11	233.23	231.66	226.88	224.87	224.00	223.63
17000	268.14	262.91	258.63	255.11	252.21	249.81	247.80	246.13	241.06	238.92	238.00	237.60
18000	283.92	278.37	273.84	270.12	267.05	264.50	262.38	260.61	255.24	252.98	252.00	251.58
19000	299.69	293.84	289.06	285.13	281.88	279.19	276.96	275.09	269.42	267.03	266.00	265.56
20000	315.46	309.30	304.27	300.13	296.72	293.89	291.53	289.57	283.60	281.08	280.00	279.53
21000	331.24	324.77	319.48	315.14	311.56	308.58	306.11	304.05	297.78	295.14	294.00	293.51
22000	347.01	340.23	334.70	330.15	326.39	323.28	320.69	318.53	311.96	309.19	308.00	307.48
23000	362.78	355.70	349.91	345.15	341.23	337.97	335.26	333.00	326.14	323.25	322.00	321.46
24000	378.55	371.16	365.12	360.16	356.06	352.67	349.84	347.48	340.32	337.30	336.00	335.44
25000	394.33	386.63	380.34	375.17	370.90	367.36	364.42	361.96	354.50	351.35	350.00	349.41
26000	410.10	402.09	395.55	390.17	385.73	382.05	378.99	376.44	368.68	365.41	364.00	363.39
27000	425.87	417.56	410.76	405.18	400.57	396.75	393.57	390.92	382.86	379.46	378.00	377.37
28000	441.65	433.02	425.97	420.19	415.41	411.44	408.15	405.39	397.04	393.52	392.00	391.34
29000	457.42	448.48	441.19	435.19	430.24	426.14	422.72	419.87	411.22	407.57	406.00	405.32
30000	473.19	463.95	456.40	450.20	445.08	440.83	437.30	434.35	425.40	421.62	420.00	419.30
31000	488.97	479.41	471.61	465.21	459.91	455.53	451.87	448.83	439.58	435.68	434.00	433.27
32000	504.74	494.88	486.83	480.21	474.75	470.22	466.45	463.31	453.76	449.73	448.00	447.25
33000	520.51	510.34	502.04	495.22	489.58	484.91	481.03	477.79	467.94	463.79	462.00	461.22
34000	536.28	525.81	517.25	510.22	504.42	499.61	495.60	492.26	482.12	477.84	476.00	475.20
35000	552.06	541.27	532.47	525.23	519.26	514.30	510.18	506.74	496.30	491.89	490.00	489.18
37500	591.49	579.94	570.50	562.75	556.35	551.04	546.62	542.94	531.75	527.03	525.00	524.12
40000	630.92	618.60	608.53	600.26	593.44	587.77	583.06	579.13	567.20	562.16	560.00	559.06
42500	670.35	657.26	646.57	637.78	630.52	624.51	619.50	615.33	602.65	597.30	595.00	594.00
45000	709.79	695.92	684.60	675.30	667.61	661.24	655.95	651.52	638.10	632.43	630.00	628.94
47500	749.22	734.58	722.63	712.81	704.70	697.98	692.39	687.72	673.55	667.57	665.00	663.88
50000	788.65	773.25	760.67	750.33	741.79	734.72	728.83	723.91	709.00	702.70	699.99	698.82
52500	828.08	811.91	798.70	787.84	778.88	771.45	765.27	760.11	744.45	737.84	734.99	733.76
55000	867.51	850.57	836.73	825.36	815.97	808.19	801.71	796.31	779.90	772.97	769.99	768.70
57500	906.95	889.23	874.76	862.88	853.06	844.92	838.15	832.50	815.35	808.11	804.99	803.65
60000	946.38	927.89	912.80	900.39	890.15	881.66	874.59	868.70	850.80	843.24	839.99	838.59
65000	1025.24	1005.22	988.86	975.43	964.33	955.13	947.47	941.09	921.70	913.51	909.99	908.47
70000	1104.11	1082.54	1064.93	1050.46	1038.51	1028.60	1020.36	1013.48	992.60	983.78	979.99	978.35
75000	1182.97	1159.87	1141.00	1125.49	1112.69	1102.07	1093.24	1085.87	1063.50	1054.05	1049.99	1048.23
80000	1261.84	1237.19	1217.06	1200.52	1186.87	1175.54	1166.12	1158.26	1134.40	1124.32	1119.99	1118.11
85000	1340.70	1314.52	1293.13	1275.55	1261.04	1249.01	1239.00	1230.65	1205.30	1194.59	1189.99	1187.99
90000	1419.57	1391.84	1369.19	1350.59	1335.22	1322.48	1311.89	1303.04	1276.20	1264.86	1259.99	1257.88
95000	1498.43	1469.16	1445.26	1425.62	1409.40	1395.95	1384.77	1375.43	1347.10	1335.13	1329.99	1327.76
100000	1577.30	1546.49	1521.33	1500.65	1483.58	1469.43	1457.65	1447.82	1418.00	1405.40	1399.98	1397.64
105000	1656.16	1623.81	1597.39	1575.68	1557.76	1542.90	1530.53	1520.22	1488.90	1475.67	1469.98	1467.52
110000	1735.02	1701.14	1673.46	1650.72	1631.94	1616.37	1603.41	1592.61	1559.80	1545.94	1539.98	1537.40
115000	1813.89	1778.46	1749.52	1725.75	1706.12	1689.84	1676.30	1665.00	1630.70	1616.21	1609.98	1607.29
120000	1892.75	1855.78	1825.59	1800.78	1780.30	1763.31	1749.18	1737.39	1701.60	1686.48	1679.98	1677.17
125000	1971.62	1933.11	1901.66	1875.81	1854.47	1836.78	1822.06	1809.78	1772.50	1756.75	1749.98	1747.05
130000	2050.48	2010.43	1977.72	1950.85	1928.65	1910.25	1894.94	1882.17	1843.40	1827.02	1819.98	1816.93
135000	2129.35	2087.76	2053.79	2025.88	2002.83	1983.72	1967.83	1954.56	1914.30	1897.29	1889.98	1886.81
140000	2208.21	2165.08	2129.85	2100.91	2077.01	2057.19	2040.71	2026.95	1985.20	1967.56	1959.98	1956.69
145000	2287.08	2242.40	2205.92	2175.94	2151.19	2130.66	2113.59	2099.34	2056.10	2037.83	2029.98	2026.58
150000	2365.94	2319.73	2281.99	2250.98	2225.37	2204.14	2186.47	2171.73	2127.00	2108.10	2099.97	2096.46
155000	2444.81	2397.05	2358.05	2326.01	2299.55	2277.61	2259.35	2244.13	2197.90	2178.37	2169.97	2166.34
160000	2523.67	2474.38	2434.12	2401.04	2373.73	2351.08	2332.24	2316.52	2268.80	2248.64	2239.97	2236.22

MONTHLY AMORTIZING PAYMENTS

AMOUNT OF LOAN	NUMBER OF YEARS IN TERM											
	1	2	3	4	5	6	7	8	9	10	11	12
$ 50	4.57	2.48	1.79	1.45	1.25	1.12	1.03	0.96	0.91	0.87	0.84	0.82
100	9.13	4.95	3.57	2.89	2.49	2.23	2.05	1.92	1.82	1.74	1.68	1.64
200	18.25	9.89	7.14	5.78	4.98	4.45	4.09	3.83	3.63	3.48	3.36	3.27
300	27.37	14.84	10.70	8.66	7.46	6.68	6.14	5.74	5.45	5.22	5.04	4.90
400	36.49	19.78	14.27	11.55	9.95	8.90	8.18	7.65	7.26	6.96	6.72	6.53
500	45.61	24.73	17.83	14.43	12.43	11.13	10.22	9.57	9.07	8.69	8.40	8.16
600	54.73	29.67	21.40	17.32	14.92	13.35	12.27	11.48	10.89	10.43	10.08	9.80
700	63.85	34.61	24.96	20.20	17.40	15.58	14.31	13.39	12.70	12.17	11.76	11.43
800	72.97	39.56	28.53	23.09	19.89	17.80	16.35	15.30	14.51	13.91	13.44	13.06
900	82.09	44.50	32.09	25.97	22.37	20.03	18.40	17.21	16.33	15.65	15.11	14.69
1000	91.21	49.45	35.66	28.86	24.86	22.25	20.44	19.13	18.14	17.38	16.79	16.32
2000	182.41	98.89	71.31	57.72	49.71	44.50	40.88	38.25	36.28	34.76	33.58	32.64
3000	273.62	148.33	106.96	86.57	74.56	66.74	61.31	57.37	54.41	52.14	50.37	48.96
4000	364.82	197.77	142.62	115.43	99.42	88.99	81.75	76.49	72.55	69.52	67.16	65.28
5000	456.03	247.22	178.27	144.28	124.27	111.24	102.18	95.61	90.69	86.90	83.95	81.60
6000	547.23	296.66	213.92	173.14	149.12	133.48	122.62	114.73	108.82	104.28	100.73	97.92
7000	638.44	346.10	249.57	201.99	173.97	155.73	143.06	133.86	126.96	121.66	117.52	114.24
8000	729.64	395.54	285.23	230.85	198.83	177.97	163.49	152.98	145.09	139.04	134.31	130.56
9000	820.85	444.99	320.88	259.70	223.68	200.22	183.93	172.10	163.23	156.42	151.10	146.88
10000	912.05	494.43	356.53	288.56	248.53	222.47	204.36	191.22	181.37	173.80	167.89	163.20
11000	1003.26	543.87	392.19	317.41	273.38	244.71	224.80	210.34	199.50	191.18	184.68	179.52
12000	1094.46	593.31	427.84	346.27	298.24	266.96	245.23	229.46	217.64	208.56	201.46	195.84
13000	1185.67	642.75	463.49	375.12	323.09	289.20	265.67	248.58	235.78	225.94	218.25	212.15
14000	1276.87	692.20	499.14	403.98	347.94	311.45	286.11	267.71	253.91	243.32	235.04	228.47
15000	1368.08	741.64	534.80	432.83	372.79	333.70	306.54	286.83	272.05	260.70	251.83	244.79
16000	1459.28	791.08	570.45	461.69	397.65	355.94	326.98	305.95	290.18	278.08	268.62	261.11
17000	1550.49	840.52	606.10	490.54	422.50	378.19	347.41	325.07	308.32	295.46	285.41	277.43
18000	1641.69	889.97	641.75	519.40	447.35	400.44	367.85	344.19	326.46	312.84	302.19	293.75
19000	1732.90	939.41	677.41	548.25	472.20	422.68	388.29	363.31	344.59	330.22	318.98	310.07
20000	1824.10	988.85	713.06	577.11	497.06	444.93	408.72	382.43	362.73	347.60	335.77	326.39
21000	1915.30	1038.29	748.71	605.96	521.91	467.17	429.16	401.56	380.86	364.98	352.56	342.71
22000	2006.51	1087.73	784.37	634.82	546.76	489.42	449.59	420.68	399.00	382.36	369.35	359.03
23000	2097.71	1137.18	820.02	663.67	571.61	511.67	470.03	439.80	417.14	399.74	386.14	375.35
24000	2188.92	1186.62	855.67	692.53	596.47	533.91	490.46	458.92	435.27	417.12	402.92	391.67
25000	2280.12	1236.06	891.32	721.38	621.32	556.16	510.90	478.04	453.41	434.50	419.71	407.99
26000	2371.33	1285.50	926.98	750.24	646.17	578.40	531.34	497.16	471.55	451.88	436.50	424.30
27000	2462.53	1334.95	962.63	779.09	671.02	600.65	551.77	516.28	489.68	469.26	453.29	440.62
28000	2553.74	1384.39	998.28	807.95	695.88	622.90	572.21	535.41	507.82	486.64	470.08	456.94
29000	2644.94	1433.83	1033.93	836.80	720.73	645.14	592.64	554.53	525.95	504.02	486.87	473.26
30000	2736.15	1483.27	1069.59	865.66	745.58	667.39	613.08	573.65	544.09	521.40	503.65	489.58
31000	2827.35	1532.72	1105.24	894.51	770.43	689.64	633.51	592.77	562.23	538.78	520.44	505.90
32000	2918.56	1582.16	1140.89	923.37	795.29	711.88	653.95	611.89	580.36	556.16	537.23	522.22
33000	3009.76	1631.60	1176.55	952.22	820.14	734.13	674.39	631.01	598.50	573.54	554.02	538.54
34000	3100.97	1681.04	1212.20	981.08	844.99	756.37	694.82	650.13	616.64	590.92	570.81	554.86
35000	3192.17	1730.48	1247.85	1009.93	869.85	778.62	715.26	669.26	634.77	608.30	587.60	571.18
37500	3420.18	1854.09	1336.98	1082.07	931.98	834.23	766.35	717.06	680.11	651.75	629.57	611.98
40000	3648.20	1977.70	1426.11	1154.21	994.11	889.85	817.44	764.86	725.45	695.20	671.54	652.77
42500	3876.21	2101.30	1515.25	1226.34	1056.24	945.47	868.53	812.67	770.79	738.65	713.51	693.57
45000	4104.22	2224.91	1604.38	1298.48	1118.37	1001.08	919.62	860.47	816.13	782.09	755.48	734.37
47500	4332.23	2348.51	1693.51	1370.62	1180.50	1056.70	970.71	908.27	861.47	825.54	797.45	775.17
50000	4560.24	2472.12	1782.64	1442.76	1242.63	1112.31	1021.80	956.08	906.81	868.99	839.42	815.97
52500	4788.25	2595.72	1871.77	1514.89	1304.77	1167.93	1072.88	1003.88	952.15	912.44	881.39	856.76
55000	5016.27	2719.33	1960.91	1587.03	1366.90	1223.54	1123.97	1051.68	997.50	955.89	923.36	897.56
57500	5244.28	2842.94	2050.04	1659.17	1429.03	1279.16	1175.06	1099.49	1042.84	999.34	965.33	938.36
60000	5472.29	2966.54	2139.17	1731.31	1491.16	1334.77	1226.15	1147.29	1088.18	1042.79	1007.30	979.16
65000	5928.31	3213.75	2317.43	1875.58	1615.42	1446.00	1328.33	1242.90	1178.86	1129.69	1091.25	1060.75
70000	6384.34	3460.96	2495.70	2019.86	1739.69	1557.23	1430.51	1338.51	1269.54	1216.59	1174.19	1142.35
75000	6840.36	3708.17	2673.96	2164.13	1863.95	1668.46	1532.69	1434.11	1360.22	1303.49	1259.13	1223.95
80000	7296.39	3955.39	2852.22	2308.41	1988.21	1779.70	1634.87	1529.72	1450.90	1390.39	1343.07	1305.54
85000	7752.41	4202.60	3030.49	2452.68	2112.47	1890.93	1737.05	1625.33	1541.58	1477.29	1427.01	1387.14
90000	8208.43	4449.81	3208.75	2596.96	2236.74	2002.16	1839.23	1720.94	1632.26	1564.18	1510.95	1468.74
95000	8664.46	4697.02	3387.01	2741.23	2361.00	2113.39	1941.41	1816.54	1722.94	1651.08	1594.90	1550.33
100000	9120.48	4944.23	3565.28	2885.51	2485.26	2224.62	2043.59	1912.15	1813.62	1737.98	1678.84	1631.93
105000	9576.50	5191.44	3743.54	3029.78	2609.53	2335.85	2145.76	2007.76	1904.30	1824.88	1762.78	1713.52
110000	10032.53	5438.65	3921.81	3174.06	2733.79	2447.08	2247.94	2103.36	1994.99	1911.78	1846.72	1795.12
115000	10488.55	5685.87	4100.07	3318.33	2858.05	2558.31	2350.12	2198.97	2085.67	1998.68	1930.66	1876.72
120000	10944.58	5933.08	4278.33	3462.61	2982.31	2669.54	2452.30	2294.58	2176.35	2085.58	2014.60	1958.31
125000	11400.60	6180.29	4456.60	3606.89	3106.58	2780.77	2554.48	2390.19	2267.03	2172.48	2098.55	2039.91
130000	11856.62	6427.50	4634.86	3751.16	3230.84	2892.00	2656.66	2485.79	2357.71	2259.37	2182.49	2121.50
135000	12312.65	6674.71	4813.12	3895.44	3355.10	3003.23	2758.84	2581.40	2448.39	2346.27	2266.43	2203.10
140000	12768.67	6921.92	4991.39	4039.71	3479.37	3114.46	2861.02	2677.01	2539.07	2433.17	2350.37	2284.70
145000	13224.69	7169.13	5169.65	4183.99	3603.63	3225.69	2963.20	2772.62	2629.75	2520.07	2434.31	2366.29
150000	13680.72	7416.34	5347.91	4328.26	3727.89	3336.92	3065.38	2868.22	2720.43	2606.97	2518.25	2447.89
155000	14136.74	7663.56	5526.18	4472.54	3852.15	3448.16	3167.55	2963.83	2811.11	2693.87	2602.19	2529.49
160000	14592.77	7910.77	5704.44	4616.81	3976.42	3559.39	3269.73	3059.44	2901.80	2780.76	2686.14	2611.08

	25	30	35	40
	0.72	0.72	0.72	0.71
	1.44	1.43	1.43	1.42
	2.88	2.86	2.85	2.84
	4.32	4.28	4.27	4.26
	5.76	5.71	5.69	5.68
	7.19	7.13	7.11	7.10
	8.63	8.56	8.53	8.51
	10.07	9.98	9.95	9.93
	11.51	11.41	11.37	11.35
	12.95	12.84	12.79	12.77
	14.38	14.26	14.21	14.19
	28.76	28.52	28.42	28.37
	43.14	42.78	42.62	42.55
	57.52	57.03	56.83	56.74
	71.89	71.29	71.03	70.92
	86.27	85.55	85.24	85.10
	100.65	99.80	99.44	99.29
	115.03	114.06	113.65	113.47
	129.41	128.32	127.85	127.65
	143.78	142.57	142.06	141.84
	158.16	156.83	156.26	156.02
	172.54	171.09	170.47	170.20
	186.92	185.34	184.67	184.39
	201.30	199.60	198.88	198.57
	215.67	213.86	213.08	212.75
	230.05	228.11	227.29	226.94
	244.43	242.37	241.49	241.12
	258.81	256.63	255.70	255.30
	273.19	270.88	269.90	269.49
	287.56	285.14	284.11	283.67
	301.94	299.40	298.32	297.85
	316.32	313.65	312.52	312.04
	330.70	327.91	326.73	326.22
	345.08	342.17	340.93	340.40
	359.45	356.42	355.14	354.59
	373.83	370.68	369.34	368.77
	388.21	384.94	383.55	382.95
	402.59	399.19	397.75	397.14
	416.97	413.45	411.96	411.32
	431.34	427.71	426.16	425.50
	445.72	441.96	440.37	439.69
	460.10	456.22	454.57	453.87
	474.48	470.48	468.78	468.05
	488.86	484.73	482.98	482.23
	503.23	498.99	497.19	496.41
	539.18	534.63	532.70	531.88
	575.12	570.28	568.22	567.33
	611.07	605.92	603.73	602.79
	647.01	641.56	639.24	638.25
	682.96	677.20	674.75	673.71
	718.90	712.84	710.27	709.17
	754.85	748.48	745.78	744.62
	790.79	784.13	781.29	780.08
	826.74	819.77	816.81	815.54
	862.68	855.41	852.32	851.00
	934.57	926.69	923.35	921.92
	1006.46	997.98	994.37	992.83
	1078.35	1069.26	1065.40	1063.75
	1150.24	1140.55	1136.43	1134.66
	1222.13	1211.83	1207.45	1205.58
	1294.02	1283.11	1278.48	1276.50
	1365.91	1354.40	1349.50	1347.41
	1437.80	1425.68	1420.53	1418.33
	1509.69	1496.96	1491.56	1489.24
	1581.58	1568.25	1562.58	1560.16
	1653.47	1639.53	1633.61	1631.08
	1725.36	1710.82	1704.64	1701.99
	1797.25	1782.10	1775.66	1772.91
	1869.14	1853.38	1846.69	1843.83
	1941.03	1924.67	1917.72	1914.74
	2012.92	1995.95	1988.74	1985.66
	2084.81	2067.23	2059.77	2056.57
	2156.70	2138.52	2130.79	2127.49
	2228.59	2209.80	2201.82	2198.41
	2300.48	2281.09	2272.85	2269.32

AMOUNT OF LOAN	1	2	3	4	5
$ 50	4.57	2.48	1.79	1.45	1
100	9.14	4.96	3.58	2.90	2
200	18.27	9.92	7.16	5.80	5
300	27.40	14.87	10.74	8.70	7
400	36.53	19.83	14.32	11.60	10
500	45.67	24.79	17.89	14.50	12
600	54.80	29.74	21.47	17.40	15
700	63.93	34.70	25.05	20.29	17
800	73.06	39.65	28.63	23.19	19
900	82.20	44.61	32.20	26.09	22
1000	91.33	49.57	35.78	28.99	24
2000	182.65	99.13	71.56	57.97	49
3000	273.98	148.69	107.34	86.96	74
4000	365.30	198.25	143.11	115.94	99
5000	456.62	247.82	178.89	144.93	124
6000	547.95	297.38	214.67	173.91	149
7000	639.27	346.94	250.45	202.90	174
8000	730.59	396.50	286.22	231.88	199
9000	821.92	446.07	322.00	260.87	224
10000	913.24	495.63	357.78	289.85	249
11000	1004.56	545.19	393.55	318.84	274
12000	1095.89	594.75	429.33	347.82	299
13000	1187.21	644.32	465.11	376.80	324
14000	1278.53	693.88	500.89	405.79	349
15000	1369.86	743.44	536.66	434.77	374
16000	1461.18	793.00	572.44	463.76	399
17000	1552.50	842.57	608.22	492.74	424
18000	1643.83	892.13	644.00	521.73	449
19000	1735.15	941.69	679.77	550.71	474
20000	1826.47	991.25	715.55	579.70	499
21000	1917.80	1040.82	751.33	608.68	524
22000	2009.12	1090.38	787.10	637.67	549
23000	2100.44	1139.94	822.88	666.65	574
24000	2191.77	1189.50	858.66	695.63	599
25000	2283.09	1239.07	894.44	724.62	624
26000	2374.41	1288.63	930.21	753.60	649
27000	2465.74	1338.19	965.99	782.59	674
28000	2557.06	1387.75	1001.77	811.57	699
29000	2648.38	1437.32	1037.55	840.56	724
30000	2739.71	1486.88	1073.32	869.54	749
31000	2831.03	1536.44	1109.10	898.53	774
32000	2922.35	1586.00	1144.88	927.51	799
33000	3013.68	1635.57	1180.65	956.50	824
34000	3105.00	1685.13	1216.43	985.48	849
35000	3196.33	1734.69	1252.21	1014.46	874
37500	3424.63	1858.60	1341.65	1086.93	937
40000	3652.94	1982.50	1431.10	1159.39	999
42500	3881.25	2106.41	1520.54	1231.85	1061
45000	4109.56	2230.32	1609.98	1304.31	1124
47500	4337.87	2354.22	1699.43	1376.77	1186
50000	4566.18	2478.13	1788.87	1449.23	1249
52500	4794.49	2602.03	1878.31	1521.69	1311
55000	5022.79	2725.94	1967.75	1594.16	1374
57500	5251.10	2849.85	2057.20	1666.62	1436
60000	5479.41	2973.75	2146.64	1739.08	1499
65000	5936.03	3221.57	2325.53	1884.00	1624
70000	6392.65	3469.38	2504.41	2028.92	1749
75000	6849.26	3717.19	2683.30	2173.85	1874
80000	7305.88	3965.00	2862.19	2318.77	1998
85000	7762.50	4212.82	3041.07	2463.69	2123
90000	8219.11	4460.63	3219.96	2608.61	2248
95000	8675.73	4708.44	3398.85	2753.54	2373
100000	9132.35	4956.25	3577.73	2898.46	2498
105000	9588.97	5204.06	3756.62	3043.38	2623
110000	10045.58	5451.88	3935.50	3188.31	2748
115000	10502.20	5699.69	4114.39	3333.23	2873
120000	10958.82	5947.50	4293.28	3478.15	2998
125000	11415.43	6195.31	4472.16	3623.07	3123
130000	11872.05	6443.13	4651.05	3768.00	3248
135000	12328.67	6690.94	4829.94	3912.92	3373
140000	12785.29	6938.75	5008.82	4057.84	3498
145000	13241.90	7186.56	5187.71	4202.76	3623
150000	13698.52	7434.38	5366.60	4347.69	3748
155000	14155.14	7682.19	5545.48	4492.61	3873
160000	14611.75	7930.00	5724.37	4637.53	3997

AMOUNT OF LOAN	NUMBER OF YEARS IN TERM											
	13	14	15	16	17	18	19	20	25	30	35	40
$ 50	0.79	0.78	0.77	0.76	0.75	0.74	0.73	0.73	0.71	0.71	0.70	0.70
100	1.58	1.55	1.53	1.51	1.49	1.47	1.46	1.45	1.42	1.41	1.40	1.40
200	3.16	3.10	3.05	3.01	2.97	2.94	2.92	2.90	2.84	2.82	2.80	2.80
300	4.74	4.64	4.57	4.51	4.46	4.41	4.38	4.35	4.26	4.22	4.20	4.20
400	6.31	6.19	6.09	6.01	5.94	5.88	5.84	5.80	5.68	5.63	5.60	5.60
500	7.89	7.74	7.61	7.51	7.42	7.35	7.29	7.24	7.09	7.03	7.00	6.99
600	9.47	9.28	9.13	9.01	8.91	8.82	8.75	8.69	8.51	8.44	8.40	8.39
700	11.05	10.83	10.65	10.51	10.39	10.29	10.21	10.14	9.93	9.84	9.80	9.79
800	12.62	12.38	12.18	12.01	11.87	11.76	11.67	11.59	11.35	11.25	11.20	11.19
900	14.20	13.92	13.70	13.51	13.36	13.23	13.12	13.04	12.77	12.65	12.60	12.58
1000	15.78	15.47	15.22	15.01	14.84	14.70	14.58	14.48	14.18	14.06	14.00	13.98
2000	31.55	30.93	30.43	30.02	29.68	29.39	29.16	28.96	28.36	28.11	28.00	27.96
3000	47.32	46.40	45.64	45.02	44.51	44.09	43.73	43.44	42.54	42.17	42.00	41.93
4000	63.10	61.86	60.86	60.03	59.35	58.78	58.31	57.92	56.72	56.22	56.00	55.91
5000	78.87	77.33	76.07	75.04	74.18	73.48	72.89	72.40	70.90	70.27	70.00	69.89
6000	94.64	92.79	91.28	90.04	89.02	88.17	87.46	86.87	85.08	84.33	84.00	83.86
7000	110.42	108.26	106.50	105.05	103.86	102.86	102.04	101.35	99.26	98.38	98.00	97.84
8000	126.19	123.72	121.71	120.06	118.69	117.56	116.62	115.83	113.44	112.44	112.00	111.82
9000	141.96	139.19	136.92	135.06	133.53	132.25	131.19	130.31	127.62	126.49	126.00	125.79
10000	157.73	154.65	152.14	150.07	148.36	146.95	145.77	144.79	141.80	140.54	140.00	139.77
11000	173.51	170.12	167.35	165.08	163.20	161.64	160.35	159.27	155.98	154.60	154.00	153.74
12000	189.28	185.58	182.56	180.08	178.03	176.34	174.92	173.74	170.16	168.65	168.00	167.72
13000	205.05	201.05	197.78	195.09	192.87	191.03	189.50	188.22	184.34	182.71	182.00	181.70
14000	220.83	216.51	212.99	210.10	207.71	205.72	204.08	202.70	198.52	196.76	196.00	195.67
15000	236.60	231.98	228.20	225.10	222.54	220.42	218.65	217.18	212.70	210.81	210.00	209.65
16000	252.37	247.44	243.42	240.11	237.38	235.11	233.23	231.66	226.88	224.87	224.00	223.63
17000	268.14	262.91	258.63	255.11	252.21	249.81	247.80	246.13	241.06	238.92	238.00	237.60
18000	283.92	278.37	273.84	270.12	267.05	264.50	262.38	260.61	255.24	252.98	252.00	251.58
19000	299.69	293.84	289.06	285.13	281.88	279.19	276.96	275.09	269.42	267.03	266.00	265.56
20000	315.46	309.30	304.27	300.13	296.72	293.89	291.53	289.57	283.60	281.08	280.00	279.53
21000	331.24	324.77	319.48	315.14	311.56	308.58	306.11	304.05	297.78	295.14	294.00	293.51
22000	347.01	340.23	334.70	330.15	326.39	323.28	320.69	318.53	311.96	309.19	308.00	307.48
23000	362.78	355.70	349.91	345.15	341.23	337.97	335.26	333.00	326.14	323.25	322.00	321.46
24000	378.55	371.16	365.12	360.16	356.06	352.67	349.84	347.48	340.32	337.30	336.00	335.44
25000	394.33	386.63	380.34	375.17	370.90	367.36	364.42	361.96	354.50	351.35	350.00	349.41
26000	410.10	402.09	395.55	390.17	385.73	382.05	378.99	376.44	368.68	365.41	364.00	363.39
27000	425.87	417.56	410.76	405.18	400.57	396.75	393.57	390.92	382.86	379.46	378.00	377.37
28000	441.65	433.02	425.97	420.19	415.41	411.44	408.15	405.39	397.04	393.52	392.00	391.34
29000	457.42	448.48	441.19	435.19	430.24	426.14	422.72	419.87	411.22	407.57	406.00	405.32
30000	473.19	463.95	456.40	450.20	445.08	440.83	437.30	434.35	425.40	421.62	420.00	419.30
31000	488.97	479.41	471.61	465.21	459.91	455.53	451.87	448.83	439.58	435.68	434.00	433.27
32000	504.74	494.88	486.83	480.21	474.75	470.22	466.45	463.31	453.76	449.73	448.00	447.25
33000	520.51	510.34	502.04	495.22	489.58	484.91	481.03	477.79	467.94	463.79	462.00	461.22
34000	536.28	525.81	517.25	510.22	504.42	499.61	495.60	492.26	482.12	477.84	476.00	475.20
35000	552.06	541.27	532.47	525.23	519.26	514.30	510.18	506.74	496.30	491.89	490.00	489.18
37500	591.49	579.94	570.50	562.75	556.35	551.04	546.62	542.94	531.75	527.03	525.00	524.12
40000	630.92	618.60	608.53	600.26	593.44	587.77	583.06	579.13	567.20	562.16	560.00	559.06
42500	670.35	657.26	646.57	637.78	630.52	624.51	619.50	615.33	602.65	597.30	595.00	594.00
45000	709.79	695.92	684.60	675.30	661.61	661.24	655.95	651.52	638.10	632.43	630.00	628.94
47500	749.22	734.58	722.63	712.81	704.70	697.98	692.39	687.72	673.55	667.57	665.00	663.88
50000	788.65	773.25	760.67	750.33	741.79	734.72	728.83	723.91	709.00	702.70	699.99	698.82
52500	828.08	811.91	798.70	787.84	778.88	771.45	765.27	760.11	744.45	737.84	734.99	733.76
55000	867.51	850.57	836.73	825.36	815.97	808.19	801.71	796.31	779.90	772.97	769.99	768.70
57500	906.95	889.23	874.76	862.88	853.06	844.92	838.15	832.50	815.35	808.11	804.99	803.65
60000	946.38	927.89	912.80	900.39	890.15	881.66	874.59	868.70	850.80	843.24	839.99	838.59
65000	1025.24	1005.22	988.86	975.43	964.33	955.13	947.47	941.09	921.70	913.51	909.99	908.47
70000	1104.11	1082.54	1064.93	1050.46	1038.51	1028.60	1020.36	1013.48	992.60	983.78	979.99	978.35
75000	1182.97	1159.87	1141.00	1125.49	1112.69	1102.07	1093.24	1085.87	1063.50	1054.05	1049.99	1048.23
80000	1261.84	1237.19	1217.06	1200.52	1186.87	1175.54	1166.12	1158.26	1134.40	1124.32	1119.99	1118.11
85000	1340.70	1314.52	1293.13	1275.55	1261.04	1249.01	1239.00	1230.65	1205.30	1194.59	1189.99	1187.99
90000	1419.57	1391.84	1369.19	1350.59	1335.22	1322.48	1311.89	1303.04	1276.20	1264.86	1259.99	1257.88
95000	1498.43	1469.16	1445.26	1425.62	1409.40	1395.95	1384.77	1375.43	1347.10	1335.13	1329.99	1327.76
100000	1577.30	1546.49	1521.33	1500.65	1483.58	1469.43	1457.65	1447.82	1418.00	1405.40	1399.98	1397.64
105000	1656.16	1623.81	1597.39	1575.68	1557.76	1542.90	1530.53	1520.22	1488.90	1475.67	1469.98	1467.52
110000	1735.02	1701.14	1673.46	1650.72	1631.94	1616.37	1603.41	1592.61	1559.80	1545.94	1539.98	1537.40
115000	1813.89	1778.46	1749.52	1725.75	1706.12	1689.84	1676.30	1665.00	1630.70	1616.21	1609.98	1607.29
120000	1892.75	1855.78	1825.59	1800.78	1780.30	1763.31	1749.18	1737.39	1701.60	1686.48	1679.98	1677.17
125000	1971.62	1933.11	1901.66	1875.81	1854.47	1836.78	1822.06	1809.78	1772.50	1756.75	1749.98	1747.05
130000	2050.48	2010.43	1977.72	1950.85	1928.65	1910.25	1894.94	1882.17	1843.40	1827.02	1819.98	1816.93
135000	2129.35	2087.76	2053.79	2025.88	2002.83	1983.72	1967.83	1954.56	1914.30	1897.29	1889.98	1886.81
140000	2208.21	2165.08	2129.85	2100.91	2077.01	2057.19	2040.71	2026.95	1985.20	1967.56	1959.98	1956.69
145000	2287.08	2242.40	2205.92	2175.94	2151.19	2130.66	2113.59	2099.34	2056.10	2037.83	2029.98	2026.58
150000	2365.94	2319.73	2281.99	2250.98	2225.37	2204.14	2186.47	2171.73	2127.00	2108.10	2099.97	2096.46
155000	2444.81	2397.05	2358.05	2326.01	2299.55	2277.61	2259.35	2244.13	2197.90	2178.37	2169.97	2166.34
160000	2523.67	2474.38	2434.12	2401.04	2373.73	2351.08	2332.24	2316.52	2268.80	2248.64	2239.97	2236.22

MONTHLY AMORTIZING PAYMENTS

AMOUNT OF LOAN	NUMBER OF YEARS IN TERM											
	1	2	3	4	5	6	7	8	9	10	11	12
$ 50	4.57	2.48	1.79	1.45	1.25	1.12	1.03	0.96	0.91	0.87	0.84	0.82
100	9.13	4.95	3.57	2.89	2.49	2.23	2.05	1.92	1.82	1.74	1.68	1.64
200	18.25	9.89	7.14	5.78	4.98	4.45	4.09	3.83	3.63	3.48	3.36	3.27
300	27.37	14.84	10.70	8.66	7.46	6.68	6.14	5.74	5.45	5.22	5.04	4.90
400	36.49	19.78	14.27	11.55	9.95	8.90	8.18	7.65	7.26	6.96	6.72	6.53
500	45.61	24.73	17.83	14.43	12.43	11.13	10.22	9.57	9.07	8.69	8.40	8.16
600	54.73	29.67	21.40	17.32	14.92	13.35	12.27	11.48	10.89	10.43	10.08	9.80
700	63.85	34.61	24.96	20.20	17.40	15.58	14.31	13.39	12.70	12.17	11.76	11.43
800	72.97	39.56	28.53	23.09	19.89	17.80	16.35	15.30	14.51	13.91	13.44	13.06
900	82.09	44.50	32.09	25.97	22.37	20.03	18.40	17.21	16.33	15.65	15.11	14.69
1000	91.21	49.45	35.66	28.86	24.86	22.25	20.44	19.13	18.14	17.38	16.79	16.32
2000	182.41	98.89	71.31	57.72	49.71	44.50	40.88	38.25	36.28	34.76	33.58	32.64
3000	273.62	148.33	106.96	86.57	74.56	66.74	61.31	57.37	54.41	52.14	50.37	48.96
4000	364.82	197.77	142.62	115.43	99.42	88.99	81.75	76.49	72.55	69.52	67.16	65.28
5000	456.03	247.22	178.27	144.28	124.27	111.24	102.18	95.61	90.69	86.90	83.95	81.60
6000	547.23	296.66	213.92	173.14	149.12	133.48	122.62	114.73	108.82	104.28	100.73	97.92
7000	638.44	346.10	249.57	201.99	173.97	155.73	143.06	133.86	126.96	121.66	117.52	114.24
8000	729.64	395.54	285.23	230.85	198.83	177.97	163.49	152.98	145.09	139.04	134.31	130.56
9000	820.85	444.99	320.88	259.70	223.68	200.22	183.93	172.10	163.23	156.42	151.10	146.88
10000	912.05	494.43	356.53	288.56	248.53	222.47	204.36	191.22	181.37	173.80	167.89	163.20
11000	1003.26	543.87	392.19	317.41	273.38	244.71	224.80	210.34	199.50	191.18	184.68	179.52
12000	1094.46	593.31	427.84	346.27	298.24	266.96	245.23	229.46	217.64	208.56	201.46	195.84
13000	1185.67	642.75	463.49	375.12	323.09	289.20	265.67	248.58	235.78	225.94	218.25	212.15
14000	1276.87	692.20	499.14	403.98	347.94	311.45	286.11	267.71	253.91	243.32	235.04	228.47
15000	1368.08	741.64	534.80	432.83	372.79	333.70	306.54	286.83	272.05	260.70	251.83	244.79
16000	1459.28	791.08	570.45	461.69	397.65	355.94	326.98	305.95	290.18	278.08	268.62	261.11
17000	1550.49	840.52	606.10	490.54	422.50	378.19	347.41	325.07	308.32	295.46	285.41	277.43
18000	1641.69	889.97	641.75	519.40	447.35	400.44	367.85	344.19	326.46	312.84	302.19	293.75
19000	1732.90	939.41	677.41	548.25	472.20	422.68	388.29	363.31	344.59	330.22	318.98	310.07
20000	1824.10	988.85	713.06	577.11	497.06	444.93	408.72	382.43	362.73	347.60	335.77	326.39
21000	1915.30	1038.29	748.71	605.96	521.91	467.17	429.16	401.56	380.86	364.98	352.56	342.71
22000	2006.51	1087.73	784.37	634.82	546.76	489.42	449.59	420.68	399.00	382.36	369.35	359.03
23000	2097.71	1137.18	820.02	663.67	571.61	511.67	470.03	439.80	417.14	399.74	386.14	375.35
24000	2188.92	1186.62	855.67	692.53	596.47	533.91	490.46	458.92	435.27	417.12	402.92	391.67
25000	2280.12	1236.06	891.32	721.38	621.32	556.16	510.90	478.04	453.41	434.50	419.71	407.99
26000	2371.33	1285.50	926.98	750.24	646.17	578.40	531.34	497.16	471.55	451.88	436.50	424.30
27000	2462.53	1334.95	962.63	779.09	671.02	600.65	551.77	516.28	489.68	469.26	453.29	440.62
28000	2553.74	1384.39	998.28	807.95	695.88	622.90	572.21	535.41	507.82	486.64	470.08	456.94
29000	2644.94	1433.83	1033.93	836.80	720.73	645.14	592.64	554.53	525.95	504.02	486.87	473.26
30000	2736.15	1483.27	1069.59	865.66	745.58	667.39	613.08	573.65	544.09	521.40	503.65	489.58
31000	2827.35	1532.72	1105.24	894.51	770.43	689.64	633.51	592.77	562.23	538.78	520.44	505.90
32000	2918.56	1582.16	1140.89	923.37	795.29	711.88	653.95	611.89	580.36	556.16	537.23	522.22
33000	3009.76	1631.60	1176.55	952.22	820.14	734.13	674.39	631.01	598.50	573.54	554.02	538.54
34000	3100.97	1681.04	1212.20	981.08	844.99	756.37	694.82	650.13	616.64	590.92	570.81	554.86
35000	3192.17	1730.48	1247.85	1009.93	869.85	778.62	715.26	669.26	634.77	608.30	587.60	571.18
37500	3420.18	1854.09	1336.98	1082.07	931.98	834.23	766.35	717.06	680.11	651.75	629.57	611.98
40000	3648.20	1977.70	1426.11	1154.21	994.11	889.85	817.44	764.86	725.45	695.20	671.54	652.77
42500	3876.21	2101.30	1515.25	1226.34	1056.24	945.47	868.53	812.67	770.79	738.65	713.51	693.57
45000	4104.22	2224.91	1604.38	1298.48	1118.37	1001.08	919.62	860.47	816.13	782.09	755.48	734.37
47500	4332.23	2348.51	1693.51	1370.62	1180.50	1056.70	970.71	908.27	861.47	825.54	797.45	775.17
50000	4560.24	2472.12	1782.64	1442.76	1242.63	1112.31	1021.80	956.08	906.81	868.99	839.42	815.97
52500	4788.25	2595.72	1871.77	1514.89	1304.77	1167.93	1072.88	1003.88	952.15	912.44	881.39	856.76
55000	5016.27	2719.33	1960.91	1587.03	1366.90	1223.54	1123.97	1051.68	997.50	955.89	923.36	897.56
57500	5244.28	2842.94	2050.04	1659.17	1429.03	1279.16	1175.06	1099.49	1042.84	999.34	965.33	938.36
60000	5472.29	2966.54	2139.17	1731.31	1491.16	1334.77	1226.15	1147.29	1088.18	1042.79	1007.30	979.16
65000	5928.31	3213.75	2317.43	1875.58	1615.42	1446.00	1328.33	1242.90	1178.86	1129.69	1091.25	1060.75
70000	6384.34	3460.96	2495.70	2019.86	1739.69	1557.23	1430.51	1338.51	1269.54	1216.59	1175.19	1142.35
75000	6840.36	3708.17	2673.96	2164.13	1863.95	1668.46	1532.69	1434.11	1360.22	1303.49	1259.13	1223.95
80000	7296.39	3955.39	2852.22	2308.41	1988.21	1779.70	1634.87	1529.72	1450.90	1390.39	1343.07	1305.54
85000	7752.41	4202.60	3030.49	2452.68	2112.47	1890.93	1737.05	1625.33	1541.58	1477.29	1427.01	1387.14
90000	8208.43	4449.81	3208.75	2596.96	2236.74	2002.16	1839.23	1720.94	1632.26	1564.18	1510.95	1468.74
95000	8664.46	4697.02	3387.01	2741.23	2361.00	2113.39	1941.41	1816.54	1722.94	1651.08	1594.90	1550.33
100000	9120.48	4944.23	3565.28	2885.51	2485.26	2224.62	2043.59	1912.15	1813.62	1737.98	1678.84	1631.93
105000	9576.50	5191.44	3743.54	3029.78	2609.53	2335.85	2145.76	2007.76	1904.30	1824.88	1762.78	1713.52
110000	10032.53	5438.65	3921.81	3174.06	2733.79	2447.08	2247.94	2103.36	1994.99	1911.78	1846.72	1795.12
115000	10488.55	5685.87	4100.07	3318.33	2858.05	2558.31	2350.12	2198.97	2085.67	1998.68	1930.66	1876.72
120000	10944.58	5933.08	4278.33	3462.61	2982.31	2669.54	2452.30	2294.58	2176.35	2085.58	2014.60	1958.31
125000	11400.60	6180.29	4456.60	3606.89	3106.58	2780.77	2554.48	2390.19	2267.03	2172.48	2098.55	2039.91
130000	11856.62	6427.50	4634.86	3751.16	3230.84	2892.00	2656.66	2485.79	2357.71	2259.37	2182.49	2121.50
135000	12312.65	6674.71	4813.12	3895.44	3355.10	3003.23	2758.84	2581.40	2448.39	2346.27	2266.43	2203.10
140000	12768.67	6921.92	4991.39	4039.71	3479.37	3114.46	2861.02	2677.01	2539.07	2433.17	2350.37	2284.70
145000	13224.69	7169.13	5169.65	4183.99	3603.63	3225.69	2963.20	2772.62	2629.75	2520.07	2434.31	2366.29
150000	13680.72	7416.34	5347.91	4328.26	3727.89	3336.92	3065.38	2868.22	2720.43	2606.97	2518.25	2447.89
155000	14136.74	7663.56	5526.18	4472.54	3852.15	3448.16	3167.55	2963.83	2811.11	2693.87	2602.19	2529.49
160000	14592.77	7910.77	5704.44	4616.81	3976.42	3559.39	3269.73	3059.44	2901.80	2780.77	2686.14	2611.08

AMOUNT OF LOAN	NUMBER OF YEARS IN TERM											
	13	14	15	16	17	18	19	20	25	30	35	40
$ 50	0.80	0.79	0.77	0.76	0.76	0.75	0.74	0.74	0.72	0.72	0.72	0.71
100	1.60	1.57	1.54	1.52	1.51	1.49	1.48	1.47	1.44	1.43	1.43	1.42
200	3.19	3.13	3.08	3.04	3.01	2.98	2.96	2.94	2.88	2.86	2.85	2.84
300	4.79	4.70	4.62	4.56	4.51	4.47	4.43	4.41	4.32	4.28	4.27	4.26
400	6.38	6.26	6.16	6.08	6.01	5.96	5.91	5.87	5.76	5.71	5.69	5.68
500	7.98	7.82	7.70	7.60	7.51	7.44	7.39	7.34	7.19	7.13	7.11	7.10
600	9.57	9.39	9.24	9.12	9.02	8.93	8.86	8.81	8.63	8.56	8.53	8.51
700	11.17	10.95	10.78	10.64	10.52	10.42	10.34	10.27	10.07	9.98	9.95	9.93
800	12.76	12.52	12.32	12.15	12.02	11.91	11.82	11.74	11.51	11.41	11.37	11.35
900	14.35	14.08	13.86	13.67	13.52	13.40	13.29	13.21	12.95	12.84	12.79	12.77
1000	15.95	15.64	15.40	15.19	15.02	14.88	14.77	14.67	14.38	14.26	14.21	14.19
2000	31.89	31.28	30.79	30.38	30.04	29.76	29.53	29.34	28.76	28.52	28.42	28.37
3000	47.83	46.92	46.18	45.56	45.06	44.64	44.30	44.01	43.14	42.78	42.62	42.55
4000	63.78	62.56	61.57	60.75	60.08	59.52	59.06	58.68	57.52	57.03	56.83	56.74
5000	79.72	78.20	76.96	75.94	75.10	74.40	73.83	73.35	71.89	71.29	71.03	70.92
6000	95.66	93.84	92.35	91.12	90.12	89.28	88.59	88.01	86.27	85.55	85.24	85.10
7000	111.61	109.47	107.74	106.31	105.13	104.16	103.35	102.68	100.65	99.80	99.44	99.29
8000	127.55	125.11	123.13	121.50	120.15	119.04	118.12	117.35	115.03	114.06	113.65	113.47
9000	143.49	140.75	138.52	136.68	135.17	133.92	132.88	132.02	129.41	128.32	127.85	127.65
10000	159.43	156.39	153.91	151.87	150.19	148.80	147.65	146.69	143.78	142.57	142.06	141.84
11000	175.38	172.03	169.30	167.05	165.21	163.68	162.41	161.35	158.16	156.83	156.26	156.02
12000	191.32	187.67	184.69	182.24	180.23	178.56	177.17	176.02	172.54	171.09	170.47	170.20
13000	207.26	203.30	200.08	197.43	195.24	193.44	191.94	190.69	186.92	185.34	184.67	184.39
14000	223.21	218.94	215.47	212.61	210.26	208.32	206.70	205.36	201.30	199.60	198.88	198.57
15000	239.15	234.58	230.86	227.80	225.28	223.20	221.47	220.03	215.67	213.86	213.08	212.75
16000	255.09	250.22	246.25	242.99	240.30	238.08	236.23	234.69	230.05	228.11	227.29	226.94
17000	271.04	265.86	261.64	258.17	255.32	252.96	250.99	249.36	244.43	242.37	241.49	241.12
18000	286.98	281.50	277.03	273.36	270.34	267.84	265.76	264.03	258.81	256.63	255.70	255.30
19000	302.92	297.13	292.42	288.55	285.36	282.72	280.52	278.70	273.19	270.88	269.90	269.49
20000	318.86	312.77	307.81	303.73	300.37	297.59	295.29	293.37	287.56	285.14	284.11	283.67
21000	334.81	328.41	323.20	318.92	315.39	312.47	310.05	308.03	301.94	299.40	298.32	297.85
22000	350.75	344.05	338.59	334.10	330.41	327.35	324.81	322.70	316.32	313.65	312.52	312.04
23000	366.69	359.69	353.98	349.29	345.43	342.23	339.58	337.37	330.70	327.91	326.73	326.22
24000	382.64	375.33	369.37	364.48	360.45	357.11	354.34	352.04	345.08	342.17	340.93	340.40
25000	398.58	390.96	384.76	379.66	375.47	371.99	369.11	366.71	359.45	356.42	355.14	354.59
26000	414.52	406.60	400.15	394.85	390.48	386.87	383.87	381.37	373.83	370.68	369.34	368.77
27000	430.46	422.24	415.54	410.04	405.50	401.75	398.64	396.04	388.21	384.94	383.55	382.95
28000	446.41	437.88	430.93	425.22	420.52	416.63	413.40	410.71	402.59	399.19	397.75	397.14
29000	462.35	453.52	446.32	440.41	435.54	431.51	428.16	425.38	416.97	413.45	411.96	411.32
30000	478.29	469.16	461.71	455.60	450.56	446.39	442.93	440.05	431.34	427.71	426.16	425.50
31000	494.24	484.79	477.10	470.78	465.58	461.27	457.69	454.71	445.72	441.96	440.37	439.69
32000	510.18	500.43	492.49	485.97	480.59	476.15	472.46	469.38	460.10	456.22	454.57	453.87
33000	526.12	516.07	507.88	501.15	495.61	491.03	487.22	484.05	474.48	470.48	468.78	468.05
34000	542.07	531.71	523.27	516.34	510.63	505.91	501.98	498.72	488.86	484.73	482.98	482.24
35000	558.01	547.35	538.66	531.53	525.65	520.79	516.75	513.39	503.23	498.99	497.19	496.42
37500	597.87	586.44	577.13	569.49	563.20	557.99	553.66	550.06	539.18	534.63	532.70	531.88
40000	637.72	625.54	615.61	607.46	600.74	595.18	590.57	586.73	575.12	570.28	568.22	567.33
42500	677.58	664.64	654.08	645.42	638.29	632.38	627.48	623.40	611.07	605.92	603.73	602.79
45000	717.44	703.73	692.56	683.39	675.83	669.58	664.39	660.07	647.01	641.56	639.24	638.25
47500	757.30	742.83	731.03	721.36	713.38	706.78	701.30	696.74	682.96	677.20	674.75	673.71
50000	797.15	781.92	769.51	759.32	750.93	743.98	738.21	733.41	718.90	712.84	710.27	709.17
52500	837.01	821.02	807.98	797.29	788.47	781.18	775.12	770.08	754.85	748.48	745.78	744.62
55000	876.87	860.12	846.46	835.25	826.02	818.38	812.03	806.75	790.79	784.13	781.29	780.08
57500	916.72	899.21	884.93	873.22	863.56	855.57	848.94	843.42	826.74	819.77	816.81	815.54
60000	956.58	938.31	923.41	911.19	901.11	892.77	885.85	880.09	862.68	855.41	852.32	851.00
65000	1036.30	1016.50	1000.36	987.12	976.20	967.17	959.67	953.43	934.57	926.69	923.35	921.92
70000	1116.01	1094.69	1077.31	1063.05	1051.30	1041.57	1033.49	1026.77	1006.46	997.98	994.37	992.83
75000	1195.73	1172.89	1154.26	1138.98	1126.39	1115.97	1107.31	1100.11	1078.35	1069.26	1065.40	1063.75
80000	1275.44	1251.08	1231.21	1214.91	1201.48	1190.36	1181.13	1173.45	1150.24	1140.55	1136.43	1134.66
85000	1355.16	1329.27	1308.16	1290.84	1276.57	1264.76	1254.95	1246.79	1222.13	1211.83	1207.45	1205.58
90000	1434.87	1407.46	1385.11	1366.78	1351.66	1339.16	1328.77	1320.13	1294.02	1283.11	1278.48	1276.50
95000	1514.59	1485.65	1462.06	1442.71	1426.76	1413.55	1402.59	1393.47	1365.91	1354.40	1349.50	1347.41
100000	1594.30	1563.84	1539.01	1518.64	1501.85	1487.95	1476.41	1466.81	1437.80	1425.68	1420.53	1418.33
105000	1674.02	1642.04	1615.96	1594.57	1576.94	1562.35	1550.23	1540.15	1509.69	1496.96	1491.56	1489.24
110000	1753.73	1720.23	1692.91	1670.50	1652.03	1636.75	1624.05	1613.49	1581.58	1568.25	1562.58	1560.16
115000	1833.44	1798.42	1769.86	1746.43	1727.12	1711.14	1697.87	1686.83	1653.47	1639.53	1633.61	1631.08
120000	1913.16	1876.61	1846.81	1822.37	1802.22	1785.54	1771.70	1760.17	1725.36	1710.82	1704.64	1701.99
125000	1992.87	1954.80	1923.76	1898.30	1877.31	1859.94	1845.52	1833.51	1797.25	1782.10	1775.66	1772.91
130000	2072.59	2032.99	2000.71	1974.23	1952.40	1934.34	1919.34	1906.85	1869.14	1853.38	1846.69	1843.83
135000	2152.30	2111.19	2077.66	2050.16	2027.49	2008.73	1993.16	1980.19	1941.03	1924.67	1917.72	1914.74
140000	2232.02	2189.38	2154.61	2126.09	2102.59	2083.13	2066.98	2053.53	2012.92	1995.95	1988.74	1985.66
145000	2311.73	2267.57	2231.56	2202.02	2177.68	2157.53	2140.80	2126.87	2084.81	2067.23	2059.77	2056.57
150000	2391.45	2345.76	2308.51	2277.96	2252.77	2231.93	2214.62	2200.21	2156.70	2138.52	2130.79	2127.49
155000	2471.16	2423.95	2385.46	2353.89	2327.86	2306.32	2288.44	2273.55	2228.59	2209.80	2201.82	2198.41
160000	2550.88	2502.15	2462.41	2429.82	2402.95	2380.72	2362.26	2346.89	2300.48	2281.09	2272.85	2269.32

MONTHLY AMORTIZING PAYMENTS

AMOUNT OF LOAN	\multicolumn{12}{c}{NUMBER OF YEARS IN TERM}

AMOUNT OF LOAN	1	2	3	4	5	6	7	8	9	10	11	12
$ 50	4.57	2.48	1.79	1.45	1.25	1.12	1.03	0.97	0.92	0.88	0.85	0.83
100	9.14	4.96	3.58	2.90	2.50	2.24	2.06	1.93	1.83	1.76	1.70	1.65
200	18.27	9.92	7.16	5.80	5.00	4.48	4.12	3.86	3.66	3.51	3.40	3.30
300	27.40	14.87	10.74	8.70	7.50	6.72	6.18	5.79	5.49	5.27	5.09	4.95
400	36.53	19.83	14.32	11.60	10.00	8.96	8.24	7.71	7.32	7.02	6.79	6.60
500	45.67	24.79	17.89	14.50	12.50	11.20	10.30	9.64	9.15	8.77	8.48	8.25
600	54.80	29.74	21.47	17.40	15.00	13.44	12.35	11.57	10.98	10.53	10.18	9.90
700	63.93	34.70	25.05	20.29	17.50	15.68	14.41	13.49	12.81	12.28	11.87	11.55
800	73.06	39.65	28.63	23.19	19.99	17.91	16.47	15.42	14.64	14.04	13.57	13.19
900	82.20	44.61	32.20	26.09	22.49	20.15	18.53	17.35	16.47	15.79	15.26	14.84
1000	91.33	49.57	35.78	28.99	24.99	22.39	20.59	19.28	18.30	17.54	16.96	16.49
2000	182.65	99.13	71.56	57.97	49.98	44.78	41.17	38.55	36.59	35.08	33.91	32.98
3000	273.98	148.69	107.34	86.96	74.97	67.16	61.75	57.82	54.88	52.62	50.86	49.46
4000	365.30	198.25	143.11	115.94	99.95	89.55	82.33	77.09	73.17	70.16	67.81	65.95
5000	456.62	247.82	178.89	144.93	124.94	111.93	102.91	96.36	91.46	87.70	84.76	82.44
6000	547.95	297.38	214.67	173.91	149.93	134.32	123.49	115.63	109.75	105.24	101.71	98.92
7000	639.27	346.94	250.45	202.90	174.92	156.71	144.07	134.90	128.04	122.77	118.66	115.41
8000	730.59	396.50	286.22	231.88	199.90	179.09	164.65	154.17	146.33	140.31	135.62	131.89
9000	821.92	446.07	322.00	260.87	224.89	201.48	185.23	173.44	164.62	157.85	152.57	148.38
10000	913.24	495.63	357.78	289.85	249.88	223.86	205.81	192.72	182.91	175.39	169.52	164.87
11000	1004.56	545.19	393.55	318.84	274.86	246.25	226.39	211.99	201.20	192.93	186.47	181.35
12000	1095.89	594.75	429.33	347.82	299.85	268.64	246.97	231.26	219.49	210.47	203.42	197.84
13000	1187.21	644.32	465.11	376.80	324.84	291.02	267.55	250.53	237.78	228.01	220.37	214.33
14000	1278.53	693.88	500.89	405.79	349.83	313.41	288.13	269.80	256.07	245.54	237.32	230.81
15000	1369.86	743.44	536.66	434.77	374.81	335.79	308.71	289.07	274.36	263.08	254.27	247.30
16000	1461.18	793.00	572.44	463.76	399.80	358.18	329.29	308.34	292.65	280.62	271.23	263.78
17000	1552.50	842.57	608.22	492.74	424.79	380.56	349.87	327.61	310.94	298.16	288.18	280.27
18000	1643.83	892.13	644.00	521.73	449.77	402.95	370.45	346.88	329.23	315.70	305.13	296.76
19000	1735.15	941.69	679.77	550.71	474.76	425.34	391.04	366.15	347.52	333.24	322.08	313.24
20000	1826.47	991.25	715.55	579.70	499.75	447.72	411.62	385.43	365.81	350.78	339.03	329.73
21000	1917.80	1040.82	751.33	608.68	524.74	470.11	432.20	404.70	384.10	368.31	355.98	346.22
22000	2009.12	1090.38	787.10	637.67	549.72	492.49	452.78	423.97	402.40	385.85	372.93	362.70
23000	2100.44	1139.94	822.88	666.65	574.71	514.88	473.36	443.24	420.69	403.39	389.88	379.19
24000	2191.77	1189.50	858.66	695.63	599.70	537.27	493.94	462.51	438.98	420.93	406.84	395.67
25000	2283.09	1239.07	894.44	724.62	624.68	559.65	514.52	481.78	457.27	438.47	423.79	412.16
26000	2374.41	1288.63	930.21	753.60	649.67	582.04	535.10	501.05	475.56	456.01	440.74	428.65
27000	2465.74	1338.19	965.99	782.59	674.66	604.42	555.68	520.32	493.85	473.54	457.69	445.13
28000	2557.06	1387.75	1001.77	811.57	699.65	626.81	576.26	539.59	512.14	491.08	474.64	461.62
29000	2648.38	1437.32	1037.55	840.56	724.63	649.19	596.84	558.87	530.43	508.62	491.59	478.11
30000	2739.71	1486.88	1073.32	869.54	749.62	671.58	617.42	578.14	548.72	526.16	508.54	494.59
31000	2831.03	1536.44	1109.10	898.53	774.61	693.97	638.00	597.41	567.01	543.70	525.50	511.08
32000	2922.35	1586.00	1144.88	927.51	799.60	716.35	658.58	616.68	585.30	561.24	542.45	527.56
33000	3013.68	1635.57	1180.65	956.50	824.58	738.74	679.16	635.95	603.59	578.78	559.40	544.05
34000	3105.00	1685.13	1216.43	985.48	849.57	761.12	699.74	655.22	621.88	596.31	576.35	560.54
35000	3196.33	1734.69	1252.21	1014.46	874.56	783.51	720.32	674.49	640.17	613.85	593.30	577.02
37500	3424.63	1858.60	1341.65	1086.93	937.02	839.47	771.78	722.67	685.90	657.70	635.68	618.24
40000	3652.94	1982.50	1431.10	1159.39	999.49	895.44	823.23	770.85	731.62	701.55	678.06	659.45
42500	3881.25	2106.41	1520.54	1231.85	1061.96	951.40	874.68	819.02	777.35	745.39	720.44	700.67
45000	4109.56	2230.32	1609.98	1304.31	1124.43	1007.37	926.13	867.20	823.08	789.24	762.81	741.88
47500	4337.87	2354.22	1699.43	1376.77	1186.90	1063.33	977.58	915.38	868.80	833.08	805.19	783.10
50000	4566.18	2478.13	1788.87	1449.23	1249.36	1119.30	1029.03	963.56	914.53	876.93	847.57	824.32
52500	4794.49	2602.03	1878.31	1521.69	1311.83	1175.26	1080.48	1011.74	960.25	920.78	889.95	865.53
55000	5022.79	2725.94	1967.75	1594.16	1374.30	1231.23	1131.93	1059.91	1005.98	964.62	932.33	906.75
57500	5251.10	2849.85	2057.20	1666.62	1436.77	1287.19	1183.39	1108.09	1051.71	1008.47	974.70	947.96
60000	5479.41	2973.75	2146.64	1739.08	1499.24	1343.16	1234.84	1156.27	1097.43	1052.32	1017.08	989.18
65000	5936.03	3221.57	2325.53	1884.00	1624.17	1455.09	1337.74	1252.62	1188.88	1140.01	1101.84	1071.61
70000	6392.65	3469.38	2504.41	2028.92	1749.11	1567.02	1440.64	1348.98	1280.34	1227.70	1186.60	1154.04
75000	6849.26	3717.19	2683.30	2173.85	1874.04	1678.94	1543.55	1445.33	1371.79	1315.39	1271.35	1236.47
80000	7305.88	3965.00	2862.19	2318.77	1998.98	1790.87	1646.45	1541.69	1463.24	1403.09	1356.11	1318.90
85000	7762.50	4212.82	3041.07	2463.69	2123.92	1902.80	1749.35	1638.04	1554.69	1490.78	1440.87	1401.33
90000	8219.11	4460.63	3219.96	2608.61	2248.85	2014.73	1852.25	1734.40	1646.15	1578.47	1525.62	1483.76
95000	8675.73	4708.44	3398.85	2753.54	2373.79	2126.66	1955.16	1830.75	1737.60	1666.16	1610.38	1566.19
100000	9132.35	4956.25	3577.73	2898.46	2498.72	2238.59	2058.06	1927.11	1829.05	1753.86	1695.13	1648.63
105000	9588.97	5204.06	3756.62	3043.38	2623.66	2350.52	2160.96	2023.47	1920.50	1841.55	1779.89	1731.06
110000	10045.58	5451.88	3935.50	3188.31	2748.60	2462.45	2263.86	2119.82	2011.96	1929.24	1864.65	1813.49
115000	10502.20	5699.69	4114.39	3333.23	2873.53	2574.38	2366.77	2216.18	2103.41	2016.93	1949.40	1895.92
120000	10958.82	5947.50	4293.28	3478.15	2998.47	2686.31	2469.67	2312.53	2194.86	2104.63	2034.16	1978.35
125000	11415.43	6195.31	4472.16	3623.07	3123.40	2798.24	2572.57	2408.89	2286.31	2192.32	2118.92	2060.78
130000	11872.05	6443.13	4651.05	3768.00	3248.34	2910.17	2675.48	2505.24	2377.76	2280.01	2203.67	2143.21
135000	12328.67	6690.94	4829.94	3912.92	3373.28	3022.10	2778.38	2601.60	2469.22	2367.70	2288.43	2225.64
140000	12785.29	6938.75	5008.82	4057.84	3498.21	3134.03	2881.28	2697.95	2560.67	2455.40	2373.19	2308.07
145000	13241.90	7186.56	5187.71	4202.76	3623.15	3245.95	2984.18	2794.31	2652.12	2543.09	2457.94	2390.51
150000	13698.52	7434.38	5366.60	4347.69	3748.08	3357.88	3087.09	2890.66	2743.57	2630.78	2542.70	2472.94
155000	14155.14	7682.19	5545.48	4492.61	3873.02	3469.81	3189.99	2987.02	2835.03	2718.47	2627.46	2555.37
160000	14611.75	7930.00	5724.37	4637.53	3997.96	3581.74	3292.89	3083.37	2926.48	2806.17	2712.21	2637.80

AMOUNT OF LOAN ·	NUMBER OF YEARS IN TERM											
	13	14	15	16	17	18	19	20	25	30	35	40
$ 50	0.81	0.80	0.78	0.77	0.77	0.76	0.75	0.75	0.73	0.73	0.73	0.72
100	1.62	1.59	1.56	1.54	1.53	1.51	1.50	1.49	1.46	1.45	1.45	1.44
200	3.23	3.17	3.12	3.08	3.05	3.02	3.00	2.98	2.92	2.90	2.89	2.88
300	4.84	4.75	4.68	4.62	4.57	4.52	4.49	4.46	4.38	4.34	4.33	4.32
400	6.45	6.33	6.23	6.15	6.09	6.03	5.99	5.95	5.84	5.79	5.77	5.76
500	8.06	7.91	7.79	7.69	7.61	7.54	7.48	7.43	7.29	7.23	7.21	7.20
600	9.67	9.49	9.35	9.23	9.13	9.04	8.98	8.92	8.75	8.68	8.65	8.64
700	11.28	11.07	10.90	10.76	10.65	10.55	10.47	10.41	10.21	10.13	10.09	10.08
800	12.90	12.66	12.46	12.30	12.17	12.06	11.97	11.89	11.67	11.57	11.53	11.52
900	14.51	14.24	14.02	13.84	13.69	13.56	13.46	13.38	13.12	13.02	12.97	12.96
1000	16.12	15.82	15.57	15.37	15.21	15.07	14.96	14.86	14.58	14.46	14.42	14.40
2000	32.23	31.63	31.14	30.74	30.41	30.14	29.91	29.72	29.16	28.92	28.83	28.79
3000	48.35	47.44	46.71	46.11	45.61	45.20	44.86	44.58	43.73	43.38	43.24	43.18
4000	64.46	63.26	62.28	61.47	60.81	60.27	59.81	59.44	58.31	57.84	57.65	57.57
5000	80.57	79.07	77.84	76.84	76.01	75.33	74.77	74.30	72.89	72.30	72.06	71.96
6000	96.69	94.88	93.41	92.21	91.22	90.40	89.72	89.16	87.46	86.76	86.47	86.35
7000	112.80	110.69	108.98	107.57	106.42	105.46	104.67	104.01	102.04	101.22	100.88	100.74
8000	128.91	126.51	124.55	122.94	121.62	120.53	119.62	118.87	116.62	115.68	115.29	115.13
9000	145.03	142.32	140.11	138.31	136.82	135.59	134.58	133.73	131.19	130.14	129.70	129.52
10000	161.14	158.13	155.68	153.67	152.02	150.66	149.53	148.59	145.77	144.60	144.11	143.91
11000	177.26	173.94	171.25	169.04	167.22	165.72	164.48	163.45	160.35	159.06	158.53	158.30
12000	193.37	189.76	186.82	184.41	182.43	180.79	179.43	178.31	174.92	173.52	172.94	172.69
13000	209.48	205.57	202.38	199.77	197.63	195.86	194.39	193.16	189.50	187.98	187.35	187.08
14000	225.60	221.38	217.95	215.14	212.83	210.92	209.34	208.02	204.07	202.44	201.76	201.47
15000	241.71	237.19	233.52	230.51	228.03	225.99	224.29	222.88	218.65	216.90	216.17	215.86
16000	257.82	253.01	249.09	245.88	243.23	241.05	239.24	237.74	233.23	231.36	230.58	230.25
17000	273.94	268.82	264.65	261.24	258.44	256.12	254.20	252.60	247.80	245.82	244.99	244.64
18000	290.05	284.63	280.22	276.61	273.64	271.18	269.15	267.46	262.38	260.28	259.40	259.03
19000	306.17	300.45	295.79	291.98	288.84	286.25	284.10	282.31	276.96	274.74	273.81	273.42
20000	322.28	316.26	311.36	307.34	304.04	301.31	299.05	297.17	291.53	289.20	288.22	287.81
21000	338.39	332.07	326.92	322.71	319.24	316.38	314.00	312.03	306.11	303.66	302.63	302.20
22000	354.51	347.88	342.49	338.08	334.44	331.44	328.96	326.89	320.69	318.12	317.05	316.59
23000	370.62	363.70	358.06	353.44	349.65	346.51	343.91	341.75	335.26	332.58	331.46	330.98
24000	386.73	379.51	373.63	368.81	364.85	361.57	358.86	356.61	349.84	347.04	345.87	345.37
25000	402.85	395.32	389.19	384.18	380.05	376.64	373.81	371.47	364.42	361.50	360.28	359.76
26000	418.96	411.13	404.76	399.54	395.25	391.71	388.77	386.32	378.99	375.96	374.69	374.15
27000	435.07	426.95	420.33	414.91	410.45	406.77	403.72	401.18	393.57	390.42	389.10	388.54
28000	451.19	442.76	435.90	430.28	425.66	421.84	418.67	416.04	408.14	404.88	403.51	402.93
29000	467.30	458.57	451.46	445.65	440.86	436.90	433.62	430.90	422.72	419.34	417.92	417.32
30000	483.42	474.38	467.03	461.01	456.06	451.97	448.58	445.76	437.30	433.80	432.33	431.71
31000	499.53	490.20	482.60	476.38	471.26	467.03	463.53	460.62	451.87	448.26	446.74	446.10
32000	515.64	506.01	498.17	491.75	486.46	482.10	478.48	475.47	466.45	462.72	461.15	460.49
33000	531.76	521.82	513.73	507.11	501.66	497.16	493.43	490.33	481.03	477.18	475.57	474.88
34000	547.87	537.63	529.30	522.48	516.87	512.23	508.39	505.19	495.60	491.64	489.98	489.27
35000	563.98	553.45	544.87	537.85	532.07	527.29	523.34	520.05	510.18	506.10	504.39	503.66
37500	604.27	592.98	583.79	576.26	570.07	564.96	560.72	557.20	546.62	542.25	540.41	539.64
40000	644.55	632.51	622.71	614.68	608.08	602.62	598.10	594.34	583.06	578.40	576.44	575.61
42500	684.84	672.04	661.63	653.10	646.08	640.28	635.48	631.49	619.50	614.55	612.47	611.59
45000	725.12	711.57	700.55	691.52	684.09	677.95	672.86	668.63	655.94	650.70	648.50	647.57
47500	765.41	751.11	739.46	729.93	722.09	715.61	710.24	705.78	692.38	686.85	684.52	683.54
50000	805.69	790.64	778.38	768.35	760.09	753.27	747.62	742.93	728.83	723.00	720.55	719.52
52500	845.97	830.17	817.30	806.77	798.10	790.94	785.00	780.07	765.27	759.15	756.58	755.49
55000	886.26	869.70	856.22	845.18	836.10	828.60	822.38	817.22	801.71	795.30	792.61	791.47
57500	926.54	909.23	895.14	883.60	874.11	866.27	859.77	854.36	838.15	831.45	828.63	827.44
60000	966.83	948.76	934.06	922.02	912.11	903.93	897.15	891.51	874.59	867.60	864.66	863.42
65000	1047.40	1027.83	1011.90	998.85	988.12	979.26	971.91	965.80	947.47	939.90	936.71	935.37
70000	1127.96	1106.89	1089.73	1075.69	1064.13	1054.58	1046.67	1040.09	1020.35	1012.20	1008.77	1007.32
75000	1208.53	1185.95	1167.57	1152.52	1140.14	1129.91	1121.43	1114.39	1093.24	1084.49	1080.82	1079.27
80000	1289.10	1265.02	1245.41	1229.36	1216.15	1205.24	1196.19	1188.68	1166.12	1156.79	1152.88	1151.22
85000	1369.67	1344.08	1323.25	1306.19	1292.16	1280.56	1270.94	1262.97	1239.00	1229.09	1224.93	1223.17
90000	1450.24	1423.14	1401.09	1383.03	1368.17	1355.89	1345.72	1337.26	1311.88	1301.39	1296.99	1295.13
95000	1530.81	1502.21	1478.92	1459.86	1444.17	1431.22	1420.48	1411.55	1384.76	1373.69	1369.04	1367.08
100000	1611.37	1581.27	1556.76	1536.69	1520.18	1506.54	1495.24	1485.85	1457.65	1445.99	1441.10	1439.03
105000	1691.94	1660.33	1634.60	1613.53	1596.19	1581.87	1570.00	1560.14	1530.53	1518.29	1513.15	1510.98
110000	1772.51	1739.40	1712.44	1690.36	1672.20	1657.20	1644.76	1634.43	1603.41	1590.59	1585.21	1582.93
115000	1853.08	1818.46	1790.28	1767.20	1748.21	1732.53	1719.53	1708.72	1676.29	1662.89	1657.26	1654.88
120000	1933.65	1897.52	1868.11	1844.03	1824.22	1807.85	1794.29	1783.02	1749.17	1735.19	1729.32	1726.83
125000	2014.22	1976.58	1945.95	1920.87	1900.23	1883.18	1869.05	1857.31	1822.06	1807.49	1801.37	1798.54
130000	2094.79	2055.65	2023.79	1997.70	1976.24	1958.51	1943.81	1931.60	1894.94	1879.79	1873.42	1870.74
135000	2175.35	2134.71	2101.63	2074.54	2052.25	2033.83	2018.57	2005.89	1967.82	1952.09	1945.48	1942.69
140000	2255.92	2213.77	2179.46	2151.37	2128.26	2109.16	2093.33	2080.18	2040.70	2024.39	2017.53	2014.64
145000	2336.49	2292.84	2257.30	2228.21	2204.26	2184.49	2168.10	2154.48	2113.59	2096.68	2089.59	2086.59
150000	2417.06	2371.90	2335.14	2305.04	2280.27	2259.81	2242.86	2228.77	2186.47	2168.98	2161.64	2158.54
155000	2497.63	2450.96	2412.98	2381.87	2356.28	2335.14	2317.62	2303.06	2259.35	2241.28	2233.70	2230.49
160000	2578.20	2530.03	2490.82	2458.71	2432.29	2410.47	2392.38	2377.35	2332.23	2313.58	2305.75	2302.44

MONTHLY AMORTIZING PAYMENTS

AMOUNT OF LOAN	NUMBER OF YEARS IN TERM											
	1	2	3	4	5	6	7	8	9	10	11	12
$ 50	4.58	2.49	1.80	1.46	1.26	1.13	1.04	0.98	0.93	0.89	0.86	0.84
100	9.15	4.97	3.60	2.92	2.52	2.26	2.08	1.95	1.85	1.77	1.72	1.67
200	18.29	9.94	7.19	5.83	5.03	4.51	4.15	3.89	3.69	3.54	3.43	3.34
300	27.44	14.91	10.78	8.74	7.54	6.76	6.22	5.83	5.54	5.31	5.14	5.00
400	36.58	19.88	14.37	11.65	10.05	9.02	8.30	7.77	7.38	7.08	6.85	6.67
500	45.73	24.85	17.96	14.56	12.57	11.27	10.37	9.72	9.23	8.85	8.56	8.33
600	54.87	29.81	21.55	17.47	15.08	13.52	12.44	11.66	11.07	10.62	10.27	10.00
700	64.01	34.78	25.14	20.39	17.59	15.77	14.51	13.60	12.92	12.39	11.99	11.66
800	73.16	39.75	28.73	23.30	20.10	18.03	16.59	15.54	14.76	14.16	13.70	13.33
900	82.30	44.72	32.32	26.21	22.61	20.28	18.66	17.48	16.61	15.93	15.41	14.99
1000	91.45	49.69	35.91	29.12	25.13	22.53	20.73	19.43	18.45	17.70	17.12	16.66
2000	182.89	99.37	71.81	58.23	50.25	45.06	41.46	38.85	36.90	35.40	34.23	33.31
3000	274.33	149.05	107.71	87.35	75.37	67.58	62.18	58.27	55.34	53.10	51.35	49.97
4000	365.77	198.74	143.61	116.46	100.49	90.11	82.91	77.69	73.79	70.80	68.46	66.62
5000	457.22	248.42	179.52	145.58	125.62	112.64	103.63	97.11	92.23	88.49	85.58	83.27
6000	548.66	298.10	215.42	174.69	150.74	135.16	124.36	116.53	110.68	106.19	102.69	99.93
7000	640.10	347.78	251.32	203.81	175.86	157.69	145.09	135.95	129.12	123.89	119.81	116.58
8000	731.54	397.47	287.22	232.92	200.98	180.21	165.81	155.37	147.57	141.59	136.92	133.24
9000	822.98	447.15	323.12	262.03	226.10	202.74	186.54	174.80	166.01	159.29	154.04	149.89
10000	914.43	496.83	359.03	291.15	251.23	225.27	207.26	194.22	184.46	176.98	171.15	166.54
11000	1005.87	546.52	394.93	320.26	276.35	247.79	227.99	213.64	202.90	194.68	188.27	183.20
12000	1097.31	596.20	430.83	349.38	301.47	270.32	248.71	233.06	221.35	212.38	205.38	199.85
13000	1188.75	645.88	466.73	378.49	326.59	292.84	269.44	252.48	239.79	230.08	222.50	216.51
14000	1280.20	695.56	502.63	407.61	351.72	315.37	290.17	271.90	258.24	247.78	239.61	233.16
15000	1371.64	745.25	538.54	436.72	376.84	337.90	310.89	291.32	276.69	265.47	256.73	249.81
16000	1463.08	794.93	574.44	465.83	401.96	360.42	331.62	310.74	295.13	283.17	273.84	266.47
17000	1554.52	844.61	610.34	494.95	427.08	382.95	352.34	330.17	313.58	300.87	290.96	283.12
18000	1645.96	894.30	646.24	524.06	452.20	405.47	373.07	349.59	332.02	318.57	308.07	299.77
19000	1737.41	943.98	682.14	553.18	477.33	428.00	393.80	369.01	350.47	336.26	325.19	316.43
20000	1828.85	993.66	718.05	582.29	502.45	450.53	414.52	388.43	368.91	353.96	342.30	333.08
21000	1920.29	1043.34	753.95	611.41	527.57	473.05	435.25	407.85	387.36	371.66	359.42	349.74
22000	2011.73	1093.03	789.85	640.52	552.69	495.58	455.97	427.27	405.80	389.36	376.53	366.39
23000	2103.18	1142.71	825.75	669.64	577.82	518.10	476.70	446.69	424.25	407.06	393.65	383.04
24000	2194.62	1192.39	861.65	698.75	602.94	540.63	497.42	466.11	442.69	424.75	410.76	399.70
25000	2286.06	1242.08	897.56	727.86	628.06	563.16	518.15	485.54	461.14	442.45	427.88	416.35
26000	2377.50	1291.76	933.46	756.98	653.18	585.68	538.88	504.96	479.58	460.15	444.99	433.01
27000	2468.94	1341.44	969.36	786.09	678.30	608.21	559.60	524.38	498.03	477.85	462.11	449.66
28000	2560.39	1391.12	1005.26	815.21	703.43	630.73	580.33	543.80	516.47	495.55	479.22	466.31
29000	2651.83	1440.81	1041.16	844.32	728.55	653.26	601.05	563.22	534.92	513.24	496.34	482.97
30000	2743.27	1490.49	1077.07	873.44	753.67	675.79	621.78	582.64	553.37	530.94	513.45	499.62
31000	2834.71	1540.17	1112.97	902.55	778.79	698.31	642.50	602.06	571.81	548.64	530.57	516.27
32000	2926.16	1589.86	1148.87	931.66	803.92	720.84	663.23	621.48	590.26	566.34	547.68	532.93
33000	3017.60	1639.54	1184.77	960.78	829.04	743.36	683.96	640.90	608.70	584.03	564.80	549.58
34000	3109.04	1689.22	1220.68	989.89	854.16	765.89	704.68	660.33	627.15	601.73	581.91	566.24
35000	3200.48	1738.90	1256.58	1019.01	879.28	788.42	725.41	679.75	645.59	619.43	599.03	582.89
37500	3429.09	1863.11	1346.33	1091.79	942.09	844.73	777.22	728.30	691.71	663.68	641.82	624.53
40000	3657.69	1987.32	1436.09	1164.58	1004.89	901.05	829.04	776.85	737.82	707.92	684.60	666.16
42500	3886.30	2111.53	1525.84	1237.37	1067.70	957.36	880.85	825.41	783.93	752.16	727.39	707.79
45000	4114.90	2235.73	1615.60	1310.15	1130.50	1013.68	932.67	873.96	830.05	796.41	770.18	749.43
47500	4343.51	2359.94	1705.35	1382.94	1193.31	1069.99	984.48	922.51	876.16	840.65	812.96	791.06
50000	4572.12	2484.15	1795.11	1455.72	1256.12	1126.31	1036.29	971.07	922.27	884.90	855.75	832.70
52500	4800.72	2608.35	1884.86	1528.51	1318.92	1182.62	1088.11	1019.62	968.39	929.14	898.54	874.33
55000	5029.33	2732.56	1974.62	1601.30	1381.73	1238.94	1139.92	1068.17	1014.50	973.39	941.33	915.97
57500	5257.93	2856.77	2064.37	1674.08	1444.53	1295.25	1191.74	1116.72	1060.61	1017.63	984.11	957.60
60000	5486.54	2980.98	2154.13	1746.87	1507.34	1351.57	1243.55	1165.28	1106.73	1061.88	1026.90	999.24
65000	5943.75	3229.39	2333.64	1892.44	1632.95	1464.20	1347.18	1262.38	1198.95	1150.37	1112.48	1082.51
70000	6400.96	3477.80	2513.15	2038.01	1758.56	1576.83	1450.81	1359.49	1291.18	1238.86	1198.05	1165.78
75000	6858.17	3726.22	2692.66	2183.58	1884.17	1689.46	1554.44	1456.60	1383.41	1327.35	1283.63	1249.05
80000	7315.38	3974.63	2872.17	2329.15	2009.78	1802.09	1658.07	1553.70	1475.63	1415.84	1369.20	1332.31
85000	7772.59	4223.05	3051.68	2474.73	2135.39	1914.72	1761.70	1650.81	1567.86	1504.32	1454.77	1415.58
90000	8229.80	4471.46	3231.19	2620.30	2261.00	2027.35	1865.33	1747.91	1660.09	1592.81	1540.35	1498.85
95000	8687.01	4719.88	3410.70	2765.87	2386.62	2139.99	1968.96	1845.02	1752.31	1681.30	1625.92	1582.12
100000	9144.23	4968.29	3590.21	2911.44	2512.23	2252.61	2072.58	1942.13	1844.54	1769.79	1711.50	1665.39
105000	9601.44	5216.70	3769.72	3057.01	2637.84	2365.24	2176.21	2039.23	1936.77	1858.28	1797.07	1748.66
110000	10058.65	5465.12	3949.23	3202.59	2763.45	2477.87	2279.84	2136.34	2028.99	1946.77	1882.65	1831.93
115000	10515.86	5713.53	4128.74	3348.16	2889.06	2590.50	2383.47	2233.44	2121.22	2035.26	1968.22	1915.20
120000	10973.07	5961.95	4308.25	3493.73	3014.67	2703.13	2487.10	2330.55	2213.45	2123.75	2053.80	1998.47
125000	11430.28	6210.36	4487.76	3639.30	3140.28	2815.76	2590.73	2427.66	2305.67	2212.24	2139.37	2081.74
130000	11887.49	6458.78	4667.27	3784.87	3265.89	2928.39	2694.36	2524.76	2397.90	2300.73	2224.95	2165.01
135000	12344.70	6707.19	4846.78	3930.45	3391.50	3041.02	2797.99	2621.87	2490.13	2389.22	2310.52	2248.28
140000	12801.91	6955.60	5026.29	4076.02	3517.11	3153.65	2901.62	2718.97	2582.35	2477.71	2396.10	2331.55
145000	13259.12	7204.02	5205.80	4221.59	3642.73	3266.28	3005.25	2816.08	2674.58	2566.20	2481.67	2414.82
150000	13716.34	7452.43	5385.31	4367.16	3768.34	3378.91	3108.87	2913.19	2766.81	2654.69	2567.25	2498.09
155000	14173.55	7700.85	5564.83	4512.73	3893.95	3491.54	3212.50	3010.29	2859.03	2743.18	2652.82	2531.35
160000	14630.76	7949.26	5744.34	4658.30	4019.56	3604.17	3316.13	3107.40	2951.26	2831.67	2738.39	2664.62

AMOUNT OF LOAN	NUMBER OF YEARS IN TERM											
	13	14	15	16	17	18	19	20	25	30	35	40
$ 50	0.82	0.80	0.79	0.78	0.77	0.77	0.76	0.76	0.74	0.74	0.74	0.73
100	1.63	1.60	1.58	1.56	1.54	1.53	1.52	1.51	1.48	1.47	1.47	1.46
200	3.26	3.20	3.15	3.11	3.08	3.06	3.03	3.01	2.96	2.94	2.93	2.92
300	4.89	4.80	4.73	4.67	4.62	4.58	4.55	4.52	4.44	4.40	4.39	4.38
400	6.52	6.40	6.30	6.22	6.16	6.11	6.06	6.02	5.92	5.87	5.85	5.84
500	8.15	8.00	7.88	7.78	7.70	7.63	7.58	7.53	7.39	7.34	7.31	7.30
600	9.78	9.60	9.45	9.33	9.24	9.16	9.09	9.03	8.87	8.80	8.78	8.76
700	11.40	11.20	11.03	10.89	10.78	10.68	10.60	10.54	10.35	10.27	10.24	10.22
800	13.03	12.80	12.60	12.44	12.31	12.21	12.12	12.04	11.83	11.74	11.70	11.68
900	14.66	14.39	14.18	14.00	13.85	13.73	13.63	13.55	13.30	13.20	13.16	13.14
1000	16.29	15.99	15.75	15.55	15.39	15.26	15.15	15.05	14.78	14.67	14.62	14.60
2000	32.58	31.98	31.50	31.10	30.78	30.51	30.29	30.10	29.56	29.33	29.24	29.20
3000	48.86	47.97	47.24	46.65	46.16	45.76	45.43	45.15	44.33	43.99	43.86	43.80
4000	65.15	63.96	62.99	62.20	61.55	61.01	60.57	60.20	59.11	58.66	58.47	58.39
5000	81.43	79.94	78.73	77.75	76.93	76.26	75.71	75.25	73.88	73.32	73.09	72.99
6000	97.72	95.93	94.48	93.29	92.32	91.52	90.85	90.30	88.66	87.98	87.71	87.59
7000	114.00	111.92	110.23	108.84	107.71	106.77	105.99	105.35	103.43	102.65	102.32	102.19
8000	130.29	127.91	125.97	124.39	123.09	122.02	121.13	120.40	118.21	117.31	116.94	116.78
9000	146.57	143.89	141.72	139.94	138.48	137.27	136.28	135.45	132.98	131.97	131.56	131.38
10000	162.86	159.88	157.46	155.49	153.86	152.52	151.42	150.50	147.76	146.64	146.17	145.98
11000	179.14	175.87	173.21	171.03	169.25	167.78	166.56	165.55	162.53	161.30	160.79	160.58
12000	195.43	191.86	188.95	186.58	184.63	183.03	181.70	180.60	177.31	175.96	175.41	175.17
13000	211.71	207.84	204.70	202.13	200.02	198.28	196.84	195.65	192.08	190.63	190.02	189.77
14000	228.00	223.83	220.45	217.68	215.41	213.53	211.98	210.70	206.86	205.29	204.64	204.37
15000	244.28	239.82	236.19	233.23	230.79	228.78	227.12	225.75	221.63	219.95	219.26	218.97
16000	260.57	255.81	251.94	248.78	246.18	244.04	242.26	240.80	236.41	234.62	233.87	233.56
17000	276.85	271.79	267.68	264.32	261.56	259.29	257.41	255.85	251.19	249.28	248.49	248.16
18000	293.14	287.78	283.43	279.87	276.95	274.54	272.55	270.89	265.96	263.94	263.11	262.76
19000	309.42	303.77	299.17	295.42	292.34	289.79	287.69	285.94	280.74	278.61	277.72	277.35
20000	325.71	319.76	314.92	310.97	307.72	305.04	302.83	300.99	295.51	293.27	292.34	291.95
21000	341.99	335.74	330.67	326.52	323.11	320.30	317.97	316.04	310.29	307.93	306.96	306.55
22000	358.28	351.73	346.41	342.06	338.49	335.55	333.11	331.09	325.06	322.60	321.57	321.15
23000	374.56	367.72	362.16	357.61	353.88	350.80	348.25	346.14	339.84	337.26	336.19	335.74
24000	390.85	383.71	377.90	373.16	369.26	366.05	363.39	361.19	354.61	351.92	350.81	350.34
25000	407.13	399.69	393.65	388.71	384.65	381.30	378.54	376.24	369.39	366.59	365.42	364.94
26000	423.42	415.68	409.40	404.26	400.04	396.56	393.68	391.29	384.16	381.25	380.04	379.54
27000	439.70	431.67	425.14	419.80	415.42	411.81	408.82	406.34	398.94	395.91	394.66	394.13
28000	455.99	447.66	440.89	435.35	430.81	427.06	423.96	421.39	413.71	410.58	409.27	408.73
29000	472.27	463.64	456.63	450.90	446.19	442.31	439.10	436.44	428.49	425.24	423.89	423.33
30000	488.56	479.63	472.38	466.45	461.58	457.56	454.24	451.49	443.26	439.90	438.51	437.93
31000	504.84	495.62	488.12	482.00	476.96	472.82	469.38	466.54	458.04	454.57	453.12	452.52
32000	521.13	511.61	503.87	497.55	492.35	488.07	484.52	481.59	472.81	469.23	467.74	467.12
33000	537.41	527.60	519.62	513.09	507.74	503.32	499.67	496.64	487.59	483.89	482.36	481.72
34000	553.70	543.58	535.36	528.64	523.12	518.57	514.81	511.69	502.37	498.56	496.97	496.31
35000	569.98	559.57	551.11	544.19	538.51	533.82	529.95	526.73	517.14	513.22	511.59	510.91
37500	610.70	599.54	590.47	583.06	576.97	571.95	567.80	564.36	554.08	549.88	548.13	547.41
40000	651.41	639.51	629.84	621.93	615.44	610.08	605.65	601.98	591.02	586.54	584.68	583.90
42500	692.12	679.48	669.20	660.80	653.90	648.21	643.51	639.61	627.96	623.19	621.22	620.39
45000	732.84	719.45	708.57	699.67	692.37	686.34	681.36	677.23	664.89	659.85	657.76	656.89
47500	773.55	759.42	747.93	738.54	730.83	724.47	719.21	714.85	701.83	696.51	694.30	693.38
50000	814.26	799.38	787.29	777.41	769.29	762.60	757.07	752.48	738.77	733.17	730.84	729.87
52500	854.97	839.35	826.66	816.28	807.76	800.73	794.92	790.10	775.71	769.83	767.38	766.37
55000	895.69	879.32	866.02	855.15	846.22	838.86	832.77	827.72	812.65	806.48	803.93	802.86
57500	936.40	919.29	905.39	894.02	884.69	876.99	870.63	865.35	849.58	843.14	840.47	839.35
60000	977.11	959.26	944.75	932.89	923.15	915.12	908.48	902.97	886.52	879.80	877.01	875.85
65000	1058.54	1039.20	1023.48	1010.63	1000.08	991.38	984.19	978.22	960.40	953.12	950.09	948.83
70000	1139.96	1119.14	1102.21	1088.37	1077.01	1067.64	1059.89	1053.46	1034.28	1026.43	1023.18	1021.82
75000	1221.39	1199.07	1180.94	1166.11	1153.94	1143.90	1135.60	1128.71	1108.15	1099.75	1096.26	1094.81
80000	1302.81	1279.01	1259.67	1243.86	1230.87	1220.16	1211.30	1203.96	1182.03	1173.07	1169.35	1167.79
85000	1384.24	1358.95	1338.40	1321.60	1307.80	1296.42	1287.01	1279.21	1255.91	1246.38	1242.43	1240.78
90000	1465.67	1438.89	1417.13	1399.34	1384.73	1372.68	1362.72	1354.45	1329.78	1319.70	1315.51	1313.77
95000	1547.09	1518.83	1495.85	1477.08	1461.66	1448.94	1438.42	1429.70	1403.66	1393.01	1388.60	1386.75
100000	1628.52	1598.76	1574.58	1554.82	1538.58	1525.20	1514.13	1504.95	1477.53	1466.33	1461.68	1459.74
105000	1709.94	1678.70	1653.31	1632.56	1615.51	1601.46	1589.84	1580.19	1551.41	1539.65	1534.76	1532.73
110000	1791.37	1758.64	1732.04	1710.30	1692.44	1677.72	1665.54	1655.44	1625.29	1612.96	1607.85	1605.71
115000	1872.79	1838.58	1810.77	1788.04	1769.37	1753.98	1741.25	1730.69	1699.16	1686.28	1680.93	1678.70
120000	1954.22	1918.52	1889.50	1865.78	1846.30	1830.24	1816.95	1805.94	1773.04	1759.60	1754.02	1751.69
125000	2035.65	1998.45	1968.23	1943.52	1923.23	1906.50	1892.66	1881.18	1846.92	1832.91	1827.10	1824.67
130000	2117.07	2078.39	2046.96	2021.26	2000.16	1982.76	1968.37	1956.43	1920.79	1906.23	1900.18	1897.66
135000	2198.50	2158.33	2125.69	2099.00	2077.09	2059.02	2044.07	2031.68	1994.67	1979.54	1973.27	1970.65
140000	2279.92	2238.27	2204.41	2176.74	2154.02	2135.28	2119.78	2106.92	2068.55	2052.86	2046.35	2043.63
145000	2361.35	2318.20	2283.14	2254.48	2230.95	2211.54	2195.48	2182.17	2142.42	2126.18	2119.43	2116.62
150000	2442.77	2398.14	2361.87	2332.22	2307.87	2287.80	2271.19	2257.42	2216.30	2199.49	2192.52	2189.61
155000	2524.20	2478.08	2440.60	2409.96	2384.80	2364.06	2346.90	2332.66	2290.18	2272.81	2265.60	2262.59
160000	2605.62	2558.02	2519.33	2487.71	2461.73	2440.32	2422.60	2407.91	2364.05	2346.13	2338.69	2335.58

MONTHLY AMORTIZING PAYMENTS

AMOUNT OF LOAN	NUMBER OF YEARS IN TERM											
	1	2	3	4	5	6	7	8	9	10	11	12
$ 50	4.58	2.50	1.81	1.47	1.27	1.14	1.05	0.98	0.94	0.90	0.87	0.85
100	9.16	4.99	3.61	2.93	2.53	2.27	2.09	1.96	1.87	1.79	1.73	1.69
200	18.32	9.97	7.21	5.85	5.06	4.54	4.18	3.92	3.73	3.58	3.46	3.37
300	27.47	14.95	10.81	8.78	7.58	6.81	6.27	5.88	5.59	5.36	5.19	5.05
400	36.63	19.93	14.42	11.70	10.11	9.07	8.35	7.83	7.45	7.15	6.92	6.73
500	45.79	24.91	18.02	14.63	12.63	11.34	10.44	9.79	9.31	8.93	8.64	8.42
600	54.94	29.89	21.62	17.55	15.16	13.61	12.53	11.75	11.17	10.72	10.37	10.10
700	64.10	34.87	25.22	20.48	17.69	15.87	14.62	13.71	13.03	12.51	12.10	11.78
800	73.25	39.85	28.83	23.40	20.21	18.14	16.70	15.66	14.89	14.29	13.83	13.46
900	82.41	44.83	32.43	26.33	22.74	20.41	18.79	17.62	16.75	16.08	15.56	15.14
1000	91.57	49.81	36.03	29.25	25.26	22.67	20.88	19.58	18.61	17.86	17.28	16.83
2000	183.13	99.61	72.06	58.49	50.52	45.34	41.75	39.15	37.21	35.72	34.56	33.65
3000	274.69	149.42	108.09	87.74	75.78	68.01	62.62	58.72	55.81	53.58	51.84	50.47
4000	366.25	199.22	144.11	116.98	101.04	90.67	83.49	78.29	74.41	71.44	69.12	67.29
5000	457.81	249.02	180.14	146.23	126.29	113.34	104.36	97.86	93.01	89.29	86.40	84.12
6000	549.37	298.83	216.17	175.47	151.55	136.01	125.23	117.44	111.61	107.15	103.68	100.94
7000	640.93	348.63	252.19	204.72	176.81	158.67	146.11	137.01	130.21	125.01	120.96	117.76
8000	732.49	398.43	288.22	233.96	202.07	181.34	166.98	156.58	148.81	142.87	138.24	134.58
9000	824.05	448.24	324.25	263.21	227.32	204.01	187.85	176.15	167.41	160.73	155.52	151.40
10000	915.62	498.04	360.28	292.45	252.58	226.67	208.72	195.72	186.01	178.58	172.80	168.23
11000	1007.18	547.84	396.30	321.69	277.84	249.34	229.59	215.30	204.61	196.44	190.08	185.05
12000	1098.74	597.65	432.33	350.94	303.10	272.01	250.46	234.87	223.21	214.30	207.36	201.87
13000	1190.30	647.45	468.36	380.18	328.35	294.67	271.34	254.44	241.82	232.16	224.64	218.69
14000	1281.86	697.25	504.38	409.43	353.61	317.34	292.21	274.01	260.42	250.02	241.91	235.52
15000	1373.42	747.06	540.41	438.67	378.87	340.01	313.08	293.58	279.02	267.87	259.19	252.34
16000	1464.98	796.86	576.44	467.92	404.13	362.67	333.95	313.16	297.62	285.73	276.47	269.16
17000	1556.54	846.66	612.47	497.16	429.38	385.34	354.82	332.73	316.22	303.59	293.75	285.98
18000	1648.10	896.47	648.49	526.41	454.64	408.01	375.69	352.30	334.82	321.45	311.03	302.80
19000	1739.67	946.27	684.52	555.65	479.90	430.67	396.56	371.87	353.42	339.30	328.31	319.63
20000	1831.23	996.07	720.55	584.90	505.16	453.34	417.44	391.44	372.02	357.16	345.59	336.45
21000	1922.79	1045.88	756.57	614.14	530.42	476.01	438.31	411.02	390.62	375.02	362.87	353.27
22000	2014.35	1095.68	792.60	643.38	555.67	498.67	459.18	430.59	409.22	392.88	380.15	370.09
23000	2105.91	1145.48	828.63	672.63	580.93	521.34	480.05	450.16	427.82	410.74	397.43	386.92
24000	2197.47	1195.29	864.66	701.87	606.19	544.01	500.92	469.73	446.42	428.59	414.71	403.74
25000	2289.03	1245.09	900.68	731.12	631.45	566.67	521.79	489.30	465.03	446.45	431.99	420.56
26000	2380.59	1294.89	936.71	760.36	656.70	589.34	542.67	508.88	483.63	464.31	449.27	437.38
27000	2472.15	1344.70	972.74	789.61	681.96	612.01	563.54	528.45	502.23	482.17	466.54	454.20
28000	2563.71	1394.50	1008.76	818.85	707.22	634.67	584.41	548.02	520.83	500.03	483.82	471.03
29000	2655.28	1444.30	1044.79	848.10	732.48	657.34	605.28	567.59	539.43	517.88	501.10	487.85
30000	2746.84	1494.11	1080.82	877.34	757.73	680.01	626.15	587.16	558.03	535.74	518.38	504.67
31000	2838.40	1543.91	1116.85	906.59	782.99	702.67	647.02	606.73	576.63	553.60	535.66	521.49
32000	2929.96	1593.71	1152.87	935.83	808.25	725.34	667.89	626.31	595.23	571.46	552.94	538.32
33000	3021.52	1643.52	1188.90	965.07	833.51	748.01	688.77	645.88	613.83	589.32	570.22	555.14
34000	3113.08	1693.32	1224.93	994.32	858.76	770.67	709.64	665.45	632.43	607.17	587.50	571.96
35000	3204.64	1743.12	1260.95	1023.56	884.02	793.34	730.51	685.02	651.03	625.03	604.78	588.78
37500	3433.54	1867.63	1351.02	1096.67	947.17	850.01	782.69	733.95	697.54	669.68	647.98	630.84
40000	3662.45	1992.14	1441.09	1169.79	1010.31	906.67	834.87	782.88	744.04	714.32	691.17	672.89
42500	3891.35	2116.65	1531.16	1242.90	1073.45	963.34	887.05	831.81	790.54	758.97	734.37	714.95
45000	4120.25	2241.16	1621.22	1316.01	1136.60	1020.01	939.23	880.74	837.04	803.61	777.57	757.00
47500	4349.16	2365.67	1711.29	1389.12	1199.74	1076.67	991.40	929.67	883.54	848.25	820.77	799.06
50000	4578.06	2490.17	1801.36	1462.23	1262.89	1133.34	1043.58	978.60	930.05	892.90	863.97	841.12
52500	4806.96	2614.68	1891.43	1535.34	1326.03	1190.01	1095.76	1027.53	976.55	937.54	907.16	883.17
55000	5035.86	2739.19	1981.50	1608.45	1389.17	1246.67	1147.94	1076.46	1023.05	982.19	950.36	925.23
57500	5264.77	2863.70	2071.56	1681.57	1452.32	1303.34	1200.12	1125.39	1069.55	1026.83	993.56	967.28
60000	5493.67	2988.21	2161.63	1754.68	1515.46	1360.01	1252.30	1174.32	1116.05	1071.48	1036.76	1009.34
65000	5951.47	3237.23	2341.77	1900.90	1641.75	1473.34	1356.66	1272.18	1209.06	1160.77	1123.16	1093.45
70000	6409.28	3486.24	2521.90	2047.12	1768.04	1586.67	1461.01	1370.04	1302.06	1250.06	1209.55	1177.56
75000	6867.08	3735.26	2702.04	2193.34	1894.33	1700.01	1565.37	1467.90	1395.07	1339.35	1295.95	1261.67
80000	7324.89	3984.28	2882.17	2339.57	2020.61	1813.34	1669.73	1565.76	1488.07	1428.64	1382.34	1345.78
85000	7782.69	4233.29	3062.31	2485.79	2146.90	1926.67	1774.09	1663.62	1581.07	1517.93	1468.74	1429.89
90000	8240.50	4482.31	3242.44	2632.01	2273.19	2040.01	1878.45	1761.48	1674.08	1607.21	1555.14	1514.00
95000	8698.31	4731.33	3422.58	2778.23	2399.48	2153.34	1982.80	1859.34	1767.08	1696.50	1641.53	1598.11
100000	9156.11	4980.34	3602.72	2924.46	2525.77	2266.67	2087.16	1957.20	1860.09	1785.79	1727.93	1682.23
105000	9613.92	5229.36	3782.85	3070.68	2652.06	2380.01	2191.52	2055.06	1953.09	1875.08	1814.32	1766.34
110000	10071.72	5478.38	3962.99	3216.90	2778.34	2493.34	2295.88	2152.92	2046.09	1964.37	1900.72	1850.45
115000	10529.53	5727.39	4143.12	3363.13	2904.63	2606.67	2400.23	2250.78	2139.10	2053.66	1987.12	1934.56
120000	10987.33	5976.41	4323.26	3509.35	3030.92	2720.01	2504.59	2348.64	2232.10	2142.95	2073.51	2018.67
125000	11445.14	6225.43	4503.39	3655.57	3157.21	2833.34	2608.95	2446.50	2325.11	2232.24	2159.91	2102.78
130000	11902.94	6474.45	4683.53	3801.79	3283.50	2946.67	2713.31	2544.36	2418.11	2321.53	2246.31	2186.89
135000	12360.75	6723.46	4863.66	3948.02	3409.78	3060.01	2817.67	2642.22	2511.11	2410.82	2332.70	2271.00
140000	12818.55	6972.48	5043.80	4094.24	3536.07	3173.34	2922.02	2740.08	2604.12	2500.11	2419.10	2355.11
145000	13276.36	7221.50	5223.94	4240.46	3662.36	3286.68	3026.38	2837.94	2697.12	2589.40	2505.49	2439.22
150000	13734.16	7470.51	5404.07	4386.68	3788.65	3400.01	3130.74	2935.79	2790.13	2678.69	2591.89	2523.34
155000	14191.97	7719.53	5584.21	4532.91	3914.94	3513.34	3235.10	3033.65	2883.13	2767.98	2678.29	2607.45
160000	14649.77	7968.55	5764.34	4679.13	4041.22	3626.68	3339.45	3131.51	2976.13	2857.27	2764.68	2691.56

AMOUNT OF LOAN	NUMBER OF YEARS IN TERM											
	13	14	15	16	17	18	19	20	25	30	35	40
$ 50	0.83	0.81	0.80	0.79	0.78	0.78	0.77	0.77	0.75	0.75	0.75	0.75
100	1.65	1.62	1.60	1.58	1.56	1.55	1.54	1.53	1.50	1.49	1.49	1.49
200	3.30	3.24	3.19	3.15	3.12	3.09	3.07	3.05	3.00	2.98	2.97	2.97
300	4.94	4.85	4.78	4.72	4.68	4.64	4.60	4.58	4.50	4.47	4.45	4.45
400	6.59	6.47	6.37	6.30	6.23	6.18	6.14	6.10	5.99	5.95	5.93	5.93
500	8.23	8.09	7.97	7.87	7.79	7.72	7.67	7.63	7.49	7.44	7.42	7.41
600	9.88	9.70	9.56	9.44	9.35	9.27	9.20	9.15	8.99	8.93	8.90	8.89
700	11.53	11.32	11.15	11.02	10.90	10.81	10.74	10.67	10.49	10.41	10.38	10.37
800	13.17	12.94	12.74	12.59	12.46	12.36	12.27	12.20	11.98	11.90	11.86	11.85
900	14.82	14.55	14.34	14.16	14.02	13.90	13.80	13.72	13.48	13.39	13.35	13.33
1000	16.46	16.17	15.93	15.74	15.58	15.44	15.34	15.25	14.98	14.87	14.83	14.81
2000	32.92	32.33	31.85	31.47	31.15	30.88	30.67	30.49	29.95	29.74	29.65	29.61
3000	49.38	48.49	47.78	47.20	46.72	46.32	46.00	45.73	44.93	44.61	44.47	44.42
4000	65.83	64.66	63.70	62.93	62.29	61.76	61.33	60.97	59.90	59.47	59.30	59.22
5000	82.29	80.82	79.63	78.66	77.86	77.20	76.66	76.21	74.88	74.34	74.12	74.03
6000	98.75	96.98	95.55	94.39	93.43	92.64	91.99	91.45	89.85	89.21	88.94	88.83
7000	115.21	113.15	111.48	110.12	109.00	108.08	107.32	106.69	104.83	104.07	103.76	103.64
8000	131.66	129.31	127.40	125.85	124.57	123.52	122.65	121.93	119.80	118.94	118.59	118.44
9000	148.12	145.47	143.33	141.58	140.14	138.96	137.98	137.17	134.78	133.81	133.41	133.25
10000	164.58	161.64	159.25	157.31	155.71	154.40	153.31	152.41	149.75	148.67	148.23	148.05
11000	181.03	177.80	175.18	173.04	171.28	169.84	168.64	167.66	164.73	163.54	163.06	162.85
12000	197.49	193.96	191.10	188.77	186.85	185.27	183.97	182.90	179.70	178.41	177.88	177.66
13000	213.95	210.13	207.03	204.50	202.42	200.71	199.30	198.14	194.67	193.27	192.70	192.46
14000	230.41	226.29	222.95	220.23	217.99	216.15	214.64	213.38	209.65	208.14	207.52	207.27
15000	246.86	242.45	238.87	235.96	233.56	231.59	229.97	228.62	224.62	223.01	222.35	222.07
16000	263.32	258.62	254.80	251.69	249.13	247.03	245.30	243.86	239.60	237.88	237.17	236.88
17000	279.78	274.78	270.72	267.42	264.70	262.47	260.63	259.10	254.57	252.74	251.99	251.68
18000	296.24	290.94	286.65	283.15	280.27	277.91	275.96	274.34	269.55	267.61	266.81	266.49
19000	312.69	307.11	302.57	298.88	295.84	293.35	291.29	289.58	284.52	282.48	281.64	281.29
20000	329.15	323.27	318.50	314.61	311.41	308.79	306.62	304.82	299.50	297.34	296.46	296.10
21000	345.61	339.43	334.42	330.34	326.98	324.23	321.95	320.07	314.47	312.21	311.28	310.90
22000	362.06	355.60	350.35	346.07	342.55	339.67	337.28	335.31	329.45	327.08	326.11	325.70
23000	378.52	371.76	366.27	361.80	358.13	355.10	352.61	350.55	344.42	341.94	340.93	340.51
24000	394.98	387.92	382.20	377.53	373.70	370.54	367.94	365.79	359.40	356.81	355.75	355.31
25000	411.44	404.09	398.12	393.26	389.27	385.98	383.27	381.03	374.37	371.68	370.57	370.12
26000	427.89	420.25	414.05	408.99	404.84	401.42	398.60	396.27	389.34	386.54	385.40	384.92
27000	444.35	436.41	429.97	424.72	420.41	416.86	413.93	411.51	404.32	401.41	400.22	399.73
28000	460.81	452.57	445.90	440.45	435.98	432.30	429.27	426.75	419.29	416.28	415.04	414.53
29000	477.26	468.74	461.82	456.18	451.55	447.74	444.60	441.99	434.27	431.15	429.86	429.34
30000	493.72	484.90	477.74	471.91	467.12	463.18	459.93	457.23	449.24	446.01	444.69	444.14
31000	510.18	501.06	493.67	487.64	482.69	478.62	475.26	472.48	464.22	460.88	459.51	458.95
32000	526.64	517.23	509.59	503.37	498.26	494.06	490.59	487.72	479.19	475.75	474.33	473.75
33000	543.09	533.39	525.52	519.10	513.83	509.50	505.92	502.96	494.17	490.61	489.16	488.55
34000	559.55	549.55	541.44	534.83	529.40	524.94	521.25	518.20	509.14	505.48	503.98	503.36
35000	576.01	565.72	557.37	550.56	544.97	540.37	536.58	533.44	524.12	520.35	518.80	518.16
37500	617.15	606.13	597.18	589.88	583.90	578.97	574.91	571.54	561.55	557.51	555.86	555.18
40000	658.29	646.53	636.99	629.21	622.82	617.57	613.23	609.64	598.99	594.68	592.92	592.19
42500	699.44	686.94	676.80	668.53	661.75	656.17	651.56	647.75	636.43	631.85	629.97	629.20
45000	740.58	727.35	716.61	707.86	700.68	694.77	689.89	685.85	673.86	669.02	667.03	666.21
47500	781.72	767.76	756.43	747.18	739.60	733.36	728.21	723.95	711.30	706.18	704.09	703.22
50000	822.87	808.17	796.24	786.51	778.53	771.96	766.54	762.05	748.73	743.35	741.14	740.23
52500	864.01	848.57	836.05	825.83	817.45	810.56	804.87	800.16	786.17	780.52	778.20	777.24
55000	905.15	888.98	875.86	865.16	856.38	849.16	843.19	838.26	823.61	817.69	815.26	814.25
57500	946.30	929.39	915.67	904.48	895.31	887.75	881.52	876.36	861.04	854.85	852.31	851.27
60000	987.44	969.80	955.48	943.81	934.23	926.35	919.85	914.46	898.48	892.02	889.37	888.28
65000	1069.73	1050.61	1035.11	1022.46	1012.08	1003.55	996.50	990.67	973.35	966.35	963.48	962.30
70000	1152.01	1131.43	1114.73	1101.11	1089.94	1080.74	1073.16	1066.87	1048.23	1040.69	1037.60	1036.32
75000	1234.30	1212.25	1194.35	1179.76	1167.79	1157.94	1149.81	1143.08	1123.10	1115.02	1111.71	1110.35
80000	1316.58	1293.06	1273.98	1258.41	1245.64	1235.14	1226.46	1219.28	1197.97	1189.36	1185.83	1184.37
85000	1398.87	1373.88	1353.60	1337.06	1323.49	1312.33	1303.12	1295.49	1272.85	1263.69	1259.94	1258.39
90000	1481.16	1454.69	1433.22	1415.71	1401.35	1389.53	1379.77	1371.69	1347.72	1338.03	1334.06	1332.41
95000	1563.44	1535.51	1512.85	1494.36	1479.20	1466.72	1456.42	1447.90	1422.59	1412.36	1408.17	1406.44
100000	1645.73	1616.33	1592.47	1573.01	1557.05	1543.92	1533.08	1524.10	1497.46	1486.70	1482.28	1480.46
105000	1728.01	1697.14	1672.09	1651.66	1634.90	1621.11	1609.73	1600.31	1572.34	1561.03	1556.39	1554.48
110000	1810.30	1777.96	1751.72	1730.31	1712.75	1698.31	1686.38	1676.51	1647.21	1635.37	1630.51	1628.50
115000	1892.59	1858.77	1831.34	1808.96	1790.61	1775.50	1763.04	1752.72	1722.08	1709.70	1704.62	1702.53
120000	1974.87	1939.59	1910.96	1887.61	1868.46	1852.70	1839.69	1828.92	1796.96	1784.04	1778.74	1776.55
125000	2057.16	2020.41	1990.59	1966.26	1946.31	1929.90	1916.34	1905.13	1871.83	1858.37	1852.85	1850.57
130000	2139.45	2101.22	2070.21	2044.91	2024.16	2007.09	1993.00	1981.33	1946.70	1932.70	1926.96	1924.59
135000	2221.73	2182.04	2149.83	2123.56	2102.02	2084.29	2069.65	2057.54	2021.58	2007.04	2001.08	1998.62
140000	2304.02	2262.85	2229.46	2202.21	2179.87	2161.48	2146.31	2133.74	2096.45	2081.37	2075.19	2072.64
145000	2386.30	2343.67	2309.08	2280.86	2257.72	2238.68	2222.96	2209.95	2171.32	2155.71	2149.30	2146.66
150000	2468.59	2424.49	2388.70	2359.51	2335.57	2315.87	2299.61	2286.15	2246.19	2230.04	2223.42	2220.69
155000	2550.88	2505.30	2468.33	2438.16	2413.42	2393.07	2376.27	2362.36	2321.07	2304.38	2297.53	2294.71
160000	2633.16	2586.12	2547.95	2516.81	2491.28	2470.27	2452.92	2438.56	2395.94	2378.71	2371.65	2368.73

18.00% MONTHLY AMORTIZING PAYMENTS

AMOUNT OF LOAN	NUMBER OF YEARS IN TERM											
	1	2	3	4	5	6	7	8	9	10	11	12
$ 50	4.59	2.50	1.81	1.47	1.27	1.15	1.06	0.99	0.94	0.91	0.88	0.85
100	9.17	5.00	3.62	2.94	2.54	2.29	2.11	1.98	1.88	1.81	1.75	1.70
200	18.34	9.99	7.24	5.88	5.08	4.57	4.21	3.95	3.76	3.61	3.49	3.40
300	27.51	14.98	10.85	8.82	7.62	6.85	6.31	5.92	5.63	5.41	5.24	5.10
400	36.68	19.97	14.47	11.75	10.16	9.13	8.41	7.89	7.51	7.21	6.98	6.80
500	45.84	24.97	18.08	14.69	12.70	11.41	10.51	9.87	9.38	9.01	8.73	8.50
600	55.01	29.96	21.70	17.63	15.24	13.69	12.62	11.84	11.26	10.82	10.47	10.20
700	64.18	34.95	25.31	20.57	17.78	15.97	14.72	13.81	13.13	12.62	12.22	11.90
800	73.35	39.94	28.93	23.50	20.32	18.25	16.82	15.78	15.01	14.42	13.96	13.60
900	82.52	44.94	32.54	26.44	22.86	20.53	18.92	17.76	16.89	16.22	15.70	15.30
1000	91.68	49.93	36.16	29.38	25.40	22.81	21.02	19.73	18.76	18.02	17.45	17.00
2000	183.36	99.85	72.31	58.75	50.79	45.62	42.04	39.45	37.52	36.04	34.89	33.99
3000	275.04	149.78	108.46	88.13	76.19	68.43	63.06	59.17	56.28	54.06	52.34	50.98
4000	366.72	199.70	144.61	117.50	101.58	91.24	84.08	78.90	75.03	72.08	69.78	67.97
5000	458.40	249.63	180.77	146.88	126.97	114.04	105.09	98.62	93.79	90.10	87.23	84.96
6000	550.08	299.55	216.92	176.25	152.37	136.85	126.11	118.34	112.55	108.12	104.67	101.95
7000	641.76	349.47	253.07	205.63	177.76	159.66	147.13	138.07	131.30	126.13	122.11	118.94
8000	733.44	399.40	289.22	235.00	203.15	182.47	168.15	157.79	150.06	144.15	139.56	135.93
9000	825.12	449.32	325.38	264.38	228.55	205.28	189.17	177.51	168.82	162.17	157.00	152.93
10000	916.80	499.25	361.53	293.75	253.94	228.08	210.18	197.24	187.57	180.19	174.45	169.92
11000	1008.48	549.17	397.68	323.13	279.33	250.89	231.20	216.96	206.33	198.21	191.89	186.91
12000	1100.16	599.09	433.83	352.50	304.73	273.70	252.22	236.68	225.09	216.23	209.34	203.90
13000	1191.84	649.02	469.99	381.88	330.12	296.51	273.24	256.41	243.84	234.25	226.78	220.89
14000	1283.52	698.94	506.14	411.25	355.51	319.31	294.25	276.13	262.60	252.26	244.22	237.88
15000	1375.20	748.87	542.29	440.63	380.91	342.12	315.27	295.85	281.36	270.28	261.67	254.87
16000	1466.88	798.79	578.44	470.00	406.30	364.93	336.29	315.58	300.12	288.30	279.11	271.86
17000	1558.56	848.71	614.60	499.38	431.69	387.74	357.31	335.30	318.87	306.32	296.56	288.86
18000	1650.24	898.64	650.75	528.75	457.09	410.55	378.33	355.02	337.63	324.34	314.00	305.85
19000	1741.92	948.56	686.90	558.13	482.48	433.35	399.34	374.75	356.39	342.36	331.44	322.84
20000	1833.60	998.49	723.05	587.50	507.87	456.16	420.36	394.47	375.14	360.38	348.89	339.83
21000	1925.28	1048.41	759.21	616.88	533.27	478.97	441.38	414.19	393.90	378.39	366.33	356.82
22000	2016.96	1098.34	795.36	646.25	558.66	501.78	462.40	433.92	412.66	396.41	383.78	373.81
23000	2108.64	1148.26	831.51	675.63	584.05	524.58	483.42	453.64	431.41	414.43	401.22	390.80
24000	2200.32	1198.18	867.66	705.00	609.45	547.39	504.43	473.36	450.17	432.45	418.67	407.79
25000	2292.00	1248.11	903.81	734.38	634.84	570.20	525.45	493.09	468.93	450.47	436.11	424.78
26000	2383.68	1298.03	939.97	763.75	660.23	593.01	546.47	512.81	487.68	468.49	453.55	441.78
27000	2475.36	1347.96	976.12	793.13	685.63	615.82	567.49	532.53	506.44	486.51	471.00	458.77
28000	2567.04	1397.88	1012.27	822.50	711.02	638.62	588.50	552.25	525.20	504.52	488.44	475.76
29000	2658.72	1447.80	1048.42	851.88	736.41	661.43	609.52	571.98	543.95	522.54	505.89	492.75
30000	2750.40	1497.73	1084.58	881.25	761.81	684.24	630.54	591.70	562.71	540.56	523.33	509.74
31000	2842.08	1547.65	1120.73	910.63	787.20	707.05	651.56	611.42	581.47	558.58	540.77	526.73
32000	2933.76	1597.58	1156.88	940.00	812.59	729.85	672.58	631.15	600.23	576.60	558.22	543.72
33000	3025.44	1647.50	1193.03	969.38	837.99	752.66	693.59	650.87	618.98	594.62	575.66	560.71
34000	3117.12	1697.42	1229.19	998.75	863.38	775.47	714.61	670.59	637.74	612.63	593.11	577.71
35000	3208.80	1747.35	1265.34	1028.13	888.77	798.28	735.63	690.32	656.50	630.65	610.55	594.70
37500	3438.00	1872.16	1355.72	1101.57	952.26	855.30	788.17	739.63	703.39	675.70	654.16	637.17
40000	3667.20	1996.97	1446.10	1175.00	1015.74	912.32	840.72	788.93	750.28	720.75	697.77	679.65
42500	3896.40	2121.78	1536.48	1248.44	1079.23	969.34	893.26	838.24	797.17	765.79	741.38	722.13
45000	4125.60	2246.59	1626.86	1321.88	1142.71	1026.36	945.81	887.55	844.06	810.84	784.99	764.61
47500	4354.80	2371.40	1717.24	1395.32	1206.19	1083.38	998.35	936.86	890.96	855.88	828.60	807.09
50000	4584.00	2496.21	1807.62	1468.75	1269.68	1140.39	1050.90	986.17	937.85	900.93	872.21	849.56
52500	4813.20	2621.02	1898.01	1542.19	1333.16	1197.41	1103.44	1035.47	984.74	945.98	915.82	892.04
55000	5042.40	2745.83	1988.39	1615.63	1396.64	1254.43	1155.99	1084.78	1031.63	991.02	959.43	934.52
57500	5271.60	2870.64	2078.77	1689.07	1460.13	1311.45	1208.53	1134.09	1078.53	1036.07	1003.05	977.00
60000	5500.80	2995.45	2169.15	1762.50	1523.61	1368.47	1261.08	1183.40	1125.42	1081.12	1046.66	1019.48
65000	5959.20	3245.07	2349.91	1909.38	1650.58	1482.51	1366.16	1282.01	1219.20	1171.21	1133.88	1104.43
70000	6417.60	3494.69	2530.67	2056.25	1777.54	1596.55	1471.25	1380.63	1312.99	1261.30	1221.10	1189.39
75000	6876.00	3744.31	2711.43	2203.13	1904.51	1710.59	1576.34	1479.25	1406.77	1351.39	1308.32	1274.34
80000	7334.40	3993.93	2892.20	2350.00	2031.48	1824.63	1681.43	1577.86	1500.56	1441.49	1395.54	1359.30
85000	7792.80	4243.55	3072.96	2496.88	2158.45	1938.67	1786.52	1676.48	1594.34	1531.58	1482.76	1444.26
90000	8251.20	4493.17	3253.72	2643.75	2285.41	2052.71	1891.61	1775.09	1688.12	1621.67	1569.98	1529.21
95000	8709.60	4742.79	3434.48	2790.63	2412.38	2166.75	1996.70	1873.71	1781.91	1711.76	1657.20	1614.17
100000	9168.00	4992.42	3615.24	2937.50	2539.35	2280.78	2101.79	1972.33	1875.69	1801.86	1744.42	1699.12
105000	9626.40	5242.04	3796.01	3084.38	2666.31	2394.82	2206.88	2070.94	1969.48	1891.95	1831.64	1784.08
110000	10084.80	5491.66	3976.77	3231.25	2793.28	2508.86	2311.97	2169.56	2063.26	1982.04	1918.86	1869.04
115000	10543.20	5741.28	4157.53	3378.13	2920.25	2622.90	2417.06	2268.17	2157.05	2072.13	2006.09	1953.99
120000	11001.60	5990.90	4338.29	3525.00	3047.22	2736.94	2522.15	2366.79	2250.83	2162.23	2093.31	2038.95
125000	11460.00	6240.52	4519.05	3671.88	3174.18	2850.98	2627.23	2465.41	2344.62	2252.32	2180.53	2123.90
130000	11918.40	6490.14	4699.82	3818.75	3301.15	2965.02	2732.32	2564.02	2438.40	2342.41	2267.75	2208.86
135000	12376.80	6739.76	4880.58	3965.63	3428.12	3079.06	2837.41	2662.64	2532.18	2432.51	2354.97	2293.82
140000	12835.20	6989.38	5061.34	4112.50	3555.08	3193.10	2942.50	2761.25	2625.97	2522.60	2442.19	2378.77
145000	13293.60	7239.00	5242.10	4259.38	3682.05	3307.13	3047.59	2859.87	2719.75	2612.69	2529.41	2463.73
150000	13752.00	7488.62	5422.86	4406.25	3809.02	3421.17	3152.68	2958.49	2813.54	2702.78	2616.63	2548.68
155000	14210.40	7738.24	5603.63	4553.13	3935.99	3535.21	3257.77	3057.10	2907.32	2792.88	2703.85	2633.64
160000	14668.80	7987.86	5784.39	4700.00	4062.95	3649.25	3362.86	3155.72	3001.11	2882.97	2791.07	2718.60

106

AMOUNT OF LOAN	NUMBER OF YEARS IN TERM											
	13	14	15	16	17	18	19	20	25	30	35	40
$ 50	0.84	0.82	0.81	0.80	0.79	0.79	0.78	0.78	0.76	0.76	0.76	0.76
100	1.67	1.64	1.62	1.60	1.58	1.57	1.56	1.55	1.52	1.51	1.51	1.51
200	3.33	3.27	3.23	3.19	3.16	3.13	3.11	3.09	3.04	3.02	3.01	3.01
300	4.99	4.91	4.84	4.78	4.73	4.69	4.66	4.63	4.56	4.53	4.51	4.51
400	6.66	6.54	6.45	6.37	6.31	6.26	6.21	6.18	6.07	6.03	6.02	6.01
500	8.32	8.17	8.06	7.96	7.88	7.82	7.77	7.72	7.59	7.54	7.52	7.51
600	9.98	9.81	9.67	9.55	9.46	9.38	9.32	9.26	9.11	9.05	9.02	9.01
700	11.65	11.44	11.28	11.14	11.03	10.94	10.87	10.81	10.63	10.55	10.53	10.51
800	13.31	13.08	12.89	12.74	12.61	12.51	12.42	12.35	12.14	12.06	12.03	12.01
900	14.97	14.71	14.50	14.33	14.19	14.07	13.97	13.89	13.66	13.57	13.53	13.52
1000	16.64	16.34	16.11	15.92	15.76	15.63	15.53	15.44	15.18	15.08	15.03	15.02
2000	33.27	32.68	32.21	31.83	31.52	31.26	31.05	30.87	30.35	30.15	30.06	30.03
3000	49.90	49.02	48.32	47.74	47.27	46.89	46.57	46.30	45.53	45.22	45.09	45.04
4000	66.53	65.36	64.42	63.66	63.03	62.51	62.09	61.74	60.70	60.29	60.12	60.05
5000	83.16	81.70	80.53	79.57	78.78	78.14	77.61	77.17	75.88	75.36	75.15	75.06
6000	99.79	98.04	96.63	95.48	94.54	93.77	93.13	92.60	91.05	90.43	90.18	90.08
7000	116.42	114.38	112.73	111.39	110.30	109.39	108.65	108.04	106.23	105.50	105.21	105.09
8000	133.05	130.72	128.84	127.31	126.05	125.02	124.17	123.47	121.40	120.57	120.24	120.10
9000	149.68	147.06	144.94	143.22	141.81	140.65	139.69	138.90	136.57	135.64	135.27	135.11
10000	166.31	163.40	161.05	159.13	157.56	156.27	155.21	154.34	151.75	150.71	150.30	150.12
11000	182.94	179.74	177.15	175.04	173.32	171.90	170.73	169.77	166.92	165.78	165.32	165.14
12000	199.57	196.08	193.26	190.96	189.07	187.53	186.25	185.20	182.10	180.86	180.35	180.15
13000	216.20	212.42	209.36	206.87	204.83	203.15	201.78	200.64	197.27	195.93	195.38	195.16
14000	232.83	228.76	225.46	222.78	220.59	218.78	217.30	216.07	212.45	211.00	210.41	210.17
15000	249.46	245.10	241.57	238.69	236.34	234.41	232.82	231.50	227.62	226.07	225.44	225.18
16000	266.09	261.44	257.67	254.61	252.10	250.04	248.34	246.93	242.79	241.14	240.47	240.19
17000	282.72	277.78	273.78	270.52	267.85	265.66	263.86	262.37	257.97	256.21	255.50	255.21
18000	299.35	294.12	289.88	286.43	283.61	281.29	279.38	277.80	273.14	271.28	270.53	270.22
19000	315.98	310.46	305.98	302.34	299.36	296.92	294.90	293.23	288.32	286.35	285.55	285.23
20000	332.61	326.80	322.09	318.26	315.12	312.54	310.42	308.67	303.49	301.42	300.58	300.24
21000	349.24	343.13	338.19	334.17	330.88	328.17	325.94	324.10	318.67	316.49	315.61	315.25
22000	365.87	359.47	354.30	350.08	346.63	343.80	341.46	339.53	333.84	331.56	330.64	330.27
23000	382.50	375.81	370.40	365.99	362.39	359.42	356.98	354.97	349.01	346.63	345.67	345.28
24000	399.13	392.15	386.51	381.91	378.14	375.05	372.50	370.40	364.19	361.71	360.70	360.29
25000	415.76	408.49	402.61	397.82	393.90	390.68	388.02	385.83	379.36	376.78	375.73	375.30
26000	432.39	424.83	418.71	413.73	409.65	406.30	403.55	401.27	394.54	391.85	390.76	390.31
27000	449.02	441.17	434.82	429.64	425.41	421.93	419.07	416.70	409.71	406.92	405.79	405.32
28000	465.65	457.51	450.92	445.56	441.17	437.56	434.59	432.13	424.89	421.99	420.81	420.34
29000	482.28	473.85	467.03	461.47	456.92	453.19	450.11	447.57	440.06	437.06	435.84	435.35
30000	498.91	490.19	483.13	477.38	472.68	468.81	465.63	463.00	455.23	452.13	450.87	450.36
31000	515.54	506.53	499.24	493.29	488.43	484.44	481.15	478.43	470.41	467.20	465.90	465.37
32000	532.17	522.87	515.34	509.21	504.19	500.07	496.67	493.86	485.58	482.27	480.93	480.38
33000	548.80	539.21	531.44	525.12	519.94	515.69	512.19	509.30	500.76	497.34	495.96	495.40
34000	565.43	555.55	547.55	541.03	535.70	531.32	527.71	524.73	515.93	512.41	510.99	510.41
35000	582.06	571.89	563.65	556.94	551.46	546.95	543.23	540.16	531.11	527.48	526.02	525.42
37500	623.63	612.74	603.91	596.73	590.84	586.01	582.03	578.75	569.04	565.16	563.59	562.95
40000	665.21	653.59	644.17	636.51	630.23	625.08	620.84	617.33	606.98	602.84	601.16	600.48
42500	706.78	694.43	684.43	676.29	669.62	664.15	659.64	655.91	644.91	640.52	638.73	638.01
45000	748.36	735.28	724.69	716.07	709.01	703.22	698.44	694.50	682.85	678.19	676.31	675.54
47500	789.93	776.13	764.95	755.85	748.40	742.28	737.24	733.08	720.78	715.87	713.88	713.07
50000	831.51	816.98	805.22	795.63	787.79	781.35	776.04	771.66	758.72	753.55	751.45	750.60
52500	873.08	857.83	845.48	835.41	827.18	820.42	814.85	810.24	796.66	791.22	789.02	788.13
55000	914.66	898.68	885.74	875.20	866.57	859.49	853.65	848.83	834.59	828.90	826.60	825.66
57500	956.23	939.53	926.00	914.98	905.96	898.55	892.45	887.41	872.53	866.58	864.17	863.18
60000	997.81	980.38	966.26	954.76	945.35	937.62	931.25	925.99	910.46	904.26	901.74	900.71
65000	1080.96	1062.07	1046.78	1034.32	1024.13	1015.75	1008.86	1003.16	986.33	979.61	976.88	975.77
70000	1164.11	1143.77	1127.30	1113.88	1102.91	1093.89	1086.46	1080.32	1062.21	1054.96	1052.03	1050.83
75000	1247.26	1224.47	1207.82	1193.45	1181.68	1172.02	1164.06	1157.49	1138.08	1130.32	1127.17	1125.89
80000	1330.41	1307.17	1288.34	1273.01	1260.46	1250.16	1241.65	1234.65	1213.95	1205.67	1202.32	1200.95
85000	1413.56	1388.86	1368.86	1352.57	1339.24	1328.29	1319.27	1311.82	1289.82	1281.03	1277.46	1276.01
90000	1496.71	1470.56	1449.38	1432.14	1418.02	1406.43	1396.88	1388.99	1365.69	1356.38	1352.61	1351.07
95000	1579.86	1552.26	1529.90	1511.70	1496.80	1484.56	1474.48	1466.15	1441.56	1431.74	1427.75	1426.13
100000	1663.01	1633.96	1610.43	1591.26	1575.58	1562.70	1552.08	1543.32	1517.43	1507.09	1502.90	1501.19
105000	1746.16	1715.65	1690.95	1670.82	1654.36	1640.83	1629.69	1620.48	1593.31	1582.44	1578.04	1576.25
110000	1829.31	1797.35	1771.47	1750.39	1733.14	1718.97	1707.29	1697.65	1669.18	1657.80	1653.19	1651.31
115000	1912.46	1879.05	1851.99	1829.95	1811.91	1797.10	1784.89	1774.81	1745.05	1733.15	1728.33	1726.36
120000	1995.61	1960.75	1932.51	1909.51	1890.69	1875.23	1862.50	1851.98	1820.92	1808.51	1803.48	1801.42
125000	2078.76	2042.44	2013.03	1989.07	1969.47	1953.37	1940.10	1929.14	1896.79	1883.86	1878.62	1876.48
130000	2161.91	2124.14	2093.55	2068.64	2048.25	2031.50	2017.71	2006.31	1972.66	1959.22	1953.76	1951.54
135000	2245.06	2205.84	2174.07	2148.20	2127.03	2109.64	2095.31	2083.48	2048.54	2034.57	2028.91	2026.60
140000	2328.21	2287.54	2254.59	2227.76	2205.81	2187.77	2172.91	2160.64	2124.41	2109.92	2104.05	2101.66
145000	2411.36	2369.23	2335.12	2307.33	2284.59	2265.91	2250.52	2237.81	2200.28	2185.28	2179.20	2176.72
150000	2494.51	2450.93	2415.64	2386.89	2363.36	2344.04	2328.12	2314.97	2276.15	2260.63	2254.34	2251.78
155000	2577.66	2532.63	2496.16	2466.45	2442.14	2422.18	2405.73	2392.14	2352.02	2335.99	2329.49	2326.84
160000	2660.81	2614.33	2576.68	2546.01	2520.92	2500.31	2483.33	2469.30	2427.89	2411.34	2404.63	2401.90

AMOUNT OF LOAN	NUMBER OF YEARS IN TERM											
	1	2	3	4	5	6	7	8	9	10	11	12
$ 50	4.59	2.51	1.82	1.48	1.28	1.15	1.06	1.00	0.95	0.91	0.89	0.86
100	9.18	5.01	3.63	2.96	2.56	2.30	2.12	1.99	1.90	1.82	1.77	1.72
200	18.36	10.01	7.26	5.91	5.11	4.59	4.24	3.98	3.79	3.64	3.53	3.44
300	27.54	15.02	10.89	8.86	7.66	6.89	6.35	5.97	5.68	5.46	5.29	5.15
400	36.72	20.02	14.52	11.81	10.22	9.18	8.47	7.96	7.57	7.28	7.05	6.87
500	45.90	25.03	18.14	14.76	12.77	11.48	10.59	9.94	9.46	9.09	8.81	8.59
600	55.08	30.03	21.77	17.71	15.32	13.77	12.70	11.93	11.35	10.91	10.57	10.30
700	64.26	35.04	25.40	20.66	17.88	16.07	14.82	13.92	13.24	12.73	12.33	12.02
800	73.44	40.04	29.03	23.61	20.43	18.36	16.94	15.91	15.14	14.55	14.09	13.73
900	82.62	45.05	32.66	26.56	22.98	20.66	19.05	17.89	17.03	16.37	15.85	15.45
1000	91.80	50.05	36.28	29.51	25.53	22.95	21.17	19.88	18.92	18.18	17.61	17.17
2000	183.60	100.09	72.56	59.02	51.06	45.90	42.33	39.76	37.83	36.36	35.22	34.33
3000	275.40	150.14	108.84	88.52	76.59	68.85	63.50	59.63	56.75	54.54	52.83	51.49
4000	367.20	200.18	145.12	118.03	102.12	91.80	84.66	79.51	75.66	72.72	70.44	68.65
5000	459.00	250.23	181.39	147.53	127.65	114.75	105.83	99.38	94.57	90.90	88.05	85.81
6000	550.80	300.27	217.67	177.04	153.18	137.70	126.99	119.26	113.49	109.08	105.66	102.97
7000	642.60	350.32	253.95	206.55	178.71	160.65	148.16	139.13	132.40	127.26	123.27	120.13
8000	734.40	400.36	290.23	236.05	204.24	183.60	169.32	159.01	151.31	145.44	140.88	137.29
9000	826.20	450.41	326.51	265.56	229.77	206.55	190.49	178.88	170.23	163.62	158.49	154.45
10000	918.00	500.45	362.78	295.06	255.30	229.50	211.65	198.76	189.14	181.80	176.10	171.61
11000	1009.79	550.50	399.06	324.57	280.83	252.45	232.82	218.63	208.05	199.98	193.71	188.77
12000	1101.59	600.54	435.34	354.07	306.36	275.40	253.98	238.51	226.97	218.16	211.32	205.94
13000	1193.39	650.59	471.62	383.58	331.89	298.35	275.15	258.38	245.88	236.34	228.93	223.10
14000	1285.19	700.63	507.90	413.09	357.42	321.30	296.31	278.26	264.79	254.52	246.54	240.26
15000	1376.99	750.68	544.17	442.59	382.95	344.25	317.47	298.13	283.71	272.70	264.15	257.42
16000	1468.79	800.72	580.45	472.10	408.48	367.19	338.64	318.01	302.62	290.88	281.76	274.58
17000	1560.59	850.77	616.73	501.60	434.01	390.14	359.80	337.88	321.54	309.06	299.37	291.74
18000	1652.39	900.81	653.01	531.11	459.54	413.09	380.97	357.76	340.45	327.24	316.98	308.90
19000	1744.19	950.86	689.29	560.62	485.07	436.04	402.13	377.63	359.36	345.42	334.59	326.06
20000	1835.99	1000.90	725.56	590.12	510.60	458.99	423.30	397.51	378.28	363.60	352.20	343.22
21000	1927.78	1050.95	761.84	619.63	536.13	481.94	444.46	417.38	397.19	381.78	369.81	360.38
22000	2019.58	1100.99	798.12	649.13	561.66	504.89	465.63	437.26	416.10	399.96	387.42	377.54
23000	2111.38	1151.04	834.40	678.64	587.19	527.84	486.79	457.13	435.02	418.14	405.03	394.70
24000	2203.18	1201.08	870.68	708.14	612.72	550.79	507.96	477.01	453.93	436.32	422.64	411.87
25000	2294.98	1251.13	906.95	737.65	638.25	573.74	529.12	496.88	472.84	454.50	440.25	429.03
26000	2386.78	1301.17	943.23	767.16	663.78	596.69	550.29	516.76	491.76	472.68	457.86	446.19
27000	2478.58	1351.22	979.51	796.66	689.30	619.64	571.45	536.63	510.67	490.86	475.47	463.35
28000	2570.38	1401.26	1015.79	826.17	714.83	642.59	592.61	556.51	529.58	509.04	493.08	480.51
29000	2662.18	1451.31	1052.07	855.67	740.36	665.54	613.78	576.38	548.50	527.22	510.69	497.67
30000	2753.98	1501.35	1088.34	885.18	765.89	688.49	634.94	596.26	567.41	545.40	528.30	514.83
31000	2845.77	1551.40	1124.62	914.68	791.42	711.43	656.11	616.13	586.33	563.58	545.91	531.99
32000	2937.57	1601.44	1160.90	944.19	816.95	734.38	677.27	636.01	605.24	581.76	563.52	549.15
33000	3029.37	1651.49	1197.18	973.70	842.48	757.33	698.44	655.88	624.15	599.94	581.13	566.31
34000	3121.17	1701.53	1233.45	1003.20	868.01	780.28	719.60	675.76	643.07	618.12	598.74	583.47
35000	3212.97	1751.58	1269.73	1032.71	893.54	803.23	740.77	695.63	661.98	636.30	616.35	600.63
37500	3442.47	1876.69	1360.43	1106.47	957.37	860.61	793.68	745.32	709.26	681.75	660.37	643.54
40000	3671.97	2001.80	1451.12	1180.24	1021.19	917.98	846.59	795.01	756.55	727.20	704.40	686.44
42500	3901.46	2126.92	1541.82	1254.00	1085.01	975.35	899.50	844.69	803.83	772.65	748.42	729.34
45000	4130.96	2252.03	1632.51	1327.77	1148.84	1032.73	952.41	894.38	851.12	818.10	792.44	772.25
47500	4360.46	2377.14	1723.21	1401.53	1212.66	1090.10	1005.32	944.07	898.40	863.54	836.47	815.15
50000	4589.96	2502.25	1813.90	1475.29	1276.49	1147.47	1058.24	993.76	945.68	908.99	880.49	858.05
52500	4819.45	2627.37	1904.60	1549.06	1340.31	1204.85	1111.15	1043.45	992.97	954.44	924.52	900.95
55000	5048.95	2752.48	1995.29	1622.82	1404.13	1262.22	1164.06	1093.13	1040.25	999.89	968.54	943.85
57500	5278.45	2877.59	2085.99	1696.59	1467.96	1319.59	1216.97	1142.82	1087.53	1045.34	1012.57	986.75
60000	5507.95	3002.70	2176.68	1770.35	1531.78	1376.97	1269.88	1192.51	1134.82	1090.79	1056.59	1029.66
65000	5966.94	3252.93	2358.07	1917.88	1659.43	1491.71	1375.71	1291.88	1229.39	1181.69	1144.64	1115.46
70000	6425.94	3503.15	2539.46	2065.41	1787.08	1606.46	1481.53	1391.26	1323.95	1272.59	1232.69	1201.26
75000	6884.93	3753.38	2720.85	2212.94	1914.73	1721.21	1587.35	1490.63	1418.52	1363.49	1320.74	1287.07
80000	7343.93	4003.60	2902.24	2360.47	2042.37	1835.95	1693.18	1590.01	1513.09	1454.39	1408.79	1372.87
85000	7802.92	4253.83	3083.63	2508.00	2170.02	1950.70	1799.00	1689.38	1607.66	1545.29	1496.84	1458.68
90000	8261.92	4504.05	3265.02	2655.53	2297.67	2065.45	1904.82	1788.76	1702.23	1636.19	1584.88	1544.48
95000	8720.91	4754.28	3446.41	2803.06	2425.32	2180.19	2010.64	1888.13	1796.79	1727.08	1672.93	1630.29
100000	9179.91	5004.50	3627.80	2950.58	2552.97	2294.94	2116.47	1987.51	1891.36	1817.98	1760.98	1716.09
105000	9638.90	5254.73	3809.19	3098.11	2680.62	2409.69	2222.29	2086.89	1985.93	1908.88	1849.03	1801.89
110000	10097.90	5504.95	3990.58	3245.64	2808.26	2524.43	2328.11	2186.26	2080.50	1999.78	1937.08	1887.70
115000	10556.89	5755.18	4171.97	3393.17	2935.91	2639.18	2433.94	2285.64	2175.06	2090.68	2025.13	1973.50
120000	11015.89	6005.40	4353.36	3540.70	3063.56	2753.93	2539.76	2385.01	2269.63	2181.58	2113.18	2059.31
125000	11474.88	6255.63	4534.75	3688.23	3191.21	2868.67	2645.58	2484.39	2364.20	2272.48	2201.23	2145.11
130000	11933.88	6505.85	4716.14	3835.76	3318.86	2983.42	2751.41	2583.76	2458.77	2363.38	2289.27	2230.91
135000	12392.87	6756.08	4897.53	3983.29	3446.50	3098.17	2857.23	2683.14	2553.34	2454.28	2377.32	2316.72
140000	12851.87	7006.30	5078.92	4130.82	3574.15	3212.91	2963.05	2782.51	2647.90	2545.17	2465.37	2402.52
145000	13310.86	7256.53	5260.31	4278.35	3701.80	3327.66	3068.88	2881.89	2742.47	2636.07	2553.42	2488.33
150000	13769.86	7506.75	5441.69	4425.87	3829.45	3442.41	3174.70	2981.26	2837.04	2726.97	2641.47	2574.13
155000	14228.85	7756.98	5623.08	4573.40	3957.10	3557.15	3280.52	3080.64	2931.61	2817.87	2729.52	2659.94
160000	14687.85	8007.20	5804.47	4720.93	4084.74	3671.90	3386.35	3180.01	3026.17	2908.77	2817.57	2745.74

AMOUNT OF LOAN	NUMBER OF YEARS IN TERM											
	13	14	15	16	17	18	19	20	25	30	35	40
$ 50	0.85	0.83	0.82	0.81	0.80	0.80	0.79	0.79	0.77	0.77	0.77	0.77
100	1.69	1.66	1.63	1.61	1.60	1.59	1.58	1.57	1.54	1.53	1.53	1.53
200	3.37	3.31	3.26	3.22	3.19	3.17	3.15	3.13	3.08	3.06	3.05	3.05
300	5.05	4.96	4.89	4.83	4.79	4.75	4.72	4.69	4.62	4.59	4.58	4.57
400	6.73	6.61	6.52	6.44	6.38	6.33	6.29	6.26	6.15	6.12	6.10	6.09
500	8.41	8.26	8.15	8.05	7.98	7.91	7.86	7.82	7.69	7.64	7.62	7.61
600	10.09	9.91	9.78	9.66	9.57	9.49	9.43	9.38	9.23	9.17	9.15	9.14
700	11.77	11.57	11.40	11.27	11.16	11.08	11.00	10.94	10.77	10.70	10.67	10.66
800	13.45	13.22	13.03	12.88	12.76	12.66	12.57	12.51	12.30	12.23	12.19	12.18
900	15.13	14.87	14.66	14.49	14.35	14.24	14.15	14.07	13.84	13.75	13.72	13.70
1000	16.81	16.52	16.29	16.10	15.95	15.82	15.72	15.63	15.38	15.28	15.24	15.22
2000	33.61	33.04	32.57	32.20	31.89	31.64	31.43	31.26	30.75	30.56	30.48	30.44
3000	50.42	49.55	48.86	48.29	47.83	47.45	47.14	46.88	46.13	45.83	45.71	45.66
4000	67.22	66.07	65.14	64.39	63.77	63.27	62.85	62.51	61.50	61.11	60.95	60.88
5000	84.02	82.59	81.43	80.48	79.71	79.08	78.56	78.13	76.88	76.38	76.18	76.10
6000	100.83	99.10	97.71	96.58	95.65	94.90	94.27	93.76	92.25	91.66	91.42	91.32
7000	117.63	115.62	114.00	112.68	111.60	110.71	109.98	109.39	107.63	106.93	106.65	106.54
8000	134.43	132.14	130.28	128.77	127.54	126.53	125.70	125.01	123.00	122.21	121.89	121.76
9000	151.24	148.65	146.56	144.87	143.48	142.34	141.41	140.64	138.37	137.48	137.12	136.98
10000	168.04	165.17	162.85	160.96	159.42	158.16	157.12	156.26	153.75	152.76	152.36	152.20
11000	184.84	181.69	179.13	177.06	175.36	173.97	172.83	171.89	169.12	168.03	167.59	167.42
12000	201.65	198.20	195.42	193.15	191.30	189.79	188.54	187.51	184.50	183.31	182.83	182.64
13000	218.45	214.72	211.70	209.25	207.25	205.60	204.25	203.14	199.87	198.58	198.06	197.85
14000	235.25	231.24	227.99	225.35	223.19	221.42	219.96	218.77	215.25	213.86	213.30	213.07
15000	252.06	247.75	244.27	241.44	239.13	237.23	235.68	234.39	230.62	229.13	228.53	228.29
16000	268.86	264.27	260.56	257.54	255.07	253.05	251.39	250.02	246.00	244.41	243.77	243.51
17000	285.66	280.78	276.84	273.63	271.01	268.86	267.10	265.64	261.37	259.68	259.00	258.73
18000	302.47	297.30	293.12	289.73	286.95	284.68	282.81	281.27	276.74	274.96	274.24	273.95
19000	319.27	313.82	309.41	305.82	302.90	300.50	298.52	296.89	292.12	290.23	289.47	289.17
20000	336.07	330.33	325.69	321.92	318.84	316.31	314.23	312.52	307.49	305.51	304.71	304.39
21000	352.88	346.85	341.98	338.02	334.78	332.13	329.94	328.15	322.87	320.78	319.94	319.61
22000	369.68	363.37	358.26	354.11	350.72	347.94	345.66	343.77	338.24	336.06	335.18	334.83
23000	386.48	379.88	374.55	370.21	366.66	363.76	361.37	359.40	353.62	351.33	350.42	350.05
24000	403.29	396.40	390.83	386.30	382.60	379.57	377.08	375.02	368.99	366.61	365.65	365.27
25000	420.09	412.92	407.12	402.40	398.55	395.39	392.79	390.65	384.36	381.88	380.89	380.48
26000	436.89	429.43	423.40	418.49	414.49	411.20	408.50	406.28	399.74	397.16	396.12	395.70
27000	453.70	445.95	439.68	434.59	430.43	427.02	424.21	421.90	415.11	412.43	411.36	410.92
28000	470.50	462.47	455.97	450.69	446.37	442.83	439.92	437.53	430.49	427.71	426.59	426.14
29000	487.30	478.98	472.25	466.78	462.31	458.65	455.64	453.15	445.86	442.98	441.83	441.36
30000	504.11	495.50	488.54	482.88	478.25	474.46	471.35	468.78	461.24	458.26	457.06	456.58
31000	520.91	512.02	504.82	498.97	494.20	490.28	487.06	484.40	476.61	473.53	472.30	471.80
32000	537.72	528.53	521.11	515.07	510.14	506.09	502.77	500.03	491.99	488.81	487.53	487.02
33000	554.52	545.05	537.39	531.16	526.08	521.91	518.48	515.66	507.36	504.08	502.77	502.24
34000	571.32	561.56	553.67	547.26	542.02	537.72	534.19	531.28	522.73	519.36	518.00	517.46
35000	588.13	578.08	569.96	563.36	557.96	553.54	549.90	546.91	538.11	534.63	533.24	532.68
37500	630.13	619.37	610.67	603.59	597.82	593.08	589.18	585.97	576.54	572.82	571.33	570.72
40000	672.14	660.66	651.38	643.83	637.67	632.62	628.46	625.04	614.98	611.01	609.41	608.77
42500	714.15	701.95	692.09	684.07	677.52	672.15	667.74	664.10	653.42	649.19	647.50	646.82
45000	756.16	743.25	732.80	724.31	717.38	711.69	707.02	703.17	691.85	687.38	685.59	684.87
47500	798.17	784.54	773.51	764.55	757.23	751.23	746.30	742.23	730.29	725.57	723.68	722.92
50000	840.18	825.83	814.23	804.79	797.09	790.77	785.58	781.29	768.72	763.76	761.77	760.96
52500	882.19	867.12	854.94	845.03	836.94	830.31	824.85	820.36	807.16	801.94	799.85	799.01
55000	924.19	908.41	895.65	885.27	876.79	869.85	864.13	859.42	845.60	840.13	837.94	837.06
57500	966.20	949.70	936.36	925.51	916.65	909.38	903.41	898.49	884.03	878.32	876.03	875.11
60000	1008.21	990.99	977.07	965.75	956.50	948.92	942.69	937.55	922.47	916.51	914.12	913.16
65000	1092.23	1073.57	1058.49	1046.23	1036.21	1028.00	1021.25	1015.68	999.34	992.88	990.29	989.25
70000	1176.25	1156.16	1139.91	1126.71	1115.92	1107.08	1099.80	1093.81	1076.21	1069.26	1066.47	1065.35
75000	1260.26	1238.74	1221.34	1207.18	1195.63	1186.15	1178.36	1171.94	1153.08	1145.63	1142.65	1141.44
80000	1344.28	1321.32	1302.76	1287.66	1275.34	1265.23	1256.92	1250.07	1229.96	1222.01	1218.82	1217.54
85000	1428.30	1403.90	1384.18	1368.14	1355.04	1344.30	1335.47	1328.20	1306.83	1298.38	1295.00	1293.64
90000	1512.32	1486.49	1465.60	1448.62	1434.75	1423.38	1414.03	1406.33	1383.70	1374.76	1371.18	1369.73
95000	1596.33	1569.07	1547.02	1529.10	1514.46	1502.46	1492.59	1484.45	1460.57	1451.13	1447.35	1445.83
100000	1680.35	1651.65	1628.45	1609.58	1594.17	1581.53	1571.15	1562.58	1537.44	1523.53	1523.53	1521.92
105000	1764.37	1734.23	1709.87	1690.06	1673.88	1660.61	1649.70	1640.71	1614.32	1603.88	1599.70	1598.02
110000	1848.38	1816.81	1791.29	1770.54	1753.58	1739.69	1728.26	1718.84	1691.19	1680.26	1675.88	1674.12
115000	1932.40	1899.40	1872.71	1851.01	1833.29	1818.76	1806.82	1796.97	1768.06	1756.63	1752.06	1750.21
120000	2016.42	1981.98	1954.13	1931.49	1913.00	1897.84	1885.37	1875.10	1844.93	1833.01	1828.23	1826.31
125000	2100.44	2064.56	2035.56	2011.97	1992.71	1976.92	1963.93	1953.23	1921.80	1909.38	1904.41	1902.40
130000	2184.45	2147.14	2116.98	2092.45	2072.42	2055.99	2042.49	2031.36	1998.68	1985.76	1980.58	1978.50
135000	2268.47	2229.73	2198.40	2172.93	2152.12	2135.07	2121.05	2109.49	2075.55	2062.13	2056.76	2054.60
140000	2352.49	2312.31	2279.82	2253.41	2231.83	2214.15	2199.60	2187.61	2152.42	2138.51	2132.94	2130.69
145000	2436.50	2394.89	2361.24	2333.89	2311.54	2293.22	2278.16	2265.74	2229.29	2214.88	2209.11	2206.79
150000	2520.52	2477.47	2442.67	2414.36	2391.25	2372.30	2356.72	2343.87	2306.16	2291.26	2285.29	2282.88
155000	2604.54	2560.06	2524.09	2494.84	2470.96	2451.38	2435.27	2422.00	2383.03	2367.64	2361.47	2358.98
160000	2688.56	2642.64	2605.51	2575.32	2550.67	2530.45	2513.83	2500.13	2459.91	2444.01	2437.64	2435.08

MONTHLY AMORTIZING PAYMENTS

AMOUNT OF LOAN	NUMBER OF YEARS IN TERM											
	1	2	3	4	5	6	7	8	9	10	11	12
$ 50	4.60	2.51	1.83	1.49	1.29	1.16	1.07	1.01	0.96	0.92	0.89	0.87
100	9.20	5.02	3.65	2.97	2.57	2.31	2.14	2.01	1.91	1.84	1.78	1.74
200	18.39	10.04	7.29	5.93	5.14	4.62	4.27	4.01	3.82	3.67	3.56	3.47
300	27.58	15.05	10.93	8.90	7.70	6.93	6.40	6.01	5.73	5.51	5.34	5.20
400	36.77	20.07	14.57	11.86	10.27	9.24	8.53	8.02	7.63	7.34	7.12	6.94
500	45.96	25.09	18.21	14.82	12.84	11.55	10.66	10.02	9.54	9.18	8.89	8.67
600	55.16	30.10	21.85	17.79	15.40	13.86	12.79	12.02	11.45	11.01	10.67	10.40
700	64.35	35.12	25.49	20.75	17.97	16.17	14.92	14.02	13.35	12.84	12.45	12.14
800	73.54	40.14	29.13	23.71	20.54	18.48	17.05	16.03	15.26	14.68	14.23	13.87
900	82.73	45.15	32.77	26.68	23.10	20.79	19.19	18.03	17.17	16.51	16.00	15.60
1000	91.92	50.17	36.41	29.64	25.67	23.10	21.32	20.03	19.08	18.35	17.78	17.34
2000	183.84	100.34	72.81	59.28	51.34	46.19	42.63	40.06	38.15	36.69	35.56	34.67
3000	275.76	150.50	109.22	88.92	77.00	69.28	63.94	60.09	57.22	55.03	53.33	52.00
4000	367.68	200.67	145.62	118.55	102.67	92.37	85.25	80.11	76.29	73.37	71.11	69.33
5000	459.60	250.84	182.02	148.19	128.34	115.46	106.56	100.14	95.36	91.71	88.88	86.66
6000	551.51	301.00	218.43	177.83	154.00	138.55	127.88	120.17	114.43	110.05	106.66	103.99
7000	643.43	351.17	254.83	207.46	179.67	161.64	149.19	140.20	133.50	128.40	124.44	121.32
8000	735.35	401.33	291.23	237.10	205.33	184.74	170.50	160.22	152.57	146.74	142.21	138.65
9000	827.27	451.50	327.64	266.74	231.00	207.83	191.81	180.25	171.64	165.08	159.99	155.99
10000	919.19	501.67	364.04	296.37	256.67	230.92	213.12	200.28	190.71	183.42	177.76	173.32
11000	1011.10	551.83	400.45	326.01	282.33	254.01	234.44	220.31	209.78	201.76	195.54	190.65
12000	1103.02	602.00	436.85	355.65	308.00	277.10	255.75	240.33	228.85	220.10	213.32	207.98
13000	1194.94	652.16	473.25	385.28	333.67	300.19	277.06	260.36	247.93	238.45	231.09	225.31
14000	1286.86	702.33	509.66	414.92	359.33	323.28	298.37	280.39	267.00	256.79	248.87	242.64
15000	1378.78	752.50	546.06	444.56	385.00	346.38	319.68	300.42	286.07	275.13	266.64	259.97
16000	1470.69	802.66	582.46	474.20	410.66	369.47	341.00	320.44	305.14	293.47	284.42	277.30
17000	1562.61	852.83	618.87	503.83	436.33	392.56	362.31	340.47	324.21	311.81	302.20	294.63
18000	1654.53	902.99	655.27	533.47	462.00	415.65	383.62	360.50	343.28	330.15	319.97	311.97
19000	1746.45	953.16	691.68	563.11	487.66	438.74	404.93	380.53	362.35	348.50	337.75	329.30
20000	1838.37	1003.33	728.08	592.74	513.33	461.83	426.24	400.55	381.42	366.84	355.52	346.63
21000	1930.29	1053.49	764.48	622.38	539.00	484.92	447.56	420.58	400.49	385.18	373.30	363.96
22000	2022.20	1103.66	800.89	652.02	564.66	508.01	468.87	440.61	419.56	403.52	391.08	381.29
23000	2114.12	1153.82	837.29	681.65	590.33	531.11	490.18	460.64	438.63	421.86	408.85	398.62
24000	2206.04	1203.99	873.69	711.29	615.99	554.20	511.49	480.66	457.70	440.20	426.63	415.95
25000	2297.96	1254.16	910.10	740.93	641.66	577.29	532.80	500.69	476.78	458.55	444.40	433.28
26000	2389.88	1304.32	946.50	770.56	667.33	600.38	554.11	520.72	495.85	476.89	462.18	450.61
27000	2481.79	1354.49	982.91	800.20	692.99	623.47	575.43	540.75	514.92	495.23	479.96	467.95
28000	2573.71	1404.65	1019.31	829.84	718.66	646.56	596.74	560.77	533.99	513.57	497.73	485.28
29000	2665.63	1454.82	1055.71	859.48	744.33	669.65	618.05	580.80	553.06	531.91	515.51	502.61
30000	2757.55	1504.99	1092.12	889.11	769.99	692.75	639.36	600.83	572.13	550.25	533.28	519.94
31000	2849.47	1555.15	1128.52	918.75	795.66	715.84	660.67	620.86	591.20	568.60	551.06	537.27
32000	2941.38	1605.32	1164.92	948.39	821.32	738.93	681.99	640.88	610.27	586.94	568.84	554.60
33000	3033.30	1655.48	1201.33	978.02	846.99	762.02	703.30	660.91	629.34	605.28	586.61	571.93
34000	3125.22	1705.65	1237.73	1007.66	872.66	785.11	724.61	680.94	648.41	623.62	604.39	589.26
35000	3217.14	1755.82	1274.14	1037.30	898.32	808.20	745.92	700.97	667.48	641.96	622.16	606.59
37500	3446.93	1881.23	1365.14	1111.39	962.49	865.93	799.20	751.03	715.16	687.82	666.60	649.92
40000	3676.73	2006.65	1456.15	1185.48	1026.65	923.66	852.48	801.10	762.84	733.67	711.04	693.25
42500	3906.52	2132.06	1547.16	1259.57	1090.82	981.39	905.76	851.17	810.51	779.53	755.48	736.58
45000	4136.32	2257.48	1638.17	1333.67	1154.98	1039.12	959.04	901.24	858.19	825.38	799.92	779.91
47500	4366.12	2382.89	1729.18	1407.76	1219.15	1096.84	1012.32	951.31	905.87	871.23	844.36	823.23
50000	4595.91	2508.31	1820.19	1481.85	1283.32	1154.57	1065.60	1001.38	953.55	917.09	888.80	866.56
52500	4825.71	2633.72	1911.20	1555.94	1347.48	1212.30	1118.88	1051.45	1001.22	962.94	933.24	909.89
55000	5055.50	2759.14	2002.21	1630.04	1411.65	1270.03	1172.16	1101.51	1048.90	1008.80	977.68	953.22
57500	5285.30	2884.55	2093.22	1704.13	1475.81	1327.76	1225.44	1151.58	1096.58	1054.65	1022.12	996.55
60000	5515.09	3009.97	2184.23	1778.22	1539.98	1385.49	1278.72	1201.65	1144.25	1100.50	1066.56	1039.87
65000	5974.68	3260.80	2366.25	1926.40	1668.31	1500.94	1385.28	1301.79	1239.61	1192.21	1155.44	1126.53
70000	6434.27	3511.63	2548.27	2074.59	1796.64	1616.40	1491.84	1401.93	1334.96	1283.92	1244.32	1213.18
75000	6893.86	3762.46	2730.28	2222.77	1924.97	1731.86	1598.40	1502.06	1430.32	1375.63	1333.20	1299.84
80000	7353.45	4013.29	2912.30	2370.96	2053.30	1847.31	1704.96	1602.20	1525.67	1467.34	1422.08	1386.50
85000	7813.04	4264.12	3094.32	2519.14	2181.63	1962.77	1811.52	1702.34	1621.02	1559.05	1510.96	1473.15
90000	8272.64	4514.95	3276.34	2667.33	2309.96	2078.23	1918.08	1802.47	1716.38	1650.75	1599.84	1559.81
95000	8732.23	4765.78	3458.36	2815.51	2438.29	2193.68	2024.64	1902.61	1811.73	1742.46	1688.72	1646.46
100000	9191.82	5016.61	3640.38	2963.70	2566.63	2309.14	2131.20	2002.75	1907.09	1834.17	1777.60	1733.12
105000	9651.41	5267.44	3822.40	3111.88	2694.96	2424.60	2237.76	2102.89	2002.44	1925.88	1866.48	1819.77
110000	10111.00	5518.27	4004.41	3260.07	2823.29	2540.05	2344.32	2203.02	2097.79	2017.59	1955.36	1906.43
115000	10570.59	5769.10	4186.43	3408.25	2951.62	2655.51	2450.88	2303.16	2193.15	2109.30	2044.24	1993.09
120000	11030.18	6019.93	4368.45	3556.43	3079.95	2770.97	2557.44	2403.30	2288.50	2201.00	2133.12	2079.74
125000	11489.77	6270.76	4550.47	3704.62	3208.28	2886.42	2663.99	2503.44	2383.86	2292.71	2222.00	2166.40
130000	11949.36	6521.59	4732.49	3852.80	3336.61	3001.88	2770.55	2603.57	2479.21	2384.42	2310.88	2253.05
135000	12408.95	6772.42	4914.51	4000.99	3464.94	3117.34	2877.11	2703.71	2574.57	2476.13	2399.76	2339.71
140000	12868.54	7023.25	5096.53	4149.17	3593.27	3232.79	2983.67	2803.85	2669.92	2567.84	2488.64	2426.36
145000	13328.13	7274.08	5278.54	4297.36	3721.61	3348.25	3090.23	2903.98	2765.27	2659.54	2577.52	2513.02
150000	13787.72	7524.91	5460.56	4445.54	3849.94	3463.71	3196.79	3004.12	2860.63	2751.25	2666.40	2599.68
155000	14247.31	7775.74	5642.58	4593.73	3978.27	3579.16	3303.35	3104.26	2955.98	2842.96	2755.28	2686.33
160000	14706.90	8026.57	5824.60	4741.91	4106.60	3694.62	3409.91	3204.40	3051.34	2934.67	2844.16	2772.99

AMOUNT OF LOAN	NUMBER OF YEARS IN TERM											
	13	14	15	16	17	18	19	20	25	30	35	40
$ 50	0.85	0.84	0.83	0.82	0.81	0.81	0.80	0.80	0.78	0.78	0.78	0.78
100	1.70	1.67	1.65	1.63	1.62	1.61	1.60	1.59	1.56	1.55	1.55	1.55
200	3.40	3.34	3.30	3.26	3.23	3.21	3.19	3.17	3.12	3.10	3.09	3.09
300	5.10	5.01	4.94	4.89	4.84	4.81	4.78	4.75	4.68	4.65	4.64	4.63
400	6.80	6.68	6.59	6.52	6.46	6.41	6.37	6.33	6.23	6.20	6.18	6.18
500	8.49	8.35	8.24	8.14	8.07	8.01	7.96	7.91	7.79	7.74	7.73	7.72
600	10.19	10.02	9.88	9.77	9.68	9.61	9.55	9.50	9.35	9.29	9.27	9.26
700	11.89	11.69	11.53	11.40	11.29	11.21	11.14	11.08	10.91	10.84	10.81	10.80
800	13.59	13.36	13.18	13.03	12.91	12.81	12.73	12.66	12.46	12.39	12.36	12.35
900	15.28	15.03	14.82	14.66	14.52	14.41	14.32	14.24	14.02	13.94	13.90	13.89
1000	16.98	16.70	16.47	16.28	16.13	16.01	15.91	15.82	15.58	15.48	15.45	15.43
2000	33.96	33.39	32.94	32.56	32.26	32.01	31.81	31.64	31.15	30.96	30.89	30.86
3000	50.94	50.09	49.40	48.84	48.39	48.02	47.71	47.46	46.73	46.44	46.33	46.28
4000	67.92	66.78	65.87	65.12	64.52	64.02	63.62	63.28	62.30	61.92	61.77	61.71
5000	84.89	83.48	82.33	81.40	80.65	80.03	79.52	79.10	77.88	77.40	77.21	77.14
6000	101.87	100.17	98.80	97.68	96.77	96.03	95.42	94.92	93.45	92.88	92.66	92.56
7000	118.85	116.86	115.26	113.96	112.90	112.03	111.32	110.74	109.03	108.36	108.10	107.99
8000	135.83	133.56	131.73	130.24	129.03	128.04	127.23	126.56	124.60	123.84	123.54	123.42
9000	152.80	150.25	148.19	146.52	145.16	144.04	143.13	142.38	140.18	139.32	138.98	138.84
10000	169.78	166.95	164.66	162.80	161.29	160.05	159.03	158.19	155.75	154.80	154.42	154.27
11000	186.76	183.64	181.12	179.08	177.41	176.05	174.93	174.01	171.33	170.28	169.86	169.70
12000	203.74	200.33	197.59	195.36	193.54	192.06	190.84	189.83	186.90	185.76	185.31	185.12
13000	220.71	217.03	214.05	211.64	209.67	208.06	206.74	205.65	202.48	201.24	200.75	200.55
14000	237.69	233.72	230.52	227.92	225.80	224.06	222.64	221.47	218.05	216.72	216.19	215.98
15000	254.67	250.42	246.98	244.20	241.93	240.07	238.54	237.29	233.63	232.20	231.63	231.40
16000	271.65	267.11	263.45	260.48	258.05	256.07	254.45	253.11	249.20	247.68	247.07	246.83
17000	288.62	283.80	279.91	276.76	274.18	272.08	270.35	268.93	264.78	263.16	262.51	262.26
18000	305.60	300.50	296.38	293.04	290.31	288.08	286.25	284.75	280.35	278.64	277.96	277.68
19000	322.58	317.19	312.84	309.32	306.44	304.09	302.15	300.57	295.93	294.11	293.40	293.11
20000	339.56	333.89	329.31	325.60	322.57	320.09	318.06	316.38	311.50	309.59	308.84	308.54
21000	356.53	350.58	345.77	341.87	338.70	336.09	333.96	332.20	327.08	325.07	324.28	323.96
22000	373.51	367.27	362.24	358.15	354.82	352.10	349.86	348.02	342.65	340.55	339.72	339.39
23000	390.49	383.97	378.71	374.43	370.95	368.10	365.76	363.84	358.23	356.03	355.16	354.82
24000	407.47	400.66	395.17	390.71	387.08	384.11	381.67	379.66	373.80	371.51	370.61	370.24
25000	424.44	417.36	411.64	406.99	403.21	400.11	397.57	395.48	389.38	386.99	386.05	385.67
26000	441.42	434.05	428.10	423.27	419.34	416.12	413.47	411.30	404.95	402.47	401.49	401.10
27000	458.40	450.74	444.57	439.55	435.46	432.12	429.38	427.12	420.53	417.95	416.93	416.52
28000	475.38	467.44	461.03	455.83	451.59	448.12	445.28	442.94	436.10	433.43	432.37	431.95
29000	492.35	484.13	477.50	472.11	467.72	464.13	461.18	458.76	451.68	448.91	447.81	447.38
30000	509.33	500.83	493.96	488.39	483.85	480.13	477.08	474.57	467.25	464.39	463.26	462.80
31000	526.31	517.52	510.43	504.67	499.98	496.14	492.99	490.39	482.83	479.87	478.70	478.23
32000	543.29	534.21	526.89	520.95	516.10	512.14	508.89	506.21	498.40	495.35	494.14	493.66
33000	560.26	550.91	543.36	537.23	532.23	528.15	524.79	522.03	513.97	510.83	509.58	509.08
34000	577.24	567.60	559.82	553.51	548.36	544.15	540.69	537.85	529.55	526.31	525.02	524.51
35000	594.22	584.30	576.29	569.79	564.49	560.15	556.60	553.67	545.12	541.79	540.46	539.94
37500	636.66	626.03	617.45	610.48	604.81	600.16	596.35	593.22	584.06	580.48	579.07	578.50
40000	679.11	667.77	658.61	651.19	645.13	640.17	636.11	632.76	623.00	619.18	617.67	617.07
42500	721.55	709.50	699.78	691.88	685.45	680.19	675.87	672.31	661.94	657.88	656.28	655.64
45000	763.99	751.24	740.94	732.58	725.77	720.20	715.62	711.86	700.87	696.58	694.88	694.20
47500	806.44	792.97	782.10	773.28	766.09	760.21	755.38	751.41	739.81	735.28	733.48	732.77
50000	848.88	834.71	823.27	813.98	806.41	800.22	795.13	790.95	778.75	773.98	772.09	771.34
52500	891.33	876.44	864.43	854.68	846.73	840.23	834.89	830.50	817.68	812.68	810.69	809.90
55000	933.77	918.18	905.59	895.38	887.05	880.24	874.65	870.05	856.62	851.37	849.30	848.47
57500	976.21	959.91	946.76	936.08	927.37	920.25	914.40	909.60	895.56	890.07	887.90	887.04
60000	1018.66	1001.65	987.92	976.78	967.69	960.26	954.16	949.14	934.50	928.77	926.51	925.60
65000	1103.54	1085.12	1070.25	1058.17	1048.33	1040.28	1033.67	1028.24	1012.37	1006.17	1003.71	1002.74
70000	1188.43	1168.59	1152.57	1139.57	1128.97	1120.30	1113.19	1107.33	1090.24	1083.57	1080.92	1079.87
75000	1273.32	1252.06	1234.90	1220.97	1209.61	1200.32	1192.70	1186.43	1168.12	1160.96	1158.13	1157.00
80000	1358.21	1335.53	1317.22	1302.37	1290.25	1280.34	1272.21	1265.52	1245.99	1238.36	1235.34	1234.14
85000	1443.10	1419.00	1399.55	1383.76	1370.90	1360.37	1351.73	1344.62	1323.87	1315.76	1312.55	1311.27
90000	1527.98	1502.47	1481.88	1465.16	1451.54	1440.39	1431.24	1423.71	1401.74	1393.16	1389.76	1388.40
95000	1612.87	1585.94	1564.20	1546.56	1532.18	1520.41	1510.75	1502.81	1479.61	1470.55	1466.96	1465.54
100000	1697.76	1669.41	1646.53	1627.96	1612.82	1600.43	1590.26	1581.90	1557.49	1547.95	1544.17	1542.67
105000	1782.65	1752.88	1728.85	1709.35	1693.46	1680.45	1669.78	1661.00	1635.36	1625.35	1621.38	1619.80
110000	1867.53	1836.35	1811.18	1790.75	1774.10	1760.47	1749.29	1740.09	1713.24	1702.74	1698.59	1696.94
115000	1952.42	1919.82	1893.51	1872.15	1854.74	1840.49	1828.80	1819.19	1791.11	1780.14	1775.80	1774.07
120000	2037.31	2003.29	1975.83	1953.55	1935.38	1920.51	1908.32	1898.28	1868.99	1857.54	1853.01	1851.20
125000	2122.20	2086.76	2058.16	2034.95	2016.02	2000.54	1987.83	1977.38	1946.86	1934.94	1930.21	1928.34
130000	2207.08	2170.23	2140.49	2116.34	2096.66	2080.56	2067.34	2056.47	2024.73	2012.33	2007.42	2005.47
135000	2291.97	2253.70	2222.81	2197.74	2177.30	2160.58	2146.86	2135.57	2102.61	2089.73	2084.63	2082.60
140000	2376.86	2337.17	2305.14	2279.14	2257.94	2240.60	2226.37	2214.66	2180.48	2167.13	2161.84	2159.74
145000	2461.75	2420.64	2387.46	2360.54	2338.58	2320.62	2305.88	2293.76	2258.36	2244.52	2239.05	2236.87
150000	2546.63	2504.11	2469.79	2441.93	2419.22	2400.64	2385.39	2372.85	2336.23	2321.92	2316.26	2314.00
155000	2631.52	2587.58	2552.12	2523.33	2499.86	2480.66	2464.91	2451.94	2414.11	2399.32	2393.46	2391.13
160000	2716.41	2671.05	2634.44	2604.73	2580.50	2560.68	2544.42	2531.04	2491.98	2476.72	2470.67	2468.27

18.75% MONTHLY AMORTIZING PAYMENTS

AMOUNT OF LOAN	\multicolumn{12}{c}{NUMBER OF YEARS IN TERM}
	1	2	3	4	5	6	7	8	9	10	11	12
$ 50	4.61	2.52	1.83	1.49	1.30	1.17	1.08	1.01	0.97	0.93	0.90	0.88
100	9.21	5.03	3.66	2.98	2.59	2.33	2.15	2.02	1.93	1.86	1.80	1.76
200	18.41	10.06	7.31	5.96	5.17	4.65	4.30	4.04	3.85	3.71	3.59	3.51
300	27.62	15.09	10.96	8.94	7.75	6.98	6.44	6.06	5.77	5.56	5.39	5.26
400	36.82	20.12	14.62	11.91	10.33	9.30	8.59	8.08	7.70	7.41	7.18	7.01
500	46.02	25.15	18.27	14.89	12.91	11.62	10.73	10.10	9.62	9.26	8.98	8.76
600	55.23	30.18	21.92	17.87	15.49	13.95	12.88	12.11	11.54	11.11	10.77	10.51
700	64.43	35.21	25.58	20.84	18.07	16.27	15.03	14.13	13.47	12.96	12.56	12.26
800	73.63	40.23	29.23	23.82	20.65	18.59	17.17	16.15	15.39	14.81	14.36	14.01
900	82.84	45.26	32.88	26.80	23.23	20.92	19.32	18.17	17.31	16.66	16.15	15.76
1000	92.04	50.29	36.53	29.77	25.81	23.24	21.46	20.19	19.23	18.51	17.95	17.51
2000	184.08	100.58	73.06	59.54	51.61	46.47	42.92	40.37	38.46	37.01	35.89	35.01
3000	276.12	150.87	109.59	89.31	77.41	69.71	64.38	60.55	57.69	55.52	53.83	52.51
4000	368.15	201.15	146.12	119.08	103.22	92.94	85.84	80.73	76.92	74.02	71.78	70.01
5000	460.19	251.44	182.65	148.85	129.02	116.17	107.30	100.91	96.15	92.53	89.72	87.52
6000	552.23	301.73	219.18	178.62	154.82	139.41	128.76	121.09	115.38	111.03	107.66	105.02
7000	644.27	352.02	255.71	208.38	180.63	162.64	150.22	141.27	134.61	129.53	125.60	122.52
8000	736.30	402.30	292.24	238.15	206.43	185.88	171.68	161.45	153.83	148.04	143.55	140.02
9000	828.34	452.59	328.77	267.92	232.23	209.11	193.14	181.63	173.06	166.54	161.49	157.52
10000	920.38	502.88	365.30	297.69	258.04	232.34	214.60	201.81	192.29	185.05	179.43	175.03
11000	1012.42	553.16	401.83	327.46	283.84	255.58	236.06	221.99	211.52	203.55	197.38	192.53
12000	1104.45	603.45	438.36	357.23	309.64	278.81	257.52	242.17	230.75	222.05	215.32	210.03
13000	1196.49	653.74	474.89	386.99	335.45	302.04	278.98	262.35	249.98	240.56	233.26	227.53
14000	1288.53	704.03	511.42	416.76	361.25	325.28	300.44	282.53	269.21	259.06	251.20	245.03
15000	1380.56	754.31	547.95	446.53	387.05	348.51	321.90	302.71	288.43	277.57	269.15	262.54
16000	1472.60	804.60	584.48	476.30	412.86	371.75	343.36	322.89	307.66	296.07	287.09	280.04
17000	1564.64	854.89	621.01	506.07	438.66	394.98	364.82	343.07	326.89	314.58	305.03	297.54
18000	1656.68	905.18	657.54	535.84	464.46	418.21	386.28	363.25	346.12	333.08	322.98	315.04
19000	1748.71	955.46	694.07	565.60	490.27	441.45	407.74	383.43	365.35	351.58	340.92	332.54
20000	1840.75	1005.75	730.60	595.37	516.07	464.68	429.20	403.61	384.58	370.09	358.86	350.05
21000	1932.79	1056.04	767.13	625.14	541.87	487.92	450.66	423.79	403.81	388.59	376.80	367.55
22000	2024.83	1106.32	803.66	654.91	567.68	511.15	472.12	443.97	423.04	407.10	394.75	385.05
23000	2116.86	1156.61	840.19	684.68	593.48	534.38	493.58	464.15	442.26	425.60	412.69	402.55
24000	2208.90	1206.90	876.72	714.45	619.28	557.62	515.04	484.33	461.49	444.10	430.63	420.05
25000	2300.94	1257.19	913.25	744.21	645.08	580.85	536.50	504.51	480.72	462.61	448.58	437.56
26000	2392.97	1307.47	949.78	773.98	670.89	604.08	557.96	524.69	499.95	481.11	466.52	455.06
27000	2485.01	1357.76	986.31	803.75	696.69	627.32	579.42	544.88	519.18	499.62	484.46	472.56
28000	2577.05	1408.05	1022.84	833.52	722.49	650.55	600.88	565.06	538.41	518.12	502.40	490.06
29000	2669.09	1458.33	1059.37	863.29	748.30	673.79	622.34	585.24	557.64	536.63	520.35	507.57
30000	2761.12	1508.62	1095.90	893.06	774.10	697.02	643.80	605.42	576.86	555.13	538.29	525.07
31000	2853.16	1558.91	1132.43	922.82	799.90	720.25	665.26	625.60	596.09	573.63	556.23	542.57
32000	2945.20	1609.20	1168.96	952.59	825.71	743.49	686.72	645.78	615.32	592.14	574.18	560.07
33000	3037.24	1659.48	1205.49	982.36	851.51	766.72	708.18	665.96	634.55	610.64	592.12	577.57
34000	3129.27	1709.77	1242.02	1012.13	877.31	789.95	729.64	686.14	653.78	629.15	610.06	595.08
35000	3221.31	1760.06	1278.55	1041.90	903.12	813.19	751.10	706.32	673.01	647.65	628.00	612.58
37500	3451.40	1885.78	1369.87	1116.32	967.62	871.27	804.74	756.77	721.08	693.91	672.86	656.33
40000	3681.50	2011.49	1461.19	1190.74	1032.13	929.36	858.39	807.22	769.15	740.17	717.72	700.09
42500	3911.59	2137.21	1552.52	1265.16	1096.64	987.44	912.04	857.67	817.22	786.43	762.58	743.84
45000	4141.68	2262.93	1643.84	1339.58	1161.15	1045.53	965.69	908.12	865.29	832.69	807.43	787.60
47500	4371.78	2388.65	1735.17	1414.00	1225.66	1103.61	1019.34	958.57	913.37	878.95	852.29	831.35
50000	4601.87	2514.37	1826.49	1488.42	1290.16	1161.70	1072.99	1009.02	961.44	925.21	897.15	875.11
52500	4831.96	2640.08	1917.82	1562.84	1354.67	1219.78	1126.64	1059.47	1009.51	971.47	942.00	918.86
55000	5062.06	2765.80	2009.14	1637.26	1419.18	1277.86	1180.29	1109.93	1057.58	1017.73	986.86	962.62
57500	5292.15	2891.52	2100.47	1711.69	1483.69	1335.95	1233.94	1160.38	1105.65	1063.99	1031.72	1006.37
60000	5522.24	3017.24	2191.79	1786.11	1548.20	1394.03	1287.59	1210.83	1153.72	1110.25	1076.58	1050.13
65000	5982.43	3268.68	2374.44	1934.95	1677.21	1510.20	1394.89	1311.73	1249.87	1202.77	1166.29	1137.64
70000	6442.62	3520.11	2557.09	2083.79	1806.23	1626.37	1502.19	1412.63	1346.01	1295.29	1256.00	1225.15
75000	6902.80	3771.55	2739.74	2232.63	1935.24	1742.54	1609.48	1513.53	1442.15	1387.82	1345.72	1312.66
80000	7362.99	4022.98	2922.38	2381.47	2064.26	1858.71	1716.78	1614.44	1538.30	1480.34	1435.43	1400.17
85000	7823.18	4274.42	3105.03	2530.32	2193.28	1974.88	1824.08	1715.34	1634.44	1572.86	1525.15	1487.68
90000	8283.36	4525.86	3287.68	2679.16	2322.29	2091.05	1931.38	1816.24	1730.58	1665.38	1614.86	1575.19
95000	8743.55	4777.29	3470.33	2828.00	2451.31	2207.22	2038.68	1917.14	1826.73	1757.90	1704.58	1662.70
100000	9203.74	5028.73	3652.98	2976.84	2580.32	2323.39	2145.98	2018.04	1922.87	1850.42	1794.29	1750.21
105000	9663.92	5280.16	3835.63	3125.68	2709.34	2439.56	2253.28	2118.94	2019.01	1942.94	1884.00	1837.72
110000	10124.11	5531.60	4018.28	3274.52	2838.36	2555.72	2360.57	2219.85	2115.16	2035.46	1973.72	1925.23
115000	10584.30	5783.04	4200.93	3423.37	2967.37	2671.89	2467.87	2320.75	2211.30	2127.98	2063.43	2012.74
120000	11044.48	6034.47	4383.57	3572.21	3096.39	2788.06	2575.17	2421.65	2307.44	2220.50	2153.15	2100.25
125000	11504.67	6285.91	4566.22	3721.05	3225.40	2904.23	2682.47	2522.55	2403.59	2313.02	2242.86	2187.76
130000	11964.85	6537.35	4748.87	3869.89	3354.42	3020.40	2789.77	2623.45	2499.73	2405.54	2332.58	2275.28
135000	12425.04	6788.78	4931.52	4018.73	3483.44	3136.57	2897.07	2724.36	2595.87	2498.06	2422.29	2362.79
140000	12885.23	7040.22	5114.17	4167.57	3612.45	3252.74	3004.37	2825.26	2692.02	2590.58	2512.00	2450.30
145000	13345.41	7291.65	5296.82	4316.42	3741.47	3368.91	3111.66	2926.16	2788.16	2683.11	2601.72	2537.81
150000	13805.60	7543.09	5479.47	4465.26	3870.48	3485.08	3218.96	3027.06	2884.30	2775.63	2691.43	2625.32
155000	14265.79	7794.53	5662.12	4614.10	3999.50	3601.25	3326.26	3127.96	2980.45	2868.15	2781.15	2712.83
160000	14725.97	8045.96	5844.76	4762.94	4128.51	3717.42	3433.56	3228.87	3076.59	2960.67	2870.86	2800.34

112

AMOUNT OF LOAN	NUMBER OF YEARS IN TERM											
	13	14	15	16	17	18	19	20	25	30	35	40
$ 50	0.86	0.85	0.84	0.83	0.82	0.81	0.81	0.81	0.79	0.79	0.79	0.79
100	1.72	1.69	1.67	1.65	1.64	1.62	1.61	1.61	1.58	1.57	1.57	1.57
200	3.44	3.38	3.33	3.30	3.27	3.24	3.22	3.21	3.16	3.14	3.13	3.13
300	5.15	5.07	5.00	4.94	4.90	4.86	4.83	4.81	4.74	4.71	4.70	4.70
400	6.87	6.75	6.66	6.59	6.53	6.48	6.44	6.41	6.32	6.28	6.26	6.26
500	8.58	8.44	8.33	8.24	8.16	8.10	8.05	8.01	7.89	7.85	7.83	7.82
600	10.30	10.13	9.99	9.88	9.79	9.72	9.66	9.61	9.47	9.42	9.39	9.39
700	12.01	11.82	11.66	11.53	11.43	11.34	11.27	11.21	11.05	10.98	10.96	10.95
800	13.73	13.50	13.32	13.18	13.06	12.96	12.88	12.82	12.63	12.55	12.52	12.51
900	15.44	15.19	14.99	14.82	14.69	14.58	14.49	14.42	14.20	14.12	14.09	14.08
1000	17.16	16.88	16.65	16.47	16.32	16.20	16.10	16.02	15.78	15.69	15.65	15.64
2000	34.31	33.75	33.30	32.93	32.64	32.39	32.19	32.03	31.56	31.37	31.30	31.27
3000	51.46	50.62	49.95	49.40	48.95	48.59	48.29	48.04	47.33	47.06	46.95	46.91
4000	68.61	67.49	66.59	65.86	65.27	64.78	64.38	64.06	63.11	62.74	62.60	62.54
5000	85.77	84.37	83.24	82.32	81.58	80.97	80.48	80.07	78.88	78.43	78.25	78.18
6000	102.92	101.24	99.89	98.79	97.90	97.17	96.57	96.08	94.66	94.11	93.89	93.81
7000	120.07	118.11	116.53	115.25	114.21	113.36	112.67	112.09	110.43	109.79	109.54	109.44
8000	137.22	134.98	133.18	131.72	130.53	129.56	128.76	128.11	126.21	125.48	125.19	125.08
9000	154.38	151.86	149.83	148.18	146.84	145.75	144.85	144.12	141.99	141.16	140.84	140.71
10000	171.53	168.73	166.47	164.64	163.16	161.94	160.95	160.13	157.76	156.85	156.49	156.35
11000	188.68	185.60	183.12	181.11	179.47	178.14	177.04	176.14	173.54	172.53	172.14	171.98
12000	205.83	202.47	199.77	197.57	195.79	194.33	193.14	192.16	189.31	188.21	187.78	187.61
13000	222.98	219.34	216.41	214.04	212.10	210.52	209.23	208.17	205.09	203.90	203.43	203.25
14000	240.14	236.22	233.06	230.50	228.42	226.72	225.33	224.18	220.86	219.58	219.08	218.88
15000	257.29	253.09	249.71	246.96	244.73	242.91	241.42	240.19	236.64	235.27	234.73	234.52
16000	274.44	269.96	266.35	263.43	261.05	259.11	257.51	256.21	252.42	250.95	250.38	250.15
17000	291.59	286.83	283.00	279.89	277.36	275.30	273.61	272.22	268.19	266.63	266.03	265.79
18000	308.75	303.71	299.65	296.36	293.68	291.49	289.70	288.23	283.97	282.32	281.67	281.42
19000	325.90	320.58	316.29	312.82	309.99	307.69	305.80	304.25	299.74	298.00	297.32	297.05
20000	343.05	337.45	332.94	329.28	326.31	323.88	321.89	320.26	315.52	313.69	312.97	312.69
21000	360.20	354.32	349.59	345.75	342.62	340.07	337.99	336.27	331.29	329.37	328.62	328.32
22000	377.35	371.20	366.23	362.21	358.94	356.27	354.08	352.28	347.07	345.05	344.27	343.96
23000	394.51	388.07	382.88	378.68	375.25	372.46	370.17	368.30	362.84	360.74	359.91	359.59
24000	411.66	404.94	399.53	395.14	391.57	388.66	386.27	384.31	378.62	376.42	375.56	375.22
25000	428.81	421.81	416.17	411.60	407.89	404.85	402.36	400.32	394.40	392.11	391.21	390.86
26000	445.96	438.68	432.82	428.07	424.20	421.04	418.46	416.33	410.17	407.79	406.86	406.49
27000	463.12	455.56	449.47	444.53	440.52	437.24	434.55	432.35	425.95	423.48	422.51	422.13
28000	480.27	472.43	466.11	460.99	456.83	453.43	450.65	448.36	441.72	439.16	438.16	437.76
29000	497.42	489.30	482.76	477.46	473.15	469.62	466.74	464.37	457.50	454.84	453.80	453.40
30000	514.57	506.17	499.41	493.92	489.46	485.82	482.83	480.38	473.27	470.53	469.45	469.03
31000	531.73	523.05	516.05	510.39	505.78	502.01	498.93	496.40	489.05	486.21	485.10	484.67
32000	548.88	539.92	532.70	526.85	522.09	518.21	515.02	512.41	504.83	501.90	500.75	500.30
33000	566.03	556.79	549.35	543.31	538.41	534.40	531.12	528.42	520.60	517.58	516.40	515.93
34000	583.18	573.66	565.99	559.78	554.72	550.59	547.21	544.44	536.38	533.26	532.05	531.57
35000	600.33	590.53	582.64	576.24	571.04	566.79	563.31	560.45	552.15	548.95	547.69	547.20
37500	643.21	632.72	624.26	617.40	611.83	607.27	603.54	600.48	591.59	588.16	586.81	586.29
40000	686.10	674.90	665.87	658.56	652.61	647.76	643.78	640.51	631.03	627.37	625.94	625.37
42500	728.98	717.08	707.49	699.72	693.40	688.24	684.01	680.54	670.47	666.58	665.06	664.46
45000	771.86	759.26	749.11	740.88	734.19	728.72	724.25	720.57	709.91	705.79	704.18	703.54
47500	814.74	801.44	790.72	782.04	774.98	769.21	764.48	760.61	749.35	745.00	743.30	742.63
50000	857.62	843.62	832.34	823.20	815.77	809.69	804.72	800.64	788.79	784.21	782.42	781.71
52500	900.50	885.80	873.96	864.36	856.55	850.18	844.96	840.67	828.23	823.42	821.54	820.80
55000	943.38	927.98	915.57	905.52	897.34	890.66	885.19	880.70	867.67	862.63	860.66	859.88
57500	986.26	970.16	957.19	946.68	938.13	931.15	925.43	920.73	907.10	901.84	899.78	898.97
60000	1029.14	1012.34	998.81	987.84	978.92	971.63	965.66	960.76	946.54	941.05	938.90	938.05
65000	1114.90	1096.70	1082.04	1070.16	1060.49	1052.60	1046.14	1040.83	1025.42	1019.47	1017.14	1016.23
70000	1200.66	1181.06	1165.27	1152.48	1142.07	1133.57	1126.61	1120.89	1104.30	1097.89	1095.38	1094.40
75000	1286.42	1265.43	1248.51	1234.80	1223.65	1214.54	1207.08	1200.95	1183.18	1176.31	1173.62	1172.57
80000	1372.19	1349.79	1331.74	1317.12	1305.22	1295.51	1287.55	1281.02	1262.06	1254.73	1251.87	1250.74
85000	1457.95	1434.15	1414.97	1399.44	1386.80	1376.48	1368.02	1361.08	1340.94	1333.15	1330.11	1328.91
90000	1543.71	1518.51	1498.21	1481.76	1468.37	1457.44	1448.49	1441.14	1419.81	1411.57	1408.35	1407.08
95000	1629.47	1602.87	1581.44	1564.08	1549.95	1538.41	1528.96	1521.21	1498.69	1489.99	1486.59	1485.25
100000	1715.23	1687.23	1664.67	1646.40	1631.53	1619.38	1609.44	1601.27	1577.57	1568.41	1564.83	1563.42
105000	1800.99	1771.59	1747.91	1728.72	1713.10	1700.35	1689.91	1681.33	1656.45	1646.83	1643.07	1641.60
110000	1886.75	1855.96	1831.14	1811.04	1794.68	1781.32	1770.38	1761.40	1735.33	1725.25	1721.31	1719.76
115000	1972.52	1940.32	1914.37	1893.36	1876.25	1862.29	1850.85	1841.46	1814.20	1803.67	1799.55	1797.93
120000	2058.28	2024.68	1997.61	1975.68	1957.83	1943.26	1931.32	1921.52	1893.08	1882.09	1877.80	1876.10
125000	2144.04	2109.04	2080.84	2058.00	2039.41	2024.23	2011.79	2001.59	1971.96	1960.52	1956.04	1954.28
130000	2229.80	2193.40	2164.07	2140.32	2120.98	2105.20	2092.27	2081.65	2050.84	2038.94	2034.28	2032.45
135000	2315.56	2277.76	2247.31	2222.64	2202.56	2186.16	2172.74	2161.71	2129.72	2117.36	2112.52	2110.62
140000	2401.32	2362.12	2330.54	2304.95	2284.13	2267.13	2253.21	2241.78	2208.60	2195.78	2190.76	2188.79
145000	2487.08	2446.49	2413.78	2387.27	2365.71	2348.10	2333.68	2321.84	2287.47	2274.20	2269.00	2266.96
150000	2572.84	2530.85	2497.01	2469.59	2447.29	2429.07	2414.15	2401.90	2366.35	2352.62	2347.24	2345.13
155000	2658.61	2615.21	2580.24	2551.91	2528.86	2510.04	2494.62	2481.97	2445.23	2431.04	2425.48	2423.30
160000	2744.37	2699.57	2663.48	2634.23	2610.44	2591.01	2575.09	2562.03	2524.11	2509.46	2503.73	2501.47

AMOUNT OF LOAN	NUMBER OF YEARS IN TERM											
	1	2	3	4	5	6	7	8	9	10	11	12
$ 50	4.61	2.53	1.84	1.50	1.30	1.17	1.09	1.02	0.97	0.94	0.91	0.89
100	9.22	5.05	3.67	3.00	2.60	2.34	2.17	2.04	1.94	1.87	1.82	1.77
200	18.44	10.09	7.34	5.99	5.19	4.68	4.33	4.07	3.88	3.74	3.63	3.54
300	27.65	15.13	11.00	8.98	7.79	7.02	6.49	6.11	5.82	5.61	5.44	5.31
400	36.87	20.17	14.67	11.97	10.38	9.36	8.65	8.14	7.76	7.47	7.25	7.07
500	46.08	25.21	18.33	14.96	12.98	11.69	10.81	10.17	9.70	9.34	9.06	8.84
600	55.30	30.25	22.00	17.95	15.57	14.03	12.97	12.21	11.64	11.21	10.87	10.61
700	64.51	35.29	25.66	20.94	18.16	16.37	15.13	14.24	13.58	13.07	12.68	12.38
800	73.73	40.33	29.33	23.93	20.76	18.71	17.29	16.27	15.51	14.94	14.49	14.14
900	82.95	45.37	33.00	26.92	23.35	21.04	19.45	18.31	17.45	16.81	16.30	15.91
1000	92.16	50.41	36.66	29.91	25.95	23.38	21.61	20.34	19.39	18.67	18.12	17.68
2000	184.32	100.82	73.32	59.81	51.89	46.76	43.22	40.67	38.78	37.34	36.23	35.35
3000	276.47	151.23	109.97	89.71	77.83	70.14	64.83	61.01	58.17	56.01	54.34	53.03
4000	368.63	201.64	146.63	119.61	103.77	93.51	86.44	81.34	77.55	74.67	72.45	70.70
5000	460.79	252.05	183.29	149.51	129.71	116.89	108.05	101.67	96.94	93.34	90.56	88.37
6000	552.94	302.46	219.94	179.41	155.65	140.27	129.65	122.01	116.33	112.01	108.67	106.05
7000	645.10	352.87	256.60	209.31	181.59	163.64	151.26	142.34	135.71	130.68	126.78	123.72
8000	737.26	403.27	293.25	239.21	207.53	187.02	172.87	162.68	155.10	149.34	144.89	141.39
9000	829.41	453.68	329.91	269.11	233.47	210.40	194.48	183.01	174.49	168.01	163.00	159.07
10000	921.57	504.09	366.57	299.01	259.41	233.77	216.09	203.34	193.88	186.68	181.11	176.74
11000	1013.73	554.50	403.22	328.91	285.35	257.15	237.69	223.68	213.26	205.34	199.22	194.42
12000	1105.88	604.90	439.88	358.81	311.29	280.53	259.30	244.01	232.65	224.01	217.33	212.09
13000	1198.04	655.32	476.53	388.71	337.23	303.90	280.91	264.35	252.04	242.68	235.44	229.76
14000	1290.20	705.73	513.19	418.61	363.17	327.28	302.52	284.68	271.42	261.35	253.55	247.44
15000	1382.35	756.13	549.85	448.51	389.11	350.66	324.13	305.01	290.81	280.01	271.66	265.11
16000	1474.51	806.54	586.50	478.41	415.05	374.03	345.73	325.35	310.20	298.68	289.77	282.78
17000	1566.67	856.95	623.16	508.31	440.99	397.41	367.34	345.68	329.59	317.35	307.88	300.46
18000	1658.82	907.36	659.81	538.21	466.93	420.79	388.95	366.01	348.97	336.02	325.99	318.13
19000	1750.98	957.77	696.47	568.11	492.88	444.16	410.56	386.35	368.36	354.68	344.10	335.80
20000	1843.14	1008.18	733.13	598.01	518.82	467.54	432.17	406.68	387.75	373.35	362.21	353.48
21000	1935.29	1058.59	769.78	627.91	544.76	490.92	453.77	427.02	407.13	392.02	380.32	371.15
22000	2027.45	1108.99	806.44	657.81	570.70	514.29	475.38	447.35	426.52	410.68	398.43	388.83
23000	2119.61	1159.40	843.09	687.71	596.64	537.67	496.99	467.68	445.91	429.35	416.54	406.50
24000	2211.76	1209.81	879.75	717.61	622.58	561.05	518.60	488.02	465.29	448.02	434.65	424.17
25000	2303.92	1260.22	916.41	747.51	648.52	584.42	540.21	508.35	484.68	466.69	452.76	441.85
26000	2396.08	1310.63	953.06	777.41	674.46	607.80	561.81	528.69	504.07	485.35	470.87	459.52
27000	2488.23	1361.04	989.72	807.31	700.40	631.18	583.42	549.02	523.46	504.02	488.98	477.19
28000	2580.39	1411.45	1026.37	837.21	726.34	654.55	605.03	569.35	542.84	522.69	507.09	494.87
29000	2672.55	1461.85	1063.03	867.11	752.28	677.93	626.64	589.69	562.23	541.35	525.20	512.54
30000	2764.70	1512.26	1099.69	897.01	778.22	701.31	648.25	610.02	581.62	560.02	543.31	530.21
31000	2856.86	1562.67	1136.34	926.91	804.16	724.68	669.85	630.35	601.00	578.69	561.43	547.89
32000	2949.02	1613.08	1173.00	956.81	830.10	748.06	691.46	650.69	620.39	597.36	579.54	565.56
33000	3041.17	1663.49	1209.65	986.71	856.04	771.44	713.07	671.02	639.78	616.02	597.65	583.24
34000	3133.33	1713.90	1246.31	1016.61	881.98	794.81	734.68	691.36	659.17	634.69	615.76	600.91
35000	3225.49	1764.31	1282.97	1046.51	907.92	818.19	756.29	711.69	678.55	653.36	633.87	618.58
37500	3455.88	1890.33	1374.61	1121.26	972.78	876.63	810.31	762.52	727.02	700.03	679.14	662.77
40000	3686.27	2016.35	1466.25	1196.01	1037.63	935.07	864.33	813.36	775.49	746.69	724.42	706.95
42500	3916.66	2142.37	1557.89	1270.76	1102.48	993.52	918.35	864.19	823.96	793.36	769.69	751.14
45000	4147.05	2268.39	1649.53	1345.51	1167.33	1051.96	972.37	915.03	872.42	840.03	814.97	795.32
47500	4377.44	2394.41	1741.17	1420.26	1232.18	1110.40	1026.39	965.86	920.89	886.70	860.25	839.50
50000	4607.83	2520.44	1832.81	1495.01	1297.03	1168.84	1080.41	1016.70	969.36	933.37	905.52	883.69
52500	4838.23	2646.46	1924.45	1569.76	1361.88	1227.28	1134.43	1067.53	1017.83	980.03	950.80	927.87
55000	5068.62	2772.48	2016.09	1644.51	1426.74	1285.72	1188.45	1118.37	1066.29	1026.70	996.07	972.06
57500	5299.01	2898.50	2107.73	1719.26	1491.59	1344.17	1242.47	1169.20	1114.76	1073.37	1041.35	1016.24
60000	5529.40	3024.52	2199.37	1794.01	1556.44	1402.61	1296.49	1220.04	1163.23	1120.04	1086.62	1060.42
65000	5990.18	3276.57	2382.65	1943.51	1686.14	1519.49	1404.53	1321.71	1260.17	1213.38	1177.18	1148.79
70000	6450.97	3528.61	2565.93	2093.01	1815.84	1636.38	1512.57	1423.38	1357.10	1306.71	1267.73	1237.16
75000	6911.75	3780.65	2749.21	2242.51	1945.55	1753.26	1620.61	1525.04	1454.04	1400.05	1358.28	1325.53
80000	7372.53	4032.69	2932.49	2392.01	2075.25	1870.14	1728.65	1626.71	1550.97	1493.38	1448.83	1413.90
85000	7833.31	4284.74	3115.77	2541.52	2204.95	1987.03	1836.69	1728.38	1647.91	1586.72	1539.38	1502.27
90000	8294.10	4536.78	3299.05	2691.02	2334.65	2103.91	1944.73	1830.05	1744.84	1680.06	1629.93	1590.63
95000	8754.88	4788.82	3482.33	2840.52	2464.36	2220.79	2052.77	1931.72	1841.78	1773.39	1720.49	1679.00
100000	9215.66	5040.87	3665.61	2990.02	2594.06	2337.68	2160.81	2033.39	1938.71	1866.73	1811.04	1767.37
105000	9676.45	5292.91	3848.89	3139.52	2723.76	2454.56	2268.85	2135.06	2035.65	1960.06	1901.59	1855.74
110000	10137.23	5544.95	4032.17	3289.02	2853.47	2571.44	2376.89	2236.73	2132.58	2053.40	1992.14	1944.11
115000	10598.01	5797.00	4215.45	3438.52	2983.17	2688.33	2484.93	2338.40	2229.52	2146.74	2082.69	2032.47
120000	11058.79	6049.04	4398.73	3588.02	3112.87	2805.21	2592.97	2440.07	2326.45	2240.07	2173.24	2120.84
125000	11519.58	6301.08	4582.01	3737.52	3242.57	2922.10	2701.01	2541.74	2423.39	2333.41	2263.80	2209.21
130000	11980.36	6553.13	4765.29	3887.02	3372.28	3038.98	2809.05	2643.41	2520.33	2426.75	2354.35	2297.58
135000	12441.14	6805.17	4948.57	4036.52	3501.98	3155.86	2917.09	2745.08	2617.26	2520.08	2444.90	2385.95
140000	12901.93	7057.21	5131.85	4186.02	3631.68	3272.75	3025.13	2846.75	2714.20	2613.42	2535.45	2474.32
145000	13362.71	7309.25	5315.13	4335.52	3761.38	3389.63	3133.17	2948.42	2811.13	2706.75	2626.00	2562.68
150000	13823.49	7561.30	5498.41	4485.02	3891.09	3506.51	3241.21	3050.08	2908.07	2800.09	2716.55	2651.05
155000	14284.27	7813.34	5681.69	4634.52	4020.79	3623.40	3349.25	3151.75	3005.00	2893.43	2807.11	2739.42
160000	14745.06	8065.38	5864.97	4784.02	4150.49	3740.28	3457.29	3253.42	3101.94	2986.76	2897.66	2827.79

AMOUNT OF LOAN	NUMBER OF YEARS IN TERM											
	13	14	15	16	17	18	19	20	25	30	35	40
$ 50	0.87	0.86	0.85	0.84	0.83	0.82	0.82	0.82	0.80	0.80	0.80	0.80
100	1.74	1.71	1.69	1.67	1.66	1.64	1.63	1.63	1.60	1.59	1.59	1.59
200	3.47	3.42	3.37	3.33	3.31	3.28	3.26	3.25	3.20	3.18	3.18	3.17
300	5.20	5.12	5.05	5.00	4.96	4.92	4.89	4.87	4.80	4.77	4.76	4.76
400	6.94	6.83	6.74	6.66	6.61	6.56	6.52	6.49	6.40	6.36	6.35	6.34
500	8.67	8.53	8.42	8.33	8.26	8.20	8.15	8.11	7.99	7.95	7.93	7.93
600	10.40	10.24	10.10	9.99	9.91	9.84	9.78	9.73	9.59	9.54	9.52	9.51
700	12.13	11.94	11.79	11.66	11.56	11.47	11.41	11.35	11.19	11.13	11.10	11.09
800	13.87	13.65	13.47	13.32	13.21	13.11	13.03	12.97	12.79	12.72	12.69	12.68
900	15.60	15.35	15.15	14.99	14.86	14.75	14.66	14.59	14.38	14.31	14.27	14.26
1000	17.33	17.06	16.83	16.65	16.51	16.39	16.29	16.21	15.98	15.89	15.86	15.85
2000	34.66	34.11	33.66	33.30	33.01	32.77	32.58	32.42	31.96	31.78	31.71	31.69
3000	51.99	51.16	50.49	49.95	49.51	49.16	48.86	48.63	47.94	47.67	47.57	47.53
4000	69.32	68.21	67.32	66.60	66.02	65.54	65.15	64.83	63.91	63.56	63.42	63.37
5000	86.64	85.26	84.15	83.25	82.52	81.92	81.44	81.04	79.89	79.45	79.28	79.21
6000	103.97	102.31	100.98	99.90	99.02	98.31	97.72	97.25	95.87	95.34	95.13	95.06
7000	121.30	119.36	117.81	116.55	115.53	114.69	114.01	113.45	111.84	111.23	110.99	110.90
8000	138.63	136.41	134.64	133.20	132.03	131.08	130.30	129.66	127.82	127.12	126.84	126.74
9000	155.95	153.46	151.46	149.85	148.53	147.46	146.58	145.87	143.80	143.01	142.70	142.58
10000	173.28	170.52	168.29	166.49	165.03	163.84	162.87	162.07	159.77	158.89	158.55	158.42
11000	190.61	187.57	185.12	183.14	181.54	180.23	179.16	178.28	175.75	174.78	174.41	174.26
12000	207.94	204.62	201.95	199.79	198.04	196.61	195.44	194.49	191.73	190.67	190.26	190.11
13000	225.26	221.67	218.78	216.44	214.54	212.99	211.73	210.69	207.70	206.56	206.12	205.95
14000	242.59	238.72	235.61	233.09	231.05	229.38	228.02	226.90	223.68	222.45	221.97	221.79
15000	259.92	255.77	252.44	249.74	247.55	245.76	244.30	243.11	239.66	238.34	237.83	237.63
16000	277.25	272.82	269.27	266.39	264.05	262.15	260.59	259.31	255.63	254.23	253.68	253.47
17000	294.57	289.87	286.09	283.04	280.55	278.53	276.88	275.52	271.61	270.12	269.54	269.31
18000	311.90	306.93	302.92	299.69	297.06	294.91	293.16	291.73	287.59	286.01	285.39	285.16
19000	329.23	323.98	319.75	316.33	313.56	311.30	309.45	307.94	303.56	301.89	301.25	301.00
20000	346.56	341.03	336.58	332.98	330.06	327.68	325.74	324.14	319.54	317.78	317.10	316.84
21000	363.89	358.08	353.41	349.63	346.57	344.07	342.02	340.35	335.52	333.67	332.96	332.68
22000	381.21	375.13	370.24	366.28	363.07	360.45	358.31	356.56	351.49	349.56	348.81	348.52
23000	398.54	392.18	387.07	382.93	379.57	376.83	374.60	372.76	367.47	365.45	364.67	364.37
24000	415.87	409.23	403.90	399.58	396.07	393.22	390.88	388.97	383.45	381.34	380.52	380.21
25000	433.20	426.28	420.72	416.23	412.58	409.60	407.17	405.18	399.43	397.23	396.38	396.05
26000	450.52	443.33	437.55	432.88	429.08	425.98	423.46	421.38	415.40	413.12	412.23	411.89
27000	467.85	460.39	454.38	449.53	445.58	442.37	439.74	437.59	431.38	429.01	428.09	427.73
28000	485.18	477.44	471.21	466.17	462.09	458.75	456.03	453.80	447.36	444.89	443.94	443.57
29000	502.51	494.49	488.04	482.82	478.59	475.14	472.32	470.00	463.33	460.78	459.80	459.42
30000	519.83	511.54	504.87	499.47	495.09	491.52	488.60	486.21	479.31	476.67	475.65	475.26
31000	537.16	528.59	521.70	516.12	511.59	507.90	504.89	502.42	495.29	492.56	491.51	491.10
32000	554.49	545.64	538.53	532.77	528.10	524.29	521.17	518.62	511.26	508.45	507.36	506.94
33000	571.82	562.69	555.35	549.42	544.60	540.67	537.46	534.83	527.24	524.34	523.22	522.78
34000	589.14	579.74	572.18	566.07	561.10	557.06	553.75	551.04	543.22	540.23	539.07	538.62
35000	606.47	596.80	589.01	582.72	577.61	573.44	570.03	567.24	559.19	556.12	554.93	554.47
37500	649.79	639.42	631.08	624.34	618.86	614.40	610.75	607.76	599.14	595.84	594.57	594.07
40000	693.11	682.05	673.16	665.96	660.12	655.36	651.47	648.28	639.08	635.56	634.20	633.67
42500	736.43	724.68	715.23	707.58	701.38	696.32	692.18	688.80	679.02	675.28	673.84	673.28
45000	779.75	767.31	757.30	749.21	742.63	737.28	732.90	729.31	718.96	715.01	713.48	712.88
47500	823.07	809.93	799.37	790.83	783.89	778.24	773.62	769.83	758.90	754.73	753.11	752.49
50000	866.39	852.56	841.44	832.45	825.15	819.20	814.33	810.35	798.85	794.45	792.75	792.09
52500	909.71	895.19	883.51	874.07	866.41	860.16	855.05	850.86	838.79	834.17	832.39	831.70
55000	953.02	937.82	925.59	915.70	907.66	901.12	895.77	891.38	878.73	873.90	872.02	871.30
57500	996.34	980.45	967.66	957.32	948.92	942.08	936.48	931.90	918.67	913.62	911.66	910.91
60000	1039.66	1023.07	1009.73	998.94	990.18	983.04	977.20	972.42	958.61	953.34	951.30	950.51
65000	1126.30	1108.33	1093.87	1082.19	1072.69	1064.95	1058.63	1053.45	1038.50	1032.79	1030.58	1029.72
70000	1212.94	1193.59	1178.02	1165.43	1155.21	1146.87	1140.06	1134.48	1118.38	1112.23	1109.85	1108.93
75000	1299.58	1278.84	1262.16	1248.67	1237.72	1228.79	1221.50	1215.52	1198.27	1191.67	1189.13	1188.14
80000	1386.21	1364.10	1346.31	1331.92	1320.24	1310.71	1302.93	1296.55	1278.15	1271.12	1268.40	1267.34
85000	1472.85	1449.35	1430.45	1415.16	1402.75	1392.63	1384.36	1377.59	1358.03	1350.56	1347.68	1346.55
90000	1559.49	1534.61	1514.59	1498.41	1485.26	1474.55	1465.79	1458.62	1437.92	1430.01	1426.95	1425.76
95000	1646.13	1619.86	1598.74	1581.65	1567.78	1556.47	1547.23	1539.66	1517.80	1509.45	1506.22	1504.97
100000	1732.77	1705.12	1682.88	1664.90	1650.29	1638.39	1628.66	1620.69	1597.69	1588.90	1585.50	1584.18
105000	1819.41	1790.38	1767.02	1748.14	1732.81	1720.31	1710.09	1701.72	1677.57	1668.34	1664.77	1663.39
110000	1906.04	1875.63	1851.17	1831.39	1815.32	1802.23	1791.53	1782.76	1757.45	1747.79	1744.05	1742.60
115000	1992.68	1960.89	1935.31	1914.63	1897.84	1884.15	1872.96	1863.79	1837.34	1827.23	1823.32	1821.81
120000	2079.32	2046.14	2019.46	1997.88	1980.35	1966.07	1954.39	1944.83	1917.22	1906.68	1902.60	1901.01
125000	2165.96	2131.40	2103.60	2081.12	2062.86	2047.99	2035.82	2025.86	1997.11	1986.12	1981.87	1980.22
130000	2252.60	2216.65	2187.74	2164.37	2145.38	2129.90	2117.26	2106.90	2076.99	2065.57	2061.15	2059.43
135000	2339.23	2301.91	2271.89	2247.61	2227.89	2211.82	2198.69	2187.93	2156.87	2145.01	2140.42	2138.64
140000	2425.87	2387.17	2356.03	2330.85	2310.41	2293.74	2280.12	2268.96	2236.76	2224.45	2219.70	2217.85
145000	2512.51	2472.42	2440.18	2414.10	2392.92	2375.66	2361.56	2350.00	2316.64	2303.90	2298.97	2297.06
150000	2599.15	2557.68	2524.32	2497.34	2475.44	2457.58	2442.99	2431.03	2396.53	2383.34	2378.25	2376.27
155000	2685.79	2642.93	2608.46	2580.59	2557.95	2539.50	2524.42	2512.07	2476.41	2462.79	2457.52	2455.48
160000	2772.42	2728.19	2692.61	2663.83	2640.47	2621.42	2605.85	2593.10	2556.29	2542.23	2536.80	2534.68

19.25% MONTHLY AMORTIZING PAYMENTS

AMOUNT OF LOAN	NUMBER OF YEARS IN TERM											
	1	2	3	4	5	6	7	8	9	10	11	12
$ 50	4.62	2.53	1.84	1.51	1.31	1.18	1.09	1.03	0.98	0.95	0.92	0.90
100	9.23	5.06	3.68	3.01	2.61	2.36	2.18	2.05	1.96	1.89	1.83	1.79
200	18.46	10.11	7.36	6.01	5.22	4.71	4.36	4.10	3.91	3.77	3.66	3.57
300	27.69	15.16	11.04	9.01	7.83	7.06	6.53	6.15	5.87	5.65	5.49	5.36
400	36.92	20.22	14.72	12.02	10.44	9.41	8.71	8.20	7.82	7.54	7.32	7.14
500	46.14	25.27	18.40	15.02	13.04	11.77	10.88	10.25	9.78	9.42	9.14	8.93
600	55.37	30.32	22.07	18.02	15.65	14.12	13.06	12.30	11.73	11.30	10.97	10.71
700	64.60	35.38	25.75	21.03	18.26	16.47	15.23	14.35	13.69	13.19	12.80	12.50
800	73.83	40.43	29.43	24.03	20.87	18.82	17.41	16.40	15.64	15.07	14.63	14.28
900	83.05	45.48	33.11	27.03	23.48	21.17	19.59	18.44	17.60	16.95	16.46	16.07
1000	92.28	50.54	36.79	30.04	26.08	23.53	21.76	20.49	19.55	18.84	18.28	17.85
2000	184.56	101.07	73.57	60.07	52.16	47.05	43.52	40.98	39.10	37.67	36.56	35.70
3000	276.83	151.60	110.35	90.10	78.24	70.57	65.28	61.47	58.64	56.50	54.84	53.54
4000	369.11	202.13	147.14	120.13	104.32	94.09	87.03	81.96	78.19	75.33	73.12	71.39
5000	461.38	252.66	183.92	150.17	130.40	117.61	108.79	102.44	97.74	94.16	91.40	89.23
6000	553.66	303.19	220.70	180.20	156.47	141.13	130.55	122.93	117.28	112.99	109.68	107.08
7000	645.94	353.72	257.48	210.23	182.55	164.65	152.30	143.42	136.83	131.82	127.95	124.93
8000	738.21	404.25	294.27	240.26	208.63	188.17	174.06	163.91	156.37	150.65	146.23	142.77
9000	830.49	454.78	331.05	270.29	234.71	211.69	195.82	184.40	175.92	169.48	164.51	160.62
10000	922.76	505.31	367.83	300.33	260.79	235.21	217.57	204.88	195.47	188.31	182.79	178.46
11000	1015.04	555.84	404.61	330.36	286.87	258.73	239.33	225.37	215.01	207.15	201.07	196.31
12000	1107.32	606.37	441.40	360.39	312.94	282.25	261.09	245.86	234.56	225.98	219.35	214.16
13000	1199.59	656.90	478.18	390.42	339.02	305.77	282.84	266.35	254.10	244.81	237.62	232.00
14000	1291.87	707.43	514.96	420.46	365.10	329.29	304.60	286.84	273.65	263.64	255.90	249.85
15000	1384.14	757.96	551.74	450.49	391.18	352.81	326.36	307.32	293.20	282.47	274.18	267.69
16000	1476.42	808.49	588.53	480.52	417.26	376.33	348.11	327.81	312.74	301.30	292.46	285.54
17000	1568.70	859.02	625.31	510.55	443.34	399.85	369.87	348.30	332.29	320.13	310.74	303.38
18000	1660.97	909.55	662.09	540.58	469.41	423.37	391.63	368.79	351.83	338.96	329.02	321.23
19000	1753.25	960.08	698.87	570.62	495.49	446.89	413.38	389.27	371.38	357.79	347.29	339.08
20000	1845.52	1010.61	735.66	600.65	521.57	470.41	435.14	409.76	390.93	376.62	365.57	356.92
21000	1937.80	1061.14	772.44	630.68	547.65	493.93	456.90	430.25	410.47	395.45	383.85	374.77
22000	2030.08	1111.67	809.22	660.71	573.73	517.45	478.66	450.74	430.02	414.29	402.13	392.61
23000	2122.35	1162.20	846.00	690.75	599.81	540.97	500.41	471.23	449.56	433.12	420.41	410.46
24000	2214.63	1212.73	882.79	720.78	625.88	564.49	522.17	491.71	469.11	451.95	438.69	428.31
25000	2306.90	1263.26	919.57	750.81	651.96	588.01	543.93	512.20	488.66	470.78	456.97	446.15
26000	2399.18	1313.79	956.35	780.84	678.04	611.53	565.68	532.69	508.20	489.61	475.24	464.00
27000	2491.46	1364.32	993.13	810.87	704.12	635.05	587.44	553.18	527.75	508.44	493.52	481.84
28000	2583.73	1414.85	1029.92	840.91	730.20	658.57	609.20	573.67	547.30	527.27	511.80	499.69
29000	2676.01	1465.38	1066.70	870.94	756.28	682.09	630.95	594.15	566.84	546.10	530.08	517.53
30000	2768.28	1515.91	1103.48	900.97	782.35	705.61	652.71	614.64	586.39	564.93	548.36	535.38
31000	2860.56	1566.44	1140.26	931.00	808.43	729.13	674.47	635.13	605.93	583.76	566.64	553.23
32000	2952.83	1616.97	1177.05	961.04	834.51	752.65	696.22	655.62	625.48	602.59	584.91	571.07
33000	3045.11	1667.50	1213.83	991.07	860.59	776.17	717.98	676.11	645.03	621.43	603.19	588.92
34000	3137.39	1718.03	1250.61	1021.10	886.67	799.69	739.74	696.59	664.57	640.26	621.47	606.76
35000	3229.66	1768.56	1287.39	1051.13	912.75	823.21	761.49	717.08	684.12	659.09	639.75	624.61
37500	3460.35	1894.89	1379.35	1126.21	977.94	882.01	815.89	768.30	732.98	706.16	685.45	669.22
40000	3691.04	2021.21	1471.31	1201.29	1043.14	940.81	870.28	819.52	781.85	753.24	731.14	713.84
42500	3921.73	2147.54	1563.26	1276.37	1108.33	999.61	924.67	870.74	830.71	800.32	776.84	758.45
45000	4152.42	2273.86	1655.22	1351.45	1173.53	1058.41	979.06	921.96	879.58	847.40	822.53	803.07
47500	4383.11	2400.19	1747.18	1426.53	1238.72	1117.21	1033.45	973.18	928.44	894.47	868.23	847.68
50000	4613.80	2526.51	1839.13	1501.62	1303.92	1176.01	1087.85	1024.40	977.31	941.55	913.93	892.30
52500	4844.49	2652.84	1931.09	1576.70	1369.12	1234.81	1142.24	1075.62	1026.17	988.63	959.62	936.91
55000	5075.18	2779.16	2023.04	1651.78	1434.31	1293.61	1196.63	1126.84	1075.04	1035.71	1005.32	981.53
57500	5305.87	2905.49	2115.00	1726.86	1499.51	1352.41	1251.02	1178.06	1123.90	1082.78	1051.01	1026.14
60000	5536.56	3031.81	2206.96	1801.94	1564.70	1411.21	1305.41	1229.28	1172.77	1129.86	1096.71	1070.76
65000	5997.94	3284.47	2390.87	1952.10	1695.09	1528.81	1414.20	1331.72	1270.50	1224.02	1188.10	1159.98
70000	6459.32	3537.12	2574.78	2102.26	1825.49	1646.41	1522.98	1434.16	1368.23	1318.17	1279.49	1249.21
75000	6920.70	3789.77	2758.70	2252.42	1955.88	1764.01	1631.77	1536.60	1465.96	1412.32	1370.89	1338.44
80000	7382.08	4042.42	2942.61	2402.58	2086.27	1881.61	1740.55	1639.04	1563.69	1506.48	1462.28	1427.67
85000	7843.46	4295.07	3126.52	2552.74	2216.66	1999.21	1849.33	1741.48	1661.42	1600.63	1553.67	1516.90
90000	8304.84	4547.72	3310.43	2702.90	2347.05	2116.81	1958.12	1843.92	1759.15	1694.79	1645.06	1606.13
95000	8766.22	4800.37	3494.35	2853.06	2477.44	2234.41	2066.90	1946.35	1856.88	1788.94	1736.45	1695.36
100000	9227.60	5053.02	3678.26	3003.23	2607.84	2352.01	2175.69	2048.79	1954.61	1883.10	1827.85	1784.59
105000	9688.98	5305.67	3862.17	3153.39	2738.23	2469.61	2284.47	2151.23	2052.34	1977.25	1919.24	1873.82
110000	10150.36	5558.32	4046.08	3303.55	2868.62	2587.21	2393.26	2253.67	2150.07	2071.41	2010.63	1963.05
115000	10611.74	5810.97	4230.00	3453.71	2999.01	2704.81	2502.04	2356.11	2247.80	2165.56	2102.02	2052.28
120000	11073.12	6063.62	4413.91	3603.87	3129.40	2822.41	2610.82	2458.55	2345.54	2259.72	2193.42	2141.51
125000	11534.50	6316.28	4597.82	3754.03	3259.79	2940.02	2719.61	2560.99	2443.27	2353.87	2284.81	2230.74
130000	11995.88	6568.93	4781.74	3904.19	3390.18	3057.62	2828.39	2663.43	2541.00	2448.03	2376.20	2319.96
135000	12457.26	6821.58	4965.65	4054.35	3520.58	3175.22	2937.18	2765.87	2638.73	2542.18	2467.59	2409.19
140000	12918.64	7074.23	5149.56	4204.51	3650.97	3292.82	3045.96	2868.31	2736.46	2636.34	2558.98	2498.42
145000	13380.02	7326.88	5333.47	4354.67	3781.36	3410.42	3154.74	2970.75	2834.19	2730.49	2650.38	2587.65
150000	13841.40	7579.53	5517.39	4504.84	3911.75	3528.02	3263.53	3073.19	2931.92	2824.64	2741.77	2676.88
155000	14302.77	7832.18	5701.30	4655.00	4042.14	3645.62	3372.31	3175.63	3029.65	2918.80	2833.16	2766.11
160000	14764.15	8084.83	5885.21	4805.16	4172.53	3763.22	3481.10	3278.07	3127.38	3012.95	2924.55	2855.34

AMOUNT OF LOAN	NUMBER OF YEARS IN TERM											
	13	14	15	16	17	18	19	20	25	30	35	40
$ 50	0.88	0.87	0.86	0.85	0.84	0.83	0.83	0.83	0.81	0.81	0.81	0.81
100	1.76	1.73	1.71	1.69	1.67	1.66	1.65	1.65	1.62	1.61	1.61	1.61
200	3.51	3.45	3.41	3.37	3.34	3.32	3.30	3.29	3.24	3.22	3.22	3.21
300	5.26	5.17	5.11	5.06	5.01	4.98	4.95	4.93	4.86	4.83	4.82	4.82
400	7.01	6.90	6.81	6.74	6.68	6.63	6.60	6.57	6.48	6.44	6.43	6.42
500	8.76	8.62	8.51	8.42	8.35	8.29	8.24	8.21	8.09	8.05	8.04	8.03
600	10.51	10.34	10.21	10.11	10.02	9.95	9.89	9.85	9.71	9.66	9.64	9.63
700	12.26	12.07	11.91	11.79	11.69	11.61	11.54	11.49	11.33	11.27	11.25	11.24
800	14.01	13.79	13.61	13.47	13.36	13.26	13.19	13.13	12.95	12.88	12.85	12.84
900	15.76	15.51	15.32	15.16	15.03	14.92	14.84	14.77	14.57	14.49	14.46	14.45
1000	17.51	17.24	17.02	16.84	16.70	16.58	16.48	16.41	16.18	16.10	16.07	16.05
2000	35.01	34.47	34.03	33.67	33.39	33.15	32.96	32.81	32.36	32.19	32.13	32.10
3000	52.52	51.70	51.04	50.51	50.08	49.73	49.44	49.21	48.54	48.29	48.19	48.15
4000	70.02	68.93	68.05	67.34	66.77	66.30	65.92	65.61	64.72	64.38	64.25	64.20
5000	87.52	86.16	85.06	84.18	83.46	82.88	82.40	82.01	80.90	80.47	80.31	80.25
6000	105.03	103.39	102.07	101.01	100.15	99.45	98.88	98.41	97.07	96.57	96.38	96.30
7000	122.53	120.62	119.09	117.85	116.84	116.03	115.36	114.82	113.25	112.66	112.44	112.35
8000	140.03	137.85	136.10	134.68	133.53	132.60	131.84	131.22	129.43	128.76	128.50	128.40
9000	157.54	155.08	153.11	151.52	150.22	149.18	148.32	147.62	145.61	144.85	144.56	144.45
10000	175.04	172.31	170.12	168.35	166.92	165.75	164.80	164.02	161.79	160.94	160.62	160.50
11000	192.54	189.54	187.13	185.18	183.61	182.32	181.28	180.42	177.97	177.04	176.68	176.55
12000	210.05	206.77	204.14	202.02	200.30	198.90	197.76	196.82	194.14	193.13	192.75	192.60
13000	227.55	224.00	221.15	218.85	216.99	215.47	214.24	213.22	210.32	209.23	208.81	208.65
14000	245.06	241.23	238.17	235.69	233.68	232.05	230.72	229.63	226.50	225.32	224.87	224.70
15000	262.56	258.46	255.18	252.52	250.37	248.62	247.19	246.03	242.68	241.41	240.93	240.75
16000	280.06	275.69	272.19	269.36	267.06	265.20	263.67	262.43	258.86	257.51	256.99	256.80
17000	297.57	292.93	289.20	286.19	283.75	281.77	280.15	278.83	275.04	273.60	273.05	272.84
18000	315.07	310.16	306.21	303.03	300.44	298.35	296.63	295.23	291.21	289.70	289.12	288.89
19000	332.57	327.39	323.22	319.86	317.14	314.92	313.11	311.63	307.39	305.79	305.18	304.94
20000	350.08	344.62	340.23	336.70	333.83	331.49	329.59	328.04	323.57	321.88	321.24	320.99
21000	367.58	361.85	357.25	353.53	350.52	348.07	346.07	344.44	339.75	337.98	337.30	337.04
22000	385.08	379.08	374.26	370.36	367.21	364.64	362.55	360.84	355.93	354.07	353.36	353.09
23000	402.59	396.31	391.27	387.20	383.90	381.22	379.03	377.24	372.11	370.17	369.43	369.14
24000	420.09	413.54	408.28	404.03	400.59	397.79	395.51	393.64	388.28	386.26	385.49	385.19
25000	437.60	430.77	425.29	420.87	417.28	414.37	411.99	410.04	404.46	402.35	401.55	401.24
26000	455.10	448.00	442.30	437.70	433.97	430.94	428.47	426.44	420.64	418.45	417.61	417.29
27000	472.60	465.23	459.31	454.54	450.66	447.52	444.95	442.85	436.82	434.54	433.67	433.34
28000	490.11	482.46	476.33	471.37	467.36	464.09	461.43	459.25	453.00	450.64	449.73	449.39
29000	507.61	499.69	493.34	488.21	484.05	480.66	477.90	475.65	469.17	466.73	465.80	465.44
30000	525.11	516.92	510.35	505.04	500.74	497.24	494.38	492.05	485.35	482.82	481.86	481.49
31000	542.62	534.15	527.36	521.87	517.43	513.81	510.86	508.45	501.53	498.92	497.92	497.54
32000	560.12	551.38	544.37	538.71	534.12	530.39	527.34	524.85	517.71	515.01	513.98	513.59
33000	577.62	568.62	561.38	555.54	550.81	546.96	543.82	541.25	533.89	531.11	530.04	529.63
34000	595.13	585.85	578.39	572.38	567.50	563.54	560.30	557.66	550.07	547.20	546.10	545.68
35000	612.63	603.08	595.41	589.21	584.19	580.11	576.78	574.06	566.24	563.29	562.17	561.73
37500	656.39	646.16	637.93	631.30	625.92	621.55	617.98	615.06	606.69	603.53	602.32	601.86
40000	700.15	689.23	680.46	673.39	667.65	662.98	659.18	656.07	647.14	643.76	642.48	641.98
42500	743.91	732.31	722.99	715.47	709.38	704.42	700.38	697.07	687.58	684.00	682.63	682.10
45000	787.67	775.38	765.52	757.56	751.10	745.86	741.57	738.07	728.03	724.23	722.78	722.23
47500	831.43	818.46	808.05	799.64	792.83	787.29	782.77	779.08	768.47	764.47	762.94	762.35
50000	875.19	861.54	850.58	841.73	834.56	828.73	823.97	820.08	808.92	804.70	803.09	802.47
52500	918.94	904.61	893.11	883.82	876.29	870.16	865.17	861.08	849.36	844.94	843.25	842.60
55000	962.70	947.69	935.63	925.90	918.02	911.60	906.37	902.09	889.81	885.17	883.40	882.72
57500	1006.46	990.77	978.16	967.99	959.74	953.04	947.56	943.09	930.26	925.41	923.56	922.85
60000	1050.22	1033.84	1020.69	1010.08	1001.47	994.47	988.76	984.10	970.70	965.64	963.71	962.97
65000	1137.74	1120.00	1105.75	1094.25	1084.93	1077.34	1071.16	1066.10	1051.59	1046.11	1044.02	1043.22
70000	1225.26	1206.15	1190.81	1178.42	1168.38	1160.22	1153.56	1148.11	1132.48	1126.58	1124.33	1123.46
75000	1312.78	1292.30	1275.86	1262.59	1251.84	1243.09	1235.95	1230.12	1213.38	1207.05	1204.64	1203.71
80000	1400.29	1378.45	1360.92	1346.77	1335.29	1325.96	1318.35	1312.13	1294.27	1287.52	1284.95	1283.96
85000	1487.81	1464.61	1445.98	1430.94	1418.75	1408.83	1400.75	1394.13	1375.16	1367.99	1365.25	1364.20
90000	1575.33	1550.76	1531.03	1515.11	1502.20	1491.71	1483.14	1476.14	1456.05	1448.46	1445.56	1444.45
95000	1662.85	1636.91	1616.09	1599.28	1585.66	1574.58	1565.54	1558.15	1536.94	1528.93	1525.87	1524.70
100000	1750.37	1723.07	1701.15	1683.46	1669.12	1657.45	1647.94	1640.16	1617.83	1609.40	1606.18	1604.94
105000	1837.88	1809.22	1786.21	1767.63	1752.57	1740.32	1730.33	1722.16	1698.72	1689.87	1686.49	1685.19
110000	1925.40	1895.37	1871.26	1851.80	1836.03	1823.19	1812.73	1804.17	1779.62	1770.34	1766.80	1765.44
115000	2012.92	1981.53	1956.32	1935.97	1919.48	1906.07	1895.12	1886.18	1860.51	1850.81	1847.11	1845.69
120000	2100.44	2067.68	2041.38	2020.15	2002.94	1988.94	1977.52	1968.19	1941.40	1931.28	1927.42	1925.93
125000	2187.96	2153.83	2126.43	2104.32	2086.39	2071.81	2059.92	2050.19	2022.29	2011.75	2007.72	2006.18
130000	2275.47	2239.99	2211.49	2188.49	2169.85	2154.68	2142.31	2132.20	2103.18	2092.22	2088.03	2086.43
135000	2362.99	2326.14	2296.55	2272.66	2253.30	2237.56	2224.71	2214.21	2184.07	2172.69	2168.34	2166.67
140000	2450.51	2412.29	2381.61	2356.84	2336.76	2320.43	2307.11	2296.22	2264.96	2253.16	2248.65	2246.92
145000	2538.03	2498.45	2466.66	2441.01	2420.21	2403.30	2389.50	2378.22	2345.85	2333.63	2328.96	2327.17
150000	2625.55	2584.60	2551.72	2525.18	2503.67	2486.17	2471.90	2460.23	2426.75	2414.10	2409.27	2407.41
155000	2713.06	2670.75	2636.78	2609.35	2587.13	2569.04	2554.30	2542.24	2507.64	2494.57	2489.58	2487.66
160000	2800.58	2756.90	2721.83	2693.53	2670.58	2651.92	2636.69	2624.25	2588.53	2575.04	2569.89	2567.91

AMOUNT OF LOAN	NUMBER OF YEARS IN TERM											
	1	2	3	4	5	6	7	8	9	10	11	12
$ 50	4.62	2.54	1.85	1.51	1.32	1.19	1.10	1.04	0.99	0.95	0.93	0.91
100	9.24	5.07	3.70	3.02	2.63	2.37	2.20	2.07	1.98	1.90	1.85	1.81
200	18.48	10.14	7.39	6.04	5.25	4.74	4.39	4.13	3.95	3.80	3.69	3.61
300	27.72	15.20	11.08	9.05	7.87	7.10	6.58	6.20	5.92	5.70	5.54	5.41
400	36.96	20.27	14.77	12.07	10.49	9.47	8.77	8.26	7.89	7.60	7.38	7.21
500	46.20	25.33	18.46	15.09	13.11	11.84	10.96	10.33	9.86	9.50	9.23	9.01
600	55.44	30.40	22.15	18.10	15.73	14.20	13.15	12.39	11.83	11.40	11.07	10.82
700	64.68	35.46	25.84	21.12	18.36	16.57	15.34	14.45	13.80	13.30	12.92	12.62
800	73.92	40.53	29.53	24.14	20.98	18.94	17.53	16.52	15.77	15.20	14.76	14.42
900	83.16	45.59	33.22	27.15	23.60	21.30	19.72	18.58	17.74	17.10	16.61	16.22
1000	92.40	50.66	36.91	30.17	26.22	23.67	21.91	20.65	19.71	19.00	18.45	18.02
2000	184.80	101.31	73.82	60.33	52.44	47.33	43.82	41.29	39.42	38.00	36.90	36.04
3000	277.19	151.96	110.73	90.50	78.65	71.00	65.72	61.93	59.12	56.99	55.35	54.06
4000	369.59	202.61	147.64	120.66	104.87	94.66	87.63	82.57	78.83	75.99	73.79	72.08
5000	461.98	253.26	184.55	150.83	131.09	118.32	109.54	103.22	98.53	94.98	92.24	90.10
6000	554.38	303.92	221.46	180.99	157.30	141.99	131.44	123.86	118.24	113.98	110.69	108.12
7000	646.77	354.57	258.37	211.16	183.52	165.65	153.35	144.50	137.94	132.97	129.13	126.14
8000	739.17	405.22	295.28	241.32	209.74	189.32	175.25	165.14	157.65	151.97	147.58	144.15
9000	831.56	455.87	332.19	271.49	235.95	212.98	197.16	185.79	177.36	170.96	166.03	162.17
10000	923.96	506.52	369.10	301.65	262.17	236.64	219.07	206.43	197.06	189.96	184.48	180.19
11000	1016.35	557.18	406.01	331.82	288.39	260.31	240.97	227.07	216.77	208.95	202.92	198.21
12000	1108.75	607.83	442.92	361.98	314.60	283.97	262.88	247.71	236.47	227.95	221.37	216.23
13000	1201.14	658.48	479.83	392.14	340.82	307.64	284.78	268.36	256.18	246.94	239.82	234.25
14000	1293.54	709.13	516.74	422.31	367.04	331.30	306.69	289.00	275.88	265.94	258.26	252.27
15000	1385.94	759.78	553.64	452.47	393.25	354.96	328.60	309.64	295.59	284.93	276.71	270.28
16000	1478.33	810.44	590.55	482.64	419.47	378.63	350.50	330.28	315.30	303.93	295.16	288.30
17000	1570.73	861.09	627.46	512.80	445.68	402.29	372.41	350.93	335.00	322.92	313.61	306.32
18000	1663.12	911.74	664.37	542.97	471.90	425.95	394.32	371.57	354.71	341.92	332.05	324.34
19000	1755.52	962.39	701.28	573.13	498.12	449.62	416.22	392.21	374.41	360.91	350.50	342.36
20000	1847.91	1013.04	738.19	603.30	524.33	473.28	438.13	412.85	394.12	379.91	368.95	360.37
21000	1940.31	1063.69	775.10	633.46	550.55	496.95	460.03	433.50	413.82	398.90	387.39	378.40
22000	2032.70	1114.35	812.01	663.63	576.77	520.61	481.94	454.14	433.53	417.90	405.84	396.42
23000	2125.10	1165.00	848.92	693.79	602.98	544.27	503.85	474.78	453.24	436.90	424.29	414.43
24000	2217.49	1215.65	885.83	723.96	629.20	567.94	525.75	495.42	472.94	455.89	442.74	432.45
25000	2309.89	1266.30	922.74	754.12	655.42	591.60	547.66	516.07	492.65	474.89	461.18	450.47
26000	2402.28	1316.95	959.65	784.28	681.63	615.27	569.56	536.71	512.35	493.88	479.63	468.49
27000	2494.68	1367.61	996.56	814.45	707.85	638.93	591.47	557.35	532.06	512.88	498.08	486.51
28000	2587.08	1418.26	1033.47	844.61	734.07	662.59	613.38	577.99	551.76	531.87	516.52	504.53
29000	2679.47	1468.91	1070.38	874.78	760.28	686.26	635.28	598.64	571.47	550.87	534.97	522.55
30000	2771.87	1519.56	1107.28	904.94	786.50	709.92	657.19	619.28	591.17	569.86	553.42	540.56
31000	2864.26	1570.21	1144.19	935.11	812.71	733.59	679.09	639.92	610.88	588.86	571.87	558.58
32000	2956.66	1620.87	1181.10	965.27	838.93	757.25	701.00	660.56	630.59	607.85	590.31	576.60
33000	3049.05	1671.52	1218.01	995.44	865.15	780.91	722.91	681.21	650.29	626.85	608.76	594.62
34000	3141.45	1722.17	1254.92	1025.60	891.36	804.58	744.81	701.85	670.00	645.84	627.21	612.64
35000	3233.84	1772.82	1291.83	1055.77	917.58	828.24	766.72	722.49	689.70	664.84	645.65	630.66
37500	3464.83	1899.45	1384.10	1131.18	983.12	887.40	821.48	774.10	738.97	712.33	691.77	675.70
40000	3695.82	2026.08	1476.38	1206.59	1048.66	946.56	876.25	825.70	788.23	759.81	737.89	720.75
42500	3926.81	2152.71	1568.65	1282.00	1114.20	1005.72	931.02	877.31	837.50	807.30	784.01	765.80
45000	4157.80	2279.34	1660.92	1357.41	1179.75	1064.88	985.78	928.92	886.76	854.79	830.13	810.84
47500	4388.79	2405.97	1753.20	1432.82	1245.29	1124.04	1040.55	980.52	936.02	902.28	876.24	855.89
50000	4619.77	2532.60	1845.47	1508.24	1310.83	1183.20	1095.31	1032.13	985.29	949.77	922.36	900.94
52500	4850.76	2659.23	1937.74	1583.65	1376.37	1242.36	1150.08	1083.73	1034.55	997.25	968.48	945.98
55000	5081.75	2785.86	2030.02	1659.06	1441.91	1301.52	1204.84	1135.34	1083.82	1044.74	1014.60	991.03
57500	5312.74	2912.49	2122.29	1734.47	1507.45	1360.68	1259.61	1186.95	1133.08	1092.23	1060.71	1036.08
60000	5543.73	3039.12	2214.56	1809.88	1572.99	1419.84	1314.37	1238.55	1182.34	1139.72	1106.83	1081.12
65000	6005.70	3292.38	2399.11	1960.70	1704.07	1538.16	1423.90	1341.76	1280.87	1234.69	1199.07	1171.22
70000	6467.68	3545.64	2583.66	2111.53	1835.16	1656.48	1533.43	1444.98	1379.40	1329.67	1291.30	1261.31
75000	6929.66	3798.90	2768.20	2262.35	1966.24	1774.80	1642.96	1548.19	1477.93	1424.65	1383.54	1351.40
80000	7391.63	4052.16	2952.75	2413.17	2097.32	1893.12	1752.49	1651.40	1576.46	1519.62	1475.78	1441.50
85000	7853.61	4305.41	3137.30	2564.00	2228.40	2011.44	1862.03	1754.61	1674.99	1614.60	1568.01	1531.59
90000	8315.59	4558.67	3321.84	2714.82	2359.49	2129.75	1971.56	1857.83	1773.51	1709.57	1660.25	1621.68
95000	8777.57	4811.93	3506.39	2865.64	2490.57	2248.07	2081.09	1961.04	1872.04	1804.55	1752.48	1711.78
100000	9239.54	5065.19	3690.94	3016.47	2621.65	2366.39	2190.62	2064.25	1970.57	1899.53	1844.72	1801.87
105000	9701.52	5318.45	3875.48	3167.29	2752.73	2484.71	2300.15	2167.46	2069.10	1994.50	1936.95	1891.96
110000	10163.50	5571.71	4060.03	3318.11	2883.81	2603.03	2409.68	2270.68	2167.63	2089.48	2029.19	1982.06
115000	10625.47	5824.97	4244.58	3468.93	3014.90	2721.35	2519.21	2373.89	2266.16	2184.46	2121.42	2072.15
120000	11087.45	6078.23	4429.12	3619.76	3145.98	2839.67	2628.74	2477.10	2364.68	2279.43	2213.66	2162.24
125000	11549.43	6331.49	4613.67	3770.58	3277.06	2957.99	2738.27	2580.31	2463.21	2374.41	2305.90	2252.34
130000	12011.40	6584.75	4798.22	3921.40	3408.14	3076.31	2847.80	2683.52	2561.74	2469.38	2398.13	2342.43
135000	12473.38	6838.01	4982.76	4072.23	3539.23	3194.63	2957.33	2786.74	2660.27	2564.36	2490.37	2432.52
140000	12935.36	7091.27	5167.31	4223.05	3670.31	3312.95	3066.86	2889.95	2758.80	2659.34	2582.60	2522.62
145000	13397.33	7344.53	5351.86	4373.87	3801.39	3431.27	3176.39	2993.16	2857.33	2754.31	2674.84	2612.71
150000	13859.31	7597.79	5536.40	4524.70	3932.47	3549.59	3285.92	3096.37	2955.85	2849.29	2767.07	2702.80
155000	14321.29	7851.05	5720.95	4675.52	4063.55	3667.91	3395.45	3199.59	3054.38	2944.26	2859.31	2792.90
160000	14783.26	8104.31	5905.49	4826.34	4194.64	3786.23	3504.98	3302.80	3152.91	3039.24	2951.55	2882.99

AMOUNT OF LOAN	\multicolumn{11}{c}{NUMBER OF YEARS IN TERM}										
	13	14	15	16	17	18	19	20	25	30	35	40
$ 50	0.89	0.88	0.86	0.86	0.85	0.84	0.84	0.83	0.82	0.82	0.82	0.82
100	1.77	1.75	1.72	1.71	1.69	1.68	1.67	1.66	1.64	1.63	1.63	1.63
200	3.54	3.49	3.44	3.41	3.38	3.36	3.34	3.32	3.28	3.26	3.26	3.26
300	5.31	5.23	5.16	5.11	5.07	5.03	5.01	4.98	4.92	4.89	4.89	4.88
400	7.08	6.97	6.88	6.81	6.76	6.71	6.67	6.64	6.56	6.52	6.51	6.51
500	8.85	8.71	8.60	8.52	8.44	8.39	8.34	8.30	8.20	8.15	8.14	8.13
600	10.61	10.45	10.32	10.22	10.13	10.06	10.01	9.96	9.83	9.78	9.77	9.76
700	12.38	12.19	12.04	11.92	11.82	11.74	11.68	11.62	11.47	11.41	11.39	11.38
800	14.15	13.93	13.76	13.62	13.51	13.42	13.34	13.28	13.11	13.04	13.02	13.01
900	15.92	15.67	15.48	15.32	15.20	15.09	15.01	14.94	14.75	14.67	14.65	14.64
1000	17.69	17.42	17.20	17.03	16.88	16.77	16.68	16.60	16.39	16.30	16.27	16.26
2000	35.37	34.83	34.39	34.05	33.76	33.54	33.35	33.20	32.77	32.60	32.54	32.52
3000	53.05	52.24	51.59	51.07	50.64	50.30	50.02	49.79	49.15	48.90	48.81	48.78
4000	70.73	69.65	68.78	68.09	67.52	67.07	66.70	66.39	65.53	65.20	65.08	65.03
5000	88.41	87.06	85.98	85.11	84.40	83.83	83.37	82.99	81.91	81.50	81.35	81.29
6000	106.09	104.47	103.17	102.13	101.28	100.60	100.04	99.58	98.29	97.80	97.62	97.55
7000	123.77	121.88	120.37	119.15	118.16	117.36	116.71	116.18	114.67	114.10	113.89	113.80
8000	141.45	139.29	137.56	136.17	135.04	134.13	133.39	132.78	131.05	130.40	130.15	130.06
9000	159.13	156.70	154.76	153.19	151.92	150.90	150.06	149.37	147.43	146.70	146.42	146.32
10000	176.81	174.11	171.95	170.21	168.80	167.66	166.73	165.97	163.81	163.00	162.69	162.58
11000	194.49	191.52	189.15	187.23	185.68	184.43	183.40	182.57	180.19	179.30	178.96	178.83
12000	212.17	208.93	206.34	204.25	202.56	201.19	200.08	199.16	196.57	195.60	195.23	195.09
13000	229.85	226.34	223.54	221.27	219.44	217.96	216.75	215.76	212.95	211.89	211.50	211.35
14000	247.53	243.75	240.73	238.29	236.32	234.72	233.42	232.36	229.33	228.19	227.77	227.60
15000	265.21	261.17	257.93	255.32	253.20	251.49	250.09	248.95	245.71	244.49	244.04	243.86
16000	282.89	278.58	275.12	272.34	270.08	268.25	266.77	265.55	262.09	260.79	260.30	260.12
17000	300.57	295.99	292.31	289.36	286.96	285.02	283.44	282.15	278.47	277.09	276.57	276.38
18000	318.25	313.40	309.51	306.38	303.84	301.79	300.11	298.74	294.85	293.39	292.84	292.63
19000	335.93	330.81	326.70	323.40	320.72	318.55	316.78	315.34	311.23	309.69	309.11	308.89
20000	353.61	348.22	343.90	340.42	337.60	335.32	333.46	331.94	327.61	325.99	325.38	325.15
21000	371.29	365.63	361.09	357.44	354.48	352.08	350.13	348.53	343.99	342.29	341.65	341.40
22000	388.97	383.04	378.29	374.46	371.36	368.85	366.80	365.13	360.37	358.59	357.92	357.66
23000	406.65	400.45	395.48	391.48	388.24	385.61	383.47	381.73	376.75	374.89	374.18	373.92
24000	424.33	417.86	412.68	408.50	405.12	402.38	400.15	398.32	393.13	391.19	390.45	390.18
25000	442.01	435.27	429.87	425.52	422.00	419.14	416.82	414.92	409.51	407.49	406.72	406.43
26000	459.69	452.68	447.07	442.54	438.88	435.91	433.49	431.52	425.89	423.78	422.99	422.69
27000	477.37	470.09	464.26	459.56	455.76	452.68	450.16	448.11	442.27	440.08	439.26	438.95
28000	495.05	487.50	481.46	476.58	472.64	469.44	466.84	464.71	458.65	456.38	455.53	455.20
29000	512.73	504.92	498.65	493.60	489.52	486.21	483.51	481.31	475.03	472.68	471.80	471.46
30000	530.41	522.33	515.85	510.63	506.40	502.97	500.18	497.90	491.41	488.98	488.07	487.72
31000	548.09	539.74	533.04	527.65	523.28	519.74	516.85	514.50	507.79	505.28	504.33	503.97
32000	565.77	557.15	550.24	544.67	540.16	536.50	533.53	531.10	524.17	521.58	520.60	520.23
33000	583.45	574.56	567.43	561.69	557.04	553.27	550.20	547.69	540.55	537.88	536.87	536.49
34000	601.13	591.97	584.62	578.71	573.92	570.03	566.87	564.29	556.93	554.18	553.14	552.75
35000	618.81	609.38	601.82	595.73	590.80	586.80	583.54	580.89	573.31	570.48	569.41	569.00
37500	663.01	652.91	644.81	638.28	633.00	628.71	625.23	622.38	614.26	611.23	610.08	609.65
40000	707.21	696.43	687.79	680.83	675.20	670.63	666.91	663.87	655.21	651.97	650.75	650.29
42500	751.41	739.96	730.78	723.38	717.40	712.54	708.59	705.36	696.16	692.72	691.42	690.93
45000	795.61	783.49	773.77	765.94	759.60	754.46	750.27	746.85	737.11	733.47	732.10	731.57
47500	839.82	827.01	816.75	808.49	801.80	796.37	791.95	788.35	778.06	774.22	772.77	772.22
50000	884.02	870.54	859.74	851.04	844.00	838.28	833.63	829.84	819.01	814.97	813.44	812.86
52500	928.22	914.07	902.73	893.59	886.20	880.20	875.31	871.33	859.96	855.71	854.11	853.50
55000	972.42	957.59	945.71	936.14	928.40	922.11	917.00	912.82	900.91	896.46	894.78	894.15
57500	1016.62	1001.12	988.70	978.69	970.60	964.03	958.68	954.31	941.86	937.21	935.45	934.79
60000	1060.82	1044.65	1031.69	1021.25	1012.80	1005.94	1000.36	995.80	982.81	977.96	976.13	975.43
65000	1149.22	1131.70	1117.66	1106.35	1097.20	1089.77	1083.72	1078.79	1064.71	1059.45	1057.47	1056.72
70000	1237.62	1218.75	1203.63	1191.45	1181.60	1173.60	1167.08	1161.77	1146.61	1140.95	1138.81	1138.00
75000	1326.02	1305.81	1289.61	1276.56	1266.00	1257.42	1250.45	1244.75	1228.51	1222.45	1220.16	1219.29
80000	1414.42	1392.86	1375.58	1361.66	1350.40	1341.25	1333.81	1327.74	1310.41	1303.94	1301.50	1300.57
85000	1502.82	1479.92	1461.55	1446.76	1434.79	1425.08	1417.17	1410.72	1392.31	1385.44	1382.84	1381.86
90000	1591.22	1566.97	1547.53	1531.87	1519.19	1508.91	1500.53	1493.70	1474.21	1466.93	1464.19	1463.14
95000	1679.63	1654.03	1633.50	1616.97	1603.59	1592.74	1583.90	1576.69	1556.11	1548.43	1545.53	1544.43
100000	1768.03	1741.08	1719.48	1702.07	1687.99	1676.56	1667.26	1659.67	1638.01	1629.93	1626.87	1625.71
105000	1856.43	1828.13	1805.45	1787.18	1772.39	1760.39	1750.62	1742.65	1719.91	1711.42	1708.22	1707.00
110000	1944.83	1915.18	1891.42	1872.28	1856.79	1844.22	1833.99	1825.64	1801.81	1792.92	1789.56	1788.29
115000	2033.23	2002.24	1977.40	1957.38	1941.19	1928.05	1917.35	1908.62	1883.71	1874.41	1870.90	1869.57
120000	2121.63	2089.29	2063.37	2042.49	2025.59	2011.87	2000.71	1991.60	1965.61	1955.91	1952.25	1950.86
125000	2210.03	2176.34	2149.34	2127.59	2109.99	2095.70	2084.07	2074.59	2047.51	2037.41	2033.59	2032.14
130000	2298.43	2263.40	2235.32	2212.69	2194.39	2179.53	2167.44	2157.57	2129.41	2118.90	2114.93	2113.43
135000	2386.83	2350.45	2321.29	2297.80	2278.79	2263.36	2250.80	2240.55	2211.31	2200.40	2196.28	2194.71
140000	2475.23	2437.50	2407.26	2382.90	2363.19	2347.19	2334.16	2323.54	2293.21	2281.89	2277.62	2276.00
145000	2563.64	2524.56	2493.24	2468.00	2447.59	2431.01	2417.52	2406.52	2375.11	2363.39	2358.96	2357.28
150000	2652.04	2611.61	2579.21	2553.11	2531.99	2514.84	2500.89	2489.50	2457.01	2444.89	2440.31	2438.57
155000	2740.44	2698.66	2665.18	2638.21	2616.39	2598.67	2584.25	2572.49	2538.91	2526.38	2521.65	2519.85
160000	2828.84	2785.72	2751.16	2723.31	2700.79	2682.50	2667.61	2655.47	2620.81	2607.88	2602.99	2601.14

MONTHLY AMORTIZING PAYMENTS

AMOUNT OF LOAN	NUMBER OF YEARS IN TERM											
	1	2	3	4	5	6	7	8	9	10	11	12
$ 50	4.63	2.54	1.86	1.52	1.32	1.20	1.11	1.04	1.00	0.96	0.94	0.91
100	9.26	5.08	3.71	3.03	2.64	2.39	2.21	2.08	1.99	1.92	1.87	1.82
200	18.51	10.16	7.41	6.06	5.28	4.77	4.42	4.16	3.98	3.84	3.73	3.64
300	27.76	15.24	11.12	9.09	7.91	7.15	6.62	6.24	5.96	5.75	5.59	5.46
400	37.01	20.31	14.82	12.12	10.55	9.53	8.83	8.32	7.95	7.67	7.45	7.28
500	46.26	25.39	18.52	15.15	13.18	11.91	11.03	10.40	9.94	9.59	9.31	9.10
600	55.51	30.47	22.23	18.18	15.82	14.29	13.24	12.48	11.92	11.50	11.17	10.92
700	64.77	35.55	25.93	21.21	18.45	16.67	15.44	14.56	13.91	13.42	13.04	12.74
800	74.02	40.62	29.63	24.24	21.09	19.05	17.65	16.64	15.90	15.33	14.90	14.56
900	83.27	45.70	33.34	27.27	23.72	21.43	19.86	18.72	17.88	17.25	16.76	16.38
1000	92.52	50.78	37.04	30.30	26.36	23.81	22.06	20.80	19.87	19.17	18.62	18.20
2000	185.03	101.55	74.08	60.60	52.71	47.62	44.12	41.60	39.74	38.33	37.24	36.39
3000	277.55	152.33	111.11	90.90	79.07	71.43	66.17	62.40	59.60	57.49	55.85	54.58
4000	370.06	203.10	148.15	121.19	105.42	95.24	88.23	83.20	79.47	76.65	74.47	72.77
5000	462.58	253.87	185.19	151.49	131.78	119.05	110.28	103.99	99.33	95.81	93.09	90.97
6000	555.09	304.65	222.22	181.79	158.13	142.85	132.34	124.79	119.20	114.97	111.70	109.16
7000	647.61	355.42	259.26	212.09	184.49	166.66	154.40	145.59	139.07	134.13	130.32	127.35
8000	740.12	406.20	296.30	242.38	210.84	190.47	176.45	166.39	158.93	153.29	148.94	145.54
9000	832.64	456.97	333.33	272.68	237.20	214.28	198.51	187.18	178.80	172.45	167.55	163.73
10000	925.15	507.74	370.37	302.98	263.55	238.09	220.56	207.98	198.66	191.61	186.17	181.93
11000	1017.67	558.52	407.40	333.28	289.91	261.89	242.62	228.78	218.53	210.77	204.79	200.12
12000	1110.18	609.29	444.44	363.57	316.26	285.70	264.68	249.58	238.39	229.93	223.40	218.31
13000	1202.70	660.06	481.48	393.87	342.62	309.51	286.73	270.37	258.26	249.09	242.02	236.50
14000	1295.21	710.84	518.51	424.17	368.97	333.32	308.79	291.17	278.13	268.25	260.64	254.69
15000	1387.73	761.61	555.55	454.46	395.33	357.13	330.84	311.97	297.99	287.41	279.25	272.89
16000	1480.24	812.39	592.59	484.76	421.68	380.94	352.90	332.77	317.86	306.57	297.87	291.08
17000	1572.76	863.16	629.62	515.06	448.04	404.74	374.96	353.56	337.72	325.73	316.48	309.27
18000	1665.27	913.93	666.66	545.36	474.39	428.55	397.01	374.36	357.59	344.89	335.10	327.46
19000	1757.79	964.71	703.70	575.65	500.75	452.36	419.07	395.16	377.46	364.05	353.72	345.65
20000	1850.30	1015.48	740.73	605.95	527.10	476.17	441.12	415.96	397.32	383.21	372.33	363.85
21000	1942.82	1066.25	777.77	636.25	553.46	499.98	463.18	436.75	417.19	402.37	390.95	382.04
22000	2035.33	1117.03	814.80	666.55	579.81	523.78	485.24	457.55	437.05	421.53	409.57	400.23
23000	2127.85	1167.80	851.84	696.84	606.17	547.59	507.29	478.35	456.92	440.69	428.18	418.42
24000	2220.36	1218.58	888.88	727.14	632.52	571.40	529.35	499.15	476.78	459.85	446.80	436.61
25000	2312.88	1269.35	925.91	757.44	658.88	595.21	551.40	519.94	496.65	479.01	465.42	454.81
26000	2405.39	1320.12	962.95	787.74	685.23	619.02	573.46	540.74	516.52	498.17	484.03	473.00
27000	2497.91	1370.90	999.99	818.03	711.59	642.82	595.51	561.54	536.38	517.33	502.65	491.19
28000	2590.42	1421.67	1037.02	848.33	737.94	666.63	617.57	582.34	556.25	536.49	521.27	509.38
29000	2682.94	1472.44	1074.06	878.63	764.30	690.44	639.63	603.13	576.11	555.65	539.88	527.57
30000	2775.45	1523.22	1111.09	908.92	790.65	714.25	661.68	623.93	595.98	574.81	558.50	545.77
31000	2867.97	1573.99	1148.13	939.22	817.01	738.06	683.74	644.73	615.84	593.97	577.11	563.96
32000	2960.48	1624.77	1185.17	969.52	843.36	761.87	705.79	665.53	635.71	613.13	595.73	582.15
33000	3053.00	1675.54	1222.20	999.82	869.72	785.67	727.85	686.32	655.58	632.29	614.35	600.34
34000	3145.51	1726.31	1259.24	1030.11	896.07	809.48	749.91	707.12	675.44	651.45	632.96	618.54
35000	3238.03	1777.09	1296.28	1060.41	922.43	833.29	771.96	727.92	695.31	670.61	651.58	636.73
37500	3469.31	1904.02	1388.87	1136.15	988.32	892.81	827.10	779.91	744.97	718.51	698.12	682.21
40000	3700.60	2030.96	1481.46	1211.90	1054.20	952.33	882.24	831.91	794.64	766.41	744.66	727.69
42500	3931.89	2157.89	1574.05	1287.64	1120.09	1011.85	937.38	883.90	844.30	814.31	791.20	773.17
45000	4163.18	2284.82	1666.64	1363.38	1185.98	1071.37	992.52	935.90	893.97	862.21	837.74	818.65
47500	4394.46	2411.76	1759.23	1439.13	1251.87	1130.89	1047.66	987.89	943.63	910.11	884.29	864.13
50000	4625.75	2538.69	1851.82	1514.87	1317.75	1190.41	1102.80	1039.88	993.29	958.01	930.83	909.61
52500	4857.04	2665.63	1944.41	1590.61	1383.64	1249.93	1157.94	1091.88	1042.96	1005.91	977.37	955.09
55000	5088.32	2792.56	2037.00	1666.36	1449.53	1309.45	1213.08	1143.87	1092.62	1053.81	1023.91	1000.57
57500	5319.61	2919.50	2129.59	1742.10	1515.42	1368.97	1268.22	1195.86	1142.29	1101.71	1070.45	1046.05
60000	5550.90	3046.43	2222.18	1817.84	1581.30	1428.49	1323.36	1247.86	1191.95	1149.61	1116.99	1091.53
65000	6013.47	3300.30	2407.37	1969.33	1713.08	1547.53	1433.64	1351.85	1291.28	1245.41	1210.07	1182.49
70000	6476.05	3554.17	2592.55	2120.82	1844.85	1666.57	1543.92	1455.83	1390.61	1341.21	1303.16	1273.45
75000	6938.62	3808.04	2777.73	2272.30	1976.63	1785.62	1654.20	1559.82	1489.94	1437.01	1396.24	1364.41
80000	7401.20	4061.91	2962.91	2423.79	2108.40	1904.66	1764.48	1663.81	1589.27	1532.81	1489.32	1455.37
85000	7863.77	4315.78	3148.09	2575.28	2240.18	2023.70	1874.76	1767.80	1688.60	1628.61	1582.40	1546.33
90000	8326.35	4569.64	3333.27	2726.76	2371.95	2142.74	1985.04	1871.79	1787.93	1724.41	1675.48	1637.29
95000	8788.92	4823.51	3518.46	2878.25	2503.73	2261.78	2095.32	1975.77	1887.26	1820.21	1768.57	1728.25
100000	9251.49	5077.38	3703.64	3029.74	2635.50	2380.82	2205.60	2079.76	1986.58	1916.02	1861.65	1819.21
105000	9714.07	5331.25	3888.82	3181.22	2767.28	2499.86	2315.88	2183.75	2085.91	2011.82	1954.73	1910.17
110000	10176.64	5585.12	4074.00	3332.71	2899.05	2618.90	2426.16	2287.74	2185.24	2107.62	2047.81	2001.13
115000	10639.22	5838.99	4259.18	3484.20	3030.83	2737.94	2536.43	2391.72	2284.57	2203.42	2140.89	2092.09
120000	11101.79	6092.86	4444.36	3635.68	3162.60	2856.98	2646.71	2495.71	2383.90	2299.22	2233.98	2183.05
125000	11564.37	6346.72	4629.55	3787.17	3294.38	2976.02	2756.99	2599.70	2483.23	2395.02	2327.06	2274.01
130000	12026.94	6600.59	4814.73	3938.66	3426.15	3095.06	2867.27	2703.69	2582.56	2490.82	2420.14	2364.97
135000	12489.52	6854.46	4999.91	4090.14	3557.93	3214.10	2977.55	2807.68	2681.89	2586.62	2513.22	2455.93
140000	12952.09	7108.33	5185.09	4241.63	3689.70	3333.14	3087.83	2911.66	2781.22	2682.42	2606.31	2546.89
145000	13414.67	7362.20	5370.27	4393.12	3821.48	3452.18	3198.11	3015.65	2880.55	2778.22	2699.39	2637.85
150000	13877.24	7616.07	5555.45	4544.60	3953.25	3571.23	3308.39	3119.64	2979.87	2874.02	2792.47	2728.82
155000	14339.81	7869.94	5740.64	4696.09	4085.03	3690.27	3418.67	3223.63	3079.20	2969.82	2885.55	2819.78
160000	14802.39	8123.81	5925.82	4847.58	4216.80	3809.31	3528.95	3327.62	3178.53	3065.62	2978.63	2910.74

AMOUNT OF LOAN	NUMBER OF YEARS IN TERM											
	13	14	15	16	17	18	19	20	25	30	35	40
$ 50	0.90	0.88	0.87	0.87	0.86	0.85	0.85	0.84	0.83	0.83	0.83	0.83
100	1.79	1.76	1.74	1.73	1.71	1.70	1.69	1.68	1.66	1.66	1.65	1.65
200	3.58	3.52	3.48	3.45	3.42	3.40	3.38	3.36	3.32	3.31	3.30	3.30
300	5.36	5.28	5.22	5.17	5.13	5.09	5.06	5.04	4.98	4.96	4.95	4.94
400	7.15	7.04	6.96	6.89	6.83	6.79	6.75	6.72	6.64	6.61	6.60	6.59
500	8.93	8.80	8.69	8.61	8.54	8.48	8.44	8.40	8.30	8.26	8.24	8.24
600	10.72	10.56	10.43	10.33	10.25	10.18	10.12	10.08	9.95	9.91	9.89	9.88
700	12.51	12.32	12.17	12.05	11.95	11.88	11.81	11.76	11.61	11.56	11.54	11.53
800	14.29	14.08	13.91	13.77	13.66	13.57	13.50	13.44	13.27	13.21	13.19	13.18
900	16.08	15.84	15.65	15.49	15.37	15.27	15.18	15.12	14.93	14.86	14.83	14.82
1000	17.86	17.60	17.38	17.21	17.07	16.96	16.87	16.80	16.59	16.51	16.48	16.47
2000	35.72	35.19	34.76	34.42	34.14	33.92	33.74	33.59	33.17	33.01	32.96	32.93
3000	53.58	52.78	52.14	51.63	51.21	50.88	50.60	50.38	49.75	49.52	49.43	49.40
4000	71.43	70.37	69.52	68.83	68.28	67.83	67.47	67.17	66.33	66.02	65.91	65.86
5000	89.29	87.96	86.90	86.04	85.35	84.79	84.34	83.97	82.92	82.53	82.38	82.33
6000	107.15	105.55	104.28	103.25	102.42	101.75	101.20	100.76	99.50	99.03	98.86	98.79
7000	125.01	123.14	121.65	120.46	119.49	118.71	118.07	117.55	116.08	115.54	115.33	115.26
8000	142.86	140.74	139.03	137.66	136.56	135.66	134.94	134.34	132.66	132.04	131.81	131.72
9000	160.72	158.33	156.41	154.87	153.63	152.62	151.80	151.14	149.24	148.55	148.29	148.19
10000	178.58	175.92	173.79	172.08	170.70	169.58	168.67	167.93	165.83	165.05	164.76	164.65
11000	196.44	193.51	191.17	189.29	187.77	186.53	185.53	184.72	182.41	181.56	181.24	181.12
12000	214.29	211.10	208.55	206.49	204.84	203.49	202.40	201.51	198.99	198.06	197.71	197.58
13000	232.15	228.69	225.93	223.70	221.90	220.45	219.27	218.30	215.57	214.56	214.19	214.05
14000	250.01	246.28	243.30	240.91	238.97	237.41	236.13	235.10	232.16	231.07	230.66	230.51
15000	267.87	263.88	260.68	258.12	256.04	254.36	253.00	251.89	248.74	247.57	247.14	246.98
16000	285.72	281.47	278.06	275.32	273.11	271.32	269.87	268.68	265.32	264.08	263.62	263.44
17000	303.58	299.06	295.44	292.53	290.18	288.28	286.73	285.47	281.90	280.58	280.09	279.91
18000	321.44	316.65	312.82	309.74	307.25	305.24	303.60	302.27	298.48	297.09	296.57	296.37
19000	339.30	334.24	330.20	326.95	324.32	322.19	320.46	319.06	315.07	313.59	313.04	312.84
20000	357.15	351.83	347.58	344.15	341.39	339.15	337.33	335.85	331.65	330.10	329.52	329.30
21000	375.01	369.42	364.95	361.36	358.46	356.11	354.20	352.64	348.23	346.60	345.99	345.77
22000	392.87	387.02	382.33	378.57	375.53	373.06	371.06	369.43	364.81	363.11	362.47	362.23
23000	410.73	404.61	399.71	395.78	392.60	390.02	387.93	386.23	381.39	379.61	378.95	378.70
24000	428.58	422.20	417.09	412.98	409.67	406.98	404.80	403.02	397.98	396.12	395.42	395.16
25000	446.44	439.79	434.47	430.19	426.73	423.94	421.66	419.81	414.56	412.62	411.90	411.63
26000	464.30	457.38	451.85	447.40	443.80	440.89	438.53	436.60	431.14	429.12	428.37	428.09
27000	482.16	474.97	469.23	464.60	460.87	457.85	455.39	453.40	447.72	445.63	444.85	444.56
28000	500.01	492.56	486.60	481.81	477.94	474.81	472.26	470.19	464.31	462.13	461.32	461.02
29000	517.87	510.16	503.98	499.02	495.01	491.76	489.13	486.98	480.89	478.64	477.80	477.49
30000	535.73	527.75	521.36	516.23	512.08	508.72	505.99	503.77	497.47	495.14	494.28	493.95
31000	553.58	545.34	538.74	533.43	529.15	525.68	522.86	520.56	514.05	511.65	510.75	510.42
32000	571.44	562.93	556.12	550.64	546.22	542.64	539.73	537.36	530.63	528.15	527.23	526.88
33000	589.30	580.52	573.50	567.85	563.29	559.59	556.59	554.15	547.22	544.66	543.70	543.34
34000	607.16	598.11	590.88	585.06	580.36	576.55	573.46	570.94	563.80	561.16	560.18	559.81
35000	625.01	615.70	608.25	602.26	597.43	593.51	590.32	587.73	580.38	577.67	576.65	576.27
37500	669.66	659.68	651.70	645.28	640.10	635.90	632.49	629.71	621.84	618.93	617.84	617.44
40000	714.30	703.66	695.15	688.30	682.77	678.29	674.66	671.69	663.29	660.19	659.03	658.60
42500	758.95	747.64	738.59	731.32	725.45	720.69	716.82	713.67	704.75	701.45	700.22	699.76
45000	803.59	791.62	782.04	774.34	768.12	763.08	758.99	755.66	746.20	742.71	741.41	740.92
47500	848.23	835.60	825.49	817.36	810.79	805.47	801.15	797.64	787.66	783.97	782.60	782.09
50000	892.88	879.57	868.93	860.37	853.46	847.87	843.32	839.62	829.11	825.24	823.79	823.25
52500	937.52	923.55	912.38	903.39	896.14	890.26	885.48	881.60	870.57	866.50	864.98	864.41
55000	982.16	967.53	955.83	946.41	938.81	932.65	927.65	923.58	912.02	907.76	906.17	905.57
57500	1026.81	1011.51	999.27	989.43	981.48	975.05	969.82	965.56	953.48	949.02	947.36	946.73
60000	1071.45	1055.49	1042.72	1032.45	1024.16	1017.44	1011.98	1007.54	994.93	990.28	988.55	987.90
65000	1160.74	1143.45	1129.61	1118.49	1109.50	1102.22	1096.31	1091.50	1077.84	1072.80	1070.92	1070.22
70000	1250.02	1231.40	1216.50	1204.53	1194.85	1187.01	1180.64	1175.46	1160.76	1155.33	1153.30	1152.54
75000	1339.31	1319.36	1303.40	1290.56	1280.19	1271.80	1264.98	1259.42	1243.67	1237.85	1235.68	1234.87
80000	1428.60	1407.32	1390.29	1376.60	1365.54	1356.58	1349.31	1343.38	1326.58	1320.37	1318.06	1317.19
85000	1517.89	1495.27	1477.18	1462.63	1450.89	1441.37	1433.64	1427.34	1409.49	1402.90	1400.44	1399.52
90000	1607.17	1583.23	1564.07	1548.67	1536.23	1526.16	1517.97	1511.31	1492.40	1485.42	1482.82	1481.84
95000	1696.46	1671.19	1650.97	1634.71	1621.58	1610.94	1602.30	1595.27	1575.31	1567.94	1565.19	1564.17
100000	1785.75	1759.14	1737.86	1720.74	1706.92	1695.73	1686.63	1679.23	1658.22	1650.47	1647.57	1646.49
105000	1875.03	1847.10	1824.75	1806.78	1792.27	1780.51	1770.96	1763.19	1741.13	1732.99	1729.95	1728.81
110000	1964.32	1935.06	1911.65	1892.82	1877.62	1865.30	1855.29	1847.15	1824.04	1815.51	1812.33	1811.14
115000	2053.61	2023.01	1998.54	1978.86	1962.96	1950.09	1939.63	1931.11	1906.95	1898.04	1894.71	1893.46
120000	2142.90	2110.97	2085.43	2064.89	2048.31	2034.87	2023.96	2015.07	1989.86	1980.56	1977.09	1975.79
125000	2232.18	2198.93	2172.32	2150.93	2133.65	2119.66	2108.29	2099.03	2072.77	2063.08	2059.47	2058.11
130000	2321.47	2286.89	2259.22	2236.97	2219.00	2204.44	2192.62	2182.99	2155.68	2145.60	2141.84	2140.43
135000	2410.76	2374.84	2346.11	2323.00	2304.35	2289.23	2276.95	2266.96	2238.59	2228.13	2224.22	2222.76
140000	2500.04	2462.80	2433.00	2409.04	2389.69	2374.02	2361.28	2350.92	2321.51	2310.65	2306.60	2305.08
145000	2589.33	2550.76	2519.89	2495.08	2475.04	2458.80	2445.61	2434.88	2404.42	2393.17	2388.98	2387.41
150000	2678.62	2638.71	2606.79	2581.11	2560.38	2543.59	2529.95	2518.84	2487.33	2475.70	2471.36	2469.73
155000	2767.90	2726.67	2693.68	2667.15	2645.73	2628.37	2614.28	2602.80	2570.24	2558.22	2553.74	2552.06
160000	2857.19	2814.63	2780.57	2753.19	2731.08	2713.16	2698.61	2686.76	2653.15	2640.74	2636.11	2634.38

MONTHLY AMORTIZING PAYMENTS

AMOUNT OF LOAN	NUMBER OF YEARS IN TERM											
	1	2	3	4	5	6	7	8	9	10	11	12
$ 50	4.64	2.55	1.86	1.53	1.33	1.20	1.12	1.05	1.01	0.97	0.94	0.92
100	9.27	5.09	3.72	3.05	2.65	2.40	2.23	2.10	2.01	1.94	1.88	1.84
200	18.53	10.18	7.44	6.09	5.30	4.80	4.45	4.20	4.01	3.87	3.76	3.68
300	27.80	15.27	11.15	9.13	7.95	7.19	6.67	6.29	6.01	5.80	5.64	5.51
400	37.06	20.36	14.87	12.18	10.60	9.59	8.89	8.39	8.02	7.74	7.52	7.35
500	46.32	25.45	18.59	15.22	13.25	11.98	11.11	10.48	10.02	9.67	9.40	9.19
600	55.59	30.54	22.30	18.26	15.90	14.38	13.33	12.58	12.02	11.60	11.28	11.02
700	64.85	35.63	26.02	21.31	18.55	16.77	15.55	14.67	14.02	13.53	13.16	12.86
800	74.11	40.72	29.74	24.35	21.20	19.17	17.77	16.77	16.03	15.47	15.03	14.70
900	83.38	45.81	33.45	27.39	23.85	21.56	19.99	18.86	18.03	17.40	16.91	16.53
1000	92.64	50.90	37.17	30.44	26.50	23.96	22.21	20.96	20.03	19.33	18.79	18.37
2000	185.27	101.80	74.33	60.87	52.99	47.91	44.42	41.91	40.06	38.66	37.58	36.74
3000	277.91	152.69	111.50	91.30	79.49	71.86	66.62	62.86	60.08	57.98	56.36	55.10
4000	370.54	203.59	148.66	121.73	105.98	95.82	88.83	83.82	80.11	77.31	75.15	73.47
5000	463.18	254.48	185.82	152.16	132.47	119.77	111.04	104.77	100.14	96.63	93.94	91.84
6000	555.81	305.38	222.99	182.59	158.97	143.72	133.24	125.72	120.16	115.96	112.72	110.20
7000	648.45	356.28	260.15	213.02	185.46	167.67	155.45	146.68	140.19	135.28	131.51	128.57
8000	741.08	407.17	297.31	243.45	211.96	191.63	177.65	167.63	160.22	154.61	150.30	146.93
9000	833.72	458.07	334.48	273.88	238.45	215.58	199.86	188.58	180.24	173.94	169.08	165.30
10000	926.35	508.96	371.64	304.31	264.94	239.53	222.07	209.54	200.27	193.26	187.87	183.67
11000	1018.98	559.86	408.80	334.74	291.44	263.49	244.27	230.49	220.30	212.59	206.65	202.03
12000	1111.62	610.75	445.97	365.17	317.93	287.44	266.48	251.44	240.32	231.91	225.44	220.40
13000	1204.25	661.65	483.13	395.60	344.43	311.39	288.69	272.40	260.35	251.24	244.23	238.76
14000	1296.89	712.55	520.30	426.03	370.92	335.34	310.89	293.35	280.38	270.56	263.01	257.13
15000	1389.52	763.44	557.46	456.46	397.41	359.30	333.10	314.30	300.40	289.89	281.80	275.50
16000	1482.16	814.34	594.62	486.89	423.91	383.25	355.30	335.26	320.43	309.21	300.59	293.86
17000	1574.79	865.23	631.79	517.32	450.40	407.20	377.51	356.21	340.46	328.54	319.37	312.23
18000	1667.43	916.13	668.95	547.75	476.89	431.16	399.72	377.16	360.48	347.87	338.16	330.59
19000	1760.06	967.03	706.11	578.18	503.39	455.11	421.92	398.12	380.51	367.19	356.95	348.96
20000	1852.70	1017.92	743.28	608.61	529.88	479.06	444.13	419.07	400.54	386.52	375.73	367.33
21000	1945.33	1068.82	780.44	639.04	556.38	503.01	466.34	440.02	420.56	405.84	394.52	385.69
22000	2037.96	1119.71	817.60	669.47	582.87	526.97	488.54	460.98	440.59	425.17	413.30	404.06
23000	2130.60	1170.61	854.77	699.90	609.36	550.92	510.75	481.93	460.61	444.49	432.09	422.42
24000	2223.23	1221.50	891.93	730.33	635.86	574.87	532.95	502.88	480.64	463.82	450.88	440.79
25000	2315.87	1272.40	929.09	760.76	662.35	598.83	555.16	523.84	500.67	483.14	469.66	459.16
26000	2408.50	1323.30	966.26	791.19	688.85	622.78	577.37	544.79	520.69	502.47	488.45	477.52
27000	2501.14	1374.19	1003.42	821.62	715.34	646.73	599.57	565.74	540.72	521.80	507.24	495.89
28000	2593.77	1425.09	1040.59	852.06	741.83	670.68	621.78	586.69	560.75	541.12	526.02	514.26
29000	2686.41	1475.98	1077.75	882.49	768.33	694.64	643.98	607.65	580.77	560.45	544.81	532.62
30000	2779.04	1526.88	1114.91	912.92	794.82	718.59	666.19	628.60	600.80	579.77	563.60	550.99
31000	2871.67	1577.77	1152.08	943.35	821.32	742.54	688.40	649.55	620.83	599.10	582.38	569.35
32000	2964.31	1628.67	1189.24	973.78	847.81	766.50	710.60	670.51	640.85	618.42	601.17	587.72
33000	3056.94	1679.57	1226.40	1004.21	874.30	790.45	732.81	691.46	660.88	637.75	619.95	606.09
34000	3149.58	1730.46	1263.57	1034.64	900.80	814.40	755.02	712.41	680.91	657.07	638.74	624.45
35000	3242.21	1781.36	1300.73	1065.07	927.29	838.35	777.22	733.37	700.93	676.40	657.53	642.82
37500	3473.80	1908.60	1393.64	1141.14	993.53	898.24	832.74	785.75	751.00	724.71	704.49	688.73
40000	3705.39	2035.84	1486.55	1217.22	1059.76	958.12	888.25	838.13	801.07	773.03	751.46	734.65
42500	3936.97	2163.08	1579.46	1293.30	1126.00	1018.00	943.77	890.52	851.13	821.34	798.42	780.56
45000	4168.56	2290.32	1672.37	1369.37	1192.23	1077.88	999.28	942.90	901.20	869.66	845.39	826.48
47500	4400.14	2417.56	1765.28	1445.45	1258.46	1137.76	1054.80	995.28	951.26	917.97	892.36	872.39
50000	4631.73	2544.80	1858.18	1521.52	1324.70	1197.65	1110.31	1047.67	1001.33	966.28	939.32	918.31
52500	4863.32	2672.03	1951.09	1597.60	1390.93	1257.53	1165.83	1100.05	1051.40	1014.60	986.29	964.22
55000	5094.90	2799.27	2044.00	1673.67	1457.17	1317.41	1221.35	1152.43	1101.46	1062.91	1033.25	1010.14
57500	5326.49	2926.51	2136.91	1749.75	1523.40	1377.29	1276.86	1204.81	1151.53	1111.23	1080.22	1056.05
60000	5558.08	3053.75	2229.82	1825.83	1589.64	1437.17	1332.38	1257.20	1201.60	1159.54	1127.19	1101.97
65000	6021.25	3308.23	2415.64	1977.98	1722.11	1556.94	1443.41	1361.96	1301.73	1256.17	1221.12	1193.80
70000	6484.42	3562.71	2601.46	2130.13	1854.58	1676.70	1554.44	1466.73	1401.86	1352.79	1315.05	1285.63
75000	6947.59	3817.19	2787.27	2282.28	1987.05	1796.47	1665.47	1571.50	1501.99	1449.42	1408.98	1377.46
80000	7410.77	4071.67	2973.09	2434.43	2119.52	1916.23	1776.50	1676.26	1602.13	1546.05	1502.91	1469.29
85000	7873.94	4326.15	3158.91	2586.59	2251.99	2036.00	1887.53	1781.03	1702.26	1642.68	1596.84	1561.12
90000	8337.11	4580.63	3344.73	2738.74	2384.45	2155.76	1998.56	1885.79	1802.39	1739.31	1690.78	1652.95
95000	8800.28	4835.11	3530.55	2890.89	2516.92	2275.52	2109.59	1990.56	1902.52	1835.93	1784.71	1744.78
100000	9263.46	5089.59	3716.36	3043.04	2649.39	2395.29	2220.62	2095.33	2002.66	1932.56	1878.64	1836.61
105000	9726.63	5344.06	3902.18	3195.19	2781.86	2515.05	2331.66	2200.09	2102.79	2029.19	1972.57	1928.44
110000	10189.80	5598.54	4088.00	3347.34	2914.33	2634.82	2442.69	2304.86	2202.92	2125.82	2066.50	2020.27
115000	10652.97	5853.02	4273.82	3499.50	3046.80	2754.58	2553.72	2409.62	2303.05	2222.45	2160.43	2112.10
120000	11116.15	6107.50	4459.64	3651.65	3179.27	2874.34	2664.75	2514.39	2403.19	2319.07	2254.37	2203.94
125000	11579.32	6361.98	4645.45	3803.80	3311.74	2994.11	2775.78	2619.16	2503.32	2415.70	2348.30	2295.77
130000	12042.49	6616.46	4831.27	3955.95	3444.21	3113.87	2886.81	2723.92	2603.45	2512.33	2442.23	2387.60
135000	12505.66	6870.94	5017.09	4108.10	3576.68	3233.64	2997.84	2828.69	2703.58	2608.96	2536.16	2479.43
140000	12968.84	7125.42	5202.91	4260.26	3709.15	3353.40	3108.87	2933.45	2803.72	2705.58	2630.09	2571.26
145000	13432.01	7379.90	5388.72	4412.41	3841.62	3473.16	3219.90	3038.22	2903.85	2802.21	2724.02	2663.09
150000	13895.18	7634.38	5574.54	4564.56	3974.09	3592.93	3330.93	3142.99	3003.98	2898.84	2817.96	2754.92
155000	14358.35	7888.85	5760.36	4716.71	4106.56	3712.69	3441.97	3247.75	3104.11	2995.47	2911.89	2846.75
160000	14821.53	8143.33	5946.18	4868.86	4239.03	3832.46	3553.00	3352.52	3204.25	3092.10	3005.82	2938.58

AMOUNT OF LOAN	NUMBER OF YEARS IN TERM											
	13	14	15	16	17	18	19	20	25	30	35	40
$ 50	0.91	0.89	0.88	0.87	0.87	0.86	0.86	0.85	0.84	0.84	0.84	0.84
100	1.81	1.78	1.76	1.74	1.73	1.72	1.71	1.70	1.68	1.68	1.67	1.67
200	3.61	3.56	3.52	3.48	3.46	3.43	3.42	3.40	3.36	3.35	3.34	3.34
300	5.42	5.34	5.27	5.22	5.18	5.15	5.12	5.10	5.04	5.02	5.01	5.01
400	7.22	7.11	7.03	6.96	6.91	6.86	6.83	6.80	6.72	6.69	6.68	6.67
500	9.02	8.89	8.79	8.70	8.63	8.58	8.54	8.50	8.40	8.36	8.35	8.34
600	10.83	10.67	10.54	10.44	10.36	10.29	10.24	10.20	10.08	10.03	10.01	10.01
700	12.63	12.45	12.30	12.18	12.09	12.01	11.95	11.90	11.75	11.70	11.68	11.68
800	14.43	14.22	14.06	13.92	13.81	13.72	13.65	13.60	13.43	13.37	13.35	13.34
900	16.24	16.00	15.81	15.66	15.54	15.44	15.36	15.29	15.11	15.04	15.02	15.01
1000	18.04	17.78	17.57	17.40	17.26	17.15	17.07	16.99	16.79	16.72	16.69	16.68
2000	36.08	35.55	35.13	34.79	34.52	34.30	34.13	33.98	33.57	33.43	33.37	33.35
3000	54.11	53.32	52.69	52.19	51.78	51.45	51.19	50.97	50.36	50.14	50.05	50.02
4000	72.15	71.10	70.26	69.58	69.04	68.60	68.25	67.96	67.14	66.85	66.74	66.70
5000	90.18	88.87	87.82	86.98	86.30	85.75	85.31	84.95	83.93	83.56	83.42	83.37
6000	108.22	106.64	105.38	104.37	103.56	102.90	102.37	101.93	100.71	100.27	100.10	100.04
7000	126.25	124.41	122.95	121.77	120.82	120.05	119.43	118.92	117.50	116.98	116.78	116.71
8000	144.29	142.19	140.51	139.16	138.08	137.20	136.49	135.91	134.28	133.69	133.47	133.39
9000	162.32	159.96	158.07	156.56	155.34	154.35	153.55	152.90	151.07	150.40	150.15	150.06
10000	180.36	177.73	175.63	173.95	172.60	171.50	170.61	169.89	167.85	167.11	166.83	166.73
11000	198.39	195.50	193.20	191.35	189.85	188.65	187.67	186.88	184.63	183.82	183.52	183.40
12000	216.43	213.28	210.76	208.74	207.11	205.80	204.73	203.86	201.42	200.53	200.20	200.08
13000	234.46	231.05	228.32	226.14	224.37	222.95	221.79	220.85	218.20	217.24	216.88	216.75
14000	252.50	248.82	245.89	243.53	241.63	240.10	238.85	237.84	234.99	233.95	233.56	233.42
15000	270.53	266.59	263.45	260.92	258.89	257.25	255.91	254.83	251.77	250.66	250.25	250.09
16000	288.57	284.37	281.01	278.32	276.15	274.39	272.97	271.82	268.56	267.37	266.93	266.77
17000	306.60	302.14	298.58	295.71	293.41	291.54	290.03	288.81	285.34	284.08	283.61	283.44
18000	324.64	319.91	316.14	313.11	310.67	308.69	307.09	305.79	302.13	300.79	300.30	300.11
19000	342.67	337.69	333.70	330.50	327.93	325.84	324.15	322.78	318.91	317.50	316.98	316.79
20000	360.71	355.46	351.26	347.90	345.19	342.99	341.21	339.77	335.70	334.21	333.66	333.46
21000	378.74	373.23	368.83	365.29	362.44	360.14	358.27	356.76	352.48	350.92	350.34	350.13
22000	396.78	391.00	386.39	382.69	379.70	377.29	375.34	373.75	369.26	367.63	367.03	366.80
23000	414.82	408.78	403.95	400.08	396.96	394.44	392.40	390.73	386.05	384.34	383.71	383.48
24000	432.85	426.55	421.52	417.48	414.22	411.59	409.46	407.72	402.83	401.05	400.39	400.15
25000	450.89	444.32	439.08	434.87	431.48	428.74	426.52	424.71	419.62	417.76	417.07	416.82
26000	468.92	462.09	456.64	452.27	448.74	445.89	443.58	441.70	436.40	434.47	433.76	433.49
27000	486.96	479.87	474.21	469.66	466.00	463.04	460.64	458.69	453.19	451.18	450.44	450.17
28000	504.99	497.64	491.77	487.06	483.26	480.19	477.70	475.68	469.97	467.89	467.12	466.84
29000	523.03	515.41	509.33	504.45	500.52	497.34	494.76	492.66	486.76	484.60	483.81	483.51
30000	541.06	533.18	526.89	521.84	517.78	514.49	511.82	509.65	503.54	501.31	500.49	500.18
31000	559.10	550.96	544.46	539.24	535.03	531.64	528.88	526.64	520.33	518.02	517.17	516.86
32000	577.13	568.73	562.02	556.63	552.29	548.78	545.94	543.63	537.11	534.73	533.85	533.53
33000	595.17	586.50	579.58	574.03	569.55	565.93	563.00	560.62	553.89	551.44	550.54	550.20
34000	613.20	604.28	597.15	591.42	586.81	583.08	580.06	577.61	570.68	568.15	567.22	566.87
35000	631.24	622.05	614.71	608.82	604.07	600.23	597.12	594.59	587.46	584.86	583.90	583.55
37500	676.33	666.48	658.62	652.30	647.22	643.11	639.77	636.99	629.42	626.64	625.61	625.23
40000	721.41	710.91	702.52	695.79	690.37	685.98	682.42	679.53	671.39	668.41	667.32	666.91
42500	766.50	755.34	746.43	739.28	733.51	728.85	725.07	722.01	713.35	710.19	709.02	708.59
45000	811.59	799.77	790.34	782.76	776.66	771.73	767.73	764.48	755.31	751.96	750.73	750.27
47500	856.68	844.21	834.25	826.25	819.81	814.60	810.38	806.95	797.27	793.74	792.44	791.96
50000	901.77	888.64	878.15	869.74	862.96	857.47	853.03	849.42	839.23	835.51	834.14	833.64
52500	946.85	933.07	922.06	913.22	906.10	900.35	895.68	891.89	881.19	877.29	875.85	875.32
55000	991.94	977.50	965.97	956.71	949.25	943.22	938.33	934.36	923.15	917.06	917.56	917.00
57500	1037.03	1021.93	1009.88	1000.20	992.40	986.09	980.98	976.83	965.11	960.84	959.27	958.68
60000	1082.12	1066.36	1053.78	1043.68	1035.55	1028.97	1023.63	1019.30	1007.08	1002.62	1000.97	1000.36
65000	1172.29	1155.23	1141.60	1130.66	1121.84	1114.71	1108.94	1104.24	1091.00	1086.17	1084.39	1083.73
70000	1262.47	1244.09	1229.41	1217.63	1208.14	1200.46	1194.24	1189.18	1174.92	1169.72	1167.80	1167.09
75000	1352.65	1332.95	1317.23	1304.60	1294.43	1286.21	1279.54	1274.12	1258.84	1253.27	1251.21	1250.45
80000	1442.82	1421.82	1405.04	1391.58	1380.73	1371.95	1364.84	1359.06	1342.77	1336.82	1334.63	1333.82
85000	1533.00	1510.68	1492.86	1478.55	1467.02	1457.70	1450.14	1444.01	1426.69	1420.37	1418.04	1417.18
90000	1623.17	1599.54	1580.67	1565.52	1553.32	1543.45	1535.45	1528.95	1510.61	1503.92	1501.46	1500.54
95000	1713.35	1688.41	1668.49	1652.50	1639.61	1629.19	1620.75	1613.89	1594.53	1587.47	1584.87	1583.91
100000	1803.53	1777.27	1756.30	1739.47	1725.91	1714.94	1706.05	1698.83	1678.46	1671.02	1668.28	1667.27
105000	1893.70	1866.13	1844.12	1826.44	1812.20	1800.69	1791.35	1783.77	1762.38	1754.57	1751.70	1750.63
110000	1983.88	1955.00	1931.93	1913.42	1898.50	1886.43	1876.66	1868.71	1846.30	1838.13	1835.11	1834.00
115000	2074.06	2043.86	2019.75	2000.39	1984.79	1972.18	1961.96	1953.65	1930.22	1921.68	1918.53	1917.36
120000	2164.23	2132.72	2107.56	2087.36	2071.09	2057.93	2047.26	2038.59	2014.15	2005.23	2001.94	2000.72
125000	2254.41	2221.59	2195.38	2174.34	2157.38	2143.68	2132.56	2123.54	2098.07	2088.78	2085.35	2084.09
130000	2344.58	2310.45	2283.19	2261.31	2243.68	2229.42	2217.87	2208.48	2181.99	2172.33	2168.77	2167.45
135000	2434.76	2399.31	2371.01	2348.28	2329.97	2315.17	2303.17	2293.42	2265.88	2255.88	2252.18	2250.81
140000	2524.94	2488.18	2458.82	2435.26	2416.27	2400.92	2388.47	2378.36	2349.84	2339.43	2335.59	2334.17
145000	2615.11	2577.04	2546.63	2522.23	2502.56	2486.66	2473.77	2463.30	2433.76	2422.98	2419.01	2417.54
150000	2705.29	2665.90	2634.45	2609.20	2588.86	2572.41	2559.07	2548.24	2517.68	2506.53	2502.42	2500.90
155000	2795.46	2754.77	2722.26	2696.18	2675.15	2658.16	2644.38	2633.18	2601.61	2590.08	2585.84	2584.26
160000	2885.64	2843.63	2810.08	2783.15	2761.45	2743.90	2729.68	2718.12	2685.53	2673.63	2669.25	2667.63

20.25% MONTHLY AMORTIZING PAYMENTS

AMOUNT OF LOAN	\multicolumn{12}{c}{NUMBER OF YEARS IN TERM}
	1	2	3	4	5	6	7	8	9	10	11	12
$ 50	4.64	2.56	1.87	1.53	1.34	1.21	1.12	1.06	1.01	0.98	0.95	0.93
100	9.28	5.11	3.73	3.06	2.67	2.41	2.24	2.12	2.02	1.95	1.90	1.86
200	18.56	10.21	7.46	6.12	5.33	4.82	4.48	4.23	4.04	3.90	3.80	3.71
300	27.83	15.31	11.19	9.17	7.99	7.23	6.71	6.34	6.06	5.85	5.69	5.57
400	37.11	20.41	14.92	12.23	10.66	9.64	8.95	8.45	8.08	7.80	7.59	7.42
500	46.38	25.51	18.65	15.29	13.32	12.05	11.18	10.56	10.10	9.75	9.48	9.28
600	55.66	30.62	22.38	18.34	15.98	14.46	13.42	12.67	12.12	11.70	11.38	11.13
700	64.93	35.72	26.11	21.40	18.65	16.87	15.65	14.78	14.14	13.65	13.27	12.98
800	74.21	40.82	29.84	24.46	21.31	19.28	17.89	16.89	16.16	15.60	15.17	14.84
900	83.48	45.92	33.57	27.51	23.97	21.69	20.13	19.00	18.17	17.55	17.07	16.69
1000	92.76	51.02	37.30	30.57	26.64	24.10	22.36	21.11	20.19	19.50	18.96	18.55
2000	185.51	102.04	74.59	61.13	53.27	48.20	44.72	42.22	40.38	38.99	37.92	37.09
3000	278.27	153.06	111.88	91.70	79.90	72.30	67.08	63.33	60.57	58.48	56.88	55.63
4000	371.02	204.08	149.17	122.26	106.54	96.40	89.43	84.44	80.76	77.97	75.83	74.17
5000	463.78	255.10	186.46	152.82	133.17	120.49	111.79	105.55	100.94	97.46	94.79	92.71
6000	556.53	306.11	223.75	183.39	159.80	144.59	134.15	126.66	121.13	116.95	113.75	111.25
7000	649.28	357.13	261.04	213.95	186.44	168.69	156.50	147.77	141.32	136.45	132.70	129.79
8000	742.04	408.15	298.33	244.51	213.07	192.79	178.86	168.88	161.51	155.94	151.66	148.33
9000	834.79	459.17	335.62	275.08	239.70	216.89	201.22	189.99	181.69	175.43	170.62	166.87
10000	927.55	510.19	372.92	305.64	266.34	240.98	223.57	211.10	201.88	194.92	189.57	185.41
11000	1020.30	561.20	410.21	336.21	292.97	265.08	245.93	232.21	222.07	214.41	208.53	203.95
12000	1113.06	612.22	447.50	366.77	319.60	289.18	268.29	253.32	242.26	233.90	227.49	222.49
13000	1205.81	663.24	484.79	397.33	346.24	313.28	290.65	274.43	262.45	253.40	246.44	241.03
14000	1298.56	714.26	522.08	427.90	372.87	337.38	313.00	295.54	282.63	272.89	265.40	259.57
15000	1391.32	765.28	559.37	458.46	399.50	361.47	335.36	316.65	302.82	292.38	284.36	278.12
16000	1484.07	816.29	596.66	489.02	426.14	385.57	357.72	337.75	323.01	311.87	303.31	296.66
17000	1576.83	867.31	633.95	519.59	452.77	409.67	380.07	358.86	343.20	331.36	322.27	315.20
18000	1669.58	918.33	671.24	550.15	479.40	433.77	402.43	379.97	363.38	350.85	341.23	333.74
19000	1762.33	969.35	708.54	580.72	506.04	457.87	424.79	401.08	383.57	370.35	360.18	352.28
20000	1855.09	1020.37	745.83	611.28	532.67	481.96	447.14	422.19	403.76	389.84	379.14	370.82
21000	1947.84	1071.38	783.12	641.84	559.30	506.06	469.50	443.30	423.95	409.33	398.10	389.36
22000	2040.60	1122.40	820.41	672.41	585.93	530.16	491.86	464.41	444.14	428.82	417.06	407.90
23000	2133.35	1173.42	857.70	702.97	612.57	554.26	514.22	485.52	464.32	448.31	436.01	426.44
24000	2226.11	1224.44	894.99	733.53	639.20	578.36	536.57	506.63	484.51	467.80	454.97	444.98
25000	2318.86	1275.46	932.28	764.10	665.83	602.45	558.93	527.74	504.70	487.30	473.93	463.52
26000	2411.61	1326.47	969.57	794.66	692.47	626.55	581.29	548.85	524.89	506.79	492.88	482.06
27000	2504.37	1377.49	1006.86	825.23	719.10	650.65	603.64	569.96	545.07	526.28	511.84	500.60
28000	2597.12	1428.51	1044.16	855.79	745.73	674.75	626.00	591.07	565.26	545.77	530.80	519.14
29000	2689.88	1479.53	1081.45	886.35	772.37	698.85	648.36	612.18	585.45	565.26	549.75	537.69
30000	2782.63	1530.55	1118.74	916.92	799.00	722.94	670.71	633.29	605.64	584.75	568.71	556.23
31000	2875.39	1581.56	1156.03	947.48	825.63	747.04	693.07	654.40	625.83	604.24	587.67	574.77
32000	2968.14	1632.58	1193.32	978.04	852.27	771.14	715.43	675.50	646.01	623.74	606.62	593.31
33000	3060.89	1683.60	1230.61	1008.61	878.90	795.24	737.79	696.61	666.20	643.23	625.58	611.85
34000	3153.65	1734.62	1267.90	1039.17	905.53	819.34	760.14	717.72	686.39	662.72	644.54	630.39
35000	3246.40	1785.64	1305.19	1069.74	932.17	843.43	782.50	738.83	706.58	682.21	663.49	648.93
37500	3478.29	1913.18	1398.42	1146.14	998.75	903.68	838.39	791.61	757.05	730.94	710.89	695.28
40000	3710.17	2040.73	1491.65	1222.55	1065.33	963.92	894.28	844.38	807.52	779.67	758.28	741.63
42500	3942.06	2168.27	1584.88	1298.96	1131.92	1024.17	950.18	897.15	857.99	828.40	805.67	787.98
45000	4173.94	2295.82	1678.10	1375.37	1198.50	1084.41	1006.07	949.93	908.45	877.13	853.06	834.34
47500	4405.83	2423.36	1771.33	1451.78	1265.08	1144.66	1061.96	1002.70	958.92	925.86	900.45	880.69
50000	4637.71	2550.91	1864.56	1528.19	1331.66	1204.90	1117.85	1055.47	1009.39	974.59	947.85	927.04
52500	4869.60	2678.45	1957.79	1604.60	1398.25	1265.15	1173.75	1108.25	1059.86	1023.31	995.24	973.39
55000	5101.49	2806.00	2051.01	1681.01	1464.83	1325.39	1229.64	1161.02	1110.33	1072.04	1042.63	1019.74
57500	5333.37	2933.54	2144.24	1757.42	1531.41	1385.64	1285.53	1213.79	1160.80	1120.77	1090.02	1066.10
60000	5565.26	3061.09	2237.47	1833.83	1598.00	1445.88	1341.42	1266.57	1211.27	1169.50	1137.42	1112.45
65000	6029.03	3316.18	2423.93	1986.65	1731.16	1566.37	1453.21	1372.11	1312.21	1266.96	1232.20	1205.15
70000	6492.80	3571.27	2610.38	2139.47	1864.33	1686.86	1564.99	1477.66	1413.15	1364.42	1326.98	1297.85
75000	6956.57	3826.36	2796.84	2292.28	1997.49	1807.35	1676.78	1583.21	1514.09	1461.88	1421.77	1390.56
80000	7420.34	4081.45	2983.29	2445.10	2130.66	1927.84	1788.56	1688.75	1615.03	1559.33	1516.55	1483.26
85000	7884.11	4336.54	3169.75	2597.92	2263.83	2048.33	1900.35	1794.30	1715.97	1656.79	1611.34	1575.96
90000	8347.88	4591.63	3356.20	2750.74	2396.99	2168.82	2012.13	1899.85	1816.90	1754.25	1706.12	1668.67
95000	8811.65	4846.72	3542.66	2903.56	2530.16	2289.31	2123.92	2005.39	1917.84	1851.71	1800.90	1761.37
100000	9275.42	5101.81	3729.11	3056.38	2663.32	2409.80	2235.70	2110.94	2018.78	1949.17	1895.69	1854.07
105000	9739.20	5356.90	3915.57	3209.20	2796.49	2530.29	2347.49	2216.49	2119.72	2046.62	1990.47	1946.78
110000	10202.97	5611.99	4102.02	3362.01	2929.65	2650.78	2459.27	2322.04	2220.66	2144.08	2085.26	2039.48
115000	10666.74	5867.08	4288.48	3514.83	3062.82	2771.27	2571.06	2427.58	2321.60	2241.54	2180.04	2132.19
120000	11130.51	6122.17	4474.94	3667.65	3195.99	2891.76	2682.84	2533.13	2422.54	2339.00	2274.83	2224.89
125000	11594.28	6377.26	4661.39	3820.47	3329.15	3012.25	2794.63	2638.68	2523.48	2436.46	2369.61	2317.59
130000	12058.05	6632.35	4847.85	3973.29	3462.32	3132.74	2906.41	2744.22	2624.41	2533.91	2464.39	2410.30
135000	12521.82	6887.44	5034.30	4126.11	3595.48	3253.23	3018.20	2849.77	2725.35	2631.37	2559.18	2503.00
140000	12985.59	7142.53	5220.76	4278.93	3728.65	3373.72	3129.98	2955.32	2826.29	2728.83	2653.96	2595.70
145000	13449.36	7397.62	5407.21	4431.74	3861.82	3494.21	3241.77	3060.86	2927.23	2826.29	2748.75	2688.41
150000	13913.13	7652.71	5593.67	4584.56	3994.98	3614.70	3353.55	3166.41	3028.17	2923.75	2843.53	2781.11
155000	14376.91	7907.80	5780.12	4737.38	4128.15	3735.19	3465.34	3271.96	3129.11	3021.20	2938.31	2873.81
160000	14840.68	8162.89	5966.58	4890.20	4261.31	3855.68	3577.12	3377.50	3230.05	3118.66	3033.10	2966.52

AMOUNT OF LOAN	NUMBER OF YEARS IN TERM											
	13	14	15	16	17	18	19	20	25	30	35	40
$ 50	0.92	0.90	0.89	0.88	0.88	0.87	0.87	0.86	0.85	0.85	0.85	0.85
100	1.83	1.80	1.78	1.76	1.75	1.74	1.73	1.72	1.70	1.70	1.69	1.69
200	3.65	3.60	3.55	3.52	3.49	3.47	3.46	3.44	3.40	3.39	3.38	3.38
300	5.47	5.39	5.33	5.28	5.24	5.21	5.18	5.16	5.10	5.08	5.07	5.07
400	7.29	7.19	7.10	7.04	6.98	6.94	6.91	6.88	6.80	6.77	6.76	6.76
500	9.11	8.98	8.88	8.80	8.73	8.68	8.63	8.60	8.50	8.46	8.45	8.45
600	10.93	10.78	10.65	10.55	10.47	10.41	10.36	10.32	10.20	10.15	10.14	10.13
700	12.75	12.57	12.43	12.31	12.22	12.14	12.09	12.03	11.90	11.85	11.83	11.82
800	14.58	14.37	14.20	14.07	13.96	13.88	13.81	13.75	13.59	13.54	13.52	13.51
900	16.40	16.16	15.98	15.83	15.71	15.61	15.53	15.47	15.29	15.23	15.21	15.20
1000	18.22	17.96	17.75	17.59	17.45	17.35	17.26	17.19	16.99	16.92	16.89	16.89
2000	36.43	35.91	35.50	35.17	34.90	34.69	34.52	34.37	33.98	33.84	33.78	33.77
3000	54.65	53.87	53.25	52.75	52.35	52.03	51.77	51.56	50.97	50.75	50.67	50.65
4000	72.86	71.82	71.00	70.33	69.80	69.37	69.03	68.74	67.95	67.67	67.56	67.53
5000	91.07	89.78	88.74	87.92	87.25	86.71	86.28	85.93	84.94	84.58	84.45	84.41
6000	109.29	107.73	106.49	105.50	104.70	104.06	103.54	103.11	101.93	101.50	101.34	101.29
7000	127.50	125.69	124.24	123.08	122.15	121.40	120.79	120.30	118.92	118.42	118.23	118.17
8000	145.71	143.64	141.99	140.66	139.60	138.74	138.05	137.48	135.90	135.33	135.12	135.05
9000	163.93	161.60	159.74	158.25	157.05	156.08	155.30	154.67	152.89	152.25	152.01	151.93
10000	182.14	179.55	177.48	175.83	174.50	173.42	172.56	171.85	169.88	169.16	168.90	168.81
11000	200.35	197.50	195.23	193.41	191.95	190.77	189.81	189.04	186.86	186.08	185.79	185.69
12000	218.57	215.46	212.98	210.99	209.40	208.11	207.07	206.22	203.85	203.00	202.68	202.57
13000	236.78	233.41	230.73	228.58	226.85	225.45	224.32	223.41	220.84	219.91	219.57	219.45
14000	255.00	251.37	248.48	246.16	244.30	242.79	241.58	240.59	237.83	236.83	236.46	236.33
15000	273.21	269.32	266.22	263.74	261.75	260.13	258.83	257.78	254.81	253.74	253.35	253.21
16000	291.42	287.28	283.97	281.32	279.20	277.48	276.09	274.96	271.80	270.66	270.24	270.09
17000	309.64	305.23	301.72	298.91	296.64	294.82	293.34	292.14	288.79	287.58	287.13	286.97
18000	327.85	323.19	319.47	316.49	314.09	312.16	310.60	309.33	305.77	304.49	304.02	303.85
19000	346.06	341.14	337.22	334.07	331.54	329.50	327.85	326.51	322.76	321.41	320.91	320.73
20000	364.28	359.09	354.96	351.65	348.99	346.84	345.11	343.70	339.75	338.32	337.80	337.61
21000	382.49	377.05	372.71	369.24	366.44	364.19	362.36	360.88	356.74	355.24	354.69	354.50
22000	400.70	395.00	390.46	386.82	383.89	381.53	379.62	378.07	373.72	372.16	371.58	371.38
23000	418.92	412.96	408.21	404.40	401.34	398.87	396.87	395.25	390.71	389.07	388.47	388.26
24000	437.13	430.91	425.96	421.98	418.79	416.21	414.13	412.44	407.70	405.99	405.36	405.14
25000	455.35	448.87	443.70	439.57	436.24	433.55	431.38	429.62	424.68	422.90	422.25	422.02
26000	473.56	466.82	461.45	457.15	453.69	450.90	448.64	446.81	441.67	439.82	439.14	438.90
27000	491.77	484.78	479.20	474.73	471.14	468.24	465.89	463.99	458.66	456.73	456.03	455.78
28000	509.99	502.73	496.95	492.31	488.59	485.58	483.15	481.18	475.65	473.65	472.92	472.66
29000	528.20	520.69	514.70	509.90	506.04	502.92	500.40	498.36	492.63	490.57	489.81	489.54
30000	546.41	538.64	532.44	527.48	523.49	520.26	517.66	515.55	509.62	507.48	506.70	506.42
31000	564.63	556.59	550.19	545.06	540.94	537.61	534.91	532.73	526.61	524.40	523.59	523.30
32000	582.84	574.55	567.94	562.64	558.39	554.95	552.17	549.92	543.59	541.31	540.48	540.18
33000	601.05	592.50	585.69	580.23	575.83	572.29	569.42	567.10	560.58	558.23	557.37	557.06
34000	619.27	610.46	603.44	597.81	593.28	589.63	586.68	584.28	577.57	575.15	574.26	573.94
35000	637.48	628.41	621.18	615.39	610.73	606.97	603.93	601.47	594.56	592.06	591.15	590.82
37500	683.02	673.30	665.55	659.35	654.36	650.33	647.07	644.43	637.02	634.35	633.38	633.02
40000	728.55	718.18	709.92	703.30	697.98	693.68	690.21	687.39	679.49	676.64	675.60	675.22
42500	774.08	763.07	754.29	747.26	741.60	737.04	733.35	730.35	721.96	718.93	717.83	717.43
45000	819.62	807.96	798.66	791.22	785.23	780.39	776.49	773.32	764.43	761.22	760.05	759.63
47500	865.15	852.84	843.03	835.17	828.85	823.75	819.62	816.28	806.90	803.51	802.28	801.83
50000	910.69	897.73	887.40	879.13	872.47	867.10	862.76	859.24	849.36	845.80	844.50	844.03
52500	956.22	942.62	931.77	923.08	916.10	910.46	905.90	902.20	891.83	888.09	886.73	886.23
55000	1001.75	987.50	976.14	967.04	959.72	953.81	949.04	945.16	934.30	930.38	928.95	928.43
57500	1047.29	1032.39	1020.51	1011.00	1003.34	997.17	992.17	988.12	976.77	972.67	971.18	970.63
60000	1092.82	1077.27	1064.88	1054.95	1046.97	1040.52	1035.31	1031.09	1019.23	1014.96	1013.40	1012.83
65000	1183.89	1167.05	1153.62	1142.87	1134.21	1127.23	1121.59	1117.01	1104.17	1099.54	1097.85	1097.24
70000	1274.96	1256.82	1242.36	1230.78	1221.46	1213.94	1207.86	1202.93	1189.11	1184.12	1182.30	1181.64
75000	1366.03	1346.59	1331.10	1318.69	1308.71	1300.65	1294.14	1288.86	1274.04	1268.70	1266.75	1266.04
80000	1457.09	1436.36	1419.84	1406.60	1395.96	1387.36	1380.41	1374.78	1358.98	1353.28	1351.20	1350.44
85000	1548.16	1526.14	1508.58	1494.51	1483.20	1474.07	1466.69	1460.70	1443.91	1437.86	1435.65	1434.85
90000	1639.23	1615.91	1597.32	1582.43	1570.45	1560.78	1552.97	1546.63	1528.85	1522.44	1520.10	1519.25
95000	1730.30	1705.68	1686.06	1670.34	1657.70	1647.49	1639.24	1632.55	1613.79	1607.02	1604.55	1603.65
100000	1821.37	1795.45	1774.80	1758.25	1744.94	1734.20	1725.52	1718.47	1698.72	1691.60	1689.00	1688.05
105000	1912.43	1885.23	1863.54	1846.16	1832.19	1820.91	1811.79	1804.40	1783.66	1776.18	1773.45	1772.46
110000	2003.50	1975.00	1952.28	1934.08	1919.44	1907.62	1898.07	1890.32	1868.60	1860.76	1857.90	1856.86
115000	2094.57	2064.77	2041.02	2021.99	2006.68	1994.33	1984.34	1976.24	1953.53	1945.34	1942.35	1941.26
120000	2185.64	2154.54	2129.76	2109.90	2093.93	2081.04	2070.62	2062.17	2038.46	2029.92	2026.80	2025.66
125000	2276.71	2244.32	2218.50	2197.81	2181.18	2167.75	2156.89	2148.09	2123.40	2114.50	2111.25	2110.07
130000	2367.77	2334.09	2307.24	2285.73	2268.42	2254.46	2243.17	2234.01	2208.34	2199.08	2195.70	2194.47
135000	2458.84	2423.86	2395.98	2373.64	2355.67	2341.17	2329.45	2319.94	2293.27	2283.65	2280.15	2278.87
140000	2549.91	2513.63	2484.72	2461.55	2442.92	2427.88	2415.72	2405.86	2378.21	2368.23	2364.60	2363.27
145000	2640.98	2603.41	2573.46	2549.46	2530.16	2514.59	2502.00	2491.78	2463.14	2452.81	2449.05	2447.67
150000	2732.05	2693.18	2662.20	2637.38	2617.41	2601.30	2588.27	2577.71	2548.08	2537.39	2533.50	2532.08
155000	2823.12	2782.95	2750.94	2725.29	2704.66	2688.01	2674.55	2663.63	2633.02	2621.97	2617.95	2616.48
160000	2914.18	2872.72	2839.68	2813.20	2791.91	2774.72	2760.82	2749.56	2717.95	2706.55	2702.40	2700.88

MONTHLY AMORTIZING PAYMENTS

AMOUNT OF LOAN	NUMBER OF YEARS IN TERM											
	1	2	3	4	5	6	7	8	9	10	11	12
$ 50	4.65	2.56	1.88	1.54	1.34	1.22	1.13	1.07	1.02	0.99	0.96	0.94
100	9.29	5.12	3.75	3.07	2.68	2.43	2.26	2.13	2.04	1.97	1.92	1.88
200	18.58	10.23	7.49	6.14	5.36	4.85	4.51	4.26	4.07	3.94	3.83	3.75
300	27.87	15.35	11.23	9.21	8.04	7.28	6.76	6.38	6.11	5.90	5.74	5.62
400	37.15	20.46	14.97	12.28	10.71	9.70	9.01	8.51	8.14	7.87	7.66	7.49
500	46.44	25.58	18.71	15.35	13.39	12.13	11.26	10.64	10.18	9.83	9.57	9.36
600	55.73	30.69	22.46	18.42	16.07	14.55	13.51	12.76	12.21	11.80	11.48	11.23
700	65.02	35.80	26.20	21.49	18.75	16.98	15.76	14.89	14.25	13.77	13.39	13.11
800	74.30	40.92	29.94	24.56	21.42	19.40	18.01	17.02	16.28	15.73	15.31	14.98
900	83.59	46.03	33.68	27.63	24.10	21.82	20.26	19.14	18.32	17.70	17.22	16.85
1000	92.88	51.15	37.42	30.70	26.78	24.25	22.51	21.27	20.35	19.66	19.13	18.72
2000	185.75	102.29	74.84	61.40	53.55	48.49	45.02	42.54	40.70	39.32	38.26	37.44
3000	278.63	153.43	112.26	92.10	80.32	72.74	67.53	63.80	61.05	58.98	57.39	56.15
4000	371.50	204.57	149.68	122.79	107.10	96.98	90.04	85.07	81.40	78.64	76.52	74.87
5000	464.37	255.71	187.10	153.49	133.87	121.22	112.55	106.34	101.75	98.30	95.64	93.58
6000	557.25	306.85	224.52	184.19	160.64	145.47	135.05	127.60	122.10	117.95	114.77	112.30
7000	650.12	357.99	261.94	214.89	187.42	169.71	157.56	148.87	142.45	137.61	133.90	131.02
8000	743.00	409.13	299.36	245.58	214.19	193.95	180.07	170.13	162.80	157.27	153.03	149.73
9000	835.87	460.27	336.77	276.28	240.96	218.20	202.58	191.40	183.15	176.93	172.16	168.45
10000	928.74	511.41	374.19	306.98	267.73	242.44	225.09	212.67	203.50	196.59	191.28	187.16
11000	1021.62	562.55	411.61	337.68	294.51	266.68	247.60	233.93	223.85	216.25	210.41	205.88
12000	1114.49	613.69	449.03	368.37	321.28	290.93	270.10	255.20	244.20	235.90	229.54	224.60
13000	1207.37	664.83	486.45	399.07	348.05	315.17	292.61	276.46	264.55	255.56	248.67	243.31
14000	1300.24	715.97	523.87	429.77	374.83	339.41	315.12	297.73	284.90	275.22	267.80	262.03
15000	1393.11	767.11	561.29	460.47	401.60	363.66	337.63	319.00	305.25	294.88	286.92	280.74
16000	1485.99	818.25	598.71	491.16	428.37	387.90	360.14	340.26	325.60	314.54	306.05	299.46
17000	1578.86	869.39	636.13	521.86	455.14	412.15	382.65	361.53	345.95	334.19	325.18	318.18
18000	1671.74	920.53	673.54	552.56	481.92	436.39	405.15	382.79	366.30	353.85	344.31	336.89
19000	1764.61	971.67	710.96	583.26	508.69	460.63	427.66	404.06	386.65	373.51	363.44	355.61
20000	1857.48	1022.81	748.38	613.95	535.46	484.88	450.17	425.33	407.00	393.17	382.56	374.32
21000	1950.36	1073.95	785.80	644.65	562.24	509.12	472.68	446.59	427.35	412.83	401.69	393.04
22000	2043.23	1125.09	823.22	675.35	589.01	533.36	495.19	467.86	447.70	432.49	420.82	411.75
23000	2136.11	1176.23	860.64	706.05	615.78	557.61	517.69	489.12	468.05	452.14	439.95	430.47
24000	2228.98	1227.37	898.06	736.74	642.55	581.85	540.20	510.39	488.40	471.80	459.07	449.19
25000	2321.85	1278.51	935.48	767.44	669.33	606.09	562.71	531.66	508.74	491.46	478.20	467.90
26000	2414.73	1329.66	972.89	798.14	696.10	630.34	585.22	552.92	529.09	511.12	497.33	486.62
27000	2507.60	1380.80	1010.31	828.83	722.87	654.58	607.73	574.19	549.44	530.78	516.46	505.33
28000	2600.48	1431.94	1047.73	859.53	749.65	678.82	630.24	595.45	569.79	550.44	535.59	524.05
29000	2693.35	1483.08	1085.15	890.23	776.42	703.07	652.74	616.72	590.14	570.09	554.71	542.77
30000	2786.22	1534.22	1122.57	920.93	803.19	727.31	675.25	637.99	610.49	589.75	573.84	561.48
31000	2879.10	1585.36	1159.99	951.62	829.96	751.55	697.76	659.25	630.84	609.41	592.97	580.20
32000	2971.97	1636.50	1197.41	982.32	856.74	775.80	720.27	680.52	651.19	629.07	612.10	598.91
33000	3064.85	1687.64	1234.83	1013.02	883.51	800.04	742.78	701.78	671.54	648.73	631.23	617.63
34000	3157.72	1738.78	1272.25	1043.72	910.28	824.29	765.29	723.05	691.89	668.38	650.35	636.35
35000	3250.59	1789.92	1309.66	1074.41	937.06	848.53	787.79	744.32	712.24	688.04	669.48	655.06
37500	3482.78	1917.77	1403.21	1151.16	1003.99	909.14	844.06	797.48	763.11	737.19	717.30	701.85
40000	3714.96	2045.61	1496.76	1227.90	1070.92	969.75	900.33	850.65	813.99	786.33	765.12	748.64
42500	3947.15	2173.47	1590.31	1304.64	1137.85	1030.36	956.61	903.81	864.86	835.48	812.94	795.43
45000	4179.33	2301.32	1683.85	1381.39	1204.78	1090.96	1012.88	956.98	915.74	884.63	860.76	842.22
47500	4411.52	2429.17	1777.40	1458.13	1271.72	1151.57	1069.15	1010.14	966.61	933.77	908.58	889.01
50000	4643.70	2557.02	1870.95	1534.87	1338.65	1212.18	1125.42	1063.31	1017.48	982.92	956.40	935.80
52500	4875.89	2684.88	1964.49	1611.62	1405.58	1272.79	1181.69	1116.47	1068.36	1032.06	1004.22	982.59
55000	5108.07	2812.73	2058.04	1688.36	1472.51	1333.40	1237.96	1169.64	1119.23	1081.21	1052.04	1029.38
57500	5340.26	2940.58	2151.59	1765.11	1539.44	1394.01	1294.23	1222.80	1170.11	1130.35	1099.86	1076.17
60000	5572.44	3068.43	2245.14	1841.85	1606.38	1454.62	1350.50	1275.97	1220.98	1179.50	1147.68	1122.96
65000	6036.81	3324.13	2432.23	1995.34	1740.24	1575.83	1463.04	1382.30	1322.73	1277.79	1243.32	1216.54
70000	6501.18	3579.83	2619.32	2148.82	1874.11	1697.05	1575.58	1488.63	1424.48	1376.08	1338.96	1310.12
75000	6965.55	3835.53	2806.42	2302.31	2007.97	1818.27	1688.12	1594.96	1526.22	1474.37	1434.60	1403.70
80000	7429.92	4091.24	2993.51	2455.80	2141.83	1939.49	1800.66	1701.29	1627.97	1572.66	1530.24	1497.28
85000	7894.29	4346.94	3180.61	2609.28	2275.70	2060.71	1913.21	1807.62	1729.72	1670.95	1625.88	1590.86
90000	8358.66	4602.64	3367.70	2762.77	2409.56	2181.92	2025.75	1913.95	1831.47	1769.25	1721.52	1684.44
95000	8823.03	4858.34	3554.79	2916.26	2543.43	2303.14	2138.29	2020.28	1933.22	1867.54	1817.16	1778.01
100000	9287.40	5114.04	3741.89	3069.74	2677.29	2424.36	2250.83	2126.61	2034.96	1965.83	1912.80	1871.59
105000	9751.77	5369.75	3928.98	3223.23	2811.16	2545.58	2363.37	2232.94	2136.71	2064.12	2008.44	1965.17
110000	10216.14	5625.45	4116.08	3376.72	2945.02	2666.79	2475.91	2339.27	2238.46	2162.41	2104.08	2058.75
115000	10680.51	5881.15	4303.17	3530.21	3078.88	2788.01	2588.45	2445.60	2340.21	2260.70	2199.72	2152.33
120000	11144.88	6136.85	4490.27	3683.69	3212.75	2909.23	2700.99	2551.93	2441.96	2358.99	2295.35	2245.91
125000	11609.25	6392.55	4677.36	3837.18	3346.61	3030.45	2813.54	2658.26	2543.70	2457.28	2390.99	2339.49
130000	12073.62	6648.26	4864.45	3990.67	3480.48	3151.66	2926.08	2764.59	2645.45	2555.57	2486.63	2433.07
135000	12537.99	6903.96	5051.55	4144.15	3614.34	3272.88	3038.62	2870.92	2747.20	2653.87	2582.27	2526.65
140000	13002.36	7159.66	5238.64	4297.64	3748.21	3394.10	3151.16	2977.25	2848.95	2752.16	2677.91	2620.23
145000	13466.73	7415.36	5425.74	4451.13	3882.07	3515.32	3263.70	3083.58	2950.69	2850.45	2773.55	2713.81
150000	13931.10	7671.06	5612.83	4604.61	4015.93	3636.54	3376.24	3189.91	3052.44	2948.74	2869.19	2807.39
155000	14395.47	7926.77	5799.92	4758.10	4149.80	3757.75	3488.78	3296.24	3154.19	3047.03	2964.83	2900.97
160000	14859.84	8182.47	5987.02	4911.59	4283.66	3878.97	3601.32	3402.57	3255.94	3145.32	3060.47	2994.55

AMOUNT OF LOAN	NUMBER OF YEARS IN TERM											
	13	14	15	16	17	18	19	20	25	30	35	40
$ 50	0.92	0.91	0.90	0.89	0.89	0.88	0.88	0.87	0.86	0.86	0.86	0.86
100	1.84	1.82	1.80	1.78	1.77	1.76	1.75	1.74	1.72	1.72	1.71	1.71
200	3.68	3.63	3.59	3.56	3.53	3.51	3.50	3.48	3.44	3.43	3.42	3.42
300	5.52	5.45	5.39	5.34	5.30	5.27	5.24	5.22	5.16	5.14	5.13	5.13
400	7.36	7.26	7.18	7.11	7.06	7.02	6.99	6.96	6.88	6.85	6.84	6.84
500	9.20	9.07	8.97	8.89	8.83	8.77	8.73	8.70	8.60	8.57	8.55	8.55
600	11.04	10.89	10.77	10.67	10.59	10.53	10.48	10.43	10.32	10.28	10.26	10.26
700	12.88	12.70	12.56	12.44	12.35	12.28	12.22	12.17	12.04	11.99	11.97	11.97
800	14.72	14.51	14.35	14.22	14.12	14.03	13.97	13.91	13.76	13.70	13.68	13.68
900	16.56	16.33	16.15	16.00	15.88	15.79	15.71	15.65	15.48	15.41	15.39	15.38
1000	18.40	18.14	17.94	17.78	17.65	17.54	17.46	17.39	17.20	17.13	17.10	17.09
2000	36.79	36.28	35.87	35.55	35.29	35.08	34.91	34.77	34.39	34.25	34.20	34.18
3000	55.18	54.42	53.81	53.32	52.93	52.61	52.36	52.15	51.58	51.37	51.30	51.27
4000	73.58	72.55	71.74	71.09	70.57	70.15	69.81	69.53	68.77	68.49	68.39	68.36
5000	91.97	90.69	89.67	88.86	88.21	87.68	87.26	86.91	85.96	85.61	85.49	85.45
6000	110.36	108.83	107.61	106.63	105.85	105.22	104.71	104.29	103.15	102.74	102.59	102.54
7000	128.75	126.96	125.54	124.40	123.49	122.75	122.16	121.68	120.34	119.86	119.69	119.62
8000	147.15	145.10	143.47	142.17	141.13	140.29	139.61	139.06	137.53	136.98	136.78	136.71
9000	165.54	163.24	161.41	159.94	158.77	157.82	157.06	156.44	154.72	154.10	153.88	153.80
10000	183.93	181.37	179.34	177.71	176.41	175.36	174.51	173.82	171.91	171.22	170.98	170.89
11000	202.32	199.51	197.27	195.48	194.05	192.89	191.96	191.20	189.10	188.34	188.07	187.98
12000	220.72	217.65	215.21	213.25	211.69	210.43	209.41	208.58	206.29	205.47	205.17	205.07
13000	239.11	235.78	233.14	231.03	229.33	227.96	226.86	225.97	223.48	222.59	222.27	222.15
14000	257.50	253.92	251.07	248.80	246.97	245.50	244.31	243.35	240.67	239.71	239.37	239.24
15000	275.89	272.06	269.01	266.57	264.61	263.03	261.76	260.73	257.86	256.83	256.46	256.33
16000	294.29	290.20	286.94	284.34	282.25	280.57	279.21	278.11	275.05	273.95	273.56	273.42
17000	312.68	308.33	304.87	302.11	299.89	298.10	296.66	295.49	292.24	291.08	290.66	290.51
18000	331.07	326.47	322.81	319.88	317.53	315.64	314.11	312.87	309.43	308.20	307.76	307.60
19000	349.46	344.61	340.74	337.65	335.17	333.17	331.56	330.25	326.62	325.32	324.85	324.68
20000	367.86	362.74	358.67	355.42	352.81	350.71	349.01	347.64	343.81	342.44	341.95	341.77
21000	386.25	380.88	376.61	373.19	370.45	368.24	366.46	365.02	361.00	359.56	359.05	358.86
22000	404.64	399.02	394.54	390.96	388.09	385.78	383.91	382.40	378.19	376.68	376.14	375.95
23000	423.03	417.15	412.47	408.73	405.73	403.31	401.36	399.78	395.38	393.81	393.24	393.04
24000	441.43	435.29	430.41	426.50	423.37	420.85	418.81	417.16	412.57	410.93	410.34	410.13
25000	459.82	453.43	448.34	444.28	441.01	438.38	436.26	434.54	429.76	428.05	427.44	427.21
26000	478.21	471.56	466.28	462.05	458.65	455.92	453.71	451.93	446.95	445.17	444.53	444.30
27000	496.60	489.70	484.21	479.82	476.29	473.45	471.16	469.31	464.14	462.29	461.63	461.39
28000	515.00	507.84	502.14	497.59	493.93	490.99	488.69	486.69	481.33	479.42	478.73	478.48
29000	533.39	525.98	520.08	515.36	511.57	508.52	506.06	504.07	498.52	496.54	495.82	495.57
30000	551.78	544.11	538.01	533.13	529.21	526.06	523.51	521.45	515.71	513.66	512.92	512.66
31000	570.18	562.25	555.94	550.90	546.85	543.59	540.96	538.83	532.90	530.78	530.02	529.74
32000	588.57	580.39	573.88	568.67	564.49	561.13	558.41	556.21	550.09	547.90	547.12	546.83
33000	606.96	598.52	591.81	586.44	582.13	578.66	575.86	573.60	567.28	565.02	564.21	563.92
34000	625.35	616.66	609.74	604.21	599.77	596.20	593.31	590.98	584.47	582.15	581.31	581.01
35000	643.75	634.80	627.68	621.98	617.41	613.73	610.76	608.36	601.66	599.27	598.41	598.10
37500	689.73	680.14	672.51	666.41	661.51	657.57	654.39	651.81	644.63	642.07	641.15	640.82
40000	735.71	725.48	717.34	710.84	705.61	701.41	698.01	695.27	687.61	684.88	683.89	683.54
42500	781.69	770.82	762.18	755.26	749.71	745.25	741.64	738.72	730.58	727.68	726.64	726.26
45000	827.67	816.17	807.01	799.69	793.82	789.08	785.26	782.17	773.56	770.49	769.38	768.98
47500	873.65	861.51	851.84	844.12	837.92	832.92	828.89	825.63	816.53	813.29	812.12	811.70
50000	919.63	906.85	896.68	888.55	882.02	876.76	872.52	869.08	859.51	856.10	854.87	854.42
52500	965.62	952.19	941.51	932.97	926.12	920.60	916.14	912.54	902.48	898.90	897.61	897.14
55000	1011.60	997.53	986.35	977.40	970.22	964.43	959.77	955.99	945.46	941.70	940.35	939.86
57500	1057.58	1042.88	1031.18	1021.83	1014.32	1008.27	1003.39	999.44	988.43	984.51	983.10	982.59
60000	1103.56	1088.22	1076.01	1066.25	1058.42	1052.11	1047.02	1042.90	1031.41	1027.31	1025.84	1025.31
65000	1195.52	1178.90	1165.68	1155.11	1146.62	1139.79	1134.27	1129.81	1117.36	1112.92	1111.33	1110.75
70000	1287.49	1269.59	1255.35	1243.96	1234.82	1227.46	1221.52	1216.71	1203.31	1198.53	1196.81	1196.19
75000	1379.45	1360.27	1345.02	1332.82	1323.02	1315.14	1308.77	1303.62	1289.26	1284.14	1282.30	1281.63
80000	1471.41	1450.96	1434.68	1421.67	1411.22	1402.81	1396.02	1390.53	1375.21	1369.75	1367.78	1367.07
85000	1563.37	1541.64	1524.35	1510.52	1499.42	1490.49	1483.27	1477.44	1461.16	1455.36	1453.27	1452.52
90000	1655.34	1632.33	1614.02	1599.38	1587.63	1578.16	1570.52	1564.34	1547.11	1540.97	1538.76	1537.96
95000	1747.30	1723.01	1703.68	1688.23	1675.83	1665.84	1657.77	1651.25	1633.06	1626.58	1624.24	1623.40
100000	1839.26	1813.70	1793.35	1777.09	1764.03	1753.51	1745.03	1738.16	1719.01	1712.19	1709.73	1708.84
105000	1931.23	1904.38	1883.02	1865.94	1852.23	1841.19	1832.28	1825.07	1804.96	1797.80	1795.22	1794.28
110000	2023.19	1995.06	1972.69	1954.79	1940.43	1928.86	1919.53	1911.97	1890.91	1883.40	1880.70	1879.72
115000	2115.15	2085.75	2062.35	2043.65	2028.63	2016.54	2006.78	1998.88	1976.86	1969.01	1966.19	1965.17
120000	2207.12	2176.43	2152.02	2132.50	2116.83	2104.21	2094.03	2085.79	2062.81	2054.62	2051.67	2050.61
125000	2299.08	2267.12	2241.69	2221.36	2205.03	2191.89	2181.28	2172.70	2148.76	2140.23	2137.16	2136.05
130000	2391.04	2357.80	2331.36	2310.21	2293.23	2279.57	2268.53	2259.61	2234.71	2225.84	2222.65	2221.49
135000	2483.00	2448.49	2421.02	2399.06	2381.44	2367.24	2355.78	2346.51	2320.66	2311.45	2308.13	2306.93
140000	2574.97	2539.17	2510.69	2487.92	2469.64	2454.92	2443.03	2433.42	2406.61	2397.06	2393.62	2392.38
145000	2666.93	2629.86	2600.36	2576.77	2557.84	2542.59	2530.28	2520.33	2492.57	2482.67	2479.10	2477.82
150000	2758.89	2720.54	2690.03	2665.63	2646.04	2630.27	2617.54	2607.24	2578.52	2568.28	2564.59	2563.26
155000	2850.86	2811.23	2779.69	2754.48	2734.24	2717.94	2704.79	2694.14	2664.47	2653.89	2650.08	2648.70
160000	2942.82	2901.91	2869.36	2843.33	2822.44	2805.62	2792.04	2781.05	2750.42	2739.49	2735.56	2734.14

MONTHLY AMORTIZING PAYMENTS

AMOUNT OF LOAN	NUMBER OF YEARS IN TERM											
	1	2	3	4	5	6	7	8	9	10	11	12
$ 50	4.65	2.57	1.88	1.55	1.35	1.22	1.14	1.08	1.03	1.00	0.97	0.95
100	9.30	5.13	3.76	3.09	2.70	2.44	2.27	2.15	2.06	1.99	1.93	1.89
200	18.60	10.26	7.51	6.17	5.39	4.88	4.54	4.29	4.11	3.97	3.86	3.78
300	27.90	15.38	11.27	9.25	8.08	7.32	6.80	6.43	6.16	5.95	5.79	5.67
400	37.20	20.51	15.02	12.34	10.77	9.76	9.07	8.57	8.21	7.94	7.72	7.56
500	46.50	25.64	18.78	15.42	13.46	12.20	11.33	10.72	10.26	9.92	9.65	9.45
600	55.80	30.76	22.53	18.50	16.15	14.64	13.60	12.86	12.31	11.90	11.58	11.34
700	65.10	35.89	26.29	21.59	18.84	17.08	15.87	15.00	14.36	13.88	13.51	13.23
800	74.40	41.02	30.04	24.67	21.54	19.52	18.13	17.14	16.41	15.87	15.44	15.12
900	83.70	46.14	33.80	27.75	24.23	21.96	20.40	19.29	18.47	17.85	17.37	17.01
1000	93.00	51.27	37.55	30.84	26.92	24.39	22.66	21.43	20.52	19.83	19.30	18.90
2000	185.99	102.53	75.10	61.67	53.83	48.78	45.32	42.85	41.03	39.66	38.60	37.79
3000	278.99	153.79	112.65	92.50	80.74	73.17	67.98	64.27	61.54	59.48	57.90	56.68
4000	371.98	205.06	150.19	123.33	107.66	97.56	90.64	85.70	82.05	79.31	77.20	75.57
5000	464.97	256.32	187.74	154.16	134.57	121.95	113.30	107.12	102.56	99.13	96.50	94.46
6000	557.97	307.58	225.29	184.99	161.48	146.34	135.96	128.54	123.08	118.96	115.80	113.36
7000	650.96	358.85	262.83	215.82	188.40	170.73	158.62	149.97	143.59	138.78	135.10	132.25
8000	743.96	410.11	300.38	246.66	215.31	195.12	181.28	171.39	164.10	158.61	154.40	151.14
9000	836.95	461.37	337.93	277.49	242.22	219.51	203.94	192.81	184.61	178.43	173.70	170.03
10000	929.94	512.63	375.47	308.32	269.13	243.90	226.60	214.24	205.12	198.26	193.00	188.92
11000	1022.94	563.90	413.02	339.15	296.05	268.29	249.26	235.66	225.64	218.08	212.30	207.81
12000	1115.93	615.16	450.57	369.98	322.96	292.68	271.92	257.08	246.15	237.91	231.60	226.71
13000	1208.92	666.42	488.11	400.81	349.87	317.07	294.58	278.51	266.66	257.74	250.90	245.60
14000	1301.92	717.69	525.66	431.64	376.79	341.46	317.24	299.93	287.17	277.56	270.20	264.49
15000	1394.91	768.95	563.21	462.48	403.70	365.85	339.90	321.35	307.68	297.39	289.50	283.38
16000	1487.91	820.21	600.75	493.31	430.61	390.24	362.56	342.78	328.20	317.21	308.80	302.27
17000	1580.90	871.47	638.30	524.14	457.52	414.63	385.22	364.20	348.71	337.04	328.10	321.16
18000	1673.89	922.74	675.85	554.97	484.44	439.02	407.88	385.62	369.22	356.86	347.40	340.06
19000	1766.89	974.00	713.39	585.80	511.35	463.41	430.54	407.05	389.73	376.69	366.70	358.95
20000	1859.88	1025.26	750.94	616.63	538.26	487.80	453.20	428.47	410.24	396.51	386.00	377.84
21000	1952.88	1076.53	788.49	647.46	565.18	512.19	475.86	449.89	430.76	416.34	405.30	396.73
22000	2045.87	1127.79	826.04	678.30	592.09	536.58	498.52	471.32	451.27	436.16	424.60	415.62
23000	2138.86	1179.05	863.58	709.13	619.00	560.96	521.18	492.74	471.78	455.99	443.90	434.51
24000	2231.86	1230.32	901.13	739.96	645.92	585.35	543.84	514.16	492.29	475.82	463.19	453.41
25000	2324.85	1281.58	938.68	770.79	672.83	609.74	566.50	535.59	512.80	495.64	482.49	472.30
26000	2417.84	1332.84	976.22	801.62	699.74	634.13	589.16	557.01	533.32	515.47	501.79	491.19
27000	2510.84	1384.10	1013.77	832.45	726.65	658.52	611.82	578.43	553.83	535.29	521.09	510.08
28000	2603.83	1435.37	1051.32	863.28	753.57	682.91	634.48	599.86	574.34	555.12	540.39	528.97
29000	2696.83	1486.63	1088.86	894.12	780.48	707.30	657.14	621.28	594.85	574.94	559.69	547.86
30000	2789.82	1537.89	1126.41	924.95	807.39	731.69	679.80	642.70	615.36	594.77	578.99	566.76
31000	2882.81	1589.16	1163.96	955.78	834.31	756.08	702.46	664.13	635.88	614.59	598.29	585.65
32000	2975.81	1640.42	1201.50	986.61	861.22	780.47	725.12	685.55	656.39	634.42	617.59	604.54
33000	3068.80	1691.68	1239.05	1017.44	888.13	804.86	747.78	706.97	676.90	654.24	636.89	623.43
34000	3161.80	1742.94	1276.60	1048.27	915.04	829.25	770.44	728.40	697.41	674.07	656.19	642.32
35000	3254.79	1794.21	1314.14	1079.10	941.96	853.64	793.10	749.82	717.92	693.89	675.49	661.21
37500	3487.27	1922.37	1408.01	1156.18	1009.24	914.61	849.75	803.38	769.20	743.46	723.74	708.44
40000	3719.76	2050.52	1501.88	1233.26	1076.52	975.59	906.40	856.94	820.48	793.02	771.99	755.67
42500	3952.24	2178.68	1595.75	1310.34	1143.80	1036.56	963.05	910.49	871.76	842.59	820.24	802.90
45000	4184.73	2306.84	1689.61	1387.42	1211.09	1097.53	1019.70	964.05	923.04	892.15	868.49	850.13
47500	4417.21	2434.99	1783.48	1464.50	1278.37	1158.51	1076.35	1017.61	974.32	941.71	916.73	897.36
50000	4649.70	2563.15	1877.35	1541.57	1345.65	1219.48	1133.00	1071.17	1025.60	991.28	964.98	944.59
52500	4882.18	2691.31	1971.21	1618.65	1412.93	1280.46	1189.65	1124.73	1076.88	1040.84	1013.23	991.82
55000	5114.67	2819.47	2065.08	1695.73	1480.22	1341.43	1246.30	1178.29	1128.16	1090.40	1061.48	1039.05
57500	5347.15	2947.62	2158.95	1772.81	1547.50	1402.40	1302.95	1231.84	1179.44	1139.97	1109.73	1086.28
60000	5579.63	3075.78	2252.81	1849.89	1614.78	1463.38	1359.60	1285.40	1230.72	1189.53	1157.98	1133.51
65000	6044.60	3332.10	2440.55	2004.05	1749.34	1585.33	1472.90	1392.52	1333.28	1288.66	1254.48	1227.96
70000	6509.57	3588.41	2628.28	2158.20	1883.91	1707.27	1586.20	1499.63	1435.84	1387.78	1350.98	1322.42
75000	6974.54	3844.73	2816.02	2312.36	2018.47	1829.22	1699.50	1606.75	1538.40	1486.91	1447.47	1416.88
80000	7439.51	4101.04	3003.75	2466.52	2153.04	1951.17	1812.80	1713.87	1640.96	1586.04	1543.97	1511.34
85000	7904.48	4357.35	3191.49	2620.67	2287.60	2073.12	1926.10	1820.98	1743.52	1685.17	1640.47	1605.80
90000	8369.45	4613.67	3379.22	2774.83	2422.17	2195.06	2039.40	1928.10	1846.08	1784.29	1736.97	1700.26
95000	8834.42	4869.98	3566.95	2928.99	2556.73	2317.01	2152.70	2035.22	1948.64	1883.42	1833.46	1794.71
100000	9299.39	5126.30	3754.69	3083.14	2691.30	2438.96	2266.00	2142.33	2051.20	1982.55	1929.96	1889.17
105000	9764.36	5382.61	3942.42	3237.30	2825.86	2560.91	2379.30	2249.45	2153.76	2081.67	2026.46	1983.63
110000	10229.33	5638.93	4130.16	3391.46	2960.43	2682.86	2492.60	2356.57	2256.32	2180.80	2122.96	2078.09
115000	10694.30	5895.24	4317.89	3545.61	3094.99	2804.80	2605.90	2463.68	2358.88	2279.93	2219.46	2172.55
120000	11159.26	6151.56	4505.62	3699.77	3229.56	2926.75	2719.20	2570.80	2461.44	2379.06	2315.95	2267.01
125000	11624.23	6407.87	4693.36	3853.93	3364.12	3048.70	2832.50	2677.91	2564.00	2478.18	2412.45	2361.46
130000	12089.20	6664.19	4881.09	4008.09	3498.68	3170.65	2945.80	2785.03	2666.56	2577.31	2508.95	2455.92
135000	12554.17	6920.50	5068.83	4162.24	3633.25	3292.59	3059.10	2892.15	2769.12	2676.44	2605.45	2550.38
140000	13019.14	7176.82	5256.56	4316.40	3767.81	3414.54	3172.40	2999.26	2871.68	2775.56	2701.95	2644.84
145000	13484.11	7433.13	5444.30	4470.56	3902.38	3536.49	3285.70	3106.38	2974.24	2874.69	2798.44	2739.30
150000	13949.08	7689.45	5632.03	4624.71	4036.94	3658.44	3399.00	3213.50	3076.80	2973.82	2894.94	2833.76
155000	14414.05	7945.76	5819.76	4778.87	4171.51	3780.38	3512.30	3320.61	3179.36	3072.94	2991.44	2928.21
160000	14879.02	8202.08	6007.50	4933.03	4306.07	3902.33	3625.60	3427.73	3281.92	3172.07	3087.94	3022.67

MONTHLY AMORTIZING PAYMENTS
20.75%

AMOUNT OF LOAN	NUMBER OF YEARS IN TERM											
	13	14	15	16	17	18	19	20	25	30	35	40
$ 50	0.93	0.92	0.91	0.90	0.90	0.89	0.89	0.88	0.87	0.87	0.87	0.87
100	1.86	1.84	1.82	1.80	1.79	1.78	1.77	1.76	1.74	1.74	1.74	1.73
200	3.72	3.67	3.63	3.60	3.57	3.55	3.53	3.52	3.48	3.47	3.47	3.46
300	5.58	5.50	5.44	5.39	5.35	5.32	5.30	5.28	5.22	5.20	5.20	5.19
400	7.43	7.33	7.25	7.19	7.14	7.10	7.06	7.04	6.96	6.94	6.93	6.92
500	9.29	9.16	9.06	8.98	8.92	8.87	8.83	8.79	8.70	8.67	8.66	8.65
600	11.15	11.00	10.88	10.78	10.70	10.64	10.59	10.55	10.44	10.40	10.39	10.38
700	13.01	12.83	12.69	12.58	12.49	12.42	12.36	12.31	12.18	12.13	12.12	12.11
800	14.86	14.66	14.50	14.37	14.27	14.19	14.12	14.07	13.92	13.87	13.85	13.84
900	16.72	16.49	16.31	16.17	16.05	15.96	15.89	15.83	15.66	15.60	15.58	15.57
1000	18.58	18.32	18.12	17.96	17.84	17.73	17.65	17.58	17.40	17.33	17.31	17.30
2000	37.15	36.64	36.24	35.92	35.67	35.46	35.30	35.16	34.79	34.66	34.61	34.60
3000	55.72	54.96	54.36	53.88	53.50	53.19	52.94	52.74	52.18	51.99	51.92	51.89
4000	74.29	73.28	72.48	71.84	71.33	70.92	70.59	70.32	69.58	69.32	69.22	69.19
5000	92.87	91.60	90.60	89.80	89.16	88.65	88.23	87.90	86.97	86.64	86.53	86.49
6000	111.44	109.92	108.72	107.76	106.99	106.38	105.88	105.48	104.36	103.97	103.83	103.78
7000	130.01	128.24	126.84	125.72	124.83	124.11	123.53	123.06	121.76	121.30	121.14	121.08
8000	148.58	146.56	144.96	143.68	142.66	141.84	141.17	140.64	139.15	138.63	138.44	138.38
9000	167.15	164.88	163.08	161.64	160.49	159.56	158.82	158.21	156.54	155.96	155.75	155.67
10000	185.73	183.20	181.20	179.60	178.32	177.29	176.46	175.79	173.94	173.28	173.05	172.97
11000	204.30	201.52	199.32	197.56	196.15	195.02	194.11	193.37	191.33	190.61	190.36	190.26
12000	222.87	219.84	217.44	215.52	213.98	212.75	211.75	210.95	208.72	207.94	207.66	207.56
13000	241.44	238.16	235.56	233.48	231.82	230.48	229.40	228.53	226.12	225.27	224.96	224.86
14000	260.01	256.48	253.68	251.44	249.65	248.21	247.05	246.11	243.51	242.59	242.27	242.15
15000	278.59	274.80	271.80	269.40	267.48	265.93	264.69	263.69	260.90	259.92	259.57	259.45
16000	297.16	293.12	289.92	287.36	285.31	283.66	282.34	281.27	278.30	277.25	276.88	276.75
17000	315.73	311.44	308.04	305.32	303.14	301.39	299.98	298.84	295.69	294.58	294.18	294.04
18000	334.30	329.76	326.16	323.28	320.97	319.12	317.63	316.42	313.08	311.91	311.49	311.34
19000	352.88	348.08	344.28	341.24	338.80	336.85	335.27	334.00	330.48	329.23	328.79	328.63
20000	371.45	366.40	362.40	359.20	356.64	354.58	352.92	351.58	347.87	346.56	346.10	345.93
21000	390.02	384.72	380.52	377.16	374.47	372.31	370.57	369.16	365.26	363.89	363.40	363.23
22000	408.59	403.04	398.63	395.12	392.30	390.03	388.21	386.74	382.66	381.22	380.71	380.52
23000	427.16	421.36	416.75	413.08	410.13	407.76	405.86	404.32	400.05	398.55	398.01	397.82
24000	445.74	439.68	434.87	431.04	427.96	425.49	423.50	421.90	417.44	415.87	415.31	415.12
25000	464.31	458.00	452.99	449.00	445.79	443.22	441.15	439.47	434.84	433.20	432.62	432.41
26000	482.88	476.32	471.11	466.96	463.63	460.95	458.79	457.05	452.23	450.53	449.92	449.71
27000	501.45	494.64	489.23	484.92	481.46	478.68	476.44	474.63	469.62	467.86	467.23	467.00
28000	520.02	512.96	507.35	502.88	499.29	496.41	494.09	492.21	487.02	485.18	484.53	484.30
29000	538.60	531.28	525.47	520.83	517.12	514.14	511.73	509.79	504.41	502.51	501.84	501.60
30000	557.17	549.60	543.59	538.79	534.95	531.86	529.38	527.37	521.80	519.84	519.14	518.89
31000	575.74	567.92	561.71	556.75	552.78	549.59	547.02	544.95	539.20	537.17	536.45	536.19
32000	594.31	586.24	579.83	574.71	570.62	567.32	564.67	562.53	556.59	554.50	553.75	553.49
33000	612.89	604.56	597.95	592.67	588.45	585.05	582.31	580.11	573.98	571.82	571.06	570.78
34000	631.46	622.88	616.07	610.63	606.28	602.78	599.96	597.68	591.37	589.15	588.36	588.08
35000	650.03	641.20	634.19	628.59	624.11	620.51	617.61	615.26	608.77	606.48	605.67	605.37
37500	696.46	687.00	679.49	673.49	668.69	664.83	661.72	659.21	652.25	649.80	648.93	648.62
40000	742.89	732.80	724.79	718.39	713.27	709.15	705.83	703.16	695.73	693.12	692.19	691.86
42500	789.32	778.60	770.09	763.29	757.85	753.47	749.95	747.10	739.22	736.44	735.45	735.10
45000	835.75	824.40	815.38	808.19	802.43	797.79	794.06	791.05	782.70	779.76	778.71	778.34
47500	882.18	870.20	860.68	853.09	847.00	842.12	838.18	835.00	826.18	823.08	821.97	821.58
50000	928.61	916.00	905.98	897.99	891.58	886.44	882.29	878.94	869.67	866.40	865.23	864.82
52500	975.04	961.80	951.28	942.89	936.16	930.76	926.41	922.89	913.15	909.72	908.50	908.06
55000	1021.47	1007.60	996.58	987.79	980.74	975.08	970.52	966.84	956.63	953.04	951.76	951.30
57500	1067.90	1053.40	1041.88	1032.68	1025.32	1019.40	1014.63	1010.79	1000.12	996.36	995.02	994.54
60000	1114.33	1099.20	1087.18	1077.58	1069.90	1063.72	1058.75	1054.73	1043.60	1039.68	1038.28	1037.78
65000	1207.19	1190.80	1177.77	1167.38	1159.06	1152.37	1146.98	1142.63	1130.56	1126.31	1124.80	1124.26
70000	1300.05	1282.40	1268.37	1257.18	1248.21	1241.01	1235.21	1230.52	1217.53	1212.95	1211.33	1210.74
75000	1392.91	1374.00	1358.97	1346.98	1337.37	1329.65	1323.43	1318.41	1304.50	1299.59	1297.85	1297.23
80000	1485.78	1465.59	1449.57	1436.78	1426.53	1418.30	1411.66	1406.31	1391.46	1386.23	1384.37	1383.71
85000	1578.64	1557.19	1540.17	1526.58	1515.69	1506.94	1499.89	1494.20	1478.43	1472.87	1470.89	1470.19
90000	1671.50	1648.79	1630.76	1616.37	1604.85	1595.58	1588.12	1582.10	1565.40	1559.51	1557.42	1556.67
95000	1764.36	1740.39	1721.36	1706.17	1694.00	1684.23	1676.35	1669.99	1652.36	1646.15	1643.94	1643.15
100000	1857.22	1831.99	1811.96	1795.97	1783.16	1772.87	1764.58	1757.88	1739.33	1732.79	1730.46	1729.63
105000	1950.08	1923.59	1902.56	1885.77	1872.32	1861.51	1852.81	1845.78	1826.29	1819.43	1816.99	1816.11
110000	2042.94	2015.19	1993.15	1975.57	1961.48	1950.15	1941.03	1933.67	1913.26	1906.07	1903.51	1902.60
115000	2135.80	2106.79	2083.75	2065.36	2050.63	2038.80	2029.26	2021.57	2000.23	1992.71	1990.03	1989.08
120000	2228.66	2198.39	2174.35	2155.16	2139.79	2127.44	2117.49	2109.46	2087.19	2079.35	2076.55	2075.56
125000	2321.52	2289.99	2264.95	2244.96	2228.95	2216.08	2205.72	2197.35	2174.16	2165.98	2163.08	2162.04
130000	2414.38	2381.59	2355.54	2334.76	2318.11	2304.73	2293.95	2285.25	2261.12	2252.62	2249.60	2248.52
135000	2507.24	2473.19	2446.14	2424.56	2407.27	2393.37	2382.18	2373.14	2348.09	2339.26	2336.12	2335.00
140000	2600.10	2564.79	2536.74	2514.36	2496.42	2482.01	2470.41	2461.04	2435.06	2425.90	2422.65	2421.48
145000	2692.96	2656.39	2627.34	2604.15	2585.58	2570.66	2558.63	2548.93	2522.02	2512.54	2509.17	2507.97
150000	2785.82	2747.99	2717.93	2693.95	2674.74	2659.30	2646.86	2636.82	2608.99	2599.18	2595.69	2594.45
155000	2878.68	2839.59	2808.53	2783.75	2763.90	2747.94	2735.09	2724.72	2695.96	2685.82	2682.21	2680.93
160000	2971.55	2931.18	2899.13	2873.55	2853.06	2836.59	2823.32	2812.61	2782.92	2772.46	2768.74	2767.41

129

MONTHLY AMORTIZING PAYMENTS

AMOUNT OF LOAN	NUMBER OF YEARS IN TERM											
	1	2	3	4	5	6	7	8	9	10	11	12
$ 50	4.66	2.57	1.89	1.55	1.36	1.23	1.15	1.08	1.04	1.00	0.98	0.96
100	9.32	5.14	3.77	3.10	2.71	2.46	2.29	2.16	2.07	2.00	1.95	1.91
200	18.63	10.28	7.54	6.20	5.42	4.91	4.57	4.32	4.14	4.00	3.90	3.82
300	27.94	15.42	11.31	9.29	8.12	7.37	6.85	6.48	6.21	6.00	5.85	5.73
400	37.25	20.56	15.08	12.39	10.83	9.82	9.13	8.64	8.27	8.00	7.79	7.63
500	46.56	25.70	18.84	15.49	13.53	12.27	11.41	10.80	10.34	10.00	9.74	9.54
600	55.87	30.84	22.61	18.58	16.24	14.73	13.69	12.95	12.41	12.00	11.69	11.45
700	65.18	35.97	26.38	21.68	18.94	17.18	15.97	15.11	14.48	14.00	13.64	13.35
800	74.50	41.11	30.15	24.78	21.65	19.63	18.25	17.27	16.54	16.00	15.58	15.26
900	83.81	46.25	33.91	27.87	24.35	22.09	20.54	19.43	18.61	18.00	17.53	17.17
1000	93.12	51.39	37.68	30.97	27.06	24.54	22.82	21.59	20.68	20.00	19.48	19.07
2000	186.23	102.78	75.36	61.94	54.11	49.08	45.63	43.17	41.35	39.99	38.95	38.14
3000	279.35	154.16	113.03	92.90	81.17	73.61	68.44	64.75	62.03	59.98	58.42	57.21
4000	372.46	205.55	150.71	123.87	108.22	98.15	91.25	86.33	82.70	79.98	77.89	76.28
5000	465.57	256.93	188.38	154.83	135.27	122.68	114.07	107.91	103.38	99.97	97.36	95.35
6000	558.69	308.32	226.06	185.80	162.33	147.22	136.88	129.49	124.05	119.96	116.84	114.41
7000	651.80	359.70	263.73	216.76	189.38	171.76	159.69	151.07	144.73	139.96	136.31	133.48
8000	744.92	411.09	301.41	247.73	216.43	196.29	182.50	172.65	165.40	159.95	155.78	152.55
9000	838.03	462.48	339.08	278.70	243.49	220.83	205.32	194.23	186.08	179.94	175.25	171.62
10000	931.14	513.86	376.76	309.66	270.54	245.36	228.13	215.82	206.75	199.94	194.72	190.69
11000	1024.26	565.25	414.43	340.63	297.59	269.90	250.94	237.40	227.43	219.93	214.19	209.75
12000	1117.37	616.63	452.11	371.59	324.65	294.44	273.75	258.98	248.10	239.92	233.67	228.82
13000	1210.48	668.02	489.78	402.56	351.70	318.97	296.56	280.56	268.78	259.92	253.14	247.89
14000	1303.60	719.40	527.46	433.52	378.75	343.51	319.38	302.14	289.45	279.91	272.61	266.96
15000	1396.71	770.79	565.13	464.49	405.81	368.04	342.19	323.72	310.13	299.90	292.08	286.03
16000	1489.83	822.18	602.81	495.46	432.86	392.58	365.00	345.30	330.80	319.90	311.55	305.09
17000	1582.94	873.56	640.48	526.42	459.91	417.12	387.81	366.88	351.48	339.89	331.03	324.16
18000	1676.05	924.95	678.16	557.39	486.97	441.65	410.63	388.46	372.15	359.88	350.50	343.23
19000	1769.17	976.33	715.83	588.35	514.02	466.19	433.44	410.04	392.83	379.88	369.97	362.30
20000	1862.28	1027.72	753.51	619.32	541.07	490.72	456.25	431.63	413.50	399.87	389.44	381.37
21000	1955.39	1079.10	791.18	650.28	568.13	515.26	479.06	453.21	434.18	419.86	408.91	400.43
22000	2048.51	1130.49	828.86	681.25	595.18	539.80	501.87	474.79	454.85	439.85	428.38	419.50
23000	2141.62	1181.87	866.53	712.22	622.23	564.33	524.69	496.37	475.53	459.85	447.86	438.57
24000	2234.74	1233.26	904.21	743.18	649.29	588.87	547.50	517.95	496.20	479.84	467.33	457.64
25000	2327.85	1284.65	941.88	774.15	676.34	613.40	570.31	539.53	516.88	499.83	486.80	476.71
26000	2420.96	1336.03	979.56	805.11	703.39	637.94	593.12	561.11	537.55	519.83	506.27	495.77
27000	2514.08	1387.42	1017.23	836.08	730.45	662.48	615.94	582.69	558.23	539.82	525.74	514.84
28000	2607.19	1438.80	1054.91	867.04	757.50	687.01	638.75	604.27	578.90	559.81	545.22	533.91
29000	2700.30	1490.19	1092.58	898.01	784.55	711.55	661.56	625.85	599.58	579.81	564.69	552.98
30000	2793.42	1541.57	1130.26	928.98	811.61	736.08	684.37	647.44	620.25	599.80	584.16	572.05
31000	2886.53	1592.96	1167.93	959.94	838.66	760.62	707.18	669.02	640.93	619.79	603.63	591.11
32000	2979.65	1644.35	1205.61	990.91	865.71	785.16	730.00	690.60	661.60	639.79	623.10	610.18
33000	3072.76	1695.73	1243.28	1021.87	892.77	809.69	752.81	712.18	682.28	659.78	642.57	629.25
34000	3165.87	1747.12	1280.96	1052.84	919.82	834.23	775.62	733.76	702.95	679.77	662.05	648.32
35000	3258.99	1798.50	1318.63	1083.80	946.87	858.76	798.43	755.34	723.63	699.77	681.52	667.39
37500	3491.77	1926.97	1412.82	1161.22	1014.51	920.10	855.46	809.29	775.31	749.75	730.20	715.06
40000	3724.56	2055.43	1507.01	1238.63	1082.14	981.44	912.49	863.25	827.00	799.73	778.88	762.73
42500	3957.34	2183.90	1601.20	1316.05	1149.77	1042.78	969.52	917.20	878.69	849.71	827.56	810.40
45000	4190.12	2312.36	1695.38	1393.46	1217.41	1104.12	1026.56	971.15	930.37	899.70	876.24	858.07
47500	4422.91	2440.82	1789.57	1470.88	1285.04	1165.46	1083.59	1025.10	982.06	949.68	924.92	905.74
50000	4655.69	2569.29	1883.76	1548.29	1352.67	1226.80	1140.62	1079.06	1033.75	999.66	973.60	953.41
52500	4888.48	2697.75	1977.95	1625.70	1420.31	1288.14	1197.65	1133.01	1085.44	1049.65	1022.27	1001.08
55000	5121.26	2826.22	2072.13	1703.12	1487.94	1349.48	1254.68	1186.96	1137.12	1099.63	1070.95	1048.75
57500	5354.05	2954.68	2166.32	1780.53	1555.57	1410.82	1311.71	1240.91	1188.81	1149.61	1119.63	1096.42
60000	5586.83	3083.14	2260.51	1857.95	1623.21	1472.16	1368.74	1294.87	1240.50	1199.60	1168.31	1144.09
65000	6052.40	3340.07	2448.88	2012.78	1758.47	1594.84	1482.80	1402.77	1343.87	1299.56	1265.67	1239.43
70000	6517.97	3597.00	2637.26	2167.60	1893.74	1717.52	1596.86	1510.68	1447.25	1399.53	1363.03	1334.77
75000	6983.54	3853.93	2825.64	2322.43	2029.01	1840.20	1710.92	1618.58	1550.62	1499.49	1460.39	1430.11
80000	7449.11	4110.86	3014.01	2477.26	2164.27	1962.88	1824.98	1726.49	1653.99	1599.46	1557.75	1525.45
85000	7914.68	4367.79	3202.39	2632.09	2299.54	2085.56	1939.04	1834.39	1757.37	1699.42	1655.11	1620.79
90000	8380.24	4624.71	3390.76	2786.92	2434.81	2208.24	2053.11	1942.30	1860.74	1799.39	1752.47	1716.13
95000	8845.81	4881.64	3579.14	2941.75	2570.07	2330.92	2167.17	2050.20	1964.12	1899.36	1849.83	1811.47
100000	9311.38	5138.57	3767.51	3096.57	2705.34	2453.60	2281.23	2158.11	2067.49	1999.32	1947.19	1906.81
105000	9776.95	5395.50	3955.89	3251.40	2840.61	2576.28	2395.29	2266.01	2170.87	2099.29	2044.54	2002.15
110000	10242.52	5652.43	4144.26	3406.23	2975.87	2698.96	2509.35	2373.92	2274.24	2199.25	2141.90	2097.49
115000	10708.09	5909.35	4332.64	3561.06	3111.14	2821.64	2623.41	2481.82	2377.61	2299.22	2239.26	2192.83
120000	11173.66	6166.28	4521.01	3715.89	3246.41	2944.32	2737.47	2589.73	2480.99	2399.19	2336.62	2288.17
125000	11639.23	6423.21	4709.39	3870.72	3381.67	3067.00	2851.53	2697.63	2584.36	2499.15	2433.98	2383.51
130000	12104.80	6680.14	4897.76	4025.55	3516.94	3189.68	2965.59	2805.54	2687.74	2599.12	2531.34	2478.85
135000	12570.36	6937.07	5086.14	4180.37	3652.21	3312.36	3079.66	2913.44	2791.11	2699.08	2628.70	2574.19
140000	13035.93	7194.00	5274.51	4335.20	3787.48	3435.04	3193.72	3021.35	2894.49	2799.05	2726.06	2669.53
145000	13501.50	7450.92	5462.89	4490.03	3922.74	3557.72	3307.78	3129.25	2997.86	2899.01	2823.42	2764.87
150000	13967.07	7707.85	5651.26	4644.86	4058.01	3680.40	3421.84	3237.16	3101.24	2998.98	2920.78	2860.21
155000	14432.64	7964.78	5839.64	4799.69	4193.28	3803.08	3535.90	3345.06	3204.61	3098.95	3018.13	2955.55
160000	14898.21	8221.71	6028.02	4954.52	4328.54	3925.76	3649.96	3452.97	3307.98	3198.91	3115.49	3050.89

MONTHLY AMORTIZING PAYMENTS 21.00%

AMOUNT OF LOAN	NUMBER OF YEARS IN TERM											
	13	14	15	16	17	18	19	20	25	30	35	40
$ 50	0.94	0.93	0.92	0.91	0.91	0.90	0.90	0.89	0.88	0.88	0.88	0.88
100	1.88	1.86	1.84	1.82	1.81	1.80	1.79	1.78	1.76	1.76	1.76	1.76
200	3.76	3.71	3.67	3.63	3.61	3.59	3.57	3.56	3.52	3.51	3.51	3.51
300	5.63	5.56	5.50	5.45	5.41	5.38	5.36	5.34	5.28	5.27	5.26	5.26
400	7.51	7.41	7.33	7.26	7.21	7.17	7.14	7.12	7.04	7.02	7.01	7.01
500	9.38	9.26	9.16	9.08	9.02	8.97	8.93	8.89	8.80	8.77	8.76	8.76
600	11.26	11.11	10.99	10.89	10.82	10.76	10.71	10.67	10.56	10.53	10.51	10.51
700	13.13	12.96	12.82	12.71	12.62	12.55	12.49	12.45	12.32	12.28	12.26	12.26
800	15.01	14.81	14.65	14.52	14.42	14.34	14.28	14.23	14.08	14.03	14.01	14.01
900	16.88	16.66	16.48	16.34	16.23	16.14	16.06	16.00	15.84	15.79	15.77	15.76
1000	18.76	18.51	18.31	18.15	18.03	17.93	17.85	17.78	17.60	17.54	17.52	17.51
2000	37.51	37.01	36.62	36.30	36.05	35.85	35.69	35.56	35.20	35.07	35.03	35.01
3000	56.26	55.52	54.92	54.45	54.08	53.77	53.53	53.33	52.79	52.61	52.54	52.52
4000	75.01	74.02	73.23	72.60	72.10	71.70	71.37	71.11	70.39	70.14	70.05	70.02
5000	93.77	92.52	91.54	90.75	90.12	89.62	89.21	88.89	87.99	87.68	87.56	87.53
6000	112.52	111.03	109.84	108.90	108.15	107.54	107.05	106.66	105.58	105.21	105.08	105.03
7000	131.27	129.53	128.15	127.05	126.17	125.46	124.90	124.44	123.18	122.74	122.59	122.53
8000	150.02	148.03	146.45	145.20	144.19	143.39	142.74	142.22	140.78	140.28	140.10	140.04
9000	168.78	166.54	164.76	163.35	162.22	161.31	160.58	159.99	158.37	157.81	157.61	157.54
10000	187.53	185.04	183.07	181.49	180.24	179.23	178.42	177.77	175.97	175.35	175.12	175.05
11000	206.28	203.54	201.37	199.64	198.26	197.15	196.26	195.55	193.57	192.88	192.64	192.55
12000	225.03	222.05	219.68	217.79	216.29	215.08	214.10	213.32	211.16	210.41	210.15	210.06
13000	243.78	240.55	237.98	235.94	234.31	233.00	231.95	231.10	228.76	227.95	227.66	227.56
14000	262.54	259.05	256.29	254.09	252.33	250.92	249.79	248.88	246.36	245.48	245.17	245.06
15000	281.29	277.56	274.60	272.24	270.36	268.84	267.63	266.65	263.95	263.02	262.68	262.57
16000	300.04	296.06	292.90	290.39	288.38	286.77	285.47	284.43	281.55	280.55	280.20	280.07
17000	318.79	314.56	311.21	308.54	306.40	304.69	303.31	302.20	299.15	298.08	297.71	297.58
18000	337.55	333.07	329.52	326.69	324.43	322.61	321.15	319.98	316.74	315.62	315.22	315.08
19000	356.30	351.57	347.82	344.84	342.45	340.54	339.00	337.76	334.34	333.15	332.73	332.59
20000	375.05	370.07	366.13	362.98	360.47	358.46	356.84	355.53	351.94	350.69	350.24	350.09
21000	393.80	388.58	384.43	381.13	378.50	376.38	374.68	373.31	369.53	368.22	367.76	367.59
22000	412.55	407.08	402.74	399.28	396.52	394.30	392.52	391.09	387.13	385.75	385.27	385.10
23000	431.31	425.58	421.05	417.43	414.54	412.23	410.36	408.86	404.73	403.29	402.78	402.60
24000	450.06	444.09	439.35	435.58	432.57	430.15	428.20	426.64	422.32	420.82	420.29	420.11
25000	468.81	462.59	457.66	453.73	450.59	448.07	446.05	444.42	439.92	438.36	437.80	437.61
26000	487.56	481.09	475.96	471.88	468.61	465.99	463.89	462.19	457.52	455.89	455.32	455.12
27000	506.32	499.60	494.27	490.03	486.64	483.92	481.73	479.97	475.11	473.42	472.83	472.62
28000	525.07	518.10	512.58	508.18	504.66	501.84	499.57	497.75	492.71	490.96	490.34	490.12
29000	543.82	536.60	530.88	526.33	522.68	519.76	517.41	515.52	510.31	508.49	507.85	507.63
30000	562.57	555.11	549.19	544.47	540.71	537.68	535.25	533.30	527.90	526.03	525.36	525.13
31000	581.32	573.61	567.49	562.62	558.73	555.61	553.10	551.07	545.50	543.56	542.88	542.64
32000	600.08	592.11	585.80	580.77	576.75	573.53	570.94	568.85	563.10	561.09	560.39	560.14
33000	618.83	610.62	604.11	598.92	594.78	591.45	588.78	586.63	580.69	578.63	577.90	577.64
34000	637.58	629.12	622.41	617.07	612.80	609.37	606.62	604.40	598.29	596.16	595.41	595.15
35000	656.33	647.62	640.72	635.22	630.82	627.30	624.46	622.18	615.89	613.70	612.92	612.65
37500	703.21	693.88	686.48	680.59	675.88	672.10	669.07	666.62	659.88	657.53	656.70	656.41
40000	750.09	740.14	732.25	725.96	720.94	716.91	713.67	711.06	703.87	701.37	700.48	700.17
42500	796.97	786.40	778.02	771.34	766.00	761.72	758.28	755.50	747.86	745.20	744.26	743.93
45000	843.86	832.66	823.78	816.71	811.06	806.52	802.88	799.94	791.85	789.04	788.04	787.70
47500	890.74	878.92	869.55	862.08	856.12	851.33	847.48	844.39	835.84	832.87	831.82	831.46
50000	937.62	925.17	915.31	907.45	901.17	896.14	892.09	888.83	879.84	876.71	875.60	875.22
52500	984.50	971.43	961.08	952.83	946.23	940.94	936.69	933.27	923.83	920.54	919.38	918.98
55000	1031.38	1017.69	1006.84	998.20	991.29	985.75	981.30	977.71	967.82	964.38	963.16	962.74
57500	1078.26	1063.95	1052.61	1043.57	1036.35	1030.56	1025.90	1022.15	1011.81	1008.21	1006.94	1006.50
60000	1125.14	1110.21	1098.37	1088.94	1081.41	1075.36	1070.50	1066.59	1055.80	1052.05	1050.72	1050.26
65000	1218.90	1202.73	1189.90	1179.69	1171.52	1164.98	1159.71	1155.47	1143.79	1139.72	1138.28	1137.78
70000	1312.66	1295.24	1281.43	1270.43	1261.64	1254.59	1248.92	1244.36	1231.77	1227.39	1225.84	1225.30
75000	1406.42	1387.76	1372.96	1361.18	1351.76	1344.20	1338.13	1333.24	1319.75	1315.06	1313.40	1312.82
80000	1500.18	1480.28	1464.49	1451.92	1441.88	1433.82	1427.34	1422.12	1407.74	1402.73	1400.96	1400.34
85000	1593.94	1572.79	1556.03	1542.67	1531.99	1523.43	1516.55	1511.00	1495.72	1490.40	1488.52	1487.86
90000	1687.71	1665.31	1647.56	1633.41	1622.11	1613.04	1605.75	1599.88	1583.70	1578.07	1576.08	1575.39
95000	1781.47	1757.83	1739.09	1724.16	1712.23	1702.66	1694.96	1688.77	1671.68	1665.74	1663.64	1662.91
100000	1875.23	1850.34	1830.62	1814.90	1802.34	1792.27	1784.17	1777.65	1759.67	1753.41	1751.20	1750.43
105000	1968.99	1942.86	1922.15	1905.65	1892.46	1881.88	1873.38	1866.53	1847.65	1841.08	1838.76	1837.95
110000	2062.75	2035.38	2013.68	1996.39	1982.58	1971.50	1962.59	1955.41	1935.63	1928.75	1926.32	1925.47
115000	2156.51	2127.89	2105.21	2087.14	2072.69	2061.11	2051.80	2044.29	2023.62	2016.42	2013.88	2012.99
120000	2250.27	2220.41	2196.74	2177.88	2162.81	2150.72	2141.00	2133.18	2111.60	2104.09	2101.44	2100.51
125000	2344.03	2312.93	2288.27	2268.63	2252.93	2240.33	2230.21	2222.06	2199.58	2191.76	2189.00	2188.03
130000	2437.79	2405.45	2379.80	2359.37	2343.04	2329.95	2319.42	2310.94	2287.57	2279.43	2276.56	2275.56
135000	2531.56	2497.96	2471.33	2450.12	2433.16	2419.56	2408.63	2399.82	2375.55	2367.10	2364.12	2363.08
140000	2625.32	2590.48	2562.86	2540.86	2523.28	2509.17	2497.84	2488.71	2463.53	2454.77	2451.68	2450.60
145000	2719.08	2683.00	2654.39	2631.61	2613.39	2598.79	2587.04	2577.59	2551.52	2542.44	2539.24	2538.12
150000	2812.84	2775.51	2745.92	2722.35	2703.51	2688.40	2676.25	2666.47	2639.50	2630.11	2626.80	2625.64
155000	2906.60	2868.03	2837.45	2813.10	2793.63	2778.01	2765.46	2755.35	2727.48	2717.78	2714.36	2713.16
160000	3000.36	2960.55	2928.98	2903.84	2883.75	2867.63	2854.67	2844.23	2815.47	2805.45	2801.92	2800.68

131

MONTHLY AMORTIZING PAYMENTS

AMOUNT OF LOAN	NUMBER OF YEARS IN TERM											
	1	2	3	4	5	6	7	8	9	10	11	12
$ 50	4.67	2.58	1.90	1.56	1.36	1.24	1.15	1.09	1.05	1.01	0.99	0.97
100	9.33	5.16	3.79	3.12	2.72	2.47	2.30	2.18	2.09	2.02	1.97	1.93
200	18.65	10.31	7.57	6.23	5.44	4.94	4.60	4.35	4.17	4.04	3.93	3.85
300	27.98	15.46	11.35	9.34	8.16	7.41	6.89	6.53	6.26	6.05	5.90	5.78
400	37.30	20.61	15.13	12.45	10.88	9.88	9.19	8.70	8.34	8.07	7.86	7.70
500	46.62	25.76	18.91	15.56	13.60	12.35	11.49	10.87	10.42	10.09	9.83	9.63
600	55.95	30.91	22.69	18.67	16.32	14.81	13.78	13.05	12.51	12.10	11.79	11.55
700	65.27	36.06	26.47	21.78	19.04	17.28	16.08	15.22	14.59	14.12	13.76	13.48
800	74.59	41.21	30.25	24.89	21.76	19.75	18.38	17.40	16.68	16.13	15.72	15.40
900	83.92	46.36	34.03	28.00	24.48	22.22	20.67	19.57	18.76	18.15	17.69	17.33
1000	93.24	51.51	37.81	31.11	27.20	24.69	22.97	21.74	20.84	20.17	19.65	19.25
2000	186.47	103.02	75.61	62.21	54.39	49.37	45.93	43.48	41.68	40.33	39.29	38.49
3000	279.71	154.53	113.42	93.31	81.59	74.05	68.90	65.22	62.52	60.49	58.94	57.74
4000	372.94	206.04	151.22	124.41	108.78	98.74	91.86	86.96	83.36	80.65	78.58	76.98
5000	466.17	257.55	189.02	155.51	135.98	123.42	114.83	108.70	104.20	100.81	98.23	96.23
6000	559.41	309.06	226.83	186.61	163.17	148.10	137.79	130.44	125.03	120.97	117.87	115.47
7000	652.64	360.56	264.63	217.71	190.36	172.79	160.76	152.18	145.87	141.14	137.52	134.72
8000	745.88	412.07	302.43	248.81	217.56	197.47	183.72	173.92	166.71	161.30	157.16	153.96
9000	839.11	463.58	340.24	279.91	244.75	222.15	206.69	195.66	187.55	181.46	176.81	173.21
10000	932.34	515.09	378.04	311.01	271.95	246.83	229.65	217.40	208.39	201.62	196.45	192.45
11000	1025.58	566.60	415.84	342.11	299.14	271.52	252.62	239.14	229.23	221.78	216.10	211.70
12000	1118.81	618.11	453.65	373.21	326.34	296.20	275.58	260.88	250.06	241.94	235.74	230.94
13000	1212.04	669.62	491.45	404.31	353.53	320.88	298.55	282.62	270.90	262.10	255.38	250.19
14000	1305.28	721.12	529.25	435.41	380.72	345.57	321.51	304.35	291.74	282.27	275.03	269.43
15000	1398.51	772.63	567.06	466.51	407.92	370.25	344.48	326.09	312.58	302.43	294.67	288.68
16000	1491.75	824.14	604.86	497.61	435.11	394.93	367.44	347.83	333.42	322.59	314.32	307.92
17000	1584.98	875.65	642.67	528.71	462.31	419.61	390.41	369.57	354.26	342.75	333.96	327.17
18000	1678.21	927.16	680.47	559.81	489.50	444.30	413.37	391.31	375.09	362.91	353.61	346.41
19000	1771.45	978.67	718.27	590.91	516.69	468.98	436.34	413.05	395.93	383.07	373.25	365.66
20000	1864.68	1030.18	756.08	622.01	543.89	493.66	459.30	434.79	416.77	403.23	392.90	384.90
21000	1957.91	1081.68	793.88	653.11	571.08	518.35	482.27	456.53	437.61	423.40	412.54	404.15
22000	2051.15	1133.19	831.68	684.21	598.28	543.03	505.23	478.27	458.45	443.56	432.19	423.39
23000	2144.38	1184.70	869.49	715.31	625.47	567.71	528.20	500.01	479.29	463.72	451.83	442.64
24000	2237.62	1236.21	907.29	746.41	652.67	592.39	551.16	521.75	500.12	483.88	471.48	461.88
25000	2330.85	1287.72	945.09	777.51	679.86	617.08	574.13	543.49	520.96	504.04	491.12	481.13
26000	2424.08	1339.23	982.90	808.61	707.05	641.76	597.09	565.23	541.80	524.20	510.76	500.37
27000	2517.32	1390.74	1020.70	839.71	734.25	666.44	620.06	586.97	562.64	544.36	530.41	519.62
28000	2610.55	1442.24	1058.50	870.81	761.44	691.13	643.02	608.70	583.48	564.53	550.05	538.86
29000	2703.79	1493.75	1096.31	901.91	788.64	715.81	665.99	630.44	604.32	584.69	569.70	558.11
30000	2797.02	1545.26	1134.11	933.01	815.83	740.49	688.95	652.18	625.15	604.85	589.34	577.35
31000	2890.25	1596.77	1171.92	964.11	843.02	765.17	711.92	673.92	645.99	625.01	608.99	596.60
32000	2983.49	1648.28	1209.72	995.22	870.22	789.86	734.88	695.66	666.83	645.17	628.63	615.84
33000	3076.72	1699.79	1247.52	1026.32	897.41	814.54	757.85	717.40	687.67	665.33	648.28	635.09
34000	3169.95	1751.29	1285.33	1057.42	924.61	839.22	780.81	739.14	708.51	685.50	667.92	654.33
35000	3263.19	1802.80	1323.13	1088.52	951.80	863.91	803.78	760.88	729.35	705.66	687.57	673.58
37500	3496.27	1931.57	1417.64	1166.27	1019.79	925.61	861.19	815.23	781.44	756.06	736.68	721.69
40000	3729.36	2060.35	1512.15	1244.02	1087.77	987.32	918.60	869.58	833.54	806.46	785.79	769.80
42500	3962.44	2189.12	1606.66	1321.77	1155.76	1049.03	976.01	923.92	885.63	856.87	834.90	817.91
45000	4195.53	2317.89	1701.16	1399.52	1223.74	1110.73	1033.43	978.27	937.73	907.27	884.01	866.03
47500	4428.61	2446.66	1795.67	1477.27	1291.73	1172.44	1090.84	1032.62	989.83	957.68	933.12	914.14
50000	4661.69	2575.43	1890.18	1555.02	1359.71	1234.15	1148.25	1086.97	1041.92	1008.08	982.23	962.25
52500	4894.78	2704.20	1984.69	1632.77	1427.70	1295.86	1205.66	1141.32	1094.02	1058.48	1031.35	1010.36
55000	5127.86	2832.97	2079.20	1710.52	1495.68	1357.56	1263.08	1195.66	1146.11	1108.89	1080.46	1058.48
57500	5360.95	2961.75	2173.71	1788.27	1563.67	1419.27	1320.49	1250.01	1198.21	1159.29	1129.57	1106.59
60000	5594.03	3090.52	2268.22	1866.02	1631.66	1480.98	1377.90	1304.36	1250.30	1209.69	1178.68	1154.70
65000	6060.20	3348.06	2457.24	2021.53	1767.63	1604.39	1492.73	1413.06	1354.50	1310.50	1276.90	1250.92
70000	6526.37	3605.60	2646.25	2177.03	1903.60	1727.81	1607.55	1521.75	1458.69	1411.31	1375.13	1347.15
75000	6992.54	3863.14	2835.27	2332.53	2039.57	1851.22	1722.38	1630.45	1562.88	1512.12	1473.35	1443.37
80000	7458.71	4120.69	3024.29	2488.03	2175.54	1974.64	1837.20	1739.15	1667.07	1612.92	1571.57	1539.60
85000	7924.88	4378.23	3213.31	2643.53	2311.51	2098.05	1952.02	1847.84	1771.26	1713.73	1669.80	1635.82
90000	8391.05	4635.77	3402.32	2799.03	2447.48	2221.46	2066.85	1956.54	1875.45	1814.54	1768.02	1732.05
95000	8857.22	4893.32	3591.34	2954.54	2583.45	2344.88	2181.67	2065.23	1979.65	1915.35	1866.24	1828.27
100000	9323.38	5150.86	3780.36	3110.04	2719.42	2468.29	2296.50	2173.93	2083.84	2016.15	1964.46	1924.50
105000	9789.55	5408.40	3969.38	3265.54	2855.39	2591.71	2411.32	2282.63	2188.03	2116.96	2062.69	2020.72
110000	10255.72	5665.94	4158.40	3421.04	2991.36	2715.12	2526.15	2391.32	2292.22	2217.77	2160.91	2116.95
115000	10721.89	5923.49	4347.41	3576.54	3127.34	2838.54	2640.97	2500.02	2396.41	2318.57	2259.13	2213.17
120000	11188.06	6181.03	4536.43	3732.04	3263.31	2961.95	2755.80	2608.72	2500.60	2419.38	2357.36	2309.40
125000	11654.23	6438.57	4725.45	3887.54	3399.28	3085.37	2870.62	2717.41	2604.80	2520.19	2455.58	2405.62
130000	12120.40	6696.11	4914.47	4043.05	3535.25	3208.78	2985.45	2826.11	2708.99	2621.00	2553.80	2501.84
135000	12586.57	6953.66	5103.48	4198.55	3671.22	3332.19	3100.27	2934.81	2813.18	2721.80	2652.02	2598.07
140000	13052.74	7211.20	5292.50	4354.05	3807.19	3455.61	3215.10	3043.50	2917.37	2822.61	2750.25	2694.29
145000	13518.91	7468.74	5481.52	4509.55	3943.16	3579.02	3329.92	3152.20	3021.56	2923.42	2848.47	2790.52
150000	13985.07	7726.28	5670.54	4665.05	4079.13	3702.44	3444.75	3260.89	3125.75	3024.23	2946.69	2886.74
155000	14451.24	7983.83	5859.56	4820.55	4215.10	3825.85	3559.57	3369.59	3229.95	3125.03	3044.92	2982.97
160000	14917.41	8241.37	6048.57	4976.06	4351.07	3949.27	3674.40	3478.29	3334.14	3225.84	3143.14	3079.19

MONTHLY AMORTIZING PAYMENTS 21.25%

AMOUNT OF LOAN	NUMBER OF YEARS IN TERM											
	13	14	15	16	17	18	19	20	25	30	35	40
$ 50	0.95	0.94	0.93	0.92	0.92	0.91	0.91	0.90	0.90	0.89	0.89	0.89
100	1.90	1.87	1.85	1.84	1.83	1.82	1.81	1.80	1.79	1.78	1.78	1.78
200	3.79	3.74	3.70	3.67	3.65	3.63	3.61	3.60	3.57	3.55	3.55	3.55
300	5.68	5.61	5.55	5.51	5.47	5.44	5.42	5.40	5.35	5.33	5.32	5.32
400	7.58	7.48	7.40	7.34	7.29	7.25	7.22	7.19	7.13	7.10	7.09	7.09
500	9.47	9.35	9.25	9.17	9.11	9.06	9.02	8.99	8.91	8.88	8.86	8.86
600	11.36	11.22	11.10	11.01	10.93	10.88	10.83	10.79	10.69	10.65	10.64	10.63
700	13.26	13.09	12.95	12.84	12.76	12.69	12.63	12.59	12.47	12.42	12.41	12.40
800	15.15	14.95	14.80	14.68	14.58	14.50	14.44	14.38	14.25	14.20	14.18	14.17
900	17.04	16.82	16.65	16.51	16.40	16.31	16.24	16.18	16.03	15.97	15.95	15.95
1000	18.94	18.69	18.50	18.34	18.22	18.12	18.04	17.98	17.81	17.75	17.72	17.72
2000	37.87	37.38	36.99	36.68	36.44	36.24	36.08	35.95	35.61	35.49	35.44	35.43
3000	56.80	56.07	55.48	55.02	54.65	54.36	54.12	53.93	53.41	53.23	53.16	53.14
4000	75.74	74.75	73.98	73.36	72.87	72.47	72.16	71.90	71.21	70.97	70.88	70.85
5000	94.67	93.44	92.47	91.70	91.08	90.59	90.19	89.88	89.01	88.71	88.60	88.57
6000	113.60	112.13	110.96	110.04	109.30	108.71	108.23	107.85	106.81	106.45	106.32	106.28
7000	132.54	130.82	129.46	128.38	127.51	126.82	126.27	125.83	124.61	124.19	124.04	123.99
8000	151.47	149.50	147.95	146.72	145.73	144.94	144.31	143.80	142.41	141.93	141.76	141.70
9000	170.40	168.19	166.44	165.05	163.95	163.06	162.35	161.77	160.21	159.67	159.48	159.41
10000	189.33	186.88	184.94	183.39	182.16	181.18	180.38	179.75	178.01	177.41	177.20	177.13
11000	208.27	205.57	203.43	201.73	200.38	199.29	198.42	197.72	195.81	195.15	194.92	194.84
12000	227.20	224.25	221.92	220.07	218.59	217.41	216.46	215.70	213.61	212.89	212.64	212.55
13000	246.13	242.94	240.42	238.41	236.81	235.53	234.50	233.67	231.41	230.63	230.36	230.26
14000	265.07	261.63	258.91	256.75	255.02	253.64	252.54	251.65	249.21	248.37	248.08	247.98
15000	284.00	280.32	277.40	275.09	273.24	271.76	270.57	269.62	267.01	266.11	265.80	265.69
16000	302.93	299.00	295.90	293.43	291.46	289.88	288.61	287.60	284.81	283.85	283.52	283.40
17000	321.86	317.69	314.39	311.77	309.67	308.00	306.65	305.57	302.61	301.59	301.24	301.11
18000	340.80	336.38	332.88	330.10	327.89	326.11	324.69	323.54	320.41	319.33	318.96	318.82
19000	359.73	355.07	351.38	348.44	346.10	344.23	342.73	341.52	338.21	337.07	336.67	336.54
20000	378.66	373.75	369.87	366.78	364.32	362.35	360.76	359.49	356.01	354.81	354.39	354.25
21000	397.60	392.44	388.36	385.12	382.53	380.46	378.80	377.47	373.81	372.55	372.11	371.96
22000	416.53	411.13	406.86	403.46	400.75	398.58	396.84	395.44	391.61	390.29	389.83	389.67
23000	435.46	429.82	425.35	421.80	418.97	416.70	414.88	413.42	409.41	408.03	407.55	407.39
24000	454.39	448.50	443.84	440.14	437.18	434.81	432.92	431.39	427.21	425.77	425.27	425.10
25000	473.33	467.19	462.34	458.48	455.40	452.93	450.95	449.37	445.01	443.51	442.99	442.81
26000	492.26	485.88	480.83	476.81	473.61	471.05	468.99	467.34	462.81	461.25	460.71	460.52
27000	511.19	504.57	499.32	495.15	491.83	489.17	487.03	485.31	480.61	478.99	478.43	478.23
28000	530.13	523.25	517.82	513.49	510.04	507.28	505.07	503.29	498.41	496.73	496.15	495.95
29000	549.06	541.94	536.31	531.83	528.26	525.40	523.11	521.26	516.21	514.47	513.87	513.66
30000	567.99	560.63	554.80	550.17	546.47	543.52	541.14	539.24	534.01	532.21	531.59	531.37
31000	586.92	579.32	573.30	568.51	564.69	561.63	559.18	557.21	551.81	549.95	549.31	549.08
32000	605.86	598.00	591.79	586.85	582.91	579.75	577.22	575.19	569.61	567.69	567.03	566.80
33000	624.79	616.69	610.28	605.19	601.12	597.87	595.26	593.16	587.41	585.43	584.75	584.51
34000	643.72	635.38	628.77	623.53	619.34	615.99	613.30	611.14	605.21	603.17	602.47	602.22
35000	662.66	654.07	647.27	641.86	637.55	634.10	631.33	629.11	623.01	620.92	620.19	619.93
37500	709.99	700.78	693.50	687.71	683.09	679.40	676.43	674.05	667.51	665.27	664.49	664.21
40000	757.32	747.50	739.73	733.56	728.63	724.69	721.52	718.98	712.02	709.62	708.78	708.49
42500	804.65	794.22	785.97	779.41	774.17	769.98	766.62	763.92	756.52	753.97	753.08	752.77
45000	851.98	840.94	832.20	825.25	819.71	815.27	811.71	808.85	801.02	798.32	797.38	797.05
47500	899.32	887.66	878.43	871.10	865.25	860.57	856.81	853.79	845.52	842.67	841.68	841.34
50000	946.65	934.38	924.67	916.95	910.79	905.86	901.90	898.73	890.02	887.02	885.98	885.62
52500	993.98	981.10	970.90	962.79	956.33	951.15	947.00	943.66	934.52	931.37	930.28	929.90
55000	1041.31	1027.81	1017.13	1008.64	1001.87	996.44	992.09	988.60	979.02	975.72	974.58	974.18
57500	1088.65	1074.53	1063.37	1054.49	1047.41	1041.74	1037.19	1033.54	1023.52	1020.07	1018.87	1018.46
60000	1135.98	1121.25	1109.60	1100.34	1092.94	1087.03	1082.28	1078.47	1068.02	1064.42	1063.17	1062.74
65000	1230.64	1214.69	1202.07	1192.03	1184.02	1177.61	1172.47	1168.34	1157.02	1153.12	1151.77	1151.30
70000	1325.31	1308.13	1294.53	1283.72	1275.10	1268.20	1262.66	1258.22	1246.02	1241.83	1240.37	1239.86
75000	1419.97	1401.56	1387.00	1375.42	1366.18	1358.79	1352.85	1348.09	1335.02	1330.53	1328.97	1328.42
80000	1514.64	1495.00	1479.46	1467.11	1457.26	1449.37	1443.04	1437.96	1424.03	1419.23	1417.56	1416.98
85000	1609.30	1588.44	1571.93	1558.81	1548.34	1539.96	1533.23	1527.83	1513.03	1507.93	1506.16	1505.54
90000	1703.96	1681.88	1664.40	1650.50	1639.41	1630.54	1623.42	1617.70	1602.03	1596.63	1594.76	1594.10
95000	1798.63	1775.31	1756.86	1742.20	1730.49	1721.13	1713.61	1707.58	1691.03	1685.33	1683.35	1682.67
100000	1893.29	1868.75	1849.33	1833.89	1821.57	1811.71	1803.80	1797.45	1780.03	1774.03	1771.95	1771.23
105000	1987.96	1962.19	1941.79	1925.58	1912.65	1902.30	1893.99	1887.32	1869.03	1862.74	1860.55	1859.79
110000	2082.62	2055.62	2034.26	2017.28	2003.73	1992.88	1984.18	1977.19	1958.03	1951.44	1949.15	1948.35
115000	2177.29	2149.06	2126.73	2108.97	2094.81	2083.47	2074.37	2067.07	2047.03	2040.14	2037.74	2036.91
120000	2271.95	2242.50	2219.19	2200.67	2185.88	2174.05	2164.56	2156.94	2136.04	2128.84	2126.34	2125.47
125000	2366.62	2335.94	2311.66	2292.36	2276.96	2264.64	2254.75	2246.81	2225.04	2217.54	2214.94	2214.03
130000	2461.28	2429.37	2404.13	2384.05	2368.04	2355.22	2344.94	2336.68	2314.04	2306.24	2303.54	2302.59
135000	2555.94	2522.81	2496.59	2475.75	2459.12	2445.81	2435.13	2426.55	2403.04	2394.94	2392.13	2391.15
140000	2650.61	2616.25	2589.06	2567.44	2550.20	2536.40	2525.32	2516.43	2492.04	2483.65	2480.73	2479.72
145000	2745.27	2709.68	2681.52	2659.14	2641.28	2626.98	2615.51	2606.30	2581.04	2572.35	2569.33	2568.28
150000	2839.94	2803.12	2773.99	2750.83	2732.35	2717.57	2705.70	2696.17	2670.04	2661.05	2657.93	2656.84
155000	2934.60	2896.56	2866.46	2842.53	2823.43	2808.15	2795.89	2786.04	2759.04	2749.75	2746.52	2745.40
160000	3029.27	2990.00	2958.92	2934.22	2914.51	2898.74	2886.08	2875.92	2848.05	2838.45	2835.12	2833.96

133

AMOUNT OF LOAN	NUMBER OF YEARS IN TERM											
	1	2	3	4	5	6	7	8	9	10	11	12
$ 50	4.67	2.59	1.90	1.57	1.37	1.25	1.16	1.10	1.06	1.02	1.00	0.98
100	9.34	5.17	3.80	3.13	2.74	2.49	2.32	2.19	2.11	2.04	1.99	1.95
200	18.68	10.33	7.59	6.25	5.47	4.97	4.63	4.38	4.21	4.07	3.97	3.89
300	28.01	15.49	11.38	9.38	8.21	7.45	6.94	6.57	6.31	6.10	5.95	5.83
400	37.35	20.66	15.18	12.50	10.94	9.94	9.25	8.76	8.41	8.14	7.93	7.77
500	46.68	25.82	18.97	15.62	13.67	12.42	11.56	10.95	10.51	10.17	9.91	9.72
600	56.02	30.98	22.76	18.75	16.41	14.90	13.88	13.14	12.61	12.20	11.90	11.66
700	65.35	36.15	26.56	21.87	19.14	17.39	16.19	15.33	14.71	14.24	13.88	13.60
800	74.69	41.31	30.35	24.99	21.87	19.87	18.50	17.52	16.81	16.27	15.86	15.54
900	84.02	46.47	34.14	28.12	24.61	22.35	20.81	19.71	18.91	18.30	17.84	17.49
1000	93.36	51.64	37.94	31.24	27.34	24.84	23.12	21.90	21.01	20.34	19.82	19.43
2000	186.71	103.27	75.87	62.48	54.68	49.67	46.24	43.80	42.01	40.67	39.64	38.85
3000	280.07	154.90	113.80	93.71	82.01	74.50	69.36	65.70	63.01	61.00	59.46	58.27
4000	373.42	206.53	151.73	124.95	109.35	99.33	92.48	87.60	84.01	81.33	79.28	77.69
5000	466.77	258.16	189.67	156.18	136.68	124.16	115.60	109.50	105.02	101.66	99.09	97.12
6000	560.13	309.79	227.60	187.42	164.02	148.99	138.71	131.39	126.02	121.99	118.91	116.54
7000	653.48	361.43	265.53	218.65	191.35	173.82	161.83	153.29	147.02	142.32	138.73	135.96
8000	746.84	413.06	303.46	249.89	218.69	198.65	184.95	175.19	168.02	162.65	158.55	155.38
9000	840.19	464.69	341.40	281.12	246.02	223.48	208.07	197.09	189.03	182.98	178.37	174.81
10000	933.54	516.32	379.33	312.36	273.36	248.31	231.19	218.99	210.03	203.31	198.18	194.23
11000	1026.90	567.95	417.26	343.59	300.69	273.14	254.30	240.88	231.03	223.64	218.00	213.65
12000	1120.25	619.58	455.19	374.83	328.03	297.97	277.42	262.78	252.03	243.97	237.82	233.07
13000	1213.61	671.22	493.12	406.06	355.36	322.80	300.54	284.68	273.04	264.30	257.64	252.50
14000	1306.96	722.85	531.06	437.30	382.70	347.63	323.66	306.58	294.04	284.63	277.46	271.92
15000	1400.31	774.48	568.99	468.53	410.04	372.46	346.78	328.48	315.04	304.96	297.27	291.34
16000	1493.67	826.11	606.92	499.77	437.37	397.29	369.90	350.37	336.04	325.29	317.09	310.76
17000	1587.02	877.74	644.85	531.00	464.71	422.12	393.01	372.27	357.04	345.62	336.91	330.19
18000	1680.38	929.37	682.79	562.24	492.04	446.95	416.13	394.17	378.05	365.95	356.73	349.61
19000	1773.73	981.00	720.72	593.47	519.38	471.78	439.25	416.07	399.05	386.28	376.55	369.03
20000	1867.08	1032.64	758.65	624.71	546.71	496.61	462.37	437.97	420.05	406.61	396.36	388.45
21000	1960.44	1084.27	796.58	655.95	574.05	521.44	485.49	459.86	441.05	426.94	416.18	407.87
22000	2053.79	1135.90	834.52	687.18	601.38	546.27	508.60	481.76	462.06	447.27	436.00	427.30
23000	2147.14	1187.53	872.45	718.42	628.72	571.10	531.72	503.66	483.06	467.60	455.82	446.72
24000	2240.50	1239.16	910.38	749.65	656.05	595.93	554.84	525.56	504.06	487.93	475.64	466.14
25000	2333.85	1290.79	948.31	780.89	683.39	620.76	577.96	547.46	525.06	508.26	495.45	485.56
26000	2427.21	1342.43	986.24	812.12	710.72	645.59	601.08	569.35	546.07	528.59	515.27	504.99
27000	2520.56	1394.06	1024.18	843.36	738.06	670.42	624.19	591.25	567.07	548.92	535.09	524.41
28000	2613.91	1445.69	1062.11	874.59	765.40	695.25	647.31	613.15	588.07	569.25	554.91	543.83
29000	2707.27	1497.32	1100.04	905.83	792.73	720.08	670.43	635.05	609.07	589.58	574.73	563.25
30000	2800.62	1548.95	1137.97	937.06	820.07	744.91	693.55	656.95	630.07	609.92	594.54	582.68
31000	2893.98	1600.58	1175.91	968.30	847.40	769.74	716.67	678.84	651.08	630.25	614.36	602.10
32000	2987.33	1652.22	1213.84	999.53	874.74	794.57	739.79	700.74	672.08	650.58	634.18	621.52
33000	3080.68	1703.85	1251.77	1030.77	902.07	819.40	762.90	722.64	693.08	670.91	654.00	640.94
34000	3174.04	1755.48	1289.70	1062.00	929.41	844.23	786.02	744.54	714.08	691.24	673.81	660.37
35000	3267.39	1807.11	1327.63	1093.24	956.74	869.06	809.14	766.44	735.09	711.57	693.63	679.79
37500	3500.78	1936.19	1422.47	1171.33	1025.08	931.14	866.94	821.18	787.59	762.39	743.18	728.34
40000	3734.16	2065.27	1517.30	1249.42	1093.42	993.21	924.73	875.93	840.10	813.22	792.72	776.90
42500	3967.55	2194.35	1612.13	1327.50	1161.76	1055.29	982.53	930.67	892.60	864.04	842.27	825.46
45000	4200.93	2323.43	1706.96	1405.59	1230.10	1117.36	1040.32	985.42	945.11	914.87	891.81	874.01
47500	4434.32	2452.50	1801.79	1483.68	1298.44	1179.44	1098.12	1040.16	997.62	965.70	941.36	922.57
50000	4667.70	2581.58	1896.62	1561.77	1366.77	1241.51	1155.91	1094.91	1050.12	1016.52	990.90	971.12
52500	4901.09	2710.66	1991.45	1639.86	1435.11	1303.59	1213.71	1149.65	1102.63	1067.35	1040.45	1019.68
55000	5134.47	2839.74	2086.28	1717.94	1503.45	1365.67	1271.50	1204.40	1155.13	1118.17	1089.99	1068.24
57500	5367.85	2968.82	2181.11	1796.03	1571.79	1427.74	1329.30	1259.14	1207.64	1169.00	1139.54	1116.79
60000	5601.24	3097.90	2275.94	1874.12	1640.13	1489.82	1387.09	1313.89	1260.14	1219.83	1189.08	1165.35
65000	6068.01	3356.06	2465.60	2030.30	1776.80	1613.97	1502.68	1423.38	1365.16	1321.48	1288.17	1262.46
70000	6534.78	3614.21	2655.26	2186.47	1913.48	1738.12	1618.27	1532.87	1470.17	1423.13	1387.26	1359.57
75000	7001.55	3872.37	2844.93	2342.65	2050.16	1862.27	1733.87	1642.36	1575.18	1524.78	1486.35	1456.68
80000	7468.32	4130.53	3034.59	2498.83	2186.84	1986.42	1849.46	1751.85	1680.19	1626.43	1585.44	1553.80
85000	7935.09	4388.69	3224.25	2655.00	2323.51	2110.57	1965.05	1861.34	1785.20	1728.08	1684.53	1650.91
90000	8401.86	4646.85	3413.91	2811.18	2460.19	2234.72	2080.64	1970.83	1890.21	1829.74	1783.62	1748.02
95000	8868.63	4905.00	3603.57	2967.35	2596.87	2358.87	2196.23	2080.32	1995.23	1931.39	1882.71	1845.13
100000	9335.40	5163.16	3793.23	3123.53	2733.54	2483.02	2311.82	2189.81	2100.24	2033.04	1981.80	1942.24
105000	9802.17	5421.32	3982.89	3279.71	2870.22	2607.18	2427.41	2299.30	2205.25	2134.69	2080.89	2039.35
110000	10268.94	5679.48	4172.56	3435.88	3006.90	2731.33	2543.00	2408.79	2310.26	2236.34	2179.98	2136.47
115000	10735.70	5937.64	4362.22	3592.06	3143.57	2855.48	2658.59	2518.28	2415.27	2337.99	2279.07	2233.58
120000	11202.47	6195.79	4551.88	3748.24	3280.25	2979.63	2774.18	2627.77	2520.28	2439.65	2378.16	2330.69
125000	11669.24	6453.95	4741.54	3904.41	3416.93	3103.78	2889.77	2737.26	2625.29	2541.30	2477.25	2427.80
130000	12136.01	6712.11	4931.20	4060.59	3553.60	3227.93	3005.36	2846.75	2730.31	2642.95	2576.34	2524.91
135000	12602.78	6970.27	5120.86	4216.76	3690.28	3352.08	3120.95	2956.24	2835.32	2744.60	2675.43	2622.03
140000	13069.55	7228.42	5310.52	4372.94	3826.96	3476.23	3236.54	3065.73	2940.33	2846.25	2774.52	2719.14
145000	13536.32	7486.58	5500.18	4529.12	3963.64	3600.38	3352.13	3175.22	3045.34	2947.90	2873.61	2816.25
150000	14003.09	7744.74	5689.85	4685.29	4100.31	3724.53	3467.73	3284.71	3150.35	3049.56	2972.70	2913.36
155000	14469.86	8002.90	5879.51	4841.47	4236.99	3848.69	3583.32	3394.20	3255.36	3151.21	3071.79	3010.47
160000	14936.63	8261.06	6069.17	4997.65	4373.67	3972.84	3698.91	3503.69	3360.38	3252.86	3170.88	3107.59

AMOUNT OF LOAN	NUMBER OF YEARS IN TERM											
	13	14	15	16	17	18	19	20	25	30	35	40
$ 50	0.96	0.95	0.94	0.93	0.93	0.92	0.92	0.91	0.91	0.90	0.90	0.90
100	1.92	1.89	1.87	1.86	1.85	1.84	1.83	1.82	1.81	1.80	1.80	1.80
200	3.83	3.78	3.74	3.71	3.69	3.67	3.65	3.64	3.61	3.59	3.59	3.59
300	5.74	5.67	5.61	5.56	5.53	5.50	5.48	5.46	5.41	5.39	5.38	5.38
400	7.65	7.55	7.48	7.42	7.37	7.33	7.30	7.27	7.21	7.18	7.18	7.17
500	9.56	9.44	9.35	9.27	9.21	9.16	9.12	9.09	9.01	8.98	8.97	8.97
600	11.47	11.33	11.21	11.12	11.05	10.99	10.95	10.91	10.81	10.77	10.76	10.76
700	13.38	13.22	13.08	12.98	12.89	12.82	12.77	12.73	12.61	12.57	12.55	12.55
800	15.30	15.10	14.95	14.83	14.73	14.65	14.59	14.54	14.41	14.36	14.35	14.34
900	17.21	16.99	16.82	16.68	16.57	16.49	16.42	16.36	16.21	16.16	16.14	16.13
1000	19.12	18.88	18.69	18.53	18.41	18.32	18.24	18.18	18.01	17.95	17.93	17.93
2000	38.23	37.75	37.37	37.06	36.82	36.63	36.47	36.35	36.01	35.90	35.86	35.85
3000	57.35	56.62	56.05	55.59	55.23	54.94	54.71	54.52	54.02	53.85	53.79	53.77
4000	76.46	75.49	74.73	74.12	73.64	73.25	72.94	72.70	72.02	71.79	71.71	71.69
5000	95.58	94.37	93.41	92.65	92.05	91.56	91.18	90.87	90.03	89.74	89.64	89.61
6000	114.69	113.24	112.09	111.18	110.46	109.88	109.41	109.04	108.03	107.69	107.57	107.53
7000	133.80	132.11	130.77	129.71	128.86	128.19	127.65	127.21	126.03	125.63	125.49	125.45
8000	152.92	150.98	149.45	148.24	147.27	146.50	145.88	145.39	144.04	143.58	143.42	143.37
9000	172.03	169.85	168.13	166.77	165.68	164.81	164.12	163.56	162.04	161.53	161.35	161.29
10000	191.15	188.73	186.81	185.30	184.09	183.12	182.35	181.73	180.05	179.47	179.28	179.21
11000	210.26	207.60	205.49	203.83	202.50	201.44	200.59	199.91	198.05	197.42	197.20	197.13
12000	229.37	226.47	224.18	222.36	220.91	219.75	218.82	218.08	216.05	215.37	215.13	215.05
13000	248.49	245.34	242.86	240.88	239.31	238.06	237.06	236.25	234.06	233.31	233.06	232.97
14000	267.60	264.21	261.54	259.41	257.72	256.37	255.29	254.42	252.06	251.26	250.98	250.89
15000	286.72	283.09	280.22	277.94	276.13	274.68	273.53	272.60	270.07	269.21	268.91	268.81
16000	305.83	301.96	298.90	296.47	294.54	293.00	291.76	290.77	288.07	287.15	286.84	286.73
17000	324.94	320.83	317.58	315.00	312.95	311.31	310.00	308.94	306.07	305.10	304.76	304.65
18000	344.06	339.70	336.26	333.53	331.36	329.62	328.23	327.12	324.08	323.05	322.69	322.57
19000	363.17	358.57	354.94	352.06	349.76	347.93	346.46	345.29	342.08	340.99	340.62	340.49
20000	382.29	377.45	373.62	370.59	368.17	366.24	364.70	363.46	360.09	358.94	358.55	358.41
21000	401.40	396.32	392.30	389.12	386.58	384.56	382.93	381.63	378.09	376.89	376.47	376.33
22000	420.51	415.19	410.98	407.65	404.99	402.87	401.17	399.81	396.10	394.83	394.40	394.25
23000	439.63	434.06	429.66	426.18	423.40	421.18	419.40	417.98	414.10	412.78	412.33	412.17
24000	458.74	452.93	448.35	444.71	441.81	439.49	437.64	436.15	432.10	430.73	430.25	430.09
25000	477.86	471.81	467.03	463.23	460.21	457.80	455.87	454.33	450.11	448.67	448.18	448.01
26000	496.97	490.68	485.71	481.76	478.62	476.12	474.11	472.50	468.11	466.62	466.11	465.93
27000	516.09	509.55	504.39	500.29	497.03	494.43	492.34	490.67	486.12	484.57	484.03	483.85
28000	535.20	528.42	523.07	518.82	515.44	512.74	510.58	508.84	504.12	502.51	501.96	501.77
29000	554.31	547.29	541.75	537.35	533.85	531.05	528.81	527.02	522.12	520.46	519.89	519.69
30000	573.43	566.17	560.43	555.88	552.26	549.36	547.05	545.19	540.13	538.41	537.82	537.61
31000	592.54	585.04	579.11	574.41	570.67	567.68	565.28	563.36	558.13	556.35	555.74	555.53
32000	611.66	603.91	597.79	592.94	589.07	585.99	583.52	581.54	576.14	574.30	573.67	573.45
33000	630.77	622.78	616.47	611.47	607.48	604.30	601.75	599.71	594.14	592.25	591.60	591.37
34000	649.88	641.65	635.15	630.00	625.89	622.61	619.99	617.88	612.14	610.19	609.52	609.29
35000	669.00	660.53	653.83	648.53	644.30	640.92	638.22	636.05	630.15	628.14	627.45	627.21
37500	716.78	707.71	700.54	694.85	690.32	686.70	683.81	681.49	675.16	673.01	672.27	672.01
40000	764.57	754.89	747.24	741.17	736.34	732.48	729.39	726.92	720.17	717.87	717.09	716.81
42500	812.35	802.07	793.94	787.49	782.36	778.26	774.98	772.35	765.18	762.74	761.90	761.61
45000	860.14	849.25	840.64	833.82	828.38	824.04	820.57	817.78	810.19	807.61	806.72	806.42
47500	907.92	896.43	887.35	880.14	874.40	869.82	866.15	863.21	855.20	852.47	851.54	851.22
50000	955.71	943.61	934.05	926.46	920.42	915.60	911.74	908.65	900.21	897.34	896.36	896.02
52500	1003.49	990.79	980.75	972.79	966.45	961.38	957.33	954.08	945.22	942.21	941.17	940.82
55000	1051.28	1037.97	1027.45	1019.11	1012.47	1007.16	1002.92	999.51	990.23	987.07	985.99	985.62
57500	1099.06	1085.15	1074.15	1065.43	1058.49	1052.94	1048.50	1044.94	1035.24	1031.94	1030.81	1030.42
60000	1146.85	1132.33	1120.86	1111.76	1104.51	1098.72	1094.09	1090.37	1080.25	1076.81	1075.63	1075.22
65000	1242.42	1226.69	1214.26	1204.40	1196.55	1190.28	1185.26	1181.24	1170.27	1166.54	1165.26	1164.82
70000	1337.99	1321.05	1307.66	1297.05	1288.59	1281.84	1276.44	1272.10	1260.29	1256.27	1254.90	1254.42
75000	1433.56	1415.41	1401.07	1389.69	1380.63	1373.40	1367.61	1362.97	1350.31	1346.01	1344.53	1344.02
80000	1529.13	1509.77	1494.47	1482.34	1472.68	1464.96	1458.78	1453.83	1440.33	1435.74	1434.17	1433.62
85000	1624.70	1604.13	1587.88	1574.98	1564.72	1556.52	1549.96	1544.69	1530.35	1525.47	1523.80	1523.22
90000	1720.27	1698.49	1681.28	1667.63	1656.76	1648.08	1641.13	1635.56	1620.37	1615.21	1613.44	1612.83
95000	1815.84	1792.85	1774.69	1760.28	1748.80	1739.64	1732.30	1726.42	1710.40	1704.94	1703.07	1702.43
100000	1911.41	1887.21	1868.09	1852.92	1840.84	1831.20	1823.48	1817.29	1800.42	1794.67	1792.71	1792.03
105000	2006.98	1981.57	1961.49	1945.57	1932.89	1922.76	1914.65	1908.15	1890.44	1884.41	1882.34	1881.63
110000	2102.55	2075.93	2054.90	2038.21	2024.93	2014.32	2005.83	1999.01	1980.46	1974.14	1971.98	1971.23
115000	2198.12	2170.29	2148.30	2130.86	2116.97	2105.88	2097.00	2089.88	2070.48	2063.88	2061.61	2060.83
120000	2293.70	2264.65	2241.71	2223.51	2209.01	2197.44	2188.17	2180.74	2160.50	2153.61	2151.25	2150.43
125000	2389.27	2359.01	2335.11	2316.15	2301.05	2289.00	2279.35	2271.61	2250.52	2243.34	2240.88	2240.03
130000	2484.84	2453.37	2428.52	2408.80	2393.10	2380.56	2370.52	2362.47	2340.54	2333.08	2330.52	2329.63
135000	2580.41	2547.73	2521.92	2501.44	2485.14	2472.12	2461.69	2453.34	2430.56	2422.81	2420.15	2419.24
140000	2675.98	2642.09	2615.32	2594.09	2577.18	2563.68	2552.87	2544.20	2520.58	2512.54	2509.79	2508.84
145000	2771.55	2736.45	2708.73	2686.73	2669.22	2655.24	2644.04	2635.06	2610.60	2602.28	2599.42	2598.44
150000	2867.12	2830.81	2802.13	2779.38	2761.26	2746.80	2735.21	2725.93	2700.62	2692.01	2689.06	2688.04
155000	2962.69	2925.17	2895.54	2872.03	2853.31	2838.36	2826.39	2816.79	2790.64	2781.74	2778.69	2777.64
160000	3058.26	3019.53	2988.94	2964.67	2945.35	2929.91	2917.56	2907.66	2880.66	2871.48	2868.33	2867.24

21.75%   MONTHLY AMORTIZING PAYMENTS

AMOUNT OF LOAN	1	2	3	4	5	6	7	8	9	10	11	12
					NUMBER OF YEARS IN TERM							
$ 50	4.68	2.59	1.91	1.57	1.38	1.25	1.17	1.11	1.06	1.03	1.00	0.99
100	9.35	5.18	3.81	3.14	2.75	2.50	2.33	2.21	2.12	2.05	2.00	1.97
200	18.70	10.36	7.62	6.28	5.50	5.00	4.66	4.42	4.23	4.10	4.00	3.93
300	28.05	15.53	11.42	9.42	8.25	7.50	6.99	6.62	6.36	6.15	6.00	5.89
400	37.39	20.71	15.23	12.55	11.00	10.00	9.31	8.83	8.47	8.20	8.00	7.85
500	46.74	25.88	19.04	15.69	13.74	12.49	11.64	11.03	10.59	10.25	10.00	9.81
600	56.09	31.06	22.84	18.83	16.49	14.99	13.97	13.24	12.71	12.30	12.00	11.77
700	65.44	36.23	26.65	21.96	19.24	17.49	16.30	15.45	14.82	14.35	14.00	13.73
800	74.78	41.41	30.45	25.10	21.99	19.99	18.62	17.65	16.94	16.40	16.00	15.69
900	84.13	46.58	34.26	28.24	24.73	22.49	20.95	19.86	19.06	18.45	18.00	17.65
1000	93.48	51.76	38.07	31.38	27.48	24.98	23.28	22.06	21.17	20.50	20.00	19.61
2000	186.95	103.51	76.13	62.75	54.96	49.96	46.55	44.12	42.34	41.00	39.99	39.21
3000	280.43	155.27	114.19	94.12	82.44	74.94	69.82	66.18	63.51	61.50	59.98	58.81
4000	373.90	207.02	152.25	125.49	109.91	99.92	93.09	88.23	84.67	82.00	79.97	78.41
5000	467.38	258.78	190.31	156.86	137.39	124.89	116.36	110.29	105.84	102.50	99.96	98.01
6000	560.85	310.53	228.37	188.23	164.87	149.87	139.64	132.35	127.01	123.00	119.96	117.61
7000	654.32	362.29	266.43	219.60	192.34	174.85	162.91	154.41	148.17	143.50	139.95	137.21
8000	747.80	414.04	304.49	250.97	219.82	199.83	186.18	176.46	169.34	164.00	159.94	156.81
9000	841.27	465.80	342.56	282.34	247.30	224.81	209.45	198.52	190.51	184.50	179.93	176.41
10000	934.75	517.55	380.62	313.71	274.77	249.78	232.72	220.58	211.67	205.00	199.92	196.01
11000	1028.22	569.31	418.68	345.08	302.25	274.76	255.99	242.64	232.84	225.50	219.92	215.61
12000	1121.69	621.06	456.74	376.45	329.73	299.74	279.27	264.69	254.01	246.00	239.91	235.21
13000	1215.17	672.82	494.80	407.82	357.21	324.72	302.54	286.75	275.17	266.50	259.90	254.81
14000	1308.64	724.57	532.86	439.19	384.68	349.70	325.81	308.81	296.34	287.00	279.89	274.41
15000	1402.12	776.33	570.92	470.56	412.16	374.67	349.08	330.86	317.51	307.50	299.88	294.01
16000	1495.59	828.08	608.98	501.93	439.64	399.65	372.35	352.92	338.67	328.00	319.87	313.61
17000	1589.06	879.84	647.05	533.30	467.11	424.63	395.63	374.98	359.84	348.50	339.87	333.21
18000	1682.54	931.59	685.11	564.67	494.59	449.61	418.90	397.04	381.01	369.00	359.86	352.81
19000	1776.01	983.35	723.17	596.04	522.07	474.59	442.17	419.09	402.18	389.50	379.85	372.41
20000	1869.49	1035.10	761.23	627.42	549.54	499.56	465.44	441.15	423.34	410.00	399.84	392.01
21000	1962.96	1086.86	799.29	658.79	577.02	524.54	488.71	463.21	444.51	430.50	419.83	411.61
22000	2056.44	1138.61	837.35	690.16	604.50	549.52	511.98	485.27	465.68	451.00	439.83	431.21
23000	2149.91	1190.36	875.41	721.53	631.98	574.50	535.26	507.32	486.84	471.50	459.82	450.81
24000	2243.38	1242.12	913.47	752.90	659.45	599.48	558.53	529.38	508.01	492.00	479.81	470.41
25000	2336.86	1293.87	951.54	784.27	686.93	624.45	581.80	551.44	529.18	512.50	499.80	490.01
26000	2430.33	1345.63	989.60	815.64	714.41	649.43	605.07	573.49	550.34	533.00	519.79	509.62
27000	2523.81	1397.38	1027.66	847.01	741.88	674.41	628.34	595.55	571.51	553.50	539.78	529.22
28000	2617.28	1449.14	1065.72	878.38	769.36	699.39	651.62	617.61	592.68	574.00	559.78	548.82
29000	2710.75	1500.89	1103.78	909.75	796.84	724.37	674.89	639.67	613.84	594.50	579.77	568.42
30000	2804.23	1552.65	1141.84	941.12	824.31	749.34	698.16	661.72	635.01	615.00	599.76	588.02
31000	2897.70	1604.40	1179.90	972.49	851.79	774.32	721.43	683.78	656.18	635.50	619.75	607.62
32000	2991.18	1656.16	1217.96	1003.86	879.27	799.30	744.70	705.84	677.34	656.00	639.74	627.22
33000	3084.65	1707.91	1256.03	1035.23	906.74	824.28	767.97	727.90	698.51	676.50	659.74	646.82
34000	3178.12	1759.67	1294.09	1066.60	934.22	849.26	791.25	749.95	719.68	697.00	679.73	666.42
35000	3271.60	1811.42	1332.15	1097.97	961.70	874.23	814.52	772.01	740.84	717.50	699.72	686.02
37500	3505.28	1940.81	1427.30	1176.40	1030.39	936.68	872.70	827.15	793.76	768.75	749.70	735.02
40000	3738.97	2070.20	1522.45	1254.83	1099.08	999.12	930.88	882.30	846.68	819.99	799.68	784.02
42500	3972.65	2199.58	1617.61	1333.25	1167.78	1061.57	989.06	937.44	899.60	871.24	849.66	833.02
45000	4206.34	2328.97	1712.76	1411.68	1236.47	1124.01	1047.24	992.58	952.51	922.49	899.64	882.02
47500	4440.02	2458.36	1807.91	1490.10	1305.16	1186.46	1105.42	1047.73	1005.43	973.74	949.62	931.02
50000	4673.71	2587.74	1903.07	1568.53	1373.85	1248.90	1163.60	1102.87	1058.35	1024.99	999.60	980.02
52500	4907.40	2717.13	1998.22	1646.96	1442.55	1311.35	1221.77	1158.01	1111.26	1076.24	1049.58	1029.03
55000	5141.08	2846.52	2093.37	1725.38	1511.24	1373.79	1279.95	1213.16	1164.18	1127.49	1099.56	1078.03
57500	5374.77	2975.90	2188.53	1803.81	1579.93	1436.24	1338.13	1268.30	1217.10	1178.74	1149.54	1127.03
60000	5608.45	3105.29	2283.68	1882.24	1648.62	1498.68	1396.31	1323.44	1270.02	1229.99	1199.52	1176.03
65000	6075.82	3364.07	2473.99	2039.09	1786.01	1623.57	1512.67	1433.73	1375.85	1332.49	1299.47	1274.03
70000	6543.19	3622.84	2664.29	2195.94	1923.39	1748.46	1629.03	1544.02	1481.68	1434.99	1399.43	1372.03
75000	7010.56	3881.61	2854.60	2352.79	2060.78	1873.35	1745.39	1654.30	1587.52	1537.49	1499.39	1470.03
80000	7477.93	4140.39	3044.90	2509.65	2198.16	1998.24	1861.75	1764.59	1693.35	1639.98	1599.35	1568.04
85000	7945.30	4399.16	3235.21	2666.50	2335.55	2123.13	1978.11	1874.88	1799.19	1742.48	1699.31	1666.04
90000	8412.67	4657.94	3425.52	2823.35	2472.93	2248.02	2094.47	1985.16	1905.02	1844.98	1799.27	1764.04
95000	8880.04	4916.71	3615.82	2980.20	2610.32	2372.91	2210.83	2095.45	2010.86	1947.48	1899.23	1862.04
100000	9347.42	5175.48	3806.13	3137.06	2747.70	2497.80	2327.19	2205.73	2116.69	2049.98	1999.19	1960.04
105000	9814.79	5434.26	3996.44	3293.91	2885.09	2622.69	2443.54	2316.02	2222.52	2152.48	2099.15	2058.05
110000	10282.16	5693.03	4186.74	3450.76	3022.47	2747.58	2559.90	2426.31	2328.36	2254.98	2199.11	2156.05
115000	10749.53	5951.80	4377.05	3607.61	3159.86	2872.47	2676.26	2536.59	2434.19	2357.48	2299.07	2254.05
120000	11216.90	6210.58	4567.35	3764.47	3297.24	2997.36	2792.62	2646.88	2540.03	2459.97	2399.03	2352.05
125000	11684.27	6469.35	4757.66	3921.32	3434.62	3122.25	2908.98	2757.17	2645.86	2562.47	2498.99	2450.05
130000	12151.64	6728.13	4947.97	4078.17	3572.01	3247.14	3025.34	2867.45	2751.69	2664.97	2598.94	2548.06
135000	12619.01	6986.90	5138.27	4235.02	3709.39	3372.03	3141.70	2977.74	2857.53	2767.47	2698.90	2646.06
140000	13086.38	7245.67	5328.58	4391.88	3846.78	3496.92	3258.06	3088.03	2963.36	2869.97	2798.86	2744.06
145000	13553.75	7504.45	5518.89	4548.73	3984.16	3621.81	3374.42	3198.31	3069.20	2972.47	2898.82	2842.06
150000	14021.12	7763.22	5709.19	4705.58	4121.55	3746.70	3490.78	3308.60	3175.03	3074.97	2998.78	2940.06
155000	14488.49	8022.00	5899.50	4862.43	4258.93	3871.59	3607.13	3418.89	3280.87	3177.46	3098.74	3038.07
160000	14955.86	8280.77	6089.80	5019.29	4396.32	3996.48	3723.49	3529.17	3386.70	3279.96	3198.70	3136.07

AMOUNT OF LOAN	NUMBER OF YEARS IN TERM											
	13	14	15	16	17	18	19	20	25	30	35	40
$ 50	0.97	0.96	0.95	0.94	0.94	0.93	0.93	0.92	0.92	0.91	0.91	0.91
100	1.93	1.91	1.89	1.88	1.87	1.86	1.85	1.84	1.83	1.82	1.82	1.82
200	3.86	3.82	3.78	3.75	3.73	3.71	3.69	3.68	3.65	3.64	3.63	3.63
300	5.79	5.72	5.67	5.62	5.59	5.56	5.53	5.52	5.47	5.45	5.45	5.44
400	7.72	7.63	7.55	7.49	7.45	7.41	7.38	7.35	7.29	7.27	7.26	7.26
500	9.65	9.53	9.44	9.36	9.31	9.26	9.22	9.19	9.11	9.08	9.07	9.07
600	11.58	11.44	11.33	11.24	11.17	11.11	11.06	11.03	10.93	10.90	10.89	10.88
700	13.51	13.34	13.21	13.11	13.03	12.96	12.91	12.87	12.75	12.71	12.70	12.69
800	15.44	15.25	15.10	14.98	14.89	14.81	14.75	14.70	14.57	14.53	14.51	14.51
900	17.37	17.16	16.99	16.85	16.75	16.66	16.59	16.54	16.39	16.34	16.33	16.32
1000	19.30	19.06	18.87	18.72	18.61	18.51	18.44	18.38	18.21	18.16	18.14	18.13
2000	38.60	38.12	37.74	37.44	37.21	37.02	36.87	36.75	36.42	36.31	36.27	36.26
3000	57.89	57.18	56.61	56.16	55.81	55.53	55.30	55.12	54.63	54.46	54.41	54.39
4000	77.19	76.23	75.48	74.88	74.41	74.03	73.73	73.49	72.84	72.62	72.54	72.52
5000	96.48	95.29	94.35	93.60	93.01	92.54	92.16	91.86	91.05	90.77	90.68	90.65
6000	115.78	114.35	113.22	112.32	111.61	111.05	110.60	110.23	109.25	108.92	108.81	108.77
7000	135.08	133.40	132.09	131.04	130.22	129.56	129.03	128.61	127.46	127.08	126.95	126.90
8000	154.37	152.46	150.96	149.76	148.82	148.06	147.46	146.98	145.67	145.23	145.08	145.03
9000	173.67	171.52	169.83	168.48	167.42	166.57	165.89	165.35	163.88	163.38	163.22	163.16
10000	192.96	190.58	188.69	187.20	186.02	185.08	184.32	183.72	182.09	181.54	181.35	181.29
11000	212.26	209.63	207.56	205.92	204.62	203.58	202.76	202.09	200.29	199.69	199.49	199.42
12000	231.55	228.69	226.43	224.64	223.22	222.09	221.19	220.46	218.50	217.84	217.62	217.54
13000	250.85	247.75	245.30	243.36	241.83	240.60	239.62	238.83	236.71	236.00	235.75	235.67
14000	270.15	266.80	264.17	262.08	260.43	259.11	258.05	257.21	254.92	254.15	253.89	253.80
15000	289.44	285.86	283.04	280.80	279.03	277.61	276.48	275.58	273.13	272.30	272.02	271.93
16000	308.74	304.92	301.91	299.52	297.63	296.12	294.91	293.95	291.34	290.46	290.16	290.06
17000	328.03	323.98	320.78	318.24	316.23	314.63	313.35	312.32	309.54	308.61	308.29	308.19
18000	347.33	343.03	339.65	336.96	334.83	333.13	331.78	330.69	327.75	326.76	326.43	326.31
19000	366.63	362.09	358.52	355.68	353.43	351.64	350.21	349.06	345.96	344.92	344.56	344.44
20000	385.92	381.15	377.38	374.40	372.04	370.15	368.64	367.44	364.17	363.07	362.70	362.57
21000	405.22	400.20	396.25	393.12	390.64	388.66	387.07	385.81	382.38	381.22	380.83	380.70
22000	424.51	419.26	415.12	411.84	409.24	407.16	405.51	404.18	400.58	399.38	398.97	398.83
23000	443.81	438.32	433.99	430.56	427.84	425.67	423.94	422.55	418.79	417.53	417.10	416.96
24000	463.10	457.38	452.86	449.28	446.44	444.18	442.37	440.92	437.00	435.68	435.24	435.08
25000	482.40	476.43	471.73	468.00	465.04	462.69	460.80	459.29	455.21	453.84	453.37	453.21
26000	501.70	495.49	490.60	486.72	483.65	481.19	479.23	477.66	473.42	471.99	471.50	471.34
27000	520.99	514.55	509.47	505.44	502.25	499.70	497.66	496.04	491.63	490.14	489.64	489.47
28000	540.29	533.60	528.34	524.16	520.85	518.21	516.10	514.41	509.83	508.30	507.77	507.60
29000	559.58	552.66	547.20	542.88	539.45	536.71	534.53	532.78	528.04	526.45	525.91	525.72
30000	578.88	571.72	566.07	561.60	558.05	555.22	552.96	551.15	546.25	544.60	544.04	543.85
31000	598.18	590.78	584.94	580.32	576.65	573.73	571.39	569.52	564.46	562.75	562.18	561.98
32000	617.47	609.83	603.81	599.04	595.26	592.24	589.82	587.89	582.67	580.91	580.31	580.11
33000	636.77	628.89	622.68	617.76	613.86	610.74	608.26	606.27	600.87	599.06	598.45	598.24
34000	656.06	647.95	641.55	636.48	632.46	629.25	626.69	624.64	619.08	617.21	616.58	616.37
35000	675.36	667.00	660.42	655.20	651.06	647.76	645.12	643.01	637.29	635.37	634.72	634.49
37500	723.60	714.65	707.59	702.00	697.56	694.03	691.20	688.94	682.81	680.75	680.05	679.81
40000	771.84	762.29	754.76	748.80	744.07	740.29	737.28	734.87	728.33	726.13	725.39	725.14
42500	820.08	809.93	801.94	795.60	790.57	786.56	783.36	780.80	773.85	771.52	770.73	770.46
45000	868.32	857.58	849.11	842.40	837.08	832.83	829.44	826.72	819.37	816.90	816.06	815.78
47500	916.56	905.22	896.28	889.20	883.58	879.10	875.52	872.65	864.89	862.28	861.40	861.10
50000	964.80	952.86	943.45	936.00	930.08	925.37	921.60	918.58	910.41	907.67	906.73	906.42
52500	1013.04	1000.50	990.63	982.80	976.59	971.63	967.68	964.51	955.93	953.05	952.07	951.74
55000	1061.28	1048.15	1037.80	1029.60	1023.09	1017.90	1013.76	1010.44	1001.45	998.43	997.41	997.06
57500	1109.51	1095.79	1084.97	1076.40	1069.60	1064.17	1059.84	1056.37	1046.97	1043.82	1042.74	1042.38
60000	1157.75	1143.43	1132.14	1123.20	1116.10	1110.44	1105.92	1102.30	1092.49	1089.20	1088.08	1087.70
65000	1254.23	1238.72	1226.49	1216.80	1209.11	1202.97	1198.07	1194.15	1183.54	1179.96	1178.75	1178.34
70000	1350.71	1334.00	1320.83	1310.40	1302.11	1295.51	1290.23	1286.01	1274.58	1270.73	1269.43	1268.98
75000	1447.19	1429.29	1415.18	1404.00	1395.12	1388.05	1382.39	1377.87	1365.62	1361.50	1360.10	1359.62
80000	1543.67	1524.57	1509.52	1497.60	1488.13	1480.58	1474.55	1469.73	1456.66	1452.26	1450.77	1450.27
85000	1640.15	1619.86	1603.87	1591.20	1581.14	1573.12	1566.71	1561.59	1547.70	1543.03	1541.45	1540.91
90000	1736.63	1715.15	1698.21	1684.80	1674.15	1665.65	1658.87	1653.44	1638.74	1633.79	1632.12	1631.55
95000	1833.11	1810.43	1792.56	1778.40	1767.15	1758.19	1751.03	1745.30	1729.78	1724.56	1722.79	1722.19
100000	1929.59	1905.72	1886.90	1872.00	1860.16	1850.73	1843.19	1837.16	1820.82	1815.33	1813.46	1812.83
105000	2026.07	2001.00	1981.25	1965.60	1953.17	1943.26	1935.35	1929.02	1911.86	1906.09	1904.14	1903.47
110000	2122.55	2096.29	2075.59	2059.20	2046.18	2035.80	2027.51	2020.87	2002.90	1996.86	1994.81	1994.11
115000	2219.02	2191.57	2169.94	2152.80	2139.19	2128.33	2119.67	2112.73	2093.94	2087.63	2085.48	2084.76
120000	2315.50	2286.86	2264.28	2246.40	2232.19	2220.87	2211.83	2204.59	2184.98	2178.39	2176.16	2175.40
125000	2411.98	2382.15	2358.63	2340.00	2325.20	2313.41	2303.99	2296.45	2276.03	2269.16	2266.83	2266.04
130000	2508.46	2477.43	2452.97	2433.60	2418.21	2405.94	2396.14	2388.30	2367.07	2359.92	2357.50	2356.68
135000	2604.94	2572.72	2547.31	2527.20	2511.22	2498.48	2488.30	2480.16	2458.11	2450.69	2448.18	2447.32
140000	2701.42	2668.00	2641.66	2620.80	2604.22	2591.01	2580.46	2572.02	2549.15	2541.46	2538.85	2537.96
145000	2797.90	2763.29	2736.00	2714.40	2697.23	2683.55	2672.62	2663.88	2640.19	2632.22	2629.52	2628.60
150000	2894.38	2858.57	2830.35	2808.00	2790.24	2776.09	2764.78	2755.74	2731.23	2722.99	2720.19	2719.24
155000	2990.86	2953.86	2924.69	2901.60	2883.25	2868.62	2856.94	2847.59	2822.27	2813.75	2810.87	2809.89
160000	3087.34	3049.14	3019.04	2995.20	2976.26	2961.16	2949.10	2939.45	2913.31	2904.52	2901.54	2900.53

MONTHLY AMORTIZING PAYMENTS

AMOUNT OF LOAN	NUMBER OF YEARS IN TERM											
	1	2	3	4	5	6	7	8	9	10	11	12
$ 50	4.68	2.60	1.91	1.58	1.39	1.26	1.18	1.12	1.07	1.04	1.01	0.99
100	9.36	5.19	3.82	3.16	2.77	2.52	2.35	2.23	2.14	2.07	2.02	1.98
200	18.72	10.38	7.64	6.31	5.53	5.03	4.69	4.45	4.27	4.14	4.04	3.96
300	28.08	15.57	11.46	9.46	8.29	7.54	7.03	6.67	6.40	6.21	6.05	5.94
400	37.44	20.76	15.28	12.61	11.05	10.06	9.38	8.89	8.54	8.27	8.07	7.92
500	46.80	25.94	19.10	15.76	13.81	12.57	11.72	11.11	10.67	10.34	10.09	9.89
600	56.16	31.13	22.92	18.91	16.58	15.08	14.06	13.34	12.80	12.41	12.10	11.87
700	65.52	36.32	26.74	22.06	19.34	17.59	16.40	15.56	14.94	14.47	14.12	13.85
800	74.88	41.51	30.56	25.21	22.10	20.11	18.75	17.78	17.07	16.54	16.14	15.83
900	84.24	46.70	34.38	28.36	24.86	22.62	21.09	20.00	19.20	18.61	18.15	17.81
1000	93.60	51.88	38.20	31.51	27.62	25.13	23.43	22.22	21.34	20.67	20.17	19.78
2000	187.19	103.76	76.39	63.02	55.24	50.26	46.86	44.44	42.67	41.34	40.34	39.56
3000	280.79	155.64	114.58	94.52	82.86	75.38	70.28	66.66	64.00	62.01	60.50	59.34
4000	374.38	207.52	152.77	126.03	110.48	100.51	93.71	88.87	85.33	82.68	80.67	79.12
5000	467.98	259.40	190.96	157.54	138.10	125.64	117.13	111.09	106.66	103.35	100.84	98.90
6000	561.57	311.27	229.15	189.04	165.72	150.76	140.56	133.31	128.00	124.02	121.00	118.68
7000	655.17	363.15	267.34	220.55	193.34	175.89	163.99	155.52	149.33	144.69	141.17	138.46
8000	748.76	415.03	305.53	252.05	220.96	201.01	187.41	177.74	170.66	165.36	161.34	158.24
9000	842.35	466.91	343.72	283.56	248.58	226.14	210.84	199.96	191.99	186.03	181.50	178.02
10000	935.95	518.79	381.91	315.07	276.19	251.27	234.26	222.18	213.32	206.70	201.67	197.79
11000	1029.54	570.66	420.10	346.57	303.81	276.39	257.69	244.39	234.66	227.37	221.83	217.57
12000	1123.14	622.54	458.29	378.08	331.43	301.52	281.12	266.61	255.99	248.04	242.00	237.35
13000	1216.73	674.42	496.48	409.58	359.05	326.64	304.54	288.83	277.32	268.71	262.17	257.13
14000	1310.33	726.30	534.67	441.09	386.67	351.77	327.97	311.04	298.65	289.38	282.33	276.91
15000	1403.92	778.18	572.86	472.60	414.29	376.90	351.39	333.26	319.98	310.05	302.50	296.69
16000	1497.52	830.06	611.05	504.10	441.91	402.02	374.82	355.48	341.32	330.72	322.67	316.47
17000	1591.11	881.93	649.24	535.61	469.53	427.15	398.25	377.70	362.65	351.39	342.83	336.25
18000	1684.70	933.81	687.43	567.11	497.15	452.28	421.67	399.91	383.98	372.06	363.00	356.03
19000	1778.30	985.69	725.62	598.62	524.76	477.40	445.10	422.13	405.31	392.73	383.16	375.80
20000	1871.89	1037.57	763.81	630.13	552.38	502.53	468.52	444.35	426.64	413.40	403.33	395.58
21000	1965.49	1089.45	802.00	661.63	580.00	527.65	491.95	466.56	447.97	434.07	423.50	415.36
22000	2059.08	1141.32	840.19	693.14	607.62	552.78	515.38	488.78	469.31	454.74	443.66	435.14
23000	2152.68	1193.20	878.39	724.64	635.24	577.91	538.80	511.00	490.64	475.41	463.83	454.92
24000	2246.27	1245.08	916.58	756.15	662.86	603.03	562.23	533.21	511.97	496.08	484.00	474.70
25000	2339.86	1296.96	954.77	787.66	690.48	628.16	585.65	555.43	533.30	516.75	504.16	494.48
26000	2433.46	1348.84	992.96	819.16	718.10	653.28	609.08	577.65	554.63	537.42	524.33	514.26
27000	2527.05	1400.72	1031.15	850.67	745.72	678.41	632.51	599.87	575.97	558.09	544.49	534.04
28000	2620.65	1452.59	1069.34	882.18	773.33	703.54	655.93	622.08	597.30	578.76	564.66	553.82
29000	2714.24	1504.47	1107.53	913.68	800.95	728.66	679.36	644.30	618.63	599.43	584.83	573.59
30000	2807.84	1556.35	1145.72	945.19	828.57	753.79	702.78	666.52	639.96	620.10	604.99	593.37
31000	2901.43	1608.23	1183.91	976.69	856.19	778.91	726.21	688.73	661.29	640.77	625.16	613.15
32000	2995.03	1660.11	1222.10	1008.20	883.81	804.04	749.64	710.95	682.63	661.44	645.33	632.93
33000	3088.62	1711.98	1260.29	1039.71	911.43	829.17	773.06	733.17	703.96	682.10	665.49	652.71
34000	3182.21	1763.86	1298.48	1071.21	939.05	854.29	796.49	755.39	725.29	702.77	685.66	672.49
35000	3275.81	1815.74	1336.67	1102.72	966.67	879.42	819.91	777.60	746.62	723.44	705.83	692.27
37500	3509.79	1945.44	1432.15	1181.48	1035.71	942.23	878.48	833.15	799.95	775.12	756.24	741.72
40000	3743.78	2075.13	1527.62	1260.25	1104.76	1005.05	937.04	888.69	853.28	826.79	806.66	791.16
42500	3977.77	2204.83	1623.10	1339.01	1173.81	1067.87	995.61	944.23	906.61	878.47	857.07	840.61
45000	4211.75	2334.52	1718.58	1417.78	1242.86	1130.68	1054.17	999.77	959.94	930.14	907.49	890.06
47500	4445.74	2464.22	1814.05	1496.54	1311.90	1193.50	1112.74	1055.32	1013.27	981.82	957.90	939.50
50000	4679.72	2593.91	1909.53	1575.31	1380.95	1256.31	1171.30	1110.86	1066.60	1033.49	1008.32	988.95
52500	4913.71	2723.61	2005.00	1654.07	1450.00	1319.13	1229.87	1166.40	1119.93	1085.16	1058.74	1038.40
55000	5147.70	2853.30	2100.48	1732.84	1519.05	1381.94	1288.43	1221.94	1173.26	1136.84	1109.15	1087.85
57500	5381.68	2983.00	2195.96	1811.60	1588.09	1444.76	1347.00	1277.49	1226.59	1188.51	1159.57	1137.29
60000	5615.67	3112.69	2291.43	1890.37	1657.14	1507.57	1405.56	1333.03	1279.92	1240.19	1209.98	1186.74
65000	6083.64	3372.09	2482.38	2047.90	1795.23	1633.20	1522.69	1444.12	1386.58	1343.53	1310.81	1285.64
70000	6551.61	3631.48	2673.34	2205.43	1933.33	1758.83	1639.82	1555.20	1493.24	1446.88	1411.65	1384.53
75000	7019.58	3890.87	2864.29	2362.96	2071.42	1884.46	1756.95	1666.29	1599.90	1550.23	1512.48	1483.43
80000	7487.56	4150.26	3055.24	2520.49	2209.52	2010.10	1874.08	1777.37	1706.56	1653.58	1613.31	1582.32
85000	7955.53	4409.65	3246.19	2678.02	2347.61	2135.73	1991.21	1888.46	1813.22	1756.93	1714.14	1681.21
90000	8423.50	4669.04	3437.15	2835.55	2485.71	2261.36	2108.34	1999.54	1919.88	1860.28	1814.97	1780.11
95000	8891.47	4928.43	3628.10	2993.08	2623.80	2386.99	2225.47	2110.63	2026.54	1963.63	1915.80	1879.00
100000	9359.44	5187.82	3819.05	3150.61	2761.90	2512.62	2342.60	2221.71	2133.20	2066.97	2016.63	1977.90
105000	9827.41	5447.21	4010.00	3308.14	2899.99	2638.25	2459.73	2332.80	2239.85	2170.32	2117.47	2076.79
110000	10295.39	5706.60	4200.95	3465.67	3038.09	2763.88	2576.86	2443.88	2346.51	2273.67	2218.30	2175.69
115000	10763.36	5965.99	4391.91	3623.20	3176.18	2889.51	2693.99	2554.97	2453.17	2377.02	2319.13	2274.58
120000	11231.33	6225.38	4582.86	3780.73	3314.27	3015.14	2811.12	2666.05	2559.83	2480.37	2419.96	2373.48
125000	11699.30	6484.77	4773.81	3938.26	3452.37	3140.77	2928.25	2777.14	2666.49	2583.72	2520.79	2472.37
130000	12167.27	6744.17	4964.76	4095.80	3590.46	3266.40	3045.38	2888.23	2773.15	2687.06	2621.62	2571.27
135000	12635.25	7003.56	5155.72	4253.33	3728.56	3392.03	3162.51	2999.31	2879.81	2790.41	2722.45	2670.16
140000	13103.22	7262.95	5346.67	4410.86	3866.65	3517.66	3279.64	3110.40	2986.47	2893.76	2823.29	2769.06
145000	13571.19	7522.34	5537.62	4568.39	4004.75	3643.29	3396.77	3221.48	3093.13	2997.11	2924.12	2867.95
150000	14039.16	7781.73	5728.57	4725.92	4142.84	3768.92	3513.90	3332.57	3199.79	3100.46	3024.95	2966.85
155000	14507.13	8041.12	5919.53	4883.45	4280.94	3894.55	3631.03	3443.65	3306.45	3203.81	3125.78	3065.74
160000	14975.11	8300.51	6110.48	5040.98	4419.03	4020.19	3748.16	3554.74	3413.11	3307.16	3226.61	3164.63

AMOUNT OF LOAN	NUMBER OF YEARS IN TERM											
	13	14	15	16	17	18	19	20	25	30	35	40
$ 50	0.98	0.97	0.96	0.95	0.94	0.94	0.94	0.93	0.93	0.92	0.92	0.92
100	1.95	1.93	1.91	1.90	1.88	1.88	1.87	1.86	1.85	1.84	1.84	1.84
200	3.90	3.85	3.82	3.79	3.76	3.75	3.73	3.72	3.69	3.68	3.67	3.67
300	5.85	5.78	5.72	5.68	5.64	5.62	5.59	5.58	5.53	5.51	5.51	5.51
400	7.80	7.70	7.63	7.57	7.52	7.49	7.46	7.43	7.37	7.35	7.34	7.34
500	9.74	9.63	9.53	9.46	9.40	9.36	9.32	9.29	9.21	9.18	9.18	9.17
600	11.69	11.55	11.44	11.35	11.28	11.23	11.18	11.15	11.05	11.02	11.01	11.01
700	13.64	13.47	13.35	13.24	13.16	13.10	13.05	13.00	12.89	12.86	12.84	12.84
800	15.59	15.40	15.25	15.13	15.04	14.97	14.91	14.86	14.73	14.69	14.68	14.67
900	17.54	17.32	17.16	17.03	16.92	16.84	16.77	16.72	16.58	16.53	16.51	16.51
1000	19.48	19.25	19.06	18.92	18.80	18.71	18.63	18.58	18.42	18.36	18.35	18.34
2000	38.96	38.49	38.12	37.83	37.60	37.41	37.26	37.15	36.83	36.72	36.69	36.68
3000	58.44	57.73	57.18	56.74	56.39	56.11	55.89	55.72	55.24	55.08	55.03	55.01
4000	77.92	76.98	76.24	75.65	75.19	74.82	74.52	74.29	73.65	73.44	73.37	73.35
5000	97.40	96.22	95.29	94.56	93.98	93.52	93.15	92.86	92.07	91.80	91.72	91.69
6000	116.87	115.46	114.35	113.47	112.78	112.22	111.78	111.43	110.48	110.16	110.06	110.02
7000	136.35	134.70	133.41	132.38	131.57	130.93	130.41	130.00	128.89	128.52	128.40	128.36
8000	155.83	153.95	152.47	151.29	150.37	149.63	149.04	148.57	147.30	146.88	146.74	146.70
9000	175.31	173.19	171.52	170.21	169.16	168.33	167.67	167.14	165.72	165.24	165.09	165.03
10000	194.79	192.43	190.58	189.12	187.96	187.03	186.30	185.71	184.13	183.60	183.43	183.37
11000	214.26	211.68	209.64	208.03	206.75	205.74	204.93	204.28	202.54	201.96	201.77	201.70
12000	233.74	230.92	228.70	226.94	225.55	224.44	223.56	222.85	220.95	220.32	220.11	220.04
13000	253.22	250.16	247.75	245.85	244.34	243.14	242.19	241.42	239.37	238.68	238.45	238.38
14000	272.70	269.40	266.81	264.76	263.14	261.85	260.82	259.99	257.78	257.04	256.78	256.71
15000	292.18	288.65	285.87	283.67	281.93	280.55	279.44	278.56	276.19	275.40	275.14	275.05
16000	311.65	307.89	304.93	302.58	300.73	299.25	298.07	297.13	294.60	293.76	293.48	293.39
17000	331.13	327.13	323.98	321.50	319.52	317.95	316.70	315.71	313.02	312.12	311.82	311.72
18000	350.61	346.37	343.04	340.41	338.32	336.66	335.33	334.28	331.43	330.48	330.17	330.06
19000	370.09	365.62	362.10	359.32	357.11	355.36	353.96	352.85	349.84	348.84	348.51	348.40
20000	389.57	384.86	381.16	378.23	375.91	374.06	372.59	371.42	368.25	367.20	366.85	366.73
21000	409.04	404.10	400.21	397.14	394.70	392.77	391.22	389.99	386.67	385.56	385.19	385.07
22000	428.52	423.35	419.27	416.05	413.50	411.47	409.85	408.56	405.08	403.92	403.53	403.40
23000	448.00	442.59	438.33	434.96	432.29	430.17	428.48	427.13	423.49	422.28	421.88	421.74
24000	467.48	461.83	457.39	453.87	451.09	448.87	447.11	445.70	441.90	440.64	440.22	440.08
25000	486.96	481.07	476.44	472.79	469.88	467.58	465.74	464.27	460.32	459.00	458.56	458.41
26000	506.44	500.32	495.50	491.70	488.68	486.28	484.37	482.84	478.73	477.36	476.90	476.75
27000	525.91	519.56	514.56	510.61	507.47	504.98	503.00	501.41	497.14	495.72	495.25	495.09
28000	545.39	538.80	533.62	529.52	526.27	523.69	521.63	519.98	515.55	514.08	513.59	513.42
29000	564.87	558.04	552.67	548.43	545.07	542.39	540.26	538.55	533.97	532.44	531.93	531.76
30000	584.35	577.29	571.73	567.34	563.86	561.09	558.88	557.12	552.38	550.80	550.27	550.09
31000	603.83	596.53	590.79	586.25	582.66	579.79	577.51	575.69	570.79	569.16	568.61	568.43
32000	623.30	615.77	609.85	605.16	601.45	598.50	596.14	594.26	589.20	587.52	586.96	586.77
33000	642.78	635.02	628.90	624.08	620.25	617.20	614.77	612.83	607.61	605.88	605.30	605.10
34000	662.26	654.26	647.96	642.99	639.04	635.90	633.40	631.41	626.03	624.24	623.64	623.44
35000	681.74	673.50	667.02	661.90	657.84	654.61	652.03	649.98	644.44	642.60	641.98	641.78
37500	730.43	721.61	714.66	709.18	704.82	701.36	698.60	696.40	690.47	688.50	687.84	687.62
40000	779.13	769.71	762.31	756.45	751.81	748.12	745.18	742.83	736.50	734.40	733.69	733.46
42500	827.82	817.82	809.95	803.73	798.80	794.88	791.75	789.26	782.53	780.30	779.55	779.30
45000	876.52	865.93	857.60	851.01	845.79	841.63	838.32	835.68	828.56	826.20	825.41	825.14
47500	925.21	914.03	905.24	898.29	892.78	888.39	884.90	882.11	874.60	872.10	871.26	870.98
50000	973.91	962.14	952.88	945.57	939.76	935.15	931.47	928.53	920.63	918.00	917.12	916.82
52500	1022.60	1010.25	1000.53	992.84	986.75	981.91	978.04	974.96	966.66	963.90	962.97	962.66
55000	1071.30	1058.36	1048.17	1040.12	1033.74	1028.66	1024.62	1021.39	1012.69	1009.80	1008.83	1008.50
57500	1120.00	1106.46	1095.81	1087.40	1080.73	1075.42	1071.19	1067.81	1058.72	1055.70	1054.68	1054.34
60000	1168.69	1154.57	1143.46	1134.68	1127.72	1122.18	1117.76	1114.24	1104.75	1101.60	1100.54	1100.18
65000	1266.08	1250.78	1238.75	1229.23	1221.69	1215.69	1210.91	1207.09	1196.81	1193.40	1192.25	1191.87
70000	1363.47	1347.00	1334.03	1323.79	1315.67	1309.21	1304.06	1299.95	1288.87	1285.19	1283.96	1283.55
75000	1460.86	1443.21	1429.32	1418.35	1409.64	1402.72	1397.20	1392.80	1380.94	1376.99	1375.67	1375.23
80000	1558.25	1539.42	1524.61	1512.90	1503.62	1496.24	1490.35	1485.65	1473.00	1468.79	1467.38	1466.91
85000	1655.64	1635.64	1619.90	1607.46	1597.60	1589.75	1583.50	1578.51	1565.06	1560.59	1559.10	1558.59
90000	1753.03	1731.85	1715.19	1702.02	1691.57	1683.26	1676.64	1671.36	1657.12	1652.39	1650.81	1650.27
95000	1850.42	1828.06	1810.47	1796.57	1785.55	1776.78	1769.79	1764.21	1749.19	1744.19	1742.52	1741.96
100000	1947.81	1924.28	1905.76	1891.13	1879.52	1870.29	1862.94	1857.06	1841.25	1835.99	1834.23	1833.64
105000	2045.20	2020.49	2001.05	1985.68	1973.50	1963.81	1956.08	1949.92	1933.31	1927.79	1925.94	1925.32
110000	2142.59	2116.71	2096.34	2080.24	2067.47	2057.32	2049.23	2042.77	2025.37	2019.59	2017.65	2017.00
115000	2239.99	2212.92	2191.62	2174.80	2161.45	2150.84	2142.38	2135.62	2117.43	2111.39	2109.36	2108.68
120000	2337.38	2309.13	2286.91	2269.35	2255.43	2244.35	2235.52	2228.48	2209.50	2203.19	2201.07	2200.36
125000	2434.77	2405.35	2382.20	2363.91	2349.40	2337.87	2328.67	2321.33	2301.56	2294.99	2292.78	2292.05
130000	2532.16	2501.56	2477.49	2458.46	2443.38	2431.38	2421.82	2414.18	2393.62	2386.79	2384.50	2383.73
135000	2629.55	2597.77	2572.78	2553.02	2537.35	2524.89	2514.96	2507.04	2485.68	2478.58	2476.21	2475.41
140000	2726.94	2693.99	2668.06	2647.58	2631.33	2618.41	2608.11	2599.89	2577.74	2570.38	2567.92	2567.09
145000	2824.33	2790.20	2763.35	2742.13	2725.30	2711.92	2701.26	2692.74	2669.81	2662.18	2659.63	2658.77
150000	2921.72	2886.41	2858.64	2836.69	2819.28	2805.44	2794.40	2785.59	2761.87	2753.98	2751.34	2750.45
155000	3019.11	2982.63	2953.93	2931.25	2913.26	2898.95	2887.55	2878.45	2853.93	2845.78	2843.05	2842.14
160000	3116.50	3078.84	3049.21	3025.80	3007.23	2992.47	2980.70	2971.30	2945.99	2937.58	2934.76	2933.82

22.25% MONTHLY AMORTIZING PAYMENTS

AMOUNT OF LOAN	\$	NUMBER OF YEARS IN TERM										
		1	2	3	4	5	6	7	8	9	10	11	12

AMOUNT OF LOAN	1	2	3	4	5	6	7	8	9	10	11	12
50	4.69	2.61	1.92	1.59	1.39	1.27	1.18	1.12	1.08	1.05	1.02	1.00
100	9.38	5.21	3.84	3.17	2.78	2.53	2.36	2.24	2.15	2.09	2.04	2.00
200	18.75	10.41	7.67	6.33	5.56	5.06	4.72	4.48	4.30	4.17	4.07	4.00
300	28.12	15.61	11.50	9.50	8.33	7.59	7.08	6.72	6.45	6.26	6.11	5.99
400	37.49	20.81	15.33	12.66	11.11	10.11	9.44	8.96	8.60	8.34	8.14	7.99
500	46.86	26.01	19.16	15.83	13.89	12.64	11.80	11.19	10.75	10.43	10.18	9.98
600	56.23	31.21	23.00	18.99	16.66	15.17	14.15	13.43	12.90	12.51	12.21	11.98
700	65.61	36.41	26.83	22.15	19.44	17.70	16.51	15.67	15.05	14.59	14.24	13.98
800	74.98	41.61	30.66	25.32	22.21	20.22	18.87	17.91	17.20	16.68	16.28	15.97
900	84.35	46.81	34.49	28.48	24.99	22.75	21.23	20.14	19.35	18.76	18.31	17.97
1000	93.72	52.01	38.32	31.65	27.77	25.28	23.59	22.38	21.50	20.85	20.35	19.96
2000	187.43	104.01	76.64	63.29	55.53	50.55	47.17	44.76	43.00	41.69	40.69	39.92
3000	281.15	156.01	114.96	94.93	83.29	75.83	70.75	67.14	64.50	62.53	61.03	59.88
4000	374.86	208.01	153.28	126.57	111.05	101.10	94.33	89.51	85.99	83.37	81.37	79.84
5000	468.58	260.01	191.60	158.21	138.81	126.38	117.91	111.89	107.49	104.21	101.71	99.80
6000	562.29	312.02	229.92	189.86	166.57	151.65	141.49	134.27	128.99	125.05	122.05	119.75
7000	656.01	364.02	268.24	221.50	194.33	176.93	165.07	156.65	150.49	145.89	142.39	139.71
8000	749.72	416.02	306.56	253.14	222.09	202.20	188.65	179.02	171.98	166.73	162.74	159.67
9000	843.44	468.02	344.88	284.78	249.86	227.48	212.23	201.40	193.48	187.57	183.08	179.63
10000	937.15	520.02	383.20	316.42	277.62	252.75	235.81	223.78	214.98	208.41	203.42	199.59
11000	1030.87	572.02	421.52	348.07	305.38	278.03	259.39	246.16	236.48	229.25	223.76	219.54
12000	1124.58	624.03	459.84	379.71	333.14	303.30	282.97	268.53	257.97	250.09	244.10	239.50
13000	1218.30	676.03	498.16	411.35	360.90	328.58	306.55	290.91	279.47	270.93	264.44	259.46
14000	1312.01	728.03	536.48	442.99	388.66	353.85	330.13	313.29	300.97	291.77	284.78	279.42
15000	1405.73	780.03	574.80	474.63	416.42	379.13	353.71	335.67	322.47	312.61	305.12	299.38
16000	1499.44	832.03	613.12	506.28	444.18	404.40	377.29	358.04	343.96	333.45	325.47	319.33
17000	1593.16	884.03	651.44	537.92	471.95	429.68	400.87	380.42	365.46	354.29	345.81	339.29
18000	1686.87	936.04	689.76	569.56	499.71	454.95	424.46	402.80	386.96	375.13	366.15	359.25
19000	1780.59	988.04	728.08	601.20	527.47	480.22	448.04	425.17	408.46	395.97	386.49	379.21
20000	1874.30	1040.04	766.40	632.84	555.23	505.50	471.62	447.55	429.95	416.81	406.83	399.17
21000	1968.01	1092.04	804.72	664.49	582.99	530.77	495.20	469.93	451.45	437.65	427.17	419.12
22000	2061.73	1144.04	843.04	696.13	610.75	556.05	518.78	492.31	472.95	458.49	447.51	439.08
23000	2155.44	1196.04	881.36	727.77	638.51	581.32	542.36	514.68	494.45	479.33	467.85	459.04
24000	2249.16	1248.05	919.68	759.41	666.27	606.60	565.94	537.06	515.94	500.17	488.20	479.00
25000	2342.87	1300.05	958.00	791.05	694.04	631.87	589.52	559.44	537.44	521.01	508.54	498.96
26000	2436.59	1352.05	996.32	822.70	721.80	657.15	613.10	581.82	558.94	541.85	528.88	518.91
27000	2530.30	1404.05	1034.64	854.34	749.56	682.42	636.68	604.19	580.44	562.69	549.22	538.87
28000	2624.02	1456.05	1072.96	885.98	777.32	707.70	660.26	626.57	601.93	583.53	569.56	558.83
29000	2717.73	1508.05	1111.28	917.62	805.08	732.97	683.84	648.95	623.43	604.37	589.90	578.79
30000	2811.45	1560.06	1149.60	949.26	832.84	758.25	707.42	671.33	644.93	625.21	610.24	598.75
31000	2905.16	1612.06	1187.92	980.91	860.60	783.52	731.00	693.70	666.43	646.05	630.58	618.70
32000	2998.88	1664.06	1226.24	1012.55	888.36	808.80	754.58	716.08	687.92	666.89	650.93	638.66
33000	3092.59	1716.06	1264.56	1044.19	916.13	834.07	778.16	738.46	709.42	687.73	671.27	658.62
34000	3186.31	1768.06	1302.88	1075.83	943.89	859.35	801.74	760.84	730.92	708.57	691.61	678.58
35000	3280.02	1820.06	1341.20	1107.47	971.65	884.62	825.32	783.21	752.42	729.41	711.95	698.54
37500	3514.31	1950.07	1437.00	1186.58	1041.05	947.81	884.28	839.16	806.16	781.51	762.80	748.43
40000	3748.59	2080.07	1532.80	1265.68	1110.45	1010.99	943.23	895.10	859.90	833.61	813.66	798.33
42500	3982.88	2210.08	1628.60	1344.79	1179.86	1074.18	1002.18	951.04	913.65	885.71	864.51	848.22
45000	4217.17	2340.08	1724.40	1423.89	1249.26	1137.37	1061.13	1006.99	967.39	937.81	915.36	898.12
47500	4451.46	2470.09	1820.20	1503.00	1318.66	1200.55	1120.08	1062.93	1021.14	989.91	966.22	948.01
50000	4685.74	2600.09	1916.00	1582.10	1388.07	1263.74	1179.03	1118.87	1074.88	1042.01	1017.07	997.91
52500	4920.03	2730.09	2011.80	1661.21	1457.47	1326.93	1237.98	1174.82	1128.62	1094.11	1067.92	1047.80
55000	5154.32	2860.10	2107.60	1740.31	1526.87	1390.12	1296.94	1230.76	1182.37	1146.21	1118.77	1097.70
57500	5388.60	2990.10	2203.40	1819.42	1596.28	1453.30	1355.89	1286.70	1236.11	1198.31	1169.63	1147.59
60000	5622.89	3120.11	2299.20	1898.52	1665.68	1516.49	1414.84	1342.65	1289.85	1250.42	1220.48	1197.49
65000	6091.46	3380.12	2490.80	2056.73	1804.49	1642.86	1532.74	1454.53	1397.34	1354.62	1322.19	1297.28
70000	6560.04	3640.12	2682.40	2214.94	1943.29	1769.24	1650.64	1566.42	1504.83	1458.82	1423.89	1397.07
75000	7028.61	3900.13	2874.00	2373.15	2082.10	1895.61	1768.55	1678.31	1612.32	1563.02	1525.60	1496.86
80000	7497.18	4160.14	3065.60	2531.36	2220.90	2021.98	1886.45	1790.19	1719.80	1667.22	1627.31	1596.65
85000	7965.76	4420.15	3257.20	2689.57	2359.71	2148.36	2004.35	1902.08	1827.29	1771.42	1729.01	1696.44
90000	8434.33	4680.16	3448.80	2847.78	2498.52	2274.73	2122.26	2013.97	1934.78	1875.62	1830.72	1796.23
95000	8902.91	4940.17	3640.40	3005.99	2637.32	2401.10	2240.16	2125.85	2042.27	1979.82	1932.43	1896.02
100000	9371.48	5200.17	3832.00	3164.20	2776.13	2527.48	2358.06	2237.74	2149.75	2084.02	2034.13	1995.81
105000	9840.05	5460.18	4023.60	3322.41	2914.94	2653.85	2475.96	2349.63	2257.24	2188.22	2135.84	2095.60
110000	10308.63	5720.19	4215.19	3480.62	3053.74	2780.23	2593.87	2461.51	2364.73	2292.42	2237.54	2195.39
115000	10777.20	5980.20	4406.79	3638.83	3192.55	2906.60	2711.77	2573.40	2472.22	2396.62	2339.25	2295.18
120000	11245.77	6240.21	4598.39	3797.04	3331.35	3032.97	2829.67	2685.29	2579.70	2500.83	2440.96	2394.97
125000	11714.35	6500.22	4789.99	3955.25	3470.16	3159.35	2947.57	2797.18	2687.19	2605.03	2542.66	2494.76
130000	12182.92	6760.23	4981.59	4113.46	3608.97	3285.72	3065.48	2909.06	2794.68	2709.23	2644.37	2594.55
135000	12651.49	7020.23	5173.19	4271.67	3747.77	3412.09	3183.38	3020.95	2902.16	2813.43	2746.08	2694.34
140000	13120.07	7280.24	5364.79	4429.88	3886.58	3538.47	3301.28	3132.84	3009.65	2917.63	2847.78	2794.13
145000	13588.64	7540.25	5556.39	4588.09	4025.39	3664.84	3419.19	3244.72	3117.14	3021.83	2949.49	2893.92
150000	14057.22	7800.26	5747.99	4746.30	4164.19	3791.22	3537.09	3356.61	3224.63	3126.03	3051.20	2993.71
155000	14525.79	8060.27	5939.59	4904.51	4303.00	3917.59	3654.99	3468.50	3332.11	3230.23	3152.90	3093.50
160000	14994.36	8320.28	6131.19	5062.72	4441.80	4043.96	3772.89	3580.38	3439.60	3334.43	3254.61	3193.29

AMOUNT OF LOAN	NUMBER OF YEARS IN TERM											
	13	14	15	16	17	18	19	20	25	30	35	40
$ 50	0.99	0.98	0.97	0.96	0.95	0.95	0.95	0.94	0.94	0.93	0.93	0.93
100	1.97	1.95	1.93	1.92	1.90	1.89	1.89	1.88	1.87	1.86	1.86	1.86
200	3.94	3.89	3.85	3.83	3.80	3.78	3.77	3.76	3.73	3.72	3.71	3.71
300	5.90	5.83	5.78	5.74	5.70	5.67	5.65	5.64	5.59	5.57	5.57	5.57
400	7.87	7.78	7.70	7.65	7.60	7.56	7.54	7.51	7.45	7.43	7.42	7.42
500	9.84	9.72	9.63	9.56	9.50	9.45	9.42	9.39	9.31	9.29	9.28	9.28
600	11.80	11.66	11.55	11.47	11.40	11.34	11.30	11.27	11.18	11.14	11.13	11.13
700	13.77	13.61	13.48	13.38	♦3.30	13.23	13.18	13.14	13.04	13.00	12.99	12.99
800	15.73	15.55	15.40	15.29	15.20	15.12	15.07	15.02	14.90	14.86	14.84	14.84
900	17.70	17.49	17.33	17.20	17.10	17.01	16.95	16.90	16.76	16.71	16.70	16.69
1000	19.67	19.43	19.25	19.11	18.99	18.90	18.83	18.77	18.62	18.57	18.55	18.55
2000	39.33	38.86	38.50	38.21	37.98	37.80	37.66	37.54	37.24	37.14	37.10	37.09
3000	58.99	58.29	57.74	57.31	56.97	56.70	56.49	56.31	55.86	55.70	55.65	55.64
4000	78.65	77.72	76.99	76.42	75.96	75.60	75.31	75.08	74.47	74.27	74.20	74.18
5000	98.31	97.15	96.24	95.52	94.95	94.50	94.14	93.85	93.09	92.84	92.75	92.73
6000	117.97	116.58	115.48	114.62	113.94	113.40	112.97	112.62	111.71	111.40	111.30	111.27
7000	137.63	136.01	134.73	133.73	132.93	132.30	131.80	131.39	130.32	129.97	129.85	129.82
8000	157.29	155.44	153.98	152.83	151.92	151.20	150.62	150.16	148.94	148.54	148.40	148.36
9000	176.95	174.86	173.22	171.93	170.91	170.10	169.45	168.93	167.56	167.10	166.95	166.90
10000	196.61	194.29	192.47	191.03	189.90	188.99	188.28	187.70	186.17	185.67	185.50	185.45
11000	216.27	213.72	211.72	210.14	208.89	207.89	207.10	206.47	204.79	204.24	204.05	203.99
12000	235.94	233.15	230.96	229.24	227.88	226.79	225.93	225.24	223.41	222.80	222.60	222.54
13000	255.60	252.58	250.21	248.34	246.86	245.69	244.76	244.01	242.02	241.37	241.15	241.08
14000	275.26	272.01	269.46	267.45	265.85	264.59	263.59	262.78	260.64	259.94	259.70	259.63
15000	294.92	291.44	288.70	286.55	284.84	283.49	282.41	281.55	279.26	278.50	278.25	278.17
16000	314.58	310.87	307.95	305.65	303.83	302.39	301.24	300.32	297.88	297.07	296.80	296.72
17000	334.24	330.30	327.20	324.75	322.82	321.29	320.07	319.09	316.49	315.64	315.35	315.26
18000	353.90	349.72	346.44	343.86	341.81	340.19	338.89	337.86	335.11	334.20	333.90	333.80
19000	373.56	369.15	365.69	362.96	360.80	359.09	357.72	356.63	353.73	352.77	352.45	352.35
20000	393.22	388.58	384.94	382.06	379.79	377.98	376.55	375.40	372.34	371.34	371.00	370.89
21000	412.88	408.01	404.18	401.17	398.78	396.88	395.38	394.17	390.96	389.90	389.55	389.44
22000	432.54	427.44	423.43	420.27	417.77	415.78	414.20	412.94	409.58	408.47	408.10	407.98
23000	452.21	446.87	442.68	439.37	436.76	434.68	433.03	431.71	428.19	427.04	426.65	426.53
24000	471.87	466.30	461.92	458.48	455.75	453.58	451.86	450.48	446.81	445.60	445.20	445.07
25000	491.53	485.73	481.17	477.58	474.74	472.48	470.68	469.25	465.43	464.17	463.75	463.62
26000	511.19	505.15	500.42	496.68	493.72	491.38	489.51	488.02	484.04	482.74	482.30	482.16
27000	530.85	524.58	519.66	515.78	512.71	510.28	508.34	506.79	502.66	501.30	500.85	500.70
28000	550.51	544.01	538.91	534.89	531.70	529.18	527.17	525.56	521.28	519.87	519.40	519.25
29000	570.17	563.44	558.16	553.99	550.69	548.07	545.99	544.33	539.89	538.44	537.95	537.79
30000	589.83	582.87	577.40	573.09	569.68	566.97	564.82	563.10	558.51	557.00	556.50	556.34
31000	609.49	602.30	596.65	592.20	588.67	585.87	583.65	581.87	577.13	575.57	575.05	574.88
32000	629.15	621.73	615.90	611.30	607.66	604.77	602.47	600.64	595.75	594.14	593.60	593.43
33000	648.81	641.16	635.14	630.40	626.65	623.67	621.30	619.41	614.36	612.70	612.15	611.97
34000	668.47	660.59	654.39	649.50	645.64	642.57	640.13	638.18	632.98	631.27	630.70	630.51
35000	688.14	680.01	673.64	668.61	664.63	661.47	658.96	656.95	651.60	649.84	649.25	649.06
37500	737.29	728.59	721.75	716.37	712.10	708.72	706.02	703.88	698.14	696.25	695.63	695.42
40000	786.44	777.16	769.87	764.12	759.57	755.96	753.09	750.80	744.68	742.67	742.00	741.78
42500	835.59	825.73	817.99	811.88	807.05	803.21	800.16	797.73	791.22	789.08	788.38	788.14
45000	884.74	874.30	866.10	859.64	854.52	850.46	847.23	844.65	837.76	835.50	834.75	834.50
47500	933.90	922.87	914.22	907.39	901.99	897.71	894.30	891.58	884.31	881.92	881.13	880.86
50000	983.05	971.45	962.34	955.15	949.47	944.95	941.36	938.50	930.85	928.33	927.50	927.23
52500	1032.20	1020.02	1010.45	1002.91	996.94	992.20	988.43	985.43	977.39	974.75	973.88	973.59
55000	1081.35	1068.59	1058.57	1050.67	1044.41	1039.45	1035.50	1032.35	1023.93	1021.17	1020.25	1019.95
57500	1130.51	1117.16	1106.69	1098.42	1091.88	1086.69	1082.57	1079.28	1070.48	1067.58	1066.63	1066.31
60000	1179.66	1165.74	1154.80	1146.18	1139.36	1133.94	1129.64	1126.20	1117.02	1114.00	1113.00	1112.67
65000	1277.96	1262.88	1251.04	1241.70	1234.30	1228.44	1223.77	1220.05	1210.10	1206.83	1205.75	1205.39
70000	1376.27	1360.02	1347.27	1337.21	1329.25	1322.93	1317.91	1313.90	1303.19	1299.67	1298.50	1298.11
75000	1474.57	1457.17	1443.50	1432.73	1424.20	1417.43	1412.04	1407.75	1396.27	1392.50	1391.25	1390.84
80000	1572.87	1554.31	1539.74	1528.24	1519.14	1511.92	1506.18	1501.60	1489.36	1485.33	1484.00	1483.56
85000	1671.18	1651.46	1635.97	1623.75	1614.09	1606.42	1600.31	1595.45	1582.44	1578.16	1576.75	1576.28
90000	1769.48	1748.60	1732.20	1719.27	1709.03	1700.91	1694.45	1689.30	1675.52	1671.00	1669.50	1669.00
95000	1867.79	1845.74	1828.44	1814.78	1803.98	1795.41	1788.59	1783.15	1768.61	1763.83	1762.25	1761.72
100000	1966.09	1942.89	1924.67	1910.30	1898.93	1889.90	1882.72	1877.00	1861.69	1856.66	1855.00	1854.45
105000	2064.40	2040.03	2020.90	2005.81	1993.87	1984.40	1976.86	1970.85	1954.78	1949.50	1947.75	1947.17
110000	2162.70	2137.18	2117.14	2101.33	2088.82	2078.89	2070.99	2064.70	2047.86	2042.33	2040.50	2039.89
115000	2261.01	2234.32	2213.37	2196.84	2183.76	2173.38	2165.13	2158.55	2140.95	2135.16	2133.25	2132.61
120000	2359.31	2331.47	2309.60	2292.36	2278.71	2267.88	2259.27	2252.40	2234.03	2227.99	2226.00	2225.33
125000	2457.61	2428.61	2405.83	2387.87	2373.66	2362.37	2353.40	2346.25	2327.11	2320.83	2318.75	2318.06
130000	2555.92	2525.75	2502.07	2483.39	2468.60	2456.87	2447.54	2440.10	2420.20	2413.66	2411.50	2410.78
135000	2654.22	2622.90	2598.30	2578.90	2563.55	2551.36	2541.67	2533.95	2513.28	2506.49	2504.25	2503.50
140000	2752.53	2720.04	2694.53	2674.42	2658.49	2645.86	2635.81	2627.80	2606.37	2599.33	2597.00	2596.22
145000	2850.83	2817.19	2790.77	2769.93	2753.44	2740.35	2729.95	2721.65	2699.45	2692.16	2689.75	2688.94
150000	2949.14	2914.33	2887.00	2865.45	2848.39	2834.85	2824.08	2815.50	2792.54	2784.99	2782.49	2781.67
155000	3047.44	3011.48	2983.23	2960.96	2943.33	2929.34	2918.22	2909.35	2885.62	2877.82	2875.24	2874.39
160000	3145.74	3108.62	3079.47	3056.47	3038.28	3023.84	3012.35	3003.20	2978.71	2970.66	2967.99	2967.11

MONTHLY AMORTIZING PAYMENTS

AMOUNT OF LOAN	NUMBER OF YEARS IN TERM											
	1	2	3	4	5	6	7	8	9	10	11	12
$ 50	4.70	2.61	1.93	1.59	1.40	1.28	1.19	1.13	1.09	1.06	1.03	1.01
100	9.39	5.22	3.85	3.18	2.80	2.55	2.38	2.26	2.17	2.11	2.06	2.02
200	18.77	10.43	7.69	6.36	5.59	5.09	4.75	4.51	4.34	4.21	4.11	4.03
300	28.16	15.64	11.54	9.54	8.38	7.63	7.13	6.77	6.50	6.31	6.16	6.05
400	37.54	20.86	15.38	12.72	11.17	10.17	9.50	9.02	8.67	8.41	8.21	8.06
500	46.92	26.07	19.23	15.89	13.96	12.72	11.87	11.27	10.84	10.51	10.26	10.07
600	56.31	31.28	23.07	19.07	16.75	15.26	14.25	13.53	13.00	12.61	12.32	12.09
700	65.69	36.49	26.92	22.25	19.54	17.80	16.62	15.78	15.17	14.71	14.37	14.10
800	75.07	41.71	30.76	25.43	22.33	20.34	18.99	18.04	17.34	16.81	16.42	16.12
900	84.46	46.92	34.61	28.61	25.12	22.89	21.37	20.29	19.50	18.92	18.47	18.13
1000	93.84	52.13	38.45	31.78	27.91	25.43	23.74	22.54	21.67	21.02	20.52	20.14
2000	187.68	104.26	76.90	63.56	55.81	50.85	47.48	45.08	43.33	42.03	41.04	40.28
3000	281.51	156.38	115.35	95.34	83.72	76.28	71.21	67.62	65.00	63.04	61.56	60.42
4000	375.35	208.51	153.80	127.12	111.62	101.70	94.95	90.16	86.66	84.05	82.07	80.56
5000	469.18	260.63	192.25	158.90	139.52	127.12	118.68	112.70	108.32	105.06	102.59	100.69
6000	563.02	312.76	230.70	190.67	167.43	152.55	142.42	135.23	129.99	126.07	123.11	120.83
7000	656.85	364.88	269.15	222.45	195.33	177.97	166.15	157.77	151.65	147.08	143.62	140.97
8000	750.69	417.01	307.60	254.23	223.24	203.40	189.89	180.31	173.31	168.09	164.14	161.11
9000	844.52	469.13	346.05	286.01	251.14	228.82	213.63	202.85	194.98	189.11	184.66	181.24
10000	938.36	521.26	384.50	317.79	279.04	254.24	237.36	225.39	216.64	210.12	205.17	201.38
11000	1032.19	573.38	422.95	349.56	306.95	279.67	261.10	247.92	238.30	231.13	225.69	221.52
12000	1126.03	625.51	461.40	381.34	334.85	305.09	284.83	270.46	259.97	252.14	246.21	241.66
13000	1219.86	677.64	499.85	413.12	362.76	330.51	308.57	293.00	281.63	273.15	266.72	261.79
14000	1313.70	729.76	538.30	444.90	390.66	355.94	332.30	315.54	303.30	294.16	287.24	281.93
15000	1407.53	781.89	576.75	476.68	418.56	381.36	356.04	338.08	324.96	315.17	307.76	302.07
16000	1501.37	834.01	615.20	508.46	446.47	406.79	379.78	360.62	346.62	336.18	328.27	322.21
17000	1595.20	886.14	653.65	540.23	474.37	432.21	403.51	383.15	368.29	357.20	348.79	342.34
18000	1689.04	938.26	692.10	572.01	502.28	457.63	427.25	405.69	389.95	378.21	369.31	362.48
19000	1782.87	990.39	730.55	603.79	530.18	483.06	450.98	428.23	411.61	399.22	389.82	382.62
20000	1876.71	1042.51	769.00	635.57	558.08	508.48	474.72	450.77	433.28	420.23	410.34	402.76
21000	1970.54	1094.64	807.45	667.35	585.99	533.90	498.45	473.31	454.94	441.24	430.86	422.90
22000	2064.38	1146.76	845.90	699.12	613.89	559.33	522.19	495.84	476.60	462.25	451.37	443.03
23000	2158.21	1198.89	884.35	730.90	641.80	584.75	545.92	518.38	498.27	483.26	471.89	463.17
24000	2252.05	1251.01	922.80	762.68	669.70	610.18	569.66	540.92	519.93	504.27	492.41	483.31
25000	2345.88	1303.14	961.25	794.46	697.60	635.60	593.40	563.46	541.59	525.28	512.92	503.45
26000	2439.72	1355.27	999.69	826.24	725.51	661.02	617.13	586.00	563.26	546.30	533.44	523.58
27000	2533.55	1407.39	1038.14	858.02	753.41	686.45	640.87	608.53	584.92	567.31	553.96	543.72
28000	2627.39	1459.52	1076.59	889.79	781.32	711.87	664.60	631.07	606.59	588.32	574.47	563.86
29000	2721.23	1511.64	1115.04	921.57	809.22	737.29	688.34	653.61	628.25	609.33	594.99	584.00
30000	2815.06	1563.77	1153.49	953.35	837.12	762.72	712.07	676.15	649.91	630.34	615.51	604.13
31000	2908.90	1615.89	1191.94	985.13	865.03	788.14	735.81	698.69	671.58	651.35	636.03	624.27
32000	3002.73	1668.02	1230.39	1016.91	892.93	813.57	759.55	721.23	693.24	672.36	656.54	644.41
33000	3096.57	1720.14	1268.84	1048.68	920.84	838.99	783.28	743.76	714.90	693.37	677.06	664.55
34000	3190.40	1772.27	1307.29	1080.46	948.74	864.41	807.02	766.30	736.57	714.39	697.58	684.68
35000	3284.24	1824.39	1345.74	1112.24	976.64	889.84	830.75	788.84	758.23	735.40	718.09	704.82
37500	3518.82	1954.71	1441.87	1191.69	1046.40	953.40	890.09	845.19	812.39	787.92	769.38	755.17
40000	3753.41	2085.02	1537.99	1271.13	1116.16	1016.96	949.43	901.53	866.55	840.45	820.68	805.51
42500	3988.00	2215.33	1634.11	1350.58	1185.92	1080.52	1008.77	957.88	920.71	892.98	871.97	855.85
45000	4222.59	2345.65	1730.24	1430.02	1255.68	1144.07	1068.11	1014.22	974.87	945.51	923.26	906.20
47500	4457.18	2475.96	1826.36	1509.47	1325.44	1207.63	1127.45	1070.57	1029.03	998.04	974.55	956.54
50000	4691.76	2606.27	1922.49	1588.91	1395.20	1271.19	1186.79	1126.91	1083.18	1050.56	1025.84	1006.89
52500	4926.35	2736.59	2018.61	1668.36	1464.96	1334.75	1246.13	1183.26	1137.34	1103.09	1077.14	1057.23
55000	5160.94	2866.90	2114.73	1747.80	1534.72	1398.31	1305.47	1239.60	1191.50	1155.62	1128.43	1107.57
57500	5395.53	2997.22	2210.86	1827.25	1604.48	1461.87	1364.80	1295.95	1245.66	1208.15	1179.72	1157.92
60000	5630.12	3127.53	2306.98	1906.69	1674.24	1525.43	1424.14	1352.29	1299.82	1260.68	1231.01	1208.26
65000	6099.29	3388.16	2499.23	2065.58	1813.76	1652.55	1542.82	1464.98	1408.14	1365.73	1333.60	1308.95
70000	6568.47	3648.78	2691.48	2224.48	1953.28	1779.67	1661.50	1577.68	1516.46	1470.79	1436.18	1409.64
75000	7037.64	3909.41	2883.73	2383.37	2092.80	1906.79	1780.18	1690.37	1624.77	1575.84	1538.76	1510.33
80000	7506.82	4170.04	3075.97	2542.26	2232.32	2033.91	1898.86	1803.06	1733.09	1680.90	1641.35	1611.01
85000	7976.00	4430.66	3268.22	2701.15	2371.84	2161.03	2017.53	1915.75	1841.41	1785.96	1743.93	1711.70
90000	8445.17	4691.29	3460.47	2860.04	2511.36	2288.14	2136.21	2028.44	1949.73	1891.01	1846.52	1812.39
95000	8914.35	4951.92	3652.72	3018.93	2650.88	2415.26	2254.89	2141.13	2058.05	1996.07	1949.10	1913.08
100000	9383.52	5212.54	3844.97	3177.82	2790.40	2542.38	2373.57	2253.82	2166.36	2101.12	2051.68	2013.77
105000	9852.70	5473.17	4037.21	3336.71	2929.92	2669.50	2492.25	2366.51	2274.68	2206.18	2154.27	2114.46
110000	10321.88	5733.80	4229.46	3495.60	3069.44	2796.62	2610.93	2479.20	2383.00	2311.24	2256.85	2215.14
115000	10791.05	5994.43	4421.71	3654.49	3208.96	2923.74	2729.60	2591.89	2491.32	2416.29	2359.44	2315.83
120000	11260.23	6255.05	4613.96	3813.38	3348.48	3050.86	2848.28	2704.58	2599.63	2521.35	2462.02	2416.52
125000	11729.40	6515.68	4806.21	3972.27	3488.00	3177.98	2966.96	2817.27	2707.95	2626.40	2564.60	2517.21
130000	12198.58	6776.31	4998.45	4131.16	3627.52	3305.09	3085.64	2929.96	2816.27	2731.46	2667.19	2617.90
135000	12667.75	7036.93	5190.70	4290.06	3767.04	3432.21	3204.32	3042.65	2924.59	2836.51	2769.77	2718.58
140000	13136.93	7297.56	5382.95	4448.95	3906.56	3559.33	3322.99	3155.35	3032.91	2941.57	2872.35	2819.27
145000	13606.11	7558.19	5575.20	4607.84	4046.08	3686.45	3441.67	3268.04	3141.22	3046.63	2974.94	2919.96
150000	14075.28	7818.81	5767.45	4766.73	4185.60	3813.57	3560.35	3380.73	3249.54	3151.68	3077.52	3020.65
155000	14544.46	8079.44	5959.69	4925.62	4325.12	3940.69	3679.03	3493.42	3357.86	3256.74	3180.11	3121.34
160000	15013.63	8340.07	6151.94	5084.51	4464.64	4067.81	3797.71	3606.11	3466.18	3361.79	3282.69	3222.02

AMOUNT OF LOAN	13	14	15	16	17	18	19	20	25	30	35	40
$ 50	1.00	0.99	0.98	0.97	0.96	0.96	0.96	0.95	0.95	0.94	0.94	0.94
100	1.99	1.97	1.95	1.93	1.92	1.91	1.91	1.90	1.89	1.88	1.88	1.88
200	3.97	3.93	3.89	3.86	3.84	3.82	3.81	3.80	3.77	3.76	3.76	3.76
300	5.96	5.89	5.84	5.79	5.76	5.73	5.71	5.70	5.65	5.64	5.63	5.63
400	7.94	7.85	7.78	7.72	7.68	7.64	7.62	7.59	7.53	7.51	7.51	7.51
500	9.93	9.81	9.72	9.65	9.60	9.55	9.52	9.49	9.42	9.39	9.38	9.38
600	11.91	11.77	11.67	11.58	11.52	11.46	11.42	11.39	11.30	11.27	11.26	11.26
700	13.90	13.74	13.61	13.51	13.43	13.37	13.32	13.28	13.18	13.15	13.14	13.13
800	15.88	15.70	15.55	15.44	15.35	15.28	15.23	15.18	15.06	15.02	15.01	15.01
900	17.86	17.66	17.50	17.37	17.27	17.19	17.13	17.08	16.94	16.90	16.89	16.88
1000	19.85	19.62	19.44	19.30	19.19	19.10	19.03	18.97	18.83	18.78	18.76	18.76
2000	39.69	39.24	38.88	38.60	38.37	38.20	38.06	37.94	37.65	37.55	37.52	37.51
3000	59.54	58.85	58.31	57.89	57.56	57.29	57.08	56.91	56.47	56.33	56.28	56.26
4000	79.38	78.47	77.75	77.19	76.74	76.39	76.11	75.88	75.29	75.10	75.04	75.02
5000	99.23	98.08	97.19	96.48	95.92	95.48	95.13	94.85	94.11	93.87	93.79	93.77
6000	119.07	117.70	116.62	115.78	115.11	114.58	114.16	113.82	112.93	112.65	112.55	112.52
7000	138.91	137.31	136.06	135.07	134.29	133.67	133.18	132.79	131.76	131.42	131.31	131.27
8000	158.76	156.93	155.49	154.37	153.47	152.77	152.21	151.76	150.58	150.19	150.07	150.03
9000	178.60	176.54	174.93	173.66	172.66	171.86	171.23	170.73	169.40	168.97	168.82	168.78
10000	198.45	196.16	194.37	192.96	191.84	190.96	190.26	189.70	188.22	187.74	187.58	187.53
11000	218.29	215.77	213.80	212.25	211.03	210.05	209.28	208.67	207.04	206.51	206.34	206.28
12000	238.14	235.39	233.24	231.55	230.21	229.15	228.31	227.64	225.86	225.29	225.10	225.04
13000	257.98	255.01	252.68	250.84	249.39	248.25	247.33	246.61	244.68	244.06	243.85	243.79
14000	277.82	274.62	272.11	270.14	268.58	267.34	266.36	265.58	263.51	262.83	262.61	262.54
15000	297.67	294.24	291.55	289.43	287.76	286.44	285.39	284.55	282.33	281.61	281.37	281.29
16000	317.51	313.85	310.98	308.73	306.94	305.53	304.41	303.52	301.15	300.38	300.13	300.05
17000	337.36	333.47	330.42	328.02	326.13	324.63	323.44	322.49	319.97	319.15	318.89	318.80
18000	357.20	353.08	349.86	347.32	345.31	343.72	342.46	341.46	338.79	337.93	337.64	337.55
19000	377.04	372.70	369.29	366.61	364.49	362.82	361.49	360.43	357.61	356.70	356.40	356.30
20000	396.89	392.31	388.73	385.91	383.68	381.91	380.51	379.40	376.44	375.47	375.16	375.06
21000	416.73	411.93	408.16	405.20	402.86	401.01	399.54	398.37	395.26	394.25	393.92	393.81
22000	436.58	431.54	427.60	424.50	422.05	420.10	418.56	417.34	414.08	413.02	412.67	412.56
23000	456.42	451.16	447.04	443.79	441.23	439.20	437.59	436.31	432.90	431.79	431.43	431.31
24000	476.27	470.78	466.47	463.09	460.41	458.29	456.61	455.28	451.72	450.57	450.19	450.07
25000	496.11	490.39	485.91	482.38	479.60	477.39	475.64	474.25	470.54	469.34	468.95	468.82
26000	515.95	510.01	505.35	501.68	498.78	496.49	494.66	493.22	489.36	488.11	487.70	487.57
27000	535.80	529.62	524.78	520.97	517.96	515.58	513.69	512.19	508.19	506.89	506.46	506.32
28000	555.64	549.24	544.22	540.27	537.15	534.68	532.72	531.16	527.01	525.66	525.22	525.08
29000	575.49	568.85	563.65	559.56	556.33	553.77	551.74	550.13	545.83	544.43	543.98	543.83
30000	595.33	588.47	583.09	578.86	575.51	572.87	570.77	569.10	564.65	563.21	562.74	562.58
31000	615.17	608.08	602.53	598.15	594.70	591.96	589.79	588.07	583.47	581.98	581.49	581.33
32000	635.02	627.70	621.96	617.45	613.88	611.06	608.82	607.04	602.29	600.75	600.25	600.09
33000	654.86	647.31	641.40	636.74	633.07	630.15	627.84	626.01	621.11	619.53	619.01	618.84
34000	674.71	666.93	660.84	656.04	652.25	649.25	646.87	644.97	639.94	638.30	637.77	637.59
35000	694.55	686.55	680.27	675.33	671.43	668.34	665.89	663.94	658.76	657.07	656.52	656.34
37500	744.16	735.58	728.86	723.57	719.39	716.08	713.46	711.37	705.81	704.01	703.42	703.22
40000	793.77	784.62	777.45	771.81	767.35	763.82	761.02	758.79	752.87	750.94	750.31	750.11
42500	843.38	833.66	826.04	820.05	815.31	811.56	808.58	806.22	799.92	797.87	797.21	796.99
45000	892.99	882.70	874.63	868.28	863.27	859.30	856.15	853.64	846.97	844.81	844.10	843.87
47500	942.60	931.74	923.22	916.52	911.23	907.04	903.71	901.07	894.03	891.74	890.99	890.75
50000	992.21	980.78	971.81	964.76	959.19	954.78	951.27	948.49	941.08	938.67	937.89	937.63
52500	1041.82	1029.82	1020.40	1013.00	1007.15	1002.51	998.84	995.91	988.13	985.61	984.78	984.51
55000	1091.43	1078.85	1068.99	1061.23	1055.11	1050.25	1046.40	1043.34	1035.19	1032.54	1031.68	1031.39
57500	1141.04	1127.89	1117.59	1109.47	1103.06	1097.99	1093.96	1090.76	1082.24	1079.48	1078.57	1078.27
60000	1190.66	1176.93	1166.18	1157.71	1151.02	1145.73	1141.53	1138.19	1129.30	1126.41	1125.47	1125.16
65000	1289.88	1275.01	1263.36	1254.19	1246.94	1241.21	1236.65	1233.04	1223.40	1220.28	1219.25	1218.92
70000	1389.10	1373.09	1360.54	1350.66	1342.86	1336.68	1331.78	1327.88	1317.51	1314.14	1313.04	1312.68
75000	1488.32	1471.16	1457.72	1447.14	1438.78	1432.16	1426.91	1422.73	1411.62	1408.01	1406.83	1406.44
80000	1587.54	1569.24	1554.90	1543.61	1534.70	1527.64	1522.03	1517.58	1505.73	1501.88	1500.62	1500.21
85000	1686.76	1667.32	1652.08	1640.09	1630.61	1623.11	1617.16	1612.43	1599.83	1595.74	1594.41	1593.97
90000	1785.98	1765.39	1749.26	1736.56	1726.53	1718.59	1712.29	1707.28	1693.94	1689.61	1688.20	1687.73
95000	1885.20	1863.47	1846.44	1833.04	1822.45	1814.07	1807.42	1802.13	1788.05	1783.48	1781.98	1781.49
100000	1984.42	1961.55	1943.62	1929.51	1918.37	1909.55	1902.54	1896.98	1882.16	1877.34	1875.77	1875.26
105000	2083.64	2059.63	2040.80	2025.99	2014.29	2005.02	1997.67	1991.82	1976.26	1971.21	1969.56	1969.02
110000	2182.86	2157.70	2137.98	2122.46	2110.21	2100.50	2092.80	2086.67	2070.37	2065.08	2063.35	2062.78
115000	2282.08	2255.78	2235.17	2218.94	2206.12	2195.98	2187.92	2181.52	2164.48	2158.95	2157.14	2156.54
120000	2381.31	2353.86	2332.35	2315.42	2302.04	2291.45	2283.05	2276.37	2258.59	2252.81	2250.93	2250.31
125000	2480.53	2451.94	2429.53	2411.89	2397.96	2386.93	2378.18	2371.22	2352.69	2346.68	2344.71	2344.07
130000	2579.75	2550.01	2526.71	2508.37	2493.88	2482.41	2473.30	2466.07	2446.80	2440.55	2438.50	2437.83
135000	2678.97	2648.09	2623.89	2604.84	2589.80	2577.88	2568.43	2560.91	2540.91	2534.41	2532.29	2531.59
140000	2778.19	2746.17	2721.07	2701.32	2685.72	2673.36	2663.56	2655.76	2635.02	2628.28	2626.08	2625.36
145000	2877.41	2844.24	2818.25	2797.79	2781.63	2768.84	2758.68	2750.61	2729.12	2722.15	2719.87	2719.12
150000	2976.63	2942.32	2915.43	2894.27	2877.55	2864.32	2853.81	2845.46	2823.23	2816.01	2813.66	2812.88
155000	3075.85	3040.40	3012.61	2990.74	2973.47	2959.79	2948.94	2940.31	2917.34	2909.88	2907.44	2906.64
160000	3175.07	3138.48	3109.79	3087.22	3069.39	3055.27	3044.06	3035.16	3011.45	3003.75	3001.23	3000.41

MONTHLY AMORTIZING PAYMENTS

AMOUNT OF LOAN	NUMBER OF YEARS IN TERM											
	1	2	3	4	5	6	7	8	9	10	11	12
$ 50	4.70	2.62	1.93	1.60	1.41	1.28	1.20	1.14	1.10	1.06	1.04	1.02
100	9.40	5.23	3.86	3.20	2.81	2.56	2.39	2.27	2.19	2.12	2.07	2.04
200	18.80	10.45	7.72	6.39	5.61	5.12	4.78	4.54	4.37	4.24	4.14	4.07
300	28.19	15.68	11.58	9.58	8.42	7.68	7.17	6.81	6.55	6.36	6.21	6.10
400	37.59	20.90	15.44	12.77	11.22	10.23	9.56	9.08	8.74	8.48	8.28	8.13
500	46.98	26.13	19.29	15.96	14.03	12.79	11.95	11.35	10.92	10.60	10.35	10.16
600	56.38	31.35	23.15	19.15	16.83	15.35	14.34	13.62	13.10	12.71	12.42	12.20
700	65.77	36.58	27.01	22.35	19.64	17.91	16.73	15.89	15.29	14.83	14.49	14.23
800	75.17	41.80	30.87	25.54	22.44	20.46	19.12	18.16	17.47	16.95	16.56	16.26
900	84.57	47.03	34.73	28.73	25.25	23.02	21.51	20.43	19.65	19.07	18.63	18.29
1000	93.96	52.25	38.58	31.92	28.05	25.58	23.90	22.70	21.84	21.19	20.70	20.32
2000	187.92	104.50	77.16	63.83	56.10	51.15	47.79	45.40	43.67	42.37	41.39	40.64
3000	281.87	156.75	115.74	95.75	84.15	76.72	71.68	68.10	65.50	63.55	62.08	60.96
4000	375.83	209.00	154.32	127.66	112.19	102.30	95.57	90.80	87.33	84.74	82.78	81.28
5000	469.78	261.25	192.90	159.58	140.24	127.87	119.46	113.50	109.16	105.92	103.47	101.59
6000	563.74	313.50	231.48	191.49	168.29	153.44	143.35	136.20	130.99	127.10	124.16	121.91
7000	657.69	365.75	270.06	223.41	196.33	179.02	167.24	158.90	152.82	148.28	144.85	142.23
8000	751.65	418.00	308.64	255.32	224.38	204.59	191.13	181.60	174.65	169.47	165.55	162.55
9000	845.61	470.25	347.22	287.24	252.43	230.16	215.03	204.30	196.48	190.65	186.24	182.86
10000	939.56	522.50	385.80	319.15	280.48	255.74	238.92	227.00	218.31	211.83	206.93	203.18
11000	1033.52	574.75	424.38	351.07	308.52	281.31	262.81	249.70	240.14	233.01	227.63	223.50
12000	1127.47	627.00	462.96	382.98	336.57	306.88	286.70	272.40	261.97	254.20	248.32	243.82
13000	1221.43	679.25	501.54	414.90	364.62	332.46	310.59	295.10	283.80	275.38	269.01	264.14
14000	1315.38	731.49	540.12	446.81	392.66	358.03	334.48	317.80	305.63	296.56	289.70	284.45
15000	1409.34	783.74	578.70	478.72	420.71	383.60	358.37	340.50	327.46	317.75	310.40	304.77
16000	1503.30	835.99	617.28	510.64	448.76	409.18	382.26	363.20	349.29	338.93	331.09	325.09
17000	1597.25	888.24	655.86	542.55	476.80	434.75	406.16	385.90	371.12	360.11	351.78	345.41
18000	1691.21	940.49	694.44	574.47	504.85	460.32	430.05	408.59	392.95	381.29	372.48	365.72
19000	1785.16	992.74	733.02	606.38	532.90	485.90	453.94	431.29	414.78	402.48	393.17	386.04
20000	1879.12	1044.99	771.60	638.30	560.95	511.47	477.83	453.99	436.61	423.66	413.86	406.36
21000	1973.07	1097.24	810.18	670.21	588.99	537.04	501.72	476.69	458.44	444.84	434.55	426.68
22000	2067.03	1149.49	848.75	702.13	617.04	562.62	525.61	499.39	480.27	466.02	455.25	447.00
23000	2160.99	1201.74	887.33	734.04	645.09	588.19	549.50	522.09	502.10	487.21	475.94	467.31
24000	2254.94	1253.99	925.91	765.96	673.13	613.76	573.39	544.79	523.93	508.39	496.63	487.63
25000	2348.90	1306.24	964.49	797.87	701.18	639.34	597.28	567.49	545.76	529.57	517.33	507.95
26000	2442.85	1358.49	1003.07	829.79	729.23	664.91	621.18	590.19	567.59	550.76	538.02	528.27
27000	2536.81	1410.74	1041.65	861.70	757.27	690.48	645.07	612.89	589.42	571.94	558.71	548.58
28000	2630.76	1462.98	1080.23	893.62	785.32	716.06	668.96	635.59	611.25	593.12	579.40	568.90
29000	2724.72	1515.23	1118.81	925.53	813.37	741.63	692.85	658.29	633.08	614.30	600.10	589.22
30000	2818.68	1567.48	1157.39	957.44	841.42	767.20	716.74	680.99	654.91	635.49	620.79	609.54
31000	2912.63	1619.73	1195.97	989.36	869.46	792.78	740.63	703.69	676.74	656.67	641.48	629.86
32000	3006.59	1671.98	1234.55	1021.27	897.51	818.35	764.52	726.39	698.57	677.85	662.18	650.17
33000	3100.54	1724.23	1273.13	1053.19	925.56	843.92	788.41	749.09	720.40	699.03	682.87	670.49
34000	3194.50	1776.48	1311.71	1085.10	953.60	869.49	812.31	771.79	742.23	720.22	703.56	690.81
35000	3288.45	1828.73	1350.29	1117.02	981.65	895.07	836.20	794.48	764.06	741.40	724.25	711.13
37500	3523.34	1959.35	1446.74	1196.80	1051.77	959.00	895.92	851.23	818.64	794.36	775.99	761.92
40000	3758.23	2089.98	1543.19	1276.59	1121.89	1022.93	955.65	907.98	873.21	847.31	827.72	812.71
42500	3993.12	2220.60	1639.64	1356.38	1192.00	1086.87	1015.38	964.73	927.79	900.27	879.45	863.51
45000	4228.01	2351.22	1736.08	1436.16	1262.12	1150.80	1075.11	1021.48	982.36	953.23	931.18	914.30
47500	4462.90	2481.85	1832.53	1515.95	1332.24	1214.73	1134.84	1078.23	1036.94	1006.18	982.91	965.10
50000	4697.79	2612.47	1928.98	1595.74	1402.36	1278.67	1194.56	1134.98	1091.51	1059.14	1034.65	1015.89
52500	4932.68	2743.09	2025.43	1675.52	1472.47	1342.60	1254.29	1191.72	1146.09	1112.10	1086.38	1066.69
55000	5167.57	2873.71	2121.88	1755.31	1542.59	1406.53	1314.02	1248.47	1200.67	1165.05	1138.11	1117.48
57500	5402.46	3004.34	2218.33	1835.10	1612.71	1470.47	1373.75	1305.22	1255.24	1218.01	1189.84	1168.28
60000	5637.35	3134.96	2314.78	1914.88	1682.83	1534.40	1433.48	1361.97	1309.82	1270.97	1241.57	1219.07
65000	6107.13	3396.21	2507.68	2074.46	1823.06	1662.26	1552.93	1475.47	1418.97	1376.88	1345.04	1320.66
70000	6576.90	3657.45	2700.57	2234.03	1963.30	1790.13	1672.39	1588.96	1528.12	1482.80	1448.50	1422.25
75000	7046.68	3918.70	2893.47	2393.60	2103.53	1918.00	1791.84	1702.46	1637.27	1588.71	1551.97	1523.84
80000	7516.46	4179.95	3086.37	2553.18	2243.77	2045.86	1911.30	1815.96	1746.42	1694.62	1655.43	1625.42
85000	7986.24	4441.19	3279.27	2712.75	2384.00	2173.73	2030.76	1929.46	1855.57	1800.54	1758.89	1727.01
90000	8456.02	4702.44	3472.16	2872.32	2524.24	2301.60	2150.21	2042.95	1964.72	1906.45	1862.36	1828.60
95000	8925.80	4963.69	3665.06	3031.90	2664.47	2429.46	2269.67	2156.45	2073.87	2012.36	1965.82	1930.19
100000	9395.58	5224.93	3857.96	3191.47	2804.71	2557.33	2389.12	2269.95	2183.02	2118.28	2069.29	2031.78
105000	9865.35	5486.18	4050.86	3351.04	2944.94	2685.19	2508.58	2383.44	2292.18	2224.19	2172.75	2133.37
110000	10335.13	5747.42	4243.75	3510.62	3085.18	2813.06	2628.04	2496.94	2401.33	2330.10	2276.22	2234.96
115000	10804.91	6008.67	4436.65	3670.19	3225.41	2940.93	2747.49	2610.44	2510.48	2436.02	2379.68	2336.55
120000	11274.69	6269.92	4629.55	3829.76	3365.65	3068.79	2866.95	2723.94	2619.63	2541.93	2483.14	2438.13
125000	11744.47	6531.16	4822.45	3989.34	3505.88	3196.66	2986.40	2837.43	2728.78	2647.85	2586.61	2539.72
130000	12214.25	6792.41	5015.35	4148.91	3646.12	3324.52	3105.86	2950.93	2837.93	2753.76	2690.07	2641.31
135000	12684.03	7053.66	5208.24	4308.48	3786.35	3452.39	3225.31	3064.43	2947.08	2859.67	2793.54	2742.90
140000	13153.80	7314.90	5401.14	4468.06	3926.59	3580.26	3344.77	3177.92	3056.23	2965.59	2897.00	2844.49
145000	13623.58	7576.15	5594.04	4627.63	4066.82	3708.12	3464.23	3291.42	3165.38	3071.50	3000.46	2946.08
150000	14093.36	7837.40	5786.94	4787.20	4207.06	3835.99	3583.68	3404.92	3274.53	3177.41	3103.93	3047.67
155000	14563.14	8098.64	5979.83	4946.78	4347.29	3963.86	3703.14	3518.42	3383.69	3283.33	3207.39	3149.26
160000	15032.92	8359.89	6172.73	5106.35	4487.53	4091.72	3822.59	3631.91	3492.84	3389.24	3310.86	3250.84

AMOUNT OF LOAN	NUMBER OF YEARS IN TERM											
	13	14	15	16	17	18	19	20	25	30	35	40
$ 50	1.01	1.00	0.99	0.98	0.97	0.97	0.97	0.96	0.96	0.95	0.95	0.95
100	2.01	1.99	1.97	1.95	1.94	1.93	1.93	1.92	1.91	1.90	1.90	1.90
200	4.01	3.97	3.93	3.90	3.88	3.86	3.85	3.84	3.81	3.80	3.80	3.80
300	6.01	5.95	5.89	5.85	5.82	5.79	5.77	5.76	5.71	5.70	5.69	5.69
400	8.02	7.93	7.86	7.80	7.76	7.72	7.69	7.67	7.62	7.60	7.59	7.59
500	10.02	9.91	9.82	9.75	9.69	9.65	9.62	9.59	9.52	9.50	9.49	9.49
600	12.02	11.89	11.78	11.70	11.63	11.58	11.54	11.51	11.42	11.39	11.38	11.38
700	14.02	13.87	13.74	13.65	13.57	13.51	13.46	13.42	13.32	13.29	13.28	13.28
800	16.03	15.85	15.71	15.60	15.51	15.44	15.38	15.34	15.23	15.19	15.18	15.17
900	18.03	17.83	17.67	17.54	17.45	17.37	17.31	17.26	17.13	17.09	17.07	17.07
1000	20.03	19.81	19.63	19.49	19.38	19.30	19.23	19.17	19.03	18.99	18.97	18.97
2000	40.06	39.61	39.26	38.98	38.76	38.59	38.45	38.34	38.06	37.97	37.94	37.93
3000	60.09	59.41	58.88	58.47	58.14	57.88	57.68	57.51	57.08	56.95	56.90	56.89
4000	80.12	79.22	78.51	77.96	77.52	77.17	76.90	76.68	76.11	75.93	75.87	75.85
5000	100.14	99.02	98.14	97.44	96.90	96.47	96.12	95.85	95.14	94.91	94.83	94.81
6000	120.17	118.82	117.76	116.93	116.28	115.76	115.35	115.02	114.16	113.89	113.80	113.77
7000	140.20	138.62	137.39	136.42	135.65	135.05	134.57	134.19	133.19	132.87	132.76	132.73
8000	160.23	158.43	157.01	155.91	155.03	154.34	153.80	153.36	152.22	151.85	151.73	151.69
9000	180.26	178.23	176.64	175.39	174.41	173.63	173.02	172.53	171.24	170.83	170.69	170.65
10000	200.28	198.03	196.27	194.88	193.79	192.93	192.24	191.70	190.27	189.81	189.66	189.61
11000	220.31	217.83	215.89	214.37	213.17	212.22	211.47	210.87	209.29	208.79	208.62	208.57
12000	240.34	237.64	235.52	233.86	232.55	231.51	230.69	230.04	228.32	227.77	227.59	227.53
13000	260.37	257.44	255.15	253.34	251.93	250.80	249.92	249.21	247.35	246.75	246.56	246.49
14000	280.40	277.24	274.77	272.83	271.30	270.10	269.14	268.38	266.37	265.73	265.52	265.45
15000	300.42	297.04	294.40	292.32	290.68	289.39	288.36	287.55	285.40	284.71	284.49	284.41
16000	320.45	316.85	314.02	311.81	310.06	308.68	307.59	306.72	304.43	303.69	303.45	303.38
17000	340.48	336.65	333.65	331.30	329.44	327.97	326.81	325.89	323.45	322.67	322.42	322.34
18000	360.51	356.45	353.28	350.78	348.82	347.26	346.04	345.06	342.48	341.65	341.38	341.30
19000	380.54	376.25	372.90	370.27	368.20	366.56	365.26	364.23	361.51	360.63	360.35	360.26
20000	400.56	396.06	392.53	389.76	387.57	385.85	384.48	383.40	380.53	379.61	379.31	379.22
21000	420.59	415.86	412.15	409.25	406.95	405.14	403.71	402.57	399.56	398.59	398.28	398.18
22000	440.62	435.66	431.78	428.73	426.33	424.43	422.93	421.74	418.58	417.57	417.24	417.14
23000	460.65	455.46	451.41	448.22	445.71	443.73	442.15	440.91	437.61	436.55	436.21	436.10
24000	480.68	475.27	471.03	467.71	465.09	463.02	461.38	460.08	456.64	455.53	455.17	455.06
25000	500.70	495.07	490.66	487.20	484.47	482.31	480.60	479.25	475.66	474.51	474.14	474.02
26000	520.73	514.87	510.29	506.68	503.85	501.60	499.83	498.42	494.69	493.49	493.11	492.98
27000	540.76	534.67	529.91	526.17	523.22	520.89	519.05	517.59	513.72	512.47	512.07	511.94
28000	560.79	554.48	549.54	545.66	542.60	540.19	538.27	536.76	532.74	531.45	531.04	530.90
29000	580.82	574.28	569.16	565.15	561.98	559.48	557.50	555.93	551.77	550.43	550.00	549.86
30000	600.84	594.08	588.79	584.63	581.36	578.77	576.72	575.10	570.79	569.41	568.97	568.82
31000	620.87	613.88	608.42	604.12	600.74	598.06	595.95	594.27	589.82	588.39	587.93	587.78
32000	640.90	633.69	628.04	623.61	620.12	617.36	615.17	613.44	608.85	607.37	606.90	606.75
33000	660.93	653.49	647.67	643.10	639.50	636.65	634.39	632.61	627.87	626.36	625.86	625.71
34000	680.96	673.29	667.30	662.59	658.87	655.94	653.62	651.78	646.90	645.34	644.83	644.67
35000	700.98	693.09	686.92	682.07	678.25	675.23	672.84	670.95	665.93	664.32	663.80	663.63
37500	751.05	742.60	735.99	730.79	726.70	723.46	720.90	718.87	713.49	711.77	711.21	711.03
40000	801.12	792.11	785.05	779.51	775.14	771.69	768.96	766.79	761.06	759.22	758.62	758.43
42500	851.19	841.61	834.12	828.23	823.59	819.92	817.02	814.72	808.62	806.67	806.04	805.83
45000	901.26	891.12	883.18	876.95	872.04	868.15	865.08	862.64	856.19	854.12	853.45	853.23
47500	951.33	940.62	932.25	925.67	920.48	916.39	913.14	910.57	903.76	901.57	900.86	900.64
50000	1001.40	990.13	981.31	974.39	968.93	964.62	961.20	958.49	951.32	949.02	948.28	948.04
52500	1051.47	1039.64	1030.38	1023.11	1017.38	1012.85	1009.26	1006.42	998.89	996.47	995.69	995.44
55000	1101.54	1089.14	1079.45	1071.83	1065.82	1061.08	1057.32	1054.34	1046.45	1043.92	1043.10	1042.84
57500	1151.61	1138.65	1128.51	1120.55	1114.27	1109.31	1105.38	1102.26	1094.02	1091.37	1090.52	1090.24
60000	1201.68	1188.16	1177.58	1169.26	1162.71	1157.54	1153.44	1150.19	1141.58	1138.82	1137.93	1137.64
65000	1301.82	1287.17	1275.71	1266.70	1259.61	1254.00	1249.56	1246.04	1236.72	1233.73	1232.76	1232.45
70000	1401.96	1386.18	1373.84	1364.14	1356.50	1350.46	1345.68	1341.89	1331.85	1328.63	1327.59	1327.25
75000	1502.10	1485.19	1471.97	1461.58	1453.39	1446.92	1441.80	1437.73	1426.98	1423.53	1422.41	1422.05
80000	1602.24	1584.21	1570.10	1559.02	1550.28	1543.38	1537.92	1533.58	1522.11	1518.43	1517.24	1516.86
85000	1702.38	1683.22	1668.23	1656.46	1647.18	1639.84	1634.04	1629.43	1617.24	1613.33	1612.07	1611.66
90000	1802.52	1782.23	1766.36	1753.89	1744.07	1736.30	1730.16	1725.28	1712.37	1708.23	1706.90	1706.46
95000	1902.66	1881.24	1864.49	1851.33	1840.96	1832.77	1826.28	1821.13	1807.51	1803.13	1801.72	1801.27
100000	2002.80	1980.26	1962.62	1948.77	1937.85	1929.23	1922.40	1916.98	1902.64	1898.04	1896.55	1896.07
105000	2102.94	2079.27	2060.75	2046.21	2034.75	2025.69	2018.51	2012.83	1997.77	1992.94	1991.38	1990.87
110000	2203.08	2178.28	2158.89	2143.65	2131.64	2122.15	2114.63	2108.67	2092.90	2087.84	2086.20	2085.68
115000	2303.22	2277.30	2257.02	2241.09	2228.53	2218.61	2210.75	2204.52	2188.03	2182.74	2181.03	2180.48
120000	2403.36	2376.31	2355.15	2338.52	2325.42	2315.07	2306.87	2300.37	2283.16	2277.64	2275.86	2275.28
125000	2503.50	2475.32	2453.28	2435.96	2422.32	2411.53	2402.99	2396.22	2378.30	2372.54	2370.69	2370.08
130000	2603.64	2574.33	2551.41	2533.40	2519.21	2507.99	2499.11	2492.07	2473.43	2467.45	2465.51	2464.89
135000	2703.78	2673.35	2649.54	2630.84	2616.10	2604.45	2595.23	2587.92	2568.56	2562.35	2560.34	2559.69
140000	2803.92	2772.36	2747.67	2728.28	2712.99	2700.92	2691.35	2683.77	2663.69	2657.26	2655.17	2654.49
145000	2904.06	2871.37	2845.80	2825.72	2809.89	2797.38	2787.47	2779.61	2758.82	2752.15	2750.00	2749.30
150000	3004.20	2970.38	2943.93	2923.15	2906.78	2893.84	2883.59	2875.46	2853.95	2847.05	2844.82	2844.10
155000	3104.34	3069.40	3042.06	3020.59	3003.67	2990.30	2979.71	2971.31	2949.08	2941.95	2939.65	2938.90
160000	3204.48	3168.41	3140.19	3118.03	3100.56	3086.76	3075.83	3067.16	3044.22	3036.85	3034.48	3033.71

23.00% MONTHLY AMORTIZING PAYMENTS

AMOUNT OF LOAN	NUMBER OF YEARS IN TERM											
	1	2	3	4	5	6	7	8	9	10	11	12
$ 50	4.71	2.62	1.94	1.61	1.41	1.29	1.21	1.15	1.10	1.07	1.05	1.03
100	9.41	5.24	3.88	3.21	2.82	2.58	2.41	2.29	2.20	2.14	2.09	2.05
200	18.82	10.48	7.75	6.42	5.64	5.15	4.81	4.58	4.40	4.28	4.18	4.10
300	28.23	15.72	11.62	9.62	8.46	7.72	7.22	6.86	6.60	6.41	6.27	6.15
400	37.64	20.95	15.49	12.83	11.28	10.29	9.62	9.15	8.80	8.55	8.35	8.20
500	47.04	26.19	19.36	16.03	14.10	12.87	12.03	11.44	11.00	10.68	10.44	10.25
600	56.45	31.43	23.23	19.24	16.92	15.44	14.43	13.72	13.20	12.82	12.53	12.30
700	65.86	36.67	27.10	22.44	19.74	18.01	16.84	16.01	15.40	14.95	14.61	14.35
800	75.27	41.90	30.97	25.65	22.56	20.58	19.24	18.29	17.60	17.09	16.70	16.40
900	84.67	47.14	34.84	28.85	25.38	23.16	21.65	20.58	19.80	19.22	18.79	18.45
1000	94.08	52.38	38.71	32.06	28.20	25.73	24.05	22.87	22.00	21.36	20.87	20.50
2000	188.16	104.75	77.42	64.11	56.39	51.45	48.10	45.73	44.00	42.71	41.74	41.00
3000	282.23	157.12	116.13	96.16	84.58	77.17	72.15	68.59	66.00	64.07	62.61	61.50
4000	376.31	209.50	154.84	128.21	112.77	102.90	96.19	91.45	87.99	85.42	83.48	82.00
5000	470.39	261.87	193.55	160.26	140.96	128.62	120.24	114.31	109.99	106.78	104.35	102.50
6000	564.46	314.24	232.26	192.31	169.15	154.34	144.29	137.17	131.99	128.13	125.22	123.00
7000	658.54	366.62	270.97	224.37	197.34	180.07	168.34	160.03	153.99	149.49	146.09	143.49
8000	752.62	418.99	309.68	256.42	225.53	205.79	192.38	182.89	175.98	170.84	166.96	163.99
9000	846.69	471.36	348.39	288.47	253.72	231.51	216.43	205.76	197.98	192.20	187.83	184.49
10000	940.77	523.74	387.10	320.52	281.91	257.24	240.48	228.62	219.98	213.55	208.70	204.99
11000	1034.84	576.11	425.81	352.57	310.10	282.96	264.52	251.48	241.98	234.91	229.57	225.49
12000	1128.92	628.48	464.52	384.62	338.29	308.68	288.57	274.34	263.97	256.26	250.44	245.99
13000	1223.00	680.86	503.23	416.67	366.48	334.41	312.62	297.20	285.97	277.62	271.31	266.48
14000	1317.07	733.23	541.94	448.73	394.67	360.13	336.67	320.06	307.97	298.97	292.18	286.98
15000	1411.15	785.60	580.65	480.78	422.86	385.85	360.71	342.92	329.96	320.33	313.05	307.48
16000	1505.23	837.98	619.36	512.83	451.05	411.57	384.76	365.78	351.96	341.68	333.92	327.98
17000	1599.30	890.35	658.07	544.88	479.24	437.30	408.81	388.65	373.96	363.04	354.78	348.48
18000	1693.38	942.72	696.78	576.93	507.43	463.02	432.85	411.51	395.96	384.39	375.65	368.98
19000	1787.46	995.10	735.49	608.98	535.62	488.74	456.90	434.37	417.95	405.75	396.52	389.47
20000	1881.53	1047.47	774.20	641.03	563.81	514.47	480.95	457.23	439.95	427.10	417.39	409.97
21000	1975.61	1099.84	812.91	673.09	592.00	540.19	505.00	480.09	461.95	448.46	438.26	430.47
22000	2069.68	1152.22	851.62	705.14	620.20	565.91	529.04	502.95	483.95	469.81	459.13	450.97
23000	2163.76	1204.59	890.33	737.19	648.39	591.64	553.09	525.81	505.94	491.16	480.00	471.47
24000	2257.84	1256.96	929.04	769.24	676.58	617.36	577.14	548.67	527.94	512.52	500.87	491.97
25000	2351.91	1309.34	967.75	801.29	704.77	643.08	601.18	571.53	549.94	533.87	521.74	512.46
26000	2445.99	1361.71	1006.46	833.34	732.96	668.81	625.23	594.40	571.94	555.23	542.61	532.96
27000	2540.07	1414.08	1045.17	865.39	761.15	694.53	649.28	617.26	593.93	576.58	563.48	553.46
28000	2634.14	1466.46	1083.88	897.45	789.34	720.25	673.33	640.12	615.93	597.94	584.35	573.96
29000	2728.22	1518.83	1122.59	929.50	817.53	745.98	697.37	662.98	637.93	619.29	605.22	594.46
30000	2822.29	1571.20	1161.30	961.55	845.72	771.70	721.42	685.84	659.92	640.65	626.09	614.96
31000	2916.37	1623.58	1200.01	993.60	873.91	797.42	745.47	708.70	681.92	662.00	646.96	635.45
32000	3010.45	1675.95	1238.72	1025.65	902.10	823.14	769.52	731.56	703.92	683.36	667.83	655.95
33000	3104.52	1728.32	1277.43	1057.70	930.29	848.87	793.56	754.42	725.92	704.71	688.69	676.45
34000	3198.60	1780.70	1316.14	1089.76	958.48	874.59	817.61	777.29	747.91	726.07	709.56	696.95
35000	3292.68	1833.07	1354.85	1121.81	986.67	900.31	841.66	800.15	769.91	747.42	730.43	717.45
37500	3527.87	1964.00	1451.62	1201.94	1057.15	964.62	901.77	857.30	824.90	800.81	782.61	768.69
40000	3763.06	2094.94	1548.39	1282.06	1127.62	1028.93	961.89	914.45	879.90	854.20	834.78	819.94
42500	3998.25	2225.87	1645.17	1362.19	1198.10	1093.24	1022.01	971.61	934.89	907.58	886.95	871.19
45000	4233.44	2356.80	1741.94	1442.32	1268.58	1157.54	1082.13	1028.76	989.88	960.97	939.13	922.43
47500	4468.63	2487.74	1838.72	1522.45	1339.05	1221.85	1142.25	1085.91	1044.88	1014.36	991.30	973.68
50000	4703.82	2618.67	1935.49	1602.58	1409.53	1286.16	1202.36	1143.06	1099.87	1067.74	1043.47	1024.92
52500	4939.01	2749.60	2032.27	1682.71	1480.00	1350.47	1262.48	1200.22	1154.86	1121.13	1095.65	1076.17
55000	5174.20	2880.54	2129.04	1762.84	1550.48	1414.78	1322.60	1257.37	1209.86	1174.52	1147.82	1127.42
57500	5409.39	3011.47	2225.81	1842.96	1620.96	1479.08	1382.72	1314.52	1264.85	1227.90	1199.99	1178.66
60000	5644.58	3142.40	2322.59	1923.09	1691.43	1543.39	1442.84	1371.68	1319.84	1281.29	1252.17	1229.91
65000	6114.97	3404.27	2516.14	2083.35	1832.39	1672.01	1563.07	1485.98	1429.83	1388.07	1356.51	1332.40
70000	6585.35	3666.14	2709.69	2243.61	1973.34	1800.62	1683.31	1600.29	1539.82	1494.84	1460.86	1434.89
75000	7055.73	3928.00	2903.23	2403.87	2114.29	1929.24	1803.54	1714.59	1649.80	1601.61	1565.21	1537.38
80000	7526.11	4189.87	3096.78	2564.12	2255.24	2057.85	1923.78	1828.90	1759.79	1708.39	1669.56	1639.87
85000	7996.49	4451.74	3290.33	2724.38	2396.20	2186.47	2044.02	1943.21	1869.78	1815.16	1773.90	1742.37
90000	8466.87	4713.60	3483.88	2884.64	2537.15	2315.08	2164.25	2057.51	1979.76	1921.94	1878.25	1844.86
95000	8937.26	4975.47	3677.43	3044.89	2678.10	2443.70	2284.49	2171.82	2089.75	2028.71	1982.60	1947.35
100000	9407.64	5237.34	3870.98	3205.15	2819.05	2572.32	2404.72	2286.12	2199.74	2135.48	2086.94	2049.84
105000	9878.02	5499.20	4064.53	3365.41	2960.00	2700.93	2524.96	2400.43	2309.72	2242.26	2191.29	2152.33
110000	10348.40	5761.07	4258.07	3525.67	3100.96	2829.55	2645.20	2514.74	2419.71	2349.03	2295.64	2254.83
115000	10818.78	6022.94	4451.62	3685.92	3241.91	2958.16	2765.43	2629.04	2529.70	2455.80	2399.98	2357.32
120000	11289.16	6284.80	4645.17	3846.18	3382.86	3086.78	2885.67	2743.35	2639.68	2562.58	2504.33	2459.81
125000	11759.55	6546.67	4838.72	4006.44	3523.81	3215.39	3005.90	2857.65	2749.67	2669.35	2608.68	2562.30
130000	12229.93	6808.53	5032.27	4166.70	3664.77	3344.01	3126.14	2971.96	2859.66	2776.13	2713.02	2664.79
135000	12700.31	7070.40	5225.82	4326.95	3805.72	3472.62	3246.38	3086.27	2969.64	2882.90	2817.37	2767.29
140000	13170.69	7332.27	5419.37	4487.21	3946.67	3601.24	3366.61	3200.57	3079.63	2989.67	2921.72	2869.78
145000	13641.07	7594.13	5612.91	4647.47	4087.62	3729.86	3486.85	3314.88	3189.62	3096.45	3026.07	2972.27
150000	14111.45	7856.00	5806.46	4807.73	4228.58	3858.47	3607.08	3429.18	3299.60	3203.22	3130.41	3074.76
155000	14581.83	8117.87	6000.01	4967.98	4369.53	3987.09	3727.32	3543.49	3409.59	3310.00	3234.76	3177.25
160000	15052.22	8379.73	6193.56	5128.24	4510.48	4115.70	3847.56	3657.80	3519.58	3416.77	3339.11	3279.74

146

AMOUNT OF LOAN	13	14	15	16	17	18	19	20	25	30	35	40
$ 50	1.02	1.00	1.00	0.99	0.98	0.98	0.98	0.97	0.97	0.96	0.96	0.96
100	2.03	2.00	1.99	1.97	1.96	1.95	1.95	1.94	1.93	1.92	1.92	1.92
200	4.05	4.00	3.97	3.94	3.92	3.90	3.89	3.88	3.85	3.84	3.84	3.84
300	6.07	6.00	5.95	5.91	5.88	5.85	5.83	5.82	5.77	5.76	5.76	5.76
400	8.09	8.00	7.93	7.88	7.83	7.80	7.77	7.75	7.70	7.68	7.67	7.67
500	10.11	10.00	9.91	9.85	9.79	9.75	9.72	9.69	9.62	9.60	9.59	9.59
600	12.13	12.00	11.89	11.81	11.75	11.70	11.66	11.63	11.54	11.52	11.51	11.51
700	14.15	14.00	13.88	13.78	13.71	13.65	13.60	13.56	13.47	13.44	13.43	13.42
800	16.17	16.00	15.86	15.75	15.66	15.60	15.54	15.50	15.39	15.35	15.34	15.34
900	18.20	18.00	17.84	17.72	17.62	17.55	17.49	17.44	17.31	17.27	17.26	17.26
1000	20.22	20.00	19.82	19.69	19.58	19.49	19.43	19.38	19.24	19.19	19.18	19.17
2000	40.43	39.99	39.64	39.37	39.15	38.98	38.85	38.75	38.47	38.38	38.35	38.34
3000	60.64	59.98	59.45	59.05	58.73	58.47	58.27	58.12	57.70	57.57	57.52	57.51
4000	80.85	79.97	79.27	78.73	78.30	77.96	77.70	77.49	76.93	76.75	76.70	76.68
5000	101.07	99.96	99.09	98.41	97.87	97.45	97.12	96.86	96.16	95.94	95.87	95.85
6000	121.28	119.95	118.90	118.09	117.45	116.94	116.54	116.23	115.39	115.13	115.04	115.02
7000	141.49	139.94	138.72	137.77	137.02	136.43	135.96	135.60	134.62	134.32	134.22	134.19
8000	161.70	159.93	158.54	157.45	156.59	155.92	155.39	154.97	153.86	153.50	153.39	153.36
9000	181.92	179.92	178.35	177.13	176.17	175.41	174.81	174.34	173.09	172.69	172.56	172.52
10000	202.13	199.91	198.17	196.81	195.74	194.90	194.23	193.71	192.32	191.88	191.74	191.69
11000	222.34	219.90	217.99	216.49	215.32	214.39	213.66	213.08	211.55	211.07	210.91	210.86
12000	242.55	239.89	237.80	236.17	234.89	233.88	233.08	232.45	230.78	230.25	230.08	230.03
13000	262.76	259.88	257.62	255.85	254.46	253.37	252.50	251.82	250.01	249.44	249.26	249.20
14000	282.98	279.87	277.44	275.53	274.04	272.86	271.92	271.19	269.24	268.63	268.43	268.37
15000	303.19	299.86	297.25	295.21	293.61	292.35	291.35	290.56	288.47	287.81	287.60	287.54
16000	323.40	319.85	317.07	314.90	313.18	311.84	310.77	309.93	307.71	307.00	306.78	306.71
17000	343.61	339.84	336.89	334.58	332.76	331.32	330.19	329.30	326.94	326.19	325.95	325.87
18000	363.83	359.83	356.70	354.26	352.33	350.81	349.61	348.67	346.17	345.38	345.12	345.04
19000	384.04	379.82	376.52	373.94	371.91	370.30	369.04	368.04	365.40	364.56	364.30	364.21
20000	404.25	399.81	396.34	393.62	391.48	389.79	388.46	387.41	384.63	383.75	383.47	383.38
21000	424.46	419.80	416.15	413.30	411.05	409.28	407.88	406.78	403.86	402.94	402.64	402.55
22000	444.67	439.79	435.97	432.98	430.63	428.77	427.31	426.15	423.09	422.13	421.82	421.72
23000	464.89	459.78	455.79	452.66	450.20	448.26	446.73	445.52	442.32	441.31	440.99	440.89
24000	485.10	479.77	475.60	472.34	469.77	467.75	466.15	464.89	461.56	460.50	460.16	460.06
25000	505.31	499.76	495.42	492.02	489.35	487.24	485.57	484.26	480.79	479.69	479.34	479.22
26000	525.52	519.75	515.24	511.70	508.92	506.73	505.00	503.63	500.02	498.88	498.51	498.39
27000	545.74	539.74	535.05	531.38	528.50	526.22	524.42	523.00	519.25	518.06	517.68	517.56
28000	565.95	559.73	554.87	551.06	548.07	545.71	543.84	542.37	538.48	537.25	536.86	536.73
29000	586.16	579.72	574.69	570.74	567.64	565.20	563.27	561.74	557.71	556.44	556.03	555.90
30000	606.37	599.71	594.50	590.42	587.22	584.69	582.69	581.11	576.94	575.62	575.20	575.07
31000	626.58	619.70	614.32	610.11	606.79	604.18	602.11	600.48	596.18	594.81	594.38	594.24
32000	646.80	639.69	634.14	629.79	626.36	623.67	621.53	619.85	615.41	614.00	613.55	613.41
33000	667.01	659.68	653.95	649.47	645.94	643.16	640.96	639.22	634.64	633.19	632.72	632.57
34000	687.22	679.67	673.77	669.15	665.51	662.64	660.38	658.59	653.87	652.37	651.90	651.74
35000	707.43	699.66	693.59	688.83	685.09	682.13	679.80	677.96	673.10	671.56	671.07	670.91
37500	757.96	749.63	743.13	738.03	734.02	730.86	728.36	726.38	721.18	719.53	719.00	718.83
40000	808.50	799.61	792.67	787.23	782.95	779.58	776.92	774.81	769.26	767.50	766.94	766.76
42500	859.03	849.58	842.21	836.43	831.89	828.30	825.47	823.23	817.34	815.47	814.87	814.68
45000	909.56	899.56	891.75	885.63	880.82	877.03	874.03	871.66	865.41	863.43	862.80	862.60
47500	960.09	949.53	941.30	934.84	929.76	925.75	922.59	920.08	913.49	911.40	910.74	910.52
50000	1010.62	999.51	990.84	984.04	978.69	974.47	971.14	968.51	961.57	959.37	958.67	958.44
52500	1061.15	1049.48	1040.38	1033.24	1027.63	1023.20	1019.70	1016.93	1009.65	1007.34	1006.60	1006.37
55000	1111.68	1099.46	1089.92	1082.44	1076.56	1071.92	1068.26	1065.36	1057.73	1055.31	1054.53	1054.29
57500	1162.21	1149.43	1139.46	1131.64	1125.49	1120.65	1116.81	1113.78	1105.80	1103.28	1102.47	1102.21
60000	1212.74	1199.41	1189.00	1180.84	1174.43	1169.37	1165.37	1162.21	1153.88	1151.25	1150.40	1150.13
65000	1313.80	1299.36	1288.09	1279.25	1272.30	1266.82	1262.48	1259.06	1250.04	1247.18	1246.27	1245.98
70000	1414.86	1399.31	1387.17	1377.65	1370.17	1364.26	1359.60	1355.91	1346.20	1343.12	1342.13	1341.82
75000	1515.92	1499.26	1486.25	1476.05	1468.03	1461.71	1456.71	1452.76	1442.35	1439.05	1438.00	1437.66
80000	1616.99	1599.21	1585.34	1574.46	1565.90	1559.16	1553.83	1549.61	1538.51	1534.99	1533.87	1533.51
85000	1718.05	1699.16	1684.42	1672.86	1663.77	1656.60	1650.94	1646.46	1634.67	1630.93	1629.73	1629.35
90000	1819.11	1799.11	1783.50	1771.26	1761.64	1754.05	1748.05	1743.31	1730.82	1726.86	1725.60	1725.20
95000	1920.17	1899.06	1882.59	1869.67	1859.51	1851.50	1845.17	1840.16	1826.98	1822.80	1821.47	1821.04
100000	2021.23	1999.01	1981.67	1968.07	1957.38	1948.94	1942.28	1937.01	1923.13	1918.74	1917.33	1916.88
105000	2122.29	2098.96	2080.75	2066.47	2055.25	2046.39	2039.40	2033.86	2019.29	2014.67	2013.20	2012.73
110000	2223.35	2198.91	2179.83	2164.88	2153.11	2143.84	2136.51	2130.71	2115.45	2110.61	2109.06	2108.57
115000	2324.41	2298.86	2278.92	2263.28	2250.98	2241.29	2233.62	2227.56	2211.60	2206.55	2204.93	2204.41
120000	2425.48	2398.81	2378.00	2361.68	2348.85	2338.73	2330.74	2324.41	2307.76	2302.48	2300.80	2300.26
125000	2526.54	2498.77	2477.08	2460.09	2446.72	2436.18	2427.85	2421.26	2403.92	2398.42	2396.66	2396.10
130000	2627.60	2598.72	2576.17	2558.49	2544.59	2533.62	2524.96	2518.11	2500.07	2494.36	2492.53	2491.95
135000	2728.66	2698.67	2675.25	2656.89	2642.46	2631.07	2622.08	2614.96	2596.23	2590.29	2588.40	2587.79
140000	2829.72	2798.62	2774.33	2755.30	2740.33	2728.52	2719.19	2711.81	2692.39	2686.23	2684.26	2683.63
145000	2930.78	2898.57	2873.42	2853.70	2838.19	2825.97	2816.31	2808.66	2788.54	2782.16	2780.13	2779.48
150000	3031.84	2998.52	2972.50	2952.10	2936.06	2923.41	2913.42	2905.51	2884.70	2878.10	2876.00	2875.32
155000	3132.90	3098.47	3071.58	3050.51	3033.93	3020.86	3010.53	3002.36	2980.86	2974.04	2971.86	2971.17
160000	3233.97	3198.42	3170.67	3148.91	3131.80	3118.31	3107.65	3099.21	3077.01	3069.97	3067.73	3067.01

MONTHLY AMORTIZING PAYMENTS

AMOUNT OF LOAN	NUMBER OF YEARS IN TERM											
	1	2	3	4	5	6	7	8	9	10	11	12
$ 50	4.71	2.63	1.95	1.61	1.42	1.30	1.22	1.16	1.11	1.08	1.06	1.04
100	9.42	5.25	3.89	3.22	2.84	2.59	2.43	2.31	2.22	2.16	2.11	2.07
200	18.84	10.50	7.77	6.44	5.67	5.18	4.85	4.61	4.44	4.31	4.21	4.14
300	28.26	15.75	11.66	9.66	8.51	7.77	7.27	6.91	6.65	6.46	6.32	6.21
400	37.68	21.00	15.54	12.88	11.34	10.35	9.69	9.21	8.87	8.62	8.42	8.28
500	47.10	26.25	19.43	16.10	14.17	12.94	12.11	11.52	11.09	10.77	10.53	10.34
600	56.52	31.50	23.31	19.32	17.01	15.53	14.53	13.82	13.30	12.92	12.63	12.41
700	65.94	36.75	27.19	22.54	19.84	18.12	16.95	16.12	15.52	15.07	14.74	14.48
800	75.36	42.00	31.08	25.76	22.67	20.70	19.37	18.42	17.74	17.23	16.84	16.55
900	84.78	47.25	34.96	28.97	25.51	23.29	21.79	20.73	19.95	19.38	18.95	18.62
1000	94.20	52.50	38.85	32.19	28.34	25.88	24.21	23.03	22.17	21.53	21.05	20.68
2000	188.40	105.00	77.69	64.38	56.67	51.75	48.41	46.05	44.33	43.06	42.10	41.36
3000	282.60	157.50	116.53	96.57	85.01	77.63	72.62	69.08	66.50	64.59	63.14	62.04
4000	376.79	210.00	155.37	128.76	113.34	103.50	96.82	92.10	88.66	86.11	84.19	82.72
5000	470.99	262.49	194.21	160.95	141.68	129.37	121.02	115.12	110.83	107.64	105.24	103.40
6000	565.19	314.99	233.05	193.14	170.01	155.25	145.23	138.15	132.99	129.17	126.28	124.08
7000	659.38	367.49	271.89	225.33	198.35	181.12	169.43	161.17	155.16	150.70	147.33	144.76
8000	753.58	419.99	310.73	257.51	226.68	206.99	193.63	184.19	177.32	172.22	168.38	165.44
9000	847.78	472.48	349.57	289.70	255.01	232.87	217.84	207.22	199.49	193.75	189.42	186.12
10000	941.98	524.98	388.41	321.89	283.35	258.74	242.04	230.24	221.65	215.28	210.47	206.80
11000	1036.17	577.48	427.25	354.08	311.68	284.61	266.25	253.26	243.82	236.81	231.52	227.48
12000	1130.37	629.98	466.09	386.27	340.02	310.49	290.45	276.29	265.98	258.33	252.56	248.16
13000	1224.57	682.47	504.93	418.46	368.35	336.36	314.65	299.31	288.15	279.86	273.61	268.84
14000	1318.76	734.97	543.77	450.65	396.69	362.23	338.86	322.33	310.31	301.39	294.66	289.52
15000	1412.96	787.47	582.61	482.83	425.02	388.11	363.06	345.36	332.48	322.92	315.70	310.20
16000	1507.16	839.97	621.45	515.02	453.35	413.98	387.26	368.38	354.64	344.44	336.75	330.88
17000	1601.35	892.46	660.29	547.21	481.69	439.85	411.47	391.40	376.81	365.97	357.79	351.56
18000	1695.55	944.96	699.13	579.40	510.02	465.73	435.67	414.43	398.97	387.50	378.84	372.24
19000	1789.75	997.46	737.97	611.59	538.36	491.60	459.87	437.45	421.14	409.02	399.89	392.92
20000	1883.95	1049.96	776.81	643.78	566.69	517.47	484.08	460.47	443.30	430.55	420.93	413.60
21000	1978.14	1102.45	815.65	675.97	595.03	543.35	508.28	483.50	465.47	452.08	441.98	434.27
22000	2072.34	1154.95	854.49	708.15	623.36	569.22	532.49	506.52	487.63	473.61	463.03	454.95
23000	2166.54	1207.45	893.33	740.34	651.69	595.09	556.69	529.54	509.80	495.13	484.07	475.63
24000	2260.73	1259.95	932.17	772.53	680.03	620.97	580.89	552.57	531.96	516.66	505.12	496.31
25000	2354.93	1312.44	971.01	804.72	708.36	646.84	605.10	575.59	554.13	538.19	526.17	516.99
26000	2449.13	1364.94	1009.85	836.91	736.70	672.71	629.30	598.61	576.29	559.72	547.21	537.67
27000	2543.32	1417.44	1048.69	869.10	765.03	698.59	653.50	621.64	598.46	581.24	568.26	558.35
28000	2637.52	1469.94	1087.53	901.29	793.37	724.46	677.71	644.66	620.62	602.77	589.31	579.03
29000	2731.72	1522.43	1126.37	933.47	821.70	750.33	701.91	667.69	642.79	624.30	610.35	599.71
30000	2825.92	1574.93	1165.21	965.66	850.03	776.21	726.11	690.71	664.95	645.83	631.40	620.39
31000	2920.11	1627.43	1204.05	997.85	878.37	802.08	750.32	713.73	687.12	667.35	652.44	641.07
32000	3014.31	1679.93	1242.89	1030.04	906.70	827.95	774.52	736.76	709.28	688.88	673.49	661.75
33000	3108.51	1732.42	1281.73	1062.23	935.04	853.83	798.73	759.78	731.45	710.41	694.54	682.43
34000	3202.70	1784.92	1320.57	1094.42	963.37	879.70	822.93	782.80	753.61	731.93	715.58	703.11
35000	3296.90	1837.42	1359.41	1126.61	991.71	905.57	847.13	805.83	775.78	753.46	736.63	723.79
37500	3532.39	1968.66	1456.51	1207.08	1062.54	970.26	907.64	863.38	831.19	807.28	789.25	775.49
40000	3767.89	2099.91	1553.61	1287.55	1133.38	1034.94	968.15	920.94	886.60	861.10	841.86	827.19
42500	4003.38	2231.15	1650.71	1368.02	1204.21	1099.63	1028.66	978.50	942.02	914.92	894.48	878.88
45000	4238.87	2362.39	1747.81	1448.49	1275.05	1164.31	1089.17	1036.06	997.43	968.74	947.10	930.58
47500	4474.36	2493.64	1844.91	1528.96	1345.88	1228.99	1149.68	1093.62	1052.84	1022.55	999.71	982.28
50000	4709.86	2624.88	1942.01	1609.43	1416.72	1293.68	1210.19	1151.18	1108.25	1076.37	1052.33	1033.98
52500	4945.35	2756.12	2039.11	1689.91	1487.56	1358.36	1270.70	1208.74	1163.67	1130.19	1104.94	1085.68
55000	5180.84	2887.37	2136.21	1770.38	1558.39	1423.04	1331.21	1266.29	1219.08	1184.01	1157.56	1137.38
57500	5416.33	3018.61	2233.31	1850.85	1629.23	1487.73	1391.72	1323.85	1274.49	1237.83	1210.18	1189.08
60000	5651.83	3149.86	2330.41	1931.32	1700.06	1552.41	1452.22	1381.41	1329.90	1291.65	1262.79	1240.78
65000	6122.81	3412.34	2524.61	2092.26	1841.73	1681.78	1573.24	1496.53	1440.73	1399.28	1368.02	1344.17
70000	6593.80	3674.83	2718.82	2253.21	1983.41	1811.14	1694.26	1611.65	1551.55	1506.92	1473.26	1447.57
75000	7064.78	3937.32	2913.02	2414.15	2125.08	1940.51	1815.28	1726.76	1662.38	1614.56	1578.49	1550.97
80000	7535.77	4199.81	3107.22	2575.09	2266.75	2069.88	1936.30	1841.88	1773.20	1722.19	1683.72	1654.37
85000	8006.75	4462.29	3301.42	2736.04	2408.42	2199.25	2057.32	1957.00	1884.03	1829.83	1788.95	1757.76
90000	8477.74	4724.78	3495.62	2896.98	2550.09	2328.61	2178.33	2072.12	1994.85	1937.46	1894.19	1861.16
95000	8948.72	4987.27	3689.82	3057.92	2691.76	2457.98	2299.35	2187.23	2105.68	2045.10	1999.42	1964.56
100000	9419.71	5249.76	3884.02	3218.86	2833.43	2587.35	2420.37	2302.35	2216.50	2152.74	2104.65	2067.96
105000	9890.69	5512.24	4078.22	3379.81	2975.11	2716.71	2541.39	2417.47	2327.33	2260.38	2209.88	2171.35
110000	10361.68	5774.73	4272.42	3540.75	3116.78	2846.08	2662.41	2532.58	2438.15	2368.01	2315.11	2274.75
115000	10832.66	6037.22	4466.62	3701.69	3258.45	2975.45	2783.43	2647.70	2548.97	2475.65	2420.35	2378.15
120000	11303.65	6299.71	4660.82	3862.64	3400.12	3104.81	2904.44	2762.82	2659.80	2583.29	2525.58	2481.55
125000	11774.63	6562.19	4855.02	4023.58	3541.79	3234.18	3025.46	2877.94	2770.62	2690.92	2630.81	2584.94
130000	12245.62	6824.68	5049.22	4184.52	3683.46	3363.55	3146.48	2993.05	2881.45	2798.56	2736.04	2688.34
135000	12716.60	7087.17	5243.42	4345.47	3825.13	3492.92	3267.50	3108.17	2992.27	2906.20	2841.28	2791.74
140000	13187.59	7349.66	5437.63	4506.41	3966.81	3622.28	3388.52	3223.29	3103.10	3013.83	2946.51	2895.14
145000	13658.57	7612.14	5631.83	4667.35	4108.48	3751.65	3509.54	3338.41	3213.92	3121.47	3051.74	2998.53
150000	14129.56	7874.63	5826.03	4828.29	4250.15	3881.02	3630.55	3453.52	3324.75	3229.11	3156.97	3101.93
155000	14600.54	8137.12	6020.23	4989.24	4391.82	4010.38	3751.57	3568.64	3435.57	3336.74	3262.20	3205.33
160000	15071.53	8399.61	6214.43	5150.18	4533.49	4139.75	3872.59	3683.76	3546.40	3444.38	3367.44	3308.73

MONTHLY AMORTIZING PAYMENTS 23.25%

AMOUNT OF LOAN	NUMBER OF YEARS IN TERM											
	13	14	15	16	17	18	19	20	25	30	35	40
$ 50	1.02	1.01	1.01	1.00	0.99	0.99	0.99	0.98	0.98	0.97	0.97	0.97
100	2.04	2.02	2.01	1.99	1.98	1.97	1.97	1.96	1.95	1.94	1.94	1.94
200	4.08	4.04	4.01	3.98	3.96	3.94	3.93	3.92	3.89	3.88	3.88	3.88
300	6.12	6.06	6.01	5.97	5.94	5.91	5.89	5.88	5.84	5.82	5.82	5.82
400	8.16	8.08	8.01	7.95	7.91	7.88	7.85	7.83	7.78	7.76	7.76	7.76
500	10.20	10.09	10.01	9.94	9.89	9.85	9.82	9.79	9.72	9.70	9.70	9.69
600	12.24	12.11	12.01	11.93	11.87	11.82	11.78	11.75	11.67	11.64	11.63	11.63
700	14.28	14.13	14.01	13.92	13.84	13.79	13.74	13.70	13.61	13.58	13.57	13.57
800	16.32	16.15	16.01	15.90	15.82	15.75	15.70	15.66	15.55	15.52	15.51	15.51
900	18.36	18.17	18.01	17.89	17.80	17.72	17.66	17.62	17.50	17.46	17.45	17.44
1000	20.40	20.18	20.01	19.88	19.77	19.69	19.63	19.58	19.44	19.40	19.39	19.38
2000	40.80	40.36	40.02	39.75	39.54	39.38	39.25	39.15	38.88	38.79	38.77	38.76
3000	61.20	60.54	60.03	59.63	59.31	59.07	58.87	58.72	58.31	58.19	58.15	58.14
4000	81.59	80.72	80.04	79.50	79.08	78.75	78.49	78.29	77.75	77.58	77.53	77.51
5000	101.99	100.90	100.04	99.38	98.85	98.44	98.11	97.86	97.19	96.98	96.91	96.89
6000	122.39	121.07	120.05	119.25	118.62	118.13	117.74	117.43	116.62	116.37	116.29	116.27
7000	142.78	141.25	140.06	139.12	138.39	137.81	137.36	137.00	136.06	135.77	135.67	135.64
8000	163.18	161.43	160.07	159.00	158.16	157.50	156.98	156.57	155.50	155.16	155.05	155.02
9000	183.58	181.61	180.07	178.87	177.93	177.19	176.60	176.14	174.93	174.55	174.44	174.40
10000	203.98	201.79	200.08	198.75	197.70	196.87	196.22	195.71	194.37	193.95	193.82	193.77
11000	224.37	221.96	220.09	218.62	217.47	216.56	215.85	215.28	213.81	213.34	213.20	213.15
12000	244.77	242.14	240.10	238.49	237.24	236.25	235.47	234.85	233.24	232.74	232.58	232.53
13000	265.17	262.32	260.10	258.37	257.01	255.93	255.09	254.42	252.68	252.13	251.96	251.91
14000	285.56	282.50	280.11	278.24	276.78	275.62	274.71	273.99	272.12	271.53	271.34	271.28
15000	305.96	302.68	300.12	298.12	296.54	295.31	294.33	293.56	291.55	290.92	290.72	290.66
16000	326.36	322.85	320.13	317.99	316.31	315.00	313.96	313.14	310.99	310.32	310.10	310.04
17000	346.75	343.03	340.13	337.86	336.08	334.68	333.58	332.71	330.42	329.71	329.48	329.41
18000	367.15	363.21	360.14	357.74	355.85	354.37	353.20	352.28	349.86	349.10	348.87	348.79
19000	387.55	383.39	380.15	377.61	375.62	374.06	372.82	371.85	369.30	368.50	368.25	368.17
20000	407.95	403.57	400.16	397.49	395.39	393.74	392.44	391.42	388.73	387.89	387.63	387.54
21000	428.34	423.75	420.16	417.36	415.16	413.43	412.07	410.99	408.17	407.29	407.01	406.92
22000	448.74	443.92	440.17	437.23	434.93	433.12	431.69	430.56	427.61	426.68	426.39	426.30
23000	469.14	464.10	460.18	457.11	454.70	452.80	451.31	450.13	447.04	446.08	445.77	445.67
24000	489.53	484.28	480.19	476.98	474.47	472.49	470.93	469.70	466.48	465.47	465.15	465.05
25000	509.93	504.46	500.19	496.86	494.24	492.18	490.55	489.27	485.92	484.86	484.53	484.43
26000	530.33	524.64	520.20	516.73	514.01	511.86	510.18	508.84	505.35	504.26	503.91	503.81
27000	550.72	544.81	540.21	536.60	533.78	531.55	529.80	528.41	524.79	523.65	523.30	523.18
28000	571.12	564.99	560.22	556.48	553.55	551.24	549.42	547.98	544.23	543.05	542.68	542.56
29000	591.52	585.17	580.22	576.35	573.32	570.93	569.04	567.55	563.66	562.44	562.06	561.94
30000	611.92	605.35	600.23	596.23	593.08	590.61	588.66	587.12	583.10	581.84	581.44	581.31
31000	632.31	625.53	620.24	616.10	612.85	610.30	608.29	606.69	602.53	601.23	600.82	600.69
32000	652.71	645.70	640.25	635.98	632.62	629.99	627.91	626.27	621.97	620.63	620.20	620.07
33000	673.11	665.88	660.26	655.85	652.39	649.67	647.53	645.84	641.41	640.02	639.58	639.44
34000	693.50	686.06	680.26	675.72	672.16	669.36	667.15	665.41	660.84	659.41	658.96	658.82
35000	713.90	706.24	700.27	695.60	691.93	689.05	686.77	684.98	680.28	678.81	678.34	678.20
37500	764.89	756.68	750.29	745.28	741.35	738.26	735.83	733.90	728.87	727.29	726.80	726.64
40000	815.89	807.13	800.31	794.97	790.78	787.48	784.88	782.83	777.46	775.78	775.25	775.08
42500	866.88	857.57	850.32	844.65	840.20	836.70	833.94	831.76	826.05	824.27	823.70	823.52
45000	917.87	908.02	900.34	894.34	889.62	885.92	882.99	880.68	874.64	872.75	872.16	871.97
47500	968.86	958.46	950.36	944.02	939.05	935.13	932.05	929.61	923.24	921.24	920.61	920.41
50000	1019.86	1008.91	1000.38	993.71	988.47	984.35	981.10	978.54	971.83	969.72	969.06	968.85
52500	1070.85	1059.36	1050.40	1043.39	1037.89	1033.57	1030.16	1027.46	1020.42	1018.21	1017.51	1017.29
55000	1121.84	1109.80	1100.42	1093.08	1087.32	1082.79	1079.21	1076.39	1069.01	1066.70	1065.97	1065.74
57500	1172.83	1160.25	1150.44	1142.76	1136.74	1132.00	1128.27	1125.32	1117.60	1115.18	1114.42	1114.18
60000	1223.83	1210.69	1200.46	1192.45	1186.16	1181.22	1177.32	1174.24	1166.19	1163.67	1162.87	1162.62
65000	1325.81	1311.58	1300.49	1291.82	1285.01	1279.65	1275.43	1272.10	1263.37	1260.64	1259.78	1259.51
70000	1427.80	1412.47	1400.53	1391.19	1383.86	1378.09	1373.54	1369.95	1360.56	1357.61	1356.68	1356.39
75000	1529.78	1513.36	1500.57	1490.56	1482.70	1476.52	1471.65	1467.80	1457.74	1454.58	1453.59	1453.28
80000	1631.77	1614.25	1600.61	1589.93	1581.55	1574.96	1569.76	1565.66	1554.92	1551.56	1550.50	1550.16
85000	1733.75	1715.14	1700.64	1689.30	1680.40	1673.39	1667.87	1663.51	1652.10	1648.53	1647.40	1647.04
90000	1835.74	1816.03	1800.68	1788.67	1779.24	1771.83	1765.98	1761.36	1749.28	1745.50	1744.31	1743.93
95000	1937.72	1916.92	1900.72	1888.04	1878.09	1870.26	1864.09	1859.22	1846.47	1842.47	1841.21	1840.81
100000	2039.71	2017.82	2000.76	1987.41	1976.94	1968.70	1962.20	1957.07	1943.65	1939.44	1938.12	1937.70
105000	2141.69	2118.71	2100.80	2086.78	2075.78	2067.13	2060.31	2054.92	2040.83	2036.42	2035.02	2034.58
110000	2243.68	2219.60	2200.83	2186.15	2174.63	2165.57	2158.42	2152.78	2138.01	2133.39	2131.93	2131.47
115000	2345.66	2320.49	2300.87	2285.52	2273.48	2264.00	2256.53	2250.63	2235.20	2230.36	2228.83	2228.35
120000	2447.65	2421.38	2400.91	2384.89	2372.32	2362.43	2354.64	2348.48	2332.38	2327.33	2325.74	2325.24
125000	2549.63	2522.27	2500.95	2484.26	2471.17	2460.87	2452.75	2446.33	2429.56	2424.30	2422.65	2422.12
130000	2651.62	2623.16	2600.98	2583.63	2570.02	2559.30	2550.86	2544.19	2526.74	2521.27	2519.55	2519.01
135000	2753.60	2724.05	2701.02	2683.00	2668.86	2657.74	2648.97	2642.04	2623.92	2618.25	2616.46	2615.89
140000	2855.59	2824.94	2801.06	2782.38	2767.71	2756.17	2747.08	2739.89	2721.11	2715.22	2713.36	2712.78
145000	2957.58	2925.83	2901.10	2881.75	2866.56	2854.61	2845.19	2837.75	2818.29	2812.19	2810.27	2809.66
150000	3059.56	3026.72	3001.13	2981.12	2965.40	2953.04	2943.30	2935.60	2915.47	2909.16	2907.17	2906.55
155000	3161.55	3127.61	3101.17	3080.49	3064.25	3051.48	3041.41	3033.45	3012.65	3006.13	3004.08	3003.43
160000	3263.53	3228.50	3201.21	3179.86	3163.10	3149.91	3139.52	3131.31	3109.83	3103.11	3100.99	3100.32

149

MONTHLY AMORTIZING PAYMENTS

AMOUNT OF LOAN	NUMBER OF YEARS IN TERM											
	1	2	3	4	5	6	7	8	9	10	11	12
$ 50	4.72	2.64	1.95	1.62	1.43	1.31	1.22	1.16	1.12	1.09	1.07	1.05
100	9.44	5.27	3.90	3.24	2.85	2.61	2.44	2.32	2.24	2.18	2.13	2.09
200	18.87	10.53	7.80	6.47	5.70	5.21	4.88	4.64	4.47	4.35	4.25	4.18
300	28.30	15.79	11.70	9.70	8.55	7.81	7.31	6.96	6.70	6.52	6.37	6.26
400	37.73	21.05	15.59	12.94	11.40	10.41	9.75	9.28	8.94	8.69	8.49	8.35
500	47.16	26.32	19.49	16.17	14.24	13.02	12.19	11.60	11.17	10.86	10.62	10.44
600	56.60	31.58	23.39	19.40	17.09	15.62	14.62	13.92	13.40	13.03	12.74	12.52
700	66.03	36.84	27.28	22.63	19.94	18.22	17.06	16.24	15.64	15.20	14.86	14.61
800	75.46	42.10	31.18	25.87	22.79	20.82	19.49	18.55	17.87	17.37	16.98	16.69
900	84.89	47.36	35.08	29.10	25.64	23.43	21.93	20.87	20.10	19.54	19.11	18.78
1000	94.32	52.63	38.98	32.33	28.48	26.03	24.37	23.19	22.34	21.71	21.23	20.87
2000	188.64	105.25	77.95	64.66	56.96	52.05	48.73	46.38	44.67	43.41	42.45	41.73
3000	282.96	157.87	116.92	96.98	85.44	78.08	73.09	69.56	67.00	65.11	63.68	62.59
4000	377.28	210.49	155.89	129.31	113.92	104.10	97.45	92.75	89.34	86.81	84.90	83.45
5000	471.59	263.11	194.86	161.64	142.40	130.13	121.81	115.94	111.67	108.51	106.13	104.31
6000	565.91	315.74	233.83	193.96	170.88	156.15	146.17	139.12	134.00	130.21	127.35	125.17
7000	660.23	368.36	272.80	226.29	199.35	182.17	170.53	162.31	156.34	151.91	148.57	146.03
8000	754.55	420.98	311.77	258.61	227.83	208.20	194.89	185.49	178.67	173.61	169.80	166.89
9000	848.87	473.60	350.74	290.94	256.31	234.22	219.25	208.68	201.00	195.31	191.02	187.76
10000	943.18	526.22	389.71	323.27	284.79	260.25	243.61	231.87	223.34	217.01	212.25	208.62
11000	1037.50	578.85	428.68	355.59	313.27	286.27	267.97	255.05	245.67	238.71	233.47	229.48
12000	1131.82	631.47	467.65	387.92	341.75	312.29	292.33	278.24	268.00	260.41	254.69	250.34
13000	1226.14	684.09	506.63	420.24	370.23	338.32	316.69	301.43	290.34	282.11	275.92	271.20
14000	1320.45	736.71	545.60	452.57	398.70	364.34	341.05	324.61	312.67	303.81	297.14	292.06
15000	1414.77	789.33	584.57	484.90	427.18	390.37	365.41	347.80	335.00	325.51	318.37	312.92
16000	1509.09	841.95	623.54	517.22	455.66	416.39	389.77	370.98	357.33	347.21	339.59	333.78
17000	1603.41	894.58	662.51	549.55	484.14	442.42	414.14	394.17	379.67	368.91	360.81	354.64
18000	1697.73	947.20	701.48	581.87	512.62	468.44	438.50	417.36	402.00	390.61	382.04	375.51
19000	1792.04	999.82	740.45	614.20	541.10	494.46	462.86	440.54	424.33	412.31	403.26	396.37
20000	1886.36	1052.44	779.42	646.53	569.57	520.49	487.22	463.73	446.67	434.01	424.49	417.23
21000	1980.68	1105.06	818.39	678.85	598.05	546.51	511.58	486.92	469.00	455.71	445.71	438.09
22000	2075.00	1157.69	857.36	711.18	626.53	572.54	535.94	510.10	491.33	477.41	466.93	458.95
23000	2169.31	1210.31	896.33	743.50	655.01	598.56	560.30	533.29	513.67	499.11	488.16	479.81
24000	2263.63	1262.93	935.30	775.83	683.49	624.58	584.66	556.47	536.00	520.82	509.38	500.67
25000	2357.95	1315.55	974.28	808.16	711.97	650.61	609.02	579.66	558.33	542.52	530.61	521.53
26000	2452.27	1368.17	1013.25	840.48	740.45	676.63	633.38	602.85	580.67	564.22	551.83	542.39
27000	2546.59	1420.80	1052.22	872.81	768.92	702.66	657.74	626.03	603.00	585.92	573.05	563.26
28000	2640.90	1473.42	1091.19	905.13	797.40	728.68	682.10	649.22	625.33	607.62	594.28	584.12
29000	2735.22	1526.04	1130.16	937.46	825.88	754.70	706.46	672.40	647.66	629.32	615.50	604.98
30000	2829.54	1578.66	1169.13	969.79	854.36	780.73	730.82	695.59	670.00	651.02	636.73	625.84
31000	2923.86	1631.28	1208.10	1002.11	882.84	806.75	755.18	718.78	692.33	672.72	657.95	646.70
32000	3018.17	1683.90	1247.07	1034.44	911.32	832.78	779.54	741.96	714.66	694.42	679.17	667.56
33000	3112.49	1736.53	1286.04	1066.76	939.79	858.80	803.90	765.15	737.00	716.12	700.40	688.42
34000	3206.81	1789.15	1325.01	1099.09	968.27	884.83	828.27	788.34	759.33	737.82	721.62	709.28
35000	3301.13	1841.77	1363.98	1131.42	996.75	910.85	852.63	811.52	781.66	759.52	742.85	730.14
37500	3536.92	1973.33	1461.41	1212.23	1067.95	975.91	913.53	869.49	837.50	813.77	795.91	782.30
40000	3772.72	2104.88	1558.84	1293.05	1139.14	1040.97	974.43	927.45	893.33	868.02	848.97	834.45
42500	4008.51	2236.43	1656.26	1373.86	1210.34	1106.03	1035.33	985.42	949.16	922.27	902.03	886.60
45000	4244.31	2367.99	1753.69	1454.68	1281.54	1171.09	1096.23	1043.38	1004.99	976.52	955.09	938.76
47500	4480.10	2499.54	1851.12	1535.49	1352.73	1236.15	1157.13	1101.35	1060.83	1030.78	1008.15	990.91
50000	4715.89	2631.10	1948.55	1616.31	1423.93	1301.21	1218.03	1159.31	1116.66	1085.03	1061.21	1043.06
52500	4951.69	2762.65	2045.97	1697.12	1495.13	1366.27	1278.94	1217.28	1172.49	1139.28	1114.27	1095.21
55000	5187.48	2894.21	2143.40	1777.94	1566.32	1431.33	1339.84	1275.25	1228.32	1193.53	1167.33	1147.37
57500	5423.28	3025.76	2240.83	1858.75	1637.52	1496.39	1400.74	1333.21	1284.16	1247.78	1220.39	1199.52
60000	5659.07	3157.32	2338.25	1939.57	1708.71	1561.45	1461.64	1391.18	1339.99	1302.03	1273.45	1251.67
65000	6130.66	3420.43	2533.11	2101.20	1851.11	1691.57	1583.44	1507.11	1451.66	1410.53	1379.57	1355.98
70000	6602.25	3683.54	2727.96	2262.83	1993.50	1821.69	1705.25	1623.04	1563.32	1519.04	1485.69	1460.28
75000	7073.84	3946.65	2922.82	2424.46	2135.89	1951.82	1827.05	1738.97	1674.99	1627.54	1591.81	1564.59
80000	7545.43	4209.75	3117.67	2586.09	2278.28	2081.94	1948.85	1854.90	1786.65	1736.04	1697.93	1668.90
85000	8017.02	4472.86	3312.52	2747.72	2420.68	2212.06	2070.66	1970.83	1898.32	1844.54	1804.05	1773.20
90000	8488.61	4735.97	3507.38	2909.35	2563.07	2342.18	2192.46	2086.76	2009.98	1953.04	1910.17	1877.51
95000	8960.20	4999.08	3702.23	3070.98	2705.46	2472.30	2314.26	2202.69	2121.65	2061.55	2016.29	1981.81
100000	9431.78	5262.19	3897.09	3232.61	2847.85	2602.42	2436.06	2318.62	2233.31	2170.05	2122.41	2086.12
105000	9903.37	5525.30	4091.94	3394.24	2990.25	2732.54	2557.87	2434.56	2344.98	2278.55	2228.53	2190.42
110000	10374.96	5788.41	4286.79	3555.87	3132.64	2862.66	2679.67	2550.49	2456.64	2387.05	2334.65	2294.73
115000	10846.55	6051.52	4481.65	3717.50	3275.03	2992.78	2801.47	2666.42	2568.31	2495.55	2440.77	2399.04
120000	11318.14	6314.63	4676.50	3879.13	3417.42	3122.90	2923.28	2782.35	2679.98	2604.06	2546.89	2503.34
125000	11789.73	6577.74	4871.36	4040.76	3559.82	3253.02	3045.08	2898.28	2791.64	2712.56	2653.01	2607.65
130000	12261.32	6840.85	5066.21	4202.39	3702.21	3383.14	3166.88	3014.21	2903.31	2821.06	2759.13	2711.95
135000	12732.91	7103.96	5261.06	4364.02	3844.60	3513.26	3288.68	3130.14	3014.97	2929.56	2865.25	2816.26
140000	13204.50	7367.07	5455.92	4525.65	3986.99	3643.38	3410.49	3246.07	3126.64	3038.07	2971.37	2920.56
145000	13676.08	7630.18	5650.77	4687.28	4129.38	3773.50	3532.29	3362.00	3238.30	3146.57	3077.49	3024.87
150000	14147.67	7893.29	5845.63	4848.91	4271.78	3903.63	3654.09	3477.93	3349.97	3255.07	3183.61	3129.18
155000	14619.26	8156.40	6040.48	5010.54	4414.17	4033.75	3775.90	3593.87	3461.63	3363.57	3289.73	3233.48
160000	15090.85	8419.50	6235.33	5172.17	4556.56	4163.87	3897.70	3709.80	3573.30	3472.07	3395.85	3337.79

AMOUNT OF LOAN	NUMBER OF YEARS IN TERM											
	13	14	15	16	17	18	19	20	25	30	35	40
$ 50	1.03	1.02	1.01	1.01	1.00	1.00	1.00	0.99	0.99	0.99	0.98	0.98
100	2.06	2.04	2.02	2.01	2.00	1.99	1.99	1.98	1.97	1.97	1.96	1.96
200	4.12	4.08	4.04	4.02	4.00	3.98	3.97	3.96	3.93	3.93	3.92	3.92
300	6.18	6.11	6.06	6.03	5.99	5.97	5.95	5.94	5.90	5.90	5.88	5.88
400	8.24	8.15	8.08	8.03	7.99	7.96	7.93	7.91	7.86	7.85	7.84	7.84
500	10.30	10.19	10.10	10.04	9.99	9.95	9.92	9.89	9.83	9.81	9.80	9.80
600	12.35	12.22	12.12	12.05	11.98	11.94	11.90	11.87	11.79	11.77	11.76	11.76
700	14.41	14.26	14.14	14.05	13.98	13.92	13.88	13.85	13.75	13.73	13.72	13.71
800	16.47	16.30	16.16	16.06	15.98	15.91	15.86	15.82	15.72	15.69	15.68	15.67
900	18.53	18.33	18.18	18.07	17.97	17.90	17.84	17.80	17.68	17.65	17.64	17.63
1000	20.59	20.37	20.20	20.07	19.97	19.89	19.83	19.78	19.65	19.61	19.59	19.59
2000	41.17	40.74	40.40	40.14	39.94	39.77	39.65	39.55	39.29	39.21	39.18	39.18
3000	61.75	61.10	60.60	60.21	59.90	59.66	59.47	59.32	58.93	58.81	58.77	58.76
4000	82.33	81.47	80.80	80.28	79.87	79.54	79.29	79.09	78.57	78.41	78.36	78.35
5000	102.92	101.84	101.00	100.34	99.83	99.43	99.11	98.86	98.21	98.01	97.95	97.93
6000	123.50	122.20	121.20	120.41	119.80	119.31	118.93	118.63	117.86	117.61	117.54	117.52
7000	144.08	142.57	141.40	140.48	139.76	139.20	138.76	138.41	137.50	137.22	137.13	137.10
8000	164.66	162.94	161.60	160.55	159.73	159.08	158.58	158.18	157.14	156.82	156.72	156.69
9000	185.25	183.30	181.79	180.62	179.69	178.97	178.40	177.95	176.78	176.42	176.31	176.27
10000	205.83	203.67	201.99	200.68	199.66	198.85	198.22	197.72	196.42	196.02	195.90	195.86
11000	226.41	224.04	222.19	220.75	219.62	218.74	218.04	217.49	216.06	215.62	215.48	215.44
12000	246.99	244.40	242.39	240.82	239.59	238.62	237.86	237.26	235.71	235.22	235.07	235.03
13000	267.57	264.77	262.59	260.89	259.55	258.51	257.68	257.03	255.35	254.82	254.66	254.61
14000	288.16	285.14	282.79	280.96	279.52	278.39	277.51	276.81	274.99	274.43	274.25	274.20
15000	308.74	305.50	302.99	301.02	299.48	298.28	297.33	296.58	294.63	294.03	293.84	293.78
16000	329.32	325.87	323.19	321.09	319.45	318.16	317.15	316.35	314.27	313.63	313.43	313.37
17000	349.90	346.24	343.39	341.16	339.42	338.05	336.97	336.12	333.91	333.23	333.02	332.95
18000	370.49	366.60	363.58	361.23	359.38	357.93	356.79	355.89	353.56	352.83	352.61	352.54
19000	391.07	386.97	383.78	381.29	379.35	377.82	376.61	375.66	373.20	372.43	372.20	372.12
20000	411.65	407.34	403.98	401.36	399.31	397.70	396.43	395.44	392.84	392.04	391.79	391.71
21000	432.23	427.70	424.18	421.43	419.28	417.59	416.25	415.21	412.48	411.64	411.37	411.29
22000	452.82	448.07	444.38	441.50	439.24	437.47	436.08	434.98	432.12	431.24	430.96	430.88
23000	473.40	468.44	464.58	461.57	459.21	457.35	455.90	454.75	451.76	450.84	450.55	450.46
24000	493.98	488.80	484.78	481.63	479.17	477.24	475.72	474.52	471.41	470.44	470.14	470.05
25000	514.56	509.17	504.98	501.70	499.14	497.12	495.54	494.29	491.05	490.04	489.73	489.63
26000	535.14	529.54	525.17	521.77	519.10	517.01	515.36	514.06	510.69	509.64	509.32	509.22
27000	555.73	549.90	545.37	541.84	539.07	536.89	535.18	533.84	530.33	529.25	528.91	528.80
28000	576.31	570.27	565.57	561.91	559.03	556.78	555.01	553.61	549.97	548.85	548.50	548.39
29000	596.89	590.64	585.77	581.97	579.00	576.66	574.83	573.38	569.62	568.45	568.09	567.97
30000	617.47	611.00	605.97	602.04	598.96	596.55	594.65	593.15	589.26	588.05	587.68	587.56
31000	638.06	631.37	626.17	622.11	618.93	616.43	614.47	612.92	608.90	607.65	607.26	607.14
32000	658.64	651.74	646.37	642.18	638.89	636.32	634.29	632.69	628.54	627.25	626.85	626.73
33000	679.22	672.10	666.57	662.25	658.86	656.20	654.11	652.47	648.18	646.86	646.44	646.31
34000	699.80	692.47	686.77	682.31	678.83	676.09	673.93	672.24	667.82	666.46	666.03	665.90
35000	720.39	712.84	706.96	702.38	698.79	695.97	693.76	692.01	687.47	686.06	685.62	685.48
37500	771.84	763.75	757.46	752.55	748.70	745.68	743.31	741.44	736.57	735.06	734.59	734.45
40000	823.30	814.67	807.96	802.72	798.62	795.40	792.86	790.87	785.67	784.07	783.57	783.41
42500	874.75	865.58	858.46	852.89	848.53	845.11	842.42	840.29	834.78	833.07	832.54	832.37
45000	926.21	916.50	908.95	903.06	898.44	894.82	891.97	889.72	883.88	882.07	881.51	881.33
47500	977.66	967.42	959.45	953.23	948.36	944.53	941.52	939.15	932.99	931.08	930.48	930.30
50000	1029.12	1018.33	1009.95	1003.40	998.27	994.24	991.08	988.58	982.09	980.08	979.46	979.26
52500	1080.58	1069.25	1060.44	1053.57	1048.18	1043.96	1040.63	1038.01	1031.20	1029.09	1028.43	1028.22
55000	1132.03	1120.17	1110.94	1103.74	1098.10	1093.67	1090.18	1087.44	1080.30	1078.09	1077.40	1077.19
57500	1183.49	1171.08	1161.44	1153.91	1148.01	1143.38	1139.74	1136.87	1129.40	1127.09	1126.37	1126.15
60000	1234.94	1222.00	1211.94	1204.08	1197.92	1193.09	1189.29	1186.30	1178.51	1176.10	1175.35	1175.11
65000	1337.85	1323.83	1312.93	1304.42	1297.75	1292.52	1288.40	1285.15	1276.72	1274.10	1273.29	1273.04
70000	1440.77	1425.67	1413.92	1404.76	1397.58	1391.94	1387.51	1384.01	1374.93	1372.11	1371.24	1370.96
75000	1543.68	1527.50	1514.92	1505.10	1497.40	1491.36	1486.61	1482.87	1473.13	1470.12	1469.18	1468.89
80000	1646.59	1629.33	1615.91	1605.44	1597.23	1590.79	1585.72	1581.73	1571.34	1568.13	1567.13	1566.81
85000	1749.50	1731.16	1716.91	1705.78	1697.06	1690.21	1684.83	1680.58	1669.55	1666.14	1665.07	1664.74
90000	1852.41	1833.00	1817.90	1806.11	1796.88	1789.64	1783.93	1779.44	1767.76	1764.14	1763.02	1762.66
95000	1955.32	1934.83	1918.90	1906.45	1896.71	1889.06	1883.04	1878.30	1865.97	1862.15	1860.96	1860.59
100000	2058.23	2036.66	2019.89	2006.79	1996.55	1988.48	1982.15	1977.16	1964.18	1960.16	1958.91	1958.52
105000	2161.15	2138.50	2120.88	2107.13	2096.38	2087.91	2081.26	2076.01	2062.39	2058.17	2056.85	2056.44
110000	2264.06	2240.33	2221.88	2207.47	2196.19	2187.33	2180.36	2174.87	2160.59	2156.17	2154.80	2154.37
115000	2366.97	2342.16	2322.87	2307.81	2296.02	2286.75	2279.47	2273.73	2258.80	2254.18	2252.74	2252.29
120000	2469.88	2443.99	2423.87	2408.15	2395.84	2386.18	2378.58	2372.59	2357.01	2352.19	2350.69	2350.22
125000	2572.79	2545.83	2524.86	2508.49	2495.67	2485.60	2477.68	2471.44	2455.22	2450.20	2448.63	2448.14
130000	2675.70	2647.66	2625.85	2608.83	2595.50	2585.03	2576.79	2570.30	2553.43	2548.20	2546.58	2546.07
135000	2778.61	2749.49	2726.85	2709.17	2695.32	2684.45	2675.90	2669.16	2651.64	2646.21	2644.52	2643.99
140000	2881.53	2851.33	2827.84	2809.51	2795.15	2783.87	2775.01	2768.02	2749.85	2744.22	2742.47	2741.92
145000	2984.44	2953.16	2928.84	2909.85	2894.98	2883.30	2874.11	2866.88	2848.06	2842.23	2840.41	2839.85
150000	3087.35	3054.99	3029.83	3010.19	2994.80	2982.72	2973.22	2965.73	2946.26	2940.24	2938.36	2937.77
155000	3190.26	3156.83	3130.83	3110.53	3094.63	3082.15	3072.33	3064.59	3044.47	3038.24	3036.30	3035.70
160000	3293.17	3258.66	3231.82	3210.87	3194.45	3181.57	3171.43	3163.45	3142.68	3136.25	3134.25	3133.62

MONTHLY AMORTIZING PAYMENTS

AMOUNT OF LOAN	NUMBER OF YEARS IN TERM											
	1	2	3	4	5	6	7	8	9	10	11	12
$ 50	4.73	2.64	1.96	1.63	1.44	1.31	1.23	1.17	1.13	1.10	1.08	1.06
100	9.45	5.28	3.92	3.25	2.87	2.62	2.46	2.34	2.26	2.19	2.15	2.11
200	18.89	10.55	7.83	6.50	5.73	5.24	4.91	4.67	4.51	4.38	4.29	4.21
300	28.34	15.83	11.74	9.74	8.59	7.86	7.36	7.01	6.76	6.57	6.43	6.32
400	37.78	21.10	15.65	12.99	11.45	10.48	9.81	9.34	9.01	8.75	8.57	8.42
500	47.22	26.38	19.56	16.24	14.32	13.09	12.26	11.68	11.26	10.94	10.71	10.53
600	56.67	31.65	23.47	19.48	17.18	15.71	14.72	14.01	13.51	13.13	12.85	12.63
700	66.11	36.93	27.38	22.73	20.04	18.33	17.17	16.35	15.76	15.32	14.99	14.74
800	75.56	42.20	31.29	25.98	22.90	20.95	19.62	18.68	18.01	17.50	17.13	16.84
900	85.00	47.48	35.20	29.22	25.77	23.56	22.07	21.02	20.26	19.69	19.27	18.94
1000	94.44	52.75	39.11	32.47	28.63	26.18	24.52	23.35	22.51	21.88	21.41	21.05
2000	188.88	105.50	78.21	64.93	57.25	52.36	49.04	46.70	45.01	43.75	42.81	42.09
3000	283.32	158.24	117.31	97.40	85.87	78.53	73.56	70.05	67.51	65.63	64.21	63.13
4000	377.76	210.99	156.41	129.86	114.50	104.71	98.08	93.40	90.01	87.50	85.61	84.18
5000	472.20	263.74	195.51	162.32	143.12	130.88	122.59	116.75	112.51	109.38	107.02	105.22
6000	566.64	316.48	234.62	194.79	171.74	157.06	147.11	140.10	135.02	131.25	128.42	126.26
7000	661.08	369.23	273.72	227.25	200.37	183.23	171.63	163.45	157.52	153.12	149.82	147.31
8000	755.51	421.98	312.82	259.72	228.99	209.41	196.15	186.80	180.02	175.00	171.22	168.35
9000	849.95	474.72	351.92	292.18	257.61	235.58	220.67	210.15	202.52	196.87	192.62	189.39
10000	944.39	527.47	391.02	324.64	286.24	261.76	245.18	233.50	225.02	218.75	214.03	210.44
11000	1038.83	580.22	430.12	357.11	314.86	287.93	269.70	256.85	247.52	240.62	235.43	231.48
12000	1133.27	632.96	469.23	389.57	343.48	314.11	294.22	280.20	270.03	262.49	256.83	252.52
13000	1227.71	685.71	508.33	422.03	372.10	340.28	318.74	303.55	292.53	284.37	278.23	273.57
14000	1322.15	738.45	547.43	454.50	400.73	366.46	343.26	326.90	315.03	306.24	299.63	294.61
15000	1416.58	791.20	586.53	486.96	429.35	392.63	367.77	350.25	337.53	328.12	321.04	315.65
16000	1511.02	843.95	625.63	519.43	457.97	418.81	392.29	373.60	360.03	349.99	342.44	336.70
17000	1605.46	896.69	664.73	551.89	486.60	444.98	416.81	396.95	382.53	371.86	363.84	357.74
18000	1699.90	949.44	703.84	584.35	515.22	471.16	441.33	420.29	405.04	393.74	385.24	378.78
19000	1794.34	1002.19	742.94	616.82	543.84	497.34	465.85	443.64	427.54	415.61	406.64	399.83
20000	1888.78	1054.93	782.04	649.28	572.47	523.51	490.36	466.99	450.04	437.49	428.05	420.87
21000	1983.22	1107.68	821.14	681.74	601.09	549.69	514.88	490.34	472.54	459.36	449.45	441.91
22000	2077.66	1160.43	860.24	714.21	629.71	575.86	539.40	513.69	495.04	481.23	470.85	462.96
23000	2172.09	1213.17	899.34	746.67	658.33	602.04	563.92	537.04	517.54	503.11	492.25	484.00
24000	2266.53	1265.92	938.45	779.14	686.96	628.21	588.44	560.39	540.05	524.98	513.66	505.04
25000	2360.97	1318.67	977.55	811.60	715.58	654.39	612.95	583.74	562.55	546.86	535.06	526.09
26000	2455.41	1371.41	1016.65	844.06	744.20	680.56	637.47	607.09	585.05	568.73	556.46	547.13
27000	2549.85	1424.16	1055.75	876.53	772.83	706.74	661.99	630.44	607.55	590.60	577.86	568.17
28000	2644.29	1476.90	1094.85	908.99	801.45	732.91	686.51	653.79	630.05	612.48	599.26	589.22
29000	2738.73	1529.65	1133.95	941.45	830.07	759.09	711.03	677.14	652.55	634.35	620.67	610.26
30000	2833.16	1582.40	1173.06	973.92	858.70	785.26	735.54	700.49	675.06	656.23	642.07	631.30
31000	2927.60	1635.14	1212.16	1006.38	887.32	811.44	760.06	723.84	697.56	678.10	663.47	652.35
32000	3022.04	1687.89	1251.26	1038.85	915.94	837.61	784.58	747.19	720.06	699.97	684.87	673.39
33000	3116.48	1740.64	1290.36	1071.31	944.57	863.79	809.10	770.54	742.56	721.85	706.27	694.43
34000	3210.92	1793.38	1329.46	1103.77	973.19	889.96	833.62	793.89	765.06	743.72	727.68	715.48
35000	3305.36	1846.13	1368.56	1136.24	1001.81	916.14	858.13	817.23	787.57	765.60	749.08	736.52
37500	3541.45	1978.00	1466.32	1217.40	1073.37	981.58	919.43	875.61	843.82	820.28	802.58	789.13
40000	3777.55	2109.86	1564.07	1298.56	1144.93	1047.02	980.72	933.98	900.07	874.97	856.09	841.74
42500	4013.65	2241.73	1661.83	1379.72	1216.48	1112.45	1042.02	992.36	956.33	929.65	909.59	894.34
45000	4249.74	2373.59	1759.58	1460.88	1288.04	1177.89	1103.31	1050.73	1012.58	984.34	963.10	946.95
47500	4485.84	2505.46	1857.34	1542.03	1359.60	1243.33	1164.61	1109.10	1068.84	1039.02	1016.60	999.56
50000	4721.94	2637.33	1955.09	1623.19	1431.16	1308.77	1225.90	1167.48	1125.09	1093.71	1070.11	1052.17
52500	4958.03	2769.19	2052.84	1704.35	1502.71	1374.21	1287.20	1225.85	1181.35	1148.39	1123.62	1104.78
55000	5194.13	2901.06	2150.60	1785.51	1574.27	1439.65	1348.49	1284.22	1237.60	1203.08	1177.12	1157.38
57500	5430.23	3032.92	2248.35	1866.67	1645.83	1505.08	1409.79	1342.60	1293.85	1257.76	1230.63	1209.99
60000	5666.32	3164.79	2346.11	1947.83	1717.39	1570.52	1471.08	1400.97	1350.11	1312.45	1284.13	1262.60
65000	6138.52	3428.52	2541.62	2110.15	1860.50	1701.40	1593.67	1517.72	1462.62	1421.82	1391.14	1367.82
70000	6610.71	3692.25	2737.12	2272.47	2003.62	1832.27	1716.26	1634.46	1575.13	1531.19	1498.15	1473.03
75000	7082.90	3955.99	2932.63	2434.79	2146.73	1963.15	1838.85	1751.21	1687.63	1640.56	1605.16	1578.25
80000	7555.10	4219.72	3128.14	2597.11	2289.85	2094.03	1961.44	1867.96	1800.14	1749.93	1712.17	1683.47
85000	8027.29	4483.45	3323.65	2759.43	2432.96	2224.90	2084.03	1984.71	1912.65	1859.30	1819.18	1788.68
90000	8499.48	4747.18	3519.16	2921.75	2576.08	2355.78	2206.62	2101.45	2025.16	1968.67	1926.19	1893.90
95000	8971.68	5010.91	3714.67	3084.06	2719.19	2486.66	2329.21	2218.20	2137.67	2078.04	2033.20	1999.11
100000	9443.87	5274.65	3910.18	3246.38	2862.31	2617.53	2451.80	2334.95	2250.18	2187.41	2140.22	2104.33
105000	9916.06	5538.38	4105.68	3408.70	3005.42	2748.41	2574.39	2451.69	2362.69	2296.78	2247.23	2209.55
110000	10388.26	5802.11	4301.19	3571.02	3148.54	2879.29	2696.98	2568.44	2475.19	2406.15	2354.24	2314.76
115000	10860.45	6065.84	4496.70	3733.34	3291.65	3010.16	2819.57	2685.19	2587.70	2515.52	2461.25	2419.98
120000	11332.64	6329.57	4692.21	3895.66	3434.77	3141.04	2942.16	2801.94	2700.21	2624.89	2568.26	2525.20
125000	11804.84	6593.31	4887.72	4057.98	3577.88	3271.91	3064.75	2918.68	2812.72	2734.26	2675.27	2630.41
130000	12277.03	6857.04	5083.23	4220.30	3721.00	3402.79	3187.34	3035.43	2925.23	2843.63	2782.28	2735.63
135000	12749.22	7120.77	5278.74	4382.62	3864.12	3533.67	3309.93	3152.18	3037.74	2953.00	2889.29	2840.84
140000	13221.42	7384.50	5474.24	4544.93	4007.23	3664.54	3432.52	3268.92	3150.25	3062.37	2996.30	2946.06
145000	13693.61	7648.23	5669.75	4707.25	4150.35	3795.42	3555.11	3385.67	3262.75	3171.74	3103.31	3051.28
150000	14165.80	7911.97	5865.26	4869.57	4293.46	3926.30	3677.70	3502.42	3375.26	3281.11	3210.32	3156.49
155000	14638.00	8175.70	6060.77	5031.89	4436.58	4057.17	3800.29	3619.17	3487.77	3390.48	3317.33	3261.71
160000	15110.19	8439.43	6256.28	5194.21	4579.69	4188.05	3922.88	3735.91	3600.28	3499.85	3424.34	3366.93

MONTHLY AMORTIZING PAYMENTS 23.75%

AMOUNT OF LOAN	NUMBER OF YEARS IN TERM										
	13	14	15	16	17	18	19	20	25	30	35	40
$ 50	1.04	1.03	1.02	1.02	1.01	1.01	1.01	1.00	1.00	1.00	0.99	0.99
100	2.08	2.06	2.04	2.03	2.02	2.01	2.01	2.00	1.99	1.99	1.98	1.98
200	4.16	4.12	4.08	4.06	4.04	4.02	4.01	4.00	3.97	3.97	3.96	3.96
300	6.24	6.17	6.12	6.08	6.05	6.03	6.01	6.00	5.96	5.95	5.94	5.94
400	8.31	8.23	8.16	8.11	8.07	8.04	8.01	7.99	7.94	7.93	7.92	7.92
500	10.39	10.28	10.20	10.14	10.09	10.05	10.02	10.02	9.93	9.91	9.90	9.90
600	12.47	12.34	12.24	12.16	12.10	12.05	12.02	11.99	11.91	11.89	11.88	11.88
700	14.54	14.39	14.28	14.19	14.12	14.06	14.02	13.99	13.90	13.87	13.86	13.86
800	16.62	16.45	16.32	16.21	16.13	16.07	16.02	15.98	15.88	15.85	15.84	15.84
900	18.70	18.50	18.36	18.24	18.15	18.08	18.02	17.98	17.87	17.83	17.82	17.82
1000	20.77	20.56	20.40	20.27	20.17	20.09	20.03	19.98	19.85	19.81	19.80	19.80
2000	41.54	41.12	40.79	40.53	40.33	40.17	40.05	39.95	39.70	39.62	39.60	39.59
3000	62.31	61.67	61.18	60.79	60.49	60.25	60.07	59.92	59.55	59.43	59.40	59.38
4000	83.08	82.23	81.57	81.05	80.65	80.34	80.09	79.90	79.39	79.24	79.19	79.18
5000	103.85	102.78	101.96	101.32	100.81	100.42	100.11	99.87	99.24	99.05	98.99	98.97
6000	124.61	123.34	122.35	121.58	120.97	120.50	120.13	119.84	119.09	118.86	118.79	118.76
7000	145.38	143.89	142.74	141.84	141.14	140.59	140.15	139.81	138.94	138.67	138.58	138.56
8000	166.15	164.45	163.13	162.10	161.30	160.67	160.17	159.79	158.78	158.48	158.38	158.35
9000	186.92	185.00	183.52	182.36	181.46	180.75	180.20	179.76	178.63	178.28	178.18	178.14
10000	207.69	205.56	203.91	202.63	201.62	200.83	200.22	199.73	198.48	198.09	197.97	197.94
11000	228.45	226.12	224.30	222.89	221.78	220.92	220.24	219.70	218.32	217.90	217.77	217.73
12000	249.22	246.67	244.69	243.15	241.94	241.00	240.26	239.68	238.17	237.71	237.57	237.52
13000	269.99	267.23	265.08	263.41	262.11	261.08	260.28	259.65	258.02	257.52	257.37	257.32
14000	290.76	287.78	285.47	283.67	282.27	281.17	280.30	279.62	277.87	277.33	277.16	277.11
15000	311.53	308.34	305.86	303.94	302.43	301.25	300.32	299.60	297.71	297.14	296.96	296.90
16000	332.29	328.89	326.25	324.20	322.59	321.33	320.34	319.57	317.56	316.95	316.76	316.70
17000	353.06	349.45	346.64	344.46	342.75	341.42	340.37	339.54	337.41	336.75	336.55	336.49
18000	373.83	370.00	367.04	364.72	362.91	361.50	360.39	359.51	357.25	356.56	356.35	356.28
19000	394.60	390.56	387.43	384.98	383.08	381.58	380.41	379.49	377.10	376.37	376.15	376.08
20000	415.37	411.12	407.82	405.25	403.24	401.66	400.43	399.46	396.95	396.18	395.94	395.87
21000	436.13	431.67	428.21	425.51	423.40	421.75	420.45	419.43	416.80	415.99	415.74	415.66
22000	456.90	452.23	448.60	445.77	443.56	441.83	440.47	439.40	436.64	435.80	435.54	435.46
23000	477.67	472.78	468.99	466.03	463.72	461.91	460.49	459.38	456.49	455.61	455.33	455.25
24000	498.44	493.34	489.38	486.30	483.88	482.00	480.51	479.35	476.34	475.42	475.13	475.04
25000	519.21	513.89	509.77	506.56	504.05	502.08	500.54	499.32	496.18	495.22	494.93	494.84
26000	539.97	534.45	530.16	526.82	524.21	522.16	520.56	519.29	516.03	515.03	514.73	514.63
27000	560.74	555.00	550.55	547.08	544.37	542.25	540.58	539.27	535.88	534.84	534.52	534.42
28000	581.51	575.56	570.94	567.34	564.53	562.33	560.60	559.24	555.73	554.65	554.32	554.22
29000	602.28	596.11	591.33	587.61	584.69	582.41	580.62	579.21	575.57	574.46	574.12	574.01
30000	623.05	616.67	611.72	607.87	604.85	602.49	600.64	599.19	595.42	594.27	593.91	593.80
31000	643.81	637.23	632.11	628.13	625.02	622.58	620.66	619.16	615.27	614.08	613.71	613.60
32000	664.58	657.78	652.50	648.39	645.18	642.66	640.68	639.13	635.11	633.89	633.51	633.39
33000	685.35	678.34	672.89	668.65	665.34	662.74	660.71	659.10	654.96	653.69	653.30	653.18
34000	706.12	698.89	693.28	688.92	685.50	682.83	680.73	679.08	674.81	673.50	673.10	672.98
35000	726.89	719.45	713.68	709.18	705.66	702.91	700.75	699.05	694.66	693.31	692.90	692.77
37500	778.81	770.84	764.65	759.83	756.07	753.12	750.80	748.98	744.27	742.83	742.39	742.25
40000	830.73	822.23	815.63	810.49	806.47	803.32	800.85	798.91	793.89	792.36	791.88	791.74
42500	882.65	873.61	866.60	861.14	856.88	853.53	850.91	848.84	843.51	841.88	841.37	841.22
45000	934.57	925.00	917.58	911.80	907.28	903.74	900.96	898.78	893.13	891.40	890.87	890.70
47500	986.49	976.39	968.56	962.45	957.68	953.95	951.01	948.71	942.75	940.92	940.36	940.19
50000	1038.41	1027.78	1019.53	1013.11	1008.09	1004.15	1001.07	998.64	992.36	990.44	989.85	989.67
52500	1090.33	1079.17	1070.51	1063.76	1058.49	1054.36	1051.12	1048.57	1041.98	1039.96	1039.34	1039.15
55000	1142.25	1130.56	1121.49	1114.42	1108.90	1104.57	1101.17	1098.50	1091.60	1089.49	1088.84	1088.64
57500	1194.17	1181.95	1172.46	1165.07	1159.30	1154.78	1151.22	1148.43	1141.22	1139.01	1138.33	1138.12
60000	1246.09	1233.34	1223.44	1215.73	1209.70	1204.98	1201.28	1198.37	1190.83	1188.53	1187.82	1187.60
65000	1349.93	1336.11	1325.39	1317.04	1310.51	1305.40	1301.38	1298.23	1290.07	1287.57	1286.81	1286.57
70000	1453.77	1438.89	1427.35	1418.35	1411.32	1405.81	1401.49	1398.09	1389.31	1386.62	1385.79	1385.54
75000	1557.61	1541.67	1529.30	1519.66	1512.13	1506.23	1501.60	1497.96	1488.54	1485.66	1484.78	1484.50
80000	1661.45	1644.45	1631.25	1620.97	1612.94	1606.64	1601.70	1597.82	1587.78	1584.71	1583.76	1583.47
85000	1765.29	1747.22	1733.20	1722.28	1713.75	1707.06	1701.81	1697.68	1687.01	1683.75	1682.74	1682.43
90000	1869.13	1850.00	1835.16	1823.59	1814.55	1807.47	1801.91	1797.55	1786.25	1782.79	1781.73	1781.40
95000	1972.97	1952.78	1937.11	1924.90	1915.36	1907.89	1902.02	1897.41	1885.49	1881.84	1880.71	1880.37
100000	2076.81	2055.56	2039.06	2026.21	2016.17	2008.30	2002.13	1997.27	1984.72	1980.88	1979.70	1979.33
105000	2180.65	2158.33	2141.02	2127.52	2116.98	2108.72	2102.23	2097.14	2083.96	2079.92	2078.68	2078.30
110000	2284.49	2261.11	2242.97	2228.83	2217.79	2209.13	2202.34	2197.00	2183.19	2178.97	2177.67	2177.27
115000	2388.33	2363.89	2344.92	2330.14	2318.60	2309.55	2302.44	2296.86	2282.43	2278.01	2276.65	2276.23
120000	2492.17	2466.67	2446.88	2431.46	2419.40	2409.96	2402.55	2396.73	2381.66	2377.06	2375.64	2375.20
125000	2596.01	2569.44	2548.83	2532.77	2520.21	2510.38	2502.66	2496.59	2480.90	2476.10	2474.62	2474.17
130000	2699.85	2672.22	2650.78	2634.08	2621.02	2610.79	2602.76	2596.45	2580.14	2575.14	2573.61	2573.13
135000	2803.69	2775.00	2752.73	2735.39	2721.83	2711.21	2702.87	2696.32	2679.37	2674.19	2672.59	2672.10
140000	2907.53	2877.78	2854.69	2836.70	2822.64	2811.62	2802.98	2796.18	2778.61	2773.23	2771.58	2771.07
145000	3011.37	2980.55	2956.64	2938.01	2923.45	2912.04	2903.08	2896.04	2877.84	2872.27	2870.56	2870.03
150000	3115.21	3083.33	3058.59	3039.32	3024.25	3012.45	3003.19	2995.91	2977.08	2971.32	2969.55	2969.00
155000	3219.05	3186.11	3160.55	3140.63	3125.06	3112.87	3103.29	3095.77	3076.32	3070.36	3068.53	3067.97
160000	3322.89	3288.89	3262.50	3241.94	3225.87	3213.28	3203.40	3195.63	3175.55	3169.41	3167.51	3166.93

24.00% MONTHLY AMORTIZING PAYMENTS

AMOUNT OF LOAN	NUMBER OF YEARS IN TERM											
	1	2	3	4	5	6	7	8	9	10	11	12
$ 50	4.73	2.65	1.97	1.64	1.44	1.32	1.24	1.18	1.14	1.11	1.08	1.07
100	9.46	5.29	3.93	3.27	2.88	2.64	2.47	2.36	2.27	2.21	2.16	2.13
200	18.92	10.58	7.85	6.53	5.76	5.27	4.94	4.71	4.54	4.41	4.32	4.25
300	28.37	15.87	11.77	9.79	8.64	7.90	7.41	7.06	6.81	6.62	6.48	6.37
400	37.83	21.15	15.70	13.05	11.51	10.54	9.88	9.41	9.07	8.82	8.64	8.50
500	47.28	26.44	19.62	16.31	14.39	13.17	12.34	11.76	11.34	11.03	10.80	10.62
600	56.74	31.73	23.54	19.57	17.27	15.80	14.81	14.11	13.61	13.23	12.95	12.74
700	66.20	37.01	27.47	22.83	20.14	18.43	17.28	16.46	15.87	15.44	15.11	14.86
800	75.65	42.30	31.39	26.09	23.02	21.07	19.75	18.82	18.14	17.64	17.27	16.99
900	85.11	47.59	35.31	29.35	25.90	23.70	22.21	21.17	20.41	19.85	19.43	19.11
1000	94.56	52.88	39.24	32.61	28.77	26.33	24.68	23.52	22.68	22.05	21.59	21.23
2000	189.12	105.75	78.47	65.21	57.54	52.66	49.36	47.03	45.35	44.10	43.17	42.46
3000	283.68	158.62	117.70	97.81	86.31	78.99	74.03	70.54	68.02	66.15	64.75	63.68
4000	378.24	211.49	156.94	130.41	115.08	105.31	98.71	94.06	90.69	88.20	86.33	84.91
5000	472.80	264.36	196.17	163.01	143.84	131.64	123.38	117.57	113.36	110.25	107.91	106.13
6000	567.36	317.23	235.40	195.62	172.61	157.97	148.06	141.08	136.03	132.29	129.49	127.36
7000	661.92	370.10	274.63	228.22	201.38	184.29	172.74	164.60	158.70	154.34	151.07	148.59
8000	756.48	422.97	313.87	260.82	230.15	210.62	197.41	188.11	181.37	176.39	172.65	169.81
9000	851.04	475.84	353.10	293.42	258.92	236.95	222.09	211.62	204.04	198.44	194.23	191.04
10000	945.60	528.72	392.33	326.02	287.68	263.27	246.76	235.14	226.71	220.49	215.81	212.26
11000	1040.16	581.59	431.57	358.63	316.45	289.60	271.44	258.65	249.38	242.53	237.39	233.49
12000	1134.72	634.46	470.80	391.23	345.22	315.93	296.11	282.16	272.06	264.58	258.97	254.72
13000	1229.28	687.33	510.03	423.83	373.99	342.25	320.79	305.68	294.73	286.63	280.55	275.94
14000	1323.84	740.20	549.26	456.43	402.76	368.58	345.47	329.19	317.40	308.68	302.13	297.17
15000	1418.40	793.07	588.50	489.03	431.52	394.91	370.14	352.70	340.07	330.73	323.72	318.39
16000	1512.96	845.94	627.73	521.63	460.29	421.23	394.82	376.22	362.74	352.77	345.30	339.62
17000	1607.52	898.81	666.96	554.24	489.06	447.56	419.49	399.73	385.41	374.82	366.88	360.84
18000	1702.08	951.68	706.20	586.84	517.83	473.89	444.17	423.24	408.08	396.87	388.46	382.07
19000	1796.64	1004.56	745.43	619.44	546.60	500.21	468.85	446.75	430.75	418.92	410.04	403.30
20000	1891.20	1057.43	784.66	652.04	575.36	526.54	493.52	470.27	453.42	440.97	431.62	424.52
21000	1985.76	1110.30	823.89	684.64	604.13	552.87	518.20	493.78	476.09	463.02	453.20	445.75
22000	2080.32	1163.17	863.13	717.25	632.90	579.20	542.87	517.29	498.76	485.06	474.78	466.97
23000	2174.88	1216.04	902.36	749.85	661.67	605.52	567.55	540.81	521.43	507.11	496.36	488.20
24000	2269.44	1268.91	941.59	782.45	690.44	631.85	592.22	564.32	544.11	529.16	517.94	509.43
25000	2363.99	1321.78	980.83	815.05	719.20	658.18	616.90	587.83	566.78	551.21	539.52	530.65
26000	2458.55	1374.65	1020.06	847.65	747.97	684.51	641.58	611.35	589.45	573.26	561.10	551.88
27000	2553.11	1427.52	1059.29	880.25	776.74	710.83	666.25	634.86	612.12	595.30	582.68	573.10
28000	2647.67	1480.40	1098.52	912.86	805.51	737.16	690.93	658.37	634.79	617.35	604.26	594.33
29000	2742.23	1533.27	1137.76	945.46	834.28	763.48	715.60	681.89	657.46	639.40	625.84	615.55
30000	2836.79	1586.14	1176.99	978.06	863.04	789.81	740.28	705.40	680.13	661.45	647.43	636.78
31000	2931.35	1639.01	1216.22	1010.66	891.81	816.14	764.96	728.91	702.80	683.50	669.01	658.01
32000	3025.91	1691.88	1255.46	1043.26	920.58	842.46	789.63	752.43	725.47	705.54	690.59	679.23
33000	3120.47	1744.75	1294.69	1075.87	949.35	868.79	814.31	775.94	748.14	727.59	712.17	700.46
34000	3215.03	1797.62	1333.92	1108.47	978.12	895.12	838.98	799.45	770.81	749.64	733.75	721.68
35000	3309.59	1850.49	1373.15	1141.07	1006.88	921.44	863.66	822.96	793.48	771.69	755.33	742.91
37500	3545.99	1982.67	1471.24	1222.57	1078.80	987.26	925.35	881.75	850.16	826.81	809.28	795.97
40000	3782.39	2114.85	1569.32	1304.08	1150.72	1053.08	987.04	940.53	906.84	881.93	863.23	849.04
42500	4018.79	2247.03	1667.40	1385.58	1222.64	1118.90	1048.73	999.31	963.52	937.05	917.18	902.10
45000	4255.19	2379.20	1765.48	1467.09	1294.56	1184.71	1110.42	1058.10	1020.19	992.17	971.14	955.17
47500	4491.59	2511.38	1863.57	1548.59	1366.48	1250.53	1172.11	1116.88	1076.87	1047.29	1025.09	1008.23
50000	4727.98	2643.56	1961.65	1630.10	1438.40	1316.35	1233.80	1175.66	1133.55	1102.41	1079.04	1061.30
52500	4964.38	2775.74	2059.73	1711.60	1510.32	1382.16	1295.49	1234.44	1190.22	1157.53	1132.99	1114.36
55000	5200.78	2907.92	2157.81	1793.11	1582.24	1447.98	1357.17	1293.23	1246.90	1212.65	1186.94	1167.43
57500	5437.18	3040.09	2255.89	1874.61	1654.16	1513.80	1418.86	1352.01	1303.58	1267.77	1240.89	1220.49
60000	5673.58	3172.27	2353.98	1956.12	1726.08	1579.61	1480.55	1410.79	1360.26	1322.89	1294.85	1273.56
65000	6146.38	3436.63	2550.14	2119.12	1869.92	1711.25	1603.93	1528.36	1473.61	1433.13	1402.75	1379.69
70000	6619.18	3700.98	2746.30	2282.13	2013.76	1842.88	1727.31	1645.92	1586.96	1543.37	1510.65	1485.82
75000	7091.97	3965.34	2942.47	2445.14	2157.60	1974.52	1850.69	1763.49	1700.32	1653.61	1618.56	1591.94
80000	7564.77	4229.69	3138.63	2608.15	2301.44	2106.15	1974.07	1881.06	1813.67	1763.85	1726.46	1698.07
85000	8037.57	4494.05	3334.80	2771.16	2445.28	2237.79	2097.45	1998.62	1927.03	1874.09	1834.36	1804.20
90000	8510.37	4758.40	3530.96	2934.17	2589.12	2369.42	2220.83	2116.19	2040.38	1984.33	1942.27	1910.33
95000	8983.17	5022.76	3727.13	3097.18	2732.96	2501.05	2344.21	2233.75	2153.74	2094.57	2050.17	2016.46
100000	9455.96	5287.11	3923.29	3260.19	2876.80	2632.69	2467.59	2351.32	2267.09	2204.81	2158.07	2122.59
105000	9928.76	5551.47	4119.45	3423.20	3020.64	2764.32	2590.97	2468.88	2380.44	2315.06	2265.98	2228.72
110000	10401.56	5815.83	4315.62	3586.21	3164.48	2895.96	2714.34	2586.45	2493.80	2425.30	2373.88	2334.85
115000	10874.36	6080.18	4511.78	3749.22	3308.32	3027.59	2837.72	2704.01	2607.15	2535.54	2481.78	2440.98
120000	11347.16	6344.54	4707.95	3912.23	3452.16	3159.22	2961.10	2821.58	2720.51	2645.78	2589.69	2547.11
125000	11819.95	6608.89	4904.11	4075.23	3596.00	3290.86	3084.48	2939.15	2833.86	2756.02	2697.59	2653.24
130000	12292.75	6873.25	5100.28	4238.24	3739.84	3422.49	3207.86	3056.71	2947.22	2866.26	2805.49	2759.37
135000	12765.55	7137.60	5296.44	4401.25	3883.68	3554.13	3331.24	3174.28	3060.57	2976.50	2913.40	2865.50
140000	13238.35	7401.96	5492.60	4564.26	4027.52	3685.76	3454.62	3291.84	3173.92	3086.74	3021.30	2971.63
145000	13711.15	7666.31	5688.77	4727.27	4171.36	3817.40	3578.00	3409.41	3287.28	3196.98	3129.20	3077.75
150000	14183.94	7930.67	5884.93	4890.28	4315.20	3949.03	3701.38	3526.97	3400.63	3307.22	3237.11	3183.88
155000	14656.74	8195.03	6081.10	5053.29	4459.04	4080.66	3824.76	3644.54	3513.99	3417.46	3345.01	3290.01
160000	15129.54	8459.38	6277.26	5216.30	4602.88	4212.30	3948.13	3762.11	3627.34	3527.70	3452.91	3396.14

154

AMOUNT OF LOAN	NUMBER OF YEARS IN TERM											
	13	14	15	16	17	18	19	20	25	30	35	40
$ 50	1.05	1.04	1.03	1.03	1.02	1.02	1.02	1.01	1.01	1.01	1.01	1.01
100	2.10	2.08	2.06	2.05	2.04	2.03	2.03	2.02	2.01	2.01	2.01	2.01
200	4.20	4.15	4.12	4.10	4.08	4.06	4.05	4.04	4.02	4.01	4.01	4.01
300	6.29	6.23	6.18	6.14	6.11	6.09	6.07	6.06	6.02	6.01	6.01	6.01
400	8.39	8.30	8.24	8.19	8.15	8.12	8.09	8.07	8.03	8.01	8.01	8.01
500	10.48	10.38	10.30	10.23	10.18	10.15	10.12	10.09	10.03	10.01	10.01	10.01
600	12.58	12.45	12.35	12.28	12.22	12.17	12.14	12.11	12.04	12.01	12.01	12.01
700	14.67	14.53	14.41	14.32	14.26	14.20	14.16	14.13	14.04	14.02	14.01	14.01
800	16.77	16.60	16.47	16.37	16.29	16.23	16.18	16.14	16.05	16.02	16.01	16.01
900	18.86	18.68	18.53	18.42	18.33	18.26	18.20	18.16	18.05	18.02	18.01	18.01
1000	20.96	20.75	20.59	20.46	20.36	20.29	20.23	20.18	20.06	20.02	20.01	20.01
2000	41.91	41.49	41.17	40.92	40.72	40.57	40.45	40.35	40.11	40.04	40.01	40.01
3000	62.87	62.24	61.75	61.38	61.08	60.85	60.67	60.53	60.16	60.05	60.02	60.01
4000	83.82	82.98	82.34	81.83	81.44	81.13	80.89	80.70	80.22	80.07	80.02	80.01
5000	104.78	103.73	102.92	102.29	101.80	101.41	101.11	100.88	100.27	100.09	100.03	100.01
6000	125.73	124.47	123.50	122.75	122.16	121.69	121.33	121.05	120.32	120.10	120.03	120.01
7000	146.68	145.22	144.08	143.20	142.51	141.98	141.55	141.22	140.37	140.12	140.04	140.02
8000	167.64	165.96	164.67	163.66	162.87	162.26	161.78	161.40	160.43	160.13	160.04	160.02
9000	188.59	186.71	185.25	184.12	183.23	182.54	182.00	181.57	180.48	180.15	180.05	180.02
10000	209.55	207.45	205.83	204.57	203.59	202.82	202.22	201.75	200.53	200.17	200.05	200.02
11000	230.50	228.20	226.42	225.03	223.95	223.10	222.44	221.92	220.59	220.18	220.06	220.02
12000	251.46	248.94	247.00	245.49	244.31	243.38	242.66	242.09	240.64	240.20	240.06	240.02
13000	272.41	269.69	267.58	265.94	264.66	263.66	262.88	262.27	260.69	260.21	260.07	260.02
14000	293.36	290.43	288.16	286.40	285.02	283.95	283.10	282.44	280.74	280.23	280.07	280.03
15000	314.32	311.18	308.75	306.86	305.38	304.23	303.32	302.62	300.80	300.25	300.08	300.03
16000	335.27	331.92	329.33	327.31	325.74	324.51	323.55	322.79	320.85	320.26	320.08	320.03
17000	356.23	352.67	349.91	347.77	346.10	344.79	343.77	342.96	340.90	340.28	340.09	340.03
18000	377.18	373.41	370.49	368.23	366.46	365.07	363.99	363.14	360.95	360.29	360.09	360.03
19000	398.14	394.16	391.08	388.68	386.81	385.35	384.21	383.31	381.01	380.31	380.10	380.03
20000	419.09	414.90	411.66	409.14	407.17	405.63	404.43	403.49	401.06	400.33	400.10	400.04
21000	440.04	435.65	432.24	429.60	427.53	425.92	424.65	423.66	421.11	420.34	420.11	420.04
22000	461.00	456.39	452.83	450.05	447.89	446.20	444.87	443.83	441.17	440.36	440.11	440.04
23000	481.95	477.14	473.41	470.51	468.25	466.48	465.09	464.01	461.22	460.37	460.12	460.04
24000	502.91	497.88	493.99	490.97	488.61	486.76	485.32	484.18	481.27	480.39	480.12	480.04
25000	523.86	518.63	514.57	511.42	508.96	507.04	505.54	504.36	501.32	500.41	500.13	500.04
26000	544.81	539.37	535.16	531.88	529.32	527.32	525.76	524.53	521.38	520.42	520.13	520.04
27000	565.77	560.12	555.74	552.34	549.68	547.61	545.98	544.71	541.43	540.44	540.14	540.05
28000	586.72	580.86	576.32	572.79	570.04	567.89	566.20	564.88	561.48	560.45	560.14	560.05
29000	607.68	601.61	596.90	593.25	590.40	588.17	586.42	585.05	581.53	580.47	580.15	580.05
30000	628.63	622.35	617.49	613.71	610.76	608.45	606.64	605.23	601.59	600.49	600.15	600.05
31000	649.59	643.10	638.07	634.16	631.11	628.73	626.87	625.40	621.64	620.50	620.16	620.05
32000	670.54	663.84	658.65	654.62	651.47	649.01	647.09	645.58	641.69	640.52	640.16	640.05
33000	691.49	684.59	679.24	675.08	671.83	669.29	667.31	665.75	660.53	660.53	660.17	660.05
34000	712.45	705.33	699.82	695.53	692.19	689.58	687.53	685.92	681.80	680.55	680.17	680.06
35000	733.40	726.08	720.40	715.99	712.55	709.86	707.75	706.10	701.85	700.57	700.18	700.06
37500	785.79	777.94	771.86	767.13	763.44	760.56	758.30	756.53	751.98	750.61	750.19	750.06
40000	838.17	829.80	823.31	818.27	814.34	811.26	808.86	806.97	802.11	800.65	800.20	800.06
42500	890.56	881.66	874.77	869.41	865.23	861.97	859.41	857.40	852.25	850.69	850.21	850.07
45000	942.94	933.52	926.23	920.56	916.13	912.67	909.96	907.84	902.38	900.73	900.22	900.07
47500	995.33	985.39	977.68	971.70	967.03	963.38	960.52	958.27	952.51	950.77	950.24	950.08
50000	1047.72	1037.25	1029.14	1022.84	1017.92	1014.08	1011.07	1008.71	1002.64	1000.81	1000.25	1000.08
52500	1100.10	1089.11	1080.60	1073.98	1068.82	1064.78	1061.62	1059.14	1052.77	1050.85	1050.26	1050.08
55000	1152.49	1140.97	1132.06	1125.12	1119.71	1115.49	1112.18	1109.58	1102.91	1100.89	1100.27	1100.09
57500	1204.87	1192.84	1183.51	1176.26	1170.61	1166.19	1162.73	1160.01	1153.04	1150.93	1150.29	1150.09
60000	1257.26	1244.70	1234.97	1227.41	1221.51	1216.89	1213.28	1210.45	1203.17	1200.97	1200.30	1200.09
65000	1362.03	1348.42	1337.88	1329.69	1323.30	1318.30	1314.39	1311.32	1303.43	1301.05	1300.32	1300.10
70000	1466.80	1452.15	1440.80	1431.97	1425.09	1419.71	1415.50	1412.19	1403.70	1401.13	1400.35	1400.11
75000	1571.57	1555.87	1543.71	1534.26	1526.88	1521.12	1516.60	1513.06	1503.96	1501.21	1500.37	1500.12
80000	1676.34	1659.59	1646.62	1636.54	1628.67	1622.52	1617.71	1613.93	1604.22	1601.29	1600.40	1600.12
85000	1781.11	1763.32	1749.54	1738.82	1730.46	1723.93	1718.81	1714.80	1704.49	1701.37	1700.42	1700.13
90000	1885.88	1867.04	1852.45	1841.11	1832.26	1825.34	1819.92	1815.67	1804.75	1801.45	1800.44	1800.14
95000	1990.66	1970.77	1955.36	1943.39	1934.05	1926.75	1921.03	1916.54	1905.02	1901.53	1900.47	1900.15
100000	2095.43	2074.49	2058.28	2045.67	2035.84	2028.15	2022.13	2017.41	2005.28	2001.61	2000.49	2000.15
105000	2200.20	2178.22	2161.19	2147.96	2137.63	2129.56	2123.24	2118.28	2105.54	2101.69	2100.52	2100.16
110000	2304.97	2281.94	2264.11	2250.24	2239.42	2230.97	2224.35	2219.15	2205.81	2201.77	2200.54	2200.17
115000	2409.74	2385.67	2367.02	2352.52	2341.22	2332.38	2325.45	2320.02	2306.07	2301.85	2300.57	2300.18
120000	2514.51	2489.39	2469.93	2454.81	2443.01	2433.78	2426.56	2420.89	2406.33	2401.93	2400.59	2400.18
125000	2619.28	2593.11	2572.85	2557.09	2544.80	2535.19	2527.67	2521.77	2506.60	2502.01	2500.62	2500.19
130000	2724.05	2696.84	2675.76	2659.37	2646.59	2636.60	2628.77	2622.64	2606.86	2602.09	2600.64	2600.20
135000	2828.82	2800.56	2778.67	2761.66	2748.38	2738.01	2729.88	2723.51	2707.12	2702.17	2700.66	2700.21
140000	2933.59	2904.29	2881.59	2863.94	2850.17	2839.41	2830.99	2824.38	2807.39	2802.25	2800.69	2800.21
145000	3038.37	3008.01	2984.50	2966.22	2951.97	2940.82	2932.09	2925.25	2907.65	2902.33	2900.71	2900.22
150000	3143.14	3111.74	3087.42	3068.51	3053.76	3042.23	3033.20	3026.12	3007.92	3002.41	3000.74	3000.23
155000	3247.91	3215.46	3190.33	3170.79	3155.55	3143.64	3134.31	3126.99	3108.18	3102.49	3100.76	3100.24
160000	3352.68	3319.18	3293.24	3273.07	3257.34	3245.04	3235.41	3227.86	3208.44	3202.57	3200.79	3200.24

MONTHLY AMORTIZING PAYMENTS

AMOUNT OF LOAN	NUMBER OF YEARS IN TERM											
	1	2	3	4	5	6	7	8	9	10	11	12
$ 50	4.74	2.65	1.97	1.64	1.45	1.33	1.25	1.19	1.15	1.12	1.09	1.08
100	9.47	5.30	3.94	3.28	2.90	2.65	2.49	2.37	2.29	2.23	2.18	2.15
200	18.94	10.60	7.88	6.55	5.79	5.30	4.97	4.74	4.57	4.45	4.36	4.29
300	28.41	15.90	11.81	9.83	8.68	7.95	7.46	7.11	6.86	6.67	6.53	6.43
400	37.88	21.20	15.75	13.10	11.57	10.60	9.94	9.48	9.14	8.89	8.71	8.57
500	47.35	26.50	19.69	16.38	14.46	13.24	12.42	11.84	11.43	11.12	10.88	10.71
600	56.81	31.80	23.62	19.65	17.35	15.89	14.91	14.21	13.71	13.34	13.06	12.85
700	66.28	37.10	27.56	22.92	20.24	18.54	17.39	16.58	15.99	15.56	15.24	14.99
800	75.75	42.40	31.50	26.20	23.14	21.19	19.87	18.95	18.28	17.78	17.41	17.13
900	85.22	47.70	35.43	29.47	26.03	23.84	22.36	21.31	20.56	20.01	19.59	19.27
1000	94.69	53.00	39.37	32.75	28.92	26.48	24.84	23.68	22.85	22.23	21.76	21.41
2000	189.37	106.00	78.73	65.49	57.83	52.96	49.67	47.36	45.69	44.45	43.52	42.82
3000	284.05	158.99	118.10	98.23	86.74	79.44	74.51	71.04	68.53	66.67	65.28	64.23
4000	378.73	211.99	157.46	130.97	115.66	105.92	99.34	94.71	91.37	88.90	87.04	85.64
5000	473.41	264.98	196.83	163.71	144.57	132.40	124.18	118.39	114.21	111.12	108.80	107.05
6000	568.09	317.98	236.19	196.45	173.48	158.88	149.01	142.07	137.05	133.34	130.56	128.46
7000	662.77	370.98	275.55	229.19	202.40	185.36	173.84	165.75	159.89	155.56	152.32	149.87
8000	757.45	423.97	314.92	261.93	231.31	211.84	198.68	189.42	182.73	177.79	174.08	171.28
9000	852.13	476.97	354.28	294.67	260.22	238.31	223.51	213.10	205.57	200.01	195.84	192.69
10000	946.81	529.96	393.65	327.41	289.14	264.79	248.35	236.78	228.41	222.23	217.60	214.09
11000	1041.49	582.96	433.01	360.15	318.05	291.27	273.18	260.46	251.25	244.45	239.36	235.50
12000	1136.17	635.96	472.38	392.89	346.96	317.75	298.01	284.13	274.09	266.68	261.12	256.91
13000	1230.85	688.95	511.74	425.63	375.88	344.23	322.85	307.81	296.93	288.90	282.88	278.32
14000	1325.53	741.95	551.10	458.37	404.79	370.71	347.68	331.49	319.77	311.12	304.64	299.73
15000	1420.21	794.94	590.47	491.11	433.70	397.19	372.52	355.16	342.61	333.35	326.40	321.14
16000	1514.89	847.94	629.83	523.85	462.62	423.67	397.35	378.84	365.45	355.57	348.16	342.55
17000	1609.58	900.94	669.20	556.59	491.53	450.14	422.18	402.52	388.29	377.79	369.92	363.96
18000	1704.26	953.93	708.56	589.33	520.44	476.62	447.02	426.20	411.13	400.01	391.68	385.37
19000	1798.94	1006.93	747.93	622.07	549.36	503.10	471.85	449.87	433.97	422.24	413.44	406.77
20000	1893.62	1059.92	787.29	654.81	578.27	529.58	496.69	473.55	456.81	444.46	435.20	428.18
21000	1988.30	1112.92	826.65	687.55	607.18	556.06	521.52	497.23	479.65	466.68	456.96	449.59
22000	2082.98	1165.92	866.02	720.29	636.10	582.54	546.36	520.91	502.50	488.90	478.72	471.00
23000	2177.66	1218.91	905.38	753.03	665.01	609.02	571.19	544.58	525.34	511.13	500.48	492.41
24000	2272.34	1271.91	944.75	785.77	693.92	635.50	596.02	568.26	548.18	533.35	522.24	513.82
25000	2367.02	1324.90	984.11	818.51	722.84	661.98	620.86	591.94	571.02	555.57	544.00	535.23
26000	2461.70	1377.90	1023.48	851.25	751.75	688.45	645.69	615.62	593.86	577.79	565.76	556.64
27000	2556.38	1430.90	1062.84	883.99	780.66	714.93	670.53	639.29	616.70	600.02	587.52	578.05
28000	2651.06	1483.89	1102.20	916.73	809.58	741.41	695.36	662.97	639.54	622.24	609.28	599.46
29000	2745.74	1536.89	1141.57	949.47	838.49	767.89	720.19	686.65	662.38	644.46	631.04	620.86
30000	2840.42	1589.88	1180.93	982.21	867.40	794.37	745.03	710.32	685.22	666.69	652.80	642.27
31000	2935.10	1642.88	1220.30	1014.95	896.32	820.85	769.86	734.00	708.06	688.91	674.56	663.68
32000	3029.78	1695.88	1259.66	1047.69	925.23	847.33	794.70	757.68	730.90	711.13	696.32	685.09
33000	3124.47	1748.87	1299.02	1080.43	954.14	873.81	819.53	781.36	753.74	733.35	718.08	706.50
34000	3219.15	1801.87	1338.39	1113.17	983.06	900.28	844.36	805.03	776.58	755.58	739.84	727.91
35000	3313.83	1854.86	1377.75	1145.91	1011.97	926.76	869.20	828.71	799.42	777.80	761.60	749.32
37500	3550.53	1987.35	1476.16	1227.76	1084.25	992.96	931.28	887.90	856.52	833.36	815.99	802.84
40000	3787.23	2119.84	1574.57	1309.61	1156.54	1059.16	993.37	947.10	913.62	888.91	870.39	856.36
42500	4023.93	2252.32	1672.99	1391.46	1228.82	1125.35	1055.45	1006.29	970.72	944.47	924.79	909.88
45000	4260.63	2384.82	1771.40	1473.31	1301.10	1191.55	1117.54	1065.48	1027.83	1000.03	979.19	963.41
47500	4497.33	2517.31	1869.81	1555.16	1373.38	1257.75	1179.62	1124.68	1084.93	1055.58	1033.59	1016.93
50000	4734.04	2649.80	1968.22	1637.01	1445.67	1323.95	1241.71	1183.87	1142.03	1111.14	1087.99	1070.45
52500	4970.74	2782.29	2066.63	1718.87	1517.95	1390.14	1303.80	1243.06	1199.13	1166.70	1142.39	1123.97
55000	5207.44	2914.78	2165.04	1800.72	1590.23	1456.34	1365.88	1302.26	1256.23	1222.25	1196.79	1177.50
57500	5444.14	3047.27	2263.45	1882.57	1662.52	1522.54	1427.97	1361.45	1313.33	1277.81	1251.19	1231.02
60000	5680.84	3179.76	2361.86	1964.42	1734.80	1588.73	1490.05	1420.64	1370.43	1333.37	1305.59	1284.54
65000	6154.25	3444.74	2558.68	2128.12	1879.37	1721.13	1614.22	1539.03	1484.64	1444.48	1414.39	1391.59
70000	6627.65	3709.72	2755.50	2291.82	2023.93	1853.52	1738.39	1657.42	1598.84	1555.59	1523.19	1498.63
75000	7101.05	3974.70	2952.32	2455.52	2168.50	1985.92	1862.56	1775.80	1713.04	1666.71	1631.98	1605.67
80000	7574.45	4239.68	3149.14	2619.22	2313.07	2118.31	1986.73	1894.19	1827.24	1777.82	1740.78	1712.72
85000	8047.86	4504.66	3345.97	2782.92	2457.63	2250.70	2110.90	2012.58	1941.44	1888.93	1849.58	1819.76
90000	8521.26	4769.64	3542.79	2946.62	2602.20	2383.10	2235.07	2130.96	2055.65	2000.05	1958.38	1926.81
95000	8994.66	5034.62	3739.61	3110.32	2746.76	2515.49	2359.24	2249.35	2169.85	2111.16	2067.18	2033.85
100000	9468.07	5299.60	3936.43	3274.02	2891.33	2647.89	2483.41	2367.74	2284.05	2222.27	2175.98	2140.90
105000	9941.47	5564.58	4133.25	3437.73	3035.90	2780.28	2607.59	2486.12	2398.25	2333.39	2284.78	2247.94
110000	10414.87	5829.56	4330.07	3601.43	3180.46	2912.67	2731.76	2604.51	2512.46	2444.50	2393.58	2354.99
115000	10888.28	6094.54	4526.89	3765.13	3325.03	3045.07	2855.93	2722.90	2626.66	2555.61	2502.37	2462.03
120000	11361.68	6359.52	4723.71	3928.83	3469.60	3177.46	2980.10	2841.28	2740.86	2666.73	2611.17	2569.08
125000	11835.08	6624.50	4920.53	4092.53	3614.16	3309.86	3104.27	2959.67	2855.06	2777.84	2719.97	2676.12
130000	12308.49	6889.48	5117.36	4256.23	3758.73	3442.25	3228.44	3078.06	2969.27	2888.95	2828.77	2783.17
135000	12781.89	7154.46	5314.18	4419.93	3903.29	3574.64	3352.61	3196.44	3083.47	3000.07	2937.57	2890.21
140000	13255.29	7419.44	5511.00	4583.63	4047.86	3707.04	3476.78	3314.83	3197.67	3111.18	3046.37	2997.26
145000	13728.70	7684.42	5707.82	4747.33	4192.43	3839.43	3600.95	3433.21	3311.87	3222.29	3155.17	3104.30
150000	14202.10	7949.40	5904.64	4911.03	4336.99	3971.83	3725.12	3551.60	3426.07	3333.41	3263.96	3211.34
155000	14675.50	8214.38	6101.46	5074.74	4481.56	4104.22	3849.29	3669.99	3540.28	3444.52	3372.76	3318.39
160000	15148.90	8479.36	6298.28	5238.44	4626.13	4236.61	3973.46	3788.37	3654.48	3555.63	3481.56	3425.43

AMOUNT OF LOAN	NUMBER OF YEARS IN TERM											
	13	14	15	16	17	18	19	20	25	30	35	40
$ 50	1.06	1.05	1.04	1.04	1.03	1.03	1.03	1.02	1.02	1.02	1.02	1.02
100	2.12	2.10	2.08	2.07	2.06	2.05	2.05	2.04	2.03	2.03	2.03	2.03
200	4.23	4.19	4.16	4.14	4.12	4.10	4.09	4.08	4.06	4.05	4.05	4.05
300	6.35	6.29	6.24	6.20	6.17	6.15	6.13	6.12	6.08	6.07	6.07	6.07
400	8.46	8.38	8.32	8.27	8.23	8.20	8.17	8.16	8.11	8.09	8.09	8.09
500	10.58	10.47	10.39	10.33	10.28	10.25	10.22	10.19	10.13	10.12	10.11	10.11
600	12.69	12.57	12.47	12.40	12.34	12.29	12.26	12.23	12.16	12.14	12.13	12.13
700	14.80	14.66	14.55	14.46	14.39	14.34	14.30	14.27	14.19	14.16	14.15	14.15
800	16.92	16.75	16.63	16.53	16.45	16.39	16.34	16.31	16.21	16.18	16.18	16.17
900	19.03	18.85	18.70	18.59	18.50	18.44	18.38	18.34	18.24	18.21	18.20	18.19
1000	21.15	20.94	20.78	20.66	20.56	20.49	20.43	20.38	20.26	20.23	20.22	20.21
2000	42.29	41.87	41.56	41.31	41.12	40.97	40.85	40.76	40.52	40.45	40.43	40.42
3000	63.43	62.81	62.33	61.96	61.67	61.45	61.27	61.13	60.78	60.68	60.64	60.63
4000	84.57	83.74	83.11	82.61	82.23	81.93	81.69	81.51	81.04	80.90	80.86	80.84
5000	105.71	104.68	103.88	103.26	102.78	102.41	102.11	101.88	101.30	101.12	101.07	101.05
6000	126.85	125.61	124.66	123.91	123.34	122.89	122.53	122.26	121.56	121.35	121.28	121.26
7000	147.99	146.55	145.43	144.57	143.89	143.37	142.96	142.64	141.81	141.57	141.50	141.47
8000	169.13	167.48	166.21	165.22	164.45	163.85	163.38	163.01	162.07	161.79	161.71	161.68
9000	190.27	188.42	186.98	185.87	185.00	184.33	183.80	183.39	182.33	182.02	181.92	181.89
10000	211.41	209.35	207.76	206.52	205.56	204.81	204.22	203.76	202.59	202.24	202.13	202.10
11000	232.55	230.29	228.53	227.17	226.11	225.29	224.64	224.14	222.85	222.46	222.35	222.31
12000	253.70	251.22	249.31	247.82	246.67	245.77	245.06	244.51	243.11	242.69	242.56	242.52
13000	274.84	272.16	270.08	268.48	267.23	266.25	265.49	264.89	263.36	262.91	262.77	262.73
14000	295.98	293.09	290.86	289.13	287.78	286.73	285.91	285.27	283.62	283.13	282.99	282.94
15000	317.12	314.03	311.63	309.78	308.34	307.21	306.33	305.64	303.88	303.36	303.20	303.15
16000	338.26	334.96	332.41	330.43	328.89	327.69	326.75	326.02	324.14	323.58	323.41	323.36
17000	359.40	355.89	353.18	351.08	349.45	348.17	347.17	346.39	344.40	343.80	343.62	343.57
18000	380.54	376.83	373.96	371.73	370.00	368.65	367.59	366.77	364.66	364.03	363.84	363.78
19000	401.68	397.76	394.74	392.39	390.56	389.13	388.02	387.14	384.92	384.25	384.05	383.99
20000	422.82	418.70	415.51	413.04	411.11	409.61	408.44	407.52	405.17	404.47	404.26	404.20
21000	443.96	439.63	436.29	433.69	431.67	430.09	428.86	427.90	425.43	424.70	424.48	424.41
22000	465.10	460.57	457.06	454.34	452.22	450.57	449.28	448.27	445.69	444.92	444.69	444.62
23000	486.24	481.50	477.84	474.99	472.78	471.05	469.70	468.65	465.95	465.14	464.90	464.83
24000	507.39	502.44	498.61	495.64	493.33	491.53	490.12	489.02	486.21	485.37	485.11	485.04
25000	528.53	523.37	519.39	516.30	513.89	512.01	510.55	509.40	506.47	505.59	505.33	505.25
26000	549.67	544.31	540.16	536.95	534.45	532.49	530.97	529.77	526.72	525.81	525.54	525.46
27000	570.81	565.24	560.94	557.60	555.00	552.97	551.39	550.15	546.98	546.04	545.75	545.67
28000	591.95	586.18	581.71	578.25	575.56	573.45	571.81	570.53	567.24	566.26	565.97	565.88
29000	613.09	607.11	602.49	598.90	596.11	593.93	592.23	590.90	587.50	586.48	586.18	586.09
30000	634.23	628.05	623.26	619.55	616.67	614.41	612.65	611.28	607.76	606.71	606.39	606.30
31000	655.37	648.98	644.04	640.21	637.22	634.89	633.08	631.65	628.02	626.93	626.60	626.51
32000	676.51	669.92	664.81	660.86	657.78	655.38	653.50	652.03	648.28	647.15	646.82	646.72
33000	697.65	690.85	685.59	681.51	678.33	675.86	673.92	672.40	668.53	667.38	667.03	666.93
34000	718.79	711.78	706.36	702.16	698.89	696.34	694.34	692.78	688.79	687.60	687.24	687.13
35000	739.93	732.72	727.14	722.81	719.44	716.82	714.76	713.16	709.05	707.82	707.46	707.34
37500	792.79	785.06	779.08	774.44	770.83	768.02	765.82	764.10	759.70	758.38	757.99	757.87
40000	845.64	837.39	831.02	826.07	822.22	819.22	816.87	815.03	810.34	808.94	808.52	808.39
42500	898.49	889.73	882.95	877.70	873.61	870.42	867.93	865.97	860.99	859.50	859.05	858.92
45000	951.34	942.07	934.89	929.33	925.00	921.62	918.98	916.91	911.64	910.06	909.58	909.44
47500	1004.20	994.40	986.83	980.96	976.39	972.82	970.03	967.85	962.28	960.62	960.12	959.97
50000	1057.05	1046.74	1038.77	1032.59	1027.77	1024.02	1021.09	1018.79	1012.93	1011.17	1010.65	1010.49
52500	1109.90	1099.08	1090.71	1084.22	1079.16	1075.22	1072.14	1069.73	1063.57	1061.73	1061.18	1061.01
55000	1162.75	1151.41	1142.65	1135.84	1130.55	1126.42	1123.20	1120.67	1114.22	1112.29	1111.71	1111.54
57500	1215.60	1203.75	1194.58	1187.47	1181.94	1177.62	1174.25	1171.61	1164.87	1162.85	1162.24	1162.06
60000	1268.46	1256.09	1246.52	1239.10	1233.33	1228.82	1225.30	1222.55	1215.51	1213.41	1212.78	1212.59
65000	1374.16	1360.76	1350.40	1342.36	1336.11	1331.23	1327.41	1324.43	1316.80	1314.53	1313.84	1313.64
70000	1479.86	1465.43	1454.28	1445.62	1438.88	1433.63	1429.52	1426.31	1418.10	1415.64	1414.91	1414.68
75000	1585.57	1570.11	1558.15	1548.88	1541.66	1536.03	1531.63	1528.19	1519.39	1516.76	1515.97	1515.73
80000	1691.27	1674.78	1662.03	1652.14	1644.43	1638.43	1633.74	1630.06	1620.68	1617.88	1617.03	1616.78
85000	1796.98	1779.45	1765.90	1755.39	1747.21	1740.83	1735.85	1731.94	1721.97	1718.99	1718.10	1717.83
90000	1902.68	1884.13	1869.78	1858.65	1849.99	1843.23	1837.95	1833.82	1823.27	1820.11	1819.16	1818.88
95000	2008.39	1988.80	1973.66	1961.91	1952.77	1945.64	1940.06	1935.70	1924.56	1921.23	1920.23	1919.93
100000	2114.09	2093.47	2077.53	2065.17	2055.54	2048.04	2042.17	2037.58	2025.85	2022.34	2021.29	2020.97
105000	2219.79	2198.15	2181.41	2168.43	2158.32	2150.44	2144.28	2139.46	2127.14	2123.46	2122.36	2122.02
110000	2325.50	2302.82	2285.29	2271.68	2261.10	2252.84	2246.39	2241.34	2228.43	2224.58	2223.42	2223.07
115000	2431.20	2407.49	2389.16	2374.94	2363.87	2355.24	2348.50	2343.22	2329.73	2325.70	2324.48	2324.12
120000	2536.91	2512.17	2493.04	2478.20	2466.65	2457.64	2450.60	2445.09	2431.02	2426.81	2425.55	2425.17
125000	2642.61	2616.84	2596.92	2581.46	2569.43	2560.04	2552.71	2546.97	2532.31	2527.93	2526.61	2526.22
130000	2748.32	2721.51	2700.79	2684.72	2672.21	2662.45	2654.82	2648.85	2633.60	2629.05	2627.68	2627.27
135000	2854.02	2826.19	2804.67	2787.97	2774.98	2764.85	2756.93	2750.73	2734.90	2730.16	2728.74	2728.31
140000	2959.72	2930.86	2908.55	2891.23	2877.76	2867.25	2859.04	2852.61	2836.19	2831.28	2829.81	2829.36
145000	3065.43	3035.53	3012.42	2994.49	2980.54	2969.65	2961.14	2954.49	2937.48	2932.40	2930.87	2930.41
150000	3171.13	3140.21	3116.30	3097.75	3083.31	3072.05	3063.25	3056.37	3038.77	3033.51	3031.93	3031.46
155000	3276.84	3244.88	3220.18	3201.01	3186.09	3174.45	3165.36	3158.25	3140.06	3134.63	3133.00	3132.51
160000	3382.54	3349.55	3324.05	3304.27	3288.87	3276.86	3267.47	3260.12	3241.36	3235.75	3234.06	3233.56

MONTHLY AMORTIZING PAYMENTS

AMOUNT OF LOAN	NUMBER OF YEARS IN TERM											
	1	2	3	4	5	6	7	8	9	10	11	12
$ 50	4.75	2.66	1.98	1.65	1.46	1.34	1.25	1.20	1.16	1.12	1.10	1.08
100	9.49	5.32	3.95	3.29	2.91	2.67	2.50	2.39	2.31	2.24	2.20	2.16
200	18.97	10.63	7.90	6.58	5.82	5.33	5.00	4.77	4.61	4.48	4.39	4.32
300	28.45	15.94	11.85	9.87	8.72	7.99	7.50	7.16	6.91	6.72	6.59	6.48
400	37.93	21.25	15.80	13.16	11.63	10.66	10.00	9.54	9.21	8.96	8.78	8.64
500	47.41	26.57	19.75	16.44	14.53	13.32	12.50	11.93	11.51	11.20	10.97	10.80
600	56.89	31.88	23.70	19.73	17.44	15.98	15.00	14.31	13.81	13.44	13.17	12.96
700	66.37	37.19	27.65	23.02	20.35	18.65	17.50	16.69	16.11	15.68	15.36	15.12
800	75.85	42.50	31.60	26.31	23.25	21.31	20.00	19.08	18.41	17.92	17.56	17.28
900	85.33	47.81	35.55	29.60	26.16	23.97	22.50	21.46	20.71	20.16	19.75	19.44
1000	94.81	53.13	39.50	32.88	29.06	26.64	25.00	23.85	23.02	22.40	21.94	21.60
2000	189.61	106.25	79.00	65.76	58.12	53.27	49.99	47.69	46.03	44.80	43.88	43.19
3000	284.41	159.37	118.49	98.64	87.18	79.90	74.98	71.53	69.04	67.20	65.82	64.78
4000	379.21	212.49	157.99	131.52	116.24	106.53	99.98	95.37	92.05	89.60	87.76	86.37
5000	474.01	265.61	197.48	164.40	145.30	133.16	124.97	119.21	115.06	111.99	109.70	107.97
6000	568.82	318.73	236.98	197.28	174.36	159.79	149.96	143.06	138.07	134.39	131.64	129.56
7000	663.62	371.85	276.48	230.16	203.42	186.42	174.95	166.90	161.08	156.79	153.58	151.15
8000	758.42	424.97	315.97	263.04	232.48	213.05	199.95	190.74	184.09	179.19	175.52	172.74
9000	853.22	478.09	355.47	295.91	261.54	239.69	224.94	214.58	207.10	201.58	197.46	194.34
10000	948.02	531.21	394.96	328.79	290.59	266.32	249.93	238.42	230.11	223.98	219.40	215.93
11000	1042.82	584.34	434.46	361.67	319.65	292.95	274.93	262.27	253.12	246.38	241.34	237.52
12000	1137.63	637.46	473.96	394.55	348.71	319.58	299.92	286.11	276.13	268.78	263.28	259.11
13000	1232.43	690.58	513.45	427.43	377.77	346.21	324.91	309.95	299.14	291.18	285.22	280.71
14000	1327.23	743.70	552.95	460.31	406.83	372.84	349.90	333.79	322.15	313.57	307.15	302.30
15000	1422.03	796.82	592.44	493.19	435.89	399.47	374.90	357.63	345.16	335.97	329.09	323.89
16000	1516.83	849.94	631.94	526.07	464.95	426.10	399.89	381.48	368.17	358.37	351.03	345.48
17000	1611.63	903.06	671.43	558.95	494.01	452.74	424.88	405.32	391.18	380.77	372.97	367.08
18000	1706.44	956.18	710.93	591.82	523.07	479.37	449.88	429.16	414.20	403.16	394.91	388.67
19000	1801.24	1009.30	750.43	624.70	552.12	506.00	474.87	453.00	437.21	425.56	416.85	410.26
20000	1896.04	1062.42	789.92	657.58	581.18	532.63	499.86	476.84	460.22	447.96	438.79	431.85
21000	1990.84	1115.55	829.42	690.46	610.24	559.26	524.85	500.69	483.23	470.36	460.73	453.45
22000	2085.64	1168.67	868.91	723.34	639.30	585.89	549.85	524.53	506.24	492.76	482.67	475.04
23000	2180.44	1221.79	908.41	756.22	668.36	612.52	574.84	548.37	529.25	515.15	504.61	496.63
24000	2275.25	1274.91	947.91	789.10	697.42	639.15	599.83	572.21	552.26	537.55	526.55	518.22
25000	2370.05	1328.03	987.40	821.98	726.48	665.78	624.83	596.05	575.27	559.95	548.49	539.82
26000	2464.85	1381.15	1026.90	854.86	755.54	692.42	649.82	619.90	598.28	582.35	570.43	561.41
27000	2559.65	1434.27	1066.39	887.73	784.60	719.05	674.81	643.74	621.29	604.74	592.37	583.00
28000	2654.45	1487.39	1105.89	920.61	813.65	745.68	699.80	667.58	644.30	627.14	614.30	604.59
29000	2749.26	1540.51	1145.38	953.49	842.71	772.31	724.80	691.42	667.31	649.54	636.24	626.19
30000	2844.06	1593.63	1184.88	986.37	871.77	798.94	749.79	715.26	690.32	671.94	658.18	647.78
31000	2938.86	1646.76	1224.38	1019.25	900.83	825.57	774.78	739.11	713.33	694.33	680.12	669.37
32000	3033.66	1699.88	1263.87	1052.13	929.89	852.20	799.78	762.95	736.34	716.73	702.06	690.96
33000	3128.46	1753.00	1303.37	1085.01	958.95	878.83	824.77	786.79	759.35	739.13	724.00	712.56
34000	3223.26	1806.12	1342.86	1117.89	988.01	905.47	849.76	810.63	782.36	761.53	745.94	734.15
35000	3318.07	1859.24	1382.36	1150.77	1017.07	932.10	874.75	834.47	805.37	783.93	767.88	755.74
37500	3555.07	1992.04	1481.10	1232.96	1089.71	998.67	937.24	894.08	862.90	839.92	822.73	809.72
40000	3792.07	2124.84	1579.84	1315.16	1162.36	1065.25	999.72	953.68	920.43	895.91	877.58	863.70
42500	4029.08	2257.65	1678.58	1397.36	1235.01	1131.83	1062.20	1013.29	977.95	951.91	932.42	917.69
45000	4266.08	2390.45	1777.32	1479.55	1307.66	1198.41	1124.68	1072.89	1035.48	1007.90	987.27	971.67
47500	4503.09	2523.25	1876.06	1561.75	1380.30	1264.99	1187.16	1132.50	1093.01	1063.90	1042.12	1025.65
50000	4740.09	2656.05	1974.80	1643.95	1452.95	1331.56	1249.65	1192.10	1150.53	1119.89	1096.97	1079.63
52500	4977.10	2788.86	2073.54	1726.15	1525.60	1398.14	1312.13	1251.71	1208.06	1175.89	1151.82	1133.61
55000	5214.10	2921.66	2172.28	1808.34	1598.25	1464.72	1374.61	1311.31	1265.59	1231.88	1206.66	1187.59
57500	5451.10	3054.46	2271.02	1890.54	1670.89	1531.30	1437.09	1370.92	1323.11	1287.87	1261.51	1241.57
60000	5688.11	3187.26	2369.76	1972.74	1743.54	1597.88	1499.58	1430.52	1380.64	1343.87	1316.36	1295.55
65000	6162.12	3452.87	2567.24	2137.13	1888.83	1731.03	1624.54	1549.73	1495.69	1455.86	1426.06	1403.52
70000	6636.13	3718.47	2764.72	2301.53	2034.13	1864.19	1749.50	1668.94	1610.74	1567.85	1535.75	1511.48
75000	7110.14	3984.08	2962.19	2465.92	2179.42	1997.34	1874.47	1788.15	1725.80	1679.83	1645.44	1619.44
80000	7584.14	4249.68	3159.67	2630.31	2324.72	2130.50	1999.43	1907.36	1840.85	1791.82	1755.15	1727.40
85000	8058.15	4515.29	3357.15	2794.71	2470.01	2263.66	2124.40	2026.57	1955.90	1903.81	1864.84	1835.37
90000	8532.16	4780.89	3554.63	2959.10	2615.31	2396.81	2249.36	2145.78	2070.96	2015.80	1974.54	1943.33
95000	9006.17	5046.50	3752.11	3123.50	2760.60	2529.97	2374.32	2264.99	2186.01	2127.79	2084.24	2051.29
100000	9480.18	5312.10	3949.59	3287.89	2905.90	2663.12	2499.29	2384.20	2301.06	2239.78	2193.93	2159.25
105000	9954.19	5577.71	4147.07	3452.29	3051.19	2796.28	2624.25	2503.41	2416.11	2351.77	2303.63	2267.21
110000	10428.20	5843.31	4344.55	3616.68	3196.49	2929.44	2749.22	2622.62	2531.17	2463.76	2413.32	2375.18
115000	10902.20	6108.92	4542.03	3781.07	3341.78	3062.59	2874.18	2741.83	2646.22	2575.74	2523.02	2483.14
120000	11376.21	6374.52	4739.51	3945.47	3487.07	3195.75	2999.15	2861.04	2761.27	2687.73	2632.72	2591.10
125000	11850.22	6640.13	4936.99	4109.86	3632.37	3328.90	3124.11	2980.25	2876.33	2799.72	2742.41	2699.06
130000	12324.23	6905.73	5134.47	4274.26	3777.66	3462.06	3249.07	3099.46	2991.38	2911.71	2852.11	2807.03
135000	12798.24	7171.34	5331.95	4438.65	3922.96	3595.21	3374.04	3218.67	3106.43	3023.70	2961.81	2914.99
140000	13272.25	7436.94	5529.43	4603.05	4068.25	3728.37	3499.00	3337.88	3221.48	3135.69	3071.50	3022.95
145000	13746.26	7702.55	5726.90	4767.44	4213.55	3861.53	3623.97	3457.09	3336.54	3247.68	3181.20	3130.91
150000	14220.27	7968.15	5924.38	4931.84	4358.84	3994.68	3748.93	3576.30	3451.59	3359.66	3290.90	3238.88
155000	14694.27	8233.76	6121.86	5096.23	4504.14	4127.84	3873.89	3695.51	3566.64	3471.65	3400.59	3346.84
160000	15168.28	8499.36	6319.34	5260.62	4649.43	4260.99	3998.86	3814.72	3681.70	3583.64	3510.29	3454.80

AMOUNT OF LOAN	NUMBER OF YEARS IN TERM											
	13	14	15	16	17	18	19	20	25	30	35	40
$ 50	1.07	1.06	1.05	1.05	1.04	1.04	1.04	1.03	1.03	1.03	1.03	1.03
100	2.14	2.12	2.10	2.09	2.08	2.07	2.07	2.06	2.05	2.05	2.05	2.05
200	4.27	4.23	4.20	4.17	4.16	4.14	4.13	4.12	4.10	4.09	4.09	4.09
300	6.40	6.34	6.30	6.26	6.23	6.21	6.19	6.18	6.14	6.13	6.13	6.13
400	8.54	8.45	8.39	8.34	8.31	8.28	8.25	8.24	8.19	8.18	8.17	8.17
500	10.67	10.57	10.49	10.43	10.38	10.34	10.32	10.29	10.24	10.22	10.22	10.21
600	12.80	12.68	12.59	12.51	12.46	12.41	12.38	12.35	12.28	12.26	12.26	12.26
700	14.93	14.79	14.68	14.60	14.53	14.48	14.44	14.41	14.33	14.31	14.30	14.30
800	17.07	16.90	16.78	16.68	16.61	16.55	16.50	16.47	16.38	16.35	16.34	16.34
900	19.20	19.02	18.88	18.77	18.68	18.62	18.57	18.52	18.42	18.39	18.38	18.38
1000	21.33	21.13	20.97	20.85	20.76	20.68	20.63	20.58	20.47	20.44	20.43	20.42
2000	42.66	42.25	41.94	41.70	41.51	41.36	41.25	41.16	40.93	40.87	40.85	40.84
3000	63.99	63.38	62.91	62.55	62.26	62.04	61.87	61.74	61.40	61.30	61.27	61.26
4000	85.32	84.50	83.88	83.39	83.02	82.72	82.49	82.32	81.86	81.73	81.69	81.68
5000	106.64	105.63	104.85	104.24	103.77	103.40	103.12	102.89	102.33	102.16	102.11	102.09
6000	127.97	126.75	125.81	125.09	124.52	124.08	123.74	123.47	122.79	122.59	122.53	122.51
7000	149.30	147.88	146.78	145.93	145.27	144.76	144.36	144.05	143.25	143.02	142.95	142.93
8000	170.63	169.00	167.75	166.78	166.03	165.44	164.98	164.63	163.72	163.45	163.37	163.35
9000	191.96	190.13	188.72	187.63	186.78	186.12	185.61	185.20	184.18	183.88	183.79	183.77
10000	213.28	211.25	209.69	208.47	207.53	206.80	206.23	205.78	204.65	204.31	204.21	204.18
11000	234.61	232.38	230.66	229.32	228.29	227.48	226.85	226.36	225.11	224.74	224.63	224.60
12000	255.94	253.50	251.62	250.17	249.04	248.16	247.47	246.94	245.58	245.17	245.06	245.02
13000	277.27	274.63	272.59	271.02	269.79	268.84	268.09	267.51	266.04	265.61	265.48	265.44
14000	298.60	295.75	293.56	291.86	290.54	289.52	288.72	288.09	286.50	286.04	285.90	285.86
15000	319.92	316.88	314.53	312.71	311.30	310.20	309.34	308.67	306.97	306.47	306.32	306.27
16000	341.25	338.00	335.50	333.56	332.05	330.88	329.96	329.25	327.43	326.90	326.74	326.69
17000	362.58	359.13	356.47	354.40	352.80	351.56	350.58	349.83	347.90	347.33	347.16	347.11
18000	383.91	380.25	377.43	375.25	373.55	372.24	371.21	370.40	368.36	367.76	367.58	367.53
19000	405.24	401.38	398.40	396.10	394.31	392.91	391.83	390.98	388.83	388.19	388.00	387.95
20000	426.56	422.50	419.37	416.94	415.06	413.59	412.45	411.56	409.29	408.62	408.42	408.36
21000	447.89	443.63	440.34	437.79	435.81	434.27	433.07	432.14	429.75	429.05	428.84	428.78
22000	469.22	464.75	461.31	458.64	456.57	454.95	453.70	452.71	450.22	449.48	449.26	449.20
23000	490.55	485.88	482.27	479.48	477.32	475.63	474.32	473.29	470.68	469.91	469.68	469.62
24000	511.88	507.00	503.24	500.33	498.07	496.31	494.94	493.87	491.15	490.34	490.11	490.03
25000	533.20	528.13	524.21	521.18	518.82	516.99	515.56	514.45	511.61	510.77	510.53	510.45
26000	554.53	549.25	545.18	542.03	539.58	537.67	536.18	535.02	532.08	531.21	530.95	530.87
27000	575.86	570.38	566.15	562.87	560.33	558.35	556.81	555.60	552.54	551.64	551.37	551.29
28000	597.19	591.50	587.12	583.72	581.08	579.03	577.43	576.18	573.00	572.07	571.79	571.71
29000	618.52	612.63	608.08	604.57	601.83	599.71	598.05	596.76	593.47	592.50	592.21	592.12
30000	639.84	633.75	629.05	625.41	622.59	620.39	618.67	617.33	613.93	612.93	612.63	612.54
31000	661.17	654.88	650.02	646.26	643.34	641.07	639.30	637.91	634.40	633.36	633.05	632.96
32000	682.50	676.00	670.99	667.11	664.09	661.75	659.92	658.49	654.86	653.79	653.47	653.38
33000	703.83	697.13	691.96	687.95	684.85	682.43	680.54	679.07	675.33	674.22	673.89	673.80
34000	725.16	718.25	712.93	708.80	705.60	703.11	701.16	699.65	695.79	694.65	694.31	694.21
35000	746.48	739.38	733.89	729.65	726.35	723.79	721.78	720.22	716.25	715.08	714.74	714.63
37500	799.80	792.19	786.31	781.77	778.23	775.48	773.34	771.67	767.42	766.16	765.79	765.68
40000	853.12	845.00	838.73	833.88	830.12	827.18	824.90	823.11	818.58	817.24	816.84	816.72
42500	906.44	897.81	891.16	886.00	882.00	878.88	876.45	874.56	869.74	868.31	867.89	867.77
45000	959.76	950.62	943.58	938.12	933.88	930.58	928.01	926.00	920.90	919.39	918.94	918.81
47500	1013.08	1003.44	996.00	990.24	985.76	982.28	979.56	977.44	972.06	970.47	970.00	969.86
50000	1066.40	1056.25	1048.42	1042.35	1037.64	1033.98	1031.12	1028.89	1023.22	1021.55	1021.05	1020.90
52500	1119.72	1109.06	1100.84	1094.47	1089.52	1085.68	1082.67	1080.33	1074.38	1072.62	1072.10	1071.95
55000	1173.04	1161.87	1153.26	1146.59	1141.41	1137.37	1134.23	1131.78	1125.54	1123.70	1123.15	1122.99
57500	1226.36	1214.69	1205.68	1198.70	1193.29	1189.07	1185.79	1183.22	1176.70	1174.78	1174.20	1174.04
60000	1279.68	1267.50	1258.10	1250.82	1245.17	1240.77	1237.34	1234.66	1227.86	1225.85	1225.26	1225.08
65000	1386.32	1373.12	1362.94	1355.06	1348.93	1344.17	1340.45	1337.55	1330.18	1328.01	1327.36	1327.17
70000	1492.96	1478.75	1467.78	1459.29	1452.70	1447.57	1443.56	1440.44	1432.50	1430.16	1429.47	1429.26
75000	1599.60	1584.37	1572.62	1563.53	1556.46	1550.96	1546.68	1543.33	1534.83	1532.32	1531.57	1531.35
80000	1706.24	1690.00	1677.46	1667.76	1660.23	1654.36	1649.79	1646.22	1637.15	1634.47	1633.67	1633.44
85000	1812.88	1795.62	1782.31	1772.00	1763.99	1757.76	1752.90	1749.11	1739.47	1736.62	1735.78	1735.53
90000	1919.52	1901.24	1887.15	1876.23	1867.75	1861.16	1856.01	1851.99	1841.79	1838.78	1837.88	1837.62
95000	2026.16	2006.87	1991.99	1980.47	1971.52	1964.55	1959.12	1954.88	1944.11	1940.93	1939.99	1939.71
100000	2132.80	2112.49	2096.83	2084.70	2075.28	2067.95	2062.23	2057.77	2046.44	2043.09	2042.09	2041.80
105000	2239.44	2218.12	2201.67	2188.93	2179.04	2171.35	2165.34	2160.66	2148.75	2145.24	2144.20	2143.89
110000	2346.08	2323.74	2306.51	2293.17	2282.81	2274.74	2268.46	2263.55	2251.08	2247.39	2246.30	2245.98
115000	2452.72	2429.37	2411.35	2397.40	2386.57	2378.14	2371.57	2366.43	2353.40	2349.55	2348.40	2348.07
120000	2559.36	2534.99	2516.19	2501.64	2490.34	2481.54	2474.68	2469.32	2455.72	2451.70	2450.51	2450.15
125000	2666.00	2640.62	2621.04	2605.87	2594.10	2584.94	2577.79	2572.21	2558.04	2553.86	2552.61	2552.24
130000	2772.64	2746.24	2725.88	2710.11	2697.86	2688.33	2680.90	2675.10	2660.36	2656.01	2654.72	2654.33
135000	2879.28	2851.86	2830.72	2814.34	2801.63	2791.73	2784.01	2777.99	2762.68	2758.16	2756.82	2756.42
140000	2985.92	2957.49	2935.56	2918.58	2905.39	2895.13	2887.12	2880.88	2865.00	2860.32	2858.93	2858.51
145000	3092.56	3063.11	3040.40	3022.81	3009.15	2998.52	2990.24	2983.76	2967.33	2962.47	2961.03	2960.60
150000	3199.20	3168.74	3145.24	3127.05	3112.92	3101.92	3093.35	3086.65	3069.65	3064.63	3063.14	3062.69
155000	3305.84	3274.36	3250.08	3231.28	3216.68	3205.32	3196.46	3189.54	3171.97	3166.78	3165.24	3164.78
160000	3412.48	3379.99	3354.92	3335.52	3320.45	3308.72	3299.57	3292.43	3274.29	3268.93	3267.34	3266.87

MONTHLY AMORTIZING PAYMENTS

AMOUNT OF LOAN	NUMBER OF YEARS IN TERM											
	1	2	3	4	5	6	7	8	9	10	11	12
$ 50	4.75	2.67	1.99	1.66	1.47	1.34	1.26	1.21	1.16	1.13	1.11	1.09
100	9.50	5.33	3.97	3.31	2.93	2.68	2.52	2.41	2.32	2.26	2.22	2.18
200	18.99	10.65	7.93	6.61	5.85	5.36	5.04	4.81	4.64	4.52	4.43	4.36
300	28.48	15.98	11.89	9.91	8.77	8.04	7.55	7.21	6.96	6.78	6.64	6.54
400	37.97	21.30	15.86	13.21	11.69	10.72	10.07	9.61	9.28	9.03	8.85	8.72
500	47.47	26.63	19.82	16.51	14.61	13.40	12.58	12.01	11.60	11.29	11.06	10.89
600	56.96	31.95	23.78	19.82	17.53	16.08	15.10	14.41	13.91	13.55	13.28	13.07
700	66.45	37.28	27.74	23.12	20.45	18.75	17.61	16.81	16.23	15.81	15.49	15.25
800	75.94	42.60	31.71	26.42	23.37	21.43	20.13	19.21	18.55	18.06	17.70	17.43
900	85.44	47.93	35.67	29.72	26.29	24.11	22.64	21.61	20.87	20.32	19.91	19.60
1000	94.93	53.25	39.63	33.02	29.21	26.79	25.16	24.01	23.19	22.58	22.12	21.78
2000	189.85	106.50	79.26	66.04	58.41	53.57	50.31	48.02	46.37	45.15	44.24	43.56
3000	284.77	159.74	118.89	99.06	87.62	80.36	75.46	72.03	69.55	67.72	66.36	65.33
4000	379.70	212.99	158.52	132.08	116.82	107.14	100.61	96.03	92.73	90.30	88.48	87.11
5000	474.62	266.24	198.14	165.09	146.03	133.92	125.77	120.04	115.91	112.87	110.60	108.89
6000	569.54	319.48	237.77	198.11	175.23	160.71	150.92	144.05	139.09	135.44	132.72	130.66
7000	664.47	372.73	277.40	231.13	204.44	187.49	176.07	168.05	162.27	158.02	154.84	152.44
8000	759.39	425.97	317.03	264.15	233.64	214.28	201.22	192.06	185.45	180.59	176.96	174.22
9000	854.31	479.22	356.65	297.17	262.85	241.06	226.37	216.07	208.64	203.16	199.08	195.99
10000	949.23	532.47	396.28	330.18	292.05	267.84	251.53	240.08	231.82	225.74	221.20	217.77
11000	1044.16	585.71	435.91	363.20	321.26	294.63	276.68	264.08	255.00	248.31	243.32	239.55
12000	1139.08	638.96	475.54	396.22	350.46	321.41	301.83	288.09	278.18	270.88	265.44	261.32
13000	1234.00	692.21	515.17	429.24	379.67	348.20	326.98	312.10	301.36	293.46	287.56	283.10
14000	1328.93	745.45	554.79	462.25	408.87	374.98	352.13	336.10	324.54	316.03	309.67	304.88
15000	1423.85	798.70	594.42	495.27	438.08	401.76	377.29	360.11	347.72	338.60	331.79	326.65
16000	1518.77	851.94	634.05	528.29	467.28	428.55	402.44	384.12	370.90	361.18	353.91	348.43
17000	1613.69	905.19	673.68	561.31	496.49	455.33	427.59	408.13	394.08	383.75	376.03	370.21
18000	1708.62	958.44	713.30	594.33	525.69	482.12	452.74	432.13	417.27	406.32	398.15	391.98
19000	1803.54	1011.68	752.93	627.34	554.90	508.90	477.89	456.14	440.45	428.90	420.27	413.76
20000	1898.46	1064.93	792.56	660.36	584.10	535.68	503.05	480.15	463.63	451.47	442.39	435.53
21000	1993.39	1118.17	832.19	693.38	613.31	562.47	528.20	504.15	486.81	474.04	464.51	457.31
22000	2088.31	1171.42	871.81	726.40	642.51	589.25	553.35	528.16	509.99	496.62	486.63	479.09
23000	2183.23	1224.67	911.44	759.42	671.72	616.04	578.50	552.17	533.17	519.19	508.75	500.86
24000	2278.16	1277.91	951.07	792.43	700.92	642.82	603.65	576.17	556.35	541.76	530.87	522.64
25000	2373.08	1331.16	990.70	825.45	730.13	669.60	628.81	600.18	579.53	564.34	552.99	544.42
26000	2468.00	1384.41	1030.33	858.47	759.33	696.39	653.96	624.19	602.71	586.91	575.11	566.19
27000	2562.92	1437.65	1069.95	891.49	788.54	723.17	679.11	648.20	625.90	609.48	597.23	587.97
28000	2657.85	1490.90	1109.58	924.50	817.74	749.96	704.26	672.20	649.08	632.06	619.34	609.75
29000	2752.77	1544.14	1149.21	957.52	846.95	776.74	729.41	696.21	672.26	654.63	641.46	631.52
30000	2847.69	1597.39	1188.84	990.54	876.15	803.52	754.57	720.22	695.44	677.20	663.58	653.30
31000	2942.62	1650.64	1228.46	1023.56	905.36	830.31	779.72	744.22	718.62	699.78	685.70	675.08
32000	3037.54	1703.88	1268.09	1056.58	934.56	857.09	804.87	768.23	741.80	722.35	707.82	696.85
33000	3132.46	1757.13	1307.72	1089.59	963.77	883.88	830.02	792.24	764.98	744.92	729.94	718.63
34000	3227.38	1810.37	1347.35	1122.61	992.97	910.66	855.17	816.25	788.16	767.50	752.06	740.41
35000	3322.31	1863.62	1386.98	1155.63	1022.18	937.44	880.33	840.25	811.34	790.07	774.18	762.18
37500	3559.61	1996.74	1486.04	1238.17	1095.19	1004.40	943.21	900.27	869.30	846.50	829.48	816.62
40000	3796.92	2129.85	1585.11	1320.72	1168.20	1071.36	1006.09	960.29	927.25	902.94	884.78	871.06
42500	4034.23	2262.97	1684.18	1403.26	1241.21	1138.32	1068.97	1020.31	985.20	959.37	940.07	925.51
45000	4271.54	2396.08	1783.25	1485.81	1314.23	1205.28	1131.85	1080.32	1043.16	1015.80	995.37	979.95
47500	4508.84	2529.20	1882.32	1568.35	1387.24	1272.24	1194.73	1140.34	1101.11	1072.24	1050.67	1034.39
50000	4746.15	2662.31	1981.39	1650.90	1460.25	1339.20	1257.61	1200.36	1159.06	1128.67	1105.97	1088.83
52500	4983.46	2795.43	2080.46	1733.44	1533.26	1406.16	1320.49	1260.38	1217.01	1185.10	1161.27	1143.27
55000	5220.77	2928.54	2179.53	1815.99	1606.28	1473.12	1383.37	1320.39	1274.97	1241.54	1216.57	1197.71
57500	5458.07	3061.66	2278.60	1898.53	1679.29	1540.08	1446.25	1380.41	1332.92	1297.97	1271.86	1252.15
60000	5695.38	3194.78	2377.67	1981.08	1752.30	1607.04	1509.13	1440.43	1390.87	1354.40	1327.16	1306.59
65000	6170.00	3461.01	2575.81	2146.16	1898.33	1740.96	1634.89	1560.47	1506.78	1467.27	1437.76	1415.48
70000	6644.61	3727.24	2773.95	2311.25	2044.35	1874.88	1760.65	1680.50	1622.68	1580.13	1548.35	1524.36
75000	7119.22	3993.47	2972.08	2476.34	2190.38	2008.80	1886.41	1800.54	1738.59	1693.00	1658.95	1633.24
80000	7593.84	4259.70	3170.22	2641.43	2336.40	2142.72	2012.17	1920.57	1854.50	1805.87	1769.55	1742.12
85000	8068.45	4525.93	3368.36	2806.52	2482.42	2276.64	2137.93	2040.61	1970.40	1918.73	1880.14	1851.01
90000	8543.07	4792.16	3566.50	2971.61	2628.45	2410.56	2263.69	2160.64	2086.31	2031.60	1990.74	1959.89
95000	9017.68	5058.39	3764.64	3136.70	2774.47	2544.48	2389.45	2280.68	2202.21	2144.47	2101.34	2068.77
100000	9492.30	5324.62	3962.78	3301.79	2920.50	2678.40	2515.21	2400.71	2318.12	2257.33	2211.93	2177.65
105000	9966.91	5590.85	4160.92	3466.88	3066.52	2812.32	2640.97	2520.75	2434.02	2370.20	2322.53	2286.53
110000	10441.53	5857.08	4359.05	3631.97	3212.55	2946.24	2766.73	2640.78	2549.93	2483.07	2433.13	2395.42
115000	10916.14	6123.31	4557.19	3797.06	3358.57	3080.16	2892.49	2760.82	2665.84	2595.93	2543.72	2504.30
120000	11390.76	6389.55	4755.33	3962.15	3504.60	3214.08	3018.25	2880.85	2781.74	2708.80	2654.32	2613.18
125000	11865.37	6655.78	4953.47	4127.24	3650.62	3348.00	3144.01	3000.89	2897.65	2821.66	2764.92	2722.06
130000	12339.99	6922.01	5151.61	4292.32	3796.65	3481.92	3269.77	3120.93	3013.55	2934.53	2875.51	2830.95
135000	12814.60	7188.24	5349.75	4457.41	3942.67	3615.84	3395.53	3240.96	3129.46	3047.40	2986.11	2939.83
140000	13289.21	7454.47	5547.89	4622.50	4088.70	3749.76	3521.29	3361.00	3245.36	3160.26	3096.70	3048.71
145000	13763.83	7720.70	5746.02	4787.59	4234.72	3883.68	3647.05	3481.03	3361.27	3273.13	3207.30	3157.59
150000	14238.44	7986.93	5944.16	4952.68	4380.75	4017.60	3772.81	3601.07	3477.18	3386.00	3317.90	3266.48
155000	14713.06	8253.16	6142.30	5117.77	4526.77	4151.52	3898.57	3721.10	3593.08	3498.86	3428.49	3375.36
160000	15187.67	8519.39	6340.44	5282.86	4672.80	4285.44	4024.33	3841.14	3708.99	3611.73	3539.09	3484.24

AMOUNT OF LOAN	NUMBER OF YEARS IN TERM											
	13	14	15	16	17	18	19	20	25	30	35	40
$ 50	1.08	1.07	1.06	1.06	1.05	1.05	1.05	1.04	1.04	1.04	1.04	1.04
100	2.16	2.14	2.12	2.11	2.10	2.09	2.09	2.08	2.07	2.07	2.07	2.07
200	4.31	4.27	4.24	4.21	4.20	4.18	4.17	4.16	4.14	4.13	4.13	4.13
300	6.46	6.40	6.35	6.32	6.29	6.27	6.25	6.24	6.21	6.20	6.19	6.19
400	8.61	8.53	8.47	8.42	8.39	8.36	8.33	8.32	8.27	8.26	8.26	8.26
500	10.76	10.66	10.59	10.53	10.48	10.44	10.42	10.39	10.34	10.32	10.32	10.32
600	12.91	12.79	12.70	12.63	12.58	12.53	12.50	12.47	12.41	12.39	12.38	12.38
700	15.07	14.93	14.82	14.73	14.67	14.62	14.58	14.55	14.47	14.45	14.45	14.44
800	17.22	17.06	16.93	16.84	16.77	16.71	16.66	16.63	16.54	16.52	16.51	16.51
900	19.37	19.19	19.05	18.94	18.86	18.80	18.75	18.71	18.61	18.58	18.57	18.57
1000	21.52	21.32	21.17	21.05	20.96	20.88	20.83	20.78	20.68	20.64	20.63	20.63
2000	43.04	42.64	42.33	42.09	41.91	41.76	41.65	41.56	41.35	41.28	41.26	41.26
3000	64.55	63.95	63.49	63.13	62.86	62.64	62.47	62.34	62.02	61.92	61.89	61.88
4000	86.07	85.27	84.65	84.18	83.81	83.52	83.30	83.12	82.69	82.56	82.52	82.51
5000	107.58	106.58	105.81	105.22	104.76	104.40	104.12	103.90	103.36	103.20	103.15	103.14
6000	129.10	127.90	126.97	126.26	125.71	125.28	124.94	124.68	124.03	123.83	123.78	123.76
7000	150.61	149.21	148.14	147.30	146.66	146.16	145.77	145.46	144.70	144.47	144.41	144.39
8000	172.13	170.53	169.30	168.35	167.61	167.04	166.59	166.24	165.37	165.11	165.04	165.01
9000	193.64	191.84	190.46	189.39	188.56	187.91	187.41	187.02	186.04	185.75	185.67	185.64
10000	215.16	213.16	211.62	210.43	209.51	208.79	208.24	207.80	206.71	206.39	206.29	206.27
11000	236.68	234.48	232.78	231.47	230.46	229.67	229.06	228.58	227.38	227.03	226.92	226.89
12000	258.19	255.79	253.94	252.52	251.41	250.55	249.88	249.36	248.05	247.66	247.55	247.52
13000	279.71	277.11	275.11	273.56	272.36	271.43	270.71	270.14	268.72	268.30	268.18	268.14
14000	301.22	298.42	296.27	294.60	293.31	292.31	291.53	290.92	289.39	288.94	288.81	288.77
15000	322.74	319.74	317.43	315.64	314.26	313.19	312.35	311.70	310.06	309.58	309.44	309.40
16000	344.25	341.05	338.59	336.69	335.21	334.07	333.18	332.48	330.73	330.22	330.07	330.02
17000	365.77	362.37	359.75	357.73	356.16	354.95	354.00	353.26	351.40	350.86	350.70	350.65
18000	387.28	383.68	380.91	378.77	377.11	375.82	374.82	374.04	372.07	371.49	371.33	371.28
19000	408.80	405.00	402.07	399.81	398.06	396.70	395.65	394.82	392.74	392.13	391.95	391.90
20000	430.31	426.32	423.24	420.86	419.01	417.58	416.47	415.60	413.41	412.77	412.58	412.53
21000	451.83	447.63	444.40	441.90	439.96	438.46	437.29	436.38	434.08	433.41	433.21	433.15
22000	473.35	468.95	465.56	462.94	460.91	459.34	458.11	457.16	454.75	454.05	453.84	453.78
23000	494.86	490.26	486.72	483.99	481.87	480.22	478.94	477.94	475.42	474.69	474.47	474.41
24000	516.38	511.58	507.88	505.03	502.82	501.10	499.76	498.72	496.09	495.32	495.10	495.03
25000	537.89	532.89	529.04	526.07	523.77	521.98	520.58	519.50	516.76	515.96	515.73	515.66
26000	559.41	554.21	550.21	547.11	544.72	542.86	541.41	540.28	537.43	536.60	536.36	536.28
27000	580.92	575.52	571.37	568.16	565.67	563.73	562.23	561.06	558.10	557.24	556.99	556.91
28000	602.44	596.84	592.53	589.20	586.62	584.61	583.05	581.84	578.78	577.88	577.61	577.54
29000	623.95	618.15	613.69	610.24	607.57	605.49	603.88	602.62	599.44	598.51	598.24	598.16
30000	645.47	639.47	634.85	631.28	628.52	626.37	624.70	623.40	620.11	619.15	618.87	618.79
31000	666.98	660.79	656.01	652.33	649.47	647.25	645.52	644.18	640.78	639.79	639.50	639.42
32000	688.50	682.10	677.18	673.37	670.42	668.13	666.35	664.96	661.45	660.43	660.13	660.04
33000	710.02	703.42	698.34	694.41	691.37	689.01	687.17	685.74	682.12	681.07	680.76	680.67
34000	731.53	724.73	719.50	715.45	712.32	709.89	707.99	706.52	702.79	701.71	701.39	701.29
35000	753.05	746.05	740.66	736.50	733.27	730.77	728.82	727.30	723.46	722.34	722.02	721.92
37500	806.84	799.34	793.56	789.10	785.65	782.96	780.87	779.25	775.14	773.94	773.59	773.49
40000	860.62	852.63	846.47	841.71	838.02	835.16	832.93	831.20	826.81	825.54	825.16	825.05
42500	914.41	905.91	899.37	894.32	890.40	887.36	884.99	883.15	878.49	877.13	876.73	876.62
45000	968.20	959.20	952.28	946.92	942.78	939.55	937.05	935.10	930.17	928.73	928.30	928.18
47500	1021.99	1012.49	1005.18	999.53	995.15	991.75	989.11	987.05	981.84	980.32	979.88	979.75
50000	1075.78	1065.78	1058.08	1052.14	1047.53	1043.95	1041.16	1038.99	1033.52	1031.92	1031.45	1031.31
52500	1129.57	1119.07	1110.99	1104.74	1099.90	1096.15	1093.22	1090.94	1085.19	1083.51	1083.02	1082.88
55000	1183.36	1172.36	1163.89	1157.35	1152.28	1148.34	1145.28	1142.89	1136.87	1135.11	1134.59	1134.44
57500	1237.15	1225.65	1216.80	1209.96	1204.66	1200.54	1197.34	1194.84	1188.54	1186.71	1186.17	1186.01
60000	1290.93	1278.94	1269.70	1262.56	1257.03	1252.74	1249.40	1246.79	1240.22	1238.30	1237.74	1237.57
65000	1398.51	1385.51	1375.51	1367.78	1361.78	1357.13	1353.51	1350.69	1343.57	1341.49	1340.88	1340.70
70000	1506.09	1492.09	1481.32	1472.99	1466.54	1461.53	1457.63	1454.59	1446.92	1444.68	1444.03	1443.84
75000	1613.67	1598.67	1587.12	1578.20	1571.29	1565.92	1561.74	1558.49	1550.27	1547.88	1547.17	1546.97
80000	1721.24	1705.25	1692.93	1683.42	1676.04	1670.31	1665.86	1662.39	1653.62	1651.07	1650.32	1650.10
85000	1828.82	1811.82	1798.74	1788.63	1780.79	1774.71	1769.98	1766.29	1756.98	1754.26	1753.46	1753.23
90000	1936.40	1918.40	1904.55	1893.84	1885.55	1879.10	1874.09	1870.19	1860.33	1857.45	1856.61	1856.36
95000	2043.98	2024.98	2010.35	1999.05	1990.30	1983.50	1978.21	1974.09	1963.68	1960.64	1959.75	1959.49
100000	2151.55	2131.56	2116.16	2104.27	2095.05	2087.89	2082.32	2077.98	2067.03	2063.83	2062.89	2062.62
105000	2259.13	2238.13	2221.97	2209.48	2199.80	2192.29	2186.44	2181.88	2170.38	2167.02	2166.04	2165.75
110000	2366.71	2344.71	2327.78	2314.69	2304.55	2296.68	2290.55	2285.78	2273.73	2270.21	2269.18	2268.88
115000	2474.29	2451.29	2433.59	2419.91	2409.31	2401.07	2394.67	2389.68	2377.08	2373.41	2372.33	2372.01
120000	2581.86	2557.87	2539.39	2525.12	2514.06	2505.47	2498.79	2493.58	2480.43	2476.60	2475.47	2475.14
125000	2689.44	2664.44	2645.20	2630.33	2618.81	2609.86	2602.90	2597.48	2583.78	2579.79	2578.62	2578.27
130000	2797.02	2771.02	2751.01	2735.55	2723.56	2714.26	2707.02	2701.38	2687.14	2682.98	2681.76	2681.40
135000	2904.59	2877.60	2856.82	2840.76	2828.32	2818.65	2811.13	2805.28	2790.49	2786.17	2784.91	2784.53
140000	3012.17	2984.18	2962.63	2945.97	2933.07	2923.05	2915.25	2909.18	2893.84	2889.36	2888.05	2887.67
145000	3119.75	3090.76	3068.43	3051.19	3037.82	3027.44	3019.37	3013.08	2997.19	2992.55	2991.19	2990.80
150000	3227.33	3197.33	3174.24	3156.40	3142.57	3131.84	3123.48	3116.97	3100.54	3095.75	3094.34	3093.93
155000	3334.90	3303.91	3280.05	3261.61	3247.33	3236.23	3227.60	3220.87	3203.89	3198.94	3197.48	3197.06
160000	3442.48	3410.49	3385.86	3366.83	3352.08	3340.62	3331.71	3324.77	3307.24	3302.13	3300.63	3300.19

MONTHLY AMORTIZING PAYMENTS

AMOUNT OF LOAN	NUMBER OF YEARS IN TERM											
	1	2	3	4	5	6	7	8	9	10	11	12
$ 50	4.76	2.67	1.99	1.66	1.47	1.35	1.27	1.21	1.17	1.14	1.12	1.10
100	9.51	5.34	3.98	3.32	2.94	2.70	2.54	2.42	2.34	2.28	2.23	2.20
200	19.01	10.68	7.96	6.64	5.88	5.39	5.07	4.84	4.68	4.55	4.46	4.40
300	28.52	16.02	11.93	9.95	8.81	8.09	7.60	7.26	7.01	6.83	6.69	6.59
400	38.02	21.35	15.91	13.27	11.75	10.78	10.13	9.67	9.35	9.10	8.92	8.79
500	47.53	26.69	19.88	16.58	14.68	13.47	12.66	12.09	11.68	11.38	11.15	10.99
600	57.03	32.03	23.86	19.90	17.62	16.17	15.19	14.51	14.02	13.65	13.38	13.18
700	66.54	37.37	27.84	23.21	20.55	18.86	17.72	16.93	16.35	15.93	15.61	15.38
800	76.04	42.70	31.81	26.53	23.49	21.55	20.25	19.34	18.69	18.20	17.84	17.57
900	85.54	48.04	35.79	29.85	26.42	24.25	22.79	21.76	21.02	20.48	20.07	19.77
1000	95.05	53.38	39.76	33.16	29.36	26.94	25.32	24.18	23.36	22.75	22.30	21.97
2000	190.09	106.75	79.52	66.32	58.71	53.88	50.63	48.35	46.71	45.50	44.60	43.93
3000	285.14	160.12	119.28	99.48	88.06	80.82	75.94	72.52	70.06	68.25	66.90	65.89
4000	380.18	213.49	159.04	132.63	117.41	107.75	101.25	96.70	93.41	91.00	89.20	87.85
5000	475.23	266.86	198.80	165.79	146.76	134.69	126.56	120.87	116.77	113.75	111.50	109.81
6000	570.27	320.23	238.56	198.95	176.11	161.63	151.87	145.04	140.12	136.50	133.80	131.77
7000	665.31	373.61	278.32	232.10	205.46	188.57	177.19	169.21	163.47	159.25	156.10	153.73
8000	760.36	426.98	318.08	265.26	234.82	215.50	202.50	193.39	186.82	182.00	178.40	175.69
9C00	855.40	480.35	357.84	298.42	264.17	242.44	227.81	217.56	210.17	204.75	200.70	197.65
10000	950.45	533.72	397.60	331.58	293.52	269.38	253.12	241.73	233.53	227.50	223.00	219.61
11000	1045.49	587.09	437.36	364.73	322.87	296.31	278.43	265.90	256.88	250.25	245.30	241.58
12000	1140.54	640.46	477.12	397.89	352.22	323.25	303.74	290.08	280.23	273.00	267.60	263.54
13000	1235.58	693.83	516.88	431.05	381.57	350.19	329.06	314.25	303.58	295.75	289.90	285.50
14000	1330.62	747.21	556.64	464.20	410.92	377.13	354.37	338.42	326.94	318.50	312.20	307.46
15000	1425.67	800.58	596.40	497.36	440.27	404.06	379.68	362.59	350.29	341.24	334.50	329.42
16000	1520.71	853.95	636.16	530.52	469.63	431.00	404.99	386.77	373.64	363.99	356.80	351.38
17000	1615.76	907.32	675.92	563.68	498.98	457.94	430.30	410.94	396.99	386.74	379.10	373.34
18000	1710.80	960.69	715.68	596.83	528.33	484.87	455.61	435.11	420.34	409.49	401.40	395.30
19000	1805.84	1014.06	755.44	629.99	557.68	511.81	480.93	459.29	443.70	432.24	423.70	417.26
20000	1900.89	1067.44	795.20	663.15	587.03	538.75	506.24	483.46	467.05	454.99	446.00	439.22
21000	1995.93	1120.81	834.96	696.30	616.38	565.69	531.55	507.63	490.40	477.74	468.30	461.18
22000	2090.98	1174.18	874.72	729.46	645.73	592.62	556.86	531.80	513.75	500.49	490.60	483.15
23000	2186.02	1227.55	914.48	762.62	675.09	619.56	582.17	555.98	537.11	523.24	512.90	505.11
24000	2281.07	1280.92	954.24	795.78	704.44	646.50	607.48	580.15	560.46	545.99	535.20	527.07
25000	2376.11	1334.29	994.00	828.93	733.79	673.43	632.80	604.32	583.81	568.74	557.50	549.03
26000	2471.15	1387.66	1033.76	862.09	763.14	700.37	658.11	628.49	607.16	591.49	579.80	570.99
27000	2566.20	1441.04	1073.52	895.25	792.49	727.31	683.42	652.67	630.51	614.24	602.10	592.95
28000	2661.24	1494.41	1113.28	928.40	821.84	754.25	708.73	676.84	653.87	636.99	624.40	614.91
29000	2756.29	1547.78	1153.04	961.56	851.19	781.18	734.04	701.01	677.22	659.73	646.70	636.87
30000	2851.33	1601.15	1192.80	994.72	880.54	808.12	759.35	725.18	700.57	682.48	669.00	658.83
31000	2946.38	1654.52	1232.56	1027.88	909.90	835.06	784.67	749.36	723.92	705.23	691.30	680.79
32000	3041.42	1707.89	1272.32	1061.03	939.25	861.99	809.98	773.53	747.28	727.98	713.60	702.75
33000	3136.46	1761.27	1312.08	1094.19	968.60	888.93	835.29	797.70	770.63	750.73	735.90	724.72
34000	3231.51	1814.64	1351.84	1127.35	997.95	915.87	860.60	821.88	793.98	773.48	758.20	746.68
35000	3326.55	1868.01	1391.60	1160.50	1027.30	942.81	885.91	846.05	817.33	796.23	780.50	768.64
37500	3564.16	2001.44	1491.00	1243.40	1100.68	1010.15	949.19	906.48	875.71	853.10	836.25	823.54
40000	3801.77	2134.87	1590.40	1326.29	1174.06	1077.49	1012.47	966.91	934.09	909.98	892.00	878.44
42500	4039.38	2268.29	1689.80	1409.18	1247.44	1144.84	1075.75	1027.34	992.47	966.85	947.74	933.34
45000	4276.99	2401.72	1789.20	1492.08	1320.81	1212.18	1139.03	1087.77	1050.85	1023.72	1003.49	988.25
47500	4514.60	2535.15	1888.60	1574.97	1394.19	1279.52	1202.31	1148.21	1109.23	1080.60	1059.24	1043.15
50000	4752.22	2668.58	1988.00	1657.86	1467.57	1346.86	1265.59	1208.64	1167.61	1137.47	1114.99	1098.05
52500	4989.83	2802.01	2087.40	1740.75	1540.95	1414.21	1328.87	1269.07	1226.00	1194.34	1170.74	1152.95
55000	5227.44	2935.44	2186.80	1823.65	1614.33	1481.55	1392.14	1329.50	1284.38	1251.22	1226.49	1207.86
57500	5465.05	3068.87	2286.19	1906.54	1687.71	1548.89	1455.42	1389.93	1342.76	1308.09	1282.24	1262.76
60000	5702.66	3202.30	2385.59	1989.43	1761.08	1616.24	1518.70	1450.36	1401.14	1364.96	1337.99	1317.66
65000	6177.88	3469.15	2584.39	2155.22	1907.84	1750.92	1645.26	1571.23	1517.90	1478.71	1449.49	1427.47
70000	6653.10	3736.01	2783.19	2321.00	2054.60	1885.61	1771.82	1692.09	1634.66	1592.46	1560.99	1537.27
75000	7128.32	4002.87	2981.99	2486.79	2201.35	2020.29	1898.38	1812.95	1751.42	1706.20	1672.49	1647.07
80000	7603.54	4269.73	3180.79	2652.58	2348.11	2154.98	2024.94	1933.82	1868.18	1819.95	1783.99	1756.88
85000	8078.76	4536.58	3379.59	2818.36	2494.87	2289.67	2151.49	2054.68	1984.94	1933.70	1895.48	1866.68
90000	8553.98	4803.44	3578.39	2984.15	2641.62	2424.35	2278.05	2175.54	2101.70	2047.44	2006.98	1976.49
95000	9029.20	5070.30	3777.19	3149.93	2788.38	2559.04	2404.61	2296.41	2218.46	2161.19	2118.48	2086.29
100000	9504.43	5337.16	3975.99	3315.72	2935.14	2693.72	2531.17	2417.27	2335.22	2274.93	2229.98	2196.10
105000	9979.65	5604.01	4174.79	3481.50	3081.89	2828.41	2657.73	2538.13	2451.99	2388.68	2341.48	2305.90
110000	10454.87	5870.87	4373.59	3647.29	3228.65	2963.09	2784.28	2659.00	2568.75	2502.43	2452.98	2415.71
115000	10930.09	6137.73	4572.38	3813.07	3375.41	3097.78	2910.84	2779.86	2685.51	2616.17	2564.48	2525.51
120000	11405.31	6404.59	4771.18	3978.86	3522.16	3232.47	3037.40	2900.72	2802.27	2729.92	2675.98	2635.32
125000	11880.53	6671.45	4969.98	4144.65	3668.92	3367.15	3163.96	3021.59	2919.03	2843.67	2787.48	2745.12
130000	12355.75	6938.30	5168.78	4310.43	3815.68	3501.84	3290.52	3142.45	3035.79	2957.41	2898.97	2854.93
135000	12830.97	7205.16	5367.58	4476.22	3962.43	3636.52	3417.08	3263.31	3152.55	3071.16	3010.47	2964.73
140000	13306.19	7472.02	5566.38	4642.00	4109.19	3771.21	3543.63	3384.18	3269.31	3184.91	3121.97	3074.54
145000	13781.41	7738.88	5765.18	4807.79	4255.95	3905.90	3670.19	3505.04	3386.07	3298.65	3233.47	3184.34
150000	14256.64	8005.73	5963.98	4973.57	4402.70	4040.58	3796.75	3625.90	3502.83	3412.40	3344.97	3294.14
155000	14731.86	8272.59	6162.78	5139.36	4549.46	4175.27	3923.31	3746.77	3619.60	3526.15	3456.47	3403.95
160000	15207.08	8539.45	6361.58	5305.15	4696.22	4309.95	4049.87	3867.63	3736.36	3639.89	3567.97	3513.75

AMOUNT OF LOAN	NUMBER OF YEARS IN TERM											
	13	14	15	16	17	18	19	20	25	30	35	40
$ 50	1.09	1.08	1.07	1.07	1.06	1.06	1.06	1.05	1.05	1.05	1.05	1.05
100	2.18	2.16	2.14	2.13	2.12	2.11	2.11	2.10	2.09	2.09	2.09	2.09
200	4.35	4.31	4.28	4.25	4.23	4.22	4.21	4.20	4.18	4.17	4.17	4.17
300	6.52	6.46	6.41	6.38	6.35	6.33	6.31	6.30	6.27	6.26	6.26	6.26
400	8.69	8.61	8.55	8.50	8.46	8.44	8.41	8.40	8.36	8.34	8.34	8.34
500	10.86	10.76	10.68	10.62	10.58	10.54	10.52	10.50	10.44	10.43	10.42	10.42
600	13.03	12.91	12.82	12.75	12.69	12.65	12.62	12.59	12.53	12.51	12.51	12.51
700	15.20	15.06	14.95	14.87	14.81	14.76	14.72	14.69	14.62	14.60	14.59	14.59
800	17.37	17.21	17.09	17.00	16.92	16.87	16.82	16.79	16.71	16.68	16.67	16.67
900	19.54	19.36	19.22	19.12	19.04	18.98	18.93	18.89	18.79	18.77	18.76	18.76
1000	21.71	21.51	21.36	21.24	21.15	21.08	21.03	20.99	20.88	20.85	20.84	20.84
2000	43.41	43.02	42.72	42.48	42.30	42.16	42.05	41.97	41.76	41.70	41.68	41.67
3000	65.12	64.52	64.07	63.72	63.45	63.24	63.08	62.95	62.63	62.54	62.52	62.51
4000	86.82	86.03	85.43	84.96	84.60	84.32	84.10	83.93	83.51	83.39	83.35	83.34
5000	108.52	107.54	106.78	106.20	105.75	105.40	105.13	104.92	104.39	104.23	104.19	104.18
6000	130.23	129.04	128.14	127.44	126.90	126.48	126.15	125.90	125.26	125.08	125.03	125.01
7000	151.93	150.55	149.49	148.68	148.04	147.56	147.18	146.88	146.14	145.93	145.86	145.85
8000	173.63	172.06	170.85	169.91	169.19	168.63	168.20	167.86	167.02	166.77	166.70	166.68
9000	195.34	193.56	192.20	191.15	190.34	189.71	189.22	188.84	187.89	187.62	187.54	187.51
10000	217.04	215.07	213.56	212.39	211.49	210.79	210.25	209.83	208.77	208.46	208.37	208.35
11000	238.74	236.58	234.91	233.63	232.64	231.87	231.27	230.81	229.64	229.31	229.21	229.18
12000	260.45	258.08	256.27	254.87	253.79	252.95	252.30	251.79	250.52	250.15	250.05	250.02
13000	282.15	279.59	277.62	276.11	274.94	274.03	273.32	272.77	271.40	271.00	270.89	270.85
14000	303.85	301.10	298.98	297.35	296.08	295.11	294.35	293.76	292.27	291.85	291.72	291.69
15000	325.56	322.60	320.33	318.58	317.23	316.18	315.37	314.74	313.15	312.69	312.56	312.52
16000	347.26	344.11	341.69	339.82	338.38	337.26	336.39	335.72	334.03	333.54	333.40	333.36
17000	368.96	365.62	363.04	361.06	359.53	358.34	357.42	356.70	354.90	354.38	354.23	354.19
18000	390.67	387.12	384.40	382.30	380.68	379.42	378.44	377.68	375.78	375.23	375.07	375.02
19000	412.37	408.63	405.76	403.54	401.83	400.50	399.47	398.67	396.65	396.07	395.91	395.86
20000	434.07	430.14	427.11	424.78	422.97	421.58	420.49	419.65	417.53	416.92	416.74	416.69
21000	455.78	451.64	448.47	446.02	444.12	442.66	441.52	440.63	438.41	437.77	437.58	437.53
22000	477.48	473.15	469.82	467.26	465.27	463.74	462.54	461.61	459.28	458.61	458.42	458.36
23000	499.18	494.66	491.18	488.49	486.42	484.81	483.56	482.59	480.16	479.46	479.25	479.20
24000	520.89	516.16	512.53	509.73	507.57	505.89	504.59	503.58	501.04	500.30	500.09	500.03
25000	542.59	537.67	533.89	530.97	528.72	526.97	525.61	524.56	521.91	521.15	520.93	520.86
26000	564.29	559.18	555.24	552.21	549.87	548.05	546.64	545.54	542.79	542.00	541.77	541.70
27000	586.00	580.68	576.60	573.45	571.01	569.13	567.66	566.52	563.67	562.84	562.60	562.53
28000	607.70	602.19	597.95	594.69	592.16	590.21	588.69	587.51	584.54	583.69	583.44	583.37
29000	629.40	623.70	619.31	615.93	613.31	611.28	609.71	608.49	605.42	604.53	604.28	604.20
30000	651.11	645.20	640.66	637.16	634.46	632.36	630.73	629.47	626.29	625.38	625.11	625.04
31000	672.81	666.71	662.02	658.40	655.61	653.44	651.76	650.45	647.17	646.22	645.95	645.87
32000	694.52	688.21	683.37	679.64	676.76	674.52	672.78	671.43	668.05	667.07	666.79	666.71
33000	716.22	709.72	704.73	700.88	697.90	695.60	693.81	692.42	688.92	687.92	687.62	687.54
34000	737.92	731.23	726.08	722.12	719.05	716.68	714.83	713.40	709.80	708.76	708.46	708.37
35000	759.63	752.73	747.44	743.36	740.20	737.76	735.86	734.38	730.68	729.61	729.30	729.21
37500	813.88	806.50	800.83	796.45	793.07	790.45	788.42	786.84	782.87	781.72	781.39	781.29
40000	868.14	860.27	854.22	849.55	845.94	843.15	840.98	839.29	835.06	833.84	833.48	833.38
42500	922.40	914.03	907.60	902.65	898.81	895.84	893.54	891.75	887.25	885.95	885.58	885.47
45000	976.66	967.80	960.99	955.74	951.69	948.54	946.10	944.20	939.44	938.07	937.67	937.55
47500	1030.92	1021.57	1014.38	1008.84	1004.56	1001.24	998.66	996.66	991.63	990.18	989.76	989.64
50000	1085.18	1075.33	1067.77	1061.94	1057.43	1053.93	1051.22	1049.11	1043.82	1042.29	1041.85	1041.72
52500	1139.44	1129.10	1121.16	1115.03	1110.30	1106.63	1103.78	1101.57	1096.01	1094.41	1093.94	1093.81
55000	1193.69	1182.87	1174.55	1168.13	1163.17	1159.33	1156.34	1154.02	1148.20	1146.52	1146.04	1145.90
57500	1247.95	1236.63	1227.93	1221.23	1216.04	1212.02	1208.90	1206.48	1200.39	1198.64	1198.13	1197.98
60000	1302.21	1290.40	1281.32	1274.32	1268.91	1264.72	1261.46	1258.93	1252.58	1250.75	1250.22	1250.07
65000	1410.73	1397.93	1388.10	1380.52	1374.66	1370.11	1366.59	1363.85	1356.96	1354.98	1354.41	1354.24
70000	1519.25	1505.46	1494.88	1486.71	1480.40	1475.51	1471.71	1468.76	1461.35	1459.21	1458.59	1458.41
75000	1627.76	1613.00	1601.65	1592.90	1586.14	1580.90	1576.83	1573.67	1565.73	1563.44	1562.78	1562.58
80000	1736.28	1720.53	1708.43	1699.10	1691.88	1686.29	1681.95	1678.58	1670.11	1667.67	1666.96	1666.76
85000	1844.80	1828.06	1815.20	1805.29	1797.62	1791.68	1787.07	1783.49	1774.49	1771.90	1771.15	1770.93
90000	1953.31	1935.59	1921.98	1911.48	1903.37	1897.08	1892.19	1888.40	1878.87	1876.13	1875.33	1875.10
95000	2061.83	2043.13	2028.76	2017.68	2009.11	2002.47	1997.32	1993.31	1983.25	1980.35	1979.51	1979.27
100000	2170.35	2150.66	2135.53	2123.87	2114.85	2107.86	2102.44	2098.22	2087.64	2084.58	2083.70	2083.44
105000	2278.87	2258.19	2242.31	2230.06	2220.59	2213.26	2207.56	2203.13	2192.02	2188.81	2187.88	2187.62
110000	2387.38	2365.73	2349.09	2336.26	2326.34	2318.65	2312.68	2308.04	2296.40	2293.04	2292.07	2291.79
115000	2495.90	2473.26	2455.86	2442.45	2432.08	2424.04	2417.80	2412.95	2400.78	2397.27	2396.25	2395.96
120000	2604.42	2580.79	2562.64	2548.64	2537.82	2529.43	2522.92	2517.86	2505.16	2501.50	2500.44	2500.13
125000	2712.94	2688.32	2669.42	2654.84	2643.56	2634.83	2628.05	2622.78	2609.54	2605.73	2604.62	2604.30
130000	2821.45	2795.86	2776.19	2761.03	2749.31	2740.22	2733.17	2727.69	2713.92	2709.96	2708.81	2708.47
135000	2929.97	2903.39	2882.97	2867.22	2855.05	2845.61	2838.29	2832.60	2818.31	2814.19	2812.99	2812.65
140000	3038.49	3010.92	2989.75	2973.42	2960.79	2951.01	2943.41	2937.51	2922.69	2918.42	2917.18	2916.82
145000	3147.00	3118.45	3096.52	3079.61	3066.53	3056.40	3048.53	3042.42	3027.07	3022.64	3021.36	3020.99
150000	3255.52	3225.99	3203.30	3185.80	3172.27	3161.79	3153.65	3147.33	3131.45	3126.87	3125.55	3125.16
155000	3364.04	3333.52	3310.07	3292.00	3278.02	3267.18	3258.78	3252.24	3235.83	3231.10	3229.73	3229.33
160000	3472.56	3441.05	3416.85	3398.19	3383.76	3372.58	3363.90	3357.15	3340.21	3335.33	3333.92	3333.51

MONTHLY AMORTIZING PAYMENTS

25.25%

AMOUNT OF LOAN	NUMBER OF YEARS IN TERM											
	1	2	3	4	5	6	7	8	9	10	11	12
$ 50	4.76	2.68	2.00	1.67	1.48	1.36	1.28	1.22	1.18	1.15	1.13	1.11
100	9.52	5.35	3.99	3.33	2.95	2.71	2.55	2.44	2.36	2.30	2.25	2.22
200	19.04	10.70	7.98	6.66	5.90	5.42	5.10	4.87	4.71	4.59	4.50	4.43
300	28.55	16.05	11.97	9.99	8.85	8.13	7.65	7.31	7.06	6.88	6.75	6.65
400	38.07	21.40	15.96	13.32	11.80	10.84	10.19	9.74	9.41	9.18	9.00	8.86
500	47.59	26.75	19.95	16.65	14.75	13.55	12.74	12.17	11.77	11.47	11.25	11.08
600	57.10	32.10	23.94	19.98	17.70	16.26	15.29	14.61	14.12	13.76	13.49	13.29
700	66.62	37.45	27.93	23.31	20.65	18.97	17.84	17.04	16.47	16.05	15.74	15.51
800	76.14	42.80	31.92	26.64	23.60	21.68	20.38	19.48	18.82	18.35	17.99	17.72
900	85.65	48.15	35.91	29.97	26.55	24.39	22.93	21.91	21.18	20.64	20.24	19.94
1000	95.17	53.50	39.90	33.30	29.50	27.10	25.48	24.34	23.53	22.93	22.49	22.15
2000	190.34	107.00	79.79	66.60	59.00	54.19	50.95	48.68	47.05	45.86	44.97	44.30
3000	285.50	160.50	119.68	99.90	88.50	81.28	76.42	73.02	70.58	68.78	67.45	66.44
4000	380.67	213.99	159.57	133.19	118.00	108.37	101.89	97.36	94.10	91.71	89.93	88.59
5000	475.83	267.49	199.47	166.49	147.50	135.46	127.36	121.70	117.62	114.63	112.41	110.73
6000	571.00	320.99	239.36	199.79	176.99	162.55	152.84	146.04	141.15	137.56	134.89	132.88
7000	666.16	374.48	279.25	233.08	206.49	189.64	178.31	170.38	164.67	160.49	157.37	155.03
8000	761.33	427.98	319.14	266.38	235.99	216.73	203.78	194.71	188.19	183.41	179.85	177.17
9000	856.50	481.48	359.03	299.68	265.49	243.82	229.25	219.05	211.72	206.34	202.33	199.32
10000	951.66	534.98	398.93	332.97	294.99	270.91	254.72	243.39	235.24	229.26	224.81	221.46
11000	1046.83	588.47	438.82	366.27	324.48	298.00	280.19	267.73	258.77	252.19	247.29	243.61
12000	1141.99	641.97	478.71	399.57	353.98	325.09	305.67	292.07	282.29	275.11	269.77	265.75
13000	1237.16	695.47	518.60	432.86	383.48	352.19	331.14	316.41	305.81	298.04	292.25	287.90
14000	1332.32	748.96	558.50	466.16	412.98	379.28	356.61	340.75	329.34	320.97	314.73	310.05
15000	1427.49	802.46	598.39	499.46	442.48	406.37	382.08	365.09	352.86	343.89	337.22	332.19
16000	1522.65	855.96	638.28	532.75	471.97	433.46	407.55	389.42	376.38	366.82	359.70	354.34
17000	1617.82	909.45	678.17	566.05	501.47	460.55	433.02	413.76	399.91	389.74	382.18	376.48
18000	1712.99	962.95	718.06	599.35	530.97	487.64	458.50	438.10	423.43	412.67	404.66	398.63
19000	1808.15	1016.45	757.96	632.64	560.47	514.73	483.97	462.44	446.96	435.59	427.14	420.78
20000	1903.32	1069.95	797.85	665.94	589.97	541.82	509.44	486.78	470.48	458.52	449.62	442.92
21000	1998.48	1123.44	837.74	699.24	619.46	568.91	534.91	511.12	494.00	481.45	472.10	465.07
22000	2093.65	1176.94	877.63	732.53	648.96	596.00	560.38	535.46	517.53	504.37	494.58	487.21
23000	2188.81	1230.44	917.52	765.83	678.46	623.09	585.85	559.80	541.05	527.30	517.06	509.36
24000	2283.98	1283.93	957.42	799.13	707.96	650.18	611.33	584.13	564.57	550.22	539.54	531.50
25000	2379.14	1337.43	997.31	832.42	737.46	677.27	636.80	608.47	588.10	573.15	562.02	553.65
26000	2474.31	1390.93	1037.20	865.72	766.95	704.37	662.27	632.81	611.62	596.08	584.50	575.80
27000	2569.48	1444.42	1077.09	899.02	796.45	731.46	687.74	657.15	635.15	619.00	606.98	597.94
28000	2664.64	1497.92	1116.99	932.31	825.95	758.55	713.21	681.49	658.67	641.93	629.46	620.09
29000	2759.81	1551.42	1156.88	965.61	855.45	785.64	738.68	705.83	682.19	664.85	651.95	642.23
30000	2854.97	1604.92	1196.77	998.91	884.95	812.73	764.16	730.17	705.72	687.78	674.43	664.38
31000	2950.14	1658.41	1236.66	1032.20	914.45	839.82	789.63	754.51	729.24	710.70	696.91	686.53
32000	3045.30	1711.91	1276.55	1065.50	943.94	866.91	815.10	778.84	752.76	733.63	719.39	708.67
33000	3140.47	1765.41	1316.45	1098.80	973.44	894.00	840.57	803.18	776.29	756.56	741.87	730.82
34000	3235.63	1818.90	1356.34	1132.09	1002.94	921.09	866.04	827.52	799.81	779.48	764.35	752.96
35000	3330.80	1872.40	1396.23	1165.39	1032.44	948.18	891.51	851.86	823.34	802.41	786.83	775.11
37500	3568.71	2006.14	1495.96	1248.63	1106.18	1015.91	955.19	912.71	882.14	859.72	843.03	830.47
40000	3806.63	2139.89	1595.69	1331.87	1179.93	1083.64	1018.87	973.55	940.95	917.04	899.23	885.84
42500	4044.54	2273.63	1695.42	1415.12	1253.67	1151.36	1082.55	1034.40	999.76	974.35	955.43	941.20
45000	4282.46	2407.37	1795.15	1498.36	1327.42	1219.09	1146.23	1095.25	1058.57	1031.67	1011.64	996.57
47500	4520.37	2541.11	1894.88	1581.60	1401.16	1286.82	1209.91	1156.09	1117.38	1088.98	1067.84	1051.93
50000	4758.28	2674.86	1994.61	1664.84	1474.91	1354.54	1273.59	1216.94	1176.19	1146.29	1124.04	1107.30
52500	4996.20	2808.60	2094.34	1748.08	1548.65	1422.27	1337.27	1277.79	1235.00	1203.61	1180.24	1162.66
55000	5234.11	2942.34	2194.07	1831.32	1622.40	1490.00	1400.95	1338.63	1293.81	1260.92	1236.44	1218.03
57500	5472.02	3076.08	2293.80	1914.57	1696.14	1557.73	1464.63	1399.48	1352.62	1318.24	1292.65	1273.39
60000	5709.94	3209.83	2393.54	1997.81	1769.89	1625.45	1528.31	1460.33	1411.43	1375.55	1348.85	1328.75
65000	6185.77	3477.31	2593.00	2164.29	1917.38	1760.91	1655.67	1582.02	1529.05	1490.18	1461.25	1439.48
70000	6661.59	3744.80	2792.46	2330.78	2064.87	1896.36	1783.02	1703.71	1646.67	1604.81	1573.65	1550.21
75000	7137.42	4012.28	2991.92	2497.26	2212.36	2031.81	1910.38	1825.41	1764.28	1719.44	1686.06	1660.94
80000	7613.25	4279.77	3191.38	2663.74	2359.85	2167.27	2037.74	1947.10	1881.90	1834.07	1798.46	1771.67
85000	8089.08	4547.25	3390.84	2830.23	2507.34	2302.72	2165.10	2068.80	1999.52	1948.70	1910.86	1882.40
90000	8564.91	4814.74	3590.30	2996.71	2654.83	2438.18	2292.46	2190.49	2117.14	2063.33	2023.27	1993.13
95000	9040.73	5082.22	3789.76	3163.19	2802.32	2573.63	2419.82	2312.18	2234.76	2177.95	2135.67	2103.86
100000	9516.56	5349.71	3989.22	3329.68	2949.81	2709.08	2547.17	2433.88	2352.38	2292.58	2248.08	2214.59
105000	9992.39	5617.19	4188.68	3496.16	3097.30	2844.54	2674.53	2555.57	2470.00	2407.21	2360.48	2325.32
110000	10468.22	5884.68	4388.14	3662.64	3244.79	2979.99	2801.89	2677.26	2587.61	2521.84	2472.88	2436.05
115000	10944.04	6152.16	4587.60	3829.13	3392.28	3115.45	2929.25	2798.96	2705.23	2636.47	2585.29	2546.78
120000	11419.87	6419.65	4787.07	3995.61	3539.77	3250.90	3056.61	2920.65	2822.85	2751.10	2697.69	2657.50
125000	11895.70	6687.13	4986.53	4162.09	3687.26	3386.35	3183.97	3042.34	2940.47	2865.73	2810.09	2768.23
130000	12371.53	6954.62	5185.99	4328.58	3834.75	3521.81	3311.33	3164.04	3058.09	2980.36	2922.50	2878.96
135000	12847.36	7222.10	5385.45	4495.06	3982.24	3657.26	3438.68	3285.73	3175.71	3094.99	3034.90	2989.69
140000	13323.18	7489.59	5584.91	4661.55	4129.73	3792.71	3566.04	3407.42	3293.33	3209.62	3147.30	3100.42
145000	13799.01	7757.08	5784.37	4828.03	4277.23	3928.17	3693.40	3529.12	3410.95	3324.24	3259.71	3211.15
150000	14274.84	8024.56	5983.83	4994.51	4424.72	4063.62	3820.76	3650.81	3528.56	3438.87	3372.11	3321.88
155000	14750.67	8292.05	6183.29	5161.00	4572.21	4199.08	3948.12	3772.51	3646.18	3553.50	3484.51	3432.61
160000	15226.50	8559.53	6382.75	5327.48	4719.70	4334.53	4075.48	3894.20	3763.80	3668.13	3596.92	3543.34

MONTHLY AMORTIZING PAYMENTS 25.25%

AMOUNT OF LOAN	NUMBER OF YEARS IN TERM											
	13	14	15	16	17	18	19	20	25	30	35	40
$ 50	1.10	1.09	1.08	1.08	1.07	1.07	1.07	1.06	1.06	1.06	1.06	1.06
100	2.19	2.17	2.16	2.15	2.14	2.13	2.13	2.12	2.11	2.11	2.11	2.11
200	4.38	4.34	4.31	4.29	4.27	4.26	4.25	4.24	4.22	4.22	4.21	4.21
300	6.57	6.51	6.47	6.44	6.41	6.39	6.37	6.36	6.33	6.32	6.32	6.32
400	8.76	8.68	8.62	8.58	8.54	8.52	8.50	8.48	8.44	8.43	8.42	8.42
500	10.95	10.85	10.78	10.72	10.68	10.64	10.62	10.60	10.55	10.53	10.53	10.53
600	13.14	13.02	12.93	12.87	12.81	12.77	12.74	12.72	12.65	12.64	12.63	12.63
700	15.33	15.19	15.09	15.01	14.95	14.90	14.86	14.83	14.76	14.74	14.74	14.73
800	17.52	17.36	17.24	17.15	17.08	17.03	16.99	16.95	16.87	16.85	16.84	16.84
900	19.71	19.53	19.40	19.30	19.22	19.16	19.11	19.07	18.98	18.95	18.95	18.94
1000	21.90	21.70	21.55	21.44	21.35	21.28	21.23	21.19	21.09	21.06	21.05	21.05
2000	43.79	43.40	43.10	42.88	42.70	42.56	42.46	42.37	42.17	42.11	42.10	42.09
3000	65.68	65.10	64.65	64.31	64.05	63.84	63.68	63.56	63.25	63.17	63.14	63.13
4000	87.57	86.80	86.20	85.75	85.39	85.12	84.91	84.74	84.33	84.22	84.19	84.18
5000	109.46	108.49	107.75	107.18	106.74	106.40	106.13	105.93	105.42	105.27	105.23	105.22
6000	131.36	130.19	129.30	128.62	128.09	127.68	127.36	127.11	126.50	126.33	126.28	126.26
7000	153.25	151.89	150.85	150.05	149.43	148.95	148.59	148.30	147.58	147.38	147.32	147.30
8000	175.14	173.59	172.40	171.49	170.78	170.23	169.81	169.48	168.66	168.43	168.37	168.35
9000	197.03	195.29	193.95	192.92	192.13	191.51	191.04	190.67	189.75	189.49	189.41	189.39
10000	218.92	216.98	215.50	214.36	213.47	212.79	212.26	211.85	210.83	210.54	210.46	210.43
11000	240.82	238.68	237.05	235.79	234.82	234.07	233.49	233.04	231.91	231.59	231.50	231.47
12000	262.71	260.38	258.60	257.23	256.17	255.35	254.71	254.22	252.99	252.65	252.55	252.52
13000	284.60	282.08	280.15	278.66	277.51	276.63	275.94	275.41	274.08	273.70	273.59	273.56
14000	306.49	303.78	301.70	300.10	298.86	297.90	297.17	296.59	295.16	294.75	294.64	294.60
15000	328.38	325.47	323.25	321.53	320.21	319.18	318.39	317.78	316.24	315.81	315.68	315.64
16000	350.27	347.17	344.79	342.97	341.55	340.46	339.62	338.96	337.32	336.86	336.73	336.69
17000	372.17	368.87	366.34	364.40	362.90	361.74	360.84	360.15	358.41	357.91	357.77	357.73
18000	394.06	390.57	387.89	385.84	384.25	383.02	382.07	381.33	379.49	378.97	378.82	378.77
19000	415.95	412.27	409.44	407.27	405.59	404.30	403.29	402.52	400.57	400.02	399.86	399.81
20000	437.84	433.96	430.99	428.71	426.94	425.58	424.52	423.70	421.65	421.07	420.91	420.86
21000	459.73	455.66	452.54	450.14	448.29	446.85	445.75	444.88	442.74	442.13	441.95	441.90
22000	481.63	477.36	474.09	471.58	469.63	468.13	466.97	466.07	463.82	463.18	463.00	462.94
23000	503.52	499.06	495.64	493.01	490.98	489.41	488.20	487.25	484.90	484.23	484.04	483.99
24000	525.41	520.76	517.19	514.45	512.33	510.69	509.42	508.44	505.98	505.29	505.09	505.03
25000	547.30	542.45	538.74	535.88	533.67	531.97	530.65	529.62	527.07	526.34	526.13	526.07
26000	569.19	564.15	560.29	557.32	555.02	553.25	551.87	550.81	548.15	547.39	547.18	547.11
27000	591.08	585.85	581.84	578.75	576.37	574.53	573.10	571.99	569.23	568.45	568.22	568.16
28000	612.98	607.55	603.39	600.19	597.71	595.80	594.33	593.18	590.31	589.50	589.27	589.20
29000	634.87	629.25	624.94	621.62	619.06	617.08	615.55	614.36	611.40	610.55	610.31	610.24
30000	656.76	650.94	646.49	643.06	640.41	638.36	636.78	635.55	632.48	631.61	631.36	631.28
31000	678.65	672.64	668.04	664.49	661.76	659.64	658.00	656.73	653.56	652.66	652.40	652.33
32000	700.54	694.34	689.58	685.93	683.10	680.92	679.23	677.92	674.64	673.71	673.45	673.37
33000	722.44	716.04	711.13	707.36	704.45	702.20	700.45	699.10	695.73	694.77	694.49	694.41
34000	744.33	737.74	732.68	728.80	725.80	723.48	721.68	720.29	716.81	715.82	715.54	715.45
35000	766.22	759.43	754.23	750.23	747.14	744.75	742.91	741.47	737.89	736.87	736.58	736.50
37500	820.95	813.68	808.11	803.82	800.51	797.95	795.97	794.43	790.60	789.51	789.19	789.10
40000	875.68	867.92	861.99	857.41	853.88	851.15	849.03	847.40	843.30	842.14	841.81	841.71
42500	930.41	922.17	915.85	910.99	907.24	904.34	902.10	900.36	896.01	894.77	894.42	894.32
45000	985.14	976.41	969.73	964.58	960.61	957.54	955.16	953.32	948.72	947.40	947.03	946.92
47500	1039.87	1030.66	1023.60	1018.17	1013.98	1010.74	1008.23	1006.28	1001.42	1000.04	999.64	999.53
50000	1094.60	1084.90	1077.47	1071.76	1067.34	1063.93	1061.29	1059.24	1054.13	1052.67	1052.26	1052.14
52500	1149.33	1139.15	1131.35	1125.34	1120.71	1117.13	1114.36	1112.20	1106.84	1105.31	1104.87	1104.74
55000	1204.06	1193.39	1185.22	1178.93	1174.08	1170.33	1167.42	1165.17	1159.54	1157.94	1157.48	1157.35
57500	1258.79	1247.64	1239.09	1232.52	1227.45	1223.52	1220.48	1218.13	1212.25	1210.57	1210.09	1209.96
60000	1313.51	1301.88	1292.97	1286.11	1280.81	1276.73	1273.55	1271.09	1264.95	1263.21	1262.71	1262.56
65000	1422.97	1410.37	1400.71	1393.28	1387.55	1383.11	1379.68	1377.01	1370.37	1368.47	1367.93	1367.78
70000	1532.43	1518.86	1508.46	1500.46	1494.28	1489.50	1485.81	1482.94	1475.78	1473.74	1473.16	1472.99
75000	1641.89	1627.35	1616.21	1607.63	1601.01	1595.90	1591.93	1588.86	1581.19	1579.01	1578.38	1578.20
80000	1751.35	1735.84	1723.95	1714.81	1707.75	1702.29	1698.06	1694.79	1686.60	1684.27	1683.61	1683.42
85000	1860.81	1844.33	1831.70	1821.98	1814.48	1808.68	1804.19	1800.71	1792.02	1789.54	1788.83	1788.63
90000	1970.27	1952.82	1939.45	1929.16	1921.22	1915.08	1910.32	1906.63	1897.43	1894.81	1894.06	1893.84
95000	2079.73	2061.31	2047.20	2036.33	2027.95	2021.47	2016.45	2012.56	2002.84	2000.07	1999.28	1999.05
100000	2189.19	2169.80	2154.94	2143.51	2134.68	2127.86	2122.58	2118.48	2108.25	2105.34	2104.51	2104.27
105000	2298.65	2278.29	2262.69	2250.68	2241.42	2234.25	2228.71	2224.40	2213.67	2210.61	2209.73	2209.48
110000	2408.11	2386.78	2370.44	2357.86	2348.15	2340.65	2334.83	2330.33	2319.08	2315.87	2314.96	2314.69
115000	2517.57	2495.27	2478.18	2465.03	2454.89	2447.04	2440.96	2436.25	2424.49	2421.14	2420.18	2419.91
120000	2627.02	2603.76	2585.93	2572.21	2561.62	2553.43	2547.09	2542.18	2529.90	2526.41	2525.41	2525.12
125000	2736.48	2712.25	2693.68	2679.38	2668.35	2659.83	2653.22	2648.10	2635.32	2631.67	2630.63	2630.33
130000	2845.94	2820.74	2801.42	2786.56	2775.09	2766.22	2759.35	2754.02	2740.73	2736.94	2735.86	2735.55
135000	2955.40	2929.23	2909.17	2893.73	2881.82	2872.61	2865.48	2859.95	2846.14	2842.21	2841.08	2840.76
140000	3064.86	3037.72	3016.92	3000.91	2988.55	2979.00	2971.61	2965.87	2951.55	2947.47	2946.31	2945.97
145000	3174.32	3146.21	3124.66	3108.08	3095.29	3085.40	3077.73	3071.79	3056.97	3052.74	3051.53	3051.19
150000	3283.78	3254.70	3232.41	3215.26	3202.02	3191.79	3183.86	3177.72	3162.38	3158.01	3156.76	3156.40
155000	3393.24	3363.19	3340.16	3322.43	3308.76	3298.18	3289.99	3283.64	3267.79	3263.27	3261.98	3261.61
160000	3502.70	3471.68	3447.90	3429.61	3415.49	3404.57	3396.12	3389.57	3373.20	3368.54	3367.21	3366.83

MONTHLY AMORTIZING PAYMENTS

AMOUNT OF LOAN	NUMBER OF YEARS IN TERM											
	1	2	3	4	5	6	7	8	9	10	11	12
$ 50	4.77	2.69	2.01	1.68	1.49	1.37	1.29	1.23	1.19	1.16	1.14	1.12
100	9.53	5.37	4.01	3.35	2.97	2.73	2.57	2.46	2.37	2.32	2.27	2.24
200	19.06	10.73	8.01	6.69	5.93	5.45	5.13	4.91	4.74	4.63	4.54	4.47
300	28.59	16.09	12.01	10.04	8.90	8.18	7.69	7.36	7.11	6.94	6.80	6.70
400	38.12	21.45	16.01	13.38	11.86	10.90	10.26	9.81	9.48	9.25	9.07	8.94
500	47.65	26.82	20.02	16.72	14.83	13.63	12.82	12.26	11.85	11.56	11.34	11.17
600	57.18	32.18	24.02	20.07	17.79	16.35	15.38	14.71	14.22	13.87	13.60	13.40
700	66.71	37.54	28.02	23.41	20.76	19.08	17.95	17.16	16.59	16.18	15.87	15.64
800	76.23	42.90	32.02	26.75	23.72	21.80	20.51	19.61	18.96	18.49	18.13	17.87
900	85.76	48.27	36.03	30.10	26.69	24.53	23.07	22.06	21.33	20.80	20.40	20.10
1000	95.29	53.63	40.03	33.44	29.65	27.25	25.64	24.51	23.70	23.11	22.67	22.34
2000	190.58	107.25	80.05	66.88	59.30	54.49	51.27	49.02	47.40	46.21	45.33	44.67
3000	285.87	160.87	120.08	100.31	88.94	81.74	76.90	73.52	71.09	69.31	67.99	67.00
4000	381.15	214.50	160.10	133.75	118.59	108.98	102.53	98.03	94.79	92.42	90.65	89.33
5000	476.44	268.12	200.13	167.19	148.23	136.23	128.17	122.53	118.48	115.52	113.32	111.66
6000	571.73	321.74	240.15	200.62	177.88	163.47	153.80	147.04	142.18	138.62	135.98	133.99
7000	667.01	375.36	280.18	234.06	207.52	190.72	179.43	171.54	165.88	161.72	158.64	156.32
8000	762.30	428.99	320.20	267.50	237.17	217.96	205.06	196.05	189.57	184.83	181.30	178.65
9000	857.59	482.61	360.23	300.93	266.81	245.21	230.69	220.55	213.27	207.93	203.96	200.99
10000	952.88	536.23	400.25	334.37	296.46	272.45	256.33	245.06	236.96	231.03	226.63	223.32
11000	1048.16	589.85	440.28	367.81	326.10	299.70	281.96	269.56	260.66	254.14	249.29	245.65
12000	1143.45	643.48	480.30	401.24	355.75	326.94	307.59	294.07	284.35	277.24	271.95	267.98
13000	1238.74	697.10	520.33	434.68	385.39	354.19	333.22	318.57	308.05	300.34	294.61	290.31
14000	1334.02	750.72	560.35	468.12	415.04	381.43	358.86	343.08	331.75	323.44	317.27	312.64
15000	1429.31	804.35	600.38	501.55	444.68	408.68	384.49	367.58	355.44	346.55	339.94	334.97
16000	1524.60	857.97	640.40	534.99	474.33	435.92	410.12	392.09	379.14	369.65	362.60	357.30
17000	1619.88	911.59	680.43	568.43	503.97	463.17	435.75	416.59	402.83	392.75	385.26	379.63
18000	1715.17	965.21	720.45	601.86	533.62	490.41	461.38	441.10	426.53	415.85	407.92	401.97
19000	1810.46	1018.84	760.48	635.30	563.26	517.66	487.02	465.60	450.22	438.96	430.59	424.30
20000	1905.75	1072.46	800.50	668.74	592.91	544.90	512.65	490.11	473.92	462.06	453.25	446.63
21000	2001.03	1126.08	840.52	702.17	622.55	572.15	538.28	514.61	497.62	485.16	475.91	468.96
22000	2096.32	1179.70	880.55	735.61	652.20	599.39	563.91	539.12	521.31	508.27	498.57	491.29
23000	2191.61	1233.33	920.57	769.05	681.84	626.64	589.55	563.62	545.01	531.37	521.23	513.62
24000	2286.89	1286.95	960.60	802.48	711.49	653.88	615.18	588.13	568.70	554.47	543.90	535.95
25000	2382.18	1340.57	1000.62	835.92	741.13	681.12	640.81	612.64	592.40	577.57	566.56	558.28
26000	2477.47	1394.20	1040.65	869.36	770.78	708.37	666.44	637.14	616.09	600.68	589.22	580.62
27000	2572.75	1447.82	1080.67	902.79	800.42	735.61	692.07	661.65	639.79	623.78	611.88	602.95
28000	2668.04	1501.44	1120.70	936.23	830.07	762.86	717.71	686.15	663.49	646.88	634.54	625.28
29000	2763.33	1555.06	1160.72	969.67	859.72	790.10	743.34	710.66	687.18	669.98	657.21	647.61
30000	2858.62	1608.69	1200.75	1003.10	889.36	817.35	768.97	735.16	710.88	693.09	679.87	669.94
31000	2953.90	1662.31	1240.77	1036.54	919.01	844.59	794.60	759.67	734.57	716.19	702.53	692.27
32000	3049.19	1715.93	1280.80	1069.98	948.65	871.84	820.24	784.17	758.27	739.29	725.19	714.60
33000	3144.48	1769.55	1320.82	1103.41	978.30	899.08	845.87	808.68	781.96	762.40	747.85	736.93
34000	3239.76	1823.18	1360.85	1136.85	1007.94	926.33	871.50	833.18	805.66	785.50	770.52	759.26
35000	3335.05	1876.80	1400.87	1170.29	1037.59	953.57	897.13	857.69	829.36	808.60	793.18	781.60
37500	3573.27	2010.86	1500.93	1253.88	1111.70	1021.68	961.21	918.59	888.59	866.36	849.83	837.42
40000	3811.49	2144.91	1600.99	1337.47	1185.81	1089.80	1025.29	980.21	947.83	924.11	906.49	893.25
42500	4049.70	2278.97	1701.06	1421.06	1259.93	1157.91	1089.37	1041.48	1007.07	981.87	963.14	949.08
45000	4287.92	2413.03	1801.12	1504.65	1334.04	1226.02	1153.45	1102.74	1066.31	1039.63	1019.80	1004.91
47500	4526.14	2547.08	1901.18	1588.24	1408.15	1294.13	1217.53	1164.00	1125.55	1097.39	1076.46	1060.74
50000	4764.36	2681.14	2001.24	1671.84	1482.26	1362.24	1281.61	1225.27	1184.79	1155.14	1133.11	1116.56
52500	5002.57	2815.20	2101.30	1755.43	1556.38	1430.36	1345.70	1286.53	1244.03	1212.90	1189.77	1172.39
55000	5240.79	2949.25	2201.37	1839.02	1630.49	1498.47	1409.78	1347.79	1303.27	1270.66	1246.42	1228.22
57500	5479.01	3083.31	2301.43	1922.61	1704.60	1566.58	1473.86	1409.05	1362.51	1328.41	1303.08	1284.05
60000	5717.23	3217.37	2401.49	2006.20	1778.72	1634.69	1537.94	1470.32	1421.75	1386.17	1359.73	1339.88
65000	6193.66	3485.48	2601.61	2173.38	1926.94	1770.92	1666.10	1592.84	1540.23	1501.68	1473.04	1451.53
70000	6670.10	3753.60	2801.74	2340.57	2075.17	1907.14	1794.26	1715.37	1658.71	1617.20	1586.35	1563.19
75000	7146.53	4021.71	3001.86	2507.75	2223.39	2043.36	1922.42	1837.90	1777.18	1732.71	1699.66	1674.84
80000	7622.97	4289.82	3201.98	2674.93	2371.62	2179.59	2050.58	1960.42	1895.66	1848.22	1812.97	1786.50
85000	8099.40	4557.94	3402.11	2842.12	2519.85	2315.81	2178.74	2082.95	2014.14	1963.74	1926.28	1898.15
90000	8575.84	4826.05	3602.23	3009.30	2668.07	2452.04	2306.90	2205.47	2132.62	2079.25	2039.59	2009.81
95000	9052.27	5094.16	3802.36	3176.48	2816.30	2588.26	2435.06	2328.00	2251.10	2194.77	2152.91	2121.47
100000	9528.71	5362.28	4002.48	3343.67	2964.52	2724.48	2563.22	2450.53	2369.58	2310.28	2266.22	2233.12
105000	10005.14	5630.39	4202.60	3510.85	3112.75	2860.71	2691.39	2573.05	2488.06	2425.79	2379.53	2344.78
110000	10481.58	5898.50	4402.73	3678.03	3260.97	2996.93	2819.55	2695.58	2606.53	2541.31	2492.84	2456.43
115000	10958.01	6166.62	4602.85	3845.22	3409.20	3133.16	2947.71	2818.10	2725.01	2656.82	2606.15	2568.09
120000	11434.45	6434.73	4802.97	4012.40	3557.43	3269.38	3075.87	2940.63	2843.49	2772.33	2719.46	2679.75
125000	11910.88	6702.84	5003.10	4179.58	3705.65	3405.60	3204.03	3063.16	2961.97	2887.85	2832.77	2791.40
130000	12387.32	6970.96	5203.22	4346.76	3853.88	3541.83	3332.19	3185.68	3080.45	3003.36	2946.08	2903.06
135000	12863.75	7239.07	5403.35	4513.95	4002.10	3678.05	3460.35	3308.21	3198.93	3118.88	3059.39	3014.71
140000	13340.19	7507.19	5603.47	4681.13	4150.33	3814.28	3588.51	3430.74	3317.41	3234.39	3172.70	3126.37
145000	13816.62	7775.30	5803.59	4848.31	4298.56	3950.50	3716.67	3553.26	3435.88	3349.90	3286.01	3238.02
150000	14293.06	8043.41	6003.72	5015.50	4446.78	4086.72	3844.83	3675.79	3554.36	3465.42	3399.32	3349.68
155000	14769.49	8311.53	6203.84	5182.68	4595.01	4222.95	3973.00	3798.31	3672.84	3580.93	3512.63	3461.34
160000	15245.93	8579.64	6403.96	5349.86	4743.23	4359.17	4101.16	3920.84	3791.32	3696.44	3625.94	3572.99

MONTHLY AMORTIZING PAYMENTS 25.50%

AMOUNT OF LOAN	NUMBER OF YEARS IN TERM											
	13	14	15	16	17	18	19	20	25	30	35	40
$ 50	1.11	1.10	1.09	1.09	1.08	1.08	1.08	1.07	1.07	1.07	1.07	1.07
100	2.21	2.19	2.18	2.17	2.16	2.15	2.15	2.14	2.13	2.13	2.13	2.13
200	4.42	4.38	4.35	4.33	4.31	4.30	4.29	4.28	4.26	4.26	4.26	4.26
300	6.63	6.57	6.53	6.49	6.47	6.45	6.43	6.42	6.39	6.38	6.38	6.38
400	8.84	8.76	8.70	8.66	8.62	8.60	8.58	8.56	8.52	8.51	8.51	8.51
500	11.05	10.95	10.88	10.82	10.78	10.74	10.72	10.70	10.65	10.64	10.63	10.63
600	13.25	13.14	13.05	12.98	12.93	12.89	12.86	12.84	12.78	12.76	12.76	12.76
700	15.46	15.33	15.23	15.15	15.09	15.04	15.00	14.98	14.91	14.89	14.88	14.88
800	17.67	17.52	17.40	17.31	17.24	17.19	17.15	17.12	17.04	17.01	17.01	17.01
900	19.88	19.71	19.57	19.47	19.40	19.34	19.29	19.25	19.16	19.14	19.13	19.13
1000	22.09	21.89	21.75	21.64	21.55	21.48	21.43	21.39	21.29	21.27	21.26	21.26
2000	44.17	43.78	43.49	43.27	43.10	42.96	42.86	42.78	42.58	42.53	42.51	42.51
3000	66.25	65.67	65.24	64.90	64.64	64.44	64.29	64.17	63.87	63.79	63.76	63.76
4000	88.33	87.56	86.98	86.53	86.19	85.92	85.71	85.56	85.16	85.05	85.02	85.01
5000	110.41	109.45	108.72	108.16	107.73	107.40	107.14	106.94	106.45	106.31	106.27	106.26
6000	132.49	131.34	130.47	129.80	129.28	128.88	128.57	128.33	127.74	127.57	127.52	127.51
7000	154.57	153.23	152.21	151.43	150.82	150.36	150.00	149.72	149.03	148.83	148.78	148.76
8000	176.65	175.12	173.96	173.06	172.37	171.84	171.42	171.11	170.32	170.09	170.03	170.01
9000	198.73	197.01	195.70	194.69	193.91	193.31	192.85	192.49	191.60	191.35	191.28	191.26
10000	220.81	218.90	217.44	216.32	215.46	214.79	214.28	213.88	212.89	212.61	212.54	212.51
11000	242.89	240.79	239.19	237.95	237.00	236.27	235.71	235.27	234.18	233.88	233.79	233.76
12000	264.97	262.68	260.93	259.59	258.55	257.75	257.13	256.66	255.47	255.14	255.04	255.02
13000	287.05	284.57	282.67	281.22	280.10	279.23	278.56	278.04	276.76	276.40	276.30	276.27
14000	309.13	306.46	304.42	302.85	301.64	300.71	299.99	299.43	298.05	297.66	297.55	297.52
15000	331.21	328.35	326.16	324.48	323.19	322.19	321.42	320.82	319.34	318.92	318.80	318.77
16000	353.30	350.24	347.91	346.11	344.73	343.67	342.84	342.21	340.63	340.18	340.05	340.02
17000	375.38	372.13	369.65	367.74	366.28	365.14	364.27	363.59	361.91	361.44	361.31	361.27
18000	397.46	394.02	391.39	389.38	387.82	386.62	385.70	384.98	383.20	382.70	382.56	382.52
19000	419.54	415.91	413.14	411.01	409.37	408.10	407.12	406.37	404.49	403.96	403.81	403.77
20000	441.62	437.80	434.88	432.64	430.91	429.58	428.55	427.76	425.78	425.22	425.07	425.02
21000	463.70	459.69	456.63	454.27	452.46	451.06	449.98	449.14	447.07	446.49	446.32	446.27
22000	485.78	481.58	478.37	475.90	474.00	472.54	471.41	470.53	468.36	467.75	467.57	467.52
23000	507.86	503.47	500.11	497.53	495.55	494.02	492.83	491.92	489.65	489.01	488.83	488.78
24000	529.94	525.36	521.86	519.17	517.09	515.50	514.26	513.31	510.94	510.27	510.08	510.03
25000	552.02	547.25	543.60	540.80	538.64	536.98	535.69	534.69	532.22	531.53	531.33	531.28
26000	574.10	569.14	565.34	562.43	560.19	558.45	557.12	556.08	553.51	552.79	552.59	552.53
27000	596.18	591.03	587.09	584.06	581.73	579.93	578.54	577.47	574.80	574.05	573.84	573.78
28000	618.26	612.92	608.83	605.69	603.28	601.41	599.97	598.86	596.09	595.31	595.09	595.03
29000	640.34	634.81	630.58	627.32	624.82	622.89	621.40	620.24	617.38	616.57	616.35	616.28
30000	662.42	656.70	652.32	648.96	646.37	644.37	642.83	641.63	638.67	637.83	637.60	637.53
31000	684.50	678.59	674.06	670.59	667.91	665.85	664.25	663.02	659.96	659.09	658.85	658.78
32000	706.59	700.48	695.81	692.22	689.46	687.33	685.68	684.41	681.25	680.36	680.10	680.03
33000	728.67	722.37	717.55	713.85	711.00	708.81	707.11	705.79	702.53	701.62	701.36	701.28
34000	750.75	744.26	739.29	735.48	732.55	730.28	728.54	727.18	723.82	722.88	722.61	722.53
35000	772.83	766.15	761.04	757.11	754.09	751.76	749.96	748.57	745.11	744.14	743.86	743.79
37500	828.03	820.87	815.40	811.19	807.96	805.46	803.53	802.04	798.33	797.29	797.00	796.91
40000	883.23	875.60	869.76	865.27	861.82	859.16	857.10	855.51	851.56	850.44	850.13	850.04
42500	938.43	930.32	924.12	919.35	915.68	912.85	910.67	908.98	904.78	903.60	903.26	903.17
45000	993.63	985.05	978.48	973.43	969.55	966.55	964.24	962.44	958.00	956.75	956.39	956.29
47500	1048.84	1039.77	1032.84	1027.51	1023.41	1020.25	1017.80	1015.91	1011.22	1009.90	1009.53	1009.42
50000	1104.04	1094.50	1087.20	1081.59	1077.28	1073.95	1071.37	1069.38	1064.44	1063.05	1062.66	1062.55
52500	1159.24	1149.22	1141.56	1135.67	1131.14	1127.64	1124.94	1122.85	1117.67	1116.21	1115.79	1115.68
55000	1214.44	1203.94	1195.91	1189.75	1185.00	1181.34	1178.51	1176.32	1170.89	1169.36	1168.93	1168.80
57500	1269.64	1258.67	1250.27	1243.83	1238.87	1235.04	1232.08	1229.79	1224.11	1222.51	1222.06	1221.93
60000	1324.84	1313.39	1304.63	1297.91	1292.73	1288.73	1285.65	1283.26	1277.33	1275.66	1275.19	1275.06
65000	1435.25	1422.84	1413.35	1406.07	1400.46	1396.13	1392.78	1390.20	1383.78	1381.97	1381.46	1381.31
70000	1545.65	1532.29	1522.07	1514.22	1508.18	1503.52	1499.92	1497.13	1490.22	1488.27	1487.72	1487.57
75000	1656.05	1641.74	1630.79	1622.38	1615.91	1610.92	1607.06	1604.07	1596.66	1594.58	1593.99	1593.82
80000	1766.46	1751.19	1739.51	1730.54	1723.64	1718.31	1714.19	1711.01	1703.11	1700.88	1700.25	1700.08
85000	1876.86	1860.64	1848.23	1838.70	1831.36	1825.70	1821.33	1817.95	1809.55	1807.19	1806.52	1806.33
90000	1987.26	1970.09	1956.95	1946.86	1939.09	1933.10	1928.47	1924.88	1915.99	1913.49	1912.78	1912.58
95000	2097.67	2079.54	2065.67	2055.02	2046.82	2040.49	2035.60	2031.82	2022.44	2019.80	2019.05	2018.84
100000	2208.07	2188.99	2174.39	2163.18	2154.55	2147.89	2142.74	2138.76	2128.88	2126.10	2125.32	2125.09
105000	2318.47	2298.44	2283.11	2271.33	2262.27	2255.28	2249.88	2245.70	2235.33	2232.41	2231.58	2231.35
110000	2428.87	2407.88	2391.82	2379.49	2370.00	2362.67	2357.01	2352.64	2341.77	2338.71	2337.85	2337.60
115000	2539.28	2517.33	2500.54	2487.65	2477.73	2470.07	2464.15	2459.57	2448.21	2445.02	2444.11	2443.86
120000	2649.68	2626.78	2609.26	2595.81	2585.45	2577.46	2571.29	2566.51	2554.66	2551.32	2550.38	2550.11
125000	2760.08	2736.23	2717.98	2703.97	2693.18	2684.86	2678.43	2673.45	2661.10	2657.63	2656.64	2656.36
130000	2870.49	2845.68	2826.70	2812.13	2800.91	2792.25	2785.56	2780.39	2767.55	2763.93	2762.91	2762.62
135000	2980.89	2955.13	2935.42	2920.29	2908.63	2899.64	2892.70	2887.32	2873.99	2870.24	2869.17	2868.87
140000	3091.29	3064.58	3044.14	3028.44	3016.36	3007.04	2999.84	2994.26	2980.43	2976.54	2975.44	2975.13
145000	3201.70	3174.03	3152.86	3136.60	3124.09	3114.43	3106.97	3101.20	3086.88	3082.85	3081.71	3081.38
150000	3312.10	3283.48	3261.58	3244.76	3231.82	3221.83	3214.11	3208.14	3193.32	3189.15	3187.97	3187.64
155000	3422.50	3392.93	3370.30	3352.92	3339.54	3329.22	3321.25	3315.08	3299.76	3295.45	3294.24	3293.89
160000	3532.91	3502.38	3479.02	3461.08	3447.27	3436.62	3428.38	3422.01	3406.21	3401.76	3400.50	3400.15

25.75% MONTHLY AMORTIZING PAYMENTS

AMOUNT OF LOAN	NUMBER OF YEARS IN TERM											
	1	2	3	4	5	6	7	8	9	10	11	12
$ 50	4.78	2.69	2.01	1.68	1.49	1.37	1.29	1.24	1.20	1.17	1.15	1.13
100	9.55	5.38	4.02	3.36	2.98	2.74	2.58	2.47	2.39	2.33	2.29	2.26
200	19.09	10.75	8.04	6.72	5.96	5.48	5.16	4.94	4.78	4.66	4.57	4.51
300	28.63	16.13	12.05	10.08	8.94	8.22	7.74	7.41	7.17	6.99	6.86	6.76
400	38.17	21.50	16.07	13.44	11.92	10.96	10.32	9.87	9.55	9.32	9.14	9.01
500	47.71	26.88	20.08	16.79	14.90	13.70	12.90	12.34	11.94	11.65	11.43	11.26
600	57.25	32.25	24.10	20.15	17.88	16.44	15.48	14.81	14.33	13.97	13.71	13.52
700	66.79	37.63	28.12	23.51	20.86	19.18	18.06	17.28	16.71	16.30	16.00	15.77
800	76.33	43.00	32.13	26.87	23.84	21.92	20.64	19.74	19.10	18.63	18.28	18.02
900	85.87	48.38	36.15	30.22	26.82	24.66	23.22	22.21	21.49	20.96	20.56	20.27
1000	95.41	53.75	40.16	33.58	29.80	27.40	25.80	24.68	23.87	23.29	22.85	22.52
2000	190.82	107.50	80.32	67.16	59.59	54.80	51.59	49.35	47.74	46.57	45.69	45.04
3000	286.23	161.25	120.48	100.74	89.38	82.20	77.38	74.02	71.61	69.85	68.54	67.56
4000	381.64	215.00	160.64	134.31	119.18	109.60	103.18	98.69	95.48	93.13	91.38	90.07
5000	477.05	268.75	200.79	167.89	148.97	137.00	128.97	123.37	119.35	116.41	114.22	112.59
6000	572.46	322.50	240.95	201.47	178.76	164.40	154.76	148.04	143.21	139.69	137.07	135.11
7000	667.86	376.24	281.11	235.04	208.55	191.80	180.56	172.71	167.08	162.97	159.91	157.62
8000	763.27	429.99	321.27	268.62	238.35	219.20	206.35	197.38	190.95	186.25	182.76	180.14
9000	858.68	483.74	361.42	302.20	268.14	246.60	232.14	222.05	214.82	209.53	205.60	202.66
10000	954.09	537.49	401.58	335.77	297.93	274.00	257.94	246.73	238.69	232.81	228.44	225.17
11000	1049.50	591.24	441.74	369.35	327.72	301.40	283.73	271.40	262.55	256.09	251.29	247.69
12000	1144.91	644.99	481.90	402.93	357.52	328.80	309.52	296.07	286.42	279.37	274.13	270.21
13000	1240.32	698.74	522.05	436.50	387.31	356.19	335.32	320.74	310.29	302.65	296.98	292.73
14000	1335.72	752.48	562.21	470.08	417.10	383.59	361.11	345.42	334.16	325.93	319.82	315.24
15000	1431.13	806.23	602.37	503.66	446.89	410.99	386.90	370.09	358.03	349.21	342.66	337.76
16000	1526.54	859.98	642.53	537.23	476.69	438.39	412.70	394.76	381.90	372.49	365.51	360.28
17000	1621.95	913.73	682.68	570.81	506.48	465.79	438.49	419.43	405.76	395.77	388.35	382.79
18000	1717.36	967.48	722.84	604.39	536.27	493.19	464.28	444.10	429.63	419.05	411.20	405.31
19000	1812.77	1021.23	763.00	637.96	566.07	520.59	490.07	468.78	453.50	442.33	434.04	427.83
20000	1908.18	1074.98	803.16	671.54	595.86	547.99	515.87	493.45	477.37	465.61	456.88	450.34
21000	2003.58	1128.72	843.31	705.12	625.65	575.39	541.66	518.12	501.24	488.89	479.73	472.86
22000	2098.99	1182.47	883.47	738.69	655.44	602.79	567.45	542.79	525.10	512.17	502.57	495.38
23000	2194.40	1236.22	923.63	772.27	685.24	630.19	593.25	567.47	548.97	535.45	525.42	517.89
24000	2289.81	1289.97	963.79	805.85	715.03	657.59	619.04	592.14	572.84	558.73	548.26	540.41
25000	2385.22	1343.72	1003.94	839.43	744.82	684.99	644.83	616.81	596.71	582.01	571.10	562.93
26000	2480.63	1397.47	1044.10	873.00	774.61	712.38	670.63	641.48	620.58	605.29	593.95	585.45
27000	2576.04	1451.22	1084.26	906.58	804.41	739.78	696.42	666.15	644.45	628.57	616.79	607.96
28000	2671.44	1504.96	1124.42	940.16	834.20	767.18	722.21	690.83	668.31	651.85	639.64	630.48
29000	2766.85	1558.71	1164.57	973.73	863.99	794.58	748.01	715.50	692.18	675.13	662.48	653.00
30000	2862.26	1612.46	1204.73	1007.31	893.78	821.98	773.80	740.17	716.05	698.41	685.32	675.51
31000	2957.67	1666.21	1244.89	1040.89	923.58	849.38	799.59	764.84	739.92	721.69	708.17	698.03
32000	3053.08	1719.96	1285.05	1074.46	953.37	876.78	825.39	789.51	763.79	744.97	731.01	720.55
33000	3148.49	1773.71	1325.20	1108.04	983.16	904.18	851.18	814.19	787.65	768.25	753.86	743.06
34000	3243.90	1827.46	1365.36	1141.62	1012.95	931.58	876.97	838.86	811.52	791.53	776.70	765.58
35000	3339.30	1881.20	1405.52	1175.19	1042.75	958.98	902.76	863.53	835.39	814.81	799.54	788.10
37500	3577.82	2015.58	1505.91	1259.14	1117.23	1027.48	967.25	925.21	895.06	873.01	856.65	844.39
40000	3816.35	2149.95	1606.31	1343.08	1191.71	1095.97	1031.73	986.89	954.73	931.21	913.76	900.68
42500	4054.87	2284.32	1706.70	1427.02	1266.19	1164.47	1096.21	1048.57	1014.40	989.41	970.87	956.97
45000	4293.39	2418.69	1807.10	1510.96	1340.67	1232.97	1160.70	1110.25	1074.07	1047.61	1027.98	1013.27
47500	4531.91	2553.06	1907.49	1594.90	1415.16	1301.47	1225.18	1171.93	1133.74	1105.81	1085.09	1069.56
50000	4770.43	2687.43	2007.88	1678.85	1489.64	1369.97	1289.66	1233.61	1193.41	1164.01	1142.09	1125.85
52500	5008.95	2821.80	2108.28	1762.79	1564.12	1438.46	1354.14	1295.29	1253.08	1222.21	1199.31	1182.14
55000	5247.47	2956.18	2208.67	1846.73	1638.60	1506.96	1418.63	1356.97	1312.75	1280.41	1256.42	1238.44
57500	5486.00	3090.55	2309.06	1930.67	1713.08	1575.46	1483.11	1418.66	1372.43	1338.61	1313.53	1294.73
60000	5724.52	3224.92	2409.46	2014.61	1787.56	1643.96	1547.59	1480.34	1432.10	1396.81	1370.64	1351.02
65000	6201.56	3493.66	2610.25	2182.50	1936.53	1780.95	1676.56	1603.70	1551.44	1513.22	1484.86	1463.61
70000	6678.60	3762.40	2811.03	2350.39	2085.49	1917.95	1805.52	1727.06	1670.78	1629.62	1599.08	1576.19
75000	7155.64	4031.15	3011.82	2518.27	2234.45	2054.95	1934.49	1850.42	1790.12	1746.02	1713.30	1688.78
80000	7632.69	4299.89	3212.61	2686.15	2383.42	2191.94	2063.46	1973.78	1909.46	1862.42	1827.52	1801.36
85000	8109.73	4568.63	3413.40	2854.03	2532.38	2328.94	2192.42	2097.14	2028.80	1978.82	1941.74	1913.94
90000	8586.77	4837.38	3614.19	3021.92	2681.34	2465.93	2321.39	2220.50	2148.14	2095.22	2055.96	2026.53
95000	9063.82	5106.12	3814.97	3189.80	2830.31	2602.93	2450.35	2343.86	2267.48	2211.62	2170.18	2139.11
100000	9540.86	5374.86	4015.76	3357.69	2979.27	2739.93	2579.32	2467.22	2386.82	2328.02	2284.40	2251.70
105000	10017.90	5643.60	4216.55	3525.57	3128.23	2876.92	2708.28	2590.58	2506.16	2444.42	2398.62	2364.28
110000	10494.94	5912.35	4417.34	3693.45	3277.20	3013.92	2837.25	2713.94	2625.50	2560.82	2512.84	2476.87
115000	10971.99	6181.09	4618.12	3861.34	3426.16	3150.91	2966.22	2837.31	2744.85	2677.22	2627.06	2589.45
120000	11449.03	6449.83	4818.91	4029.22	3575.12	3287.91	3095.18	2960.67	2864.19	2793.62	2741.28	2702.04
125000	11926.07	6718.57	5019.70	4197.11	3724.09	3424.91	3224.15	3084.03	2983.53	2910.03	2855.50	2814.62
130000	12403.11	6987.32	5220.49	4364.99	3873.05	3561.90	3353.11	3207.39	3102.87	3026.43	2969.72	2927.21
135000	12880.16	7256.06	5421.28	4532.87	4022.01	3698.90	3482.08	3330.75	3222.21	3142.83	3083.94	3039.79
140000	13357.20	7524.80	5622.06	4700.76	4170.98	3835.90	3611.04	3454.11	3341.55	3259.23	3198.16	3152.38
145000	13834.24	7793.55	5822.85	4868.64	4319.94	3972.89	3740.01	3577.47	3460.89	3375.63	3312.38	3264.96
150000	14311.28	8062.29	6023.64	5036.53	4468.90	4109.89	3868.97	3700.83	3580.23	3492.03	3426.60	3377.55
155000	14788.33	8331.03	6224.43	5204.41	4617.86	4246.88	3997.94	3824.19	3699.57	3608.43	3540.82	3490.13
160000	15265.37	8599.77	6425.22	5372.29	4766.83	4383.88	4126.91	3947.55	3818.91	3724.83	3655.04	3602.72

168

AMOUNT OF LOAN	NUMBER OF YEARS IN TERM											
	13	14	15	16	17	18	19	20	25	30	35	40
$ 50	1.12	1.11	1.10	1.10	1.09	1.09	1.09	1.08	1.08	1.08	1.08	1.08
100	2.23	2.21	2.20	2.19	2.18	2.17	2.17	2.16	2.15	2.15	2.15	2.15
200	4.46	4.42	4.39	4.37	4.35	4.34	4.33	4.32	4.30	4.30	4.30	4.30
300	6.69	6.63	6.59	6.55	6.53	6.51	6.49	6.48	6.45	6.45	6.44	6.44
400	8.91	8.84	8.78	8.74	8.70	8.68	8.66	8.64	8.60	8.59	8.59	8.59
500	11.14	11.05	10.97	10.92	10.88	10.84	10.82	10.80	10.75	10.74	10.74	10.73
600	13.37	13.25	13.17	13.10	13.05	13.01	12.98	12.96	12.90	12.89	12.88	12.88
700	15.59	15.46	15.36	15.29	15.23	15.18	15.15	15.12	15.05	15.03	15.03	15.03
800	17.82	17.67	17.56	17.47	17.40	17.35	17.31	17.28	17.20	17.18	17.17	17.17
900	20.05	19.88	19.75	19.65	19.57	19.52	19.47	19.44	19.35	19.33	19.32	19.32
1000	22.27	22.09	21.94	21.83	21.75	21.68	21.63	21.60	21.50	21.47	21.47	21.46
2000	44.54	44.17	43.88	43.66	43.49	43.36	43.26	43.19	43.00	42.94	42.93	42.92
3000	66.81	66.25	65.82	65.49	65.24	65.04	64.89	64.78	64.49	64.41	64.39	64.38
4000	89.08	88.33	87.76	87.32	86.98	86.72	86.52	86.37	85.99	85.88	85.85	85.84
5000	111.35	110.42	109.70	109.15	108.73	108.40	108.15	107.96	107.48	107.35	107.31	107.30
6000	133.62	132.50	131.64	130.98	130.47	130.08	129.78	129.55	128.98	128.82	128.77	128.76
7000	155.89	154.58	153.58	152.81	152.22	151.76	151.41	151.14	150.47	150.29	150.23	150.22
8000	178.16	176.66	175.51	174.63	173.96	173.44	173.04	172.73	171.97	171.75	171.69	171.68
9000	200.43	198.74	197.45	196.46	195.70	195.12	194.67	194.32	193.46	193.22	193.16	193.14
10000	222.70	220.83	219.39	218.29	217.45	216.80	216.30	215.91	214.96	214.69	214.62	214.60
11000	244.97	242.91	241.33	240.12	239.19	238.48	237.93	237.50	236.45	236.16	236.08	236.06
12000	267.24	264.99	263.27	261.95	260.94	260.16	259.56	259.09	257.95	257.63	257.54	257.51
13000	289.51	287.07	285.21	283.78	282.68	281.84	281.18	280.68	279.44	279.10	279.00	278.97
14000	311.78	309.15	307.15	305.61	304.43	303.52	302.81	302.27	300.94	300.57	300.46	300.43
15000	334.05	331.24	329.08	327.44	326.17	325.19	324.44	323.86	322.43	322.03	321.92	321.89
16000	356.32	353.32	351.02	349.26	347.91	346.87	346.07	345.45	343.93	343.50	343.38	343.35
17000	378.59	375.40	372.96	371.09	369.66	368.55	367.70	367.04	365.42	364.97	364.85	364.81
18000	400.86	397.48	394.90	392.92	391.40	390.23	389.33	388.64	386.92	386.44	386.31	386.27
19000	423.13	419.56	416.84	414.75	413.15	411.91	410.96	410.23	408.41	407.91	407.77	407.73
20000	445.40	441.65	438.78	436.58	434.89	433.59	432.59	431.82	429.91	429.38	429.23	429.19
21000	467.67	463.73	460.72	458.41	456.64	455.27	454.22	453.41	451.40	450.85	450.69	450.65
22000	489.94	485.81	482.65	480.24	478.38	476.95	475.85	475.00	472.90	472.31	472.15	472.11
23000	512.21	507.89	504.59	502.07	500.12	498.63	497.48	496.59	494.39	493.78	493.61	493.57
24000	534.48	529.97	526.53	523.89	521.87	520.31	519.11	518.18	515.89	515.25	515.07	515.02
25000	556.75	552.06	548.47	545.72	543.61	541.99	540.74	539.77	537.38	536.72	536.54	536.48
26000	579.02	574.14	570.41	567.55	565.36	563.67	562.36	561.36	558.88	558.19	558.00	557.94
27000	601.29	596.22	592.35	589.38	587.10	585.35	583.99	582.95	580.37	579.66	579.46	579.40
28000	623.56	618.30	614.29	611.21	608.85	607.03	605.62	604.54	601.87	601.13	600.92	600.86
29000	645.83	640.38	636.22	633.04	630.59	628.71	627.25	626.13	623.36	622.60	622.38	622.32
30000	668.10	662.47	658.16	654.87	652.33	650.38	648.88	647.72	644.86	644.06	643.84	643.78
31000	690.37	684.55	680.10	676.70	674.08	672.06	670.51	669.31	666.35	665.53	665.30	665.24
32000	712.64	706.63	702.04	698.52	695.82	693.74	692.14	690.90	687.85	687.00	686.76	686.70
33000	734.91	728.71	723.98	720.35	717.57	715.42	713.77	712.49	709.35	708.47	708.22	708.16
34000	757.18	750.79	745.92	742.18	739.31	737.10	735.40	734.08	730.84	729.94	729.69	729.62
35000	779.45	772.88	767.86	764.01	761.06	758.78	757.03	755.67	752.34	751.41	751.15	751.07
37500	835.12	828.08	822.70	818.58	815.42	812.98	811.10	809.65	806.07	805.08	804.80	804.72
40000	890.80	883.29	877.55	873.15	869.78	867.18	865.17	863.63	859.81	858.75	858.45	858.37
42500	946.47	938.49	932.40	927.73	924.14	921.38	919.25	917.60	913.55	912.42	912.11	912.02
45000	1002.15	993.70	987.24	982.30	978.50	975.57	973.32	971.58	967.29	966.09	965.76	965.67
47500	1057.82	1048.90	1042.09	1036.87	1032.86	1029.77	1027.39	1025.56	1021.03	1019.76	1019.41	1019.31
50000	1113.50	1104.11	1096.94	1091.44	1087.22	1083.97	1081.47	1079.53	1074.76	1073.44	1073.07	1072.96
52500	1169.17	1159.31	1151.78	1146.01	1141.58	1138.17	1135.54	1133.51	1128.50	1127.11	1126.72	1126.61
55000	1224.85	1214.52	1206.63	1200.58	1195.94	1192.37	1189.61	1187.49	1182.24	1180.78	1180.37	1180.26
57500	1280.52	1269.72	1261.48	1255.16	1250.30	1246.57	1243.69	1241.46	1235.98	1234.45	1234.02	1233.91
60000	1336.20	1324.93	1316.32	1309.73	1304.66	1300.76	1297.76	1295.44	1289.71	1288.12	1287.68	1287.55
65000	1447.54	1435.34	1426.01	1418.87	1413.39	1409.16	1405.90	1403.39	1397.19	1395.47	1394.98	1394.85
70000	1558.89	1545.75	1535.71	1528.02	1522.11	1517.56	1514.05	1511.34	1504.67	1502.81	1502.29	1502.14
75000	1670.24	1656.16	1645.40	1637.16	1630.83	1625.95	1622.20	1619.30	1612.14	1610.15	1609.60	1609.44
80000	1781.59	1766.57	1755.09	1746.30	1739.55	1734.35	1730.34	1727.25	1719.62	1717.49	1716.90	1716.74
85000	1892.94	1876.98	1864.79	1855.45	1848.27	1842.75	1838.49	1835.20	1827.09	1824.84	1824.21	1824.03
90000	2004.29	1987.39	1974.48	1964.59	1956.99	1951.14	1946.64	1943.16	1934.57	1932.18	1931.51	1931.33
95000	2115.64	2097.80	2084.17	2073.73	2065.71	2059.54	2054.78	2051.11	2042.05	2039.52	2038.82	2038.62
100000	2226.99	2208.21	2193.87	2182.88	2174.44	2167.94	2162.93	2159.06	2149.52	2146.87	2146.13	2145.92
105000	2338.34	2318.62	2303.56	2292.02	2283.16	2276.33	2271.07	2267.01	2257.00	2254.21	2253.43	2253.21
110000	2449.69	2429.03	2413.25	2401.16	2391.88	2384.73	2379.22	2374.97	2364.47	2361.55	2360.74	2360.51
115000	2561.03	2539.44	2522.95	2510.31	2500.60	2493.13	2487.37	2482.92	2471.95	2468.90	2468.04	2467.81
120000	2672.39	2649.85	2632.64	2619.45	2609.32	2601.52	2595.51	2590.87	2579.42	2576.24	2575.35	2575.10
125000	2783.74	2760.26	2742.33	2728.60	2718.04	2709.92	2703.66	2698.82	2686.90	2683.58	2682.66	2682.40
130000	2895.08	2870.67	2852.02	2837.74	2826.77	2818.32	2811.80	2806.78	2794.38	2790.93	2789.96	2789.69
135000	3006.43	2981.08	2961.72	2946.88	2935.49	2926.71	2919.95	2914.73	2901.85	2898.27	2897.27	2896.99
140000	3117.78	3091.49	3071.41	3056.03	3044.21	3035.11	3028.10	3022.68	3009.33	3005.61	3004.57	3004.28
145000	3229.13	3201.90	3181.10	3165.17	3152.93	3143.51	3136.24	3130.64	3116.80	3112.96	3111.88	3111.58
150000	3340.48	3312.31	3290.80	3274.31	3261.65	3251.90	3244.39	3238.59	3224.28	3220.30	3219.19	3218.88
155000	3451.83	3422.72	3400.49	3383.46	3370.37	3360.30	3352.54	3346.54	3331.75	3327.64	3326.49	3326.17
160000	3563.18	3533.13	3510.18	3492.60	3479.09	3468.70	3460.68	3454.49	3439.23	3434.98	3433.80	3433.47

MONTHLY AMORTIZING PAYMENTS

AMOUNT OF LOAN	NUMBER OF YEARS IN TERM											
	1	2	3	4	5	6	7	8	9	10	11	12
$ 50	4.78	2.70	2.02	1.69	1.50	1.38	1.30	1.25	1.21	1.18	1.16	1.14
100	9.56	5.39	4.03	3.38	3.00	2.76	2.60	2.49	2.41	2.35	2.31	2.28
200	19.11	10.78	8.06	6.75	5.99	5.52	5.20	4.97	4.81	4.70	4.61	4.55
300	28.66	16.17	12.09	10.12	8.99	8.27	7.79	7.46	7.22	7.04	6.91	6.82
400	38.22	21.55	16.12	13.49	11.98	11.03	10.39	9.94	9.62	9.39	9.22	9.09
500	47.77	26.94	20.15	16.86	14.98	13.78	12.98	12.42	12.03	11.73	11.52	11.36
600	57.32	32.33	24.18	20.24	17.97	16.54	15.58	14.91	14.43	14.08	13.82	13.63
700	66.88	37.72	28.21	23.61	20.96	19.29	18.17	17.39	16.83	16.43	16.12	15.90
800	76.43	43.10	32.24	26.98	23.96	22.05	20.77	19.88	19.24	18.77	18.43	18.17
900	85.98	48.49	36.27	30.35	26.95	24.80	23.36	22.36	21.64	21.12	20.73	20.44
1000	95.54	53.88	40.30	33.72	29.95	27.56	25.96	24.84	24.05	23.46	23.03	22.71
2000	191.07	107.75	80.59	67.44	59.89	55.11	51.91	49.68	48.09	46.92	46.06	45.41
3000	286.60	161.63	120.88	101.16	89.83	82.67	77.87	74.52	72.13	70.38	69.08	68.11
4000	382.13	215.50	161.17	134.87	119.77	110.22	103.82	99.36	96.17	93.84	92.11	90.82
5000	477.66	269.38	201.46	168.59	149.71	137.78	129.78	124.20	120.21	117.30	115.14	113.52
6000	573.19	323.25	241.75	202.31	179.65	165.33	155.73	149.04	144.25	140.75	138.16	136.22
7000	668.72	377.13	282.04	236.03	209.59	192.88	181.69	173.88	168.29	164.21	161.19	158.93
8000	764.25	431.00	322.33	269.74	239.53	220.44	207.64	198.72	192.33	187.67	184.21	181.63
9000	859.78	484.88	362.62	303.46	269.47	247.99	233.60	223.56	216.37	211.13	207.24	204.33
10000	955.31	538.75	402.91	337.18	299.41	275.55	259.55	248.40	240.42	234.59	230.27	227.04
11000	1050.84	592.63	443.20	370.90	329.35	303.10	285.50	273.24	264.46	258.04	253.29	249.74
12000	1146.37	646.50	483.49	404.61	359.29	330.65	311.46	298.08	288.50	281.50	276.32	272.44
13000	1241.90	700.37	523.78	438.33	389.23	358.21	337.41	322.92	312.54	304.96	299.35	295.15
14000	1337.43	754.25	564.07	472.05	419.17	385.76	363.37	347.76	336.58	328.42	322.37	317.85
15000	1432.96	808.12	604.36	505.76	449.11	413.32	389.32	372.60	360.62	351.88	345.40	340.55
16000	1528.49	862.00	644.65	539.48	479.05	440.87	415.28	397.44	384.66	375.33	368.42	363.26
17000	1624.02	915.87	684.95	573.20	508.99	468.42	441.23	422.28	408.70	398.79	391.45	385.96
18000	1719.55	969.75	725.24	606.92	538.93	495.98	467.19	447.12	432.74	422.25	414.48	408.66
19000	1815.08	1023.62	765.53	640.63	568.87	523.53	493.14	471.96	456.79	445.71	437.50	431.36
20000	1910.61	1077.50	805.82	674.35	598.81	551.09	519.09	496.80	480.83	469.17	460.53	454.07
21000	2006.14	1131.37	846.11	708.07	628.75	578.64	545.05	521.64	504.87	492.62	483.56	476.77
22000	2101.67	1185.25	886.40	741.79	658.70	606.19	571.00	546.48	528.91	516.08	506.58	499.47
23000	2197.20	1239.12	926.69	775.50	688.64	633.75	596.96	571.32	552.95	539.54	529.61	522.18
24000	2292.73	1292.99	966.98	809.22	718.58	661.30	622.91	596.16	576.99	563.00	552.63	544.88
25000	2388.26	1346.87	1007.27	842.94	748.52	688.86	648.87	620.99	601.03	586.46	575.66	567.58
26000	2483.79	1400.74	1047.56	876.65	778.46	716.41	674.82	645.83	625.07	609.91	598.69	590.29
27000	2579.32	1454.62	1087.85	910.37	808.40	743.96	700.78	670.67	649.11	633.37	621.71	612.99
28000	2674.85	1508.49	1128.14	944.09	838.34	771.52	726.73	695.51	673.16	656.83	644.74	635.69
29000	2770.38	1562.37	1168.43	977.81	868.28	799.07	752.69	720.35	697.20	680.29	667.77	658.40
30000	2865.91	1616.24	1208.72	1011.52	898.22	826.63	778.64	745.19	721.24	703.75	690.79	681.10
31000	2961.44	1670.12	1249.01	1045.24	928.16	854.18	804.59	770.03	745.28	727.20	713.82	703.80
32000	3056.97	1723.99	1289.30	1078.96	958.10	881.73	830.55	794.87	769.32	750.66	736.84	726.51
33000	3152.50	1777.87	1329.60	1112.68	988.04	909.29	856.50	819.71	793.36	774.12	759.87	749.21
34000	3248.03	1831.74	1369.89	1146.39	1017.98	936.84	882.46	844.55	817.40	797.58	782.90	771.91
35000	3343.56	1885.61	1410.18	1180.11	1047.92	964.40	908.41	869.39	841.44	821.04	805.92	794.61
37500	3582.39	2020.30	1510.90	1264.40	1122.77	1033.28	973.30	931.49	901.55	879.68	863.49	851.37
40000	3821.21	2154.99	1611.63	1348.70	1197.62	1102.17	1038.18	993.59	961.65	938.33	921.05	908.13
42500	4060.04	2289.67	1712.36	1432.99	1272.47	1171.05	1103.07	1055.69	1021.75	996.97	978.62	964.89
45000	4298.86	2424.36	1813.08	1517.28	1347.33	1239.94	1167.96	1117.79	1081.85	1055.62	1036.19	1021.65
47500	4537.69	2559.05	1913.81	1601.58	1422.18	1308.82	1232.84	1179.89	1141.96	1114.26	1093.75	1078.40
50000	4776.51	2693.73	2014.54	1685.87	1497.03	1377.71	1297.73	1241.98	1202.06	1172.91	1151.32	1135.16
52500	5015.34	2828.42	2115.26	1770.16	1571.88	1446.59	1362.62	1304.08	1262.16	1231.55	1208.88	1191.92
55000	5254.16	2963.11	2215.99	1854.46	1646.73	1515.48	1427.50	1366.18	1322.26	1290.20	1266.45	1248.68
57500	5492.99	3097.79	2316.72	1938.75	1721.58	1584.36	1492.39	1428.28	1382.37	1348.84	1324.01	1305.44
60000	5731.81	3232.48	2417.44	2023.04	1796.43	1653.25	1557.27	1490.38	1442.47	1407.49	1381.58	1362.19
65000	6209.46	3501.85	2618.90	2191.63	1946.14	1791.02	1687.05	1614.58	1562.68	1524.78	1496.71	1475.71
70000	6687.11	3771.22	2820.35	2360.22	2095.84	1928.79	1816.82	1738.78	1682.88	1642.07	1611.84	1589.22
75000	7164.77	4040.60	3021.80	2528.80	2245.54	2066.56	1946.59	1862.97	1803.09	1759.36	1726.97	1702.74
80000	7642.42	4309.97	3223.25	2697.39	2395.24	2204.33	2076.36	1987.17	1923.29	1876.65	1842.10	1816.26
85000	8120.07	4579.34	3424.71	2865.98	2544.94	2342.10	2206.14	2111.37	2043.50	1993.94	1957.24	1929.77
90000	8597.72	4848.72	3626.16	3034.56	2694.65	2479.87	2335.91	2235.57	2163.70	2111.23	2072.37	2043.29
95000	9075.37	5118.09	3827.61	3203.15	2844.35	2617.64	2465.68	2359.77	2283.91	2228.52	2187.50	2156.80
100000	9553.02	5387.46	4029.07	3371.74	2994.05	2755.41	2595.45	2483.96	2404.11	2345.81	2302.63	2270.32
105000	10030.67	5656.83	4230.52	3540.32	3143.75	2893.18	2725.23	2608.16	2524.32	2463.10	2417.76	2383.83
110000	10508.32	5926.21	4431.97	3708.91	3293.46	3030.95	2855.00	2732.36	2644.52	2580.39	2532.89	2497.35
115000	10985.97	6195.58	4633.43	3877.50	3443.16	3168.72	2984.77	2856.56	2764.73	2697.68	2648.02	2610.87
120000	11463.62	6464.95	4834.88	4046.08	3592.86	3306.49	3114.54	2980.76	2884.94	2814.97	2763.15	2724.38
125000	11941.27	6734.33	5036.33	4214.67	3742.56	3444.26	3244.32	3104.95	3005.14	2932.26	2878.29	2837.90
130000	12418.92	7003.70	5237.79	4383.25	3892.27	3582.03	3374.09	3229.15	3125.35	3049.55	2993.42	2951.41
135000	12896.57	7273.07	5439.24	4551.84	4041.97	3719.80	3503.86	3353.35	3245.56	3166.84	3108.55	3064.93
140000	13374.22	7542.44	5640.69	4720.43	4191.67	3857.57	3633.63	3477.55	3365.76	3284.13	3223.68	3178.44
145000	13851.88	7811.82	5842.14	4889.01	4341.37	3995.34	3763.41	3601.74	3485.96	3401.42	3338.81	3291.96
150000	14329.53	8081.19	6043.60	5057.60	4491.08	4133.11	3893.18	3725.94	3606.17	3518.71	3453.94	3405.48
155000	14807.18	8350.56	6245.05	5226.19	4640.78	4270.88	4022.95	3850.14	3726.37	3636.00	3569.07	3518.99
160000	15284.83	8619.94	6446.50	5394.77	4790.48	4408.65	4152.72	3974.34	3846.58	3753.29	3684.20	3632.51

AMOUNT OF LOAN	NUMBER OF YEARS IN TERM											
	13	14	15	16	17	18	19	20	25	30	35	40
$ 50	1.13	1.12	1.11	1.11	1.10	1.10	1.10	1.09	1.09	1.09	1.09	1.09
100	2.25	2.23	2.22	2.21	2.20	2.19	2.19	2.18	2.18	2.17	2.17	2.17
200	4.50	4.46	4.43	4.41	4.39	4.38	4.37	4.36	4.35	4.34	4.34	4.34
300	6.74	6.69	6.65	6.61	6.59	6.57	6.55	6.54	6.52	6.51	6.51	6.51
400	8.99	8.91	8.86	8.82	8.78	8.76	8.74	8.72	8.69	8.68	8.67	8.67
500	11.23	11.14	11.07	11.02	10.98	10.95	10.92	10.90	10.86	10.84	10.84	10.84
600	13.48	13.37	13.29	13.22	13.17	13.13	13.10	13.08	13.03	13.01	13.01	13.01
700	15.73	15.60	15.50	15.42	15.37	15.32	15.29	15.26	15.20	15.18	15.17	15.17
800	17.97	17.82	17.71	17.63	17.56	17.51	17.47	17.44	17.37	17.35	17.34	17.34
900	20.22	20.05	19.93	19.83	19.75	19.70	19.65	19.62	19.54	19.51	19.51	19.51
1000	22.46	22.28	22.14	22.03	21.95	21.89	21.84	21.80	21.71	21.68	21.67	21.67
2000	44.92	44.55	44.27	44.06	43.89	43.77	43.67	43.59	43.41	43.36	43.34	43.34
3000	67.38	66.83	66.41	66.08	65.84	65.65	65.50	65.39	65.11	65.03	65.01	65.01
4000	89.84	89.10	88.54	88.11	87.78	87.53	87.33	87.18	86.81	86.71	86.68	86.67
5000	112.30	111.38	110.67	110.14	109.72	109.41	109.16	108.97	108.51	108.39	108.35	108.34
6000	134.76	133.65	132.81	132.16	131.67	131.29	130.99	130.77	130.21	130.06	130.02	130.01
7000	157.22	155.93	154.94	154.19	153.61	153.17	152.82	152.56	151.92	151.74	151.69	151.68
8000	179.68	178.20	177.08	176.21	175.55	175.05	174.66	174.36	173.62	173.42	173.36	173.34
9000	202.14	200.48	199.21	198.24	197.50	196.93	196.49	196.15	195.32	195.09	195.03	195.01
10000	224.60	222.75	221.34	220.27	219.44	218.81	218.32	217.94	217.02	216.77	216.70	216.68
11000	247.06	245.03	243.48	242.29	241.38	240.69	240.15	239.74	238.72	238.44	238.37	238.35
12000	269.52	267.30	265.61	264.32	263.33	262.57	261.98	261.53	260.42	260.12	260.04	260.01
13000	291.98	289.57	287.74	286.34	285.27	284.45	283.81	283.32	282.13	281.80	281.71	281.68
14000	314.44	311.85	309.88	308.37	307.21	306.33	305.64	305.12	303.83	303.47	303.38	303.35
15000	336.90	334.12	332.01	330.40	329.16	328.21	327.47	326.91	325.53	325.15	325.05	325.02
16000	359.36	356.40	354.15	352.42	351.10	350.09	349.31	348.71	347.23	346.83	346.71	346.68
17000	381.82	378.67	376.28	374.45	373.04	371.97	371.14	370.50	368.93	368.50	368.38	368.35
18000	404.28	400.95	398.41	396.47	394.99	393.85	392.97	392.29	390.63	390.18	390.05	390.02
19000	426.73	423.22	420.55	418.50	416.93	415.73	414.80	414.09	412.34	411.86	411.72	411.69
20000	449.19	445.50	442.68	440.53	438.88	437.61	436.63	435.88	434.04	433.53	433.39	433.35
21000	471.65	467.77	464.81	462.55	460.82	459.49	458.46	457.67	455.74	455.21	455.06	455.02
22000	494.11	490.05	486.95	484.58	482.76	481.37	480.29	479.47	477.44	476.88	476.73	476.69
23000	516.57	512.32	509.08	506.60	504.71	503.25	502.13	501.26	499.14	498.56	498.40	498.36
24000	539.03	534.60	531.22	528.63	526.65	525.13	523.96	523.06	520.84	520.24	520.07	520.02
25000	561.49	556.87	553.35	550.66	548.59	547.01	545.79	544.85	542.55	541.91	541.74	541.69
26000	583.95	579.14	575.48	572.68	570.54	568.89	567.62	566.64	564.25	563.59	563.41	563.36
27000	606.41	601.42	597.62	594.71	592.48	590.77	589.45	588.44	585.95	585.27	585.08	585.02
28000	628.87	623.69	619.75	616.73	614.42	612.65	611.28	610.23	607.65	606.94	606.75	606.69
29000	651.33	645.97	641.88	638.76	636.37	634.53	633.11	632.02	629.35	628.62	628.42	628.36
30000	673.79	668.24	664.02	660.79	658.31	656.41	654.94	653.82	651.05	650.30	650.09	650.03
31000	696.25	690.52	686.15	682.81	680.25	678.29	676.78	675.61	672.76	671.97	671.75	671.69
32000	718.71	712.79	708.29	704.84	702.20	700.17	698.61	697.41	694.46	693.65	693.42	693.36
33000	741.17	735.07	730.42	726.86	724.14	722.05	720.44	719.20	716.16	715.32	715.09	715.03
34000	763.63	757.34	752.55	748.89	746.08	743.93	742.27	740.99	737.86	737.00	736.76	736.70
35000	786.09	779.62	774.69	770.92	768.03	765.81	764.10	762.79	759.56	758.68	758.43	758.36
37500	842.23	835.30	830.02	825.98	822.89	820.51	818.68	817.27	813.82	812.87	812.61	812.53
40000	898.38	890.99	885.36	881.05	877.75	875.21	873.26	871.76	868.07	867.06	866.78	866.70
42500	954.53	946.68	940.69	936.11	932.60	929.91	927.84	926.24	922.32	921.25	920.95	920.87
45000	1010.68	1002.36	996.02	991.18	987.46	984.61	982.41	980.72	976.58	975.44	975.13	975.04
47500	1066.83	1058.05	1051.36	1046.24	1042.32	1039.31	1036.99	1035.21	1030.83	1029.63	1029.30	1029.21
50000	1122.98	1113.74	1106.69	1101.31	1097.18	1094.01	1091.57	1089.69	1085.09	1083.82	1083.47	1083.38
52500	1179.13	1169.42	1162.03	1156.37	1152.04	1148.71	1146.15	1144.18	1139.34	1138.01	1137.65	1137.54
55000	1235.28	1225.11	1217.36	1211.44	1206.90	1203.41	1200.73	1198.66	1193.60	1192.20	1191.82	1191.71
57500	1291.42	1280.79	1272.70	1266.50	1261.76	1258.11	1255.31	1253.15	1247.85	1246.39	1245.99	1245.88
60000	1347.57	1336.48	1328.03	1321.57	1316.62	1312.81	1309.88	1307.63	1302.10	1300.58	1300.17	1300.05
65000	1459.87	1447.85	1438.70	1431.70	1426.33	1422.21	1419.04	1416.60	1410.61	1408.97	1408.51	1408.39
70000	1572.17	1559.23	1549.37	1541.83	1536.05	1531.61	1528.20	1525.57	1519.12	1517.35	1516.86	1516.72
75000	1684.46	1670.60	1660.04	1651.96	1645.77	1641.01	1637.35	1634.54	1627.63	1625.73	1625.21	1625.06
80000	1796.76	1781.97	1770.71	1762.09	1755.49	1750.41	1746.51	1743.51	1736.14	1734.11	1733.55	1733.40
85000	1909.06	1893.35	1881.37	1872.22	1865.20	1859.81	1855.67	1852.47	1844.64	1842.49	1841.90	1841.73
90000	2021.36	2004.72	1992.04	1982.35	1974.92	1969.21	1964.82	1961.44	1953.15	1950.87	1950.25	1950.07
95000	2133.65	2116.09	2102.71	2092.48	2084.64	2078.61	2073.98	2070.41	2061.66	2059.26	2058.59	2058.41
100000	2245.95	2227.47	2213.38	2202.61	2194.36	2188.01	2183.14	2179.38	2170.17	2167.64	2166.94	2166.75
105000	2358.25	2338.84	2324.05	2312.74	2304.07	2297.42	2292.29	2288.35	2278.68	2276.02	2275.29	2275.08
110000	2470.55	2450.21	2434.72	2422.87	2413.79	2406.82	2401.45	2397.32	2387.19	2384.40	2383.63	2383.42
115000	2582.84	2561.58	2545.39	2533.00	2523.51	2516.22	2510.61	2506.29	2495.69	2492.78	2491.98	2491.76
120000	2695.14	2672.96	2656.06	2643.13	2633.23	2625.62	2619.76	2615.26	2604.20	2601.16	2600.33	2600.09
125000	2807.44	2784.33	2766.72	2753.26	2742.94	2735.02	2728.92	2724.22	2712.71	2709.54	2708.67	2708.43
130000	2919.73	2895.70	2877.39	2863.39	2852.66	2844.42	2838.08	2833.19	2821.22	2817.93	2817.02	2816.77
135000	3032.03	3007.08	2988.06	2973.52	2962.38	2953.82	2947.23	2942.16	2929.73	2926.31	2925.37	2925.10
140000	3144.33	3118.45	3098.73	3083.65	3072.10	3063.22	3056.39	3051.13	3038.23	3034.69	3033.71	3033.44
145000	3256.63	3229.82	3209.40	3193.78	3181.81	3172.62	3165.55	3160.10	3146.74	3143.07	3142.06	3141.78
150000	3368.92	3341.20	3320.07	3303.91	3291.53	3282.02	3274.70	3269.07	3255.25	3251.45	3250.41	3250.12
155000	3481.22	3452.57	3430.74	3414.04	3401.25	3391.42	3383.86	3378.04	3363.76	3359.83	3358.75	3358.45
160000	3593.52	3563.94	3541.41	3524.17	3510.97	3500.82	3493.02	3487.01	3472.27	3468.22	3467.10	3466.79

MONTHLY AMORTIZING PAYMENTS

AMOUNT OF LOAN	NUMBER OF YEARS IN TERM											
	1	2	3	4	5	6	7	8	9	10	11	12
$ 50	4.79	2.71	2.03	1.70	1.51	1.39	1.31	1.26	1.22	1.19	1.17	1.15
100	9.57	5.41	4.05	3.39	3.01	2.78	2.62	2.51	2.43	2.37	2.33	2.29
200	19.14	10.81	8.09	6.78	6.02	5.55	5.23	5.01	4.85	4.73	4.65	4.58
300	28.70	16.21	12.13	10.16	9.03	8.32	7.84	7.51	7.27	7.10	6.97	6.87
400	38.27	21.61	16.17	13.55	12.04	11.09	10.45	10.01	9.69	9.46	9.29	9.16
500	47.83	27.01	20.22	16.93	15.05	13.86	13.06	12.51	12.11	11.82	11.61	11.45
600	57.40	32.41	24.26	20.32	18.06	16.63	15.67	15.01	14.53	14.19	13.93	13.74
700	66.96	37.81	28.30	23.71	21.07	19.40	18.29	17.51	16.96	16.55	16.25	16.03
800	76.53	43.21	32.34	27.09	24.08	22.17	20.90	20.01	19.38	18.91	18.57	18.32
900	86.09	48.61	36.39	30.48	27.08	24.94	23.51	22.51	21.80	21.28	20.89	20.61
1000	95.66	54.01	40.43	33.86	30.09	27.71	26.12	25.01	24.22	23.64	23.21	22.89
2000	191.31	108.01	80.85	67.72	60.18	55.42	52.24	50.02	48.43	47.28	46.42	45.78
3000	286.96	162.01	121.28	101.58	90.27	83.13	78.35	75.03	72.65	70.91	69.63	68.67
4000	382.61	216.01	161.70	135.44	120.36	110.84	104.47	100.03	96.86	94.55	92.84	91.56
5000	478.26	270.01	202.12	169.30	150.45	138.55	130.59	125.04	121.08	118.19	116.05	114.45
6000	573.92	324.01	242.55	203.15	180.54	166.26	156.70	150.05	145.29	141.82	139.26	137.34
7000	669.57	378.01	282.97	237.01	210.63	193.97	182.82	175.06	169.51	165.46	162.47	160.23
8000	765.22	432.01	323.40	270.87	240.71	221.68	208.94	200.06	193.72	189.10	185.68	183.12
9000	860.87	486.01	363.82	304.73	270.80	249.39	235.05	225.07	217.94	212.73	208.89	206.01
10000	956.52	540.01	404.24	338.59	300.89	277.10	261.17	250.08	242.15	236.37	232.09	228.90
11000	1052.18	594.01	444.67	372.44	330.98	304.81	287.28	275.09	266.36	260.00	255.30	251.79
12000	1147.83	648.01	485.09	406.30	361.07	332.52	313.40	300.09	290.58	283.64	278.51	274.68
13000	1243.48	702.01	525.52	440.16	391.16	360.23	339.52	325.10	314.79	307.28	301.72	297.57
14000	1339.13	756.02	565.94	474.02	421.25	387.93	365.63	350.11	339.01	330.91	324.93	320.46
15000	1434.78	810.02	606.36	507.88	451.33	415.64	391.75	375.12	363.22	354.55	348.14	343.35
16000	1530.43	864.02	646.79	541.73	481.42	443.35	417.87	400.12	387.44	378.19	371.35	366.24
17000	1626.09	918.02	687.21	575.59	511.51	471.06	443.98	425.13	411.65	401.82	394.56	389.13
18000	1721.74	972.02	727.64	609.45	541.60	498.77	470.10	450.14	435.87	425.46	417.77	412.02
19000	1817.39	1026.02	768.06	643.31	571.69	526.48	496.21	475.15	460.08	449.10	440.98	434.91
20000	1913.04	1080.02	808.48	677.17	601.78	554.19	522.33	500.15	484.29	472.73	464.18	457.80
21000	2008.69	1134.02	848.91	711.03	631.87	581.90	548.45	525.16	508.51	496.37	487.39	480.69
22000	2104.35	1188.02	889.33	744.88	661.96	609.61	574.56	550.17	532.72	520.00	510.60	503.58
23000	2200.00	1242.02	929.76	778.74	692.04	637.32	600.68	575.18	556.94	543.64	533.81	526.47
24000	2295.65	1296.02	970.18	812.60	722.13	665.03	626.80	600.18	581.15	567.28	557.02	549.36
25000	2391.30	1350.02	1010.60	846.46	752.22	692.74	652.91	625.19	605.37	590.91	580.23	572.25
26000	2486.95	1404.02	1051.03	880.32	782.31	720.45	679.03	650.20	629.58	614.55	603.44	595.14
27000	2582.60	1458.02	1091.45	914.17	812.40	748.15	705.14	675.21	653.80	638.19	626.65	618.03
28000	2678.26	1512.01	1131.87	948.03	842.49	775.86	731.26	700.21	678.01	661.82	649.86	640.92
29000	2773.91	1566.01	1172.30	981.89	872.58	803.57	757.38	725.22	702.22	685.46	673.07	663.81
30000	2869.56	1620.01	1212.72	1015.75	902.66	831.28	783.49	750.23	726.44	709.10	696.27	686.70
31000	2965.21	1674.03	1253.15	1049.61	932.75	858.99	809.61	775.24	750.65	732.73	719.48	709.59
32000	3060.86	1728.03	1293.57	1083.46	962.84	886.70	835.73	800.24	774.87	756.37	742.69	732.48
33000	3156.52	1782.03	1333.99	1117.32	992.93	914.41	861.84	825.25	799.08	780.00	765.90	755.37
34000	3252.17	1836.03	1374.42	1151.18	1023.02	942.12	887.96	850.26	823.30	803.64	789.11	778.26
35000	3347.82	1890.03	1414.84	1185.04	1053.11	969.83	914.08	875.27	847.51	827.28	812.32	801.15
37500	3586.95	2025.03	1515.90	1269.68	1128.33	1039.10	979.37	937.78	908.05	886.37	870.34	858.37
40000	3826.08	2160.03	1616.96	1354.33	1203.55	1108.37	1044.66	1000.30	968.58	945.46	928.36	915.60
42500	4065.21	2295.04	1718.02	1438.97	1278.77	1177.65	1109.95	1062.82	1029.12	1004.55	986.39	972.82
45000	4304.34	2430.04	1819.08	1523.62	1353.99	1246.92	1175.24	1125.34	1089.66	1063.64	1044.41	1030.04
47500	4543.47	2565.04	1920.14	1608.27	1429.22	1316.19	1240.53	1187.86	1150.19	1122.73	1102.43	1087.27
50000	4782.60	2700.04	2021.20	1692.91	1504.44	1385.47	1305.82	1250.38	1210.73	1181.82	1160.45	1144.49
52500	5021.73	2835.04	2122.26	1777.56	1579.66	1454.74	1371.11	1312.90	1271.26	1240.91	1218.48	1201.72
55000	5260.86	2970.05	2223.32	1862.20	1654.88	1524.01	1436.40	1375.41	1331.80	1300.00	1276.50	1258.94
57500	5499.99	3105.05	2324.38	1946.85	1730.10	1593.29	1501.69	1437.93	1392.34	1359.10	1334.52	1316.17
60000	5739.11	3240.05	2425.44	2031.49	1805.32	1662.56	1566.98	1500.45	1452.87	1418.19	1392.54	1373.39
65000	6217.37	3510.05	2627.56	2200.78	1955.77	1801.11	1697.56	1625.49	1573.94	1536.37	1508.59	1487.84
70000	6695.63	3780.06	2829.68	2370.07	2106.21	1939.65	1828.15	1750.53	1695.02	1654.55	1624.63	1602.29
75000	7173.89	4050.06	3031.80	2539.36	2256.65	2078.20	1958.73	1875.56	1816.09	1772.73	1740.68	1716.74
80000	7652.15	4320.06	3233.92	2708.65	2407.10	2216.74	2089.31	2000.60	1937.16	1890.91	1856.72	1831.19
85000	8130.41	4590.07	3436.04	2877.94	2557.54	2355.29	2219.89	2125.64	2058.23	2009.10	1972.77	1945.63
90000	8608.67	4860.07	3638.16	3047.23	2707.98	2493.84	2350.47	2250.67	2179.31	2127.28	2088.81	2060.08
95000	9086.93	5130.08	3840.28	3216.53	2858.43	2632.38	2481.05	2375.71	2300.38	2245.46	2204.86	2174.53
100000	9565.19	5400.08	4042.40	3385.82	3008.87	2770.93	2611.63	2500.75	2421.45	2363.64	2320.90	2288.98
105000	10043.45	5670.08	4244.52	3555.11	3159.31	2909.48	2742.22	2625.79	2542.52	2481.82	2436.95	2403.43
110000	10521.71	5940.09	4446.64	3724.40	3309.76	3048.02	2872.80	2750.82	2663.60	2600.00	2552.99	2517.88
115000	10999.97	6210.09	4648.76	3893.69	3460.20	3186.57	3003.38	2875.86	2784.67	2718.19	2669.04	2632.33
120000	11478.22	6480.09	4850.87	4062.98	3610.64	3325.11	3133.96	3000.90	2905.74	2836.37	2785.08	2746.78
125000	11956.48	6750.10	5052.99	4232.27	3761.09	3463.66	3264.54	3125.94	3026.81	2954.55	2901.13	2861.22
130000	12434.74	7020.10	5255.11	4401.56	3911.53	3602.21	3395.12	3250.97	3147.88	3072.73	3017.17	2975.67
135000	12913.00	7290.10	5457.23	4570.85	4061.97	3740.75	3525.70	3376.01	3268.96	3190.91	3133.22	3090.12
140000	13391.26	7560.11	5659.35	4740.14	4212.42	3879.30	3656.29	3501.05	3390.03	3309.10	3249.26	3204.57
145000	13869.52	7830.11	5861.47	4909.43	4362.86	4017.85	3786.87	3626.08	3511.10	3427.28	3365.31	3319.02
150000	14347.78	8100.12	6063.59	5078.72	4513.30	4156.39	3917.45	3751.12	3632.17	3545.46	3481.35	3433.47
155000	14826.04	8370.12	6265.71	5248.01	4663.75	4294.94	4048.03	3876.16	3753.25	3663.64	3597.40	3547.92
160000	15304.30	8640.12	6467.83	5417.30	4814.19	4433.48	4178.61	4001.20	3874.32	3781.82	3713.44	3662.37

AMOUNT OF LOAN	NUMBER OF YEARS IN TERM											
	13	14	15	16	17	18	19	20	25	30	35	40
$ 50	1.14	1.13	1.12	1.12	1.11	1.11	1.11	1.10	1.10	1.10	1.10	1.10
100	2.27	2.25	2.24	2.23	2.22	2.21	2.21	2.20	2.20	2.19	2.19	2.19
200	4.53	4.50	4.47	4.45	4.43	4.42	4.41	4.40	4.39	4.38	4.38	4.38
300	6.80	6.75	6.70	6.67	6.65	6.63	6.62	6.60	6.58	6.57	6.57	6.57
400	9.06	8.99	8.94	8.89	8.86	8.84	8.82	8.80	8.77	8.76	8.76	8.76
500	11.33	11.24	11.17	11.12	11.08	11.05	11.02	11.00	10.96	10.95	10.94	10.94
600	13.59	13.49	13.40	13.34	13.29	13.25	13.23	13.20	13.15	13.14	13.13	13.13
700	15.86	15.73	15.64	15.56	15.51	15.46	15.43	15.40	15.34	15.32	15.32	15.32
800	18.12	17.98	17.87	17.78	17.72	17.67	17.63	17.60	17.53	17.51	17.51	17.51
900	20.39	20.23	20.10	20.01	19.93	19.88	19.84	19.80	19.72	19.70	19.69	19.69
1000	22.65	22.47	22.33	22.23	22.15	22.09	22.04	22.00	21.91	21.89	21.88	21.88
2000	45.30	44.94	44.66	44.45	44.29	44.17	44.07	44.00	43.82	43.77	43.76	43.76
3000	67.95	67.41	66.99	66.68	66.43	66.25	66.11	66.00	65.73	65.66	65.64	65.63
4000	90.60	89.88	89.32	88.90	88.58	88.33	88.14	87.99	87.64	87.54	87.51	87.51
5000	113.25	112.34	111.65	111.12	110.72	110.41	110.17	109.99	109.55	109.43	109.39	109.38
6000	135.90	134.81	133.98	133.35	132.86	132.49	132.21	131.99	131.45	131.31	131.27	131.26
7000	158.55	157.28	156.31	155.57	155.01	154.57	154.24	153.99	153.36	153.19	153.15	153.13
8000	181.20	179.75	178.64	177.79	177.15	176.65	176.27	175.98	175.27	175.08	175.02	175.01
9000	203.85	202.21	200.97	200.02	199.29	198.74	198.31	197.98	197.18	196.96	196.90	196.89
10000	226.50	224.68	223.30	222.24	221.43	220.82	220.34	219.98	219.09	218.85	218.78	218.76
11000	249.15	247.15	245.63	244.47	243.58	242.90	242.37	241.97	241.00	240.73	240.66	240.64
12000	271.80	269.62	267.96	266.69	265.72	264.98	264.41	263.97	262.90	262.61	262.53	262.51
13000	294.45	292.08	290.28	288.91	287.86	287.06	286.44	285.97	284.81	284.50	284.41	284.39
14000	317.10	314.55	312.61	311.14	310.01	309.14	308.48	307.97	306.72	306.38	306.29	306.26
15000	339.75	337.02	334.94	333.36	332.15	331.22	330.51	329.96	328.63	328.27	328.17	328.14
16000	362.40	359.49	357.27	355.58	354.29	353.30	352.54	351.96	350.54	350.15	350.04	350.02
17000	385.05	381.95	379.60	377.81	376.44	375.38	374.58	373.96	372.44	372.03	371.92	371.89
18000	407.70	404.42	401.93	400.03	398.58	397.47	396.61	395.95	394.35	393.92	393.80	393.77
19000	430.34	426.89	424.26	422.26	420.72	419.55	418.64	417.95	416.26	415.80	415.68	415.64
20000	452.99	449.36	446.59	444.48	442.86	441.63	440.68	439.95	438.17	437.69	437.55	437.52
21000	475.64	471.82	468.92	466.70	465.01	463.71	462.71	461.95	460.08	459.57	459.43	459.39
22000	498.29	494.29	491.25	488.93	487.15	485.79	484.74	483.94	481.99	481.45	481.31	481.27
23000	520.94	516.76	513.58	511.15	509.29	507.87	506.78	505.94	503.89	503.34	503.19	503.15
24000	543.59	539.23	535.91	533.37	531.44	529.95	528.81	527.94	525.80	525.22	525.06	525.02
25000	566.24	561.69	558.24	555.60	553.58	552.03	550.85	549.93	547.71	547.11	546.94	546.90
26000	588.89	584.16	580.56	577.82	575.72	574.11	572.88	571.93	569.62	568.99	568.82	568.77
27000	611.54	606.63	602.89	600.04	597.87	596.20	594.91	593.93	591.53	590.87	590.70	590.65
28000	634.19	629.10	625.22	622.27	620.01	618.28	616.95	615.93	613.43	612.76	612.57	612.52
29000	656.84	651.56	647.55	644.49	642.15	640.36	638.98	637.92	635.34	634.64	634.45	634.40
30000	679.49	674.03	669.88	666.72	664.29	662.44	661.01	659.92	657.25	656.53	656.33	656.28
31000	702.14	696.50	692.21	688.94	686.44	684.52	683.05	681.92	679.16	678.41	678.21	678.15
32000	724.79	718.97	714.54	711.16	708.58	706.60	705.08	703.91	701.07	700.29	700.08	700.03
33000	747.44	741.43	736.87	733.39	730.72	728.68	727.11	725.91	722.98	722.18	721.96	721.90
34000	770.09	763.90	759.20	755.61	752.87	750.76	749.15	747.91	744.88	744.06	743.84	743.78
35000	792.74	786.37	781.53	777.83	775.01	772.84	771.18	769.91	766.79	765.95	765.72	765.65
37500	849.36	842.54	837.35	833.39	830.37	828.05	826.27	824.90	821.56	820.66	820.41	820.34
40000	905.98	898.71	893.17	888.95	885.72	883.25	881.35	879.89	876.33	875.37	875.10	875.03
42500	962.61	954.88	949.00	944.51	941.08	938.45	936.43	934.88	931.10	930.08	929.80	929.72
45000	1019.23	1011.05	1004.82	1000.07	996.44	993.66	991.52	989.88	985.87	984.79	984.49	984.41
47500	1075.85	1067.21	1060.64	1055.63	1051.80	1048.86	1046.60	1044.87	1040.64	1039.50	1039.18	1039.10
50000	1132.48	1123.38	1116.47	1111.19	1107.15	1104.06	1101.69	1099.86	1095.42	1094.21	1093.88	1093.79
52500	1189.10	1179.55	1172.29	1166.75	1162.51	1159.26	1156.77	1154.86	1150.19	1148.92	1148.57	1148.48
55000	1245.73	1235.72	1228.11	1222.31	1217.87	1214.47	1211.85	1209.85	1204.96	1203.63	1203.27	1203.17
57500	1302.35	1291.89	1283.94	1277.87	1273.23	1269.67	1266.94	1264.84	1259.73	1258.34	1257.96	1257.86
60000	1358.97	1348.06	1339.76	1333.43	1328.58	1324.87	1322.02	1319.83	1314.50	1313.05	1312.65	1312.55
65000	1472.22	1460.40	1451.40	1444.55	1439.30	1435.28	1432.19	1429.82	1424.04	1422.47	1422.04	1421.92
70000	1585.47	1572.73	1563.05	1555.66	1550.01	1545.68	1542.36	1539.81	1533.58	1531.89	1531.43	1531.30
75000	1698.72	1685.07	1674.70	1666.78	1660.73	1656.09	1652.53	1649.79	1643.12	1641.31	1640.82	1640.68
80000	1811.96	1797.41	1786.34	1777.90	1771.44	1766.49	1762.70	1759.78	1752.66	1750.73	1750.20	1750.06
85000	1925.21	1909.75	1897.99	1889.02	1882.16	1876.90	1872.86	1869.76	1862.20	1860.15	1859.59	1859.44
90000	2038.46	2022.09	2009.64	2000.14	1992.87	1987.31	1983.03	1979.75	1971.74	1969.57	1968.98	1968.82
95000	2151.70	2134.42	2121.28	2111.26	2103.59	2097.71	2093.20	2089.73	2081.28	2078.99	2078.36	2078.19
100000	2264.95	2246.76	2232.93	2222.37	2214.30	2208.12	2203.37	2199.72	2190.83	2188.41	2187.75	2187.57
105000	2378.20	2359.10	2344.57	2333.49	2325.02	2318.52	2313.54	2309.71	2300.37	2297.83	2297.14	2296.95
110000	2491.45	2471.44	2456.22	2444.61	2435.73	2428.93	2423.70	2419.69	2409.91	2407.25	2406.53	2406.33
115000	2604.69	2583.77	2567.87	2555.73	2546.45	2539.33	2533.87	2529.68	2519.45	2516.67	2515.91	2515.71
120000	2717.94	2696.11	2679.51	2666.85	2657.16	2649.74	2644.04	2639.66	2628.99	2626.09	2625.30	2625.09
125000	2831.19	2808.45	2791.16	2777.97	2767.88	2760.14	2754.21	2749.65	2738.53	2735.51	2734.69	2734.46
130000	2944.44	2920.79	2902.80	2889.09	2878.59	2870.55	2864.38	2859.63	2848.07	2844.93	2844.08	2843.84
135000	3057.68	3033.13	3014.45	3000.20	2989.31	2980.96	2974.55	2969.62	2957.61	2954.35	2953.46	2953.22
140000	3170.93	3145.46	3126.10	3111.32	3100.02	3091.36	3084.71	3079.61	3067.15	3063.77	3062.85	3062.60
145000	3284.18	3257.80	3237.74	3222.44	3210.74	3201.77	3194.88	3189.59	3176.70	3173.19	3172.24	3171.98
150000	3397.43	3370.14	3349.39	3333.56	3321.45	3312.17	3305.05	3299.58	3286.24	3282.61	3281.63	3281.36
155000	3510.67	3482.48	3461.04	3444.68	3432.17	3422.58	3415.22	3409.56	3395.78	3392.03	3391.01	3390.73
160000	3623.92	3594.81	3572.68	3555.80	3542.88	3532.99	3525.39	3519.55	3505.32	3501.45	3500.40	3500.11

AMOUNT OF LOAN	NUMBER OF YEARS IN TERM											
	1	2	3	4	5	6	7	8	9	10	11	12
$ 50	4.79	2.71	2.03	1.70	1.52	1.40	1.32	1.26	1.22	1.20	1.17	1.16
100	9.58	5.42	4.06	3.40	3.03	2.79	2.63	2.52	2.44	2.39	2.34	2.31
200	19.16	10.83	8.12	6.80	6.05	5.58	5.26	5.04	4.88	4.77	4.68	4.62
300	28.74	16.24	12.17	10.20	9.08	8.36	7.89	7.56	7.32	7.15	7.02	6.93
400	38.31	21.66	16.23	13.60	12.10	11.15	10.52	10.08	9.76	9.53	9.36	9.24
500	47.89	27.07	20.28	17.00	15.12	13.94	13.14	12.59	12.20	11.91	11.70	11.54
600	57.47	32.48	24.34	20.40	18.15	16.72	15.77	15.11	14.64	14.29	14.04	13.85
700	67.05	37.89	28.40	23.80	21.17	19.51	18.40	17.63	17.08	16.68	16.38	16.16
800	76.62	43.31	32.45	27.20	24.19	22.30	21.03	20.15	19.52	19.06	18.72	18.47
900	86.20	48.72	36.51	30.60	27.22	25.08	23.66	22.66	21.95	21.44	21.06	20.77
1000	95.78	54.13	40.56	34.00	30.24	27.87	26.28	25.18	24.39	23.82	23.40	23.08
2000	191.55	108.26	81.12	68.00	60.48	55.73	52.56	50.36	48.78	47.64	46.79	46.16
3000	287.33	162.39	121.68	102.00	90.72	83.60	78.84	75.53	73.17	71.45	70.18	69.24
4000	383.10	216.51	162.23	136.00	120.95	111.46	105.12	100.71	97.56	95.27	93.57	92.31
5000	478.87	270.64	202.79	170.00	151.19	139.33	131.40	125.88	121.95	119.08	116.97	115.39
6000	574.65	324.77	243.35	204.00	181.43	167.19	157.68	151.06	146.33	142.90	140.36	138.47
7000	670.42	378.89	283.91	238.00	211.67	195.06	183.95	176.24	170.72	166.71	163.75	161.54
8000	766.19	433.02	324.46	272.00	241.90	222.92	210.23	201.41	195.11	190.53	187.14	184.62
9000	861.97	487.15	365.02	306.00	272.14	250.79	236.51	226.59	219.50	214.34	210.53	207.70
10000	957.74	541.28	405.58	340.00	302.38	278.65	262.79	251.76	243.89	238.16	233.93	230.77
11000	1053.51	595.40	446.14	374.00	332.61	306.52	289.07	276.94	268.28	261.97	257.32	253.85
12000	1149.29	649.53	486.69	408.00	362.85	334.38	315.35	302.11	292.66	285.79	280.71	276.93
13000	1245.06	703.66	527.25	441.99	393.09	362.25	341.63	327.29	317.05	309.60	304.10	300.00
14000	1340.84	757.78	567.81	475.99	423.33	390.11	367.90	352.47	341.44	333.42	327.50	323.08
15000	1436.61	811.91	608.37	509.99	453.56	417.98	394.18	377.64	365.83	357.23	350.89	346.16
16000	1532.38	866.04	648.92	543.99	483.80	445.84	420.46	402.82	390.22	381.05	374.28	369.23
17000	1628.16	920.17	689.48	577.99	514.04	473.71	446.74	427.99	414.61	404.86	397.67	392.31
18000	1723.93	974.29	730.04	611.99	544.27	501.57	473.02	453.17	438.99	428.68	421.06	415.39
19000	1819.70	1028.42	770.60	645.99	574.51	529.44	499.30	478.34	463.38	452.49	444.46	438.46
20000	1915.48	1082.55	811.15	679.99	604.75	557.30	525.58	503.52	487.77	476.31	467.85	461.54
21000	2011.25	1136.67	851.71	713.99	634.99	585.17	551.85	528.70	512.16	500.12	491.24	484.62
22000	2107.02	1190.80	892.27	747.99	665.22	613.03	578.13	553.87	536.55	523.94	514.63	507.69
23000	2202.80	1244.93	932.83	781.99	695.46	640.90	604.41	579.05	560.94	547.75	538.02	530.77
24000	2298.57	1299.05	973.38	815.99	725.70	668.76	630.69	604.22	585.32	571.57	561.42	553.85
25000	2394.35	1353.18	1013.94	849.99	755.93	696.63	656.97	629.40	609.71	595.38	584.81	576.92
26000	2490.12	1407.31	1054.50	883.98	786.17	724.49	683.25	654.57	634.10	619.20	608.20	600.00
27000	2585.89	1461.44	1095.06	917.98	816.41	752.36	709.52	679.75	658.49	643.01	631.59	623.08
28000	2681.67	1515.56	1135.61	951.98	846.65	780.22	735.80	704.93	682.88	666.83	654.99	646.16
29000	2777.44	1569.69	1176.17	985.98	876.88	808.09	762.08	730.10	707.26	690.64	678.38	669.23
30000	2873.21	1623.82	1216.73	1019.98	907.12	835.95	788.36	755.28	731.65	714.46	701.77	692.31
31000	2968.99	1677.94	1257.29	1053.98	937.36	863.82	814.64	780.45	756.04	738.27	725.16	715.39
32000	3064.76	1732.07	1297.84	1087.98	967.60	891.68	840.92	805.63	780.43	762.09	748.55	738.46
33000	3160.53	1786.20	1338.40	1121.98	997.83	919.55	867.20	830.80	804.82	785.90	771.95	761.54
34000	3256.31	1840.33	1378.96	1155.98	1028.07	947.41	893.47	855.98	829.21	809.72	795.34	784.62
35000	3352.08	1894.45	1419.52	1189.98	1058.31	975.28	919.75	881.16	853.59	833.53	818.73	807.69
37500	3591.52	2029.77	1520.91	1274.98	1133.90	1044.94	985.45	944.10	914.57	893.07	877.21	865.38
40000	3830.95	2165.09	1622.30	1359.97	1209.49	1114.60	1051.15	1007.03	975.54	952.61	935.69	923.08
42500	4070.38	2300.41	1723.70	1444.97	1285.09	1184.26	1116.84	1069.97	1036.51	1012.15	994.17	980.77
45000	4309.82	2435.72	1825.09	1529.97	1360.68	1253.92	1182.54	1132.91	1097.48	1071.69	1052.65	1038.46
47500	4549.25	2571.04	1926.48	1614.97	1436.27	1323.59	1248.23	1195.85	1158.45	1131.22	1111.13	1096.15
50000	4788.69	2706.36	2027.88	1699.97	1511.86	1393.25	1313.93	1258.79	1219.42	1190.76	1169.61	1153.84
52500	5028.12	2841.68	2129.27	1784.96	1587.46	1462.91	1379.63	1321.73	1280.39	1250.30	1228.09	1211.54
55000	5267.55	2976.99	2230.66	1869.96	1663.05	1532.57	1445.32	1384.67	1341.36	1309.84	1286.57	1269.23
57500	5506.99	3112.31	2332.06	1954.96	1738.64	1602.23	1511.02	1447.61	1402.33	1369.37	1345.05	1326.92
60000	5746.42	3247.63	2433.45	2039.96	1814.24	1671.90	1576.72	1510.55	1463.30	1428.91	1403.53	1384.61
65000	6225.29	3518.26	2636.24	2209.95	1965.42	1811.22	1708.11	1636.43	1585.24	1547.99	1520.49	1500.00
70000	6704.16	3788.90	2839.03	2379.95	2116.61	1950.55	1839.50	1762.31	1707.18	1667.06	1637.46	1615.38
75000	7183.03	4059.54	3041.81	2549.95	2267.79	2089.87	1970.89	1888.19	1829.13	1786.14	1754.42	1730.76
80000	7661.89	4330.17	3244.60	2719.94	2418.98	2229.19	2102.29	2014.06	1951.07	1905.22	1871.38	1846.15
85000	8140.76	4600.81	3447.39	2889.94	2570.17	2368.52	2233.68	2139.94	2073.01	2024.29	1988.34	1961.53
90000	8619.63	4871.44	3650.17	3059.93	2721.35	2507.84	2365.07	2265.82	2194.95	2143.37	2105.30	2076.92
95000	9098.50	5142.08	3852.96	3229.93	2872.54	2647.17	2496.46	2391.70	2316.89	2262.44	2222.26	2192.30
100000	9577.37	5412.71	4055.75	3399.93	3023.72	2786.49	2627.86	2517.58	2438.83	2381.52	2339.22	2307.68
105000	10056.23	5683.35	4258.54	3569.92	3174.91	2925.82	2759.25	2643.46	2560.77	2500.59	2456.18	2423.07
110000	10535.10	5953.98	4461.32	3739.92	3326.10	3065.14	2890.64	2769.34	2682.72	2619.67	2573.14	2538.45
115000	11013.97	6224.62	4664.11	3909.91	3477.28	3204.46	3022.03	2895.22	2804.66	2738.74	2690.10	2653.84
120000	11492.84	6495.25	4866.90	4079.91	3628.47	3343.79	3153.43	3021.09	2926.60	2857.82	2807.06	2769.22
125000	11971.71	6765.89	5069.69	4249.91	3779.65	3483.11	3284.82	3146.97	3048.54	2976.90	2924.02	2884.60
130000	12450.57	7036.52	5272.47	4419.90	3930.84	3622.44	3416.21	3272.85	3170.48	3095.97	3040.98	2999.99
135000	12929.44	7307.16	5475.26	4589.90	4082.03	3761.76	3547.60	3398.73	3292.42	3215.05	3157.94	3115.37
140000	13408.31	7577.80	5678.05	4759.90	4233.21	3901.09	3679.00	3524.61	3414.36	3334.12	3274.91	3230.76
145000	13887.18	7848.43	5880.83	4929.89	4384.40	4040.41	3810.39	3650.49	3536.30	3453.20	3391.87	3346.14
150000	14366.05	8119.07	6083.62	5099.89	4535.58	4179.73	3941.78	3776.37	3658.25	3572.27	3508.83	3461.52
155000	14844.91	8389.70	6286.41	5269.88	4686.77	4319.06	4073.18	3902.24	3780.19	3691.35	3625.79	3576.91
160000	15323.78	8660.34	6489.20	5439.88	4837.96	4458.38	4204.57	4028.12	3902.13	3810.43	3742.75	3692.30

AMOUNT OF LOAN	NUMBER OF YEARS IN TERM											
	13	14	15	16	17	18	19	20	25	30	35	40
$ 50	1.15	1.14	1.13	1.13	1.12	1.12	1.12	1.12	1.11	1.11	1.11	1.11
100	2.29	2.27	2.26	2.25	2.24	2.23	2.23	2.23	2.22	2.21	2.21	2.21
200	4.57	4.54	4.51	4.49	4.47	4.46	4.45	4.45	4.43	4.42	4.42	4.42
300	6.86	6.80	6.76	6.73	6.71	6.69	6.68	6.67	6.64	6.63	6.63	6.63
400	9.14	9.07	9.02	8.97	8.94	8.92	8.90	8.89	8.85	8.84	8.84	8.84
500	11.42	11.34	11.27	11.22	11.18	11.15	11.12	11.11	11.06	11.05	11.05	11.05
600	13.71	13.60	13.52	13.46	13.41	13.37	13.35	13.33	13.27	13.26	13.26	13.26
700	15.99	15.87	15.77	15.70	15.64	15.60	15.57	15.55	15.49	15.47	15.46	15.46
800	18.28	18.13	18.03	17.94	17.88	17.83	17.79	17.77	17.70	17.68	17.67	17.67
900	20.56	20.40	20.28	20.18	20.11	20.06	20.02	19.99	19.91	19.89	19.88	19.88
1000	22.84	22.67	22.53	22.43	22.35	22.29	22.24	22.21	22.12	22.10	22.09	22.09
2000	45.68	45.33	45.06	44.85	44.69	44.57	44.48	44.41	44.23	44.19	44.18	44.17
3000	68.52	67.99	67.58	67.27	67.03	66.85	66.71	66.61	66.35	66.28	66.26	66.26
4000	91.36	90.65	90.11	89.69	89.38	89.13	88.95	88.81	88.46	88.37	88.35	88.34
5000	114.20	113.31	112.63	112.11	111.72	111.42	111.19	111.01	110.58	110.46	110.43	110.42
6000	137.04	135.97	135.16	134.53	134.06	133.70	133.42	133.21	132.69	132.56	132.52	132.51
7000	159.88	158.63	157.68	156.96	156.40	155.98	155.66	155.41	154.81	154.65	154.60	154.59
8000	182.72	181.29	180.21	179.38	178.75	178.26	177.89	177.61	176.92	176.74	176.69	176.68
9000	205.56	203.95	202.73	201.80	201.09	200.55	200.13	199.81	199.04	198.83	198.78	198.76
10000	228.40	226.61	225.26	224.22	223.43	222.83	222.37	222.01	221.15	220.92	220.86	220.84
11000	251.24	249.27	247.78	246.64	245.77	245.11	244.60	244.21	243.27	243.02	242.95	242.93
12000	274.08	271.94	270.31	269.06	268.12	267.39	266.84	266.41	265.38	265.11	265.03	265.01
13000	296.92	294.60	292.83	291.49	290.46	289.68	289.08	288.61	287.50	287.20	287.12	287.10
14000	319.76	317.26	315.36	313.91	312.80	311.96	311.31	310.82	309.61	309.29	309.20	309.18
15000	342.60	339.92	337.88	336.33	335.15	334.24	333.55	333.02	331.73	331.38	331.29	331.26
16000	365.44	362.58	360.41	358.75	357.49	356.52	355.78	355.22	353.84	353.47	353.37	353.35
17000	388.28	385.24	382.93	381.17	379.83	378.81	378.02	377.42	375.96	375.57	375.46	375.43
18000	411.12	407.90	405.46	403.59	402.17	401.09	400.26	399.62	398.07	397.66	397.55	397.52
19000	433.96	430.56	427.98	426.02	424.52	423.37	422.49	421.82	420.19	419.75	419.63	419.60
20000	456.80	453.22	450.51	448.44	446.86	445.65	444.73	444.02	442.30	441.84	441.72	441.68
21000	479.64	475.88	473.03	470.86	469.20	467.93	466.96	466.22	464.42	463.93	463.80	463.77
22000	502.48	498.54	495.56	493.28	491.54	490.22	489.20	488.42	486.53	486.03	485.89	485.85
23000	525.32	521.20	518.08	515.70	513.89	512.50	511.44	510.62	508.65	508.12	507.97	507.94
24000	548.16	543.87	540.61	538.12	536.23	534.78	533.67	532.82	530.76	530.21	530.06	530.02
25000	571.00	566.53	563.13	560.55	558.57	557.06	555.91	555.02	552.88	552.30	552.15	552.10
26000	593.84	589.19	585.66	582.97	580.92	579.35	578.15	577.22	574.99	574.39	574.23	574.19
27000	616.68	611.85	608.18	605.39	603.26	601.63	600.38	599.42	597.11	596.48	596.32	596.27
28000	639.52	634.51	630.71	627.81	625.60	623.91	622.62	621.63	619.22	618.58	618.40	618.36
29000	662.36	657.17	653.23	650.23	647.94	646.19	644.85	643.83	641.34	640.67	640.49	640.44
30000	685.20	679.83	675.76	672.65	670.29	668.48	667.09	666.03	663.45	662.76	662.57	662.52
31000	708.04	702.49	698.28	695.08	692.63	690.76	689.33	688.23	685.57	684.85	684.66	684.61
32000	730.88	725.15	720.81	717.50	714.97	713.04	711.56	710.43	707.68	706.94	706.74	706.69
33000	753.72	747.81	743.33	739.92	737.31	735.32	733.80	732.63	729.80	729.04	728.83	728.78
34000	776.56	770.47	765.86	762.34	759.66	757.61	756.03	754.83	751.91	751.13	750.92	750.86
35000	799.40	793.14	788.38	784.76	782.00	779.89	778.27	777.03	774.03	773.22	773.00	772.94
37500	856.50	849.79	844.69	840.82	837.86	835.59	833.86	832.53	829.31	828.45	828.21	828.15
40000	913.60	906.44	901.01	896.87	893.71	891.30	889.45	888.03	884.60	883.68	883.43	883.36
42500	970.70	963.09	957.32	952.92	949.57	947.01	945.04	943.54	939.89	938.91	938.64	938.57
45000	1027.80	1019.74	1013.63	1008.98	1005.43	1002.71	1000.63	999.04	995.17	994.14	993.86	993.78
47500	1084.90	1076.40	1069.94	1065.03	1061.28	1058.42	1056.22	1054.54	1050.46	1049.37	1049.07	1048.99
50000	1142.00	1133.05	1126.26	1121.09	1117.14	1114.12	1111.81	1110.04	1105.75	1104.60	1104.29	1104.20
52500	1199.10	1189.70	1182.57	1177.14	1173.00	1169.83	1167.40	1165.54	1161.04	1159.83	1159.50	1159.41
55000	1256.20	1246.35	1238.88	1233.19	1228.85	1225.53	1222.99	1221.05	1216.32	1215.06	1214.71	1214.62
57500	1313.30	1303.00	1295.19	1289.25	1284.71	1281.24	1278.58	1276.55	1271.61	1270.29	1269.93	1269.83
60000	1370.40	1359.66	1351.51	1345.30	1340.57	1336.95	1334.17	1332.05	1326.90	1325.51	1325.14	1325.04
65000	1484.60	1472.96	1464.13	1457.41	1452.28	1448.36	1445.36	1443.05	1437.47	1435.97	1435.57	1435.46
70000	1598.80	1586.27	1576.76	1569.52	1563.99	1559.77	1556.54	1554.06	1548.05	1546.43	1546.00	1545.88
75000	1713.00	1699.57	1689.38	1681.63	1675.71	1671.18	1667.72	1665.06	1658.62	1656.89	1656.43	1656.30
80000	1827.19	1812.87	1802.01	1793.74	1787.42	1782.59	1778.90	1776.06	1769.19	1767.35	1766.85	1766.72
85000	1941.39	1926.18	1914.63	1905.84	1899.14	1894.01	1890.08	1887.07	1879.77	1877.81	1877.28	1877.14
90000	2055.59	2039.48	2027.26	2017.95	2010.85	2005.42	2001.26	1998.07	1990.34	1988.27	1987.71	1987.56
95000	2169.79	2152.79	2139.88	2130.06	2122.57	2116.83	2112.44	2109.07	2100.92	2098.73	2098.14	2097.98
100000	2283.99	2266.09	2252.51	2242.17	2234.28	2228.24	2223.62	2220.08	2211.49	2209.19	2208.57	2208.40
105000	2398.19	2379.40	2365.13	2354.28	2345.99	2339.65	2334.80	2331.08	2322.07	2319.65	2319.00	2318.82
110000	2512.39	2492.70	2477.76	2466.38	2457.70	2451.06	2445.98	2442.09	2432.64	2430.11	2429.42	2429.24
115000	2626.59	2606.01	2590.38	2578.49	2569.42	2562.47	2557.16	2553.09	2543.21	2540.57	2539.85	2539.66
120000	2740.79	2719.31	2703.01	2690.60	2681.13	2673.89	2668.34	2664.09	2653.79	2651.02	2650.28	2650.08
125000	2854.99	2832.61	2815.63	2802.71	2792.84	2785.30	2779.52	2775.10	2764.36	2761.48	2760.71	2760.50
130000	2969.19	2945.92	2928.26	2914.82	2904.56	2896.71	2890.71	2886.10	2874.94	2871.94	2871.14	2870.92
135000	3083.39	3059.22	3040.88	3026.92	3016.27	3008.12	3001.89	2997.10	2985.51	2982.40	2981.56	2981.34
140000	3197.59	3172.53	3153.51	3139.03	3127.98	3119.54	3113.07	3108.11	3096.09	3092.86	3091.99	3091.76
145000	3311.79	3285.83	3266.14	3251.14	3239.70	3230.95	3224.25	3219.11	3206.66	3203.32	3202.42	3202.18
150000	3425.99	3399.13	3378.76	3363.25	3351.41	3342.36	3335.43	3330.11	3317.24	3313.78	3312.85	3312.60
155000	3540.18	3512.44	3491.39	3475.36	3463.12	3453.77	3446.61	3441.12	3427.81	3424.24	3423.28	3423.02
160000	3654.38	3625.74	3604.01	3587.47	3574.84	3565.18	3557.79	3552.12	3538.38	3534.70	3533.70	3533.44

MONTHLY AMORTIZING PAYMENTS

AMOUNT OF LOAN	NUMBER OF YEARS IN TERM											
	1	2	3	4	5	6	7	8	9	10	11	12
$ 50	4.80	2.72	2.04	1.71	1.52	1.41	1.33	1.27	1.23	1.20	1.18	1.17
100	9.59	5.43	4.07	3.42	3.04	2.81	2.65	2.54	2.46	2.40	2.36	2.33
200	19.18	10.86	8.14	6.83	6.08	5.61	5.29	5.07	4.92	4.80	4.72	4.66
300	28.77	16.28	12.21	10.25	9.12	8.41	7.94	7.61	7.37	7.20	7.08	6.98
400	38.36	21.71	16.28	13.66	12.16	11.21	10.58	10.14	9.83	9.60	9.44	9.31
500	47.95	27.13	20.35	17.08	15.20	14.02	13.23	12.68	12.29	12.00	11.79	11.64
600	57.54	32.56	24.42	20.49	18.24	16.82	15.87	15.21	14.74	14.40	14.15	13.96
700	67.13	37.98	28.49	23.90	21.28	19.62	18.51	17.75	17.20	16.80	16.51	16.29
800	76.72	43.41	32.56	27.32	24.31	22.42	21.16	20.28	19.66	19.20	18.87	18.62
900	86.31	48.83	36.63	30.73	27.35	25.22	23.80	* 22.82	22.11	21.60	21.22	20.94
1000	95.90	54.26	40.70	34.15	30.39	28.03	26.45	25.35	24.57	24.00	23.58	23.27
2000	191.80	108.51	81.39	68.29	60.78	56.05	52.89	50.69	49.13	47.99	47.16	46.53
3000	287.69	162.77	122.08	102.43	91.16	84.07	79.33	76.04	73.69	71.99	70.73	69.80
4000	383.59	217.02	162.77	136.57	121.55	112.09	105.77	101.38	98.26	95.98	94.31	93.06
5000	479.48	271.27	203.46	170.71	151.94	140.11	132.21	126.73	122.82	119.98	117.88	116.33
6000	575.38	325.53	244.15	204.85	182.32	168.13	158.65	152.07	147.38	143.97	141.46	139.59
7000	671.27	379.78	284.84	238.99	212.71	196.15	185.09	177.42	171.94	167.97	165.04	162.85
8000	767.17	434.03	325.53	273.13	243.09	224.17	211.53	202.76	196.51	191.96	188.61	186.12
9000	863.06	488.29	366.23	307.27	273.48	252.19	237.98	228.11	221.07	215.95	212.19	209.38
10000	958.96	542.54	406.92	341.41	303.87	280.21	264.42	253.45	245.63	239.95	235.76	232.65
11000	1054.86	596.79	447.61	375.55	334.25	308.23	290.86	278.79	270.19	263.94	259.34	255.91
12000	1150.75	651.05	488.30	409.69	364.64	336.26	317.30	304.14	294.76	287.94	282.91	279.18
13000	1246.65	705.30	528.99	443.83	395.02	364.28	343.74	329.48	319.32	311.93	306.49	302.44
14000	1342.54	759.55	569.68	477.97	425.41	392.30	370.18	354.83	343.88	335.93	330.07	325.70
15000	1438.44	813.81	610.37	512.11	455.80	420.32	396.62	380.17	368.44	359.92	353.64	348.97
16000	1534.33	868.06	651.06	546.25	486.18	448.34	423.06	405.52	393.01	383.91	377.22	372.23
17000	1630.23	922.32	691.76	580.40	516.57	476.36	449.50	430.86	417.57	407.91	400.79	395.50
18000	1726.12	976.57	732.45	614.54	546.95	504.38	475.95	456.21	442.13	431.90	424.37	418.76
19000	1822.02	1030.82	773.14	648.68	577.34	532.40	502.39	481.55	466.69	455.90	447.94	442.03
20000	1917.91	1085.08	813.83	682.82	607.73	560.42	528.83	506.89	491.26	479.89	471.52	465.29
21000	2013.81	1139.33	854.52	716.96	638.11	588.44	555.27	532.24	515.82	503.89	495.10	488.55
22000	2109.71	1193.58	895.21	751.10	668.50	616.46	581.71	557.58	540.38	527.88	518.67	511.82
23000	2205.60	1247.84	935.90	785.24	698.88	644.49	608.15	582.93	564.94	551.87	542.25	535.08
24000	2301.50	1302.09	976.59	819.38	729.27	672.51	634.59	608.27	589.51	575.87	565.82	558.35
25000	2397.39	1356.34	1017.29	853.52	759.66	700.53	661.03	633.62	614.07	599.86	589.40	581.61
26000	2493.29	1410.60	1057.98	887.66	790.04	728.55	687.48	658.96	638.63	623.86	612.97	604.87
27000	2589.18	1464.85	1098.67	921.80	820.43	756.57	713.92	684.31	663.19	647.85	636.55	628.14
28000	2685.08	1519.10	1139.36	955.94	850.82	784.59	740.36	709.65	687.76	671.85	660.13	651.40
29000	2780.97	1573.36	1180.05	990.08	881.20	812.61	766.80	735.00	712.32	695.84	683.70	674.67
30000	2876.87	1627.61	1220.74	1024.22	911.59	840.63	793.24	760.34	736.88	719.84	707.28	697.93
31000	2972.76	1681.87	1261.43	1058.36	941.97	868.65	819.68	785.68	761.44	743.83	730.85	721.20
32000	3068.66	1736.12	1302.12	1092.50	972.36	896.67	846.12	811.03	786.01	767.82	754.43	744.46
33000	3164.56	1790.37	1342.81	1126.65	1002.75	924.69	872.56	836.37	810.57	791.82	778.00	767.72
34000	3260.45	1844.63	1383.51	1160.79	1033.13	952.71	899.00	861.72	835.13	815.81	801.58	790.99
35000	3356.35	1898.88	1424.20	1194.93	1063.52	980.74	925.45	887.06	859.69	839.81	825.16	814.25
37500	3596.08	2034.51	1525.93	1280.28	1139.48	1050.79	991.55	950.42	921.10	899.79	884.10	872.41
40000	3835.82	2170.15	1627.65	1365.63	1215.45	1120.84	1057.65	1013.78	982.51	959.78	943.03	930.57
42500	4075.56	2305.78	1729.38	1450.98	1291.41	1190.89	1123.75	1077.15	1043.91	1019.76	1001.97	988.73
45000	4315.30	2441.42	1831.11	1536.33	1367.38	1260.94	1189.86	1140.51	1105.32	1079.75	1060.91	1046.89
47500	4555.04	2577.05	1932.84	1621.68	1443.34	1331.00	1255.96	1203.87	1166.73	1139.74	1119.85	1105.06
50000	4794.78	2712.68	2034.57	1707.04	1519.31	1401.05	1322.06	1267.23	1228.13	1199.72	1178.79	1163.22
52500	5034.52	2848.32	2136.29	1792.39	1595.27	1471.10	1388.17	1330.59	1289.54	1259.71	1237.73	1221.38
55000	5274.26	2983.95	2238.02	1877.74	1671.24	1541.15	1454.27	1393.95	1350.94	1319.69	1296.67	1279.54
57500	5513.99	3119.59	2339.75	1963.09	1747.20	1611.21	1520.37	1457.31	1412.35	1379.68	1355.61	1337.70
60000	5753.73	3255.22	2441.48	2048.44	1823.17	1681.26	1586.47	1520.67	1473.76	1439.67	1414.55	1395.86
65000	6233.21	3526.49	2644.93	2219.15	1975.10	1821.36	1718.68	1647.40	1596.57	1559.64	1532.43	1512.18
70000	6712.69	3797.75	2848.39	2389.85	2127.03	1961.47	1850.89	1774.12	1719.38	1679.61	1650.31	1628.50
75000	7192.16	4069.02	3051.85	2560.55	2278.94	2101.57	1983.09	1900.84	1842.20	1799.58	1768.19	1744.82
80000	7671.64	4340.29	3255.30	2731.25	2430.89	2241.67	2115.30	2027.56	1965.01	1919.55	1886.06	1861.14
85000	8151.12	4611.56	3458.76	2901.96	2582.82	2381.78	2247.51	2154.29	2087.82	2039.52	2003.94	1977.46
90000	8630.60	4882.83	3662.21	3072.66	2734.75	2521.88	2379.71	2281.01	2210.63	2159.50	2121.82	2093.78
95000	9110.07	5154.09	3865.67	3243.36	2886.68	2661.99	2511.92	2407.73	2333.45	2279.47	2239.70	2210.11
100000	9589.55	5425.36	4069.13	3414.07	3038.61	2802.09	2644.12	2534.45	2456.26	2399.44	2357.58	2328.43
105000	10069.03	5696.63	4272.58	3584.77	3190.54	2942.20	2776.33	2661.18	2579.07	2519.41	2475.46	2442.75
110000	10548.51	5967.90	4476.04	3755.47	3342.47	3082.30	2908.53	2787.90	2701.88	2639.38	2593.34	2559.07
115000	11027.98	6239.17	4679.49	3926.18	3494.40	3222.41	3040.74	2914.62	2824.70	2759.35	2711.21	2675.39
120000	11507.46	6510.43	4882.95	4096.88	3646.33	3362.51	3172.94	3041.34	2947.51	2879.33	2829.09	2791.71
125000	11986.94	6781.70	5086.41	4267.58	3798.27	3502.61	3305.15	3168.07	3070.32	2999.30	2946.97	2908.03
130000	12466.42	7052.97	5289.86	4438.29	3950.20	3642.72	3437.36	3294.79	3193.14	3119.27	3064.85	3024.35
135000	12945.89	7324.24	5493.32	4608.99	4102.13	3782.82	3569.56	3421.51	3315.95	3239.24	3182.73	3140.67
140000	13425.37	7595.50	5696.77	4779.69	4254.06	3922.93	3701.77	3548.23	3438.76	3359.21	3300.61	3257.00
145000	13904.85	7866.77	5900.23	4950.40	4405.99	4063.03	3833.97	3674.96	3561.57	3479.18	3418.49	3373.32
150000	14384.32	8138.04	6103.69	5121.10	4557.92	4203.14	3966.18	3801.68	3684.39	3599.16	3536.37	3489.64
155000	14863.80	8409.31	6307.14	5291.80	4709.85	4343.24	4098.39	3928.40	3807.20	3719.13	3654.24	3605.96
160000	15343.28	8680.58	6510.60	5462.50	4861.78	4483.34	4230.59	4055.12	3930.01	3839.10	3772.12	3722.28

AMOUNT OF LOAN	NUMBER OF YEARS IN TERM											
	13	14	15	16	17	18	19	20	25	30	35	40
$ 50	1.16	1.15	1.14	1.14	1.13	1.13	1.13	1.13	1.12	1.12	1.12	1.12
100	2.31	2.29	2.28	2.27	2.26	2.25	2.25	2.25	2.24	2.23	2.23	2.23
200	4.61	4.58	4.55	4.53	4.51	4.50	4.49	4.49	4.47	4.46	4.46	4.46
300	6.91	6.86	6.82	6.79	6.77	6.75	6.74	6.73	6.70	6.69	6.69	6.69
400	9.22	9.15	9.09	9.05	9.02	9.00	8.98	8.97	8.93	8.92	8.92	8.92
500	11.52	11.43	11.37	11.31	11.28	11.25	11.22	11.21	11.17	11.15	11.15	11.15
600	13.82	13.72	13.64	13.58	13.53	13.50	13.47	13.45	13.40	13.38	13.38	13.38
700	16.13	16.00	15.91	15.84	15.78	15.74	15.71	15.69	15.63	15.61	15.61	15.61
800	18.43	18.29	18.18	18.10	18.04	17.99	17.96	17.93	17.86	17.84	17.84	17.84
900	20.73	20.57	20.45	20.36	20.29	20.24	20.20	20.17	20.09	20.07	20.07	20.07
1000	23.04	22.86	22.73	22.62	22.55	22.49	22.44	22.41	22.33	22.30	22.30	22.30
2000	46.07	45.71	45.45	45.24	45.09	44.97	44.88	44.81	44.65	44.60	44.59	44.59
3000	69.10	68.57	68.17	67.86	67.63	67.46	67.32	67.22	66.97	66.90	66.89	66.88
4000	92.13	91.42	90.89	90.48	90.18	89.94	89.76	89.62	89.29	89.20	89.18	89.17
5000	115.16	114.28	113.61	113.10	112.72	112.42	112.20	112.03	111.61	111.50	111.47	111.47
6000	138.19	137.13	136.33	135.72	135.26	134.91	134.64	134.43	133.93	133.80	133.77	133.76
7000	161.22	159.99	159.05	158.34	157.80	157.39	157.08	156.84	156.26	156.10	156.06	156.05
8000	184.25	182.84	181.77	180.96	180.35	179.88	179.52	179.24	178.58	178.40	178.36	178.34
9000	207.28	205.70	204.50	203.58	202.89	202.36	201.95	201.65	200.90	200.70	200.65	200.64
10000	230.31	228.55	227.22	226.20	225.43	224.84	224.39	224.05	223.22	223.00	222.94	222.93
11000	253.34	251.40	249.94	248.82	247.97	247.33	246.83	246.45	245.54	245.30	245.24	245.22
12000	276.37	274.26	272.66	271.44	270.52	269.81	269.27	268.86	267.86	267.60	267.53	267.51
13000	299.40	297.11	295.38	294.06	293.06	292.30	291.71	291.26	290.19	289.90	289.82	289.80
14000	322.43	319.97	318.10	316.68	315.60	314.78	314.15	313.67	312.51	312.20	312.12	312.10
15000	345.46	342.82	340.82	339.30	338.15	337.26	336.59	336.07	334.83	334.50	334.41	334.39
16000	368.50	365.68	363.54	361.92	360.69	359.75	359.03	358.48	357.15	356.80	356.71	356.68
17000	391.53	388.53	386.26	384.54	383.23	382.23	381.47	380.88	379.47	379.10	379.00	378.97
18000	414.56	411.39	408.99	407.16	405.77	404.71	403.90	403.29	401.79	401.40	401.29	401.27
19000	437.59	434.24	431.71	429.78	428.32	427.20	426.34	425.69	424.12	423.70	423.59	423.56
20000	460.62	457.10	454.43	452.40	450.86	449.68	448.78	448.09	446.44	446.00	445.88	445.85
21000	483.65	479.95	477.15	475.02	473.40	472.17	471.22	470.50	468.76	468.30	468.17	468.14
22000	506.68	502.80	499.87	497.64	495.94	494.65	493.66	492.90	491.08	490.60	490.47	490.43
23000	529.71	525.66	522.59	520.26	518.49	517.13	516.10	515.31	513.40	512.90	512.76	512.73
24000	552.74	548.51	545.31	542.88	541.03	539.62	538.54	537.71	535.72	535.20	535.05	535.02
25000	575.77	571.37	568.03	565.50	563.57	562.10	560.98	560.12	558.05	557.50	557.35	557.31
26000	598.80	594.22	590.76	588.12	586.12	584.59	583.42	582.52	580.37	579.80	579.64	579.60
27000	621.83	617.08	613.48	610.74	608.66	607.07	605.85	604.93	602.69	602.10	601.94	601.90
28000	644.86	639.93	636.20	633.36	631.20	629.55	628.29	627.33	625.01	624.39	624.23	624.19
29000	667.89	662.79	658.92	655.98	653.74	652.04	650.73	649.74	647.33	646.69	646.52	646.48
30000	690.92	685.64	681.64	678.60	676.29	674.52	673.17	672.14	669.65	668.99	668.82	668.77
31000	713.96	708.50	704.36	701.22	698.83	697.00	695.61	694.54	691.97	691.29	691.11	691.06
32000	736.99	731.35	727.08	723.84	721.37	719.49	718.05	716.95	714.30	713.59	713.41	713.36
33000	760.02	754.20	749.80	746.46	743.91	741.97	740.49	739.35	736.62	735.89	735.70	735.65
34000	783.05	777.06	772.52	769.08	766.46	764.46	762.93	761.76	758.94	758.19	757.99	757.94
35000	806.08	799.91	795.25	791.70	789.00	786.94	785.37	784.16	781.26	780.49	780.29	780.23
37500	863.65	857.05	852.05	848.25	845.36	843.15	841.46	840.17	837.07	836.24	836.02	835.96
40000	921.23	914.19	908.85	904.80	901.71	899.36	897.56	896.18	892.87	891.99	891.76	891.69
42500	978.81	971.32	965.65	961.35	958.07	955.57	953.66	952.20	948.67	947.74	947.49	947.42
45000	1036.38	1028.46	1022.46	1017.90	1014.43	1011.78	1009.75	1008.21	1004.48	1003.49	1003.23	1003.16
47500	1093.96	1085.60	1079.26	1074.45	1070.78	1067.99	1065.85	1064.22	1060.28	1059.24	1058.96	1058.89
50000	1151.54	1142.73	1136.06	1131.00	1127.14	1124.20	1121.95	1120.23	1116.09	1114.99	1114.69	1114.62
52500	1209.11	1199.87	1192.87	1187.55	1183.50	1180.41	1178.05	1176.24	1171.89	1170.74	1170.43	1170.35
55000	1266.69	1257.00	1249.67	1244.10	1239.85	1236.62	1234.14	1232.25	1227.69	1226.48	1226.16	1226.08
57500	1324.27	1314.14	1306.47	1300.65	1296.21	1292.83	1290.24	1288.26	1283.50	1282.23	1281.90	1281.81
60000	1381.84	1371.28	1363.27	1357.20	1352.57	1349.04	1346.34	1344.27	1339.30	1337.98	1337.63	1337.54
65000	1497.00	1485.55	1476.88	1470.30	1465.28	1461.46	1458.53	1456.30	1450.91	1449.48	1449.10	1449.00
70000	1612.15	1599.82	1590.49	1583.39	1577.99	1573.87	1570.73	1568.32	1562.52	1560.98	1560.57	1560.46
75000	1727.30	1714.09	1704.09	1696.49	1690.71	1686.29	1682.92	1680.34	1674.13	1672.48	1672.04	1671.92
80000	1842.46	1828.37	1817.70	1809.59	1803.42	1798.71	1795.12	1792.36	1785.73	1783.98	1783.51	1783.38
85000	1957.61	1942.64	1931.30	1922.69	1916.14	1911.13	1907.31	1904.39	1897.34	1895.47	1894.98	1894.84
90000	2072.76	2056.91	2044.91	2035.79	2028.85	2023.55	2019.50	2016.41	2008.95	2006.97	2006.45	2006.31
95000	2187.92	2171.19	2158.52	2148.89	2141.56	2135.97	2131.70	2128.43	2120.56	2118.47	2117.91	2117.77
100000	2303.07	2285.46	2272.12	2261.99	2254.28	2248.39	2243.89	2240.45	2232.17	2229.97	2229.38	2229.23
105000	2418.22	2399.73	2385.73	2375.09	2366.99	2360.81	2356.09	2352.48	2343.77	2341.47	2340.85	2340.69
110000	2533.38	2514.00	2499.33	2488.19	2479.70	2473.23	2468.28	2464.50	2455.38	2452.96	2452.32	2452.15
115000	2648.53	2628.28	2612.94	2601.29	2592.42	2585.65	2580.48	2576.52	2566.99	2564.46	2563.79	2563.61
120000	2763.68	2742.55	2726.54	2714.39	2705.13	2698.07	2692.67	2688.54	2678.60	2675.96	2675.26	2675.07
125000	2878.84	2856.82	2840.15	2827.49	2817.84	2810.49	2804.86	2800.57	2790.21	2787.46	2786.73	2786.53
130000	2993.99	2971.09	2953.76	2940.59	2930.56	2922.91	2917.06	2912.59	2901.81	2898.96	2898.20	2898.00
135000	3109.14	3085.37	3067.36	3053.69	3043.27	3035.32	3029.25	3024.61	3013.42	3010.46	3009.67	3009.46
140000	3224.30	3199.64	3180.97	3166.78	3155.98	3147.74	3141.45	3136.63	3125.03	3121.95	3121.14	3120.92
145000	3339.45	3313.91	3294.57	3279.88	3268.70	3260.16	3253.64	3248.66	3236.64	3233.45	3232.60	3232.38
150000	3454.60	3428.18	3408.18	3392.98	3381.41	3372.58	3365.84	3360.68	3348.25	3344.95	3344.07	3343.84
155000	3569.76	3542.46	3521.79	3506.08	3494.12	3485.00	3478.03	3472.70	3459.85	3456.45	3455.54	3455.30
160000	3684.91	3656.73	3635.39	3619.18	3606.84	3597.42	3590.23	3584.72	3571.46	3567.95	3567.01	3566.76

MONTHLY AMORTIZING PAYMENTS

AMOUNT OF LOAN	NUMBER OF YEARS IN TERM											
	1	2	3	4	5	6	7	8	9	10	11	12
$ 50	4.81	2.72	2.05	1.72	1.53	1.41	1.34	1.28	1.24	1.21	1.19	1.18
100	9.61	5.44	4.09	3.43	3.06	2.82	2.67	2.56	2.48	2.42	2.38	2.35
200	19.21	10.88	8.17	6.86	6.11	5.64	5.33	5.11	4.95	4.84	4.76	4.70
300	28.81	16.32	12.25	10.29	9.17	8.46	7.99	7.66	7.43	7.26	7.13	7.04
400	38.41	21.76	16.34	13.72	12.22	11.28	10.65	10.21	9.90	9.67	9.51	9.39
500	48.01	27.20	20.42	17.15	15.27	14.09	13.31	12.76	12.37	12.09	11.88	11.73
600	57.62	32.63	24.50	20.57	18.33	16.91	15.97	15.31	14.85	14.51	14.26	14.08
700	67.22	38.07	28.58	24.00	21.38	19.73	18.63	17.86	17.32	16.93	16.64	16.42
800	76.82	43.51	32.67	27.43	24.43	22.55	21.29	20.42	19.79	19.34	19.01	18.77
900	86.42	48.95	36.75	30.86	27.49	25.36	23.95	22.97	22.27	21.76	21.39	21.11
1000	96.02	54.39	40.83	34.29	30.54	28.18	26.61	25.52	24.74	24.18	23.76	23.46
2000	192.04	108.77	81.66	68.57	61.08	56.36	53.21	51.03	49.48	48.35	47.52	46.91
3000	288.06	163.15	122.48	102.85	91.61	84.54	79.82	76.55	74.22	72.53	71.28	70.36
4000	384.07	217.53	163.31	137.13	122.15	112.71	106.42	102.06	98.95	96.70	95.04	93.81
5000	480.09	271.91	204.13	171.42	152.68	140.89	133.03	127.57	123.69	120.87	118.80	117.27
6000	576.11	326.29	244.96	205.70	183.22	169.07	159.63	153.09	148.43	145.05	142.56	140.72
7000	672.13	380.67	285.78	239.98	213.75	197.25	186.23	178.60	173.17	169.22	166.32	164.17
8000	768.14	435.05	326.61	274.26	244.29	225.42	212.84	204.11	197.90	193.40	190.08	187.62
9000	864.16	489.43	367.43	308.55	274.82	253.60	239.44	229.63	222.64	217.57	213.84	211.07
10000	960.18	543.81	408.26	342.83	305.36	281.78	266.05	255.14	247.38	241.74	237.60	234.53
11000	1056.20	598.19	449.08	377.11	335.89	309.96	292.65	280.66	272.11	265.92	261.36	257.98
12000	1152.21	652.57	489.91	411.39	366.43	338.13	319.26	306.17	296.85	290.09	285.12	281.43
13000	1248.23	706.95	530.73	445.68	396.96	366.31	345.86	331.68	321.59	314.27	308.88	304.88
14000	1344.25	761.33	571.56	479.96	427.50	394.49	372.46	357.20	346.33	338.44	332.64	328.33
15000	1440.27	815.71	612.38	514.24	458.03	422.66	399.07	382.71	371.06	362.61	356.40	351.79
16000	1536.28	870.09	653.21	548.52	488.57	450.84	425.67	408.22	395.80	386.79	380.16	375.24
17000	1632.30	924.47	694.03	582.80	519.11	479.02	452.28	433.74	420.54	410.96	403.92	398.69
18000	1728.32	978.85	734.86	617.09	549.64	507.20	478.88	459.25	445.28	435.14	427.68	422.14
19000	1824.34	1033.23	775.68	651.37	580.18	535.37	505.49	484.76	470.01	459.31	451.44	445.59
20000	1920.35	1087.61	816.51	685.65	610.71	563.55	532.09	510.28	494.75	483.48	475.20	469.05
21000	2016.37	1141.99	857.33	719.93	641.25	591.73	558.69	535.79	519.49	507.66	498.96	492.50
22000	2112.39	1196.37	898.16	754.22	671.78	619.91	585.30	561.31	544.22	531.83	522.72	515.95
23000	2208.41	1250.75	938.98	788.50	702.32	648.08	611.90	586.82	568.96	556.01	546.48	539.40
24000	2304.42	1305.13	979.81	822.78	732.85	676.26	638.51	612.33	593.70	580.18	570.24	562.85
25000	2400.44	1359.51	1020.64	857.06	763.39	704.44	665.11	637.85	618.44	604.35	594.00	586.31
26000	2496.46	1413.89	1061.46	891.35	793.92	732.61	691.72	663.36	643.17	628.53	617.76	609.76
27000	2592.47	1468.27	1102.29	925.63	824.46	760.79	718.32	688.87	667.91	652.70	641.52	633.21
28000	2688.49	1522.65	1143.11	959.91	854.99	788.97	744.92	714.39	692.65	676.88	665.28	656.66
29000	2784.51	1577.03	1183.94	994.19	885.53	817.15	771.53	739.90	717.39	701.05	689.04	680.11
30000	2880.53	1631.41	1224.76	1028.47	916.06	845.32	798.13	765.41	742.12	725.22	712.80	703.57
31000	2976.54	1685.79	1265.59	1062.76	946.60	873.50	824.74	790.93	766.86	749.40	736.56	727.02
32000	3072.56	1740.17	1306.41	1097.04	977.14	901.68	851.34	816.44	791.60	773.57	760.32	750.47
33000	3168.58	1794.55	1347.24	1131.32	1007.67	929.86	877.94	841.96	816.33	797.75	784.08	773.92
34000	3264.60	1848.93	1388.06	1165.60	1038.21	958.03	904.55	867.47	841.07	821.92	807.84	797.37
35000	3360.61	1903.31	1428.89	1199.89	1068.74	986.21	931.15	892.98	865.81	846.09	831.60	820.83
37500	3600.66	2039.26	1530.95	1285.59	1145.08	1056.65	997.66	956.77	927.65	906.53	891.00	879.46
40000	3840.70	2175.21	1633.01	1371.30	1221.42	1127.10	1064.17	1020.55	989.49	966.96	950.39	938.09
42500	4080.74	2311.16	1735.08	1457.00	1297.76	1197.54	1130.68	1084.34	1051.34	1027.40	1009.79	996.72
45000	4320.79	2447.12	1837.14	1542.71	1374.09	1267.98	1197.20	1148.12	1113.18	1087.83	1069.19	1055.35
47500	4560.83	2583.07	1939.20	1628.42	1450.43	1338.43	1263.71	1211.90	1175.02	1148.27	1128.59	1113.98
50000	4800.88	2719.02	2041.27	1714.12	1526.77	1408.87	1330.22	1275.69	1236.87	1208.70	1187.99	1172.61
52500	5040.92	2854.97	2143.33	1799.83	1603.11	1479.31	1396.73	1339.47	1298.71	1269.14	1247.39	1231.24
55000	5280.96	2990.92	2245.39	1885.53	1679.45	1549.76	1463.24	1403.26	1360.55	1329.57	1306.79	1289.87
57500	5521.01	3126.87	2347.45	1971.24	1755.79	1620.20	1529.75	1467.04	1422.40	1390.01	1366.19	1348.50
60000	5761.05	3262.82	2449.52	2056.94	1832.12	1690.64	1596.26	1530.82	1484.24	1450.44	1425.59	1407.13
65000	6241.14	3534.72	2653.64	2228.36	1984.80	1831.53	1729.28	1658.39	1607.93	1571.31	1544.39	1524.39
70000	6721.22	3806.62	2857.77	2399.77	2137.48	1972.41	1862.30	1785.96	1731.61	1692.18	1663.19	1641.65
75000	7201.31	4078.52	3061.90	2571.18	2290.15	2113.30	1995.32	1913.53	1855.30	1813.05	1781.99	1758.91
80000	7681.40	4350.42	3266.02	2742.59	2442.83	2254.19	2128.34	2041.10	1978.98	1933.92	1900.78	1876.17
85000	8161.48	4622.32	3470.15	2914.00	2595.51	2395.07	2261.36	2168.67	2102.67	2054.79	2019.58	1993.43
90000	8641.57	4894.23	3674.27	3085.41	2748.18	2535.96	2394.39	2296.23	2226.36	2175.66	2138.38	2110.69
95000	9121.66	5166.13	3878.40	3256.83	2900.86	2676.85	2527.41	2423.80	2350.04	2296.53	2257.18	2227.95
100000	9601.75	5438.03	4082.53	3428.24	3053.54	2817.73	2660.43	2551.37	2473.73	2417.40	2375.98	2345.21
105000	10081.83	5709.93	4286.65	3599.65	3206.21	2958.62	2793.45	2678.94	2597.42	2538.27	2494.78	2462.47
110000	10561.92	5981.83	4490.78	3771.06	3358.89	3099.51	2926.47	2806.51	2721.10	2659.14	2613.58	2579.73
115000	11042.01	6253.73	4694.90	3942.47	3511.57	3240.39	3059.49	2934.08	2844.79	2780.01	2732.38	2696.99
120000	11522.09	6525.63	4899.03	4113.88	3664.24	3381.28	3192.51	3061.64	2968.47	2900.88	2851.17	2814.25
125000	12002.18	6797.53	5103.16	4285.30	3816.92	3522.16	3325.53	3189.21	3092.16	3021.75	2969.97	2931.51
130000	12482.27	7069.43	5307.28	4456.71	3969.60	3663.05	3458.56	3316.78	3215.85	3142.62	3088.77	3048.77
135000	12962.35	7341.34	5511.41	4628.12	4122.27	3803.94	3591.58	3444.35	3339.53	3263.49	3207.57	3166.03
140000	13442.44	7613.24	5715.54	4799.53	4274.95	3944.82	3724.60	3571.92	3463.22	3384.36	3326.37	3283.29
145000	13922.53	7885.14	5919.66	4970.94	4427.63	4085.71	3857.62	3699.49	3586.91	3505.23	3445.17	3400.55
150000	14402.62	8157.04	6123.79	5142.35	4580.30	4226.60	3990.64	3827.05	3710.59	3626.10	3563.97	3517.81
155000	14882.70	8428.94	6327.91	5313.77	4732.98	4367.48	4123.66	3954.62	3834.28	3746.97	3682.77	3635.07
160000	15362.79	8700.84	6532.04	5485.18	4885.66	4508.37	4256.68	4082.19	3957.96	3867.84	3801.56	3752.33

AMOUNT OF LOAN	NUMBER OF YEARS IN TERM											
	13	14	15	16	17	18	19	20	25	30	35	40
$ 50	1.17	1.16	1.15	1.15	1.14	1.14	1.14	1.14	1.13	1.13	1.13	1.13
100	2.33	2.31	2.30	2.29	2.28	2.27	2.27	2.27	2.26	2.26	2.26	2.26
200	4.65	4.61	4.59	4.57	4.55	4.54	4.53	4.53	4.51	4.51	4.51	4.51
300	6.97	6.92	6.88	6.85	6.83	6.81	6.80	6.79	6.76	6.76	6.76	6.76
400	9.29	9.22	9.17	9.13	9.10	9.08	9.06	9.05	9.02	9.01	9.01	9.01
500	11.62	11.53	11.46	11.41	11.38	11.35	11.33	11.31	11.27	11.26	11.26	11.26
600	13.94	13.83	13.76	13.70	13.65	13.62	13.59	13.57	13.52	13.51	13.51	13.51
700	16.26	16.14	16.05	15.98	15.93	15.88	15.85	15.83	15.77	15.76	15.76	15.76
800	18.58	18.44	18.34	18.26	18.20	18.15	18.12	18.09	18.03	18.01	18.01	18.01
900	20.90	20.75	20.63	20.54	20.47	20.42	20.38	20.35	20.28	20.26	20.26	20.26
1000	23.23	23.05	22.92	22.82	22.75	22.69	22.65	22.61	22.53	22.51	22.51	22.51
2000	46.45	46.10	45.84	45.64	45.49	45.38	45.29	45.22	45.06	45.02	45.01	45.01
3000	69.67	69.15	68.76	68.46	68.23	68.06	67.93	67.83	67.59	67.53	67.51	67.51
4000	92.89	92.20	91.68	91.28	90.98	90.75	90.57	90.44	90.12	90.03	90.01	90.01
5000	116.11	115.25	114.59	114.10	113.72	113.43	113.21	113.05	112.65	112.54	112.51	112.51
6000	139.34	138.30	137.51	136.92	136.46	136.12	135.86	135.66	135.18	135.05	135.02	135.01
7000	162.56	161.34	160.43	159.73	159.21	158.80	158.50	158.26	157.70	157.56	157.52	157.51
8000	185.78	184.39	183.35	182.55	181.95	181.49	181.14	180.87	180.23	180.06	180.02	180.01
9000	209.00	207.44	206.26	205.37	204.69	204.17	203.78	203.48	202.76	202.57	202.52	202.51
10000	232.22	230.49	229.18	228.19	227.43	226.86	226.42	226.09	225.29	225.08	225.02	225.01
11000	255.44	253.54	252.10	251.01	250.18	249.55	249.06	248.70	247.82	247.59	247.53	247.51
12000	278.67	276.59	275.02	273.83	272.92	272.23	271.71	271.31	270.35	270.09	270.03	270.01
13000	301.89	299.64	297.93	296.64	295.66	294.92	294.35	293.91	292.87	292.60	292.53	292.51
14000	325.11	322.68	320.85	319.46	318.41	317.60	316.99	316.52	315.40	315.11	315.03	315.01
15000	348.33	345.73	343.77	342.28	341.15	340.29	339.63	339.13	337.93	337.62	337.53	337.51
16000	371.55	368.78	366.69	365.10	363.89	362.97	362.27	361.74	360.46	360.12	360.04	360.01
17000	394.78	391.83	389.60	387.92	386.64	385.66	384.92	384.35	382.99	382.63	382.54	382.51
18000	418.00	414.88	412.52	410.74	409.38	408.34	407.56	406.96	405.52	405.14	405.04	405.01
19000	441.22	437.93	435.44	433.55	432.12	431.03	430.20	429.56	428.05	427.65	427.54	427.51
20000	464.44	460.98	458.36	456.37	454.86	453.72	452.84	452.17	450.57	450.15	450.04	450.02
21000	487.66	484.02	481.27	479.19	477.61	476.40	475.48	474.78	473.10	472.66	472.55	472.52
22000	510.88	507.07	504.19	502.01	500.35	499.09	498.12	497.39	495.63	495.17	495.05	495.02
23000	534.11	530.12	527.11	524.83	523.09	521.77	520.77	520.00	518.16	517.68	517.55	517.52
24000	557.33	553.17	550.03	547.65	545.84	544.46	543.41	542.61	540.69	540.18	540.05	540.02
25000	580.55	576.22	572.95	570.46	568.58	567.14	566.05	565.22	563.22	562.69	562.55	562.52
26000	603.77	599.27	595.86	593.28	591.32	589.83	588.69	587.82	585.74	585.20	585.06	585.02
27000	626.99	622.32	618.78	616.10	614.06	612.51	611.33	610.43	608.27	607.71	607.56	607.52
28000	650.22	645.36	641.70	638.92	636.81	635.20	633.98	633.04	630.80	630.21	630.06	630.02
29000	673.44	668.41	664.62	661.74	659.55	657.89	656.62	655.65	653.33	652.72	652.56	652.52
30000	696.66	691.46	687.53	684.56	682.29	680.57	679.26	678.26	675.86	675.23	675.06	675.02
31000	719.88	714.51	710.45	707.37	705.04	703.26	701.90	700.87	698.39	697.74	697.57	697.52
32000	743.10	737.56	733.37	730.19	727.78	725.94	724.54	723.47	720.91	720.24	720.07	720.02
33000	766.32	760.61	756.29	753.01	750.52	748.63	747.18	746.08	743.44	742.75	742.57	742.52
34000	789.55	783.66	779.20	775.83	773.27	771.31	769.83	768.69	765.97	765.26	765.07	765.02
35000	812.77	806.70	802.12	798.65	796.01	794.00	792.47	791.30	788.50	787.77	787.57	787.52
37500	870.82	864.33	859.42	855.69	852.87	850.71	849.07	847.82	844.82	844.04	843.83	843.77
40000	928.88	921.95	916.71	912.74	909.72	907.43	905.68	904.34	901.14	900.30	900.08	900.03
42500	986.93	979.57	974.00	969.79	966.58	964.14	962.28	960.86	957.46	956.57	956.33	956.28
45000	1044.99	1037.19	1031.30	1026.83	1023.44	1020.85	1018.89	1017.38	1013.78	1012.84	1012.59	1012.53
47500	1103.04	1094.81	1088.59	1083.88	1080.30	1077.57	1075.49	1073.90	1070.11	1069.11	1068.85	1068.78
50000	1161.10	1152.43	1145.89	1140.92	1137.15	1134.28	1132.09	1130.43	1126.43	1125.38	1125.10	1125.03
52500	1219.15	1210.05	1203.18	1197.97	1194.01	1191.00	1188.70	1186.95	1182.75	1181.65	1181.36	1181.28
55000	1277.20	1267.67	1260.47	1255.02	1250.87	1247.71	1245.30	1243.47	1239.07	1237.92	1237.61	1237.53
57500	1335.26	1325.30	1317.77	1312.06	1307.73	1304.42	1301.91	1299.99	1295.39	1294.18	1293.87	1293.78
60000	1393.31	1382.92	1375.06	1369.11	1364.58	1361.14	1358.51	1356.51	1351.71	1350.45	1350.12	1350.04
65000	1509.42	1498.16	1489.65	1483.20	1478.30	1474.57	1471.72	1469.55	1464.35	1462.99	1462.63	1462.54
70000	1625.53	1613.40	1604.24	1597.29	1592.01	1587.99	1584.93	1582.59	1576.99	1575.53	1575.14	1575.04
75000	1741.64	1728.65	1718.83	1711.38	1705.73	1701.42	1698.14	1695.64	1689.64	1688.07	1687.65	1687.54
80000	1857.75	1843.89	1833.41	1825.47	1819.44	1814.85	1811.35	1808.68	1802.28	1800.60	1800.16	1800.05
85000	1973.86	1959.13	1948.00	1939.57	1933.16	1928.28	1924.56	1921.72	1914.92	1913.14	1912.67	1912.55
90000	2089.97	2074.37	2062.59	2053.66	2046.87	2041.70	2037.77	2034.76	2027.56	2025.68	2025.18	2025.05
95000	2206.08	2189.62	2177.18	2167.75	2160.59	2155.13	2150.98	2147.80	2140.21	2138.21	2137.69	2137.55
100000	2322.19	2304.86	2291.77	2281.84	2274.30	2268.56	2264.18	2260.85	2252.85	2250.75	2250.20	2250.06
105000	2438.29	2420.10	2406.35	2395.93	2388.02	2381.99	2377.39	2373.89	2365.49	2363.29	2362.71	2362.56
110000	2554.40	2535.34	2520.94	2510.03	2501.73	2495.42	2490.60	2486.93	2478.13	2475.83	2475.22	2475.06
115000	2670.51	2650.59	2635.53	2624.12	2615.45	2608.84	2603.81	2599.97	2590.77	2588.36	2587.73	2587.56
120000	2786.62	2765.83	2750.12	2738.21	2729.16	2722.27	2717.02	2713.01	2703.42	2700.90	2700.24	2700.07
125000	2902.73	2881.07	2864.71	2852.30	2842.87	2835.70	2830.23	2826.06	2816.06	2813.44	2812.75	2812.57
130000	3018.84	2996.31	2979.29	2966.39	2956.59	2949.13	2943.44	2939.10	2928.70	2925.98	2925.26	2925.07
135000	3134.95	3111.56	3093.88	3080.48	3070.30	3062.55	3056.65	3052.14	3041.34	3038.51	3037.77	3037.57
140000	3251.06	3226.80	3208.47	3194.58	3184.02	3175.98	3169.86	3165.18	3153.98	3151.05	3150.28	3150.08
145000	3367.17	3342.04	3323.06	3308.67	3297.73	3289.41	3283.07	3278.22	3266.63	3263.59	3262.79	3262.58
150000	3483.28	3457.29	3437.65	3422.76	3411.45	3402.84	3396.27	3391.27	3379.27	3376.13	3375.30	3375.08
155000	3599.38	3572.53	3552.23	3536.85	3525.16	3516.27	3509.48	3504.31	3491.91	3488.66	3487.81	3487.58
160000	3715.49	3687.77	3666.82	3650.94	3638.88	3629.69	3622.69	3617.35	3604.55	3601.20	3600.32	3600.09

MONTHLY AMORTIZING PAYMENTS

AMOUNT OF LOAN	NUMBER OF YEARS IN TERM											
	1	2	3	4	5	6	7	8	9	10	11	12
$ 50	4.81	2.73	2.05	1.73	1.54	1.42	1.34	1.29	1.25	1.22	1.20	1.19
100	9.62	5.46	4.10	3.45	3.07	2.84	2.68	2.57	2.50	2.44	2.40	2.37
200	19.23	10.91	8.20	6.89	6.14	5.67	5.36	5.14	4.99	4.88	4.79	4.73
300	28.85	16.36	12.29	10.33	9.21	8.51	8.04	7.71	7.48	7.31	7.19	7.10
400	38.46	21.81	16.39	13.77	12.28	11.34	10.71	10.28	9.97	9.75	9.58	9.46
500	48.07	27.26	20.48	17.22	15.35	14.17	13.39	12.85	12.46	12.18	11.98	11.83
600	57.69	32.71	24.58	20.66	18.42	17.01	16.07	15.41	14.95	14.62	14.37	14.19
700	67.30	38.16	28.68	24.10	21.48	19.84	18.74	17.98	17.44	17.05	16.77	16.55
800	76.92	43.61	32.77	27.54	24.55	22.67	21.42	20.55	19.93	19.49	19.16	18.92
900	86.53	49.06	36.87	30.99	27.62	25.51	24.10	23.12	22.43	21.92	21.55	21.28
1000	96.14	54.51	40.96	34.43	30.69	28.34	26.77	25.69	24.92	24.36	23.95	23.65
2000	192.28	109.02	81.92	68.85	61.37	56.67	53.54	51.37	49.83	48.71	47.89	47.29
3000	288.42	163.53	122.88	103.28	92.06	85.01	80.31	77.05	74.74	73.07	71.84	70.93
4000	384.56	218.03	163.84	137.70	122.74	113.34	107.08	102.74	99.65	97.42	95.78	94.57
5000	480.70	272.54	204.80	172.13	153.43	141.68	133.84	128.42	124.57	121.78	119.73	118.21
6000	576.84	327.05	245.76	206.55	184.11	170.01	160.61	154.10	149.48	146.13	143.67	141.85
7000	672.98	381.55	286.72	240.98	214.80	198.34	187.38	179.79	174.39	170.48	167.61	165.49
8000	769.12	436.06	327.68	275.40	245.48	226.68	214.15	205.47	199.30	194.84	191.56	189.13
9000	865.26	490.57	368.64	309.82	276.17	255.01	240.91	231.15	224.22	219.19	215.50	212.77
10000	961.40	545.08	409.60	344.25	306.85	283.35	267.68	256.84	249.13	243.55	239.45	236.41
11000	1057.54	599.58	450.56	378.67	337.54	311.68	294.45	282.52	274.04	267.90	263.39	260.05
12000	1153.68	654.09	491.52	413.10	368.22	340.01	321.22	308.20	298.95	292.25	287.34	283.69
13000	1249.82	708.60	532.48	447.52	398.91	368.35	347.99	333.89	323.87	316.61	311.28	307.33
14000	1345.96	763.10	573.44	481.95	429.59	396.68	374.75	359.57	348.78	340.96	335.22	330.97
15000	1442.10	817.61	614.40	516.37	460.28	425.02	401.52	385.25	373.69	365.32	359.17	354.61
16000	1538.24	872.12	655.36	550.79	490.96	453.35	428.29	410.94	398.60	389.67	383.11	378.25
17000	1634.38	926.62	696.32	585.22	521.65	481.68	455.06	436.62	423.52	414.02	407.06	401.89
18000	1730.51	981.13	737.28	619.64	552.33	510.02	481.82	462.30	448.43	438.38	431.00	425.53
19000	1826.65	1035.64	778.23	654.07	583.02	538.35	508.59	487.99	473.34	462.73	454.94	449.17
20000	1922.79	1090.15	819.19	688.49	613.70	566.69	535.36	513.67	498.25	487.09	478.89	472.81
21000	2018.93	1144.65	860.15	722.92	644.39	595.02	562.13	539.35	523.17	511.44	502.83	496.45
22000	2115.07	1199.16	901.11	757.34	675.07	623.35	588.89	565.04	548.08	535.79	526.78	520.09
23000	2211.21	1253.67	942.07	791.76	705.76	651.69	615.66	590.72	572.99	560.15	550.72	543.73
24000	2307.35	1308.17	983.03	826.19	736.44	680.02	642.43	616.40	597.90	584.50	574.67	567.37
25000	2403.49	1362.68	1023.99	860.61	767.13	708.36	669.20	642.09	622.81	608.86	598.61	591.01
26000	2499.63	1417.19	1064.95	895.04	797.81	736.69	695.97	667.77	647.73	633.21	622.55	614.65
27000	2595.77	1471.70	1105.91	929.46	828.50	765.03	722.73	693.45	672.64	657.56	646.50	638.29
28000	2691.91	1526.20	1146.87	963.89	859.18	793.36	749.50	719.14	697.55	681.92	670.44	661.93
29000	2788.05	1580.71	1187.83	998.31	889.87	821.69	776.27	744.82	722.46	706.27	694.39	685.57
30000	2884.19	1635.22	1228.79	1032.74	920.55	850.03	803.04	770.50	747.38	730.63	718.33	709.21
31000	2980.33	1689.72	1269.75	1067.16	951.24	878.36	829.80	796.19	772.29	754.98	742.27	732.85
32000	3076.47	1744.23	1310.71	1101.58	981.92	906.70	856.57	821.87	797.20	779.33	766.22	756.49
33000	3172.61	1798.74	1351.67	1136.01	1012.61	935.03	883.34	847.55	822.11	803.69	790.16	780.13
34000	3268.75	1853.24	1392.63	1170.43	1043.29	963.36	910.11	873.24	847.03	828.04	814.11	803.77
35000	3364.88	1907.75	1433.59	1204.86	1073.98	991.70	936.88	898.92	871.94	852.40	838.05	827.42
37500	3605.23	2044.02	1535.98	1290.92	1150.69	1062.53	1003.79	963.13	934.22	913.28	897.91	886.52
40000	3845.58	2180.29	1638.38	1376.98	1227.40	1133.37	1070.71	1027.34	996.50	974.17	957.77	945.62
42500	4085.93	2316.55	1740.78	1463.04	1304.11	1204.20	1137.63	1091.54	1058.78	1035.05	1017.63	1004.72
45000	4326.28	2452.82	1843.18	1549.10	1380.83	1275.04	1204.55	1155.75	1121.06	1095.94	1077.49	1063.82
47500	4566.63	2589.09	1945.58	1635.16	1457.54	1345.87	1271.47	1219.96	1183.34	1156.82	1137.35	1122.92
50000	4806.98	2725.36	2047.98	1721.22	1534.25	1416.71	1338.39	1284.17	1245.62	1217.71	1197.21	1182.02
52500	5047.32	2861.63	2150.38	1807.28	1610.96	1487.54	1405.31	1348.38	1307.91	1278.59	1257.07	1241.12
55000	5287.67	2997.89	2252.78	1893.34	1687.68	1558.38	1472.23	1412.58	1370.19	1339.48	1316.93	1300.22
57500	5528.02	3134.16	2355.17	1979.40	1764.39	1629.21	1539.15	1476.79	1432.47	1400.36	1376.80	1359.32
60000	5768.37	3270.43	2457.57	2065.47	1841.10	1700.05	1606.07	1541.00	1494.75	1461.25	1436.66	1418.42
65000	6249.07	3542.96	2662.37	2237.59	1994.53	1841.72	1739.91	1669.42	1619.31	1583.02	1556.38	1536.62
70000	6729.76	3815.50	2867.17	2409.71	2147.95	1983.39	1873.75	1797.83	1743.87	1704.79	1676.10	1654.83
75000	7210.46	4088.03	3071.96	2581.83	2301.37	2125.06	2007.58	1926.25	1868.43	1826.56	1795.82	1773.03
80000	7691.16	4360.57	3276.76	2753.95	2454.80	2266.73	2141.42	2054.67	1993.00	1948.33	1915.54	1891.23
85000	8171.86	4633.10	3481.56	2926.07	2608.22	2408.40	2275.26	2183.08	2117.56	2070.10	2035.26	2009.43
90000	8652.55	4905.64	3686.36	3098.20	2761.65	2550.07	2409.10	2311.50	2242.12	2191.87	2154.98	2127.63
95000	9133.25	5178.17	3891.15	3270.32	2915.07	2691.74	2542.94	2439.92	2366.68	2313.64	2274.70	2245.83
100000	9613.95	5450.71	4095.95	3442.44	3068.50	2833.41	2676.78	2568.33	2491.24	2435.41	2394.42	2364.03
105000	10094.64	5723.25	4300.75	3614.56	3221.92	2975.08	2810.62	2696.75	2615.81	2557.18	2514.14	2482.24
110000	10575.34	5995.78	4505.55	3786.68	3375.35	3116.75	2944.45	2825.16	2740.37	2678.95	2633.86	2600.44
115000	11056.04	6268.32	4710.34	3958.80	3528.77	3258.42	3078.29	2953.58	2864.93	2800.72	2753.59	2718.64
120000	11536.74	6540.85	4915.14	4130.93	3682.20	3400.09	3212.13	3082.00	2989.49	2922.49	2873.31	2836.84
125000	12017.43	6813.39	5119.94	4303.05	3835.62	3541.76	3345.97	3210.41	3114.05	3044.26	2993.03	2955.04
130000	12498.13	7085.92	5324.73	4475.17	3989.05	3683.43	3479.81	3338.83	3238.61	3166.03	3112.75	3073.24
135000	12978.83	7358.46	5529.53	4647.29	4142.47	3825.11	3613.65	3467.25	3363.18	3287.80	3232.47	3191.44
140000	13459.52	7630.99	5734.33	4819.41	4295.89	3966.78	3747.49	3595.66	3487.74	3409.57	3352.19	3309.65
145000	13940.22	7903.53	5939.13	4991.53	4449.32	4108.45	3881.32	3724.08	3612.30	3531.34	3471.91	3427.85
150000	14420.92	8176.06	6143.92	5163.66	4602.74	4250.12	4015.16	3852.50	3736.86	3653.11	3591.63	3546.05
155000	14901.62	8448.60	6348.72	5335.78	4756.17	4391.79	4149.00	3980.91	3861.42	3774.88	3711.35	3664.25
160000	15382.31	8721.13	6553.52	5507.90	4909.59	4533.46	4282.84	4109.33	3985.99	3896.65	3831.07	3782.45

AMOUNT OF LOAN	NUMBER OF YEARS IN TERM											
	13	14	15	16	17	18	19	20	25	30	35	40
$ 50	1.18	1.17	1.16	1.16	1.15	1.15	1.15	1.15	1.14	1.14	1.14	1.14
100	2.35	2.33	2.32	2.31	2.30	2.29	2.29	2.29	2.28	2.28	2.28	2.28
200	4.69	4.65	4.63	4.61	4.59	4.58	4.57	4.57	4.55	4.55	4.55	4.55
300	7.03	6.98	6.94	6.91	6.89	6.87	6.86	6.85	6.83	6.82	6.82	6.82
400	9.37	9.30	9.25	9.21	9.18	9.16	9.14	9.13	9.10	9.09	9.09	9.09
500	11.71	11.63	11.56	11.51	11.48	11.45	11.43	11.41	11.37	11.36	11.36	11.36
600	14.05	13.95	13.87	13.82	13.77	13.74	13.71	13.69	13.65	13.63	13.63	13.63
700	16.39	16.28	16.19	16.12	16.07	16.03	16.00	15.97	15.92	15.91	15.90	15.90
800	18.74	18.60	18.50	18.42	18.36	18.31	18.28	18.26	18.19	18.18	18.17	18.17
900	21.08	20.92	20.81	20.72	20.65	20.60	20.57	20.54	20.47	20.45	20.44	20.44
1000	23.42	23.25	23.12	23.02	22.95	22.89	22.85	22.82	22.74	22.72	22.72	22.71
2000	46.83	46.49	46.23	46.04	45.89	45.78	45.69	45.63	45.48	45.44	45.43	45.42
3000	70.24	69.73	69.35	69.06	68.84	68.67	68.54	68.44	68.21	68.15	68.14	68.13
4000	93.66	92.98	92.46	92.07	91.78	91.55	91.38	91.26	90.95	90.87	90.85	90.84
5000	117.07	116.22	115.58	115.09	114.72	114.44	114.23	114.07	113.68	113.58	113.56	113.55
6000	140.48	139.46	138.69	138.11	137.67	137.33	137.07	136.88	136.42	136.30	136.27	136.26
7000	163.90	162.71	161.81	161.13	160.61	160.22	159.92	159.69	159.15	159.01	158.98	158.97
8000	187.31	185.95	184.92	184.14	183.55	183.10	182.76	182.51	181.89	181.73	181.69	181.68
9000	210.72	209.19	208.03	207.16	206.50	205.99	205.61	205.32	204.62	204.44	204.40	204.38
10000	234.14	232.43	231.15	230.18	229.44	228.88	228.45	228.13	227.36	227.16	227.11	227.09
11000	257.55	255.68	254.26	253.19	252.38	251.77	251.30	250.94	250.09	249.87	249.82	249.80
12000	280.96	278.92	277.38	276.21	275.33	274.65	274.15	273.76	272.83	272.59	272.53	272.51
13000	304.38	302.16	300.49	299.23	298.27	297.54	296.99	296.57	295.56	295.30	295.24	295.22
14000	327.79	325.41	323.61	322.25	321.21	320.43	319.83	319.38	318.30	318.02	317.95	317.93
15000	351.20	348.65	346.72	345.26	344.16	343.32	342.68	342.19	341.03	340.74	340.66	340.64
16000	374.62	371.89	369.83	368.28	367.10	366.20	365.52	365.01	363.77	363.45	363.37	363.35
17000	398.03	395.13	392.95	391.30	390.04	389.09	388.37	387.82	386.51	386.17	386.08	386.05
18000	421.44	418.38	416.06	414.31	412.99	411.98	411.21	410.63	409.24	408.88	408.79	408.76
19000	444.86	441.62	439.18	437.33	435.93	434.87	434.06	433.44	431.98	431.60	431.50	431.47
20000	468.27	464.86	462.29	460.35	458.87	457.75	456.90	456.26	454.71	454.31	454.21	454.18
21000	491.68	488.11	485.41	483.37	481.82	480.64	479.75	479.07	477.45	477.03	476.92	476.89
22000	515.10	511.35	508.52	506.39	504.76	503.53	502.59	501.88	500.18	499.74	499.63	499.60
23000	538.51	534.59	531.64	529.40	527.70	526.42	525.44	524.69	522.92	522.46	522.34	522.31
24000	561.92	557.83	554.75	552.42	550.65	549.30	548.28	547.51	545.65	545.17	545.05	545.02
25000	585.34	581.08	577.86	575.43	573.59	572.19	571.13	570.32	568.39	567.89	567.76	567.73
26000	608.75	604.32	600.98	598.45	596.53	595.08	593.97	593.13	591.12	590.60	590.47	590.43
27000	632.16	627.56	624.09	621.47	619.48	617.97	616.82	615.94	613.86	613.32	613.18	613.14
28000	655.58	650.81	647.21	644.49	642.42	640.85	639.66	638.76	636.59	636.03	635.89	635.85
29000	678.99	674.05	670.32	667.50	665.37	663.74	662.51	661.57	659.33	658.75	658.60	658.56
30000	702.40	697.29	693.44	690.52	688.31	686.63	685.35	684.38	682.06	681.47	681.31	681.27
31000	725.82	720.53	716.55	713.54	711.25	709.52	708.20	707.19	704.80	704.18	704.02	703.98
32000	749.23	743.78	739.66	736.55	734.20	732.40	731.04	730.01	727.54	726.90	726.73	726.69
33000	772.64	767.02	762.78	759.57	757.14	755.29	753.89	752.82	750.27	749.61	749.44	749.40
34000	796.06	790.26	785.89	782.59	780.08	778.18	776.73	775.63	773.01	772.33	772.15	772.10
35000	819.47	813.51	809.01	805.61	803.03	801.07	799.58	798.44	795.74	795.04	794.86	794.81
37500	878.00	871.61	866.79	863.15	860.38	858.29	856.69	855.47	852.58	851.83	851.64	851.59
40000	936.54	929.72	924.58	920.69	917.74	915.50	913.80	912.51	909.42	908.62	908.41	908.36
42500	995.07	987.83	982.37	978.23	975.10	972.72	970.91	969.54	966.26	965.41	965.19	965.13
45000	1053.60	1045.93	1040.15	1035.78	1032.46	1029.94	1028.03	1026.57	1023.09	1022.20	1021.96	1021.90
47500	1112.14	1104.04	1097.94	1093.32	1089.82	1087.16	1085.14	1083.60	1079.93	1078.98	1078.74	1078.67
50000	1170.67	1162.15	1155.72	1150.86	1147.18	1144.38	1142.25	1140.63	1136.77	1135.77	1135.51	1135.45
52500	1229.20	1220.26	1213.51	1208.41	1204.54	1201.60	1199.36	1197.66	1193.61	1192.56	1192.29	1192.22
55000	1287.74	1278.36	1271.30	1265.95	1261.90	1258.82	1256.48	1254.69	1250.45	1249.35	1249.06	1248.99
57500	1346.27	1336.47	1329.08	1323.49	1319.25	1316.04	1313.59	1311.72	1307.29	1306.14	1305.84	1305.76
60000	1404.80	1394.58	1386.87	1381.03	1376.61	1373.25	1370.70	1368.76	1364.12	1362.93	1362.61	1362.53
65000	1521.87	1510.79	1502.44	1496.12	1491.33	1487.69	1484.92	1482.82	1477.80	1476.50	1476.17	1476.08
70000	1638.94	1627.01	1618.01	1611.21	1606.05	1602.13	1599.15	1596.88	1591.48	1590.08	1589.72	1589.62
75000	1756.00	1743.22	1733.58	1726.29	1720.76	1716.57	1713.37	1710.94	1705.15	1703.66	1703.27	1703.17
80000	1873.07	1859.44	1849.15	1841.38	1835.48	1831.00	1827.60	1825.01	1818.83	1817.23	1816.82	1816.71
85000	1990.14	1975.65	1964.73	1956.46	1950.20	1945.44	1941.82	1939.07	1932.51	1930.81	1930.37	1930.25
90000	2107.20	2091.86	2080.30	2071.55	2064.92	2059.88	2056.05	2053.13	2046.18	2044.39	2043.92	2043.80
95000	2224.27	2208.08	2195.87	2186.63	2179.63	2174.32	2170.27	2167.19	2159.86	2157.96	2157.47	2157.34
100000	2341.34	2324.29	2311.44	2301.72	2294.35	2288.75	2284.50	2281.26	2273.54	2271.54	2271.02	2270.89
105000	2458.40	2440.51	2427.01	2416.81	2409.07	2403.19	2398.72	2395.32	2387.21	2385.12	2384.57	2384.43
110000	2575.47	2556.72	2542.59	2531.89	2523.79	2517.63	2512.95	2509.38	2500.89	2498.69	2498.12	2497.97
115000	2692.54	2672.94	2658.16	2646.98	2638.50	2632.07	2627.17	2623.44	2614.57	2612.27	2611.67	2611.52
120000	2809.60	2789.15	2773.73	2762.06	2753.22	2746.50	2741.39	2737.51	2728.24	2725.85	2725.22	2725.06
125000	2926.67	2905.37	2889.30	2877.15	2867.94	2860.94	2855.62	2851.57	2841.92	2839.42	2838.77	2838.61
130000	3043.74	3021.58	3004.87	2992.24	2982.65	2975.38	2969.84	2965.63	2955.60	2953.00	2952.33	2952.15
135000	3160.80	3137.79	3120.44	3107.32	3097.37	3089.81	3084.07	3079.69	3069.27	3066.58	3065.88	3065.69
140000	3277.87	3254.01	3236.02	3222.41	3212.09	3204.25	3198.29	3193.76	3182.95	3180.15	3179.43	3179.24
145000	3394.94	3370.22	3351.59	3337.49	3326.81	3318.69	3312.52	3307.82	3296.63	3293.73	3292.98	3292.78
150000	3512.00	3486.44	3467.16	3452.58	3441.52	3433.13	3426.74	3421.88	3410.30	3407.31	3406.53	3406.33
155000	3629.07	3602.65	3582.73	3567.66	3556.24	3547.56	3540.97	3535.94	3523.98	3520.88	3520.08	3519.87
160000	3746.14	3718.87	3698.30	3682.75	3670.96	3662.00	3655.19	3650.01	3637.66	3634.46	3633.63	3633.41

MONTHLY AMORTIZING PAYMENTS

AMOUNT OF LOAN	NUMBER OF YEARS IN TERM											
	1	2	3	4	5	6	7	8	9	10	11	12
$ 50	4.82	2.74	2.06	1.73	1.55	1.43	1.35	1.30	1.26	1.23	1.21	1.20
100	9.63	5.47	4.11	3.46	3.09	2.85	2.70	2.59	2.51	2.46	2.42	2.39
200	19.26	10.93	8.22	6.92	6.17	5.70	5.39	5.18	5.02	4.91	4.83	4.77
300	28.88	16.40	12.33	10.37	9.26	8.55	8.08	7.76	7.53	7.37	7.24	7.15
400	38.51	21.86	16.44	13.83	12.34	11.40	10.78	10.35	10.04	9.82	9.66	9.54
500	48.14	27.32	20.55	17.29	15.42	14.25	13.47	12.93	12.55	12.27	12.07	11.92
600	57.76	32.79	24.66	20.74	18.51	17.10	16.16	15.52	15.06	14.73	14.48	14.30
700	67.39	38.25	28.77	24.20	21.59	19.95	18.86	18.10	17.57	17.18	16.90	16.69
800	77.01	43.71	32.88	27.66	24.67	22.80	21.55	20.69	20.08	19.63	19.31	19.07
900	86.64	49.18	36.99	31.11	27.76	25.65	24.24	23.27	22.58	22.09	21.72	21.45
1000	96.27	54.64	41.10	34.57	30.84	28.50	26.94	25.86	25.09	24.54	24.13	23.83
2000	192.53	109.27	82.19	69.14	61.67	56.99	53.87	51.71	50.18	49.07	48.26	47.66
3000	288.79	163.91	123.29	103.70	92.51	85.48	80.80	77.56	75.27	73.61	72.39	71.49
4000	385.05	218.54	164.38	138.27	123.34	113.97	107.73	103.42	100.36	98.14	96.52	95.32
5000	481.31	273.18	205.47	172.84	154.18	142.46	134.66	129.27	125.44	122.68	120.65	119.15
6000	577.57	327.81	246.57	207.40	185.01	170.95	161.59	155.12	150.53	147.21	144.78	142.98
7000	673.84	382.44	287.66	241.97	215.85	199.44	188.53	180.98	175.62	171.75	168.91	166.81
8000	770.10	437.08	328.76	276.54	246.68	227.94	215.46	206.83	200.71	196.28	193.04	190.64
9000	866.36	491.71	369.85	311.10	277.52	256.43	242.39	232.68	225.80	220.82	217.17	214.47
10000	962.62	546.35	410.94	345.67	308.35	284.92	269.32	258.54	250.88	245.35	241.30	238.29
11000	1058.88	600.98	452.04	380.24	339.19	313.41	296.25	284.39	275.97	269.89	265.42	262.12
12000	1155.14	655.61	493.13	414.80	370.02	341.90	323.18	310.24	301.06	294.42	289.55	285.95
13000	1251.40	710.25	534.23	449.37	400.86	370.39	350.12	336.10	326.15	318.95	313.68	309.78
14000	1347.67	764.88	575.32	483.94	431.69	398.88	377.05	361.95	351.24	343.49	337.81	333.61
15000	1443.93	819.52	616.41	518.50	462.53	427.37	403.98	387.80	376.32	368.02	361.94	357.44
16000	1540.19	874.15	657.51	553.07	493.36	455.87	430.91	413.66	401.41	392.56	386.07	381.27
17000	1636.45	928.78	698.60	587.64	524.20	484.36	457.84	439.51	426.50	417.09	410.20	405.10
18000	1732.71	983.42	739.70	622.20	555.03	512.85	484.77	465.36	451.59	441.63	434.33	428.93
19000	1828.97	1038.05	780.79	656.77	585.87	541.34	511.71	491.22	476.68	466.16	458.46	452.76
20000	1925.24	1092.69	821.88	691.34	616.70	569.83	538.64	517.07	501.76	490.70	482.59	476.58
21000	2021.50	1147.32	862.98	725.90	647.54	598.32	565.57	542.92	526.85	515.23	506.71	500.41
22000	2117.76	1201.95	904.07	760.47	678.37	626.81	592.50	568.78	551.94	539.77	530.84	524.24
23000	2214.02	1256.59	945.17	795.04	709.21	655.30	619.43	594.63	577.03	564.30	554.97	548.07
24000	2310.28	1311.22	986.26	829.60	740.04	683.80	646.36	620.48	602.12	588.83	579.10	571.90
25000	2406.54	1365.86	1027.35	864.17	770.88	712.29	673.30	646.34	627.20	613.37	603.23	595.73
26000	2502.80	1420.49	1068.45	898.74	801.71	740.78	700.23	672.19	652.29	637.90	627.36	619.56
27000	2599.07	1475.12	1109.54	933.30	832.55	769.27	727.16	698.04	677.38	662.44	651.49	643.39
28000	2695.33	1529.76	1150.64	967.87	863.38	797.76	754.09	723.90	702.47	686.97	675.62	667.21
29000	2791.59	1584.39	1191.73	1002.44	894.22	826.25	781.02	749.75	727.56	711.51	699.75	691.04
30000	2887.85	1639.03	1232.82	1037.00	925.05	854.74	807.95	775.60	752.64	736.04	723.88	714.87
31000	2984.11	1693.66	1273.92	1071.57	955.89	883.23	834.89	801.46	777.73	760.58	748.00	738.70
32000	3080.37	1748.29	1315.01	1106.14	986.72	911.73	861.82	827.31	802.82	785.11	772.13	762.53
33000	3176.64	1802.93	1356.10	1140.70	1017.56	940.22	888.75	853.16	827.91	809.65	796.26	786.36
34000	3272.90	1857.56	1397.20	1175.27	1048.39	968.71	915.68	879.02	853.00	834.18	820.39	810.19
35000	3369.16	1912.20	1438.29	1209.84	1079.23	997.20	942.61	904.87	878.08	858.71	844.52	834.02
37500	3609.81	2048.78	1541.03	1296.25	1156.31	1068.43	1009.94	969.50	940.80	920.05	904.84	893.59
40000	3850.47	2185.37	1643.76	1382.67	1233.40	1139.66	1077.27	1034.14	1003.52	981.39	965.17	953.16
42500	4091.12	2321.95	1746.50	1469.09	1310.49	1210.88	1144.60	1098.77	1066.24	1042.72	1025.49	1012.73
45000	4331.77	2458.54	1849.23	1555.50	1387.57	1282.11	1211.93	1163.40	1128.96	1104.06	1085.81	1072.31
47500	4572.43	2595.12	1951.97	1641.92	1464.66	1353.34	1279.26	1228.04	1191.68	1165.40	1146.13	1131.88
50000	4813.08	2731.71	2054.70	1728.34	1541.75	1424.57	1346.59	1292.67	1254.40	1226.73	1206.46	1191.45
52500	5053.74	2868.29	2157.44	1814.75	1618.84	1495.80	1413.92	1357.30	1317.12	1288.07	1266.78	1251.02
55000	5294.39	3004.88	2260.17	1901.17	1695.92	1567.02	1481.24	1421.94	1379.84	1349.41	1327.10	1310.59
57500	5535.04	3141.46	2362.91	1987.59	1773.01	1638.25	1548.57	1486.57	1442.56	1410.74	1387.42	1370.17
60000	5775.70	3278.05	2465.64	2074.00	1850.10	1709.48	1615.90	1551.20	1505.28	1472.08	1447.75	1429.74
65000	6257.00	3551.22	2671.11	2246.84	2004.27	1851.94	1750.56	1680.47	1630.72	1594.75	1568.39	1548.88
70000	6738.31	3824.59	2876.58	2419.67	2158.45	1994.39	1885.22	1809.74	1756.16	1717.42	1689.04	1668.03
75000	7219.62	4097.56	3082.05	2592.50	2312.62	2136.85	2019.88	1939.00	1881.60	1840.10	1809.68	1787.17
80000	7700.93	4370.73	3287.52	2765.34	2466.79	2279.31	2154.54	2068.27	2007.04	1962.77	1930.33	1906.32
85000	8182.24	4643.90	3492.99	2938.17	2620.97	2421.76	2289.19	2197.54	2132.48	2085.44	2050.97	2025.46
90000	8663.54	4917.07	3698.46	3111.00	2775.14	2564.22	2423.85	2326.80	2257.92	2208.11	2171.62	2144.61
95000	9144.85	5190.24	3903.93	3283.84	2929.32	2706.67	2558.51	2456.07	2383.36	2330.79	2292.26	2263.75
100000	9626.16	5463.41	4109.40	3456.67	3083.49	2849.13	2693.17	2585.34	2508.80	2453.46	2412.91	2382.90
105000	10107.47	5736.58	4314.87	3629.50	3237.67	2991.59	2827.83	2714.60	2634.24	2576.13	2533.55	2502.04
110000	10588.77	6009.75	4520.34	3802.34	3391.84	3134.04	2962.48	2843.87	2759.68	2698.81	2654.20	2621.18
115000	11070.08	6282.92	4725.81	3975.17	3546.02	3276.50	3097.14	2973.14	2885.12	2821.48	2774.84	2740.33
120000	11551.39	6556.09	4931.28	4148.00	3700.19	3418.96	3231.80	3102.40	3010.56	2944.15	2895.49	2859.47
125000	12032.70	6829.26	5136.75	4320.84	3854.36	3561.41	3366.46	3231.67	3136.00	3066.82	3016.13	2978.62
130000	12514.00	7102.43	5342.22	4493.67	4008.54	3703.87	3501.12	3360.94	3261.44	3189.50	3136.78	3097.76
135000	12995.31	7375.60	5547.69	4666.50	4162.71	3846.33	3635.77	3490.20	3386.88	3312.17	3257.42	3216.91
140000	13476.62	7648.77	5753.16	4839.33	4316.89	3988.78	3770.43	3619.47	3512.32	3434.84	3378.07	3336.05
145000	13957.93	7921.94	5958.62	5012.17	4471.06	4131.24	3905.09	3748.74	3637.76	3557.51	3498.71	3455.20
150000	14439.23	8195.11	6164.09	5185.00	4625.24	4273.69	4039.75	3878.00	3763.20	3680.19	3619.36	3574.34
155000	14920.54	8468.28	6369.56	5357.83	4779.41	4416.15	4174.41	4007.27	3888.64	3802.86	3740.00	3693.48
160000	15401.85	8741.45	6575.03	5530.67	4933.58	4558.61	4309.07	4136.54	4014.08	3925.53	3860.65	3812.63

MONTHLY AMORTIZING PAYMENTS 27.50%

AMOUNT OF LOAN	NUMBER OF YEARS IN TERM											
	13	14	15	16	17	18	19	20	25	30	35	40
$ 50	1.19	1.18	1.17	1.17	1.16	1.16	1.16	1.16	1.15	1.15	1.15	1.15
100	2.37	2.35	2.34	2.33	2.32	2.31	2.31	2.31	2.30	2.30	2.30	2.30
200	4.73	4.69	4.67	4.65	4.63	4.62	4.61	4.61	4.59	4.59	4.59	4.59
300	7.09	7.04	7.00	6.97	6.95	6.93	6.92	6.91	6.89	6.88	6.88	6.88
400	9.45	9.38	9.33	9.29	9.26	9.24	9.22	9.21	9.18	9.17	9.17	9.17
500	11.81	11.72	11.66	11.61	11.58	11.55	11.53	11.51	11.48	11.47	11.46	11.46
600	14.17	14.07	13.99	13.93	13.89	13.86	13.83	13.82	13.77	13.76	13.76	13.76
700	16.53	16.41	16.32	16.26	16.21	16.17	16.14	16.12	16.06	16.05	16.05	16.05
800	18.89	18.76	18.65	18.58	18.52	18.48	18.44	18.42	18.36	18.34	18.34	18.34
900	21.25	21.10	20.99	20.90	20.83	20.79	20.75	20.72	20.65	20.64	20.63	20.63
1000	23.61	23.44	23.32	23.22	23.15	23.09	23.05	23.02	22.95	22.93	22.92	22.92
2000	47.22	46.88	46.63	46.44	46.29	46.18	46.10	46.04	45.89	45.85	45.84	45.84
3000	70.82	70.32	6♦.94	69.65	69.44	69.27	69.15	69.06	68.83	68.77	68.76	68.76
4000	94.43	93.76	93.25	92.87	92.58	92.36	92.20	92.07	91.77	91.70	91.68	91.67
5000	118.03	117.19	116.56	116.09	115.73	115.45	115.25	115.09	114.72	114.62	114.60	114.59
6000	141.64	140.63	139.87	139.30	138.87	138.54	138.29	138.11	137.66	137.54	137.52	137.51
7000	165.24	164.07	163.18	162.52	162.01	161.63	161.34	161.12	160.60	160.47	160.43	160.42
8000	188.85	187.51	186.50	185.73	185.16	184.72	184.39	184.14	183.54	183.39	183.35	183.34
9000	212.45	210.94	209.81	208.95	208.30	207.81	207.44	207.16	206.49	206.31	206.27	206.26
10000	236.06	234.38	233.12	232.17	231.45	230.90	230.49	230.17	229.43	229.24	229.19	229.18
11000	259.66	257.82	256.43	255.38	254.59	253.99	253.54	253.19	252.37	252.16	252.11	252.09
12000	283.27	281.26	279.74	278.60	277.74	277.08	276.58	276.21	275.31	275.08	275.03	275.01
13000	306.87	304.69	303.05	301.82	300.88	300.17	299.63	299.22	298.25	298.01	297.94	297.93
14000	330.48	328.13	326.36	325.03	324.02	323.26	322.68	322.24	321.20	320.93	320.86	320.84
15000	354.08	351.57	349.68	348.25	347.17	346.35	345.73	345.26	344.14	343.85	343.78	343.76
16000	377.69	375.01	372.99	371.46	370.31	369.44	368.78	368.27	367.08	366.78	366.70	366.68
17000	401.29	398.44	396.30	394.68	393.46	392.53	391.82	391.29	390.02	389.70	389.62	389.60
18000	424.90	421.88	419.61	417.90	416.60	415.62	414.87	414.31	412.97	412.62	412.54	412.51
19000	448.50	445.32	442.92	441.11	439.74	438.71	437.92	437.32	435.91	435.55	435.45	435.43
20000	472.11	468.76	466.23	464.33	462.89	461.80	460.97	460.34	458.85	458.47	458.37	458.35
21000	495.71	492.19	489.54	487.55	486.03	484.89	484.02	483.36	481.79	481.39	481.29	481.26
22000	519.32	515.63	512.86	510.76	509.18	507.98	507.07	506.38	504.74	504.32	504.21	504.18
23000	542.92	539.07	536.17	533.98	532.32	531.07	530.11	529.39	527.68	527.24	527.13	527.10
24000	566.53	562.51	559.48	557.19	555.47	554.16	553.16	552.41	550.62	550.16	550.05	550.02
25000	590.14	585.94	582.79	580.41	578.61	577.25	576.21	575.42	573.56	573.09	572.96	572.93
26000	613.74	609.38	606.10	603.63	601.75	600.34	599.26	598.44	596.50	596.01	595.88	595.85
27000	637.35	632.82	629.41	626.84	624.90	623.42	622.31	621.46	619.45	618.93	618.80	618.77
28000	660.95	656.26	652.72	650.06	648.04	646.51	645.35	644.47	642.39	641.86	641.72	641.68
29000	684.56	679.69	676.04	673.28	671.19	669.60	668.40	667.49	665.33	664.78	664.64	664.60
30000	708.16	703.13	699.35	696.49	694.33	692.69	691.45	690.51	688.27	687.70	687.56	687.52
31000	731.77	726.57	722.66	719.71	717.47	715.78	714.50	713.52	711.22	710.63	710.47	710.44
32000	755.37	750.01	745.97	742.92	740.62	738.87	737.55	736.54	734.16	733.55	733.39	733.35
33000	778.98	773.44	769.28	766.14	763.76	761.96	760.60	759.56	757.10	756.47	756.31	756.27
34000	802.58	796.88	792.59	789.36	786.91	785.05	783.64	782.57	780.04	779.40	779.23	779.19
35000	826.19	820.32	815.90	812.57	810.05	808.14	806.69	805.59	802.98	802.32	802.15	802.10
37500	885.20	878.91	874.18	870.61	867.91	865.87	864.31	863.13	860.34	859.63	859.44	859.40
40000	944.21	937.51	932.46	928.65	925.77	923.59	921.93	920.68	917.70	916.93	916.74	916.69
42500	1003.23	996.10	990.74	986.69	983.63	981.31	979.55	978.22	975.05	974.24	974.04	973.98
45000	1062.24	1054.70	1049.02	1044.73	1041.49	1039.04	1037.17	1035.76	1032.41	1031.55	1031.33	1031.27
47500	1121.25	1113.29	1107.30	1102.78	1099.35	1096.76	1094.79	1093.30	1089.76	1088.86	1088.63	1088.57
50000	1180.27	1171.88	1165.58	1160.82	1157.21	1154.49	1152.42	1150.84	1147.12	1146.17	1145.92	1145.86
52500	1239.28	1230.48	1223.85	1218.86	1215.08	1212.21	1210.04	1208.38	1204.47	1203.48	1203.22	1203.15
55000	1298.29	1289.07	1282.13	1276.90	1272.94	1269.93	1267.66	1265.93	1261.83	1260.78	1260.51	1260.45
57500	1357.30	1347.66	1340.41	1334.94	1330.80	1327.66	1325.28	1323.47	1319.19	1318.09	1317.81	1317.74
60000	1416.32	1406.26	1398.69	1392.98	1388.66	1385.38	1382.90	1381.01	1376.54	1375.40	1375.11	1375.03
65000	1534.34	1523.45	1515.25	1509.06	1504.38	1500.83	1498.14	1496.09	1491.25	1490.02	1489.70	1489.62
70000	1652.37	1640.63	1631.80	1625.14	1620.10	1616.28	1613.38	1611.18	1605.96	1604.63	1604.29	1604.20
75000	1770.40	1757.82	1748.36	1741.22	1735.82	1731.73	1728.62	1726.26	1720.68	1719.25	1718.88	1718.79
80000	1888.42	1875.01	1864.92	1857.30	1851.54	1847.17	1843.86	1841.35	1835.39	1833.86	1833.47	1833.37
85000	2006.45	1992.20	1981.48	1973.38	1967.26	1962.62	1959.10	1956.43	1950.10	1948.47	1948.07	1947.96
90000	2124.47	2109.39	2098.03	2089.46	2082.98	2078.07	2074.34	2071.51	2064.81	2063.10	2062.66	2062.54
95000	2242.50	2226.57	2214.59	2205.55	2198.70	2193.52	2189.58	2186.60	2179.52	2177.71	2177.25	2177.13
100000	2360.53	2343.76	2331.15	2321.63	2314.42	2308.97	2304.83	2301.68	2294.23	2292.33	2291.84	2291.72
105000	2478.55	2460.95	2447.70	2437.71	2430.15	2424.41	2420.07	2416.76	2408.94	2406.95	2406.43	2406.30
110000	2596.58	2578.14	2564.26	2553.79	2545.87	2539.86	2535.31	2531.85	2523.66	2521.56	2521.02	2520.89
115000	2714.60	2695.32	2680.82	2669.87	2661.59	2655.31	2650.55	2646.93	2638.37	2636.18	2635.62	2635.47
120000	2832.63	2812.51	2797.38	2785.95	2777.31	2770.76	2765.79	2762.02	2753.08	2750.79	2750.21	2750.06
125000	2950.66	2929.70	2913.93	2902.03	2893.03	2886.21	2881.03	2877.10	2867.79	2865.41	2864.80	2864.64
130000	3068.68	3046.89	3030.49	3018.11	3008.75	3001.66	2996.27	2992.18	2982.50	2980.03	2979.39	2979.23
135000	3186.71	3164.08	3147.05	3134.19	3124.47	3117.10	3111.51	3107.27	3097.21	3094.64	3093.98	3093.81
140000	3304.73	3281.26	3263.60	3250.27	3240.19	3232.55	3226.75	3222.35	3211.92	3209.26	3208.57	3208.40
145000	3422.76	3398.45	3380.16	3366.34	3355.91	3348.00	3342.00	3337.43	3326.64	3323.87	3323.17	3322.98
150000	3540.79	3515.64	3496.72	3482.44	3471.63	3463.45	3457.24	3452.52	3441.35	3438.49	3437.76	3437.57
155000	3658.81	3632.83	3613.27	3598.52	3587.35	3578.90	3572.48	3567.60	3556.06	3553.11	3552.35	3552.16
160000	3776.84	3750.01	3729.83	3714.60	3703.08	3694.34	3687.72	3682.69	3670.77	3667.72	3666.94	3666.74

183

MONTHLY AMORTIZING PAYMENTS

AMOUNT OF LOAN	NUMBER OF YEARS IN TERM											
	1	2	3	4	5	6	7	8	9	10	11	12
$ 50	4.82	2.74	2.07	1.74	1.55	1.44	1.36	1.31	1.27	1.24	1.22	1.21
100	9.64	5.48	4.13	3.48	3.10	2.87	2.71	2.61	2.53	2.48	2.44	2.41
200	19.28	10.96	8.25	6.95	6.20	5.73	5.42	5.21	5.06	4.95	4.87	4.81
300	28.92	16.43	12.37	10.42	9.30	8.60	8.13	7.81	7.58	7.42	7.30	7.21
400	38.56	21.91	16.50	13.89	12.40	11.46	10.84	10.41	10.11	9.89	9.73	9.61
500	48.20	27.39	20.62	17.36	15.50	14.33	13.55	13.02	12.64	12.36	12.16	12.01
600	57.84	32.86	24.74	20.83	18.60	17.19	16.26	15.62	15.16	14.83	14.59	14.42
700	67.47	38.34	28.87	24.30	21.69	20.06	18.97	18.22	17.69	17.31	17.02	16.82
800	77.11	43.81	32.99	27.77	24.79	22.92	21.68	20.82	20.22	19.78	19.46	19.22
900	86.75	49.29	37.11	31.24	27.89	25.79	24.39	23.43	22.74	22.25	21.89	21.62
1000	96.39	54.77	41.23	34.71	30.99	28.65	27.10	26.03	25.27	24.72	24.32	24.02
2000	192.77	109.53	82.46	69.42	61.98	57.30	54.20	52.05	50.53	49.44	48.63	48.04
3000	289.16	164.29	123.69	104.13	92.96	85.95	81.29	78.08	75.80	74.15	72.95	72.06
4000	385.54	219.05	164.92	138.84	123.95	114.60	108.39	104.10	101.06	98.87	97.26	96.08
5000	481.92	273.81	206.15	173.55	154.93	143.25	135.48	130.12	126.32	123.58	121.58	120.09
6000	578.31	328.57	247.38	208.26	185.92	171.90	162.58	156.15	151.59	148.30	145.89	144.11
7000	674.69	383.33	288.61	242.97	216.90	200.55	189.68	182.17	176.85	173.01	170.20	168.13
8000	771.07	438.09	329.83	277.68	247.89	229.20	216.77	208.20	202.12	197.73	194.52	192.15
9000	867.46	492.86	371.06	312.39	278.87	257.84	243.87	234.22	227.38	222.44	218.83	216.17
10000	963.84	547.62	412.29	347.10	309.86	286.49	270.96	260.24	252.64	247.16	243.15	240.18
11000	1060.23	602.38	453.52	381.81	340.84	315.14	298.06	286.27	277.91	271.88	267.46	264.20
12000	1156.61	657.14	494.75	416.52	371.83	343.79	325.16	312.29	303.17	296.59	291.78	288.22
13000	1252.99	711.90	535.98	451.23	402.81	372.44	352.25	338.31	328.44	321.31	316.09	312.24
14000	1349.38	766.66	577.21	485.93	433.80	401.09	379.35	364.34	353.70	346.02	340.40	336.26
15000	1445.76	821.42	618.43	520.64	464.78	429.74	406.44	390.36	378.96	370.74	364.72	360.27
16000	1542.14	876.18	659.66	555.35	495.77	458.39	433.54	416.39	404.23	395.45	389.03	384.29
17000	1638.53	930.95	700.89	590.06	526.75	487.04	460.64	442.41	429.49	420.17	413.35	408.31
18000	1734.91	985.71	742.12	624.77	557.74	515.68	487.73	468.43	454.76	444.88	437.66	432.33
19000	1831.30	1040.47	783.35	659.48	588.72	544.33	514.83	494.46	480.02	469.60	461.98	456.35
20000	1927.68	1095.23	824.58	694.19	619.71	572.98	541.92	520.48	505.28	494.31	486.29	480.36
21000	2024.06	1149.99	865.81	728.90	650.69	601.63	569.02	546.50	530.55	519.03	510.60	504.38
22000	2120.45	1204.75	907.04	763.61	681.68	630.28	596.12	572.53	555.81	543.75	534.92	528.40
23000	2216.83	1259.51	948.26	798.32	712.66	658.93	623.21	598.55	581.08	568.46	559.23	552.42
24000	2313.21	1314.27	989.49	833.03	743.65	687.58	650.31	624.58	606.34	593.18	583.55	576.43
25000	2409.60	1369.03	1030.72	867.74	774.63	716.23	677.40	650.60	631.60	617.89	607.86	600.45
26000	2505.98	1423.80	1071.95	902.45	805.62	744.87	704.50	676.62	656.87	642.61	632.18	624.47
27000	2602.37	1478.56	1113.18	937.15	836.60	773.52	731.60	702.65	682.13	667.32	656.49	648.49
28000	2698.75	1533.32	1154.41	971.86	867.59	802.17	758.69	728.67	707.40	692.04	680.80	672.51
29000	2795.13	1588.08	1195.64	1006.57	898.58	830.82	785.79	754.69	732.66	716.75	705.12	696.52
30000	2891.52	1642.84	1236.86	1041.28	929.56	859.47	812.88	780.72	757.92	741.47	729.43	720.54
31000	2987.90	1697.60	1278.09	1075.99	960.55	888.12	839.98	806.74	783.19	766.18	753.75	744.56
32000	3084.28	1752.36	1319.32	1110.70	991.53	916.77	867.08	832.77	808.45	790.90	778.06	768.58
33000	3180.67	1807.12	1360.55	1145.41	1022.52	945.42	894.17	858.79	833.72	815.62	802.38	792.60
34000	3277.05	1861.89	1401.78	1180.12	1053.50	974.07	921.27	884.81	858.98	840.33	826.69	816.61
35000	3373.44	1916.65	1443.01	1214.83	1084.49	1002.71	948.36	910.84	884.24	865.05	851.00	840.63
37500	3614.39	2053.55	1546.08	1301.60	1161.95	1074.34	1016.10	975.90	947.40	926.84	911.79	900.68
40000	3855.35	2190.45	1649.15	1388.37	1239.41	1145.96	1083.84	1040.96	1010.56	988.62	972.57	960.72
42500	4096.31	2327.36	1752.22	1475.15	1316.87	1217.58	1151.58	1106.02	1073.72	1050.41	1033.36	1020.77
45000	4337.27	2464.26	1855.29	1561.92	1394.34	1289.20	1219.32	1171.08	1136.88	1112.20	1094.15	1080.81
47500	4578.23	2601.16	1958.37	1648.69	1471.80	1360.82	1287.06	1236.13	1200.04	1173.99	1154.93	1140.86
50000	4819.19	2738.06	2061.44	1735.47	1549.26	1432.45	1354.80	1301.19	1263.20	1235.78	1215.72	1200.90
52500	5060.15	2874.97	2164.51	1822.24	1626.73	1504.07	1422.54	1366.25	1326.36	1297.57	1276.50	1260.94
55000	5301.11	3011.87	2267.58	1909.01	1704.19	1575.69	1490.28	1431.31	1389.52	1359.36	1337.29	1320.99
57500	5542.07	3148.77	2370.65	1995.79	1781.65	1647.31	1558.02	1496.37	1452.68	1421.14	1398.07	1381.03
60000	5783.03	3285.68	2473.72	2082.56	1859.12	1718.94	1625.76	1561.43	1515.84	1482.93	1458.86	1441.08
65000	6264.95	3559.48	2679.87	2256.11	2014.04	1862.18	1761.24	1691.55	1642.16	1606.51	1580.43	1561.17
70000	6746.87	3833.29	2886.01	2429.65	2168.97	2005.42	1896.72	1821.67	1768.48	1730.09	1702.00	1681.25
75000	7228.78	4107.09	3092.15	2603.20	2323.89	2148.67	2032.20	1951.79	1894.80	1853.67	1823.57	1801.35
80000	7710.70	4380.90	3298.30	2776.74	2478.82	2291.91	2167.68	2081.91	2021.12	1977.24	1945.14	1921.44
85000	8192.62	4654.71	3504.44	2950.29	2633.74	2435.16	2303.16	2212.03	2147.44	2100.82	2066.72	2041.53
90000	8674.54	4928.51	3710.58	3123.84	2788.67	2578.40	2438.64	2342.15	2273.76	2224.40	2188.29	2161.62
95000	9156.46	5202.32	3916.73	3297.38	2943.60	2721.64	2574.12	2472.26	2400.08	2347.97	2309.86	2281.71
100000	9638.38	5476.12	4122.87	3470.93	3098.52	2864.89	2709.60	2602.38	2526.40	2471.55	2431.43	2401.79
105000	10120.30	5749.93	4329.01	3644.48	3253.45	3008.13	2845.08	2732.50	2652.72	2595.13	2553.00	2521.88
110000	10602.21	6023.74	4535.16	3818.02	3408.37	3151.38	2980.56	2862.62	2779.04	2718.71	2674.57	2641.97
115000	11084.13	6297.54	4741.30	3991.57	3563.30	3294.62	3116.04	2992.74	2905.36	2842.28	2796.14	2762.06
120000	11566.05	6571.35	4947.44	4165.11	3718.23	3437.87	3251.52	3122.86	3031.68	2965.86	2917.71	2882.15
125000	12047.97	6845.15	5153.59	4338.66	3873.15	3581.11	3387.00	3252.98	3158.00	3089.44	3039.29	3002.24
130000	12529.89	7118.96	5359.73	4512.21	4028.08	3724.35	3522.48	3383.10	3284.32	3213.02	3160.86	3122.33
135000	13011.81	7392.77	5565.87	4685.75	4183.00	3867.60	3657.96	3513.22	3410.64	3336.59	3282.43	3242.42
140000	13493.73	7666.57	5772.01	4859.30	4337.93	4010.84	3793.44	3643.33	3536.96	3460.17	3404.00	3362.51
145000	13975.64	7940.38	5978.16	5032.85	4492.86	4154.09	3928.92	3773.45	3663.28	3583.75	3525.57	3482.60
150000	14457.56	8214.18	6184.30	5206.39	4647.78	4297.33	4064.40	3903.57	3789.60	3707.33	3647.14	3602.69
155000	14939.48	8487.99	6390.44	5379.94	4802.71	4440.57	4199.88	4033.69	3915.92	3830.90	3768.71	3722.78
160000	15421.40	8761.79	6596.59	5553.48	4957.63	4583.82	4335.36	4163.81	4042.24	3954.48	3890.28	3842.87

AMOUNT OF LOAN	NUMBER OF YEARS IN TERM											
	13	14	15	16	17	18	19	20	25	30	35	40
$ 50	1.19	1.19	1.18	1.18	1.17	1.17	1.17	1.17	1.16	1.16	1.16	1.16
100	2.38	2.37	2.36	2.35	2.34	2.33	2.33	2.33	2.32	2.32	2.32	2.32
200	4.76	4.73	4.71	4.69	4.67	4.66	4.66	4.65	4.63	4.63	4.63	4.63
300	7.14	7.09	7.06	7.03	7.01	6.99	6.98	6.97	6.95	6.94	6.94	6.94
400	9.52	9.46	9.41	9.37	9.34	9.32	9.31	9.29	9.26	9.26	9.26	9.26
500	11.90	11.82	11.76	11.71	11.68	11.65	11.63	11.62	11.58	11.57	11.57	11.57
600	14.28	14.18	14.11	14.05	14.01	13.98	13.96	13.94	13.89	13.88	13.88	13.88
700	16.66	16.55	16.46	16.40	16.35	16.31	16.28	16.26	16.21	16.20	16.19	16.19
800	19.04	18.91	18.81	18.74	18.68	18.64	18.61	18.58	18.52	18.51	18.51	18.51
900	21.42	21.27	21.16	21.08	21.02	20.97	20.93	20.90	20.84	20.82	20.82	20.82
1000	23.80	23.64	23.51	23.42	23.35	23.30	23.26	23.23	23.15	23.14	23.13	23.13
2000	47.60	47.27	47.02	46.84	46.70	46.59	46.51	46.45	46.30	46.27	46.26	46.26
3000	71.40	70.90	70.53	70.25	70.04	69.88	69.76	69.67	69.45	69.40	69.38	69.38
4000	95.19	94.54	94.04	93.67	93.39	93.17	93.01	92.89	92.60	92.53	92.51	92.51
5000	118.99	118.17	117.55	117.08	116.73	116.46	116.26	116.11	115.75	115.66	115.64	115.63
6000	142.79	141.80	141.06	140.50	140.08	139.76	139.52	139.33	138.90	138.79	138.76	138.76
7000	166.59	165.43	164.57	163.91	163.42	163.05	162.77	162.55	162.05	161.92	161.89	161.88
8000	190.38	189.07	188.08	187.33	186.77	186.34	186.02	185.77	185.20	185.05	185.02	185.01
9000	214.18	212.70	211.58	210.74	210.11	209.63	209.27	209.00	208.35	208.19	208.14	208.13
10000	237.98	236.33	235.09	234.16	233.46	232.92	232.52	232.22	231.50	231.32	231.27	231.26
11000	261.78	259.96	258.60	257.58	256.80	256.22	255.77	255.44	254.65	254.45	254.40	254.38
12000	285.57	283.60	282.11	280.99	280.15	279.51	279.03	278.66	277.80	277.58	277.52	277.51
13000	309.37	307.23	305.62	304.41	303.49	302.80	302.28	301.88	300.95	300.71	300.65	300.64
14000	333.17	330.86	329.13	327.82	326.84	326.09	325.53	325.10	324.10	323.84	323.78	323.76
15000	356.97	354.49	352.64	351.24	350.18	349.38	348.78	348.32	347.24	346.97	346.90	346.89
16000	380.76	378.13	376.15	374.65	373.53	372.68	372.03	371.54	370.39	370.10	370.03	370.01
17000	404.56	401.76	399.65	398.07	396.87	395.97	395.28	394.76	393.54	393.23	393.16	393.14
18000	428.36	425.39	423.16	421.48	420.22	419.26	418.54	417.99	416.69	416.37	416.28	416.26
19000	452.16	449.02	446.67	444.90	443.56	442.55	441.79	441.21	439.84	439.50	439.41	439.39
20000	475.95	472.66	470.18	468.32	466.91	465.84	465.04	464.43	462.99	462.63	462.54	462.51
21000	499.75	496.29	493.69	491.73	490.25	489.14	488.29	487.65	486.14	485.76	485.66	485.64
22000	523.55	519.92	517.20	515.15	513.60	512.43	511.54	510.87	509.29	508.89	508.79	508.76
23000	547.35	543.55	540.71	538.56	536.94	535.72	534.79	534.09	532.44	532.02	531.92	531.89
24000	571.14	567.19	564.22	561.98	560.29	559.01	558.05	557.31	555.59	555.15	555.04	555.01
25000	594.94	590.82	587.72	585.39	583.63	582.30	581.30	580.53	578.74	578.28	578.17	578.14
26000	618.74	614.45	611.23	608.81	606.98	605.60	604.55	603.76	601.89	601.42	601.30	601.27
27000	642.54	638.08	634.74	632.22	630.32	628.89	627.80	626.98	625.04	624.55	624.42	624.39
28000	666.33	661.72	658.25	655.64	653.67	652.18	651.05	650.20	648.19	647.68	647.55	647.52
29000	690.13	685.35	681.76	679.06	677.01	675.47	674.30	673.42	671.34	670.81	670.68	670.64
30000	713.93	708.98	705.27	702.47	700.36	698.76	697.56	696.64	694.48	693.94	693.80	693.77
31000	737.73	732.61	728.78	725.89	723.71	722.06	720.81	719.86	717.63	717.07	716.93	716.89
32000	761.52	756.25	752.29	749.30	747.05	745.35	744.06	743.08	740.78	740.20	740.06	740.02
33000	785.32	779.88	775.79	772.72	770.40	768.64	767.31	766.30	763.93	763.33	763.18	763.14
34000	809.12	803.51	799.30	796.13	793.74	791.93	790.56	789.52	787.08	786.46	786.31	786.27
35000	832.92	827.14	822.81	819.55	817.09	815.22	813.81	812.75	810.23	809.60	809.43	809.39
37500	892.41	886.23	881.58	878.09	875.45	873.45	871.94	870.80	868.10	867.42	867.25	867.21
40000	951.90	945.31	940.36	936.63	933.81	931.68	930.07	928.85	925.98	925.25	925.07	925.02
42500	1011.40	1004.39	999.13	995.17	992.17	989.91	988.20	986.90	983.85	983.08	982.88	982.83
45000	1070.89	1063.47	1057.90	1053.70	1050.54	1048.14	1046.33	1044.96	1041.72	1040.91	1040.70	1040.65
47500	1130.38	1122.55	1116.67	1112.24	1108.90	1106.37	1104.46	1103.01	1099.60	1098.74	1098.52	1098.46
50000	1189.88	1181.63	1175.44	1170.78	1167.26	1164.60	1162.59	1161.06	1157.47	1156.56	1156.33	1156.27
52500	1249.37	1240.71	1234.22	1229.32	1225.63	1222.83	1220.72	1219.12	1215.34	1214.39	1214.15	1214.09
55000	1308.86	1299.80	1292.99	1287.86	1283.99	1281.06	1278.85	1277.17	1273.22	1272.22	1271.97	1271.90
57500	1368.36	1358.88	1351.76	1346.40	1342.35	1339.29	1336.98	1335.22	1331.09	1330.05	1329.78	1329.72
60000	1427.85	1417.96	1410.53	1404.94	1400.71	1397.52	1395.11	1393.27	1388.96	1387.87	1387.60	1387.53
65000	1546.84	1536.12	1528.07	1522.01	1517.44	1513.98	1511.36	1509.38	1504.71	1503.53	1503.23	1503.16
70000	1665.83	1654.28	1645.62	1639.09	1634.17	1630.44	1627.62	1625.49	1620.46	1619.19	1618.86	1618.78
75000	1784.81	1772.45	1763.16	1756.17	1750.89	1746.90	1743.88	1741.59	1736.20	1734.84	1734.50	1734.41
80000	1903.80	1890.61	1880.71	1873.25	1867.62	1863.36	1860.14	1857.70	1851.95	1850.50	1850.13	1850.04
85000	2022.79	2008.77	1998.25	1990.33	1984.34	1979.82	1976.40	1973.80	1967.70	1966.15	1965.76	1965.66
90000	2141.77	2126.94	2115.79	2107.40	2101.07	2096.28	2092.66	2089.91	2083.44	2081.81	2081.40	2081.29
95000	2260.76	2245.10	2233.34	2224.48	2217.80	2212.74	2208.91	2206.02	2199.19	2197.47	2197.03	2196.92
100000	2379.75	2363.26	2350.88	2341.56	2334.52	2329.20	2325.17	2322.12	2314.94	2313.12	2312.66	2312.54
105000	2498.74	2481.42	2468.43	2458.64	2451.25	2445.66	2441.43	2438.23	2430.68	2428.78	2428.29	2428.17
110000	2617.72	2599.59	2585.97	2575.71	2567.97	2562.12	2557.69	2554.33	2546.43	2544.43	2543.93	2543.80
115000	2736.71	2717.75	2703.51	2692.79	2684.70	2678.58	2673.95	2670.44	2662.18	2660.09	2659.56	2659.43
120000	2855.70	2835.91	2821.06	2809.87	2801.42	2795.04	2790.21	2786.54	2777.92	2775.74	2775.19	2775.05
125000	2974.69	2954.08	2938.60	2926.95	2918.15	2911.50	2906.47	2902.65	2893.67	2891.40	2890.83	2890.68
130000	3093.67	3072.24	3056.14	3044.02	3034.88	3027.96	3022.72	3018.76	3009.42	3007.06	3006.46	3006.31
135000	3212.66	3190.40	3173.69	3161.10	3151.60	3144.42	3138.98	3134.86	3125.16	3122.71	3122.09	3121.93
140000	3331.65	3308.56	3291.23	3278.18	3268.33	3260.88	3255.24	3250.97	3240.91	3238.37	3237.72	3237.56
145000	3450.63	3426.73	3408.78	3395.26	3385.05	3377.34	3371.50	3367.07	3356.66	3354.02	3353.36	3353.19
150000	3569.62	3544.89	3526.32	3512.33	3501.78	3493.80	3487.76	3483.18	3472.40	3469.68	3468.99	3468.81
155000	3688.61	3663.05	3643.86	3629.41	3618.51	3610.26	3604.02	3599.28	3588.15	3585.34	3584.62	3584.44
160000	3807.60	3781.22	3761.41	3746.49	3735.23	3726.72	3720.27	3715.39	3703.90	3700.99	3700.26	3700.07

MONTHLY AMORTIZING PAYMENTS

AMOUNT OF LOAN	NUMBER OF YEARS IN TERM											
	1	2	3	4	5	6	7	8	9	10	11	12
$ 50	4.83	2.75	2.07	1.75	1.56	1.45	1.37	1.31	1.28	1.25	1.23	1.22
100	9.66	5.49	4.14	3.49	3.12	2.89	2.73	2.62	2.55	2.49	2.45	2.43
200	19.31	10.98	8.28	6.98	6.23	5.77	5.46	5.24	5.09	4.98	4.90	4.85
300	28.96	16.47	12.41	10.46	9.35	8.65	8.18	7.86	7.64	7.47	7.35	7.27
400	38.61	21.96	16.55	13.95	12.46	11.53	10.91	10.48	10.18	9.96	9.80	9.69
500	48.26	27.45	20.69	17.43	15.57	14.41	13.64	13.10	12.73	12.45	12.25	12.11
600	57.91	32.94	24.82	20.92	18.69	17.29	16.36	15.72	15.27	14.94	14.70	14.53
700	67.56	38.43	28.96	24.40	21.80	20.17	19.09	18.34	17.81	17.43	17.15	16.95
800	77.21	43.92	33.10	27.89	24.91	23.05	21.81	20.96	20.36	19.92	19.60	19.37
900	86.86	49.40	37.23	31.37	28.03	25.93	24.54	23.58	22.90	22.41	22.05	21.79
1000	96.51	54.89	41.37	34.86	31.14	28.81	27.27	26.20	25.45	24.90	24.50	24.21
2000	193.02	109.78	82.73	69.71	62.28	57.62	54.53	52.39	50.89	49.80	49.00	48.42
3000	289.52	164.67	124.10	104.56	93.41	86.43	81.79	78.59	76.33	74.70	73.50	72.63
4000	386.03	219.56	165.46	139.41	124.55	115.23	109.05	104.78	101.77	99.59	98.00	96.83
5000	482.53	274.45	206.82	174.27	155.68	144.04	136.31	130.98	127.21	124.49	122.50	121.04
6000	579.04	329.34	248.19	209.12	186.82	172.85	163.57	157.17	152.65	149.39	147.00	145.25
7000	675.55	384.22	289.55	243.97	217.96	201.65	190.83	183.37	178.09	174.28	171.50	169.46
8000	772.05	439.11	330.91	278.82	249.09	230.46	218.09	209.56	203.53	199.18	196.00	193.66
9000	868.56	494.00	372.28	313.67	280.23	259.27	245.35	235.76	228.97	224.08	220.50	217.87
10000	965.06	548.89	413.64	348.53	311.36	288.07	272.61	261.95	254.41	248.97	245.00	242.08
11000	1061.57	603.78	455.00	383.38	342.50	316.88	299.87	288.15	279.85	273.87	269.50	266.28
12000	1158.08	658.67	496.37	418.23	373.63	345.69	327.13	314.34	305.29	298.77	294.00	290.49
13000	1254.58	713.56	537.73	453.08	404.77	374.49	354.39	340.54	330.73	323.66	318.50	314.70
14000	1351.09	768.44	579.10	487.94	435.91	403.30	381.65	366.73	356.17	348.56	343.00	338.91
15000	1447.59	823.33	620.46	522.79	467.04	432.11	408.92	392.93	381.61	373.46	367.50	363.11
16000	1544.10	878.22	661.82	557.64	498.18	460.91	436.18	419.12	407.05	398.35	392.00	387.32
17000	1640.61	933.11	703.19	592.49	529.31	489.72	463.44	445.31	432.49	423.25	416.50	411.53
18000	1737.11	988.00	744.55	627.34	560.45	518.53	490.70	471.51	457.93	448.15	441.00	435.74
19000	1833.62	1042.89	785.91	662.20	591.59	547.33	517.96	497.70	483.37	473.04	465.50	459.94
20000	1930.12	1097.77	827.28	697.05	622.72	576.14	545.22	523.90	508.81	497.94	490.00	484.15
21000	2026.63	1152.66	868.64	731.90	653.86	604.95	572.48	550.09	534.25	522.84	514.50	508.36
22000	2123.14	1207.55	910.00	766.75	684.99	633.75	599.74	576.29	559.69	547.73	539.00	532.56
23000	2219.64	1262.44	951.37	801.60	716.13	662.56	627.00	602.48	585.13	572.63	563.50	556.77
24000	2316.15	1317.33	992.73	836.46	747.26	691.37	654.26	628.68	610.57	597.53	588.00	580.98
25000	2412.65	1372.22	1034.09	871.31	778.40	720.17	681.52	654.87	636.01	622.43	612.50	605.19
26000	2509.16	1427.11	1075.46	906.16	809.54	748.98	708.78	681.07	661.45	647.32	637.00	629.39
27000	2605.67	1481.99	1116.82	941.01	840.67	777.79	736.04	707.26	686.90	672.22	661.50	653.60
28000	2702.17	1536.88	1158.19	975.87	871.81	806.60	763.30	733.46	712.34	697.12	686.00	677.81
29000	2798.68	1591.77	1199.55	1010.72	902.94	835.40	790.56	759.65	737.78	722.01	710.50	702.02
30000	2895.18	1646.66	1240.91	1045.57	934.08	864.21	817.83	785.85	763.22	746.91	735.00	726.22
31000	2991.69	1701.55	1282.28	1080.42	965.22	893.02	845.09	812.04	788.66	771.81	759.50	750.43
32000	3088.20	1756.44	1323.64	1115.27	996.35	921.82	872.35	838.23	814.10	796.70	784.00	774.64
33000	3184.70	1811.33	1365.00	1150.13	1027.49	950.63	899.61	864.43	839.54	821.60	808.50	798.84
34000	3281.21	1866.21	1406.37	1184.98	1058.62	979.44	926.87	890.62	864.98	846.50	833.00	823.05
35000	3377.71	1921.10	1447.73	1219.83	1089.76	1008.24	954.13	916.82	890.42	871.39	857.50	847.26
37500	3618.98	2058.32	1551.14	1306.96	1167.60	1080.26	1022.28	982.31	954.02	933.64	918.75	907.78
40000	3860.24	2195.54	1654.55	1394.09	1245.44	1152.28	1090.43	1047.79	1017.62	995.88	980.00	968.30
42500	4101.51	2332.77	1757.96	1481.22	1323.28	1224.29	1158.58	1113.28	1081.22	1058.12	1041.25	1028.81
45000	4342.77	2469.99	1861.37	1568.35	1401.12	1296.31	1226.74	1178.77	1144.82	1120.36	1102.50	1089.33
47500	4584.04	2607.21	1964.78	1655.48	1478.96	1368.33	1294.89	1244.25	1208.42	1182.60	1163.75	1149.85
50000	4825.30	2744.43	2068.18	1742.61	1556.80	1440.34	1363.04	1309.74	1272.02	1244.85	1225.00	1210.37
52500	5066.57	2881.65	2171.59	1829.74	1634.64	1512.36	1431.19	1375.23	1335.63	1307.09	1286.25	1270.89
55000	5307.83	3018.87	2275.00	1916.87	1712.48	1584.38	1499.34	1440.71	1399.23	1369.33	1347.50	1331.40
57500	5549.10	3156.09	2378.41	2004.00	1790.31	1656.40	1567.49	1506.20	1462.83	1431.57	1408.75	1391.92
60000	5790.36	3293.31	2481.82	2091.13	1868.15	1728.41	1635.65	1571.69	1526.43	1493.81	1470.00	1452.44
65000	6272.89	3567.76	2688.64	2265.39	2023.83	1872.45	1771.95	1702.66	1653.63	1618.30	1592.50	1573.48
70000	6755.42	3842.20	2895.46	2439.66	2179.51	2016.48	1908.25	1833.63	1780.83	1742.78	1715.00	1694.51
75000	7237.95	4116.64	3102.27	2613.92	2335.19	2160.51	2044.56	1964.61	1908.03	1867.27	1837.50	1815.55
80000	7720.48	4391.08	3309.09	2788.18	2490.87	2304.55	2180.86	2095.58	2035.24	1991.75	1960.00	1936.59
85000	8203.01	4665.53	3515.91	2962.44	2646.55	2448.58	2317.16	2226.55	2162.44	2116.23	2082.50	2057.62
90000	8685.54	4939.97	3722.73	3136.70	2802.23	2592.62	2453.47	2357.53	2289.64	2240.72	2204.99	2178.66
95000	9168.07	5214.41	3929.55	3310.96	2957.91	2736.65	2589.77	2488.50	2416.84	2365.20	2327.49	2299.70
100000	9650.60	5488.85	4136.36	3485.22	3113.59	2880.68	2726.07	2619.47	2544.04	2489.69	2449.99	2420.73
105000	10133.13	5763.30	4343.18	3659.48	3269.27	3024.72	2862.38	2750.45	2671.25	2614.17	2572.49	2541.77
110000	10615.66	6037.74	4550.00	3833.74	3424.95	3168.75	2998.68	2881.42	2798.45	2738.65	2694.99	2662.80
115000	11098.19	6312.18	4756.82	4008.00	3580.62	3312.79	3134.98	3012.39	2925.65	2863.14	2817.49	2783.84
120000	11580.72	6586.62	4963.64	4182.26	3736.30	3456.82	3271.29	3143.37	3052.85	2987.62	2939.99	2904.88
125000	12063.25	6861.07	5170.45	4356.52	3891.98	3600.85	3407.59	3274.34	3180.05	3112.11	3062.49	3025.91
130000	12545.78	7135.51	5377.27	4530.78	4047.66	3744.89	3543.89	3405.31	3307.25	3236.59	3184.99	3146.95
135000	13028.31	7409.95	5584.09	4705.04	4203.34	3888.92	3680.20	3536.29	3434.46	3361.07	3307.49	3267.99
140000	13510.84	7684.39	5790.91	4879.31	4359.02	4032.96	3816.50	3667.26	3561.66	3485.56	3429.99	3389.02
145000	13993.37	7958.84	5997.73	5053.57	4514.70	4176.99	3952.80	3798.23	3688.86	3610.04	3552.49	3510.06
150000	14475.90	8233.28	6204.54	5227.83	4670.38	4321.02	4089.11	3929.21	3816.06	3734.53	3674.99	3631.10
155000	14958.43	8507.72	6411.36	5402.09	4826.06	4465.06	4225.41	4060.18	3943.26	3859.01	3797.49	3752.13
160000	15440.96	8782.16	6618.18	5576.35	4981.74	4609.09	4361.71	4191.15	4070.47	3983.49	3919.99	3873.17

AMOUNT OF LOAN	NUMBER OF YEARS IN TERM											
	13	14	15	16	17	18	19	20	25	30	35	40
$ 50	1.20	1.20	1.19	1.19	1.18	1.18	1.18	1.18	1.17	1.17	1.17	1.17
100	2.40	2.39	2.38	2.37	2.36	2.35	2.35	2.35	2.34	2.34	2.34	2.34
200	4.80	4.77	4.75	4.73	4.71	4.70	4.70	4.69	4.68	4.67	4.67	4.67
300	7.20	7.15	7.12	7.09	7.07	7.05	7.04	7.03	7.01	7.01	7.01	7.01
400	9.60	9.54	9.49	9.45	9.42	9.40	9.39	9.38	9.35	9.34	9.34	9.34
500	12.00	11.92	11.86	11.81	11.78	11.75	11.73	11.72	11.68	11.67	11.67	11.67
600	14.40	14.30	14.23	14.17	14.13	14.10	14.08	14.06	14.02	14.01	14.01	14.01
700	16.80	16.68	16.60	16.54	16.49	16.45	16.42	16.40	16.35	16.34	16.34	16.34
800	19.20	19.07	18.97	18.90	18.84	18.80	18.77	18.75	18.69	18.68	18.67	18.67
900	21.60	21.45	21.34	21.26	21.20	21.15	21.11	21.09	21.03	21.01	21.01	21.01
1000	24.00	23.83	23.71	23.62	23.55	23.50	23.46	23.43	23.36	23.34	23.34	23.34
2000	47.99	47.66	47.42	47.24	47.10	46.99	46.92	46.86	46.72	46.68	46.67	46.67
3000	71.98	71.49	71.12	70.85	70.64	70.49	70.37	70.28	70.07	70.02	70.01	70.01
4000	95.97	95.32	94.83	94.47	94.19	93.98	93.83	93.71	93.43	93.36	93.34	93.34
5000	119.96	119.14	118.54	118.08	117.74	117.48	117.28	117.13	116.79	116.70	116.68	116.67
6000	143.95	142.97	142.24	141.70	141.28	140.97	140.74	140.56	140.14	140.04	140.01	140.01
7000	167.94	166.80	165.95	165.31	164.83	164.47	164.19	163.99	163.50	163.38	163.35	163.34
8000	191.93	190.63	189.66	188.93	188.38	187.96	187.65	187.41	186.86	186.72	186.68	186.67
9000	215.92	214.46	213.36	212.54	211.92	211.46	211.10	210.84	210.21	210.06	210.02	210.01
10000	239.91	238.28	237.07	236.16	235.47	234.95	234.56	234.26	233.57	233.40	233.35	233.34
11000	263.90	262.11	260.78	259.77	259.01	258.44	258.01	257.69	256.93	256.74	256.69	256.68
12000	287.89	285.94	284.48	283.39	282.56	281.94	281.47	281.11	280.28	280.07	280.02	280.01
13000	311.88	309.77	308.19	307.00	306.11	305.43	304.92	304.54	303.64	303.41	303.36	303.34
14000	335.87	333.60	331.89	330.62	329.65	328.93	328.38	327.97	326.99	326.75	326.69	326.68
15000	359.86	357.42	355.60	354.23	353.20	352.42	351.83	351.39	350.35	350.09	350.03	350.01
16000	383.85	381.25	379.31	377.85	376.75	375.92	375.29	374.82	373.71	373.43	373.36	373.34
17000	407.84	405.08	403.01	401.46	400.29	399.41	398.75	398.24	397.06	396.77	396.70	396.68
18000	431.83	428.91	426.72	425.08	423.84	422.91	422.20	421.67	420.42	420.11	420.03	420.01
19000	455.82	452.73	450.43	448.69	447.39	446.40	445.66	445.09	443.78	443.45	443.37	443.35
20000	479.81	476.56	474.13	472.31	470.93	469.89	469.11	468.52	467.13	466.79	466.70	466.68
21000	503.80	500.39	497.84	495.92	494.48	493.39	492.57	491.95	490.49	490.13	490.04	490.01
22000	527.79	524.22	521.55	519.54	518.02	516.88	516.02	515.37	513.85	513.47	513.37	513.35
23000	551.78	548.05	545.25	543.15	541.57	540.38	539.48	538.80	537.20	536.80	536.70	536.68
24000	575.77	571.87	568.96	566.77	565.12	563.87	562.93	562.22	560.56	560.14	560.04	560.01
25000	599.76	595.70	592.66	590.38	588.66	587.37	586.39	585.65	583.92	583.48	583.37	583.35
26000	623.75	619.53	616.37	614.00	612.21	610.86	609.84	609.07	607.27	606.82	606.71	606.68
27000	647.74	643.36	640.08	637.61	635.76	634.36	633.30	632.50	630.63	630.16	630.04	630.01
28000	671.73	667.19	663.78	661.23	659.30	657.85	656.75	655.93	653.98	653.50	653.38	653.35
29000	695.72	691.01	687.49	684.84	682.85	681.35	680.21	679.35	677.34	676.84	676.71	676.68
30000	719.71	714.84	711.20	708.46	706.40	704.84	703.66	702.78	700.70	700.18	700.05	700.02
31000	743.70	738.67	734.90	732.07	729.94	728.33	727.12	726.20	724.05	723.52	723.38	723.35
32000	767.69	762.50	758.61	755.69	753.49	751.83	750.58	749.63	747.41	746.86	746.72	746.68
33000	791.68	786.33	782.32	779.31	777.03	775.32	774.03	773.05	770.77	770.20	770.05	770.02
34000	815.67	810.15	806.02	802.92	800.58	798.82	797.49	796.48	794.12	793.53	793.39	793.35
35000	839.66	833.98	829.73	826.53	824.13	822.31	820.94	819.91	817.48	816.87	816.72	816.68
37500	899.63	893.55	888.99	885.57	882.99	881.05	879.58	878.47	875.87	875.22	875.06	875.02
40000	959.61	953.12	948.26	944.61	941.86	939.78	938.22	937.03	934.26	933.57	933.40	933.35
42500	1019.58	1012.69	1007.53	1003.65	1000.73	998.52	996.86	995.60	992.65	991.92	991.73	991.69
45000	1079.56	1072.26	1066.79	1062.68	1059.59	1057.26	1055.49	1054.16	1051.04	1050.27	1050.07	1050.02
47500	1139.53	1131.83	1126.06	1121.72	1118.46	1115.99	1114.13	1112.73	1109.43	1108.61	1108.41	1108.36
50000	1199.51	1191.40	1185.32	1180.76	1177.32	1174.73	1172.77	1171.29	1167.83	1166.96	1166.74	1166.69
52500	1259.48	1250.97	1244.59	1239.80	1236.19	1233.47	1231.41	1229.86	1226.22	1225.31	1225.08	1225.02
55000	1319.46	1310.54	1303.86	1298.84	1295.05	1292.20	1290.05	1288.42	1284.61	1283.66	1283.42	1283.36
57500	1379.43	1370.11	1363.12	1357.87	1353.92	1350.94	1348.69	1346.98	1343.00	1342.00	1341.75	1341.69
60000	1439.41	1429.68	1422.39	1416.91	1412.79	1409.67	1407.32	1405.55	1401.39	1400.35	1400.09	1400.03
65000	1559.36	1548.82	1540.92	1534.99	1530.52	1527.15	1524.60	1522.68	1518.17	1517.05	1516.77	1516.70
70000	1679.31	1667.96	1659.45	1653.06	1648.25	1644.62	1641.88	1639.81	1634.95	1633.74	1633.44	1633.36
75000	1799.26	1787.10	1777.98	1771.14	1765.98	1762.09	1759.15	1756.93	1751.74	1750.44	1750.11	1750.03
80000	1919.21	1906.24	1896.52	1889.21	1883.71	1879.56	1876.43	1874.06	1868.52	1867.13	1866.79	1866.70
85000	2039.16	2025.37	2015.05	2007.29	2001.45	1997.04	1993.71	1991.19	1985.30	1983.83	1983.46	1983.37
90000	2159.11	2144.51	2133.58	2125.36	2119.18	2114.51	2110.98	2108.32	2102.08	2100.53	2100.14	2100.04
95000	2279.06	2263.65	2252.11	2243.44	2236.91	2231.98	2228.26	2225.45	2218.86	2217.22	2216.81	2216.71
100000	2399.01	2382.79	2370.64	2361.52	2354.64	2349.45	2345.54	2342.58	2335.65	2333.92	2333.48	2333.37
105000	2518.96	2501.93	2489.18	2479.59	2472.37	2466.93	2462.81	2459.71	2452.43	2450.61	2450.16	2450.04
110000	2638.91	2621.07	2607.71	2597.67	2590.10	2584.40	2580.09	2576.83	2569.21	2567.31	2566.83	2566.71
115000	2758.86	2740.21	2726.24	2715.74	2707.84	2701.87	2697.37	2693.96	2685.99	2684.00	2683.50	2683.38
120000	2878.81	2859.35	2844.77	2833.82	2825.57	2819.34	2814.64	2811.09	2802.77	2800.70	2800.18	2800.05
125000	2998.76	2978.49	2963.30	2951.89	2943.30	2936.82	2931.92	2928.22	2919.56	2917.39	2916.85	2916.72
130000	3118.71	3097.63	3081.84	3069.97	3061.03	3054.29	3049.20	3045.35	3036.34	3034.09	3033.53	3033.39
135000	3238.66	3216.77	3200.37	3188.04	3178.76	3171.76	3166.47	3162.48	3153.12	3150.79	3150.20	3150.05
140000	3358.61	3335.91	3318.90	3306.12	3296.50	3289.23	3283.75	3279.61	3269.90	3267.48	3266.87	3266.72
145000	3478.56	3455.05	3437.43	3424.20	3414.23	3406.71	3401.03	3396.73	3386.69	3384.18	3383.55	3383.39
150000	3598.51	3574.19	3555.96	3542.27	3531.96	3524.18	3518.30	3513.86	3503.47	3500.87	3500.22	3500.06
155000	3718.46	3693.33	3674.50	3660.35	3649.69	3641.65	3635.58	3630.99	3620.25	3617.57	3616.90	3616.73
160000	3838.41	3812.47	3793.03	3778.42	3767.42	3759.12	3752.86	3748.12	3737.03	3734.26	3733.57	3733.40

MONTHLY AMORTIZING PAYMENTS

AMOUNT OF LOAN	NUMBER OF YEARS IN TERM											
	1	2	3	4	5	6	7	8	9	10	11	12
$ 50	4.84	2.76	2.08	1.75	1.57	1.45	1.38	1.32	1.29	1.26	1.24	1.22
100	9.67	5.51	4.15	3.50	3.13	2.90	2.75	2.64	2.57	2.51	2.47	2.44
200	19.33	11.01	8.30	7.00	6.26	5.80	5.49	5.28	5.13	5.02	4.94	4.88
300	28.99	16.51	12.45	10.50	9.39	8.69	8.23	7.91	7.69	7.53	7.41	7.32
400	38.66	22.01	16.60	14.00	12.52	11.59	10.98	10.55	10.25	10.04	9.88	9.76
500	48.32	27.51	20.75	17.50	15.65	14.49	13.72	13.19	12.81	12.54	12.35	12.20
600	57.98	33.01	24.90	21.00	18.78	17.38	16.46	15.82	15 38	15.05	14.82	14.64
700	67.64	38.52	29.05	24.50	21.91	20.28	19.20	18.46	17.94	17.56	17.29	17.08
800	77.31	44.02	33.20	28.00	25.03	23.18	21.95	21.10	20.50	20.07	19.75	19.52
900	86.97	49.52	37.35	31.50	28.16	26.07	24.69	23.73	23.06	22.58	22.22	21.96
1000	96.63	55.02	41.50	35.00	31.29	28.97	27.43	26.37	25.62	25.08	24.69	24.40
2000	193.26	110.04	83.00	70.00	62.58	57.94	54.86	52.74	51.24	50.16	49.38	48.80
3000	289.89	165.05	124.50	104.99	93.87	86.90	82.28	79.10	76.86	75.24	74.06	73.20
4000	386.52	220.07	166.00	139.99	125.15	115.87	109.71	105.47	102.47	100.32	98.75	97.59
5000	483.15	275.08	207.50	174.98	156.44	144.83	137.13	131.83	128.09	125.40	123.43	121.99
6000	579.78	330.10	249.00	209.98	187.73	173.80	164.56	158.20	153.71	150.48	148.12	146.39
7000	676.40	385.12	290.50	244.97	219.01	202.76	191.99	184.57	179.33	175.55	172.81	170.78
8000	773.03	440.13	332.00	279.97	250.30	231.73	219.41	210.93	204.94	200.63	197.49	195.18
9000	869.66	495.15	373.49	314.96	281.59	260.69	246.84	237.30	230.56	225.71	222.18	219.58
10000	966.29	550.16	414.99	349.96	312.87	289.66	274.26	263.66	256.18	250.79	246.86	243.98
11000	1062.92	605.18	456.49	384.95	344.16	318.62	301.69	290.03	281.79	275.87	271.55	268.37
12000	1159.55	660.20	497.99	419.95	375.45	347.59	329.11	316.40	307.41	300.95	296.24	292.77
13000	1256.17	715.21	539.49	454.94	406.73	376.55	356.54	342.76	333.03	326.03	320.92	317.17
14000	1352.80	770.23	580.99	489.94	438.02	405.52	383.97	369.13	358.65	351.10	345.61	341.56
15000	1449.43	825.24	622.49	524.94	469.31	434.48	411.39	395.49	384.26	376.18	370.29	365.96
16000	1546.06	880.26	663.99	559.93	500.59	463.45	438.82	421.86	409.88	401.26	394.98	390.36
17000	1642.69	935.28	705.48	594.93	531.88	492.41	466.24	448.23	435.50	426.34	419.67	414.75
18000	1739.32	990.29	746.98	629.92	563.17	521.38	493.67	474.59	461.12	451.42	444.35	439.15
19000	1835.94	1045.31	788.48	664.92	594.45	550.34	521.10	500.96	486.73	476.50	469.04	463.55
20000	1932.57	1100.32	829.98	699.91	625.74	579.31	548.52	527.32	512.35	501.58	493.72	487.95
21000	2029.20	1155.34	871.48	734.91	657.03	608.27	575.95	553.69	537.97	526.65	518.41	512.34
22000	2125.83	1210.36	912.98	769.90	688.31	637.24	603.37	580.06	563.58	551.73	543.10	536.74
23000	2222.46	1265.37	954.48	804.90	719.60	666.20	630.80	606.42	589.20	576.81	567.78	561.14
24000	2319.09	1320.39	995.98	839.89	750.89	695.17	658.22	632.79	614.82	601.89	592.47	585.53
25000	2415.71	1375.40	1037.47	874.89	782.18	724.13	685.65	659.15	640.44	626.97	617.15	609.93
26000	2512.34	1430.42	1078.97	909.88	813.46	753.10	713.08	685.52	666.05	652.05	641.84	634.33
27000	2608.97	1485.44	1120.47	944.88	844.75	782.06	740.50	711.89	691.67	677.13	666.52	658.72
28000	2705.60	1540.45	1161.97	979.87	876.04	811.03	767.93	738.25	717.29	702.20	691.21	683.12
29000	2802.23	1595.47	1203.47	1014.87	907.32	839.99	795.35	764.62	742.90	727.28	715.90	707.52
30000	2898.86	1650.48	1244.97	1049.87	938.61	868.96	822.78	790.98	768.52	752.36	740.58	731.92
31000	2995.48	1705.50	1286.47	1084.86	969.90	897.92	850.21	817.35	794.14	777.44	765.27	756.31
32000	3092.11	1760.52	1327.97	1119.86	1001.18	926.89	877.63	843.72	819.76	802.52	789.95	780.71
33000	3188.74	1815.53	1369.46	1154.85	1032.47	955.85	905.06	870.08	845.37	827.60	814.64	805.11
34000	3285.37	1870.55	1410.96	1189.85	1063.76	984.82	932.48	896.45	870.99	852.68	839.33	829.50
35000	3382.00	1925.56	1452.46	1224.84	1095.04	1013.79	959.91	922.81	896.61	877.75	864.01	853.90
37500	3623.57	2063.10	1556.21	1312.33	1173.26	1086.20	1028.47	988.73	960.65	940.45	925.73	914.89
40000	3865.14	2200.64	1659.96	1399.82	1251.48	1158.61	1097.04	1054.64	1024.69	1003.15	987.44	975.89
42500	4106.71	2338.18	1763.70	1487.31	1329.69	1231.02	1165.60	1120.56	1088.74	1065.84	1049.16	1036.88
45000	4348.28	2475.72	1867.45	1574.80	1407.91	1303.44	1234.17	1186.47	1152.78	1128.54	1110.87	1097.87
47500	4589.85	2613.26	1971.20	1662.28	1486.13	1375.85	1302.73	1252.39	1216.82	1191.24	1172.59	1158.86
50000	4831.42	2750.80	2074.94	1749.77	1564.35	1448.26	1371.30	1318.30	1280.87	1253.93	1234.30	1219.86
52500	5072.99	2888.34	2178.69	1837.26	1642.56	1520.68	1439.86	1384.22	1344.91	1316.63	1296.02	1280.85
55000	5314.56	3025.88	2282.44	1924.75	1720.78	1593.09	1508.42	1450.13	1408.95	1379.32	1357.73	1341.84
57500	5556.13	3163.42	2386.18	2012.24	1799.00	1665.50	1576.99	1516.05	1473.00	1442.02	1419.45	1402.83
60000	5797.71	3300.96	2489.93	2099.73	1877.21	1737.91	1645.55	1581.96	1537.04	1504.72	1481.16	1463.83
65000	6280.85	3576.04	2697.42	2274.70	2033.65	1882.74	1782.68	1713.79	1665.12	1630.11	1604.59	1585.81
70000	6763.99	3851.12	2904.92	2449.68	2190.08	2027.57	1919.81	1845.62	1793.21	1755.50	1728.02	1707.80
75000	7247.13	4126.20	3112.41	2624.66	2346.52	2172.39	2056.94	1977.45	1921.30	1880.90	1851.45	1829.78
80000	7730.27	4401.28	3319.91	2799.63	2502.95	2317.22	2194.07	2109.28	2049.38	2006.29	1974.88	1951.77
85000	8213.41	4676.36	3527.40	2974.61	2659.38	2462.04	2331.20	2241.11	2177.47	2131.68	2098.31	2073.75
90000	8696.56	4951.44	3734.89	3149.59	2815.82	2606.87	2468.33	2372.94	2305.56	2257.07	2221.74	2195.74
95000	9179.70	5226.52	3942.39	3324.56	2972.25	2751.69	2605.46	2504.77	2433.64	2382.47	2345.17	2317.72
100000	9662.84	5501.60	4149.88	3499.54	3128.69	2896.52	2742.59	2636.60	2561.73	2507.86	2468.60	2439.71
105000	10145.98	5776.68	4357.38	3674.52	3285.12	3041.35	2879.72	2768.43	2689.81	2633.25	2592.03	2561.69
110000	10629.12	6051.76	4564.87	3849.49	3441.55	3186.17	3016.84	2900.26	2817.90	2758.64	2715.46	2683.68
115000	11112.26	6326.84	4772.36	4024.47	3597.99	3331.00	3153.97	3032.09	2945.99	2884.04	2838.89	2805.66
120000	11595.41	6601.92	4979.86	4199.45	3754.42	3475.82	3291.10	3163.92	3074.07	3009.43	2962.31	2927.65
125000	12078.55	6877.00	5187.35	4374.42	3910.86	3620.65	3428.23	3295.75	3202.16	3134.82	3085.74	3049.63
130000	12561.69	7152.08	5394.84	4549.40	4067.29	3765.47	3565.36	3427.58	3330.24	3260.22	3209.17	3171.62
135000	13044.83	7427.16	5602.34	4724.38	4223.73	3910.30	3702.49	3559.41	3458.33	3385.61	3332.60	3293.60
140000	13527.97	7702.24	5809.83	4899.35	4380.16	4055.13	3839.62	3691.24	3586.42	3511.00	3456.03	3415.59
145000	14011.11	7977.32	6017.33	5074.33	4536.59	4199.95	3976.75	3823.07	3714.50	3636.39	3579.46	3537.57
150000	14494.26	8252.40	6224.82	5249.31	4693.03	4344.78	4113.88	3954.90	3842.59	3761.79	3702.89	3659.56
155000	14977.40	8527.48	6432.31	5424.28	4849.46	4489.60	4251.01	4086.73	3970.68	3887.18	3826.32	3781.54
160000	15460.54	8802.56	6639.81	5599.26	5005.90	4634.43	4388.13	4218.56	4098.76	4012.57	3949.75	3903.53

AMOUNT OF LOAN	NUMBER OF YEARS IN TERM											
	13	14	15	16	17	18	19	20	25	30	35	40
$ 50	1.21	1.21	1.20	1.20	1.19	1.19	1.19	1.19	1.18	1.18	1.18	1.18
100	2.42	2.41	2.40	2.39	2.38	2.37	2.37	2.37	2.36	2.36	2.36	2.36
200	4.84	4.81	4.79	4.77	4.75	4.74	4.74	4.73	4.72	4.71	4.71	4.71
300	7.26	7.21	7.18	7.15	7.13	7.11	7.10	7.09	7.07	7.07	7.07	7.07
400	9.68	9.61	9.57	9.53	9.50	9.48	9.47	9.46	9.43	9.42	9.42	9.42
500	12.10	12.02	11.96	11.91	11.88	11.85	11.83	11.82	11.79	11.78	11.78	11.78
600	14.51	14.42	14.35	14.29	14.25	14.22	14.20	14.18	14.14	14.13	14.13	14.13
700	16.93	16.82	16.74	16.68	16.63	16.59	16.57	16.55	16.50	16.49	16.49	16.48
800	19.35	19.22	19.13	19.06	19.00	18.96	18.93	18.91	18.86	18.84	18.84	18.84
900	21.77	21.63	21.52	21.44	21.38	21.33	21.30	21.27	21.21	21.20	21.19	21.19
1000	24.19	24.03	23.91	23.82	23.75	23.70	23.66	23.64	23.57	23.55	23.55	23.55
2000	48.37	48.05	47.81	47.63	47.50	47.40	47.32	47.27	47.13	47.10	47.09	47.09
3000	72.55	72.08	71.72	71.45	71.25	71.10	70.98	70.90	70.70	70.65	70.63	70.63
4000	96.74	96.10	95.62	95.26	95.00	94.79	94.64	94.53	94.26	94.19	94.18	94.17
5000	120.92	120.12	119.53	119.08	118.74	118.49	118.30	118.16	117.82	117.74	117.72	117.71
6000	145.10	144.15	143.43	142.89	142.49	142.19	141.96	141.79	141.39	141.29	141.26	141.26
7000	169.29	168.17	167.34	166.71	166.24	165.89	165.62	165.42	164.95	164.83	164.81	164.80
8000	193.47	192.19	191.24	190.52	189.99	189.58	189.28	189.05	188.51	188.38	188.35	188.34
9000	217.65	216.22	215.14	214.34	213.73	213.28	212.94	212.68	212.08	211.93	211.89	211.88
10000	241.83	240.24	239.05	238.15	237.48	236.98	236.60	236.31	235.64	235.48	235.44	235.42
11000	266.02	264.26	262.95	261.97	261.23	260.67	260.26	259.94	259.20	259.02	258.98	258.97
12000	290.20	288.29	286.86	285.78	284.98	284.37	283.91	283.57	282.77	282.57	282.52	282.51
13000	314.38	312.31	310.76	309.60	308.73	308.07	307.57	307.20	306.33	306.11	306.06	306.05
14000	338.57	336.33	334.67	333.41	332.47	331.77	331.23	330.83	329.90	329.66	329.61	329.59
15000	362.75	360.36	358.57	357.23	356.22	355.46	354.89	354.46	353.46	353.21	353.15	353.13
16000	386.93	384.38	382.47	381.04	379.97	379.16	378.55	378.09	377.02	376.76	376.69	376.68
17000	411.12	408.40	406.38	404.86	403.72	402.86	402.21	401.72	400.59	400.31	400.24	400.22
18000	435.30	432.43	430.28	428.67	427.46	426.56	425.87	425.35	424.15	423.85	423.78	423.76
19000	459.48	456.45	454.19	452.49	451.21	450.25	449.53	448.98	447.71	447.40	447.32	447.30
20000	483.66	480.48	478.09	476.30	474.96	473.95	473.19	472.61	471.28	470.95	470.87	470.84
21000	507.85	504.50	502.00	500.12	498.71	497.65	496.85	496.24	494.84	494.49	494.41	494.39
22000	532.03	528.52	525.90	523.93	522.46	521.34	520.51	519.87	518.40	518.04	517.95	517.93
23000	556.21	552.55	549.80	547.75	546.20	545.04	544.17	543.50	541.97	541.59	541.49	541.47
24000	580.40	576.57	573.71	571.56	569.95	568.74	567.82	567.13	565.53	565.13	565.04	565.01
25000	604.58	600.59	597.61	595.38	593.70	592.44	591.48	590.77	589.09	588.68	588.58	588.55
26000	628.76	624.62	621.52	619.19	617.45	616.13	615.14	614.40	612.66	612.23	612.12	612.10
27000	652.94	648.64	645.42	643.01	641.19	639.83	638.80	638.03	636.22	635.77	635.67	635.64
28000	677.13	672.66	669.33	666.82	664.94	663.53	662.46	661.66	659.79	659.32	659.21	659.18
29000	701.31	696.69	693.23	690.64	688.69	687.22	686.12	685.29	683.35	682.87	682.75	682.72
30000	725.49	720.71	717.13	714.45	712.44	710.92	709.78	708.92	706.91	706.42	706.30	706.26
31000	749.68	744.73	741.04	738.27	736.19	734.62	733.44	732.55	730.48	729.96	729.84	729.81
32000	773.86	768.76	764.94	762.08	759.93	758.32	757.10	756.18	754.04	753.51	753.38	753.35
33000	798.04	792.78	788.85	785.90	783.68	782.01	780.76	779.81	777.60	777.06	776.92	776.89
34000	822.23	816.80	812.75	809.71	807.43	805.71	804.42	803.44	801.17	800.61	800.47	800.43
35000	846.41	840.83	836.66	833.53	831.18	829.41	828.07	827.07	824.73	824.15	824.01	823.97
37500	906.87	900.89	896.42	893.07	890.55	888.65	887.22	886.15	883.64	883.02	882.87	882.83
40000	967.32	960.95	956.18	952.60	949.92	947.89	946.37	945.22	942.55	941.89	941.73	941.68
42500	1027.78	1021.00	1015.94	1012.14	1009.29	1007.14	1005.52	1004.30	1001.46	1000.76	1000.58	1000.54
45000	1088.24	1081.06	1075.70	1071.68	1068.65	1066.38	1064.67	1063.37	1060.37	1059.62	1059.44	1059.39
47500	1148.69	1141.12	1135.46	1131.21	1128.02	1125.62	1123.81	1122.45	1119.27	1118.49	1118.30	1118.25
50000	1209.15	1201.18	1195.22	1190.75	1187.39	1184.87	1182.96	1181.53	1178.18	1177.36	1177.16	1177.10
52500	1269.61	1261.24	1254.98	1250.29	1246.76	1244.11	1242.11	1240.60	1237.09	1236.23	1236.01	1235.96
55000	1330.07	1321.30	1314.74	1309.83	1306.13	1303.35	1301.26	1299.68	1296.00	1295.09	1294.87	1294.81
57500	1390.52	1381.36	1374.50	1369.36	1365.50	1362.60	1360.41	1358.75	1354.91	1353.96	1353.73	1353.67
60000	1450.98	1441.42	1434.26	1428.90	1424.87	1421.84	1419.55	1417.83	1413.82	1412.83	1412.59	1412.52
65000	1571.90	1561.53	1553.79	1547.98	1543.61	1540.32	1537.85	1535.98	1531.64	1530.57	1530.30	1530.23
70000	1692.81	1681.65	1673.31	1667.05	1662.35	1658.81	1656.14	1654.13	1649.46	1648.30	1648.02	1647.94
75000	1813.73	1801.77	1792.83	1786.13	1781.09	1777.30	1774.44	1772.29	1767.27	1766.04	1765.73	1765.65
80000	1934.64	1921.89	1912.35	1905.20	1899.83	1895.78	1892.74	1890.44	1885.09	1883.77	1883.45	1883.36
85000	2055.56	2042.00	2031.87	2024.27	2018.57	2014.27	2011.03	2008.59	2002.91	2001.51	2001.16	2001.07
90000	2176.47	2162.12	2151.39	2143.35	2137.30	2132.76	2129.33	2126.74	2120.73	2119.24	2118.88	2118.78
95000	2297.38	2282.24	2270.91	2262.42	2256.04	2251.24	2247.62	2244.89	2238.54	2236.98	2236.59	2236.49
100000	2418.30	2402.36	2390.44	2381.50	2374.78	2369.73	2365.92	2363.05	2356.35	2354.71	2354.31	2354.20
105000	2539.21	2522.47	2509.96	2500.57	2493.52	2488.21	2484.21	2481.20	2474.18	2472.45	2472.02	2471.91
110000	2660.13	2642.59	2629.48	2619.65	2612.26	2606.70	2602.51	2599.35	2592.00	2590.18	2589.74	2589.62
115000	2781.04	2762.71	2749.00	2738.72	2731.00	2725.19	2720.81	2717.50	2709.82	2707.92	2707.45	2707.33
120000	2901.96	2882.83	2868.52	2857.80	2849.74	2843.67	2839.10	2835.65	2827.63	2825.66	2825.17	2825.04
125000	3022.87	3002.94	2988.04	2976.87	2968.48	2962.16	2957.40	2953.81	2945.45	2943.39	2942.88	2942.75
130000	3143.79	3123.06	3107.57	3095.95	3087.22	3080.64	3075.69	3071.96	3063.27	3061.13	3060.60	3060.46
135000	3264.70	3243.18	3227.09	3215.02	3205.95	3199.13	3193.99	3190.11	3181.09	3178.86	3178.31	3178.17
140000	3385.62	3363.30	3346.61	3334.10	3324.69	3317.62	3312.28	3308.26	3298.91	3296.60	3296.03	3295.88
145000	3506.53	3483.41	3466.13	3453.17	3443.43	3436.10	3430.58	3426.41	3416.72	3414.33	3413.74	3413.59
150000	3627.45	3603.53	3585.65	3572.25	3562.17	3554.59	3548.88	3544.57	3534.54	3532.07	3531.46	3531.30
155000	3748.36	3723.65	3705.17	3691.32	3680.91	3673.08	3667.17	3662.72	3652.36	3649.80	3649.17	3649.01
160000	3869.28	3843.77	3824.69	3810.39	3799.65	3791.56	3785.47	3780.87	3770.18	3767.54	3766.89	3766.72

MONTHLY AMORTIZING PAYMENTS

AMOUNT OF LOAN	NUMBER OF YEARS IN TERM											
	1	2	3	4	5	6	7	8	9	10	11	12
$ 50	4.84	2.76	2.09	1.76	1.58	1.46	1.38	1.33	1.29	1.27	1.25	1.23
100	9.68	5.52	4.17	3.52	3.15	2.92	2.76	2.66	2.58	2.53	2.49	2.46
200	19.36	11.03	8.33	7.03	6.29	5.83	5.52	5.31	5.16	5.06	4.98	4.92
300	29.03	16.55	12.50	10.55	9.44	8.74	8.28	7.97	7.74	7.58	7.47	7.38
400	38.71	22.06	16.66	14.06	12.58	11.65	11.04	10.62	10.32	10.11	9.95	9.84
500	48.38	27.58	20.82	17.57	15.72	14.57	13.80	13.27	12.90	12.64	12.44	12.30
600	58.06	33.09	24.99	21.09	18.87	17.48	16.56	15.93	15.48	15.16	14.93	14.76
700	67.73	38.61	29.15	24.60	22.01	20.39	19.32	18.58	18.06	17.69	17.42	17.22
800	77.41	44.12	33.31	28.12	25.16	23.30	22.08	21.24	20.64	20.21	19.90	19.67
900	87.08	49.63	37.48	31.63	28.30	26.22	24.84	23.89	23.22	22.74	22.39	22.13
1000	96.76	55.15	41.64	35.14	31.44	29.13	27.60	26.54	25.80	25.27	24.88	24.59
2000	193.51	110.29	83.27	70.28	62.88	58.25	55.19	53.08	51.59	50.53	49.75	49.18
3000	290.26	165.44	124.91	105.42	94.32	87.38	82.78	79.62	77.39	75.79	74.62	73.77
4000	387.01	220.58	166.54	140.56	125.76	116.50	110.37	106.16	103.18	101.05	99.49	98.35
5000	483.76	275.72	208.18	175.70	157.20	145.62	137.96	132.69	128.98	126.31	124.37	122.94
6000	580.51	330.87	249.81	210.84	188.63	174.75	165.55	159.23	154.77	151.57	149.24	147.53
7000	677.26	386.01	291.44	245.98	220.07	203.87	193.14	185.77	180.57	176.83	174.11	172.11
8000	774.01	441.15	333.08	281.12	251.51	233.00	220.74	212.31	206.36	202.09	198.98	196.70
9000	870.76	496.30	374.71	316.25	282.95	262.12	248.33	238.84	232.16	227.35	223.86	221.29
10000	967.51	551.44	416.35	351.39	314.39	291.24	275.92	265.38	257.95	252.61	248.73	245.88
11000	1064.26	606.58	457.98	386.53	345.82	320.37	303.51	291.92	283.74	277.87	273.60	270.46
12000	1161.01	661.73	499.62	421.67	377.26	349.49	331.10	318.46	309.54	303.13	298.47	295.05
13000	1257.77	716.87	541.25	456.81	408.70	378.62	358.69	345.00	335.33	328.39	323.35	319.64
14000	1354.52	772.02	582.88	491.95	440.14	407.74	386.28	371.53	361.13	353.65	348.22	344.22
15000	1451.27	827.16	624.52	527.09	471.58	436.86	413.88	398.07	386.92	378.92	373.09	368.81
16000	1548.02	882.30	666.15	562.23	503.02	465.99	441.47	424.61	412.72	404.18	397.96	393.40
17000	1644.77	937.45	707.79	597.37	534.45	495.11	469.06	451.15	438.51	429.44	422.83	417.99
18000	1741.52	992.59	749.42	632.50	565.89	524.23	496.65	477.68	464.31	454.70	447.71	442.57
19000	1838.27	1047.73	791.05	667.64	597.33	553.36	524.24	504.22	490.10	479.96	472.58	467.16
20000	1935.02	1102.88	832.69	702.78	628.77	582.48	551.83	530.76	515.89	505.22	497.45	491.75
21000	2031.77	1158.02	874.32	737.92	660.21	611.61	579.42	557.30	541.69	530.48	522.32	516.33
22000	2128.52	1213.16	915.96	773.06	691.64	640.73	607.01	583.83	567.48	555.74	547.20	540.92
23000	2225.27	1268.31	957.59	808.20	723.08	669.85	634.61	610.37	593.28	581.00	572.07	565.51
24000	2322.02	1323.45	999.23	843.34	754.52	698.98	662.20	636.91	619.07	606.26	596.94	590.10
25000	2418.77	1378.60	1040.86	878.48	785.96	728.10	689.79	663.45	644.87	631.52	621.81	614.68
26000	2515.53	1433.74	1082.49	913.61	817.40	757.23	717.38	689.99	670.66	656.78	646.69	639.27
27000	2612.28	1488.88	1124.13	948.75	848.84	786.35	744.97	716.52	696.46	682.04	671.56	663.86
28000	2709.03	1544.03	1165.76	983.89	880.27	815.47	772.56	743.06	722.25	707.30	696.43	688.44
29000	2805.78	1599.17	1207.40	1019.03	911.71	844.60	800.15	769.60	748.05	732.57	721.30	713.03
30000	2902.53	1654.31	1249.03	1054.17	943.15	873.72	827.75	796.14	773.84	757.83	746.17	737.62
31000	2999.28	1709.46	1290.66	1089.31	974.59	902.85	855.34	822.67	799.63	783.09	771.05	762.21
32000	3096.03	1764.60	1332.30	1124.45	1006.03	931.97	882.93	849.21	825.43	808.35	795.92	786.79
33000	3192.78	1819.74	1373.93	1159.59	1037.46	961.09	910.52	875.75	851.22	833.61	820.79	811.38
34000	3289.53	1874.89	1415.57	1194.73	1068.90	990.22	938.11	902.29	877.02	858.87	845.66	835.97
35000	3386.28	1930.03	1457.20	1229.86	1100.34	1019.34	965.70	928.82	902.81	884.13	870.54	860.55
37500	3628.16	2067.89	1561.29	1317.71	1178.94	1092.15	1034.68	995.17	967.30	947.28	932.72	922.02
40000	3870.04	2205.75	1665.37	1405.56	1257.53	1164.96	1103.66	1061.51	1031.78	1010.43	994.90	983.49
42500	4111.91	2343.61	1769.46	1493.41	1336.13	1237.77	1172.64	1127.86	1096.27	1073.58	1057.08	1044.96
45000	4353.79	2481.47	1873.54	1581.25	1414.72	1310.58	1241.62	1194.20	1160.76	1136.74	1119.26	1106.43
47500	4595.67	2619.33	1977.63	1669.10	1493.32	1383.39	1310.59	1260.55	1225.24	1199.89	1181.44	1167.89
50000	4837.54	2757.19	2081.71	1756.95	1571.91	1456.20	1379.57	1326.89	1289.73	1263.04	1243.62	1229.36
52500	5079.42	2895.04	2185.80	1844.79	1650.51	1529.01	1448.55	1393.23	1354.22	1326.19	1305.80	1290.83
55000	5321.30	3032.90	2289.89	1932.64	1729.10	1601.82	1517.53	1459.58	1418.70	1389.34	1367.98	1352.30
57500	5563.17	3170.76	2393.97	2020.49	1807.70	1674.63	1586.51	1525.92	1483.19	1452.49	1430.16	1413.76
60000	5805.05	3308.62	2498.06	2108.34	1886.29	1747.44	1655.49	1592.27	1547.67	1515.65	1492.34	1475.23
65000	6288.81	3584.34	2706.23	2284.03	2043.49	1893.06	1793.44	1724.96	1676.65	1641.95	1616.71	1598.17
70000	6772.56	3860.06	2914.40	2459.72	2200.68	2038.68	1931.40	1857.64	1805.62	1768.25	1741.07	1721.10
75000	7256.31	4135.78	3122.57	2635.42	2357.87	2184.30	2069.36	1990.33	1934.59	1894.56	1865.43	1844.04
80000	7740.07	4411.49	3330.74	2811.11	2515.06	2329.91	2207.31	2123.02	2063.56	2020.86	1989.79	1966.97
85000	8223.82	4687.21	3538.91	2986.81	2672.25	2475.53	2345.27	2255.71	2192.54	2147.16	2114.15	2089.91
90000	8707.58	4962.93	3747.08	3162.50	2829.44	2621.15	2483.23	2388.40	2321.51	2273.47	2238.51	2212.85
95000	9191.33	5238.65	3955.25	3338.19	2986.63	2766.77	2621.18	2521.09	2450.48	2399.77	2362.88	2335.78
100000	9675.08	5514.37	4163.42	3513.89	3143.82	2912.39	2759.14	2653.78	2579.45	2526.07	2487.24	2458.72
105000	10158.84	5790.08	4371.59	3689.58	3301.01	3058.01	2897.10	2786.46	2708.43	2652.38	2611.60	2581.65
110000	10642.59	6065.80	4579.77	3865.28	3458.20	3203.63	3035.05	2919.15	2837.40	2778.68	2735.96	2704.59
115000	11126.34	6341.52	4787.94	4040.97	3615.39	3349.25	3173.01	3051.84	2966.37	2904.98	2860.32	2827.52
120000	11610.10	6617.24	4996.11	4216.67	3772.58	3494.87	3310.97	3184.53	3095.34	3031.29	2984.68	2950.46
125000	12093.85	6892.96	5204.28	4392.36	3929.77	3640.49	3448.92	3317.22	3224.32	3157.59	3109.05	3073.39
130000	12577.61	7168.67	5412.45	4568.05	4086.97	3786.11	3586.88	3449.91	3353.29	3283.89	3233.41	3196.33
135000	13061.36	7444.39	5620.62	4743.75	4244.16	3931.73	3724.84	3582.60	3482.26	3410.20	3357.77	3319.27
140000	13545.11	7720.11	5828.79	4919.44	4401.35	4077.35	3862.79	3715.28	3611.23	3536.50	3482.13	3442.20
145000	14028.87	7995.83	6036.96	5095.14	4558.54	4222.97	4000.75	3847.97	3740.21	3662.81	3606.49	3565.14
150000	14512.62	8271.55	6245.13	5270.83	4715.73	4368.59	4138.71	3980.66	3869.18	3789.11	3730.85	3688.07
155000	14996.38	8547.26	6453.30	5446.53	4872.92	4514.21	4276.66	4113.35	3998.15	3915.41	3855.22	3811.01
160000	15480.13	8822.98	6661.47	5622.22	5030.11	4659.82	4414.62	4246.04	4127.12	4041.72	3979.58	3933.94

MONTHLY AMORTIZING PAYMENTS   28.50%

AMOUNT OF LOAN	\NUMBER OF YEARS IN TERM											
	13	14	15	16	17	18	19	20	25	30	35	40
$ 50	1.22	1.22	1.21	1.21	1.20	1.20	1.20	1.20	1.19	1.19	1.19	1.19
100	2.44	2.43	2.42	2.41	2.40	2.40	2.39	2.39	2.38	2.38	2.38	2.38
200	4.88	4.85	4.83	4.81	4.79	4.79	4.78	4.77	4.76	4.76	4.76	4.76
300	7.32	7.27	7.24	7.21	7.19	7.18	7.16	7.16	7.14	7.13	7.13	7.13
400	9.76	9.69	9.65	9.61	9.58	9.57	9.55	9.54	9.51	9.51	9.51	9.51
500	12.19	12.11	12.06	12.01	11.98	11.96	11.94	11.92	11.89	11.88	11.88	11.88
600	14.63	14.54	14.47	14.41	14.37	14.35	14.32	14.31	14.27	14.26	14.26	14.26
700	17.07	16.96	16.88	16.82	16.77	16.74	16.71	16.69	16.64	16.63	16.63	16.63
800	19.51	19.38	19.29	19.22	19.16	19.13	19.10	19.07	19.02	19.01	19.01	19.01
900	21.94	21.80	21.70	21.62	21.56	21.52	21.48	21.46	21.40	21.38	21.38	21.38
1000	24.38	24.22	24.11	24.02	23.95	23.91	23.87	23.84	23.78	23.76	23.76	23.76
2000	48.76	48.44	48.21	48.04	47.90	47.81	47.73	47.68	47.55	47.52	47.51	47.51
3000	73.13	72.66	72.31	72.05	71.85	71.71	71.59	71.51	71.32	71.27	71.26	71.26
4000	97.51	96.88	96.41	96.07	95.80	95.61	95.46	95.35	95.09	95.03	95.01	95.01
5000	121.89	121.10	120.52	120.08	119.75	119.51	119.32	119.18	118.86	118.78	118.76	118.76
6000	146.26	145.32	144.62	144.10	143.70	143.41	143.18	143.02	142.63	142.54	142.51	142.51
7000	170.64	169.54	168.72	168.11	167.65	167.31	167.05	166.85	166.40	166.29	166.26	166.26
8000	195.01	193.76	192.82	192.13	191.60	191.21	190.91	190.69	190.17	190.05	190.01	190.01
9000	219.39	217.98	216.93	216.14	215.55	215.11	214.77	214.52	213.94	213.80	213.77	213.76
10000	243.77	242.20	241.03	240.16	239.50	239.01	238.64	238.36	237.71	237.56	237.52	237.51
11000	268.14	266.42	265.13	264.17	263.45	262.91	262.50	262.19	261.48	261.31	261.27	261.26
12000	292.52	290.64	289.23	288.19	287.40	286.81	286.36	286.03	285.25	285.07	285.02	285.01
13000	316.90	314.86	313.34	312.20	311.35	310.71	310.23	309.86	309.03	308.82	308.77	308.76
14000	341.27	339.08	337.44	336.22	335.30	334.61	334.09	333.70	332.80	332.58	332.52	332.51
15000	365.65	363.30	361.54	360.23	359.25	358.51	357.95	357.53	356.57	356.33	356.27	356.26
16000	390.02	387.52	385.64	384.25	383.20	382.41	381.81	381.37	380.34	380.09	380.02	380.01
17000	414.40	411.74	409.75	408.26	407.14	406.31	405.68	405.20	404.11	403.84	403.78	403.76
18000	438.78	435.96	433.85	432.28	431.09	430.21	429.54	429.04	427.88	427.60	427.53	427.51
19000	463.15	460.17	457.95	456.29	455.04	454.11	453.40	452.87	451.65	451.35	451.28	451.26
20000	487.53	484.39	482.05	480.31	478.99	478.01	477.27	476.71	475.42	475.11	475.03	475.01
21000	511.91	508.61	506.16	504.32	502.94	501.91	501.13	500.55	499.19	498.86	498.78	498.76
22000	536.28	532.83	530.26	528.34	526.89	525.81	524.99	524.38	522.96	522.62	522.53	522.51
23000	560.66	557.05	554.36	552.35	550.84	549.71	548.86	548.22	546.73	546.37	546.28	546.26
24000	585.03	581.27	578.46	576.37	574.79	573.61	572.72	572.05	570.50	570.13	570.03	570.01
25000	609.41	605.49	602.57	600.38	598.74	597.51	596.58	595.89	594.27	593.88	593.79	593.76
26000	633.79	629.71	626.67	624.40	622.69	621.41	620.45	619.72	618.05	617.64	617.54	617.51
27000	658.16	653.93	650.77	648.41	646.64	645.31	644.31	643.56	641.82	641.39	641.29	641.26
28000	682.54	678.15	674.87	672.43	670.59	669.21	668.17	667.39	665.59	665.15	665.04	665.01
29000	706.91	702.37	698.98	696.44	694.54	693.11	692.04	691.23	689.36	688.90	688.79	688.76
30000	731.29	726.59	723.08	720.46	718.49	717.01	715.90	715.06	713.13	712.66	712.54	712.51
31000	755.67	750.81	747.18	744.47	742.44	740.91	739.76	738.90	736.90	736.41	736.29	736.26
32000	780.04	775.03	771.28	768.49	766.39	764.81	763.62	762.73	760.67	760.17	760.04	760.01
33000	804.42	799.25	795.39	792.50	790.34	788.71	787.49	786.57	784.44	783.92	783.80	783.77
34000	828.80	823.47	819.49	816.52	814.28	812.61	811.35	810.40	808.21	807.68	807.55	807.52
35000	853.17	847.69	843.59	840.53	838.23	836.51	835.21	834.24	831.98	831.43	831.30	831.27
37500	914.11	908.23	903.85	900.57	898.11	896.26	894.87	893.83	891.41	890.82	890.68	890.64
40000	975.05	968.78	964.10	960.61	957.98	956.01	954.53	953.41	950.84	950.21	950.05	950.02
42500	1035.99	1029.33	1024.36	1020.64	1017.85	1015.76	1014.19	1013.00	1010.26	1009.60	1009.43	1009.39
45000	1096.93	1089.88	1084.62	1080.68	1077.73	1075.51	1073.85	1072.59	1069.69	1068.98	1068.81	1068.77
47500	1157.87	1150.43	1144.87	1140.72	1137.60	1135.26	1133.50	1132.18	1129.12	1128.37	1128.19	1128.14
50000	1218.82	1210.98	1205.13	1200.75	1197.48	1195.01	1193.16	1191.77	1188.54	1187.76	1187.57	1187.52
52500	1279.76	1271.53	1265.39	1260.79	1257.35	1254.76	1252.82	1251.36	1247.97	1247.15	1246.95	1246.90
55000	1340.70	1332.07	1325.64	1320.83	1317.22	1314.51	1312.48	1310.94	1307.40	1306.53	1306.33	1306.27
57500	1401.64	1392.62	1385.90	1380.87	1377.10	1374.26	1372.13	1370.53	1366.83	1365.92	1365.70	1365.65
60000	1462.58	1453.17	1446.15	1440.91	1436.97	1434.01	1431.79	1430.12	1426.25	1425.31	1425.08	1425.02
65000	1584.46	1574.27	1566.67	1560.98	1556.72	1553.51	1551.11	1549.30	1545.11	1544.09	1543.84	1543.77
70000	1706.34	1695.37	1687.18	1681.06	1676.46	1673.02	1670.42	1668.47	1663.96	1662.86	1662.59	1662.53
75000	1828.22	1816.46	1807.69	1801.13	1796.21	1792.52	1789.74	1787.65	1782.81	1781.64	1781.35	1781.28
80000	1950.10	1937.56	1928.20	1921.21	1915.96	1912.02	1909.05	1906.82	1901.67	1900.41	1900.10	1900.03
85000	2071.98	2058.66	2048.72	2041.28	2035.70	2031.52	2028.37	2026.00	2020.52	2019.19	2018.86	2018.78
90000	2193.86	2179.76	2169.23	2161.36	2155.45	2151.02	2147.69	2145.18	2139.38	2137.96	2137.62	2137.53
95000	2315.74	2300.85	2289.74	2281.43	2275.20	2270.52	2267.00	2264.35	2258.23	2256.74	2256.37	2256.28
100000	2437.63	2421.95	2410.25	2401.51	2394.95	2390.02	2386.32	2383.53	2377.08	2375.51	2375.13	2375.04
105000	2559.51	2543.05	2530.77	2521.58	2514.69	2509.52	2505.63	2502.71	2495.94	2494.29	2493.89	2493.79
110000	2681.39	2664.14	2651.28	2641.66	2634.44	2629.02	2624.95	2621.88	2614.79	2613.06	2612.64	2612.54
115000	2803.27	2785.24	2771.79	2761.73	2754.19	2748.52	2744.26	2741.06	2733.65	2731.84	2731.40	2731.29
120000	2925.15	2906.34	2892.30	2881.81	2873.93	2868.02	2863.58	2860.23	2852.50	2850.61	2850.15	2850.04
125000	3047.03	3027.44	3012.82	3001.88	2993.68	2987.52	2982.89	2979.41	2971.35	2969.39	2968.91	2968.79
130000	3168.91	3148.53	3133.33	3121.96	3113.43	3107.02	3102.21	3098.59	3090.21	3088.17	3087.67	3087.54
135000	3290.79	3269.63	3253.84	3242.03	3233.17	3226.52	3221.53	3217.76	3209.06	3206.94	3206.42	3206.30
140000	3412.67	3390.73	3374.35	3362.11	3352.92	3346.03	3340.84	3336.94	3327.92	3325.72	3325.18	3325.05
145000	3534.55	3511.82	3494.87	3482.18	3472.67	3465.53	3460.16	3456.12	3446.77	3444.49	3443.94	3443.80
150000	3656.44	3632.92	3615.38	3602.26	3592.42	3585.03	3579.47	3575.29	3565.62	3563.27	3562.69	3562.55
155000	3778.32	3754.02	3735.89	3722.33	3712.16	3704.53	3698.79	3694.47	3684.48	3682.04	3681.45	3681.30
160000	3900.20	3875.12	3856.40	3842.41	3831.91	3824.03	3818.10	3813.64	3803.33	3800.82	3800.20	3800.05

191

28.75% MONTHLY AMORTIZING PAYMENTS

AMOUNT OF LOAN	NUMBER OF YEARS IN TERM											
	1	2	3	4	5	6	7	8	9	10	11	12
$ 50	4.85	2.77	2.09	1.77	1.58	1.47	1.39	1.34	1.30	1.28	1.26	1.24
100	9.69	5.53	4.18	3.53	3.16	2.93	2.78	2.68	2.60	2.55	2.51	2.48
200	19.38	11.06	8.36	7.06	6.32	5.86	5.56	5.35	5.20	5.09	5.02	4.96
300	29.07	16.59	12.54	10.59	9.48	8.79	8.33	8.02	7.80	7.64	7.52	7.44
400	38.75	22.11	16.71	14.12	12.64	11.72	11.11	10.69	10.39	10.18	10.03	9.92
500	48.44	27.64	20.89	17.65	15.80	14.65	13.88	13.36	12.99	12.73	12.53	12.39
600	58.13	33.17	25.07	21.17	18.96	17.57	16.66	16.03	15.59	15.27	15.04	14.87
700	67.82	38.69	29.24	24.70	22.12	20.50	19.44	18.70	18.19	17.82	17.55	17.35
800	77.50	44.22	33.42	28.23	25.28	23.43	22.21	21.37	20.78	20.36	20.05	19.83
900	87.19	49.75	37.60	31.76	28.44	26.36	24.99	24.04	23.38	22.90	22.56	22.30
1000	96.88	55.28	41.77	35.29	31.59	29.29	27.76	26.71	25.98	25.45	25.06	24.78
2000	193.75	110.55	83.54	70.57	63.18	58.57	55.52	53.42	51.95	50.89	50.12	49.56
3000	290.62	165.82	125.31	105.85	94.77	87.85	83.28	80.13	77.92	76.33	75.18	74.34
4000	387.50	221.09	167.08	141.14	126.36	117.14	111.03	106.84	103.89	101.78	100.24	99.12
5000	484.37	276.36	208.85	176.42	157.95	146.42	138.79	133.55	129.87	127.22	125.30	123.89
6000	581.24	331.63	250.62	211.70	189.54	175.70	166.55	160.26	155.84	152.66	150.36	148.67
7000	678.12	386.90	292.39	246.98	221.13	204.99	194.31	186.97	181.81	178.11	175.42	173.45
8000	774.99	442.18	334.16	282.27	252.72	234.27	222.06	213.68	207.78	203.55	200.48	198.23
9000	871.86	497.45	375.93	317.55	284.31	263.55	249.82	240.39	233.75	228.99	225.54	223.00
10000	968.74	552.72	417.70	352.83	315.90	292.83	277.58	267.10	259.73	254.44	250.60	247.78
11000	1065.61	607.99	459.47	388.11	347.49	322.12	305.34	293.81	285.70	279.88	275.66	272.56
12000	1162.48	663.26	501.24	423.40	379.08	351.40	333.09	320.52	311.67	305.32	300.71	297.34
13000	1259.36	718.53	543.01	458.68	410.67	380.68	360.85	347.23	337.64	330.77	325.77	322.11
14000	1356.23	773.80	584.78	493.96	442.26	409.97	388.61	373.94	363.62	356.21	350.83	346.89
15000	1453.10	829.08	626.55	529.24	473.85	439.25	416.36	400.65	389.59	381.65	375.89	371.67
16000	1549.98	884.35	668.32	564.53	505.44	468.53	444.12	427.36	415.56	407.10	400.95	396.45
17000	1646.85	939.62	710.09	599.81	537.03	497.82	471.88	454.07	441.53	432.54	426.01	421.22
18000	1743.72	994.89	751.86	635.09	568.62	527.10	499.64	480.78	467.50	457.98	451.07	446.00
19000	1840.60	1050.16	793.63	670.38	600.21	556.38	527.39	507.49	493.48	483.43	476.13	470.78
20000	1937.47	1105.43	835.40	705.66	631.80	585.66	555.15	534.20	519.45	508.87	501.19	495.56
21000	2034.34	1160.70	877.17	740.94	663.39	614.95	582.91	560.91	545.42	534.31	526.25	520.33
22000	2131.22	1215.98	918.94	776.22	694.98	644.23	610.67	587.62	571.39	559.76	551.31	545.11
23000	2228.09	1271.25	960.71	811.51	726.57	673.51	638.42	614.33	597.36	585.20	576.36	569.89
24000	2324.96	1326.52	1002.48	846.79	758.16	702.80	666.18	641.04	623.34	610.64	601.42	594.67
25000	2421.84	1381.79	1044.25	882.07	789.75	732.08	693.94	667.75	649.31	636.09	626.48	619.44
26000	2518.71	1437.06	1086.02	917.35	821.34	761.36	721.69	694.46	675.28	661.53	651.54	644.22
27000	2615.58	1492.33	1127.79	952.64	852.93	790.65	749.45	721.17	701.25	686.97	676.60	669.00
28000	2712.46	1547.60	1169.56	987.92	884.52	819.93	777.21	747.88	727.23	712.42	701.66	693.78
29000	2809.33	1602.88	1211.33	1023.20	916.11	849.21	804.97	774.59	753.20	737.86	726.72	718.55
30000	2906.20	1658.15	1253.10	1058.48	947.70	878.49	832.72	801.30	779.17	763.30	751.78	743.33
31000	3003.08	1713.42	1294.87	1093.77	979.29	907.78	860.48	828.01	805.14	788.75	776.84	768.11
32000	3099.95	1768.69	1336.64	1129.05	1010.88	937.06	888.24	854.72	831.11	814.19	801.90	792.89
33000	3196.82	1823.96	1378.41	1164.33	1042.47	966.34	916.00	881.43	857.09	839.63	826.96	817.66
34000	3293.70	1879.23	1420.18	1199.61	1074.06	995.63	943.75	908.14	883.06	865.08	852.02	842.44
35000	3390.57	1934.50	1461.95	1234.90	1105.65	1024.91	971.51	934.85	909.03	890.52	877.07	867.22
37500	3632.75	2072.68	1566.37	1323.10	1184.62	1098.12	1040.90	1001.62	973.96	954.13	939.72	929.16
40000	3874.94	2210.86	1670.80	1411.31	1263.60	1171.32	1110.30	1068.40	1038.89	1017.73	1002.37	991.11
42500	4117.12	2349.04	1775.22	1499.52	1342.57	1244.53	1179.69	1135.17	1103.82	1081.34	1065.02	1053.05
45000	4359.30	2487.22	1879.65	1587.72	1421.55	1317.74	1249.08	1201.95	1168.75	1144.95	1127.67	1115.00
47500	4601.49	2625.40	1984.07	1675.93	1500.52	1390.95	1318.48	1268.72	1233.68	1208.56	1190.31	1176.94
50000	4843.67	2763.58	2088.50	1764.14	1579.50	1464.15	1387.87	1335.50	1298.61	1272.17	1252.96	1238.88
52500	5085.85	2901.75	2192.92	1852.34	1658.47	1537.36	1457.26	1402.27	1363.54	1335.77	1315.61	1300.83
55000	5328.04	3039.93	2297.35	1940.55	1737.45	1610.57	1526.66	1469.05	1428.47	1399.38	1378.26	1362.77
57500	5570.22	3178.11	2401.77	2028.76	1816.42	1683.78	1596.05	1535.82	1493.40	1462.99	1440.90	1424.72
60000	5812.40	3316.29	2506.19	2116.96	1895.40	1756.98	1665.44	1602.60	1558.33	1526.60	1503.55	1486.66
65000	6296.77	3592.65	2715.04	2293.38	2053.34	1903.40	1804.23	1736.15	1688.20	1653.82	1628.85	1610.55
70000	6781.14	3869.00	2923.89	2469.79	2211.29	2049.81	1943.02	1869.69	1818.06	1781.03	1754.14	1734.43
75000	7265.50	4145.36	3132.74	2646.20	2369.24	2196.23	2081.80	2003.24	1947.92	1908.25	1879.44	1858.32
80000	7749.87	4421.72	3341.59	2822.62	2527.19	2342.64	2220.59	2136.79	2077.78	2035.46	2004.73	1982.21
85000	8234.24	4698.07	3550.44	2999.03	2685.14	2489.06	2359.38	2270.34	2207.64	2162.68	2130.03	2106.10
90000	8718.60	4974.43	3759.29	3175.44	2843.09	2635.47	2498.16	2403.89	2337.50	2289.90	2255.33	2229.99
95000	9202.97	5250.79	3968.14	3351.86	3001.04	2781.89	2636.95	2537.44	2467.36	2417.11	2380.62	2353.87
100000	9687.33	5527.15	4176.99	3528.27	3158.99	2928.30	2775.73	2670.99	2597.22	2544.33	2505.92	2477.76
105000	10171.70	5803.50	4385.84	3704.68	3316.94	3074.72	2914.52	2804.54	2727.08	2671.54	2631.21	2601.65
110000	10656.07	6079.86	4594.69	3881.09	3474.89	3221.13	3053.31	2938.09	2856.94	2798.76	2756.51	2725.54
115000	11140.43	6356.22	4803.54	4057.51	3632.84	3367.55	3192.09	3071.64	2986.80	2925.98	2881.80	2849.43
120000	11624.80	6632.57	5012.38	4233.92	3790.79	3513.96	3330.88	3205.19	3116.66	3053.19	3007.10	2973.31
125000	12109.17	6908.93	5221.23	4410.33	3948.74	3660.38	3469.67	3338.74	3246.52	3180.41	3132.40	3097.20
130000	12593.53	7185.29	5430.08	4586.75	4106.68	3806.79	3608.45	3472.29	3376.39	3307.63	3257.69	3221.09
135000	13077.90	7461.64	5638.93	4763.16	4264.63	3953.21	3747.24	3605.85	3506.25	3434.84	3382.99	3344.98
140000	13562.27	7738.00	5847.78	4939.57	4422.58	4099.62	3886.03	3739.38	3636.11	3562.06	3508.28	3468.86
145000	14046.63	8014.36	6056.63	5115.99	4580.53	4246.04	4024.81	3872.93	3765.97	3689.27	3633.58	3592.75
150000	14531.00	8290.72	6265.48	5292.40	4738.48	4392.45	4163.60	4006.48	3895.83	3816.49	3758.87	3716.64
155000	15015.37	8567.07	6474.33	5468.81	4896.43	4538.87	4302.39	4140.03	4025.69	3943.71	3884.17	3840.53
160000	15499.73	8843.43	6683.18	5645.23	5054.38	4685.28	4441.17	4273.58	4155.55	4070.92	4009.46	3964.42

192

AMOUNT OF LOAN	NUMBER OF YEARS IN TERM											
	13	14	15	16	17	18	19	20	25	30	35	40
$ 50	1.23	1.23	1.22	1.22	1.21	1.21	1.21	1.21	1.20	1.20	1.20	1.20
100	2.46	2.45	2.44	2.43	2.42	2.42	2.41	2.41	2.40	2.40	2.40	2.40
200	4.92	4.89	4.87	4.85	4.84	4.83	4.82	4.81	4.80	4.80	4.80	4.80
300	7.38	7.33	7.30	7.27	7.25	7.24	7.23	7.22	7.20	7.19	7.19	7.19
400	9.83	9.77	9.73	9.69	9.67	9.65	9.63	9.62	9.60	9.59	9.59	9.59
500	12.29	12.21	12.16	12.11	12.08	12.06	12.04	12.03	11.99	11.99	11.98	11.98
600	14.75	14.65	14.59	14.53	14.50	14.47	14.45	14.43	14.39	14.38	14.38	14.38
700	17.20	17.10	17.02	16.96	16.91	16.88	16.85	16.83	16.79	16.78	16.78	16.78
800	19.66	19.54	19.45	19.38	19.33	19.29	19.26	19.24	19.19	19.18	19.17	19.17
900	22.12	21.98	21.88	21.80	21.74	21.70	21.67	21.64	21.59	21.57	21.57	21.57
1000	24.57	24.42	24.31	24.22	24.16	24.11	24.07	24.05	23.98	23.97	23.96	23.96
2000	49.14	48.84	48.61	48.44	48.31	48.21	48.14	48.09	47.96	47.93	47.92	47.92
3000	73.71	73.25	72.91	72.65	72.46	72.31	72.21	72.13	71.94	71.89	71.88	71.88
4000	98.28	97.67	97.21	96.87	96.61	96.42	96.27	96.17	95.92	95.86	95.84	95.84
5000	122.85	122.08	121.51	121.08	120.76	120.52	120.34	120.21	119.90	119.82	119.80	119.80
6000	147.42	146.50	145.81	145.30	144.91	144.62	144.41	144.25	143.87	143.78	143.76	143.76
7000	171.99	170.91	170.11	169.51	169.06	168.73	168.48	168.29	167.85	167.75	167.72	167.72
8000	196.56	195.33	194.41	193.73	193.21	192.83	192.54	192.33	191.83	191.71	191.68	191.67
9000	221.13	219.75	218.71	217.94	217.37	216.93	216.61	216.37	215.81	215.67	215.64	215.63
10000	245.70	244.16	243.01	242.16	241.52	241.04	240.68	240.41	239.79	239.64	239.60	239.59
11000	270.27	268.58	267.32	266.37	265.67	265.14	264.74	264.45	263.76	263.60	263.56	263.55
12000	294.84	292.99	291.62	290.59	289.82	289.24	288.81	288.49	287.74	287.56	287.52	287.51
13000	319.41	317.41	315.92	314.80	313.97	313.35	312.88	312.53	311.72	311.53	311.48	311.47
14000	343.98	341.82	340.22	339.02	338.12	337.45	336.95	336.57	335.70	335.49	335.44	335.43
15000	368.55	366.24	364.52	363.23	362.27	361.55	361.01	360.61	359.68	359.45	359.40	359.38
16000	393.12	390.66	388.82	387.45	386.42	385.66	385.08	384.65	383.65	383.41	383.36	383.34
17000	417.69	415.07	413.12	411.67	410.58	409.76	409.15	408.69	407.63	407.38	407.32	407.30
18000	442.26	439.49	437.42	435.88	434.73	433.86	433.22	432.73	431.61	431.34	431.28	431.26
19000	466.83	463.90	461.72	460.10	458.88	457.97	457.28	456.77	455.59	455.30	455.24	455.22
20000	491.40	488.32	486.02	484.31	483.03	482.07	481.35	480.81	479.57	479.27	479.19	479.18
21000	515.97	512.73	510.33	508.53	507.18	506.17	505.42	504.85	503.54	503.23	503.15	503.14
22000	540.54	537.15	534.63	532.74	531.33	530.28	529.48	528.89	527.52	527.19	527.11	527.09
23000	565.11	561.57	558.93	556.96	555.48	554.38	553.55	552.93	551.50	551.16	551.07	551.05
24000	589.68	585.98	583.23	581.17	579.63	578.48	577.62	576.97	575.48	575.12	575.03	575.01
25000	614.25	610.40	607.53	605.39	603.79	602.59	601.69	601.01	599.46	599.08	598.99	598.97
26000	638.82	634.81	631.83	629.60	627.94	626.69	625.75	625.05	623.43	623.05	622.95	622.93
27000	663.39	659.23	656.13	653.82	652.09	650.79	649.82	649.09	647.41	647.01	646.91	646.89
28000	687.96	683.64	680.43	678.03	676.24	674.90	673.89	673.13	671.39	670.97	670.87	670.85
29000	712.53	708.06	704.73	702.25	700.39	699.00	697.96	697.17	695.37	694.93	694.83	694.80
30000	737.10	732.48	729.03	726.46	724.54	723.10	722.02	721.21	719.35	718.90	718.79	718.76
31000	761.67	756.89	753.33	750.68	748.69	747.21	746.09	745.25	743.32	742.86	742.75	742.72
32000	786.24	781.31	777.64	774.89	772.84	771.31	770.16	769.29	767.30	766.82	766.71	766.68
33000	810.81	805.72	801.94	799.11	797.00	795.41	794.22	793.33	791.28	790.79	790.67	790.64
34000	835.38	830.14	826.24	823.33	821.15	819.52	818.29	817.37	815.26	814.75	814.63	814.60
35000	859.95	854.55	850.54	847.54	845.30	843.62	842.36	841.41	839.24	838.71	838.59	838.56
37500	921.37	915.59	911.29	908.08	905.68	903.88	902.53	901.51	899.18	898.62	898.49	898.45
40000	982.80	976.63	972.04	968.62	966.05	964.13	962.69	961.61	959.13	958.53	958.38	958.35
42500	1044.22	1037.67	1032.80	1029.16	1026.43	1024.39	1022.86	1021.71	1019.07	1018.44	1018.28	1018.25
45000	1105.65	1098.71	1093.55	1089.69	1086.81	1084.65	1083.03	1081.81	1079.02	1078.34	1078.18	1078.14
47500	1167.07	1159.75	1154.30	1150.23	1147.19	1144.91	1143.20	1141.92	1138.96	1138.25	1138.08	1138.04
50000	1228.49	1220.79	1215.05	1210.77	1207.57	1205.17	1203.37	1202.02	1198.91	1198.16	1197.98	1197.94
52500	1289.92	1281.83	1275.81	1271.31	1267.95	1265.43	1263.54	1262.12	1258.85	1258.07	1257.88	1257.83
55000	1351.34	1342.87	1336.56	1331.85	1328.32	1325.68	1323.70	1322.22	1318.80	1317.98	1317.78	1317.73
57500	1412.77	1403.91	1397.31	1392.39	1388.70	1385.94	1383.87	1382.32	1378.74	1377.88	1377.68	1377.63
60000	1474.19	1464.95	1458.06	1452.92	1449.08	1446.20	1444.04	1442.42	1438.69	1437.79	1437.57	1437.52
65000	1597.04	1587.02	1579.57	1574.00	1569.84	1566.72	1564.38	1562.62	1558.58	1557.61	1557.37	1557.31
70000	1719.89	1709.10	1701.07	1695.08	1690.59	1687.23	1684.71	1682.82	1678.47	1677.42	1677.17	1677.11
75000	1842.74	1831.18	1822.58	1816.15	1811.35	1807.75	1805.05	1803.02	1798.36	1797.24	1796.97	1796.90
80000	1965.59	1953.26	1944.08	1937.23	1932.10	1928.26	1925.38	1923.22	1918.25	1917.05	1916.76	1916.69
85000	2088.44	2075.34	2065.59	2058.31	2052.86	2048.78	2045.72	2043.42	2038.14	2036.86	2036.56	2036.49
90000	2211.29	2197.42	2187.09	2179.38	2173.62	2169.30	2166.06	2163.62	2158.03	2156.68	2156.36	2156.28
95000	2334.13	2319.49	2308.60	2300.46	2294.37	2289.81	2286.39	2283.83	2277.92	2276.50	2276.16	2276.07
100000	2456.98	2441.57	2430.10	2421.54	2415.13	2410.33	2406.73	2404.03	2397.81	2396.31	2395.95	2395.87
105000	2579.83	2563.65	2551.61	2542.61	2535.89	2530.85	2527.07	2524.23	2517.70	2516.13	2515.75	2515.66
110000	2702.68	2685.73	2673.11	2663.69	2656.64	2651.36	2647.40	2644.43	2637.59	2635.95	2635.55	2635.45
115000	2825.53	2807.81	2794.61	2784.77	2777.40	2771.88	2767.74	2764.63	2757.48	2755.76	2755.35	2755.25
120000	2948.38	2929.89	2916.12	2905.84	2898.15	2892.39	2888.07	2884.83	2877.37	2875.58	2875.14	2875.04
125000	3071.23	3051.96	3037.62	3026.92	3018.91	3012.91	3008.41	3005.03	2997.26	2995.39	2994.94	2994.83
130000	3194.08	3174.04	3159.13	3148.00	3139.67	3133.43	3128.75	3125.23	3117.15	3115.21	3114.74	3114.62
135000	3316.93	3296.12	3280.63	3269.07	3260.42	3253.94	3249.08	3245.43	3237.04	3235.02	3234.54	3234.42
140000	3439.78	3418.20	3402.14	3390.15	3381.18	3374.46	3369.42	3365.64	3356.93	3354.84	3354.33	3354.21
145000	3562.62	3540.28	3523.64	3511.22	3501.94	3494.98	3489.76	3485.84	3476.82	3474.65	3474.13	3474.00
150000	3685.47	3662.36	3645.15	3632.30	3622.69	3615.49	3610.09	3606.04	3596.71	3594.47	3593.93	3593.80
155000	3808.32	3784.44	3766.65	3753.38	3743.45	3736.01	3730.43	3726.24	3716.60	3714.28	3713.73	3713.59
160000	3931.17	3906.51	3888.16	3874.45	3864.20	3856.52	3850.76	3846.44	3836.50	3834.10	3833.52	3833.38

TABLE 2. PAYMENT REQUIRED TO AMORTIZE A $1,000 LOAN

Use this Table to find the payment amount required to completely pay off a $1,000 loan amount over a given loan term at a fixed rate of interest. By simple proportion, you can find the payments for other loan amounts. There are sections for monthly, quarterly, semiannual, and annual payments. In order to ensure complete amortization, each payment entry is rounded up to the next highest cent.

Example: What quarterly payment is needed to pay off a loan amount of $15,500 over a ten-year term at 10.5% interest? Within the quarterly payment section of the Table, find the 10.5% interest rate column on page 205. Read down this column to the 10-year loan term row. The entry is $40.68. Since this entry is the payment for a $1,000 loan, multiply 40.68 by 15.5 ($15,500 divided by $1,000) to get the required quarterly payment of $630.54.

MONTHLY
PAYMENT REQUIRED TO AMORTIZE A $1,000.00 LOAN

TERM IN YEARS	INTEREST RATES											
	5.00%	5.25%	5.50%	5.75%	6.00%	6.25%	6.50%	6.75%	7.00%	7.25%	7.50%	7.75%
0.5	169.11	169.23	169.36	169.48	169.60	169.72	169.85	169.97	170.09	170.21	170.34	170.46
1.0	85.61	85.73	85.84	85.96	86.07	86.19	86.30	86.42	86.53	86.65	86.76	86.88
1.5	57.79	57.90	58.01	58.12	58.24	58.35	58.46	58.58	58.69	58.80	58.92	59.03
2.0	43.88	43.99	44.10	44.21	44.33	44.44	44.55	44.66	44.78	44.89	45.00	45.12
2.5	35.53	35.65	35.76	35.87	35.98	36.10	36.21	36.32	36.44	36.55	36.66	36.78
3.0	29.98	30.09	30.20	30.31	30.43	30.54	30.65	30.77	30.88	31.00	31.11	31.23
3.5	26.01	26.12	26.23	26.35	26.46	26.58	26.69	26.80	26.92	27.03	27.15	27.27
4.0	23.03	23.15	23.26	23.38	23.49	23.60	23.72	23.84	23.95	24.07	24.18	24.30
4.5	20.72	20.84	20.95	21.07	21.18	21.30	21.41	21.53	21.65	21.76	21.88	22.00
5.0	18.88	18.99	19.11	19.22	19.34	19.45	19.57	19.69	19.81	19.92	20.04	20.16
5.5	17.37	17.48	17.60	17.71	17.83	17.95	18.07	18.18	18.30	18.42	18.54	18.66
6.0	16.11	16.23	16.34	16.46	16.58	16.70	16.81	16.93	17.05	17.17	17.30	17.42
6.5	15.05	15.16	15.28	15.40	15.52	15.64	15.76	15.88	16.00	16.12	16.24	16.37
7.0	14.14	14.26	14.38	14.49	14.61	14.73	14.85	14.98	15.10	15.22	15.34	15.47
7.5	13.35	13.47	13.59	13.71	13.83	13.95	14.07	14.20	14.32	14.44	14.57	14.69
8.0	12.66	12.78	12.90	13.03	13.15	13.27	13.39	13.51	13.64	13.76	13.89	14.01
8.5	12.06	12.18	12.30	12.42	12.54	12.67	12.79	12.92	13.04	13.17	13.29	13.42
9.0	11.52	11.64	11.76	11.89	12.01	12.13	12.26	12.39	12.51	12.64	12.77	12.89
9.5	11.04	11.16	11.29	11.41	11.53	11.66	11.79	11.91	12.04	12.17	12.30	12.43
10.0	10.61	10.73	10.86	10.98	11.11	11.23	11.36	11.49	11.62	11.75	11.88	12.01
10.5	10.22	10.35	10.47	10.60	10.72	10.85	10.98	11.10	11.23	11.36	11.50	11.63
11.0	9.87	9.99	10.12	10.25	10.37	10.50	10.63	10.76	10.89	11.02	11.15	11.29
11.5	9.55	9.67	9.80	9.93	10.05	10.18	10.31	10.44	10.58	10.71	10.84	10.98
12.0	9.25	9.38	9.51	9.63	9.76	9.89	10.02	10.16	10.29	10.42	10.56	10.69
12.5	8.98	9.11	9.24	9.37	9.50	9.63	9.76	9.89	10.03	10.16	10.30	10.43
13.0	8.74	8.86	8.99	9.12	9.25	9.38	9.52	9.65	9.79	9.92	10.06	10.20
13.5	8.51	8.63	8.76	8.89	9.03	9.16	9.29	9.43	9.56	9.70	9.84	9.98
14.0	8.29	8.42	8.55	8.68	8.82	8.95	9.09	9.22	9.36	9.50	9.64	9.78
14.5	8.10	8.23	8.36	8.49	8.62	8.76	8.89	9.03	9.17	9.31	9.45	9.59
15.0	7.91	8.04	8.18	8.31	8.44	8.58	8.72	8.85	8.99	9.13	9.28	9.42
15.5	7.74	7.87	8.01	8.14	8.28	8.41	8.55	8.69	8.83	8.97	9.11	9.26
16.0	7.58	7.71	7.85	7.98	8.12	8.26	8.40	8.54	8.68	8.82	8.96	9.11
16.5	7.43	7.57	7.70	7.84	7.97	8.11	8.25	8.39	8.53	8.68	8.82	8.97
17.0	7.29	7.43	7.56	7.70	7.84	7.98	8.12	8.26	8.40	8.55	8.69	8.84
17.5	7.16	7.29	7.43	7.57	7.71	7.85	7.99	8.13	8.28	8.42	8.57	8.72
18.0	7.04	7.17	7.31	7.45	7.59	7.73	7.87	8.01	8.16	8.31	8.45	8.60
18.5	6.92	7.05	7.19	7.33	7.47	7.62	7.76	7.90	8.05	8.20	8.35	8.50
19.0	6.81	6.95	7.08	7.22	7.37	7.51	7.65	7.80	7.95	8.10	8.25	8.40
19.5	6.70	6.84	6.98	7.12	7.26	7.41	7.55	7.70	7.85	8.00	8.15	8.30
20.0	6.60	6.74	6.88	7.03	7.17	7.31	7.46	7.61	7.76	7.91	8.06	8.21
20.5	6.51	6.65	6.79	6.93	7.08	7.22	7.37	7.52	7.67	7.82	7.98	8.13
21.0	6.42	6.56	6.70	6.85	6.99	7.14	7.29	7.44	7.59	7.74	7.90	8.05
21.5	6.34	6.48	6.62	6.77	6.91	7.06	7.21	7.36	7.51	7.67	7.82	7.98
22.0	6.26	6.40	6.54	6.69	6.84	6.98	7.13	7.29	7.44	7.59	7.75	7.91
22.5	6.18	6.32	6.47	6.62	6.76	6.91	7.06	7.22	7.37	7.53	7.68	7.84
23.0	6.11	6.25	6.40	6.54	6.69	6.84	7.00	7.15	7.30	7.46	7.62	7.78
23.5	6.04	6.18	6.33	6.48	6.63	6.78	6.93	7.09	7.24	7.40	7.56	7.72
24.0	5.97	6.12	6.27	6.41	6.56	6.72	6.87	7.03	7.18	7.34	7.50	7.66
24.5	5.91	6.06	6.20	6.35	6.50	6.66	6.81	6.97	7.13	7.29	7.45	7.61
25.0	5.85	6.00	6.15	6.30	6.45	6.60	6.76	6.91	7.07	7.23	7.39	7.56
25.5	5.79	5.94	6.09	6.24	6.39	6.55	6.70	6.86	7.02	7.18	7.35	7.51
26.0	5.74	5.89	6.04	6.19	6.34	6.50	6.65	6.81	6.97	7.14	7.30	7.46
26.5	5.69	5.83	5.99	6.14	6.29	6.45	6.61	6.77	6.93	7.09	7.25	7.42
27.0	5.64	5.78	5.94	6.09	6.24	6.40	6.56	6.72	6.88	7.05	7.21	7.38
27.5	5.59	5.74	5.89	6.04	6.20	6.36	6.52	6.68	6.84	7.01	7.17	7.34
28.0	5.54	5.69	5.84	6.00	6.16	6.31	6.48	6.64	6.80	6.97	7.13	7.30
28.5	5.50	5.65	5.80	5.96	6.11	6.27	6.44	6.60	6.76	6.93	7.10	7.27
29.0	5.45	5.61	5.76	5.92	6.08	6.24	6.40	6.56	6.73	6.89	7.06	7.23
29.5	5.41	5.57	5.72	5.88	6.04	6.20	6.36	6.53	6.69	6.86	7.03	7.20
30.0	5.37	5.53	5.68	5.84	6.00	6.16	6.33	6.49	6.66	6.83	7.00	7.17
31.0	5.30	5.45	5.61	5.77	5.93	6.10	6.26	6.43	6.60	6.77	6.94	7.11
32.0	5.23	5.39	5.55	5.71	5.87	6.03	6.20	6.37	6.54	6.71	6.88	7.06
33.0	5.17	5.32	5.48	5.65	5.81	5.98	6.14	6.31	6.49	6.66	6.83	7.01
34.0	5.11	5.27	5.43	5.59	5.76	5.92	6.09	6.26	6.44	6.61	6.79	6.97
35.0	5.05	5.21	5.38	5.54	5.71	5.88	6.05	6.22	6.39	6.57	6.75	6.93
36.0	5.00	5.16	5.33	5.49	5.66	5.83	6.00	6.18	6.35	6.53	6.71	6.89
37.0	4.95	5.12	5.28	5.45	5.62	5.79	5.96	6.14	6.32	6.49	6.67	6.86
38.0	4.91	5.07	5.24	5.41	5.58	5.75	5.93	6.10	6.28	6.46	6.64	6.83
39.0	4.87	5.03	5.20	5.37	5.54	5.72	5.89	6.07	6.25	6.43	6.61	6.80
40.0	4.83	4.99	5.16	5.33	5.51	5.68	5.86	6.04	6.22	6.40	6.59	6.77

MONTHLY
PAYMENT REQUIRED TO AMORTIZE A $1,000.00 LOAN

TERM IN YEARS	INTEREST RATES											
	8.00%	8.25%	8.50%	8.75%	9.00%	9.25%	9.50%	9.75%	10.00%	10.25%	10.50%	10.75%
0.5	170.58	170.70	170.83	170.95	171.07	171.20	171.32	171.44	171.57	171.69	171.81	171.94
1.0	86.99	87.11	87.22	87.34	87.46	87.57	87.69	87.80	87.92	88.04	88.15	88.27
1.5	59.15	59.26	59.37	59.49	59.60	59.72	59.83	59.95	60.06	60.18	60.29	60.41
2.0	45.23	45.35	45.46	45.58	45.69	45.80	45.92	46.03	46.15	46.27	46.38	46.50
2.5	36.89	37.01	37.12	37.24	37.35	37.47	37.58	37.70	37.82	37.93	38.05	38.17
3.0	31.34	31.46	31.57	31.69	31.80	31.92	32.04	32.15	32.27	32.39	32.51	32.63
3.5	27.38	27.50	27.62	27.73	27.85	27.97	28.09	28.20	28.32	28.44	28.56	28.68
4.0	24.42	24.54	24.65	24.77	24.89	25.01	25.13	25.25	25.37	25.49	25.61	25.73
4.5	22.12	22.24	22.36	22.47	22.59	22.71	22.84	22.96	23.08	23.20	23.32	23.44
5.0	20.28	20.40	20.52	20.64	20.76	20.88	21.01	21.13	21.25	21.38	21.50	21.62
5.5	18.78	18.90	19.03	19.15	19.27	19.39	19.52	19.64	19.76	19.89	20.01	20.14
6.0	17.54	17.66	17.78	17.91	18.03	18.15	18.28	18.41	18.53	18.66	18.78	18.91
6.5	16.49	16.61	16.74	16.86	16.99	17.11	17.24	17.36	17.49	17.62	17.75	17.88
7.0	15.59	15.72	15.84	15.97	16.09	16.22	16.35	16.48	16.61	16.74	16.87	17.00
7.5	14.82	14.94	15.07	15.20	15.32	15.45	15.58	15.71	15.84	15.97	16.11	16.24
8.0	14.14	14.27	14.40	14.53	14.66	14.79	14.92	15.05	15.18	15.31	15.45	15.58
8.5	13.55	13.68	13.81	13.94	14.07	14.20	14.33	14.46	14.60	14.73	14.87	15.00
9.0	13.02	13.15	13.28	13.42	13.55	13.68	13.81	13.95	14.08	14.22	14.36	14.49
9.5	12.56	12.69	12.82	12.95	13.09	13.22	13.36	13.49	13.63	13.76	13.90	14.04
10.0	12.14	12.27	12.40	12.54	12.67	12.81	12.94	13.08	13.22	13.36	13.50	13.64
10.5	11.76	11.89	12.03	12.16	12.30	12.44	12.58	12.71	12.85	12.99	13.14	13.28
11.0	11.42	11.56	11.69	11.83	11.97	12.10	12.24	12.38	12.52	12.67	12.81	12.95
11.5	11.11	11.25	11.38	11.52	11.66	11.80	11.94	12.08	12.23	12.37	12.51	12.66
12.0	10.83	10.97	11.11	11.24	11.39	11.53	11.67	11.81	11.96	12.10	12.25	12.39
12.5	10.57	10.71	10.85	10.99	11.13	11.28	11.42	11.56	11.71	11.86	12.00	12.15
13.0	10.34	10.48	10.62	10.76	10.90	11.05	11.19	11.34	11.48	11.63	11.78	11.93
13.5	10.12	10.26	10.40	10.55	10.69	10.83	10.98	11.13	11.28	11.43	11.58	11.73
14.0	9.92	10.06	10.20	10.35	10.49	10.64	10.79	10.94	11.09	11.24	11.39	11.54
14.5	9.73	9.88	10.02	10.17	10.31	10.46	10.61	10.76	10.91	11.06	11.22	11.37
15.0	9.56	9.71	9.85	10.00	10.15	10.30	10.45	10.60	10.75	10.90	11.06	11.21
15.5	9.40	9.55	9.70	9.84	9.99	10.14	10.30	10.45	10.60	10.76	10.91	11.07
16.0	9.25	9.40	9.55	9.70	9.85	10.00	10.15	10.31	10.46	10.62	10.78	10.94
16.5	9.12	9.26	9.41	9.57	9.72	9.87	10.02	10.18	10.34	10.49	10.65	10.81
17.0	8.99	9.14	9.29	9.44	9.59	9.75	9.90	10.06	10.22	10.38	10.54	10.70
17.5	8.87	9.02	9.17	9.32	9.48	9.63	9.79	9.95	10.11	10.27	10.43	10.59
18.0	8.75	8.91	9.06	9.21	9.37	9.53	9.68	9.84	10.00	10.16	10.33	10.49
18.5	8.65	8.80	8.96	9.11	9.27	9.43	9.59	9.75	9.91	10.07	10.23	10.40
19.0	8.55	8.70	8.86	9.02	9.17	9.33	9.49	9.65	9.82	9.98	10.15	10.31
19.5	8.46	8.61	8.77	8.93	9.09	9.25	9.41	9.57	9.73	9.90	10.06	10.23
20.0	8.37	8.53	8.68	8.84	9.00	9.16	9.33	9.49	9.66	9.82	9.99	10.16
20.5	8.29	8.44	8.60	8.76	8.92	9.09	9.25	9.42	9.58	9.75	9.92	10.09
21.0	8.21	8.37	8.53	8.69	8.85	9.01	9.18	9.35	9.51	9.68	9.85	10.02
21.5	8.14	8.30	8.46	8.62	8.78	8.95	9.11	9.28	9.45	9.62	9.79	9.96
22.0	8.07	8.23	8.39	8.55	8.72	8.88	9.05	9.22	9.39	9.56	9.73	9.90
22.5	8.00	8.16	8.33	8.49	8.66	8.82	8.99	9.16	9.33	9.50	9.68	9.85
23.0	7.94	8.10	8.27	8.43	8.60	8.77	8.93	9.11	9.28	9.45	9.62	9.80
23.5	7.88	8.04	8.21	8.38	8.54	8.71	8.88	9.05	9.23	9.40	9.58	9.75
24.0	7.83	7.99	8.16	8.32	8.49	8.66	8.83	9.01	9.18	9.35	9.53	9.71
24.5	7.77	7.94	8.11	8.27	8.44	8.61	8.79	8.96	9.13	9.31	9.49	9.67
25.0	7.72	7.89	8.06	8.23	8.40	8.57	8.74	8.92	9.09	9.27	9.45	9.63
25.5	7.68	7.84	8.01	8.18	8.35	8.53	8.70	8.88	9.05	9.23	9.41	9.59
26.0	7.63	7.80	7.97	8.14	8.31	8.49	8.66	8.84	9.01	9.19	9.37	9.55
26.5	7.59	7.76	7.93	8.10	8.27	8.45	8.62	8.80	8.98	9.16	9.34	9.52
27.0	7.55	7.72	7.89	8.06	8.24	8.41	8.59	8.77	8.95	9.13	9.31	9.49
27.5	7.51	7.68	7.85	8.03	8.20	8.38	8.56	8.73	8.91	9.10	9.28	* 9.46
28.0	7.47	7.64	7.82	7.99	8.17	8.35	8.52	8.70	8.88	9.07	9.25	9.43
28.5	7.44	7.61	7.78	7.96	8.14	8.31	8.49	8.67	8.86	9.04	9.22	9.41
29.0	7.40	7.58	7.75	7.93	8.11	8.29	8.47	8.65	8.83	9.01	9.20	9.38
29.5	7.37	7.55	7.72	7.90	8.08	8.26	8.44	8.62	8.80	8.99	9.17	9.36
30.0	7.34	7.52	7.69	7.87	8.05	8.23	8.41	8.60	8.78	8.97	9.15	9.34
31.0	7.29	7.46	7.64	7.82	8.00	8.18	8.37	8.55	8.74	8.92	9.11	9.30
32.0	7.24	7.41	7.59	7.77	7.96	8.14	8.32	8.51	8.70	8.89	9.07	9.26
33.0	7.19	7.37	7.55	7.73	7.92	8.10	8.29	8.47	8.66	8.85	9.04	9.23
34.0	7.15	7.33	7.51	7.69	7.88	8.06	8.25	8.44	8.63	8.82	9.01	9.21
35.0	7.11	7.29	7.47	7.66	7.84	8.03	8.22	8.41	8.60	8.79	8.99	9.18
36.0	7.07	7.26	7.44	7.63	7.81	8.00	8.19	8.38	8.58	8.77	8.96	9.16
37.0	7.04	7.22	7.41	7.60	7.79	7.98	8.17	8.36	8.55	8.75	8.94	9.14
38.0	7.01	7.20	7.38	7.57	7.76	7.95	8.15	8.34	8.53	8.73	8.92	9.12
39.0	6.98	7.17	7.36	7.55	7.74	7.93	8.12	8.32	8.51	8.71	8.91	9.10
40.0	6.96	7.15	7.34	7.53	7.72	7.91	8.11	8.30	8.50	8.69	8.89	9.09

MONTHLY
PAYMENT REQUIRED TO AMORTIZE A $1,000.00 LOAN

TERM IN YEARS	INTEREST RATES											
	11.00%	11.25%	11.50%	11.75%	12.00%	12.25%	12.50%	12.75%	13.00%	13.25%	13.50%	13.75%
0.5	172.06	172.18	172.31	172.43	172.55	172.68	172.80	172.92	173.05	173.17	173.30	173.42
1.0	88.39	88.50	88.62	88.74	88.85	88.97	89.09	89.21	89.32	89.44	89.56	89.67
1.5	60.52	60.64	60.76	60.87	60.99	61.10	61.22	61.34	61.45	61.57	61.69	61.80
2.0	46.61	46.73	46.85	46.96	47.08	47.20	47.31	47.43	47.55	47.66	47.78	47.90
2.5	38.28	38.40	38.52	38.64	38.75	38.87	38.99	39.11	39.23	39.35	39.46	39.58
3.0	32.74	32.86	32.98	33.10	33.22	33.34	33.46	33.58	33.70	33.82	33.94	34.06
3.5	28.80	28.92	29.04	29.16	29.28	29.40	29.52	29.65	29.77	29.89	30.01	30.14
4.0	25.85	25.97	26.09	26.22	26.34	26.46	26.58	26.71	26.83	26.96	27.08	27.21
4.5	23.57	23.69	23.81	23.94	24.06	24.19	24.31	24.44	24.56	24.69	24.82	24.94
5.0	21.75	21.87	22.00	22.12	22.25	22.38	22.50	22.63	22.76	22.89	23.01	23.14
5.5	20.27	20.39	20.52	20.65	20.78	20.90	21.03	21.16	21.29	21.42	21.55	21.68
6.0	19.04	19.17	19.30	19.43	19.56	19.69	19.82	19.95	20.08	20.21	20.34	20.48
6.5	18.01	18.14	18.27	18.40	18.53	18.66	18.79	18.93	19.06	19.20	19.33	19.47
7.0	17.13	17.26	17.39	17.52	17.66	17.79	17.93	18.06	18.20	18.33	18.47	18.61
7.5	16.37	16.50	16.64	16.77	16.91	17.04	17.18	17.32	17.45	17.59	17.73	17.87
8.0	15.71	15.85	15.98	16.12	16.26	16.40	16.53	16.67	16.81	16.95	17.09	17.23
8.5	15.14	15.27	15.41	15.55	15.69	15.83	15.97	16.11	16.25	16.39	16.54	16.68
9.0	14.63	14.77	14.91	15.05	15.19	15.33	15.47	15.62	15.76	15.90	16.05	16.19
9.5	14.18	14.32	14.46	14.60	14.75	14.89	15.03	15.18	15.32	15.47	15.62	15.76
10.0	13.78	13.92	14.06	14.21	14.35	14.50	14.64	14.79	14.94	15.08	15.23	15.38
10.5	13.42	13.56	13.71	13.85	14.00	14.15	14.29	14.44	14.59	14.74	14.89	15.04
11.0	13.10	13.24	13.39	13.54	13.68	13.83	13.98	14.13	14.28	14.43	14.58	14.74
11.5	12.81	12.95	13.10	13.25	13.40	13.55	13.70	13.85	14.00	14.16	14.31	14.46
12.0	12.54	12.69	12.84	12.99	13.14	13.29	13.44	13.60	13.75	13.91	14.06	14.22
12.5	12.30	12.45	12.60	12.75	12.90	13.06	13.21	13.37	13.52	13.68	13.84	14.00
13.0	12.08	12.23	12.38	12.54	12.69	12.85	13.00	13.16	13.32	13.48	13.63	13.80
13.5	11.88	12.03	12.19	12.34	12.50	12.65	12.81	12.97	13.13	13.29	13.45	13.61
14.0	11.70	11.85	12.01	12.16	12.32	12.48	12.64	12.80	12.96	13.12	13.28	13.45
14.5	11.53	11.68	11.84	12.00	12.16	12.32	12.48	12.64	12.80	12.96	13.13	13.29
15.0	11.37	11.53	11.69	11.85	12.01	12.17	12.33	12.49	12.66	12.82	12.99	13.15
15.5	11.23	11.39	11.55	11.71	11.87	12.03	12.20	12.36	12.53	12.69	12.86	13.03
16.0	11.10	11.26	11.42	11.58	11.74	11.91	12.07	12.24	12.40	12.57	12.74	12.91
16.5	10.97	11.13	11.30	11.46	11.63	11.79	11.96	12.13	12.29	12.46	12.63	12.80
17.0	10.86	11.02	11.19	11.35	11.52	11.68	11.85	12.02	12.19	12.36	12.53	12.71
17.5	10.75	10.92	11.08	11.25	11.42	11.59	11.75	11.93	12.10	12.27	12.44	12.62
18.0	10.66	10.82	10.99	11.16	11.32	11.49	11.67	11.84	12.01	12.18	12.36	12.53
18.5	10.56	10.73	10.90	11.07	11.24	11.41	11.58	11.75	11.93	12.10	12.28	12.46
19.0	10.48	10.65	10.82	10.99	11.16	11.33	11.50	11.68	11.85	12.03	12.21	12.39
19.5	10.40	10.57	10.74	10.91	11.08	11.26	11.43	11.61	11.78	11.96	12.14	12.32
20.0	10.33	10.50	10.67	10.84	11.02	11.19	11.37	11.54	11.72	11.90	12.08	12.26
20.5	10.26	10.43	10.60	10.78	10.95	11.13	11.30	11.48	11.66	11.84	12.02	12.20
21.0	10.19	10.37	10.54	10.72	10.89	11.07	11.25	11.43	11.61	11.79	11.97	12.15
21.5	10.13	10.31	10.48	10.66	10.84	11.01	11.19	11.37	11.55	11.74	11.92	12.10
22.0	10.08	10.25	10.43	10.61	10.78	10.96	11.14	11.33	11.51	11.69	11.87	12.06
22.5	10.02	10.20	10.38	10.56	10.74	10.92	11.10	11.28	11.46	11.65	11.83	12.02
23.0	9.98	10.15	10.33	10.51	10.69	10.87	11.05	11.24	11.42	11.61	11.79	11.98
23.5	9.93	10.11	10.29	10.47	10.65	10.83	11.01	11.20	11.38	11.57	11.76	11.94
24.0	9.89	10.06	10.25	10.43	10.61	10.79	10.98	11.16	11.35	11.53	11.72	11.91
24.5	9.84	10.02	10.21	10.39	10.57	10.76	10.94	11.13	11.31	11.50	11.69	11.88
25.0	9.81	9.99	10.17	10.35	10.54	10.72	10.91	11.10	11.28	11.47	11.66	11.85
25.5	9.77	9.95	10.14	10.32	10.50	10.69	10.88	11.07	11.25	11.44	11.63	11.83
26.0	9.74	9.92	10.10	10.29	10.47	10.66	10.85	11.04	11.23	11.42	11.61	11.80
26.5	9.70	9.89	10.07	10.26	10.45	10.63	10.82	11.01	11.20	11.39	11.58	11.78
27.0	9.67	9.86	10.05	10.23	10.42	10.61	10.80	10.99	11.18	11.37	11.56	11.76
27.5	9.65	9.83	10.02	10.21	10.39	10.58	10.77	10.97	11.16	11.35	11.54	11.74
28.0	9.62	9.81	9.99	10.18	10.37	10.56	10.75	10.94	11.14	11.33	11.52	11.72
28.5	9.59	9.78	9.97	10.16	10.35	10.54	10.73	10.92	11.12	11.31	11.51	11.70
29.0	9.57	9.76	9.95	10.14	10.33	10.52	10.71	10.91	11.10	11.29	11.49	11.68
29.5	9.55	9.74	9.93	10.12	10.31	10.50	10.69	10.89	11.08	11.28	11.47	11.67
30.0	9.53	9.72	9.91	10.10	10.29	10.48	10.68	10.87	11.07	11.26	11.46	11.66
31.0	9.49	9.68	9.87	10.06	10.26	10.45	10.65	10.84	11.04	11.24	11.43	11.63
32.0	9.46	9.65	9.84	10.03	10.23	10.42	10.62	10.82	11.01	11.21	11.41	11.61
33.0	9.43	9.62	9.81	10.01	10.20	10.40	10.60	10.79	10.99	11.19	11.39	11.59
34.0	9.40	9.59	9.79	9.98	10.18	10.38	10.58	10.77	10.97	11.17	11.37	11.57
35.0	9.37	9.57	9.77	9.96	10.16	10.36	10.56	10.76	10.96	11.16	11.36	11.56
36.0	9.35	9.55	9.75	9.94	10.14	10.34	10.54	10.74	10.94	11.14	11.35	11.55
37.0	9.33	9.53	9.73	9.93	10.13	10.33	10.53	10.73	10.93	11.13	11.33	11.54
38.0	9.32	9.51	9.71	9.91	10.11	10.31	10.51	10.72	10.92	11.12	11.32	11.53
39.0	9.30	9.50	9.70	9.90	10.10	10.30	10.50	10.71	10.91	11.11	11.32	11.52
40.0	9.29	9.49	9.69	9.89	10.09	10.29	10.49	10.70	10.90	11.10	11.31	11.51

MONTHLY
PAYMENT REQUIRED TO AMORTIZE A $1,000.00 LOAN

TERM IN YEARS	14.00%	14.25%	14.50%	14.75%	15.00%	15.25%	15.50%	15.75%	16.00%	16.25%	16.50%	16.75%
0.5	173.54	173.67	173.79	173.91	174.04	174.16	174.29	174.41	174.54	174.66	174.78	174.91
1.0	89.79	89.91	90.03	90.15	90.26	90.38	90.50	90.62	90.74	90.85	90.97	91.09
1.5	61.92	62.04	62.15	62.27	62.39	62.51	62.63	62.74	62.86	62.98	63.10	63.22
2.0	48.02	48.14	48.25	48.37	48.49	48.61	48.73	48.85	48.97	49.09	49.21	49.33
2.5	39.70	39.82	39.94	40.06	40.18	40.30	40.42	40.55	40.67	40.79	40.91	41.03
3.0	34.18	34.30	34.43	34.55	34.67	34.79	34.92	35.04	35.16	35.29	35.41	35.53
3.5	30.26	30.38	30.51	30.63	30.75	30.88	31.00	31.13	31.25	31.38	31.51	31.63
4.0	27.33	27.46	27.58	27.71	27.84	27.96	28.09	28.22	28.35	28.47	28.60	28.73
4.5	25.07	25.20	25.33	25.45	25.58	25.71	25.84	25.97	26.10	26.23	26.36	26.49
5.0	23.27	23.40	23.53	23.66	23.79	23.93	24.06	24.19	24.32	24.46	24.59	24.72
5.5	21.82	21.95	22.08	22.21	22.35	22.48	22.61	22.75	22.88	23.02	23.15	23.29
6.0	20.61	20.74	20.88	21.01	21.15	21.29	21.42	21.56	21.70	21.83	21.97	22.11
6.5	19.60	19.74	19.87	20.01	20.15	20.29	20.43	20.57	20.71	20.85	20.99	21.13
7.0	18.75	18.88	19.02	19.16	19.30	19.44	19.58	19.72	19.87	20.01	20.15	20.30
7.5	18.01	18.15	18.29	18.43	18.58	18.72	18.86	19.01	19.15	19.30	19.44	19.59
8.0	17.38	17.52	17.66	17.81	17.95	18.10	18.24	18.39	18.53	18.68	18.83	18.98
8.5	16.82	16.97	17.11	17.26	17.41	17.55	17.70	17.85	18.00	18.15	18.30	18.45
9.0	16.34	16.49	16.63	16.78	16.93	17.08	17.23	17.38	17.53	17.68	17.83	17.99
9.5	15.91	16.06	16.21	16.36	16.51	16.66	16.81	16.97	17.12	17.27	17.43	17.58
10.0	15.53	15.68	15.83	15.99	16.14	16.29	16.45	16.60	16.76	16.91	17.07	17.23
10.5	15.19	15.35	15.50	15.65	15.81	15.96	16.12	16.28	16.43	16.59	16.75	16.91
11.0	14.89	15.05	15.20	15.36	15.51	15.67	15.83	15.99	16.15	16.31	16.47	16.63
11.5	14.62	14.78	14.93	15.09	15.25	15.41	15.57	15.73	15.89	16.05	16.22	16.38
12.0	14.38	14.53	14.69	14.85	15.01	15.18	15.34	15.50	15.66	15.83	15.99	16.16
12.5	14.16	14.32	14.48	14.64	14.80	14.96	15.13	15.29	15.46	15.62	15.79	15.96
13.0	13.96	14.12	14.28	14.44	14.61	14.77	14.94	15.10	15.27	15.44	15.61	15.78
13.5	13.77	13.94	14.10	14.27	14.43	14.60	14.77	14.94	15.10	15.27	15.44	15.62
14.0	13.61	13.78	13.94	14.11	14.28	14.44	14.61	14.78	14.95	15.12	15.30	15.47
14.5	13.46	13.63	13.79	13.96	14.13	14.30	14.47	14.64	14.82	14.99	15.16	15.34
15.0	13.32	13.49	13.66	13.83	14.00	14.17	14.34	14.52	14.69	14.87	15.04	15.22
15.5	13.20	13.37	13.54	13.71	13.88	14.05	14.23	14.40	14.58	14.76	14.93	15.11
16.0	13.08	13.25	13.43	13.60	13.77	13.95	14.12	14.30	14.48	14.65	14.83	15.01
16.5	12.98	13.15	13.32	13.50	13.67	13.85	14.03	14.20	14.38	14.56	14.74	14.92
17.0	12.88	13.05	13.23	13.41	13.58	13.76	13.94	14.12	14.30	14.48	14.66	14.84
17.5	12.79	12.97	13.14	13.32	13.50	13.68	13.86	14.04	14.22	14.40	14.58	14.77
18.0	12.71	12.89	13.06	13.24	13.42	13.60	13.78	13.96	14.15	14.33	14.51	14.70
18.5	12.63	12.81	12.99	13.17	13.35	13.53	13.72	13.90	14.08	14.27	14.45	14.64
19.0	12.56	12.74	12.92	13.10	13.29	13.47	13.65	13.84	14.02	14.21	14.39	14.58
19.5	12.50	12.68	12.86	13.04	13.23	13.41	13.60	13.78	13.97	14.15	14.34	14.53
20.0	12.44	12.62	12.80	12.99	13.17	13.36	13.54	13.73	13.92	14.11	14.29	14.48
20.5	12.39	12.57	12.75	12.94	13.12	13.31	13.50	13.68	13.87	14.06	14.25	14.44
21.0	12.33	12.52	12.70	12.89	13.08	13.26	13.45	13.64	13.83	14.02	14.21	14.40
21.5	12.29	12.47	12.66	12.85	13.03	13.22	13.41	13.60	13.79	13.98	14.17	14.37
22.0	12.24	12.43	12.62	12.81	12.99	13.18	13.37	13.56	13.75	13.95	14.14	14.33
22.5	12.20	12.39	12.58	12.77	12.96	13.15	13.34	13.53	13.72	13.91	14.11	14.30
23.0	12.17	12.35	12.54	12.73	12.92	13.12	13.31	13.50	13.69	13.89	14.08	14.27
23.5	12.13	12.32	12.51	12.70	12.89	13.08	13.28	13.47	13.66	13.86	14.05	14.25
24.0	12.10	12.29	12.48	12.67	12.86	13.06	13.25	13.44	13.64	13.83	14.03	14.23
24.5	12.07	12.26	12.45	12.64	12.84	13.03	13.23	13.42	13.62	13.81	14.01	14.20
25.0	12.04	12.23	12.43	12.62	12.81	13.01	13.20	13.40	13.59	13.79	13.99	14.18
25.5	12.02	12.21	12.40	12.60	12.79	12.99	13.18	13.38	13.57	13.77	13.97	14.17
26.0	11.99	12.19	12.38	12.57	12.77	12.97	13.16	13.36	13.56	13.75	13.95	14.15
26.5	11.97	12.16	12.36	12.55	12.75	12.95	13.14	13.34	13.54	13.74	13.94	14.14
27.0	11.95	12.14	12.34	12.54	12.73	12.93	13.13	13.32	13.52	13.72	13.92	14.12
27.5	11.93	12.13	12.32	12.52	12.72	12.91	13.11	13.31	13.51	13.71	13.91	14.11
28.0	11.91	12.11	12.31	12.50	12.70	12.90	13.10	13.30	13.50	13.70	13.90	14.10
28.5	11.90	12.09	12.29	12.49	12.69	12.88	13.08	13.28	13.48	13.68	13.89	14.09
29.0	11.88	12.08	12.28	12.47	12.67	12.87	13.07	13.27	13.47	13.67	13.87	14.08
29.5	11.87	12.06	12.26	12.46	12.66	12.86	13.06	13.26	13.46	13.66	13.87	14.07
30.0	11.85	12.05	12.25	12.45	12.65	12.85	13.05	13.25	13.45	13.65	13.86	14.06
31.0	11.83	12.03	12.23	12.43	12.63	12.83	13.03	13.23	13.44	13.64	13.84	14.04
32.0	11.81	12.01	12.21	12.41	12.61	12.81	13.02	13.22	13.42	13.62	13.83	14.03
33.0	11.79	11.99	12.19	12.39	12.60	12.80	13.00	13.21	13.41	13.61	13.82	14.02
34.0	11.78	11.98	12.18	12.38	12.58	12.79	12.99	13.19	13.40	13.60	13.81	14.01
35.0	11.76	11.96	12.17	12.37	12.57	12.78	12.98	13.19	13.39	13.59	13.80	14.00
36.0	11.75	11.95	12.16	12.36	12.56	12.77	12.97	13.18	13.38	13.59	13.79	14.00
37.0	11.74	11.94	12.15	12.35	12.56	12.76	12.97	13.17	13.38	13.58	13.79	13.99
38.0	11.73	11.93	12.14	12.34	12.55	12.75	12.96	13.16	13.37	13.58	13.78	13.99
39.0	11.72	11.93	12.13	12.34	12.54	12.75	12.95	13.16	13.37	13.57	13.78	13.98
40.0	11.72	11.92	12.13	12.33	12.54	12.74	12.95	13.16	13.36	13.57	13.77	13.98

MONTHLY
PAYMENT REQUIRED TO AMORTIZE A $1,000.00 LOAN

TERM IN YEARS	17.00%	17.25%	17.50%	17.75%	18.00%	18.25%	18.50%	18.75%	19.00%	19.25%	19.50%	19.75%
0.5	175.03	175.16	175.28	175.41	175.53	175.65	175.78	175.90	176.03	176.15	176.28	176.40
1.0	91.21	91.33	91.45	91.57	91.68	91.80	91.92	92.04	92.16	92.28	92.40	92.52
1.5	63.34	63.45	63.57	63.69	63.81	63.93	64.05	64.17	64.29	64.41	64.53	64.65
2.0	49.45	49.57	49.69	49.81	49.93	50.05	50.17	50.29	50.41	50.54	50.66	50.78
2.5	41.15	41.28	41.40	41.52	41.64	41.77	41.89	42.01	42.14	42.26	42.39	42.51
3.0	35.66	35.78	35.91	36.03	36.16	36.28	36.41	36.53	36.66	36.79	36.91	37.04
3.5	31.76	31.89	32.01	32.14	32.27	32.40	32.53	32.65	32.78	32.91	33.04	33.17
4.0	28.86	28.99	29.12	29.25	29.38	29.51	29.64	29.77	29.91	30.04	30.17	30.30
4.5	26.63	26.76	26.89	27.02	27.16	27.29	27.42	27.56	27.69	27.83	27.96	28.10
5.0	24.86	24.99	25.13	25.26	25.40	25.53	25.67	25.81	25.95	26.08	26.22	26.36
5.5	23.43	23.56	23.70	23.84	23.98	24.12	24.26	24.40	24.54	24.68	24.82	24.96
6.0	22.25	22.39	22.53	22.67	22.81	22.95	23.10	23.24	23.38	23.53	23.67	23.81
6.5	21.27	21.41	21.55	21.70	21.84	21.99	22.13	22.28	22.42	22.57	22.71	22.86
7.0	20.44	20.59	20.73	20.88	21.02	21.17	21.32	21.46	21.61	21.76	21.91	22.06
7.5	19.73	19.88	20.03	20.18	20.33	20.48	20.63	20.78	20.93	21.08	21.23	21.38
8.0	19.13	19.28	19.43	19.58	19.73	19.88	20.03	20.19	20.34	20.49	20.65	20.80
8.5	18.60	18.75	18.90	19.06	19.21	19.37	19.52	19.68	19.83	19.99	20.15	20.30
9.0	18.14	18.30	18.45	18.61	18.76	18.92	19.08	19.23	19.39	19.55	19.71	19.87
9.5	17.74	17.90	18.05	18.21	18.37	18.53	18.69	18.85	19.01	19.17	19.33	19.49
10.0	17.38	17.54	17.70	17.86	18.02	18.18	18.35	18.51	18.67	18.84	19.00	19.17
10.5	17.07	17.23	17.39	17.56	17.72	17.88	18.05	18.21	18.38	18.54	18.71	18.88
11.0	16.79	16.96	17.12	17.28	17.45	17.61	17.78	17.95	18.12	18.28	18.45	18.62
11.5	16.55	16.71	16.88	17.04	17.21	17.38	17.55	17.71	17.88	18.05	18.23	18.40
12.0	16.32	16.49	16.66	16.83	17.00	17.17	17.34	17.51	17.68	17.85	18.02	18.20
12.5	16.13	16.29	16.46	16.63	16.81	16.98	17.15	17.32	17.50	17.67	17.84	18.02
13.0	15.95	16.12	16.29	16.46	16.64	16.81	16.98	17.16	17.33	17.51	17.69	17.86
13.5	15.79	15.96	16.13	16.31	16.48	16.66	16.83	17.01	17.19	17.36	17.54	17.72
14.0	15.64	15.82	15.99	16.17	16.34	16.52	16.70	16.88	17.06	17.24	17.42	17.60
14.5	15.51	15.69	15.87	16.04	16.22	16.40	16.58	16.76	16.94	17.12	17.30	17.48
15.0	15.40	15.57	15.75	15.93	16.11	16.29	16.47	16.65	16.83	17.02	17.20	17.38
15.5	15.29	15.47	15.65	15.83	16.01	16.19	16.37	16.56	16.74	16.92	17.11	17.29
16.0	15.19	15.37	15.55	15.74	15.92	16.10	16.28	16.47	16.65	16.84	17.03	17.21
16.5	15.10	15.29	15.47	15.65	15.84	16.02	16.20	16.39	16.58	16.76	16.95	17.14
17.0	15.02	15.21	15.39	15.58	15.76	15.95	16.13	16.32	16.51	16.70	16.88	17.07
17.5	14.95	15.14	15.32	15.51	15.69	15.88	16.07	16.26	16.45	16.63	16.82	17.02
18.0	14.88	15.07	15.26	15.44	15.63	15.82	16.01	16.20	16.39	16.58	16.77	16.96
18.5	14.82	15.01	15.20	15.39	15.58	15.77	15.96	16.15	16.34	16.53	16.72	16.91
19.0	14.77	14.96	15.15	15.34	15.53	15.72	15.91	16.10	16.29	16.48	16.68	16.87
19.5	14.72	14.91	15.10	15.29	15.48	15.67	15.86	16.06	16.25	16.44	16.64	16.83
20.0	14.67	14.86	15.05	15.25	15.44	15.63	15.82	16.02	16.21	16.41	16.60	16.80
20.5	14.63	14.82	15.01	15.21	15.40	15.59	15.79	15.98	16.18	16.37	16.57	16.77
21.0	14.59	14.79	14.98	15.17	15.37	15.56	15.76	15.95	16.15	16.34	16.54	16.74
21.5	14.56	14.75	14.94	15.14	15.33	15.53	15.73	15.92	16.12	16.32	16.51	16.71
22.0	14.53	14.72	14.91	15.11	15.31	15.50	15.70	15.90	16.09	16.29	16.49	16.69
22.5	14.50	14.69	14.89	15.08	15.28	15.48	15.67	15.87	16.07	16.27	16.47	16.67
23.0	14.47	14.67	14.86	15.06	15.26	15.45	15.65	15.85	16.05	16.25	16.45	16.65
23.5	14.45	14.64	14.84	15.04	15.23	15.43	15.63	15.83	16.03	16.23	16.43	16.63
24.0	14.42	14.62	14.82	15.02	15.21	15.41	15.61	15.81	16.01	16.21	16.41	16.61
24.5	14.40	14.60	14.80	15.00	15.20	15.40	15.60	15.80	16.00	16.20	16.40	16.60
25.0	14.38	14.58	14.78	14.98	15.18	15.38	15.58	15.78	15.98	16.18	16.39	16.59
25.5	14.37	14.56	14.76	14.96	15.16	15.36	15.57	15.77	15.97	16.17	16.37	16.58
26.0	14.35	14.55	14.75	14.95	15.15	15.35	15.55	15.75	15.96	16.16	16.36	16.56
26.5	14.34	14.54	14.74	14.94	15.14	15.34	15.54	15.74	15.95	16.15	16.35	16.56
27.0	14.32	14.52	14.72	14.92	15.13	15.33	15.53	15.73	15.94	16.14	16.34	16.55
27.5	14.31	14.51	14.71	14.91	15.12	15.32	15.52	15.72	15.93	16.13	16.33	16.54
28.0	14.30	14.50	14.70	14.90	15.11	15.31	15.51	15.72	15.92	16.12	16.33	16.53
28.5	14.29	14.49	14.69	14.89	15.10	15.30	15.50	15.71	15.91	16.12	16.32	16.53
29.0	14.28	14.48	14.68	14.89	15.09	15.29	15.50	15.70	15.91	16.11	16.31	16.52
29.5	14.27	14.47	14.68	14.88	15.08	15.29	15.49	15.69	15.90	16.10	16.31	16.51
30.0	14.26	14.46	14.67	14.87	15.08	15.28	15.48	15.69	15.89	16.10	16.30	16.51
31.0	14.25	14.45	14.66	14.86	15.06	15.27	15.47	15.68	15.88	16.09	16.30	16.50
32.0	14.24	14.44	14.64	14.85	15.05	15.26	15.47	15.67	15.88	16.08	16.29	16.49
33.0	14.23	14.43	14.64	14.84	15.05	15.25	15.46	15.66	15.87	16.08	16.28	16.49
34.0	14.22	14.42	14.63	14.83	15.04	15.25	15.45	15.66	15.86	16.07	16.28	16.48
35.0	14.21	14.42	14.62	14.83	15.03	15.24	15.45	15.65	15.86	16.07	16.27	16.48
36.0	14.20	14.41	14.62	14.82	15.03	15.24	15.44	15.65	15.86	16.06	16.27	16.48
37.0	14.20	14.41	14.61	14.82	15.03	15.23	15.44	15.65	15.85	16.06	16.27	16.48
38.0	14.19	14.40	14.61	14.81	15.02	15.23	15.44	15.64	15.85	16.06	16.27	16.47
39.0	14.19	14.40	14.60	14.81	15.02	15.23	15.43	15.64	15.85	16.06	16.26	16.47
40.0	14.19	14.40	14.60	14.81	15.02	15.22	15.43	15.64	15.85	16.05	16.26	16.47

MONTHLY
PAYMENT REQUIRED TO AMORTIZE A $1,000.00 LOAN

TERM IN YEARS	20.00%	20.25%	20.50%	20.75%	21.00%	21.25%	21.50%	21.75%	22.00%	22.25%	22.50%	22.75%
				INTEREST RATES								
0.5	176.53	176.65	176.78	176.90	177.03	177.15	177.28	177.40	177.53	177.65	177.78	177.90
1.0	92.64	92.76	92.88	93.00	93.12	93.24	93.36	93.48	93.60	93.72	93.84	93.96
1.5	64.77	64.89	65.01	65.13	65.25	65.37	65.49	65.61	65.73	65.85	65.98	66.10
2.0	50.90	51.02	51.15	51.27	51.39	51.51	51.64	51.76	51.88	52.01	52.13	52.25
2.5	42.63	42.76	42.88	43.01	43.13	43.26	43.39	43.51	43.64	43.76	43.89	44.02
3.0	37.17	37.30	37.42	37.55	37.68	37.81	37.94	38.07	38.20	38.32	38.45	38.58
3.5	33.30	33.43	33.56	33.69	33.83	33.96	34.09	34.22	34.35	34.49	34.62	34.75
4.0	30.44	30.57	30.70	30.84	30.97	31.11	31.24	31.38	31.51	31.65	31.78	31.92
4.5	28.23	28.37	28.51	28.64	28.78	28.92	29.06	29.20	29.33	29.47	29.61	29.75
5.0	26.50	26.64	26.78	26.92	27.06	27.20	27.34	27.48	27.62	27.77	27.91	28.05
5.5	25.10	25.24	25.39	25.53	25.67	25.82	25.96	26.11	26.25	26.40	26.54	26.69
6.0	23.96	24.10	24.25	24.39	24.54	24.69	24.84	24.98	25.13	25.28	25.43	25.58
6.5	23.01	23.16	23.30	23.45	23.60	23.75	23.90	24.05	24.21	24.36	24.51	24.66
7.0	22.21	22.36	22.51	22.66	22.82	22.97	23.12	23.28	23.43	23.59	23.74	23.90
7.5	21.54	21.69	21.84	22.00	22.15	22.31	22.46	22.62	22.78	22.94	23.09	23.25
8.0	20.96	21.11	21.27	21.43	21.59	21.74	21.90	22.06	22.22	22.38	22.54	22.70
8.5	20.46	20.62	20.78	20.94	21.10	21.26	21.42	21.58	21.75	21.91	22.07	22.24
9.0	20.03	20.19	20.35	20.52	20.68	20.84	21.01	21.17	21.34	21.50	21.67	21.84
9.5	19.66	19.82	19.99	20.15	20.32	20.48	20.65	20.82	20.98	21.15	21.32	21.49
10.0	19.33	19.50	19.66	19.83	20.00	20.17	20.34	20.50	20.67	20.85	21.02	21.19
10.5	19.04	19.21	19.38	19.55	19.72	19.89	20.06	20.23	20.41	20.58	20.75	20.93
11.0	18.79	18.96	19.13	19.30	19.48	19.65	19.82	20.00	20.17	20.35	20.52	20.70
11.5	18.57	18.74	18.91	19.09	19.26	19.44	19.61	19.79	19.97	20.14	20.32	20.50
12.0	18.37	18.55	18.72	18.90	19.07	19.25	19.43	19.61	19.78	19.96	20.14	20.32
12.5	18.20	18.37	18.55	18.73	18.91	19.08	19.26	19.44	19.62	19.81	19.99	20.17
13.0	18.04	18.22	18.40	18.58	18.76	18.94	19.12	19.30	19.48	19.67	19.85	20.03
13.5	17.90	18.08	18.26	18.44	18.63	18.81	18.99	19.17	19.36	19.54	19.73	19.91
14.0	17.78	17.96	18.14	18.32	18.51	18.69	18.88	19.06	19.25	19.43	19.62	19.81
14.5	17.67	17.85	18.03	18.22	18.40	18.59	18.78	18.96	19.15	19.34	19.53	19.71
15.0	17.57	17.75	17.94	18.12	18.31	18.50	18.69	18.87	19.06	19.25	19.44	19.63
15.5	17.48	17.67	17.85	18.04	18.23	18.42	18.61	18.80	18.99	19.18	19.37	19.56
16.0	17.40	17.59	17.78	17.96	18.15	18.34	18.53	18.72	18.92	19.11	19.30	19.49
16.5	17.33	17.52	17.71	17.90	18.09	18.28	18.47	18.66	18.85	19.05	19.24	19.43
17.0	17.26	17.45	17.65	17.84	18.03	18.22	18.41	18.61	18.80	18.99	19.19	19.38
17.5	17.21	17.40	17.59	17.78	17.98	18.17	18.36	18.56	18.75	18.95	19.14	19.34
18.0	17.15	17.35	17.54	17.73	17.93	18.12	18.32	18.51	18.71	18.90	19.10	19.30
18.5	17.11	17.30	17.50	17.69	17.88	18.08	18.28	18.47	18.67	18.87	19.06	19.26
19.0	17.07	17.26	17.46	17.65	17.85	18.04	18.24	18.44	18.63	18.83	19.03	19.23
19.5	17.03	17.22	17.42	17.62	17.81	18.01	18.21	18.41	18.60	18.80	19.00	19.20
20.0	16.99	17.19	17.39	17.58	17.78	17.98	18.18	18.38	18.58	18.77	18.97	19.17
20.5	16.96	17.16	17.36	17.56	17.75	17.95	18.15	18.35	18.55	18.75	18.95	19.15
21.0	16.93	17.13	17.33	17.53	17.73	17.93	18.13	18.33	18.53	18.73	18.93	19.13
21.5	16.91	17.11	17.31	17.51	17.71	17.91	18.11	18.31	18.51	18.71	18.91	19.11
22.0	16.89	17.09	17.29	17.49	17.69	17.89	18.09	18.29	18.49	18.69	18.90	19.10
22.5	16.87	17.07	17.27	17.47	17.67	17.87	18.07	18.27	18.48	18.68	18.88	19.08
23.0	16.85	17.05	17.25	17.45	17.65	17.85	18.06	18.26	18.46	18.66	18.87	19.07
23.5	16.83	17.03	17.23	17.44	17.64	17.84	18.04	18.25	18.45	18.65	18.86	19.06
24.0	16.82	17.02	17.22	17.42	17.62	17.83	18.03	18.23	18.44	18.64	18.84	19.05
24.5	16.80	17.00	17.21	17.41	17.61	17.82	18.02	18.22	18.43	18.63	18.83	19.04
25.0	16.79	16.99	17.20	17.40	17.60	17.81	18.01	18.21	18.42	18.62	18.83	19.03
25.5	16.78	16.98	17.18	17.39	17.59	17.80	18.00	18.20	18.41	18.61	18.82	19.02
26.0	16.77	16.97	17.18	17.38	17.58	17.79	17.99	18.20	18.40	18.61	18.81	19.02
26.5	16.76	16.96	17.17	17.37	17.58	17.78	17.99	18.19	18.40	18.60	18.81	19.01
27.0	16.75	16.95	17.16	17.36	17.57	17.77	17.98	18.18	18.39	18.59	18.80	19.01
27.5	16.74	16.95	17.15	17.36	17.56	17.77	17.97	18.18	18.38	18.59	18.80	19.00
28.0	16.74	16.94	17.15	17.35	17.56	17.76	17.97	18.17	18.38	18.59	18.79	19.00
28.5	16.73	16.94	17.14	17.35	17.55	17.76	17.96	18.17	18.38	18.58	18.79	18.99
29.0	16.72	16.93	17.14	17.34	17.55	17.75	17.96	18.17	18.37	18.58	18.79	18.99
29.5	16.72	16.93	17.13	17.34	17.54	17.75	17.96	18.16	18.37	18.57	18.78	18.99
30.0	16.72	16.92	17.13	17.33	17.54	17.75	17.95	18.16	18.36	18.57	18.78	18.99
31.0	16.71	16.91	17.12	17.33	17.53	17.74	17.95	18.15	18.36	18.57	18.77	18.98
32.0	16.70	16.91	17.11	17.32	17.53	17.73	17.94	18.15	18.36	18.56	18.77	18.98
33.0	16.70	16.90	17.11	17.32	17.52	17.73	17.94	18.14	18.35	18.56	18.77	18.97
34.0	16.69	16.90	17.11	17.31	17.52	17.73	17.93	18.14	18.35	18.56	18.76	18.97
35.0	16.69	16.89	17.10	17.31	17.52	17.72	17.93	18.14	18.35	18.55	18.76	18.97
36.0	16.68	16.89	17.10	17.31	17.51	17.72	17.93	18.14	18.35	18.55	18.76	18.97
37.0	16.68	16.89	17.10	17.31	17.51	17.72	17.93	18.14	18.34	18.55	18.76	18.97
38.0	16.68	16.89	17.10	17.30	17.51	17.72	17.93	18.13	18.34	18.55	18.76	18.97
39.0	16.68	16.89	17.09	17.30	17.51	17.72	17.93	18.13	18.34	18.55	18.76	18.97
40.0	16.68	16.89	17.09	17.30	17.51	17.72	17.93	18.13	18.34	18.55	18.76	18.97

MONTHLY
PAYMENT REQUIRED TO AMORTIZE A $1,000.00 LOAN

TERM IN YEARS	INTEREST RATES											
	23.00%	23.25%	23.50%	23.75%	24.00%	24.25%	24.50%	24.75%	25.00%	25.25%	25.50%	25.75%
0.5	178.03	178.15	178.28	178.41	178.53	178.66	178.78	178.91	179.03	179.16	179.28	179.41
1.0	94.08	94.20	94.32	94.44	94.56	94.69	94.81	94.93	95.05	95.17	95.29	95.41
1.5	66.22	66.34	66.46	66.58	66.71	66.83	66.95	67.07	67.20	67.32	67.44	67.57
2.0	52.38	52.50	52.63	52.75	52.88	53.00	53.13	53.25	53.38	53.50	53.63	53.75
2.5	44.14	44.27	44.40	44.53	44.65	44.78	44.91	45.04	45.17	45.30	45.43	45.56
3.0	38.71	38.85	38.98	39.11	39.24	39.37	39.50	39.63	39.76	39.90	40.03	40.16
3.5	34.89	35.02	35.15	35.29	35.42	35.56	35.69	35.83	35.96	36.10	36.24	36.37
4.0	32.06	32.19	32.33	32.47	32.61	32.75	32.88	33.02	33.16	33.30	33.44	33.58
4.5	29.89	30.03	30.17	30.32	30.46	30.60	30.74	30.88	31.03	31.17	31.31	31.46
5.0	28.20	28.34	28.48	28.63	28.77	28.92	29.06	29.21	29.36	29.50	29.65	29.80
5.5	26.84	26.98	27.13	27.28	27.43	27.57	27.72	27.87	28.02	28.17	28.32	28.48
6.0	25.73	25.88	26.03	26.18	26.33	26.48	26.64	26.79	26.94	27.10	27.25	27.40
6.5	24.81	24.97	25.12	25.28	25.43	25.59	25.74	25.90	26.05	26.21	26.37	26.53
7.0	24.05	24.21	24.37	24.52	24.68	24.84	25.00	25.16	25.32	25.48	25.64	25.80
7.5	23.41	23.57	23.73	23.89	24.05	24.21	24.37	24.54	24.70	24.86	25.03	25.19
8.0	22.87	23.03	23.19	23.35	23.52	23.68	23.85	24.01	24.18	24.34	24.51	24.68
8.5	22.40	22.57	22.73	22.90	23.06	23.23	23.40	23.57	23.74	23.90	24.07	24.24
9.0	22.00	22.17	22.34	22.51	22.68	22.85	23.02	23.19	23.36	23.53	23.70	23.87
9.5	21.66	21.83	22.00	22.17	22.34	22.51	22.69	22.86	23.03	23.21	23.38	23.56
10.0	21.36	21.53	21.71	21.88	22.05	22.23	22.40	22.58	22.75	22.93	23.11	23.29
10.5	21.10	21.28	21.45	21.63	21.80	21.98	22.16	22.34	22.51	22.69	22.87	23.05
11.0	20.87	21.05	21.23	21.41	21.59	21.76	21.94	22.12	22.30	22.49	22.67	22.85
11.5	20.68	20.86	21.04	21.22	21.40	21.58	21.76	21.94	22.12	22.31	22.49	22.67
12.0	20.50	20.68	20.87	21.05	21.23	21.41	21.60	21.78	21.97	22.15	22.34	22.52
12.5	20.35	20.53	20.72	20.90	21.09	21.27	21.46	21.64	21.83	22.02	22.20	22.39
13.0	20.22	20.40	20.59	20.77	20.96	21.15	21.33	21.52	21.71	21.90	22.09	22.27
13.5	20.10	20.29	20.47	20.66	20.85	21.04	21.22	21.41	21.60	21.79	21.98	22.17
14.0	20.00	20.18	20.37	20.56	20.75	20.94	21.13	21.32	21.51	21.70	21.89	22.09
14.5	19.90	20.09	20.28	20.47	20.66	20.85	21.05	21.24	21.43	21.62	21.82	22.01
15.0	19.82	20.01	20.20	20.40	20.59	20.78	20.97	21.17	21.36	21.55	21.75	21.94
15.5	19.75	19.94	20.13	20.33	20.52	20.71	20.91	21.10	21.30	21.49	21.69	21.89
16.0	19.69	19.88	20.07	20.27	20.46	20.66	20.85	21.05	21.24	21.44	21.64	21.83
16.5	19.63	19.82	20.02	20.21	20.41	20.61	20.80	21.00	21.20	21.39	21.59	21.79
17.0	19.58	19.77	19.97	20.17	20.36	20.56	20.76	20.96	21.15	21.35	21.55	21.75
17.5	19.53	19.73	19.93	20.12	20.32	20.52	20.72	20.92	21.12	21.32	21.51	21.71
18.0	19.49	19.69	19.89	20.09	20.29	20.49	20.68	20.88	21.08	21.28	21.48	21.68
18.5	19.46	19.66	19.86	20.06	20.25	20.45	20.65	20.85	21.05	21.26	21.46	21.66
19.0	19.43	19.63	19.83	20.03	20.23	20.43	20.63	20.83	21.03	21.23	21.43	21.63
19.5	19.40	19.60	19.80	20.00	20.20	20.40	20.60	20.81	21.01	21.21	21.41	21.61
20.0	19.38	19.58	19.78	19.98	20.18	20.38	20.58	20.78	20.99	21.19	21.39	21.60
20.5	19.35	19.55	19.76	19.96	20.16	20.36	20.56	20.77	20.97	21.17	21.38	21.58
21.0	19.33	19.54	19.74	19.94	20.14	20.34	20.55	20.75	20.95	21.16	21.36	21.57
21.5	19.32	19.52	19.72	19.92	20.13	20.33	20.53	20.74	20.94	21.14	21.35	21.55
22.0	19.30	19.50	19.71	19.91	20.11	20.32	20.52	20.72	20.93	21.13	21.34	21.54
22.5	19.29	19.49	19.69	19.90	20.10	20.30	20.51	20.71	20.92	21.12	21.33	21.53
23.0	19.27	19.48	19.68	19.89	20.09	20.29	20.50	20.70	20.91	21.11	21.32	21.52
23.5	19.26	19.47	19.67	19.88	20.08	20.29	20.49	20.70	20.90	21.11	21.31	21.52
24.0	19.25	19.46	19.66	19.87	20.07	20.28	20.48	20.69	20.89	21.10	21.30	21.51
24.5	19.24	19.45	19.65	19.86	20.06	20.27	20.48	20.68	20.89	21.09	21.30	21.51
25.0	19.24	19.44	19.65	19.85	20.06	20.26	20.47	20.68	20.88	21.09	21.29	21.50
25.5	19.23	19.43	19.64	19.85	20.05	20.26	20.46	20.67	20.88	21.08	21.29	21.50
26.0	19.22	19.43	19.63	19.84	20.05	20.25	20.46	20.67	20.87	21.08	21.29	21.49
26.5	19.22	19.42	19.63	19.84	20.04	20.25	20.45	20.66	20.87	21.07	21.28	21.49
27.0	19.21	19.42	19.62	19.83	20.04	20.24	20.45	20.66	20.86	21.07	21.28	21.49
27.5	19.21	19.41	19.62	19.83	20.03	20.24	20.45	20.65	20.86	21.07	21.28	21.48
28.0	19.20	19.41	19.62	19.82	20.03	20.24	20.44	20.65	20.86	21.07	21.27	21.48
28.5	19.20	19.41	19.61	19.82	20.03	20.23	20.44	20.65	20.86	21.06	21.27	21.48
29.0	19.20	19.40	19.61	19.82	20.03	20.23	20.44	20.65	20.85	21.06	21.27	21.48
29.5	19.19	19.40	19.61	19.82	20.02	20.23	20.44	20.64	20.85	21.06	21.27	21.48
30.0	19.19	19.40	19.61	19.81	20.02	20.23	20.44	20.64	20.85	21.06	21.27	21.47
31.0	19.19	19.40	19.60	19.81	20.02	20.23	20.43	20.64	20.85	21.06	21.26	21.47
32.0	19.18	19.39	19.60	19.81	20.01	20.22	20.43	20.64	20.85	21.05	21.26	21.47
33.0	19.18	19.39	19.60	19.81	20.01	20.22	20.43	20.64	20.84	21.05	21.26	21.47
34.0	19.18	19.39	19.60	19.80	20.01	20.22	20.43	20.63	20.84	21.05	21.26	21.47
35.0	19.18	19.39	19.59	19.80	20.01	20.22	20.43	20.63	20.84	21.05	21.26	21.47
36.0	19.18	19.38	19.59	19.80	20.01	20.22	20.42	20.63	20.84	21.05	21.26	21.47
37.0	19.18	19.38	19.59	19.80	20.01	20.22	20.42	20.63	20.84	21.05	21.26	21.47
38.0	19.17	19.38	19.59	19.80	20.01	20.22	20.42	20.63	20.84	21.05	21.26	21.46
39.0	19.17	19.38	19.59	19.80	20.01	20.22	20.42	20.63	20.84	21.05	21.26	21.46
40.0	19.17	19.38	19.59	19.80	20.01	20.21	20.42	20.63	20.84	21.05	21.26	21.46

MONTHLY
PAYMENT REQUIRED TO AMORTIZE A $1,000.00 LOAN

TERM IN YEARS	INTEREST RATES											
	26.00%	26.25%	26.50%	26.75%	27.00%	27.25%	27.50%	27.75%	28.00%	28.25%	28.50%	28.75%
0.5	179.54	179.66	179.79	179.91	180.04	180.17	180.29	180.42	180.54	180.67	180.80	180.92
1.0	95.54	95.66	95.78	95.90	96.02	96.14	96.27	96.39	96.51	96.63	96.76	96.88
1.5	67.69	67.81	67.94	68.06	68.18	68.31	68.43	68.55	68.68	68.80	68.93	69.05
2.0	53.88	54.01	54.13	54.26	54.39	54.51	54.64	54.77	54.89	55.02	55.15	55.28
2.5	45.68	45.81	45.94	46.07	46.20	46.33	46.47	46.60	46.73	46.86	46.99	47.12
3.0	40.30	40.43	40.56	40.70	40.83	40.96	41.10	41.23	41.37	41.50	41.64	41.77
3.5	36.51	36.65	36.78	36.92	37.06	37.20	37.34	37.47	37.61	37.75	37.89	38.03
4.0	33.72	33.86	34.00	34.15	34.29	34.43	34.57	34.71	34.86	35.00	35.14	35.29
4.5	31.60	31.75	31.89	32.04	32.18	32.33	32.47	32.62	32.77	32.91	33.06	33.21
5.0	.29.95	30.09	30.24	30.39	30.54	30.69	30.84	30.99	31.14	31.29	31.44	31.59
5.5	28.63	28.78	28.93	29.08	29.24	29.39	29.54	29.70	29.85	30.01	30.16	30.32
6.0	27.56	27.71	27.87	28.03	28.18	28.34	28.50	28.65	28.81	28.97	29.13	29.29
6.5	26.68	26.84	27.00	27.16	27.32	27.48	27.64	27.80	27.96	28.13	28.29	28.45
7.0	25.96	26.12	26.28	26.45	26.61	26.77	26.94	27.10	27.27	27.43	27.60	27.76
7.5	25.35	25.52	25.68	25.85	26.02	26.18	26.35	26.52	26.69	26.85	27.02	27.19
8.0	24.84	25.01	25.18	25.35	25.52	25.69	25.86	26.03	26.20	26.37	26.54	26.71
8.5	24.41	24.58	24.76	24.93	25.10	25.27	25.44	25.62	25.79	25.97	26.14	26.31
9.0	24.05	24.22	24.39	24.57	24.74	24.92	25.09	25.27	25.45	25.62	25.80	25.98
9.5	23.73	23.91	24.08	24.26	24.44	24.62	24.79	24.97	25.15	25.33	25.51	25.69
10.0	23.46	23.64	23.82	24.00	24.18	24.36	24.54	24.72	24.90	25.08	25.27	25.45
10.5	23.23	23.41	23.59	23.77	23.96	24.14	24.32	24.50	24.69	24.87	25.06	25.24
11.0	23.03	23.21	23.40	23.58	23.76	23.95	24.13	24.32	24.50	24.69	24.88	25.06
11.5	22.86	23.04	23.23	23.41	23.60	23.79	23.97	24.16	24.35	24.54	24.72	24.91
12.0	22.71	22.89	23.08	23.27	23.46	23.65	23.83	24.02	24.21	24.40	24.59	24.78
12.5	22.58	22.77	22.95	23.14	23.33	23.52	23.71	23.90	24.10	24.29	24.48	24.67
13.0	22.46	22.65	22.84	23.04	23.23	23.42	23.61	23.80	24.00	24.19	24.38	24.57
13.5	22.37	22.56	22.75	22.94	23.13	23.33	23.52	23.71	23.91	24.10	24.30	24.49
14.0	22.28	22.47	22.67	22.86	23.05	23.25	23.44	23.64	23.83	24.03	24.22	24.42
14.5	22.20	22.40	22.59	22.79	22.98	23.18	23.38	23.57	23.77	23.96	24.16	24.36
15.0	22.14	22.33	22.53	22.73	22.92	23.12	23.32	23.51	23.71	23.91	24.11	24.31
15.5	22.08	22.28	22.47	22.67	22.87	23.07	23.27	23.46	23.66	23.86	24.06	24.26
16.0	22.03	22.23	22.43	22.62	22.82	23.02	23.22	23.42	23.62	23.82	24.02	24.22
16.5	21.99	22.19	22.38	22.58	22.78	22.98	23.18	23.38	23.58	23.78	23.98	24.19
17.0	21.95	22.15	22.35	22.55	22.75	22.95	23.15	23.35	23.55	23.75	23.95	24.16
17.5	21.91	22.11	22.32	22.52	22.72	22.92	23.12	23.32	23.52	23.73	23.93	24.13
18.0	21.89	22.09	22.29	22.49	22.69	22.89	23.09	23.30	23.50	23.70	23.91	24.11
18.5	21.86	22.06	22.26	22.46	22.67	22.87	23.07	23.28	23.48	23.68	23.89	24.09
19.0	21.84	22.04	22.24	22.44	22.65	22.85	23.05	23.26	23.46	23.66	23.87	24.07
19.5	21.82	22.02	22.22	22.43	22.63	22.83	23.04	23.24	23.44	23.65	23.85	24.06
20.0	21.80	22.00	22.21	22.41	22.61	22.82	23.02	23.23	23.43	23.64	23.84	24.05
20.5	21.78	21.99	22.19	22.40	22.60	22.80	23.01	23.21	23.42	23.62	23.83	24.03
21.0	21.77	21.97	22.18	22.38	22.59	22.79	23.00	23.20	23.41	23.61	23.82	24.02
21.5	21.76	21.96	22.17	22.37	22.58	22.78	22.99	23.19	23.40	23.60	23.81	24.02
22.0	21.75	21.95	22.16	22.36	22.57	22.77	22.98	23.19	23.39	23.60	23.80	24.01
22.5	21.74	21.94	22.15	22.35	22.56	22.77	22.97	23.18	23.38	23.59	23.80	24.00
23.0	21.73	21.94	22.14	22.35	22.55	22.76	22.97	23.17	23.38	23.58	23.79	24.00
23.5	21.72	21.93	22.14	22.34	22.55	22.75	22.96	23.17	23.37	23.58	23.79	23.99
24.0	21.72	21.92	22.13	22.34	22.54	22.75	22.96	23.16	23.37	23.58	23.78	23.99
24.5	21.71	21.92	22.12	22.33	22.54	22.74	22.95	23.16	23.36	23.57	23.78	23.99
25.0	21.71	21.91	22.12	22.33	22.53	22.74	22.95	23.15	23.36	23.57	23.78	23.98
25.5	21.70	21.91	22.12	22.32	22.53	22.74	22.94	23.15	23.36	23.56	23.77	23.98
26.0	21.70	21.91	22.11	22.32	22.53	22.73	22.94	23.15	23.35	23.56	23.77	23.98
26.5	21.70	21.90	22.11	22.32	22.52	22.73	22.94	23.15	23.35	23.56	23.77	23.98
27.0	21.69	21.90	22.11	22.31	22.52	22.73	22.94	23.14	23.35	23.56	23.77	23.97
27.5	21.69	21.90	22.10	22.31	22.52	22.73	22.93	23.14	23.35	23.56	23.77	23.97
28.0	21.69	21.90	22.10	22.31	22.52	22.73	22.93	23.14	23.35	23.56	23.76	23.97
28.5	21.69	21.89	22.10	22.31	22.52	22.72	22.93	23.14	23.35	23.55	23.76	23.97
29.0	21.68	21.89	22.10	22.31	22.51	22.72	22.93	23.14	23.35	23.55	23.76	23.97
29.5	21.68	21.89	22.10	22.31	22.51	22.72	22.93	23.14	23.34	23.55	23.76	23.97
30.0	21.68	21.89	22.10	22.30	22.51	22.72	22.93	23.14	23.34	23.55	23.76	23.97
31.0	21.68	21.89	22.09	22.30	22.51	22.72	22.93	23.13	23.34	23.55	23.76	23.97
32.0	21.68	21.89	22.09	22.30	22.51	22.72	22.93	23.13	23.34	23.55	23.76	23.97
33.0	21.68	21.88	22.09	22.30	22.51	22.72	22.92	23.13	23.34	23.55	23.76	23.97
34.0	21.68	21.88	22.09	22.30	22.51	22.72	22.92	23.13	23.34	23.55	23.76	23.96
35.0	21.67	21.88	22.09	22.30	22.51	22.72	22.92	23.13	23.34	23.55	23.76	23.96
36.0	21.67	21.88	22.09	22.30	22.51	22.71	22.92	23.13	23.34	23.55	23.76	23.96
37.0	21.67	21.88	22.09	22.30	22.51	22.71	22.92	23.13	23.34	23.55	23.76	23.96
38.0	21.67	21.88	22.09	22.30	22.51	22.71	22.92	23.13	23.34	23.55	23.76	23.96
39.0	21.67	21.88	22.09	22.30	22.51	22.71	22.92	23.13	23.34	23.55	23.76	69.96
40.0	21.67	21.88	22.09	22.30	22.51	22.71	22.92	23.13	23.34	23.55	23.76	23.96

QUARTERLY
PAYMENT REQUIRED TO AMORTIZE A $1,000.00 LOAN

TERM IN YEARS	INTEREST RATES											
	5.00%	5.25%	5.50%	5.75%	6.00%	6.25%	6.50%	6.75%	7.00%	7.25%	7.50%	7.75%
0.5	509.40	509.87	510.34	510.81	511.28	511.75	512.23	512.70	513.17	513.64	514.11	514.58
1.0	257.87	258.26	258.66	259.05	259.45	259.85	260.24	260.64	261.04	261.43	261.83	262.23
1.5	174.04	174.41	174.78	175.16	175.53	175.90	176.28	176.65	177.03	177.40	177.78	178.15
2.0	132.14	132.50	132.86	133.23	133.59	133.95	134.32	134.68	135.05	135.41	135.78	136.15
2.5	107.01	107.36	107.72	108.08	108.44	108.80	109.16	109.52	109.88	110.24	110.60	110.97
3.0	90.26	90.62	90.97	91.33	91.68	92.04	92.40	92.76	93.12	93.48	93.84	94.20
3.5	78.31	78.66	79.02	79.37	79.73	80.09	80.44	80.80	81.16	81.52	81.88	82.24
4.0	69.35	69.70	70.06	70.41	70.77	71.13	71.49	71.84	72.20	72.57	72.93	73.29
4.5	62.39	62.74	63.10	63.45	63.81	64.17	64.53	64.89	65.25	65.61	65.98	66.34
5.0	56.83	57.18	57.54	57.89	58.25	58.61	58.97	59.33	59.70	60.06	60.43	60.79
5.5	52.28	52.63	52.99	53.35	53.71	54.07	54.43	54.80	55.16	55.53	55.90	56.27
6.0	48.49	48.85	49.21	49.57	49.93	50.29	50.66	51.02	51.39	51.76	52.13	52.50
6.5	45.29	45.65	46.01	46.37	46.74	47.10	47.47	47.84	48.21	48.58	48.95	49.33
7.0	42.55	42.91	43.28	43.64	44.01	44.37	44.74	45.11	45.49	45.86	46.24	46.62
7.5	40.18	40.55	40.91	41.28	41.64	42.01	42.39	42.76	43.13	43.51	43.89	44.27
8.0	38.11	38.48	38.84	39.21	39.58	39.95	40.33	40.70	41.08	41.46	41.85	42.23
8.5	36.29	36.66	37.02	37.39	37.77	38.14	38.52	38.90	39.28	39.66	40.05	40.43
9.0	34.67	35.04	35.41	35.78	36.16	36.53	36.91	37.30	37.68	38.07	38.45	38.85
9.5	33.22	33.60	33.97	34.34	34.72	35.10	35.48	35.87	36.25	36.64	37.04	37.43
10.0	31.93	32.30	32.67	33.05	33.43	33.81	34.20	34.59	34.98	35.37	35.76	36.16
10.5	30.75	31.13	31.51	31.89	32.27	32.65	33.04	33.43	33.83	34.22	34.62	35.02
11.0	29.69	30.07	30.45	30.83	31.22	31.60	31.99	32.39	32.78	33.18	33.58	33.99
11.5	28.72	29.10	29.48	29.87	30.26	30.65	31.04	31.44	31.84	32.24	32.64	33.05
12.0	27.84	28.22	28.60	28.99	29.38	29.77	30.17	30.57	30.97	31.38	31.78	32.19
12.5	27.02	27.41	27.79	28.18	28.58	28.97	29.37	29.77	30.18	30.59	31.00	31.41
13.0	26.27	26.66	27.05	27.44	27.84	28.24	28.64	29.04	29.45	29.86	30.28	30.69
13.5	25.58	25.97	26.36	26.76	27.16	27.56	27.96	28.37	28.78	29.20	29.61	30.03
14.0	24.94	25.33	25.73	26.13	26.53	26.93	27.34	27.75	28.16	28.58	29.00	29.42
14.5	24.35	24.74	25.14	25.54	25.94	26.35	26.76	27.17	27.59	28.01	28.43	28.86
15.0	23.79	24.19	24.59	24.99	25.40	25.81	26.22	26.64	27.06	27.48	27.91	28.34
15.5	23.28	23.68	24.08	24.48	24.89	25.30	25.72	26.14	26.56	26.99	27.42	27.85
16.0	22.80	23.20	23.60	24.01	24.42	24.84	25.25	25.68	26.10	26.53	26.97	27.40
16.5	22.35	22.75	23.15	23.56	23.98	24.40	24.82	25.24	25.67	26.11	26.54	26.98
17.0	21.92	22.33	22.74	23.15	23.57	23.99	24.41	24.84	25.27	25.71	26.15	26.59
17.5	21.52	21.93	22.34	22.76	23.18	23.60	24.03	24.46	24.89	25.33	25.78	26.22
18.0	21.15	21.56	21.97	22.39	22.81	23.24	23.67	24.10	24.54	24.98	25.43	25.88
18.5	20.80	21.21	21.62	22.05	22.47	22.90	23.33	23.77	24.21	24.65	25.10	25.56
19.0	20.46	20.88	21.30	21.72	22.15	22.58	23.01	23.45	23.90	24.34	24.80	25.25
19.5	20.15	20.57	20.99	21.41	21.84	22.28	22.71	23.16	23.60	24.05	24.51	24.97
20.0	19.85	20.27	20.69	21.12	21.55	21.99	22.43	22.88	23.33	23.78	24.24	24.70
20.5	19.57	19.99	20.42	20.85	21.28	21.72	22.16	22.61	23.06	23.52	23.98	24.45
21.0	19.30	19.72	20.15	20.59	21.02	21.46	21.91	22.36	22.82	23.28	23.74	24.21
21.5	19.05	19.47	19.90	20.34	20.78	21.22	21.67	22.13	22.58	23.05	23.51	23.98
22.0	18.81	19.23	19.67	20.10	20.55	20.99	21.45	21.90	22.36	22.83	23.30	23.77
22.5	18.58	19.01	19.44	19.88	20.33	20.78	21.23	21.69	22.15	22.62	23.09	23.57
23.0	18.36	18.79	19.23	19.67	20.12	20.57	21.03	21.49	21.95	22.42	22.90	23.38
23.5	18.15	18.58	19.02	19.47	19.92	20.37	20.83	21.30	21.77	22.24	22.72	23.20
24.0	17.95	18.39	18.83	19.28	19.73	20.19	20.65	21.11	21.59	22.06	22.54	23.03
24.5	17.76	18.20	18.64	19.09	19.55	20.01	20.47	20.94	21.42	21.89	22.38	22.87
25.0	17.58	18.02	18.47	18.92	19.38	19.84	20.30	20.78	21.25	21.74	22.22	22.71
25.5	17.41	17.85	18.30	18.75	19.21	19.68	20.15	20.62	21.10	21.58	22.07	22.57
26.0	17.24	17.69	18.14	18.59	19.05	19.52	19.99	20.47	20.95	21.44	21.93	22.43
26.5	17.08	17.53	17.98	18.44	18.90	19.37	19.85	20.33	20.81	21.30	21.80	22.30
27.0	16.93	17.38	17.83	18.30	18.76	19.23	19.71	20.19	20.68	21.17	21.67	22.17
27.5	16.78	17.24	17.69	18.16	18.63	19.10	19.58	20.06	20.55	21.05	21.55	22.05
28.0	16.64	17.10	17.56	18.02	18.49	18.97	19.45	19.94	20.43	20.93	21.43	21.94
28.5	16.51	16.97	17.43	17.90	18.37	18.85	19.33	19.82	20.32	20.82	21.32	21.83
29.0	16.38	16.84	17.30	17.77	18.25	18.73	19.22	19.71	20.20	20.71	21.21	21.72
29.5	16.26	16.72	17.18	17.66	18.13	18.62	19.11	19.60	20.10	20.60	21.11	21.63
30.0	16.14	16.60	17.07	17.54	18.02	18.51	19.00	19.50	20.00	20.50	21.02	21.53
31.0	15.91	16.38	16.85	17.33	17.82	18.31	18.80	19.30	19.81	20.32	20.84	21.36
32.0	15.71	16.18	16.65	17.14	17.63	18.12	18.62	19.13	19.64	20.15	20.67	21.20
33.0	15.51	15.99	16.47	16.96	17.45	17.95	18.45	18.96	19.48	20.00	20.52	21.05
34.0	15.34	15.81	16.30	16.79	17.29	17.79	18.30	18.81	19.33	19.86	20.38	20.92
35.0	15.17	15.65	16.14	16.63	17.14	17.64	18.16	18.67	19.20	19.72	20.26	20.80
36.0	15.01	15.50	15.99	16.49	17.00	17.51	18.02	18.55	19.07	19.61	20.14	20.68
37.0	14.87	15.36	15.86	16.36	16.87	17.38	17.90	18.43	18.96	19.50	20.04	20.58
38.0	14.73	15.23	15.73	16.23	16.75	17.27	17.79	18.32	18.85	19.39	19.94	20.49
39.0	14.61	15.10	15.61	16.12	16.64	17.16	17.69	18.22	18.76	19.30	19.85	20.40
40.0	14.49	14.99	15.50	16.01	16.53	17.06	17.59	18.13	18.67	19.21	19.77	20.32

QUARTERLY
PAYMENT REQUIRED TO AMORTIZE A $1,000.00 LOAN

TERM IN YEARS	INTEREST RATES											
	8.00%	8.25%	8.50%	8.75%	9.00%	9.25%	9.50%	9.75%	10.00%	10.25%	10.50%	10.75%
0.5	515.05	515.53	516.00	516.47	516.94	517.41	517.89	518.36	518.83	519.30	519.78	520.25
1.0	262.63	263.03	263.43	263.82	264.22	264.62	265.02	265.42	265.82	266.22	266.62	267.02
1.5	178.53	178.91	179.28	179.66	180.04	180.42	180.80	181.18	181.55	181.93	182.31	182.70
2.0	136.51	136.88	137.25	137.62	137.99	138.36	138.73	139.10	139.47	139.84	140.22	140.59
2.5	111.33	111.70	112.06	112.43	112.79	113.16	113.53	113.90	114.26	114.63	115.00	115.37
3.0	94.56	94.93	95.29	95.66	96.02	96.39	96.76	97.12	97.49	97.86	98.23	98.60
3.5	82.61	82.97	83.34	83.70	84.07	84.43	84.80	85.17	85.54	85.91	86.28	86.66
4.0	73.66	74.02	74.39	74.75	75.12	75.49	75.86	76.23	76.60	76.98	77.35	77.73
4.5	66.71	67.07	67.44	67.81	68.18	68.55	68.93	69.30	69.68	70.05	70.43	70.81
5.0	61.16	61.53	61.90	62.27	62.65	63.02	63.40	63.77	64.15	64.53	64.91	65.29
5.5	56.64	57.01	57.38	57.76	58.13	58.51	58.89	59.27	59.65	60.03	60.42	60.80
6.0	52.88	53.25	53.63	54.01	54.39	54.77	55.15	55.53	55.92	56.30	56.69	57.08
6.5	49.70	50.08	50.46	50.84	51.23	51.61	52.00	52.38	52.77	53.16	53.56	53.95
7.0	46.99	47.38	47.76	48.14	48.53	48.92	49.31	49.70	50.09	50.49	50.88	51.28
7.5	44.65	45.04	45.43	45.81	46.20	46.60	46.99	47.39	47.78	48.18	48.58	48.99
8.0	42.62	43.00	43.39	43.79	44.18	44.57	44.97	45.37	45.77	46.18	46.58	46.99
8.5	40.82	41.22	41.61	42.00	42.40	42.80	43.20	43.61	44.01	44.42	44.83	45.24
9.0	39.24	39.63	40.03	40.43	40.83	41.23	41.64	42.05	42.46	42.87	43.28	43.70
9.5	37.83	38.22	38.62	39.03	39.43	39.84	40.25	40.66	41.08	41.49	41.91	42.33
10.0	36.56	36.96	37.37	37.77	38.18	38.59	39.01	39.42	39.84	40.26	40.68	41.11
10.5	35.42	35.83	36.24	36.65	37.06	37.47	37.89	38.31	38.73	39.16	39.59	40.02
11.0	34.39	34.80	35.21	35.63	36.04	36.46	36.88	37.31	37.74	38.16	38.60	39.03
11.5	33.46	33.87	34.29	34.70	35.12	35.55	35.97	36.40	36.83	37.27	37.70	38.14
12.0	32.61	33.02	33.44	33.86	34.29	34.71	35.14	35.58	36.01	36.45	36.89	37.33
12.5	31.83	32.25	32.67	33.10	33.52	33.95	34.39	34.82	35.26	35.70	36.15	36.60
13.0	31.11	31.54	31.96	32.39	32.82	33.26	33.70	34.14	34.58	35.03	35.47	35.93
13.5	30.46	30.88	31.31	31.75	32.18	32.62	33.06	33.51	33.95	34.40	34.86	35.31
14.0	29.85	30.28	30.71	31.15	31.59	32.03	32.48	32.93	33.38	33.83	34.29	34.75
14.5	29.29	29.73	30.16	30.60	31.04	31.49	31.94	32.39	32.85	33.31	33.77	34.23
15.0	28.77	29.21	29.65	30.09	30.54	30.99	31.44	31.90	32.36	32.82	33.29	33.75
15.5	28.29	28.73	29.18	29.62	30.07	30.53	30.98	31.44	31.91	32.37	32.84	33.31
16.0	27.84	28.29	28.73	29.19	29.64	30.10	30.56	31.02	31.49	31.96	32.43	32.91
16.5	27.43	27.87	28.32	28.78	29.24	29.70	30.16	30.63	31.10	31.57	32.05	32.53
17.0	27.04	27.49	27.94	28.40	28.86	29.32	29.79	30.26	30.74	31.22	31.70	32.18
17.5	26.67	27.13	27.58	28.05	28.51	28.98	29.45	29.92	30.40	30.88	31.37	31.86
18.0	26.33	26.79	27.25	27.71	28.18	28.65	29.13	29.61	30.09	30.57	31.06	31.55
18.5	26.01	26.47	26.94	27.40	27.88	28.35	28.83	29.31	29.80	30.29	30.78	31.27
19.0	25.71	26.18	26.64	27.11	27.59	28.07	28.55	29.04	29.52	30.02	30.51	31.01
19.5	25.43	25.90	26.37	26.84	27.32	27.80	28.29	28.78	29.27	29.77	30.26	30.77
20.0	25.17	25.64	26.11	26.59	27.07	27.55	28.04	28.54	29.03	29.53	30.03	30.54
20.5	24.92	25.39	25.87	26.35	26.83	27.32	27.81	28.31	28.81	29.31	29.82	30.33
21.0	24.68	25.16	25.64	26.12	26.61	27.10	27.60	28.10	28.60	29.10	29.61	30.13
21.5	24.46	24.94	25.42	25.91	26.40	26.89	27.39	27.90	28.40	28.91	29.42	29.94
22.0	24.25	24.73	25.22	25.71	26.20	26.70	27.20	27.71	28.22	28.73	29.25	29.76
22.5	24.05	24.54	25.03	25.52	26.02	26.52	27.02	27.53	28.04	28.56	29.08	29.60
23.0	23.86	24.35	24.84	25.34	25.84	26.34	26.85	27.36	27.88	28.40	28.92	29.45
23.5	23.69	24.18	24.67	25.17	25.68	26.18	26.69	27.21	27.73	28.25	28.77	29.30
24.0	23.52	24.01	24.51	25.01	25.52	26.03	26.54	27.06	27.58	28.11	28.63	29.17
24.5	23.36	23.86	24.36	24.86	25.37	25.88	26.40	26.92	27.45	27.97	28.50	29.04
25.0	23.21	23.71	24.21	24.72	25.23	25.75	26.27	26.79	27.32	27.85	28.38	28.92
25.5	23.06	23.57	24.07	24.58	25.10	25.62	26.14	26.67	27.20	27.73	28.27	28.81
26.0	22.93	23.43	23.94	24.46	24.97	25.49	26.02	26.55	27.08	27.62	28.16	28.70
26.5	22.80	23.31	23.82	24.33	24.85	25.38	25.91	26.44	26.97	27.51	28.05	28.60
27.0	22.68	23.19	23.70	24.22	24.74	25.27	25.80	26.33	26.87	27.41	27.96	28.51
27.5	22.56	23.07	23.59	24.11	24.64	25.16	25.70	26.23	26.78	27.32	27.87	28.42
28.0	22.45	22.96	23.48	24.01	24.53	25.07	25.60	26.14	26.68	27.23	27.78	28.33
28.5	22.34	22.86	23.38	23.91	24.44	24.97	25.51	26.05	26.60	27.15	27.70	28.25
29.0	22.24	22.76	23.29	23.81	24.35	24.88	25.42	25.97	26.52	27.07	27.62	28.18
29.5	22.14	22.67	23.19	23.73	24.26	24.80	25.34	25.89	26.44	26.99	27.55	28.11
30.0	22.05	22.58	23.11	23.64	24.18	24.72	25.27	25.81	26.37	26.92	27.48	28.04
31.0	21.88	22.41	22.95	23.48	24.03	24.57	25.12	25.68	26.23	26.79	27.36	27.92
32.0	21.73	22.26	22.80	23.34	23.89	24.44	24.99	25.55	26.11	26.68	27.24	27.81
33.0	21.59	22.12	22.67	23.21	23.76	24.32	24.88	25.44	26.00	26.57	27.14	27.72
34.0	21.46	22.00	22.55	23.10	23.65	24.21	24.77	25.34	25.91	26.48	27.05	27.63
35.0	21.34	21.89	22.44	22.99	23.55	24.11	24.68	25.25	25.82	26.39	26.97	27.55
36.0	21.23	21.78	22.34	22.89	23.46	24.02	24.59	25.16	25.74	26.32	26.90	27.48
37.0	21.13	21.69	22.24	22.81	23.37	23.94	24.51	25.09	25.67	26.25	26.83	27.42
38.0	21.04	21.60	22.16	22.73	23.30	23.87	24.44	25.02	25.61	26.19	26.78	27.37
39.0	20.96	21.52	22.09	22.65	23.23	23.80	24.38	24.96	25.55	26.13	26.72	27.32
40.0	20.88	21.45	22.02	22.59	23.16	23.74	24.32	24.91	25.50	26.09	26.68	27.27

QUARTERLY
PAYMENT REQUIRED TO AMORTIZE A $1,000.00 LOAN

TERM IN YEARS	INTEREST RATES											
	11.00%	11.25%	11.50%	11.75%	12.00%	12.25%	12.50%	12.75%	13.00%	13.25%	13.50%	13.75%
0.5	520.72	521.20	521.67	522.14	522.62	523.09	523.56	524.04	524.51	524.98	525.46	525.93
1.0	267.43	267.83	268.23	268.63	269.03	269.43	269.84	270.24	270.64	271.05	271.45	271.85
1.5	183.08	183.46	183.84	184.22	184.60	184.99	185.37	185.75	186.13	186.52	186.90	187.29
2.0	140.96	141.34	141.71	142.09	142.46	142.84	143.21	143.59	143.97	144.35	144.72	145.10
2.5	115.74	116.12	116.49	116.86	117.24	117.61	117.98	118.36	118.74	119.11	119.49	119.87
3.0	98.97	99.35	99.72	100.09	100.47	100.84	101.22	101.59	101.97	102.35	102.73	103.11
3.5	87.03	87.40	87.78	88.15	88.53	88.91	89.29	89.67	90.05	90.43	90.81	91.19
4.0	78.10	78.48	78.86	79.24	79.62	80.00	80.38	80.76	81.15	81.53	81.92	82.30
4.5	71.19	71.57	71.95	72.33	72.71	73.10	73.48	73.87	74.26	74.65	75.04	75.43
5.0	65.68	66.06	66.45	66.83	67.22	67.61	68.00	68.39	68.78	69.18	69.57	69.97
5.5	61.19	61.58	61.97	62.36	62.75	63.15	63.54	63.94	64.33	64.73	65.13	65.53
6.0	57.47	57.87	58.26	58.66	59.05	59.45	59.85	60.25	60.65	61.06	61.46	61.87
6.5	54.35	54.74	55.14	55.54	55.94	56.35	56.75	57.16	57.56	57.97	58.38	58.80
7.0	51.68	52.08	52.49	52.89	53.30	53.71	54.12	54.53	54.94	55.35	55.77	56.19
7.5	49.39	49.80	50.20	50.61	51.02	51.44	51.85	52.27	52.69	53.11	53.53	53.95
8.0	47.40	47.81	48.22	48.64	49.05	49.47	49.89	50.31	50.73	51.16	51.59	52.02
8.5	45.65	46.07	46.49	46.91	47.33	47.75	48.18	48.60	49.03	49.46	49.89	50.33
9.0	44.12	44.54	44.96	45.38	45.81	46.24	46.67	47.10	47.53	47.97	48.41	48.85
9.5	42.75	43.18	43.60	44.03	44.46	44.90	45.33	45.77	46.21	46.65	47.09	47.54
10.0	41.54	41.97	42.40	42.83	43.27	43.71	44.15	44.59	45.03	45.48	45.93	46.38
10.5	40.45	40.88	41.32	41.76	42.20	42.64	43.09	43.53	43.98	44.43	44.89	45.34
11.0	39.47	39.90	40.35	40.79	41.23	41.68	42.13	42.59	43.04	43.50	43.96	44.42
11.5	38.58	39.02	39.47	39.92	40.37	40.82	41.28	41.73	42.19	42.66	43.12	43.59
12.0	37.78	38.22	38.67	39.13	39.58	40.04	40.50	40.96	41.43	41.90	42.37	42.84
12.5	37.05	37.50	37.95	38.41	38.87	39.33	39.80	40.27	40.74	41.21	41.68	42.16
13.0	36.38	36.84	37.30	37.76	38.22	38.69	39.16	39.63	40.11	40.58	41.06	41.54
13.5	35.77	36.23	36.69	37.16	37.63	38.10	38.58	39.05	39.53	40.02	40.50	40.99
14.0	35.21	35.68	36.14	36.62	37.09	37.57	38.04	38.53	39.01	39.50	39.99	40.48
14.5	34.70	35.17	35.64	36.12	36.59	37.07	37.56	38.04	38.53	39.02	39.52	40.01
15.0	34.23	34.70	35.18	35.66	36.14	36.62	37.11	37.60	38.09	38.59	39.09	39.59
15.5	33.79	34.27	34.75	35.23	35.72	36.21	36.70	37.20	37.69	38.19	38.70	39.20
16.0	33.39	33.87	34.35	34.84	35.33	35.83	36.32	36.82	37.32	37.83	38.34	38.85
16.5	33.01	33.50	33.99	34.48	34.98	35.47	35.97	36.48	36.98	37.49	38.00	38.52
17.0	32.67	33.16	33.65	34.15	34.65	35.15	35.65	36.16	36.67	37.18	37.70	38.22
17.5	32.35	32.84	33.34	33.84	34.34	34.85	35.36	35.87	36.38	36.90	37.42	37.94
18.0	32.05	32.55	33.05	33.55	34.06	34.57	35.08	35.60	36.12	36.64	37.16	37.69
18.5	31.77	32.27	32.78	33.29	33.80	34.31	34.83	35.35	35.87	36.39	36.92	37.45
19.0	31.51	32.02	32.53	33.04	33.55	34.07	34.59	35.11	35.64	36.17	36.70	37.23
19.5	31.27	31.78	32.29	32.81	33.33	33.85	34.37	34.90	35.43	35.96	36.50	37.03
20.0	31.05	31.56	32.08	32.60	33.12	33.64	34.17	34.70	35.23	35.77	36.31	36.85
20.5	30.84	31.35	31.87	32.40	32.92	33.45	33.98	34.51	35.05	35.59	36.13	36.67
21.0	30.64	31.16	31.68	32.21	32.74	33.27	33.80	34.34	34.88	35.42	35.97	36.52
21.5	30.46	30.98	31.51	32.04	32.57	33.10	33.64	34.18	34.72	35.27	35.82	36.37
22.0	30.29	30.81	31.34	31.87	32.41	32.95	33.49	34.03	34.58	35.13	35.68	36.23
22.5	30.13	30.66	31.19	31.72	32.26	32.80	33.35	33.89	34.44	34.99	35.55	36.10
23.0	29.98	30.51	31.04	31.58	32.12	32.67	33.21	33.76	34.31	34.87	35.43	35.99
23.5	29.83	30.37	30.91	31.45	31.99	32.54	33.09	33.64	34.20	34.75	35.31	35.88
24.0	29.70	30.24	30.78	31.32	31.87	32.42	32.97	33.53	34.09	34.65	35.21	35.77
24.5	29.58	30.12	30.66	31.21	31.76	32.31	32.87	33.42	33.98	34.55	35.11	35.68
25.0	29.46	30.00	30.55	31.10	31.65	32.21	32.76	33.33	33.89	34.45	35.02	35.59
25.5	29.35	29.90	30.44	31.00	31.55	32.11	32.67	33.23	33.80	34.37	34.94	35.51
26.0	29.25	29.79	30.35	30.90	31.46	32.02	32.58	33.15	33.72	34.29	34.86	35.43
26.5	29.15	29.70	30.25	30.81	31.37	31.93	32.50	33.07	33.64	34.21	34.79	35.36
27.0	29.06	29.61	30.17	30.73	31.29	31.86	32.42	32.99	33.57	34.14	34.72	35.30
27.5	28.97	29.53	30.09	30.65	31.21	31.78	32.35	32.92	33.50	34.08	34.65	35.24
28.0	28.89	29.45	30.01	30.57	31.14	31.71	32.28	32.86	33.43	34.01	34.60	35.18
28.5	28.81	29.37	29.94	30.50	31.07	31.65	32.22	32.80	33.38	33.96	34.54	35.13
29.0	28.74	29.30	29.87	30.44	31.01	31.58	32.16	32.74	33.32	33.90	34.49	35.08
29.5	28.67	29.24	29.81	30.38	30.95	31.53	32.11	32.69	33.27	33.85	34.44	35.03
30.0	28.61	29.18	29.75	30.32	30.89	31.47	32.05	32.64	33.22	33.81	34.40	34.99
31.0	28.49	29.06	29.64	30.21	30.79	31.37	31.96	32.54	33.13	33.72	34.31	34.91
32.0	28.39	28.96	29.54	30.12	30.70	31.29	31.88	32.46	33.06	33.65	34.24	34.84
33.0	28.29	28.87	29.45	30.04	30.62	31.21	31.80	32.39	32.99	33.58	34.18	34.78
34.0	28.21	28.79	29.38	29.96	30.55	31.14	31.74	32.33	32.93	33.53	34.13	34.73
35.0	28.14	28.72	29.31	29.90	30.49	31.09	31.68	32.28	32.88	33.48	34.08	34.69
36.0	28.07	28.66	29.25	29.84	30.44	31.03	31.63	32.23	32.83	33.44	34.04	34.65
37.0	28.01	28.60	29.19	29.79	30.39	30.99	31.59	32.19	32.79	33.40	34.01	34.61
38.0	27.96	28.55	29.15	29.74	30.34	30.95	31.55	32.15	32.76	33.37	33.97	34.58
39.0	27.91	28.51	29.10	29.70	30.31	30.91	31.51	32.12	32.73	33.34	33.95	34.56
40.0	27.87	28.47	29.07	29.67	30.27	30.88	31.48	32.09	32.70	33.31	33.92	34.53

QUARTERLY
PAYMENT REQUIRED TO AMORTIZE A $1,000.00 LOAN

TERM IN YEARS	14.00%	14.25%	14.50%	14.75%	15.00%	15.25%	15.50%	15.75%	16.00%	16.25%	16.50%	16.75%
0.5	526.41	526.88	527.35	527.83	528.30	528.78	529.25	529.73	530.20	530.68	531.15	531.63
1.0	272.26	272.66	273.06	273.47	273.87	274.28	274.68	275.09	275.50	275.90	276.31	276.71
1.5	187.67	188.06	188.44	188.83	189.22	189.60	189.99	190.38	190.77	191.16	191.54	191.93
2.0	145.48	145.86	146.24	146.62	147.00	147.39	147.77	148.15	148.53	148.92	149.30	149.68
2.5	120.25	120.63	121.01	121.39	121.77	122.15	122.53	122.91	123.30	123.68	124.06	124.45
3.0	103.49	103.87	104.25	104.63	105.02	105.40	105.79	106.17	106.56	106.94	107.33	107.72
3.5	91.58	91.96	92.35	92.73	93.12	93.51	93.89	94.28	94.67	95.07	95.46	95.85
4.0	82.69	83.08	83.47	83.86	84.25	84.64	85.04	85.43	85.82	86.22	86.62	87.02
4.5	75.82	76.22	76.61	77.01	77.40	77.80	78.20	78.60	79.00	79.40	79.80	80.21
5.0	70.37	70.76	71.16	71.57	71.97	72.37	72.77	73.18	73.59	73.99	74.40	74.81
5.5	65.94	66.34	66.75	67.15	67.56	67.97	68.38	68.79	69.20	69.62	70.03	70.45
6.0	62.28	62.69	63.10	63.51	63.92	64.34	64.76	65.17	65.59	66.01	66.43	66.86
6.5	59.21	59.63	60.04	60.46	60.88	61.30	61.72	62.15	62.57	63.00	63.43	63.86
7.0	56.61	57.03	57.45	57.87	58.30	58.73	59.16	59.59	60.02	60.45	60.89	61.32
7.5	54.38	54.80	55.23	55.66	56.09	56.53	56.96	57.40	57.84	58.27	58.72	59.16
8.0	52.45	52.88	53.31	53.75	54.19	54.63	55.07	55.51	55.95	56.40	56.85	57.30
8.5	50.76	51.20	51.64	52.08	52.53	52.97	53.42	53.87	54.32	54.77	55.23	55.68
9.0	49.29	49.73	50.18	50.63	51.08	51.53	51.98	52.44	52.89	53.35	53.81	54.27
9.5	47.99	48.44	48.89	49.34	49.80	50.25	50.71	51.17	51.64	52.10	52.57	53.04
10.0	46.83	47.29	47.74	48.20	48.66	49.13	49.59	50.06	50.53	51.00	51.47	51.95
10.5	45.80	46.26	46.73	47.19	47.66	48.13	48.60	49.07	49.55	50.02	50.50	50.98
11.0	44.88	45.35	45.82	46.29	46.76	47.23	47.71	48.19	48.67	49.15	49.64	50.12
11.5	44.06	44.53	45.00	45.48	45.95	46.43	46.92	47.40	47.89	48.38	48.87	49.36
12.0	43.31	43.79	44.27	44.75	45.23	45.72	46.20	46.69	47.19	47.68	48.18	48.67
12.5	42.64	43.12	43.60	44.09	44.58	45.07	45.56	46.06	46.56	47.05	47.56	48.06
13.0	42.03	42.52	43.01	43.50	43.99	44.49	44.98	45.48	45.99	46.49	47.00	47.51
13.5	41.48	41.97	42.46	42.96	43.46	43.96	44.46	44.97	45.47	45.98	46.50	47.01
14.0	40.97	41.47	41.97	42.47	42.97	43.48	43.99	44.50	45.01	45.52	46.04	46.56
14.5	40.51	41.01	41.52	42.02	42.53	43.04	43.56	44.07	44.59	45.11	45.63	46.15
15.0	40.09	40.60	41.11	41.62	42.13	42.65	43.16	43.68	44.21	44.73	45.26	45.79
15.5	39.71	40.22	40.73	41.25	41.77	42.29	42.81	43.33	43.86	44.39	44.92	45.45
16.0	39.36	39.87	40.39	40.91	41.43	41.96	42.48	43.01	43.54	44.08	44.61	45.15
16.5	39.04	39.55	40.08	40.60	41.13	41.65	42.19	42.72	43.25	43.79	44.33	44.87
17.0	38.74	39.26	39.79	40.32	40.85	41.38	41.91	42.45	42.99	43.53	44.08	44.62
17.5	38.47	38.99	39.52	40.06	40.59	41.13	41.67	42.21	42.75	43.30	43.84	44.39
18.0	38.21	38.75	39.28	39.82	40.35	40.89	41.44	41.98	42.53	43.08	43.63	44.18
18.5	37.98	38.52	39.06	39.60	40.14	40.68	41.23	41.78	42.33	42.88	43.44	43.99
19.0	37.77	38.31	38.85	39.39	39.94	40.49	41.04	41.59	42.14	42.70	43.26	43.82
19.5	37.57	38.11	38.66	39.21	39.76	40.31	40.86	41.42	41.97	42.53	43.10	43.66
20.0	37.39	37.94	38.48	39.03	39.59	40.14	40.70	41.26	41.82	42.38	42.95	43.51
20.5	37.22	37.77	38.32	38.88	39.43	39.99	40.55	41.11	41.68	42.24	42.81	43.38
21.0	37.07	37.62	38.17	38.73	39.29	39.85	40.41	40.98	41.55	42.11	42.69	43.26
21.5	36.92	37.48	38.03	38.59	39.16	39.72	40.29	40.85	41.43	42.00	42.57	43.15
22.0	36.79	37.35	37.91	38.47	39.03	39.60	40.17	40.74	41.31	41.89	42.47	43.04
22.5	36.66	37.22	37.79	38.35	38.92	39.49	40.06	40.64	41.21	41.79	42.37	42.95
23.0	36.55	37.11	37.68	38.25	38.82	39.39	39.96	40.54	41.12	41.70	42.28	42.86
23.5	36.44	37.01	37.58	38.15	38.72	39.30	39.87	40.45	41.03	41.62	42.20	42.78
24.0	36.34	36.91	37.48	38.06	38.63	39.21	39.79	40.37	40.95	41.54	42.12	42.71
24.5	36.25	36.82	37.40	37.97	38.55	39.13	39.71	40.30	40.88	41.47	42.06	42.65
25.0	36.16	36.74	37.32	37.89	38.47	39.06	39.64	40.23	40.81	41.40	41.99	42.58
25.5	36.08	36.66	37.24	37.82	38.40	38.99	39.57	40.16	40.75	41.34	41.93	42.53
26.0	36.01	36.59	37.17	37.75	38.34	38.92	39.51	40.10	40.69	41.29	41.88	42.48
26.5	35.94	36.52	37.11	37.69	38.28	38.87	39.46	40.05	40.64	41.24	41.83	42.43
27.0	35.88	36.46	37.05	37.63	38.22	38.81	39.40	40.00	40.59	41.19	41.79	42.38
27.5	35.82	36.40	36.99	37.58	38.17	38.76	39.36	39.95	40.55	41.15	41.74	42.34
28.0	35.76	36.35	36.94	37.53	38.12	38.72	39.31	39.91	40.51	41.11	41.71	42.31
28.5	35.71	36.30	36.89	37.48	38.08	38.67	39.27	39.87	40.47	41.07	41.67	42.27
29.0	35.66	36.25	36.85	37.44	38.04	38.63	39.23	39.83	40.43	41.03	41.64	42.24
29.5	35.62	36.21	36.81	37.40	38.00	38.60	39.20	39.80	40.40	41.00	41.61	42.21
30.0	35.58	36.17	36.77	37.36	37.96	38.56	39.16	39.77	40.37	40.97	41.58	42.19
31.0	35.50	36.10	36.70	37.30	37.90	38.50	39.11	39.71	40.32	40.92	41.53	42.14
32.0	35.44	36.04	36.64	37.24	37.84	38.45	39.06	39.66	40.27	40.88	41.49	42.10
33.0	35.38	35.98	36.59	37.19	37.80	38.41	39.01	39.62	40.23	40.84	41.45	42.07
34.0	35.33	35.94	36.54	37.15	37.76	38.37	38.98	39.59	40.20	40.81	41.42	42.04
35.0	35.29	35.90	36.50	37.11	37.72	38.33	38.95	39.56	40.17	40.78	41.40	42.01
36.0	35.25	35.86	36.47	37.08	37.69	38.31	38.92	39.53	40.15	40.76	41.38	41.99
37.0	35.22	35.83	36.44	37.05	37.67	38.28	38.90	39.51	40.13	40.74	41.36	41.98
38.0	35.19	35.81	36.42	37.03	37.64	38.26	38.88	39.49	40.11	40.73	41.34	41.96
39.0	35.17	35.78	36.40	37.01	37.63	38.24	38.86	39.48	40.09	40.71	41.33	41.95
40.0	35.15	35.76	36.38	36.99	37.61	38.23	38.84	39.46	40.08	40.70	41.32	41.94

QUARTERLY
PAYMENT REQUIRED TO AMORTIZE A $1,000.00 LOAN

TERM IN YEARS	INTEREST RATES 17.00%	17.25%	17.50%	17.75%	18.00%	18.25%	18.50%	18.75%	19.00%	19.25%	19.50%	19.75%
0.5	532.10	532.58	533.05	533.53	534.00	534.48	534.95	535.43	535.91	536.38	536.86	537.33
1.0	277.12	277.53	277.93	278.34	278.75	279.16	279.56	279.97	280.38	280.79	281.20	281.61
1.5	192.32	192.71	193.10	193.49	193.88	194.27	194.67	195.06	195.45	195.84	196.24	196.63
2.0	150.07	150.46	150.84	151.23	151.61	152.00	152.39	152.78	153.17	153.56	153.95	154.34
2.5	124.84	125.22	125.61	126.00	126.38	126.77	127.16	127.55	127.94	128.33	128.72	129.12
3.0	108.11	108.50	108.89	109.28	109.67	110.06	110.46	110.85	111.25	111.64	112.04	112.43
3.5	96.24	96.64	97.03	97.43	97.83	98.22	98.62	99.02	99.42	99.82	100.22	100.63
4.0	87.42	87.82	88.22	88.62	89.02	89.42	89.83	90.23	90.64	91.05	91.46	91.86
4.5	80.61	81.02	81.42	81.83	82.24	82.65	83.06	83.48	83.89	84.30	84.72	85.13
5.0	75.22	75.64	76.05	76.47	76.88	77.30	77.72	78.14	78.56	78.98	79.40	79.82
5.5	70.87	71.29	71.71	72.13	72.55	72.97	73.40	73.83	74.25	74.68	75.11	75.54
6.0	67.28	67.71	68.13	68.56	68.99	69.42	69.86	70.29	70.72	71.16	71.60	72.04
6.5	64.29	64.72	65.15	65.59	66.03	66.46	66.90	67.34	67.79	68.23	68.68	69.12
7.0	61.76	62.20	62.64	63.08	63.53	63.97	64.42	64.87	65.32	65.77	66.22	66.67
7.5	59.60	60.05	60.50	60.95	61.40	61.85	62.30	62.76	63.21	63.67	64.13	64.59
8.0	57.75	58.20	58.65	59.11	59.57	60.03	60.49	60.95	61.41	61.88	62.35	62.82
8.5	56.14	56.60	57.06	57.52	57.99	58.45	58.92	59.39	59.86	60.33	60.81	61.28
9.0	54.74	55.20	55.67	56.14	56.61	57.08	57.56	58.03	58.51	58.99	59.47	59.96
9.5	53.51	53.98	54.45	54.93	55.41	55.89	56.37	56.85	57.33	57.82	58.31	58.80
10.0	52.42	52.90	53.38	53.86	54.35	54.83	55.32	55.81	56.30	56.79	57.29	57.79
10.5	51.46	51.95	52.44	52.92	53.41	53.91	54.40	54.90	55.39	55.89	56.39	56.90
11.0	50.61	51.10	51.60	52.09	52.59	53.08	53.58	54.09	54.59	55.09	55.60	56.11
11.5	49.85	50.35	50.85	51.35	51.85	52.35	52.86	53.37	53.88	54.39	54.90	55.42
12.0	49.17	49.68	50.18	50.69	51.19	51.70	52.22	52.73	53.24	53.76	54.28	54.80
12.5	48.57	49.07	49.58	50.09	50.61	51.12	51.64	52.16	52.68	53.20	53.73	54.25
13.0	48.02	48.53	49.05	49.56	50.08	50.60	51.13	51.65	52.18	52.70	53.23	53.77
13.5	47.53	48.04	48.56	49.09	49.61	50.14	50.66	51.19	51.73	52.26	52.79	53.33
14.0	47.08	47.60	48.13	48.66	49.19	49.72	50.25	50.78	51.32	51.86	52.40	52.94
14.5	46.68	47.21	47.74	48.27	48.80	49.34	49.88	50.42	50.96	51.50	52.05	52.59
15.0	46.32	46.85	47.38	47.92	48.46	49.00	49.54	50.09	50.63	51.18	51.73	52.28
15.5	45.99	46.52	47.06	47.60	48.15	48.69	49.24	49.79	50.34	50.89	51.44	52.00
16.0	45.69	46.23	46.77	47.32	47.87	48.42	48.97	49.52	50.07	50.63	51.19	51.75
16.5	45.42	45.96	46.51	47.06	47.61	48.16	48.72	49.28	49.83	50.40	50.96	51.52
17.0	45.17	45.72	46.27	46.82	47.38	47.94	48.50	49.06	49.62	50.18	50.75	51.32
17.5	44.94	45.50	46.05	46.61	47.17	47.73	48.29	48.86	49.42	49.99	50.56	51.13
18.0	44.74	45.30	45.86	46.42	46.98	47.54	48.11	48.68	49.25	49.82	50.39	50.97
18.5	44.55	45.11	45.68	46.24	46.81	47.37	47.94	48.52	49.09	49.66	50.24	50.82
19.0	44.38	44.95	45.51	46.08	46.65	47.22	47.79	48.37	48.94	49.52	50.10	50.68
19.5	44.23	44.79	45.36	45.93	46.51	47.08	47.66	48.23	48.81	49.39	49.97	50.56
20.0	44.08	44.65	45.23	45.80	46.38	46.95	47.53	48.11	48.69	49.28	49.86	50.45
20.5	43.95	44.53	45.10	45.68	46.26	46.84	47.42	48.00	48.59	49.17	49.76	50.35
21.0	43.83	44.41	44.99	45.57	46.15	46.73	47.32	47.90	48.49	49.08	49.67	50.26
21.5	43.72	44.30	44.88	45.47	46.05	46.64	47.22	47.81	48.40	48.99	49.58	50.18
22.0	43.62	44.21	44.79	45.37	45.96	46.55	47.14	47.73	48.32	48.91	49.51	50.10
22.5	43.53	44.12	44.70	45.29	45.88	46.47	47.06	47.65	48.25	48.84	49.44	50.03
23.0	43.45	44.04	44.62	45.21	45.80	46.40	46.99	47.58	48.18	48.78	49.37	49.97
23.5	43.37	43.96	44.55	45.14	45.73	46.33	46.92	47.52	48.12	48.72	49.32	49.92
24.0	43.30	43.89	44.48	45.08	45.67	46.27	46.87	47.46	48.06	48.66	49.27	49.87
24.5	43.24	43.83	44.42	45.02	45.62	46.21	46.81	47.41	48.01	48.62	49.22	49.82
25.0	43.18	43.77	44.37	44.97	45.56	46.16	46.76	47.37	47.97	48.57	49.18	49.78
25.5	43.12	43.72	44.32	44.92	45.52	46.12	46.72	47.32	47.93	48.53	49.14	49.74
26.0	43.07	43.67	44.27	44.87	45.47	46.07	46.68	47.28	47.89	48.50	49.10	49.71
26.5	43.03	43.63	44.23	44.83	45.43	46.04	46.64	47.25	47.85	48.46	49.07	49.68
27.0	42.98	43.59	44.19	44.79	45.40	46.00	46.61	47.22	47.82	48.43	49.04	49.65
27.5	42.95	43.55	44.15	44.76	45.36	45.97	46.58	47.19	47.79	48.41	49.02	49.63
28.0	42.91	43.51	44.12	44.73	45.33	45.94	46.55	47.16	47.77	48.38	48.99	49.60
28.5	42.88	43.48	44.09	44.70	45.30	45.91	46.52	47.13	47.75	48.36	48.97	49.58
29.0	42.85	43.45	44.06	44.67	45.28	45.89	46.50	47.11	47.72	48.34	48.95	49.56
29.5	42.82	43.43	44.04	44.65	45.26	45.87	46.48	47.09	47.70	48.32	48.93	49.55
30.0	42.79	43.40	44.01	44.62	45.23	45.85	46.46	47.07	47.68	48.30	48.92	49.53
31.0	42.75	43.36	43.97	44.58	45.20	45.81	46.43	47.04	47.66	48.27	48.89	49.51
32.0	42.71	43.32	43.94	44.55	45.17	45.78	46.40	47.01	47.63	48.25	48.87	49.48
33.0	42.68	43.29	43.91	44.52	45.14	45.76	46.37	46.99	47.61	48.23	48.85	49.47
34.0	42.65	43.27	43.88	44.50	45.12	45.74	46.35	46.97	47.59	48.21	48.83	49.45
35.0	42.63	43.25	43.86	44.48	45.10	45.72	46.34	46.96	47.58	48.20	48.82	49.44
36.0	42.61	43.23	43.85	44.47	45.08	45.70	46.32	46.94	47.56	48.19	48.81	49.43
37.0	42.59	43.21	43.83	44.45	45.07	45.69	46.31	46.93	47.55	48.18	48.80	49.42
38.0	42.58	43.20	43.82	44.44	45.06	45.68	46.30	46.92	47.55	48.17	48.79	49.41
39.0	42.57	43.19	43.81	44.43	45.05	45.67	46.30	46.92	47.54	48.16	48.78	49.41
40.0	42.56	43.18	43.80	44.42	45.04	45.67	46.29	46.91	47.53	48.16	48.78	49.40

QUARTERLY
PAYMENT REQUIRED TO AMORTIZE A $1,000.00 LOAN

TERM IN YEARS	INTEREST RATES											
	20.00%	20.25%	20.50%	20.75%	21.00%	21.25%	21.50%	21.75%	22.00%	22.25%	22.50%	22.75%
0.5	537.81	538.29	538.76	539.24	539.72	540.19	540.67	541.15	541.62	542.10	542.58	543.05
1.0	282.02	282.43	282.84	283.25	283.66	284.07	284.48	284.89	285.30	285.71	286.12	286.53
1.5	197.02	197.42	197.81	198.21	198.60	199.00	199.39	199.79	200.18	200.58	200.98	201.38
2.0	154.73	155.12	155.51	155.90	156.29	156.69	157.08	157.47	157.87	158.26	158.66	159.06
2.5	129.51	129.90	130.30	130.69	131.09	131.48	131.88	132.28	132.67	133.07	133.47	133.87
3.0	112.83	113.23	113.63	114.03	114.43	114.83	115.23	115.63	116.03	116.44	116.84	117.25
3.5	101.03	101.43	101.84	102.24	102.65	103.06	103.47	103.87	104.28	104.69	105.11	105.52
4.0	92.27	92.69	93.10	93.51	93.92	94.34	94.75	95.17	95.59	96.01	96.42	96.84
4.5	85.55	85.97	86.39	86.81	87.23	87.65	88.08	88.50	88.92	89.35	89.78	90.21
5.0	80.25	80.67	81.10	81.53	81.96	82.39	82.82	83.25	83.68	84.12	84.55	84.99
5.5	75.98	76.41	76.84	77.28	77.72	78.15	78.59	79.03	79.48	79.92	80.36	80.81
6.0	72.48	72.92	73.36	73.80	74.25	74.69	75.14	75.59	76.04	76.49	76.94	77.40
6.5	69.57	70.02	70.47	70.92	71.37	71.83	72.28	72.74	73.20	73.66	74.12	74.58
7.0	67.13	67.58	68.04	68.50	68.96	69.42	69.89	70.35	70.82	71.29	71.76	72.23
7.5	65.06	65.52	65.99	66.45	66.92	67.39	67.86	68.34	68.81	69.29	69.76	70.24
8.0	63.29	63.76	64.23	64.70	65.18	65.66	66.14	66.62	67.10	67.58	68.07	68.55
8.5	61.76	62.24	62.72	63.20	63.69	64.17	64.66	65.15	65.63	66.13	66.62	67.11
9.0	60.44	60.93	61.41	61.90	62.39	62.89	63.38	63.87	64.37	64.87	65.37	65.87
9.5	59.29	59.78	60.28	60.77	61.27	61.77	62.27	62.77	63.28	63.78	64.29	64.80
10.0	58.28	58.78	59.28	59.79	60.29	60.80	61.31	61.81	62.33	62.84	63.35	63.87
10.5	57.40	57.91	58.41	58.92	59.43	59.95	60.46	60.98	61.49	62.01	62.53	63.06
11.0	56.62	57.13	57.65	58.16	58.68	59.20	59.72	60.24	60.77	61.29	61.82	62.35
11.5	55.93	56.45	56.97	57.49	58.02	58.54	59.07	59.60	60.13	60.66	61.19	61.73
12.0	55.32	55.85	56.37	56.90	57.43	57.96	58.49	59.03	59.56	60.10	60.64	61.18
12.5	54.78	55.31	55.84	56.38	56.91	57.45	57.99	58.53	59.07	59.61	60.15	60.70
13.0	54.30	54.83	55.37	55.91	56.45	56.99	57.54	58.08	58.63	59.17	59.72	60.28
13.5	53.87	54.41	54.95	55.50	56.04	56.59	57.14	57.69	58.24	58.79	59.34	59.90
14.0	53.49	54.03	54.58	55.13	55.68	56.23	56.78	57.34	57.89	58.45	59.01	59.57
14.5	53.14	53.69	54.24	54.80	55.35	55.91	56.46	57.02	57.59	58.15	58.71	59.28
15.0	52.83	53.39	53.94	54.50	55.06	55.62	56.18	56.75	57.31	57.88	58.45	59.02
15.5	52.56	53.12	53.68	54.24	54.80	55.37	55.93	56.50	57.07	57.64	58.21	58.78
16.0	52.31	52.87	53.44	54.00	54.57	55.14	55.71	56.28	56.85	57.43	58.00	58.58
16.5	52.09	52.65	53.22	53.79	54.36	54.93	55.51	56.08	56.66	57.24	57.82	58.40
17.0	51.88	52.46	53.03	53.60	54.17	54.75	55.33	55.91	56.49	57.07	57.65	58.23
17.5	51.70	52.28	52.85	53.43	54.01	54.59	55.17	55.75	56.33	56.92	57.50	58.09
18.0	51.54	52.12	52.70	53.28	53.86	54.44	55.02	55.61	56.19	56.78	57.37	57.96
18.5	51.39	51.97	52.56	53.14	53.72	54.31	54.90	55.48	56.07	56.66	57.25	57.84
19.0	51.26	51.85	52.43	53.02	53.60	54.19	54.78	55.37	55.96	56.55	57.15	57.74
19.5	51.14	51.73	52.32	52.90	53.49	54.08	54.68	55.27	55.86	56.46	57.05	57.65
20.0	51.03	51.62	52.21	52.80	53.40	53.99	54.58	55.18	55.77	56.37	56.97	57.57
20.5	50.94	51.53	52.12	52.71	53.31	53.90	54.50	55.10	55.70	56.29	56.89	57.50
21.0	50.85	51.44	52.04	52.63	53.23	53.83	54.42	55.02	55.62	56.23	56.83	57.43
21.5	50.77	51.36	51.96	52.56	53.16	53.76	54.36	54.96	55.56	56.16	56.77	57.37
22.0	50.70	51.29	51.89	52.49	53.09	53.69	54.30	54.90	55.50	56.11	56.71	57.32
22.5	50.63	51.23	51.83	52.43	53.04	53.64	54.24	54.85	55.45	56.06	56.67	57.27
23.0	50.57	51.17	51.78	52.38	52.98	53.59	54.19	54.80	55.41	56.01	56.62	57.23
23.5	50.52	51.12	51.73	52.33	52.94	53.54	54.15	54.76	55.37	55.98	56.59	57.20
24.0	50.47	51.08	51.68	52.29	52.89	53.50	54.11	54.72	55.33	55.94	56.55	57.16
24.5	50.43	51.03	51.64	52.25	52.86	53.46	54.07	54.69	55.30	55.91	56.52	57.13
25.0	50.39	51.00	51.60	52.21	52.82	53.43	54.04	54.65	55.27	55.88	56.49	57.11
25.5	50.35	50.96	51.57	52.18	52.79	53.40	54.01	54.63	55.24	55.85	56.47	57.08
26.0	50.32	50.93	51.54	52.15	52.76	53.38	53.99	54.60	55.22	55.83	56.45	57.06
26.5	50.29	50.90	51.51	52.12	52.74	53.35	53.96	54.58	55.19	55.81	56.43	57.04
27.0	50.26	50.88	51.49	52.10	52.71	53.33	53.94	54.56	55.17	55.79	56.41	57.03
27.5	50.24	50.85	51.47	52.08	52.69	53.31	53.93	54.54	55.16	55.77	56.39	57.01
28.0	50.22	50.83	51.45	52.06	52.68	53.29	53.91	54.52	55.14	55.76	56.38	57.00
28.5	50.20	50.81	51.43	52.04	52.66	53.28	53.89	54.51	55.13	55.75	56.37	56.98
29.0	50.18	50.80	51.41	52.03	52.64	53.26	53.88	54.50	55.12	55.73	56.35	56.97
29.5	50.16	50.78	51.40	52.01	52.63	53.25	53.87	54.49	55.10	55.72	56.34	56.96
30.0	50.15	50.77	51.38	52.00	52.62	53.24	53.86	54.47	55.09	55.71	56.33	56.95
31.0	50.12	50.74	51.36	51.98	52.60	53.22	53.84	54.46	55.08	55.70	56.32	56.94
32.0	50.10	50.72	51.34	51.96	52.58	53.20	53.82	54.44	55.06	55.68	56.31	56.93
33.0	50.08	50.70	51.32	51.95	52.57	53.19	53.81	54.43	55.05	55.67	56.30	56.92
34.0	50.07	50.69	51.31	51.93	52.55	53.18	53.80	54.42	55.04	55.67	56.29	56.91
35.0	50.06	50.68	51.30	51.92	52.55	53.17	53.79	54.41	55.04	55.66	56.28	56.90
36.0	50.05	50.67	51.29	51.92	52.54	53.16	53.78	54.41	55.03	55.65	56.28	56.90
37.0	50.04	50.66	51.29	51.91	52.53	53.16	53.78	54.40	55.02	55.65	56.27	56.90
38.0	50.04	50.66	51.28	51.90	52.53	53.15	53.77	54.40	55.02	55.64	56.27	56.89
39.0	50.03	50.65	51.28	51.90	52.52	53.15	53.77	54.39	55.02	55.64	56.27	56.89
40.0	50.03	50.65	51.27	51.90	52.52	53.14	53.77	54.39	55.02	55.64	56.26	56.89

QUARTERLY
PAYMENT REQUIRED TO AMORTIZE A $1,000.00 LOAN

TERM IN YEARS	23.00%	23.25%	23.50%	23.75%	24.00%	24.25%	24.50%	24.75%	25.00%	25.25%	25.50%	25.75%
0.5	543.53	544.01	544.49	544.96	545.44	545.92	546.40	546.88	547.35	547.83	548.31	548.79
1.0	286.95	287.36	287.77	288.18	288.60	289.01	289.42	289.84	290.25	290.66	291.08	291.49
1.5	201.77	202.17	202.57	202.97	203.37	203.77	204.17	204.57	204.97	205.37	205.77	206.17
2.0	159.45	159.85	160.25	160.64	161.04	161.44	161.84	162.24	162.64	163.04	163.44	163.84
2.5	134.27	134.67	135.07	135.47	135.87	136.28	136.68	137.08	137.49	137.89	138.30	138.70
3.0	117.65	118.06	118.47	118.87	119.28	119.69	120.10	120.51	120.92	121.33	121.75	122.16
3.5	105.93	106.34	106.76	107.17	107.59	108.01	108.42	108.84	109.26	109.68	110.10	110.52
4.0	97.27	97.69	98.11	98.53	98.96	99.38	99.81	100.24	100.66	101.09	101.52	101.95
4.5	90.64	91.07	91.50	91.93	92.36	92.80	93.23	93.67	94.10	94.54	94.98	95.42
5.0	85.43	85.87	86.31	86.75	87.19	87.63	88.08	88.52	88.97	89.41	89.86	90.31
5.5	81.25	81.70	82.15	82.60	83.05	83.50	83.96	84.41	84.86	85.32	85.78	86.24
6.0	77.85	78.31	78.77	79.22	79.68	80.14	80.61	81.07	81.53	82.00	82.47	82.93
6.5	75.04	75.51	75.97	76.44	76.91	77.38	77.85	78.32	78.79	79.27	79.74	80.22
7.0	72.70	73.17	73.65	74.12	74.60	75.08	75.56	76.04	76.52	77.00	77.49	77.97
7.5	70.72	71.20	71.68	72.17	72.65	73.14	73.63	74.12	74.61	75.10	75.59	76.09
8.0	69.04	69.53	70.02	70.51	71.01	71.50	72.00	72.50	72.99	73.49	74.00	74.50
8.5	67.61	68.10	68.60	69.10	69.60	70.11	70.61	71.11	71.62	72.13	72.64	73.15
9.0	66.37	66.88	67.38	67.89	68.40	68.91	69.42	69.93	70.45	70.96	71.48	72.00
9.5	65.31	65.82	66.33	66.85	67.36	67.88	68.40	68.92	69.44	69.96	70.49	71.01
10.0	64.38	64.90	65.42	65.94	66.47	66.99	67.52	68.04	68.57	69.10	69.63	70.16
10.5	63.58	64.10	64.63	65.16	65.69	66.22	66.75	67.29	67.82	68.36	68.89	69.43
11.0	62.88	63.41	63.94	64.48	65.01	65.55	66.09	66.63	67.17	67.71	68.25	68.80
11.5	62.26	62.80	63.34	63.88	64.42	64.96	65.51	66.05	66.60	67.15	67.70	68.25
12.0	61.72	62.26	62.81	63.36	63.90	64.45	65.00	65.55	66.11	66.66	67.22	67.77
12.5	61.25	61.79	62.35	62.90	63.45	64.00	64.56	65.12	65.67	66.23	66.79	67.36
13.0	60.83	61.38	61.94	62.49	63.05	63.61	64.17	64.73	65.30	65.86	66.43	66.99
13.5	60.46	61.02	61.58	62.14	62.70	63.27	63.83	64.40	64.96	65.53	66.10	66.68
14.0	60.13	60.69	61.26	61.83	62.39	62.96	63.53	64.10	64.67	65.25	65.82	66.40
14.5	59.84	60.41	60.98	61.55	62.12	62.69	63.27	63.84	64.42	65.00	65.57	66.15
15.0	59.59	60.16	60.73	61.31	61.88	62.46	63.04	63.61	64.19	64.78	65.36	65.94
15.5	59.36	59.93	60.51	61.09	61.67	62.25	62.83	63.41	64.00	64.58	65.17	65.75
16.0	59.16	59.74	60.32	60.90	61.48	62.07	62.65	63.24	63.82	64.41	65.00	65.59
16.5	58.98	59.56	60.14	60.73	61.32	61.90	62.49	63.08	63.67	64.26	64.85	65.45
17.0	58.82	59.40	59.99	60.58	61.17	61.76	62.35	62.94	63.53	64.13	64.72	65.32
17.5	58.68	59.27	59.86	60.45	61.04	61.63	62.22	62.82	63.42	64.01	64.61	65.21
18.0	58.55	59.14	59.73	60.33	60.92	61.52	62.11	62.71	63.31	63.91	64.51	65.11
18.5	58.44	59.03	59.63	60.22	60.82	61.42	62.02	62.62	63.22	63.82	64.42	65.02
19.0	58.34	58.93	59.53	60.13	60.73	61.33	61.93	62.53	63.13	63.74	64.34	64.95
19.5	58.25	58.85	59.45	60.05	60.65	61.25	61.85	62.46	63.06	63.67	64.27	64.88
20.0	58.17	58.77	59.37	59.97	60.58	61.18	61.79	62.39	63.00	63.61	64.21	64.82
20.5	58.10	58.70	59.30	59.90	60.51	61.12	61.73	62.33	62.94	63.55	64.16	64.77
21.0	58.03	58.64	59.24	59.85	60.46	61.07	61.67	62.28	62.89	63.50	64.11	64.72
21.5	57.98	58.58	59.19	59.80	60.41	61.02	61.63	62.24	62.85	63.46	64.07	64.68
22.0	57.93	58.54	59.14	59.75	60.36	60.97	61.58	62.20	62.81	63.42	64.03	64.65
22.5	57.88	58.49	59.10	59.71	60.32	60.93	61.55	62.16	62.77	63.39	64.00	64.62
23.0	57.84	58.45	59.06	59.68	60.29	60.90	61.51	62.13	62.74	63.36	63.97	64.59
23.5	57.81	58.42	59.03	59.64	60.26	60.87	61.49	62.10	62.72	63.33	63.95	64.56
24.0	57.77	58.39	59.00	59.61	60.23	60.84	61.46	62.07	62.69	63.31	63.92	64.54
24.5	57.75	58.36	58.97	59.59	60.20	60.82	61.44	62.05	62.67	63.29	63.90	64.52
25.0	57.72	58.34	58.95	59.57	60.18	60.80	61.42	62.03	62.65	63.27	63.89	64.51
25.5	57.70	58.31	58.93	59.55	60.16	60.78	61.40	62.02	62.63	63.25	63.87	64.49
26.0	57.68	58.29	58.91	59.53	60.15	60.76	61.38	62.00	62.62	63.24	63.86	64.48
26.5	57.66	58.28	58.89	59.51	60.13	60.75	61.37	61.99	62.61	63.23	63.85	64.47
27.0	57.64	58.26	58.88	59.50	60.12	60.74	61.35	61.97	62.59	63.22	63.84	64.46
27.5	57.63	58.25	58.87	59.48	60.10	60.72	61.34	61.96	62.58	63.21	63.83	64.45
28.0	57.61	58.23	58.85	59.47	60.09	60.71	61.33	61.95	62.58	63.20	63.82	64.44
28.5	57.60	58.22	58.84	59.46	60.08	60.70	61.32	61.95	62.57	63.19	63.81	64.43
29.0	57.59	58.21	58.83	59.45	60.07	60.70	61.32	61.94	62.56	63.18	63.80	64.43
29.5	57.58	58.20	58.82	59.45	60.07	60.69	61.31	61.93	62.55	63.18	63.80	64.42
30.0	57.58	58.20	58.82	59.44	60.06	60.68	61.30	61.93	62.55	63.17	63.79	64.42
31.0	57.56	58.18	58.80	59.43	60.05	60.67	61.29	61.92	62.54	63.16	63.78	64.41
32.0	57.55	58.17	58.79	59.42	60.04	60.66	61.29	61.91	62.53	63.15	63.78	64.40
33.0	57.54	58.16	58.79	59.41	60.03	60.66	61.28	61.90	62.53	63.15	63.77	64.40
34.0	57.53	58.16	58.78	59.40	60.03	60.65	61.27	61.90	62.52	63.15	63.77	64.39
35.0	57.53	58.15	58.77	59.40	60.02	60.65	61.27	61.89	62.52	63.14	63.77	64.39
36.0	57.52	58.15	58.77	59.39	60.02	60.64	61.27	61.89	62.52	63.14	63.76	64.39
37.0	57.52	58.14	58.77	59.39	60.02	60.64	61.26	61.89	62.51	63.14	63.76	64.39
38.0	57.52	58.14	58.77	59.39	60.01	60.64	61.26	61.89	62.51	63.14	63.76	64.38
39.0	57.51	58.14	58.76	59.39	60.01	60.64	61.26	61.89	62.51	63.13	63.76	64.38
40.0	57.51	58.14	58.76	59.39	60.01	60.63	61.26	61.88	62.51	63.13	63.76	64.38

QUARTERLY
PAYMENT REQUIRED TO AMORTIZE A $1,000.00 LOAN

TERM IN YEARS	INTEREST RATES 26.00%	26.25%	26.50%	26.75%	27.00%	27.25%	27.50%	27.75%	28.00%	28.25%	28.50%	28.75%
0.5	549.27	549.74	550.22	550.70	551.18	551.66	552.14	552.62	553.10	553.58	554.06	554.53
1.0	291.91	292.32	292.74	293.15	293.57	293.98	294.40	294.82	295.23	295.65	296.07	296.48
1.5	206.57	206.98	207.38	207.78	208.18	208.58	208.99	209.40	209.80	210.21	210.61	211.02
2.0	164.24	164.64	165.05	165.45	165.85	166.26	166.66	167.07	167.47	167.88	168.28	168.69
2.5	139.11	139.52	139.92	140.33	140.74	141.15	141.56	141.97	142.38	142.79	143.21	143.62
3.0	122.57	122.99	123.40	123.82	124.23	124.65	125.07	125.49	125.91	126.33	126.75	127.17
3.5	110.95	111.37	111.79	112.22	112.64	113.07	113.49	113.92	114.35	114.78	115.21	115.64
4.0	102.38	102.81	103.25	103.68	104.12	104.55	104.99	105.42	105.86	106.30	106.74	107.18
4.5	95.86	96.30	96.74	97.19	97.63	98.08	98.52	98.97	99.42	99.87	100.32	100.77
5.0	90.76	91.21	91.66	92.12	92.57	93.03	93.48	93.94	94.40	94.86	95.32	95.78
5.5	86.70	87.16	87.62	88.08	88.55	89.01	89.48	89.94	90.41	90.88	91.35	91.82
6.0	83.40	83.87	84.34	84.82	85.29	85.76	86.24	86.72	87.19	87.67	88.15	88.63
6.5	80.70	81.18	81.66	82.14	82.82	83.11	83.59	84.08	84.57	85.05	85.54	86.03
7.0	78.46	78.95	79.44	79.93	80.42	80.91	81.41	81.90	82.40	82.89	83.39	83.89
7.5	76.58	77.08	77.58	78.08	78.58	79.08	79.58	80.09	80.59	81.10	81.61	82.11
8.0	75.00	75.51	76.01	76.52	77.03	77.54	78.05	78.56	79.08	79.59	80.11	80.63
8.5	73.66	74.17	74.69	75.20	75.72	76.24	76.76	77.28	77.80	78.32	78.85	79.37
9.0	72.52	73.04	73.56	74.08	74.61	75.14	75.66	76.19	76.72	77.25	77.78	78.32
9.5	71.54	72.07	72.60	73.13	73.66	74.19	74.73	75.26	75.80	76.34	76.88	77.42
10.0	70.70	71.23	71.77	72.31	72.85	73.39	73.93	74.47	75.01	75.56	76.11	76.65
10.5	69.97	70.52	71.06	71.60	72.15	72.69	73.24	73.79	74.34	74.89	75.44	76.00
11.0	69.35	69.89	70.44	70.99	71.54	72.10	72.65	73.21	73.76	74.32	74.88	75.44
11.5	68.80	69.36	69.91	70.47	71.02	71.58	72.14	72.70	73.26	73.83	74.39	74.96
12.0	68.33	68.89	69.45	70.01	70.57	71.14	71.70	72.27	72.84	73.40	73.97	74.54
12.5	67.92	68.48	69.05	69.62	70.18	70.75	71.32	71.89	72.46	73.04	73.61	74.19
13.0	67.56	68.13	68.70	69.27	69.84	70.42	70.99	71.57	72.14	72.72	73.30	73.88
13.5	67.25	67.82	68.40	68.97	69.55	70.13	70.71	71.29	71.87	72.45	73.03	73.61
14.0	66.97	67.55	68.13	68.71	69.29	69.87	70.46	71.04	71.63	72.21	72.80	73.38
14.5	66.73	67.32	67.90	68.48	69.07	69.65	70.24	70.83	71.42	72.01	72.60	73.19
15.0	66.53	67.11	67.70	68.28	68.87	69.46	70.05	70.64	71.23	71.83	72.42	73.01
15.5	66.34	66.93	67.52	68.11	68.70	69.29	69.89	70.48	71.08	71.67	72.27	72.87
16.0	66.18	66.77	67.37	67.96	68.55	69.15	69.74	70.34	70.94	71.54	72.14	72.74
16.5	66.04	66.63	67.23	67.83	68.42	69.02	69.62	70.22	70.82	71.42	72.02	72.62
17.0	65.92	66.51	67.11	67.71	68.31	68.91	69.51	70.11	70.72	71.32	71.92	72.53
17.5	65.81	66.41	67.01	67.61	68.21	68.81	68.81	69.42	70.02	70.62	71.23	71.84	72.44
18.0	65.71	66.31	66.92	67.52	68.12	68.73	69.33	69.94	70.55	71.15	71.76	72.37
18.5	65.63	66.23	66.83	67.44	68.05	68.65	69.26	69.87	70.48	71.09	71.70	72.31
19.0	65.55	66.16	66.76	67.37	67.98	68.59	69.20	69.81	70.42	71.03	71.64	72.25
19.5	65.49	66.09	66.70	67.31	67.92	68.53	69.14	69.75	70.36	70.98	71.59	72.20
20.0	65.43	66.04	66.65	67.26	67.87	68.48	69.09	69.71	70.32	70.93	71.55	72.16
20.5	65.38	65.99	66.60	67.21	67.83	68.44	69.05	69.66	70.28	70.89	71.51	72.12
21.0	65.33	65.95	66.56	67.17	67.79	68.40	69.01	69.63	70.24	70.86	71.48	72.09
21.5	65.30	65.91	66.52	67.14	67.75	68.37	68.98	69.60	70.21	70.83	71.45	72.06
22.0	65.26	65.88	66.49	67.11	67.72	68.34	68.95	69.57	70.19	70.80	71.42	72.04
22.5	65.23	65.85	66.46	67.08	67.69	68.31	68.93	69.55	70.16	70.78	71.40	72.02
23.0	65.20	65.82	66.44	67.05	67.67	68.29	68.91	69.53	70.14	70.76	71.38	72.00
23.5	65.18	65.80	66.41	67.03	67.65	68.27	68.89	69.51	70.13	70.75	71.37	71.99
24.0	65.16	65.78	66.40	67.01	67.63	68.25	68.87	69.49	70.11	70.73	71.35	71.97
24.5	65.14	65.76	66.38	67.00	67.62	68.24	68.86	69.48	70.10	70.72	71.34	71.96
25.0	65.12	65.74	66.36	66.98	67.60	68.22	68.84	69.46	70.09	70.71	71.33	71.95
25.5	65.11	65.72	66.35	66.97	67.59	68.21	68.83	69.45	70.08	70.70	71.32	71.94
26.0	65.10	65.72	66.34	66.96	67.58	68.20	68.82	69.44	70.07	70.69	71.31	71.93
26.5	65.09	65.71	66.33	66.95	67.57	68.19	68.81	69.44	70.06	70.68	71.30	71.93
27.0	65.08	65.70	66.32	66.94	67.56	68.19	68.81	69.43	70.05	70.67	71.30	71.92
27.5	65.07	65.69	66.31	66.93	67.56	68.18	68.80	69.42	70.05	70.67	71.29	71.91
28.0	65.06	65.68	66.31	66.92	67.55	68.17	68.80	69.42	70.04	70.66	71.29	71.91
28.5	65.05	65.68	66.30	66.92	67.54	68.17	68.79	69.41	70.04	70.66	71.28	71.91
29.0	65.05	65.67	66.29	66.92	67.54	68.16	68.79	69.41	70.03	70.66	71.28	71.90
29.5	65.04	65.67	66.29	66.91	67.54	68.16	68.78	69.41	70.03	70.65	71.28	71.90
30.0	65.04	65.66	66.29	66.91	67.53	68.16	68.78	69.40	70.03	70.65	71.27	71.90
31.0	65.03	65.65	66.28	66.90	67.53	68.15	68.77	69.40	70.02	70.64	71.27	71.89
32.0	65.03	65.65	66.27	66.90	67.52	68.14	68.77	69.39	70.01	70.64	71.27	71.89
33.0	65.02	65.64	66.27	66.89	67.52	68.14	68.77	69.39	70.01	70.64	71.26	71.89
34.0	65.02	65.64	66.27	66.89	67.51	68.14	68.76	69.39	70.01	70.64	71.26	71.88
35.0	65.01	65.64	66.26	66.89	67.51	68.14	68.76	69.39	70.01	70.64	71.26	71.88
36.0	65.01	65.64	66.26	66.89	67.51	68.14	68.76	69.38	70.01	70.63	71.26	71.88
37.0	65.01	65.64	66.26	66.88	67.51	68.13	68.76	69.38	70.01	70.63	71.26	71.88
38.0	65.01	65.63	66.26	66.88	67.51	68.13	68.76	69.38	70.01	70.63	71.26	71.88
39.0	65.01	65.63	66.26	66.88	67.51	68.13	68.76	69.38	70.01	70.63	71.26	71.88
40.0	65.01	65.63	66.26	66.88	67.51	68.13	68.76	69.38	70.01	70.63	71.26	71.88

SEMI-ANNUAL
PAYMENT REQUIRED TO AMORTIZE A $1,000.00 LOAN

TERM IN YEARS	INTEREST RATES											
	5.00%	5.25%	5.50%	5.75%	6.00%	6.25%	6.50%	6.75%	7.00%	7.25%	7.50%	7.75%
0.5	1025.00	1026.25	1027.50	1028.75	1030.00	1031.25	1032.50	1033.75	1035.00	1036.25	1037.50	1038.75
1.0	518.83	519.78	520.72	521.67	522.62	523.56	524.51	525.46	526.41	527.35	528.30	529.25
1.5	350.14	350.99	351.84	352.69	353.54	354.39	355.24	356.09	356.94	357.79	358.65	359.50
2.0	265.82	266.62	267.43	268.23	269.03	269.84	270.64	271.45	272.26	273.06	273.87	274.68
2.5	215.25	216.03	216.80	217.58	218.36	219.14	219.92	220.70	221.49	222.27	223.06	223.84
3.0	181.55	182.31	183.08	183.84	184.60	185.37	186.13	186.90	187.67	188.44	189.22	189.99
3.5	157.50	158.25	159.00	159.76	160.51	161.27	162.03	162.79	163.55	164.31	165.08	165.85
4.0	139.47	140.22	140.96	141.71	142.46	143.21	143.97	144.72	145.48	146.24	147.00	147.77
4.5	125.46	126.20	126.95	127.69	128.44	129.19	129.94	130.69	131.45	132.21	132.97	133.73
5.0	114.26	115.00	115.74	116.49	117.24	117.98	118.74	119.49	120.25	121.01	121.77	122.53
5.5	105.11	105.85	106.59	107.34	108.08	108.83	109.58	110.34	111.10	111.86	112.62	113.39
6.0	97.49	98.23	98.97	99.72	100.47	101.22	101.97	102.73	103.49	104.25	105.02	105.79
6.5	91.05	91.79	92.54	93.28	94.03	94.79	95.54	96.30	97.07	97.83	98.60	99.37
7.0	85.54	86.28	87.03	87.78	88.53	89.29	90.05	90.81	91.58	92.35	93.12	93.89
7.5	80.77	81.52	82.26	83.02	83.77	84.53	85.29	86.06	86.83	87.60	88.38	89.16
8.0	76.60	77.35	78.10	78.86	79.62	80.38	81.15	81.92	82.69	83.47	84.25	85.04
8.5	72.93	73.68	74.44	75.20	75.96	76.72	77.49	78.27	79.05	79.83	80.62	81.41
9.0	69.68	70.43	71.19	71.95	72.71	73.48	74.26	75.04	75.82	76.61	77.40	78.20
9.5	66.77	67.52	68.28	69.05	69.82	70.59	71.37	72.16	72.95	73.74	74.54	75.34
10.0	64.15	64.91	65.68	66.45	67.22	68.00	68.78	69.57	70.37	71.16	71.97	72.77
10.5	61.79	62.56	63.32	64.10	64.88	65.66	66.45	67.24	68.04	68.85	69.65	70.47
11.0	59.65	60.42	61.19	61.97	62.75	63.54	64.33	65.13	65.94	66.75	67.56	68.38
11.5	57.70	58.47	59.25	60.03	60.82	61.61	62.41	63.21	64.02	64.84	65.66	66.48
12.0	55.92	56.69	57.47	58.26	59.05	59.85	60.65	61.46	62.28	63.10	63.92	64.76
12.5	54.28	55.06	55.84	56.64	57.43	58.24	59.04	59.86	60.68	61.51	62.34	63.17
13.0	52.77	53.56	54.35	55.14	55.94	56.75	57.56	58.38	59.21	60.04	60.88	61.72
13.5	51.38	52.17	52.96	53.76	54.57	55.38	56.20	57.03	57.86	58.69	59.54	60.39
14.0	50.09	50.88	51.68	52.49	53.30	54.12	54.94	55.77	56.61	57.45	58.30	59.16
14.5	48.90	49.69	50.49	51.30	52.12	52.94	53.77	54.61	55.45	56.30	57.15	58.02
15.0	47.78	48.58	49.39	50.20	51.02	51.85	52.69	53.53	54.38	55.23	56.09	56.96
15.5	46.74	47.55	48.36	49.18	50.00	50.84	51.68	52.52	53.38	54.24	55.11	55.98
16.0	45.77	46.58	47.40	48.22	49.05	49.89	50.73	51.59	52.45	53.31	54.19	55.07
16.5	44.86	45.68	46.50	47.33	48.16	49.00	49.85	50.71	51.58	52.45	53.33	54.22
17.0	44.01	44.83	45.65	46.49	47.33	48.18	49.03	49.89	50.76	51.64	52.53	53.42
17.5	43.21	44.03	44.86	45.70	46.54	47.40	48.26	49.13	50.00	50.89	51.78	52.68
18.0	42.46	43.28	44.12	44.96	45.81	46.67	47.53	48.41	49.29	50.18	51.08	51.98
18.5	41.75	42.58	43.41	44.26	45.12	45.98	46.85	47.73	48.62	49.51	50.42	51.33
19.0	41.08	41.91	42.75	43.60	44.46	45.33	46.21	47.09	47.99	48.89	49.80	50.71
19.5	40.44	41.28	42.13	42.98	43.85	44.72	45.60	46.49	47.39	48.30	49.21	50.14
20.0	39.84	40.68	41.54	42.40	43.27	44.15	45.03	45.93	46.83	47.74	48.66	49.59
20.5	39.27	40.12	40.98	41.84	42.72	43.60	44.49	45.39	46.30	47.22	48.15	49.08
21.0	38.73	39.59	40.45	41.32	42.20	43.09	43.98	44.89	45.80	46.73	47.66	48.60
21.5	38.22	39.08	39.94	40.82	41.70	42.60	43.50	44.41	45.33	46.26	47.20	48.14
22.0	37.74	38.60	39.47	40.35	41.23	42.13	43.04	43.96	44.88	45.82	46.76	47.71
22.5	37.27	38.14	39.01	39.90	40.79	41.69	42.61	43.53	44.46	45.40	46.35	47.30
23.0	36.83	37.70	38.58	39.47	40.37	41.28	42.19	43.12	44.06	45.00	45.95	46.92
23.5	36.41	37.29	38.17	39.06	39.97	40.88	41.80	42.73	43.67	44.62	45.58	46.55
24.0	36.01	36.89	37.78	38.67	39.58	40.50	41.43	42.37	43.31	44.27	45.23	46.20
24.5	35.63	36.51	37.40	38.31	39.22	40.14	41.07	42.02	42.97	43.93	44.90	45.88
25.0	35.26	36.15	37.05	37.95	38.87	39.80	40.74	41.68	42.64	43.60	44.58	45.56
25.5	34.91	35.80	36.71	37.62	38.54	39.47	40.41	41.37	42.33	43.30	44.28	45.27
26.0	34.58	35.47	36.38	37.30	38.22	39.16	40.11	41.06	42.03	43.01	43.99	44.98
26.5	34.26	35.16	36.07	36.99	37.92	38.86	39.81	40.77	41.75	42.73	43.72	44.72
27.0	33.95	34.86	35.77	36.69	37.63	38.58	39.53	40.50	41.48	42.46	43.46	44.46
27.5	33.66	34.57	35.48	36.41	37.35	38.30	39.27	40.24	41.22	42.21	43.21	44.22
28.0	33.38	34.29	35.21	36.14	37.09	38.04	39.01	39.99	40.97	41.97	42.97	43.99
28.5	33.11	34.02	34.95	35.89	36.84	37.80	38.77	39.75	40.74	41.74	42.75	43.77
29.0	32.85	33.77	34.70	35.64	36.59	37.56	38.53	39.52	40.51	41.52	42.53	43.56
29.5	32.60	33.52	34.46	35.40	36.36	37.33	38.31	39.30	40.30	41.31	42.33	43.36
30.0	32.36	33.29	34.23	35.18	36.14	37.11	38.09	39.09	40.09	41.11	42.13	43.16
31.0	31.91	32.84	33.79	34.75	35.72	36.70	37.69	38.70	39.71	40.73	41.77	42.81
32.0	31.49	32.43	33.39	34.35	35.33	36.32	37.32	38.34	39.36	40.39	41.43	42.48
33.0	31.10	32.05	33.01	33.99	34.98	35.97	36.98	38.00	39.04	40.08	41.13	42.19
34.0	30.74	31.70	32.67	33.65	34.65	35.65	36.67	37.70	38.74	39.79	40.85	41.91
35.0	30.40	31.37	32.35	33.34	34.34	35.36	36.38	37.42	38.47	39.52	40.59	41.67
36.0	30.09	31.06	32.05	33.05	34.06	35.08	36.12	37.16	38.21	39.28	40.35	41.44
37.0	29.80	30.78	31.77	32.78	33.80	34.83	35.87	36.92	37.98	39.06	40.14	41.23
38.0	29.52	30.51	31.51	32.53	33.55	34.59	35.64	36.70	37.77	38.85	39.94	41.04
39.0	29.27	30.26	31.27	32.29	33.33	34.37	35.43	36.50	37.57	38.66	39.76	40.86
40.0	29.03	30.03	31.05	32.08	33.12	34.17	35.23	36.31	37.39	38.48	39.59	40.70

SEMI-ANNUAL
PAYMENT REQUIRED TO AMORTIZE A $1,000.00 LOAN

TERM IN YEARS	INTEREST RATES											
	8.00%	8.25%	8.50%	8.75%	9.00%	9.25%	9.50%	9.75%	10.00%	10.25%	10.50%	10.75%
0.5	1040.00	1041.25	1042.50	1043.75	1045.00	1046.25	1047.50	1048.75	1050.00	1051.25	1052.50	1053.75
1.0	530.20	531.15	532.10	533.05	534.00	534.95	535.91	536.86	537.81	538.76	539.72	540.67
1.5	360.35	361.21	362.06	362.92	363.78	364.64	365.49	366.35	367.21	368.07	368.94	369.80
2.0	275.50	276.31	277.12	277.93	278.75	279.56	280.38	281.20	282.02	282.84	283.66	284.48
2.5	224.63	225.42	226.21	227.00	227.80	228.59	229.39	230.18	230.98	231.78	232.58	233.38
3.0	190.77	191.54	192.32	193.10	193.88	194.67	195.45	196.24	197.02	197.81	198.60	199.39
3.5	166.61	167.39	168.16	168.93	169.71	170.48	171.26	172.04	172.82	173.61	174.39	175.18
4.0	148.53	149.30	150.07	150.84	151.61	152.39	153.17	153.95	154.73	155.51	156.29	157.08
4.5	134.50	135.27	136.03	136.81	137.58	138.36	139.13	139.91	140.70	141.48	142.27	143.05
5.0	123.30	124.06	124.84	125.61	126.38	127.16	127.94	128.72	129.51	130.30	131.09	131.88
5.5	114.15	114.92	115.70	116.47	117.25	118.03	118.82	119.60	120.39	121.19	121.98	122.78
6.0	106.56	107.33	108.11	108.89	109.67	110.46	111.25	112.04	112.83	113.63	114.43	115.23
6.5	100.15	100.93	101.71	102.49	103.28	104.07	104.86	105.66	106.46	107.26	108.07	108.88
7.0	94.67	95.46	96.24	97.03	97.83	98.62	99.42	100.22	101.03	101.84	102.65	103.47
7.5	89.95	90.73	91.53	92.32	93.12	93.92	94.73	95.53	96.35	97.16	97.98	98.80
8.0	85.82	86.62	87.42	88.22	89.02	89.83	90.64	91.46	92.27	93.10	93.92	94.75
8.5	82.20	83.00	83.81	84.61	85.42	86.24	87.06	87.88	88.70	89.53	90.37	91.21
9.0	79.00	79.80	80.61	81.42	82.24	83.06	83.89	84.72	85.55	86.39	87.23	88.08
9.5	76.14	76.95	77.77	78.59	79.41	80.24	81.07	81.91	82.75	83.60	84.44	85.30
10.0	73.59	74.40	75.22	76.05	76.88	77.72	78.56	79.40	80.25	81.10	81.96	82.82
10.5	71.29	72.11	72.94	73.77	74.61	75.45	76.29	77.15	78.00	78.86	79.73	80.60
11.0	69.20	70.03	70.87	71.71	72.55	73.40	74.25	75.11	75.98	76.84	77.72	78.59
11.5	67.31	68.15	68.99	69.84	70.69	71.54	72.40	73.27	74.14	75.02	75.90	76.78
12.0	65.59	66.43	67.28	68.13	68.99	69.86	70.72	71.60	72.48	73.36	74.25	75.14
12.5	64.02	64.87	65.72	66.58	67.44	68.31	69.19	70.07	70.96	71.85	72.75	73.65
13.0	62.57	63.43	64.29	65.15	66.03	66.90	67.79	68.68	69.57	70.47	71.37	72.28
13.5	61.24	62.11	62.97	63.85	64.72	65.61	66.50	67.40	68.30	69.20	70.12	71.03
14.0	60.02	60.89	61.76	62.64	63.53	64.42	65.32	66.22	67.13	68.04	68.96	69.89
14.5	58.88	59.76	60.64	61.53	62.42	63.32	64.22	65.13	66.05	66.97	67.90	68.83
15.0	57.84	58.72	59.60	60.49	61.40	62.30	63.21	64.13	65.06	65.99	66.92	67.86
15.5	56.86	57.75	58.64	59.54	60.45	61.36	62.28	63.21	64.14	65.07	66.02	66.97
16.0	55.95	56.85	57.75	58.65	59.57	60.49	61.41	62.35	63.29	64.23	65.18	66.14
16.5	55.11	56.01	56.92	57.83	58.75	59.68	60.61	61.55	62.50	63.45	64.41	65.37
17.0	54.32	55.23	56.14	57.06	57.99	58.92	59.86	60.81	61.76	62.72	63.69	64.66
17.5	53.58	54.50	55.41	56.34	57.28	58.22	59.16	60.12	61.08	62.04	63.02	63.99
18.0	52.89	53.81	54.74	55.67	56.61	57.56	58.51	59.47	60.44	61.41	62.39	63.38
18.5	52.24	53.17	54.10	55.04	55.99	56.94	57.90	58.87	59.84	60.83	61.81	62.81
19.0	51.64	52.57	53.51	54.45	55.41	56.37	57.33	58.31	59.29	60.28	61.27	62.27
19.5	51.07	52.00	52.95	53.90	54.86	55.83	56.80	57.78	58.77	59.76	60.76	61.77
20.0	50.53	51.47	52.42	53.38	54.35	55.32	56.30	57.29	58.28	59.28	60.29	61.31
20.5	50.02	50.97	51.93	52.89	53.87	54.85	55.83	56.83	57.83	58.83	59.85	60.87
21.0	49.55	50.50	51.46	52.44	53.41	54.40	55.39	56.39	57.40	58.41	59.43	60.46
21.5	49.09	50.06	51.03	52.00	52.99	53.98	54.98	55.98	57.00	58.02	59.05	60.08
22.0	48.67	49.64	50.61	51.60	52.59	53.58	54.59	55.60	56.62	57.65	58.68	59.72
22.5	48.27	49.24	50.22	51.21	52.21	53.21	54.22	55.24	56.27	57.30	58.34	59.38
23.0	47.89	48.87	49.85	50.85	51.85	52.86	53.88	54.90	55.93	56.97	58.02	59.07
23.5	47.53	48.51	49.50	50.50	51.51	52.53	53.55	54.58	55.62	56.66	57.71	58.77
24.0	47.19	48.18	49.17	50.18	51.19	52.22	53.24	54.28	55.32	56.37	57.43	58.49
24.5	46.86	47.86	48.86	49.87	50.89	51.92	52.95	54.00	55.04	56.10	57.16	58.23
25.0	46.56	47.56	48.57	49.58	50.61	51.64	52.68	53.73	54.78	55.84	56.91	57.99
25.5	46.26	47.27	48.28	49.31	50.34	51.38	52.42	53.47	54.53	55.60	56.67	57.75
26.0	45.99	47.00	48.02	49.05	50.08	51.13	52.18	53.23	54.30	55.37	56.45	57.54
26.5	45.72	46.74	47.77	48.80	49.84	50.89	51.94	53.01	54.08	55.16	56.24	57.33
27.0	45.47	46.50	47.53	48.56	49.61	50.66	51.73	52.79	53.87	54.95	56.04	57.14
27.5	45.24	46.26	47.30	48.34	49.39	50.45	51.52	52.59	53.67	54.76	55.85	56.95
28.0	45.01	46.04	47.08	48.13	49.19	50.25	51.32	52.40	53.49	54.58	55.68	56.78
28.5	44.79	45.83	46.88	47.93	48.99	50.06	51.13	52.22	53.31	54.41	55.51	56.62
29.0	44.59	45.63	46.68	47.74	48.80	49.88	50.96	52.05	53.14	54.24	55.35	56.46
29.5	44.39	45.44	46.49	47.56	48.63	49.71	50.79	51.88	52.98	54.09	55.20	56.32
30.0	44.21	45.26	46.32	47.38	48.46	49.54	50.63	51.73	52.83	53.94	55.06	56.18
31.0	43.86	44.92	45.99	47.06	48.15	49.24	50.34	51.44	52.56	53.68	54.80	55.93
32.0	43.54	44.61	45.69	46.77	47.87	48.97	50.07	51.19	52.31	53.44	54.57	55.71
33.0	43.25	44.33	45.42	46.51	47.61	48.72	49.83	50.96	52.09	53.22	54.36	55.51
34.0	42.99	44.08	45.17	46.27	47.38	48.50	49.62	50.75	51.88	53.03	54.17	55.33
35.0	42.75	43.84	44.94	46.05	47.17	48.29	49.42	50.56	51.70	52.85	54.01	55.17
36.0	42.53	43.63	44.74	45.86	46.98	48.11	49.25	50.39	51.54	52.70	53.86	55.02
37.0	42.33	43.44	44.55	45.68	46.81	47.94	49.09	50.24	51.39	52.56	53.72	54.90
38.0	42.14	43.26	44.38	45.51	46.65	47.79	48.94	50.10	51.26	52.43	53.60	54.78
39.0	41.97	43.10	44.23	45.36	46.51	47.66	48.81	49.97	51.14	52.32	53.49	54.68
40.0	41.82	42.95	44.08	45.23	46.38	47.53	48.69	49.86	51.03	52.21	53.40	54.58

213

SEMI-ANNUAL
PAYMENT REQUIRED TO AMORTIZE A $1,000.00 LOAN

TERM IN YEARS	INTEREST RATES											
	11.00%	11.25%	11.50%	11.75%	12.00%	12.25%	12.50%	12.75%	13.00%	13.25%	13.50%	13.75%
0.5	1055.00	1056.25	1057.50	1058.75	1060.00	1061.25	1062.50	1063.75	1065.00	1066.25	1067.50	1068.75
1.0	541.62	542.58	543.53	544.49	545.44	546.40	547.35	548.31	549.27	550.22	551.18	552.14
1.5	370.66	371.52	372.39	373.25	374.11	374.98	375.85	376.71	377.58	378.45	379.32	380.19
2.0	285.30	286.12	286.95	287.77	288.60	289.42	290.25	291.08	291.91	292.74	293.57	294.40
2.5	234.18	234.98	235.79	236.59	237.40	238.21	239.02	239.83	240.64	241.45	242.27	243.08
3.0	200.18	200.98	201.77	202.57	203.37	204.17	204.97	205.77	206.57	207.38	208.18	208.99
3.5	175.97	176.76	177.55	178.34	179.14	179.94	180.73	181.53	182.34	183.14	183.94	184.75
4.0	157.87	158.66	159.45	160.25	161.04	161.84	162.64	163.44	164.24	165.05	165.85	166.66
4.5	143.84	144.64	145.43	146.23	147.03	147.83	148.63	149.44	150.24	151.05	151.86	152.68
5.0	132.67	133.47	134.27	135.07	135.87	136.68	137.49	138.30	139.11	139.92	140.74	141.56
5.5	123.58	124.38	125.18	125.99	126.80	127.61	128.42	129.24	130.06	130.88	131.71	132.53
6.0	116.03	116.84	117.65	118.47	119.28	120.10	120.92	121.75	122.57	123.40	124.23	125.07
6.5	109.69	110.50	111.32	112.14	112.97	113.79	114.62	115.45	116.29	117.13	117.97	118.81
7.0	104.28	105.11	105.93	106.76	107.59	108.42	109.26	110.10	110.95	111.79	112.64	113.49
7.5	99.63	100.46	101.29	102.13	102.97	103.81	104.66	105.51	106.36	107.21	108.07	108.93
8.0	95.59	96.42	97.27	98.11	98.96	99.81	100.66	101.52	102.38	103.25	104.12	104.99
8.5	92.05	92.89	93.74	94.59	95.45	96.31	97.17	98.04	98.91	99.79	100.66	101.55
9.0	88.92	89.78	90.64	91.50	92.36	93.23	94.10	94.98	95.86	96.74	97.63	98.52
9.5	86.16	87.02	87.88	88.75	89.63	90.50	91.39	92.27	93.16	94.05	94.95	95.85
10.0	83.68	84.55	85.43	86.31	87.19	88.08	88.97	89.86	90.76	91.66	92.57	93.48
10.5	81.47	82.35	83.23	84.12	85.01	85.91	86.81	87.71	88.62	89.53	90.45	91.37
11.0	79.48	80.36	81.25	82.15	83.05	83.96	84.86	85.78	86.70	87.62	88.55	89.48
11.5	77.67	78.57	79.47	80.37	81.28	82.20	83.12	84.04	84.97	85.90	86.83	87.77
12.0	76.04	76.94	77.85	78.77	79.68	80.61	81.53	82.47	83.40	84.34	85.29	86.24
12.5	74.55	75.47	76.38	77.30	78.23	79.16	80.10	81.04	81.99	82.94	83.89	84.85
13.0	73.20	74.12	75.04	75.97	76.91	77.85	78.79	79.74	80.70	81.66	82.62	83.59
13.5	71.96	72.89	73.82	74.76	75.70	76.65	77.61	78.56	79.53	80.50	81.47	82.45
14.0	70.82	71.76	72.70	73.65	74.60	75.56	76.52	77.49	78.46	79.44	80.42	81.41
14.5	69.77	70.72	71.67	72.62	73.58	74.55	75.52	76.50	77.48	78.47	79.46	80.45
15.0	68.81	69.76	70.72	71.68	72.65	73.63	74.61	75.59	76.58	77.58	78.58	79.58
15.5	67.92	68.88	69.85	70.82	71.80	72.78	73.77	74.76	75.76	76.76	77.77	78.78
16.0	67.10	68.07	69.04	70.02	71.01	72.00	72.99	74.00	75.00	76.01	77.03	78.05
16.5	66.34	67.32	68.30	69.28	70.28	71.28	72.28	73.29	74.30	75.32	76.35	77.38
17.0	65.63	66.62	67.61	68.60	69.60	70.61	71.62	72.64	73.66	74.69	75.72	76.76
17.5	64.98	65.97	66.97	67.97	68.98	69.99	71.01	72.04	73.07	74.10	75.14	76.19
18.0	64.37	65.37	66.37	67.38	68.40	69.42	70.45	71.48	72.52	73.56	74.61	75.66
18.5	63.80	64.81	65.82	66.84	67.86	68.89	69.93	70.97	72.01	73.06	74.12	75.18
19.0	63.28	64.29	65.31	66.33	67.36	68.40	69.44	70.49	71.54	72.60	73.66	74.73
19.5	62.78	63.80	64.83	65.86	66.90	67.94	68.99	70.04	71.10	72.17	73.24	74.31
20.0	62.33	63.35	64.38	65.42	66.47	67.52	68.57	69.63	70.70	71.77	72.85	73.93
20.5	61.90	62.93	63.97	65.01	66.06	67.12	68.18	69.25	70.32	71.40	72.48	73.57
21.0	61.49	62.53	63.58	64.63	65.69	66.75	67.82	68.89	69.97	71.06	72.15	73.24
21.5	61.12	62.16	63.22	64.27	65.34	66.41	67.48	68.56	69.65	70.74	71.83	72.94
22.0	60.77	61.82	62.88	63.94	65.01	66.09	67.17	68.25	69.35	70.44	71.54	72.65
22.5	60.44	61.49	62.56	63.63	64.71	65.79	66.87	67.97	69.06	70.17	71.28	72.39
23.0	60.13	61.19	62.26	63.34	64.42	65.51	66.60	67.70	68.80	69.91	71.02	72.14
23.5	59.84	60.91	61.98	63.06	64.15	65.25	66.34	67.45	68.56	69.67	70.79	71.91
24.0	59.56	60.64	61.72	62.81	63.90	65.00	66.11	67.22	68.33	69.45	70.57	71.70
24.5	59.31	60.39	61.48	62.57	63.67	64.77	65.88	67.00	68.12	69.24	70.37	71.51
25.0	59.07	60.15	61.25	62.35	63.45	64.56	65.67	66.79	67.92	69.05	70.18	71.32
25.5	58.84	59.93	61.03	62.13	63.24	64.36	65.48	66.60	67.73	68.87	70.01	71.15
26.0	58.63	59.72	60.83	61.94	63.05	64.17	65.30	66.43	67.56	68.70	69.84	70.99
26.5	58.43	59.53	60.64	61.75	62.87	64.00	65.12	66.26	67.40	68.54	69.69	70.84
27.0	58.24	59.34	60.46	61.58	62.70	63.83	64.96	66.10	67.25	68.40	69.55	70.71
27.5	58.06	59.17	60.29	61.41	62.54	63.68	64.81	65.96	67.11	68.26	69.42	70.58
28.0	57.89	59.01	60.13	61.26	62.39	63.53	64.67	65.82	66.97	68.13	69.29	70.46
28.5	57.73	58.86	59.98	61.11	62.25	63.39	64.54	65.69	66.85	68.01	69.18	70.34
29.0	57.59	58.71	59.84	60.98	62.12	63.27	64.42	65.57	66.73	67.90	69.07	70.24
29.5	57.44	58.57	59.71	60.85	62.00	63.15	64.30	65.46	66.63	67.79	68.97	70.14
30.0	57.31	58.45	59.59	60.73	61.88	63.04	64.19	65.36	66.53	67.70	68.87	70.05
31.0	57.07	58.21	59.36	60.51	61.67	62.83	64.00	65.17	66.34	67.52	68.70	69.89
32.0	56.85	58.00	59.16	60.32	61.48	62.65	63.82	65.00	66.18	67.37	68.55	69.74
33.0	56.66	57.82	58.98	60.14	61.32	62.49	63.67	64.85	66.04	67.23	68.42	69.62
34.0	56.49	57.65	58.82	59.99	61.17	62.35	63.53	64.72	65.92	67.11	68.31	69.51
35.0	56.33	57.50	58.68	59.86	61.04	62.22	63.42	64.61	65.81	67.01	68.21	69.42
36.0	56.19	57.37	58.55	59.73	60.92	62.11	63.31	64.51	65.71	66.92	68.12	69.33
37.0	56.07	57.25	58.44	59.63	60.82	62.02	63.22	64.42	65.63	66.83	68.05	69.26
38.0	55.96	57.15	58.34	59.53	60.73	61.93	63.13	64.34	65.55	66.76	67.98	69.20
39.0	55.86	57.05	58.25	59.45	60.65	61.85	63.06	64.27	65.49	66.70	67.92	69.14
40.0	55.77	56.97	58.17	59.37	60.58	61.79	63.00	64.21	65.43	66.65	67.87	69.09

SEMI-ANNUAL
PAYMENT REQUIRED TO AMORTIZE A $1,000.00 LOAN

TERM IN YEARS	14.00%	14.25%	14.50%	14.75%	15.00%	15.25%	15.50%	15.75%	16.00%	16.25%	16.50%	16.75%
0.5	1070.00	1071.25	1072.50	1073.75	1075.00	1076.25	1077.50	1078.75	1080.00	1081.25	1082.50	1083.75
1.0	553.10	554.06	555.01	555.97	556.93	557.89	558.85	559.81	560.77	561.74	562.70	563.66
1.5	381.06	381.93	382.80	383.67	384.54	385.42	386.29	387.16	388.04	388.91	389.79	390.67
2.0	295.23	296.07	296.90	297.74	298.57	299.41	300.25	301.09	301.93	302.77	303.61	304.45
2.5	243.90	244.71	245.53	246.35	247.17	247.99	248.81	249.64	250.46	251.29	252.11	252.94
3.0	209.80	210.61	211.42	212.24	213.05	213.87	214.68	215.50	216.32	217.14	217.96	218.79
3.5	185.56	186.37	187.18	187.99	188.81	189.62	190.44	191.26	192.08	192.90	193.72	194.55
4.0	167.47	168.28	169.10	169.91	170.73	171.55	172.37	173.20	174.02	174.85	175.67	176.50
4.5	153.49	154.31	155.13	155.95	156.77	157.60	158.42	159.25	160.08	160.92	161.75	162.59
5.0	142.38	143.21	144.03	144.86	145.69	146.52	147.36	148.20	149.03	149.88	150.72	151.56
5.5	133.36	134.19	135.03	135.86	136.70	137.54	138.39	139.23	140.08	140.93	141.78	142.64
6.0	125.91	126.75	127.59	128.43	129.28	130.13	130.99	131.84	132.70	133.56	134.42	135.29
6.5	119.66	120.50	121.36	122.21	123.07	123.93	124.79	125.66	126.53	127.40	128.27	129.15
7.0	114.35	115.21	116.07	116.93	117.80	118.67	119.55	120.42	121.30	122.18	123.07	123.96
7.5	109.80	110.67	111.54	112.41	113.29	114.17	115.06	115.94	116.83	117.73	118.62	119.52
8.0	105.86	106.74	107.62	108.51	109.40	110.29	111.18	112.08	112.98	113.89	114.79	115.70
8.5	102.43	103.32	104.21	105.11	106.01	106.91	107.81	108.72	109.63	110.55	111.47	112.39
9.0	99.42	100.32	101.22	102.12	103.03	103.95	104.86	105.78	106.71	107.63	108.56	109.50
9.5	96.76	97.67	98.58	99.50	100.42	101.34	102.27	103.20	104.13	105.07	106.01	106.96
10.0	94.40	95.32	96.24	97.17	98.10	99.03	99.97	100.91	101.86	102.81	103.76	104.72
10.5	92.29	93.22	94.16	95.09	96.03	96.98	97.93	98.88	99.84	100.80	101.76	102.73
11.0	90.41	91.35	92.29	93.24	94.19	95.15	96.11	97.07	98.04	99.01	99.98	100.96
11.5	88.72	89.67	90.62	91.58	92.54	93.51	94.48	95.45	96.43	97.41	98.39	99.38
12.0	87.19	88.15	89.12	90.08	91.06	92.03	93.01	93.99	94.98	95.98	96.97	97.97
12.5	85.82	86.78	87.76	88.73	89.72	90.70	91.69	92.69	93.68	94.69	95.69	96.70
13.0	84.57	85.54	86.53	87.51	88.50	89.50	90.50	91.50	92.51	93.52	94.54	95.56
13.5	83.43	84.42	85.41	86.41	87.41	88.41	89.42	90.44	91.45	92.48	93.50	94.53
14.0	82.40	83.39	84.39	85.40	86.41	87.42	88.44	89.47	90.49	91.53	92.56	93.60
14.5	81.45	82.46	83.47	84.48	85.50	86.53	87.55	88.59	89.62	90.66	91.71	92.76
15.0	80.59	81.61	82.62	83.65	84.68	85.71	86.75	87.79	88.83	89.88	90.94	91.99
15.5	79.80	80.82	81.85	82.88	83.92	84.96	86.01	87.06	88.11	89.17	90.23	91.30
16.0	79.08	80.11	81.15	82.19	83.23	84.28	85.33	86.39	87.46	88.52	89.59	90.67
16.5	78.41	79.45	80.50	81.55	82.60	83.66	84.72	85.79	86.86	87.93	89.01	90.09
17.0	77.80	78.85	79.90	80.96	82.02	83.09	84.16	85.23	86.31	87.39	88.48	89.57
17.5	77.24	78.29	79.35	80.42	81.49	82.56	83.64	84.72	85.81	86.90	87.99	89.09
18.0	76.72	77.78	78.85	79.92	81.00	82.08	83.17	84.26	85.35	86.45	87.55	88.66
18.5	76.24	77.31	78.39	79.47	80.55	81.64	82.73	83.83	84.93	86.03	87.14	88.26
19.0	75.80	76.88	77.96	79.05	80.14	81.23	82.33	83.44	84.54	85.66	86.77	87.89
19.5	75.39	76.48	77.56	78.66	79.76	80.86	81.96	83.08	84.19	85.31	86.43	87.56
20.0	75.01	76.11	77.20	78.30	79.41	80.51	81.63	82.74	83.87	84.99	86.12	87.25
20.5	74.66	75.76	76.86	77.97	79.08	80.20	81.32	82.44	83.57	84.70	85.83	86.97
21.0	74.34	75.44	76.55	77.67	78.78	79.90	81.03	82.16	83.29	84.43	85.57	86.71
21.5	74.04	75.15	76.27	77.38	78.51	79.63	80.77	81.90	83.04	84.18	85.33	86.48
22.0	73.76	74.88	76.00	77.12	78.25	79.38	80.52	81.66	82.81	83.95	85.11	86.26
22.5	73.50	74.63	75.75	76.88	78.02	79.15	80.30	81.44	82.59	83.75	84.90	86.06
23.0	73.26	74.39	75.52	76.66	77.80	78.94	80.09	81.24	82.39	83.55	84.71	85.88
23.5	73.04	74.17	75.31	76.45	77.60	78.75	79.90	81.05	82.21	83.38	84.54	85.71
24.0	72.84	73.97	75.11	76.26	77.41	78.56	79.72	80.88	82.05	83.21	84.38	85.56
24.5	72.64	73.79	74.93	76.08	77.24	78.40	79.56	80.72	81.89	83.06	84.24	85.41
25.0	72.46	73.61	74.76	75.92	77.08	78.24	79.41	80.58	81.75	82.92	84.10	85.28
25.5	72.30	73.45	74.61	75.77	76.93	78.10	79.27	80.44	81.62	82.80	83.98	85.16
26.0	72.14	73.30	74.46	75.62	76.79	77.96	79.14	80.31	81.49	82.68	83.86	85.05
26.5	72.00	73.16	74.32	75.49	76.66	77.84	79.02	80.20	81.38	82.57	83.76	84.95
27.0	71.87	73.03	74.20	75.37	76.55	77.72	78.91	80.09	81.28	82.47	83.66	84.86
27.5	71.74	72.91	74.08	75.26	76.44	77.62	78.80	79.99	81.18	82.38	83.57	84.77
28.0	71.63	72.80	73.97	75.15	76.33	77.52	78.71	79.90	81.09	82.29	83.49	84.69
28.5	71.52	72.69	73.87	75.05	76.24	77.43	78.62	79.82	81.01	82.21	83.41	84.62
29.0	71.42	72.60	73.78	74.96	76.15	77.35	78.54	79.74	80.94	82.14	83.34	84.55
29.5	71.32	72.50	73.69	74.88	76.07	77.27	78.46	79.66	80.87	82.07	83.28	84.49
30.0	71.23	72.42	73.61	74.80	76.00	77.19	78.39	79.60	80.80	82.01	83.22	84.43
31.0	71.08	72.27	73.46	74.66	75.86	77.06	78.27	79.48	80.69	81.90	83.11	84.33
32.0	70.94	72.14	73.34	74.54	75.74	76.95	78.16	79.38	80.59	81.81	83.02	84.24
33.0	70.82	72.02	73.23	74.43	75.64	76.86	78.07	79.29	80.51	81.73	82.95	84.17
34.0	70.72	71.92	73.13	74.34	75.56	76.77	77.99	79.21	80.43	81.66	82.88	84.11
35.0	70.62	71.84	73.05	74.26	75.48	76.70	77.92	79.15	80.37	81.60	82.83	84.06
36.0	70.55	71.76	72.98	74.20	75.42	76.64	77.87	79.09	80.32	81.55	82.78	84.01
37.0	70.48	71.70	72.92	74.14	75.36	76.59	77.82	79.04	80.27	81.51	82.74	83.97
38.0	70.42	71.64	72.86	74.09	75.31	76.54	77.77	79.00	80.24	81.47	82.70	83.94
39.0	70.36	71.59	72.81	74.04	75.27	76.50	77.74	78.97	80.20	81.44	82.68	83.91
40.0	70.32	71.55	72.77	74.00	75.24	76.47	77.70	78.94	80.17	81.41	82.65	83.89

215

TERM IN YEARS	17.00%	17.25%	17.50%	17.75%	18.00%	18.25%	18.50%	18.75%	19.00%	19.25%	19.50%	19.75%
0.5	1085.00	1086.25	1087.50	1088.75	1090.00	1091.25	1092.50	1093.75	1095.00	1096.25	1097.50	1098.75
1.0	564.62	565.58	566.55	567.51	568.47	569.44	570.40	571.37	572.33	573.30	574.26	575.23
1.5	391.54	392.42	393.30	394.18	395.06	395.94	396.82	397.70	398.58	399.47	400.35	401.24
2.0	305.29	306.14	306.98	307.83	308.67	309.52	310.37	311.22	312.07	312.92	313.77	314.62
2.5	253.77	254.60	255.43	256.26	257.10	257.93	258.77	259.60	260.44	261.28	262.12	262.96
3.0	219.61	220.44	221.27	222.09	222.92	223.76	224.59	225.42	226.26	227.09	227.93	228.77
3.5	195.37	196.20	197.03	197.86	198.70	199.53	200.37	201.20	202.04	202.88	203.72	204.57
4.0	177.34	178.17	179.00	179.84	180.68	181.52	182.36	183.21	184.05	184.90	185.75	186.60
4.5	163.43	164.27	165.11	165.96	166.80	167.65	168.50	169.36	170.21	171.07	171.92	172.78
5.0	152.41	153.26	154.11	154.97	155.83	156.68	157.54	158.41	159.27	160.14	161.01	161.88
5.5	143.50	144.36	145.22	146.08	146.95	147.82	148.69	149.57	150.44	151.32	152.20	153.08
6.0	136.16	137.03	137.90	138.78	139.66	140.54	141.42	142.30	143.19	144.08	144.98	145.87
6.5	130.03	130.91	131.79	132.68	133.57	134.46	135.36	136.26	137.16	138.06	138.97	139.87
7.0	124.85	125.74	126.64	127.54	128.44	129.34	130.25	131.16	132.07	132.99	133.91	134.83
7.5	120.43	121.33	122.24	123.15	124.06	124.98	125.90	126.82	127.75	128.68	129.61	130.54
8.0	116.62	117.54	118.46	119.38	120.30	121.23	122.17	123.10	124.04	124.98	125.92	126.87
8.5	113.32	114.25	115.18	116.11	117.05	117.99	118.94	119.89	120.84	121.79	122.75	123.71
9.0	110.44	111.38	112.32	113.27	114.22	115.17	116.13	117.09	118.05	119.02	119.99	120.96
9.5	107.91	108.86	109.81	110.77	111.74	112.70	113.67	114.64	115.62	116.60	117.58	118.56
10.0	105.68	106.64	107.61	108.58	109.55	110.53	111.51	112.49	113.48	114.47	115.47	116.46
10.5	103.70	104.68	105.65	106.64	107.62	108.61	109.60	110.60	111.60	112.60	113.61	114.62
11.0	101.94	102.93	103.92	104.91	105.91	106.91	107.91	108.92	109.93	110.95	111.96	112.99
11.5	100.38	101.37	102.37	103.38	104.39	105.40	106.41	107.43	108.45	109.48	110.51	111.54
12.0	98.97	99.98	100.99	102.01	103.03	104.05	105.08	106.11	107.14	108.18	109.21	110.26
12.5	97.72	98.73	99.76	100.78	101.81	102.84	103.88	104.92	105.96	107.01	108.06	109.12
13.0	96.59	97.61	98.65	99.68	100.72	101.76	102.81	103.86	104.91	105.97	107.03	108.10
13.5	95.57	96.60	97.64	98.69	99.74	100.79	101.85	102.91	103.97	105.04	106.11	107.19
14.0	94.64	95.69	96.74	97.80	98.86	99.92	100.99	102.06	103.13	104.21	105.29	106.37
14.5	93.81	94.87	95.93	96.99	98.06	99.13	100.21	101.29	102.37	103.46	104.54	105.64
15.0	93.06	94.12	95.19	96.26	97.34	98.42	99.51	100.59	101.69	102.78	103.88	104.98
15.5	92.37	93.44	94.52	95.60	96.69	97.78	98.87	99.97	101.07	102.17	103.28	104.39
16.0	91.75	92.83	93.92	95.01	96.10	97.20	98.30	99.40	100.51	101.62	102.74	103.86
16.5	91.18	92.27	93.37	94.46	95.57	96.67	97.78	98.89	100.01	101.13	102.25	103.38
17.0	90.66	91.76	92.87	93.97	95.08	96.19	97.31	98.43	99.55	100.68	101.81	102.94
17.5	90.19	91.30	92.41	93.52	94.64	95.76	96.89	98.01	99.14	100.28	101.41	102.55
18.0	89.77	90.88	92.00	93.12	94.24	95.37	96.50	97.63	98.77	99.91	101.05	102.20
18.5	89.37	90.49	91.62	92.74	93.88	95.01	96.15	97.29	98.43	99.58	100.73	101.88
19.0	89.01	90.14	91.27	92.41	93.54	94.68	95.83	96.97	98.12	99.28	100.43	101.59
19.5	88.69	89.82	90.96	92.10	93.24	94.39	95.54	96.69	97.85	99.00	100.17	101.33
20.0	88.39	89.53	90.67	91.82	92.96	94.12	95.27	96.43	97.59	98.76	99.92	101.09
20.5	88.11	89.26	90.41	91.56	92.71	93.87	95.03	96.20	97.36	98.53	99.70	100.88
21.0	87.86	89.01	90.17	91.32	92.48	93.65	94.81	95.98	97.15	98.33	99.50	100.68
21.5	87.63	88.79	89.95	91.11	92.27	93.44	94.61	95.79	96.96	98.14	99.32	100.51
22.0	87.42	88.58	89.74	90.91	92.08	93.25	94.43	95.61	96.79	97.97	99.16	100.35
22.5	87.22	88.39	89.56	90.73	91.91	93.08	94.26	95.45	96.63	97.82	99.01	100.20
23.0	87.05	88.22	89.39	90.57	91.75	92.93	94.11	95.30	96.49	97.68	98.87	100.07
23.5	86.88	88.06	89.24	90.42	91.60	92.79	93.97	95.17	96.36	97.55	98.75	99.95
24.0	86.73	87.91	89.09	90.28	91.47	92.66	93.85	95.04	96.24	97.44	98.64	99.84
24.5	86.60	87.78	88.96	90.15	91.34	92.54	93.73	94.93	96.13	97.33	98.54	99.74
25.0	86.47	87.66	88.85	90.04	91.23	92.43	93.63	94.83	96.03	97.24	98.44	99.65
25.5	86.35	87.54	88.74	89.93	91.13	92.33	93.53	94.74	95.94	97.15	98.36	99.57
26.0	86.24	87.44	88.64	89.83	91.04	92.24	93.44	94.65	95.86	97.07	98.28	99.50
26.5	86.15	87.34	88.54	89.75	90.95	92.16	93.36	94.57	95.79	97.00	98.21	99.43
27.0	86.06	87.26	88.46	89.66	90.87	92.08	93.29	94.50	95.72	96.93	98.15	99.37
27.5	85.97	87.18	88.38	89.59	90.80	92.01	93.22	94.44	95.65	96.87	98.09	99.31
28.0	85.90	87.10	88.31	89.52	90.73	91.95	93.16	94.38	95.60	96.82	98.04	99.26
28.5	85.83	87.03	88.24	89.46	90.67	91.89	93.11	94.33	95.55	96.77	97.99	99.22
29.0	85.76	86.97	88.18	89.40	90.62	91.83	93.05	94.28	95.50	96.72	97.95	99.18
29.5	85.70	86.91	88.13	89.35	90.57	91.79	93.01	94.23	95.46	96.68	97.91	99.14
30.0	85.65	86.86	88.08	89.30	90.52	91.74	92.97	94.19	95.42	96.64	97.87	99.10
31.0	85.55	86.77	87.99	89.21	90.44	91.66	92.89	94.12	95.35	96.58	97.81	99.04
32.0	85.47	86.69	87.91	89.14	90.37	91.60	92.83	94.06	95.29	96.52	97.76	98.99
33.0	85.40	86.62	87.85	89.08	90.31	91.54	92.78	94.01	95.24	96.48	97.72	98.95
34.0	85.34	86.57	87.80	89.03	90.26	91.50	92.73	93.97	95.20	96.44	97.68	98.92
35.0	85.29	86.52	87.75	88.99	90.22	91.46	92.69	93.93	95.17	96.41	97.65	98.89
36.0	85.24	86.48	87.71	88.95	90.19	91.43	92.66	93.90	95.14	96.38	97.63	98.87
37.0	85.21	86.44	87.68	88.92	90.16	91.40	92.64	93.88	95.12	96.36	97.60	98.85
38.0	85.18	86.42	87.65	88.89	90.13	91.37	92.62	93.86	95.10	96.34	97.59	98.83
39.0	85.15	86.39	87.63	88.87	90.11	91.36	92.60	93.84	95.09	96.33	97.57	98.82
40.0	85.13	86.37	87.61	88.85	90.10	91.34	92.58	93.83	95.07	96.32	97.56	98.81

SEMI-ANNUAL
PAYMENT REQUIRED TO AMORTIZE A $1,000.00 LOAN

TERM IN YEARS	INTEREST RATES											
	20.00%	20.25%	20.50%	20.75%	21.00%	21.25%	21.50%	21.75%	22.00%	22.25%	22.50%	22.75%
0.5	1100.00	1101.25	1102.50	1103.75	1105.00	1106.25	1107.50	1108.75	1110.00	1111.25	1112.50	1113.75
1.0	576.20	577.16	578.13	579.10	580.06	581.03	582.00	582.97	583.94	584.91	585.88	586.85
1.5	402.12	403.01	403.89	404.78	405.66	406.55	407.44	408.33	409.22	410.11	411.00	411.89
2.0	315.48	316.33	317.18	318.04	318.90	319.75	320.61	321.47	322.33	323.19	324.05	324.92
2.5	263.80	264.65	265.49	266.33	267.18	268.03	268.88	269.73	270.58	271.43	272.28	273.13
3.0	229.61	230.45	231.30	232.14	232.99	233.83	234.68	235.53	236.38	237.23	238.09	238.94
3.5	205.41	206.26	207.10	207.95	208.80	209.66	210.51	211.36	212.22	213.08	213.94	214.80
4.0	187.45	188.30	189.16	190.02	190.87	191.73	192.60	193.46	194.33	195.19	196.06	196.93
4.5	173.65	174.51	175.37	176.24	177.11	177.98	178.86	179.73	180.61	181.49	182.37	183.25
5.0	162.75	163.63	164.50	165.38	166.26	167.15	168.03	168.92	169.81	170.70	171.59	172.49
5.5	153.97	154.86	155.74	156.64	157.53	158.43	159.32	160.22	161.13	162.03	162.94	163.85
6.0	146.77	147.67	148.57	149.47	150.38	151.29	152.20	153.12	154.03	154.95	155.87	156.79
6.5	140.78	141.70	142.61	143.53	144.45	145.37	146.30	147.23	148.16	149.09	150.02	150.96
7.0	135.75	136.68	137.61	138.54	139.47	140.41	141.35	142.29	143.23	144.18	145.13	146.08
7.5	131.48	132.42	133.36	134.31	135.25	136.20	137.16	138.11	139.07	140.03	140.99	141.96
8.0	127.82	128.77	129.73	130.69	131.65	132.61	133.58	134.55	135.52	136.50	137.47	138.45
8.5	124.67	125.63	126.60	127.58	128.55	129.53	130.51	131.49	132.48	133.47	134.46	135.45
9.0	121.94	122.91	123.90	124.88	125.87	126.86	127.85	128.85	129.85	130.85	131.85	132.86
9.5	119.55	120.54	121.54	122.54	123.54	124.54	125.55	126.56	127.57	128.58	129.60	130.62
10.0	117.46	118.47	119.48	120.49	121.50	122.51	123.53	124.56	125.58	126.61	127.64	128.67
10.5	115.63	116.65	117.66	118.69	119.71	120.74	121.77	122.81	123.84	124.88	125.93	126.97
11.0	114.01	115.04	116.07	117.10	118.14	119.18	120.22	121.27	122.32	123.37	124.43	125.48
11.5	112.58	113.62	114.66	115.70	116.75	117.80	118.86	119.92	120.98	122.04	123.11	124.18
12.0	111.30	112.35	113.41	114.46	115.52	116.59	117.65	118.72	119.79	120.87	121.94	123.02
12.5	110.17	111.23	112.30	113.36	114.43	115.51	116.58	117.66	118.75	119.83	120.92	122.01
13.0	109.16	110.23	111.31	112.39	113.47	114.55	115.64	116.73	117.82	118.91	120.01	121.11
13.5	108.26	109.34	110.43	111.51	112.60	113.70	114.79	115.89	116.99	118.10	119.21	120.32
14.0	107.46	108.55	109.64	110.74	111.83	112.94	114.04	115.15	116.26	117.38	118.49	119.61
14.5	106.73	107.83	108.93	110.04	111.15	112.26	113.37	114.49	115.61	116.73	117.86	118.99
15.0	106.08	107.19	108.30	109.42	110.53	111.65	112.78	113.90	115.03	116.16	117.29	118.43
15.5	105.50	106.62	107.74	108.86	109.98	111.11	112.24	113.38	114.51	115.65	116.79	117.94
16.0	104.98	106.10	107.23	108.36	109.49	110.63	111.76	112.90	114.05	115.19	116.34	117.49
16.5	104.50	105.64	106.77	107.91	109.05	110.19	111.34	112.48	113.63	114.79	115.94	117.10
17.0	104.08	105.22	106.36	107.50	108.65	109.80	110.95	112.11	113.26	114.42	115.59	116.75
17.5	103.69	104.84	105.99	107.14	108.29	109.45	110.61	111.77	112.93	114.10	115.27	116.44
18.0	103.35	104.50	105.65	106.81	107.97	109.13	110.30	111.47	112.64	113.81	114.98	116.16
18.5	103.03	104.19	105.35	106.52	107.68	108.85	110.02	111.19	112.37	113.55	114.73	115.91
19.0	102.75	103.92	105.08	106.25	107.42	108.60	109.77	110.95	112.13	113.31	114.50	115.68
19.5	102.50	103.67	104.84	106.01	107.19	108.37	109.55	110.73	111.92	113.10	114.29	115.48
20.0	102.26	103.44	104.62	105.79	106.98	108.16	109.35	110.53	111.72	112.92	114.11	115.30
20.5	102.05	103.23	104.42	105.60	106.79	107.97	109.16	110.36	111.55	112.75	113.95	115.14
21.0	101.86	103.05	104.24	105.42	106.61	107.81	109.00	110.20	111.40	112.60	113.80	115.00
21.5	101.69	102.88	104.07	105.26	106.46	107.66	108.85	110.05	111.26	112.46	113.67	114.87
22.0	101.54	102.73	103.92	105.12	106.32	107.52	108.72	109.93	111.13	112.34	113.55	114.76
22.5	101.40	102.59	103.79	104.99	106.19	107.40	108.60	109.81	111.02	112.23	113.44	114.65
23.0	101.27	102.47	103.67	104.87	106.08	107.29	108.49	109.71	110.92	112.13	113.35	114.56
23.5	101.15	102.36	103.56	104.77	105.98	107.19	108.40	109.61	110.83	112.04	113.26	114.48
24.0	101.05	102.25	103.46	104.67	105.88	107.10	108.31	109.53	110.74	111.96	113.18	114.40
24.5	100.95	102.16	103.37	104.58	105.80	107.01	108.23	109.45	110.67	111.89	113.11	114.34
25.0	100.86	102.08	103.29	104.51	105.72	106.94	108.16	109.38	110.60	111.83	113.05	114.28
25.5	100.79	102.00	103.22	104.43	105.65	106.87	108.10	109.32	110.54	111.77	113.00	114.22
26.0	100.71	101.93	103.15	104.37	105.59	106.82	108.04	109.26	110.49	111.72	112.95	114.18
26.5	100.65	101.87	103.09	104.31	105.54	106.76	107.99	109.21	110.44	111.67	112.90	114.13
27.0	100.59	101.81	103.04	104.26	105.49	106.71	107.94	109.17	110.40	111.63	112.86	114.09
27.5	100.54	101.76	102.99	104.21	105.44	106.67	107.90	109.13	110.36	111.59	112.83	114.06
28.0	100.49	101.71	102.94	104.17	105.40	106.63	107.86	109.09	110.32	111.56	112.79	114.03
28.5	100.44	101.67	102.90	104.13	105.36	106.59	107.82	109.06	110.29	111.53	112.76	114.00
29.0	100.40	101.63	102.86	104.09	105.33	106.56	107.79	109.03	110.26	111.50	112.74	113.98
29.5	100.37	101.60	102.83	104.06	105.30	106.53	107.77	109.00	110.24	111.48	112.71	113.95
30.0	100.33	101.57	102.80	104.03	105.27	106.50	107.74	108.98	110.22	111.45	112.69	113.93
31.0	100.28	101.51	102.75	103.98	105.22	106.46	107.70	108.94	110.18	111.42	112.66	113.90
32.0	100.23	101.47	102.70	103.94	105.18	106.42	107.66	108.90	110.14	111.39	112.63	113.87
33.0	100.19	101.43	102.67	103.91	105.15	106.39	107.63	108.87	110.12	111.36	112.60	113.85
34.0	100.16	101.40	102.64	103.88	105.12	106.37	107.61	*108.85	110.10	111.34	112.58	113.83
35.0	100.13	101.37	102.62	103.86	105.10	106.35	107.59	108.83	110.08	111.32	112.57	113.82
36.0	100.11	101.35	102.60	103.84	105.08	106.33	107.57	108.82	110.07	111.31	112.56	113.80
37.0	100.09	101.34	102.58	103.82	105.07	106.32	107.56	108.81	110.05	111.30	112.55	113.79
38.0	100.08	101.32	102.57	103.81	105.06	106.30	107.55	108.80	110.04	111.29	112.54	113.79
39.0	100.06	101.31	102.56	103.80	105.05	106.30	107.54	108.79	110.04	111.28	112.53	113.78
40.0	100.05	101.30	102.55	103.79	105.04	106.29	107.54	108.78	110.03	111.28	112.53	113.78

217

SEMI-ANNUAL
PAYMENT REQUIRED TO AMORTIZE A $1,000.00 LOAN

TERM IN YEARS	INTEREST RATES											
	23.00%	23.25%	23.50%	23.75%	24.00%	24.25%	24.50%	24.75%	25.00%	25.25%	25.50%	25.75%
0.5	1115.00	1116.25	1117.50	1118.75	1120.00	1121.25	1122.50	1123.75	1125.00	1126.25	1127.50	1128.75
1.0	587.82	588.79	589.76	590.73	591.70	592.68	593.65	594.62	595.59	596.57	597.54	598.51
1.5	412.78	413.67	414.57	415.46	416.35	417.25	418.14	419.04	419.94	420.83	421.73	422.63
2.0	325.78	326.64	327.51	328.37	329.24	330.11	330.97	331.84	332.71	333.58	334.45	335.33
2.5	273.99	274.84	275.70	276.56	277.41	278.27	279.13	280.00	280.86	281.72	282.59	283.45
3.0	239.80	240.65	241.51	242.37	243.23	244.09	244.96	245.82	246.68	247.55	248.42	249.29
3.5	215.66	216.52	217.39	218.25	219.12	219.99	220.86	221.73	222.61	223.48	224.36	225.24
4.0	197.80	198.68	199.55	200.43	201.31	202.19	203.07	203.95	204.84	205.72	206.61	207.50
4.5	184.13	185.02	185.90	186.79	187.68	188.58	189.47	190.37	191.27	192.16	193.07	193.97
5.0	173.38	174.28	175.18	176.08	176.99	177.90	178.80	179.71	180.63	181.54	182.46	183.37
5.5	164.76	165.67	166.58	167.50	168.42	169.34	170.26	171.19	172.12	173.05	173.98	174.91
6.0	157.72	158.65	159.58	160.51	161.44	162.38	163.32	164.26	165.20	166.14	167.09	168.04
6.5	151.90	152.84	153.79	154.73	155.68	156.63	157.59	158.54	159.50	160.46	161.42	162.39
7.0	147.04	147.99	148.95	149.91	150.88	151.84	152.81	153.78	154.76	155.73	156.71	157.69
7.5	142.93	143.90	144.87	145.85	146.83	147.81	148.79	149.78	150.77	151.76	152.75	153.75
8.0	139.44	140.42	141.41	142.40	143.40	144.39	145.39	146.39	147.39	148.40	149.41	150.42
8.5	136.45	137.45	138.45	139.45	140.46	141.47	142.48	143.50	144.52	145.54	146.56	147.59
9.0	133.87	134.89	135.90	136.92	137.94	138.97	139.99	141.02	142.05	143.09	144.12	145.16
9.5	131.65	132.67	133.70	134.73	135.77	136.81	137.85	138.89	139.93	140.98	142.03	143.08
10.0	129.71	130.75	131.79	132.84	133.88	134.93	135.99	137.04	138.10	139.16	140.22	141.29
10.5	128.02	129.07	130.13	131.19	132.25	133.31	134.37	135.44	136.51	137.58	138.66	139.74
11.0	126.54	127.61	128.67	129.74	130.82	131.89	132.97	134.05	135.13	136.21	137.30	138.39
11.5	125.25	126.32	127.40	128.48	129.56	130.65	131.74	132.83	133.92	135.02	136.12	137.22
12.0	124.11	125.19	126.28	127.37	128.47	129.57	130.66	131.77	132.87	133.98	135.09	136.20
12.5	123.10	124.20	125.30	126.40	127.50	128.61	129.72	130.83	131.95	133.07	134.18	135.31
13.0	122.22	123.32	124.43	125.54	126.66	127.77	128.89	130.01	131.14	132.27	133.39	134.53
13.5	121.43	122.55	123.66	124.79	125.91	127.04	128.16	129.29	130.43	131.56	132.70	133.84
14.0	120.73	121.86	122.99	124.12	125.25	126.38	127.52	128.66	129.80	130.95	132.09	133.24
14.5	120.12	121.25	122.39	123.52	124.67	125.81	126.95	128.10	129.25	130.40	131.56	132.71
15.0	119.57	120.71	121.85	123.00	124.15	125.30	126.45	127.61	128.77	129.92	131.09	132.25
15.5	119.08	120.23	121.38	122.54	123.69	124.85	126.01	127.17	128.34	129.50	130.67	131.84
16.0	118.65	119.80	120.96	122.12	123.29	124.45	125.62	126.79	127.96	129.13	130.31	131.48
16.5	118.26	119.42	120.59	121.76	122.93	124.10	125.27	126.45	127.62	128.80	129.98	131.17
17.0	117.92	119.09	120.26	121.43	122.61	123.78	124.96	126.14	127.33	128.51	129.70	130.89
17.5	117.61	118.78	119.96	121.14	122.32	123.50	124.69	125.88	127.06	128.25	129.45	130.64
18.0	117.34	118.52	119.70	120.88	122.07	123.26	124.45	125.64	126.83	128.03	129.22	130.42
18.5	117.09	118.28	119.46	120.65	121.84	123.04	124.23	125.43	126.63	127.83	129.03	130.23
19.0	116.87	118.06	119.26	120.45	121.64	122.84	124.04	125.24	126.44	127.65	128.85	130.06
19.5	116.68	117.87	119.07	120.27	121.47	122.67	123.87	125.08	126.28	127.49	128.70	129.91
20.0	116.50	117.70	118.90	120.10	121.31	122.51	123.72	124.93	126.14	127.35	128.56	129.78
20.5	116.35	117.55	118.75	119.96	121.17	122.38	123.59	124.80	126.01	127.23	128.44	129.66
21.0	116.21	117.41	118.62	119.83	121.04	122.25	123.47	124.68	125.90	127.12	128.34	129.56
21.5	116.08	117.29	118.50	119.72	120.93	122.15	123.36	124.58	125.80	127.02	128.24	129.46
22.0	115.97	117.18	118.40	119.61	120.83	122.05	123.27	124.49	125.71	126.93	128.16	129.38
22.5	115.87	117.09	118.30	119.52	120.74	121.96	123.18	124.41	125.63	126.86	128.08	129.31
23.0	115.78	117.00	118.22	119.44	120.66	121.89	123.11	124.34	125.56	126.79	128.02	129.25
23.5	115.70	116.92	118.14	119.37	120.59	121.82	123.04	124.27	125.50	126.73	127.96	129.19
24.0	115.63	116.85	118.08	119.30	120.53	121.76	122.98	124.21	125.44	126.68	127.91	129.14
24.5	115.56	116.79	118.02	119.24	120.47	121.70	122.93	124.16	125.40	126.63	127.86	129.10
25.0	115.50	116.73	117.96	119.19	120.42	121.65	122.89	124.12	125.35	126.59	127.82	129.06
25.5	115.45	116.68	117.91	119.14	120.38	121.61	122.84	124.08	125.31	126.55	127.79	129.02
26.0	115.41	116.64	117.87	119.10	120.34	121.57	122.81	124.04	125.28	126.52	127.75	128.99
26.5	115.37	116.60	117.83	119.07	120.30	121.54	122.77	124.01	125.25	126.49	127.73	128.97
27.0	115.33	116.56	117.80	119.03	120.27	121.51	122.74	123.98	125.22	126.46	127.70	128.94
27.5	115.29	116.53	117.77	119.00	120.24	121.48	122.72	123.96	125.20	126.44	127.68	128.92
28.0	115.26	116.50	117.74	118.98	120.22	121.46	122.69	123.94	125.18	126.42	127.66	128.90
28.5	115.24	116.48	117.71	118.95	120.19	121.43	122.67	123.92	125.16	126.40	127.64	128.88
29.0	115.21	116.45	117.69	118.93	120.17	121.41	122.66	123.90	125.14	126.38	127.63	128.87
29.5	115.19	116.43	117.67	118.91	120.15	121.40	122.64	123.88	125.13	126.37	127.61	128.86
30.0	115.17	116.41	117.65	118.90	120.14	121.38	122.62	123.87	125.11	126.36	127.60	128.84
31.0	115.14	116.38	117.62	118.87	120.11	121.36	122.60	123.84	125.09	126.33	127.58	128.83
32.0	115.11	116.36	117.60	118.85	120.09	121.33	122.58	123.83	125.07	126.32	127.56	128.81
33.0	115.09	116.34	117.58	118.83	120.07	121.32	122.56	123.81	125.06	126.30	127.55	128.80
34.0	115.08	116.32	117.57	118.81	120.06	121.31	122.55	123.80	125.05	126.29	127.54	128.79
35.0	115.06	116.31	117.55	118.80	120.05	121.30	122.54	123.79	125.04	126.29	127.53	128.78
36.0	115.05	116.30	117.54	118.79	120.04	121.29	122.53	123.78	125.03	126.28	127.53	128.78
37.0	115.04	116.29	117.54	118.78	120.03	121.28	122.53	123.78	125.03	126.27	127.52	128.77
38.0	115.03	116.28	117.53	118.78	120.03	121.28	122.52	123.77	125.02	126.27	127.52	128.77
39.0	115.03	116.28	117.53	118.77	120.02	121.27	122.52	123.77	125.02	126.27	127.52	128.77
40.0	115.02	116.27	117.52	118.77	120.02	121.27	122.52	123.77	125.02	126.26	127.51	128.76

218

SEMI-ANNUAL
PAYMENT REQUIRED TO AMORTIZE A $1,000.00 LOAN

TERM IN YEARS	26.00%	26.25%	26.50%	26.75%	27.00%	27.25%	27.50%	27.75%	28.00%	28.25%	28.50%	28.75%
0.5	1130.00	1131.25	1132.50	1133.75	1135.00	1136.25	1137.50	1138.75	1140.00	1141.25	1142.50	1143.75
1.0	599.49	600.46	601.44	602.41	603.39	604.37	605.34	606.32	607.29	608.27	609.25	610.23
1.5	423.53	424.43	425.33	426.23	427.13	428.03	428.93	429.83	430.74	431.64	432.54	433.45
2.0	336.20	337.07	337.95	338.82	339.70	340.57	341.45	342.33	343.21	344.09	344.97	345.85
2.5	284.32	285.19	286.06	286.93	287.80	288.67	289.54	290.41	291.29	292.16	293.04	293.92
3.0	250.16	251.03	251.90	252.78	253.65	254.53	255.40	256.28	257.16	258.04	258.93	259.81
3.5	226.12	227.00	227.88	228.76	229.65	230.53	231.42	232.31	233.20	234.09	234.98	235.88
4.0	208.39	209.28	210.18	211.07	211.97	212.87	213.77	214.67	215.58	216.48	217.39	218.29
4.5	194.87	195.78	196.69	197.60	198.51	199.42	200.34	201.26	202.17	203.09	204.01	204.94
5.0	184.29	185.22	186.14	187.06	187.99	188.92	189.85	190.78	191.72	192.65	193.59	194.53
5.5	175.85	176.78	177.72	178.66	179.61	180.55	181.50	182.45	183.40	184.35	185.31	186.26
6.0	168.99	169.94	170.90	171.86	172.82	173.78	174.74	175.71	176.67	177.64	178.62	179.59
6.5	163.36	164.32	165.30	166.27	167.24	168.22	169.20	170.18	171.17	172.15	173.14	174.13
7.0	158.67	159.66	160.64	161.63	162.63	163.62	164.62	165.61	166.61	167.62	168.62	169.63
7.5	154.75	155.75	156.75	157.75	158.76	159.77	160.78	161.80	162.81	163.83	164.85	165.88
8.0	151.43	152.45	153.46	154.48	155.51	156.53	157.56	158.59	159.62	160.65	161.69	162.73
8.5	148.61	149.64	150.68	151.71	152.75	153.79	154.83	155.87	156.92	157.97	159.02	160.07
9.0	146.21	147.25	148.30	149.35	150.40	151.45	152.51	153.57	154.63	155.69	156.75	157.82
9.5	144.14	145.20	146.26	147.32	148.38	149.45	150.52	151.59	152.67	153.74	154.82	155.90
10.0	142.36	143.43	144.50	145.58	146.66	147.74	148.82	149.90	150.99	152.08	153.17	154.27
10.5	140.82	141.90	142.99	144.08	145.17	146.26	147.35	148.45	149.55	150.65	151.76	152.86
11.0	139.48	140.58	141.68	142.78	143.88	144.98	146.09	147.20	148.31	149.42	150.54	151.65
11.5	138.32	139.43	140.54	141.65	142.76	143.88	144.99	146.11	147.24	148.36	149.49	150.61
12.0	137.31	138.43	139.55	140.67	141.79	142.92	144.05	145.18	146.31	147.44	148.58	149.72
12.5	136.43	137.56	138.69	139.82	140.95	142.09	143.22	144.36	145.50	146.65	147.79	148.94
13.0	135.66	136.80	137.93	139.07	140.22	141.36	142.51	143.65	144.81	145.96	147.11	148.27
13.5	134.98	136.13	137.28	138.42	139.57	140.73	141.88	143.04	144.20	145.36	146.52	147.68
14.0	134.39	135.54	136.70	137.86	139.02	140.18	141.34	142.50	143.67	144.84	146.01	147.18
14.5	133.87	135.03	136.20	137.36	138.53	139.69	140.86	142.04	143.21	144.38	145.56	146.74
15.0	133.42	134.58	135.75	136.92	138.10	139.27	140.45	141.63	142.81	143.99	145.17	146.36
15.5	133.01	134.19	135.36	136.54	137.72	138.90	140.09	141.27	142.46	143.65	144.83	146.03
16.0	132.66	133.84	135.02	136.21	137.39	138.58	139.77	140.96	142.15	143.35	144.54	145.74
16.5	132.35	133.54	134.72	135.91	137.10	138.30	139.49	140.69	141.88	143.08	144.28	145.48
17.0	132.08	133.27	134.46	135.66	136.85	138.05	139.25	140.45	141.65	142.85	144.06	145.26
17.5	131.83	133.03	134.23	135.43	136.63	137.83	139.04	140.24	141.45	142.65	143.86	145.07
18.0	131.62	132.82	134.02	135.23	136.43	137.64	138.85	140.06	141.27	142.48	143.69	144.91
18.5	131.43	132.64	133.85	135.05	136.26	137.47	138.68	139.90	141.11	142.33	143.54	144.76
19.0	131.27	132.48	133.69	134.90	136.11	137.33	138.54	139.76	140.97	142.19	143.41	144.63
19.5	131.12	132.33	133.55	134.76	135.98	137.20	138.42	139.63	140.86	142.08	143.30	144.52
20.0	130.99	132.21	133.42	134.64	135.86	137.08	138.30	139.53	140.75	141.97	143.20	144.43
20.5	130.88	132.10	133.32	134.54	135.76	136.98	138.21	139.43	140.66	141.88	143.11	144.34
21.0	130.78	132.00	133.22	134.44	135.67	136.90	138.12	139.35	140.58	141.81	143.04	144.27
21.5	130.69	131.91	133.14	134.36	135.59	136.82	138.05	139.28	140.51	141.74	142.97	144.20
22.0	130.61	131.84	133.06	134.29	135.52	136.75	137.98	139.21	140.45	141.68	142.91	144.15
22.5	130.54	131.77	133.00	134.23	135.46	136.69	137.92	139.16	140.39	141.63	142.86	144.10
23.0	130.48	131.71	132.94	134.17	135.40	136.64	137.87	139.11	140.34	141.58	142.82	144.06
23.5	130.42	131.66	132.89	134.12	135.36	136.59	137.83	139.06	140.30	141.54	142.78	144.02
24.0	130.37	131.61	132.84	134.08	135.32	136.55	137.79	139.03	140.27	141.50	142.74	143.98
24.5	130.33	131.57	132.80	134.04	135.28	136.52	137.75	138.99	140.23	141.47	142.71	143.95
25.0	130.29	131.53	132.77	134.01	135.25	136.48	137.72	138.96	140.21	141.45	142.69	143.93
25.5	130.26	131.50	132.74	133.98	135.22	136.46	137.70	138.94	140.18	141.42	142.66	143.91
26.0	130.23	131.47	132.71	133.95	135.19	136.43	137.67	138.92	140.16	141.40	142.64	143.89
26.5	130.21	131.45	132.69	133.93	135.17	136.41	137.65	138.90	140.14	141.38	142.63	143.87
27.0	130.18	131.42	132.67	133.91	135.15	136.39	137.64	138.88	140.12	141.37	142.61	143.86
27.5	130.16	131.40	132.65	133.89	135.13	136.38	137.62	138.86	140.11	141.35	142.60	143.84
28.0	130.14	131.39	132.63	133.87	135.12	136.36	137.61	138.85	140.10	141.34	142.59	143.83
28.5	130.13	131.37	132.62	133.86	135.10	136.35	137.59	138.84	140.08	141.33	142.58	143.82
29.0	130.11	131.36	132.60	133.85	135.09	136.34	137.58	138.83	140.08	141.32	142.57	143.81
29.5	130.10	131.35	132.59	133.84	135.08	136.33	137.57	138.82	140.07	141.31	142.56	143.81
30.0	130.09	131.34	132.58	133.83	135.07	136.32	137.57	138.81	140.06	141.31	142.55	143.80
31.0	130.07	131.32	132.56	133.81	135.06	136.30	137.55	138.80	140.05	141.29	142.54	143.79
32.0	130.06	131.30	132.55	133.80	135.05	136.29	137.54	138.79	140.04	141.29	142.53	143.78
33.0	130.05	131.29	132.54	133.79	135.04	136.28	137.53	138.78	140.03	141.28	142.53	143.78
34.0	130.04	131.28	132.53	133.78	135.03	136.28	137.53	138.78	140.02	141.27	142.52	143.77
35.0	130.03	131.28	132.53	133.78	135.02	136.27	137.52	138.77	140.02	141.27	142.52	143.77
36.0	130.02	131.27	132.52	133.77	135.02	136.27	137.52	138.76	140.02	141.26	142.51	143.76
37.0	130.02	131.27	132.52	133.77	135.02	136.27	137.51	138.76	140.01	141.26	142.51	143.76
38.0	130.02	131.27	132.52	133.76	135.01	136.26	137.51	138.76	140.01	141.26	142.51	143.76
39.0	130.01	131.26	132.51	133.76	135.01	136.26	137.51	138.76	140.01	141.26	142.51	143.76
40.0	130.01	131.26	132.51	133.76	135.01	136.26	137.51	138.76	140.01	141.26	142.51	143.76

ANNUAL
PAYMENT REQUIRED TO AMORTIZE A $1,000.00 LOAN

TERM IN YEARS	INTEREST RATES											
	5.00%	5.25%	5.50%	5.75%	6.00%	6.25%	6.50%	6.75%	7.00%	7.25%	7.50%	7.75%
1	1050.00	1052.50	1055.00	1057.50	1060.00	1062.50	1065.00	1067.50	1070.00	1072.50	1075.00	1077.50
2	537.81	539.72	541.62	543.53	545.44	547.35	549.27	551.18	553.10	555.01	556.93	558.85
3	367.21	368.94	370.66	372.39	374.11	375.85	377.58	379.32	381.06	382.80	384.54	386.29
4	282.02	283.66	285.30	286.95	288.60	290.25	291.91	293.57	295.23	296.90	298.57	300.25
5	230.98	232.58	234.18	235.79	237.40	239.02	240.64	242.27	243.90	245.53	247.17	248.81
6	197.02	198.60	200.18	201.77	203.37	204.97	206.57	208.18	209.80	211.42	213.05	214.68
7	172.82	174.39	175.97	177.55	179.14	180.73	182.34	183.94	185.56	187.18	188.81	190.44
8	154.73	156.29	157.87	159.45	161.04	162.64	164.24	165.85	167.47	169.10	170.73	172.37
9	140.70	142.27	143.84	145.43	147.03	148.63	150.24	151.86	153.49	155.13	156.77	158.42
10	129.51	131.09	132.67	134.27	135.87	137.49	139.11	140.74	142.38	144.03	145.69	147.36
11	120.39	121.98	123.58	125.18	126.80	128.42	130.06	131.71	133.36	135.03	136.70	138.39
12	112.83	114.43	116.03	117.65	119.28	120.92	122.57	124.23	125.91	127.59	129.28	130.99
13	106.46	108.07	109.69	111.32	112.97	114.62	116.29	117.97	119.66	121.36	123.07	124.79
14	101.03	102.65	104.28	105.93	107.59	109.26	110.95	112.64	114.35	116.07	117.80	119.55
15	96.35	97.98	99.63	101.29	102.97	104.66	106.36	108.07	109.80	111.54	113.29	115.06
16	92.27	93.92	95.59	97.27	98.96	100.66	102.38	104.12	105.86	107.62	109.40	111.18
17	88.70	90.37	92.05	93.74	95.45	97.17	98.91	100.66	102.43	104.21	106.01	107.81
18	85.55	87.23	88.92	90.64	92.36	94.10	95.86	97.63	99.42	101.22	103.03	104.86
19	82.75	84.44	86.16	87.88	89.63	91.39	93.16	94.95	96.76	98.58	100.42	102.27
20	80.25	81.96	83.68	85.43	87.19	88.97	90.76	92.57	94.40	96.24	98.10	99.97
21	78.00	79.73	81.47	83.23	85.01	86.81	88.62	90.45	92.29	94.16	96.03	97.93
22	75.98	77.72	79.48	81.25	83.05	84.86	86.70	88.55	90.41	92.29	94.19	96.11
23	74.14	75.90	77.67	79.47	81.28	83.12	84.97	86.83	88.72	90.62	92.54	94.48
24	72.48	74.25	76.04	77.85	79.68	81.53	83.40	85.29	87.19	89.12	91.06	93.01
25	70.96	72.75	74.55	76.38	78.23	80.10	81.99	83.89	85.82	87.76	89.72	91.69
26	69.57	71.37	73.20	75.04	76.91	78.79	80.70	82.62	84.57	86.53	88.50	90.50
27	68.30	70.12	71.96	73.82	75.70	77.61	79.53	81.47	83.43	85.41	87.41	89.42
28	67.13	68.96	70.82	72.70	74.60	76.52	78.46	80.42	82.40	84.39	86.41	88.44
29	66.05	67.90	69.77	71.67	73.58	75.52	77.48	79.46	81.45	83.47	85.50	87.55
30	65.06	66.92	68.81	70.72	72.65	74.61	76.58	78.58	80.59	82.62	84.68	86.75
31	64.14	66.02	67.92	69.85	71.80	73.77	75.76	77.77	79.80	81.85	83.92	86.01
32	63.29	65.18	67.10	69.04	71.01	72.99	75.00	77.03	79.08	81.15	83.23	85.33
33	62.50	64.41	66.34	68.30	70.28	72.28	74.30	76.35	78.41	80.50	82.60	84.72
34	61.76	63.69	65.63	67.61	69.60	71.62	73.66	75.72	77.80	79.90	82.02	84.16
35	61.08	63.02	64.98	66.97	68.98	71.01	73.07	75.14	77.24	79.35	81.49	83.64
36	60.44	62.39	64.37	66.37	68.40	70.45	72.52	74.61	76.72	78.85	81.00	83.17
37	59.84	61.81	63.80	65.82	67.86	69.93	72.01	74.12	76.24	78.39	80.55	82.73
38	59.29	61.27	63.28	65.31	67.36	69.44	71.54	73.66	75.80	77.96	80.14	82.33
39	58.77	60.76	62.78	64.83	66.90	68.99	71.10	73.24	75.39	77.56	79.76	81.96
40	58.28	60.29	62.33	64.38	66.47	68.57	70.70	72.85	75.01	77.20	79.41	81.63
41	57.83	59.85	61.90	63.97	66.06	68.18	70.32	72.48	74.66	76.86	79.08	81.32
42	57.40	59.43	61.49	63.58	65.69	67.82	69.97	72.15	74.34	76.55	78.78	81.03
43	57.00	59.05	61.12	63.22	65.34	67.48	69.65	71.83	74.04	76.27	78.51	80.77
44	56.62	58.68	60.77	62.88	65.01	67.17	69.35	71.54	73.76	76.00	78.25	80.52
45	56.27	58.34	60.44	62.56	64.71	66.87	69.06	71.28	73.50	75.75	78.02	80.30
46	55.93	58.02	60.13	62.26	64.42	66.60	68.80	71.02	73.26	75.52	77.80	80.09
47	55.62	57.71	59.84	61.98	64.15	66.34	68.56	70.79	73.04	75.31	77.60	79.90
48	55.32	57.43	59.56	61.72	63.90	66.11	68.33	70.57	72.84	75.11	77.41	79.72
49	55.04	57.16	59.31	61.48	63.67	65.88	68.12	70.37	72.64	74.93	77.24	79.56
50	54.78	56.91	59.07	61.25	63.45	65.67	67.92	70.18	72.46	74.76	77.08	79.41

ANNUAL
PAYMENT REQUIRED TO AMORTIZE A $1,000.00 LOAN

TERM IN YEARS	INTEREST RATES											
	8.00%	8.25%	8.50%	8.75%	9.00%	9.25%	9.50%	9.75%	10.00%	10.25%	10.50%	10.75%
1	1080.00	1082.50	1085.00	1087.50	1090.00	1092.50	1095.00	1097.50	1100.00	1102.50	1105.00	1107.50
2	560.77	562.70	564.62	566.55	568.47	570.40	572.33	574.26	576.20	578.13	580.06	582.00
3	388.04	389.79	391.54	393.30	395.06	396.82	398.58	400.35	402.12	403.89	405.66	407.44
4	301.93	303.61	305.29	306.98	308.67	310.37	312.07	313.77	315.48	317.18	318.90	320.61
5	250.46	252.11	253.77	255.43	257.10	258.77	260.44	262.12	263.80	265.49	267.18	268.88
6	216.32	217.96	219.61	221.27	222.92	224.59	226.26	227.93	229.61	231.30	232.99	234.68
7	192.08	193.72	195.37	197.03	198.70	200.37	202.04	203.72	205.41	207.10	208.80	210.51
8	174.02	175.67	177.34	179.00	180.68	182.36	184.05	185.75	187.45	189.16	190.87	192.60
9	160.08	161.75	163.43	165.11	166.80	168.50	170.21	171.92	173.65	175.37	177.11	178.86
10	149.03	150.72	152.41	154.11	155.83	157.54	159.27	161.01	162.75	164.50	166.26	168.03
11	140.08	141.78	143.50	145.22	146.95	148.69	150.44	152.20	153.97	155.74	157.53	159.32
12	132.70	134.42	136.16	137.90	139.66	141.42	143.19	144.98	146.77	148.57	150.38	152.20
13	126.53	128.27	130.03	131.79	133.57	135.36	137.16	138.97	140.78	142.61	144.45	146.30
14	121.30	123.07	124.85	126.64	128.44	130.25	132.07	133.91	135.75	137.61	139.47	141.35
15	116.83	118.62	120.43	122.24	124.06	125.90	127.75	129.61	131.48	133.36	135.25	137.16
16	112.98	114.79	116.62	118.46	120.30	122.17	124.04	125.92	127.82	129.73	131.65	133.58
17	109.63	111.47	113.32	115.18	117.05	118.94	120.84	122.75	124.67	126.60	128.55	130.51
18	106.71	108.56	110.44	112.32	114.22	116.13	118.05	119.99	121.94	123.90	125.87	127.85
19	104.13	106.01	107.91	109.81	111.74	113.67	115.62	117.58	119.55	121.54	123.54	125.55
20	101.86	103.76	105.68	107.61	109.55	111.51	113.48	115.47	117.46	119.48	121.50	123.53
21	99.84	101.76	103.70	105.65	107.62	109.60	111.60	113.61	115.63	117.66	119.71	121.77
22	98.04	99.98	101.94	103.92	105.91	107.91	109.93	111.96	114.01	116.07	118.14	120.22
23	96.43	98.39	100.38	102.37	104.39	106.41	108.45	110.51	112.58	114.66	116.75	118.86
24	94.98	96.97	98.97	100.99	103.03	105.08	107.14	109.21	111.30	113.41	115.52	117.65
25	93.68	95.69	97.72	99.76	101.81	103.88	105.96	108.06	110.17	112.30	114.43	116.58
26	92.51	94.54	96.59	98.65	100.72	102.81	104.91	107.03	109.16	111.31	113.47	115.64
27	91.45	93.50	95.57	97.64	99.74	101.85	103.97	106.11	108.26	110.43	112.60	114.79
28	90.49	92.56	94.64	96.74	98.86	100.99	103.13	105.29	107.46	109.64	111.83	114.04
29	89.62	91.71	93.81	95.93	98.06	100.21	102.37	104.54	106.73	108.93	111.15	113.37
30	88.83	90.94	93.06	95.19	97.34	99.51	101.69	103.88	106.08	108.30	110.53	112.78
31	88.11	90.23	92.37	94.52	96.69	98.87	101.07	103.28	105.50	107.74	109.98	112.24
32	87.46	89.59	91.75	93.92	96.10	98.30	100.51	102.74	104.98	107.23	109.49	111.76
33	86.86	89.01	91.18	93.37	95.57	97.78	100.01	102.25	104.50	106.77	109.05	111.34
34	86.31	88.48	90.66	92.87	95.08	97.31	99.55	101.81	104.08	106.36	108.65	110.95
35	85.81	87.99	90.19	92.41	94.64	96.89	99.14	101.41	103.69	105.99	108.29	110.61
36	85.35	87.55	89.77	92.00	94.24	96.50	98.77	101.05	103.35	105.65	107.97	110.30
37	84.93	87.14	89.37	91.62	93.88	96.15	98.43	100.73	103.03	105.35	107.68	110.02
38	84.54	86.77	89.01	91.27	93.54	95.83	98.12	100.43	102.75	105.08	107.42	109.77
39	84.19	86.43	88.69	90.96	93.24	95.54	97.85	100.17	102.50	104.84	107.19	109.55
40	83.87	86.12	88.39	90.67	92.96	95.27	97.59	99.92	102.26	104.62	106.98	109.35
41	83.57	85.83	88.11	90.41	92.71	95.03	97.36	99.70	102.05	104.42	106.79	109.16
42	83.29	85.57	87.86	90.17	92.48	94.81	97.15	99.50	101.86	104.24	106.61	109.00
43	83.04	85.33	87.63	89.95	92.27	94.61	96.96	99.32	101.69	104.07	106.46	108.85
44	82.81	85.11	87.42	89.74	92.08	94.43	96.79	99.16	101.54	103.92	106.32	108.72
45	82.59	84.90	87.22	89.56	91.91	94.26	96.63	99.01	101.40	103.79	106.19	108.60
46	82.39	84.71	87.05	89.39	91.75	94.11	96.49	98.87	101.27	103.67	106.08	108.49
47	82.21	84.54	86.88	89.24	91.60	93.97	96.36	98.75	101.15	103.56	105.98	108.40
48	82.05	84.38	86.73	89.09	91.47	93.85	96.24	98.64	101.05	103.46	105.88	108.31
49	81.89	84.24	86.60	88.96	91.34	93.73	96.13	98.54	100.95	103.37	105.80	108.23
50	81.75	84.10	86.47	88.85	91.23	93.63	96.03	98.44	100.86	103.29	105.72	108.16

TERM IN YEARS	INTEREST RATES											
	11.00%	11.25%	11.50%	11.75%	12.00%	12.25%	12.50%	12.75%	13.00%	13.25%	13.50%	13.75%
1	1110.00	1112.50	1115.00	1117.50	1120.00	1122.50	1125.00	1127.50	1130.00	1132.50	1135.00	1137.50
2	583.94	585.88	587.82	589.76	591.70	593.65	595.59	597.54	599.49	601.44	603.39	605.34
3	409.22	411.00	412.78	414.57	416.35	418.14	419.94	421.73	423.53	425.33	427.13	428.93
4	322.33	324.05	325.78	327.51	329.24	330.97	332.71	334.45	336.20	337.95	339.70	341.45
5	270.58	272.28	273.99	275.70	277.41	279.13	280.86	282.59	284.32	286.06	287.80	289.54
6	236.38	238.09	239.80	241.51	243.23	244.96	246.68	248.42	250.16	251.90	253.65	255.40
7	212.22	213.94	215.66	217.39	219.12	220.86	222.61	224.36	226.12	227.88	229.65	231.42
8	194.33	196.06	197.80	199.55	201.31	203.07	204.84	206.61	208.39	210.18	211.97	213.77
9	180.61	182.37	184.13	185.90	187.68	189.47	191.27	193.07	194.87	196.69	198.51	200.34
10	169.81	171.59	173.38	175.18	176.99	178.80	180.63	182.46	184.29	186.14	187.99	189.85
11	161.13	162.94	164.76	166.58	168.42	170.26	172.12	173.98	175.85	177.72	179.61	181.50
12	154.03	155.87	157.72	159.58	161.44	163.32	165.20	167.09	168.99	170.90	172.82	174.74
13	148.16	150.02	151.90	153.79	155.68	157.59	159.50	161.42	163.36	165.30	167.24	169.20
14	143.23	145.13	147.04	148.95	150.88	152.81	154.76	156.71	158.67	160.64	162.63	164.62
15	139.07	140.99	142.93	144.87	146.83	148.79	150.77	152.75	154.74	156.75	158.76	160.78
16	135.52	137.47	139.44	141.41	143.40	145.39	147.39	149.41	151.43	153.46	155.51	157.56
17	132.48	134.46	136.45	138.45	140.46	142.48	144.52	146.56	148.61	150.68	152.75	154.83
18	129.85	131.85	133.87	135.90	137.94	139.99	142.05	144.12	146.21	148.30	150.40	152.51
19	127.57	129.60	131.65	133.70	135.77	137.85	139.93	142.03	144.14	146.26	148.38	150.52
20	125.58	127.64	129.71	131.79	133.88	135.99	138.10	140.22	142.36	144.50	146.66	148.82
21	123.84	125.93	128.02	130.13	132.25	134.37	136.51	138.66	140.82	142.99	145.17	147.35
22	122.32	124.43	126.54	128.67	130.82	132.97	135.13	137.30	139.48	141.68	143.88	146.09
23	120.98	123.11	125.25	127.40	129.56	131.74	133.92	136.12	138.32	140.54	142.76	144.99
24	119.79	121.94	124.11	126.28	128.47	130.66	132.87	135.09	137.31	139.55	141.79	144.05
25	118.75	120.92	123.10	125.30	127.50	129.72	131.95	134.18	136.43	138.69	140.95	143.22
26	117.82	120.01	122.22	124.43	126.66	128.89	131.14	133.39	135.66	137.93	140.22	142.51
27	116.99	119.21	121.43	123.66	125.91	128.16	130.43	132.70	134.98	137.28	139.57	141.88
28	116.26	118.49	120.73	122.99	125.25	127.52	129.80	132.09	134.39	136.70	139.02	141.34
29	115.61	117.86	120.12	122.39	124.67	126.95	129.25	131.56	133.87	136.20	138.53	140.86
30	115.03	117.29	119.57	121.85	124.15	126.45	128.77	131.09	133.42	135.75	138.10	140.45
31	114.51	116.79	119.08	121.38	123.69	126.01	128.34	130.67	133.01	135.36	137.72	140.09
32	114.05	116.34	118.65	120.96	123.29	125.62	127.96	130.31	132.66	135.02	137.39	139.77
33	113.63	115.94	118.26	120.59	122.93	125.27	127.62	129.98	132.35	134.72	137.10	139.49
34	113.26	115.59	117.92	120.26	122.61	124.96	127.33	129.70	132.08	134.46	136.85	139.25
35	112.93	115.27	117.61	119.96	122.32	124.69	127.06	129.45	131.83	134.23	136.63	139.04
36	112.64	114.98	117.34	119.70	122.07	124.45	126.83	129.22	131.62	134.02	136.43	138.85
37	112.37	114.73	117.09	119.46	121.84	124.23	126.63	129.03	131.43	133.85	136.26	138.68
38	112.13	114.50	116.87	119.26	121.64	124.04	126.44	128.85	131.27	133.69	136.11	138.54
39	111.92	114.29	116.68	119.07	121.47	123.87	126.28	128.70	131.12	133.55	135.98	138.42
40	111.72	114.11	116.50	118.90	121.31	123.72	126.14	128.56	130.99	133.42	135.86	138.30
41	111.55	113.95	116.35	118.75	121.17	123.59	126.01	128.44	130.88	133.32	135.76	138.21
42	111.40	113.80	116.21	118.62	121.04	123.47	125.90	128.34	130.78	133.22	135.67	138.12
43	111.26	113.67	116.08	118.50	120.93	123.36	125.80	128.24	130.69	133.14	135.59	138.05
44	111.13	113.55	115.97	118.40	120.83	123.27	125.71	128.16	130.61	133.06	135.52	137.98
45	111.02	113.44	115.87	118.30	120.74	123.18	125.63	128.08	130.54	133.00	135.46	137.92
46	110.92	113.35	115.78	118.22	120.66	123.11	125.56	128.02	130.48	132.94	135.40	137.87
47	110.83	113.26	115.70	118.14	120.59	123.04	125.50	127.96	130.42	132.89	135.36	137.83
48	110.74	113.18	115.63	118.08	120.53	122.98	125.44	127.91	130.37	132.84	135.32	137.79
49	110.67	113.11	115.56	118.02	120.47	122.93	125.40	127.86	130.33	132.80	135.28	137.75
50	110.60	113.05	115.50	117.96	120.42	122.89	125.35	127.82	130.29	132.77	135.25	137.72

ANNUAL
PAYMENT REQUIRED TO AMORTIZE A $1,000.00 LOAN

TERM IN YEARS	INTEREST RATES											
	14.00%	14.25%	14.50%	14.75%	15.00%	15.25%	15.50%	15.75%	16.00%	16.25%	16.50%	16.75%
1	1140.00	1142.50	1145.00	1147.50	1150.00	1152.50	1155.00	1157.50	1160.00	1162.50	1165.00	1167.50
2	607.29	609.25	611.21	613.16	615.12	617.08	619.04	621.00	622.97	624.93	626.90	628.87
3	430.74	432.54	434.35	436.17	437.98	439.80	441.62	443.44	445.26	447.09	448.92	450.75
4	343.21	344.97	346.73	348.50	350.27	352.04	353.82	355.60	357.38	359.17	360.95	362.74
5	291.29	293.04	294.80	296.56	298.32	300.09	301.86	303.64	305.41	307.20	308.98	310.77
6	257.16	258.93	260.69	262.47	264.24	266.02	267.81	269.60	271.39	273.19	275.00	276.81
7	233.20	234.98	236.77	238.57	240.37	242.17	243.98	245.80	247.62	249.44	251.27	253.11
8	215.58	217.39	219.20	221.03	222.86	224.69	226.53	228.38	230.23	232.09	233.95	235.82
9	202.17	204.01	205.86	207.72	209.58	211.45	213.32	215.20	217.09	218.98	220.88	222.78
10	191.72	193.59	195.47	197.36	199.26	201.16	203.07	204.98	206.91	208.84	210.77	212.71
11	183.40	185.31	187.22	189.14	191.07	193.01	194.96	196.91	198.87	200.83	202.80	204.78
12	176.67	178.62	180.56	182.52	184.49	186.46	188.44	190.43	192.42	194.42	196.43	198.45
13	171.17	173.14	175.13	177.12	179.12	181.12	183.14	185.16	187.19	189.23	191.27	193.32
14	166.61	168.62	170.64	172.66	174.69	176.73	178.78	180.84	182.90	184.97	187.05	189.14
15	162.81	164.85	166.90	168.96	171.02	173.10	175.18	177.27	179.36	181.47	183.58	185.70
16	159.62	161.69	163.77	165.86	167.95	170.06	172.17	174.29	176.42	178.55	180.70	182.85
17	156.92	159.02	161.13	163.25	165.37	167.51	169.65	171.80	173.96	176.12	178.30	180.48
18	154.63	156.75	158.89	161.04	163.19	165.35	167.52	169.70	171.89	174.08	176.29	178.49
19	152.67	154.82	156.99	159.16	161.34	163.53	165.73	167.93	170.15	172.37	174.60	176.83
20	150.99	153.17	155.36	157.56	159.77	161.98	164.20	166.43	168.67	170.92	173.17	175.43
21	149.55	151.76	153.97	156.19	158.42	160.66	162.91	165.16	167.42	169.69	171.96	174.25
22	148.31	150.54	152.77	155.02	157.27	159.53	161.80	164.08	166.36	168.65	170.94	173.25
23	147.24	149.49	151.74	154.01	156.28	158.56	160.85	163.15	165.45	167.76	170.08	172.40
24	146.31	148.58	150.86	153.14	155.43	157.74	160.04	162.36	164.68	167.01	169.34	171.68
25	145.50	147.79	150.09	152.39	154.70	157.02	159.35	161.68	164.02	166.36	168.71	171.07
26	144.81	147.11	149.43	151.75	154.07	156.41	158.75	161.10	163.45	165.81	168.18	170.55
27	144.20	146.52	148.85	151.19	153.53	155.88	158.24	160.60	162.97	165.34	167.72	170.10
28	143.67	146.01	148.35	150.70	153.06	155.43	157.80	160.17	162.55	164.94	167.33	169.73
29	143.21	145.56	147.92	150.29	152.66	155.03	157.42	159.80	162.20	164.59	167.00	169.40
30	142.81	145.17	147.54	149.92	152.31	154.69	157.09	159.49	161.89	164.30	166.71	169.13
31	142.46	144.83	147.22	149.61	152.00	154.40	156.81	159.21	161.63	164.05	166.47	168.89
32	142.15	144.54	146.93	149.33	151.74	154.15	156.56	158.98	161.40	163.83	166.26	168.69
33	141.88	144.28	146.69	149.10	151.51	153.93	156.35	158.78	161.21	163.64	166.08	168.52
34	141.65	144.06	146.47	148.89	151.31	153.74	156.17	158.60	161.04	163.48	165.93	168.38
35	141.45	143.86	146.28	148.71	151.14	153.57	156.01	158.45	160.90	163.35	165.80	168.25
36	141.27	143.69	146.12	148.55	150.99	153.43	155.88	158.32	160.77	163.23	165.68	168.14
37	141.11	143.54	145.98	148.42	150.86	153.31	155.76	158.21	160.67	163.13	165.59	168.05
38	140.97	143.41	145.85	148.30	150.75	153.20	155.66	158.11	160.58	163.04	165.50	167.97
39	140.86	143.30	145.75	148.20	150.65	153.11	155.57	158.03	160.50	162.96	165.43	167.90
40	140.75	143.20	145.65	148.11	150.57	153.03	155.49	157.96	160.43	162.90	165.37	167.85
41	140.66	143.11	145.57	148.03	150.49	152.96	155.43	157.90	160.37	162.84	165.32	167.80
42	140.58	143.04	145.50	147.96	150.43	152.90	155.37	157.84	160.32	162.80	165.28	167.76
43	140.51	142.97	145.44	147.90	150.37	152.85	155.32	157.80	160.28	162.76	165.24	167.72
44	140.45	142.91	145.38	147.85	150.33	152.80	155.28	157.76	160.24	162.72	165.20	167.69
45	140.39	142.86	145.33	147.81	150.28	152.76	155.24	157.72	160.21	162.69	165.18	167.66
46	140.34	142.82	145.29	147.77	150.25	152.73	155.21	157.69	160.18	162.66	165.15	167.64
47	140.30	142.78	145.26	147.73	150.22	152.70	155.18	157.67	160.15	162.64	165.13	167.62
48	140.27	142.74	145.22	147.71	150.19	152.67	155.16	157.65	160.13	162.62	165.11	167.60
49	140.23	142.71	145.20	147.68	150.16	152.65	155.14	157.63	160.12	162.61	165.10	167.59
50	140.21	142.69	145.17	147.66	150.14	152.63	155.12	157.61	160.10	162.59	165.08	167.58

223

ANNUAL
PAYMENT REQUIRED TO AMORTIZE A $1,000.00 LOAN

TERM IN YEARS	INTEREST RATES											
	17.00%	17.25%	17.50%	17.75%	18.00%	18.25%	18.50%	18.75%	19.00%	19.25%	19.50%	19.75%
1	1170.00	1172.50	1175.00	1177.50	1180.00	1182.50	1185.00	1187.50	1190.00	1192.50	1195.00	1197.50
2	630.83	632.80	634.78	636.75	638.72	640.70	642.67	644.65	646.63	648.61	650.59	652.57
3	452.58	454.41	456.25	458.09	459.93	461.77	463.62	465.46	467.31	469.16	471.02	472.87
4	364.54	366.34	368.14	369.94	371.74	373.55	375.36	377.18	379.00	380.82	382.64	384.47
5	312.57	314.37	316.17	317.97	319.78	321.60	323.41	325.23	327.06	328.88	330.71	332.55
6	278.62	280.44	282.26	284.08	285.92	287.75	289.59	291.43	293.28	295.13	296.99	298.85
7	254.95	256.80	258.65	260.51	262.37	264.23	266.10	267.98	269.86	271.75	273.64	275.53
8	237.69	239.58	241.46	243.35	245.25	247.15	249.06	250.97	252.89	254.81	256.74	258.68
9	224.70	226.61	228.54	230.46	232.40	234.34	236.29	238.24	240.20	242.16	244.13	246.10
10	214.66	216.62	218.58	220.55	222.52	224.50	226.49	228.48	230.48	232.48	234.49	236.51
11	206.77	208.76	210.76	212.77	214.78	216.80	218.83	220.86	222.90	224.94	226.99	229.05
12	200.47	202.50	204.54	206.58	208.63	210.69	212.75	214.82	216.90	218.98	221.07	223.17
13	195.38	197.45	199.52	201.60	203.69	205.79	207.89	209.99	212.11	214.23	216.35	218.49
14	191.24	193.34	195.45	197.56	199.68	201.81	203.95	206.09	208.24	210.39	212.56	214.72
15	187.83	189.96	192.10	194.25	196.41	198.57	200.74	202.91	205.10	207.29	209.48	211.68
16	185.01	187.18	189.35	191.53	193.72	195.91	198.11	200.32	202.53	204.75	206.97	209.20
17	182.67	184.86	187.06	189.27	191.49	193.71	195.94	198.18	200.42	202.67	204.92	207.18
18	180.71	182.93	185.16	187.40	189.64	191.89	194.15	196.41	198.68	200.95	203.23	205.52
19	179.07	181.32	183.58	185.84	188.11	190.38	192.66	194.95	197.24	199.54	201.84	204.15
20	177.70	179.97	182.25	184.53	186.82	189.12	191.43	193.74	196.05	198.37	200.70	203.03
21	176.54	178.83	181.13	183.44	185.75	188.07	190.39	192.72	195.06	197.40	199.74	202.09
22	175.56	177.87	180.19	182.52	184.85	187.19	189.53	191.88	194.23	196.59	198.96	201.32
23	174.73	177.06	179.40	181.74	184.10	186.45	188.81	191.18	193.55	195.92	198.30	200.68
24	174.02	176.38	178.73	181.09	183.46	185.83	188.21	190.59	192.97	195.36	197.75	200.15
25	173.43	175.79	178.17	180.54	182.92	185.31	187.70	190.09	192.49	194.89	197.30	199.71
26	172.92	175.30	177.69	180.08	182.47	184.87	187.27	189.68	192.09	194.50	196.92	199.34
27	172.49	174.89	177.28	179.69	182.09	184.50	186.92	189.33	191.75	194.18	196.61	199.04
28	172.13	174.53	176.94	179.35	181.77	184.19	186.61	189.04	191.47	193.91	196.34	198.78
29	171.81	174.23	176.65	179.07	181.50	183.93	186.36	188.80	191.24	193.68	196.12	198.57
30	171.55	173.97	176.40	178.83	181.27	183.71	186.15	188.59	191.04	193.49	195.94	198.39
31	171.32	173.76	176.19	178.63	181.08	183.52	185.97	188.42	190.87	193.33	195.79	198.25
32	171.13	173.57	176.02	178.46	180.91	183.36	185.82	188.28	190.73	193.20	195.66	198.12
33	170.97	173.41	175.86	178.32	180.77	183.23	185.69	188.15	190.62	193.08	195.55	198.02
34	170.83	173.28	175.74	178.19	180.65	183.12	185.58	188.05	190.52	192.99	195.46	197.94
35	170.71	173.16	175.63	178.09	180.56	183.02	185.49	187.96	190.44	192.91	195.39	197.87
36	170.60	173.07	175.53	178.00	180.47	182.94	185.42	187.89	190.37	192.85	195.33	197.81
37	170.52	172.98	175.45	177.93	180.40	182.88	185.35	187.83	190.31	192.79	195.27	197.76
38	170.44	172.91	175.39	177.86	180.34	182.82	185.30	187.78	190.26	192.74	195.23	197.71
39	170.38	172.85	175.33	177.81	180.29	182.77	185.25	187.74	190.22	192.71	195.19	197.68
40	170.32	172.80	175.28	177.76	180.25	182.73	185.21	187.70	190.19	192.67	195.16	197.65
41	170.28	172.76	175.24	177.72	180.21	182.69	185.18	187.67	190.16	192.65	195.14	197.63
42	170.24	172.72	175.21	177.69	180.18	182.66	185.15	187.64	190.13	192.62	195.11	197.61
43	170.20	172.69	175.18	177.66	180.15	182.64	185.13	187.62	190.11	192.60	195.09	197.59
44	170.18	172.66	175.15	177.64	180.13	182.62	185.11	187.60	190.10	192.59	195.08	197.58
45	170.15	172.64	175.13	177.62	180.11	182.60	185.09	187.59	190.08	192.57	195.07	197.56
46	170.13	172.62	175.11	177.60	180.09	182.59	185.08	187.57	190.07	192.56	195.06	197.55
47	170.11	172.60	175.09	177.59	180.08	182.57	185.07	187.56	190.06	192.55	195.05	197.55
48	170.10	172.59	175.08	177.57	180.07	182.56	185.06	187.55	190.05	192.55	195.04	197.54
49	170.08	172.58	175.07	177.56	180.06	182.55	185.05	187.55	190.04	192.54	195.04	197.53
50	170.07	172.57	175.06	177.56	180.05	182.55	185.04	187.54	190.04	192.53	195.03	197.53

224

ANNUAL
PAYMENT REQUIRED TO AMORTIZE A $1,000.00 LOAN

TERM IN YEARS	\multicolumn{12}{c}{INTEREST RATES}											
	20.00%	20.25%	20.50%	20.75%	21.00%	21.25%	21.50%	21.75%	22.00%	22.25%	22.50%	22.75%
1	1200.00	1202.50	1205.00	1207.50	1210.00	1212.50	1215.00	1217.50	1220.00	1222.50	1225.00	1227.50
2	654.55	656.53	658.52	660.51	662.49	664.48	666.47	668.46	670.46	672.45	674.44	676.44
3	474.73	476.59	478.45	480.31	482.18	484.05	485.92	487.79	489.66	491.54	493.42	495.30
4	386.29	388.13	389.96	391.80	393.64	395.48	397.33	399.17	401.03	402.88	404.74	406.59
5	334.38	336.23	338.07	339.92	341.77	343.63	345.48	347.35	349.21	351.08	352.95	354.83
6	300.71	302.58	304.45	306.33	308.21	310.09	311.98	313.87	315.77	317.67	319.57	321.48
7	277.43	279.33	281.24	283.15	285.07	286.99	288.92	290.85	292.79	294.73	296.67	298.62
8	260.61	262.56	264.51	266.46	268.42	270.38	272.35	274.33	276.30	278.29	280.27	282.27
9	248.08	250.07	252.06	254.06	256.06	258.07	260.08	262.09	264.12	266.14	268.18	270.21
10	238.53	240.55	242.59	244.63	246.67	248.72	250.77	252.83	254.90	256.97	259.05	261.13
11	231.11	233.18	235.25	237.33	239.42	241.51	243.60	245.70	247.81	249.92	252.04	254.17
12	225.27	227.38	229.49	231.61	233.73	235.87	238.00	240.14	242.29	244.44	246.60	248.76
13	220.63	222.77	224.92	227.08	229.24	231.41	233.58	235.76	237.94	240.13	242.33	244.53
14	216.90	219.08	221.26	223.45	225.65	227.85	230.06	232.28	234.50	236.72	238.95	241.18
15	213.89	216.10	218.32	220.54	222.77	225.01	227.25	229.49	231.74	234.00	236.26	238.53
16	211.44	213.68	215.93	218.19	220.45	222.71	224.98	227.25	229.53	231.82	234.11	236.40
17	209.45	211.72	213.99	216.27	218.56	220.85	223.15	225.45	227.76	230.07	232.38	234.70
18	207.81	210.11	212.41	214.71	217.03	219.34	221.66	223.99	226.32	228.65	230.99	233.33
19	206.47	208.79	211.11	213.44	215.77	218.11	220.45	222.80	225.15	227.51	229.87	232.23
20	205.36	207.70	210.05	212.40	214.75	217.11	219.47	221.84	224.21	226.58	228.96	231.34
21	204.45	206.81	209.17	211.54	213.91	216.29	218.67	221.05	223.44	225.83	228.22	230.62
22	203.69	206.07	208.45	210.83	213.22	215.61	218.01	220.41	222.81	225.22	227.62	230.04
23	203.07	205.46	207.86	210.25	212.66	215.06	217.47	219.88	222.30	224.72	227.14	229.56
24	202.55	204.96	207.37	209.78	212.19	214.61	217.03	219.46	221.88	224.31	226.74	229.18
25	202.12	204.54	206.96	209.38	211.81	214.24	216.67	219.10	221.54	223.98	226.42	228.87
26	201.77	204.19	206.62	209.06	211.49	213.93	216.37	218.82	221.26	223.71	226.16	228.61
27	201.47	203.91	206.35	208.79	211.23	213.68	216.13	218.58	221.03	223.49	225.95	228.41
28	201.23	203.67	206.12	208.57	211.02	213.47	215.93	218.39	220.85	223.31	225.77	228.24
29	201.02	203.47	205.93	208.38	210.84	213.30	215.77	218.23	220.70	223.16	225.63	228.10
30	200.85	203.31	205.77	208.23	210.70	213.16	215.63	218.10	220.57	223.04	225.52	227.99
31	200.71	203.17	205.64	208.11	210.58	213.05	215.52	217.99	220.47	222.95	225.42	227.90
32	200.59	203.06	205.53	208.00	210.48	212.95	215.43	217.91	220.38	222.86	225.35	227.83
33	200.49	202.97	205.44	207.92	210.40	212.87	215.35	217.83	220.32	222.80	225.28	227.77
34	200.41	202.89	205.37	207.85	210.33	212.81	215.29	217.78	220.26	222.75	225.23	227.72
35	200.34	202.82	205.31	207.79	210.27	212.76	215.24	217.73	220.21	222.70	225.19	227.68
36	200.29	202.77	205.25	207.74	210.22	212.71	215.20	217.69	220.18	222.67	225.16	227.65
37	200.24	202.73	205.21	207.70	210.19	212.68	215.16	217.65	220.15	222.64	225.13	227.62
38	200.20	202.69	205.18	207.67	210.16	212.65	215.14	217.63	220.12	222.61	225.11	227.60
39	200.17	202.66	205.15	207.64	210.13	212.62	215.11	217.61	220.10	222.59	225.09	227.58
40	200.14	202.63	205.12	207.62	210.11	212.60	215.09	217.59	220.08	222.58	225.07	227.57
41	200.12	202.61	205.10	207.60	210.09	212.58	215.08	217.57	220.07	222.56	225.06	227.56
42	200.10	202.59	205.09	207.58	210.08	212.57	215.07	217.56	220.06	222.55	225.05	227.55
43	200.08	202.58	205.07	207.57	210.06	212.56	215.05	217.55	220.05	222.54	225.04	227.54
44	200.07	202.57	205.06	207.56	210.05	212.55	215.05	217.54	220.04	222.54	225.03	227.53
45	200.06	202.56	205.05	207.55	210.04	212.54	215.04	217.54	220.03	222.53	225.03	227.53
46	200.05	202.55	205.04	207.54	210.04	212.54	215.03	217.53	220.03	222.53	225.02	227.52
47	200.04	202.54	205.04	207.53	210.03	212.53	215.03	217.53	220.02	222.52	225.02	227.52
48	200.04	202.53	205.03	207.53	210.03	212.53	215.02	217.52	220.02	222.52	225.02	227.52
49	200.03	202.53	205.03	207.53	210.02	212.52	215.02	217.52	220.02	222.52	225.02	227.51
50	200.03	202.53	205.02	207.52	210.02	212.52	215.02	217.52	220.02	222.51	225.01	227.51

ANNUAL
PAYMENT REQUIRED TO AMORTIZE A $1,000.00 LOAN

TERM IN YEARS	INTEREST RATES											
	23.00%	23.25%	23.50%	23.75%	24.00%	24.25%	24.50%	24.75%	25.00%	25.25%	25.50%	25.75%
1	1230.00	1232.50	1235.00	1237.50	1240.00	1242.50	1245.00	1247.50	1250.00	1252.50	1255.00	1257.50
2	678.44	680.43	682.43	684.43	686.43	688.44	690.44	692.44	694.45	696.46	698.46	700.47
3	497.18	499.06	500.95	502.83	504.72	506.61	508.51	510.40	512.30	514.20	516.10	518.00
4	408.46	410.32	412.19	414.06	415.93	417.81	419.68	421.56	423.45	425.33	427.22	429.11
5	356.71	358.59	360.47	362.36	364.25	366.15	368.05	369.95	371.85	373.76	375.67	377.58
6	323.39	325.31	327.23	329.15	331.08	333.01	334.94	336.88	338.82	340.77	342.72	344.67
7	300.57	302.53	304.49	306.46	308.43	310.40	312.38	314.36	316.35	318.34	320.33	322.33
8	284.26	286.27	288.27	290.28	292.30	294.32	296.34	298.37	300.40	302.44	304.48	306.53
9	272.25	274.30	276.35	278.41	280.47	282.54	284.61	286.68	288.76	290.85	292.93	295.03
10	263.21	265.30	267.40	269.50	271.61	273.72	275.83	277.95	280.08	282.21	284.34	286.48
11	256.29	258.43	260.57	262.71	264.86	267.01	269.17	271.33	273.50	275.67	277.85	280.03
12	250.93	253.10	255.28	257.47	259.65	261.85	264.04	266.25	268.45	270.66	272.88	275.10
13	246.73	248.94	251.16	253.38	255.60	257.83	260.07	262.31	264.55	266.80	269.05	271.30
14	243.42	245.67	247.92	250.17	252.43	254.69	256.96	259.23	261.51	263.79	266.07	268.36
15	240.80	243.07	245.35	247.64	249.92	252.22	254.51	256.82	259.12	261.43	263.75	266.06
16	238.70	241.01	243.31	245.62	247.94	250.26	252.59	254.91	257.25	259.58	261.92	264.26
17	237.03	239.35	241.69	244.02	246.36	248.71	251.06	253.41	255.76	258.12	260.49	262.85
18	235.68	238.03	240.39	242.74	245.11	247.47	249.84	252.22	254.59	256.97	259.35	261.74
19	234.60	236.97	239.34	241.72	244.10	246.49	248.88	251.27	253.66	256.06	258.46	260.86
20	233.73	236.11	238.51	240.90	243.30	245.70	248.10	250.51	252.92	255.33	257.75	260.17
21	233.02	235.42	237.83	240.24	242.65	245.07	247.49	249.91	252.33	254.76	257.19	259.62
22	232.45	234.87	237.29	239.71	242.14	244.56	247.00	249.43	251.86	254.30	256.74	259.18
23	231.99	234.42	236.85	239.28	241.72	244.16	246.60	249.04	251.49	253.94	256.39	258.84
24	231.62	234.06	236.50	238.94	241.39	243.84	246.29	248.74	251.19	253.65	256.10	258.56
25	231.31	233.76	236.21	238.66	241.12	243.57	246.03	248.49	250.95	253.42	255.88	258.35
26	231.07	233.52	235.98	238.44	240.90	243.37	245.83	248.30	250.76	253.23	255.70	258.17
27	230.87	233.33	235.79	238.26	240.73	243.20	245.67	248.14	250.61	253.08	255.56	258.04
28	230.71	233.17	235.64	238.12	240.59	243.06	245.54	248.01	250.49	252.97	255.45	257.93
29	230.57	233.05	235.52	238.00	240.47	242.95	245.43	247.91	250.39	252.87	255.36	257.84
30	230.47	232.95	235.42	237.90	240.38	242.87	245.35	247.83	250.31	252.80	255.29	257.77
31	230.38	232.86	235.34	237.83	240.31	242.79	245.28	247.77	250.25	252.74	255.23	257.72
32	230.31	232.79	235.28	237.76	240.25	242.74	245.23	247.71	250.20	252.69	255.18	257.67
33	230.25	232.74	235.23	237.71	240.20	242.69	245.18	247.67	250.16	252.65	255.15	257.64
34	230.21	232.70	235.18	237.67	240.17	242.66	245.15	247.64	250.13	252.62	255.12	257.61
35	230.17	232.66	235.15	237.64	240.13	242.63	245.12	247.61	250.11	252.60	255.09	257.59
36	230.14	232.63	235.12	237.62	240.11	242.60	245.10	247.59	250.09	252.58	255.08	257.57
37	230.11	232.61	235.10	237.59	240.09	242.58	245.08	247.57	250.07	252.57	255.06	257.56
38	230.09	232.59	235.08	237.58	240.07	242.57	245.06	247.56	250.06	252.55	255.05	257.55
39	230.08	232.57	235.07	237.56	240.06	242.56	245.05	247.55	250.05	252.54	255.04	257.54
40	230.06	232.56	235.06	237.55	240.05	242.55	245.04	247.54	250.04	252.54	255.03	257.53
41	230.05	232.55	235.05	237.54	240.04	242.54	245.04	247.53	250.03	252.53	255.03	257.53
42	230.04	232.54	235.04	237.54	240.03	242.53	245.03	247.53	250.02	252.52	255.02	257.52
43	230.04	232.53	235.03	237.53	240.03	242.52	245.02	247.52	250.02	252.52	255.02	257.52
44	230.03	232.53	235.03	237.53	240.02	242.52	245.02	247.52	250.02	252.52	255.02	257.52
45	230.03	232.52	235.02	237.52	240.02	242.52	245.02	247.52	250.02	252.52	255.01	257.51
46	230.02	232.52	235.02	237.52	240.02	242.51	245.02	247.51	250.01	252.51	255.01	257.51
47	230.02	232.52	235.02	237.52	240.01	242.51	245.01	247.51	250.01	252.51	255.01	257.51
48	230.02	232.51	235.01	237.51	240.01	242.51	245.01	247.51	250.01	252.51	255.01	257.51
49	230.01	232.51	235.01	237.51	240.01	242.51	245.01	247.51	250.01	252.51	255.01	257.51
50	230.01	232.51	235.01	237.51	240.01	242.51	245.01	247.51	250.01	252.51	255.01	257.51

ANNUAL
PAYMENT REQUIRED TO AMORTIZE A $1,000.00 LOAN

TERM IN YEARS	26.00%	26.25%	26.50%	26.75%	27.00%	27.25%	27.50%	27.75%	28.00%	28.25%	28.50%	28.75%
					INTEREST RATES							
1	1260.00	1262.50	1265.00	1267.50	1270.00	1272.50	1275.00	1277.50	1280.00	1282.50	1285.00	1287.50
2	702.48	704.49	706.51	708.52	710.53	712.55	714.57	716.58	718.60	720.62	722.64	724.66
3	519.91	521.81	523.72	525.63	527.54	529.46	531.37	533.29	535.21	537.13	539.06	540.98
4	431.00	432.90	434.80	436.70	438.60	440.51	442.42	444.33	446.24	448.16	450.07	452.00
5	379.50	381.42	383.34	385.27	387.20	389.13	391.07	393.01	394.95	396.89	398.84	400.79
6	346.63	348.59	350.55	352.52	354.49	356.46	358.44	360.42	362.41	364.39	366.38	368.38
7	324.33	326.34	328.35	330.36	332.38	334.40	336.43	338.45	340.49	342.52	344.56	346.61
8	308.58	310.63	312.69	314.75	316.82	318.89	320.96	323.04	325.12	327.21	329.30	331.39
9	297.12	299.23	301.33	303.44	305.56	307.67	309.80	311.92	314.05	316.19	318.33	320.47
10	288.62	290.77	292.92	295.08	297.24	299.40	301.57	303.74	305.92	308.10	310.28	312.47
11	282.21	284.40	286.60	288.79	291.00	293.20	295.41	297.63	299.85	302.07	304.30	306.53
12	277.32	279.55	281.79	284.02	286.26	288.51	290.76	293.01	295.27	297.53	299.80	302.06
13	273.56	275.83	278.10	280.37	282.65	284.93	287.21	289.50	291.79	294.09	296.38	298.69
14	270.65	272.95	275.25	277.55	279.86	282.17	284.49	286.81	289.13	291.45	293.78	296.11
15	268.38	270.71	273.04	275.37	277.71	280.04	282.39	284.73	287.08	289.43	291.79	294.15
16	266.61	268.96	271.31	273.67	276.03	278.40	280.76	283.13	285.50	287.88	290.26	292.64
17	265.22	267.59	269.97	272.35	274.73	277.11	279.50	281.89	284.28	286.68	289.08	291.48
18	264.13	266.52	268.91	271.31	273.71	276.11	278.52	280.93	283.34	285.75	288.16	290.58
19	263.27	265.67	268.08	270.50	272.91	275.33	277.75	280.18	282.60	285.03	287.46	289.89
20	262.59	265.01	267.43	269.86	272.29	274.72	277.16	279.59	282.03	284.47	286.91	289.35
21	262.05	264.48	266.92	269.36	271.80	274.24	276.69	279.14	281.58	284.03	286.48	288.94
22	261.63	264.07	266.52	268.97	271.42	273.87	276.32	278.78	281.24	283.70	286.16	288.62
23	261.29	263.74	266.20	268.66	271.12	273.58	276.04	278.50	280.97	283.43	285.90	288.37
24	261.02	263.48	265.95	268.41	270.88	273.35	275.81	278.28	280.76	283.23	285.70	288.17
25	260.81	263.28	265.75	268.22	270.69	273.17	275.64	278.11	280.59	283.07	285.55	288.02
26	260.65	263.12	265.59	268.07	270.55	273.02	275.50	277.98	280.46	282.94	285.43	287.91
27	260.51	262.99	265.47	267.95	270.43	272.91	275.40	277.88	280.36	282.85	285.33	287.82
28	260.41	262.89	265.37	267.86	270.34	272.83	275.31	277.80	280.28	282.77	285.26	287.75
29	260.32	262.81	265.30	267.78	270.27	272.76	275.24	277.73	280.22	282.71	285.20	287.69
30	260.26	262.75	265.23	267.72	270.21	272.70	275.19	277.68	280.18	282.67	285.16	287.65
31	260.21	262.70	265.19	267.68	270.17	272.66	275.15	277.65	280.14	282.63	285.12	287.62
32	260.16	262.66	265.15	267.64	270.13	272.63	275.12	277.61	280.11	282.60	285.10	287.59
33	260.13	262.62	265.12	267.61	270.11	272.60	275.10	277.59	280.09	282.58	285.08	287.57
34	260.11	262.60	265.09	267.59	270.08	272.58	275.08	277.57	280.07	282.56	285.06	287.56
35	260.08	262.58	265.08	267.57	270.07	272.56	275.06	277.56	280.05	282.55	285.05	287.55
36	260.07	262.56	265.06	267.55	270.05	272.55	275.05	277.55	280.04	282.54	285.04	287.54
37	260.06	262.55	265.05	267.55	270.04	272.54	275.04	277.53	280.04	282.53	285.03	287.53
38	260.04	262.54	265.04	267.54	270.04	272.53	275.03	277.53	280.03	282.53	285.03	287.52
39	260.04	262.53	265.03	267.53	270.03	272.53	275.03	277.52	280.02	282.52	285.02	287.52
40	260.03	262.53	265.03	267.53	270.02	272.52	275.02	277.52	280.02	282.52	285.02	287.52
41	260.02	262.52	265.02	267.52	270.02	272.52	275.02	277.52	280.02	282.52	285.01	287.51
42	260.02	262.52	265.02	267.52	270.02	272.52	275.02	277.51	280.01	282.51	285.01	287.51
43	260.02	262.52	265.02	267.52	270.01	272.51	275.01	277.51	280.01	282.51	285.01	287.51
44	260.01	262.51	265.01	267.51	270.01	272.51	275.01	277.51	280.01	282.51	285.01	287.51
45	260.01	262.51	265.01	267.51	270.01	272.51	275.01	277.51	280.01	282.51	285.01	287.51
46	260.01	262.51	265.01	267.51	270.01	272.51	275.01	277.51	280.01	282.51	285.01	287.51
47	260.01	262.51	265.01	267.51	270.01	272.51	275.01	277.51	280.01	282.51	285.01	287.51
48	260.01	262.51	265.01	267.51	270.01	272.51	275.01	277.51	280.01	282.51	285.01	287.51
49	260.01	262.51	265.01	267.51	270.01	272.51	275.01	277.51	280.01	282.51	285.01	287.51
50	260.01	262.51	265.01	267.51	270.01	272.51	275.01	277.51	280.01	282.51	285.01	287.51

TABLE 3. LOAN PROGRESS CHART

Use this Table to find the fraction of an original loan amount that remains unpaid at various times during the life of the loan. You need to know the current age of the loan, the interest rate, and the original loan term.

Example: A $20,000 original loan amount has an original loan term of 25 years and an interest rate of 12.5%. What is the principal balance remaining on this loan at the end of 10 years?

Find the 12.5% interest rate on page 245. Find the column with an original loan term of 25 years. Read down this column to the 10-year age of loan row. Find the entry 0.8847. Multiply 0.8847 by the $20,000 original loan amount to get a remaining balance of $17,694.

Asterisk entries in the Table simply indicate that the remaining loan amount is virtually the same as the original loan amount.

LOAN PROGRESS CHART

5.00%

AGE OF LOAN	ORIGINAL TERM IN YEARS															
	1	2	3	4	5	6	7	8	9	10	15	20	25	30	35	40
1	.0000	.5125	.6832	.7684	.8194	.8534	.8776	.8957	.9097	.9209	.9541	.9701	.9794	.9852	.9892	.9920
2		.0000	.3501	.5249	.6297	.6993	.7490	.7861	.8149	.8378	.9058	.9387	.9577	.9697	.9778	.9835
3			.0000	.2690	.4301	.5374	.6137	.6709	.7151	.7504	.8550	.9057	.9349	.9534	.9659	.9746
4				.0000	.2204	.3671	.4716	.5497	.6103	.6586	.8017	.8710	.9110	.9363	.9533	.9653
5					.0000	.1881	.3222	.4224	.5001	.5620	.7456	.8345	.8858	.9183	.9401	.9554
6						.0000	.1651	.2886	.3843	.4606	.6866	.7962	.8593	.8994	.9263	.9451
7							.0000	.1479	.2625	.3539	.6246	.7559	.8315	.8795	.9117	.9343
8								.0000	.1345	.2418	.5595	.7136	.8023	.8585	.8964	.9228
9									.0000	.1239	.4910	.6690	.7716	.8365	.8803	.9109
10										.0000	.4190	.6222	.7392	.8134	.8633	.8982
11											.3434	.5730	.7053	.7891	.8455	.8850
12											.2639	.5213	.6696	.7636	.8268	.8711
13											.1803	.4669	.6321	.7367	.8071	.8564
14											.0924	.4098	.5926	.7085	.7865	.8410
15											.0000	.3497	.5512	.6788	.7647	.8248
16												.2866	.5076	.6477	.7419	.8078
17												.2202	.4618	.6149	.7179	.7900
18												.1504	.4136	.5804	.6926	.7712
19												.0771	.3630	.5442	.6661	.7514
20												.0000	.3098	.5061	.6382	.7306
21													.2538	.4661	.6089	.7088
22													.1951	.4240	.5781	.6859
23													.1333	.3798	.5457	.6618
24													.0683	.3333	.5116	.6364
25													.0000	.2845	.4758	.6098
26														.2331	.4382	.5818
27														.1791	.3986	.5523
28														.1224	.3571	.5214
29														.0627	.3134	.4888
30														.0000	.2674	.4546
35															.0000	.2555
40																.0000

5.25%

AGE OF LOAN	ORIGINAL TERM IN YEARS															
	1	2	3	4	5	6	7	8	9	10	15	20	25	30	35	40
1	.0000	.5131	.6840	.7693	.8204	.8544	.8786	.8967	.9107	.9219	.9550	.9709	.9801	.9859	.9898	.9925
2		.0000	.3509	.5262	.6311	.7009	.7506	.7878	.8166	.8396	.9075	.9403	.9592	.9710	.9790	.9845
3			.0000	.2700	.4317	.5392	.6158	.6731	.7175	.7528	.8575	.9081	.9371	.9554	.9676	.9761
4				.0000	.2215	.3688	.4737	.5522	.6130	.6614	.8048	.8741	.9138	.9389	.9556	.9673
5					.0000	.1892	.3240	.4248	.5029	.5651	.7492	.8382	.8893	.9215	.9430	.9580
6						.0000	.1663	.2905	.3869	.4636	.6907	.8005	.8635	.9032	.9297	.9482
7							.0000	.1491	.2646	.3566	.6290	.7607	.8362	.8839	.9157	.9379
8								.0000	.1358	.2439	.5641	.7188	.8075	.8635	.9010	.9270
9									.0000	.1252	.4956	.6746	.7773	.8421	.8854	.9155
10										.0000	.4234	.6280	.7454	.8195	.8690	.9034
11											.3474	.5790	.7119	.7957	.8517	.8907
12											.2672	.5273	.6765	.7706	.8335	.8773
13											.1828	.4728	.6392	.7441	.8143	.8631
14											.0938	.4154	.5999	.7163	.7941	.8482
15											.0000	.3549	.5585	.6869	.7728	.8325
16												.2912	.5149	.6560	.7503	.8159
17												.2240	.4689	.6234	.7267	.7985
18												.1532	.4205	.5890	.7017	.7801
19												.0786	.3694	.5528	.6755	.7607
20												.0000	.3156	.5147	.6478	.7403
21													.2589	.4745	.6186	.7188
22													.1992	.4321	.5879	.6962
23													.1362	.3875	.5555	.6723
24													.0699	.3404	.5213	.6471
25													.0000	.2908	.4854	.6206
26														.2386	.4474	.5926
27														.1836	.4075	.5632
28														.1255	.3654	.5321
29														.0644	.3210	.4994
30														.0000	.2743	.4650
35															.0000	.2628
40																.0000

LOAN PROGRESS CHART

5.50%

AGE OF LOAN	ORIGINAL TERM IN YEARS															
	1	2	3	4	5	6	7	8	9	10	15	20	25	30	35	40
1	.0000	.5137	.6848	.7702	.8213	.8553	.8796	.8977	.9117	.9228	.9558	.9717	.9808	.9865	.9903	.9929
2		.0000	.3518	.5274	.6326	.7025	.7523	.7895	.8184	.8413	.9092	.9419	.9606	.9723	.9801	.9855
3			.0000	.2709	.4332	.5411	.6179	.6753	.7198	.7552	.8599	.9104	.9392	.9573	.9693	.9776
4				.0000	.2225	.3705	.4759	.5547	.6157	.6643	.8079	.8771	.9166	.9414	.9579	.9692
5					.0000	.1903	.3259	.4272	.5057	.5682	.7529	.8419	.8927	.9246	.9458	.9604
6						.0000	.1674	.2925	.3895	.4666	.6948	.8047	.8675	.9069	.9331	.9511
7							.0000	.1503	.2667	.3594	.6334	.7654	.8409	.8882	.9196	.9413
8								.0000	.1370	.2461	.5686	.7240	.8127	.8684	.9054	.9309
9									.0000	.1264	.5001	.6801	.7830	.8475	.8904	.9200
10										.0000	.4278	.6338	.7516	.8254	.8745	.9084
11											.3513	.5849	.7184	.8021	.8577	.8961
12											.2706	.5333	.6833	.7775	.8400	.8832
13											.1853	.4787	.6463	.7514	.8213	.8696
14											.0952	.4210	.6072	.7239	.8016	.8551
15											.0000	.3601	.5658	.6949	.7807	.8399
16												.2958	.5222	.6642	.7586	.8238
17												.2278	.4761	.6318	.7353	.8068
18												.1560	.4273	.5976	.7107	.7888
19												.0801	.3759	.5614	.6847	.7698
20												.0000	.3215	.5232	.6572	.7498
21													.2641	.4828	.6282	.7286
22													.2034	.4402	.5976	.7062
23													.1393	.3951	.5652	.6826
24													.0715	.3475	.5310	.6576
25													.0000	.2973	.4948	.6312
26														.2441	.4566	.6034
27														.1880	.4163	.5739
28														.1288	.3737	.5428
29														.0661	.3287	.5100
30														.0000	.2811	.4752
35															.0000	.2700
40																.0000

5.75%

AGE OF LOAN	1	2	3	4	5	6	7	8	9	10	15	20	25	30	35	40
1	.0000	.5143	.6856	.7711	.8223	.8563	.8805	.8986	.9126	.9238	.9567	.9725	.9815	.9871	.9908	.9934
2		.0000	.3526	.5286	.6340	.7041	.7540	.7912	.8201	.8431	.9109	.9434	.9620	.9735	.9811	.9864
3			.0000	.2719	.4347	.5429	.6200	.6775	.7221	.7576	.8623	.9126	.9412	.9591	.9709	.9789
4				.0000	.2236	.3722	.4780	.5571	.6183	.6671	.8109	.8800	.9193	.9438	.9600	.9711
5					.0000	.1914	.3277	.4296	.5084	.5712	.7565	.8455	.8961	.9276	.9485	.9628
6						.0000	.1686	.2945	.3920	.4697	.6989	.8089	.8714	.9105	.9363	.9539
7							.0000	.1515	.2688	.3622	.6378	.7701	.8454	.8923	.9233	.9446
8								.0000	.1382	.2483	.5731	.7291	.8178	.8731	.9097	.9347
9									.0000	.1277	.5047	.6856	.7885	.8528	.8952	.9242
10										.0000	.4321	.6396	.7576	.8312	.8798	.9131
11											.3553	.5909	.7248	.8084	.8636	.9014
12											.2740	.5392	.6901	.7842	.8464	.8890
13											.1878	.4846	.6533	.7586	.8281	.8758
14											.0966	.4267	.6144	.7315	.8088	.8618
15											.0000	.3653	.5731	.7028	.7884	.8471
16												.3004	.5294	.6723	.7667	.8314
17												.2316	.4832	.6401	.7438	.8148
18												.1588	.4342	.6060	.7195	.7973
19												.0817	.3823	.5699	.6938	.7787
20												.0000	.3274	.5316	.6665	.7590
21													.2692	.4911	.6377	.7382
22													.2076	.4482	.6071	.7161
23													.1423	.4028	.5748	.6927
24													.0732	.3546	.5405	.6679
25													.0000	.3037	.5042	.6417
26														.2497	.4658	.6139
27														.1925	.4251	.5845
28														.1320	.3820	.5534
29														.0679	.3364	.5204
30														.0000	.2880	.4855
35															.0000	.2773
40																.0000

LOAN PROGRESS CHART

6.00%

AGE OF LOAN	ORIGINAL TERM IN YEARS															
	1	2	3	4	5	6	7	8	9	10	15	20	25	30	35	40
1	.0000	.5150	.6864	.7720	.8232	.8572	.8815	.8996	.9136	.9247	.9576	.9733	.9822	.9877	.9913	.9938
2		.0000	.3535	.5299	.6355	.7057	.7556	.7929	.8218	.8448	.9126	.9450	.9633	.9747	.9821	.9872
3			.0000	.2729	.4362	.5448	.6220	.6797	.7244	.7600	.8647	.9149	.9432	.9608	.9724	.9802
4				.0000	.2246	.3739	.4802	.5596	.6210	.6699	.8140	.8829	.9219	.9461	.9620	.9728
5					.0000	.1926	.3296	.4320	.5112	.5743	.7601	.8490	.8993	.9305	.9510	.9650
6						.0000	.1697	.2965	.3946	.4727	.7029	.8130	.8753	.9140	.9393	.9566
7							.0000	.1527	.2709	.3649	.6421	.7748	.8498	.8964	.9270	.9477
8								.0000	.1395	.2505	.5776	.7342	.8228	.8777	.9138	.9383
9									.0000	.1290	.5092	.6911	.7940	.8579	.8998	.9283
10										.0000	.4365	.6453	.7635	.8369	.8850	.9177
11											.3593	.5967	.7311	.8145	.8692	.9064
12											.2774	.5452	.6968	.7908	.8525	.8945
13											.1904	.4904	.6602	.7656	.8347	.8818
14											.0980	.4323	.6215	.7389	.8159	.8683
15											.0000	.3706	.5803	.7105	.7959	.8540
16												.3051	.5367	.6804	.7746	.8388
17												.2355	.4903	.6484	.7521	.8226
18												.1616	.4410	.6144	.7281	.8055
19												.0832	.3888	.5783	.7027	.7873
20												.0000	.3333	.5400	.6757	.7680
21													.2743	.4994	.6470	.7475
22													.2118	.4562	.6166	.7257
23													.1454	.4104	.5843	.7026
24													.0749	.3618	.5500	.6781
25													.0000	.3101	.5136	.6520
26														.2553	.4749	.6244
27														.1971	.4339	.5950
28														.1353	.3903	.5638
29														.0697	.3440	.5307
30														.0000	.2949	.4956
35															.0000	.2846
40																.0000

6.25%

AGE OF LOAN	1	2	3	4	5	6	7	8	9	10	15	20	25	30	35	40
1	.0000	.5156	.6872	.7729	.8241	.8582	.8824	.9005	.9145	.9257	.9584	.9741	.9829	.9883	.9918	.9942
2		.0000	.3543	.5311	.6369	.7073	.7573	.7946	.8235	.8465	.9142	.9464	.9646	.9758	.9831	.9880
3			.0000	.2738	.4377	.5466	.6241	.6820	.7267	.7623	.8671	.9170	.9452	.9625	.9738	.9815
4				.0000	.2257	.3756	.4823	.5620	.6237	.6727	.8170	.8858	.9245	.9484	.9640	.9745
5					.0000	.1937	.3315	.4344	.5140	.5773	.7636	.8525	.9025	.9334	.9535	.9671
6						.0000	.1709	.2985	.3972	.4758	.7069	.8170	.8791	.9174	.9423	.9592
7							.0000	.1539	.2730	.3677	.6465	.7793	.8542	.9003	.9304	.9507
8								.0000	.1407	.2527	.5821	.7392	.8276	.8822	.9178	.9418
9									.0000	.1303	.5137	.6965	.7994	.8629	.9043	.9322
10										.0000	.4409	.6510	.7694	.8424	.8900	.9221
11											.3633	.6026	.7374	.8205	.8747	.9113
12											.2808	.5511	.7033	.7973	.8585	.8998
13											.1930	.4963	.6671	.7725	.8412	.8875
14											.0995	.4379	.6286	.7461	.8228	.8745
15											.0000	.3758	.5875	.7181	.8032	.8606
16												.3097	.5438	.6883	.7824	.8459
17												.2394	.4974	.6565	.7602	.8302
18												.1645	.4479	.6227	.7366	.8135
19												.0848	.3952	.5867	.7114	.7957
20												.0000	.3392	.5484	.6847	.7767
21													.2795	.5076	.6562	.7566
22													.2160	.4642	.6259	.7351
23													.1485	.4180	.5937	.7123
24													.0765	.3689	.5594	.6880
25													.0000	.3166	.5229	.6621
26														.2609	.4840	.6346
27														.2016	.4426	.6053
28														.1386	.3986	.5741
29														.0714	.3517	.5410
30														.0000	.3019	.5056
35															.0000	.2919
40																.0000

LOAN PROGRESS CHART

6.50%

AGE OF LOAN	ORIGINAL TERM IN YEARS															
	1	2	3	4	5	6	7	8	9	10	15	20	25	30	35	40
1	.0000	.5162	.6880	.7738	.8251	.8591	.8834	.9015	.9155	.9266	.9593	.9748	.9835	.9888	.9923	.9946
2		.0000	.3552	.5324	.6384	.7088	.7589	.7963	.8253	.8482	.9158	.9479	.9659	.9769	.9840	.9888
3			.0000	.2748	.4392	.5485	.6262	.6842	.7290	.7647	.8694	.9192	.9471	.9642	.9752	.9826
4				.0000	.2267	.3774	.4845	.5645	.6263	.6755	.8200	.8886	.9270	.9506	.9659	.9761
5					.0000	.1948	.3333	.4368	.5167	.5803	.7672	.8559	.9056	.9361	.9558	.9691
6						.0000	.1721	.3005	.3998	.4788	.7108	.8210	.8828	.9207	.9452	.9616
7							.0000	.1551	.2751	.3705	.6507	.7838	.8584	.9042	.9338	.9536
8								.0000	.1420	.2549	.5866	.7441	.8324	.8866	.9216	.9451
9									.0000	.1316	.5182	.7018	.8047	.8678	.9086	.9360
10										.0000	.4452	.6566	.7751	.8478	.8948	.9263
11											.3673	.6084	.7435	.8264	.8800	.9159
12											.2842	.5570	.7099	.8036	.8642	.9049
13											.1956	.5021	.6739	.7793	.8474	.8931
14											.1009	.4435	.6356	.7533	.8295	.8805
15											.0000	.3811	.5946	.7256	.8103	.8671
16												.3144	.5510	.6960	.7899	.8528
17												.2433	.5044	.6645	.7681	.8375
18												.1674	.4547	.6309	.7448	.8212
19												.0864	.4017	.5950	.7200	.8038
20												.0000	.3451	.5567	.6935	.7852
21													.2847	.5158	.6653	.7654
22													.2203	.4722	.6352	.7443
23													.1516	.4257	.6030	.7218
24													.0782	.3760	.5687	.6977
25													.0000	.3230	.5321	.6721
26														.2665	.4930	.6447
27														.2062	.4513	.6155
28														.1419	.4069	.5843
29														.0732	.3594	.5511
30														.0000	.3088	.5156
35															.0000	.2992
40																.0000

6.75%

AGE OF LOAN	1	2	3	4	5	6	7	8	9	10	15	20	25	30	35	40
1	.0000	.5168	.6888	.7746	.8260	.8601	.8843	.9024	.9164	.9275	.9601	.9755	.9841	.9893	.9927	.9949
2		.0000	.3560	.5336	.6398	.7104	.7606	.7980	.8269	.8499	.9174	.9493	.9671	.9779	.9849	.9895
3			.0000	.2758	.4407	.5503	.6282	.6863	.7313	.7670	.8717	.9213	.9489	.9657	.9766	.9837
4				.0000	.2278	.3791	.4866	.5669	.6290	.6783	.8229	.8913	.9295	.9527	.9676	.9776
5					.0000	.1959	.3352	.4392	.5195	.5834	.7707	.8593	.9087	.9388	.9581	.9709
6						.0000	.1732	.3025	.4024	.4818	.7148	.8250	.8864	.9238	.9479	.9639
7							.0000	.1563	.2772	.3733	.6550	.7883	.8626	.9079	.9370	.9563
8								.0000	.1433	.2571	.5911	.7491	.8371	.8908	.9253	.9482
9									.0000	.1329	.5227	.7071	.8099	.8725	.9128	.9395
10										.0000	.4496	.6622	.7808	.8530	.8994	.9302
11											.3713	.6142	.7496	.8321	.8851	.9203
12											.2877	.5628	.7163	.8098	.8698	.9097
13											.1981	.5079	.6806	.7859	.8535	.8984
14											.1024	.4491	.6425	.7603	.8360	.8863
15											.0000	.3863	.6017	.7330	.8173	.8733
16												.3191	.5581	.7037	.7972	.8594
17												.2472	.5114	.6724	.7758	.8445
18												.1703	.4615	.6389	.7529	.8287
19												.0880	.4081	.6032	.7284	.8117
20												.0000	.3510	.5649	.7022	.7935
21													.2899	.5239	.6742	.7741
22													.2246	.4801	.6442	.7533
23													.1547	.4332	.6122	.7311
24													.0800	.3831	.5779	.7073
25													.0000	.3295	.5412	.6818
26														.2722	.5020	.6546
27														.2108	.4600	.6255
28														.1452	.4151	.5944
29														.0751	.3671	.5611
30														.0000	.3157	.5255
35															.0000	.3065
40																.0000

LOAN PROGRESS CHART
7.00%

AGE OF LOAN	ORIGINAL TERM IN YEARS

AGE OF LOAN	1	2	3	4	5	6	7	8	9	10	15	20	25	30	35	40
1	.0000	.5174	.6896	.7755	.8269	.8610	.8853	.9033	.9173	.9284	.9609	.9762	.9847	.9898	.9931	.9953
2		.0000	.3569	.5348	.6413	.7120	.7622	.7997	.8286	.8516	.9190	.9507	.9683	.9789	.9857	.9902
3			.0000	.2767	.4423	.5522	.6303	.6885	.7335	.7693	.8740	.9233	.9507	.9673	.9778	.9848
4				.0000	.2288	.3808	.4888	.5693	.6316	.6810	.8258	.8940	.9318	.9547	.9693	.9790
5					.0000	.1970	.3371	.4415	.5223	.5864	.7741	.8626	.9116	.9413	.9602	.9727
6						.0000	.1744	.3045	.4050	.4849	.7187	.8288	.8899	.9269	.9505	.9660
7							.0000	.1576	.2793	.3760	.6593	.7927	.8667	.9115	.9400	.9589
8								.0000	.1445	.2593	.5955	.7539	.8417	.8949	.9288	.9512
9									.0000	.1342	.5272	.7123	.8150	.8772	.9168	.9429
10										.0000	.4539	.6677	.7863	.8581	.9039	.9341
11											.3754	.6199	.7556	.8377	.8901	.9246
12											.2911	.5687	.7226	.8158	.8752	.9144
13											.2008	.5137	.6873	.7923	.8593	.9035
14											.1039	.4547	.6494	.7672	.8423	.8918
15											.0000	.3915	.6087	.7402	.8240	.8792
16												.3238	.5651	.7112	.8044	.8658
17												.2511	.5184	.6802	.7834	.8514
18												.1732	.4683	.6469	.7609	.8359
19												.0896	.4146	.6113	.7367	.8193
20												.0000	.3569	.5730	.7108	.8015
21													.2952	.5320	.6830	.7825
22													.2289	.4880	.6532	.7620
23													.1579	.4408	.6212	.7401
24													.0817	.3902	.5870	.7166
25													.0000	.3360	.5502	.6914
26														.2778	.5108	.6643
27														.2155	.4686	.6354
28														.1486	.4233	.6043
29														.0769	.3747	.5710
30														.0000	.3226	.5352
35															.0000	.3138
40																.0000

7.25%

AGE OF LOAN	1	2	3	4	5	6	7	8	9	10	15	20	25	30	35	40
1	.0000	.5181	.6904	.7764	.8278	.8619	.8862	.9043	.9182	.9293	.9617	.9769	.9853	.9903	.9935	.9956
2		.0000	.3577	.5361	.6427	.7135	.7638	.8013	.8303	.8533	.9205	.9521	.9695	.9799	.9865	.9909
3			.0000	.2777	.4438	.5540	.6323	.6907	.7358	.7716	.8763	.9254	.9524	.9687	.9790	.9858
4				.0000	.2299	.3825	.4909	.5718	.6342	.6838	.8287	.8967	.9342	.9567	.9710	.9803
5					.0000	.1982	.3390	.4439	.5250	.5894	.7776	.8658	.9145	.9438	.9623	.9744
6						.0000	.1756	.3065	.4076	.4879	.7226	.8327	.8934	.9299	.9530	.9681
7							.0000	.1588	.2815	.3788	.6635	.7970	.8707	.9150	.9430	.9613
8								.0000	.1458	.2616	.6000	.7587	.8463	.8989	.9322	.9540
9									.0000	.1355	.5317	.7175	.8200	.8817	.9207	.9461
10										.0000	.4583	.6732	.7918	.8631	.9082	.9377
11											.3794	.6256	.7615	.8432	.8949	.9286
12											.2946	.5745	.7289	.8217	.8805	.9189
13											.2034	.5195	.6938	.7987	.8650	.9084
14											.1054	.4603	.6562	.7739	.8484	.8971
15											.0000	.3968	.6157	.7473	.8306	.8850
16												.3285	.5721	.7187	.8114	.8720
17												.2550	.5254	.6879	.7908	.8580
18												.1761	.4751	.6548	.7686	.8429
19												.0912	.4210	.6193	.7448	.8267
20												.0000	.3629	.5811	.7191	.8093
21													.3004	.5400	.6916	.7906
22													.2332	.4958	.6620	.7705
23													.1610	.4484	.6302	.7489
24													.0834	.3973	.5959	.7257
25													.0000	.3425	.5592	.7007
26														.2835	.5196	.6739
27														.2201	.4771	.6450
28														.1520	.4315	.6140
29														.0787	.3823	.5807
30														.0000	.3296	.5449
35															.0000	.3211
40																.0000

LOAN PROGRESS CHART
7.50%

AGE OF LOAN	ORIGINAL TERM IN YEARS															
	1	2	3	4	5	6	7	8	9	10	15	20	25	30	35	40
1	.0000	.5187	.6913	.7773	.8287	.8629	.8871	.9052	.9191	.9302	.9625	.9776	.9858	.9908	.9939	.9959
2		.0000	.3585	.5373	.6442	.7151	.7655	.8030	.8320	.8550	.9221	.9534	.9706	.9808	.9873	.9915
3			.0000	.2787	.4453	.5558	.6344	.6929	.7381	.7739	.8785	.9273	.9541	.9701	.9802	.9867
4				.0000	.2310	.3842	.4931	.5742	.6368	.6865	.8316	.8993	.9364	.9586	.9725	.9816
5					.0000	.1993	.3409	.4463	.5278	.5924	.7810	.8690	.9173	.9462	.9643	.9760
6						.0000	.1768	.3085	.4102	.4909	.7264	.8364	.8967	.9328	.9554	.9700
7							.0000	.1600	.2836	.3816	.6677	.8013	.8746	.9183	.9458	.9636
8								.0000	.1471	.2638	.6044	.7634	.8507	.9028	.9355	.9567
9									.0000	.1368	.5362	.7226	.8249	.8860	.9244	.9492
10										.0000	.4626	.6787	.7972	.8679	.9124	.9412
11											.3834	.6313	.7673	.8485	.8995	.9325
12											.2980	.5802	.7350	.8275	.8855	.9231
13											.2060	.5252	.7003	.8049	.8705	.9131
14											.1069	.4659	.6629	.7805	.8544	.9022
15											.0000	.4020	.6226	.7543	.8370	.8905
16												.3332	.5791	.7260	.8182	.8779
17												.2590	.5323	.6955	.7979	.8643
18												.1790	.4818	.6626	.7761	.8497
19												.0929	.4274	.6272	.7526	.8339
20												.0000	.3688	.5891	.7273	.8169
21													.3056	.5479	.7000	.7986
22													.2376	.5036	.6706	.7788
23													.1642	.4559	.6390	.7575
24													.0852	.4044	.6048	.7346
25													.0000	.3489	.5680	.7099
26														.2892	.5284	.6833
27														.2248	.4856	.6546
28														.1554	.4396	.6236
29														.0806	.3900	.5903
30														.0000	.3365	.5544
35															.0000	.3284
40																.0000

7.75%

AGE OF LOAN	1	2	3	4	5	6	7	8	9	10	15	20	25	30	35	40
1	.0000	.5193	.6921	.7782	.8296	.8638	.8880	.9061	.9200	.9311	.9633	.9782	.9864	.9912	.9942	.9962
2		.0000	.3594	.5385	.6456	.7166	.7671	.8046	.8336	.8566	.9236	.9547	.9717	.9817	.9880	.9920
3			.0000	.2797	.4468	.5577	.6364	.6950	.7403	.7762	.8807	.9293	.9558	.9715	.9813	.9876
4				.0000	.2320	.3859	.4952	.5766	.6395	.6893	.8344	.9018	.9386	.9604	.9740	.9827
5					.0000	.2004	.3427	.4487	.5305	.5954	.7843	.8722	.9201	.9485	.9662	.9775
6						.0000	.1780	.3105	.4128	.4940	.7303	.8401	.9000	.9356	.9577	.9719
7							.0000	.1613	.2857	.3844	.6719	.8055	.8784	.9216	.9485	.9658
8								.0000	.1484	.2660	.6088	.7681	.8550	.9065	.9386	.9592
9									.0000	.1381	.5406	.7277	.8297	.8903	.9279	.9521
10										.0000	.4670	.6841	.8025	.8727	.9164	.9445
11											.3874	.6369	.7730	.8537	.9039	.9362
12											.3015	.5860	.7411	.8331	.8904	.9272
13											.2086	.5309	.7067	.8110	.8759	.9175
14											.1084	.4715	.6695	.7870	.8601	.9071
15											.0000	.4073	.6294	.7611	.8431	.8958
16												.3379	.5860	.7331	.8248	.8836
17												.2629	.5391	.7029	.8049	.8704
18												.1820	.4885	.6703	.7835	.8562
19												.0945	.4338	.6350	.7604	.8408
20												.0000	.3747	.5970	.7354	.8242
21													.3109	.5558	.7083	.8062
22													.2419	.5114	.6792	.7869
23													.1674	.4633	.6476	.7659
24													.0869	.4115	.6136	.7433
25													.0000	.3554	.5768	.7188
26														.2949	.5370	.6924
27														.2295	.4941	.6639
28														.1588	.4477	.6331
29														.0825	.3975	.5998
30														.0000	.3434	.5638
35															.0000	.3357
40																.0000

LOAN PROGRESS CHART

8.00%

AGE OF LOAN	ORIGINAL TERM IN YEARS

AGE OF LOAN	1	2	3	4	5	6	7	8	9	10	15	20	25	30	35	40
1	.0000	.5199	.6929	.7791	.8306	.8647	.8890	.9070	.9209	.9319	.9640	.9789	.9869	.9916	.9946	.9964
2		.0000	.3602	.5398	.6471	.7182	.7687	.8063	.8353	.8582	.9251	.9560	.9727	.9826	.9887	.9926
3			.0000	.2806	.4483	.5595	.6384	.6972	.7425	.7784	.8829	.9312	.9574	.9728	.9823	.9884
4				.0000	.2331	.3877	.4974	.5791	.6421	.6920	.8372	.9043	.9407	.9622	.9754	.9839
5					.0000	.2016	.3446	.4511	.5333	.5984	.7877	.8753	.9227	.9507	.9680	.9790
6						.0000	.1792	.3126	.4155	.4970	.7341	.8438	.9032	.9383	.9599	.9736
7							.0000	.1625	.2879	.3872	.6760	.8097	.8821	.9248	.9511	.9679
8								.0000	.1497	.2683	.6131	.7727	.8592	.9102	.9416	.9617
9									.0000	.1395	.5451	.7327	.8345	.8944	.9314	.9549
10										.0000	.4713	.6894	.8076	.8772	.9202	.9476
11											.3915	.6425	.7786	.8587	.9082	.9397
12											.3050	.5917	.7471	.8386	.8952	.9311
13											.2113	.5367	.7130	.8169	.8810	.9218
14											.1099	.4771	.6761	.7933	.8657	.9118
15											.0000	.4125	.6361	.7678	.8491	.9009
16												.3426	.5929	.7402	.8312	.8891
17												.2669	.5460	.7103	.8118	.8763
18												.1849	.4952	.6779	.7907	.8625
19												.0962	.4402	.6428	.7679	.8475
20												.0000	.3806	.6048	.7432	.8313
21													.3162	.5636	.7165	.8137
22													.2463	.5191	.6875	.7947
23													.1707	.4708	.6562	.7741
24													.0887	.4185	.6222	.7517
25													.0000	.3619	.5854	.7276
26														.3006	.5456	.7014
27														.2342	.5024	.6731
28														.1622	.4557	.6423
29														.0844	.4051	.6091
30														.0000	.3503	.5731
35															.0000	.3429
40																.0000

8.25%

AGE OF LOAN	1	2	3	4	5	6	7	8	9	10	15	20	25	30	35	40
1	.0000	.5205	.6937	.7799	.8315	.8656	.8899	.9079	.9218	.9328	.9648	.9795	.9874	.9921	.9949	.9967
2		.0000	.3611	.5410	.6485	.7197	.7703	.8079	.8369	.8599	.9265	.9572	.9738	.9834	.9893	.9931
3			.0000	.2816	.4498	.5614	.6405	.6993	.7447	.7807	.8850	.9330	.9589	.9741	.9833	.9892
4				.0000	.2342	.3894	.4995	.5815	.6447	.6947	.8399	.9068	.9428	.9639	.9768	.9849
5					.0000	.2027	.3465	.4535	.5360	.6013	.7910	.8783	.9253	.9528	.9697	.9803
6						.0000	.1804	.3146	.4181	.5000	.7378	.8473	.9064	.9409	.9620	.9753
7							.0000	.1638	.2900	.3900	.6801	.8138	.8858	.9278	.9536	.9699
8								.0000	.1510	.2705	.6175	.7773	.8634	.9137	.9445	.9639
9									.0000	.1408	.5495	.7377	.8391	.8984	.9347	.9575
10										.0000	.4756	.6947	.8127	.8817	.9240	.9506
11											.3955	.6480	.7841	.8636	.9123	.9430
12											.3085	.5974	.7530	.8440	.8997	.9348
13											.2140	.5423	.7193	.8227	.8860	.9259
14											.1114	.4826	.6826	.7995	.8711	.9162
15											.0000	.4178	.6428	.7744	.8550	.9058
16												.3474	.5996	.7471	.8374	.8944
17												.2709	.5528	.7175	.8184	.8820
18												.1879	.5018	.6853	.7977	.8685
19												.0978	.4466	.6504	.7753	.8540
20												.0000	.3866	.6125	.7509	.8381
21													.3214	.5714	.7245	.8209
22													.2507	.5267	.6957	.8023
23													.1739	.4782	.6646	.7820
24													.0905	.4255	.6307	.7600
25													.0000	.3683	.5939	.7361
26														.3063	.5540	.7102
27														.2389	.5107	.6820
28														.1657	.4637	.6515
29														.0862	.4126	.6183
30														.0000	.3572	.5822
35															.0000	.3501
40																.0000

LOAN PROGRESS CHART

8.50%

AGE OF LOAN	1	2	3	4	5	6	7	8	9	10	15	20	25	30	35	40
							ORIGINAL TERM IN YEARS									
1	.0000	.5212	.6945	.7808	.8324	.8665	.8908	.9088	.9227	.9337	.9655	.9801	.9879	.9924	.9952	.9969
2		.0000	.3619	.5422	.6499	.7213	.7719	.8095	.8385	.8615	.9280	.9584	.9747	.9842	.9900	.9935
3			.0000	.2826	.4514	.5632	.6425	.7015	.7469	.7829	.8871	.9349	.9604	.9753	.9843	.9899
4				.0000	.2352	.3911	.5017	.5839	.6473	.6974	.8426	.9092	.9448	.9655	.9781	.9859
5					.0000	.2038	.3484	.4559	.5388	.6043	.7942	.8813	.9279	.9549	.9713	.9816
6						.0000	.1816	.3166	.4207	.5030	.7416	.8509	.9094	.9434	.9640	.9768
7							.0000	.1650	.2921	.3928	.6842	.8178	.8893	.9308	.9560	.9717
8								.0000	.1523	.2728	.6218	.7818	.8674	.9171	.9473	.9661
9									.0000	.1422	.5539	.7426	.8436	.9022	.9378	.9600
10										.0000	.4800	.6999	.8177	.8860	.9275	.9534
11											.3995	.6535	.7895	.8684	.9163	.9462
12											.3119	.6030	.7588	.8492	.9041	.9384
13											.2166	.5480	.7254	.8283	.8908	.9298
14											.1129	.4881	.6890	.8056	.8764	.9205
15											.0000	.4230	.6495	.7808	.8606	.9104
16												.3521	.6064	.7539	.8435	.8994
17												.2749	.5595	.7246	.8248	.8874
18												.1909	.5085	.6927	.8046	.8744
19												.0995	.4529	.6580	.7825	.8602
20												.0000	.3925	.6202	.7584	.8448
21													.3267	.5790	.7323	.8279
22													.2551	.5343	.7038	.8096
23													.1771	.4855	.6728	.7897
24													.0923	.4325	.6391	.7680
25													.0000	.3748	.6024	.7445
26														.3120	.5624	7188
27														.2436	.5189	.6908
28														.1692	.4716	.6604
29														.0882	.4201	.6273
30														.0000	.3640	.5913
35															.0000	.3573
40																.0000

8.75%

AGE OF LOAN	1	2	3	4	5	6	7	8	9	10	15	20	25	30	35	40
1	.0000	.5218	.6953	.7817	.8333	.8674	.8917	.9097	.9236	.9345	.9662	.9807	.9884	.9928	.9955	.9971
2		.0000	.3628	.5435	.6514	.7228	.7735	.8111	.8401	.8631	.9294	.9596	.9757	.9850	.9905	.9940
3			.0000	.2836	.4529	.5650	.6445	.7036	.7491	.7851	.8892	.9366	.9619	.9764	.9852	.9906
4				.0000	.2363	.3928	.5038	.5863	.6498	.7001	.8453	.9116	.9468	.9671	.9793	.9868
5					.0000	.2050	.3503	.4583	.5415	.6073	.7975	.8842	.9303	.9569	.9729	.9828
6						.0000	.1828	.3186	.4233	.5060	.7453	.8543	.9124	.9458	.9659	.9783
7							.0000	.1663	.2943	.3956	.6883	.8218	.8928	.9336	.9583	.9735
8								.0000	.1536	.2750	.6261	.7862	.8714	.9204	.9499	.9682
9									.0000	.1435	.5583	.7474	.8481	.9060	.9408	.9624
10										.0000	.4843	.7051	.8226	.8902	.9309	.9561
11											.4035	.6590	.7948	.8730	.9201	.9492
12											.3154	.6086	.7645	.8543	.9083	.9417
13											.2193	.5536	.7314	.8338	.8955	.9336
14											.1144	.4936	.6954	.8115	.8814	.9246
15											.0000	.4282	.6560	.7871	.8661	.9149
16												.3568	.6130	.7606	.8494	.9043
17												.2789	.5662	.7316	.8311	.8927
18												.1939	.5150	.6999	.8112	.8800
19												.1012	.4593	.6654	.7895	.8662
20												.0000	.3984	.6277	.7658	.8512
21													.3320	.5866	.7399	.8347
22													.2595	.5418	.7117	.8168
23													.1804	.4928	.6809	.7972
24													.0941	.4395	.6473	.7759
25													.0000	.3812	.6107	.7526
26														.3176	.5707	.7272
27														.2483	.5271	.6994
28														.1726	.4795	.6692
29														.0901	.4275	.6362
30														.0000	.3709	.6002
35															.0000	.3645
40																.0000

LOAN PROGRESS CHART

9.00%

AGE OF LOAN	ORIGINAL TERM IN YEARS															
	1	2	3	4	5	6	7	8	9	10	15	20	25	30	35	40
1	.0000	.5224	.6961	.7826	.8342	.8684	.8926	.9106	.9244	.9354	.9669	.9813	.9888	.9932	.9957	.9973
2		.0000	.3636	.5447	.6528	.7244	.7751	.8127	.8417	.8647	.9308	.9608	.9766	.9857	.9911	.9944
3			.0000	.2846	.4544	.5668	.6465	.7057	.7513	.7873	.8912	.9384	.9633	.9775	.9860	.9912
4				.0000	.2374	.3946	.5060	.5887	.6524	.7028	.8480	.9139	.9487	.9686	.9804	.9877
5					.0000	.2061	.3522	.4607	.5442	.6102	.8007	.8871	.9327	.9588	.9744	.9839
6						.0000	.1840	.3207	.4259	.5090	.7489	.8577	.9153	.9481	.9677	.9797
7							.0000	.1675	.2964	.3984	.6923	.8257	.8962	.9364	.9604	.9751
8								.0000	.1549	.2773	.6304	.7906	.8753	.9236	.9525	.9701
9									.0000	.1449	.5627	.7522	.8524	.9096	.9437	.9647
10										.0000	.4886	.7103	.8274	.8943	.9342	.9587
11											.4076	.6644	.8000	.8775	.9238	.9521
12											.3190	.6141	.7701	.8592	.9124	.9449
13											.2220	.5592	.7374	.8392	.8999	.9371
14											.1160	.4991	.7016	.8173	.8863	.9285
15											.0000	.4334	.6625	.7933	.8714	.9192
16												.3616	.6197	.7671	.8551	.9089
17												.2829	.5728	.7384	.8372	.8977
18												.1969	.5216	.7070	.8177	.8854
19												.1029	.4656	.6727	.7963	.8720
20												.0000	.4043	.6352	.7730	.8573
21													.3372	.5941	.7474	.8413
22													.2639	.5492	.7195	.8237
23													.1837	.5001	.6889	.8045
24													.0960	.4464	.6555	.7835
25													.0000	.3876	.6189	.7605
26														.3233	.5789	.7354
27														.2530	.5351	.7079
28														.1761	.4873	.6778
29														.0920	.4349	.6449
30														.0000	.3777	.6089
35															.0000	.3716
40																.0000

9.25%

AGE OF LOAN	1	2	3	4	5	6	7	8	9	10	15	20	25	30	35	40
1	.0000	.5230	.6969	.7834	.8351	.8693	.8935	.9114	.9253	.9362	.9676	.9818	.9893	.9935	.9960	.9975
2		.0000	.3645	.5459	.6542	.7259	.7766	.8143	.8433	.8662	.9322	.9619	.9775	.9864	.9916	.9948
3			.0000	.2855	.4559	.5687	.6485	.7079	.7535	.7895	.8933	.9401	.9647	.9786	.9868	.9918
4				.0000	.2384	.3963	.5081	.5911	.6550	.7054	.8506	.9161	.9505	.9700	.9815	.9885
5					.0000	.2073	.3541	.4631	.5469	.6132	.8039	.8899	.9351	.9606	.9758	.9849
6						.0000	.1852	.3227	.4285	.5121	.7526	.8611	.9181	.9504	.9694	.9810
7							.0000	.1688	.2986	.4012	.6963	.8295	.8994	.9391	.9625	.9767
8								.0000	.1562	.2796	.6347	.7949	.8790	.9267	.9549	.9720
9									.0000	.1462	.5671	.7570	.8566	.9131	.9465	.9668
10										.0000	.4929	.7153	.8321	.8982	.9374	.9611
11											.4116	.6697	.8052	.8819	.9273	.9548
12											.3225	.6197	.7757	.8640	.9163	.9480
13											.2247	.5648	.7433	.8444	.9042	.9405
14											.1175	.5046	.7078	.8229	.8910	.9323
15											.0000	.4386	.6689	.7993	.8765	.9233
16												.3663	.6262	.7735	.8606	.9134
17												.2870	.5794	.7451	.8431	.9025
18												.2000	.5281	.7140	.8240	.8906
19												.1046	.4718	.6799	.8030	.8776
20												.0000	.4101	.6426	.7800	.8633
21													.3425	.6016	.7547	.8476
22													.2683	.5566	.7271	.8304
23													.1870	.5073	.6967	.8116
24													.0978	.4533	.6635	.7909
25													.0000	.3940	.6270	.7682
26														.3290	.5870	.7434
27														.2578	.5431	.7161
28														.1796	.4950	.6862
29														.0939	.4423	.6535
30														.0000	.3845	.6175
35															.0000	.3787
40																.0000

LOAN PROGRESS CHART

9.50%

AGE OF LOAN	1	2	3	4	5	6	7	8	9	10	15	20	25	30	35	40
															ORIGINAL TERM IN YEARS	
1	.0000	.5236	.6977	.7843	.8360	.8701	.8944	.9123	.9261	.9370	.9683	.9824	.9897	.9938	.9962	.9977
2		.0000	.3653	.5472	.6556	.7274	.7782	.8159	.8449	.8678	.9335	.9630	.9784	.9871	.9921	.9952
3			.0000	.2865	.4574	.5705	.6506	.7100	.7557	.7917	.8953	.9418	.9660	.9796	.9876	.9924
4				.0000	.2395	.3980	.5102	.5935	.6575	.7081	.8532	.9184	.9523	.9714	.9826	.9893
5					.0000	.2084	.3560	.4655	.5497	.6161	.8070	.8927	.9373	.9624	.9771	.9859
6						.0000	.1864	.3248	.4311	.5151	.7562	.8644	.9208	.9525	.9711	.9822
7							.0000	.1701	.3008	.4040	.7003	.8333	.9027	.9416	.9645	.9782
8								.0000	.1575	.2818	.6389	.7992	.8827	.9297	.9572	.9737
9									.0000	.1476	.5714	.7616	.8608	.9165	.9492	.9688
10										.0000	.4972	.7204	.8367	.9021	.9404	.9634
11											.4156	.6750	.8102	.8862	.9307	.9574
12											.3260	.6251	.7811	.8687	.9201	.9509
13											.2274	.5703	.7491	.8495	.9084	.9437
14											.1191	.5101	.7139	.8284	.8956	.9358
15											.0000	.4438	.6752	.8052	.8814	.9272
16												.3710	.6327	.7797	.8659	.9176
17												.2910	.5859	.7517	.8488	.9071
18												.2030	.5346	.7209	.8301	.8956
19												.1063	.4781	.6870	.8095	.8830
20												.0000	.4160	.6498	.7868	.8690
21													.3478	.6089	.7619	.8537
22													.2727	.5639	.7345	.8369
23													.1903	.5145	.7044	.8184
24													.0996	.4601	.6713	.7981
25													.0000	.4004	.6350	.7758
26														.3347	.5950	.7512
27														.2625	.5510	.7242
28														.1831	.5027	.6945
29														.0959	.4496	.6619
30														.0000	.3912	.6260
35															.0000	.3857
40																.0000

9.75%

AGE OF LOAN	1	2	3	4	5	6	7	8	9	10	15	20	25	30	35	40
1	.0000	.5243	.6985	.7852	.8368	.8710	.8952	.9132	.9270	.9378	.9690	.9829	.9901	.9941	.9965	.9979
2		.0000	.3662	.5484	.6571	.7289	.7798	.8175	.8465	.8694	.9349	.9641	.9793	.9877	.9926	.9955
3			.0000	.2875	.4589	.5723	.6526	.7121	.7578	.7939	.8972	.9434	.9673	.9806	.9883	.9929
4				.0000	.2406	.3997	.5124	.5959	.6601	.7107	.8558	.9205	.9541	.9727	.9836	.9900
5					.0000	.2096	.3579	.4679	.5524	.6191	.8101	.8954	.9395	.9641	.9784	.9869
6						.0000	.1876	.3268	.4337	.5181	.7597	.8676	.9235	.9546	.9727	.9834
7							.0000	.1713	.3029	.4068	.7043	.8371	.9058	.9441	.9663	.9796
8								.0000	.1588	.2841	.6431	.8034	.8863	.9326	.9594	.9753
9									.0000	.1489	.5757	.7662	.8649	.9198	.9517	.9707
10										.0000	.5015	.7253	.8412	.9058	.9433	.9656
11											.4197	.6802	.8151	.8903	.9340	.9599
12											.3295	.6306	.7864	.8733	.9237	.9537
13											.2301	.5758	.7548	.8545	.9124	.9468
14											.1207	.5155	.7199	.8338	.8999	.9392
15											.0000	.4490	.6815	.8110	.8862	.9309
16												.3758	.6391	.7859	.8711	.9217
17												.2950	.5924	.7582	.8544	.9116
18												.2061	.5410	.7277	.8360	.9004
19												.1080	.4843	.6941	.8158	.8881
20												.0000	.4219	.6570	.7935	.8746
21													.3530	.6162	.7689	.8597
22													.2772	.5712	.7418	.8432
23													.1936	.5216	.7120	.8251
24													.1015	.4669	.6791	.8051
25													.0000	.4067	.6428	.7831
26														.3404	.6028	.7588
27														.2672	.5588	.7321
28														.1867	.5103	.7026
29														.0979	.4568	.6701
30														.0000	.3979	.6344
35															.0000	.3927
40																.0000

LOAN PROGRESS CHART
10.00%

AGE OF LOAN	ORIGINAL TERM IN YEARS															
	1	2	3	4	5	6	7	8	9	10	15	20	25	30	35	40
1	.0000	.5249	.6993	.7860	.8377	.8719	.8961	.9140	.9278	.9387	.9697	.9835	.9905	.9944	.9967	.9980
2		.0000	.3670	.5496	.6585	.7304	.7813	.8191	.8481	.8709	.9362	.9652	.9801	.9883	.9930	.9958
3			.0000	.2885	.4604	.5741	.6546	.7142	.7599	.7960	.8992	.9450	.9685	.9815	.9890	.9934
4				.0000	.2417	.4015	.5145	.5983	.6626	.7133	.8583	.9227	.9557	.9740	.9845	.9907
5					.0000	.2107	.3598	.4703	.5551	.6220	.8132	.8980	.9416	.9657	.9796	.9878
6						.0000	.1888	.3288	.4363	.5210	.7633	.8708	.9261	.9566	.9742	.9845
7							.0000	.1726	.3051	.4096	.7082	.8407	.9088	.9465	.9681	.9809
8								.0000	.1601	.2864	.6473	.8075	.8898	.9353	.9615	.9769
9									.0000	.1503	.5801	.7708	.8688	.9230	.9542	.9725
10										.0000	.5058	.7302	.8456	.9094	.9460	.9676
11											.4237	.6854	.8200	.8943	.9371	.9622
12											.3330	.6360	.7917	.8777	.9272	.9563
13											.2329	.5813	.7604	.8593	.9163	.9497
14											.1222	.5209	.7258	.8391	.9042	.9425
15											.0000	.4542	.6876	.8166	.8908	.9345
16												.3805	.6454	.7919	.8761	.9256
17												.2991	.5988	.7645	.8598	.9158
18												.2091	.5474	.7343	.8418	.9050
19												.1098	.4905	.7009	.8219	.8931
20												.0000	.4277	.6641	.8000	.8799
21													.3583	.6233	.7757	.8654
22													.2816	.5783	.7489	.8493
23													.1969	.5286	.7193	.8315
24													.1034	.4737	.6866	.8119
25													.0000	.4130	.6505	.7902
26														.3460	.6106	.7662
27														.2720	.5665	.7398
28														.1902	.5178	.7105
29														.0998	.4640	.6782
30														.0000	.4046	.6426
35															.0000	.3997
40																.0000

10.25%

AGE OF LOAN	1	2	3	4	5	6	7	8	9	10	15	20	25	30	35	40
1	.0000	.5255	.7001	.7869	.8386	.8728	.8970	.9149	.9286	.9395	.9703	.9840	.9909	.9947	.9969	.9982
2		.0000	.3679	.5509	.6599	.7320	.7829	.8206	.8496	.8724	.9375	.9662	.9809	.9889	.9935	.9961
3			.0000	.2895	.4620	.5760	.6565	.7163	.7621	.7982	.9011	.9465	.9697	.9824	.9896	.9939
4				.0000	.2428	.4032	.5166	.6007	.6651	.7159	.8608	.9248	.9574	.9752	.9854	.9914
5					.0000	.2119	.3617	.4727	.5578	.6249	.8162	.9006	.9437	.9673	.9808	.9886
6						.0000	.1901	.3309	.4389	.5240	.7668	.8739	.9286	.9585	.9756	.9855
7							.0000	.1739	.3073	.4124	.7121	.8443	.9118	.9488	.9699	.9821
8								.0000	.1615	.2887	.6515	.8116	.8933	.9380	.9635	.9783
9									.0000	.1517	.5844	.7753	.8727	.9261	.9565	.9742
10										.0000	.5100	.7351	.8499	.9129	.9487	.9696
11											.4277	.6906	.8247	.8982	.9401	.9644
12											.3366	.6413	.7968	.8820	.9305	.9588
13											.2356	.5867	.7659	.8641	.9200	.9525
14											.1238	.5263	.7316	.8442	.9083	.9456
15											.0000	.4594	.6937	.8221	.8953	.9379
16												.3852	.6517	.7978	.8809	.9293
17												.3031	.6052	.7708	.8650	.9199
18												.2122	.5537	.7408	.8474	.9095
19												.1115	.4967	.7077	.8279	.8979
20												.0000	.4335	.6710	.8063	.8851
21													.3635	.6304	.7824	.8709
22													.2861	.5854	.7559	.8552
23													.2003	.5356	.7266	.8377
24													.1052	.4804	.6941	.8185
25													.0000	.4193	.6581	.7971
26														.3516	.6183	.7735
27														.2767	.5742	.7473
28														.1937	.5253	.7183
29														.1018	.4712	.6862
30														.0000	.4113	.6506
35															.0000	.4066
40																.0000

10.50%

AGE OF LOAN	ORIGINAL TERM IN YEARS															
	1	2	3	4	5	6	7	8	9	10	15	20	25	30	35	40
1	.0000	.5261	.7008	.7877	.8395	.8737	.8978	.9157	.9295	.9403	.9710	.9845	.9913	.9950	.9971	.9983
2		.0000	.3687	.5521	.6613	.7335	.7844	.8222	.8511	.8739	.9388	.9672	.9816	.9894	.9939	.9964
3			.0000	.2905	.4635	.5778	.6585	.7183	.7642	.8003	.9030	.9481	.9709	.9833	.9903	.9943
4				.0000	.2438	.4049	.5188	.6030	.6677	.7185	.8633	.9268	.9590	.9764	.9863	.9919
5					.0000	.2130	.3636	.4750	.5605	.6278	.8192	.9032	.9457	.9688	.9818	.9894
6						.0000	.1913	.3329	.4415	.5270	.7703	.8770	.9310	.9604	.9769	.9865
7							.0000	.1752	.3094	.4152	.7159	.8479	.9147	.9510	.9715	.9833
8								.0000	.1628	.2910	.6556	.8156	.8966	.9406	.9654	.9797
9									.0000	.1531	.5886	.7797	.8765	.9290	.9587	.9758
10										.0000	.5143	.7399	.8542	.9162	.9512	.9714
11											.4317	.6957	.8294	.9020	.9429	.9665
12											.3401	.6466	.8019	.8862	.9337	.9611
13											.2384	.5921	.7713	.8686	.9235	.9551
14											.1254	.5316	.7374	.8491	.9122	.9485
15											.0000	.4645	.6997	.8275	.8996	.9411
16												.3899	.6579	.8035	.8856	.9329
17												.3072	.6115	.7768	.8701	.9238
18												.2153	.5600	.7473	.8529	.9137
19												.1133	.5028	.7144	.8337	.9025
20												.0000	.4393	.6779	.8125	.8900
21													.3688	.6374	.7889	.8762
22													.2905	.5924	.7627	.8608
23													.2036	.5425	.7337	.8438
24													.1071	.4871	.7014	.8249
25													.0000	.4256	.6656	.8038
26														.3573	.6258	.7805
27														.2814	.5817	.7546
28														.1972	.5327	.7259
29														.1038	.4783	.6940
30														.0000	.4179	.6585
35															.0000	.4134
40																.0000

10.75%

AGE OF LOAN	1	2	3	4	5	6	7	8	9	10	15	20	25	30	35	40
1	.0000	.5267	.7016	.7886	.8404	.8746	.8987	.9166	.9303	.9410	.9716	.9849	.9916	.9953	.9973	.9984
2		.0000	.3696	.5533	.6627	.7350	.7860	.8237	.8527	.8754	.9400	.9682	.9823	.9900	.9942	.9967
3			.0000	.2914	.4650	.5796	.6605	.7204	.7663	.8024	.9049	.9495	.9720	.9841	.9908	.9947
4				.0000	.2449	.4067	.5209	.6054	.6702	.7211	.8657	.9288	.9605	.9775	.9871	.9925
5					.0000	.2142	.3655	.4774	.5632	.6307	.8222	.9057	.9477	.9703	.9829	.9901
6						.0000	.1925	.3350	.4441	.5300	.7737	.8800	.9334	.9622	.9782	.9874
7							.0000	.1764	.3116	.4180	.7198	.8514	.9175	.9531	.9730	.9844
8								.0000	.1641	.2933	.6597	.8195	.8998	.9431	.9672	.9810
9									.0000	.1545	.5929	.7841	.8802	.9319	.9608	.9773
10										.0000	.5185	.7446	.8583	.9195	.9537	.9731
11											.4358	.7007	.8339	.9056	.9457	.9685
12											.3436	.6519	.8068	.8902	.9368	.9634
13											.2411	.5975	.7766	.8731	.9269	.9576
14											.1270	.5370	.7430	.8540	.9160	.9513
15											.0000	.4696	.7057	.8328	.9037	.9442
16												.3947	.6641	.8091	.8901	.9363
17												.3112	.6178	.7828	.8750	.9275
18												.2184	.5662	.7535	.8581	.9177
19												.1150	.5089	.7209	.8394	.9069
20												.0000	.4450	.6847	.8185	.8948
21													.3740	.6443	.7953	.8813
22													.2949	.5994	.7694	.8663
23													.2069	.5494	.7406	.8496
24													.1090	.4937	.7086	.8311
25													.0000	.4318	.6730	.8104
26														.3629	.6333	.7874
27														.2862	.5891	.7618
28														.2008	.5400	.7333
29														.1058	.4853	.7016
30														.0000	.4244	.6663
35															.0000	.4202
40																.0000

LOAN PROGRESS CHART
11.00%

AGE OF LOAN	ORIGINAL TERM IN YEARS															
	1	2	3	4	5	6	7	8	9	10	15	20	25	30	35	40
1	.0000	.5273	.7024	.7894	.8412	.8754	.8996	.9174	.9311	.9418	.9722	.9854	.9920	.9955	.9974	.9985
2		.0000	.3704	.5545	.6641	.7365	.7875	.8253	.8542	.8769	.9413	.9691	.9831	.9905	.9946	.9969
3			.0000	.2924	.4665	.5814	.6625	.7225	.7684	.8045	.9067	.9510	.9731	.9849	.9914	.9951
4				.0000	.2460	.4084	.5230	.6078	.6727	.7237	.8681	.9307	.9620	.9786	.9878	.9930
5					.0000	.2154	.3674	.4798	.5659	.6336	.8251	.9081	.9495	.9716	.9839	.9908
6						.0000	.1937	.3370	.4467	.5330	.7771	.8829	.9357	.9639	.9794	.9882
7							.0000	.1777	.3138	.4208	.7236	.8548	.9203	.9552	.9745	.9854
8								.0000	.1655	.2956	.6638	.8234	.9030	.9455	.9690	.9822
9									.0000	.1559	.5971	.7884	.8838	.9347	.9628	.9787
10										.0000	.5228	.7493	.8623	.9226	.9560	.9748
11											.4398	.7057	.8384	.9092	.9483	.9704
12											.3472	.6571	.8117	.8942	.9398	.9655
13											.2439	.6028	.7819	.8774	.9302	.9600
14											.1286	.5423	.7486	.8587	.9196	.9539
15											.0000	.4747	.7115	.8379	.9077	.9471
16												.3994	.6701	.8146	.8945	.9395
17												.3153	.6239	.7887	.8797	.9311
18												.2215	.5724	.7597	.8633	.9216
19												.1168	.5149	.7274	.8449	.9111
20												.0000	.4508	.6913	.8244	.8993
21													.3792	.6511	.8015	.8862
22													.2994	.6063	.7759	.8716
23													.2103	.5562	.7474	.8553
24													.1109	.5003	.7157	.8371
25													.0000	.4380	.6802	.8167
26														.3685	.6406	.7941
27														.2909	.5965	.7688
28														.2043	.5472	.7405
29														.1078	.4923	.7090
30														.0000	.4309	.6739
35															.0000	.4270
40																.0000

11.25%

AGE OF LOAN	ORIGINAL TERM IN YEARS															
	1	2	3	4	5	6	7	8	9	10	15	20	25	30	35	40
1	.0000	.5280	.7032	.7903	.8421	.8763	.9004	.9182	.9319	.9426	.9728	.9859	.9923	.9957	.9976	.9986
2		.0000	.3713	.5558	.6655	.7379	.7890	.8268	.8557	.8784	.9425	.9701	.9837	.9910	.9949	.9971
3			.0000	.2934	.4680	.5832	.6645	.7245	.7705	.8066	.9085	.9524	.9741	.9856	.9919	.9954
4				.0000	.2471	.4101	.5251	.6101	.6752	.7263	.8705	.9326	.9634	.9797	.9886	.9935
5					.0000	.2165	.3693	.4822	.5686	.6364	.8280	.9105	.9514	.9730	.9848	.9914
6						.0000	.1950	.3391	.4494	.5359	.7805	.8858	.9379	.9655	.9806	.9890
7							.0000	.1790	.3160	.4236	.7273	.8582	.9229	.9572	.9759	.9863
8								.0000	.1668	.2979	.6679	.8272	.9061	.9478	.9706	.9834
9									.0000	.1573	.6014	.7926	.8873	.9374	.9648	.9800
10										.0000	.5270	.7539	.8663	.9257	.9582	.9763
11											.4438	.7107	.8427	.9126	.9508	.9721
12											.3507	.6623	.8164	.8980	.9426	.9675
13											.2466	.6081	.7870	.8816	.9334	.9623
14											.1302	.5476	.7541	.8633	.9231	.9564
15											.0000	.4798	.7173	.8429	.9116	.9499
16												.4041	.6761	.8200	.8987	.9426
17												.3193	.6301	.7944	.8843	.9345
18												.2246	.5785	.7657	.8682	.9254
19												.1186	.5209	.7337	.8502	.9152
20												.0000	.4565	.6979	.8300	.9037
21													.3844	.6578	.8075	.8910
22													.3038	.6130	.7823	.8767
23													.2136	.5629	.7541	.8607
24													.1128	.5069	.7226	.8429
25													.0000	.4442	.6873	.8229
26														.3740	.6478	.8005
27														.2956	.6037	.7756
28														.2079	.5544	.7476
29														.1097	.4992	.7163
30														.0000	.4374	.6814
35															.0000	.4336
40																.0000

LOAN PROGRESS CHART

11.50%

AGE OF LOAN	ORIGINAL TERM IN YEARS															
	1	2	3	4	5	6	7	8	9	10	15	20	25	30	35	40
1	.0000	.5286	.7040	.7912	.8430	.8772	.9013	.9191	.9327	.9434	.9734	.9863	.9926	.9960	.9978	.9987
2		.0000	.3721	.5570	.6669	.7394	.7906	.8283	.8572	.8799	.9437	.9710	.9844	.9914	.9952	.9973
3			.0000	.2944	.4695	.5850	.6664	.7266	.7726	.8086	.9103	.9538	.9751	.9863	.9924	.9957
4				.0000	.2482	.4118	.5272	.6125	.6777	.7288	.8729	.9345	.9648	.9806	.9892	.9940
5					.0000	.2177	.3712	.4846	.5713	.6393	.8309	.9129	.9532	.9742	.9857	.9920
6						.0000	.1962	.3411	.4520	.5389	.7838	.8887	.9401	.9671	.9817	.9898
7							.0000	.1803	.3182	.4264	.7311	.8615	.9255	.9590	.9772	.9873
8								.0000	.1682	.3002	.6719	.8310	.9091	.9500	.9722	.9844
9									.0000	.1587	.6056	.7968	.8907	.9399	.9666	.9813
10										.0000	.5312	.7585	.8701	.9286	.9603	.9778
11											.4478	.7155	.8470	.9159	.9532	.9738
12											.3543	.6674	.8211	.9017	.9453	.9694
13											.2494	.6134	.7921	.8857	.9364	.9644
14											.1318	.5528	.7595	.8678	.9265	.9588
15											.0000	.4849	.7230	.8477	.9153	.9526
16												.4088	.6820	.8252	.9028	.9456
17												.3234	.6361	.8000	.8887	.9377
18												.2277	.5846	.7717	.8730	.9289
19												.1203	.5269	.7399	.8554	.9190
20												.0000	.4622	.7044	.8356	.9080
21													.3896	.6645	.8134	.8955
22													.3082	.6197	.7885	.8816
23													.2170	.5696	.7606	.8660
24													.1147	.5133	.7293	.8485
25													.0000	.4503	.6943	.8289
26														.3796	.6549	.8069
27														.3003	.6109	.7822
28														.2114	.5614	.7545
29														.1118	.5060	.7235
30														.0000	.4438	.6887
35															.0000	.4403
40																.0000

11.75%

AGE OF LOAN	1	2	3	4	5	6	7	8	9	10	15	20	25	30	35	40
1	.0000	.5292	.7048	.7920	.8438	.8780	.9021	.9199	.9335	.9441	.9740	.9868	.9930	.9962	.9979	.9988
2		.0000	.3730	.5582	.6683	.7409	.7921	.8298	.8587	.8813	.9449	.9719	.9850	.9919	.9955	.9975
3			.0000	.2954	.4710	.5868	.6684	.7286	.7746	.8107	.9120	.9551	.9761	.9870	.9929	.9961
4				.0000	.2493	.4136	.5294	.6148	.6801	.7313	.8752	.9363	.9661	.9816	.9899	.9944
5					.0000	.2189	.3731	.4870	.5739	.6421	.8337	.9152	.9549	.9755	.9865	.9925
6						.0000	.1974	.3432	.4546	.5419	.7871	.8914	.9422	.9686	.9827	.9904
7							.0000	.1816	.3204	.4292	.7348	.8647	.9280	.9609	.9785	.9881
8								.0000	.1695	.3025	.6759	.8347	.9120	.9522	.9737	.9855
9									.0000	.1601	.6097	.8009	.8941	.9424	.9683	.9825
10										.0000	.5354	.7630	.8739	.9314	.9623	.9792
11											.4518	.7204	.8512	.9191	.9555	.9754
12											.3578	.6725	.8257	.9052	.9479	.9712
13											.2522	.6186	.7970	.8897	.9393	.9664
14											.1335	.5580	.7648	.8721	.9297	.9611
15											.0000	.4900	.7286	.8524	.9189	.9551
16												.4135	.6879	.8303	.9067	.9484
17												.3275	.6421	.8054	.8930	.9408
18												.2308	.5907	.7775	.8777	.9323
19												.1221	.5328	.7460	.8604	.9228
20												.0000	.4678	.7107	.8409	.9120
21													.3948	.6710	.8191	.8999
22													.3127	.6263	.7946	.8864
23													.2204	.5762	.7670	.8711
24													.1166	.5198	.7360	.8540
25													.0000	.4564	.7011	.8347
26														.3851	.6619	.8130
27														.3050	.6179	.7886
28														.2150	.5684	.7613
29														.1138	.5128	.7305
30														.0000	.4502	.6959
35															.0000	.4469
40																.0000

LOAN PROGRESS CHART

12.00%

AGE OF LOAN	ORIGINAL TERM IN YEARS															
	1	2	3	4	5	6	7	8	9	10	15	20	25	30	35	40
1	.0000	.5298	.7056	.7928	.8447	.8789	.9029	.9207	.9343	.9449	.9746	.9872	.9932	.9964	.9980	.9989
2		.0000	.3738	.5594	.6697	.7424	.7936	.8313	.8602	.8827	.9460	.9727	.9856	.9923	.9958	.9977
3			.0000	.2964	.4725	.5886	.6703	.7306	.7767	.8127	.9138	.9565	.9771	.9877	.9933	.9963
4				.0000	.2504	.4153	.5315	.6172	.6826	.7339	.8775	.9381	.9674	.9825	.9905	.9948
5					.0000	.2200	.3750	.4893	.5766	.6450	.8365	.9174	.9565	.9766	.9873	.9931
6						.0000	.1987	.3453	.4572	.5448	.7904	.8942	.9443	.9700	.9837	.9911
7							.0000	.1829	.3226	.4320	.7384	.8679	.9305	.9626	.9797	.9889
8								.0000	.1709	.3048	.6799	.8383	.9149	.9542	.9751	.9864
9									.0000	.1615	.6139	.8050	.8973	.9448	.9700	.9836
10										.0000	.5395	.7675	.8776	.9342	.9642	.9804
11											.4558	.7252	.8553	.9222	.9577	.9769
12											.3613	.6775	.8302	.9087	.9504	.9729
13											.2550	.6237	.8019	.8935	.9421	.9684
14											.1351	.5632	.7700	.8764	.9328	.9633
15											.0000	.4950	.7341	.8571	.9223	.9575
16												.4181	.6936	.8353	.9105	.9511
17												.3315	.6480	.8108	.8972	.9438
18												.2339	.5966	.7832	.8822	.9356
19												.1239	.5387	.7520	.8652	.9263
20												.0000	.4735	.7169	.8462	.9159
21													.4000	.6774	.8247	.9042
22													.3171	.6329	.8005	.8909
23													.2237	.5827	.7732	.8760
24													.1185	.5261	.7425	.8592
25													.0000	.4624	.7078	.8403
26														.3906	.6688	.8190
27														.3097	.6248	.7949
28														.2185	.5753	.7678
29														.1158	.5195	.7373
30														.0000	.4565	.7029
35															.0000	.4534
40																.0000

12.25%

AGE OF LOAN	1	2	3	4	5	6	7	8	9	10	15	20	25	30	35	40
1	.0000	.5304	.7064	.7937	.8456	.8797	.9038	.9215	.9350	.9456	.9752	.9876	.9935	.9966	.9982	.9990
2		.0000	.3747	.5606	.6711	.7439	.7951	.8328	.8616	.8842	.9471	.9736	.9862	.9927	.9961	.9979
3			.0000	.2974	.4741	.5904	.6723	.7327	.7787	.8148	.9155	.9577	.9780	.9883	.9937	.9966
4				.0000	.2515	.4170	.5336	.6195	.6851	.7364	.8797	.9399	.9687	.9833	.9911	.9952
5					.0000	.2212	.3769	.4917	.5793	.6478	.8393	.9196	.9581	.9777	.9880	.9935
6						.0000	.1999	.3473	.4598	.5478	.7936	.8968	.9463	.9714	.9847	.9917
7							.0000	.1842	.3248	.4348	.7421	.8710	.9328	.9643	.9808	.9896
8								.0000	.1723	.3071	.6838	.8419	.9176	.9562	.9765	.9873
9									.0000	.1629	.6180	.8090	.9005	.9471	.9716	.9840
10										.0000	.5437	.7719	.8812	.9368	.9661	.9817
11											.4597	.7299	.8593	.9252	.9598	.9783
12											.3649	.6824	.8346	.9121	.9528	.9745
13											.2577	.6289	.8067	.8972	.9448	.9702
14											.1367	.5684	.7752	.8805	.9358	.9653
15											.0000	.5000	.7395	.8615	.9256	.9598
16												.4228	.6993	.8402	.9141	.9536
17												.3356	.6539	.8160	.9012	.9466
18												.2370	.6026	.7887	.8865	.9387
19												.1257	.5446	.7579	.8700	.9298
20												.0000	.4791	.7231	.8512	.9196
21													.4051	.6838	.8301	.9082
22													.3215	.6393	.8063	.8953
23													.2271	.5891	.7793	.8808
24													.1205	.5325	.7488	.8643
25													.0000	.4684	.7144	.8458
26														.3961	.6756	.8248
27														.3144	.6317	.8010
28														.2221	.5821	.7743
29														.1178	.5261	.7440
30														.0000	.4628	.7098
35															.0000	.4598
40																.0000

LOAN PROGRESS CHART

12.50%

AGE OF LOAN	ORIGINAL TERM IN YEARS															
	1	2	3	4	5	6	7	8	9	10	15	20	25	30	35	40
1	.0000	.5310	.7072	.7945	.8464	.8806	.9046	.9223	.9358	.9463	.9757	.9880	.9938	.9967	.9983	.9991
2		.0000	.3755	.5619	.6725	.7453	.7966	.8343	.8631	.8856	.9483	.9744	.9868	.9931	.9963	.9980
3			.0000	.2984	.4756	.5922	.6742	.7347	.7807	.8168	.9172	.9590	.9789	.9889	.9941	.9969
4				.0000	.2526	.4188	.5357	.6219	.6875	.7389	.8819	.9416	.9699	.9842	.9916	.9955
5					.0000	.2224	.3788	.4941	.5819	.6506	.8420	.9218	.9597	.9788	.9888	.9940
6						.0000	.2012	.3494	.4624	.5507	.7968	.8994	.9482	.9728	.9856	.9923
7							.0000	.1855	.3270	.4375	.7457	.8741	.9351	.9659	.9819	.9903
8								.0000	.1736	.3094	.6877	.8454	.9203	.9581	.9778	.9881
9									.0000	.1643	.6221	.8130	.9036	.9493	.9731	.9856
10										.0000	.5478	.7762	.8847	.9394	.9678	.9828
11											.4637	.7345	.8632	.9281	.9618	.9796
12											.3684	.6874	.8389	.9153	.9550	.9760
13											.2605	.6340	.8114	.9008	.9474	.9719
14											.1384	.5735	.7802	.8845	.9387	.9673
15											.0000	.5050	.7449	.8659	.9288	.9620
16												.4274	.7049	.8449	.9177	.9560
17												.3396	.6597	.8211	.9050	.9493
18												.2402	.6084	.7942	.8907	.9417
19												.1275	.5504	.7637	.8745	.9330
20												.0000	.4846	.7291	.8562	.9232
21													.4102	.6900	.8354	.9121
22													.3259	.6457	.8119	.8996
23													.2305	.5955	.7852	.8854
24													.1224	.5387	.7551	.8693
25													.0000	.4744	.7209	.8510
26														.4015	.6822	.8304
27														.3190	.6384	.8070
28														.2256	.5888	.7805
29														.1198	.5327	.7505
30														.0000	.4690	.7166
35															.0000	.4662
40																.0000

12.75%

AGE OF LOAN	1	2	3	4	5	6	7	8	9	10	15	20	25	30	35	40
1	.0000	.5317	.7079	.7954	.8473	.8814	.9054	.9231	.9366	.9471	.9763	.9884	.9941	.9969	.9984	.9991
2		.0000	.3764	.5631	.6739	.7468	.7981	.8358	.8645	.8870	.9494	.9752	.9873	.9934	.9965	.9982
3			.0000	.2994	.4771	.5940	.6762	.7367	.7828	.8188	.9188	.9602	.9797	.9895	.9945	.9971
4				.0000	.2536	.4205	.5378	.6242	.6899	.7413	.8841	.9432	.9710	.9850	.9921	.9958
5					.0000	.2236	.3807	.4965	.5846	.6534	.8447	.9239	.9612	.9798	.9894	.9944
6						.0000	.2024	.3515	.4650	.5536	.8000	.9020	.9500	.9740	.9864	.9928
7							.0000	.1869	.3292	.4403	.7493	.8771	.9374	.9674	.9829	.9910
8								.0000	.1750	.3117	.6916	.8489	.9230	.9600	.9790	.9889
9									.0000	.1657	.6262	.8168	.9066	.9515	.9745	.9866
10										.0000	.5520	.7804	.8881	.9418	.9695	.9839
11											.4677	.7391	.8670	.9309	.9637	.9809
12											.3720	.6922	.8431	.9185	.9572	.9774
13											.2633	.6390	.8160	.9044	.9498	.9735
14											.1400	.5786	.7851	.8883	.9414	.9691
15											.0000	.5100	.7502	.8702	.9319	.9641
16												.4321	.7105	.8495	.9210	.9584
17												.3437	.6654	.8261	.9087	.9519
18												.2433	.6142	.7995	.8948	.9445
19												.1294	.5561	.7693	.8789	.9362
20												.0000	.4902	.7350	.8610	.9267
21													.4153	.6961	.8405	.9159
22													.3303	.6520	.8174	.9037
23													.2339	.6018	.7911	.8898
24													.1243	.5449	.7612	.8740
25													.0000	.4803	.7273	.8562
26														.4069	.6888	.8359
27														.3237	.6451	.8128
28														.2291	.5955	.7866
29														.1218	.5392	.7569
30														.0000	.4752	.7232
35															.0000	.4726
40																.0000

LOAN PROGRESS CHART

13.00%

AGE OF LOAN	ORIGINAL TERM IN YEARS															
	1	2	3	4	5	6	7	8	9	10	15	20	25	30	35	40
1	.0000	.5323	.7087	.7962	.8481	.8823	.9062	.9239	.9373	.9478	.9768	.9888	.9943	.9971	.9985	.9992
2		.0000	.3772	.5643	.6753	.7483	.7995	.8373	.8660	.8884	.9504	.9760	.9879	.9938	.9968	.9983
3			.0000	.3004	.4786	.5958	.6781	.7387	.7848	.8208	.9204	.9614	.9805	.9900	.9948	.9973
4				.0000	.2547	.4222	.5399	.6265	.6924	.7438	.8863	.9448	.9722	.9857	.9926	.9961
5					.0000	.2248	.3827	.4988	.5872	.6562	.8474	.9260	.9627	.9808	.9901	.9948
6						.0000	.2037	.3535	.4675	.5566	.8031	.9045	.9518	.9753	.9872	.9933
7							.0000	.1882	.3314	.4431	.7528	.8801	.9395	.9689	.9839	.9916
8								.0000	.1764	.3141	.6955	.8523	.9255	.9617	.9801	.9897
9									.0000	.1672	.6303	.8207	.9096	.9535	.9759	.9874
10										.0000	.5561	.7847	.8914	.9442	.9711	.9849
11											.4716	.7437	.8707	.9336	.9656	.9820
12											.3755	.6971	.8472	.9215	.9593	.9788
13											.2661	.6440	.8205	.9078	.9522	.9751
14											.1417	.5836	.7900	.8921	.9440	.9708
15											.0000	.5149	.7554	.8743	.9348	.9660
16												.4367	.7159	.8540	.9243	.9605
17												.3477	.6710	.8310	.9123	.9543
18												.2464	.6200	.8047	.8987	.9472
19												.1312	.5618	.7749	.8832	.9391
20												.0000	.4957	.7409	.8656	.9300
21													.4204	.7022	.8455	.9195
22													.3347	.6582	.8227	.9076
23													.2372	.6081	.7967	.8941
24													.1263	.5511	.7672	.8786
25													.0000	.4862	.7335	.8611
26														.4123	.6952	.8412
27														.3283	.6516	.8184
28														.2327	.6020	.7926
29														.1239	.5456	.7632
30														.0000	.4813	.7297
35															.0000	.4788
40																.0000

13.25%

AGE OF LOAN	1	2	3	4	5	6	7	8	9	10	15	20	25	30	35	40
1	.0000	.5329	.7095	.7970	.8490	.8831	.9071	.9247	.9381	.9485	.9773	.9891	.9946	.9972	.9986	.9993
2		.0000	.3781	.5655	.6767	.7497	.8010	.8387	.8674	.8897	.9515	.9767	.9884	.9941	.9970	.9984
3			.0000	.3014	.4801	.5976	.6800	.7407	.7868	.8227	.9220	.9626	.9813	.9905	.9951	.9975
4				.0000	.2558	.4240	.5420	.6288	.6948	.7462	.8884	.9464	.9733	.9864	.9930	.9964
5					.0000	.2259	.3846	.5012	.5899	.6590	.8500	.9280	.9641	.9818	.9906	.9952
6						.0000	.2049	.3556	.4701	.5595	.8062	.9070	.9536	.9764	.9879	.9938
7							.0000	.1895	.3336	.4459	.7563	.8830	.9416	.9703	.9848	.9922
8								.0000	.1778	.3164	.6993	.8556	.9280	.9634	.9812	.9903
9									.0000	.1686	.6343	.8244	.9124	.9555	.9772	.9883
10										.0000	.5602	.7888	.8946	.9465	.9726	.9859
11											.4756	.7482	.8744	.9362	.9673	.9832
12											.3790	.7018	.8513	.9244	.9613	.9801
13											.2689	.6490	.8249	.9110	.9544	.9765
14											.1433	.5886	.7948	.8958	.9466	.9725
15											.0000	.5198	.7605	.8783	.9376	.9679
16												.4413	.7213	.8584	.9274	.9626
17												.3518	.6766	.8357	.9158	.9566
18												.2496	.6256	.8098	.9025	.9498
19												.1330	.5675	.7803	.8874	.9420
20												.0000	.5012	.7466	.8701	.9331
21													.4255	.7081	.8504	.9230
22													.3391	.6643	.8279	.9114
23													.2406	.6142	.8023	.8982
24													.1282	.5571	.7730	.8831
25													.0000	.4920	.7396	.8659
26														.4177	.7015	.8463
27														.3329	.6581	.8239
28														.2362	.6085	.7984
29														.1259	.5519	.7693
30														.0000	.4874	.7360
35															.0000	.4851
40																.0000

LOAN PROGRESS CHART
13.50%

AGE OF LOAN	ORIGINAL TERM IN YEARS															
	1	2	3	4	5	6	7	8	9	10	15	20	25	30	35	40
1	.0000	.5335	.7103	.7979	.8498	.8839	.9079	.9254	.9388	.9492	.9779	.9895	.9948	.9974	.9987	.9993
2		.0000	.3789	.5667	.6781	.7512	.8025	.8402	.8688	.8911	.9526	.9774	.9889	.9944	.9972	.9986
3			.0000	.3024	.4816	.5993	.6820	.7426	.7887	.8247	.9236	.9637	.9821	.9910	.9954	.9977
4				.0000	.2569	.4257	.5441	.6311	.6972	.7487	.8905	.9480	.9743	.9871	.9935	.9967
5					.0000	.2271	.3865	.5036	.5925	.6618	.8526	.9300	.9654	.9826	.9912	.9955
6						.0000	.2062	.3577	.4727	.5624	.8093	.9094	.9553	.9775	.9886	.9942
7							.0000	.1908	.3358	.4487	.7598	.8858	.9437	.9717	.9857	.9927
8								.0000	.1791	.3187	.7031	.8589	.9304	.9650	.9823	.9910
9									.0000	.1700	.6383	.8281	.9152	.9574	.9784	.9890
10										.0000	.5642	.7929	.8978	.9487	.9740	.9868
11											.4795	.7526	.8779	.9387	.9689	.9842
12											.3826	.7066	.8552	.9273	.9632	.9813
13											.2717	.6539	.8292	.9142	.9566	.9779
14											.1450	.5936	.7995	.8993	.9490	.9740
15											.0000	.5247	.7655	.8822	.9403	.9696
16												.4459	.7266	.8627	.9304	.9646
17												.3558	.6821	.8404	.9191	.9589
18												.2527	.6313	.8148	.9062	.9523
19												.1348	.5731	.7856	.8914	.9447
20												.0000	.5066	.7522	.8745	.9361
21													.4305	.7140	.8551	.9263
22													.3435	.6703	.8330	.9150
23													.2440	.6203	.8077	.9021
24													.1302	.5632	.7787	.8874
25													.0000	.4978	.7456	.8706
26														.4230	.7077	.8513
27														.3375	.6644	.8293
28														.2397	.6149	.8040
29														.1279	.5582	.7752
30														.0000	.4934	.7423
35															.0000	.4912
40																.0000

13.75%

AGE OF LOAN	1	2	3	4	5	6	7	8	9	10	15	20	25	30	35	40
1	.0000	.5341	.7111	.7987	.8507	.8848	.9087	.9262	.9395	.9499	.9784	.9898	.9950	.9975	.9988	.9994
2		.0000	.3798	.5679	.6794	.7526	.8039	.8416	.8702	.8925	.9536	.9782	.9893	.9947	.9974	.9987
3			.0000	.3033	.4831	.6011	.6839	.7446	.7907	.8266	.9251	.9648	.9828	.9915	.9957	.9979
4				.0000	.2580	.4274	.5462	.6334	.6996	.7511	.8926	.9495	.9753	.9878	.9939	.9969
5					.0000	.2283	.3884	.5059	.5951	.6645	.8552	.9319	.9668	.9835	.9917	.9958
6						.0000	.2075	.3597	.4753	.5653	.8123	.9117	.9569	.9786	.9893	.9946
7							.0000	.1921	.3380	.4515	.7632	.8886	.9456	.9730	.9865	.9932
8								.0000	.1805	.3211	.7069	.8621	.9327	.9666	.9833	.9916
9									.0000	.1715	.6423	.8317	.9179	.9592	.9796	.9897
10										.0000	.5683	.7969	.9009	.9508	.9754	.9876
11											.4834	.7570	.8814	.9411	.9705	.9852
12											.3861	.7112	.8591	.9300	.9650	.9824
13											.2746	.6587	.8335	.9173	.9586	.9792
14											.1466	.5986	.8041	.9027	.9513	.9755
15											.0000	.5296	.7704	.8860	.9429	.9713
16												.4505	.7318	.8669	.9333	.9665
17												.3598	.6876	.8449	.9223	.9610
18												.2559	.6368	.8197	.9097	.9546
19												.1367	.5787	.7908	.8953	.9474
20												.0000	.5120	.7577	.8787	.9390
21													.4355	.7198	.8597	.9295
22													.3479	.6762	.8379	.9185
23													.2473	.6263	.8129	.9060
24													.1321	.5691	.7843	.8916
25													.0000	.5035	.7515	.8751
26														.4283	.7138	.8561
27														.3421	.6706	.8344
28														.2433	.6212	.8096
29														.1299	.5644	.7810
30														.0000	.4994	.7483
35															.0000	.4973
40																.0000

LOAN PROGRESS CHART
14.00%

AGE OF LOAN	ORIGINAL TERM IN YEARS															
	1	2	3	4	5	6	7	8	9	10	15	20	25	30	35	40
1	.0000	.5347	.7118	.7995	.8515	.8856	.9095	.9270	.9403	.9506	.9789	.9902	.9953	.9977	.9988	.9994
2		.0000	.3807	.5691	.6808	.7541	.8054	.8430	.8716	.8938	.9546	.9789	.9898	.9950	.9975	.9988
3			.0000	.3043	.4846	.6029	.6858	.7466	.7927	.8285	.9267	.9659	.9835	.9919	.9960	.9980
4				.0000	.2591	.4292	.5483	.6357	.7020	.7535	.8946	.9509	.9763	.9884	.9942	.9971
5					.0000	.2295	.3903	.5083	.5977	.6673	.8577	.9338	.9680	.9843	.9922	.9961
6						.0000	.2087	.3618	.4779	.5682	.8153	.9140	.9585	.9796	.9899	.9950
7							.0000	.1935	.3402	.4543	.7666	.8913	.9476	.9743	.9873	.9937
8								.0000	.1819	.3234	.7106	.8653	.9350	.9681	.9842	.9922
9									.0000	.1729	.6463	.8353	.9205	.9610	.9807	.9904
10										.0000	.5723	.8009	.9039	.9528	.9767	.9884
11											.4873	.7613	.8848	.9435	.9720	.9861
12											.3897	.7158	.8628	.9327	.9667	.9835
13											.2774	.6636	.8376	.9203	.9606	.9804
14											.1483	.6035	.8086	.9061	.9535	.9769
15											.0000	.5344	.7753	.8897	.9454	.9729
16												.4551	.7370	.8709	.9361	.9683
17												.3638	.6930	.8493	.9254	.9630
18												.2590	.6423	.8245	.9132	.9569
19												.1385	.5842	.7959	.8990	.9499
20												.0000	.5173	.7631	.8828	.9418
21													.4405	.7254	.8642	.9325
22													.3522	.6821	.8427	.9219
23													.2507	.6323	.8181	.9096
24													.1341	.5750	.7897	.8956
25													.0000	.5092	.7572	.8794
26														.4336	.7198	.8608
27														.3467	.6768	.8395
28														.2468	.6274	.8149
29														.1320	.5706	.7867
30														.0000	.5053	.7543
35															.0000	.5033
40																.0000

14.25%

AGE OF LOAN	1	2	3	4	5	6	7	8	9	10	15	20	25	30	35	40
1	.0000	.5354	.7126	.8004	.8523	.8864	.9102	.9277	.9410	.9513	.9794	.9905	.9955	.9978	.9989	.9995
2		.0000	.3815	.5704	.6822	.7555	.8068	.8445	.8730	.8951	.9556	.9795	.9902	.9953	.9977	.9989
3			.0000	.3053	.4861	.6047	.6877	.7485	.7946	.8304	.9282	.9669	.9842	.9923	.9963	.9982
4				.0000	.2603	.4309	.5504	.6380	.7043	.7559	.8966	.9524	.9773	.9890	.9946	.9974
5					.0000	.2307	.3922	.5106	.6003	.6700	.8602	.9356	.9693	.9851	.9927	.9964
6						.0000	.2100	.3639	.4805	.5711	.8183	.9163	.9600	.9806	.9905	.9953
7							.0000	.1948	.3424	.4571	.7700	.8940	.9494	.9755	.9880	.9941
8								.0000	.1833	.3257	.7144	.8684	.9372	.9695	.9851	.9927
9									.0000	.1744	.6502	.8388	.9231	.9627	.9818	.9910
10										.0000	.5764	.8048	.9068	.9548	.9779	.9892
11											.4912	.7656	.8881	.9457	.9735	.9870
12											.3932	.7204	.8665	.9353	.9683	.9845
13											.2802	.6683	.8417	.9232	.9625	.9816
14											.1500	.6084	.8131	.9093	.9557	.9782
15											.0000	.5392	.7801	.8933	.9478	.9744
16												.4596	.7421	.8749	.9388	.9700
17												.3679	.6983	.8536	.9284	.9649
18												.2621	.6478	.8291	.9165	.9590
19												.1403	.5897	.8009	.9027	.9522
20												.0000	.5227	.7684	.8868	.9444
21													.4455	.7310	.8685	.9355
22													.3565	.6878	.8474	.9251
23													.2541	.6381	.8231	.9132
24													.1360	.5809	.7951	.8994
25													.0000	.5149	.7628	.8836
26														.4388	.7257	.8654
27														.3512	.6828	.8444
28														.2503	.6335	.8201
29														.1340	.5766	.7922
30														.0000	.5111	.7601
35															.0000	.5093
40																.0000

LOAN PROGRESS CHART

14.50%

AGE OF LOAN	ORIGINAL TERM IN YEARS															
	1	2	3	4	5	6	7	8	9	10	15	20	25	30	35	40
1	.0000	.5360	.7134	.8012	.8532	.8872	.9110	.9285	.9417	.9519	.9798	.9908	.9957	.9979	.9990	.9995
2		.0000	.3824	.5716	.6835	.7569	.8083	.8459	.8743	.8964	.9565	.9802	.9906	.9955	.9978	.9989
3			.0000	.3063	.4876	.6064	.6896	.7505	.7966	.8323	.9296	.9679	.9849	.9927	.9965	.9983
4				.0000	.2614	.4326	.5525	.6403	.7067	.7583	.8986	.9537	.9782	.9895	.9949	.9975
5					.0000	.2319	.3941	.5130	.6029	.6728	.8627	.9374	.9704	.9858	.9932	.9967
6						.0000	.2113	.3660	.4831	.5740	.8212	.9185	.9615	.9815	.9911	.9957
7							.0000	.1961	.3446	.4599	.7733	.8966	.9512	.9766	.9887	.9945
8								.0000	.1847	.3281	.7180	.8714	.9393	.9709	.9859	.9932
9									.0000	.1758	.6542	.8423	.9256	.9643	.9828	.9916
10										.0000	.5804	.8087	.9097	.9567	.9791	.9899
11											.4951	.7698	.8913	.9479	.9748	.9878
12											.3967	.7249	.8701	.9377	.9699	.9854
13											.2830	.6731	.8457	.9260	.9642	.9827
14											.1517	.6132	.8174	.9124	.9577	.9795
15											.0000	.5440	.7848	.8968	.9501	.9758
16												.4641	.7470	.8787	.9414	.9716
17												.3719	.7035	.8578	.9313	.9667
18												.2653	.6532	.8337	.9197	.9610
19												.1422	.5951	.8058	.9062	.9545
20												.0000	.5279	.7736	.8906	.9470
21													.4504	.7365	.8727	.9383
22													.3609	.6935	.8519	.9282
23													.2574	.6439	.8280	.9166
24													.1380	.5866	.8003	.9032
25													.0000	.5205	.7683	.8877
26														.4440	.7314	.8698
27														.3558	.6888	.8491
28														.2538	.6395	.8252
29														.1360	.5826	.7976
30														.0000	.5169	.7658
35															.0000	.5152
40																.0000

14.75%

AGE OF LOAN	1	2	3	4	5	6	7	8	9	10	15	20	25	30	35	40
1	.0000	.5366	.7142	.8020	.8540	.8880	.9118	.9292	.9424	.9526	.9803	.9911	.9959	.9980	.9991	.9996
2		.0000	.3832	.5728	.6849	.7584	.8097	.8473	.8757	.8977	.9575	.9808	.9910	.9958	.9980	.9990
3			.0000	.3073	.4891	.6082	.6915	.7524	.7985	.8342	.9311	.9689	.9855	.9931	.9967	.9984
4				.0000	.2625	.4344	.5546	.6425	.7091	.7606	.9005	.9551	.9790	.9901	.9953	.9977
5					.0000	.2331	.3961	.5153	.6055	.6755	.8651	.9391	.9716	.9865	.9936	.9969
6						.0000	.2125	.3680	.4856	.5768	.8241	.9206	.9630	.9824	.9916	.9960
7							.0000	.1975	.3468	.4626	.7766	.8992	.9530	.9777	.9894	.9949
8								.0000	.1861	.3304	.7217	.8744	.9414	.9722	.9867	.9936
9									.0000	.1773	.6580	.8457	.9280	.9659	.9837	.9922
10										.0000	.5843	.8124	.9124	.9585	.9802	.9905
11											.4990	.7739	.8945	.9500	.9761	.9886
12											.4002	.7294	.8737	.9401	.9714	.9863
13											.2858	.6778	.8496	.9287	.9660	.9837
14											.1534	.6180	.8217	.9155	.9596	.9807
15											.0000	.5488	.7894	.9002	.9523	.9772
16												.4686	.7520	.8824	.9439	.9731
17												.3759	.7086	.8619	.9341	.9684
18												.2684	.6585	.8381	.9227	.9630
19												.1440	.6004	.8106	.9096	.9567
20												.0000	.5332	.7787	.8944	.9494
21													.4553	.7418	.8768	.9410
22													.3652	.6991	.8564	.9312
23													.2608	.6496	.8327	.9199
24													.1399	.5923	.8054	.9068
25													.0000	.5260	.7737	.8916
26														.4492	.7371	.8741
27														.3603	.6946	.8537
28														.2573	.6455	.8302
29														.1381	.5885	.8029
30														.0000	.5226	.7713
35															.0000	.5210
40																.0000

LOAN PROGRESS CHART
15.00%

AGE OF LOAN	ORIGINAL TERM IN YEARS															
	1	2	3	4	5	6	7	8	9	10	15	20	25	30	35	40
1	.0000	.5372	.7149	.8028	.8548	.8888	.9126	.9300	.9431	.9533	.9808	.9914	.9960	.9981	.9991	.9996
2		.0000	.3841	.5740	.6863	.7598	.8111	.8487	.8771	.8990	.9584	.9814	.9914	.9960	.9981	.9991
3			.0000	.3083	.4906	.6100	.6934	.7543	.8004	.8361	.9325	.9699	.9861	.9935	.9969	.9985
4				.0000	.2636	.4361	.5567	.6448	.7114	.7630	.9024	.9564	.9799	.9906	.9956	.9979
5					.0000	.2343	.3980	.5177	.6081	.6782	.8675	.9408	.9727	.9872	.9940	.9971
6						.0000	.2138	.3701	.4882	.5797	.8270	.9227	.9643	.9833	.9921	.9963
7							.0000	.1988	.3491	.4654	.7799	.9017	.9546	.9787	.9900	.9953
8								.0000	.1875	.3327	.7253	.8773	.9434	.9735	.9875	.9941
9									.0000	.1787	.6619	.8490	.9303	.9674	.9846	.9927
10										.0000	.5883	.8162	.9151	.9602	.9812	.9911
11											.5029	.7780	.8975	.9520	.9774	.9893
12											.4037	.7338	.8771	.9424	.9728	.9871
13											.2887	.6824	.8534	.9313	.9676	.9847
14											.1551	.6227	.8259	.9184	.9615	.9818
15											.0000	.5535	.7939	.9034	.9545	.9784
16												.4731	.7568	.8861	.9463	.9746
17												.3799	.7137	.8659	.9367	.9701
18												.2716	.6638	.8425	.9257	.9648
19												.1459	.6057	.8153	.9129	.9588
20												.0000	.5384	.7837	.8980	.9517
21													.4602	.7471	.8807	.9436
22													.3695	.7046	.8607	.9341
23													.2642	.6553	.8374	.9230
24													.1419	.5980	.8104	.9103
25													.0000	.5315	.7790	.8954
26														.4543	.7426	.8782
27														.3648	.7004	.8582
28														.2608	.6513	.8350
29														.1401	.5944	.8081
30														.0000	.5283	.7768
35															.0000	.5268
40																.0000

15.25%

AGE OF LOAN	ORIGINAL TERM IN YEARS															
	1	2	3	4	5	6	7	8	9	10	15	20	25	30	35	40
1	.0000	.5378	.7157	.8037	.8556	.8896	.9134	.9307	.9438	.9539	.9812	.9917	.9962	.9982	.9992	.9996
2		.0000	.3849	.5752	.6876	.7612	.8125	.8501	.8784	.9003	.9594	.9820	.9918	.9962	.9982	.9992
3			.0000	.3093	.4922	.6117	.6952	.7562	.8023	.8379	.9339	.9708	.9867	.9938	.9971	.9987
4				.0000	.2647	.4378	.5587	.6471	.7137	.7653	.9043	.9577	.9807	.9911	.9958	.9981
5					.0000	.2355	.3999	.5200	.6107	.6809	.8699	.9425	.9738	.9878	.9943	.9974
6						.0000	.2151	.3722	.4908	.5826	.8298	.9248	.9657	.9841	.9926	.9965
7							.0000	.2002	.3513	.4682	.7832	.9042	.9563	.9798	.9906	.9956
8								.0000	.1889	.3351	.7289	.8802	.9453	.9747	.9882	.9945
9									.0000	.1802	.6657	.8523	.9326	.9688	.9855	.9932
10										.0000	.5923	.8199	.9178	.9619	.9823	.9917
11											.5067	.7821	.9005	.9539	.9785	.9900
12											.4073	.7381	.8805	.9447	.9742	.9879
13											.2915	.6870	.8571	.9338	.9692	.9856
14											.1568	.6275	.8300	.9213	.9633	.9828
15											.0000	.5582	.7983	.9066	.9565	.9797
16												.4776	.7616	.8896	.9485	.9759
17												.3838	.7188	.8698	.9393	.9716
18												.2747	.6690	.8467	.9286	.9666
19												.1477	.6110	.8199	.9160	.9608
20												.0000	.5436	.7886	.9015	.9539
21													.4651	.7523	.8846	.9460
22													.3738	.7100	.8648	.9368
23													.2675	.6608	.8419	.9261
24													.1439	.6036	.8152	.9136
25													.0000	.5370	.7842	.8991
26														.4594	.7480	.8822
27														.3692	.7060	.8626
28														.2643	.6571	.8397
29														.1421	.6002	.8131
30														.0000	.5339	.7821
35															.0000	.5325
40																.0000

LOAN PROGRESS CHART

15.50%

AGE OF LOAN	ORIGINAL TERM IN YEARS															
	1	2	3	4	5	6	7	8	9	10	15	20	25	30	35	40
1	.0000	.5384	.7165	.8045	.8564	.8904	.9141	.9314	.9445	.9546	.9817	.9920	.9964	.9983	.9992	.9996
2		.0000	.3858	.5764	.6890	.7626	.8140	.8515	.8797	.9016	.9603	.9826	.9922	.9964	.9983	.9992
3			.0000	.3103	.4937	.6135	.6971	.7581	.8042	.8398	.9353	.9717	.9872	.9942	.9973	.9988
4				.0000	.2658	.4396	.5608	.6493	.7161	.7676	.9062	.9590	.9815	.9915	.9961	.9982
5					.0000	.2367	.4018	.5224	.6133	.6835	.8722	.9441	.9748	.9885	.9947	.9975
6						.0000	.2163	.3743	.4934	.5854	.8326	.9268	.9670	.9849	.9930	.9968
7							.0000	.2015	.3535	.4709	.7864	.9066	.9579	.9807	.9911	.9959
8								.0000	.1903	.3374	.7324	.8830	.9472	.9758	.9889	.9949
9									.0000	.1817	.6695	.8555	.9348	.9702	.9863	.9937
10										.0000	.5962	.8235	.9203	.9635	.9832	.9922
11											.5106	.7861	.9034	.9558	.9796	.9906
12											.4108	.7424	.8838	.9468	.9755	.9887
13											.2943	.6915	.8608	.9363	.9707	.9864
14											.1585	.6321	.8340	.9240	.9650	.9838
15											.0000	.5629	.8027	.9097	.9584	.9808
16												.4821	.7662	.8930	.9507	.9772
17												.3878	.7237	.8736	.9418	.9731
18												.2779	.6741	.8508	.9313	.9683
19												.1496	.6162	.8244	.9191	.9626
20												.0000	.5487	.7935	.9049	.9561
21													.4699	.7574	.8883	.9484
22													.3780	.7154	.8689	.9395
23													.2709	.6663	.8463	.9290
24													.1458	.6091	.8200	.9169
25													.0000	.5423	.7892	.9027
26														.4645	.7534	.8861
27														.3737	.7116	.8668
28														.2677	.6628	.8442
29														.1442	.6059	.8180
30														.0000	.5395	.7873
35															.0000	.5381
40																.0000

15.75%

AGE OF LOAN	1	2	3	4	5	6	7	8	9	10	15	20	25	30	35	40
1	.0000	.5390	.7173	.8053	.8573	.8912	.9149	.9322	.9452	.9552	.9821	.9923	.9965	.9984	.9993	.9997
2		.0000	.3866	.5776	.6903	.7640	.8154	.8528	.8810	.9028	.9611	.9832	.9925	.9966	.9985	.9993
3			.0000	.3114	.4952	.6152	.6990	.7600	.8061	.8416	.9366	.9726	.9878	.9945	.9975	.9989
4				.0000	.2669	.4413	.5629	.6516	.7184	.7700	.9080	.9602	.9822	.9920	.9963	.9983
5					.0000	.2379	.4037	.5247	.6158	.6862	.8745	.9457	.9758	.9890	.9950	.9977
6						.0000	.2176	.3763	.4959	.5882	.8353	.9288	.9682	.9856	.9935	.9970
7							.0000	.2029	.3557	.4737	.7895	.9090	.9594	.9816	.9916	.9962
8								.0000	.1917	.3398	.7360	.8858	.9490	.9770	.9895	.9952
9									.0000	.1832	.6733	.8587	.9370	.9715	.9870	.9941
10										.0000	.6001	.8270	.9228	.9651	.9841	.9928
11											.5144	.7900	.9063	.9576	.9807	.9912
12											.4143	.7467	.8870	.9489	.9767	.9894
13											.2971	.6960	.8643	.9386	.9721	.9873
14											.1602	.6368	.8379	.9267	.9666	.9848
15											.0000	.5675	.8070	.9127	.9603	.9819
16												.4865	.7709	.8964	.9528	.9785
17												.3918	.7286	.8772	.9441	.9745
18												.2810	.6792	.8549	.9340	.9699
19												.1515	.6214	.8287	.9221	.9644
20												.0000	.5538	.7982	.9082	.9581
21													.4747	.7624	.8919	.9507
22													.3823	.7206	.8729	.9420
23													.2742	.6717	.8506	.9318
24													.1478	.6145	.8246	.9200
25													.0000	.5477	.7942	.9061
26														.4695	.7586	.8899
27														.3781	.7170	.8709
28														.2712	.6684	.8487
29														.1462	.6115	.8227
30														.0000	.5450	.7924
35															.0000	.5437
40																.0000

LOAN PROGRESS CHART

16.00%

AGE OF LOAN	1	2	3	4	5	6	7	8	9	10	15	20	25	30	35	40
							ORIGINAL TERM IN YEARS									
1	.0000	.5397	.7180	.8061	.8581	.8920	.9156	.9329	.9458	.9558	.9825	.9925	.9967	.9985	.9993	.9997
2		.0000	.3875	.5788	.6917	.7654	.8168	.8542	.8823	.9041	.9620	.9837	.9928	.9968	.9986	.9994
3			.0000	.3124	.4967	.6170	.7008	.7619	.8079	.8434	.9380	.9735	.9883	.9948	.9976	.9989
4				.0000	.2680	.4430	.5650	.6538	.7207	.7722	.9098	.9614	.9830	.9924	.9966	.9985
5					.0000	.2391	.4057	.5270	.6184	.6888	.8768	.9473	.9767	.9896	.9953	.9979
6						.0000	.2189	.3784	.4985	.5911	.8380	.9307	.9694	.9863	.9939	.9972
7							.0000	.2042	.3579	.4765	.7927	.9113	.9609	.9825	.9921	.9965
8								.0000	.1932	.3421	.7395	.8885	.9508	.9780	.9901	.9955
9									.0000	.1846	.6771	.8618	.9390	.9727	.9877	.9945
10										.0000	.6040	.8305	.9252	.9666	.9850	.9932
11											.5182	.7939	.9090	.9593	.9817	.9918
12											.4178	.7509	.8901	.9509	.9779	.9900
13											.3000	.7005	.8678	.9409	.9734	.9880
14											.1619	.6414	.8418	.9293	.9682	.9857
15											.0000	.5721	.8112	.9156	.9621	.9829
16												.4909	.7754	.8996	.9549	.9797
17												.3957	.7334	.8808	.9464	.9758
18												.2841	.6842	.8588	.9365	.9714
19												.1533	.6265	.8330	.9249	.9662
20												.0000	.5588	.8028	.9113	.9600
21													.4795	.7673	.8954	.9528
22													.3865	.7258	.8767	.9444
23													.2775	.6770	.8548	.9346
24													.1498	.6199	.8291	.9230
25													.0000	.5530	.7990	.9094
26														.4745	.7637	.8935
27														.3825	.7224	.8749
28														.2746	.6739	.8530
29														.1482	.6170	.8274
30														.0000	.5504	.7973
35															.0000	.5492
40																.0000

16.25%

AGE OF LOAN	1	2	3	4	5	6	7	8	9	10	15	20	25	30	35	40
1	.0000	.5403	.7188	.8069	.8589	.8928	.9164	.9336	.9465	.9565	.9829	.9928	.9968	.9986	.9994	.9997
2		.0000	.3883	.5800	.6930	.7668	.8182	.8555	.8836	.9053	.9629	.9843	.9931	.9970	.9987	.9994
3			.0000	.3134	.4982	.6187	.7027	.7638	.8098	.8452	.9393	.9743	.9888	.9950	.9978	.9990
4				.0000	.2691	.4448	.5670	.6560	.7230	.7745	.9116	.9626	.9837	.9928	.9968	.9986
5					.0000	.2403	.4076	.5294	.6209	.6915	.8790	.9488	.9777	.9901	.9956	.9980
6						.0000	.2202	.3805	.5010	.5939	.8407	.9326	.9706	.9870	.9942	.9974
7							.0000	.2056	.3601	.4792	.7958	.9135	.9623	.9833	.9926	.9967
8								.0000	.1946	.3445	.7429	.8912	.9525	.9790	.9907	.9959
9									.0000	.1861	.6808	.8649	.9411	.9740	.9884	.9948
10										.0000	.6078	.8340	.9276	.9680	.9858	.9937
11											.5220	.7977	.9117	.9610	.9827	.9923
12											.4212	.7550	.8931	.9528	.9790	.9907
13											.3028	.7049	.8713	.9431	.9747	.9887
14											.1636	.6459	.8456	.9318	.9697	.9865
15											.0000	.5767	.8153	.9184	.9638	.9839
16												.4953	.7798	.9027	.9568	.9808
17												.3997	.7381	.8843	.9486	.9771
18												.2873	.6891	.8627	.9390	.9728
19												.1552	.6315	.8372	.9277	.9678
20												.0000	.5638	.8073	.9144	.9619
21													.4842	.7722	.8988	.9549
22													.3907	.7308	.8804	.9468
23													.2809	.6823	.8589	.9372
24													.1517	.6253	.8335	.9259
25													.0000	.5582	.8038	.9126
26														.4795	.7688	.8970
27														.3869	.7276	.8787
28														.2781	.6793	.8572
29														.1502	.6225	.8319
30														.0000	.5558	.8022
35															.0000	.5547
40																.0000

LOAN PROGRESS CHART

16.50%

AGE OF LOAN	ORIGINAL TERM IN YEARS

AGE OF LOAN	1	2	3	4	5	6	7	8	9	10	15	20	25	30	35	40
1	.0000	.5409	.7196	.8077	.8597	.8936	.9171	.9343	.9472	.9571	.9833	.9930	.9970	.9987	.9994	.9997
2		.0000	.3892	.5812	.6944	.7682	.8195	.8569	.8849	.9065	.9637	.9848	.9934	.9971	.9987	.9994
3			.0000	.3144	.4997	.6205	.7045	.7657	.8116	.8469	.9406	.9751	.9893	.9953	.9979	.9991
4				.0000	.2703	.4465	.5691	.6582	.7252	.7768	.9133	.9637	.9843	.9932	.9970	.9987
5					.0000	.2415	.4095	.5317	.6235	.6941	.8812	.9503	.9785	.9906	.9959	.9982
6						.0000	.2215	.3826	.5036	.5967	.8434	.9344	.9717	.9877	.9946	.9976
7							.0000	.2069	.3624	.4820	.7988	.9158	.9637	.9841	.9930	.9969
8								.0000	.1960	.3468	.7463	.8938	.9542	.9800	.9912	.9961
9									.0000	.1876	.6845	.8679	.9430	.9751	.9891	.9952
10										.0000	.6116	.8374	.9299	.9694	.9866	.9941
11											.5258	.8014	.9144	.9626	.9836	.9928
12											.4247	.7591	.8961	.9546	.9801	.9912
13											.3056	.7092	.8746	.9453	.9760	.9894
14											.1653	.6504	.8493	.9342	.9711	.9873
15											.0000	.5812	.8194	.9212	.9654	.9848
16												.4997	.7842	.9058	.9587	.9818
17												.4036	.7428	.8877	.9507	.9783
18												.2904	.6940	.8664	.9414	.9742
19												.1571	.6365	.8413	.9303	.9694
20												.0000	.5688	.8117	.9174	.9636
21													.4889	.7769	.9021	.9569
22													.3949	.7358	.8841	.9490
23													.2842	.6875	.8628	.9397
24													.1537	.6305	.8378	.9287
25													.0000	.5634	.8084	.9157
26														.4844	.7737	.9004
27														.3912	.7328	.8825
28														.2815	.6847	.8613
29														.1523	.6279	.8363
30														.0000	.5611	.8069
35															.0000	.5601
40																.0000

16.75%

AGE OF LOAN	1	2	3	4	5	6	7	8	9	10	15	20	25	30	35	40
1	.0000	.5415	.7203	.8085	.8605	.8944	.9179	.9350	.9478	.9577	.9837	.9933	.9971	.9988	.9995	.9998
2		.0000	.3901	.5824	.6957	.7696	.8209	.8582	.8862	.9077	.9645	.9853	.9937	.9973	.9988	.9995
3			.0000	.3154	.5012	.6222	.7064	.7675	.8134	.8487	.9418	.9759	.9897	.9956	.9981	.9992
4				.0000	.2714	.4482	.5711	.6605	.7275	.7790	.9150	.9648	.9850	.9935	.9972	.9988
5					.0000	.2427	.4114	.5340	.6260	.6967	.8834	.9517	.9794	.9911	.9961	.9983
6						.0000	.2228	.3847	.5061	.5995	.8460	.9362	.9728	.9883	.9949	.9978
7							.0000	.2083	.3646	.4847	.8019	.9179	.9650	.9849	.9935	.9972
8								.0000	.1974	.3492	.7497	.8963	.9558	.9809	.9917	.9964
9									.0000	.1891	.6882	.8708	.9449	.9762	.9897	.9955
10										.0000	.6155	.8407	.9321	.9707	.9873	.9945
11											.5296	.8051	.9169	.9642	.9845	.9932
12											.4282	.7631	.8990	.9564	.9811	.9918
13											.3084	.7135	.8779	.9473	.9771	.9901
14											.1670	.6549	.8529	.9365	.9725	.9880
15											.0000	.5857	.8234	.9238	.9670	.9856
16												.5040	.7885	.9088	.9604	.9828
17												.4075	.7474	.8910	.9527	.9795
18												.2935	.6988	.8701	.9437	.9755
19												.1590	.6414	.8453	.9329	.9708
20												.0000	.5737	.8161	.9202	.9653
21													.4936	.7815	.9053	.9588
22													.3991	.7408	.8876	.9511
23													.2875	.6926	.8667	.9421
24													.1557	.6357	.8420	.9314
25													.0000	.5686	.8129	.9187
26														.4892	.7785	.9038
27														.3956	.7379	.8861
28														.2849	.6899	.8653
29														.1543	.6333	.8406
30														.0000	.5664	.8116
35															.0000	.5654
40																.0000

LOAN PROGRESS CHART
17.00%

AGE OF LOAN	ORIGINAL TERM IN YEARS															
	1	2	3	4	5	6	7	8	9	10	15	20	25	30	35	40
1	.0000	.5421	.7211	.8093	.8613	.8951	.9186	.9357	.9485	.9583	.9841	.9935	.9973	.9988	.9995	.9998
2		.0000	.3909	.5836	.6971	.7710	.8223	.8595	.8875	.9089	.9653	.9858	.9940	.9974	.9989	.9995
3			.0000	.3164	.5027	.6240	.7082	.7694	.8153	.8505	.9431	.9767	.9902	.9958	.9982	.9992
4				.0000	.2725	.4499	.5732	.6627	.7298	.7812	.9167	.9659	.9856	.9939	.9974	.9989
5					.0000	.2439	.4133	.5363	.6285	.6993	.8855	.9531	.9802	.9916	.9964	.9984
6						.0000	.2241	.3867	.5087	.6023	.8486	.9379	.9738	.9888	.9952	.9979
7							.0000	.2097	.3668	.4875	.8049	.9200	.9663	.9856	.9938	.9974
8								.0000	.1989	.3515	.7531	.8988	.9574	.9818	.9922	.9967
9									.0000	.1906	.6918	.8737	.9468	.9773	.9903	.9958
10										.0000	.6193	.8440	.9342	.9720	.9880	.9948
11											.5334	.8088	.9194	.9656	.9853	.9937
12											.4317	.7671	.9018	.9581	.9821	.9923
13											.3113	.7178	.8810	.9493	.9783	.9907
14											.1687	.6594	.8564	.9388	.9738	.9887
15											.0000	.5902	.8273	.9264	.9685	.9865
16												.5083	.7928	.9117	.9621	.9838
17												.4114	.7519	.8942	.9547	.9805
18												.2967	.7036	.8736	.9459	.9768
19												.1608	.6463	.8492	.9354	.9723
20												.0000	.5785	.8203	.9230	.9670
21													.4983	.7861	.9084	.9607
22													.4033	.7456	.8910	.9532
23													.2908	.6976	.8705	.9444
24													.1576	.6409	.8461	.9339
25													.0000	.5737	.8173	.9216
26														.4941	.7833	.9070
27														.3999	.7429	.8896
28														.2884	.6951	.8691
29														.1563	.6385	.8448
30														.0000	.5716	.8161
35															.0000	.5707
40																.0000

17.25%

AGE OF LOAN	1	2	3	4	5	6	7	8	9	10	15	20	25	30	35	40
1	.0000	.5427	.7219	.8101	.8621	.8959	.9194	.9364	.9491	.9589	.9845	.9937	.9974	.9989	.9995	.9998
2		.0000	.3918	.5848	.6984	.7723	.8236	.8609	.8887	.9101	.9661	.9863	.9943	.9976	.9990	.9996
3			.0000	.3174	.5042	.6257	.7101	.7712	.8171	.8522	.9443	.9774	.9906	.9960	.9983	.9993
4				.0000	.2736	.4517	.5752	.6649	.7320	.7835	.9184	.9669	.9862	.9942	.9975	.9990
5					.0000	.2451	.4152	.5386	.6310	.7019	.8876	.9544	.9810	.9920	.9966	.9986
6						.0000	.2254	.3888	.5112	.6051	.8511	.9397	.9749	.9894	.9955	.9981
7							.0000	.2110	.3690	.4902	.8078	.9221	.9675	.9863	.9942	.9975
8								.0000	.2003	.3539	.7564	.9013	.9589	.9827	.9927	.9969
9									.0000	.1920	.6954	.8765	.9486	.9783	.9908	.9961
10										.0000	.6230	.8472	.9363	.9732	.9886	.9952
11											.5371	.8124	.9218	.9671	.9861	.9941
12											.4351	.7710	.9046	.9598	.9830	.9928
13											.3141	.7220	.8842	.9512	.9793	.9912
14											.1705	.6637	.8599	.9410	.9750	.9894
15											.0000	.5946	.8311	.9288	.9699	.9872
16												.5126	.7969	.9144	.9638	.9846
17												.4153	.7564	.8974	.9566	.9816
18												.2998	.7083	.8771	.9480	.9779
19												.1627	.6511	.8530	.9378	.9736
20												.0000	.5834	.8245	.9257	.9685
21													.5029	.7906	.9114	.9624
22													.4074	.7503	.8943	.9552
23													.2941	.7026	.8741	.9466
24													.1596	.6459	.8501	.9364
25													.0000	.5787	.8217	.9244
26														.4989	.7879	.9100
27														.4042	.7478	.8930
28														.2918	.7002	.8729
29														.1583	.6438	.8489
30														.0000	.5767	.8205
35															.0000	.5759
40																.0000

LOAN PROGRESS CHART
17.50%

AGE OF LOAN	ORIGINAL TERM IN YEARS															
	1	2	3	4	5	6	7	8	9	10	15	20	25	30	35	40
1	.0000	.5433	.7226	.8109	.8629	.8967	.9201	.9371	.9498	.9595	.9849	.9939	.9975	.9990	.9996	.9998
2		.0000	.3926	.5860	.6997	.7737	.8250	.8622	.8900	.9113	.9669	.9867	.9945	.9977	.9990	.9996
3			.0000	.3184	.5057	.6274	.7119	.7731	.8188	.8539	.9455	.9781	.9910	.9963	.9984	.9993
4				.0000	.2747	.4534	.5773	.6671	.7342	.7857	.9200	.9679	.9868	.9945	.9977	.9990
5					.0000	.2463	.4172	.5409	.6335	.7045	.8897	.9558	.9818	.9924	.9968	.9987
6						.0000	.2267	.3909	.5138	.6079	.8536	.9413	.9758	.9899	.9958	.9982
7							.0000	.2124	.3713	.4929	.8108	.9241	.9687	.9870	.9946	.9977
8								.0000	.2017	.3562	.7597	.9037	.9603	.9835	.9931	.9971
9									.0000	.1935	.6990	.8793	.9503	.9793	.9913	.9964
10										.0000	.6268	.8504	.9384	.9743	.9893	.9955
11											.5408	.8159	.9242	.9684	.9868	.9945
12											.4386	.7749	.9073	.9614	.9839	.9932
13											.3169	.7261	.8872	.9530	.9804	.9918
14											.1722	.6681	.8633	.9431	.9762	.9900
15											.0000	.5990	.8349	.9312	.9713	.9880
16												.5169	.8010	.9172	.9654	.9855
17												.4192	.7608	.9004	.9584	.9826
18												.3029	.7129	.8805	.9500	.9791
19												.1646	.6559	.8568	.9401	.9749
20												.0000	.5881	.8285	.9283	.9700
21													.5075	7950	.9143	.9641
22													.4115	.7550	.8976	.9571
23													.2974	.7075	.8777	.9488
24													.1616	.6509	.8540	.9388
25													.0000	.5837	.8259	.9271
26														.5036	.7924	.9130
27														.4084	.7526	.8964
28														.2951	.7052	.8765
29														.1604	.6489	.8529
30														.0000	.5818	.8248
35															.0000	.5811
40																.0000

17.75%

AGE OF LOAN	1	2	3	4	5	6	7	8	9	10	15	20	25	30	35	40
1	.0000	.5439	.7234	.8117	.8637	.8974	.9208	.9377	.9504	.9601	.9852	.9941	.9976	.9990	.9996	.9998
2		.0000	.3935	.5872	.7011	.7751	.8263	.8635	.8912	.9124	.9676	.9872	.9948	.9979	.9991	.9996
3			.0000	.3194	.5071	.6292	.7137	.7749	.8206	.8556	.9466	.9788	.9914	.9965	.9985	.9994
4				.0000	.2759	.4551	.5793	.6693	.7364	.7878	.9216	.9689	.9873	.9948	.9978	.9991
5					.0000	.2476	.4191	.5433	.6360	.7070	.8917	.9571	.9825	.9928	.9970	.9988
6						.0000	.2280	.3930	.5163	.6106	.8561	.9429	.9768	.9904	.9961	.9984
7							.0000	.2138	.3735	.4957	.8136	.9261	.9699	.9876	.9949	.9979
8								.0000	.2032	.3586	.7630	.9060	.9617	.9843	.9935	.9973
9									.0000	.1950	.7026	.8820	.9520	.9802	.9918	.9966
10										.0000	.6305	.8535	.9403	.9755	.9899	.9958
11											.5445	.8194	.9265	.9697	.9875	.9948
12											.4420	.7787	.9099	.9629	.9847	.9937
13											.3198	.7302	.8902	.9548	.9813	.9923
14											.1739	.6724	.8666	.9451	.9773	.9906
15											.0000	.6034	.8385	.9336	.9726	.9886
16												.5212	.8051	.9198	.9669	.9863
17												.4230	.7651	.9034	.9601	.9835
18												.3060	.7175	.8838	.9520	.9801
19												.1665	.6606	.8604	.9423	.9761
20												.0000	.5929	.8325	.9308	.9714
21													.5120	.7993	.9171	.9657
22													.4156	.7596	.9007	.9589
23													.3007	.7123	.8811	.9508
24													.1635	.6559	.8578	.9412
25													.0000	.5886	.8300	.9297
26														.5084	.7969	.9159
27														.4127	.7573	.8996
28														.2985	.7102	.8801
29														.1624	.6539	.8568
30														.0000	.5869	.8290
35															.0000	.5861
40																.0000

LOAN PROGRESS CHART

18.00%

AGE OF LOAN	ORIGINAL TERM IN YEARS															
	1	2	3	4	5	6	7	8	9	10	15	20	25	30	35	40
1	.0000	.5445	.7241	.8125	.8645	.8982	.9215	.9384	.9510	.9606	.9856	.9944	.9977	.9991	.9996	.9998
2		.0000	.3943	.5884	.7024	.7764	.8277	.8648	.8924	.9136	.9684	.9876	.9950	.9980	.9992	.9997
3			.0000	.3204	.5086	.6309	.7155	.7767	.8224	.8573	.9478	.9795	.9918	.9967	.9986	.9994
4				.0000	.2770	.4568	.5814	.6714	.7387	.7900	.9232	.9699	.9879	.9951	.9980	.9992
5					.0000	.2488	.4210	.5456	.6385	.7096	.8938	.9583	.9832	.9932	.9972	.9989
6						.0000	.2293	.3951	.5188	.6134	.8586	.9445	.9777	.9909	.9963	.9985
7							.0000	.2151	.3757	.4984	.8165	.9280	.9710	.9882	.9952	.9980
8								.0000	.2046	.3609	.7662	.9083	.9631	.9850	.9939	.9975
9									.0000	.1965	.7061	.8847	.9536	.9811	.9923	.9969
10										.0000	.6342	.8565	.9423	.9765	.9904	.9961
11											.5482	.8228	.9287	.9710	.9882	.9952
12											.4455	.7825	.9125	.9644	.9855	.9941
13											.3226	.7343	.8931	.9565	.9823	.9927
14											.1757	.6767	.8699	.9471	.9784	.9912
15											.0000	.6078	.8422	.9358	.9738	.9893
16												.5254	.8090	.9224	.9683	.9870
17												.4269	.7694	.9062	.9617	.9844
18												.3091	.7220	.8870	.9539	.9811
19												.1683	.6653	.8639	.9445	.9773
20												.0000	.5976	.8364	.9332	.9727
21													.5166	.8035	.9198	.9672
22													.4197	.7641	.9037	.9606
23													.3039	.7171	.8845	.9528
24													.1655	.6608	.8615	.9434
25													.0000	.5935	.8341	.9322
26														.5131	.8012	.9187
27														.4169	.7620	.9027
28														.3019	.7151	.8835
29														.1644	.6589	.8606
30														.0000	.5918	.8331
35															.0000	.5912
40																.0000

18.25%

AGE OF LOAN	1	2	3	4	5	6	7	8	9	10	15	20	25	30	35	40
1	.0000	.5452	.7249	.8133	.8652	.8989	.9222	.9391	.9516	.9612	.9860	.9945	.9978	.9991	.9996	.9999
2		.0000	.3952	.5896	.7037	.7778	.8290	.8660	.8936	.9147	.9691	.9880	.9952	.9981	.9992	.9997
3			.0000	.3214	.5101	.6326	.7173	.7785	.8241	.8590	.9489	.9802	.9921	.9968	.9987	.9995
4				.0000	.2781	.4586	.5834	.6736	.7408	.7922	.9247	.9708	.9884	.9953	.9981	.9992
5					.0000	.2500	.4229	.5479	.6410	.7121	.8957	.9596	.9839	.9935	.9974	.9989
6						.0000	.2306	.3971	.5214	.6161	.8610	.9461	.9785	.9914	.9965	.9986
7							.0000	.2165	.3779	.5011	.8193	.9299	.9721	.9888	.9955	.9982
8								.0000	.2060	.3633	.7694	.9105	.9644	.9857	.9942	.9977
9									.0000	.1980	.7096	.8873	.9552	.9820	.9927	.9971
10										.0000	.6379	.8595	.9441	.9776	.9909	.9963
11											.5519	.8262	.9309	.9722	.9888	.9955
12											.4489	.7862	.9150	.9658	.9862	.9944
13											.3254	.7383	.8959	.9582	.9831	.9932
14											.1774	.6809	.8731	.9490	.9794	.9917
15											.0000	.6121	.8457	.9380	.9750	.9899
16												.5296	.8129	.9248	.9697	.9878
17												.4307	.7736	.9090	.9633	.9852
18												.3122	.7264	.8901	.9557	.9821
19												.1702	.6699	.8674	.9465	.9784
20												.0000	.6022	.8402	.9356	.9740
21													.5211	.8076	.9224	.9687
22													.4238	.7686	.9067	.9623
23													.3072	.7217	.8878	.9547
24													.1675	.6656	.8652	.9455
25													.0000	.5983	.8380	.9346
26														.5177	.8055	.9215
27														.4211	.7666	.9057
28														.3052	.7198	.8869
29														.1664	.6639	.8642
30														.0000	.5968	.8371
35															.0000	.5961
40																.0000

LOAN PROGRESS CHART
18.50%

AGE OF LOAN	1	2	3	4	5	6	7	8	9	10	15	20	25	30	35	40
						ORIGINAL TERM IN YEARS										
1	.0000	.5458	.7257	.8141	.8660	.8997	.9229	.9397	.9522	.9618	.9863	.9947	.9979	.9992	.9997	.9999
2		.0000	.3960	.5908	.7050	.7791	.8303	.8673	.8948	.9158	.9698	.9884	.9954	.9982	.9993	.9997
3			.0000	.3224	.5116	.6343	.7191	.7803	.8259	.8606	.9500	.9808	.9925	.9970	.9988	.9995
4				.0000	.2792	.4603	.5854	.6758	.7430	.7943	.9263	.9717	.9889	.9956	.9982	.9993
5					.0000	.2512	.4248	.5501	.6435	.7146	.8977	.9607	.9846	.9939	.9976	.9990
6						.0000	.2319	.3992	.5239	.6189	.8634	.9476	.9794	.9918	.9967	.9987
7							.0000	.2179	.3802	.5038	.8221	.9318	.9732	.9894	.9958	.9983
8								.0000	.2075	.3656	.7726	.9127	.9657	.9864	.9946	.9978
9									.0000	.1995	.7130	.8899	.9567	.9828	.9932	.9973
10										.0000	.6415	.8625	.9459	.9785	.9914	.9966
11											.5556	.8295	.9330	.9734	.9894	.9958
12											.4523	.7899	.9174	.9672	.9869	.9948
13											.3282	.7423	.8987	.9598	.9840	.9938
14											.1791	.6851	.8762	.9509	.9804	.9922
15											.0000	.6163	.8492	.9401	.9761	.9905
16												.5338	.8167	.9272	.9710	.9884
17												.4345	.7777	.9118	.9648	.9860
18												.3153	.7308	.8932	.9574	.9830
19												.1721	.6745	.8708	.9485	.9795
20												.0000	.6068	.8440	.9378	.9752
21													.5255	.8117	.9250	.9701
22													.4278	.7729	.9095	.9639
23													.3105	.7263	.8910	.9565
24													.1694	.6704	.8687	.9476
25													.0000	.6031	.8419	.9369
26														.5223	.8097	.9241
27														.4252	.7710	.9087
28														.3086	.7246	.8901
29														.1684	.6687	.8678
30														.0000	.6016	.8411
35															.0000	.6010
40																.0000

18.75%

AGE OF LOAN	1	2	3	4	5	6	7	8	9	10	15	20	25	30	35	40
1	.0000	.5464	.7264	.8149	.8668	.9004	.9236	.9404	.9528	.9623	.9866	.9949	.9980	.9992	.9997	.9999
2		.0000	.3969	.5920	.7064	.7805	.8317	.8686	.8960	.9169	.9705	.9888	.9957	.9983	.9993	.9997
3			.0000	.3234	.5131	.6360	.7209	.7821	.8276	.8623	.9511	.9815	.9928	.9972	.9989	.9996
4				.0000	.2804	.4620	.5875	.6779	.7452	.7964	.9278	.9726	.9893	.9958	.9984	.9994
5					.0000	.2524	.4267	.5524	.6459	.7171	.8996	.9619	.9852	.9942	.9977	.9991
6						.0000	.2332	.4013	.5264	.6216	.8657	.9491	.9802	.9922	.9969	.9988
7							.0000	.2193	.3824	.5066	.8249	.9336	.9742	.9899	.9960	.9984
8								.0000	.2089	.3680	.7757	.9149	.9669	.9870	.9949	.9980
9									.0000	.2011	.7165	.8924	.9582	.9836	.9935	.9975
10										.0000	.6451	.8654	.9477	.9795	.9919	.9968
11											.5592	.8327	.9350	.9745	.9900	.9960
12											.4557	.7935	.9197	.9685	.9876	.9951
13											.3310	.7462	.9014	.9613	.9848	.9940
14											.1809	.6892	.8792	.9526	.9814	.9927
15											.0000	.6206	.8525	.9422	.9772	.9910
16												.5379	.8204	.9296	.9723	.9891
17												.4383	.7817	.9144	.9663	.9867
18												.3184	.7351	.8961	.9591	.9839
19												.1740	.6790	.8741	.9505	.9805
20												.0000	.6114	.8476	.9400	.9764
21													.5299	.8157	.9275	.9714
22													.4319	.7772	.9123	.9654
23													.3137	.7309	.8941	.9583
24													.1714	.6751	.8721	.9496
25													.0000	.6078	.8457	.9392
26														.5269	.8138	.9266
27														.4294	.7754	.9115
28														.3119	.7292	.8933
29														.1704	.6735	.8713
30														.0000	.6064	.8449
35															.0000	.6059
40																.0000

LOAN PROGRESS CHART

19.00%

AGE OF LOAN	ORIGINAL TERM IN YEARS															
	1	2	3	4	5	6	7	8	9	10	15	20	25	30	35	40
1	.0000	.5470	.7272	.8157	.8676	.9012	.9243	.9410	.9534	.9629	.9870	.9951	.9981	.9993	.9997	.9999
2		.0000	.3978	.5932	.7077	.7818	.8330	.8698	.8972	.9180	.9712	.9892	.9959	.9984	.9994	.9998
3			.0000	.3244	.5146	.6377	.7227	.7839	.8293	.8639	.9522	.9821	.9931	.9973	.9990	.9996
4				.0000	.2815	.4637	.5895	.6801	.7474	.7985	.9292	.9734	.9898	.9960	.9985	.9994
5					.0000	.2537	.4287	.5547	.6484	.7196	.9015	.9630	.9858	.9945	.9979	.9992
6						.0000	.2345	.4034	.5289	.6243	.8680	.9505	.9810	.9926	.9971	.9989
7							.0000	.2206	.3846	.5093	.8276	.9353	.9752	.9904	.9963	.9985
8								.0000	.2104	.3703	.7788	.9170	.9681	.9876	.9952	.9981
9									.0000	.2026	.7199	.8949	.9596	.9844	.9939	.9976
10										.0000	.6487	.8682	.9494	.9804	.9924	.9970
11											.5628	.8360	.9370	.9756	.9905	.9963
12											.4591	.7970	.9220	.9698	.9883	.9954
13											.3338	.7500	.9040	.9628	.9855	.9944
14											.1826	.6933	.8822	.9544	.9823	.9931
15											.0000	.6248	.8559	.9442	.9783	.9915
16												.5420	.8241	.9318	.9735	.9897
17												.4421	.7857	.9170	.9677	.9874
18												.3215	.7394	.8990	.9607	.9847
19												.1759	.6834	.8773	.9523	.9814
20												.0000	.6159	.8512	.9421	.9775
21													.5343	.8196	.9298	.9727
22													.4359	.7814	.9150	.9669
23													.3169	.7353	.8971	.9599
24													.1734	.6797	.8755	.9515
25													.0000	.6125	.8493	.9413
26														.5314	.8178	.9291
27														.4335	.7797	.9142
28														.3152	.7338	.8963
29														.1724	.6782	.8747
30														.0000	.6112	.8486
35															.0000	.6107
40																.0000

19.25%

AGE OF LOAN	1	2	3	4	5	6	7	8	9	10	15	20	25	30	35	40
1	.0000	.5476	.7279	.8165	.8683	.9019	.9250	.9417	.9540	.9634	.9873	.9953	.9982	.9993	.9997	.9999
2		.0000	.3986	.5943	.7090	.7832	.8343	.8711	.8984	.9191	.9719	.9896	.9960	.9985	.9994	.9998
3			.0000	.3255	.5161	.6394	.7244	.7856	.8310	.8655	.9532	.9827	.9934	.9975	.9990	.9996
4				.0000	.2826	.4655	.5915	.6822	.7495	.8006	.9307	.9743	.9902	.9963	.9986	.9994
5					.0000	.2549	.4306	.5570	.6508	.7221	.9034	.9641	.9864	.9948	.9980	.9992
6						.0000	.2358	.4055	.5314	.6270	.8703	.9519	.9817	.9930	.9973	.9990
7							.0000	.2220	.3868	.5120	.8303	.9370	.9761	.9908	.9965	.9986
8								.0000	.2118	.3727	.7819	.9191	.9693	.9882	.9955	.9983
9									.0000	.2041	.7233	.8973	.9610	.9851	.9943	.9978
10										.0000	.6523	.8710	.9510	.9812	.9928	.9972
11											.5664	.8391	.9389	.9766	.9910	.9965
12											.4625	.8005	.9243	.9710	.9889	.9957
13											.3367	.7539	.9066	.9642	.9863	.9947
14											.1844	.6973	.8851	.9560	.9831	.9935
15											.0000	.6289	.8591	.9461	.9793	.9920
16												.5461	.8277	.9340	.9747	.9903
17												.4459	.7897	.9195	.9691	.9881
18												.3246	.7436	.9018	.9623	.9855
19												.1777	.6878	.8805	.9541	.9823
20												.0000	.6204	.8547	.9442	.9785
21													.5387	.8234	.9322	.9739
22													.4398	.7855	.9176	.9683
23													.3202	.7397	.9000	.9616
24													.1753	.6843	.8787	.9534
25													.0000	.6171	.8529	.9434
26														.5359	.8217	.9314
27														.4375	.7840	.9169
28														.3185	.7382	.8993
29														.1744	.6829	.8781
30														.0000	.6159	.8523
35															.0000	.6154
40																.0000

LOAN PROGRESS CHART

19.50%

AGE OF LOAN	ORIGINAL TERM IN YEARS															
	1	2	3	4	5	6	7	8	9	10	15	20	25	30	35	40
1	.0000	.5482	.7287	.8173	.8691	.9026	.9257	.9423	.9546	.9639	.9876	.9954	.9983	.9994	.9998	.9999
2		.0000	.3995	.5955	.7103	.7845	.8356	.8723	.8996	.9202	.9725	.9899	.9962	.9986	.9995	.9998
3			.0000	.3265	.5176	.6411	.7262	.7874	.8327	.8671	.9543	.9832	.9937	.9976	.9991	.9997
4				.0000	.2837	.4672	.5935	.6843	.7517	.8027	.9321	.9751	.9907	.9965	.9987	.9995
5					.0000	.2561	.4325	.5593	.6533	.7246	.9052	.9652	.9870	.9951	.9981	.9993
6						.0000	.2371	.4075	.5339	.6297	.8726	.9532	.9825	.9934	.9975	.9990
7							.0000	.2234	.3890	.5146	.8330	.9387	.9770	.9913	.9967	.9987
8								.0000	.2133	.3750	.7849	.9211	.9704	.9888	.9957	.9984
9									.0000	.2056	.7266	.8997	.9624	.9858	.9946	.9979
10										.0000	.6559	.8737	.9526	.9821	.9932	.9974
11											.5700	.8422	.9408	.9776	.9915	.9968
12											.4659	.8040	.9265	.9722	.9894	.9960
13											.3395	.7576	.9091	.9656	.9869	.9950
14											.1861	.7013	.8879	.9576	.9839	.9939
15											.0000	.6331	.8623	.9479	.9802	.9925
16												.5502	.8312	.9362	.9758	.9908
17												.4497	.7935	.9219	.9704	.9887
18												.3277	.7477	.9046	.9638	.9862
19												.1796	.6922	.8836	.9558	.9832
20												.0000	.6248	.8581	.9461	.9795
21													.5430	.8271	.9344	.9751
22													.4438	.7896	.9202	.9697
23													.3234	.7440	.9029	.9631
24													.1773	.6888	.8819	.9551
25													.0000	.6217	.8565	.9455
26														.5403	.8256	.9337
27														.4416	.7881	.9195
28														.3218	.7427	.9022
29														.1764	.6875	.8813
30														.0000	.6206	.8559
35															.0000	.6201
40																.0000

19.75%

AGE OF LOAN	1	2	3	4	5	6	7	8	9	10	15	20	25	30	35	40
1	.0000	.5488	.7294	.8180	.8699	.9034	.9264	.9429	.9552	.9645	.9879	.9956	.9984	.9994	.9998	.9999
2		.0000	.4003	.5967	.7116	.7858	.8369	.8735	.9007	.9213	.9732	.9903	.9964	.9987	.9995	.9998
3			.0000	.3275	.5191	.6428	.7280	.7891	.8344	.8687	.9553	.9838	.9940	.9978	.9992	.9997
4				.0000	.2849	.4689	.5955	.6864	.7538	.8048	.9335	.9759	.9911	.9967	.9987	.9995
5					.0000	.2573	.4344	.5615	.6557	.7270	.9070	.9663	.9875	.9953	.9982	.9993
6						.0000	.2384	.4096	.5364	.6324	.8748	.9546	.9832	.9937	.9976	.9991
7							.0000	.2248	.3913	.5173	.8356	.9404	.9779	.9917	.9969	.9988
8								.0000	.2147	.3774	.7879	.9231	.9715	.9893	.9960	.9985
9									.0000	.2071	.7299	.9020	.9637	.9864	.9949	.9981
10										.0000	.6594	.8764	.9542	.9829	.9936	.9976
11											.5736	.8453	.9426	.9786	.9920	.9970
12											.4692	.8074	.9286	.9733	.9900	.9962
13											.3423	.7613	.9115	.9669	.9876	.9953
14											.1878	.7053	.8907	.9592	.9847	.9943
15											.0000	.6372	.8655	.9497	.9811	.9929
16												.5542	.8347	.9382	.9768	.9913
17												.4534	.7973	.9242	.9716	.9893
18												.3307	.7518	.9072	.9652	.9870
19												.1815	.6965	.8866	.9575	.9840
20												.0000	.6292	.8614	.9480	.9805
21													.5473	.8308	.9366	.9762
22													.4477	.7936	.9226	.9710
23													.3266	.7483	.9057	.9646
24													.1792	.6932	.8850	.9568
25													.0000	.6262	.8599	.9474
26														.5448	.8293	.9360
27														.4456	.7922	.9220
28														.3251	.7470	.9051
29														.1784	.6920	.8844
30														.0000	.6251	.8593
35															.0000	.6247
40																.0000

LOAN PROGRESS CHART

20.00%

AGE OF LOAN	ORIGINAL TERM IN YEARS															
	1	2	3	4	5	6	7	8	9	10	15	20	25	30	35	40
1	.0000	.5494	.7302	.8188	.8706	.9041	.9271	.9436	.9558	.9650	.9882	.9958	.9984	.9994	.9998	.9999
2		.0000	.4012	.5979	.7129	.7871	.8382	.8748	.9018	.9223	.9738	.9906	.9966	.9987	.9995	.9998
3			.0000	.3285	.5206	.6445	.7297	.7909	.8361	.8703	.9563	.9843	.9943	.9979	.9992	.9997
4				.0000	.2860	.4706	.5975	.6886	.7559	.8068	.9349	.9766	.9914	.9968	.9988	.9996
5					.0000	.2586	.4363	.5638	.6581	.7294	.9088	.9673	.9880	.9956	.9984	.9994
6						.0000	.2397	.4117	.5389	.6351	.8770	.9559	.9838	.9940	.9978	.9992
7							.0000	.2262	.3935	.5200	.8382	.9419	.9787	.9921	.9971	.9989
8								.0000	.2162	.3797	.7909	.9250	.9725	.9898	.9962	.9986
9									.0000	.2086	.7332	.9043	.9649	.9870	.9952	.9982
10										.0000	.6629	.8791	.9557	.9836	.9939	.9978
11											.5772	.8483	.9444	.9795	.9924	.9972
12											.4726	.8108	.9307	.9744	.9905	.9965
13											.3451	.7650	.9139	.9682	.9882	.9956
14											.1896	.7092	.8934	.9607	.9854	.9946
15											.0000	.6412	.8685	.9514	.9820	.9933
16												.5583	.8381	.9402	.9779	.9918
17												.4571	.8010	.9265	.9728	.9899
18												.3338	.7558	.9098	.9666	.9876
19												.1834	.7007	.8895	.9591	.9848
20												.0000	.6335	.8647	.9499	.9814
21													.5516	.8344	.9387	.9773
22													.4516	.7975	.9250	.9722
23													.3298	.7525	.9083	.9660
24													.1812	.6976	.8880	.9585
25													.0000	.6307	.8632	.9493
26														.5491	.8330	.9381
27														.4496	.7962	.9244
28														.3283	.7513	.9078
29														.1804	.6965	.8875
30														.0000	.6297	.8627
35															.0000	.6293
40																.0000

20.25%

AGE OF LOAN	1	2	3	4	5	6	7	8	9	10	15	20	25	30	35	40
1	.0000	.5500	.7309	.8196	.8714	.9048	.9278	.9442	.9563	.9655	.9885	.9959	.9985	.9995	.9998	.9999
2		.0000	.4020	.5991	.7142	.7884	.8394	.8760	.9030	.9234	.9744	.9909	.9967	.9988	.9996	.9998
3			.0000	.3295	.5220	.6462	.7315	.7926	.8377	.8718	.9572	.9848	.9945	.9980	.9993	.9997
4				.0000	.2871	.4723	.5995	.6907	.7580	.8088	.9362	.9774	.9918	.9970	.9989	.9996
5					.0000	.2598	.4382	.5661	.6605	.7319	.9105	.9683	.9885	.9958	.9985	.9994
6						.0000	.2410	.4138	.5414	.6377	.8791	.9571	.9845	.9943	.9979	.9992
7							.0000	.2276	.3957	.5227	.8408	.9435	.9795	.9925	.9973	.9990
8								.0000	.2176	.3821	.7938	.9269	.9735	.9903	.9965	.9987
9									.0000	.2101	.7365	.9065	.9661	.9876	.9955	.9983
10										.0000	.6664	.8816	.9571	.9844	.9943	.9979
11											.5807	.8512	.9461	.9803	.9928	.9974
12											.4759	.8141	.9327	.9754	.9910	.9967
13											.3479	.7686	.9162	.9694	.9888	.9959
14											.1913	.7131	.8961	.9621	.9861	.9949
15											.0000	.6452	.8715	.9531	.9829	.9937
16												.5623	.8415	.9422	.9788	.9923
17												.4608	.8047	.9288	.9739	.9905
18												.3368	.7598	.9124	.9679	.9883
19												.1853	.7049	.8923	.9606	.9856
20												.0000	.6378	.8679	.9517	.9823
21													.5558	.8379	.9407	.9783
22													.4555	.8013	.9273	.9734
23													.3330	.7566	.9110	.9674
24													.1831	.7020	.8910	.9601
25													.0000	.6351	.8665	.9511
26														.5535	.8366	.9402
27														.4536	.8001	.9268
28														.3316	.7555	.9105
29														.1824	.7009	.8905
30														.0000	.6342	.8660
35															.0000	.6338
40																.0000

LOAN PROGRESS CHART
20.50%

AGE OF LOAN	| ORIGINAL TERM IN YEARS															
	1	2	3	4	5	6	7	8	9	10	15	20	25	30	35	40
1	.0000	.5506	.7317	.8204	.8722	.9055	.9284	.9448	.9569	.9660	.9888	.9961	.9986	.9995	.9998	.9999
2		.0000	.4029	.6003	.7155	.7898	.8407	.8772	.9041	.9244	.9750	.9912	.9969	.9989	.9996	.9999
3			.0000	.3305	.5235	.6479	.7332	.7943	.8394	.8734	.9582	.9853	.9948	.9981	.9993	.9998
4				.0000	.2883	.4741	.6015	.6928	.7601	.8109	.9376	.9781	.9922	.9972	.9990	.9996
5					.0000	.2610	.4401	.5683	.6629	.7343	.9123	.9692	.9890	.9960	.9986	.9995
6						.0000	.2424	.4158	.5438	.6404	.8813	.9584	.9851	.9946	.9981	.9993
7							.0000	.2290	.3979	.5254	.8433	.9450	.9803	.9929	.9974	.9991
8								.0000	.2191	.3844	.7968	.9287	.9745	.9908	.9967	.9988
9									.0000	.2117	.7397	.9087	.9673	.9882	.9957	.9985
10										.0000	.6698	.8842	.9585	.9851	.9946	.9980
11											.5842	.8541	.9478	.9812	.9932	.9975
12											.4793	.8173	.9346	.9764	.9915	.9969
13											.3507	.7722	.9185	.9706	.9894	.9962
14											.1931	.7170	.8987	.9635	.9868	.9952
15											.0000	.6492	.8744	.9547	.9836	.9941
16												.5662	.8447	.9440	.9798	.9927
17												.4645	.8083	.9309	.9750	.9910
18												.3399	.7637	.9148	.9692	.9889
19												.1872	.7091	.8951	.9621	.9863
20												.0000	6421	.8710	.9534	.9831
21													.5600	.8414	.9427	.9793
22													.4594	.8051	.9296	.9745
23													.3361	.7607	.9135	.9687
24													.1851	.7062	.8938	.9616
25													.0000	.6395	.8697	.9529
26														.5578	.8402	.9422
27														.4576	.8040	.9291
28														.3348	.7596	.9130
29														.1844	.7052	.8934
30														.0000	.6386	.8693
35															.0000	.6383
40																.0000

20.75%

AGE OF LOAN	1	2	3	4	5	6	7	8	9	10	15	20	25	30	35	40
1	.0000	.5513	.7324	.8211	.8729	.9062	.9291	.9454	.9575	.9665	.9891	.9962	.9987	.9995	.9998	.9999
2		.0000	.4038	.6014	.7168	.7911	.8420	.8784	.9052	.9254	.9756	.9915	.9970	.9989	.9996	.9999
3			.0000	.3315	.5250	.6496	.7350	.7960	.8410	.8749	.9591	.9858	.9950	.9982	.9994	.9998
4				.0000	.2894	.4758	.6035	.6949	.7622	.8129	.9389	.9788	.9925	.9973	.9990	.9997
5					.0000	.2623	.4420	.5706	.6653	.7367	.9140	.9702	.9894	.9962	.9987	.9995
6						.0000	.2437	.4179	.5463	.6430	.8834	.9595	.9857	.9949	.9982	.9993
7							.0000	.2304	.4001	.5280	.8458	.9465	.9811	.9933	.9976	.9991
8								.0000	.2206	.3867	.7996	.9305	.9754	.9912	.9969	.9989
9									.0000	.2132	.7429	.9108	.9685	.9888	.9960	.9986
10										.0000	.6733	.8867	.9599	.9857	.9949	.9982
11											.5877	.8570	.9494	.9820	.9936	.9977
12											.4826	.8205	.9365	.9774	.9919	.9971
13											.3535	.7758	.9207	.9718	.9899	.9964
14											.1948	.7208	.9012	.9648	.9874	.9955
15											.0000	.6532	.8773	.9563	.9844	.9944
16												.5702	.8480	.9458	.9807	.9931
17												.4682	.8119	.9330	.9761	.9915
18												.3429	.7676	.9172	.9704	.9894
19												.1890	.7131	.8978	.9635	.9870
20												.0000	.6463	.8740	.9550	.9839
21													.5641	.8448	.9446	.9802
22													.4632	.8088	.9318	.9756
23													.3393	.7647	.9160	.9700
24													.1870	.7105	.8966	.9631
25													.0000	.6438	.8728	.9546
26														.5620	.8436	.9441
27														.4615	.8077	.9313
28														.3380	.7637	.9156
29														.1863	.7095	.8962
30														.0000	.6430	.8724
35															.0000	.6427
40																.0000

LOAN PROGRESS CHART

21.00%

AGE OF LOAN	\multicolumn{16}{ORIGINAL TERM IN YEARS}

AGE OF LOAN	1	2	3	4	5	6	7	8	9	10	15	20	25	30	35	40
1	.0000	.5519	.7332	.8219	.8737	.9069	.9297	.9460	.9580	.9670	.9893	.9963	.9987	.9996	.9998	.9999
2		.0000	.4046	.6026	.7181	.7924	.8432	.8796	.9063	.9264	.9762	.9918	.9971	.9990	.9996	.9999
3			.0000	.3326	.5265	.6513	.7367	.7977	.8426	.8764	.9600	.9863	.9952	.9983	.9994	.9998
4				.0000	.2905	.4775	.6055	.6969	.7642	.8149	.9401	.9795	.9928	.9975	.9991	.9997
5					.0000	.2635	.4439	.5728	.6677	.7390	.9156	.9711	.9899	.9964	.9987	.9996
6						.0000	.2450	.4200	.5488	.6457	.8854	.9607	.9863	.9952	.9983	.9994
7							.0000	.2318	.4023	.5307	.8483	.9480	.9818	.9936	.9977	.9992
8								.0000	.2220	.3891	.8025	.9323	.9763	.9917	.9971	.9990
9									.0000	.2147	.7461	.9129	.9696	.9893	.9962	.9987
10										.0000	.6767	.8891	.9612	.9864	.9952	.9983
11											.5912	.8598	.9510	.9828	.9939	.9979
12											.4859	.8237	.9384	.9783	.9924	.9973
13											.3562	.7793	.9228	.9728	.9904	.9966
14											.1966	.7245	.9037	.9661	.9880	.9958
15											.0000	.6571	.8801	.9578	.9851	.9947
16												.5741	.8511	.9476	.9815	.9935
17												.4718	.8154	.9350	.9771	.9919
18												.3459	.7714	.9196	.9716	.9900
19												.1909	.7172	.9005	.9649	.9876
20												.0000	.6504	.8770	.9566	.9847
21													.5683	.8481	.9464	.9811
22													.4671	.8125	.9339	.9767
23													.3424	.7686	.9184	.9712
24													.1890	.7146	.8994	.9645
25													.0000	.6481	.8759	.9562
26														.5662	.8470	.9460
27														.4654	.8115	.9334
28														.3412	.7677	.9180
29														.1883	.7137	.8990
30														.0000	.6473	.8755
35															.0000	.6470
40																.0000

21.25%

AGE OF LOAN	1	2	3	4	5	6	7	8	9	10	15	20	25	30	35	40
1	.0000	.5525	.7339	.8227	.8744	.9077	.9304	.9466	.9586	.9675	.9896	.9965	.9988	.9996	.9999	.9999
2		.0000	.4055	.6038	.7194	.7937	.8445	.8807	.9074	.9274	.9768	.9921	.9973	.9991	.9997	.9999
3			.0000	.3336	.5280	.6529	.7384	.7994	.8442	.8779	.9609	.9868	.9954	.9984	.9994	.9998
4				.0000	.2917	.4792	.6075	.6990	.7663	.8168	.9414	.9801	.9931	.9976	.9992	.9997
5					.0000	.2647	.4458	.5751	.6700	.7414	.9173	.9719	.9903	.9966	.9988	.9996
6						.0000	.2463	.4221	.5512	.6483	.8875	.9618	.9868	.9954	.9984	.9994
7							.0000	.2332	.4046	.5333	.8507	.9494	.9825	.9939	.9979	.9993
8								.0000	.2235	.3914	.8053	.9340	.9772	.9921	.9972	.9990
9									.0000	.2162	.7492	.9150	.9706	.9898	.9964	.9988
10										.0000	.6800	.8915	.9625	.9870	.9955	.9984
11											.5946	.8626	.9525	.9835	.9942	.9980
12											.4892	.8268	.9402	.9792	.9928	.9975
13											.3590	.7827	.9249	.9739	.9909	.9968
14											.1984	.7282	.9061	.9674	.9886	.9960
15											.0000	.6610	.8829	.9593	.9858	.9951
16												.5780	.8542	.9493	.9823	.9938
17												.4755	.8188	.9370	.9781	.9923
18												.3490	.7751	.9218	.9728	.9905
19												.1928	.7212	.9031	.9662	.9882
20												.0000	.6546	.8799	.9582	.9854
21													.5723	.8513	.9482	.9819
22													.4709	.8160	.9359	.9777
23													.3456	.7725	.9207	.9724
24													.1909	.7187	.9020	.9658
25													.0000	.6524	.8789	.9578
26														.5704	.8503	.9478
27														.4693	.8151	.9355
28														.3444	.7716	.9204
29														.1903	.7179	.9016
30														.0000	.6516	.8785
35															.0000	.6513
40																.0000

LOAN PROGRESS CHART

21.50%

AGE OF LOAN	ORIGINAL TERM IN YEARS															
	1	2	3	4	5	6	7	8	9	10	15	20	25	30	35	40
1	.0000	.5531	.7347	.8234	.8751	.9084	.9310	.9472	.9591	.9680	.9899	.9966	.9988	.9996	.9999	*****
2		.0000	.4063	.6050	.7206	.7949	.8457	.8819	.9085	.9284	.9773	.9924	.9974	.9991	.9997	.9999
3			.0000	.3346	.5294	.6546	.7401	.8011	.8458	.8794	.9618	.9872	.9956	.9985	.9995	.9998
4				.0000	.2928	.4809	.6095	.7011	.7683	.8188	.9426	.9808	.9934	.9977	.9992	.9997
5					.0000	.2660	.4478	.5773	.6724	.7437	.9189	.9728	.9907	.9968	.9989	.9996
6						.0000	.2476	.4241	.5537	.6509	.8895	.9630	.9874	.9957	.9985	.9995
7							.0000	.2346	.4068	.5360	.8531	.9508	.9832	.9942	.9980	.9993
8								.0000	.2250	.3938	.8081	.9357	.9780	.9925	.9974	.9991
9									.0000	.2178	.7523	.9170	.9717	.9903	.9967	.9988
10										.0000	.6834	.8939	.9638	.9876	.9957	.9985
11											.5981	.8653	.9540	.9842	.9946	.9981
12											.4925	.8299	.9419	.9801	.9931	.9976
13											.3618	.7861	.9270	.9749	.9914	.9970
14											.2001	.7319	.9085	.9686	.9892	.9963
15											.0000	.6648	.8856	.9607	.9865	.9953
16												.5818	.8572	.9510	.9831	.9942
17												.4791	.8222	.9389	.9790	.9928
18												.3520	.7788	.9240	.9738	.9910
19												.1947	.7251	.9056	.9675	.9888
20												.0000	.6586	.8828	.9596	.9861
21													.5764	.8545	.9499	.9828
22													.4746	.8196	.9379	.9786
23													.3487	.7763	.9230	.9735
24													.1929	.7228	.9046	.9671
25													.0000	.6565	.8818	.9593
26														.5746	.8536	.9496
27														.4731	.8187	.9375
28														.3476	.7755	.9227
29														.1922	.7220	.9042
30														.0000	.6558	.8815
35															.0000	.6556
40																.0000

21.75%

AGE OF LOAN	ORIGINAL TERM IN YEARS															
	1	2	3	4	5	6	7	8	9	10	15	20	25	30	35	40
1	.0000	.5537	.7354	.8242	.8759	.9091	.9317	.9478	.9596	.9685	.9901	.9967	.9989	.9996	.9999	*****
2		.0000	.4072	.6061	.7219	.7962	.8470	.8831	.9095	.9294	.9779	.9927	.9975	.9992	.9997	.9999
3			.0000	.3356	.5309	.6563	.7418	.8028	.8474	.8809	.9627	.9876	.9958	.9986	.9995	.9998
4				.0000	.2940	.4826	.6114	.7031	.7703	.8207	.9438	.9814	.9937	.9979	.9993	.9998
5					.0000	.2672	.4497	.5795	.6747	.7461	.9204	.9736	.9911	.9970	.9990	.9997
6						.0000	.2490	.4262	.5561	.6535	.8914	.9640	.9879	.9959	.9986	.9995
7							.0000	.2360	.4090	.5386	.8555	.9521	.9838	.9945	.9981	.9994
8								.0000	.2264	.3961	.8108	.9373	.9789	.9928	.9976	.9992
9									.0000	.2193	.7554	.9190	.9727	.9907	.9968	.9989
10										.0000	.6867	.8962	.9650	.9881	.9960	.9986
11											.6015	.8679	.9555	.9849	.9949	.9983
12											.4958	.8329	.9436	.9809	.9935	.9978
13											.3646	.7894	.9290	.9759	.9918	.9972
14											.2019	.7355	.9108	.9697	.9897	.9965
15											.0000	.6686	.8882	.9621	.9871	.9956
16												.5856	.8602	.9526	.9839	.9945
17												.4827	.8255	.9408	.9799	.9931
18												.3550	.7824	.9262	.9749	.9915
19												.1965	.7290	.9080	.9687	.9894
20												.0000	.6627	.8855	.9611	.9868
21													.5804	.8576	.9516	.9835
22													.4784	.8230	.9398	.9795
23													.3518	.7801	.9252	.9746
24													.1948	.7268	.9071	.9684
25													.0000	.6607	.8846	.9607
26														.5787	.8567	.9513
27														.4769	.8222	.9395
28														.3508	.7793	.9249
29														.1942	.7260	.9068
30														.0000	.6600	.8843
35															.0000	.6598
40																.0000

LOAN PROGRESS CHART

22.00%

AGE OF LOAN	ORIGINAL TERM IN YEARS															
	1	2	3	4	5	6	7	8	9	10	15	20	25	30	35	40
1	.0000	.5543	.7362	.8250	.8766	.9097	.9323	.9484	.9602	.9690	.9904	.9968	.9989	.9996	.9999	.....
2		.0000	.4080	.6073	.7232	.7975	.8482	.8842	.9106	.9304	.9784	.9929	.9976	.9992	.9997	.9999
3			.0000	.3366	.5324	.6579	.7435	.8044	.8490	.8823	.9635	.9881	.9960	.9987	.9996	.9998
4				.0000	.2951	.4843	.6134	.7052	.7724	.8226	.9450	.9820	.9940	.9980	.9993	.9998
5					.0000	.2685	.4516	.5817	.6771	.7484	.9220	.9744	.9915	.9971	.9990	.9997
6						.0000	.2503	.4283	.5586	.6561	.8934	.9651	.9884	.9961	.9987	.9996
7							.0000	.2374	.4112	.5412	.8578	.9534	.9845	.9948	.9983	.9994
8								.0000	.2279	.3984	.8135	.9389	.9796	.9932	.9977	.9992
9									.0000	.2208	.7585	.9209	.9736	.9912	.9970	.9990
10										.0000	.6900	.8984	.9661	.9887	.9962	.9987
11											.6049	.8706	.9569	.9855	.9951	.9984
12											.4990	.8359	.9453	.9817	.9938	.9979
13											.3674	.7927	.9309	.9768	.9922	.9974
14											.2036	.7391	.9130	.9708	.9902	.9967
15											.0000	.6724	.8908	.9634	.9877	.9959
16												.5894	.8631	.9541	.9846	.9948
17												.4863	.8288	.9426	.9807	.9935
18												.3580	.7860	.9283	.9759	.9919
19												.1984	.7328	.9104	.9699	.9899
20												.0000	.6667	.8882	.9625	.9874
21													.5844	.8607	.9532	.9843
22													.4821	.8264	.9417	.9804
23													.3549	.7837	.9274	.9756
24													.1967	.7307	.9095	.9696
25													.0000	.6648	.8874	.9622
26														.5827	.8599	.9529
27														.4807	.8256	.9414
28														.3539	.7830	.9271
29														.1962	.7300	.9093
30														.0000	.6641	.8871
35															.0000	.6639
40																.0000

22.25%

AGE OF LOAN	1	2	3	4	5	6	7	8	9	10	15	20	25	30	35	40
1	.0000	.5549	.7369	.8257	.8774	.9104	.9330	.9490	.9607	.9694	.9906	.9970	.9990	.9997	.9999	.....
2		.0000	.4089	.6085	.7245	.7988	.8494	.8854	.9117	.9313	.9789	.9932	.9978	.9993	.9998	.9999
3			.0000	.3376	.5339	.6596	.7452	.8061	.8506	.8838	.9644	.9885	.9962	.9987	.9996	.9999
4				.0000	.2962	.4860	.6154	.7072	.7744	.8245	.9462	.9826	.9943	.9981	.9994	.9998
5					.0000	.2697	.4535	.5840	.6794	.7507	.9235	.9752	.9918	.9973	.9991	.9997
6						.0000	.2516	.4303	.5610	.6586	.8953	.9661	.9888	.9963	.9988	.9996
7							.0000	.2388	.4134	.5438	.8601	.9547	.9851	.9951	.9984	.9995
8								.0000	.2294	.4008	.8162	.9405	.9804	.9935	.9978	.9993
9									.0000	.2224	.7615	.9228	.9746	.9916	.9972	.9991
10										.0000	.6933	.9007	.9673	.9892	.9964	.9988
11											.6083	.8731	.9582	.9862	.9954	.9985
12											.5023	.8388	.9469	.9824	.9942	.9981
13											.3701	.7960	.9328	.9777	.9926	.9975
14											.2054	.7426	.9152	.9719	.9907	.9969
15											.0000	.6761	.8933	.9647	.9883	.9961
16												.5932	.8660	.9556	.9853	.9951
17												.4898	.8320	.9443	.9815	.9939
18												.3609	.7895	.9303	.9769	.9923
19												.2003	.7366	.9128	.9711	.9904
20												.0000	.6706	.8909	.9638	.9880
21													.5884	.8637	.9548	.9850
22													.4858	.8297	.9435	.9812
23													.3580	.7874	.9294	.9766
24													.1987	.7346	.9119	.9708
25													.0000	.6688	.8901	.9635
26														.5868	.8629	.9545
27														.4845	.8290	.9432
28														.3570	.7867	.9292
29														.1981	.7339	.9117
30														.0000	.6682	.8898
35															.0000	.6680
40																.0000

LOAN PROGRESS CHART

22.50%

AGE OF LOAN	1	2	3	4	5	6	7	8	9	10	15	20	25	30	35	40
						ORIGINAL TERM IN YEARS										
1	.0000	.5555	.7376	.8265	.8781	.9111	.9336	.9495	.9612	.9699	.9909	.9971	.9990	.9997	.9999	*****
2		.0000	.4098	.6096	.7257	.8000	.8506	.8865	.9127	.9322	.9794	.9934	.9979	.9993	.9998	.9999
3			.0000	.3387	.5353	.6612	.7469	.8077	.8521	.8852	.9652	.9888	.9964	.9988	.9996	.9999
4				.0000	.2974	.4877	.6173	.7092	.7764	.8264	.9473	.9831	.9945	.9982	.9994	.9998
5					.0000	.2709	.4554	.5862	.6817	.7530	.9250	.9760	.9922	.9974	.9992	.9997
6						.0000	.2530	.4324	.5634	.6612	.8972	.9671	.9893	.9965	.9989	.9996
7							.0000	.2402	.4156	.5465	.8624	.9559	.9857	.9953	.9985	.9995
8								.0000	.2309	.4031	.8189	.9420	.9811	.9938	.9980	.9993
9									.0000	.2239	.7645	.9246	.9755	.9920	.9974	.9991
10										.0000	.6965	.9028	.9684	.9897	.9966	.9989
11											.6116	.8756	.9595	.9868	.9957	.9986
12											.5055	.8417	.9485	.9831	.9945	.9982
13											.3729	.7992	.9346	.9786	.9930	.9977
14											.2071	.7461	.9174	.9730	.9911	.9971
15											.0000	.6798	.8958	.9659	.9888	.9963
16												.5969	.8688	.9571	.9859	.9954
17												.4934	.8351	.9460	.9823	.9942
18												.3639	.7930	.9323	.9778	.9927
19												.2022	.7403	.9150	.9721	.9909
20												.0000	.6745	.8935	.9651	.9886
21													.5923	.8666	.9563	.9857
22													.4895	.8330	.9452	.9820
23													.3611	.7909	.9315	.9775
24													.2006	.7384	.9143	.9719
25													.0000	.6728	.8927	.9648
26														.5908	.8659	.9560
27														.4883	.8323	.9450
28														.3602	.7903	.9312
29														.2001	.7378	.9140
30														.0000	.6722	.8925
35															.0000	.6720
40																.0000

22.75%

AGE OF LOAN	1	2	3	4	5	6	7	8	9	10	15	20	25	30	35	40
1	.0000	.5561	.7384	.8272	.8788	.9118	.9342	.9501	.9617	.9703	.9911	.9972	.9991	.9997	.9999	*****
2		.0000	.4106	.6108	.7270	.8013	.8518	.8876	.9137	.9332	.9799	.9937	.9980	.9993	.9998	.9999
3			.0000	.3397	.5368	.6629	.7486	.8093	.8536	.8866	.9660	.9892	.9965	.9989	.9996	.9999
4				.0000	.2985	.4894	.6193	.7113	.7783	.8283	.9485	.9837	.9948	.9983	.9995	.9998
5					.0000	.2722	.4573	.5884	.6840	.7553	.9265	.9767	.9925	.9976	.9992	.9997
6						.0000	.2543	.4344	.5658	.6637	.8990	.9680	.9897	.9967	.9989	.9997
7							.0000	.2416	.4178	.5491	.8646	.9571	.9862	.9955	.9986	.9995
8								.0000	.2323	.4054	.8215	.9435	.9818	.9941	.9981	.9994
9									.0000	.2255	.7675	.9264	.9763	.9923	.9975	.9992
10										.0000	.6998	.9050	.9694	.9901	.9968	.9990
11											.6150	.8781	.9608	.9873	.9959	.9987
12											.5087	.8445	.9500	.9838	.9948	.9983
13											.3756	.8024	.9364	.9795	.9933	.9978
14											.2089	.7496	.9195	.9740	.9916	.9973
15											.0000	.6835	.8982	.9671	.9893	.9965
16												.6007	.8716	.9585	.9866	.9956
17												.4969	.8382	.9477	.9831	.9945
18												.3669	.7964	.9342	.9787	.9931
19												.2040	.7440	.9172	.9732	.9913
20												.0000	.6784	.8960	.9663	.9891
21													.5962	.8695	.9577	.9863
22													.4932	.8362	.9469	.9828
23													.3641	.7944	.9334	.9784
24													.2025	.7422	.9165	.9730
25													.0000	.6767	.8953	.9661
26														.5947	.8688	.9575
27														.4920	.8355	.9467
28														.3633	.7938	.9332
29														.2020	.7416	.9163
30														.0000	.6762	.8951
35															.0000	.6760
40																.0000

LOAN PROGRESS CHART

23.00%

AGE OF LOAN	ORIGINAL TERM IN YEARS															
	1	2	3	4	5	6	7	8	9	10	15	20	25	30	35	40
1	.0000	.5567	.7391	.8280	.8795	.9125	.9348	.9507	.9622	.9708	.9913	.9973	.9991	.9997	.9999	*****
2		.0000	.4115	.6120	.7283	.8026	.8530	.8887	.9148	.9341	.9804	.9939	.9981	.9994	.9998	.9999
3			.0000	.3407	.5383	.6645	.7503	.8110	.8552	.8880	.9667	.9896	.9967	.9989	.9997	.9999
4				.0000	.2997	.4911	.6212	.7133	.7803	.8302	.9496	.9842	.9950	.9984	.9995	.9998
5					.0000	.2734	.4591	.5906	.6863	.7575	.9280	.9775	.9928	.9977	.9993	.9998
6						.0000	.2556	.4365	.5683	.6663	.9009	.9690	.9901	.9969	.9990	.9997
7							.0000	.2430	.4200	.5517	.8668	.9583	.9868	.9958	.9986	.9996
8								.0000	.2338	.4077	.8241	.9450	.9825	.9944	.9982	.9994
9									.0000	.2270	.7704	.9282	.9772	.9927	.9977	.9993
10										.0000	.7030	.9071	.9705	.9906	.9970	.9990
11											.6183	.8806	.9620	.9879	.9961	.9988
12											.5119	.8473	.9515	.9845	.9950	.9984
13											.3784	.8055	.9382	.9803	.9937	.9980
14											.2106	.7530	.9215	.9749	.9920	.9974
15											.0000	.6871	.9006	.9682	.9898	.9967
16												.6043	.8743	.9598	.9872	.9959
17												.5004	.8412	.9493	.9838	.9948
18												.3698	.7997	.9360	.9795	.9935
19												.2059	.7476	.9194	.9742	.9917
20												.0000	.6822	.8985	.9675	.9896
21													.6000	.8723	.9591	.9869
22													.4968	.8393	.9486	.9835
23													.3672	.7979	.9354	.9793
24													.2044	.7459	.9187	.9740
25													.0000	.6806	.8978	.9673
26														.5986	.8716	.9589
27														.4957	.8387	.9484
28														.3664	.7973	.9351
29														.2040	.7454	.9185
30														.0000	.6801	.8976
35															.0000	.6800
40																.0000

23.25%

AGE OF LOAN	1	2	3	4	5	6	7	8	9	10	15	20	25	30	35	40
1	.0000	.5573	.7398	.8287	.8803	.9131	.9355	.9512	.9627	.9712	.9915	.9974	.9992	.9997	.9999	*****
2		.0000	.4123	.6131	.7295	.8038	.8542	.8898	.9158	.9350	.9809	.9941	.9981	.9994	.9998	.9999
3			.0000	.3417	.5397	.6662	.7519	.8126	.8567	.8894	.9675	.9899	.9968	.9990	.9997	.9999
4				.0000	.3008	.4929	.6232	.7153	.7823	.8320	.9506	.9847	.9952	.9985	.9995	.9998
5					.0000	.2747	.4610	.5928	.6886	.7598	.9294	.9782	.9931	.9978	.9993	.9998
6						.0000	.2569	.4386	.5707	.6688	.9027	.9699	.9905	.9970	.9991	.9997
7							.0000	.2444	.4222	.5543	.8690	.9595	.9873	.9960	.9987	.9996
8								.0000	.2353	.4101	.8266	.9464	.9832	.9947	.9983	.9995
9									.0000	.2285	.7733	.9299	.9780	.9931	.9978	.9993
10										.0000	.7061	.9091	.9715	.9910	.9972	.9991
11											.6216	.8830	.9632	.9884	.9963	.9988
12											.5151	.8500	.9529	.9851	.9953	.9985
13											.3811	.8086	.9399	.9810	.9940	.9981
14											.2124	.7564	.9235	.9759	.9924	.9976
15											.0000	.6907	.9029	.9694	.9903	.9969
16												.6080	.8769	.9612	.9877	.9961
17												.5039	.8442	.9508	.9845	.9951
18												.3728	.8030	.9379	.9804	.9938
19												.2078	.7512	.9215	.9752	.9922
20												.0000	.6860	.9009	.9687	.9901
21													.6038	.8750	.9605	.9875
22													.5004	.8424	.9502	.9843
23													.3702	.8013	.9372	.9802
24													.2063	.7496	.9209	.9750
25													.0000	.6845	.9003	.9685
26														.6025	.8744	.9603
27														.4993	.8418	.9500
28														.3694	.8008	.9370
29														.2059	.7491	.9207
30														.0000	.6840	.9001
35															.0000	.6839
40																.0000

LOAN PROGRESS CHART
23.50%

AGE OF LOAN	ORIGINAL TERM IN YEARS															
	1	2	3	4	5	6	7	8	9	10	15	20	25	30	35	40
1	.0000	.5579	.7406	.8295	.8810	.9138	.9361	.9518	.9632	.9717	.9918	.9975	.9992	.9998	.9999	*****
2		.0000	.4132	.6143	.7308	.8051	.8554	.8909	.9168	.9359	.9814	.9943	.9982	.9994	.9998	.9999
3			.0000	.3427	.5412	.6678	.7536	.8142	.8582	.8908	.9683	.9903	.9970	.9991	.9997	.9999
4				.0000	.3019	.4945	.6251	.7173	.7842	.8339	.9517	.9852	.9954	.9986	.9996	.9999
5					.0000	.2759	.4629	.5950	.6909	.7620	.9308	.9788	.9934	.9980	.9994	.9998
6						.0000	.2583	.4406	.5731	.6713	.9044	.9708	.9909	.9972	.9991	.9997
7							.0000	.2458	.4244	.5568	.8712	.9606	.9878	.9962	.9988	.9996
8								.0000	.2368	.4124	.8292	.9478	.9838	.9949	.9984	.9995
9									.0000	.2301	.7762	.9316	.9788	.9934	.9979	.9994
10										.0000	.7093	.9111	.9724	.9914	.9973	.9992
11											.6248	.8853	.9644	.9889	.9965	.9989
12											.5183	.8527	.9543	.9858	.9956	.9986
13											.3838	.8116	.9415	.9818	.9943	.9982
14											.2142	.7597	.9254	.9768	.9927	.9977
15											.0000	.6943	.9051	.9704	.9908	.9971
16												.6116	.8795	.9624	.9883	.9963
17												.5073	.8471	.9523	.9851	.9954
18												.3757	.8063	.9396	.9812	.9941
19												.2096	.7548	.9236	.9761	.9925
20												.0000	.6897	.9033	.9698	.9906
21													.6076	.8777	.9618	.9881
22													.5040	.8454	.9517	.9849
23													.3733	.8046	.9390	.9810
24													.2083	.7532	.9230	.9759
25													.0000	.6883	.9027	.9696
26														.6064	.8771	.9616
27														.5030	.8449	.9516
28														.3725	.8041	.9388
29														.2078	.7527	.9228
30														.0000	.6879	.9025
35															.0000	.6877
40																.0000

23.75%

AGE OF LOAN	1	2	3	4	5	6	7	8	9	10	15	20	25	30	35	40
1	.0000	.5585	.7413	.8302	.8817	.9145	.9367	.9523	.9637	.9721	.9920	.9976	.9993	.9998	.9999	*****
2		.0000	.4140	.6155	.7320	.8063	.8566	.8920	.9178	.9368	.9818	.9945	.9983	.9995	.9998	*****
3			.0000	.3438	.5427	.6694	.7552	.8158	.8597	.8922	.9690	.9906	.9971	.9991	.9997	.9999
4				.0000	.3031	.4962	.6270	.7192	.7861	.8357	.9527	.9857	.9956	.9987	.9996	.9999
5					.0000	.2772	.4648	.5971	.6931	.7642	.9322	.9795	.9937	.9981	.9994	.9998
6						.0000	.2596	.4427	.5755	.6738	.9062	.9716	.9913	.9973	.9992	.9997
7							.0000	.2472	.4266	.5594	.8733	.9617	.9883	.9964	.9989	.9997
8								.0000	.2383	.4147	.8317	.9491	.9844	.9952	.9985	.9995
9									.0000	.2316	.7790	.9332	.9795	.9937	.9981	.9994
10										.0000	.7124	.9131	.9733	.9918	.9975	.9992
11											.6281	.8876	.9655	.9894	.9967	.9990
12											.5215	.8554	.9557	.9863	.9958	.9987
13											.3866	.8146	.9432	.9825	.9946	.9983
14											.2159	.7630	.9273	.9776	.9931	.9979
15											.0000	.6978	.9073	.9715	.9912	.9973
16												.6152	.8820	.9637	.9888	.9965
17												.5108	.8500	.9538	.9858	.9956
18												.3787	.8095	.9413	.9819	.9944
19												.2115	.7582	.9256	.9770	.9929
20												.0000	.6934	.9056	.9709	.9910
21													.6114	.8803	.9631	.9886
22													.5076	.8484	.9532	.9856
23													.3763	.8079	.9408	.9817
24													.2102	.7568	.9250	.9769
25													.0000	.6921	.9050	.9707
26														.6102	.8798	.9629
27														.5066	.8479	.9531
28														.3755	.8074	.9406
29														.2098	.7563	.9248
30														.0000	.6916	.9049
35															.0000	.6915
40																.0000

LOAN PROGRESS CHART
24.00%

AGE OF LOAN	ORIGINAL TERM IN YEARS															
	1	2	3	4	5	6	7	8	9	10	15	20	25	30	35	40
1	.0000	.5591	.7420	.8310	.8824	.9151	.9373	.9529	.9642	.9725	.9922	.9977	.9993	.9998	.9999	*****
2		.0000	.4149	.6166	.7333	.8075	.8578	.8931	.9187	.9377	.9823	.9947	.9984	.9995	.9999	*****
3			.0000	.3448	.5441	.6710	.7569	.8173	.8611	.8935	.9697	.9909	.9973	.9992	.9997	.9999
4				.0000	.3042	.4979	.6290	.7212	.7881	.8375	.9538	.9862	.9958	.9987	.9996	.9999
5					.0000	.2784	.4667	.5993	.6954	.7664	.9335	.9801	.9940	.9982	.9994	.9998
6						.0000	.2610	.4447	.5779	.6763	.9079	.9725	.9917	.9975	.9992	.9998
7							.0000	.2487	.4288	.5620	.8754	.9628	.9887	.9966	.9990	.9997
8								.0000	.2398	.4170	.8341	.9504	.9850	.9954	.9986	.9996
9									.0000	.2332	.7818	.9348	.9803	.9940	.9982	.9994
10										.0000	.7155	.9150	.9743	.9922	.9976	.9993
11											.6313	.8899	.9666	.9898	.9969	.9991
12											.5246	.8580	.9570	.9869	.9960	.9988
13											.3893	.8176	.9447	.9832	.9949	.9984
14											.2177	.7663	.9292	.9785	.9934	.9980
15											.0000	.7013	.9095	.9725	.9916	.9974
16												.6188	.8845	.9649	.9893	.9967
17												.5142	.8528	.9552	.9864	.9958
18												.3816	.8126	.9430	.9826	.9947
19												.2133	.7617	.9275	.9779	.9933
20												.0000	.6971	.9078	.9719	.9914
21													.6151	.8829	.9643	.9891
22													.5111	.8513	.9547	.9862
23													.3793	.8112	.9425	.9825
24													.2121	.7603	.9270	.9777
25													.0000	.6958	.9073	.9718
26														.6140	.8824	.9642
27														.5102	.8508	.9545
28														.3786	.8107	.9423
29														.2117	.7599	.9268
30														.0000	.6954	.9072
35															.0000	.6953
40																.0000

24.25%

AGE OF LOAN	1	2	3	4	5	6	7	8	9	10	15	20	25	30	35	40
1	.0000	.5597	.7428	.8317	.8831	.9158	.9379	.9534	.9647	.9730	.9924	.9978	.9993	.9998	.9999	*****
2		.0000	.4158	.6178	.7345	.8088	.8589	.8942	.9197	.9386	.9827	.9949	.9985	.9995	.9999	*****
3			.0000	.3458	.5456	.6727	.7585	.8189	.8626	.8948	.9704	.9913	.9974	.9992	.9998	.9999
4				.0000	.3054	.4996	.6309	.7232	.7900	.8393	.9548	.9866	.9960	.9988	.9996	.9999
5					.0000	.2797	.4686	.6015	.6976	.7686	.9349	.9808	.9942	.9983	.9995	.9998
6						.0000	.2623	.4468	.5802	.6788	.9096	.9733	.9920	.9976	.9993	.9998
7							.0000	.2501	.4310	.5645	.8774	.9638	.9892	.9967	.9990	.9997
8								.0000	.2412	.4193	.8366	.9517	.9856	.9957	.9987	.9996
9									.0000	.2347	.7846	.9364	.9810	.9943	.9983	.9995
10										.0000	.7185	.9169	.9751	.9925	.9978	.9993
11											.6345	.8921	.9677	.9903	.9971	.9991
12											.5278	.8606	.9583	.9875	.9962	.9989
13											.3920	.8205	.9463	.9838	.9951	.9985
14											.2194	.7695	.9310	.9793	.9938	.9981
15											.0000	.7047	.9116	.9734	.9920	.9976
16												.6223	.8870	.9660	.9898	.9969
17												.5176	.8556	.9566	.9869	.9961
18												.3845	.8158	.9446	.9833	.9950
19												.2152	.7651	.9294	.9788	.9936
20												.0000	.7007	.9100	.9729	.9919
21													.6188	.8854	.9655	.9896
22													.5146	.8541	.9561	.9868
23													.3823	.8143	.9441	.9832
24													.2140	.7638	.9289	.9786
25													.0000	.6995	.9096	.9728
26														.6177	.8850	.9654
27														.5138	.8537	.9560
28														.3816	.8139	.9440
29														.2136	.7634	.9288
30														.0000	.6991	.9094
35															.0000	.6990
40																.0000

LOAN PROGRESS CHART

24.50%

AGE OF LOAN	ORIGINAL TERM IN YEARS															
	1	2	3	4	5	6	7	8	9	10	15	20	25	30	35	40
1	.0000	.5603	.7435	.8325	.8838	.9165	.9385	.9540	.9651	.9734	.9926	.9978	.9994	.9998	.9999	*****
2		.0000	.4166	.6189	.7357	.8100	.8601	.8953	.9207	.9394	.9831	.9951	.9985	.9996	.9999	*****
3			.0000	.3468	.5470	.6743	.7601	.8205	.8640	.8962	.9711	.9916	.9975	.9993	.9998	.9999
4				.0000	.3065	.5013	.6328	.7251	.7919	.8410	.9557	.9871	.9962	.9989	.9997	.9999
5					.0000	.2809	.4705	.6037	.6999	.7708	.9362	.9814	.9945	.9984	.9995	.9999
6						.0000	.2636	.4488	.5826	.6812	.9112	.9741	.9923	.9977	.9993	.9998
7							.0000	.2515	.4332	.5671	.8795	.9648	.9896	.9969	.9991	.9997
8								.0000	.2427	.4216	.8390	.9530	.9861	.9959	.9988	.9996
9									.0000	.2363	.7874	.9379	.9816	.9945	.9984	.9995
10										.0000	.7216	.9187	.9760	.9929	.9979	.9994
11											.6377	.8943	.9687	.9907	.9972	.9992
12											.5309	.8631	.9595	.9880	.9964	.9989
13											.3947	.8233	.9478	.9845	.9954	.9986
14											.2212	.7727	.9328	.9800	.9941	.9982
15											.0000	.7081	.9137	.9744	.9924	.9977
16												.6259	.8893	.9671	.9902	.9971
17												.5210	.8583	.9579	.9875	.9963
18												.3874	.8188	.9462	.9840	.9952
19												.2171	.7684	.9312	.9796	.9939
20												.0000	.7042	.9122	.9739	.9922
21													.6224	.8879	.9667	.9901
22													.5181	.8569	.9575	.9874
23													.3852	.8175	.9457	.9839
24													.2159	.7672	.9308	.9794
25													.0000	.7031	.9117	.9738
26														.6214	.8875	.9665
27														.5173	.8565	.9573
28														.3846	.8171	.9456
29														.2155	.7668	.9307
30														.0000	.7027	.9116
35															.0000	.7026
40																.0000

24.75%

AGE OF LOAN	ORIGINAL TERM IN YEARS															
	1	2	3	4	5	6	7	8	9	10	15	20	25	30	35	40
1	.0000	.5609	.7442	.8332	.8845	.9171	.9391	.9545	.9656	.9738	.9928	.9979	.9994	.9998	.9999	*****
2		.0000	.4175	.6201	.7370	.8112	.8612	.8963	.9216	.9403	.9836	.9953	.9986	.9996	.9999	*****
3			.0000	.3478	.5485	.6759	.7618	.8220	.8655	.8975	.9718	.9919	.9976	.9993	.9998	.9999
4				.0000	.3077	.5030	.6347	.7271	.7937	.8428	.9567	.9875	.9963	.9989	.9997	.9999
5					.0000	.2822	.4724	.6058	.7021	.7729	.9375	.9820	.9947	.9985	.9995	.9999
6						.0000	.2650	.4509	.5850	.6837	.9129	.9749	.9927	.9978	.9994	.9998
7							.0000	.2529	.4354	.5696	.8815	.9658	.9900	.9971	.9991	.9997
8								.0000	.2442	.4239	.8413	.9542	.9866	.9961	.9988	.9997
9									.0000	.2378	.7901	.9394	.9823	.9948	.9985	.9996
10										.0000	.7246	.9205	.9768	.9932	.9980	.9994
11											.6409	.8964	.9697	.9911	.9974	.9992
12											.5340	.8656	.9607	.9885	.9966	.9990
13											.3974	.8262	.9492	.9851	.9956	.9987
14											.2229	.7758	.9345	.9808	.9944	.9983
15											.0000	.7115	.9157	.9753	.9927	.9979
16												.6294	.8917	.9682	.9907	.9973
17												.5244	.8610	.9592	.9880	.9965
18												.3903	.8218	.9477	.9847	.9955
19												.2189	.7717	.9330	.9803	.9942
20												.0000	.7078	.9143	.9748	.9926
21													.6260	.8903	.9678	.9905
22													.5216	.8597	.9588	.9879
23													.3882	.8205	.9473	.9845
24													.2178	.7705	.9326	.9802
25													.0000	.7067	.9139	.9747
26														.6251	.8899	.9677
27														.5208	.8593	.9587
28														.3876	.8202	.9472
29														.2174	.7702	.9325
30														.0000	.7063	.9137
35															.0000	.7063
40																.0000

LOAN PROGRESS CHART

25.00%

AGE OF LOAN	ORIGINAL TERM IN YEARS															
	1	2	3	4	5	6	7	8	9	10	15	20	25	30	35	40
1	.0000	.5615	.7450	.8339	.8852	.9178	.9397	.9550	.9661	.9742	.9930	.9980	.9994	.9998	*****	*****
2		.0000	.4183	.6213	.7382	.8124	.8624	.8974	.9226	.9411	.9840	.9954	.9987	.9996	.9999	*****
3			.0000	.3489	.5499	.6775	.7634	.8236	.8669	.8988	.9724	.9921	.9977	.9993	.9998	.9999
4				.0000	.3088	.5047	.6366	.7290	.7956	.8445	.9576	.9879	.9965	.9990	.9997	.9999
5					.0000	.2834	.4743	.6080	.7043	.7751	.9387	.9825	.9950	.9985	.9996	.9999
6						.0000	.2663	.4529	.5873	.6861	.9145	.9756	.9930	.9980	.9994	.9998
7							.0000	.2543	.4375	.5722	.8834	.9668	.9904	.9972	.9992	.9998
8								.0000	.2457	.4262	.8437	.9554	.9871	.9963	.9989	.9997
9									.0000	.2394	.7928	.9409	.9829	.9951	.9986	.9996
10										.0000	.7276	.9223	.9776	.9935	.9981	.3995
11											.6441	.8985	.9707	.9915	.9975	.9993
12											.5371	.8680	.9619	.9890	.9968	.9991
13											.4001	.8290	.9506	.9857	.9958	.9988
14											.2247	.7789	.9362	.9815	.9946	.9984
15											.0000	.7149	.9177	.9761	.9931	.9980
16												.6328	.8940	.9693	.9911	.9974
17												.5277	.8636	.9605	.9885	.9967
18												.3931	.8248	.9492	.9853	.9957
19												.2208	.7750	.9348	.9811	.9945
20												.0000	.7113	.9163	.9757	.9930
21													.6296	.8927	.9689	.9910
22													.5251	.8624	.9601	.9884
23													.3912	.8236	.9488	.9851
24													.2196	.7739	.9344	.9810
25													.0000	.7102	.9159	.9756
26														.6287	.8923	.9687
27														.5243	.8620	.9600
28														.3906	.8232	.9487
29														.2193	.7735	.9343
30														.0000	.7099	.9158
35															.0000	.7098
40																.0000

25.25%

AGE OF LOAN	1	2	3	4	5	6	7	8	9	10	15	20	25	30	35	40
1	.0000	.5621	.7457	.8347	.8859	.9184	.9402	.9555	.9665	.9746	.9932	.9981	.9994	.9998	*****	*****
2		.0000	.4192	.6224	.7394	.8136	.8635	.8984	.9235	.9419	.9844	.9956	.9987	.9996	.9999	*****
3			.0000	.3499	.5514	.6791	.7650	.8251	.8683	.9000	.9731	.9924	.9978	.9994	.9998	.9999
4				.0000	.3100	.5064	.6385	.7310	.7975	.8463	.9586	.9883	.9967	.9990	.9997	.9999
5					.0000	.2847	.4761	.6101	.7065	.7772	.9400	.9831	.9952	.9986	.9996	.9999
6						.0000	.2677	.4550	.5897	.6885	.9161	.9763	.9933	.9981	.9994	.9998
7							.0000	.2558	.4397	.5747	.8854	.9677	.9908	.9974	.9992	.9998
8								.0000	.2472	.4285	.8460	.9566	.9876	.9965	.9990	.9997
9									.0000	.2409	.7955	.9424	.9836	.9953	.9987	.9996
10										.0000	.7305	.9241	.9783	.9938	.9982	.9995
11											.6472	.9006	.9716	.9919	.9977	.9993
12											.5402	.8704	.9630	.9894	.9970	.9991
13											.4028	.8317	.9520	.9863	.9961	.9989
14											.2264	.7820	.9378	.9822	.9949	.9985
15											.0000	.7182	.9196	.9770	.9934	.9981
16												.6362	.8962	.9703	.9915	.9976
17												.5311	.8662	.9617	.9890	.9969
18												.3960	.8277	.9507	.9859	.9959
19												.2226	.7782	.9365	.9818	.9948
20												.0000	.7147	.9183	.9766	.9933
21													.6332	.8950	.9699	.9914
22													.5285	.8650	.9613	.9889
23													.3941	.8265	.9503	.9858
24													.2215	.7771	.9361	.9817
25													.0000	.7137	.9180	.9765
26														.6323	.8946	.9698
27														.5278	.8647	.9612
28														.3935	.8262	.9502
29														.2212	.7768	.9360
30														.0000	.7134	.9179
35															.0000	.7134
40																.0000

LOAN PROGRESS CHART

25.50%

AGE OF LOAN	ORIGINAL TERM IN YEARS															
	1	2	3	4	5	6	7	8	9	10	15	20	25	30	35	40
1	.0000	.5627	.7464	.8354	.8866	.9190	.9408	.9560	.9670	.9750	.9933	.9981	.9995	.9999	*****	*****
2		.0000	.4200	.6236	.7407	.8148	.8646	.8994	.9245	.9428	.9847	.9958	.9988	.9997	.9999	*****
3			.0000	.3509	.5528	.6807	.7666	.8266	.8697	.9013	.9737	.9927	.9979	.9994	.9998	*****
4				.0000	.3111	.5081	.6404	.7329	.7993	.8480	.9595	.9887	.9968	.9991	.9997	.9999
5					.0000	.2859	.4780	.6123	.7087	.7793	.9412	.9836	.9954	.9987	.9996	.9999
6						.0000	.2690	.4570	.5920	.6909	.9176	.9771	.9935	.9982	.9995	.9999
7							.0000	.2572	.4419	.5772	.8873	.9686	.9912	.9975	.9993	.9998
8								.0000	.2487	.4308	.8483	.9577	.9881	.9966	.9990	.9997
9									.0000	.2425	.7981	.9438	.9841	.9955	.9987	.9996
10										.0000	.7335	.9258	.9791	.9941	.9983	.9995
11											.6503	.9026	.9725	.9922	.9978	.9994
12											.5433	.8728	.9641	.9899	.9971	.9992
13											.4055	.8344	.9533	.9868	.9963	.9989
14											.2282	.7850	.9394	.9829	.9951	.9986
15											.0000	.7215	.9215	.9778	.9937	.9982
16												.6396	.8984	.9713	.9919	.9977
17												.5344	.8687	.9629	.9895	.9970
18												.3989	.8305	.9521	.9864	.9962
19												.2245	.7814	.9382	.9825	.9950
20												.0000	.7181	.9203	.9774	.9936
21													.6367	.8972	.9709	.9918
22													.5319	.8676	.9625	.9894
23													.3970	.8295	.9517	.9863
24													.2234	.7804	.9378	.9824
25													.0000	.7172	.9199	.9773
26														.6359	.8969	.9708
27														.5312	.8673	.9624
28														.3965	.8292	.9516
29														.2231	.7801	.9377
30														.0000	.7169	.9198
35															.0000	.7168
40																.0000

25.75%

AGE OF LOAN	1	2	3	4	5	6	7	8	9	10	15	20	25	30	35	40
1	.0000	.5634	.7471	.8361	.8873	.9197	.9414	.9565	.9674	.9754	.9935	.9982	.9995	.9999	*****	*****
2		.0000	.4209	.6247	.7419	.8160	.8658	.9005	.9254	.9436	.9851	.9959	.9989	.9997	.9999	*****
3			.0000	.3519	.5543	.6823	.7682	.8281	.8711	.9026	.9743	.9929	.9980	.9994	.9998	*****
4				.0000	.3123	.5098	.6423	.7348	.8011	.8497	.9604	.9891	.9970	.9992	.9998	.9999
5					.0000	.2872	.4799	.6144	.7109	.7814	.9424	.9841	.9956	.9988	.9997	.9999
6						.0000	.2703	.4590	.5944	.6933	.9192	.9777	.9938	.9983	.9995	.9999
7							.0000	.2586	.4441	.5797	.8892	.9695	.9915	.9976	.9993	.9998
8								.0000	.2502	.4331	.8506	.9589	.9885	.9968	.9991	.9997
9									.0000	.2440	.8007	.9451	.9847	.9957	.9988	.9997
10										.0000	.7364	.9274	.9798	.9944	.9984	.9996
11											.6534	.9046	.9734	.9926	.9979	.9994
12											.5463	.8751	.9652	.9903	.9973	.9992
13											.4082	.8371	.9546	.9873	.9965	.9990
14											.2299	.7880	.9410	.9835	.9954	.9987
15											.0000	.7247	.9233	.9786	.9940	.9983
16												.6430	.9006	.9722	.9922	.9978
17												.5376	.8712	.9640	.9899	.9972
18												.4017	.8334	.9534	.9870	.9964
19												.2263	.7845	.9398	.9832	.9953
20												.0000	.7215	.9222	.9782	.9939
21													.6402	.8995	.9719	.9921
22													.5353	.8702	.9637	.9898
23													.3999	.8323	.9531	.9869
24													.2253	.7835	.9395	.9831
25													.0000	.7206	.9219	.9781
26														.6394	.8992	.9718
27														.5346	.8699	.9636
28														.3994	.8321	.9530
29														.2250	.7833	.9394
30														.0000	.7204	.9218
35															.0000	.7203
40																.0000

LOAN PROGRESS CHART
26.00%

AGE OF LOAN	1	2	3	4	5	6	7	8	9	10	15	20	25	30	35	40
									ORIGINAL TERM IN YEARS							
1	.0000	.5640	.7479	.8369	.8880	.9203	.9419	.9570	.9679	.9757	.9937	.9983	.9995	.9999	*****	*****
2		.0000	.4218	.6258	.7431	.8172	.8669	.9015	.9263	.9444	.9855	.9961	.9989	.9997	.9999	*****
3			.0000	.3529	.5557	.6839	.7698	.8296	.8725	.9038	.9749	.9932	.9981	.9995	.9999	*****
4				.0000	.3134	.5114	.6442	.7367	.8030	.8513	.9612	.9895	.9971	.9992	.9998	.9999
5					.0000	.2884	.4818	.6165	.7130	.7835	.9435	.9846	.9958	.9988	.9997	.9999
6						.0000	.2717	.4611	.5967	.6957	.9207	.9784	.9941	.9984	.9995	.9999
7							.0000	.2600	.4462	.5822	.8911	.9704	.9918	.9977	.9994	.9998
8								.0000	.2517	.4354	.8528	.9599	.9890	.9970	.9992	.9998
9									.0000	.2456	.8033	.9465	.9853	.9959	.9989	.9997
10										.0000	.7393	.9291	.9805	.9946	.9985	.9996
11											.6565	.9065	.9743	.9929	.9980	.9995
12											.5494	.8774	.9663	.9907	.9974	.9993
13											.4108	.8397	.9559	.9878	.9966	.9991
14											.2317	.7909	.9425	.9841	.9956	.9988
15											.0000	.7279	.9251	.9793	.9943	.9984
16												.6464	.9027	.9731	.9926	.9979
17												.5409	.8737	.9651	.9904	.9973
18												.4045	.8361	.9548	.9875	.9965
19												.2281	.7876	.9414	.9838	.9955
20												.0000	.7248	.9240	.9790	.9942
21													.6436	.9016	.9728	.9925
22													.5386	.8727	.9648	.9903
23													.4028	.8352	.9545	.9874
24													.2272	.7867	.9411	.9837
25													.0000	.7240	.9237	.9789
26														.6429	.9013	.9727
27														.5380	.8724	.9647
28														.4023	.8349	.9544
29														.2269	.7864	.9410
30														.0000	.7237	.9237
35															.0000	.7237
40																.0000

26.25%

AGE OF LOAN	1	2	3	4	5	6	7	8	9	10	15	20	25	30	35	40
1	.0000	.5646	.7486	.8376	.8887	.9209	.9425	.9575	.9683	.9761	.9938	.9983	.9995	.9999	*****	*****
2		.0000	.4226	.6270	.7443	.8184	.8680	.9025	.9272	.9452	.9859	.9962	.9990	.9997	.9999	*****
3			.0000	.3540	.5572	.6855	.7713	.8311	.8739	.9050	.9755	.9934	.9982	.9995	.9999	*****
4				.0000	.3146	.5131	.6461	.7386	.8048	.8530	.9621	.9898	.9972	.9992	.9998	.9999
5					.0000	.2897	.4836	.6186	.7152	.7856	.9447	.9851	.9960	.9989	.9997	.9999
6						.0000	.2730	.4631	.5990	.6981	.9221	.9791	.9943	.9984	.9996	.9999
7							.0000	.2614	.4484	.5847	.8929	.9712	.9922	.9979	.9994	.9998
8								.0000	.2532	.4377	.8550	.9610	.9894	.9971	.9992	.9998
9									.0000	.2471	.8058	.9478	.9858	.9961	.9989	.9997
10										.0000	.7421	.9306	.9811	.9949	.9986	.9996
11											.6595	.9084	.9751	.9932	.9981	.9995
12											.5524	.8796	.9673	.9911	.9976	.9993
13											.4135	.8423	.9571	.9883	.9968	.9991
14											.2334	.7939	.9440	.9847	.9958	.9989
15											.0000	.7311	.9269	.9801	.9946	.9985
16												.6497	.9048	.9740	.9929	.9981
17												.5442	.8761	.9662	.9908	.9975
18												.4073	.8389	.9561	.9880	.9967
19												.2300	.7906	.9429	.9844	.9957
20												.0000	.7281	.9259	.9798	.9945
21													.6471	.9038	.9737	.9928
22													.5420	.8751	.9659	.9907
23													.4057	.8379	.9558	.9879
24													.2290	.7898	.9426	.9843
25													.0000	.7273	.9256	.9797
26														.6463	.9035	.9737
27														.5414	.8748	.9658
28														.4053	.8377	.9557
29														.2288	.7895	.9426
30														.0000	.7271	.9255
35															.0000	.7270
40																.0000

LOAN PROGRESS CHART
26.50%

AGE OF LOAN	ORIGINAL TERM IN YEARS															
	1	2	3	4	5	6	7	8	9	10	15	20	25	30	35	40
1	.0000	.5652	.7493	.8383	.8893	.9215	.9431	.9580	.9687	.9765	.9940	.9984	.9996	.9999	*****	*****
2		.0000	.4235	.6281	.7455	.8196	.8691	.9035	.9281	.9460	.9862	.9963	.9990	.9997	.9999	*****
3			.0000	.3550	.5586	.6870	.7729	.8326	.8752	.9063	.9761	.9936	.9983	.9995	.9999	*****
4				.0000	.3157	.5148	.6479	.7405	.8066	.8547	.9629	.9901	.9974	.9993	.9998	.9999
5					.0000	.2909	.4855	.6207	.7173	.7876	.9458	.9856	.9961	.9990	.9997	.9999
6						.0000	.2744	.4651	.6013	.7005	.9236	.9797	.9945	.9985	.9996	.9999
7							.0000	.2629	.4506	.5872	.8947	.9720	.9925	.9980	.9995	.9999
8								.0000	.2546	.4400	.8572	.9620	.9898	.9973	.9993	.9998
9									.0000	.2487	.8084	.9491	.9863	.9963	.9990	.9997
10										.0000	.7449	.9322	.9818	.9951	.9987	.9996
11											.6625	.9103	.9759	.9935	.9983	.9995
12											.5554	.8818	.9683	.9914	.9977	.9994
13											.4162	.8448	.9583	.9888	.9970	.9992
14											.2352	.7967	.9454	.9853	.9960	.9989
15											.0000	.7342	.9286	.9808	.9948	.9986
16												.6530	.9068	.9749	.9932	.9982
17												.5474	.8784	.9672	.9912	.9976
18												.4102	.8416	.9573	.9885	.9969
19												.2318	.7936	.9444	.9850	.9960
20												.0000	.7314	.9276	.9805	.9947
21													.6505	.9058	.9746	.9932
22													.5453	.8775	.9670	.9911
23													.4086	.8407	.9570	.9884
24													.2309	.7928	.9441	.9849
25													.0000	.7306	.9274	.9804
26														.6498	.9056	.9745
27														.5447	.8773	.9669
28														.4081	.8404	.9570
29														.2307	.7926	.9441
30														.0000	.7304	.9273
35															.0000	.7304
40																.0000

26.75%

AGE OF LOAN	1	2	3	4	5	6	7	8	9	10	15	20	25	30	35	40
1	.0000	.5658	.7500	.8390	.8900	.9222	.9436	.9585	.9691	.9769	.9942	.9985	.9996	.9999	*****	*****
2		.0000	.4243	.6293	.7467	.8207	.8702	.9045	.9290	.9467	.9866	.9965	.9991	.9998	.9999	*****
3			.0000	.3560	.5601	.6885	.7745	.8341	.8766	.9075	.9767	.9939	.9984	.9996	.9999	*****
4				.0000	.3169	.5165	.6498	.7424	.8083	.8563	.9638	.9905	.9975	.9993	.9998	*****
5					.0000	.2922	.4874	.6228	.7195	.7896	.9469	.9861	.9963	.9990	.9997	.9999
6						.0000	.2757	.4671	.6036	.7028	.9250	.9803	.9948	.9986	.9996	.9999
7							.0000	.2643	.4527	.5897	.8965	.9728	.9928	.9981	.9995	.9999
8								.0000	.2561	.4423	.8593	.9630	.9902	.9974	.9993	.9998
9									.0000	.2502	.8109	.9503	.9868	.9965	.9991	.9998
10										.0000	.7477	.9337	.9824	.9953	.9988	.9997
11											.6655	.9121	.9767	.9938	.9983	.9996
12											.5584	.8840	.9692	.9918	.9978	.9994
13											.4188	.8473	.9595	.9892	.9971	.9992
14											.2369	.7996	.9468	.9858	.9962	.9990
15											.0000	.7373	.9303	.9814	.9951	.9987
16												.6562	.9088	.9757	.9935	.9983
17												.5506	.8807	.9683	.9915	.9977
18												.4130	.8442	.9585	.9890	.9971
19												.2336	.7966	.9459	.9856	.9962
20												.0000	.7346	.9294	.9812	.9950
21													.6538	.9079	.9755	.9935
22													.5486	.8799	.9680	.9915
23													.4114	.8434	.9583	.9889
24													.2328	.7958	.9456	.9855
25													.0000	.7339	.9291	.9811
26														.6532	.9076	.9754
27														.5480	.8796	.9679
28														.4110	.8431	.9582
29														.2325	.7956	.9456
30														.0000	.7337	.9291
35															.0000	.7336
40																.0000

LOAN PROGRESS CHART

27.00%

AGE OF LOAN	\multicolumn{16}{ORIGINAL TERM IN YEARS}															
	1	2	3	4	5	6	7	8	9	10	15	20	25	30	35	40
1	.0000	.5664	.7507	.8397	.8907	.9228	.9442	.9590	.9696	.9772	.9943	.9985	.9996	.9999	*****	*****
2		.0000	.4252	.6304	.7480	.8219	.8713	.9055	.9298	.9475	.9869	.9966	.9991	.9998	.9999	*****
3			.0000	.3570	.5615	.6902	.7760	.8355	.8779	.9087	.9772	.9941	.9984	.9996	.9999	*****
4				.0000	.3180	.5182	.6517	.7442	.8101	.8579	.9646	.9908	.9976	.9994	.9998	*****
5					.0000	.2935	.4892	.6249	.7216	.7917	.9480	.9865	.9965	.9991	.9998	.9999
6						.0000	.2771	.4692	.6059	.7051	.9264	.9809	.9950	.9987	.9997	.9999
7							.0000	.2657	.4549	.5921	.8982	.9736	.9931	.9982	.9995	.9999
8								.0000	.2576	.4445	.8614	.9640	.9906	.9975	.9993	.9998
9									.0000	.2518	.8133	.9515	.9873	.9967	.9991	.9998
10										.0000	.7505	.9352	.9830	.9955	.9988	.9997
11											.6685	.9139	.9774	.9941	.9984	.9996
12											.5614	.8861	.9701	.9922	.9979	.9995
13											.4214	.8498	.9606	.9896	.9973	.9993
14											.2387	.8024	.9482	.9864	.9964	.9991
15											.0000	.7404	.9319	.9821	.9953	.9988
16												.6595	.9107	.9765	.9938	.9984
17												.5538	.8830	.9692	.9919	.9979
18												.4157	.8468	.9597	.9894	.9972
19												.2355	.7995	.9473	.9861	.9964
20												.0000	.7378	.9311	.9819	.9952
21													.6571	.9099	.9763	.9938
22													.5518	.8822	.9690	.9918
23													.4143	.8460	.9595	.9893
24													.2346	.7988	.9471	.9861
25													.0000	.7371	.9308	.9818
26														.6565	.9096	.9762
27														.5513	.8820	.9689
28														.4139	.8458	.9594
29														.2344	.7986	.9470
30														.0000	.7369	.9308
35															.0000	.7369
40																.0000

27.25%

AGE OF LOAN	1	2	3	4	5	6	7	8	9	10	15	20	25	30	35	40
1	.0000	.5670	.7515	.8404	.8914	.9234	.9447	.9595	.9700	.9776	.9945	.9986	.9996	.9999	*****	*****
2		.0000	.4260	.6316	.7492	.8231	.8723	.9064	.9307	.9482	.9872	.9967	.9992	.9998	.9999	*****
3			.0000	.3581	.5630	.6918	.7776	.8370	.8792	.9098	.9778	.9943	.9985	.9996	.9999	*****
4				.0000	.3192	.5198	.6535	.7461	.8119	.8595	.9653	.9911	.9977	.9994	.9998	*****
5					.0000	.2947	.4911	.6270	.7237	.7937	.9491	.9869	.9966	.9991	.9998	.9999
6						.0000	.2784	.4712	.6082	.7075	.9278	.9815	.9952	.9988	.9997	.9999
7							.0000	.2671	.4570	.5946	.9000	.9743	.9934	.9983	.9996	.9999
8								.0000	.2591	.4468	.8635	.9650	.9909	.9976	.9994	.9998
9									.0000	.2533	.8158	.9527	.9878	.9968	.9992	.9998
10										.0000	.7533	.9367	.9836	.9957	.9989	.9997
11											.6715	.9157	.9782	.9943	.9985	.9996
12											.5643	.8882	.9710	.9925	.9980	.9995
13											.4241	.8522	.9617	.9901	.9974	.9993
14											.2404	.8051	.9495	.9869	.9966	.9991
15											.0000	.7434	.9335	.9827	.9955	.9988
16												.6627	.9126	.9773	.9941	.9985
17												.5570	.8852	.9702	.9923	.9980
18												.4185	.8494	.9609	.9898	.9974
19												.2373	.8024	.9487	.9867	.9965
20												.0000	.7409	.9327	.9825	.9955
21													.6604	.9118	.9771	.9940
22													.5551	.8844	.9700	.9922
23													.4171	.8486	.9607	.9898
24													.2365	.8017	.9485	.9866
25													.0000	.7403	.9325	.9825
26														.6599	.9116	.9770
27														.5546	.8842	.9699
28														.4167	.8484	.9606
29														.2363	.8015	.9484
30														.0000	.7401	.9324
35															.0000	.7401
40																.0000

274

LOAN PROGRESS CHART
27.50%

AGE OF LOAN	ORIGINAL TERM IN YEARS															
	1	2	3	4	5	6	7	8	9	10	15	20	25	30	35	40
1	.0000	.5676	.7522	.8412	.8920	.9240	.9453	.9600	.9704	.9779	.9946	.9986	.9997	.9999	*****	*****
2		.0000	.4269	.6327	.7504	.8242	.8734	.9074	.9315	.9490	.9876	.9968	.9992	.9998	.9999	*****
3			.0000	.3591	.5644	.6933	.7791	.8384	.8805	.9110	.9783	.9945	.9986	.9996	.9999	*****
4				.0000	.3203	.5215	.6554	.7479	.8136	.8611	.9661	.9914	.9978	.9994	.9999	*****
5					.0000	.2960	.4929	.6291	.7258	.7957	.9501	.9874	.9968	.9992	.9998	.9999
6						.0000	.2798	.4732	.6105	.7098	.9292	.9820	.9954	.9988	.9997	.9999
7							.0000	.2686	.4592	.5970	.9017	.9751	.9936	.9984	.9996	.9999
8								.0000	.2606	.4491	.8656	.9659	.9913	.9978	.9994	.9999
9									.0000	.2549	.8182	.9539	.9882	.9970	.9992	.9998
10										.0000	.7560	.9381	.9842	.9959	.9990	.9997
11											.6744	.9174	.9789	.9946	.9986	.9996
12											.5673	.8903	.9719	.9928	.9982	.9995
13											.4267	.8546	.9628	.9905	.9975	.9994
14											.2422	.8079	.9508	.9874	.9968	.9992
15											.0000	.7465	.9351	.9833	.9957	.9989
16												.6659	.9145	.9781	.9944	.9986
17												.5601	.8874	.9711	.9926	.9981
18												.4213	.8519	.9620	.9902	.9975
19												.2391	.8052	.9500	.9872	.9967
20												.0000	.7440	.9343	.9831	.9957
21													.6637	.9137	.9778	.9943
22													.5583	.8867	.9709	.9925
23													.4199	.8512	.9618	.9902
24													.2383	.8046	.9498	.9871
25													.0000	.7434	.9341	.9831
26														.6632	.9135	.9778
27														.5578	.8865	.9708
28														.4196	.8510	.9617
29														.2381	.8044	.9498
30														.0000	.7433	.9341
35															.0000	.7432
40																.0000

27.75%

AGE OF LOAN	1	2	3	4	5	6	7	8	9	10	15	20	25	30	35	40
1	.0000	.5682	.7529	.8419	.8927	.9246	.9458	.9604	.9708	.9783	.9948	.9987	.9997	.9999	*****	*****
2		.0000	.4278	.6338	.7515	.8254	.8745	.9084	.9324	.9497	.9879	.9970	.9992	.9998	.9999	*****
3			.0000	.3601	.5658	.6949	.7807	.8399	.8818	.9121	.9788	.9947	.9987	.9997	.9999	*****
4				.0000	.3215	.5232	.6572	.7498	.8154	.8627	.9669	.9917	.9979	.9995	.9999	*****
5					.0000	.2972	.4948	.6312	.7279	.7977	.9512	.9878	.9969	.9992	.9998	.9999
6						.0000	.2811	.4752	.6128	.7121	.9305	.9826	.9956	.9989	.9997	.9999
7							.0000	.2700	.4613	.5995	.9034	.9758	.9939	.9984	.9996	.9999
8								.0000	.2621	.4513	.8676	.9668	.9916	.9979	.9995	.9999
9									.0000	.2564	.8206	.9550	.9886	.9971	.9993	.9998
10										.0000	.7587	.9395	.9847	.9961	.9990	.9998
11											.6773	.9191	.9796	.9948	.9987	.9997
12											.5702	.8923	.9728	.9931	.9982	.9996
13											.4293	.8570	.9638	.9908	.9977	.9994
14											.2439	.8105	.9521	.9879	.9969	.9992
15											.0000	.7494	.9366	.9839	.9959	.9990
16												.6690	.9163	.9788	.9946	.9986
17												.5632	.8895	.9720	.9929	.9982
18												.4240	.8543	.9631	.9906	.9976
19												.2409	.8080	.9513	.9877	.9969
20												.0000	.7471	.9359	.9837	.9959
21													.6669	.9156	.9786	.9946
22													.5615	.8888	.9718	.9928
23													.4227	.8537	.9629	.9906
24													.2402	.8074	.9512	.9876
25													.0000	.7465	.9357	.9837
26														.6664	.9154	.9785
27														.5610	.8887	.9718
28														.4224	.8535	.9628
29														.2400	.8072	.9511
30														.0000	.7464	.9357
35															.0000	.7463
40																.0000

LOAN PROGRESS CHART
28.00%

AGE OF LOAN	ORIGINAL TERM IN YEARS															
	1	2	3	4	5	6	7	8	9	10	15	20	25	30	35	40
1	.0000	.5688	.7536	.8426	.8934	.9252	.9463	.9609	.9712	.9786	.9949	.9987	.9997	.9999	*****	*****
2		.0000	.4286	.6350	.7527	.8265	.8755	.9093	.9332	.9505	.9882	.9971	.9993	.9998	*****	*****
3			.0000	.3611	.5673	.6964	.7822	.8413	.8831	.9133	.9793	.9949	.9987	.9997	.9999	*****
4				.0000	.3226	.5248	.6591	.7516	.8171	.8643	.9676	.9920	.9980	.9995	.9999	*****
5					.0000	.2985	.4967	.6333	.7300	.7996	.9522	.9882	.9970	.9993	.9998	*****
6						.0000	.2825	.4772	.6150	.7144	.9318	.9831	.9958	.9989	.9997	.9999
7							.0000	.2714	.4635	.6019	.9050	.9765	.9941	.9985	.9996	.9999
8								.0000	.2636	.4536	.8696	.9677	.9919	.9980	.9995	.9999
9									.0000	.2580	.8229	.9562	.9890	.9973	.9993	.9998
10										.0000	.7614	.9409	.9852	.9963	.9991	.9998
11											.6802	.9208	.9802	.9950	.9988	.9997
12											.5731	.8943	.9736	.9934	.9983	.9996
13											.4319	.8593	.9649	.9912	.9978	.9994
14											.2456	.8132	.9533	.9883	.9971	.9993
15											.0000	.7524	.9381	.9845	.9961	.9990
16												.6721	.9181	.9795	.9949	.9987
17												.5663	.8916	.9729	.9932	.9983
18												.4268	.8568	.9641	.9910	.9977
19												.2427	.8108	.9526	.9881	.9970
20												.0000	.7501	.9374	.9843	.9961
21													.6702	.9174	.9793	.9948
22													.5647	.8910	.9727	.9932
23													.4255	.8561	.9640	.9910
24													.2420	.8102	.9524	.9881
25													.0000	.7496	.9373	.9843
26														.6697	.9172	.9793
27														.5642	.8908	.9726
28														.4252	.8560	.9639
29														.2418	.8100	.9524
30														.0000	.7495	.9372
35															.0000	.7494
40																.0000

28.25%

AGE OF LOAN	1	2	3	4	5	6	7	8	9	10	15	20	25	30	35	40
1	.0000	.5694	.7543	.8433	.8940	.9258	.9469	.9614	.9716	.9790	.9950	.9988	.9997	.9999	*****	*****
2		.0000	.4295	.6361	.7539	.8277	.8766	.9103	.9341	.9512	.9885	.9972	.9993	.9998	*****	*****
3			.0000	.3622	.5687	.6980	.7837	.8427	.8844	.9144	.9798	.9951	.9988	.9997	.9999	*****
4				.0000	.3238	.5265	.6609	.7534	.8188	.8658	.9683	.9923	.9981	.9995	.9999	*****
5					.0000	.2998	.4985	.6353	.7320	.8016	.9532	.9885	.9972	.9993	.9998	*****
6						.0000	.2838	.4792	.6173	.7166	.9331	.9836	.9960	.9990	.9998	.9999
7							.0000	.2729	.4656	.6043	.9066	.9772	.9944	.9986	.9997	.9999
8								.0000	.2651	.4558	.8716	.9686	.9922	.9981	.9995	.9999
9									.0000	.2595	.8253	.9572	.9894	.9974	.9994	.9998
10										.0000	.7640	.9423	.9857	.9965	.9991	.9998
11											.6831	.9224	.9809	.9953	.9988	.9997
12											.5760	.8962	.9744	.9937	.9984	.9996
13											.4345	.8616	.9658	.9915	.9979	.9995
14											.2474	.8158	.9545	.9888	.9972	.9993
15											.0000	.7553	.9396	.9851	.9963	.9991
16												.6752	.9198	.9802	.9951	.9988
17												.5694	.8937	.9737	.9935	.9984
18												.4295	.8592	.9652	.9914	.9979
19												.2445	.8135	.9539	.9886	.9972
20												.0000	.7531	.9389	.9849	.9963
21													.6733	.9192	.9800	.9950
22													.5678	.8931	.9735	.9934
23													.4283	.8586	.9650	.9913
24													.2439	.8129	.9537	.9885
25													.0000	.7526	.9388	.9848
26														.6729	.9190	.9800
27														.5674	.8929	.9735
28														.4280	.8584	.9650
29														.2437	.8128	.9537
30														.0000	.7525	.9387
35															.0000	.7525
40																.0000

LOAN PROGRESS CHART
28.50%

AGE OF LOAN	1	2	3	4	5	6	7	8	9	10	15	20	25	30	35	40
						ORIGINAL TERM IN YEARS										
1	.0000	.5700	.7550	.8440	.8947	.9264	.9474	.9618	.9720	.9793	.9952	.9988	.9997	.9999	*****	*****
2		.0000	.4303	.6372	.7551	.8288	.8776	.9112	.9349	.9519	.9888	.9973	.9993	.9998	*****	*****
3			.0000	.3632	.5701	.6995	.7852	.8441	.8857	.9155	.9803	.9952	.9988	.9997	.9999	*****
4				.0000	.3249	.5281	.6627	.7552	.8205	.8674	.9690	.9925	.9982	.9996	.9999	*****
5					.0000	.3010	.5004	.6374	.7341	.8035	.9542	.9889	.9973	.9993	.9998	
6						.0000	.2852	.4812	.6196	.7189	.9344	.9841	.9961	.9991	.9998	.9999
7							.0000	.2743	.4678	.6067	.9082	.9778	.9946	.9987	.9997	.9999
8								.0000	.2666	.4581	.8736	.9694	.9925	.9982	.9996	.9999
9									.0000	.2611	.8276	.9583	.9898	.9975	.9994	.9999
10										.0000	.7667	.9436	.9862	.9966	.9992	.9998
11											.6859	.9240	.9815	.9955	.9989	.9997
12											.5789	.8982	.9752	.9939	.9985	.9996
13											.4371	.8639	.9668	.9919	.9980	.9995
14											.2491	.8184	.9557	.9892	.9974	.9994
15											.0000	.7582	.9410	.9856	.9965	.9991
16												.6783	.9215	.9808	.9953	.9989
17												.5725	.8957	.9745	.9938	.9985
18												.4322	.8615	.9662	.9917	.9980
19												.2464	.8162	.9551	.9890	.9973
20												.0000	.7561	.9404	.9854	.9964
21													.6765	.9209	.9807	.9953
22													.5709	.8951	.9744	.9937
23													.4311	.8610	.9660	.9917
24													.2457	.8157	.9549	.9890
25													.0000	.7556	.9402	.9854
26														.6760	.9208	.9806
27														.5706	.8950	.9743
28														.4308	.8608	.9660
29														.2455	.8155	.9549
30														.0000	.7555	.9402
35															.0000	.7555
40																.0000

28.75%

AGE OF LOAN	1	2	3	4	5	6	7	8	9	10	15	20	25	30	35	40
1	.0000	.5706	.7557	.8447	.8953	.9270	.9479	.9623	.9724	.9796	.9953	.9989	.9997	.9999	*****	*****
2		.0000	.4312	.6384	.7563	.8300	.8787	.9121	.9357	.9526	.9891	.9974	.9994	.9998	*****	*****
3			.0000	.3642	.5715	.7011	.7867	.8455	.8869	.9166	.9808	.9954	.9989	.9997	.9999	*****
4				.0000	.3261	.5298	.6645	.7570	.8222	.8689	.9697	.9928	.9983	.9996	.9999	*****
5					.0000	.3023	.5022	.6395	.7361	.8054	.9551	.9893	.9974	.9994	.9998	
6						.0000	.2865	.4832	.6218	.7211	.9357	.9846	.9963	.9991	.9998	.9999
7							.0000	.2757	.4699	.6091	.9098	.9784	.9948	.9987	.9997	.9999
8								.0000	.2681	.4603	.8755	.9702	.9928	.9983	.9996	.9999
9									.0000	.2626	.8299	.9593	.9902	.9976	.9994	.9999
10										.0000	.7693	.9449	.9867	.9968	.9992	.9998
11											.6888	.9256	.9821	.9957	.9990	.9997
12											.5818	.9001	.9759	.9942	.9986	.9997
13											.4397	.8661	.9677	.9922	.9981	.9995
14											.2509	.8210	.9569	.9896	.9975	.9994
15											.0000	.7610	.9424	.9861	.9966	.9992
16												.6814	.9232	.9815	.9955	.9989
17												.5755	.8977	.9753	.9940	.9986
18												.4349	.8638	.9671	.9921	.9981
19												.2482	.8188	.9563	.9894	.9974
20												.0000	.7590	.9418	.9859	.9966
21													.6796	.9226	.9813	.9955
22													.5741	.8972	.9752	.9940
23													.4338	.8633	.9670	.9920
24													.2475	.8183	.9561	.9894
25													.0000	.7586	.9417	.9859
26														.6792	.9225	.9813
27														.5737	.8970	.9751
28														.4336	.8632	.9669
29														.2474	.8182	.9561
30														.0000	.7585	.9416
35															.0000	.7584
40																.0000

TABLE 4. PRORATION

Use this Table to find either the exact number of elapsed days from January 1st to any given date, or the exact number of elapsed days from a given date to December 31st. The Table also indicates the fraction of one year (expressed as a percentage) represented by the number of elapsed days.

There are two sections to the Proration Table, one for a 360-day financial calendar, and one for an actual 365-day calendar.

Example: A property with an annual tax bill of $1,075 transfers from seller to buyer on June 21st. What percentage of the tax bill is chargeable to the seller if an actual 365-day calendar is used for the proration?

Turn to page 282. Locate the June column in the Prorations from January 1st to Proration Date Table. Read down this column to the 21st row. Find the two entries 172 and 47.12. There are 172 elapsed days between January 1st and June 21st. No allowance is made for leap year. The seller is charged 47.12% of the $1,075 tax bill or $506.54.

PRORATIONS FROM JAN. 1st TO PRORATION DATE

DATE	JAN DAYS PAST	JAN % OF 360	FEB DAYS PAST	FEB % OF 360	MAR DAYS PAST	MAR % OF 360	APR DAYS PAST	APR % OF 360	MAY DAYS PAST	MAY % OF 360	JUN DAYS PAST	JUN % OF 360	DATE
1	1	0.28	31	8.61	61	16.94	91	25.28	121	33.61	151	41.94	1
2	2	0.56	32	8.89	62	17.22	92	25.56	122	33.89	152	42.22	2
3	3	0.83	33	9.17	63	17.50	93	25.83	123	34.17	153	42.50	3
4	4	1.11	34	9.44	64	17.78	94	26.11	124	34.44	154	42.78	4
5	5	1.39	35	9.72	65	18.06	95	26.39	125	34.72	155	43.06	5
6	6	1.67	36	10.00	66	18.33	96	26.67	126	35.00	156	43.33	6
7	7	1.94	37	10.28	67	18.61	97	26.94	127	35.28	157	43.61	7
8	8	2.22	38	10.56	68	18.89	98	27.22	128	35.56	158	43.89	8
9	9	2.50	39	10.83	69	19.17	99	27.50	129	35.83	159	44.17	9
10	10	2.78	40	11.11	70	19.44	100	27.78	130	36.11	160	44.44	10
11	11	3.06	41	11.39	71	19.72	101	28.06	131	36.39	161	44.72	11
12	12	3.33	42	11.67	72	20.00	102	28.33	132	36.67	162	45.00	12
13	13	3.61	43	11.94	73	20.28	103	28.61	133	36.94	163	45.28	13
14	14	3.89	44	12.22	74	20.56	104	28.89	134	37.22	164	45.56	14
15	15	4.17	45	12.50	75	20.83	105	29.17	135	37.50	165	45.83	15
16	16	4.44	46	12.78	76	21.11	106	29.44	136	37.78	166	46.11	16
17	17	4.72	47	13.06	77	21.39	107	29.72	137	38.06	167	46.39	17
18	18	5.00	48	13.33	78	21.67	108	30.00	138	38.33	168	46.67	18
19	19	5.28	49	13.61	79	21.94	109	30.28	139	38.61	169	46.94	19
20	20	5.56	50	13.89	80	22.22	110	30.56	140	38.89	170	47.22	20
21	21	5.83	51	14.17	81	22.50	111	30.83	141	39.17	171	47.50	21
22	22	6.11	52	14.44	82	22.78	112	31.11	142	39.44	172	47.78	22
23	23	6.39	53	14.72	83	23.06	113	31.39	143	39.72	173	48.06	23
24	24	6.67	54	15.00	84	23.33	114	31.67	144	40.00	174	48.33	24
25	25	6.94	55	15.28	85	23.61	115	31.94	145	40.28	175	48.61	25
26	26	7.22	56	15.56	86	23.89	116	32.22	146	40.56	176	48.89	26
27	27	7.50	57	15.83	87	24.17	117	32.50	147	40.83	177	49.17	27
28	28	7.78	58	16.11	88	24.44	118	32.78	148	41.11	178	49.44	28
29	29	8.06	59	16.39	89	24.72	119	33.06	149	41.39	179	49.72	29
30	30	8.33	60	16.67	90	25.00	120	33.33	150	41.67	180	50.00	30
31													31

PRORATIONS FROM PRORATION DATE TO DEC 31st

DATE	JAN DAYS TO COME	JAN % OF 360	FEB DAYS TO COME	FEB % OF 360	MAR DAYS TO COME	MAR % OF 360	APR DAYS TO COME	APR % OF 360	MAY DAYS TO COME	MAY % OF 360	JUN DAYS TO COME	JUN % OF 360	DATE
1	360	100.00	330	91.67	300	83.33	270	75.00	240	66.67	210	58.33	1
2	359	99.72	329	91.39	299	83.06	269	74.72	239	66.39	209	58.06	2
3	358	99.44	328	91.11	298	82.78	268	74.44	238	66.11	208	57.78	3
4	357	99.17	327	90.83	297	82.50	267	74.17	237	65.83	207	57.50	4
5	356	98.89	326	90.56	296	82.22	266	73.89	236	65.56	206	57.22	5
6	355	98.61	325	90.28	295	81.94	265	73.61	235	65.28	205	56.94	6
7	354	98.33	324	90.00	294	81.67	264	73.33	234	65.00	204	56.67	7
8	353	98.06	323	89.72	293	81.39	263	73.06	233	64.72	203	56.39	8
9	352	97.78	322	89.44	292	81.11	262	72.78	232	64.44	202	56.11	9
10	351	97.50	321	89.17	291	80.83	261	72.50	231	64.17	201	55.83	10
11	350	97.22	320	88.89	290	80.56	260	72.22	230	63.89	200	55.56	11
12	349	96.94	319	88.61	289	80.28	259	71.94	229	63.61	199	55.28	12
13	348	96.67	318	88.33	288	80.00	258	71.67	228	63.33	198	55.00	13
14	347	96.39	317	88.06	287	79.72	257	71.39	227	63.06	197	54.72	14
15	346	96.11	316	87.78	286	79.44	256	71.11	226	62.78	196	54.44	15
16	345	95.83	315	87.50	285	79.17	255	70.83	225	62.50	195	54.17	16
17	344	95.56	314	87.22	284	78.89	254	70.56	224	62.22	194	53.89	17
18	343	95.28	313	86.94	283	78.61	253	70.28	223	61.94	193	53.61	18
19	342	95.00	312	86.67	282	78.33	252	70.00	222	61.67	192	53.33	19
20	341	94.72	311	86.39	281	78.06	251	69.72	221	61.39	191	53.06	20
21	340	94.44	310	86.11	280	77.78	250	69.44	220	61.11	190	52.78	21
22	339	94.17	309	85.83	279	77.50	249	69.17	219	60.83	189	52.50	22
23	338	93.89	308	85.56	278	77.22	248	68.89	218	60.56	188	52.22	23
24	337	93.61	307	85.28	277	76.94	247	68.61	217	60.28	187	51.94	24
25	336	93.33	306	85.00	276	76.67	246	68.33	216	60.00	186	51.67	25
26	335	93.06	305	84.72	275	76.39	245	68.06	215	59.72	185	51.39	26
27	334	92.78	304	84.44	274	76.11	244	67.78	214	59.44	184	51.11	27
28	333	92.50	303	84.17	273	75.83	243	67.50	213	59.17	183	50.83	28
29	332	92.22	302	83.89	272	75.56	242	67.22	212	58.89	182	50.56	29
30	331	91.94	301	83.61	271	75.28	241	66.94	211	58.61	181	50.28	30
31													31

PRORATIONS FROM JAN. 1st TO PRORATION DATE

DATE	JUL DAYS PAST	% OF 360	AUG DAYS PAST	% OF 360	SEP DAYS PAST	% OF 360	OCT DAYS PAST	% OF 360	NOV DAYS PAST	% OF 360	DEC DAYS PAST	% OF 360	DATE
1	181	50.28	211	58.61	241	66.94	271	75.28	301	83.61	331	91.94	1
2	182	50.56	212	58.89	242	67.22	272	75.56	302	83.89	332	92.22	2
3	183	50.83	213	59.17	243	67.50	273	75.83	303	84.17	333	92.50	3
4	184	51.11	214	59.44	244	67.78	274	76.11	304	84.44	334	92.78	4
5	185	51.39	215	59.72	245	68.06	275	76.39	305	84.72	335	93.06	5
6	186	51.67	216	60.00	246	68.33	276	76.67	306	85.00	336	93.33	6
7	187	51.94	217	60.28	247	68.61	277	76.94	307	85.28	337	93.61	7
8	188	52.22	218	60.56	248	68.89	278	77.22	308	85.56	338	93.89	8
9	189	52.50	219	60.83	249	69.17	279	77.50	309	85.83	339	94.17	9
10	190	52.78	220	61.11	250	69.44	280	77.78	310	86.11	340	94.44	10
11	191	53.06	221	61.39	251	69.72	281	78.06	311	86.39	341	94.72	11
12	192	53.33	222	61.67	252	70.00	282	78.33	312	86.67	342	95.00	12
13	193	53.61	223	61.94	253	70.28	283	78.61	313	86.94	343	95.28	13
14	194	53.89	224	62.22	254	70.56	284	78.89	314	87.22	344	95.56	14
15	195	54.17	225	62.50	255	70.83	285	79.17	315	87.50	345	95.83	15
16	196	54.44	226	62.78	256	71.11	286	79.44	316	87.78	346	96.11	16
17	197	54.72	227	63.06	257	71.39	287	79.72	317	88.06	347	96.39	17
18	198	55.00	228	63.33	258	71.67	288	80.00	318	88.33	348	96.67	18
19	199	55.28	229	63.61	259	71.94	289	80.28	319	88.61	349	96.94	19
20	200	55.56	230	63.89	260	72.22	290	80.56	320	88.89	350	97.22	20
21	201	55.83	231	64.17	261	72.50	291	80.83	321	89.17	351	97.50	21
22	202	56.11	232	64.44	262	72.78	292	81.11	322	89.44	352	97.78	22
23	203	56.39	233	64.72	263	73.06	293	81.39	323	89.72	353	98.06	23
24	204	56.67	234	65.00	264	73.33	294	81.67	324	90.00	354	98.33	24
25	205	56.94	235	65.28	265	73.61	295	81.94	325	90.28	355	98.61	25
26	206	57.22	236	65.56	266	73.89	296	82.22	326	90.56	356	98.89	26
27	207	57.50	237	65.83	267	74.17	297	82.50	327	90.83	357	99.17	27
28	208	57.78	238	66.11	268	74.44	298	82.78	328	91.11	358	99.44	28
29	209	58.06	239	66.39	269	74.72	299	83.06	329	91.39	359	99.72	29
30	210	58.33	240	66.67	270	75.00	300	83.33	330	91.67	360	100.00	30
31													31

PRORATIONS FROM PRORATION DATE TO DEC 31st

DATE	JUL DAYS TO COME	% OF 360	AUG DAYS TO COME	% OF 360	SEP DAYS TO COME	% OF 360	OCT DAYS TO COME	% OF 360	NOV DAYS TO COME	% OF 360	DEC DAYS TO COME	% OF 360	DATE
1	180	50.00	150	41.67	120	33.33	90	25.00	60	16.67	30	8.33	1
2	179	49.72	149	41.39	119	33.06	89	24.72	59	16.39	29	8.06	2
3	178	49.44	148	41.11	118	32.78	88	24.44	58	16.11	28	7.78	3
4	177	49.17	147	40.83	117	32.50	87	24.17	57	15.83	27	7.50	4
5	176	48.89	146	40.56	116	32.22	86	23.89	56	15.56	26	7.22	5
6	175	48.61	145	40.28	115	31.94	85	23.61	55	15.28	25	6.94	6
7	174	48.33	144	40.00	114	31.67	84	23.33	54	15.00	24	6.67	7
8	173	48.06	143	39.72	113	31.39	83	23.06	53	14.72	23	6.39	8
9	172	47.78	142	39.44	112	31.11	82	22.78	52	14.44	22	6.11	9
10	171	47.50	141	39.17	111	30.83	81	22.50	51	14.17	21	5.83	10
11	170	47.22	140	38.89	110	30.56	80	22.22	50	13.89	20	5.56	11
12	169	46.94	139	38.61	109	30.28	79	21.94	49	13.61	19	5.28	12
13	168	46.67	138	38.33	108	30.00	78	21.67	48	13.33	18	5.00	13
14	167	46.39	137	38.06	107	29.72	77	21.39	47	13.06	17	4.72	14
15	166	46.11	136	37.78	106	29.44	76	21.11	46	12.78	16	4.44	15
16	165	45.83	135	37.50	105	29.17	75	20.83	45	12.50	15	4.17	16
17	164	45.56	134	37.22	104	28.89	74	20.56	44	12.22	14	3.89	17
18	163	45.28	133	36.94	103	28.61	73	20.28	43	11.94	13	3.61	18
19	162	45.00	132	36.67	102	28.33	72	20.00	42	11.67	12	3.33	19
20	161	44.72	131	36.39	101	28.06	71	19.72	41	11.39	11	3.06	20
21	160	44.44	130	36.11	100	27.78	70	19.44	40	11.11	10	2.78	21
22	159	44.17	129	35.83	99	27.50	69	19.17	39	10.83	9	2.50	22
23	158	43.89	128	35.56	98	27.22	68	18.89	38	10.56	8	2.22	23
24	157	43.61	127	35.28	97	26.94	67	18.61	37	10.28	7	1.94	24
25	156	43.33	126	35.00	96	26.67	66	18.33	36	10.00	6	1.67	25
26													26
27	155	43.06	125	34.72	95	26.39	65	18.06	35	9.72	5	1.39	27
28	154	42.78	124	34.44	94	26.11	64	17.78	34	9.44	4	1.11	28
29	153	42.50	123	34.17	93	25.83	63	17.50	33	9.17	3	0.83	29
30	152	42.22	122	33.89	92	25.56	62	17.22	32	8.89	2	0.56	30
31	151	41.94	121	33.61	91	25.28	61	16.94	31	8.61	1	0.28	31

PRORATIONS FROM JAN. 1st TO PRORATION DATE

DATE	JAN DAYS PAST	JAN % OF 365	FEB DAYS PAST	FEB % OF 365	MAR DAYS PAST	MAR % OF 365	APR DAYS PAST	APR % OF 365	MAY DAYS PAST	MAY % OF 365	JUN DAYS PAST	JUN % OF 365	DATE
1	1	0.27	32	8.77	60	16.44	91	24.93	121	33.15	152	41.64	1
2	2	0.55	33	9.04	61	16.71	92	25.21	122	33.42	153	41.92	2
3	3	0.82	34	9.32	62	16.99	93	25.48	123	33.70	154	42.19	3
4	4	1.10	35	9.59	63	17.26	94	25.75	124	33.97	155	42.47	4
5	5	1.37	36	9.86	64	17.53	95	26.03	125	34.25	156	42.74	5
6	6	1.64	37	10.14	65	17.81	96	26.30	126	34.52	157	43.01	6
7	7	1.92	38	10.41	66	18.08	97	26.58	127	34.79	158	43.29	7
8	8	2.19	39	10.68	67	18.36	98	26.85	128	35.07	159	43.56	8
9	9	2.47	40	10.96	68	18.63	99	27.12	129	35.34	160	43.84	9
10	10	2.74	41	11.23	69	18.90	100	27.40	130	35.62	161	44.11	10
11	11	3.01	42	11.51	70	19.18	101	27.67	131	35.89	162	44.38	11
12	12	3.29	43	11.78	71	19.45	102	27.95	132	36.16	163	44.66	12
13	13	3.56	44	12.05	72	19.73	103	28.22	133	36.44	164	44.93	13
14	14	3.84	45	12.33	73	20.00	104	28.49	134	36.71	165	45.21	14
15	15	4.11	46	12.60	74	20.27	105	28.77	135	36.99	166	45.48	15
16	16	4.38	47	12.88	75	20.55	106	29.04	136	37.26	167	45.75	16
17	17	4.66	48	13.15	76	20.82	107	29.32	137	37.53	168	46.03	17
18	18	4.93	49	13.42	77	21.10	108	29.59	138	37.81	169	46.30	18
19	19	5.21	50	13.70	78	21.37	109	29.86	139	38.08	170	46.58	19
20	20	5.48	51	13.97	79	21.64	110	30.14	140	38.36	171	46.85	20
21	21	5.75	52	14.25	80	21.92	111	30.41	141	38.63	172	47.12	21
22	22	6.03	53	14.52	81	22.19	112	30.68	142	38.90	173	47.40	22
23	23	6.30	54	14.79	82	22.47	113	30.96	143	39.18	174	47.67	23
24	24	6.58	55	15.07	83	22.74	114	31.23	144	39.45	175	47.95	24
25	25	6.85	56	15.34	84	23.01	115	31.51	145	39.73	176	48.22	25
26	26	7.12	57	15.62	85	23.29	116	31.78	146	40.00	177	48.49	26
27	27	7.40	58	15.89	86	23.56	117	32.05	147	40.27	178	48.77	27
28	28	7.67	59	16.16	87	23.84	118	32.33	148	40.55	179	49.04	28
29	29	7.95			88	24.11	119	32.60	149	40.82	180	49.32	29
30	30	8.22			89	24.38	120	32.88	150	41.10	181	49.59	30
31	31	8.49			90	24.66			151	41.37			31

PRORATIONS FROM PRORATION DATE TO DEC 31st

DATE	JAN DAYS TO COME	JAN % OF 365	FEB DAYS TO COME	FEB % OF 365	MAR DAYS TO COME	MAR % OF 365	APR DAYS TO COME	APR % OF 365	MAY DAYS TO COME	MAY % OF 365	JUN DAYS TO COME	JUN % OF 365	DATE
1	365	100.00	334	91.51	306	83.84	275	75.34	245	67.12	214	58.63	1
2	364	99.73	333	91.23	305	83.56	274	75.07	244	66.85	213	58.36	2
3	363	99.45	332	90.96	304	83.29	273	74.79	243	66.58	212	58.08	3
4	362	99.18	331	90.68	303	83.01	272	74.52	242	66.30	211	57.81	4
5	361	98.90	330	90.41	302	82.74	271	74.25	241	66.03	210	57.53	5
6	360	98.63	329	90.14	301	82.47	270	73.97	240	65.75	209	57.26	6
7	359	98.36	328	89.86	300	82.19	269	73.70	239	65.48	208	56.99	7
8	358	98.08	327	89.59	299	81.92	268	73.42	238	65.21	207	56.71	8
9	357	97.81	326	89.32	298	81.64	267	73.15	237	64.93	206	56.44	9
10	356	97.53	325	89.04	297	81.37	266	72.88	236	64.66	205	56.16	10
11	355	97.26	324	88.77	296	81.10	265	72.60	235	64.38	204	55.89	11
12	354	96.99	323	88.49	295	80.82	264	72.33	234	64.11	203	55.62	12
13	353	96.71	322	88.22	294	80.55	263	72.05	233	63.84	202	55.34	13
14	352	96.44	321	87.95	293	80.27	262	71.78	232	63.56	201	55.07	14
15	351	96.16	320	87.67	292	80.00	261	71.51	231	63.29	200	54.79	15
16	350	95.89	319	87.40	291	79.73	260	71.23	230	63.01	199	54.52	16
17	349	95.62	318	87.12	290	79.45	259	70.96	229	62.74	198	54.25	17
18	348	95.34	317	86.85	289	79.18	258	70.68	228	62.47	197	53.97	18
19	347	95.07	316	86.58	288	78.90	257	70.41	227	62.19	196	53.70	19
20	346	94.79	315	86.30	287	78.63	256	70.14	226	61.92	195	53.42	20
21	345	94.52	314	86.03	286	78.36	255	69.86	225	61.64	194	53.15	21
22	344	94.25	313	85.75	285	78.08	254	69.59	224	61.37	193	52.88	22
23	343	93.97	312	85.48	284	77.81	253	69.32	223	61.10	192	52.60	23
24	342	93.70	311	85.21	283	77.53	252	69.04	222	60.82	191	52.33	24
25	341	93.42	310	84.93	282	77.26	251	68.77	221	60.55	190	52.05	25
26	340	93.15	309	84.66	281	76.99	250	68.49	220	60.27	189	51.78	26
27	339	92.88	308	84.38	280	76.71	249	68.22	219	60.00	188	51.51	27
28	338	92.60	307	84.11	279	76.44	248	67.95	218	59.73	187	51.23	28
29	337	92.33			278	76.16	247	67.67	217	59.45	186	50.96	29
30	336	92.05			277	75.89	246	67.40	216	59.18	185	50.68	30
31	335	91.78			276	75.62			215	58.90			31

PRORATIONS FROM JAN. 1st TO PRORATION DATE

DATE	JUL DAYS PAST	JUL % OF 365	AUG DAYS PAST	AUG % OF 365	SEP DAYS PAST	SEP % OF 365	OCT DAYS PAST	OCT % OF 365	NOV DAYS PAST	NOV % OF 365	DEC DAYS PAST	DEC % OF 365	DATE
1	182	49.86	213	58.36	244	66.85	274	75.07	305	83.56	335	91.78	1
2	183	50.14	214	58.63	245	67.12	275	75.34	306	83.84	336	92.05	2
3	184	50.41	215	58.90	246	67.40	276	75.62	307	84.11	337	92.33	3
4	185	50.68	216	59.18	247	67.67	277	75.89	308	84.38	338	92.60	4
5	186	50.96	217	59.45	248	67.95	278	76.16	309	84.66	339	92.88	5
6	187	51.23	218	59.73	249	68.22	279	76.44	310	84.93	340	93.15	6
7	188	51.51	219	60.00	250	68.49	280	76.71	311	85.21	341	93.42	7
8	189	51.78	220	60.27	251	68.77	281	76.99	312	85.48	342	93.70	8
9	190	52.05	221	60.55	252	69.04	282	77.26	313	85.75	343	93.97	9
10	191	52.33	222	60.82	253	69.32	283	77.53	314	86.03	344	94.25	10
11	192	52.60	223	61.10	254	69.59	284	77.81	315	86.30	345	94.52	11
12	193	52.88	224	61.37	255	69.86	285	78.08	316	86.58	346	94.79	12
13	194	53.15	225	61.64	256	70.14	286	78.36	317	86.85	347	95.07	13
14	195	53.42	226	61.92	257	70.41	287	78.63	318	87.12	348	95.34	14
15	196	53.70	227	62.19	258	70.68	288	78.90	319	87.40	349	95.62	15
16	197	53.97	228	62.47	259	70.96	289	79.18	320	87.67	350	95.89	16
17	198	54.25	229	62.74	260	71.23	290	79.45	321	87.95	351	96.16	17
18	199	54.52	230	63.01	261	71.51	291	79.73	322	88.22	352	96.44	18
19	200	54.79	231	63.29	262	71.78	292	80.00	323	88.49	353	96.71	19
20	201	55.07	232	63.56	263	72.05	293	80.27	324	88.77	354	96.99	20
21	202	55.34	233	63.84	264	72.33	294	80.55	325	89.04	355	97.26	21
22	203	55.62	234	64.11	265	72.60	295	80.82	326	89.32	356	97.53	22
23	204	55.89	235	64.38	266	72.88	296	81.10	327	89.59	357	97.81	23
24	205	56.16	236	64.66	267	73.15	297	81.37	328	89.86	358	98.08	24
25	206	56.44	237	64.93	268	73.42	298	81.64	329	90.14	359	98.36	25
26	207	56.71	238	65.21	269	73.70	299	81.92	330	90.41	360	98.63	26
27	208	56.99	239	65.48	270	73.97	300	82.19	331	90.68	361	98.90	27
28	209	57.26	240	65.75	271	74.25	301	82.47	332	90.96	362	99.18	28
29	210	57.53	241	66.03	272	74.52	302	82.74	333	91.23	363	99.45	29
30	211	57.81	242	66.30	273	74.79	303	83.01	334	91.51	364	99.73	30
31	212	58.08	243	66.58			304	83.29			365	100.00	31

PRORATIONS FROM PRORATION DATE TO DEC 31st

DATE	JUL DAYS TO COME	JUL % OF 365	AUG DAYS TO COME	AUG % OF 365	SEP DAYS TO COME	SEP % OF 365	OCT DAYS TO COME	OCT % OF 365	NOV DAYS TO COME	NOV % OF 365	DEC DAYS TO COME	DEC % OF 365	DATE
1	184	50.41	153	41.92	122	33.42	92	25.21	61	16.71	31	8.49	1
2	183	50.14	152	41.64	121	33.15	91	24.93	60	16.44	30	8.22	2
3	182	49.86	151	41.37	120	32.88	90	24.66	59	16.16	29	7.95	3
4	181	49.59	150	41.10	119	32.60	89	24.38	58	15.89	28	7.67	4
5	180	49.32	149	40.82	118	32.33	88	24.11	57	15.62	27	7.40	5
6	179	49.04	148	40.55	117	32.05	87	23.84	56	15.34	26	7.12	6
7	178	48.77	147	40.27	116	31.78	86	23.56	55	15.07	25	6.85	7
8	177	48.49	146	40.00	115	31.51	85	23.29	54	14.79	24	6.58	8
9	176	48.22	145	39.73	114	31.23	84	23.01	53	14.52	23	6.30	9
10	175	47.95	144	39.45	113	30.96	83	22.74	52	14.25	22	6.03	10
11	174	47.67	143	39.18	112	30.68	82	22.47	51	13.97	21	5.75	11
12	173	47.40	142	38.90	111	30.41	81	22.19	50	13.70	20	5.48	12
13	172	47.12	141	38.63	110	30.14	80	21.92	49	13.42	19	5.21	13
14	171	46.85	140	38.36	109	29.86	79	21.64	48	13.15	18	4.93	14
15	170	46.58	139	38.08	108	29.59	78	21.37	47	12.88	17	4.66	15
16	169	46.30	138	37.81	107	29.32	77	21.10	46	12.60	16	4.38	16
17	168	46.03	137	37.53	106	29.04	76	20.82	45	12.33	15	4.11	17
18	167	45.75	136	37.26	105	28.77	75	20.55	44	12.05	14	3.84	18
19	166	45.48	135	36.99	104	28.49	74	20.27	43	11.78	13	3.56	19
20	165	45.21	134	36.71	103	28.22	73	20.00	42	11.51	12	3.29	20
21	164	44.93	133	36.44	102	27.95	72	19.73	41	11.23	11	3.01	21
22	163	44.66	132	36.16	101	27.67	71	19.45	40	10.96	10	2.74	22
23	162	44.38	131	35.89	100	27.40	70	19.18	39	10.68	9	2.47	23
24	161	44.11	130	35.62	99	27.12	69	18.90	38	10.41	8	2.19	24
25	160	43.84	129	35.34	98	26.85	68	18.63	37	10.14	7	1.92	25
26	159	43.56	128	35.07	97	26.58	67	18.36	36	9.86	6	1.64	26
27	158	43.29	127	34.79	96	26.30	66	18.08	35	9.59	5	1.37	27
28	157	43.01	126	34.52	95	26.03	65	17.81	34	9.32	4	1.10	28
29	156	42.74	125	34.25	94	25.75	64	17.53	33	9.04	3	0.82	29
30	155	42.47	124	33.97	93	25.48	63	17.26	32	8.77	2	0.55	30
31	154	42.19	123	33.70			62	16.99			1	0.27	31